Contractual Duties: Performance, Breach, Termination and Remedies

CONTRACTUAL DUTIES: PERFORMANCE, BREACH, TERMINATION AND REMEDIES

FOURTH EDITION

PROFESSOR NEIL ANDREWS
Professor of Civil Justice and Private Law

PROFESSOR ANDREW TETTENBORN
Professor of Commercial Law

PROFESSOR GRAHAM VIRGO KC (HONORIS CAUSA)
Professor of English Private Law

SWEET & MAXWELL

THOMSON REUTERS

Published in 2023 by Thomson Reuters, trading as Sweet & Maxwell.
Thomson Reuters is registered in England & Wales, Company No.1679046.
Registered Office and address for service: 5 Canada Square, Canary Wharf,
London, E14 5AQ.

For further information on our products and services, visit *http://
www.sweetandmaxwell.co.uk*.

Computerset by Sweet & Maxwell.
Printed and bound by CPI Group (UK) Ltd, Croydon, CR0 4YY.
A CIP catalogue record of this book is available for the British Library.
For orders and enquiries, go to:
http://www.tr.com/uki-legal-contact; Tel: 0345 600 9355.

ISBN (print): 978-0-414-11397-8

ISBN (e-book): 978-0-414-11398-5

ISBN (print and ebook): 978-0-414-11399-2

FOREWORD

Books on the law of contract conventionally start with sections on contract formation—addressing topics such as offer and acceptance, consideration, intention to contract, formalities and capacity. While those topics are of interest to some academics, they are also of largely academic interest in the sense that they seldom arise in practice. Such works then typically proceed to discuss the contents of contracts, about which there is only limited scope for generalisation. This book bypasses these shallow waters and jumps straight in at the deep end of contract law, with the principles governing contractual performance, breach, rescission and remedies. These are subjects of great practical importance because in those commercial contract disputes which turn on more than the meaning of particular contractual language, the law discussed in this book determines when, how and with what consequences a party may exit their bargain.

The authors' specific focus on this important area enables them to engage in a depth and detail of analysis not to be found in more general works. Exegesis of notable cases is accompanied by identification of points on which the relevant law is unsettled or unsatisfactory and explanation of rival views, leavened with the authors' own incisive opinions. This recipe makes the book of real value to any lawyer looking for intellectual assistance in grappling with a practical problem.

The three authors of this work are all leading legal scholars with a profound knowledge of their subject. It is a testament to their commitment that they have once again not only updated this book to reflect the latest relevant legal developments—itself no small task when the speed of legal change continues to increase—but have also made other revisions to the text in order to further refine and improve it. I believe their erudition will benefit anyone who consults this valuable work.

George Leggatt
Supreme Court, Parliament Square
July 2023

PREFACE

Since the publication of our third edition in 2020 the law of contract and contract remedies has developed significantly. Our preface to that edition noted that it had been completed during lockdown following the pandemic. Sure enough, as we might have foreseen, one recurring theme has been the impact of this exact pandemic on contracts.

In Pt I there have been significant developments, particularly in two decisions of the Privy Council (*Nature Resorts Ltd v First Citizens Bank Ltd* [2022] UKPC 10 on undue influence, and *Moses v Moses* [2022] UKPC 42 on rights of third parties). There have also been important considerations of duress (*Times Travel (UK) Ltd v Pakistan International Airlines Corp* [2021] UKSC 40 and *Law Debenture Trust Corp Plc v Ukraine* [2023] UKSC 11); on misrepresentation (*SK Shipping Europe Ltd v Capital VLCC 3 Corp* [2022] EWCA Civ 231); and on the identification of fiduciary duties (*Children's Investment Fund Foundation (UK) v Attorney General* [2020] UKSC 33).

In Pt II (breach and performance) cases of note include the following: renunciation, *AI Giorgis Oil Trading Ltd v AG Shipping and Energy Pte Ltd* [2021] EWHC 2319 (Comm); *Olympic Council of Asia v Novans Jets LLP* [2022] EWHC 88 (Comm); repudiation, *EMFC Loan Syndications LLP v Resort Group Plc* [2021] EWCA Civ 844; *SK Shipping Europe Plc v Capital VLCC 3 Corp* [2020] EWHC 3448 (Comm) (not disturbed on appeal, [2022] EWCA Civ 231); identifying conditions, *Duchy Farm Kennels Ltd v Steels* [2020] EWHC 1208 (QB); *Galtrade Ltd v BP Oil International Ltd* [2021] EWHC 1796 (Comm); *EMFC Loan* case [2021] EWCA Civ 844; *Pharmapac (UK) Ltd v HBS Healthcare Ltd* [2022] EWHC 23 (Comm); innominate terms, *DD Classics Ltd v Chen* [2022] EWHC 1357 (Comm); *Neath Port Talbot (Recycling) Ltd v James Heys and Sons Ltd* [2021] EWHC 3157 (Comm); *Galtrade* case [2021] EWHC 1796 (Comm); the process of terminating for breach, *Pharmapac* case [2022] EWHC 23 (Comm); *DD Classics* case [2022] EWHC 1357 (Comm); the entire obligation rule, *Donovan v Grainmarket Asset Management LLP* [2021] EWCA Civ 686.

In Pt III (frustration), case law on force majeure clauses includes: *Target Rich International Ltd v Forex Capital Markets Ltd* [2020] EWHC 1544 (Comm); *Delta Petroleum (Caribbean) Ltd v British Virgin Islands Electricity Corp* [2020] UKPC 23; *NKD Maritime Ltd v Bart Maritime (No. 2) Inc* [2022] EWHC 1615 (Comm); *Billy Graham Evangelistic Association v Scottish Event Campus Ltd* (2021) (Scotland: 2021 S.L.T. (Sh Ct) 185); *Dwyer (UK Franchising) Ltd v Fredbar Ltd* [2021] EWHC 1218 (Ch); *MUR Shipping BV v RTI Ltd* [2022] EWCA Civ 1406. Cases concerning the doctrine of frustration include: *Dayah v Partners of Bushloe Street Surgery* [2020] EWHC 1375 (QB); *Bank of New York Mellon (International) Ltd v Cine-UK Ltd* [2022] EWCA Civ 1021; *Wilmington Trust SP Services (Dublin) Ltd v Spicejet Ltd* [2021] EWHC 1117 (Comm); *Banco San Juan Internacional Inc v Petroleos de Venezuela SA* [2020] EWHC 2937 (Comm); *London Trocadero (2015) LLP v Picturehouse Cinemas Ltd* [2021] EWHC 2591 (Ch); *Salam Air SAOC v Latam Airlines Groups SA* [2020] EWHC 2414 (Comm).

Lastly, in Pt IV, dealing with remedies where things go wrong, we have seen some interesting developments on damages for late payment of debts (*Sagicor Bank Jamaica Ltd v Seaton* [2022] UKPC 48); on the relation between recoverable financial loss and the insolvency laws (*Stanford International Bank Ltd (In*

Liquidation) v HSBC Plc [2022] UKSC 34); and—perhaps inevitably—on the remedies for failure to pay cryptocurrencies like Ether or Bitcoin.

As ever, we owe heartfelt thanks to the staff at Thomson Reuters for their support and encouragement. We have endeavoured to state the law as at 1 May 2023, though a few later developments have been incorporated. All errors of course remain ours.

Neil Andrews

Andrew Tettenborn

Graham Virgo

May 2023

TABLE OF CONTENTS

PART I RESCISSION

1   THE NATURE OF RESCISSION

2   THE GROUNDS FOR RESCISSION

PART III FRUSTRATION: DISCHARGE BY IMPOSSIBILITY, ILLEGAILITY OR FRUSTRATION

16 CORE FEATURES OF FRUSTRATION: LEGAL BASIS, RISK ALLOCATION AND "SELF-INDUCEMENT"

TABLE OF CASES

TABLE OF STATUTES

TABLE OF STATUTORY INSTRUMENTS

PART I RESCISSION

By Professor Graham Virgo KC (honoris causa)

CHAPTER 1

THE NATURE OF RESCISSION

I.   GENERAL PRINCIPLES

The essence of rescission   Where there is a flaw in the making of a contract which   **1-001**
renders that contract voidable, rescission is a remedy which enables the contract to
be retrospectively treated as though it had never come into existence.[1] The essence of the remedy of rescission was usefully summarised by Master Matthews
in *Bainbridge v Bainbridge*[2] as being

> "available in appropriate circumstances to undo (or set aside) otherwise consensual
> transactions between two or more parties where there is a factor or element vitiating
> consent"

If a voidable contract is not rescinded it remains effective but can still be rescinded,
save where one of the bars to rescission applies.[3] A contract can be rescinded if there
was some relevant flaw at the time the contract was made, which can be considered
as a matter of law to have impaired the consent of one of the parties to the contract
so that their consent to enter into the contract can be treated as vitiated. Relevant
vitiating factors include misrepresentation which induced the contract to be made,[4]
or duress[5] or undue influence[6] of the claimant to enter into the contract. Once a
contract is rescinded it is nullified and everything which has been done under the
contract is liable to be undone[7] by operation of law rather than agreement, so that
the parties are restored to their original pre-contractual position; there is a giving
and a taking back on both sides.[8] For example, where money has been paid under
a contract which is subsequently rescinded, the recipient of the payment will be liable to return the money or its value to the payer. This is effected by reference to
the law of unjust enrichment rather than the law of contract.[9] Once the contract has
been rescinded any unperformed obligations will be extinguished and any liability

---

[1]   *Johnson v Agnew* [1980] A.C. 367 at 393 (Lord Wilberforce); *AC v DC* [2012] EWHC 2032 (Fam)
      at [30] (Mostyn J). See generally N. McBride, "Rescission" in G. Virgo and S. Worthington (eds),
      Commercial Remedies: Resolving Controversies (Cambridge: Cambridge University Press, 2017),
      Ch.7.
[2]   [2016] EWHC 898 (Ch) at [2].
[3]   See Ch.3.
[4]   See para.2-002.
[5]   See para.2-023.
[6]   See para.2-029.
[7]   *Manifest Shipping Co Ltd v Uni-Polaris Insurance Co Ltd (The Star Sea)* [2003] 1 A.C. 469 at [51]
      (Lord Hobhouse).
[8]   *Shalson v Russo* [2003] EWHC 1637 (Ch); [2005] Ch. 281 at [122] (Rimer J).
[9]   *Manifest Shipping Co Ltd v Uni-Polaris Insurance Co Ltd (The Star Sea)* [2003] 1 A.C. 469 at [51]
      (Lord Hobhouse). See further para.4-012.

to pay damages which had already accrued will be discharged, because the contract will be treated as never having been made so that there can be no liability for breach of that contract, although there may still be liability under a collateral contract which was unaffected by the vitiating factor. Rescission can be sought without the party who seeks the remedy also being required to plead a claim for damages as well.[10]

1-002 **Distinction between rescission and discharge for breach** Sometimes the discharge of a contract for breach has been described as rescission *de futuro*,[11] since the effect of termination of the contract is prospective, (with discharge of primary obligations and substitution for them of secondary obligations to compensate[12]) and termination triggered by a defect operating at the time the contract was made is described as rescission *ab initio*, since the termination of the contract is retrospective. But this dual use of the term "rescission" is incorrect.[13] Rescission is concerned with the termination of a contract as a result of a defect which was operating at the time the contract was made, whereas discharge for breach is a response to a defect in the subsequent performance of the contract.[14] Using the language of rescission to describe both situations is liable to confuse[15] and the use of the term "rescission" should be confined to the retrospective termination of contracts for defects in the making of the contract.[16]

1-003 The effects of termination of a contract by rescission and discharge of a contract for breach are fundamentally different. Where a contract is rescinded it is treated as though it was void from the start. Consequently, all unperformed obligations are extinguished as are any secondary obligations to pay damages for breach. Where a contract is terminated for breach, any future obligations which have not yet accrued are terminated but those obligations which have accrued continue to be enforceable, as will any liability to pay damages for a breach which has already occurred.[17] Termination for breach will not usually result in title to property being revested or money paid being recovered, but these are common consequences of a

---

[10] *Ruttle Plant Hire Ltd v Secretary of State for the Environment Food and Rural Affairs* [2007] EWHC 2870 (TCC) at [86] (Ramsey J).

[11] See *Peyman v Lanjani* [1985] Ch. 457.

[12] *HEB Enterprises Ltd v Richards* [2023] UKPC 7 at [48].

[13] *Heyman v Darwins Ltd* [1942] A.C. 356 at 399 (Lord Porter); *Johnson v Agnew* [1980] A.C. 367 at 393 (Lord Wilberforce); *Hurst v Bryk* [2002] 1 A.C. 185 at 194 (Lord Millett); *Manifest Shipping Co Ltd v Uni-Polaris Insurance Co Ltd (The Star Sea)* [2003] 1 A.C. 469 at [51] (Lord Hobhouse); *Howard-Jones v Tate* [2011] EWCA Civ 1330 at [15] (Kitchin LJ). S. Williston, "Repudiation of Contracts" (1901) 14 Harv. L.R. 421 at 425.

[14] See Ch.5.

[15] *Johnson v Agnew* [1980] A.C. 367 at 392 (Lord Wilberforce); *Hurst v Bryck* [2002] 1 A.C. 185 at 194 (Lord Millett).

[16] In *Patel v Mirza* [2016] UKSC 42; [2017] A.C. 467 some of the Justices used the language of rescission to describe the restitutionary consequences of an illegal contract being void: at [197] and [200] (Lord Mance) at [210] (Lord Clarke) and at [253] (Lord Sumption). This too is incorrect: an illegal contract is void so there is nothing to be rescinded. Further, restitution can arise as a result of rescission and is distinct from it. See para.4-012 ff.

[17] *McDonald v Denys Lascelles Ltd* (1933) 48 C.L.R. 476–477 (Sir Owen Dixon). See further Ch.20. See *Hardy v Griffiths* [2014] EWHC 3947 (Ch); [2015] Ch. 417 where it was held that rescission of a contract for the sale of land did not vitiate the purchaser's liability to pay a deposit, because the vendor's right to receive the deposit had already accrued before rescission. But this should have been treated as a case where the contract was discharged for breach since, had it been rescinded, the purchaser's liability would have been discharged as well.

contract being rescinded by virtue of the principle that everything done under a contract which has been rescinded is liable to be undone.[18]

Distinction between rescission and frustration It is also important to distinguish   **1-004**
between rescission *ab initio* of contracts and frustration of contracts.[19] Where a contract is frustrated it is terminated prospectively and automatically, so that the parties are released from obligations which would have fallen due after the frustrating event but remain bound by obligations which have already accrued,[20] whereas rescission operates retrospectively releasing the parties from all obligations arising from the contract. Where, however, a contract could not be performed from the moment it was made, the distinction between rescission and frustration is more difficult to discern because no contractual obligations will have accrued. But it remains important to distinguish between rescission and frustration for two reasons. First, because a contract which is liable to be rescinded remains valid until rescission has occurred, whereas a frustrated contract will automatically be terminated by virtue of the frustrating event. Secondly, because the factors which trigger rescission relate to the validity of a contracting party's consent to enter into a contract, whereas a contract will be frustrated by a change of circumstances which would make performance of the contract radically different.[21]

Distinction between rescission and termination The essence of rescission is that   **1-005**
a party to a contract has a right to avoid the contract because of some defect at the time the contract was made. The language of rescission is also sometimes used where a party terminates a contract by virtue of a clause in the contract permitting such termination.[22] This involves a misuse of the language of rescission because the contract is not avoided *ab initio*. Consequently, the language of rescission should not be used to describe the contractual right to terminate the contract. Rescission is a remedy which arises by operation of law and cannot be provided for by the contract. That termination by virtue of a contractual term does not involve the law of rescission matters because it follows that the complexities of the law relating to the machinery of rescission[23] and the bars to rescission[24] will not apply.

Void and voidable contracts In determining when a contract is liable to be   **1-006**
rescinded it is important to draw a distinction between contracts which are void and those which are voidable. There are various defects which may affect the intention of a contracting party to enter into a contract. In some cases these defects are regarded as so significant that the contracting party cannot be considered to have agreed to enter into the contract at all, so that no contract was made. A contract will be void because, for example, of a fundamental common mistake made by the parties[25] or because of the doctrine of *non est factum*, by virtue of which a party's signature to a document can be considered to have been mistaken because they

---

[18] See para.4-001.
[19] See Ch.17.
[20] Subject to the operation of the Law Reform (Frustrated Contracts) Act 1943 s.1(2). See para.18-028.
[21] See para.17-002.
[22] See, e.g. *BDW Trading Ltd (t/a Barratt North London) v JM Rowe (Investments) Ltd* [2011] EWCA Civ 548.
[23] See para.1-009 ff.
[24] See Ch.3.
[25] *Great Peace Shipping Ltd v Tsalviris Salvage (International) Ltd* [2003] Q.B. 679.

thought that they were signing a document which was fundamentally different from that which they had contemplated.[26] In other circumstances the defect which operates at the time the contract was made will not be regarded as so significant that it cannot be said that no contract had been made. Consequently, the parties will be considered to have entered into a valid contract, but the effect of the defect in the making of the contract is such that the party whose consent to enter into the contract has been compromised has the option of seeking to get the contract rescinded and, once rescinded, it will be treated as though it was void. Until a voidable contract is rescinded it remains effective to confer rights, to create obligations and to pass title to property.

1-007　**Ineffective contracts**　A further distinction should be drawn between contracts which are voidable and contracts which are ineffective. A voidable contract remains valid until rescinded. An ineffective contract is invalid but may be validated by subsequent ratification. So, for example, where an agent enters into an agreement on behalf of their principal but without authority to do so, the agreement will be ineffective to create any rights or obligations. But if the principal ratifies the contract, it will be retrospectively validated from the time the agreement was made.[27] Ratification can be considered to be the mirror image of rescission; ratification retrospectively validates whereas rescission retrospectively invalidates a contract.

1-008　**Rescission of other transactions**　Rescission is primarily relevant to the setting aside of contracts. But the language of rescission has also been used as regards other transactions, including deeds of gift and other voluntary settlements such as wills[28] or a disposition to trusts.[29] Rescission is not necessary to enable the recovery of gifts where there is no deed, since there is no transaction which needs to be set aside. Where a gift has been effected by deed and there is some defect in the making of the deed, that deed will need to be rescinded before the gift can be recovered, with the same grounds of rescission operating as apply to rescission of a contract.[30] So, for example, a deed can be rescinded for duress[31] or mistake.[32] Where a voluntary transfer has been made by mistake, for example where a disposition has been made to a trust, there is an equitable jurisdiction to set aside the transfer, which will be held on trust for the transferor.[33] The transfer can only be avoided in Equity if the transferor was mistaken at the time of the transfer; the mistake was sufficiently serious; and the mistake was of such gravity that it would be unjust or unconscionable for the transferee to retain it. At one time it was assumed that a mistaken gift not transferred pursuant to a deed could be recovered at Common Law under the law

---

[26]　See *Saunders v Anglia Building Society* [1971] A.C. 1004.
[27]　*Bolton Partners v Lambert* (1888) 41 Ch D. 295.
[28]　*Re Edwards (deceased)* [2007] EWHC 1119 (Ch).
[29]　*Pitt v Holt; Futter v Futter* [2013] UKSC 26; [2013] 2 A.C. 108.
[30]　See Ch.2.
[31]　*Whelpdale's case* (1604) 5 Co. Rep. 119; 77 E.R. 239 at 240. Cf. *Barton v Armstrong* [1976] A.C. 104 at 120 where it was recognised that duress rendered the deed void. See further, para.2-024.
[32]　*Fender v National Westminster Bank Plc* [2008] EWHC 2242 (Ch).
[33]　*Pitt v Holt; Futter v Futter* [2013] UKSC 26; [2013] 2 A.C. 108; *Kennedy v Kennedy* [2014] EWHC 4129 (Ch); *Wright v National Westminster Bank Plc* [2014] EWHC 3158 (Ch); [2015] W.T.L.R. 547; *Freedman v Freedman* [2015] EWHC 1457 (Ch); [2015] W.T.L.R. 118; *Bainbridge v Bainbridge* [2016] EWHC 898 (Ch); [2016] W.T.L.R. 943; *Rogge v Rogge* [2019] EWHC 1949 (Ch); [2019] W.T.L.R. 1305.

of unjust enrichment, simply because the mistake caused the transfer to be made.[34] More recently, however, it has been assumed that the stricter test for recovering mistaken gifts in Equity will extend to the Common Law as well.[35]

II.   THE PROCESS OF RESCISSION

Rescission at Common Law and in Equity   The process of rescinding a contract depends on whether rescission occurs at Common Law or in Equity.[36] This reflects the historical origins of the law of rescission, which developed across the jurisdictional divide of the Common Law and chancery courts and which survives despite the fusion of the administration of the law following the Judicature Acts 1873 and 1875.[37] Whether rescission is effected at Common Law or in Equity will depend on the type of vitiating factor which is engaged. The Common Law recognises far fewer vitiating factors than Equity. All the factors which are recognised at Common Law are also recognised in Equity by virtue of Equity's concurrent jurisdiction, so the party who wishes a contract to be rescinded may have a choice as to whether to seek rescission at Common Law or in Equity. Depending on the facts of the case there may be certain advantages in seeking rescission at Common Law or in Equity, although usually equitable rescission will be preferable, both because of the more extensive vitiating factors[38] and the less restrictive approach to the bars on rescission,[39] especially as regards the determination of whether the parties can be restored to their original position. Further, the remedial consequences arising from rescission in Equity are more likely to be beneficial to the party who seeks rescission of the contract.[40]

1-009

Fundamental features of rescission at Common Law   Rescission at Common Law is properly characterised as a self-help remedy which takes effect by the act of the party seeking rescission and does not require intervention of the court.[41] The existence of a vitiating factor which is recognised at Common Law gives the claimant the power to rescind the contract. Rescission takes effect automatically on the rescinding party exercising the power of rescission, which is usually effected by communication to the other party to the contract and without requiring a court order to effect rescission.[42] Once the claimant has announced that they have rescinded the contract it will be treated as invalid *ab initio*. If the contract was executory there

1-010

---

34   *Kleinwort Benson Ltd v Lincoln CC* [1999] 2 A.C. 349. But note *Deutsche Morgan Grenfell Group Plc v IRC* [2006] UKHL 49; [2007] 1 A.C. 558, where Lord Scott at [87] expressed doubts about the appropriateness of a "but for" test of causation for restitution of mistaken gifts.
35   *Pagel v Farman* [2013] EWHC 2210 (Comm); *Spaul v Spaul* [2014] EWCA Civ 679 at [52] (Rimer LJ); *Van der Merwe v Goldman* [2016] EWHC 790 (Ch); [2016] 4 W.L.R. 71 at [26] and [31] (Morgan J). See further para.2-022.
36   J. O'Sullivan, "Rescission as a self-help remedy: a critical analysis" (2000) 59 C.L.J. 509.
37   For analysis of the historical origins of rescission see D. O'Sullivan, S. Elliott and R. Zakrzewski, *The Law of Rescission*, 3rd edn (Oxford: Oxford University Press, 2023), Ch.3.
38   See Ch.2.
39   See Ch.3.
40   See Ch.4.
41   *Halpern v Halpern (No.2)* [2006] EWHC 1728 (Comm); [2007] Q.B. 88 at [26] (Nigel Teare QC). This was not considered by the Court of Appeal: [2007] EWCA Civ 291; [2008] Q.B. 195, although the gist of that court's obiter consideration of rescission was that there should be no difference between rescission at Common Law and in Equity. See para.1-028. See also *Revenue and Customs Commissioners v IGE USA Investments Ltd* [2021] EWCA Civ 534; [2021] Ch. 423.
42   *Abram Steamship Co Ltd v Westville Shipping Co Ltd* [1923] A.C. 773 at 781 (Lord Atkinson);

will be no other consequences. If any part of the contract has been executed by the claimant they will then be able to bring an action to recover what has been transferred to the other party, and vice versa.[43]

1-011   The role of the court is limited to determining whether the conditions for the exercise of the self-help power were satisfied so that the contract has effectively been avoided and to give effect to the consequences of rescission by ensuring that the parties are restored to the position they occupied before the contract was made.[44] Crucially, rescission at Common Law does not depend on the exercise of judicial discretion, unlike rescission in Equity,[45] with the consequence that terms cannot be attached as a condition of rescission at Common Law. If one party challenges the other's right to rescind the contract that other party may bring an action to enforce the right to rescind. If the court confirms that the claimant has validly elected to rescind the contract, the judgment does not effect the rescission but simply confirms that the election was effective.[46]

1-012   Rescission at Common Law is available where the rescinding party was induced to enter into the contract as the result of a fraudulent (but not negligent or innocent) misrepresentation,[47] or non-disclosure[48] in respect of certain types of contract, or duress,[49] or where the rescinding party's consent to enter into the contract has been impaired by incapacity.[50]

1-013   **Communication of election to rescind**   Typically a party will rescind a contract at Common Law by communicating their election to rescind to the other party to the contract, either through words or conduct,[51] so that the intention to rescind is unequivocally or clearly demonstrated or made manifest.[52] So, for example, sending a letter to the other party to the contract stating that the rescinding party wishes to call off the transaction or that they are no longer bound by it will be sufficient to rescind the contract.

1-014   A rescinding party will also have communicated an intention to treat the contract as rescinded through the assertion of rights which are incompatible with the contract subsisting. So, for example, demanding the return of money may suffice for the communication of the election to rescind. In *Re Eastgate*[53] repossessing furniture and other chattels was sufficient to rescind a contract of sale which had been induced by fraud. If, however, one party to the contract takes possession of property and it is then discovered that they had no right to rescind the contract at Common Law, the act of taking possession will constitute the tort of conversion by interfering with another party's proprietary or possessory rights. If the contracting party did

---

Horsler v Zorro [1975] 1 Ch. 302 at 310 (Megarry J); *Car and Universe Finance Co Ltd v Caldwell* [1965] 1 Q.B. 525 at 532 (Lord Denning MR); *Brotherton v Aseguradora Cobeguros (No.2)* [2003] EWCA Civ 705; [2003] 3 All E.R. (Comm.) 298 at [27] (Mance LJ) at [45] (Buxton LJ).

[43]   See para.4-012 ff.

[44]   *Abram Steamship Co Ltd v Westville Shipping Co Ltd* [1923] A.C. 773 at 781 (Lord Atkinson). Cf. *Islington LBC v UKCAC* [2006] EWCA Civ 340 where Dyson LJ at [26], assumed that all rescission is effected by an order of the court.

[45]   See para.1-021.

[46]   *Abram Steamship Co Ltd v Westville Shipping Co Ltd* [1923] A.C. 773 at 781 (Lord Atkinson).

[47]   See para.2-011.

[48]   See para.2-017.

[49]   See para.2-023.

[50]   See para.2-038.

[51]   *Clough v London and North Western Railway Co* (1871) L.R. 7 Ex. 26 at 34 (Mellor J).

[52]   *Car and Universal Finance Co Ltd v Caldwell* [1965] 1 Q.B. 525 at 550 (Sellers LJ).

[53]   [1905] 1 K.B. 465.

have a right to rescind which was effected through repossessing property, the tort of conversion will not have been committed, because the act of repossession will rescind the contract so that legal title to the property would be restored to that person.[54] The issue of pleadings may constitute a sufficient act to rescind the contract, but only if the pleadings expressed an unequivocal intention to treat the contract as terminated, such as where the claimant seeks the recovery of property transferred under the contract, but not where the claimant seeks to recover the price for property which had been transferred.[55] Alternatively, if there is a dispute about the right to rescind and the claimant commences judicial proceedings to resolve the matter, the statement in the particulars of claim that the transaction has been or should be set aside will in itself be sufficient to rescind the contract.[56] Resisting an action for specific performance or damages and making a counterclaim will also rescind the contract.[57]

Where a party's conduct is equivocal as to whether or not they have elected to affirm or disaffirm the contract, subsequent conduct may be sufficient to resolve the ambiguity. In *Drake Insurance Plc v Provident Insurance Plc*[58] the claimant insurance company had purported to rescind a contract in respect of one of two vehicles which were insured with it. It is not possible to rescind a contract in part,[59] so it was consequently unclear whether or not the contract of insurance had been rescinded. Since, however, the claimant had issued a certificate of insurance and continued to receive insurance premiums in respect of both vehicles it was held that the contract of insurance had not been unequivocally rescinded.   **1-015**

As a general rule, the election to rescind must be communicated to the other party or parties to the contract[60] and communication to a third party will not be sufficient. So, for example, in *Moyce v Newington*[61] contacting the police was not an effective communication of the election to rescind a contract of sale to enable the vendor to recover title to a flock of sheep.   **1-016**

Exceptionally, however, a contract can be rescinded at Common Law even though there has been no effective communication of the election to the other party to the contract. This was recognised in *Car and Universal Finance Co Ltd v Caldwell*[62] where Caldwell wished to rescind a contract to sell a car which he had been induced to sell as the result of a fraudulent misrepresentation, but he could not trace the purchaser of the vehicle who had deliberately absconded. It was held to be sufficient to rescind the contract that he had notified both the Automobile Association (AA) and the police that he wished them to assist him in finding the car. Such dispensation of the requirement of communication to the other party to the   **1-017**

---

54 See para.4-024. If the claimant has a right to rescind in Equity, repossession of the property would still constitute conversion because the claimant would not have an immediate legal right to the possession of the property in such circumstances.
55 *Clough v London and North Western Railway Co* (1871) L.R. 7 Ex. 26 at 36 (Mellor J).
56 *TSB Bank Plc v Camfield* [1995] 1 W.L.R. 430 at 438 (Roch LJ).
57 *Clough v London and North Western Railway Co* (1871) L.R. 7 Ex. 26.
58 [2003] EWCA Civ 1834; [2004] 1 Lloyd's Rep. 268 at [98] (Rix LJ) at [183] (Pill LJ) CA.
59 [2004] 1 Lloyd's Rep. 268 at [103] (Rix LJ). See para.4-008.
60 *Reese River Silver Mining Co Ltd v Smith* (1869) 4 H.L. 64 at 74 (Lord Hatherley); *Scarfe v Jardine* (1882) 7 App. Cas. 345 at 361 (Lord Blackburn); *Car and Universal Finance Co Ltd v Caldwell* [1965] 1 Q.B. 525 at 549 (Sellers LJ).
61 (1878) 4 Q.B.D. 32.
62 [1965] 1 Q.B. 525. See also *Newtons of Wembley Ltd v Williams* [1965] 1 Q.B. 560.

contract will only be possible if three conditions are satisfied:[63]

(i) communication to the other party to the contract must be impracticable, such as where the other party has disappeared;[64]

(ii) the misconduct of the other party to the contract prevents them from asserting a right to receive communication of the decision to rescind the contract; and

(iii) once the party who wishes to rescind the contract has discovered the facts which give them the right to rescind they must act promptly and take all reasonable steps to demonstrate a public unequivocal intention to rescind the contract.

1-018   These conditions were satisfied in *Car and Universal Finance Co Ltd v Caldwell* because the purchaser of the car had defrauded the vendor and, by absconding, had made it impossible for the vendor to communicate with him. Communication to the police and the AA was regarded as sufficient notification to the world at large.

1-019   Although the rule in *Car and Universal Finance Co Ltd v Caldwell* is exceptional, it is unclear when it will be engaged. It might simply be confined to where the vitiating factor which justifies rescission of the contract is fraudulent misrepresentation, because the misconduct of the defendant justifies the removal of the obligation to communicate the election to rescind.[65] A rule insisting on communication of the decision to rescind in such circumstances would mean that a fraudster could easily avoid rescission of the contract by avoiding contact with the claimant.[66] Even where a contract is voidable by virtue of fraudulent misrepresentation, the disapplication of the communication requirement protects the vendor of the property from the consequences of fraud at the expense of a third party purchaser from the fraudster, although such a purchaser would be protected from the consequences of rescission if they had purchased the property in good faith before the contract had been rescinded.[67]

1-020   A party will retain the right to rescind the contract at Common Law as long as there has been no election either to affirm or disaffirm the contract[68] and rescission is not otherwise barred. Once a party has elected to rescind the contract, the election is irrevocable.[69]

1-021   **Fundamental features of rescission in Equity**   Rescission in Equity is a remedy[70] which is conferred by the court in the exercise of judicial discretion.[71] Although a claimant must still elect for the contract to be rescinded, this is simply a decision

---

[63] [1965] 1 Q.B. 525 at 550 (Sellers LJ).

[64] See *Empresa Cubana de Fletes v Lagonisi Shipping Co Ltd* [1971] Q.B. 488 at 505 (Lord Denning MR).

[65] *Spriggs v Wessington Court School Ltd* [2005] 1 Lloyd's Rep. I.R. 474 at 483 (Stanley Burnton J).

[66] *Car and Universal Finance Co Ltd v Caldwell* [1965] 1 Q.B. 525 at 550 (Sellers LJ).

[67] See para.3-040.

[68] *Clough v London and North Western Railway Co* (1871) L.R. 7 Ex 26 at 35 (Mellor J).

[69] *Clough v London and North Western Railway Co* (1871) L.R. 7 Ex 26 at 34 (Mellor J).

[70] *Dunbar Bank Plc v Nadeem* [1998] 3 All E.R. 876 at 884 (Millett LJ).

[71] *Spence v Crawford* [1939] 3 All E.R. 271 at 288 (Lord Wright). Cf. *Shalson v Russo* [2003] EWHC 1637 (Ch); [2005] Ch. 281 at [122] where Rimer J assumed that even rescission in Equity is an act of the parties, rather than depending on an order of the court being made. In *SK Shipping Europe Ltd v Capital VLCC 3 Corp* [2022] EWCA Civ 231; [2022] 2 All E.R. (Comm) 784 at [89] Males LJ noted that it was controversial that rescission for misrepresentation was not a self-help remedy. But rescission for negligent misrepresentation, which was in issue in that case, occurs in Equity rather than at Common Law. Nonetheless, damages in lieu of rescission by s.2(2) of the Misrepresenta-

made by the claimant as to whether an application should be made to the court. Rescission in Equity can only be effected by order of the court, although once the order has been made it will operate retrospectively to nullify the contract *ab initio*. When making an application to the court the claimant can either expressly ask for the court to rescind the contract or this may be implicit, for example in an application to commence proceeding to recover property from the defendant.[72]

It follows that strictly there is no right to rescind a contract in Equity, as compared **1-022** with the Common Law. Rescission in Equity is a form of equitable relief which is determined and effected by the court.[73] The judge has a discretion both as to whether to order rescission and, if so, as to the nature and extent of that relief, which might be subject to conditions.[74] In exercising this discretion, however, the courts are not simply concerned to reach a just result. The discretion is exercised with reference to recognised principles, so it is still correct to describe the claimant as having a right to rescission if an equitable vitiating factor is identified and none of the bars to rescission apply.[75]

Exceptionally even in Equity the claimant may elect to rescind a contract and the **1-023** rescission will take effect automatically. This will only be relevant where the claimant has been induced to enter into the contract as the result of a fraudulent misrepresentation.[76] Since the jurisdiction to rescind a contract in Equity for fraudulent misrepresentation is concurrent with the jurisdiction to rescind a contract at Common Law, it should follow that communication of the election to rescind should automatically be effective to rescind the contract in Equity as well.[77] On communicating an election to rescind such a contract, an equitable proprietary interest will be created in the property which had been transferred to the defendant pursuant to the contract so that the property will be held on trust for the claimant.[78] It should also follow that rescission in Equity for duress should be automatic following communication of the intention to rescind.

In addition to Equity's concurrent jurisdiction to recognise rescission on the **1-024** grounds recognised at Common Law, there is an exclusive equitable jurisdiction of rescission in Equity where a contract has been induced by non-fraudulent misrepresentation,[79] or undue influence,[80] or where the defendant has procured the

---

tion Act 1967 (see para.3-44, below) is available for innocent or negligent misrepresentation where the contract "has been" rescinded, presumably by one of the parties as a self-help remedy.

72   *Shalson v Russo* [2003] EWHC 1637 (Ch); [2005] Ch. 281 at [120] (Rimer J).

73   *Erlanger v New Sombrero Phosphate Co* (1878) 3 App. Cas. 1218 at 1278 (Lord Blackburn); *Spence v Crawford* [1939] 3 All E.R. 271 at 288 (Lord Wright).

74   *Cheese v Thomas* [1994] 1 W.L.R. 129 at 137 (Sir Donald Nicholls VC); *Johnson v EBS Pensioner Trustees Ltd* [2002] Lloyd's Rep. P.N. 309 at [79] (Dyson LJ); *Hurstanger Ltd v Wilson* [2007] EWCA Civ 299 at [38]; [2007] 1 W.L.R. 2351 at [48] (Tuckey LJ).

75   *Lagunas Nitrate Co v Lagunas Syndicate* [1899] 2 Ch. 392 at 457 (Rigby LJ); *Spence v Crawford* [1939] 3 All E.R. 271 at 281 (Lord Thankerton).

76   *TSB Bank Plc v Camfield* [1995] 1 W.L.R. 430 at 438–439 (Roch LJ): although that case concerned non-fraudulent misrepresentation it was assumed that rescission took effect by the claimant's act of election. But the jurisdiction to rescind for non-fraudulent misrepresentation lies in the exclusive rather than concurrent jurisdiction of the court and should not be automatic following communication.

77   This is the position in Australia. See *Alati v Kruger* (1955) 94 C.L.R. 216 at 223 (Dixon CJ).

78   *El Ajou v Dollar Land Holdings Plc* [1993] 3 All E.R. 717 at 734 (Millett J). See further para.4-026.

79   See para.2-014.

80   See para.2-029.

contract in breach of the defendant's fiduciary duty,[81] or where the contract can be considered to be an unconscionable bargain.[82]

1-025 Before the contract is rescinded by the court the claimant will only have an equity to rescind if one of the equitable vitiating factors applies. This gives the claimant an entitlement to apply to the court for an order to rescind the contract.[83] Where the contract is rescinded in Equity by the court a condition will be imposed to ensure that the parties are restored substantially to their original positions.

1-026 **Fusion of rescission at Common Law and in Equity** It is clear that the orthodox analysis of the law of rescission is that the rules relating to rescission differ depending on whether the jurisdiction to rescind is asserted at Common Law or in Equity. Following the enactment of the Judicature Acts of 1873 and 1875 the administration of Common Law and Equity was fused, but this was not intended to effect a fusion of the substantive rules. Since the enactment of the Judicature Acts, numerous cases have recognised the continued difference between the operation of rescission at Common Law and Equity.[84] The key difference in the application of these rules is that rescission at Common Law is effected by the election of the party seeking rescission of the contract,[85] whereas rescission in Equity is effected by a court order, with the court having a discretion to determine whether rescission is appropriate and, if it is, what the conditions for rescission should be.[86] Further, different grounds for rescission at Common Law and in Equity continue to exist.[87]

1-027 Despite this continued recognition of the different rules on rescission dependent on whether the right to rescind is asserted at Common Law or in Equity, there are cases where the courts have assumed that all cases of rescission involve self-help,[88] so that rescission is effective on the claimant's election even if the trigger for rescission occurs in Equity. This analysis has been extended to rescission for fraudulent or non-fraudulent misrepresentation, even though rescission for the latter ground forms part of the court's exclusive rather than concurrent jurisdiction.[89]

1-028 In fact, the Judicature Act 1873 itself might have operated to ensure that the equitable rules of rescission prevailed over those of the Common Law, so that all rescission would be effected by order of the court. This is because that Act provided that where there is a conflict or variance between the rules of Equity and the Com-

---

[81] See para.2-042.

[82] See para.2-034.

[83] *Phillips v Phillips* (1861) 4 De G. F. and J. 208 at 218; 45 E.R. 1164 at 1167 (Lord Westbury); *Goldsworthy v Bricknell* [1987] Ch. 378 at 409 (Nourse LJ).

[84] Including *Erlanger v The New Sombrero Phosphate Co* (1878) 3 App. Cas. 1218 at 1278 (Lord Blackburn); *Spence v Crawford* [1939] 3 All E.R. 271 at 290 (Lord Wright); *O'Sullivan v Management Agency and Music Ltd* [1985] Q.B. 428 at 457 (Dunn LJ).

[85] *Car and Universal Finance Co Ltd v Caldwell* [1965] 1 Q.B. 525.

[86] *Lagunas Nitrate Co v Lagunas Syndicate* [1899] 2 Ch. 392 at 457 (Rigby LJ); *Spence v Crawford* [1939] 3 All E.R. 271 at 280 (Lord Thankerton); *Johnson v EBS Pensioner Trustees Ltd* [2002] Lloyd's Rep. P.N. 309 at [79] (Dyson LJ); *Drake Insurance Plc v Provident Insurance Plc* [2003] Lloyd's Rep. 781 at 788 (Moore-Bick J). *Hurstanger Ltd v Wilson* [2007] EWCA Civ 299 at [48] (Tuckey LJ).

[87] But note *Halpern v Halpern (No.2)* [2008] Q.B. 88 at [70] where Carnwath LJ acknowledged that there should be no difference in the operation of the vitiating factors regardless of whether rescission occurred at Common Law or in Equity.

[88] See *O'Sullivan v Management Agency and Music Ltd* [1985] Q.B. 428 at 457 where Dunn LJ approved a dictum of Dixon CJ in the Australian case of *Alati v Kruger* (1955) 94 C.L.R. 216 at 223; *Shalson v Russo* [2003] EWHC 1637 (Ch); [2005] Ch. 281 at [122] (Rimer J).

[89] *TSB Bank Plc v Camfield* [1995] 1 W.L.R. 430 at 438–439 (Roch LJ); *Shalson v Russo* [2003] EWHC 1637 (Ch); [2005] Ch. 281 at [122] (Rimer J).

mon Law with reference to the same matter, the rules of Equity will prevail.[90] This could be interpreted to mean that, where there is a concurrent jurisdiction to rescind in Equity and the Common Law, the equitable rules should apply to the extent that they conflict. This interpretation of the legislation was acknowledged by Carnwath LJ in *Halpern v Halpern (No.2)*[91] where, in a case concerning rescission of a contract for duress, it was recognised that rescission for duress, which takes place at Common Law, should be subject to the more flexible, equitable interpretation of the bar that rescission will be denied if the claimant cannot restore the defendant to the defendant's pre-contractual position, so that rescission would not be barred if the claimant could restore the defendant substantially to their pre-contractual position.[92]

Some commentators have suggested that the rules of rescission at Common Law and in Equity should be considered to have been fused, with the Common Law rules prevailing, so that rescission is always a self-help remedy.[93] Although the matter remains controversial, it appears that the state of English law is such that a distinction is preserved between rescission at Common Law and in Equity. It has been suggested that this distinction survives the Judicature Acts because the differences between the two jurisdictions is not a consequence of differences in the application of rules but are simply consequences of the different mechanisms employed by the Common Law and Equity to effect rescission, so that there is no reason for the equitable rules of rescission to prevail over those of the Common Law.[94] The more restrictive approach to rescission at Common Law has been defended as proportionate and justified,[95] because such self-help rescission is defensible where the defendant's conduct is particularly bad or the commercial context calls for this mechanism of rescission without the need for rescission to be effected by the court.[96] Nevertheless, the limitations of rescission at Common Law are difficult to defend, especially when compared with the more flexible equitable jurisdiction. Consequently, the equitable jurisdiction should be preferred, so that all rescission should be effected by means of a judicial order to which terms can be attached if necessary, rather than be treated simply as a self-help remedy.[97] This is not, however, the state of the law of recission yet.

1-029

---

[90] Judicature Act 1873 s.25(11). See now Senior Courts Act 1981 s.49.

[91] [2008] Q.B. 88 at [70].

[92] See para.3-014. In *Ruttle Plant Hire Ltd v Secretary of State for the Environment Food and Rural Affairs* [2007] EWHC 2870 (TCC) at [90], Ramsay J recognised that the claimant could pursue a claim for duress without being required to offer counter-restitution as a condition of the claimant seeking rescission. He appeared to assume that rescission would arise in Equity for duress because the grant of the remedy of rescission and the requirement of counter-restitution is a matter for the court. See also *Islington LBC v UKCAC* [2006] EWCA Civ 340 at [26] (Dyson LJ).

[93] See, e.g. A. Burrows, *The Law of Restitution*, 3rd edn (Oxford: Oxford University Press, 2011), p.15.

[94] D. O'Sullivan, S. Elliott and R. Zakrzewski, *The Law of Rescission*, 3rd edn (Oxford: Oxford University Press, 2023), para.10.13.

[95] D. O'Sullivan, S. Elliott and R. Zakrzewski, *The Law of Rescission*, 3rd edn (Oxford: Oxford University Press, 2023), para.10.17.

[96] Cf. J. O'Sullivan, "Rescission as a Self-Help Remedy: A Critical Analysis" (2000) 59 C.L.J. 509 at 528 who argues that self-help rescission at Common Law should be abolished and the equitable approach should replace it.

[97] This was assumed by Dyson LJ in *Islington LBC v UKCAC* [2006] EWCA Civ 340 at [26]. The distinction between rescission at Common Law and in Equity would continue to be relevant, however, even if the mechanism for rescission was assimilated, because the proprietary consequences of rescission at Common Law and in Equity are distinct. See para.4-023.

CHAPTER 2

THE GROUNDS FOR RESCISSION

Impaired consent   In *Johnson v Agnew*[1] Lord Wilberforce recognised that rescis-   **2-001**
sion may arise in cases of mistake, fraud or lack of consent. But if a party did not
consent to enter into a contract they cannot be regarded as being a party to that
contract, since the key requirement for participation in a contract, namely voluntari-
ness, will be absent; consequently the contract will be rendered void.[2] The preferable view is that a contract will be voidable where a party has factually consented
to enter into the transaction but their consent can be considered to have been
impaired by virtue of some defect operating at the time the contract was formed,
so that the contract may not have been properly made. This may be due to mistake
or fraud, as Lord Wilberforce recognised, but also for a number of other reasons.

I.   MISREPRESENTATION

Key features of misrepresentation[3]   A contract will be voidable for misrepre-   **2-002**
sentation where an untrue statement or assertion is made by one party, which is
relied on by the representee, who is induced to enter into a contract as a result. The
representee can rescind the contract in Equity for misrepresentation regardless of
whether the misrepresentation was made fraudulently, negligently or innocently,
although, as will be seen, the representor's state of mind will affect what needs to
be established before the contract can be rescinded.[4] A contract can only be
rescinded at Common Law for fraudulent misrepresentation.[5] The contract can be
rescinded for misrepresentation even where it has been executed as long as the
representee would otherwise be entitled to do so without proving fraud.[6] The courts
should not be too ready to find a misrepresentation, in part because of the drastic
consequences of a contract being rescinded.[7]

Misrepresentation as term of contract   If the representation is incorporated as   **2-003**
a term of the contract, the representee can either rescind the contract, if they would

---

[1]   [1980] A.C. 367 at 392.
[2]   See para.2-038.
[3]   For more detailed analysis of the law on misrepresentation see J. Cartwright, *Misrepresentation,
      Mistake and Non-Disclosure*, 6th edn (London: Sweet & Maxwell, 2022), Pt I; D. O'Sullivan, S. El-
      liott and R. Zakrzewski, *The Law of Rescission*, 3rd edn (Oxford: Oxford University Press, 2023),
      Ch.4; H.G. Beale (ed), *Chitty on Contracts*, 35th edn (London: Sweet & Maxwell, 2023), Ch.9.
[4]   See para.2-007.
[5]   See para.2-011.
[6]   Misrepresentation Act 1967 s.1(b).
[7]   *SK Shipping Europe Ltd v Capital VLCC 3 Corp* [2022] EWCA Civ 231; [2022] 2 All E.R. (Comm)
      784 at [34] (Males LJ).

be entitled to do so without proving fraud,[8] or sue for damages for breach of the term.[9]

2-004 **Consequences other than rescission** Where the term has not been incorporated as a term of the contract, the representee will have other claims as well as for rescission. Where the misrepresentation was fraudulent the representee could sue the representor for damages in the tort of deceit.[10] Where the misrepresentation was negligent, the representee may sue the representor for damages for negligent misrepresentation[11] or by virtue of the Misrepresentation Act 1967 s.2(1), which applies where the misrepresentation was made other than fraudulently, save where the misrepresentor can prove that they had reasonable grounds for believing and did believe up to the time when the contract was made that the representation was true. Where the representation was made innocently the representee has no right to damages, but damages may be awarded through the exercise of a judicial discretion in lieu of rescission.[12]

2-005 **Ambit of rescission** Typically, only the contract which has been made as a result of the misrepresentation will be voidable, but in some contexts other contracts may be voidable as well. So, for example, where a purchaser acquires two lots of property at an auction, having been induced to bid for one lot as the result of an innocent misrepresentation, usually only that contract will be voidable, save where both contracts were to the knowledge of both parties interdependent.[13] Where an original contract has been induced by misrepresentation, a substitute contract may be avoided as well where, for example, the original representation can be considered to have been repeated and so induced the substitute contract also.[14]

2-006 **Representation** A representation is a statement or assertion of an existing fact.[15] It appears that a representation as to the law will also suffice,[16] since a mistake of law has now been recognised as a ground of restitution within the law of unjust enrichment.[17] The representation may be express or implied. For example, in *Laurence v Lexcourt Holdings Ltd*,[18] a reference to premises as "offices" implied the existence of planning permission to use the property for that purpose. A statement that a vendor is not aware of a defect in title implies that the vendor has taken reasonable steps to ascertain whether any defects existed.[19] Silence will generally not constitute a representation because there is generally no duty of disclosure,[20] even if the party who remained silent was aware of the other party's

---

8   Misrepresentation Act 1967 s.1(a). See para.2-014, for analysis of when a contract can be rescinded for a non-fraudulent misrepresentation.
9   See Ch.20.
10 *Derry v Peek* (1899) 14 App. Cas. 337; *Doyle v Olby (Ironmongers) Ltd* [1969] 2 Q.B. 158; *Weir v Area Estates Ltd* [2010] EWHC 398 (QB).
11 *Hedley Byrne and Co Ltd v Heller and Partners Ltd* [1964] A.C. 465.
12 Misrepresentation Act 1967 s.2(2). See para.3-044.
13 *Holliday v Lockwood* [1917] 2 Ch. 47.
14 *Yorkshire Bank Plc v Tinsley* [2004] EWCA Civ 816 at [18] (Longmore LJ).
15 *Spence v Crawford* [1939] 3 All E.R. 271.
16 *Pankhania v Hackney LBC* [2002] EWHC 2441 (Ch) at [58] (Rex Tedd QC); *Brennan v Bolt Burdon* [2005] Q.B. 303 at 317 (Bodey J).
17 *Kleinwort Benson Ltd v Lincoln CC* [1999] 2 A.C. 349.
18 [1978] 1 W.L.R. 1128. See also *Deutsche Bank v Unitech Global Ltd* [2013] EWCA Civ. 1372.
19 *William Sindall Plc v Cambridgeshire CC* [1994] 1 W.L.R. 1016 at 1025 (Hoffmann LJ).
20 *Turner v Green* [1895] 2 Ch. 205 at 209 (Chitty J). See para.2-017.

misapprehension. Where, however, there is a continuing representation which is subsequently falsified, silence on the part of the representor may then constitute a misrepresentation.[21] A representation made by a third party will be relevant if a party to the contract can be considered to have approved and adopted it and communicated this to the other party to the contract.[22]

Limits of representation   As a general rule sales talk, statements of opinion and statements as to the future are not relevant representations because they are not statements of existing fact. But in certain circumstances such statements will be treated as misrepresentations if untrue. So, for example, a fraudulent statement about the representor's opinion will constitute a misrepresentation because it relates to the fact of the representor's state of mind at the time the statement is made.[23] Similarly, a statement of opinion by a party who is in a good position to know the true facts might constitute an implied representation that that party knows of facts which justify the opinion[24] or has better access to the facts which justify the opinion,[25] but there is no general rule that by a party offering to contract they impliedly represent that they are able and willing to perform the contract.[26] In *Qatar Investment and Projects Development Holding Co v John Eskenazi Ltd*[27] a representation that the representor believed that ancient objects were authentic was held to be a misrepresentation because there was an absence of reasonable grounds for the expression of an emphatic or unqualified opinion. A statement as to the future will generally not be treated as a misrepresentation if the representation becomes untrue, because this cannot operate retrospectively to convert a misprediction as to the future into a misrepresentation of existing fact. Where, however, the representor makes a misrepresentation as to acts he will do in the future, knowing at the time the representation is made that they do not intend to perform such acts, this will constitute a misrepresentation of their present intention. So, in *Edgington v Fitzmaurice*[28] a statement in a company's prospectus that funds raised from the issue of shares would be used to complete building projects and to develop the company's business was a misrepresentation of the representor's intention at the time, since the representor actually intended the money to be used to enable the directors to discharge pressing liabilities.

2-007

False representation   The representation must be false at the time the representee relied on it to enter into the contract; it is not sufficient that the representation is

2-008

---

[21] See para.2-008. For consideration of the implications of a representation being continuous see *Cramaso LLP v Ogilvie-Grant* [2014] UKSC 9; [2014] A.C. 1093 (contract made between representor and a third party but the original representee acted as agent for the third party so that the representation continued to be made to him, but in a different capacity).

[22] *Vald Nielsen Holding A/S v Baldorino* [2019] EWHC 1926 (Comm) at [382] (Jacobs J); *Ivy Technology Ltd v Martin* [2022] EWHC 1218 (Comm) at [351] (Henshaw J).

[23] *Edgington v Fitzmaurice* (1885) 29 Ch D. 459 at 483 (Bowen LJ).

[24] *Smith v Land and House Property Corp* (1884) 28 Ch D. 7 at 15 (Bowen LJ); *Foodco UK LLP (t/a Muffin Break) v Henry Root Developments Ltd* [2010] EWHC 358 (Ch) at [202] (Lewison J).

[25] *Brown v Raphael* [1958] Ch. 636 at 642 (Lord Evershed MR).

[26] *SK Shipping Europe Ltd v Capital VLCC 3 Corp* [2022] EWCA Civ 231; [2022] 2 All E.R. (Comm) 784 at [48] (Males LJ). Sometimes there may be an implied representation as to the representor's honesty in relation to the transaction: [2022] EWCA Civ 231 at [51] (Males LJ).

[27] [2022] EWHC 3023 (Comm).

[28] *Edgington v Fitzmaurice* (1885) 29 Ch D. 459.

false when it was made, if it had become true by the time the contract was made.[29] If the representation was substantially true at the time the contract was made it will not be a misrepresentation,[30] provided that the difference between what was represented and what was true would not have induced a reasonable person in the position of the claimant to enter into the contract.[31] A contract cannot be rescinded if a representation became false after the contract was made, because the representee will not have been induced to enter into the contract by reason of a misrepresentation.[32] If the representation was true when made but was then rendered false before the contract was made, this will constitute a relevant misrepresentation if the representation can be considered to have continued.[33] For example, in *With v O'Flanagan*[34] a true representation was made about the turnover of a medical practice. Before the purchasers signed the contract of sale the turnover had fallen due to changes of circumstances, but these were not disclosed to the purchasers. The representation was held to continue until the contract was signed and, since at that point it had been falsified by the change of circumstances, a misrepresentation could be identified and the contract could be rescinded. A representation made in the course of contractual negotiations will normally continue until the contract has been concluded.[35]

2-009 **Reliance** A misrepresentation will only be relevant where the representee relied on it to enter into the contract. This is a subjective test which has regard to the effect of the representation on the representee who relied on it. Reliance will not be established where, for example, the representee knew that the representation was false by the time the contract was made, perhaps because the representor had corrected the error;[36] the representee was unaware that the representation, whether express or implied from conduct, had been made;[37] the representee had forgotten about the representation by the time the contract was made; the representee had interpreted the representation in such a way that it was actually true;[38] the representee relied on their own assumptions as to the interpretation of the representation[39] or relied on the assessment of a third party as to the accuracy of the representation.[40] The negligence of the representee in failing to discover the truth will not generally prevent the representee from rescinding the contract, regardless

---

[29] *Briess v Woolley* [1954] A.C. 333 at 353 (Lord Tucker).
[30] *Mckeown v Boudard-Peveril Gear Co* (1896) 65 L.J. Ch. 735; *With v O'Flanagan* [1936] Ch. 575 at 581 (Lord Wright MR); *Ivy Technology Ltd v Martin* [2022] EWHC 1218 (Comm) at [357] (Henshaw J).
[31] *Avon Insurance v Swire Fraser Ltd* [2000] EWHC 230 (Comm); [2000] 1 All E.R. (Comm) 573 at [17] (Rix J).
[32] *Manifest Shipping Co Ltd v Uni-Polaris Insurance Co Ltd (The Star Sea)* [2003] 1 A.C. 469.
[33] *Briess v Woolley* [1954] A.C. 333. See also *Erlson Precision Holdings Ltd (formerly GG132 Ltd) v Hampson Industries Plc* [2011] EWHC 1137 (Comm).
[34] [1936] Ch. 575.
[35] *Ivy Technology Ltd v Martin* [2022] EWHC 1218 (Comm) at [355] (Henshaw J).
[36] *Assicurazioni Generali v Arab Insurance Group* [2002] EWCA Civ 1642; [2003] 1 All E.R. (Comm) 140 at [63] (Clarke LJ).
[37] *Marme Inversiones 2007 SL v Natwest Markets Plc* [2019] EWHC 366 (Comm); *Leeds City Council v Barclays Bank Plc* [2021] EWHC 363 (Comm); [2021] Q.B. 1027 at [102] (Cockerill J).
[38] *Smith v Chadwick* (1884) 9 App. Cas. 187.
[39] *Peekay Intermark Ltd v Australia and New Zealand Banking Group Ltd* [2006] EWCA Civ 386 at [52] (Moore-Bick LJ).
[40] *Attwood v Small* (1836) 6 Cl. and F. 232; 7 E.R. 684.

of whether the representation was made fraudulently or innocently.[41] Where the representee was suspicious about the truth of the representation but failed to investigate they will not be considered to have relied on the representation.[42] In *Zurich Insurance Co Plc v Hayward*,[43] however, the insurer to a compromise settlement was able to rescind it on the ground that the claims made by the other party were fraudulent, even though the insurer had not believed that the claims were true but feared that the court might believe them. This was because it was held that it was not a specific requirement that the representee believed that the representation was true. It was sufficient that the representation had induced the settlement to be made, and this could be established on the facts because of the insurer's belief that a judge might believe the misrepresentation.

Representation induced the contract   The representation must have operated as   **2-010**
a material inducement for the representee to enter into the contract;[44] this involves a causal link between the representation by the defendant and the conduct of the claimant in entering into the contract.[45] The key question is not what the representee would have done if they had known the truth, but what they would have done had the representation not been made at all.[46] It is sufficient that the representation was an inducement without it necessarily being the sole or predominant inducement,[47] but it must be shown that the representee would not have entered into the contract but for the misrepresentation,[48] save where the representation was fraudulent.[49] Whether a person who entered into a contract was induced to do so by the representation is a question of fact, but inducement can be inferred once the representation has been proved to be false, if the representation would objectively have been likely to induce a person to enter into the contract.[50] The burden is then placed on the misrepresentor to prove that the misrepresentee had not relied on the misrepresentation.[51] If the representation is considered to have been of no real

---

[41] *Standard Chartered Bank v Pakistan National Shipping Corp (No.2)* [2003] 1 A.C. 959 at 967 (Lord Hoffmann).

[42] *Redgrave v Hurd* (1881) 20 Ch D. 1 at 14 (Jessel MR); 23 (Baggallay LJ).

[43] [2016] UKSC 48; [2017] A.C. 142. See P.S. Davies and W.Day, "A mistake in the law of misrepresentation" [2019] L.M.C.L.Q. 390

[44] *Ross River Ltd v Cambridge City Football Club Ltd* [2007] EWHC 2115 (Ch) at [193] (Briggs J).

[45] *Leeds City Council v Barclays Bank Plc* [2021] EWHC 363 (Comm), [2021] Q.B. 1027 at [144] (Cockerill J). See generally N. Verbatsen, "Causation in misrepresentation: historical or counterfactual? And 'but for' what?" (2021) 137 L.Q.R. 503.

[46] *SK Shipping Europe Ltd v Capital VLCC 3 Corp* [2022] EWCA Civ 231; [2022] 2 All E.R. (Comm) 784 at [61] (Males LJ).

[47] *Attwood v Small* (1836) 6 Cl. and F. 232; 7 E.R. 684; *Edgington v Fitzmaurice* (1885) 29 Ch. D. 458; *Assicurazioni Generali v Arab Insurance Group* [2002] EWCA Civ 1642; [2003] 1 All E.R. (Comm) 140 at [59] (Clarke LJ); *SK Shipping Europe Ltd v Capital VLCC 3 Corp* [2022] EWCA Civ 231; [2022] 2 All E.R. (Comm) 784 at [61] (Males LJ)

[48] *Assicurazioni Generali v Arab Insurance Group* [2002] EWCA Civ 1642; [2003] 1 All E.R. (Comm) 140.

[49] *BV Nederlandse Industrie Van Eiprodukten v Rembrandt Enterprises Inc* [2019] EWCA Civ 596; [2020] Q.B. 551. See para.2-013.

[50] *Smith v Chadwick* (1884) 9 App. Cas. 187 at 196 (Lord Blackburn); *Ross River Ltd v Cambridge City Football Club Ltd* [2007] EWHC 2115 (Ch) at [200] (Briggs J); *SK Shipping Europe Ltd v Capital VLCC 3 Corp* [2022] EWCA Civ 231; [2022] 2 All E.R. (Comm) 784 at [62] (Males LJ).

[51] *Smith v Chadwick* (1884) 9 App. Cas. 187 at 196 (Lord Blackburn); *Standard Chartered Bank v Pakistan National Shipping Corp (No.2)* [2003] 1 A.C. 959 at 967 (Lord Hoffmann); *Ross River Ltd v Cambridge City Football Club Ltd* [2007] EWHC 2115 (Ch); [2008] 1 All E.R. 1004 at [200] (Briggs J); *Dadourian v Simms* [2009] EWCA Civ 169; [2009] 1 Lloyd's Rep. 601 at [99] (Arden

significance the court will decline to hold that it was one of the reasons which induced the contract.[52]

2-011   **Fraudulent misrepresentation**   It is important to distinguish between fraudulent and non-fraudulent misrepresentations. This is because rescission will be more readily available where the representation was fraudulent because of a policy of deterring such misconduct on the part of the representor. Fraud for these purposes means that the representor knew that the representation was untrue, had no belief in the truth of the representation, was wilfully blind, suspected that it might be untrue or was indifferent[53] as to whether or not it was true.[54] A representation will be fraudulent even though the representor had no intention to cheat or injure the representee and does not require proof of dishonesty in a criminal sense.[55] A representation will not be fraudulent if the representor honestly believed it to be true, although if this is an unreasonable belief the representation is more likely to be treated as fraudulent.[56] A transaction will be voidable for fraud even though the transaction was initially legitimate and the fraud arose subsequently.[57] A fraudulent misrepresentation constitutes a ground for rescission both at Common Law and in Equity.[58]

2-012   If a misrepresentation was made fraudulently it is more likely that representations of opinion and intention will be treated as grounds for rescission because the representor's conscious untruth makes it more likely that they had made a misrepresentation as to the state of their own mind.[59] A failure to reveal that a true representation of fact is no longer true will be fraudulent if the representor knew of the change of facts and their significance.[60] Where the contract is rescinded at Common Law for fraudulent misrepresentation it is not necessary to communicate the intention to rescind to the representee.[61] The statutory discretion to award damages in lieu of rescission under the Misrepresentation Act 1967 is not available where the representation is fraudulent.[62] The bars to rescission are

---

LJ); *Raffeisen Zentralbank Österreich AG v The Royal Bank of Scotland Plc* [2010] EWHC 1392 (Comm) at [153] (Christopher Clarke J).

52   *Vald Nielsen Holding A/S v Baldorino* [2019] EWHC 1926 (Comm) at [157] (Jacobs J).

53   *Pisante v Logothetis* [2022] EWHC 161 (Comm) at [35] (Andrew Baker J) (reckless indifference encompasses both indifference as to the truth of the representation and as to how it will be understood by the other party).

54   *Derry v Peek* (1889) 14 App. Cas. 337 at 374 (Lord Herschell). See *Greenridge Luton One Ltd v Kempton Investments Ltd* [2016] EWHC 91 (Ch).

55   *Vald Nielsen Holding A/S v Baldorino* [2019] EWHC 1926 (Comm) at [147] (Jacobs J); *Bell v Singh* [2022] EWHC 3272 (Comm) at [154] (Nigel Cooper KC).

56   *Derry v Peek* (1889) 14 App. Cas. 337 at 375–376 (Lord Herschell).

57   *The National Crime Agency v Robb* [2014] EWHC 4384 (Ch); [2015] Ch. 520 at [5] (Etherton C).

58   See para.1-010 and para.1-021 for analysis of the different processes of rescission at Law and in Equity.

59   *Edgington v Fitzmaurice* (1885) 29 Ch D. 458 at 483 (Bowen LJ); *West London Commercial Bank v Kitson* (1884) 13 Q.B.D. 360 at 363 (Bowen LJ).

60   *Foodco UK LLP (t/a Muffin Break) v Henry Root Developments Ltd* [2010] EWHC 358 (Ch) at [2014] (Lewison J).

61   *Car and Universal Finance Co Ltd v Caldwell* [1965] Q.B. 525. See para.1-017.

62   See para.3-044.

interpreted more restrictively where the representation is fraudulent.[63] The right to rescind cannot be excluded where the representation was fraudulent.[64]

The representee must prove by reference to the ordinary civil standard of proof **2-013** that a fraudulent misrepresentation has been made and that the representee was induced to enter the contract by virtue of the fraudulent representation,[65] although, since the allegation of fraud is very serious, strong and clear evidence of the fraud must be adduced.[66] Where the representation was fraudulent the misrepresentation must have materially influenced the representee's decision to enter into the contract, in the sense that the representation has been actively present in the representee's mind, but it need not be a but for cause of the representee having entered into the contract; it is sufficient that it influenced the representee.[67] There is an evidential presumption of fact, which is difficult to rebut,[68] that the representee was induced by the fraudulent misrepresentation to enter into the contract if the representor intended the representee to enter into the contract,[69] but this only applies where the claimant has established that they were aware of the representation being made.[70]

Non-fraudulent misrepresentation Where the representor made the representa- **2-014** tion negligently or innocently, with no conscious awareness that the representation was untrue, rescission of the contract will only be possible in Equity.[71] A contract induced by a non-fraudulent representation can be rescinded even though the representor did not intend the representation to induce the contract to be made, since it is not even necessary to show that the representor was aware that they had made a representation.[72]

The right to rescind for non-fraudulent misrepresentation can be excluded by the **2-015** contract[73] or the contract may prevent the conditions from arising to enable the representee to rescind, such as a clause which states that no representations had been made[74] or that there had not been any reliance on any representation.[75] Any such clause which purports to exclude rescission for misrepresentation either expressly

---

63 See, e.g. para.3-013.
64 *HIH Casualty and General Insurance v Chase Manhattan Bank* [2003] UKHL 6; [2003] 2 Lloyd's Rep. 61 at [16] (Lord Bingham of Cornhill) and [121] (Lord Scott of Foscote).
65 *BV Nederlandse Industrie Van Eiprodukten v Rembrandt Enterprises Inc* [2019] EWCA Civ 596; [2020] Q.B. 551.
66 *Smith New Court Securities Ltd v Scrimgeour Vickers (Asset Management) Ltd* [1997] A.C. 254 at 274 (Lord Steyn). Before a finding of fraud can be made it must be pleaded and put in cross-examination to the person who is accused of having made the representation: *Haringey LBC v Hines* [2010] EWCA Civ 1111; [2011] H.L.R.6.
67 *BV Nederlandse Industrie Van Eiprodukten v Rembrandt Enterprises Inc* [2019] EWCA Civ 596; [2020] Q.B. 551 at [32] (Longmore LJ).
68 *BV Nederlandse Industrie Van Eiprodukten v Rembrandt Enterprises Inc* [2019] EWCA Civ 596; [2020] Q.B. 551 at [44] (Longmore LJ); *Bell v Singh* [2022] EWHC 3272 (Comm) at [213] (Nigel Cooper KC).
69 *BV Nederlandse Industrie Van Eiprodukten v Rembrandt Enterprises Inc* [2019] EWCA Civ 596; [2020] Q.B. 551 at [25] (Longmore LJ).
70 *Leeds City Council v Barclays Bank Plc* [2021] EWHC 363 (Comm); [2021] Q.B. 1027 at [140] (Cockerill J).
71 *Redgrave v Hurd* (1881) 20 Ch D. 1.
72 *Spice Girls Ltd v Apilla World Services BV* [2002] EWCA Civ 15 at [57].
73 *HIH Casualty and General Insurance Ltd v Chase Manhattan Bank* [2003] 2 Lloyd's Rep. 61 at [9] (Lord Bingham).
74 *Cremdean Properties Ltd v Nash* (1977) 244 E.G. 547 at 551 (Bridge LJ). Cf. *William Sindall Plc v Cambridgeshire CC* [1994] 1 W.L.R. 1016 at 1034 (Hoffmann LJ) where clauses in a contract did not purport to exclude liability but related to whether there was a misrepresentation in the first place and so were not caught by the Misrepresentation Act 1967 s.3.

or impliedly will only be effective if it is fair and reasonable to have been included in the contract having regard to the circumstances which were, or ought reasonably to have been, known to or in the contemplation of the parties when the contract was made.[76] In determining what is fair and reasonable relevant factors include the relative strength of the bargaining position of the parties and whether the representee knew or ought to have known about the clause.[77] If the clause excluding rescission purports to exclude rescission for fraudulent misrepresentation it will not be reasonable as a whole; it cannot be interpreted in such a way as to confine its operation to excluding rescission for non-fraudulent misrepresentations only.[78] But such a clause is likely to be interpreted as not being intended to extend to fraudulent representations.[79] If the clause is a term in a consumer contract its validity is controlled by the Consumer Rights Act 2015 and turns on whether the clause is unfair within s.62 of that Act, by virtue of a significant imbalance in the parties' rights and obligations under the contract to the detriment of the consumer, and having regard to the subject matter of the contract, all the circumstances which existed when the term was agreed and to other terms and contracts.

2-016   **Misrepresentation and third parties**   Where the representee enters into a contract with the defendant as the result of a misrepresentation made by a third party, that contract can be rescinded if the representee can establish that the defendant had actual or constructive notice of the misrepresentation.[80] So, for example, where a wife has been induced to agree to the matrimonial home being used as security for a loan made by a bank to her husband, as a result of a misrepresentation made by the husband to the wife, the security transaction with the bank can be rescinded if it can be considered to have constructive notice of the misrepresentation because the transaction is not on its face to the wife's advantage and there was a substantial risk that the husband had made a misrepresentation to induce the wife to enter into the transaction.[81] Where, however, the bank can show that it had taken reasonable steps to ensure that the wife had not been induced to act by a misrepresentation then the contract cannot be rescinded, such as where it receives confirmation from a solicitor that the wife received legal advice before she entered into the transaction.[82]

II. NON-DISCLOSURE

2-017   **General principles**   Usually a failure by one party to a contract to disclose material facts to the other will not enable that other party to rescind the contract,[83] even if the first party is aware of the misapprehension of the other. This is consistent with

---

[75]   *Government of Zanzibar v British Aerospace (Lancaster House) Ltd* [2000] 1 W.L.R. 2333 at 2347 (Judge Raymond Jack QC).

[76]   Misrepresentation Act 1967 s.3. Reasonableness is defined by the Unfair Contract Terms Act 1977 s.11(1) and Sch.2. See *Walker v Boyle* [1982] 1 W.L.R. 495 at 507 (Dillon LJ).

[77]   Unfair Contract Terms Act 1977 Sch.2. See *FoodCo UK LLP v Henry Boot Developments Ltd* [2010] EWHC 358 (Ch); *Cleaver v Schyde Investments Ltd* [2011] EWCA Civ 929 at [38] (Etherton LJ).

[78]   *Thomas Witter Ltd v TBP Industries Ltd* [1996] 2 All E.R. 573 at 598 (Jacob J).

[79]   Cf. *Government of Zanzibar v British Aerospace (Lancaster House) Ltd* [2000] 1 W.L.R. 2333 at 2346 (Judge Raymond Jack QC).

[80]   *Barclays Bank Plc v O'Brien* [1994] 1 A.C. 180.

[81]   *Royal Bank of Scotland v Etridge (No.2)* [2002] A.C. 773.

[82]   *Royal Bank of Scotland v Etridge (No.2)* [2002] A.C. 773.

[83]   See *Smith v Hughes* (1871) L.R. 6 Q.B. 597; *Bell v Lever Bros Ltd* [1932] A.C. 161 at 227 (Lord Atkin).

fundamental principles of the law that there is no liability for an omission to act. There are, however, certain circumstances where non-disclosure may trigger the application of particular grounds of rescission. For example, where there is a continuing representation which is subsequently falsified, silence on the part of the representor may then constitute a misrepresentation;[84] a contract made with a fiduciary may be voidable for breach of fiduciary duty save where the fiduciary has disclosed material facts to the principal.[85] A contract can be rescinded specifically for non-disclosure where there is a duty of disclosure and the failure to disclose significant facts induced the other party to enter into the contract. The duty of disclosure will only arise in limited circumstances, notably sometimes in respect of contracts of insurance and surety contracts, but is also applicable as between people who are negotiating their entry into a partnership who are required to disclose all material facts.[86]

Contracts of insurance   Contracts of insurance have traditionally been described   **2-018** as *uberrimae fidei*, meaning that there was a duty of utmost good faith on the part of both the insurer and the insured, such that they must both disclose facts which were material to the decision to place or accept the risk or the insurer's assessment of the premium. Legislation has significantly adumbrated this duty of disclosure, such that there is now no duty of disclosure on the insurer and none on a consumer insured.[87] For the non-consumer insured there is now a duty to make a fair presentation of the risk to the insurer.[88] This requires the insured to dislose every material circumstance which they know or ought to know or, failing that, give the insurer sufficient information to put a prudent insurer on notice that it needs to make further enquiries for the purpose of revealing those material circumstances.[89] If this duty is breached and the breach was deliberate or reckless the insurer may rescind the policy and refuse any claims under it and need not repay the premiums;[90] in other cases the insurer may avoid the contract and refuse any claims only if, in the absence of the breach, they would not have entered the contract on any terms; but if the contract is avoided the premiums must be repaid.[91]

Surety contracts   Surety contracts are not regarded as *uberrimae fide* so that a   **2-019** creditor usually owes no duty to disclose material facts to an intended surety.[92] A creditor is, however, under a duty to disclose unusual features[93] of the transaction between the debtor and the creditor, or between the creditor and other creditors of the debtor, which make the contract materially different in a potentially disadvantageous way from that which the surety would naturally expect,[94] in that the matter makes the risk taken by the surety creditor more onerous. Failure to disclose unusual

---

[84] See para.2-008.
[85] *Gamatronic (UK) Ltd v Hamilton* [2016] EWHC 2225 (QB); [2017] B.C.C. 670. See para.2-045.
[86] *Conlon v Simms* [2006] EWCA Civ 1749; [2008] 1 W.L.R. 484 at [127]–[129] (Jonathan Parker LJ).
[87] Insurance Act 2015 s.2.
[88] Insurance Act 2015 s.3(1).
[89] Insurance Act 2015 s.3(4).
[90] Insurance Act 2015 Sch.1 para.2.
[91] Insurance Act 2015 Sch.1 para.4.
[92] *Seaton v Heath* [1899] 1 Q.B. 782 at 792 (Romer LJ); *North Shore Ventures Ltd v Anstead Holdings Inc* [2011] EWCA Civ 230; [2012] Ch. 31 at [29] (Sir Andrew Morritt C).
[93] See *North Shore Ventures Ltd v Anstead Holdings Inc* [2011] EWCA Civ 230; [2012] Ch. 31.
[94] *Hamilton v Watson* (1845) 12 Cl. and F. 109, 119 (Lord Campbell); *Lee v Jones* (1864) 17 C.B.N.S. 482 at 503 (Blackburn J); *Royal Bank of Scotland Plc v Etridge (No.2)* [2002] 2 A.C. 773 at [81] (Lord Nicholls) at [188] (Lord Scott); *Estate of Imorette Palmer (decd) v Cornerstone Investments*

facts will render the contract voidable at the option of the surety.[95] The creditor is not required to disclose facts or matters which are not unusual features of the contractual relationship between the creditor and the debtor or the creditor and other creditors of the debtor,[96] even if they are material and would have influenced the surety's decision to enter into the contract.[97] In *North Shore Ventures Ltd v Anstead Holdings Inc*[98] the creditor was consequently not under any obligation to disclose to the prospective surety that the creditor was under investigation by the Swiss authorities or that there was a risk that any funds associated with him might be frozen. There is no duty to disclose any unusual matters if the surety already knew of it, because the non-disclosure could not have induced the surety to enter into the contract.[99] But the creditor will not be excused from the duty to disclose an unusual matter simply because he reasonably believed that the surety already knew of it.[100]

III.   MISTAKE

2-020 **Mistake rendering contract void**   Where a contract has been made as a result of a fundamental common mistake shared by the parties, where the non-existence of a state of affairs which was assumed to exist renders the performance of the contract impossible, the contract will be void at Common Law.[101] Where one party has made a unilateral mistake as to the identity of the other party to the contract or the subject matter of the contract,[102] that contract will also be void;[103] and similarly where the mistake related to the terms of the contract, but only then if the other party knew of the mistake.[104]

2-021 **Mistake in Equity**   For many years there was an equitable jurisdiction to rescind a contract for a common mistake which could be regarded as fundamental.[105] But this equitable jurisdiction was rejected by the Court of Appeal in *Great Peace Shipping Ltd v Tsalviris Salvage (International) Ltd*.[106] Certain cases decided before *Great Peace* had recognised an equitable jurisdiction to rescind a contract for a unilateral mistake where the other party had engaged in sharp practice or unconscionable conduct.[107] The existence of this jurisdiction to rescind for unilateral

---

95 *and Finance Co Ltd* [2007] UKPC 49 at [40]; *North Shore Ventures Ltd v Anstead Holdings Inc* [2011] EWCA Civ 230; [2012] Ch. 31 at [14] (Sir Andrew Morritt C).

95 *Royal Bank of Scotland Plc v Etridge (No.2)* [2002] 2 A.C. 773 at [350] (Lord Scott).

96 *North Shore Ventures Ltd v Anstead Holdings Inc* [2011] EWCA Civ 230; [2012] Ch. 31 at [31] (Sir Andrew Morritt C).

97 *North Shore Ventures Ltd v Anstead Holdings Inc* [2011] EWCA Civ 230; [2012] Ch. 31 at [14] (Sir Andrew Morritt C).

98 [2011] EWCA Civ 230; [2012] Ch. 31.

99 *North Shore Ventures Ltd v Anstead Holdings Inc* [2011] EWCA Civ 230; [2012] Ch. 31 at [33] (Sir Andrew Morritt C).

100 *North Shore Ventures Ltd v Anstead Holdings Inc* [2011] EWCA Civ 230; [2012] Ch. 31 at [33] (Sir Andrew Morritt VC).

101 *Great Peace Shipping Ltd v Tsalviris Salvage (International) Ltd* [2003] Q.B. 679; *British Red Cross v Werry* [2017] EWHC 875 (Ch).

102 *Raffles v Wichelhaus* (1864) 2 H & C 906; 159 E.R. 375.

103 *Shogun Finance Ltd v Hudson* [2003] UKHL 62; [2004] 1 A.C. 919.

104 *Smith v Hughes* (1871) L.R. 6 Q.B. 597; *Hartog v Colin & Shields* [1939] 3 All E.R. 566.

105 *Solle v Butcher* [1950] 1 K.B. 671; *Grist v Bailey* [1967] Ch. 532.

106 [2003] Q.B. 679.

107 *OT Africa Ltd v Vickers Plc* [1996] 1 Lloyd's Rep. 700 at 704 (Mance J); *Huyton v Dipasa* [2003]

mistake in Equity was, however, rejected[108] and, following the decision in *Great Peace*, the preferable view is that there is no jurisdiction in Equity to rescind a contract for any mistake, whether common or unilateral.[109] There is, however, a continuing equitable jurisdiction to rescind a contract which had been induced by a misrepresentation.[110] That a common fundamental mistake renders the contract void rather than voidable at Common Law was criticised by the Court of Appeal in *Great Peace Shipping Ltd v Tsavliris Salvage Ltd*,[111] where it was recognised that an equitable jurisdiction to grant rescission on terms for such a mistake is preferable because it gives greater flexibility as to the appropriate result. It was considered, however, that it was a matter for Parliament rather than the courts to introduce such a flexible regime, by analogy with the Law Reform (Frustrated Contracts) Act 1943.[112]

Voluntary dispositions   There is an equitable jurisdiction to set aside deeds,[113]   **2-022**
gifts and voluntary dispositions to trusts which have been made by mistake.[114] This jurisdiction is available where the mistake was sufficiently serious[115] and was of such gravity as to make it objectively unjust or unconscionable for the donee to retain the property transferred.[116] The mistake will typically only be sufficiently serious where it related to the legal character or nature of a transaction or as to a matter of fact or law which was basic to the transaction.[117] Where the defendant has given consideration, the common law rule on mistake will apply, rendering the contract void, but where no consideration has been provided, as in a voluntary transaction, the equitable jurisdiction is applicable, rendering the transaction voidable.[118]

[footnote] 2 Lloyd's Rep. 780 at 838 (Andrew Smith J). See also *Thames Trains Ltd v Adams* [2006] EWHC 3291 at [56] (Nelson J), which was decided after *Great Peace*.

[108] *Riverlate Properties Ltd v Paul* [1975] Ch. 133 at 144 (Russell LJ).

[109] *Statoil ASA v Louis Dreyfus Energy Services LP, The Harriette N* [2008] EWHC 2257 (Comm).

[110] See para.2-014.

[111] [2002] EWCA Civ 1407; [2003] A.C. 679 at [161].

[112] See para.18-025.

[113] *Moses v Moses* [2022] UKPC 42.

[114] *Pitt v Holt; Futter v Futter* [2013] UKSC 26; [2013] 2 A.C. 108. See *Hopes v Burton* [2022] EWHC 2770 (Ch); [2023] W.T.L.R. 187.

[115] The stricter test for setting aside a voluntary disposition in Equity was rejected by the Jersey Royal Court (*Re R* [2011] J.R.C. 117), where it was held to be sufficient that the mistake was a "but for" cause of the transfer.

[116] *Pitt v Holt; Futter v Futter* [2013] UKSC 26; [2013] 2 A.C. 108. See *Van Der Merwe v Goldman* [2016] EWHC 790 (Ch); [2016] 4 W.L.R. 71; *Bainbridge v Bainbridge* [2016] EWHC 898 (Ch); [2016] W.T.L.R. 943; *Rogge v Rogge* [2019] EWHC 1949 (Ch); [2019] W.T.L.R. 1305; *JTC Employer Ser Trustees v Ramin Khadem* [2021] EWHC 2929 (Ch).

[117] *Pitt v Holt; Futter v Futter* [2013] UKSC 26; [2013] 2 A.C. 108 at [122] (Lord Walker).

[118] *Pagel v Farman* [2013] EWHC 2210 (Comm); [2013] W.T.L.R. 1575; *Spaul v Spaul* [2014] EWCA Civ 679 at [52] (Rimer LJ); *Van der Merwe v Goldman* [2016] EWHC 790 (Ch); [2016] 4 W.L.R. 71. The equitable jurisdiction is not, however, engaged where the transaction was neither a gift nor a voluntary disposition: *Mackay v Wesley* [2020] EWHC 1215 (Ch) at [139] (Henderson J). Nevertheless, in *Fattal v Fattal* [2022] EWHC 950 (Ch); [2022] 2 P. & C.R. DG19 the doctrine was considered to be applicable where the claimant had transferred property to the defendant in the mistaken belief that the defendant had already paid for it. But this had not been intended to be a voluntary disposition since the mistake related to payment. Further, in *Middleton v Middleton* 22 March 2022 the equitable doctrine was extended to rescind a loan (albeit for no interest) on the ground that the loan had purported to avoid taxation and had actually incurred a significant inherit-

IV. DURESS

2-023 **General principles** A contract which was made as a result of duress being exerted on one of the parties is voidable at Common Law.[119] Duress involves the application of illegitimate pressure or the making of an illegitimate threat,[120] which coerces a party to enter into a contract in circumstances where that party had no practical choice to act differently.[121] The pressure or threat may be explicit or implicit[122] and involves a demand backed by a threat of harm within the control of the party exerting the pressure; rather than a warning made by a person who has no control over whether the unwelcome consequence will occur,[123] or a request. Duress does not require proof of bad faith, but the threat or pressure must usually[124] be unlawful,[125] such as a threat or pressure to commit a crime or a tort or to breach a contract. A contract made as a result of duress can be rescinded only; there is no right to damages or injunctive relief, save where a separate claim for tort, such as the tort of intimidation, is available.[126] The right to rescind a contract made under duress cannot be excluded by a term of the contract.[127] Duress takes three forms: duress of the person, duress of property and economic duress.

2-024 **Duress of the person** Duress of the person involves actual or threatened unauthorised interference with the person, whether by endangering life, personal safety or liberty,[128] such as a threat to kill, to injure or imprison[129] if the contract is not made. It is sufficient that the duress was an operative cause of the contract being made without being a cause but for which the contract would not have been made,[130] but it is still necessary to show that the duress was an inducement of the contract being made.[131] So, in *Barton v Armstrong*[132] a contract to purchase shares was avoided following threats to kill, even though the purchaser would have bought

---

ance tax liability. But a loan cannot sensibly be analysed as a voluntary transaction, and this should also be rejected as an unnecessary extension of the equitable jurisdiction.

[119] *Whelpdale's case* (1605) 5 Co Rep. 119a; 77 E.R. 239; *The Universe Sentinel* [1983] 1 A.C. 366 at 383 (Lord Diplock) and 400 (Lord Scarman); *The Evia Luck* [1992] 2 A.C. 52 at 168 (Lord Goff); *Halpern v Halpern* [2008] Q.B. 195; *Al Nehayan v Kent* [2018] EWHC 333 (Comm) at [217] (Leggatt LJ]. In *Barton v Armstrong* [1976] A.C. 104 at 120, the Privy Council found that threats to kill the claimant rendered a deed, which was entered into as a result of the threats, to be void. This decision is explicable either because of the extreme nature of the threats or, more likely, because the claimant had sought a declaration that the deed was void and the form of the declaration which was granted had not been challenged by the defendant. Cf. D.J. Lanham, "Duress and Void Contracts" (1966) 29 M.L.R. 615.

[120] *Barton v Armstrong* [1976] A.C. 104 at 121 (Lord Wilberforce and Simon); *The Universe Sentinel* [1983] 1 A.C. 366 at 384 (Lord Diplock); *Times Travel (UK) Ltd v Pakistan International Airlines Corp* [2021] UKSC 40; [2023] A.C. 101 at [62] (Lord Burrows).

[121] *The Universe Sentinel* [1983] 1 A.C. 366 at 400 (Lord Scarman).

[122] *The Alev* [1989] 1 Lloyd's Rep. 138 at 142 (Hobhouse J).

[123] S. Smith, "Contracting Under Pressure: A Theory of Duress" (1997) 56 C.L.J. 343 at 346.

[124] See further para.2-026.

[125] *Mutual Finance Ltd v John Wetton and Sons Ltd* [1937] 2 K.B. 389 at 395 (Porter J).

[126] See para.4-038.

[127] *Borelli v Ting* [2010] UKPC 21 at [40].

[128] *Law Debenture Trust Corp Plc v Ukraine* [2023] UKSC 11 at [194]; [2023] 2 W.L.R. 699 (threats of use of physical violence towards a nation's armed forces and civilians).

[129] But not if it involves proper use of the legal process: *Al Saif Group v Cable* [2022] EWHC 271 (QB) at [195] (Griffiths J). This may exceptionally constitute lawful act duress. See para.2-026, below.

[130] *Barton v Armstrong* [1976] A.C. 104.

[131] *BV Nederlandse Industrie Van Eiprodukten v Rembrandt Enterprises Inc* [2019] EWCA Civ 596; [2020] Q.B. 551 at [45] (Longmore LJ).

the shares for commercial reasons even had no threats been made. Lord Cross in that case did suggest that there is a presumption that the threats caused the contract to be made, with the burden being placed on the threatener to show that they had no effect on the decision to enter into the contract.[133] This is consistent with the approach adopted as regards the effect of a fraudulent misrepresentation on the contract being made.[134]

Duress of property   An old rule that only duress of the person could be relied on to set aside any contract which was entered into as a result of the threats[135] is no longer valid.[136] Consequently, a contract made as the result of a threat to seize or to retain property which belongs to the other party or in which they have a proprietary interest[137] can be rescinded.[138] Although no case has specifically considered the test of causation for duress of property, the preferable view is that the operative cause test of causation as recognised in *Barton v Armstrong*[139] will apply.   **2-025**

Economic duress   Economic duress arises where the defendant resorts to express or implied illegitimate[140] commercial pressure or threats to compel the claimant to enter into a contract or to vary an existing one.[141] The threats or pressure will usually be unlawful[142] and typically will involve threats to break a contract[143] or to commit a tort.[144] Exceptionally, lawful threats or pressure will be sufficient to establish duress if it is illegitimate since it involves reprehensible or unconscionable conduct which renders the enforcement of the contract unconscionable;[145] this requires consideration of the behaviour of the threatening party (including their motive), the   **2-026**

---

[132] [1976] A.C. 104.

[133] *Barton v Armstrong* [1976] A.C. 104 at 120.

[134] See para.2-013.

[135] *Skeate v Beale* (1841) 11 Ad. and E. 983; 113 E.R. 688.

[136] *Occidental Worldwide Investment Corp v Skibs A/S Avanti (The Siboen and The Sibotre)* [1976] 1 Lloyd's Rep. 293 at 335 (Kerr J); *The Atlantic Baron* [1979] Q.B. 705 at 719 (Mocatta J); *Pao On v Lau Yiu Long* [1980] A.C. 614 at 636 (Lord Scarman); *Vantage Navigation Corporation v Suhail and Saud Bahwan Building Materials (The Alev)* [1989] 1 Lloyd's Rep. 138 at 145 (Hobhouse J); *The Evia Luck* [1992] 2 A.C. 152 at 165 (Lord Goff).

[137] In *Fell v Whittaker* (1871) L.R. 7 Q.B. 120 it was sufficient that the claimant had possession of the property that had been seized.

[138] *Law Debenture Trust Corp Plc v Ukraine* [2023] UKSC 11 at [194]; [2023] 2 W.L.R. 699.

[139] [1976] A.C. 104. See para.2-024.

[140] *Universe Tankships Inc of Monrovia v International Transport Workers Federation* [1983] A.C. 366 at 400 (Lord Scarman); *DSND Subsea Ltd v PGS Offshore Technology AS* [2000] B.L.R. 530 at [131] (Dyson J); *Times Travel (UK) Ltd v Pakistan International Airlines Corp* [2021] UKSC 40; [2023] A.C. 101; *Heritage Travel and Tourism Ltd v Windhorst* [2021] EWHC 2380 (Comm) at [34] (Salter QC).

[141] *The Siboen and The Sibotre* [1976] 1 Lloyd's Rep. 293.

[142] *CTN Cash and Carry Ltd v Gallaher Ltd* [1994] 4 All E.R. 714, where a threat to withdraw credit facilities in the future was not considered to be an unlawful threat.

[143] *The Atlantic Baron* [1979] Q.B. 705.

[144] *The Universe Sentinel* [1983] A.C. 366; *The Evia Luck* [1992] 2 A.C. 152.

[145] *Times Travel (UK) Ltd v Pakistan International Airlines Corp* [2021] UKSC 40; [2023] A.C. 101. See W. Day (2022) 138 L.Q.R. 194. See also *Law Debenture Trust Corp Plc v Ukraine* [2023] UKSC 11; [2023] 2 W.L.R. 699. In *Times Travel* the offer of a new contract on terms that existing claims were waived did not constitute lawful act duress because the defendant genuinely believed that it was entitled to make such a demand, even though the defendant occupied a monopoly position. Such lawful act duress is preferably analysed as involving the distinct equitable doctrine of undue pressure, see para.2-028. See *Australia and New Zealand Banking Group Ltd v Karam* (2005) 64 N.S.W.L.R. 149. Lawful act duress was not established in *Heritage Travel and Tourism Ltd v*

nature of the threat and the circumstances of the threatened party. A demand motivated by commercial self-interest will usually be legitimate. A prior question before economic duress is examined is whether any consideration was provided for the contract made as a result of the duress, since, without new consideration, the new contract or variation of an existing one will be void.[146] This is particularly significant where the defendant has threatened not to perform an existing contract unless its terms are renegotiated. It has been recognised that the performance of an existing promise will constitute good consideration for the renegotiated contract since this is of practical benefit to the other party.[147] It follows that there is a much more significant role for the doctrine of economic duress.[148]

2-027   The illegitimate threat or pressure must have caused the other party to enter into the contract. This is assessed by determining whether the threats or pressure coerced the victim's will so their decision to enter into the contract cannot be considered to be voluntary in that it was not exercised freely.[149] The relevant test of causation is that the threat or pressure was the pre-dominant or the "but for" cause of the contract being made.[150] Relevant factors in determining whether the victim's will has been coerced include whether the victim protested at the time the contract was made or varied,[151] whether the victim received independent legal advice and whether the victim took any steps to avoid the contract after it had been made.[152] A third requirement to establish economic duress is whether the victim of the threats or pressure had a reasonable alternative course of action available to them rather than to submit to the threat or pressure.[153] Whereas the test of causation is a subjective test, the test of whether there was any reasonable alternative is an objective test which is assessed by reference to what the reasonable person would have done had

---

Windhorst [2021] EWHC 2380 (Comm) (threats to enforce contractual rights were not illegitimate) and *Al-Subaihi v Al-Sanea* [2021] EWHC 2609 (Comm) at [188] (Ross Cranston J)(lawful threats to cease to act as lawyer, bringing proceedings to claim fees, enforce promissor notes and apply for travel bans for family members were considered legitimate).

[146] *D and C Builders v Rees* [1966] 2 Q.B. 617.

[147] *Williams v Roffey Bros and Nicholls (Contractors) Ltd* [1991] 1 Q.B. 1.

[148] *Williams v Roffey Bros and Nicholls (Contractors) Ltd* [1991] 1 Q.B. 1 at 13 (Glidewell LJ), 21 (Purchas LJ).

[149] *The Siboen and The Sibotre* [1976] 1 Lloyd's Rep. 293 at 336 (Kerr J); *Pao On v Lau Yiu Long* [1980] A.C. 614 at 635 (Lord Scarman); *Hennessy v Craigmoyle and Co Ltd* [1986] I.C.R. 461 at 468 (Sir John Donaldson MR); *The Alev* [1989] 1 Lloyd's Rep. 138 at 145 (Hobhouse J).

[150] *The Evia Luck* [1992] 2 A.C. 152 at 165 (Lord Goff); *Huyton v Peter Cremer* [1999] 1 Lloyd's Rep. 620; *Carillion Construction Ltd v Felix (UK) Ltd* [2001] B.L.R. 1; *Kolmar Group AG v Traxpo Enterprises Pvt Ltd* [2010] EWHC 113 (Comm) at [92] (Christopher Clarke J). In *DSND Subsea Ltd v PGS Offshore Technology AS* [2000] B.L.R. 530 at [131] Dyson J used the language of a "significant cause". Cf. D. O'Sullivan, S. Elliott and R. Zakrzewski, *The Law of Rescission*, 3rd edn (New York: Oxford University Press, 2023), para.6.68 who assert that an operative cause test should be sufficient, because the victim also needs to show that the threat was illegitimate and that no practical alternative was available.

[151] *The Siboen and The Sibotre* [1976] 1 Lloyd's Rep. 293 at 336 (Kerr J).

[152] *Pao On v Lau Yiu Long* [1980] A.C. 614 at 635 (Lord Scarman); *The Universe Sentinel* [1983] A.C. 366 at 400 (Lord Scarman).

[153] *Pao On v Lau Yiu Long* [1980] A.C. 614 at 635 (Lord Scarman); *Times Travel (UK) Ltd v Pakistan International Airlines Corp* [2021] UKSC 40; [2023] A.C. 101 at [79] (Lord Burrows). In *DSND Subsea Ltd v PGS Offshore Technology AS* [2000] B.L.R. 530 at [136] Dyson J described this as "no realistic practical alternative but to concede" to the pressure.

they been in the victim's position.[154] A reasonable alternative might include contracting with somebody else or seeking legal redress.[155]

V.   UNDUE PRESSURE

The essence of undue pressure   Whereas duress traditionally involved a contract being made or renegotiated as the result of an unlawful threat or unlawful pressure so that the contract was voidable at Common Law, the doctrine of undue pressure was recognised in Equity where what the defendant threatened to do was lawful but their conduct could be characterised as unconscionable, typically because of inequality between the parties so that the defendant can be considered to have taken unfair advantage of the claimant.[156] The lawful threat may be a threat to invoke the criminal process if a contract is not made, in circumstances where the person who might be prosecuted has actually committed a crime;[157] or a threat to commence civil proceedings,[158] or to publish information.[159] Threats to prosecute would now fall within the category of lawful act duress and, following the confirmation of that doctrine by the Supreme Court,[160] it seems likely that the doctrine of undue pressure has been assimilated into lawful act duress. But, since lawful act duress operates at Common Law it is unfortunate that the equitable doctrine of undue pressure appears now to have no independent existence.

2-028

VI.   UNDUE INFLUENCE

General principles   Where the claimant can be considered to have entered into a contract with the defendant as the result of the actual or presumed exercise of undue influence, the contract is voidable in Equity, because the claimant did not exercise a free judgment, independent of the defendant.[161] The essential feature of undue influence is that the relationship between the defendant and the claimant is one of ascendancy and dependency[162] and the defendant either abuses that relationship or is presumed to have abused it to induce the claimant to enter into a contract

2-029

---

[154] *B&S Contracts and Design Ltd v Victor Green Publications Ltd* [1984] I.C.R. 419. Cf. *The Universe Sentinel* [1983] 1 A.C. 366 at 400 (Lord Scarman).

[155] *B&S Contracts and Design Ltd v Victor Green Publications Ltd* [1984] I.C.R. 419 at 428 (Kerr J); *The Alev* [1989] 1 Lloyd's Rep. 138 at 147 (Hobhouse J). See *Hennessy v Craigmyle and Co Ltd* [1986] I.C.R. 461.

[156] *Williams v Bayley* (1866) L.R. 1 HL 200 at 214 (Lord Chelmsford), 216 (Lord Westbury); *Lloyd's Bank v Bundy* [1975] Q.B. 326 at 338–339 (Lord Denning MR).

[157] *Williams v Bayley* (1866) L.R. 1 H.L. 200; *Mutual Finance Ltd v John Wetton and Sons Ltd* [1937] 2 K.B. 389.

[158] *Unwin v Leaper* (1840) 1 Man. and G. 747; 133 E.R. 533.

[159] *Norreys v Zeffert* [1939] 2 All E.R. 187.

[160] *Times Travel (UK) Ltd v Pakistan International Airlines Corp* [2021] UKSC 40; [2023] A.C. 101. See para.2-026, above. See *Al Saif Group v Cable* [2022] EWHC 271 (QB) at [205] (Griffiths J). But it is doubtful whether lawful act duress could be established when the threat of prosecution by due process was used to obtain an agreement from the person liable to the prosecution and in respect of sums which were lawfully due from that person: *Al Saif Group v Cable* [2022] EWHC 271 (QB) at [208] (Griffiths J). See also *Flower v Sadler* (1882) 10 Q.B.D. 572 at 576 (Cotton LJ).

[161] *Nature Resorts Ltd v First Citizens Bank Ltd* [2022] UKPC 10; [2022] 1 W.L.R. 2788 at [10] (Lords Briggs and Burrows).

[162] *Royal Bank of Scotland Plc v Etridge (No.2)* [2002] 2 A.C. 773 at 795 (Lord Nicholls); *National Commercial Bank (Jamaica) Ltd v Hew's Executors* [2003] UKPC 51 at [31]. Where there is no relationship of influence between the parties, a transaction may still be set aside on the alternative ground of the defendant's unconscionable conduct. See para.2-034.

with the defendant.[163] Such a contract may be rescinded because the defendant's ability to exploit the claimant's weaker position means that the claimant cannot be considered to have entered into the contract voluntarily so that the claimant's intention to enter into the contract may have been vitiated.[164] Unlike the ground of duress the doctrine of undue influence does not require the defendant to have threatened or pressurised the claimant to enter into the contract; the ability to influence is sufficient.[165] There is one single concept of undue influence, but there are two different ways of establishing it, known as actual and presumed undue influence.[166] Actual undue influence involves the proof of influence unduly exerted. Where undue influence is presumed the burden shifts to the defendant to rebut the presumption, usually by showing that the claimant obtained independent advice. But both forms are founded on the same notion of undue influence, namely that there is a relationship which is capable of giving rise to the necessary influence and that this influence had been abused.[167] Where the claimant has entered into a substitute contract to replace the original contract which was vitiated for undue influence, the substitute may also be vitiated, either because of continuing undue influence or because of the continuing effect of the original undue influence.[168]

2-030   **Actual undue influence**   Actual undue influence will be established where the relationship between the claimant and the defendant was such that the claimant trusted and had confidence in the defendant;[169] the defendant exercised influence over the claimant; the exercise can be characterised as undue,[170] such as by tricking the claimant to enter into a contract, and the undue influence caused the claimant to enter into the contract. Although it has sometimes been suggested that the test of causation is that the influence was a predominant or "but for" cause of the claimant entering the contract,[171] the better view is that it is sufficient that the undue influence was an operative cause by analogy with the test of causation for fraudulent misrepresentation, [172] since actual undue influence can be considered to be a form of fraud.[173] Consequently, the contract can be avoided for actual undue influence even if the claimant would have entered into it had there not been undue influence. It is not necessary to show that the defendant was aware that they had exerted undue

---

163 *CIBC Mortgages Plc v Pitt* [1994] 1 A.C. 200 at 209 (Lord Browne-Wilkinson); *Royal Bank of Scotland Plc v Etridge (No.2)* [2002] 2 A.C. 773 at 795 (Lord Nicholls); *Daniel v Drew* [2005] EWCA Civ 507 at [36] (Ward LJ).

164 *National Westminster Bank Plc v Morgan* [1985] A.C. 686 at 705 (Lord Scarman), relying on a dictum of Lindley LJ in *Allcard v Skinner* (1887) 36 Ch D. 145 at 182; *Royal Bank of Scotland Plc v Etridge (No.2)* [2002] 2 A.C. 773 at 795 (Lord Nicholls); *Hammond v Osborn* [2002] EWCA Civ 885; [2002] W.T.L.R. 1125 at [60] (Ward LJ); *Hurley v Darjan Estate Co Plc* [2012] EWHC 189 (Ch); [2012] 1 W.L.R. 1782 at [40] (Miss Geraldine Andrews QC).

165 *Dunbar Bank Plc v Nadeem* [1998] 3 All E.R. 876 at 883 (Millett LJ); *Nature Resorts Ltd v First Citizens Bank Ltd* [2022] UKPC 10; [2022] 1 W.L.R. 2788 at [10] (Lords Briggs and Burrows).

166 *Nature Resorts Ltd v First Citizens Bank Ltd* [2022] UKPC 10; [2022] 1 W.L.R. 2788 at [11] (Lords Briggs and Burrows). See K. Lewison, "Under the Influence" [2011] R.L.R. 19.

167 *Royal Bank of Scotland Plc v Etridge (No.2)* [2002] 2 A.C. 773 at 795 (Lord Nicholls); *National Commercial Bank (Jamaica) Ltd v Hew's Executors* [2003] UKPC 51 at [30].

168 *Yorkshire Bank Plc v Tinsley* [2004] EWCA Civ 816; [2004] 1 W.L.R. 2380; *Samuel v Wadlow* [2007] EWCA Civ 155 at [49] (Toulson LJ). If a mutual wills contract is avoided for undue influence there is no basis for Equity to intervene: *Naidoo v Barton* [2023] EWHC 500 (Ch).

169 *Morley v Laughnan* [1893] 1 Ch. 736.

170 *Dunbar Bank Plc v Nadeem* [1998] 3 All E.R. 876 at 883 (Millett LJ).

171 *BCCI v Aboody* [1990] 1 Q.B. 923 at 971 (Slade LJ).

172 See para.2-010.

173 *UCB Group Ltd v Hedworth* [2003] EWCA Civ 1717 at [77].

influence on the claimant.[174] Although at one time there was a requirement that the transaction was manifestly and unfairly disadvantageous to the claimant,[175] this was rejected by the House of Lords,[176] so it is not necessary to consider the substantive fairness of the contract when determining whether it is voidable for undue influence. The focus is placed instead on the process by which the claimant's consent to enter into the contract was obtained.[177]

Presumed undue influence   Where it is not possible for the claimant to establish   **2-031** that they were unduly influenced to enter into the contract, it may be possible to establish a presumption of undue influence which caused the claimant to enter into the contract, if two conditions are satisfied.[178] First, the relationship between the parties must be a relationship of influence. Certain relationships are always treated as relationships of influence by virtue of a legal rule,[179] without the claimant needing to prove that they placed particular trust and confidence in the defendant, such as the relationship of solicitor and client.[180] Other relationships can be treated as relationships of influence on the facts by the claimant showing that they placed such a degree of trust and confidence in the defendant that the claimant was under the defendant's influence so that the defendant could take advantage of the claimant, such as the relationship between husband and wife[181] and between a junior employee and her employer's agent.[182] Such a relationship of influence has even been recognised between a bank and a potential guarantor of debts owed to the bank, where the assistant bank manager had gone beyond the normal commercial role of the bank and had advised on general matters relating to the wisdom of a particular transaction.[183] Secondly, the nature of the transaction is such that it is not readily explicable on ordinary motives, such as a contract which is substantively unfair to the claimant.[184] It is this second condition which triggers the presumption that the influence which was presumed to have been exerted was undue,[185] because, for example, the terms of the transaction make it disadvantageous to the claimant, such as a sale at an undervalue[186] or a liability as surety beyond the means

---

[174] *Papous v Gibson-West* [2004] EWHC 396.

[175] *BCCI v Aboody* [1990] 1 Q.B. 923.

[176] *CIBC Mortgages Plc v Pitt* [1994] 1 A.C. 200.

[177] *CIBC Mortgages Plc v Pitt* [1994] 1 A.C. 200 at 209 (Lord Browne-Wilkinson).

[178] *Royal Bank of Scotland Plc v Etridge (No.2)* [2001] UKHL 44; [2002] 2 A.C. 773 at 796 (Lord Nicholls of Birkenhead); *Nature Resorts Ltd v First Citizens Bank Ltd* [2022] UKPC 10; [2022] 1 W.L.R. 2788 at [12] (Lords Briggs and Burrows).

[179] *Nature Resorts Ltd v First Citizens Bank Ltd* [2022] UKPC 10; [2022] 1 W.L.R. 2788 at [12] (Lords Briggs and Burrows). For the valid criticism of the recognition of these relations of influence as the product of a very different social context, see K. Lewison, "Under the Influence" [2011] R.L.R. 19.

[180] *Wright v Carter* [1903] 1 Ch. 27.

[181] *National Westminster Bank Plc v Morgan* [1985] A.C. 686 at 703 (Lord Scarman); *Barclays Bank Plc v O'Brien* [1994] 1 A.C. 180 at 190 (Lord Browne-Wilkinson); *Royal Bank of Scotland Plc v Etridge (No.2)* [2001] UKHL 44; [2002] 2 A.C. 773 at 797 (Lord Nicholls of Birkenhead).

[182] *Crédit Lyonnais Bank Nederland NV v Burch* [1997] 1 All E.R. 144.

[183] *Lloyd's Bank Ltd v Bundy* [1975] 1 Q.B. 326. Cf. *National Westminster Bank Plc v Morgan* [1985] A.C. 686.

[184] *Nature Resorts Ltd v First Citizens Bank Ltd* [2022] UKPC 10; [2022] 1 W.L.R. 2788 at [12] (Lords Briggs and Burrows). See *Fielder v Smith* [2005] All E.R. (D) 264 (guarantee of company's liability for disbursements given by client to solicitor upheld as it did not call for an explanation).

[185] *BCCI v Aboody* [1990] 1 Q.B. 923 at 957 (Slade LJ).

[186] *Leeder v Stevens* [2005] EWCA Civ 50. See also *Hammond v Osborn* [2002] EWCA Civ 885 and *Goodchild v Bradley* [2006] EWCA Civ 1868 involving substantial gifts.

of the claimant.[187] This is an objective test,[188] which is applied by considering whether an ordinary person would have entered into the transaction unless they had been unduly influenced to do so,[189] having regard to such matters as the nature of the relationship between the parties, their respective circumstances and the nature of the transaction. The identity and circumstances of the claimant will be relevant when determining whether the transaction requires explanation. In *Nature Resorts Ltd v First Citizens Bank Ltd*[190] the Privy Council recognised that an ordinary commercial transaction, such as a mortgage entered into by the claimant who is engaged in business, would rarely be regarded as a transaction that is not readily explicable by ordinary motives merely because it turns out to be disadvantageous. This will especially be the case, as occurred on the facts, where the claimant derived a substantial benefit from the transaction. In that case the sole shareholder of the claimant company had signed a deed of charge over the company's property as security for a loan to enable third parties to buy shares in the company, the purpose being to raise capital for the company. When the third parties defaulted on the loan, the claimant sought to rescind the deed on the ground that the lawyer who had facilitated the transaction had exercised undue influence. The Court of Appeal of Trinidad and Tobago had held that the presumption of undue influence had been established but it was rebutted because it was found that the sole shareholder had exercised a free and independent judgment. This finding was affirmed by the Privy Council, but the Board went on to conclude that the presumption should not have been triggered because the transaction was readily explicable as one which a business person would enter into, since it facilitated a capital injection into the company, even though it turned out to be disadvantageous.

2-032   Once the presumption of undue influence has been triggered, the burden shifts to the defendant to rebut it, by showing that the claimant entered into the contract voluntarily and was not induced to do so by the defendant's influence.[191] This is usually established by showing that the claimant entered into the contract having obtained independent, relevant and competent[192] advice from a qualified person, often a lawyer, who was independent of any influence from the defendant[193] and who advised that the claimant should enter into the contract, having explained the nature and effect of the transaction to the claimant.[194] It does not follow from the fact that advice about the transaction has been given by a lawyer that the presumption of undue influence will necessarily be rebutted, since this will depend on the quality of the advice and whether it can be considered to have negatived the undue

---

[187] *Crédit Lyonnais Bank Nederland NV v Burch* [1997] 1 All E.R. 144.

[188] *Vale v Armstrong* [2004] EWHC 1160 at [44] (Evans-Lombe J).

[189] *Turkey v Awadh* [2005] EWCA Civ 382 at [39] (Chadwick LJ).

[190] [2022] UKPC 10; [2022] 1 W.L.R. 2788 at [27] (Lords Briggs and Burrows).

[191] *Allcard v Skinner* (1887) 36 Ch D. 145 at 171 (Cotton LJ); *Nature Resorts Ltd v First Citizens Bank Ltd* [2022] UKPC 10; [2022] 1 W.L.R. 2788 at [13] (Lords Briggs and Burrows) (proof that the other party exercised a free and independent judgment).

[192] *Wright v Carter* [1903] 1 Ch. 27.

[193] *Inche Noriah v Shaik Allie Bin Omar* [1929] A.C. 127 at 135 (Lord Hailsham LC). The adviser will not be considered to be independent if they were presumed to have exercised the undue influence: *Nature Resorts Ltd v First Citizens Bank Ltd* [2022] UKPC 10; [2022] 1 W.L.R. 2788 at [13] (Lords Briggs and Burrows).

[194] *Niersmans v Pesticcio* [2004] EWCA Civ 372 at [23] (Mummery LJ); *Randall v Randall* [2004] EWHC 2258 at [37] (Edward Bartley Jones QC).

influence.[195] The fact that the defendant's own conduct is unimpeachable is not sufficient to rebut the presumption of undue influence.[196]

Undue influence and third parties   Where the claimant has entered into a   **2-033**
contract with the defendant as the result of actual or presumed undue influence
exerted by a third party, as a general rule the contract cannot be rescinded, save in
two circumstances:[197] first, where the defendant can be considered to have acted as
agent for the third party; secondly, where the defendant had actual[198] or constructive notice of the undue influence.[199] A defendant will have constructive notice if,
having regard to the relationship between the parties, the transaction could not be
explained by the ordinary motives of the parties. The defendant would then be put
on inquiry about the possibility of undue influence.[200] If the defendant is put on
inquiry, they will only avoid being fixed with constructive notice of the undue influence if they had taken reasonable steps to ensure that the claimant was not affected by undue influence at the time the contract was signed. These reasonable
steps would typically involve the defendant arranging a private meeting to ensure
that the claimant was properly advised about the nature and effect of the transaction in the absence of the third party.[201]

VII.   UNCONSCIONABLE CONDUCT

General principles   Contracts and gifts[202] can be rescinded in Equity where the   **2-034**
claimant's consent to enter into the contract can be considered to have been
procured by unconscionable conduct,[203] or what is sometimes described as constructive or equitable fraud.[204] Unlike the ground of undue influence, a contract can be
rescinded for unconscionable conduct without needing to identify an existing
relationship of influence or dependency between the parties and it is different from

---

[195] *Vale v Armstrong* [2004] EWHC 1160 at [55] (Evans-Lombe J).
[196] *Hammond v Osborn* [2002] EWCA Civ 85 at [32] (Nourse LJ); *Jennings v Cairns* [2003] EWCA Civ 1935 at [40] (Arden LJ).
[197] *Royal Bank of Scotland Plc v Etridge (No.2)* [2002] 2 A.C. 773 at [144] (Lord Scott). See also where the contract was induced by a third party's misrepresentation. See para.2-016.
[198] Where the relationship between the person who has been unduly influenced and the person who has unduly influenced that person is a standard contractual relationship, such as a joint tenancy under a lease, rather than a suretyship, actual knowledge of the undue influence on the part of the third party is required: *Darjan Estate Co Plc v Hurley (No.2)* [2012] EWHC 189 (Ch); [2012] 1 W.L.R. 1782.
[199] *Barclays Bank Plc v O'Brien* [1994] 1 A.C. 180; *Royal Bank of Scotland Plc v Etridge (No.2)* [2002] 2 A.C. 773. It appears that constructive notice is only relevant where the transaction is a suretyship because the person who has been unduly influenced to become a surety is unlikely to derive a direct benefit from such a transaction and requires additional protection: *Darjan Estate Co Plc v Hurley (No. 2)* [2012] EWHC 189 (Ch); [2012] 1 W.L.R. 1782 at [34] (Geraldine Andrews QC).
[200] *Chater v Mortgage Agency Services Number Two Ltd* [2003] EWCA Civ 490 at [67] (Scott Baker LJ).
[201] *Royal Bank of Scotland Plc v Etridge (No.2)* [2002] 2 A.C. 773. See *Padden v Bevan Ashford Solicitors* [2011] EWCA Civ 1616; [2012] 1 W.L.R. 1759.
[202] *Evans v Lloyd* [2013] EWHC 1725 (Ch); [2013] W.T.L.R. 1137.
[203] *Hart v O'Connor* [1985] A.C. 1000; *Credit Lyonnais Bank Nederland NV v Burch* [1997] 1 All E.R. 144 at 151 (Nourse LJ). This is also known as "unconscionable bargains": *Times Travel (UK) Ltd v Pakistan International Airlines Corp* [2021] UKSC 40; [2023] A.C. 101 at [77] (Lord Burrows). See N. Bamforth, "Unconscionability as a Vitiating Factor" [1995] L.M.C.L.Q. 538 and D. Capper, "Unconscionable Bargains" in N. Dawson, D. Greer and P. Ingrams (eds), *One Hundred and Fifty Years of Irish Law* (Dublin; SLS/Round Hall Sweet & Maxwell, 1996), p.45
[204] Earl of Chesterfield and Others Executors of *John Spencer v Sir Abraham Janssen* (1751) 2 Ves. Sen. 125 at 157; 28 E.R. 82 at 101 (Lord Hardwicke); *Hart v O'Connor* [1985] A.C. 1000.

duress because no illegitimate threats or pressure need be established.[205] Unconscionable conduct will be established where the defendant has unconscientiously exploited their superior bargaining position to the detriment of the claimant who is in a much weaker position.[206] A distinct ground of rescission of inequality of bargaining power is not recognised.[207]

2-035 **Conditions for establishing unconscionable conduct** The defendant will be considered to have unconscionably exploited the claimant if the following conditions are satisfied:

(i) The claimant suffered from a special disability or disadvantage which placed them in a disadvantageous position as against the defendant, so that there was a reasonable degree of inequality between the parties.[208] This includes contracts made with somebody who is poor and ignorant,[209] although this is now interpreted as meaning a member of the lower income group and somebody who is less highly educated;[210] contracts made with expectant heirs who expect to receive an inheritance in the future and who are particularly vulnerable to exploitation by virtue of inexperience and immaturity;[211] contracts made with people suffering from infirmity of body or mind or some other disadvantage, which has been held to encompass a claimant who was illiterate and had a poor command of English.[212] Exceptionally, a gross inequality of bargaining power between the parties may also constitute a special disadvantage.[213] Such inequality may even arise in a purely commercial context.[214]

(ii) The defendant acted unconscientiously[215] in exploiting the claimant's disadvantage in a morally culpable manner, having regard to the defendant's knowledge of that disadvantage. This is a requirement of procedural unconscionability. But simple exploitation of the inequality of

---

[205] *Times Travel (UK) Ltd v Pakistan International Airlines Corp* [2021] UKSC 40; [2023] A.C. 101 at [77] (Lord Burrows).

[206] *Lloyds Bank Ltd v Bundy* [1975] Q.B. 326 at 337.

[207] *Times Travel (UK) Ltd v International Airlines Corp* [2021] UKSC 40; [2023] A.C. 101 at [25] (Lord Hodge).

[208] *Cresswell v Potter* [1978] 1 W.L.R. 255; *Irvani v Irvani* [2000] 1 Lloyd's Rep. 412 at 425 (Buxton LJ).

[209] *Fry v Lane* (1888) 40 Ch. D. 312. See also *Evans v Llewellin* (1787) 1 Cox Eq. Cas. 333; 29 E.R. 1191.

[210] *Cresswell v Potter* [1978] 1 W.L.R. 255. See also *Credit Lyonnais Bank Nederland NV v Burch* [1997] 1 All E.R. 144; *Portman Building Society v Dusangh* [2000] 2 All E.R. (Comm) 221, where being old, illiterate and with a low income was characterised as being the modern equivalent of "poor and ignorant"; *Chagos Islanders v Attorney General* [2003] EWHC 2222 (QB) at [580] (Ouseley J).

[211] *Earl of Aylesford v Morris* (1872-73) L.R. 8 Ch. App. 484.

[212] *Singla v Bashir* [2002] EWHC 883 (Ch) at [1] (Park J). See also *Commercial Bank of Australia Ltd v Amadio* (1983) 151 C.L.R. 447.

[213] *Backhouse v Backhouse* [1978] 1 W.L.R. 243 (divorcing couple); *Strydom v Vendside Ltd* [2009] EWHC 2130 (QB) (trade union and a member).

[214] *Multiservice Bookbinding Ltd v Marden* [1979] Ch. 84 at 110 (Browne-Wilkinson J); *Alec Lobb Garages Ltd v Total Oil Great Britain Ltd* [1983] 1 W.L.R. 87 at 95 (Peter Millett QC), affirmed CA [1985] 1 W.L.R. 173.

[215] *Alec Lobb Garages Ltd v Total Oil Great Britain Ltd* [1985] 1 W.L.R. 173 at 182 (Dillon LJ).

bargaining power between the parties is not sufficient.[216] The defendant needs to have acted in a morally reprehensible manner,[217] either because they actually knew of the claimant's special disability or disadvantage or should have known this since the defendant was aware of particular facts which would have put the reasonable person on notice that the claimant had a special disability or disadvantage.[218] In *Hart v O'Connor*[219] the Privy Council recognised that a transaction for the sale of land could not be set aside, even though the vendor was suffering from senile dementia, because the purchaser was not aware of her condition and there was nothing to put him on notice of this, since it appeared that the vendor was acting in accordance with the most full and careful legal advice. The potential for abuse as regards contracts with the poor and ignorant and with expectant heirs might be so great that unconscionability on the part of the defendant may even be presumed, at least where the transaction is oppressive, such as a sale at a significant undervalue.[220]

(iii) The contract must have been clearly disadvantageous to the claimant, rather than being simply harsh or improvident,[221] for example because a contract of sale was at a substantial undervalue. This requirement focuses on the substantive unconscionability of the transaction.

The contract will not be voidable where the defendant can establish that it was fair, just and reasonable.[222] The defendant will be able to establish this by showing, for example, that the claimant had obtained independent legal advice, since this places the parties on equal terms.[223] But obtaining such advice will only be relevant if its effect really is to place the parties on equal terms. So, for example, in *Boustany v Pigott*[224] a renegotiated lease was set aside by reason of the defendant's unconscionable conduct, even though the disadvantages of the transaction had been forcibly pointed out to the claimant by a barrister, because the defendant was present and was taking advantage of the claimant whilst the advice was taken.   **2-036**

Unconscionable conduct and third parties Where the claimant is induced to enter into a transaction with the defendant as a result of the unconscionable conduct   **2-037**

---

[216] *National Westminster Bank Plc v Morgan* [1985] A.C. 686 at 708 (Lord Scarman). Cf. *Lloyds Bank Ltd v Bundy* [1975] Q.B. 326 at 339 (Lord Denning MR).

[217] *Yorkshire Bank Plc v Tinsley* [2004] EWCA Civ 816; [2004] 1 W.L.R. 2380; *Portman Building Society v Dusangh* [2000] 2 All E.R. (Comm) 221; (2000) 80 P. & C.R. D20; *Jones v Morgan* [2001] EWCA Civ 995 at [35]; [2001] Lloyd's Rep. Bank. 323 (Chadwick LJ).

[218] *John Owen and J. M. Gutch v Sarah Homan* (1853) 4 H.L. Cas. 997 at 1035; *10 E.R. 752* at 761 (Lord Carnworth LC); *Commercial Bank of Australia Ltd v Amadio* (1983) 151 C.L.R. 447 at 467 (Mason J); *Nichols v Jessup* [1986] 1 N.Z.L.R. 226 at 236 (Somers J). Cf. *Louth v Diprose* (1992) 175 C.L.R. 621 and *Kakavas v Crown Melbourne Ltd* [2013] H.C.A. 25 where the High Court of Australia adopted a subjective test of fault.

[219] [1985] A.C. 1000.

[220] *Fry v Lane* (1888) 40 Ch. D. 312 at 321 (Kay J); *Alec Lobb Garages Ltd v Total Oil Great Britain Ltd* [1985] 1 W.L.R. 173 at 182 (Dillon LJ).

[221] *Alec Lobb Garages Ltd v Total Oil Great Britain Ltd* [1983] 1 W.L.R. 87 at 95 (Peter Millett QC) affirmed CA [1985] 1 W.L.R. 173; *Portman Building Society v Dusangh* [2000] 2 All E.R. (Comm) 221; [2000] Lloyd's Rep. Bank. 197; *Times Travel (UK) Ltd v International Airlines Corp* [2021] UKSC 40; [2023] A.C. 101 at [25] (Lord Hodge).

[222] *Earl of Aylesford v Morris* (1872-73) L.R. 8 Ch. App. 484 at 491 (Lord Selborne LC); *Portman Building Society v Dusangh* [2000] 2 All E.R. (Comm) 221.

[223] *Fry v Lane* (1888) 40 Ch. D. 312.

[224] (1995) 69 P. & C.R. 298.

of a third party, and the defendant's own conduct cannot be characterised as unconscionable, the defendant will be able to enforce the transaction unless they had notice, whether actual or constructive, of the claimant's equity to set the transaction aside.[225] So, for example, if an employer induces an employee to provide security for the employer's debts in favour of a bank and this can be characterised as unconscionable by virtue of the employer's conduct, the bank will still be able to enforce the security unless it has notice of the employer's impropriety.[226]

VIII.   IMPAIRED CAPACITY

2-038   **General principles**   Where a person lacks capacity to enter into a contract any agreement made by that person will be void. But there will be circumstances where a person's capacity to contract can be considered to be impaired rather than absent. In such circumstances, the contract will be voidable[227] at Common Law if the other party to the contract is aware of the impairment[228] and regardless of the fairness of the contract.[229] Whether a person's capacity to contract can be considered to be impaired rather than absent is a matter of degree.

2-039   **Mental infirmity**   A contract made by a party who lacks mental capacity will be void, save that the incapacitated person must pay a reasonable price for necessary goods and services supplied.[230] Where a person suffers from a mental infirmity short of mental incapacity any contract made by such a person will be voidable if they were unable to appreciate the general nature and effect of the contract[231] when they entered into it and the other party knew of their infirmity.[232] Knowledge refers to actual or constructive notice, so it is sufficient that the defendant had sufficient awareness of the facts which would indicate to the honest and reasonable person that the other party to the contract was suffering from mental infirmity.[233]

2-040   **Intoxication**   In extreme cases the intoxication of one party will render a contract void where that person was unaware of what they were doing. In less extreme cases, intoxication by drink or drugs will render the contract voidable if the effect of the intoxication is to impair the capacity of the person to understand the nature and effect of the contract[234] and the other party knew that the person with whom they were

---

[225] See *Yorkshire Bank Plc v Tinsley* [2004] EWCA Civ 816; [2004] 1 W.L.R. 2380.

[226] See *Credit Lyonnais Bank Nederland NV v Burch* [1997] 1 All E.R. 144 at 153 (Millett LJ).

[227] *Imperial Loan Co Ltd v Stone* [1892] 1 Q.B. 599 at 602 (Lopes LJ) and *Gibbons v Wright* (1954) 91 C.L.R. 423. Cf. *Daily Telegraph Newspaper Co Ltd v McLaughlin* [1904] A.C. 776 and *Simpson v Simpson* [1989] Fam. Law 20 where impaired capacity was held to render the contract void, although those cases involved such severe incapacity that the defendant did not know what he was doing.

[228] Save where the impaired capacity arises from the party to the contract being a child: see para.2-041.

[229] *Hart v O'Connor* [1985] A.C. 1000. Cf. the distinct equitable doctrine of unconscionable conduct, para.2-034, where the contract will be voidable where the defendant can be considered to have taken unfair advantage of the claimant's disability or disadvantage.

[230] Mental Capacity Act 2005 s.7.

[231] See *Re Beaney* [1978] 1 W.L.R. 770 (gift of house to daughter by a woman suffering from senile dementia).

[232] *Imperial Loan Co v Stone* [1892] 1 Q.B. 599 at 601 (Lord Esher MR); *Hart v O'Connor* [1985] A.C. 1000.

[233] *Hassard v Smith* (1872) I.R. 6 Eq. 429.

[234] *Irvani v Irvani* [2000] 1 Lloyd's Rep. 412 at 425 (Buxton LJ).

contracting was intoxicated at the time.[235] Where the intoxicated person is supplied with necessaries they must pay a reasonable price for them.[236]

Minority   Contracts made with a minor, who is defined as a child under 18,[237] **2-041** generally do not bind the minor unless they are ratified within a reasonable time after attaining the age of majority. If, however, the contract is one which purports to give the minor an interest of a permanent or continuous nature, such as contracts for the acquisition of interests in land or shares in a company,[238] it is valid and binding until the minor rescinds it at Common Law whilst still a minor or within a reasonable time of having attained the age of majority.[239] The contract is voidable even if the other party to it is unaware that the claimant was a child when the contract was made.

IX.   BREACH OF FIDUCIARY DUTY

General principles   A fiduciary relationship is a relationship whereby one party **2-042** places trust and confidence in the other. Since many transactions involve one party reposing trust and confidence in another without creating a fiduciary relationship,[240] it is preferable to focus on whether a person is responsible for managing the property or affairs of another.[241] Notable fiduciary relationships include, the relationship between solicitor and client,[242] trustee and beneficiary and agent and principal.[243] The key obligation of a fiduciary is one of loyalty, in that the principal is entitled to the single-minded loyalty of the fiduciary in denial of their own self-interest.[244] No fiduciary can enter into a transaction where their personal interest conflicts with the duties which they owe to the principal.[245] Where a fiduciary finds themself in a position where their personal interest does conflict with their duty to the principal, or may conflict in a real and sensible manner,[246] the fiduciary must prefer the duty to the principal to their personal interest,[247] save where the principal has given their free and fully informed consent to enable the fiduciary to prefer their own interest. Two specific rules are founded on the no-conflict rule, namely the self-

---

[235] *Gore v Gibson* (1845) 13 M. and W. 623; 153 E.R. 260; *Molton v Camroux* (1849) 4 Ex. 17; 154 E.R. 1107; *Matthews v Baxter* (1873) L.R. 8 Exch. 132.

[236] Sale of Goods Act 1979 s.3(2).

[237] Family Law Reform Act 1969 s.1.

[238] *Steinberg v Scala (Leeds) Ltd* [1923] 2 Ch. 452 at 462 (Warrington LJ); 463 (Younger LJ).

[239] *Lovell and Christmas v Beauchamp* [1894] A.C. 607 at 611 (Lord Herschell LC).

[240] *Secretariat Consulting Pte Ltd v A Company* [2021] EWCA Civ 6; [2021] 4 W.L.R. 20 at [65] (Coulson LJ).

[241] *Al Nehayan v Kent* [2018] EWHC 333 (Comm) at [159]; [2018] 1 C.L.C. 216 (Leggatt LJ). See S. Worthington, "Fiduciaries then and now" (2021) 80 C.L.J. s154 at [163].

[242] See *Wright v Carter* [1903] 1 Ch. 27.

[243] Not every agent will owe fiduciary duties: *Prince Eze v Conway* [2019] EWCA Civ 88 at [39] (Asplin LJ).

[244] *Children's Investment Fund Foundation (UK) v Attorney General* [2020] UKSC 33; [2022] A.C. 155 at [44] (Lady Arden). See S. Worthington, "Fiduciaries: when is self-denial obligatory?" (1999) 58(3) C.L.J. 500; M. Conaglen, "The nature and function of fiduciary loyalty" (2005) 121 L.Q.R. 452.

[245] *Aberdeen Railway Co v Blaikie Bros* (1854) 1 Macq 461 at 471 (Lord Cranworth). As regards fiduciary duties owed by directors to companies, the no-conflict rule is enacted in the Companies Act 2006 s.175(1).

[246] *Boardman v Phipps* [1967] 2 A.C. 46 at 124 (Lord Upjohn).

[247] *Swain v The Law Society* [1982] 1 W.L.R. 17 at 36 (Oliver LJ).

dealing and the fair-dealing rules.[248] Any contract made between the principal and the fiduciary in breach of fiduciary duty is liable to be rescinded in Equity.

2-043 The identification of a fiduciary relationship may alternatively be sufficient to establish actual or presumed undue influence.[249] The boundary between breach of fiduciary duty and undue influence is uncertain,[250] particularly because where there is a relationship of trust and confidence there will also be the potential for undue influence. So, typically both may be pleaded on the same set of facts. But although the two principles overlap, they do not coincide.[251] The doctrine of breach of fiduciary duty has two advantages over actual or presumed undue influence, namely that it is not necessary to prove that the claimant was under the influence of the defendant and neither is it necessary to establish that the resulting contract requires explanation. Once the fiduciary relationship has been identified the need for an explanation is assumed and the burden is placed on the fiduciary to show that the principal had given their fully informed consent to the transaction. The heavy burden of proving consent is borne by the fiduciary because of the potential for abuse of such relationships by the fiduciary.[252]

2-044 **Self-dealing rule** The self-dealing rule will be breached where a fiduciary deals on behalf of themselves and the principal in the same transaction.[253] So, for example, a trustee, cannot sell trust property to themselves[254] or obtain a lease of trust property for themselves.[255] Neither can the trustee sell their own property to the trust.[256] Breach of this rule renders the transaction voidable[257] so that the principal can rescind it without needing to prove that the transaction was unfair.[258] The self-dealing rule can be excluded by the relevant instrument which governs the fiduciary relationship.[259] The rationale behind the rule is that the risk of conflict between personal interest and duty to the principal is such that the principal can rescind the contract, regardless of the fairness of the transaction.[260]

2-045 The contract will not, however, be voidable where the fiduciary has obtained the consent of the court or the fully informed consent of the principal to the transaction.[261] The fairness of the transaction may be a relevant evidential factor when assessing whether the consent was fully informed. Since the principal will not have been a party to the transaction, clear evidence of consent to the transaction will need to be adduced before the court will be able to conclude that the principal had

---

[248] *Tito v Waddell (No.2)* [1977] Ch 106 at 241.

[249] See paras 2-030 and 2-031.

[250] *CICB Mortgages Plc v Pitt* [1994] 1 A.C. 200 at 209 (Lord Browne-Wilkinson).

[251] *B.C.C.I. v Aboody* [1990] Q.B. 923 at 962 (Slade LJ). In *Moody v Cox and Hatt* [1917] 2 Ch 71 at 79 Lord Cozens-Hardy MR specifically held that relief in Equity was given by reason of breach of fiduciary duty and not for undue influence.

[252] *B.C.C.I. v Aboody* [1990] Q.B. 923 at 963 (Slade LJ); *CICB Mortgages Plc v Pitt* [1994] 1 A.C. 200 at 209 (Lord Browne-Wilkinson).

[253] *Tito v Waddell (No.2)* [1977] Ch 106 at 241 (Sir Robert Megarry VC).

[254] *Ex p. Lacey* (1802) 6 Ves. 625 at 626 (Lord Eldon LC); *Ex p. James* (1803) 8 Ves. 337 at 345 (Lord Eldon LC).

[255] *Re Thompson's Settlement* [1986] Ch 99.

[256] *Armstrong v Jackson* [1917] 2 K.B. 822 at 824 (McCardie J).

[257] *Holder v Holder* [1968] 1 Ch 353 at 398; *Caldicott v Richards* [2020] EWHC 767 (Ch).

[258] *Tito v Waddell (No.2)* [1977] Ch 106 at 241 (Sir Robert Megarry VC).

[259] *Sargeant v National Westminster Bank Plc* (1990) 61 P. & C.R. 518.

[260] *Wright v Morgan* [1926] A.C. 788.

[261] *Ex p. James* (1803) 8 Ves 337 at 353 (Lord Eldon LC); *Tito v Waddell (No.2)* [1977] 1 Ch 106 at 225 (Megarry VC).

indeed consented to it. It has sometimes been recognised that the court has a discretion to uphold a contract even though it was made in breach of the self-dealing rule.[262]

Fair-dealing rule　The fair-dealing rule will be breached where a fiduciary contracts with the principal in their own right. This will render the contract voidable,[263] save where the fiduciary can show that they took no advantage of their fiduciary position, that the transaction was fair[264] and that there had been full disclosure of everything which was or might be material to the principal's decision to enter into the transaction.[265] So, for example, if a trustee purchases a beneficiary's interest in trust property, the contract can be set aside by the beneficiary unless the trustee can establish the fairness of the transaction and that the trustee had not taken advantage of the principal.[266] Although a purchase from the beneficiary can be valid therefore, it remains a hazardous transaction because the negotiations and the final agreement must be completely above board and reasonable, with no hint of fraud, concealment or advantage of the principal taken by the fiduciary.[267] The rationale behind the rule is that any contract between the principal and fiduciary is suspect because of the conflict between the fiduciary's personal interest and duty to the principal.

2-046

Acting for more than one principal　Fiduciaries should avoid placing themselves in a position where their duty to one principal conflicts with their duty to another principal, [268] save where both principals have given their fully informed consent to such a conflict.[269] Such consent may be given expressly or may be implied where the principal was aware that the fiduciary was acting for another principal.[270] If such fully informed consent has not been obtained, where the interests of the two principals come into conflict any contract entered into by the fiduciary on behalf of one or both of the principals will be voidable,[271] although rescission will only be possible if the other principal with whom the transaction was made knew of the double employment.[272] The rationale behind this recognition of a breach of duty is that the conflict of duty means that the fiduciary is unable to provide undivided

2-047

---

262 *Holder v Holder* [1968] Ch 353 at 398 (Danckwerts LJ); *Hillsdown Holdings Plc v Pensions Ombudsman* [1997] 1 All E.R. 862 at 895 (Knox J).

263 *Re Cape Breton Co* (1885) 29 Ch D. 795 at 803 (Cotton LJ); *Burland v Earle* [1902] A.C. 83 at 99 (Lord Davey).

264 *Moody v Cox and Hatt* [1917] 2 Ch 71; *Tito v Waddell (No.2)* [1977] Ch 106 at 241 (Megarry VC).

265 *Demerara Bauxite Co Ltd v Hubbard* [1923] A.C. 673.

266 See *Thomson v Eatswood* (1877) 2 App. Cas. 215 at 236 (Lord Cairns LC). Conaglen has argued that fairness should simply be an evidential factor taken into account by the court in determining whether the principal gave his fully informed consent to the transaction: M. Conaglen, "A Reappraisal of the fiduciary self-dealing and fair-dealing Rules" (2006) C.L.J. 366 at [368].

267 See *Coles v Trecothick* (1804) 9 Ves. 234 at 247 (Lord Eldon LC).

268 *Clarke Boyce v Mouat* [1994] 1 A.C. 428; *Marks and Spencer Plc v Freshfields Bruckhaus Deringer (a firm)* [2004] EWHC 1337 (Ch); [2004] 1 W.L.R. 2331.

269 *Clark Boyce v Mouat* [1994] 1 A.C. 428 at 435.

270 *Bristol and West Building Society v Mothew* [1998] Ch 1 at 19 (Millett LJ).

271 *North and South Trust Co v Berkeley* [1971] 1 W.L.R. 470 at 485 (Donaldson J).

272 *Transvaal Land Co v New Belgium (Transvaal) Land and Development Co* [1914] 2 Ch 488; *North and South Trust Co v Berkeley* [1971] 1 W.L.R. 470 at 485 (Donaldson J). M. Conaglen, *Fiduciary Loyalty: Protecting the Due Performance of Non-Fiduciary Duties* (Oxford: Hart Publishing, 2010), p.159. It would not be appropriate to impute the fiduciary's knowledge of the double-employment to the principal: M. Conaglen, *Fiduciary Loyalty: Protecting the Due Performance of Non-Fiduciary Duties* (Oxford: Hart Publishing, 2010), p.161.

loyalty to each principal. It is no defence that making full disclosure to one principal will involve breach of the duty owed to the other,[273] since the fiduciary should not put themselves in a position where the duties conflict.[274] Liability for a conflict of duties owed to different principals can be avoided by an express or implied term in the contract of appointment which allows the fiduciary to act for other principals.[275]

2-048   **Bribery**   Bribery is committed where a third party either makes or agrees to make a payment or gift to a fiduciary, such as an agent, without the knowledge and consent of his principal. There is no need to prove that any of the parties were consciously aware that they were doing anything wrong for a payment to be characterised as a bribe.[276] Where a fiduciary enters into a contract with another on behalf of the principal as a result of the third party bribing the fiduciary,[277] the contract will be void because of the fiduciary's absence of authority to bind the principal.[278] Where, however, a principal is induced to enter into a contract with another party as a result of the fiduciary being bribed, either by the other party or somebody else, the contract may be voidable in Equity by virtue of breach of the no-conflict rule,[279] there being an irrebuttable presumption that the agent was influenced by the bribe.[280] The contract will only be voidable, however, if the conscience of the other party to the contract was affected in some way.[281] This will be established if the other party to the contract knew[282] that the principal was deprived of the fiduciary's disinterested advice,[283] that the principal neither knew nor consented to the payment to the fiduciary[284] and that the bribe was paid or

---

[273] *Moody v Cox and Hatt* [1917] 2 Ch 71.
[274] *Hilton v Barker, Booth and Eastwood* [2005] UKHL 8; [2005] 1 W.L.R. 567 at [44] (Lord Walker).
[275] *Kelly v Cooper* [1993] A.C. 205.
[276] *Ross River Ltd v Cambridge City Football Club Ltd* [2007] EWHC 2115 (Ch); [2008] 1 All E.R. 1004 at [218] (Briggs J).
[277] Or where the fiduciary has or will obtain a secret commission: *Logicrose Ltd v Southend United Football Club* [1988] 1 W.L.R. 1256 at 1260 (Millett J).
[278] *Heinl v Jykse Bank (Gibraltar) Ltd* [1999] Lloyd's Rep. Bank 511 at 521 (Nourse LJ).
[279] *Logicrose Ltd v Southend United Football Club* [1988] 1 W.L.R. 1256 at 1260 (Millett J). See also *Panama and South Pacific Telegraph Co v India Rubber, Gutta Percha, and Telegraph Works Co* (1875) L.R. 10 Ch. App. 515; *Grant v Gold Exploration and Development Syndicate Ltd* [1900] 1 Q.B. 233 at 249 (Collins LJ); *Armagas Ltd v Mundogas SA* [1986] A.C. 717 at 142 (Robert Goff LJ); *Hurstanger Ltd v Wilson* [2007] EWCA Civ 299 at [38]; [2007] 4 All E.R. 1118 at [38] (Tuckey LJ).
[280] *Hovenden and Sons v Millhof* (1900) 83 L.T. 41 at 43 (Romer LJ). See also *UBS AG v Depfa Bank Plc* [2017] EWCA Civ 1567; [2017] 2 Lloyd's Rep. 621 at [155] (Lord Briggs and Hamblen LJ).
[281] *UBS AG v Depfa Bank Plc* [2017] EWCA Civ 1567; [2017] 2 Lloyd's Rep. 621.
[282] *Logicrose Ltd v Southend United Football Club* [1988] 1 W.L.R. 1256 at 1261 (Millett J); *Chancery Client Partners Ltd v MRC 957 Ltd* [2016] EWHC 2142 (Ch). This includes Nelsonian blindness (turning a blind eye): *Logicrose Ltd v Southend United Football Club* [1988] 1 W.L.R. 1256 at 1261 (Millett J).
[283] *Logicrose Ltd v Southend United Football Club* [1988] 1 W.L.R. 1256 at 1261 (Millett J).
[284] *Ross River Ltd v Cambridge City Football Club Ltd* [2007] EWHC 2115 (Ch); [2008] 1 All E.R. 1004 at [203] (Briggs J); *Hurstanger Ltd v Wilson* [2007] EWCA Civ 299; [2007] 1 W.L.R. 2351 *Medsted Associates Ltd v Canaccord Genuity Wealth (International) Ltd* [2019] EWCA Civ 83; [2019] 1 W.L.R. 4481. Where the principal is a company it is the knowledge and consent of the directors rather than the shareholders which is relevant: *Ross River Ltd v Cambridge City Football Club Ltd* [2007] EWHC 2115 (Ch); [2008] 1 All E.R. 1004 at [207] (Briggs J). Disclosure of the bribe must be made to all the directors at a properly convened broad meeting attended by a sufficient quorum: *Ross River Ltd v Cambridge City Football Club Ltd* [2007] EWHC 2115 (Ch); [2008] 1 All E.R. 1004 at [214].

mentioned before the contract was made.[285] If the principal was aware of the possibility of the bribe but did not give their informed consent to its receipt, the consequent contract may still be rescinded if it would be just and proportionate to do so, having regard to questions of improper intent and motive.[286] It has been recognised that the other contracting party's conscience will be affected if they had dealt with the fiduciary secretly and behind the back of the principal and dishonestly assisted the fiduciary to abuse their position to make the contract, even if the fiduciary breached their duty in some other way.[287] Consequently in *UBS AG v Depfa Bank Plc*,[288] the principal could rescind a contract where the other contracting party knew of the fiduciary's conflict of interest but did not know that the fiduciary had been bribed by a third party.[289] If the other contracting party acts honestly they will not be affected by what they do not know provided that they do not turn a blind eye to the truth.

X.   BRIBERY

It was recognised in *Wood v Commercial First Business Ltd; Business Mortgage Finance 4 Plc v Pengelly*[290] that a contract may be voidable at Common Law where an agent of the claimant received a bribe[291] from the other party to the contract, even though the bribe was not received in breach of fiduciary duty. The contract will be voidable simply by showing that the recipient was under a legal duty to provide information, advice or a recommendation on an impartial or disinterested basis. If it is possible to establish that the agent did receive the bribe in breach of fiduciary duty, then rescission will be available in Equity,[292] but it was considered that it was not necessary to establish a fiduciary relationship as a pre-condition of civil liability.[293] In *Pengelly* a borrower successfully sought rescission of a loan transaction where the borrower's broker had received an undisclosed commission from the

2-049

---

[285] *Ross River Ltd v Cambridge City Football Club Ltd* [2007] EWHC 2115 (Ch); [2008] 1 All E.R. 1004 at [228] (Briggs J). Cf. *Panama and South Pacific Telegraph Co v India Rubber, Gutta Percha, and Telegraph Works Co* (1875) L.R. 10 Ch. App. 515 at 527 (James LJ) and 332 where Mellish LJ assumed the case involved termination for a repudiatory breach of contract.

[286] See *Johnson v EBS Pensioner Trustees Ltd* [2002] Lloyds Rep. P.N. 309; *Hurstanger Ltd v Wilson* [2007] EWCA Civ 299; [2007] 4 All E.R. 1118 at [50] (Tuckey LJ).

[287] *UBS AG v Depfa Bank Plc* [2017] EWCA Civ 1567; [2017] 2 Lloyd's Rep. 621. See P. Kelisher, "Rescission and attribution of knowledge in multi-party cases of dishonest assistance" (2018) 134 L.Q.R. 363.

[288] [2017] EWCA Civ 1567; [2017] 2 Lloyd's Rep. 621.

[289] Gloster LJ dissented on the ground that this interpretation of conscience was impracticable and introduced the 'moral standards of the vicarage' into commercial transactions: [2017] EWCA Civ 1567; [2017] 2 Lloyd's Rep. 621 at [347].

[290] [2021] EWCA Civ 471; [2022] Ch. 123. See A. Taylor (2021) 80 C.L.J. 452; J. Grower (2022) 138 L.Q.R. 15.

[291] This includes a "half-secret commission" where the principal is aware that a commission might be paid but is unaware of the amount and the agent breaches an obligation to inform the principal of the amount: *Wood v Commercial First Business Ltd* [2021] EWCA Civ 471; [2022] Ch. 123 at [128] (David Richards LJ).

[292] See para.2-048, above. Rescission in Equity might be preferable by virtue of the interpretation of the bars on rescission in Equity (see chapter 3) and the remedies following rescission (see chapter 4).

[293] That a fiduciary duty could not be established is somewhat artificial, especially because the court recognised that an agent subject to such a legal duty could be characterised as owing a fiduciary duty of loyalty ([2021] EWCA Civ 471; [2022] Ch. 123 at [102]), but it was recognised that courts should avoid the complex analysis of the nature of a fiduciary relationship or the duties associated with such a relationship.

lender, and even though the broker was not considered to have breached a fiduciary duty owed to the borrower. It was also recognised that the lender could be liable to the borrower not as an accessory to breach of fiduciary duty but as primary wrongdoer for the actionable wrong at Common Law of bribery, which is a species of fraud,[294] for which the remedies of money had and received and damages would be available.

---

[294] *Wood v Commercial First Business Ltd* [2021] EWCA Civ 471; [2022] Ch. 123 at [94] (David Richards LJ).

CHAPTER 3

BARS TO RESCISSION

The claimant's right to rescind a voidable contract may be barred in certain **3-001**
circumstances. Various bars to rescission have been recognised, which generally apply regardless of the ground for rescission and regardless of whether rescission occurs at Common Law or in Equity. The bars are, however, interpreted differently depending on the jurisdiction for rescission; being interpreted more restrictively at Common Law than in Equity. The bars also apply to claims to rescind voluntary dispositions and are interpreted even more liberally in that context than when seeking rescission of a contract.[1] The burden of establishing these bars is borne by the party who wishes to challenge rescission. In addition, where rescission is sought in Equity, the court has a discretion as to whether the remedy will be awarded and that discretion will not be exercised if the consequences of rescission are considered to be unfair and disproportionate,[2] or if another remedy is more appropriate[3] or if the party seeking rescission does not come to the court "with clean hands".[4]

I.   COMPLETE RESTORATION NOT POSSIBLE

General principles   Rescission of the contract will be barred if it would not be **3-002**
possible to restore the defendant to the position which they occupied before the contract was made.[5] This is also called the bar of *restitutio in integrum* being impossible, or the obligation to make counter-restitution.[6] The bar operates as a defence so that, once the claimant has established a right to rescind the contract, the burden shifts to the defendant to establish that it is not possible to restore them to their pre-contractual position.[7] The justification for this bar is both to ensure that the claimant is not unjustly enriched at the expense of the defendant,[8] which would occur if the claimant was able to recover benefits from the defendant but was not required

---

[1]   *Rogge v Rogge* [2019] EWHC 1949 (Ch); [2019] W.T.L.R. 1305 at [164.1] (Deputy Master Henderson).

[2]   *Hurstanger Ltd v Wilson* [2007] EWCA Civ 299; [2007] 1 W.L.R. 2351.

[3]   *UBS AG v Depfa Bank Plc* [2017] EWCA Civ 1567; [2017] 2 Lloyd's Rep. 621 at [157] (Lord Briggs and Hamblen LJ).

[4]   *Royal Bank of Scotland Plc v Highland Financial Partners LP* [2013] EWCA Civ 328 at [158] (Aikens LJ); *UBS AG v Depfa Bank Plc* [2017] EWCA Civ 1567; [2017] 2 Lloyd's Rep. 621.

[5]   *Clarke v Dickson* (1858) El. Bl. and El. 148, 120 E.R. 463; *Western Bank of Scotland v Addie* (1867) L.R. 1 Sc. and Div. 145; *Spence v Crawford* [1939] 3 All E.R. 271 at 288–289 (Lord Wright); *Smith New Court Securities Ltd v Scrimgeour Vickers (Asset Management) Ltd* [1994] 1 W.L.R. 1271 at 1280 (Nourse LJ); *Halpern v Halpern (Nos 1 and 2)* [2007] EWCA Civ 291; [2008] Q.B. 195.

[6]   *Dunbar Bank Plc v Nadeem* [1998] 3 All E.R. 876 at 884 (Millett LJ).

[7]   *Erlanger v The New Sombrero Phosphate Co* (1878) 3 App. Cas. 1218 at 1283 (Lord Blackburn).

[8]   *Spence v Crawford* [1939] 3 All E.R. 271 at 288–289 (Lord Wright); *Banwaitt v Dewji* [2013] EWHC 879 (QB) at [86] (Patten LJ).

to restore benefits received from the defendant, and also to protect the defendant from being in a worse position following the rescission of the contract than the defendant occupied before the contract was made.[9] Although the doctrine of *restitutio in integrum* is often described as requiring both parties to be restored to their pre-contractual position,[10] the doctrine only operates as a bar to rescission when the defendant cannot be restored to their original position.[11] The fact that a claimant cannot be restored to their pre-contractual position precisely will not bar rescission,[12] presumably because the claimant has elected to rescind the contract and takes the risk of not being restored precisely to their pre-contractual position. If the defendant can be restored to their original position but the claimant is unwilling to do so, rescission will be barred.[13]

3-003   The *restitutio in integrum* being impossible bar only applies as regards the rights and obligations which had been created by the contract.[14] The fact that a contracting party has incurred losses to third parties by relying on the validity of the contract does not mean that *restitutio in integrum* cannot be achieved.[15] The bar will not operate to defeat rescission where the contract is executory, since the effect of rescission will simply be to terminate future contractual obligations and the claimant will not have received any benefit from the defendant so that there is nothing to return.[16] The bar is typically engaged where the claimant has received a benefit under the contract which they are not able to restore to the defendant. The most controversial issue relating to this bar concerns whether the claimant is required to restore the defendant to his pre-contract position precisely or whether substantial restoration is sufficient. The bar also applies where circumstances have irreversibly changed so that the defendant would be unjustifiably prejudiced if the contract was rescinded.[17]

3-004   Where the claimant has received a benefit from the defendant pursuant to the contract there are a variety of mechanisms for ensuring that the defendant can be restored to their pre-contract position. Where the claimant has received property from the defendant then returning that property, or its traceable substitute,[18] to the defendant will satisfy the *restitutio in integrum* requirement. In *Salt v Stratstone Specialist Ltd*[19] it was recognised that a contract for the purchase of a car could be rescinded for misrepresentation that the car was new, even though title to the car had been registered with the claimant, because the *restitutio in integrum* bar was concerned with changes in the car as a physical entity, rather than its legal condition. Further, the fact that the car had depreciated in value or the claimant had intermittently used it did not bar rescission, but could be reflected in a compensatory award

---

9   E. Bant, *The Change of Position Defence* (Oxford: Hart Publishing, 2009), p.118
10   See, e.g. *Erlanger v The New Sombrero Phosphate Co* (1878) 3 App. Cas. 1218 at 1278 (Lord Blackburn).
11   *Spence v Crawford* [1939] 3 All E.R. 271 at 289 (Lord Wright).
12   *Spence v Crawford* [1939] 3 All E.R. 271 at 279 (Lord Thankerton); *Halpern v Halpern* [2007] EWCA Civ 291, [2008] Q.B. 195 at [75] (Carnwath LJ).
13   *Gamatronic (UK) Ltd v Hamilton* [2016] EWHC 2225 (QB) at [224] (Akhlaq Choudhury QC).
14   *Newbigging v Adam* (1886) 34 Ch D. 582 at 593 (Bowen LJ).
15   *UBS AG v Depfa Bank Plc* [2017] EWCA Civ 1567; [2017] 2 Lloyd's Rep. 621 at [225] (Lord Briggs and Hamblen LJ).
16   *National Commercial Bank (Jamaica) Ltd v Hew's Executors* [2003] UKPC 51 at [43] (contract of guarantee).
17   See para.3-018.
18   See further para.4-028.
19   [2015] EWCA Civ 745; [2015] 2 C.L.C. 269.

for the other party if practical justice required this.[20] Similarly, the requirement will be satisfied if title to the property or its traceable substitute has been transferred to the defendant so that they have a claim to recover the property or its value. Finally, the requirement will be satisfied if the defendant has a personal claim for money paid to the claimant, since the court can then enforce the claim.[21] Where, however, the claimant has received shares from the defendant, the claimant must tender the shares to the defendant because title to the shares can only be revested in the defendant if the register of members is altered.[22]

Where the claimant has received a benefit from the defendant, the claimant will **3-005** not always be required to restore this benefit to the defendant before rescission can be effected. For example, the bar of *restitutio in integrum* being impossible will not apply where the benefit was not obtained by the claimant under the contract which the claimant wishes to rescind;[23] where the benefit cannot be returned because of the defendant's wrongdoing, such as where the defendant fraudulently communicated information to the claimant which cannot be restored;[24] where the benefit received by the claimant corresponded with a benefit received by the defendant, so that one can be set off against the other;[25] where the benefit to the claimant was worthless;[26] where the defendant had sought the destruction of property which had been transferred to the claimant;[27] or where property was transferred to the claimant which was forfeited but only after the claimant had notified the defendant of the election to rescind the contract, because the defendant then bears the risk of such forfeiture.[28]

Where the ground of rescission is dependent on the fault of the defendant, such **3-006** as where the defendant has induced the contract by fraud, the fact that the defendant cannot be restored to their pre-contractual position may not necessarily defeat rescission,[29] at least where the reason why *restitutio in integrum* is not possible is because of the defendant's own fraudulent conduct. So, in *Spence v Crawford*[30] rescission was not barred by the fact that the defendant could not be restored to his pre-contractual position of sharing the controlling interest in a company with the claimant, where the reason why *restitutio in integrum* was not possible was because of the defendant's fraudulent misconduct in inducing the claimant to sell shares to him. Similarly, an insurer is not required to return premiums to the assured where the insurer seeks to rescind the contract for the assured's fraudulent misrepresentation.[31]

Restitution at Common Law   At Common Law the claimant is under a duty of **3-007**

---

20 *Salt v Stratstone Specialist Ltd* [2015] EWCA Civ 745; [2015] 2 C.L.C. 269 at [24] (Longmore LJ).
21 See below, paras 4-018 and 4-020, for the more complicated scenario where the claimant has benefited from the use of goods received from the defendant or from the receipt of services.
22 *Clarke v Dickson* (1858) El. Bl. & El. 148; 120 E.R. 463; *Kennedy v Panama New Zealand & Australian Royal Mail Co* (1866–67) L.R. 2 Q.B. 580. See D. O'Sullivan, S. Elliott and R. Zakrzewski, *The Law of Rescission*, 3rd edn (Oxford: Oxford University Press, 2023), para.14.59.
23 *Logicrose Ltd v Southend United Football Club Ltd* [1988] 1 W.L.R. 1256 at 1264 (Millett J).
24 *Rees v De Bernardy* [1896] 2 Ch. 437 at 446 (Romer J).
25 *Hulton v Hulton* [1917] 1 K.B. 813 at 826 (Scrutton LJ).
26 *Halpern v Halpern* [2007] EWCA Civ 291, [2008] Q.B. 195 at [74] (Carnwath LJ).
27 *Hulton v Hulton* [1917] 1 K.B. 813 at 825 (Scrutton LJ): destruction of documents at the request of the defendant was not a bar to rescission.
28 *Maturin v Tredinnick* (1864) 10 L.T. (N.S.) 331.
29 *Lagunas Nitrate Co v Lagunas Syndicate* [1899] 2 Ch. 392 at 434 (Lindley MR); *Spence v Crawford* [1939] 3 All E.R. 271 at 281 (Lord Thankerton).
30 [1939] 3 All E.R. 271.
31 Marine Insurance Act 1906 s.84(3)(a).

making *restitutio in integrum* before the contract can be rescinded.[32] At Common Law the bar is interpreted strictly, so that if the claimant is unable to restore the defendant precisely to the position the defendant occupied before the contract was made, rescission will be barred.[33] So, for example, if the claimant has consumed[34] or disposed[35] of property which was received from the defendant under a voidable contract, the claimant will be barred from rescinding the contract because the property cannot be restored,[36] such as where documents have been received under the contract, which are then destroyed.[37] Similarly, rescission will be barred at Common Law where the claimant has received property the nature of which substantially alters other than due to an inherent defect, such as where the claimant has bought live cattle which are then slaughtered or obtains shares in a company which is in the process of being wound up at the time rescission is sought.[38]

3-008   The reason why the requirement to make *restitutio in integrum* is interpreted so strictly at Common Law is because the Common Law lacks the adjudicative machinery to make financial adjustments on rescission, so that it is unable to value benefits received,[39] even though this now regularly occurs within the law of unjust enrichment.[40] But it is also a function of the nature of rescission at Common Law that it occurs automatically once the claimant has given notice of his intention to rescind.[41] At the point when the intention to rescind is communicated the defendant must be restored to their pre-contractual position either by recovering any benefits transferred to the claimant or by acquiring a right to recover the benefits, such as a claim in unjust enrichment to recover money the defendant had paid to the claimant.[42] It follows that there is no scope for the application of judicial discretion to authorise substantial restoration of the defendant to their pre-contractual position.

3-009   The Common Law does not recognise a claim to recover the reasonable value of an asset as being a sufficient substitute for the recovery of the asset itself.[43] Where chattels have been transferred to the claimant under the contract, the claimant will

---

[32] *Abram Steamship Co Ltd v Westville Shipping Co Ltd* [1923] A.C. 773 at 781 (Lord Atkinson). For the defence of counter-restitution to claims in unjust enrichment, see para.4-013.

[33] *Clarke v Dickson* (1858) El. Bl. and El. 148; 120 E.R. 463; *Erlanger v The New Sombrero Phosphate Co* (1878) 3 App. Cas. 1218 at 1278 (Lord Blackburn); *O'Sullivan v Management Agency and Music Ltd* [1985] Q.B. 428 at 465 (Fox LJ); *Smith New Court Securities Ltd v Scrimgeour Vickers (Asset Management) Ltd* [1994] 1 W.L.R. 1271 at 1280 (Nourse LJ).

[34] *Clarke v Dickson* (1858) El. Bl. and El. 148 at 153; 120 E.R. 463 at 466 (Crompton J).

[35] *Ladywell Mining Co v Brookes* (1887) 35 Ch D. 400 at 414 (Lindley LJ).

[36] *Street v Blay* (1831) 2 B. & Ad. 456; 109 E.R. 1212 and *The Sheffield Nickel and Silver Plating Co Ltd v Unwin* (1877) 2 Q.B.D. 214 at 224 (Lush J). See also *Capcon Holdings Plc v Edwards* [2007] EWHC 2662 (Ch) where *restitutio in integrum* in respect of a contract for the purchase of shares was held not to be possible because the purchaser's conduct had caused the shares to depreciate in value.

[37] See *Halpern v Halpern (Nos 1 and 2)* [2007] EWCA Civ 291, [2008] Q.B. 195. Although Carnwath LJ did recognise at [75], that it would be surprising if the law could not provide a suitable remedy in such circumstances, possibly in Equity (by virtue of fusion of the law on *restitutio in integrum*) or by the identification of a tortious claim.

[38] *Clarke v Dickson* (1858) El. Bl. and Bl. 148 at 153; 120 E.R. 463 at 466 (Crompton J).

[39] *Erlanger v The New Sombrero Phosphate Co* (1878) 3 App. Cas. 1218 at 1278 (Lord Blackburn).

[40] See para.4-012.

[41] D. O'Sullivan, S. Elliott and R. Zakrzewski, *The Law of Rescission*, 3rd edn (Oxford: Oxford University Press, 2023), para.18.25.

[42] See para.4-012.

[43] *Smith New Court Securities Ltd v Scrimgeour Vickers (Asset Management) Ltd* [1994] 1 W.L.R. 1271. See para.3-010.

only be able to make *restitutio in integrum* if the chattels are returned to the defendant in the same condition as when they had been received, but the claimant is not required to account for the benefit arising from the use of the asset.[44] Sometimes the fact that the claimant has benefited from the use of property will bar rescission, although this will depend on the nature of the property received. In *Hunt v Silk*[45] the claimant had entered into possession of land after the contract had been made and was barred from rescinding the contract because, having enjoyed the benefit of the land, he could not restore this benefit to the defendant; the agreement having been partly executed.

In *Smith New Court Securities Ltd v Scrimgeour Vickers (Asset Management)* **3-010** *Ltd*[46] the claimant had been induced to buy shares as a result of the defendant's fraudulent misrepresentation. Although the case turned on the assessment of damages for fraud, Nourse LJ recognised that the claimant would have been unable to rescind the contract and recover the full purchase price of the shares from the defendant, because the claimant had sold the shares to a third party and so was unable to make "substantial restitution *in specie* of the property" which it had received.[47] It would not have been sufficient that the claimant could pay to the defendant the value of the purchase price for the shares which had been received from the third party, presumably because rescission at Common Law is a self-help remedy which operates automatically on election[48] so that there is no scope for the benefit to be valued. Nourse LJ described this as a hard rule. On appeal to the House of Lords, Lord Browne-Wilkinson did state, obiter, that if rescission was barred because the actual property received could not be returned, the law would need to be reviewed.[49] But he did recognise that, where shares in a public quoted company had been purchased and then sold to a third party, substantial *restitutio in integrum* could be made by purchasing identical shares in the market and transferring them to the defendant.[50] Such a result would be available if rescission occurred in Equity.[51] In *Halpern v Halpern (Nos 1 and 2)*[52] Carnwath LJ expressed a willingness to adopt a much more flexible approach to the *restitutio in integrum* requirement at Common Law, an approach which is consistent with that which is adopted in Equity.[53]

Restoration of the defendant to their pre-contractual position means that the **3-011** claimant either restores property which had been transferred by the defendant or the defendant acquires a right to recover the benefit transferred. Where the defendant has transferred money to the claimant pursuant to the contract, the defendant will have a claim to recover the value of that money at Common Law, [54] which will usually be a claim in unjust enrichment founded on total failure of basis, with the total failure arising from the retrospective invalidity of the contract following its

---

[44] *Street v Blay* (1831) 2 B. & Ad. 456 at 461; 109 E.R. 1212 at 1214 (Lord Tenterden CJ).
[45] (1804) 5 East 44; 102 E.R. 1142; *Blackburn v Smith* (1848) 2 Ex. 783; 154 E.R. 707.
[46] [1994] 1 W.L.R. 1271.
[47] [1994] 1 W.L.R. 1271 at 1280 (Nourse LJ).
[48] See para.1-010.
[49] [1997] A.C. 254 at 262.
[50] [1997] A.C. 254 at 262.
[51] See para.3-014.
[52] [2007] EWCA Civ 291, [2008] Q.B. 195 at [74]. See also *Sabah Shipyard (Pakistan) Ltd v Pakistan* [2007] EWHC 2602 (Comm) at [131] (Clarke J).
[53] See para.1-028.
[54] *Clough v The London and North Western Railway Co* (1871) L.R. 7 Ex. 26 at 37 (Mellor J).

rescission.[55] But a personal claim in unjust enrichment for the value of property transferred will not suffice to enable *restitutio in integrum* to be effected, because this would require the property to be valued and this is something which the Common Law is not generally willing to do. It has, however, been recognised that where the claimant wishes to rescind a contract for the provision of services after those services had been provided by the defendant, the claimant might be required to pay for their reasonable value, but only if they were of benefit to the claimant.[56] This is consistent with the law of unjust enrichment which recognises restitutionary claims for the value of services,[57] and also for the value of property too.

3-012   Whether it is possible to restore the defendant to their pre-contractual position is to be assessed at the time the claimant elects to rescind the contract.[58] Since rescission occurs automatically at Common Law by the election of the claimant the court will only have a role subsequently to determine whether the contract has been effectively rescinded. If the court concludes that the defendant had not been and cannot be restored to their pre-contractual position it follows that the contract will not have been effectively rescinded.[59]

3-013   If the claim for rescission is barred at Common Law because of the strict interpretation of *restitutio in integrum* then the claimant should seek rescission in Equity, since there is a concurrent jurisdiction to rescind both at Common Law and in Equity so that all factors triggering rescission which are recognised at Common Law are also recognised in Equity.[60]

3-014   **Restitution in Equity**   Where rescission is sought in Equity the *restitutio in integrum* requirement can be justified by reference to the maxim that a claimant who seeks Equity must do Equity.[61]

    Whereas the Common Law requires the defendant to be restored precisely to the position they occupied before the contract was made, Equity does not require precise restoration; it is sufficient that the defendant can be restored substantially to their pre-contractual position, by reference to a more flexible criterion of "practical justice".[62] It follows that the bar of *restitutio in integrum* being impossible is of much more limited significance in Equity. Equity effects this substantial restitution by directing accounts and making allowances.[63]

3-015   Since rescission in Equity occurs by order of the court it is possible for the court to value the benefit which has been received by the claimant and to ensure that the

---

55 See further para.4-014.

56 *Halpern v Halpern* [2007] EWCA Civ 291; [2008] Q.B. 195 at [74] (Carnwath LJ).

57 *Benedetti v Sawiris* [2013] UKSC 50; [2014] A.C. 938.

58 *Alati v Kruger* (1955) 94 C.L.R. 216 at 223 (Dixon CJ) (High Court of Australia).

59 *Abram Steamship Co Ltd v Westville Shipping Co Ltd* [1923] A.C. 773 at 781 (Lord Atkinson).

60 *Newbigging v Adam* (1886) 34 Ch D. 582 at 592 (Bowen LJ). See *Spence v Crawford* [1939] 3 All E.R. 271 at 288 (Lord Wright).

61 *Sturgis v Champneys* (1839) 5 My. and Cr. 97 at 102; 41 E.R. 308 at 310 (Lord Cottenham LC); *Hulton v Hulton* [1917] 1 K.B. 813 at 825 (Scrutton LJ); *O'Sullivan v Management Agency and Music Ltd* [1985] 1 Q.B. 428 at 458 (Dunn LJ).

62 *Erlanger v New Sombrero Phosphate Co* (1878) 3 App. Cas. 1218 at 1278 (Lord Blackburn); *Lagunas Nitrate Co v Lagunas Syndicate* [1899] 2 Ch. 392 at 457 (Rigby LJ); *Compagnie Francaise des Chemins de Fer Paris-Orleans v Leeston Shipping Co Ltd* [1919] 1 Lloyd's Rep. 235 at 238 (Roche J); *Spence v Crawford* [1939] 3 All E.R. 271 at 279 (Lord Thankerton) at 288 (Lord Wright); *O'Sullivan v Management Agency and Music Ltd* [1985] 1 Q.B. 428 at 458 (Dunn LJ) at 466 (Fox LJ); *Halpern v Halpern (Nos 1 and 2)* [2007] EWCA Civ 291; [2008] Q.B. 195 at [61] (Carnwath LJ).

63 *Cheese v Thomas* [1994] 1 W.L.R. 129 at 136 (Sir Donald Nicholls VC).

defendant is restored to their original position financially if not *in specie*; the right to rescission is conditional on counter-restitution being made.[64] So, rescission will still be possible in Equity where the defendant had transferred property to the claimant who had disposed of or destroyed it,[65] or where services had been provided by the defendant to the claimant,[66] because the claimant will be required to pay to the defendant the reasonable value of the property or service as assessed at the time the order for rescission is made. So, for example, in *Erlanger v New Sombrero Phosphate Co*[67] the claimant sought to rescind a contract for the purchase of a phosphate mine on the ground of non-disclosure of a material fact by the defendant. Since the mine had been worked by the claimant it was held the contract could only be rescinded if the claimant returned the mine to the defendant and accounted for the profits made from working it. Lord Blackburn recognised that a court of Equity would grant relief "whenever, by the use of its powers, it can do what is practically just, though it cannot restore the parties precisely to the state they were in before the contract".[68] In the exercise of this power the court will also be prepared to grant the defendant an allowance in respect of the deterioration in value of any property which is returned to the defendant, to compensate the defendant for any loss suffered,[69] or to compensate the defendant for incurring a liability to a third party,[70] in each case to ensure that the defendant is restored to their pre-contractual position.

That the inability to make precise restitution to the defendant will not bar rescission in Equity has been recognised in a number of different contexts. **3-016**

(i) Where the claimant has received fungible assets which have been disposed of, such as publicly quoted shares, it is sufficient that the claimant can obtain identical assets in the market and restore them to the defendant.[71] Care must be taken in such circumstances to ensure that the claimant does not profit from this transaction of obtaining the substitute shares, which would occur where the substitute shares are purchased for a lower price than the shares which the claimant had sold.[72] This might be dealt with by requiring the claimant to account to the defendant for any profit made, by paying to the defendant the difference between the price at which the claimant sold the original shares and the price paid for the substitute shares.[73]

(ii) Where the claimant has received property from the defendant which has

---

[64] *Dunbar Bank Plc v Nadeem* [1998] 3 All E.R. 876 at 884 (Millett LJ). In *Ruttle Plant Hire Ltd v Secretary of State for the Environment Food and Rural Affairs* [2007] EWHC 2870 (TCC), Ramsey J recognised at [90], that the claimant is not required to provide the security of full counter-restitution before being allowed to proceed with an application to the court for rescission of the contract.

[65] *Erlanger v New Sombrero Phosphate Co* (1878) 3 App. Cas. 1218 at 1278 (Lord Blackburn).

[66] *O'Sullivan v Management Agency and Music Ltd* [1985] 1 Q.B. 428. See also *Atlantic Lines and Navigation Co Inc v Hallam Ltd* [1983] 1 Lloyd's Rep. 188 at 202 (Mustill J) and *Guinness Plc v Saunders* [1990] 2 A.C. 693 at 698 (Lord Goff).

[67] (1878) 3 App. Cas. 1218.

[68] *Erlanger v New Sombrero Phosphate Co* (1878) 3 App. Cas. 1218 at 1278.

[69] *Erlanger v New Sombrero Phosphate Co* (1878) 3 App. Cas. 1218 at 1278 (Lord Blackburn); *Lagunas Nitrate Co v Lagunas Syndicate* [1899] 2 Ch. 392 at 457 (Rigby LJ).

[70] *Spence v Crawford* [1939] 3 All E.R. 271 at 283 (Lord Thankerton).

[71] *Smith New Court Securities Ltd v Scrimgeour Vickers (Asset Management) Ltd* [1997] A.C. 254 at 262 (Lord Browne-Wilkinson).

[72] See R. Halson, "Rescission for Misrepresentation" [1997] R.L.R. 89 at 92.

[73] See R. Halson, "Rescission for Misrepresentation" [1997] R.L.R. 89 at 92.

been sold, it will be sufficient for the claimant to account for the proceeds of sale.[74]

(iii) Where the asset has been dissipated but can be valued, that value should be transferred to the defendant. This was recognised in *Mahoney v Purnell*[75] where shares had been sold and their value was awarded to the defendant as a condition of rescission.

(iv) Where the claimant has used the asset, they will be required to account for the value of that use by paying the reasonable value of the use to the defendant.[76]

(v) Where the property has deteriorated Equity can give relief for the fall in value[77] and will even be willing to apportion the loss between the claimant and the defendant.[78]

(vi) Where the defendant improved property which was transferred under the contract the claimant may be required to pay for that improvement before the property can be recovered.[79]

3-017   Rescission will, however, be barred in Equity if it is not possible to restore the defendant to their pre-contractual position because it is not possible to value the property or the service which had been transferred with any degree of accuracy,[80] or because the property which had been transferred to the claimant had changed in its nature so that it is no longer identifiable in any reasonable sense,[81] other than due to an inherent vice in the nature of the property which existed at the time it was transferred to the claimant.[82] So, for example, in *Thomas Witter Ltd v TBP Industries Ltd*[83] rescission was barred as being impractical where a company had been sold to the claimant but the nature of the business changed from being the operator of licensed premises to a property holding company and there had been numerous changes of staff. In *Adam v Newbigging*,[84] however, the claimant sought to rescind a contract by virtue of which he became a partner in the defendant's business, on the ground of non-fraudulent misrepresentation. Whilst the claimant was partner the business became insolvent, but this was held not to bar rescission because it was due to an inherent vice in the business which already existed when the contract was made between the claimant and the defendant. Where the change in the asset arises after the claimant has learned of their right to rescind the contract, rescission will be barred.[85]

3-018   **Irreversible change of circumstances**   Although one function of the *restitutio in*

---

[74] *Savary v King* (1856) 5 HLC 627 at 667; 10 E.R. 1046 at 1063.

[75] [1996] 3 All E.R. 61. See para.4-019. See also *Securities and Investments Board v Pantell SA (No.2)* [1993] Ch. 256 at 283 (Steyn LJ).

[76] *Compagnie Francaise des Chemins de Fer Paris-Orleans v Leeston Shipping Co Ltd* [1919] 1 Lloyd's Rep. 235; *Alati v Kruger* (1955) 94 C.L.R. 216 at 224 (Dixon CJ).

[77] *Erlanger v New Sombrero Phosphate Co* (1878) 3 App. Cas. 1218 at 1278 (Lord Blackburn).

[78] *Cheese v Thomas* [1994] 1 W.L.R. 129 at 136 (Sir Donald Nicholls VC).

[79] *O'Sullivan v Management Agency and Music Ltd* [1985] Q.B. 428 at 466 (Fox LJ).

[80] This will be rare but see *Dunbar Bank Plc v Nadeem* [1998] 3 All E.R. 876 at 888 where Morritt LJ contemplated that the wife would have been unable to restore a benefit to her husband because it had become encumbered by a subsequent charge.

[81] *Spence v Crawford* [1939] 3 All E.R. 271 at 279 (Lord Thankerton).

[82] *Adam v Newbigging* (1888) 13 App. Cas. 308.

[83] [1996] 2 All E.R. 573 at 587 (Jacob J). See also *Boyd and Forrest v Glasgow and South Western Railway Co* [1915] S.C. (HL) 20 (land could not be restored to its original condition).

[84] (1888) 13 App. Cas. 308.

[85] *Lagunas Nitrate Co v Lagunas Syndicate* [1899] 2 Ch. 392 at 433–434.

integrum bar is to ensure that the claimant is not unjustly enriched at the expense of the defendant, by requiring the claimant to make restitution to the defendant of benefits received, the bar also operates in Equity to ensure that rescission will not unjustifiably prejudice the defendant, for otherwise rescission will cause injustice.[86] So, even if the claimant has offered to return benefits to the defendant, rescission may still be barred if the circumstances are such that rescission of the contract would be to the defendant's prejudice. This was recognised by Lord Blackburn in *Erlanger v New Sombrero Phosphate Co*[87] as regards either irreversible changes in the state of the property which had been transferred to the claimant or changes in the position of the parties. So, for example, in *Holder v Holder*[88] rescission was barred in Equity because the defendant had incurred liabilities which he could not recoup, so that *restitutio in integrum* was not possible. Although in *De Molestina v Ponton*[89] Colman J did recognise that the remedy of rescission was "not fettered by some overriding equitable test as to whether the consequences would work unfairly to the misrepresentor" and preferred to focus instead on whether substantial restitution was possible, there are certainly circumstances where rescission is barred because of the unfairness which would result to the defendant. But the identification of such unfairness is often inextricably linked with the claimant's delay in seeking rescission, [90] this being a separate bar to rescission.[91]

Where the trigger for rescission is founded on the defendant's conscious wrongdoing, such as fraud, rescission is less likely to be barred on the ground that the effect of rescission will be to prejudice the defendant.[92] So, in *Spence v Crawford* the fact that the defendant would lose control of a company if a contract of sale of shares was avoided did not bar rescission because it was a consequence of the defendant's fraud. But it was recognised that had the contract been voidable for innocent misrepresentation the fact that the defendant could not be placed in his original position of controlling a company might bar rescission. Rescission will still be barred, however, even though the defendant has participated in conscious wrongdoing, where the claimant has delayed seeking rescission after they were aware of the right to rescind and in the meantime there has been such a change of circumstances that rescission would prejudice the defendant.[93] In such circumstances the claimant's delay in seeking rescission counteracts the defendant's fault in triggering the ground of rescission in the first place. **3-019**

Depreciation in the value of the asset due to changes in the market will generally not constitute a significant change in the nature of the asset to bar rescission,[94] save where the depreciation occurred after the claimant had become aware of their right to rescind the contract and had delayed rescission. This is because the claimant cannot speculate with the value of the property which had been transferred under **3-020**

---

86 See D. O'Sullivan, S. Elliott and R. Zakrzewski, *The Law of Rescission*, 3rd edn (Oxford: Oxford University Press, 2023), para.18.06.
87 (1878) 3 App. Cas. 1218 at 1279 (Lord Blackburn).
88 [1968] Ch. 353 at 395 (Harman LJ).
89 [2002] 1 Lloyd's Rep. 271 at 287.
90 *Armstrong v Jackson* [1917] 2 K.B. 822 at 829 (McCardie J).
91 See para.3-033.
92 *Spence v Crawford* [1939] 3 All E.R. 271 at 281–282 (Lord Thankerton).
93 *Clough v The London and North Western Railway Co* (1871) 7 L.R. Ex. 26 at 35 (Mellor J).
94 *Armstrong v Jackson* [1917] K.B. 822 at 829 (McCardie J); *Cheese v Thomas* [1994] 1 W.L.R. 129 at 136 (Sir Donald Nicholls VC); *Salt v Stratstone Specialist Ltd* [2015] EWCA Civ 745; [2015] 2 C.L.C. 269 at [24] (Longmore LJ).

the contract, with the decision whether to rescind the contract turning on whether or not the value of the property had changed.[95]

3-021   Where rescission is sought in Equity and the effect of rescinding the contract may be to cause the defendant prejudice by virtue of a change of circumstances, the court may be able to make pecuniary adjustments to reduce the prejudicial consequences,[96] such as by apportioning losses between the claimant and the defendant following depreciation in the value of property.[97]

3-022   **Rationalisation of the bar**   There is no longer any reason why rescission at Common Law should be barred because the parties cannot be restored precisely to their initial position. It should be sufficient that the parties can be restored substantially by virtue of receiving equivalent property to that which had been transferred or receiving the reasonable value of the property or services which had been transferred to the other party. This is consistent with the Senior Courts Act 1981 s.49,[98] which states that, where there is a conflict or variance between the rules of the Common Law and Equity, the rules of Equity should prevail. Since the bar that *restitutio in integrum* is impossible is founded on the same principles at Common Law and in Equity it should follow that, to the extent they conflict, the equitable interpretation should prevail. Consequently, in all cases of rescission it should be sufficient that the claimant can restore the defendant substantially to the position the defendant occupied before the contract was made.[99]

II.   AFFIRMATION

3-023   **General principles**   The right to rescission will be waived if the person entitled to rescind elects to waive the right and affirms the contract.[100] A contract will only have been affirmed if the claimant knew of the circumstances which enabled them to rescind the transaction and the claimant had unequivocally manifested an intention to affirm the contract once they were free from the effects of the vitiating factor which gave rise to the right to rescind in the first place.[101]

3-024   Where the contract is affirmed it remains effective, but the claimant can still sue the defendant for its breach.[102] The burden of proving that the right to rescind has been waived is borne by the defendant who asserts that the claimant affirmed the contract.[103] This bar to rescission operates in the same way regardless of whether the right to rescind arises at Common Law or in Equity.

3-025   The bar of affirmation applies regardless of the effect of the affirmation on the defendant, who is not required to prove any detrimental reliance on the act of affirmation or even awareness that it had occurred, since affirmation depends on an

---

[95]   *Erlanger v The New Sombrero Phosphate Co* (1878) 3 App. Cas. 1218 at 1281 (Lord Blackburn).

[96]   *Erlanger v New Sombrero Phosphate Co* (1878) 3 App. Cas. 1218 at 1278 (Lord Blackburn); *Lagunas Nitrate Co v Lagunas Syndicate* [1899] 2 Ch. 392 at 457 (Rigby LJ).

[97]   *Cheese v Thomas* [1994] 1 W.L.R. 129 at 136 (Sir Donald Nicholls VC).

[98]   Which effectively reproduces Judicature Act 1873 s.25(11). See para.1-028.

[99]   *Halpern v Halpern (Nos 1 and 2)* [2007] EWCA Civ 291 [2008] Q.B. 195 at [76] (Carnwath LJ).

[100]   *SK Shipping Europe Ltd v Capital VLCC 3 Corp* [2022] EWCA Civ 231; [2022] 2 All E.R. (Comm) 784 at [73] (Males LJ).

[101]   *Leeds City Council Council v Barclays Bank Plc* [2021] EWHC 363 (Comm); [2021] Q.B. 1027 at [165] (Cockerill J).

[102]   *Car and Universe Finance Co Ltd v Caldwell* [1965] 1 Q.B. 525 at 550 (Sellers LJ).

[103]   *Erlanger v The New Sombrero Phosphate Co* (1878) 3 App. Cas. 1218 at 1283 (Lord Blackburn).

objective manifestation of a choice to affirm by the party who has a right to rescind.[104]

Once the claimant has elected to affirm the contract this is usually irrevocable, [105] even if the defendant has not relied on the election. If, however, the claimant discovers a new ground of rescission, such as a new misrepresentation or an additional material fact which was not disclosed, the affirmation may be avoided and the right to rescind revived.[106]

3-026

Knowledge of circumstances   The claimant can only be considered to have affirmed the contract if they knew of the facts which gave rise to the right to rescind the contract.[107] So, for example, where the claimant had been induced to enter into the contract as the result of a misrepresentation, they will not have affirmed the contract if they had not discovered the material facts,[108] although it is not necessary for the claimant to know all aspects or incidents of the facts,[109] it being sufficient that the claimant knows the facts which would be needed to plead the case.[110] Similarly, where the claimant entered into the contract as the result of a nondisclosure of a material fact, the claimant can only affirm the contract once they knew of the material fact which had not been disclosed.[111] Rescission will not be barred if the claimant merely had the means of discovering that there was a ground for rescinding the transaction, even if this could have been discovered with due diligence;[112] constructive knowledge will not suffice.[113] Suspicion of the facts which relate to the identification of the vitiating factor will not bar rescission either.[114] It has, however, been recognised that deliberately failing to investigate the truth will

3-027

---

[104]   *ICCI Ltd v The Royal Hotel Ltd* [1998] Lloyd's Rep. I.R. 151 at 163 (Mance J); *Spriggs v Wessington Court School Ltd* [2005] 1 Lloyd's Rep. I.R. 474 at 480 (Stanley Burnton J).

[105]   *Clough v London & North Western Railway Co* (1871–72) L.R. 7 Ex. 26 at 34 (Mellor J); *Johnson v Agnew* [1980] A.C. 367 at 399 (Lord Wilberforce); *Peyman v Lanjani* [1985] Ch. 457 at 494 (May LJ); *Drake Insurance Plc (In Provisional Liquidation) v Provident Insurance Plc* [2003] Lloyd's Rep. I.R. 781 at [35] (Moore-Bick J); *SK Shipping Europe Ltd v Capital VLCC 3 Corp* [2022] EWCA Civ 231; [2022] 2 All E.R. (Comm) 784 at [79] (Males LJ). See also *Sargent v ASL Developments Ltd* (1974) 131 C.L.R. 634 (High Court of Australia).

[106]   *The London and Provincial Electric Lighting and Power Generating Co Ltd, Ex p. Hale* (1887) 55 L.T. (N.S.) 670; *Spriggs v Wessington Court School Ltd* [2005] 1 Lloyd's Rep. I.R. 474 at 489 (Stanley Burnton J).

[107]   *Clough v London & North Western Railway Co* (1871–72) L.R. 7 Ex. 26 at 34 (Mellor J); *ICCI Ltd v The Royal Hotel Ltd* [1998] Lloyd's Rep. I.R. 151 at 161 (Mance J).

[108]   *Greenwood v Leather Shod Wheel Co* [1900] 1 Ch. 421 at 437 (Lindley MR); *Occidental Worldwide Investment Corp v Skibs A/S Avanti (The Siboen and the Sibotre)* [1976] 1 Lloyd's Rep. 293 at 325 (Kerr J).

[109]   *Campbell v Fleming* (1834) 1 A. and E. 40 at 42, 110 E.R. 1122 at 1123 (Littledale J); *Law v Law* [1905] 1 Ch. 140 at 158 (Cozens-Hardy LJ); *ICCI Ltd v The Royal Hotel Ltd* [1998] Lloyd's Rep. I.R. 151 at 161 (Mance J).

[110]   *Leeds City Council v Barclays Bank Plc* [2021] EWHC 363 (Comm); [2021] Q.B. 1027 at [174] (Cockerill J).

[111]   For contracts of insurance see *Container Transport International Inc and Reliance Group Inc v Oceanus Mutual Underwriting Assoc (Bermuda) Ltd* [1984] 1 Lloyd's Rep. 476 at 498 (Kerr J); *Black King Shipping Corp and Wayang (Panama) S.A. v Mark Ranald Massie (The Litsion Pride)* [1985] 1 Lloyd's Rep. 437 at 516 (Hirst J); *ICCI Ltd v The Royal Hotel Ltd* [1998] Lloyd's Rep. I.R. 151 at 161 (Mance J); *Spriggs v Wessington Court Schools Ltd* [2005] 1 Lloyd's Rep. I.R. 474 at 479 (Stanley Burnton J).

[112]   *Redgrave v Hurd* (1881) 20 Ch D. 1 at 23 (Baggallay LJ). Cf. *Seddon v The North Eastern Salt Co Ltd* [1905] 1 Ch. 326 at 334 (Joyce J).

[113]   *ICCI Ltd v The Royal Hotel Ltd* [1998] Lloyd's Rep. I.R. 151 at 161 (Mance J).

[114]   *Aaron's Reefs Ltd v Twiss* [1896] A.C. 273 at 290 (Lord Watson); *Container Transport International Inc and Reliance Group Inc v Oceanus Mutual Underwriting Assoc (Bermuda) Ltd* [1984] 1 Lloyd's

mean that the claimant is treated as knowing the true circumstances and this may be sufficient to constitute an affirmation of the contract if the other requirements are satisfied.[115]

3-028   It has been recognised that it is not enough that the claimant knows of the facts which enable a ground of rescission to be established; the claimant must also know of their legal right to rescind[116] or deliberately decide not to investigate these rights.[117] But this rule is difficult to defend.[118] It is inconsistent with general principles of the law, particularly that ignorance of the law is no defence, and also with the objective test of affirmation.[119] It also makes it much more difficult for the defendant to discharge the burden of proving that the contract has been affirmed by the claimant, since the defendant would be required to prove that the claimant knew of the right to rescind.[120] It follows that the preferable view is that it is enough that the claimant knows of the facts which trigger the ground of rescission without it being necessary to prove that the claimant was aware that they had a choice whether or not to affirm the contract. Nevertheless, the preponderance of authority is in favour of the defendant being required to establish both that the claimant was aware of the facts which trigger the vitiating factor and of the right to rescind. It remains unclear whether the knowledge of a solicitor about the right to rescind can be attributed to their client, or when the availability of legal knowledge raises a presumption that the claimant knew of the right to rescind and how this can be rebutted.[121] Where the claimant did not know of the right to rescind but by their conduct represented that they had affirmed the contract, and if the other party relies on this representation, the claimant will be estopped from seeking rescission of the contract.[122]

3-029   **Affirming party free from effects of vitiating factor**   The claimant can only be considered to have affirmed the contract once they were free from the effects of the vitiating factor which gave them the right to rescind the contract in the first place. If the claimant continues to be affected by the vitiating factor, they cannot be

---

Rep. 476 at 498 (Kerr J); *Black King Shipping Corp and Wuyang (Panama) S.A. v Mark Ranald Massie (The Litsion Pride)* [1985] 1 Lloyd's Rep. 437 at 516 (Hirst J).

[115] *ICCI Ltd v The Royal Hotel Ltd* [1998] Lloyd's Rep. I.R. 151 at 162 (Mance J).

[116] *Evans v Bartlam* [1937] A.C. 473 at 479 (Lord Atkin); *Peyman v Lanjani* [1985] Ch. 457 at 487 (Stephenson LJ), 501 (Slade LJ); *Moore Large and Co Ltd v Hermes Credit and Guarantee Plc* [2003] 1 Lloyd's Rep. I.R. 315 at 334 (Colman J); *ICCI Ltd v The Royal Hotel Ltd* [1998] Lloyd's Rep. I.R. 151 at 161 (Mance J); *Spriggs v Wessington Court School Ltd* [2005] 1 Lloyd's Rep. I.R. 474 at 479 (Stanley Burnton J). Cf. *Clough v London & North Western Railway Co* (1871–72) L.R. 7 Ex. 26 at 34 (Mellor J); *Car and Universal Finance Co Ltd v Caldwell* [1965] 1 Q.B. 525, 550 (Sellers LJ), 554 (Upjohn LJ); *Kammins Ballrooms Co Ltd v Zenith Investments (Torquay) Ltd* [1971] A.C. 850 at 878 (Lord Pearson); *Capcon Holdings Plc v Edwards* [2007] EWHC 2662 (Ch) at [55]; *Sabah Shipyard (Pakistan) Ltd v Pakistan* [2007] EWHC 2602 (Comm) at [131] (Clarke J).

[117] *Allcard v Skinner* (1887) 36 Ch D. 145 at 188 (Lindley LJ), 192 (Bowen LJ).

[118] See D. O'Sullivan, S. Elliott and R. Zakrzewski, *The Law of Rescission*, 3rd edn (Oxford: Oxford University Press, 2023), para.23.51. In Singapore it has been recognised that knowledge of the right to rescind is not required for affirmation: *Strait Colonies Pte Ltd v SMRT Alpha Pte Ltd* [2018] SGCA 36.

[119] See para.3-025.

[120] *Moore Large and Co Ltd v Hermes Credit and Guarantee Plc* [2003] 1 Lloyd's Rep. I.R. 315 at 335 (Colman J).

[121] *Peyman v Lanjani* [1985] 1 Ch. 457 at 487 (Stephenson LJ); *ICCI Ltd v The Royal Hotel Ltd* [1998] Lloyd's Rep. I.R. 151 at 171–172 (Mance J); *Moore Large and Co Ltd v Hermes Credit and Guarantee Plc* [2003] 1 Lloyd's Rep. I.R. 315 at [98]–[105] (Colman J). The issue was left open in *Capcon Holdings Plc v Edwards* [2007] EWHC 2662 (Ch) at [60].

[122] *Peyman v Lanjani* [1985] 1 Ch. 457 at 488 (Stephenson LJ).

considered to have affirmed the contract voluntarily. So, for example, if the claimant is still actually or presumably unduly influenced by the defendant, the claimant cannot be considered to have affirmed any contract made with the defendant.[123] Similarly where the claimant was compelled to enter into a contract with the defendant[124] or where the claimant continued to be affected by mental impairment.[125]

Act of affirmation   The defendant must show that the claimant had decided not **3-030** to rescind the contract and had expressed this by clear words, unequivocal conduct or necessary implication.[126] To determine that the claimant has elected to affirm the contract involves an objective test as to whether the claimant has made an informed choice not to rescind the contract being aware of the right to rescind. This election may be accidental[127] and does not require proof of a subjective intention to affirm the contract.[128]

Usually the claimant will have communicated this election to the defendant by **3-031** words,[129] but in the same way that it is not necessary to communicate an election to rescind at Common Law to the defendant,[130] communication to the defendant of the election to affirm is not required; affirmation by conduct suffices.[131] This choice may be established in a variety of ways. For example: the claimant may have asserted a right arising under the contract;[132] continued to operate a business where the claimant has a choice as to whether or not to do so;[133] refused to repay money which would have been repayable on rescission;[134] received payments under the contract;[135] made payments under the contract;[136] continued to use property received

---

[123] *Allcard v Skinner* (1887) 36 Ch D. 145 at 187 (Lindley LJ).

[124] *North Ocean Shipping Co Ltd v Hyundai Construction Co Ltd (Atlantic Baron)* [1979] 1 Q.B. 705 at 721 (Mocatta J); *DSND Subsea Ltd v Petroleum Geo-services ASA* [2000] 1 B.L.R. 530 at 548 (Dyson J).

[125] *Matthews v Baxter* (1873) L.R. 8 Exch. 132 at 133 (Kelly CB).

[126] *Clough v London & North Western Railway Co* (1871–72) L.R. 7 Ex. 26 at 34 (Mellor J); *Abram Steamship Co Ltd (In Liquidation) v Westville Shipping Co Ltd (In Liquidation)* [1923] A.C. 773 at 789 (Lord Atkinson); *SK Shipping Europe Ltd v Capital VLCC 3 Corp* [2022] EWCA Civ 231; [2022] 2 All E.R. (Comm) 784 at [73] (Males J).

[127] *North Ocean Shipping Co Ltd v Hyundai Construction Co Ltd (Atlantic Baron)* [1979] 1 Q.B. 705 at 721 (Mocatta J).

[128] *Scarfe v Jardine* (1882) 7 App. Cas. 345 at 361 (Lord Blackburn); *Kammin Ballrooms Co Ltd v Zenith Investments (Torquay) Ltd* [1971] A.C. 850 at 883 (Lord Diplock).

[129] *Peyman v Lanjani* [1985] Ch. 457 at 494 (May LJ); *ICCI Ltd v The Royal Hotel Ltd* [1998] Lloyd's Rep. I.R. 151 at 162 (Mance J).

[130] *Car and Universe Finance Co Ltd v Caldwell* [1965] 1 Q.B. 525. See para.1-017.

[131] *Clough v London & North Western Railway Co* (1871–72) L.R. 7 Ex. 26. This has also been recognised as regards insurance contracts: *ICCI Ltd v The Royal Hotel Ltd* [1998] Lloyd's Rep. I.R. 151 at 162 (Mance J); *Spriggs v Wessington Court School Ltd* [2005] 1 Lloyd's Rep. I.R. 474 at 484 (Stanley Burnton J).

[132] *Mint Security Ltd v Blair* [1982] 1 Lloyd's Rep. 188 at 198 (Staughton J); *Iron Trades Mutual Insurance Co Ltd v Companhia de Seguros Imperio* [1992] 1 Lloyd's Rep. I.R. 213 at 225 (Hirst J); *Strive Shipping Corp v Hellenic Mutual War Risks Assoc (The Grecia Express)* [2002] 2 Lloyd's Rep. 88 at 163 (Colman J); *WISE (Underwriting Agency) Ltd v Grupo Nacional Provincial SA* [2004] 2 Lloyd's Rep. 483 at [83] (Rix LJ).

[133] *Erlanger v The New Sombrero Phosphate Co* (1878) 3 App. Cas. 1218 at 1261 (Lord Selborne); *Lagunas Nitrate Co v Lagunas Syndicate* [1899] 2 Ch. 392 at 464 (Collins LJ).

[134] *Clough v London & North Western Railway Co* (1871–72) L.R. 7 Ex. 26 at 37 (Mellor J).

[135] *Spriggs v Wesington Court School Ltd* [2005] 1 Lloyd's Rep. I.R. 474 at 479 (Stanley Burnton J).

[136] *North Ocean Shipping Co Ltd v Hyundai Construction Co Ltd (Atlantic Baron)* [1979] 1 Q.B. 705 at 721 (Mocatta J); *Svenska Handeslbanken v Sun Alliance and London Insurance Plc* [1996] 1 Lloyd's Rep. 519 at 569 (Rix J).

under the contract;[137] or sued the defendant for damages for breach of contract.[138] But a claimant will only have affirmed the contract by conduct where that conduct unequivocally manifests an intention to affirm.[139] In *Sharpley v Louth and East Coast Rly Co*[140] the claimant was induced by a misrepresentation of the defendant company to purchase shares in that company. The claimant sought to rescind the contract but was unable to do so because, having discovered that the defendant's representations had been untrue, he continued to act as a shareholder, for example by attending general meetings of the company. This was conduct which was considered to show that he intended to affirm the contract. It may even be possible to affirm a contract by inaction, such as by failing to protest.[141]

3-032   There may be circumstances, however, which are inconsistent with the claimant having elected to affirm the contract. So, for example, in *Spriggs v Wesington Court School Ltd*[142] it was held that the claimant insurer had not elected to affirm the contract of insurance, even though it had continued to accept premiums from the assured, because the insurer had indicated that it was seeking further information about the terms of the policy. The claimant will not have elected to affirm the contract by pleading rescission in the alternative to a claim for damages for breach of contract.[143] Similarly, where the claimant expressly reserves their right to rescind the contract, this will usually prevent the affirmation bar from being raised, although this will depend on the circumstances of the case.[144]

III.   LAPSE OF TIME

3-033   **General principles**   As a matter of principle, the claimant may be barred from rescinding a contract if a substantial period of time has elapsed before they sought to rescind it.[145] What constitutes a substantial period of time is a question of fact which depends on the particular circumstances of the case. The time should only begin to run once the claimant was aware of the material facts which trigger the ground of rescission[146] and where the claimant is free from the effects of any pressure or exploitation.[147]

3-034   This bar is recognised because it is unreasonable and unjust for the claimant to seek to rescind a contract after a substantial period of time has passed, since delay enables the claimant to speculate whether it is beneficial for them to rescind the

---

[137] *Long v Lloyd* [1958] 1 W.L.R. 753.

[138] *ICCI Ltd v The Royal Hotel Ltd* [1998] Lloyd's Rep. I.R. 151 at 174 (Mance J).

[139] *Clough v London & North Western Railway Co* (1871–72) L.R. 7 Ex .26 at 34 (Mellor J); *Car and Universe Finance Co Ltd v Caldwell* [1965] 1 Q.B. 525 at 550 (Sellers LJ).

[140] (1876) 2 Ch D. 663.

[141] *North Ocean Shipping Co Ltd v Hyundai Construction Co Ltd (Atlantic Baron)* [1979] 1 Q.B. 705 at 721 (Mocatta J).

[142] [2005] 1 Lloyd's Rep. I.R. 474 at 488 (Stanley Burnton J).

[143] *Clough v London & North Western Railway Co* (1871–72) L.R. 7 Ex. 26 at 38 (Mellor J).

[144] *SK Shipping Europe Ltd v Capital VLCC 3 Corp* [2022] EWCA Civ 231; [2022] 2 All E.R. (Comm) 784 at [75] (Males LJ).

[145] *Leaf v International Galleries* [1950] 2 K.B. 86.

[146] At least where the ground of rescission involves fraud: *Redgrave v Hurd* (1881) 20 Ch D. 1 at 13 (Sir George Jessel MR). But note *Leaf v International Galleries* [1950] 2 K.B. 86 where the claim for rescission on the ground of innocent misrepresentation was barred after five years, even though the claimant had not been aware that a misrepresentation had been made for most of that time.

[147] *Allcard v Skinner* (1887) 36 Ch D. 145 at 192 (Bowen LJ).

contract.[148] This bar is often difficult to distinguish from the bar of affirmation since, if the claimant delays for a substantial period of time before they seek to rescind the transaction, this might also be treated as an implied affirmation of it because of an irrebuttable presumption of waiver of the right to rescind.[149] However, such affirmation will only be recognised where the claimant was aware of the right to rescind.[150] The bar of lapse of time is, however, distinct from affirmation and comprises a number of specific bars to rescission.[151]

Laches Where the claimant seeks to rescind the contract in Equity they will be   **3-035**
prevented from doing so by the doctrine of laches, which applies where there has been such a period of delay that allowing rescission would mean that the defendant would suffer an unfair prejudice or detriment.[152] The fact that the claimant is aware that the delay will cause prejudice to the defendant is a relevant factor to take into account.[153] It is not necessary to show that the claimant was aware that they had a right to rescind,[154] but the claimant must be aware of the facts which trigger the ground of rescission, such as the fact that a contract has been induced by misrepresentation.[155] Where the ground of rescission is undue influence, laches can only be established once the claimant is free from the effect of the exploitation.[156] Where the vitiating factor is fraud, it is unclear whether delay in seeking rescission before the rescinding party was aware of their legal right to rescind can be material to laches,[157] but in principle it should be irrelevant.

Acquiescence Alternatively, the claimant may be barred from rescinding the   **3-036**
contract on the ground that the unreasonable delay in seeking rescission means that the claimant is considered to have acquiesced so that the contract will continue to operate. The doctrine of acquiescence is different from that of affirmation because the claimant need not be aware of the right to rescind,[158] and may not even need to be aware of the facts which trigger the right to rescind.[159] Although the doctrine of acquiescence is similar to that of laches, and both doctrines may arise on the same facts,[160] acquiescence is distinct because the operation of the bar does not depend on prejudice or detriment being suffered by the defendant as a result of the delay. In determining whether the doctrine of acquiescence applies, ultimately the court has to look at the whole of the circumstances and decide whether on balance it is

---

[148] *Erlanger v The New Sombrero Phosphate Co* (1878) 3 App. Cas. 1218 at 1279 (Lord Blackburn).

[149] *Clough v London & North Western Railway Co* (1871–72) L.R. 7 Ex. 26 at 35 (Mellor J).

[150] See para.3-028.

[151] Although the bars of acquiescence and laches have both been described as involving implied affirmation of the contract: *Goldsworthy v Brickell* [1987] Ch. 378 at 410 (Nourse LJ).

[152] *Lindsay Petroleum Co v Hurd* (1873–74) L.R. 5 P.C. 221 at 240 (Sir Barnes Peacock); *Erlanger v New Sombrero Phosphate Co* (1878) 3 App. Cas. 1218 at 1230 (Lord Penzance) at 1279 (Lord Blackburn). It is for this reason that the doctrine of laches may overlap with the interpretation of *restitutio in integrum* being impossible. See para.3-002.

[153] *Nelson v Rye* [1996] 1 W.L.R. 1378 at 1392 (Laddie J).

[154] *Samuels v Wadlow* [2007] EWCA Civ 155 at [66] (Toulson LJ).

[155] *Erlanger v The New Sombrero Phosphate Co* (1878) 3 App. Cas. 1218 at 1261 (Lord Selborne) at 1279 (Lord Blackburn).

[156] *Allcard v Skinner* (1887) 36 Ch D. 145 at 187 (Lindley LJ).

[157] The issue was left open in *Capcon Holdings Plc v Edwards* [2007] EWHC 2662 (Ch) at [61].

[158] *Holder v Holder* [1968] Ch. 353 at 394 (Harman LJ); *Goldsworthy v Brickell* [1987] 1 Ch. 378 at 411 (Nourse LJ); *Samuels v Wadlow* [2007] EWCA Civ 155 at [66] (Toulson LJ). This matter was raised but left open in *Capcon Holdings Plc v Edwards* [2007] EWHC 2662 (Ch) at [61].

[159] *Leaf v International Galleries* [1950] 2 K.B. 86.

[160] See, for example, *Allcard v Skinner* (1887) 36 Ch D. 145.

just that the agreement should be set aside.[161] Relevant factors in assessing what is an unreasonable period of time to seek rescission include: the damage which would be suffered by the defendant if delayed rescission was allowed;[162] the conduct of the defendant in triggering the ground for rescission;[163] the conduct of the claimant before rescission is sought, especially as to whether the claimant's conduct has damaged property transferred under the contract with the defendant[164] or where the claimant has delayed rescission to speculate as to whether the property transferred would increase or fall in value;[165] or simply because an inordinate period of time has passed.[166] It is not unreasonable to delay rescission pending the outcome of an investigation by an expert as to the options available to the claimant.[167]

3-037   **Limitation periods**   The statutory limitation periods identified by the Limitation Act 1980 do not apply to bar the right to rescind at Common Law.[168] However, the consequences of rescission may be barred after a period of six years. So, for example, the claimant's right to restitution of a benefit transferred to the defendant under the contract will be barred after six years.[169]

3-038   The right to rescission in Equity may, however, be barred by the application of the statutory limitation period by analogy.[170] So, for example, a claim to rescind for fraudulent misrepresentation will be barred after six years, since the statutory limitation period which applies to claims for the tort of deceit[171] will be applied by analogy.[172] Similarly a claim to rescind a contract for dishonest breach of fiduciary duty will be subject to a six-year limitation period by analogy with the statutory limitation period.[173] Where, however, there is a claim for breach of fiduciary duty without proof of dishonesty, the statutory limitation period which applies for breach

---

[161] *John v James* [1991] F.S.R. 397 at 459 (Nicholls J) and *Goldsworthy v Brickell* [1987] Ch. 378 at 412 (Nourse LJ) at 416 (Parker LJ).

[162] *Erlanger v The New Sombrero Phosphate Co* (1878) 3 App. Cas. 1218 at 1247 (Lord Hatherley).

[163] *Erlanger v The New Sombrero Phosphate Co* (1878) 3 App. Cas. 1218 at 1248 (Lord Hatherley).

[164] *Erlanger v The New Sombrero Phosphate Co* (1878) 3 App. Cas. 1218 at 1261 (Lord Selborne); *Lagunas Nitrate Co v Lagunas Syndicate* [1899] 2 Ch. 392 at 464 (Collins LJ).

[165] *Erlanger v The New Sombrero Phosphate Co* (1878) 3 App. Cas. 1218 at 1281 (Lord Blackburn).

[166] *Allcard v Skinner* (1887) 36 Ch. D. 145 at 192 (Bowen LJ). In *Leaf v International Galleries* [1950] 2 K.B. 86 rescission of a contract to buy a picture was barred after five years, although the claimant was only aware of the misrepresentation shortly before the proceedings were commenced. It is difficult to characterise the delay in such circumstances as unreasonable. See *Salt v Stratstone Specialist Ltd (t/a Stratstone Cadillac Newcastle)* [2015] EWCA Civ 745; [2015] 2 C.L.C. 269 where it was considered that the decision turned on the equation of the lapse of time bar with the contractual right to reject goods, an equation which is no longer appropriate: at [49] (Roth J).

[167] *Fiona Trust and Holding Corp v Privalov* [2006] EWHC 2583 at [36] (Morison J).

[168] *Revenue and Customs Commissioners v IGE USA Investments Ltd* [2021] EWCA Civ 534; [2021] Ch. 423 at [20] (Henderson LJ).

[169] Limitation Act 1980 s.5. A similar limitation period applies to claims to recover property: Limitation Act 1980 ss.2 and 3.

[170] Limitation Act 1980 s.36(1).

[171] Under s.2 of the Limitation Act 1980.

[172] *Molloy v Mutual Reserve Life Insurance Co* (1906) 94 L.T. 756; *Revenue and Customs Commissioners v IGE USA Investments Ltd* [2021] EWCA Civ 534; [2021] Ch. 423. But the limitation priod will not start until the claimant has discovered the fraud, or could have discovered it with reasonable diligence: Limitation Act 1980 s.32(1).

[173] *Armstrong v Jackson* [1917] 2 K.B. 822 at 831 (McCardie J).

of trust will not be applied by analogy[174] and similarly where rescission is triggered by undue influence.[175]

Promissory estoppel Where the effect of the delay is to constitute a clear and unequivocal representation that the claimant would not set the contract aside, that representation was made with the knowledge or intention that it would be acted on by the defendant and the defendant did rely on it to their detriment or in some other way to make it inequitable for the claimant to seek rescission, the claimant will be estopped from seeking rescission of the contract.[176] It will, however, be difficult to identify such a knowing representation from the simple fact of delay in seeking rescission.

3-039

IV. THIRD PARTY RIGHTS

Nature of the bar Rescission is also traditionally barred where the effect of rescission of the contract would be to harm the rights of third parties.[177] In particular, the right of rescission will be barred if a third party subsequently acquires a legal[178] or equitable interest in property which had been transferred to the defendant under a voidable contract, if the third party had acquired the property for value and without notice of the defect which provides the reason for the claimant wishing to rescind it.

3-040

Critique of the bar The existence of the third party rights bar is difficult to defend. Whilst it is correct that, if a third party has acquired proprietary rights in good faith and for value, the claimant should not be able to bring a claim against the third party to recover the property, it does not follow that the acquisition of third party proprietary rights should necessarily prevent the claimant from rescinding the contract with the defendant[179] and so protect the defendant. Although an effect of rescission is traditionally to revest title to property to the claimant,[180] it would not be appropriate for rescission to have this effect where a third party has acquired rights in the property transferred for value; the security of the third party's receipt is then paramount. But there is no reason why this should bar rescission completely since rescission has other consequences, such as to avoid future contractual obligations and to enable the claimant to recover the value of the property transferred to the defendant.[181] This can still occur, however, and the third party's proprietary right can be left unaffected.[182] This was recognised by the Privy Council in *Moses v*

3-041

---

[174] *Tito v Waddell (No.2)* [1977] Ch. 106 at 250 (Megarry VC).

[175] *Allcard v Skinner* (1887) 36 Ch D. 145.

[176] *Allcard v Skinner* (1887) 36 Ch D. 145 at 192 (Bowen LJ); *Holder v Holder* [1968] Ch. 353 at 403 (Sachs LJ); *Goldsworthy v Brickell* [1987] Ch. 378 at 410 (Nourse LJ).

[177] *Tennent v The City of Glasgow Bank and Liquidators* (1879) 4 App. Cas. 615 at 621 (Earl Cairns LC); *Society of Lloyds v Leighs* [1997] EWCA Civ 2283.

[178] *White v Garden* (1851) 10 C.B. 919, 138 E.R. 364; *Clough v The London and North Western Rly Co* (1871) L.R. 7 Ex. 26 at 35; *Phillips v Brooks Ltd* [1919] 2 K.B. 243.

[179] N.Y. Nahan, "Rescission: A Case For Rejecting the Classical Model?" (1997) 27 Univ. W.A.L.R. 66 at 74.

[180] See para.4-023. Cf. W. Swadling, "Rescission, Property, and the Common Law" (2005) 121 L.Q.R. 123.

[181] See para.4-018.

[182] B. Häcker, "Rescission and Third Party Rights" [2006] R.L.R. 21 at 36.

Moses[183] where land had been mistakenly conveyed to the defendant. It was recognised that the deed of conveyance could be rescinded, even though the defendant had sold the land to a third party. Rescission did not affect the third party's rights because he was a bona fide purchaser for value. However, the defendant was liable to pay to the claimant the value of the land received, by virtue of a Common Law claim in unjust enrichment.

3-042   The only justification for a bar to rescission relating to the acquisition of rights by a third party is where rescission of the contract between the claimant and the defendant would destroy or necessarily frustrate the rights which were acquired by the third party for value and in reliance on the validity of the contract between the claimant and the defendant. So, for example, in *Society of Lloyds v Leighs*[184] a contract could not be rescinded for fraudulent misrepresentation since the effect of rescission would have been to revoke the authority of the rescinding parties to enter into contracts with third parties.

3-043   **Winding up**   The bankruptcy of the other party to the contract will not bar rescission.[185] It has, however, been recognised that the winding up of a company will bar rescission of the statutory contract between the shareholder and the company, typically where rescission is sought for misrepresentation. [186] It follows that the shareholder who owns partly paid shares is unable to rescind the contract once the winding up has commenced, in order to avoid liability as a contributory to the creditors of the company. The bar will also operate to prevent a shareholder from recovering the price paid for shares issued by the company.[187] It appears that the bar is only available where the person seeking rescission is a shareholder.[188] The function of this bar is to protect creditors whose rights would be defeated by the rescission,[189] by ensuring that shareholders do not avoid their liability to creditors by avoiding their contract. But the bar is of much less significance now since partly paid shares are less common and the shareholder will be able to obtain a pecuniary remedy for the misrepresentation where it was made fraudulently or negligently.[190]

V.   Damages in Lieu of Rescission

3-044   **General principles**   Whilst the bars which have been considered so far are of general application regardless of the reason for rescission, there is one specific bar which is potentially applicable only where a contract has been induced by non-fraudulent misrepresentation. In such circumstances s.2(2) of the Misrepresentation Act 1967 provides that the court has a discretion to declare that the contract is

---

[183] [2022] UKPC 42.
[184] [1997] EWCA Civ 2283. See also *Crystal Palace FC (2000) Ltd v Dowie* [2007] EWHC 1392 (QB) at [216] (Tugendhat J) (rescission would have revived an employment contract of a football manager who was now employed by another football club).
[185] *Load v Green* (1846) 15 M. and W. 216; 153 E.R. 828.
[186] *Oakes v Turquand and Harding* (1867) L.R. 2 HL 325; *Stone v The City and Country Bank Ltd* (1877) 3 C.P.D. 282; *Tennent v City of Glasgow Bank* (1879) 4 All Cas 615; *Soden v British and Commonwealth Holdings Plc* [1998] A.C. 298 at 324 (Lord Browne-Wilkinson).
[187] *Stone v The City and Country Bank Ltd* (1877) 3 C.P.D. 282.
[188] *Re Yorke Street Mezzanine Pty Ltd* [2007] F.C.A. 922 (Federal Court of Australia) at [39]. At [40] it is suggested that this is probably the position in England as well.
[189] *Tennent v City of Glasgow Bank* (1879) 4 All Cas 615 at 621 (Earl Cairns LC).
[190] See para.2-004.

subsisting and to award damages in lieu of rescission. This discretionary bar to rescission can only apply where rescission would otherwise be available and where the court considers it to be equitable to award damages instead of rescinding the contract. This is an exceptional bar, with rescission being the normal remedy.[191]

Conditions for exercise of discretion   The court only has jurisdiction to award   3-045
damages in lieu of rescission where the contract has been induced by a non-fraudulent misrepresentation.[192] Although in one case it was recognised that the court has the power to award damages as long as the claimant had the right to rescind the contract, even if that right has since been barred, [193] the language of the statute has been interpreted as requiring the claimant still to be entitled to rescind the contract, so the jurisdiction to award damages will not be available if rescission is barred.[194] Section 2(2) of the Misrepresentation Act 1967 identifies certain factors which should be considered by the court when determining whether it is equitable to award damages instead of rescission, namely: the nature of the misrepresentation, the loss to the representee if the contract was not rescinded and the loss to the representor which would arise from rescission. Consequently, the court is more likely to award damages in lieu of rescission where the misrepresentation can be characterised as trivial or where the harm to the representor arising from rescission outweighs any advantages of rescission to the representee.[195] The court may declare the contract to be subsisting even though the claimant has suffered no relevant loss such that no damages will be awarded in lieu of rescission.[196]

Assessment of damages   Once the court has determined that damages should be   3-046
awarded in lieu of rescission the damages operate to compensate[197] the claimant for the loss caused by the misrepresentation as a result of rescission being barred, rather than the loss caused by entering into the contract.[198] This is assessed by comparing the claimant's present position with the position the claimant would have occupied had the misrepresentation been true.[199] Consequently, where the contract was for the purchase of property by the claimant, the damages would be assessed with

---

[191] *SK Shipping Europe Ltd v Capital VLCC 3 Corp* [2022] EWCA Civ 231; [2022] 2 All E.R. (Comm) 784 at [86] (Males LJ).

[192] *Government of Zanzibar v British Aerospace (Lancaster House) Ltd* [2000] 1 W.L.R. 2333 at 2342 (Judge Raymond Jack QC).

[193] *Thomas Witter Ltd v TBP Industries Ltd* [1996] 2 All E.R. 573 at 590 (Jacob J).

[194] *Atlantic Lines and Navigation Co Inc v Hallam (The Lucy)* [1983] 1 Lloyd's Rep. 188 at 202 (Mustill J); *William Sindall Plc v Cambridgeshire CC* [1994] 1 W.L.R. 1016 at 1044 (Evans LJ); *Floods of Queensferry Ltd v Shand Construction Ltd* [2000] B.L.R. 81 at 92 (Judge Humphrey Lloyd QC); *Government of Zanzibar v British Aerospace (Lancaster House) Ltd* [2000] 1 W.L.R. 2333 at 2343 (Judge Raymond Jack QC); *Pankhania v Hackney London BC* [2002] EWHC 2441 (Ch) at [76] (Judge Rex Tedd QC); *Salt v Stratstone Specialist Ltd* [2015] EWCA Civ 745; [2015] 2 C.L.C. 269 at [17] (Longmore LJ). See H. Beale, "Points on Misrepresentation" (1995) 111 L.Q.R. 385; D. Malet, "Section 2(2) of the Misrepresentation Act 1967" (2001) 117 L.Q.R. 524; J. O'Sullivan, "Remedies for misrepresentation: up in the air again" (2001) C.L.J. 239.

[195] See *William Sindall Plc v Cambridgeshire CC* [1994] 1 W.L.R. 1016 at 1036–1038 (Hoffmann LJ).

[196] *Huyton SA v Distribuidora Internacional de Productos Agricolas SA de CV* [2003] 2 Lloyd's Rep. 780 at 846.

[197] Cf. P. Birks, "Unjust Factors and Wrongs: Pecuniary Rescission for Undue Influence" [1997] R.L.R. 72 at 75 who considered that the function of the pecuniary remedy was restitutionary to reverse the defendant's unjust enrichment, rather than as a remedy for the unknown wrong of innocent misrepresentation.

[198] *William Sindall Plc v Cambridgeshire CC* [1994] 1 W.L.R. 1016 at 1037 (Hoffmann LJ).

[199] In *William Sindall Plc v Cambridgeshire CC* [1994] 1 W.L.R. 1016 at 1045–1046 (Evans LJ) this

reference to the difference between the actual value of the property at the time of the purchase and the value of the property as it was represented to be.[200] But the damages should not exceed the sum which would have been awarded had the representation been a term of the contract.[201] If the claimant would not have been in any better position had the representation been true then there will be no loss and no damages will be awarded but rescission may still be barred.[202]

3-047   The claimant cannot be compensated for loss which was not caused by the misrepresentation.[203] So the claimant will not be compensated for consequential loss arising from a fall in the value of the property which the claimant had purchased from the defendant.[204]

3-048   **Impact on contract**   Where the court exercises the discretion not to rescind the contract it follows that the contract is declared to be subsisting. In *SK Shipping Europe Plc v Capital VLCC 3 Corp*,[205] Foxton J recognised that a consequence of the exercise of the discretion not to rescind would be that purported rescission by one of the parties to a contract would be a repudiatory breach, for which damages could be awarded and it would not be possible to indemnify for this under s.2(2), since the liability would not have arisen from the reason for rescission but by virtue of the court's decision to award damages in lieu. In the Court of Appeal[206] the approach of the judge was not endorsed, but the issue was left to be resolved in the future. Males LJ did, however, note that it would not be appropriate to treat the contract as subsisting where the contract had naturally come to an end by the time of the court's adjudication; that in practice the contract would be terminated following the purported rescission by the other party's acceptance of the rescission as a repudiatory breach; and further that the uncertainty relating to the exercise of the court's discretion creates insuperable difficulties for commercial parties. It follows that the decision to award damages in lieu of rescission need not necessarily mean that the contract continues to subsist. As part of the exercise of the court's discretion it would be appropriate to consider whether the party who sought rescission should be indemnified for any liability owed to the other party arising from the court's decision not to rescind.

---

was described as the "contract measure", since the function of the damages is to place the claimant in the position they would have been in had the representation been true, rather than a "tort measure", which would return the claimant to the position before the contract was made, which would operate like pecuniary rescission.

[200] *William Sindall Plc v Cambridgeshire CC* [1994] 1 W.L.R. 1016 at 1037 (Hoffmann LJ).

[201] *William Sindall Plc v Cambridgeshire CC* [1994] 1 W.L.R. 1016 at 1038 (Hoffmann LJ).

[202] *UCB Corporate Services Ltd v Thomason* [2004] EWHC 1164 (Ch); [2004] 2 All E.R. (Comm) 774 at [68] (Pumfrey J).

[203] *William Sindall Plc v Cambridgeshire CC* [1994] 1 W.L.R. 1016 at 1037 (Hoffmann LJ).

[204] *William Sindall Plc v Cambridgeshire CC* [1994] 1 W.L.R. 1016 at 1045 (Evans LJ). Where the defendant had no reasonable grounds for believing the truth of the representation, the claimant could instead sue for damages under Misrepresentation Act 1967 s.2(1), where damages are assessed by reference to the tortious measure so that consequential losses are recoverable: *Royscot Trust Ltd v Rogerson* [1991] 2 Q.B. 297.

[205] [2020] EWHC 3448 (Comm).

[206] *SK Shipping Europe Ltd v Capital VLCC 3 Corp* [2022] EWCA Civ 231; [2022] 2 All E.R. (Comm) 784 at [85] (Males LJ).

CHAPTER 4

THE CONSEQUENCES OF RESCISSION

General principles Once the claimant has identified a ground of rescission, has **4-001**
elected to rescind the contract and no bar to rescission applies the contract will be
set aside, either automatically at Common Law or by order of the court in Equity.[1]
A number of consequences may follow from the rescission of the contract. Primarily all future obligations will be revoked. But there will also be mutual restitutionary consequences since the claimant can recover "the property with which he has
parted under the contract and [must return] the benefit which he received" to the
defendant.[2] This restitutionary consequence is available once the claimant has satisfied the conditions for setting the contract aside, as recognised by Millett LJ in *Portman BS v Hamlyn Taylor and Neck*:[3]

> "The obligation to make restitution must flow from the ineffectiveness of the transaction
> under which the money was paid and not from a mistake or misrepresentation which
> induced it…If the payer exercises his right of rescission in time and before the recipient
> deals with the money in accordance with his instructions, the obligation to make restitu-
> tion may follow."

This restitutionary consequence follows automatically from the rescission of the **4-002**
transaction, but it is also a condition of rescission, since the transaction cannot be
set aside if the defendant cannot be restored to their original position.[4] A key issue
relating to this restitutionary consequence is whether the parties have a personal or
a proprietary right to property which has been transferred pursuant to the contract.

Where an executory contract is rescinded it has been suggested that the **4-003**
consequences of rescission are restitutionary by virtue of the fact that the parties
are required to restore those rights which derived from the contract.[5] These personal
rights could be considered to be benefits which were obtained under the contract
and, if the contract is to be rescinded, they need to be restored. The better view,
however, is that this does not involve restitution because there is no revesting of the
benefit of contractual rights; rather those rights simply cease to exist at the moment of rescission. The consequences of rescission will be restitutionary only if

---

[1] See para.1-009.
[2] *Smith New Court Securities Ltd v Scrimgeour Vickers (Asset Management) Ltd* [1994] 2 B.C.L.C.
   212 at 221 (Nourse LJ).
[3] [1998] 4 All E.R. 202 at 208.
[4] See para.3-002.
[5] N.Y. Nahan, "Rescission: A Case For Rejecting the Classical Model?" (1997) 27 Univ. W.A.L.R.
   66, 72; A. Burrows, *The Law of Restitution*, 3rd edn (Oxford: Oxford University Press, 2011), p.17;
   A.V.M. Lodder, *Enrichment in the Law of Restitution and Unjust Enrichment* (Oxford: Hart Publishing, 2012), Ch.3.

there is some valuable benefit to be restored to the claimant.[6] This is significant because it may affect the operation of defences, notably that of change of position.[7]

I. EXTINCTION OF THE CONTRACT

4-004   **General principles**   The most significant consequence of the contract being rescinded is that it is treated as never having come into existence.[8] It follows that all future contractual obligations are terminated, even if they should already have been performed.[9] Equitable remedies such as specific performance and injunctions will no longer be available once the contract has been rescinded.

4-005   Rescission will also destroy the secondary obligation to pay damages for breach of contractual obligation because this secondary obligation arises from the contract, and if the contract is considered never to have existed then neither can the obligation to pay damages.[10] If the transfer of property or money under the contract is conditional, the rescission of the contract will terminate the contractual obligation to return the property or the money, although there may be an independent claim founded on the vindication of property rights or unjust enrichment to obtain restitution of the property or money.

4-006   If a variation of contract is rescinded the original contract will be automatically revived.[11] A substitute contract may also be voidable if the factor which vitiated the original contract continues to operate,[12] although the substitute contract is not automatically treated as voidable simply because the original contract was voidable.[13] Where a compromise agreement has been rescinded the rights and obligations which had been compromised will revive.[14]

4-007   Certain aspects of the contract will survive rescission. In particular arbitration clauses survive rescission of the main contract[15] because they are treated as an independent contract between the parties; although the arbitration clause itself might be independently void or voidable and not merely as a consequence of the invalidity of the main contract.[16] Similarly, exclusive jurisdiction clauses have been held

---

[6]   See *National Commercial Bank (Jamaica) Ltd v Hew's Executors* [2003] UKPC 51 at [43]. In *Criterion Properties Plc v Stratford UK Properties LLC* [2004] 1 W.L.R. 1846 at [1855] (Lord Scott) recognised that the creation of contractual rights through an executory contract does not constitute the receipt of an asset and therefore cannot constitute an enrichment.

[7]   See para.4-022.

[8]   *Johnson v Agnew* [1980] A.C. 367 at 393 (Lord Wilberforce).

[9]   *Hurst v Bryk* [2002] 1 A.C. 185 at 200 (Lord Millett). Accrued obligations which have not yet been performed are not terminated if the contract is discharged for breach. See para.5-027.

[10]   See *Johnson v Agnew* [1980] A.C. 367 at 394 (Lord Wilberforce). It does not follow that a pecuniary award cannot be made in addition to rescission to ensure that the claimant is restored to their pre-contractual position. See para.4-037.

[11]   *Occidental Worldwide Investment Corp v Skibs A/S Avanti (The Siboen and the Sibotre)* [1976] 1 Lloyd's Rep. 293 at 337 (Kerr J); *Crystal Palace FC (2000) Ltd v Dowie* [2007] EWHC 1392 (QB) at [209] (Tugendhat J).

[12]   *Yorkshire Bank Plc v Tinsley* [2004] EWCA Civ 816; [2004] 1 W.L.R. 2380 at [18] (Longmore LJ).

[13]   *Samuel v Wadlow* [2007] EWCA Civ 155 at [57] (Toulson LJ). The vitiating factor may only affect a side agreement, leaving the main agreement valid: *British Nuclear Group Sellafield Ltd v Kernkraftwerk Brokdorf GMBH & Co OHG* [2007] EWHC 2245 (Ch).

[14]   *Magee v Penine Insurance* [1969] 2 Q.B. 507; *Samuel v Wadlow* [2007] EWCA Civ 155 at [65] (Toulson LJ).

[15]   Arbitration Act 1996 s.7.

[16]   *Vee Networks Ltd v Econet Wireless International Ltd* [2005] 1 Lloyd's Rep. 192 at [20] (Colman

to survive rescission,[17] although this is difficult to justify because such clauses cannot be considered to have an independent contractual existence.[18]

Rescission of entire contract   Where a contract is rescinded it can only be set   **4-008**
aside in its entirety and not so that part of the transaction remains effective,[19] except
where part of the contract is properly severable from the rest.[20] For example, in *TSB
Bank Plc v Camfield*[21] a mortgage was set aside completely as a result of a
husband's misrepresentation and was not treated as valid to the extent of the liability which the wife had intended to accept.[22] A contract which forms an
inseparable part of a larger transaction cannot be separately rescinded.[23] It has also
been recognised that it is possible to rescind a self-contained and severable part of
a non-contractual voluntary transaction, such as a disposition to a trust made by a
deed which is voidable for mistake.[24] This has been justified on the unconvincing
ground that in such a transaction there is no need to restore both parties to their
original position since, being a voluntary disposition, only the recipient will have
received a benefit which needs to be reversed. Rescission of the whole contract is
available even if the claimant would have entered into the contract, albeit on different terms, had there not been an operating vitiating factor.

Rescission on terms   Rescission of a contract on terms differs from partial rescis-   **4-009**

J); *Premium Nafta Product Ltd v Fili Shipping Co Ltd* [2007] UKHL 40; [2007] 4 All E.R. 951 at
[19] (Lord Hoffmann).

[17]   *Mackender v Feldia* [1967] 2 Q.B. 590 at 598 (Lord Denning MR); *Brit Syndicates Ltd v Grant
Thornton* [2006] EWHC 341 (Comm) at [22] (Langley J).

[18]   D. O'Sullivan, S. Elliott and R. Zakrzewski, *The Law of Rescission*, 3rd edn (Oxford: Oxford
University Press, 2023), para.1.16. In *Mackender v Feldia AG* [1967] 2 Q.B. 590 at 598 (Lord Denning MR) and 603 (Diplock LJ), assumed that avoidance only took effect from the moment of avoidance and that it did not operate retrospectively. But this was to confuse rescission with termination
for breach. See para.1-002.

[19]   *The Sheffield Nickel and Silver Plating Co Ltd v Unwin* (1877) 2 Q.B.D. 214 at 223 (Lush J); *TSB
Bank Plc v Camfield* [1995] 1 W.L.R. 430 at 436 (Nourse LJ); *Drake Insurance Plc v Provident
Insurance Plc* [2004] 1 Lloyd's Rep. 268 at [103] (Rix LJ); *Potter v Dyer* [2011] EWCA Civ. 1417
at [58] (Etherton LJ); *Kennedy v Kennedy* [2014] EWHC 4129 (Ch); [2015] W.T.L.R. 837 at [46]
(Etherton C); *NGM Sustainable Developments Ltd v Wallis* [2015] EWHC 2089 (Ch) at [226] (Peter
Smith J).

[20]   *Barclays Bank Plc v Caplan* [1998] 1 F.L.R. 532 at 546; *De Molestina v Ponton* [2002] 1 Lloyd's
Rep. 271; *Drake Insurance Plc v Provident Insurance Plc* [2004] 1 Lloyd's Rep. 268 at [103] (Rix
LJ). In certain circumstances it may be possible to rectify the contract where, for example, a
misrepresentation has been incorporated as a term of the contract.

[21]   [1995] 1 W.L.R. 430. See also *Bank Melli Iran v Samadi-Rad* [1995] 2 F.L.R. 367; *De Molestina v
Ponton* [2002] 1 All E.R. (Comm) 587. In Australia partial rescission is accepted: *Vadasz v Pioneer
Concrete (SA) Pty Ltd* (1995) 184 C.L.R. 102, rescission of guarantee for fraudulent misrepresentation relating to past but not future indebtedness since the claimant agreed to accept liability for future
indebtedness. The matter was left open by the Privy Council in an appeal from New Zealand: See
generally *Far Eastern Shipping Co Public Ltd v Scales Trading Ltd* [2001] 1 All E.R. (Comm) 319
at 326. L. Proksch, "Rescission on Terms" [1996] R.L.R. 71; J. Poole and A. Keyser, "Justifying
Partial Rescission in English Law" (2005) 121 L.Q.R. 273. Cf. *Maguire v Makaronis* (1996) 188
C.L.R. 449 at 472 where rescission on terms was not awarded for breach of fiduciary duty.

[22]   In *Yorkshire Bank Plc v Tinsley* [2004] EWCA Civ 816; [2004] 1 W.L.R. 2380, where a replacement mortgage was taken out as a condition of discharging an earlier mortgage which was voidable for undue influence, the replacement mortgage was also voidable, at least where the two
mortgages were taken out with the same lender.

[23]   *Al Nehayan v Kent* [2018] EWHC 333 (Comm) at [220] (Leggatt LJ).

[24]   *Kennedy v Kennedy* [2014] EWHC 4129 (Ch); [2015] W.T.L.R. 837; *Bainbridge v Bainbridge* [2016]
EWHC 898 (Ch); [2016] W.T.L.R. 943.

sion in that rescission on terms involves the contract being rescinded *ab initio* and the court imposing terms as a condition of this rescission being ordered. Such terms may include that a new, fairer contract replaces the original one. Rescission on terms is generally prohibited in English law.[25] This general principle against rescission on terms is, however, subject to an apparent exception in Equity where the order for rescission is made conditional on the defendant making restitution to the claimant and the claimant making counter-restitution to the defendant of any benefits received under the transaction to prevent unjust enrichment.[26] But this is consistent with rescission operating to set the transaction aside completely so that both parties are restored to the position they occupied before entering into the transaction, by ensuring that they return any benefits received, or the value of any benefits received, to the other party.[27]

4-010   In fact, rescission on terms has been recognised more generally, such as where a claimant wishes to rescind a transaction in Equity for mistake[28] or undue influence.[29] In *West Sussex Properties Ltd v Chichester DC*[30] Morritt LJ recognised that the court had jurisdiction to impose terms when ordering rescission in Equity, such as to exclude restitution following avoidance of the contract, although the jurisdiction was not exercised in that case against a public authority defendant. The recognition of this general jurisdiction to rescind on terms would mean that, for example, if the claimant entered into a transaction as a result of misrepresentation thinking that they had entered into a surety transaction for £5,000 but in fact the transaction was for £50,000, the actual surety transaction should be rescinded but terms be imposed that a £5,000 surety transaction should be substituted since this is the amount which the claimant actually consented to guarantee. The effect of this would be to partially rescind the contract, although the mechanism adopted would be complete rescission of the contract and then judicial construction of a new contract.

4-011   The failure to recognise partial rescission and rescission on terms can be justified at Common Law by virtue of the essential nature of Common Law rescission, which arises automatically on the claimant's election,[31] so that there is no scope for the exercise of judicial discretion;[32] either the claimant is or is not entitled to rescind the transaction in question. The rule can also be justified more generally on the ground that the function of rescission is to restore the parties to the position they

---

[25] *Zamet v Hyman* [1961] 1 W.L.R. 1442 at 1451 (Lord Evershed MR).

[26] *Barclays Bank Plc v Caplan* [1998] 1 F.L.R. 532 at 546 (Jonathan Sumption QC). For an example of such conditional rescission see *Midland Bank Plc v Greene* [1994] 2 F.L.R. 82. See further para.4-012.

[27] See J. Poole and A. Keyser, "Justifying Partial Rescission in English Law" (2005) 121 L.Q.R. 273 who argue that partial rescission and rescission on terms is distinct from the equitable jurisdiction to secure restitution and counter-restitution, since partial rescission and rescission on terms is concerned with fulfilling the parties' expectations, where those expectations were not affected by the operating vitiating factor.

[28] *Hopes v Burton* [2022] EWHC 2770 (Ch) at [66] (Master Clark). In some of the cases on rescission in Equity for mistake the claimant was permitted to rescind the transaction but only on condition that a new contract was made: *Solle v Butcher* [1950] 1 K.B. 671 and *Grist v Bailey* [1967] Ch. 532. Today, rescission in Equity would not be allowed for mistake in such cases: *Great Peace Shipping Ltd v Tsalviris Salvage (International) Ltd* [2002] EWCA Civ 1407; [2003] Q.B. 679. See para.2-021.

[29] *Cheese v Thomas* [1994] 1 W.L.R. 129. See para.4-036.

[30] [2000] EWCA Civ 205 at [35].

[31] See para.1-010.

[32] *TSB Bank Plc v Camfield* [1995] 1 W.L.R 430 at 438–439 (Roch LJ).

would have occupied had there not been a contract.[33] But it could just as easily be concluded that the function of rescission is to restore the parties to the position they would have occupied had there not been a vitiating factor operating. So, where there was a misrepresentation but there was evidence that the claimant would have entered into a different contract had there not been a misrepresentation, it would be appropriate to alter the contract accordingly. This could only occur in Equity where the judicial order for rescission can be made conditional on the new contract being accepted.[34] Such flexibility of rescission would be consistent with the rationale of rescission in Equity, which is to seek practical justice,[35] and so rescission on terms, which might effect partial rescission, should be recognised in Equity.

II.   RESTITUTION TO PREVENT UNJUST ENRICHMENT

General principles   It is a fundamental consequence of rescission that the parties are restored to their pre-contractual position. It follows that the defendant must make restitution to the claimant of any benefits which the defendant has received pursuant to the transaction and the claimant will be required to make counter-restitution to the defendant of the value of any benefit which the claimant has received.[36] If the claimant is unable to restore the defendant to their pre-contractual position, rescission will be barred,[37] although the fact that the defendant is unable to restore the claimant to the claimant's pre-contractual position does not operate as bar to rescission. The claimant will be required to make counter-restitution to the defendant even if the defendant procured the contract by fraud or duress.[38] The claimant must give credit to the defendant for benefits received which are sufficiently closely connected to the benefit which the claimant provided to the defendant.[39] Failure to make counter-restitution is a defence to a claim in unjust enrichment.[40] Various rationales for this defence have been recognised,[41] including that the receipt of the benefit by the claimant reduces or eliminates the defendant's enrichment; the receipt of that benefit qualifies the injustice of the defendant's receipt; the defence incorporates a cross-claim by the defendant against

4-012

---

[33]   See generally D. O'Sullivan, S. Elliott and R. Zakrzewski, *The Law of Rescission*, 3rd edn (Oxford: Oxford University Press, 2023), Ch.19.

[34]   But presumably not where a contract is voidable for fraudulent misrepresentation since, even in Equity, rescission is the act of the claimant since the equitable jurisdiction to rescind for fraud is a concurrent jurisdiction with the Common Law. See *Alati v Kruger* (1955) 94 C.L.R. 216 at 224 (Dixon CJ), para.1-027. Cf. *Vadasz v Pioneer Concrete (S.A.) Pty Ltd* (1995) 69 A.L.J.R. 678. See D. O'Sullivan, "Partial Rescission for Misrepresentation in Australia" (1997) 113 L.Q.R. 16 at 17. Compare with rescission for non-fraudulent representation where the equitable jurisdiction to rescind is exclusive.

[35]   *Erlanger v The New Sombrero Phosphate Co* (1878) 3 App. Cas. 1218 at 1278 (Lord Blackburn). See also *Vadasz v Pioneer Concrete (S.A.) Pty Ltd* (1995) 69 A.L.J.R. 678 at 684.

[36]   *Clough v London & North Western Railway Co* (1871–72) L.R. 7 Ex. 26 at 37 (Mellor J); *O'Sullivan v Management Agency and Music Ltd* [1985] Q.B. 428; *Cheese v Thomas* [1994] 1 W.L.R. 129; *Mahoney v Purnell* [1996] 3 All E.R. 61; *School Facility Management Ltd v Governing Body of Christ the King College* [2021] EWCA Civ 1053; [2021] 1 W.L.R. 6129.

[37]   See para.3-002.

[38]   *Halpern v Halpern (Nos 1 and 2)* [2007] EWCA Civ 291; [2008] Q.B. 195 at 223 (Carnwath LJ).

[39]   *School Facility Management Ltd v Governing Body of Christ the King College* [2021] EWCA Civ 1053; [2021] 1 W.L.R. 6129 at [83] (Popplewell LJ).

[40]   *School Facility Management Ltd v Governing Body of Christ the King College* [2021] EWCA Civ 1053; [2021] 1 W.L.R. 6129 at [84] (Popplewell LJ).

[41]   *School Facility Management Ltd v Governing Body of Christ the King College* [2021] EWCA Civ 1053; [2021] 1 W.L.R. 6129 at [34] (Popplewell LJ).

the claimant; or the application of the defence is a condition of the claimant obtaining restitution. In *School Facility Management Ltd v Governing Body of Christ the King College*,[42] no concluded view was expressed as to the conceptual basis of the defence, with the Court recognising that one or more of these rationales may be relevant to the facts of the particular case.

4-013   The restitutionary consequence of rescission may operate in two different ways. First, the claimant or the defendant may have a proprietary claim to recover property by vindicating their property rights. This is considered later.[43] Secondly, the claimant or the defendant may have a personal claim for the value of benefits transferred to the other. Whether rescission has occurred at Common Law or in Equity, this personal claim for the value of the benefits received is preferably analysed as being founded on unjust enrichment. This is because, if the value of the benefits were not restored to the other party after the contract had been rescinded, the party who received the benefit would be unjustly enriched at the expense of the other.[44] It is to prevent such unjust enrichment from arising that restitution and counter-restitution will be required. This is only a personal claim,[45] with restitution in monetary form,[46] and the claim will be defeated by the insolvency of the party who had been unjustly enriched. Where both the claimant and the defendant have a personal claim against the other for the restitution of the value of the benefits transferred, one claim may be set against the other with a liability to pay only the outstanding amount.

4-014   Where rescission occurs by election of the claimant at Common Law, restitution of benefits should follow automatically, but if the party who has received a benefit does not make restitution of it, the other party will have a claim in unjust enrichment for restitution which can be enforced by the court. To establish this claim, it must be established that the other party has received a valuable enrichment, whether it is money, property or services; this was received directly at the expense of the claimant; and that one of the recognised grounds for restitution apply.[47] Although the ground for rescission might replicate the ground for unjust enrichment, such as misrepresentation, undue influence or duress, the most likely ground of restitution is that of total failure of basis, since if the effect of rescission is that the contract will be treated as void *ab initio* it follows that the basis for the transfer of the enrichment to the other party will be vitiated, so that the basis for the transfer of the enrichment will have failed totally.

4-015   Where rescission occurs in Equity, in principle the claimant or the defendant will have a separate claim in unjust enrichment for the recovery of the value of benefits transferred. Since, however, rescission occurs by order of the court, the court will require restitution and counter-restitution of the value of benefits transferred as a condition of the contract being rescinded, so a separate claim in unjust enrichment will not need to be pursued. But the requirement to make restitution and counter-restitution can still be analysed in terms of the need to prevent one party being unjustly enriched at the expense of the other.

---

[42] [2021] EWCA Civ 1053; [2021] 1 W.L.R. 6129.

[43] See para.4-023.

[44] *National Commercial Bank (Jamaica) Ltd v Hew's Executors* [2003] UKPC 51 at [43] (Lord Millett).

[45] *Lawton v Elmore* (1858) 27 LJR Exch. (N.S.) 141.

[46] This has been described as pecuniary rescission: P. Birks, "Unjust Factors and Wrongs: Pecuniary Rescission for Undue Influence" [1997] R.L.R. 72. This is misleading. Rescission involves setting aside the contract; the pecuniary element relates to restitution following rescission, albeit often as a condition of rescission.

[47] The general requirements of a claim in unjust enrichment were identified in *Banque Financière de la Cité v Parc (Battersea) Ltd* [1999] 1 A.C. 221 at 227 (Lord Steyn).

English law only requires the parties to the contract to make restitution to each **4-016** other. If a third party has received a benefit under the transaction, as will be the case where a bank has lent money to a third party as a result of the claimant agreeing to act as surety, the guarantee can be rescinded for non-disclosure[48] even though the bank cannot recover what it had lent to the third party.[49] This is because the benefit obtained by the third party arises from a separate transaction, albeit that the bank will have relied on the validity of the contract in lending the money. Although, by lending the money the bank will have changed its position in reliance on the validity of the contract and change of position is a defence to claims founded on unjust enrichment,[50] the bank's change of position cannot be relevant because rescission of the contract of guarantee will not require the bank to return any benefits to the surety.[51]

Personal claim for money transferred Where one party has transferred money **4-017** to the other pursuant to the contract which is then rescinded, the payer will be able to recover the value of the money from the recipient.[52] This is sometimes described as the action for money had and received, although it is preferably analysed simply as a claim in unjust enrichment for the value of money paid. For example, in *Newbigging v Adam*,[53] where the claimant sought to rescind a contract for misrepresentation, it was held that the defendant was required to make restitution in respect of all the benefits which he had received under the transaction. Consequently, the defendant was required to repay to the claimant the money which the claimant had put into a partnership business, as well as the money he had paid to discharge the debts of the business, minus those sums which the claimant had received from the partnership. Where the claimant has paid money to obtain an asset which has then fallen in value this will have no effect on the restitutionary claim for recovery of the value of the money.[54] Where an insurance policy is avoided by the insurer, there is a statutory obligation to return the premium to the assured save if the assured had acted fraudulently or illegally.[55] The parties will be required to restore the value of the benefit which they had received even if this is greater than what the other party had lost. So, in *Banwaitt v Dewji*[56] the claimant had been induced to pay the defendant £318,650 but this was required by the contract to be converted into dollars, so that the defendant received $750,000. The defendant was required to restore this amount to the claimant even though the value of the dollar had increased, so that the claimant received more than he had lost, for otherwise the defendant would have been unjustly enriched at the claimant's expense.

Personal claim for value of asset Where one party has transferred an asset to the **4-018**

---

48 See para.2-019.
49 *Mackenzie v Royal Bank of Canada* [1934] A.C. 468 at 476 (Lord Atkin).
50 See para.4-022.
51 The bank in such circumstances might seek an indemnity from the surety in respect of the benefit transferred to the third party, but this will only be available if the obligation to transfer the benefit arose under the contract of guarantee, which would be unlikely. See further para.4-031.
52 *Erlanger v New Sombrero Phosphate Co* (1878) 3 App. Cas. 1218.
53 (1886) 34 Ch D. 582. See also *Redgrave v Hurd* (1881) 20 Ch D. 1 (recovery of deposit); *With v O'Flanagan* [1936] Ch. 575 (recovery of purchase price).
54 *Cheese v Thomas* [1994] 1 W.L.R. 129, 135 (Sir Donald Nicholls VC). There may be some circumstances, however, where the loss is apportioned between the claimant and the defendant. See para.4-036.
55 Marine Insurance Act 1906 s.84(3)(a).
56 [2013] EWHC 879 (QB).

other pursuant to the contract, which is then rescinded, the transferor of the asset may not be able to recover it because, for example, it may have been dissipated or transferred and can no longer be identified. In such circumstances the transferor of the asset will be able to recover its reasonable value; sometimes known as *quantum valebat*.[57] The recipient of the asset will also be liable to account for any benefits derived from the use of the asset, such as dividends paid in respect of shares[58] or rent received.[59] There may also be a liability to pay for the use of land or chattels.[60] This should be assessed with reference to the objective market value for the use of the property. But the defendant will not be required to make restitution of indirect benefits since these will not have been obtained at the expense of the claimant. So, in *Moses v Moses*[61] land, which had been conveyed by mistake, was sold by the defendant for $300,000. The defendant then repurchased part of the land and sold it later for $320,000. It was held that the defendant was not liable to make restitution of this profit since it had not been made directly at the expense of the claimant.

4-019   The operation of this personal restitutionary remedy for goods received is illustrated by the difficult case of *Mahoney v Purnell*[62] where the claimant had sold shares in a company to the defendant. This transaction was liable to be set aside for presumed undue influence. It was not, however, possible to restore the parties to their precise pre-contractual position because the shares were in a company which was subsequently wound up. It was held that this barred rescission but that the court had power to award "equitable compensation" to the claimant, which was assessed as the value of the shares at the time of the sale. Awarding the remedy of "equitable compensation" suggests that the defendant had committed a wrong, but undue influence is not characterised as a wrong.[63] The case is better analysed as one where rescission was not barred, but, since the shares could not be restored because of the corporate insolvency, the claimant had a personal claim for the value of the shares which had been received by the defendant, with the relevant value being the value of the shares at the time of their receipt by the defendant. The remedy is consequently restitutionary, assessed by reference to the defendant's benefit, rather than compensating the claimant for loss suffered, although the claimant's loss reflects the defendant's gain. The result is consistent with key principles of the law of rescission, namely that where specific restitution is not possible, the benefit received by the defendant will be valued at the time the shares were sold and this value will be paid to the claimant, with the claimant giving credit for any payment received from the defendant for the shares. The monetary award was not made in lieu of rescission but was a condition of rescission to ensure that the parties were returned to the position they occupied before entering into the transaction.[64] It follows that the defendant in that case bore the risk of the shares becoming worthless, but this is an inevitable consequence of the effect of rescission being to restore the parties to their pre-contractual position. If the shares cannot be restored to the

---

[57] See *Moses v Moses* [2022] UKPC 42.

[58] *Spence v Crawford* [1939] 3 All E.R. 271 at 284 (Lord Thankerton).

[59] *Erlanger v New Sombrero Phosphate Co* (1878) 3 App. Cas. 1218 at 1278 (Lord Blackburn).

[60] *Cheese v Thomas* [1994] 1 W.L.R. 129 (liability to pay rent for use of land by the claimant).

[61] [2022] UKPC 42.

[62] [1996] 3 All E.R. 61.

[63] *Nature Resorts Ltd v First Citizen Bank Ltd* [2022] UKPC 10; [2022] 1 W.L.R. 2788 at [15] (Lords Briggs and Burrows). The trial judge in *Mahoney v Purnell* had characterised the relationship as fiduciary so the award of a compensatory remedy might have been awarded for breach of fiduciary duty.

[64] J. O'Sullivan, "Rescission as a Self-help Remedy: A Critical Analysis" (2000) 59 C.L.J. 509 at 510.

claimant, they will recover the value of the shares, with the defendant recovering any payment made to the claimant for the shares.

Personal claim for value of services   Where one party has provided a service pursuant to a contract, which is then rescinded, and the other party has benefited[65] from the provision of the service, the former will have a personal claim for the reasonable value of that service;[66] sometimes known as *quantum meruit*.[67]   **4-020**

Interest   The claimant can also recover interest in respect of the value of the benefit received,[68] to ensure that the other party is liable to give up all benefits obtained from the receipt of that benefit. Interest is assessed from the date of receipt of the benefit, rather than the date when the election to rescind was made.[69]   **4-021**

Change of position   A consequence of analysing the personal claim for restitution and counter-restitution as being founded on the reversal of the defendant's unjust enrichment is that the other party who has received the benefit will have a defence to the extent that they have changed their position in good faith as a result of receiving the benefit in circumstances where the change of position can be considered to be extraordinary.[70] So, for example, if the claimant has paid money to the defendant under the contract which is then avoided, the defendant should have a defence to the extent that they changed their position in good faith by spending the money on something which they would not otherwise have purchased from their own resources. The defence will not, however, be available if the defendant is a wrongdoer, such as where the defendant has acted fraudulently or in breach of fiduciary duty.[71]   **4-022**

III.   PROPRIETARY CONSEQUENCES

General principles[72]   Where one party has transferred an asset to the other party pursuant to a contract which is voidable, title to the asset will be transferred to the other party.[73] Once the transaction is rescinded at Common Law legal title to the asset will automatically be revested in the claimant, who will have a legal proprietary interest in the asset.[74] Where the transaction has been rescinded in Equity, the asset will be held on trust for the claimant, who will have an equitable   **4-023**

---

[65] See *Benedetti v Sawaris* [2013] UKSC 50; [2014] A.C. 938 for identification and valuation of beneficial services.

[66] *Atlantic Lines and Navigation Co Inc v Hallam Ltd (The Lucy)* [1983] 1 Lloyd's Rep. 188 at 202 (Mustill J).

[67] *O'Sullivan v Management Agency and Music Ltd* [1985] A.C. 686. See *Selway v Fogg* (1839) 5 M. and W. 83; 151 E.R. 36 which contemplated that, where services had been provided pursuant to a contract induced by fraud, the claimant could bring a separate claim for the tort of deceit.

[68] *National Commercial Bank (Jamaica) Ltd v Hew's Executors* [2003] UKPC 51 at [43] (Lord Millett).

[69] *Erlanger v The New Sombrero Phosphate Co* (1876) 5 Ch D. 73 at 125 (Jessel MR); *Adam v Newbigging* (1886) 34 Ch D. 582 at 585; *Re Metropolitan Coal Consumers' Association (Karberg's Case)* [1892] 3 Ch. 1 at 17.

[70] *Lipkin Gorman (a firm) v Karpnale Ltd* [1991] 2 A.C. 548 at 580 (Lord Goff).

[71] *Lipkin Gorman (a firm) v Karpnale Ltd* [1991] 2 A.C. 548 at 580 (Lord Goff).

[72] See generally S. Worthington, "The Proprietary Consequences of Rescission" [2002] R.L.R. 28.

[73] *Load v Green* (1846) 15 M. and W. 216 at 221; 153 E.R. 828 at 830 (Parke B).

[74] *Car & Universal Finance Co Ltd v Caldwell* [1965] 1 Q.B. 525.

proprietary interest in it.[75] In both cases the claimant will be able to bring a proprietary claim to vindicate their proprietary right in the asset. Property claims at Common Law are very limited and the claimant will usually only be able to pursue a personal claim for the value of the asset. In Equity, proprietary claims are much more extensive and, in some circumstances, enable the claimant to recover the asset itself. Since all cases of rescission at Common Law can also be effected in Equity, but not vice versa,[76] there are consequently advantages in seeking rescission in Equity.

4-024 **Rescission at Common Law** Once the claimant has elected to rescind the transaction at Common Law the legal title to the asset, whether land, chattels or money, which had been transferred to the defendant, will automatically revest in the claimant.[77] So, for example, where the claimant was induced to transfer property to the defendant as a result of a fraudulent representation, the effect of rescission of the contract to transfer the property will be to revest legal title in the claimant.[78] Rescission at Common Law will not, however, revest title in shares, because the revesting of legal title depends on the register of members being amended, nor in the revesting of title in unregistered or registered land because a formal conveyance of the property is required.[79] Neither will legal title in property revest in the claimant where the property has become irretrievably mixed with other property, since it is not possible to trace into a mixture at Common Law.[80] In all these circumstances the claimant should seek rescission in Equity. Rescission will be barred if the property transferred under the contract has been acquired by a *bona fide* purchaser for value,[81] so it will not be possible to revest legal title in the claimant. In particular, if goods are sold by a seller who has voidable title but that title has not yet been avoided at the time of the sale, the buyer will acquire good title to the goods provided that they were bought in good faith and without notice of the defect in title.[82] It is for the person seeking rescission of the contract to prove that the third party purchaser had actual or constructive notice of the defect in title.[83] But rescission at Common Law will be effective to revest title even though the

---

[75] *El Ajou v Dollar Land Holdings Plc* [1993] 3 All E.R. 717 at 734 (Millett LJ).

[76] See para.1-023 ff.

[77] *Street v Blay* (1831) 2 B. and Ad. 456; 109 E.R. 1212; *Murray v Mann* (1848) 2 Ex. 538, 154 E.R. 605; *Car & Universal Finance Co Ltd v Caldwell* [1965] 1 Q.B. 525; *O'Sullivan v Management Agency and Music Ltd* [1985] Q.B. 428 at 457 (Dunn LJ). See also *Alati v Kruger* (1955) 94 C.L.R. 216 at 223 (Dixon CJ). This is criticised by W. Swadling, "Rescission, Property and the Common Law" (2005) 121 L.Q.R. 123 who argues that rescission at Common Law should not result in legal title to the property transferred revesting in the claimant. Cf. B. Häcker, "Rescission of a Contract and Revesting of Title: A Reply to Mr Swadling" [2006] R.L.R. 106. See also S. Worthington, *Proprietary Interests in Commercial Transactions* (New York: Clarendon Press, 1996), p.132.

[78] *Clough v London and North Western Rly Co* (1871) L.R. 7 Ex. 26 at 32 (Mellor J). Presumably the same will be true where a contract has been rescinded for duress.

[79] It has been recognised in Australia in such circumstances that the property will be held on constructive trust for the other party to the contract: *Alati v Kruger* (1995) 94 C.L.R. 216 at 224 (Dixon CJ).

[80] *Agip (Africa) Ltd v Jackson* [1990] Ch. 265 at 286 (Millett J); [1991] Ch. 547 at 566 (Fox LJ); *El Ajou v Dollar Land Holdings Plc* [1993] 3 All E.R. 717 at 733 (Millett J).

[81] *Phillips v Brooks Ltd* [1919] 2 K.B. 243. See para.3-040.

[82] Sale of Goods Act 1979 s.23.

[83] *Whitehorn Bros v Davison* [1911] 1 K.B. 463; *Barclays Bank Plc v Boulter* [1999] 1 W.L.R. 1919 at 1925 (Lord Hoffmann).

property sold under the contract has been purchased by a *bona fide* purchaser for value after the contract has been rescinded.[84]

Where legal title to an asset has been revested in the claimant they can assert a proprietary claim against the asset. The claimant will gain priority over the defendant's unsecured creditors.[85] The claimant can also assert a proprietary interest in a substitute asset through the law of tracing save where its identity is lost through irretrievable mixing.[86] The Common Law lacks a mechanism, however, to enable the claimant to recover the asset itself, save for the action of ejectment to recover land. Consequently, the claimant might take the property back without recourse to the court.[87] Or the claimant might bring a claim for money had and received in respect of the proceeds of sale of the property which had been transferred.[88] Alternatively, since the defendant who has the possession of the claimant's property will have committed the tort of conversion in not returning the property, the claimant may sue the defendant for that tort. The court has a discretion to award either damages to compensate the claimant for the loss suffered or may order specific recovery of the asset.[89]

4-025

Rescission in Equity Where a contract is rescinded in Equity the court will recognise that the party who has rescinded the contract has an equitable proprietary interest in the property which was transferred to the defendant, who will consequently hold this property on trust for the rescinding party, assuming that it is possible to identify the transferred property or its traceable proceeds in the hands of the defendant.[90] The trust has variously been analysed as a resulting trust[91] or, preferably, as a constructive trust,[92] although nothing turns on this characterisation. Since rescission in Equity only takes effect on the order of the court, it follows that

4-026

---

84 *Car & Universal Finance Co Ltd v Caldwell* [1965] 1 Q.B. 525. In a commercial context, third party purchasers of goods from a seller with defective title might be protected by Sale of Goods Act 1979 s.25 since a sale to the defendant will be with the consent of the seller, albeit that this consent is voidable. But s.25 only applies if the third party purchaser acted in good faith and without notice of the defect in title. See *Newtons of Wembley Ltd v Williams* [1965] 1 Q.B. 560.

85 *Load v Green* (1846) 15 M. and W. 216; 153 E.R. 828; *Re Eastgate* [1905] 1 K.B. 465; *Tilley v Bowman Ltd* [1910] 1 K.B. 745.

86 *Agip (Africa) Ltd v Jackson* [1990] Ch. 265 at 286 (Millett J); [1991] Ch. 547 at 566 (Fox LJ); *El Ajou v Dollar Land Holdings Plc* [1993] 3 All E.R. 717 at 733 (Millett J).

87 *Re Eastgate* [1905] 1 K.B. 465.

88 *Lipkin Gorman (a firm) v Karpnale Ltd* [1991] 2 A.C. 546.

89 Torts (Interference with Goods) Act 1977.

90 *Lonrho Plc v Fayed (No.2)* [1992] 1 W.L.R. 1 at 11–12 (Millett J); *El Ajou v Dollar Land Holdings Plc* [1993] 3 All E.R. 717 at 734 (Millett J); *Bristol and West Building Society v Mothew* [1998] Ch. 1 at 22–23 (Millett LJ); *Shalson v Russo* [2005] Ch. 281 at 316 at [122] (Rimer J); *The National Crime Agency v Robb* [2014] EWHC 4384 (Ch), [2015] Ch. 520 at [51] (Etherton C); *ED and F Man Capital Markets v Come Harvest Holdings Ltd* [2022] EWHC 229 (Comm) at [614] (Calver J).

91 *El Ajou v Dollar Land Holdings Plc* [1993] 3 All E.R. 717 at 734 (Millett J).

92 *Daly v Sydney Stock Exchange Ltd* (1986) 160 C.L.R. 371 at 388 (Brennan J); *Lonrho Plc v Al-Fayed (No.2)* [1992] 1 W.L.R. 1 at 11–12 (Millett J); *Twinsectra Ltd v Yardley* [1999] Lloyd's Rep. Bank. 438 at 461 (Potter LJ); *National Crime Agency v Robb* [2014] EWHC 4384 (Ch); [2015] Ch. 520. See P.J. Millett, "Restitution and Constructive Trusts" (1998) 114 L.Q.R. 399, para.416. This is an institutional constructive trust. The remedial constructive trust, which responds to the exercise of judicial discretion, is not recognised in England and Wales: *FHR European Ventures LLP v Cedar Capital Partners LLC* [2014] UKSC 45; [2015] A.C. 250 at [44] (Lord Neuberger); *Angove Pty Ltd v Bailey* [2016] UKSC 47; [2016] 1 W.L.R. 3179 at [27] (Lord Sumption); *Crown Prosecution Service v Aquila Advisory Ltd* [2021] UKSC 49; [2021] 1 W.L.R. 5666 at [88] (Lord Stephens). See also *Re Polly Peck International Plc (In Administration) (No.5)* [1998] 3 All E.R. 812 at 830 (Nourse LJ); *Cobbold v Bakewell Management Ltd* [2003] EWHC 2289 (Ch) at [17] (Rimer J); *Shalson v*

the claimant has no equitable proprietary interest in the property until the court order is made, which will have the effect of vesting equitable title in the claimant who can then recover the property.[93] Before the court order is made the claimant only has a mere equity to rescind the contract, which creates an entitlement to the equitable relief which is conferred by the order of the court. [94] However, it has been recognised that where the contract was induced by fraud, the claimant will obtain an equitable proprietary interest in the property transferred from the point at which the claimant makes the election to rescind,[95] and this operates retrospectively to the date when the Equity to rescind arose.[96] But rescission will not invalidate or render wrongful transactions which had taken place on the faith of the receipt.[97] In particular, although the recipient of the property will hold it on trust for the person who sought rescission of the contract, the recipient cannot be liable for breach of fiduciary duty before the rescission was effective. Neither will the recipient be liable for knowing receipt following rescission, despite the retrospective vesting of the equitable interest in the claimant.[98]

4-027   The creation of equitable proprietary interests following rescission of the contract in Equity has been recognised for a variety of grounds of rescission, including fraudulent misrepresentation[99] and undue influence.[100] Where a fiduciary has obtained a profit in breach of fiduciary duty that profit will be held on constructive trust for the principal.[101] This will be the case even where the fiduciary's profit derived from a third party, such as where the fiduciary has received a bribe.[102]

4-028   Once the claimant has established an equitable proprietary interest in property received by the defendant, the claimant will be able to assert a claim to recover that asset. Where the asset has been replaced by a substitute asset the claimant can trace into that asset and assert a claim against it also.[103] Even where value from the claimant's asset has been mixed with another asset, the claimant will be able to trace

---

Russo [2005] Ch. 281 at [118] (Rimer J). *Re Farepak Food and Gifts Ltd (In Administration)* [2006] EWHC 3272 (Ch) at [38] (Mann J); *Sinclair Investments (UK) Ltd v Versailles Trade Finance Ltd* [2011] EWCA Civ 347; [2012] Ch. 453 at [37] (Lord Neuberger MR). In *ED & F Man Capital Markets v Come Harvest Holdings Ltd* [2022] EWHC 229 (Comm) at [614] Calver J described this as a "rescission trust".

93 *Daly v Sydney Stock Exchange Ltd* (1986) 160 C.L.R. 371 389–390 (Brennan J); *Bristol and West Building Society v Mothew* [1998] 1 Ch. 1 at 23 (Millett LJ).

94 *Phillips v Phillips* (1861) 4 De G.F. & J. 208 at 218; 45 E.R. 1164 at 1167 (Lord Westbury); *National Crime Agency v Robb* [2014] EWHC 4384 (Ch); [2015] Ch 520 at [80] (Etherton C).

95 *Small v Attwood* (1832) You. 407 at 535; 159 E.R. 1103; *Banque Belge pur l'Etranger v Hambrouck* [1921] 1 K.B. 321 at 332 (Atkin LJ); *Lonrho Plc v Fayed (No.2)* [1992] 1 W.L.R. 1 at 12 (Millett J); *El Ajou v Dollar Land Holdings Plc* [1993] 3 All E.R. 717 at 734 (Millett J); *Collings v Lee* [2001] 2 All E.R. 332 at 337 (Nourse LJ); *Shalson v Russo* [2005] Ch. 281 at 316 [122] (Rimer J).

96 P.J. Millett, "Restitution and Constructive Trusts" (1998) 114 L.Q.R. 399 at 416.

97 *Bolton Partners v Lambert* (1889) 41 Ch D. 295 at 307 (Cotton LJ); *Lipkin Gorman (a firm) v Karpnale Ltd* [1991] 2 A.C. 548 at 573 (Lord Goff).

98 *ED and F Man Capital Markets v Come Harvest Holdings Ltd* [2022] EWHC 229 (Comm) at [635] (Calver J).

99 *Lonrho Plc v Fayed (No.2)* [1992] 1 W.L.R. 1; *El Ajou v Dollar Land Holdings Plc* [1993] 3 All E.R. 717 at 735 (Millett J); *Shalson v Russo* [2005] Ch. 281.

100 *Allcard v Skinner* (1887) 36 Ch D. 145 at 172 (Cotton LJ); *Smith v Cooper* [2010] EWCA Civ 722; [2010] 2 F.C.R. 551.

101 *FHR European Ventures LLP v Cedar Capital Partners LLC* [2014] UKSC 45; [2015] A.C. 250.

102 *FHR European Ventures LLP v Cedar Capital Partners LLC* [2014] UKSC 45; [2015] A.C. 250. See para.4-041.

103 *Bainbridge v Bainbridge* [2016] EWHC 898 (Ch); [2016] W.T.L.R. 943.

into the mixture.[104] So, for example, where money in which the claimant has an equitable proprietary interest is mixed with money belonging to the defendant, the claimant will be able to assert a claim against the mixture, a proportion of which will be held on trust for the claimant. A claimant with an equitable proprietary right is not able to sue the party in possession of the property for the tort of conversion, since equitable title is not sufficient to establish such a claim.[105]

The equity to rescind which enables the claimant to recover property on rescis-   **4-029** sion is preferably treated as an inchoate or prospective proprietary right.[106] The equity to rescind can be enforced against any party who receives the property from the defendant, other than a *bona fide* purchaser for value; it is a right which can be left in a will and passes on death; it can be conveyed and assigned but only in connection with the property to which it relates;[107] it can be traced through substitute property. Once rescission is barred so that the contract can no longer be set aside, the equity to rescind will be defeated and the claimant will not be able to assert a proprietary claim to recover property.[108] Where a chose in action is purchased the purchaser takes the chose in action subject to all prior claims upon it, including the equity to rescind.[109]

Where property has been transferred to the defendant pursuant to a contract   **4-030** which is voidable in Equity and the property is transferred to a third party, the claimant can assert the equity to rescind against the third party, save if the defendant or third party was a good faith purchaser of the legal title to the property for value, since such a purchaser acquires the property free from all equitable proprietary interests in it.[110] Consequently, the claimant's equitable proprietary claim will be defeated.[111] The purchaser will not have acted in good faith if they had actual or constructive notice of the claimant's equitable proprietary right.[112] The purchaser will have constructive notice if they failed to make inquiries which would have been

---

[104] *El-Ajou v Dollar Land Holdings Plc (No.1)* [1993] B.C.L.C. 735 at 753 (Millett J). It is also possible to trace into an asset which was already in the defendant's possession: *Brazil v Durant International Corp* [2015] UKPC 35; [2016] A.C. 297. But such "backwards tracing" has been recognised only in exceptional and narrow situations where a strict insistence on the chronological sequence would not reflect the substance of the situation: *Serious Fraud Office v Hotel Portfolio II UK Ltd* [2021] EWHC 1273 (Comm) at [45]–[46] (Foxton J).

[105] *MCC Proceeds Inc v Lehman Bros International Europe* [1998] 4 All E.R. 675.

[106] See *Global Currency Exchange Network Ltd v Osago 1 Ltd* [2019] EWHC 1375 (Comm); [2019] 1 W.L.R. 5865 at [52] (Andrew Henshaw QC). In *Re Crown Holdings (London) Ltd* [2015] EWHC 1876 (Ch) at [38] MH Rosen QC held that the equity to rescind was a personal right which did not give any proprietary rights, consequently customers' money paid to a company which had gone into insolvent liquidation was available to the company's creditors despite the existence of an equity to rescind. See generally A. Reilly, "Is the 'mere equity' to rescind a legal power? Unpacking Hohfeld's concept of 'volitional control'" (2019) 39 O.J.L.S. 779.

[107] *Investors Compensation Scheme Ltd v West Bromwich Building Society* [1998] 1 W.L.R. 896 at 916 (Lord Hoffmann).

[108] *Lonrho Plc v Fayed (No.2)* [1992] 1 W.L.R. 1 at 12 (Millett J).

[109] *Cockell v Taylor* (1852) 15 Beav. 103 at 118; 51 E.R. 475 at 481 (Sir John Romilly MR).

[110] *Pilcher v Rawlins* (1871–72) L.R. 7 Ch. App. 259 at 266 (Lord Hatherley LC). In *Ward v Savill* [2021] EWCA Civ 1378 it was held that an earlier judgment declaring that a transaction was avoided, and which also made a declaration as to proprietary rights and beneficial interests as between the parties to the judgment, did not bind a third party recipient of proprietary rights. Consequently, the claimant had to establish the elements of any proprietary claim against the third party, namely that the claimant was beneficially interested in the fund and could trace the value in the fund into the third party's property.

[111] *Daly v Sydney Stock Exchange* (1985) 160 C.L.R. 371 at 388 (Brennan J); *Twinsectra Ltd v Yardley* [1999] Lloyd's Rep. Bank. 438 at 461 (Potter LJ).

[112] *Credit Agricole Corp and Investment Bank v Papadimitriou* [2015] UKPC 13; [2015] 1 W.L.R. 4265.

made by a reasonable person in the purchaser's position.[113] Such inquiries should be made if there is a serious possibility of someone else having a proprietary right or if the facts known to the purchaser would give a reasonable person in the position of the purchaser serious cause to question the propriety of the transaction involving the transfer of property.[114] Where a third party acquires an equitable interest in the property for value and in good faith, this too will defeat the claimant's mere equity to rescind the contract.[115] The burden of proving that the purchaser took the property with notice of the circumstances of the claimant's claim is borne by the claimant who seeks rescission.[116] In fact, where a third party acquires either a legal or an equitable interest in the property in good faith and for value, rescission will be barred,[117] so it will not be possible to assert an equitable proprietary interest in the property. Where the transaction involving the transfer of property to the good faith purchaser is itself rescinded, the transaction will be a nullity so that the recipient will be converted into a volunteer and the prior equitable proprietary interest will be resurrected.[118]

IV. INDEMNITY

4-031 **General principles** A further consequence of rescission of the contract in Equity is that both parties to the contract acquire a right to be indemnified for any detriment or disadvantage which they suffered under the contract, but only where they were required to suffer the detriment or disadvantage by the contract or, perhaps, where the detriment was necessarily incurred in carrying out the contract in circumstances where, had the contract not been made, the other party would have been liable for the expense.[119] For example, if either party had incurred a necessary expense in performing the contract, or conferred a benefit on another or incurred a liability to another under the contract, that party can be indemnified by the other for the value of the benefit or the liability incurred.[120] Although the matter is not free from doubt, the rationale behind an indemnity award is not to compensate one party for loss suffered in carrying out the contract, but to ensure that the other party is liable for benefits obtained from the first party's performance, for otherwise the other party will be unjustly enriched at the expense of the first party following rescission of the contract. This restitutionary analysis of indemnity is possible because an enrichment can encompass the saving of an inevitable expense which would otherwise be borne by the defendant, either through the discharge of a liability owed to a third party or by work for which the defendant would have had to pay had the claimant not done so.

---

[113] *Credit Agricole Corp and Investment Bank v Papadimitriou* [2015] UKPC 13; [2015] 1 W.L.R. 4265 at [20] (Lord Clarke).

[114] *Credit Agricole Corp and Investment Bank v Papadimitriou* [2015] UKPC 13; [2015] 1 W.L.R. 4265 at [20] (Lord Clarke).

[115] *Phillips v Phillips* (1861) 4 De G.F. & J. 208 at 218; 45 E.R. 1164 at 1167 (Lord Westbury). See D.B. O'Sullivan, "The Rule in *Phillips v Phillips*" (2002) 118 L.Q.R. 296.

[116] *Re Nisbet and Potts Contract* [1905] 1 Ch. 391 at 398; *Barclays Bank Plc v Boulter* [1999] 1 W.L.R. 1919 at 1924 (Lord Hoffmann).

[117] See para.3-040.

[118] *Independent Trustees Service Ltd v GP Noble Trustees Ltd* [2012] EWCA Civ 195; [2013] Ch. 91.

[119] D. O'Sullivan, S. Elliott and R. Zakrzewski, *The Law of Rescission*, 3rd edn (Oxford: Oxford University Press, 2023), para.17.24.

[120] *Newbigging v Adam* (1886) 34 Ch D. 582 at 589 (Cotton LJ), 595 (Bowen LJ), affirmed as *Adam v Newbigging* (1888) 13 App. Cas. 308; *Whittington v Seale-Hayne* (1900) 82 L.T. 49 at 51 (Farwell LJ).

That the right to indemnity can be analysed in restitutionary terms is illustrated **4-032** by *Whittington v Seale-Hayne*[121] where the defendant had let a poultry farm to the claimant, having represented it as being in good condition when the buildings were in disrepair and it was in an insanitary state. The claimant rescinded the lease of the farm. In addition to recovery of the rent paid to the defendant, he was also indemnified for rates paid to the local authority and the cost of repair work made to the farm which he carried out as a result of an order made by the local authority. This was justified because the obligation to make these payments could be considered to have been created by the contract. But both of these payments can also be considered to have enriched the defendant even though the money was paid to a third party. This was because the payments were incontrovertibly beneficial to the defendant since the claimant had discharged a liability which the defendant would otherwise have inevitably incurred, and so a failure to indemnify the claimant for these payments would have unjustly enriched the defendant. The claimant could not, however, be indemnified for the loss of pigs which had died as a result of the farm's insanitary state, nor for loss of profits in running the business. This can be justified because these losses did not correspond with any gain to the defendant.[122]

V. COMPENSATION

Where a party has suffered loss in carrying out the contract before it is rescinded **4-033** then, as a function of the need to restore the parties substantially to their pre-contractual position, the other party will be required to compensate for this loss.[123] So, for example, the claimant can recover compensation for improvements or repairs to property purchased under the contract.[124] Where the claimant is required by the contract to make such repairs or improvements they will be able to seek an indemnity for the cost of the work.[125] Compensation for loss will be available where the claimant was not contractually obliged to do the work. For example, where a house is sold to another as a result of undue influence and that other party voluntarily spent money on improving it, credit could be given for the improvements.[126] Where a party has incurred expense in repairing property transferred under the voidable contract, that party cannot be compensated for this loss if they were aware that

---

[121] (1900) 82 L.T. 49.

[122] The claimant might instead bring a claim in tort to recover damages for such losses, but only where the misrepresentation was fraudulent, so the tort of deceit would be engaged, or negligent, so the tort of negligent misstatement would apply (*Hedley Byrne and Co Ltd v Heller and Partners Ltd* [1964] A.C. 465) or alternatively a claim under the Misrepresentation Act 1967 s.2(1). Where the misrepresentation is innocent, there will be no tort claim. Where there is a claim in tort the damages which are available to compensate for loss suffered are likely to be just as extensive as an indemnity award.

[123] This must be loss suffered by the contracting party rather than a company in which the party has an interest, by virtue of the reflective loss principle: *Burnford v Automobile Association Developments Ltd* [2022] EWCA Civ 1943 at [42] (Newey LJ).

[124] *Mill v Hill* (1852) 3 HLC 828 at 869; 10 E.R. 330 at 346 (Lord Truro); *Ex p. Bennett* (1805) 10 Ves. 381 at 400; 32 E.R. 893 at 900 (Lord Eldon LC); *Lagunas Nitrate Co v Lagunas Syndicate* [1899] 2 Ch. 293 at 456 (Rigby LJ).

[125] See para.4-031.

[126] *O'Sullivan v Management Agency and Music Ltd* [1985] Q.B. 428 at 466 (Fox LJ). If the improvements can be characterised as an enrichment for the defendant then there may be a claim in unjust enrichment instead for the reasonable value of the claimant's services. See para.4-020.

the contract was voidable or if they were a wrongdoer, such as a fraudster.[127] Where a party has repaired the property, the measure of compensation should be the cost of the work as reflecting the increase in the market value of the property.[128]

4-034   But the claimant cannot be compensated for consequential losses which they were not obliged to incur by the contract. So, for example, in *Redgrave v Hurd*,[129] where the claimant had been induced to purchase a solicitor's practice as the result of an innocent misrepresentation, he could not recover costs incurred in preparing to perform the contract, such as moving expenses.[130] Similarly, it is not possible to obtain compensation for loss suffered in foregoing other opportunities.[131]

4-035   Where property is transferred to the claimant pursuant to a voidable contract and the property falls in value, either as a result of deterioration or depreciation, compensation can only be awarded if the loss arose from acts of the defendant.[132] It follows that ordinary wear and tear is not compensatable. Neither is depreciation due to market forces[133] nor due to an inherent defect in the property.[134]

VI.   APPORTIONMENT OF LOSS

4-036   Although normally a consequence of rescission is to require one party to make restitution of gains to the other, there will sometimes be circumstances where the contract has resulted in a loss and the court may seek to allocate the loss between the parties. This is illustrated by *Cheese v Thomas*[135] where a contract for the joint purchase of a house was rescinded for presumed undue influence. Both the claimant and the defendant had contributed to the purchase of the property, which had fallen in value. Rather than setting aside the transaction in its entirety and requiring the defendant to make restitution of the claimant's contribution, the court imposed a condition on rescission,[136] namely that the loss should be apportioned between the parties in proportion to their contribution to the purchase price. This was justified because the parties were considered to have entered into a joint venture so that they should be treated as equal participants and so share the loss between them, although this joint venture analysis is difficult to defend because the defendant's presumed undue influence meant that the parties should have been treated as unequal participants.[137]

---

[127] *Kenny v Browne* (1796) 3 Ridge P.C. 462 at 518.

[128] *Ex p. Bennett* (1805) 10 Ves 381 at 400; 32 E.R. 893 at 900 (Lord Eldon LC). See also *Holder v Holder* [1968] Ch. 353 at 373 (Cross J).

[129] (1881) 20 Ch D. 1.

[130] Such damages for consequential loss may now be available under the Misrepresentation Act 1967 s.2(1), save where the defendant can prove that they had acted reasonably in making the representation.

[131] *Newbigging v Adam* (1886) 34 Ch D. 582 at 589 (Cotton LJ).

[132] *Ex p. Bennett* (1805) 10 Ve.s 381 at 401; 32 E.R. 894 at 900 (Lord Eldon LC); *Lagunas Nitrate Co v Lagunas Syndicate* [1899] 2 Ch. 392 at 456–457 (Rigby LJ); *Spence v Crawford* [1939] 3 All E.R. 271 at 280 (Lord Thankerton). Cf. *Erlanger v New Sombrero Phosphate Co* (1878) 3 App. Cas. 1218 at 1278 where Lord Blackburn made no reference to the significance of the defendant's fault as a reason for the deterioration in the property.

[133] *Cheese v Thomas* [1994] 1 W.L.R. 129 at 135 (Sir Donald Nicholls VC).

[134] *Adam v Newbigging* (1888) 13 App. Cas. 308.

[135] [1994] 1 W.L.R. 129.

[136] See para.4-009 for analysis of rescission on terms.

[137] Cf. M. Chen-Wishart, "Loss-Sharing, Undue Influence and Manifest Disadvantage" (1994) 110 L.Q.R. 173 who analyses the case as involving an implicit application of the defence of change of position.

VII.   CONCURRENT CLAIMS

General principles   There will sometimes be circumstances where, either in ad-   **4-037**
dition to or as an alternative to a right to rescind the contract, the claimant will have
a concurrent claim either at Common Law or in Equity by virtue of which the claimant may obtain a compensatory or disgorgement remedy, not as a consequence of
the contract being rescinded but for some distinct cause of action.

Common Law claims   Where the claimant has a right to rescind the contract at   **4-038**
Common Law there will not be an additional claim for compensatory damages for
breach of contract because, following rescission, there will be no contract which
could have been breached. But the claimant may have a concurrent claim in tort,
such as the tort of deceit for fraudulent misrepresentation or the tort of negligent
misstatement where there has been a negligent misrepresentation, [138] for which the
claimant can obtain damages. [139] In such circumstances the claimant can claim both
rescission and damages for the tort.[140] If rescission is barred, the claimant can simply
sue for damages with a claim founded on the relevant tort, or, where appropriate,
for breach of contract.

Equitable compensation   Where the claimant seeks rescission in Equity they may   **4-039**
also have a concurrent claim in Equity for wrongdoing, typically for breach of
fiduciary duty for which a pecuniary award may be made to compensate the claimant for loss suffered as a result of the breach of duty, such as consequential financial
loss.[141] If rescission is barred then the claimant could simply seek equitable
compensation for the wrong.[142]

Disgorgement   Where a fiduciary has entered into a contract on behalf of the   **4-040**
principal in breach of fiduciary duty[143] and obtains a profit as a result, if the contract
is rescinded the fiduciary will also be liable to account for the profits made in breach
of fiduciary duty. Where, however, the contract cannot be rescinded because one
of the bars to rescission applies, it has been recognised that the fiduciary cannot be
liable to account for profits made from breach of fiduciary duty, at least where the
fiduciary sold property to the principal which the fiduciary had obtained before they
were in a fiduciary relationship with the principal and the breach of duty involved
the failure to disclose that interest to the principal.[144] But this is unjustifiable. In the
same way that the claim for rescission and the tort of deceit are distinct claims, so

---

[138] *Hedley Byrne and Co Ltd v Heller and Partners Ltd* [1964] A.C. 465. Also note the claim for damages under Misrepresentation Act 1967 s.2(1) where there has been a misrepresentation which the
misrepresentor could not prove that he had reasonable grounds to believe that it was true.

[139] Where the claimant has been compelled to enter into a contract there may be a claim for the tort of
intimidation: *Halpern v Halpern (Nos 1 and 2)* [2007] EWCA Civ 291; [2008] Q.B. at 195 at [59]
(Carnwath LJ).

[140] *Adam v Newbigging* (1886) 34 Ch D. 582.

[141] *Nocton v Lord Ashburton* [1914] A.C. 932; *Mahoney v Purnell* [1996] 3 All E.R. 61; *Swindle v Harrison* [1997] 4 All E.R. 705 at 718 (Evans LJ), 726 (Hobhouse LJ), 733 (Mummery LJ); *Bristol and
West Building Society v Mothew* [1998] Ch. 1 at 17 (Millett LJ); *Longstaff v Birtles* [2002] 1 W.L.R.
470 at [36] (Mummery LJ). M. Conaglen, "Equitable Compensation for Breach of Fiduciary Dealing Rules" (2003) 119 L.Q.R. 246.

[142] *Cavendish Bentinck v Fenn* (1887) 12 App. Cas. 652; *Re Leeds and Hanley Theatres of Varieties
Ltd* [1902] 2 Ch. 809; *JJ Harrison (Properties) Ltd v Harrison* [2001] 1 B.C.L.C. 158.

[143] See para.2-042.

[144] *Re Cape Breton Co* (1885) 29 Ch D. 795; *Ladywell Minding Co v Brookes* (1887) 35 Ch D. 400 at

too should be the claim for rescission and a claim for profits made in breach of fiduciary duty. And the fact that rescission is barred should not bar a claim for an account of profits.[145] There are situations, however, where it has been recognised that a principal, who has entered into a contract with a fiduciary involving breach of the fiduciary's duties as a fiduciary, can seek disgorgement from the fiduciary regardless of whether the contract has been rescinded, such as where the fiduciary sells an asset to the principal which was the principal's property;[146] where the breach of fiduciary duty was dishonest;[147] or where the impossibility of rescission was due to the acts of the fiduciary.[148]

4-041   Where a fiduciary has received a bribe or a secret commission as a result of which the principal enters into a contract with a third party, the principal can require the fiduciary to disgorge the value of the bribe or the secret commission by seeking a personal remedy of an account of profits for breach of fiduciary duty without needing to rescind the contract.[149] Alternatively, the bribe or secret commission will be held on constructive trust for the principal, who can bring a proprietary restitutionary claim to vindicate their equitable proprietary right.[150]

---

408 (Cotton LJ); *Burland v Earle* [1902] A.C. 83 at 99 (Lord Davey); *Jacobus Marler Estates Ltd v Marler* (1916) 114 L.T. 640n. The fiduciary might still be liable to compensate the principal for the difference between the price paid by the principal and the market value at the time of the sale: *Re Cape Breton Co* (1885) 29 Ch D. 795 at 805 (Cotton LJ); *Cavendish Bentinck v Fenn* (1887) 12 App. Cas. 652 (on appeal from *Re Cape Breton Co*). See M. Conaglen, *Fiduciary Loyalty: Protecting the Due Performance of Non-Fiduciary Duties* (Oxford: Hart Publishing, 2010), p.89.

[145] See *Re Cape Breton Co* (1885) 29 Ch D. 795 at 808–809 (Bowen LJ, dissenting).

[146] *Re Cape Breton Co* (1885) 29 Ch D. 795 at 811 (Fry LJ); *Gluckstein v Barnes* [1900] A.C. 240; *Jacobus Marler Estates Ltd v Marler* (1916) 114 L.T. 640n.

[147] *Gwembe Valley Development Co v Koshy* [2004] 1 B.C.L.C. 131 at 177 (Mummery LJ).

[148] *Re Cape Breton Co* (1885) 29 Ch D. 795 at 811 (Fry LJ).

[149] *Lister and Co v Stubbs* (1890) 45 Ch D. 1; *Sinclair Investments (UK) Ltd v Versailles Trade Finance Ltd* [2011] EWCA Civ 347; [2012] Ch. 453.

[150] *FHR European Ventures LLP v Cedar Capital Partners LLC* [2014] UKSC 45; [2015] A.C. 250. See para.4-027.

PART II BREACH AND PERFORMANCE

By Professor Neil Andrews

CHAPTER 5

BREACH: INTRODUCTION[1]

I. FUNDAMENTAL ASPECTS

Breach might be a one-off default, or it might be recurrent or persistent, or it **5-001**
might be continuous (in the last case, for example, when a promise not to build on
land is breached and left unremedied by the promisor).

Breach can occur by declaration (see category (i) below) or misconduct (or omis- **5-002**
sion) (see categories (ii) and (iii) below).

(i) *Explicit or implicit renunciation:* If, whether before or at the time of **5-003**
     performance, a party (a) declares or (b) indicates by conduct that he does not
     intend to perform, the other party can "elect" to end the contract straightaway
     and sue for compensation.
(ii) *Culpably rendering future performance impossible:* Before the performance **5-004**
      is due, a party might have culpably (that is, without lawful excuse) prevented
      the contract from being performed.
(iii) *Defective performance:* Performance can be defective in a myriad of ways: **5-005**
       total non-performance; the tender or supply of wrong or shoddy subject-
       matter or useless or unsatisfactory services; performance might be delayed
       or too slow; or the guilty party might do that which he promised not to do,
       for example, by working for a rival company in breach of an obligation to
       perform exclusively for the claimant's benefit.

Of these three forms of breach, the most common is (iii); (i) is the next most com- **5-006**
mon; mode (ii) is quite uncommon because the innocent party here takes the risk
that he might have misperceived the situation and that instead the other party might
yet have retrieved the situation.

Breach is to be distinguished from the situation where a party's prima facie **5-007**
default is in fact excusable. The three possible grounds of excuse (as opposed to a
shield[2] against liability for default or ex post facto waiver)[3] might be:

- the law of frustration (Pt III at Chs 16–18); or
- an exculpatory clause, such as a force majeure clause (stipulating that a

---

[1] Pt II, Chs 5–15, are by N. Andrews.
[2] Strictly speaking, an exclusion clause will not prevent a breach from occurring, but merely exclude
     or restrict liability arising from breach.
[3] If the innocent party waives his rights to complain about the relevant breach, the breach did occur,
     but it has ceased to be a ground of compliant.

party will be released from his obligation by reason of freak and excusable supervening events);[4] or

- the fact that the other party's default excuses the current party from performing (Ch.15).

5-008   Breach (if unexcused: for sources of excuse see the preceding paragraph) exposes the guilty party to a claim for damages, or debt, or specific performance, or an injunction or, at least, a declaration that breach has occurred (on these remedies, Pt IV).

5-009   Every breach entitles the innocent party to recover at least "nominal damages" (a token sum signifying the fact that there has been a technical legal wrong: for example, sums of £5 or £10).[5] For example, in *Multi Veste 226 BV v NI Summer Row Unitholder BV* (2011)[6] Lewison J held that the claimant had failed to establish substantial loss. In fact, early collapse of the deal had saved the claimant from a multi-million eventual loss. Nominal damages of £2 were awarded.

5-010   *De Minimis Default in Loan Repayment: Default Judgment Set Aside for Reconsideration on the Merits.* In *Lombard North Central Plc v European Skyjets Ltd* (2020)[7] Freedman J (setting aside a default judgment, despite a four year delay) said that there was an arguable case that the claimant lender could not show default on the part of the borrower, there having been a mere $179 dollar underpayment (the loan agreement contained an acceleration clause which the creditor alleged had been triggered by default). The de minimis point was left open for eventual decision.[8]

5-011   *Entitlement to Terminate for Breach.* At Common Law the innocent party is entitled to terminate a contract for breach if: (i) the other party has shown a clear unwillingness to satisfy his contract; this category should be identified as "renunciation", which is normally express, that is verbal, but occasionally it can be implied; category (i), confusingly, is sometimes known as "repudiatory breach", but see (v) below; or (ii) performance has been rendered impossible by the default of the guilty party; or there has been a breach of (iii) an important term (a "condition") or (iv) of another term which can give rise to termination, depending on the seriousness of the breach (an "innominate term") or (v) there has been a breach or set of breaches constituting repudiatory breach that goes to the root of the expected performance. As for category (iii), there are three types of promissory obligation: conditions; innominate (or "intermediate") terms; and warranties,[9] but there is no

---

[4]   K. Lewison, *Interpretation of Contracts*, 7th edn (London: Sweet & Maxwell, 2020), Ch.13; E. McKendrick (ed), *Force Majeure and Frustration of Contract*, 2nd edn (London: Informa, 1995); G. McMeel, *The Construction of Contracts: Interpretation, Implication and Rectification*, 3rd edn (Oxford: Oxford University Press, 2017), 22.35 ff; E. Peel, *Frustration and Force Majeure*, 4th edn (London: Sweet & Maxwell, 2021), para.12-035 ff (such cases are examined in N. Andrews, *Contract Rules: Decoding English Law* (Cambridge: Intersentia, 2016), 266–269); Ben Symons, *Force Majeure and Frustration in Commercial Contracts*, (London: Bloomsbury Professional, 2022); *Tennants (Lancashire) Ltd v CS Wilson & Co Ltd* [1917] A.C. 495 HL and *Great Elephant Corp v Trafigura Beheer BV* [2013] EWCA Civ 905; [2013] 2 All E.R. (Comm) 992; on force majeure clauses and notification requirements, *Scottish Power UK Plc v BP Exploration Operating Co Ltd* [2015] EWHC 2658 (Comm); [2016] 1 All E.R. (Comm) 536 at [194] ff per (Leggatt J); decision affirmed [2016] EWCA Civ 1043; and see para.16-044 ff on force majeure clauses.

[5]   J. Edelman (ed) *McGregor on Damages*, 21st edn (London: Sweet & Maxwell, 2021), Ch.12.

[6]   [2011] EWHC 2026 (Ch); 139 Con. L.R. 23 at [275].

[7]   [2020] EWHC 679 (QB).

[8]   [2020] EWHC 679 (QB) at [44] and [45].

[9]   On the history of warranties and conditions, D.J. Ibbetson, *A Historical Introduction to the Law of*

fourth category of "fundamental term",[10] even though some judges persist in using that now largely abandoned terminology.[11] In addition to these Common Law grounds for treating the contract as discharged for breach, that is terminating for breach, it is possible that the contract might contain a termination for breach clause, specifying that the innocent party is entitled in certain circumstances to treat the contract as terminated for breach (on such clauses see Ch.9).

A "condition" (that is, condition in the sense of a promissory obligation) will arise **5-012** when statute so provides, or if the relevant obligation is expressed to be a "condition", or it is subject to a clause entitling the innocent party to terminate the contract for failure to satisfy the obligation, or if the court construes a neutral term as a condition.

Express use of the word "condition" is not decisive because, exceptionally, the **5-013** courts are prepared to "construe away" this word, taking the view that the parties did not intend this word to bear the technical meaning just mentioned (see *Schuler v Wickman*, on which para.10.39 ff). There is also a qualification in the Sale of Goods Act 1979 s.15A.

Faced by the other party's renunciation, serious breach or repudiation, the in- **5-014** nocent party has a choice (para.7-082 ff): he can accept the renunciation etc and thus terminate the contract and sue for damages, or he can affirm the contract and sue for damages.[12] This is known as the right of "election". (For (i) an exception, however, where the contract has become incapable of being sustained, and it has been terminated by breach, see the Court of Appeal in *MSC Mediterranean Shipping Co SA v Cottonex Anstalt* (para.7-098–7-100 ff);[13] and (ii) for the situation where an innocent party cannot continue because the other party's co-operation is required, see para.7-087 ff; and (iii) see para.7-091 ff for the situation where a party affirms the contract and completes performance, but his claim in debt is barred on the ground that the innocent party lacks a "legitimate interest" in presenting such a claim).

Termination or discharge for breach operates to end the contract from that point **5-015** in time, but only prospectively. The effect is that both parties' primary obligations cease to apply. But such termination does not annihilate the contract retrospectively (para.13-001 ff). The innocent party retains the right to sue in respect of preceding breaches. The term "rescission" (or the verb "rescind") is now confined to the quite distinct process of setting aside retrospectively a contract that is vitiated by reason of misrepresentation or duress or undue influence, and restoring the parties to the original position *as though the contract had never existed*.

Obligations (Oxford: Oxford University Press, 1999), 83–87; G.H. Jones (with P. Schlechtriem) "Breach of Contract" in *International Encyclopaedia of Comparative Law*, Vol.VII (Contracts in General), (Tübingen: Mohr Siebeck, 1999), 15–129 ff; M. Lobban, in W. Cornish, *The Oxford History of the Laws of England*, Vol.XII (1820–1914: Private Law) (Oxford: Oxford University Press, 2010), 485 ff.

[10] *Suisse Atlantique Societe d'Armement SA v NV Rotterdamsche Kolen Centrale* [1967] 1 A.C. 361 HL; *Photo Production Ltd v Securicor Transport Ltd* [1980] A.C. 827 HL; on the fundamental breach saga, H. Beale (ed), *Chitty on Contracts*, 34th edn (London: Sweet & Maxwell, 2021), paras 17-023–17-027; 27-023–27-025.

[11] e.g. *Future Publishing Ltd v Edge Interactive Media Inc* [2011] EWHC 1489 (Ch); [2011] E.T.M.R. 50 at [59], [60], [61], [62], [63], [66], [68] per Proudman J, where the epithet "fundamental" is used repeatedly as a synonym for "repudiatory".

[12] *Fermometal SARL v Mediterranean Shipping Co SA "The Simona"* [1989] A.C. 788 HL; *Vitol SA v Norelf Ltd, "The Santa Clara"* [1996] A.C. 800 HL.

[13] [2016] EWCA Civ 789; [2017] 1 All E.R. (Comm) 483, notably at [41]–[43] per Moore-Bick LJ, and at [61] per Tomlinson LJ.

5-016   The question of breach is technically distinct from the right to refuse performance if the other side has failed to complete performance of an obligation, where the parties' obligations are "dependent" (see Ch.15). As Carter explains, giving a concrete example:[14]

> "the law distinguishes one party's right to terminate (for breach of a contractual term) from the other party's inability to enforce a dependent obligation to perform. Thus, under a sale of goods contract requiring payment in exchange for the goods, the seller's obligation to deliver is dependent on the buyer's readiness to pay. If the buyer is not ready and willing to pay on the appointed day, the seller is not bound to deliver the goods. However, this does not mean that the seller is necessarily able to terminate the performance of the contract because of a breach by the buyer of the term providing for payment on the appointed day. Such a term is not presumed to be a condition even though the seller's obligation to perform will be, presumptively, a dependent obligation."

II.   "RENUNCIATION" AND "REPUDIATION" BY ACTUAL BREACH: QUESTIONS OF TERMINOLOGY

5-017   In *Heyman v Darwins Ltd*, Lord Wright said: "The word 'repudiation' has also led to difficulties because it is an ambiguous word constantly used without precise definition in contract law".[15] However, an attempt will be made here to use it more precisely, and to distinguish it from "renunciation" (this distinction between "repudiation" by actual breach and "renunciation" by declaring unwillingness to perform was emphasised by Popplewell J in the *Spar Shipping* case, passage cited at para.10-080).[16]

5-018   The source of this terminological confusion is that the expression "repudiation" (or "repudiatory breach") is sometimes used in a generic sense to embrace all types of breach which justify termination. In this wide sense, the word expresses the conclusion that termination is an option available to the innocent party. That right to terminate for breach arises in various situations, namely: (i) an anticipatory breach by renunciation, or renunciation at the time of expected performance; (ii) anticipatory breach by self-created impossibility; or (iii) substantial breach justifying termination (a repudiatory breach, or breach of a condition or serious breach of an intermediate term, or a serious pattern of default (para.10-060 on *Rice v Great Yarmouth BC*).[17] It is suggested that "renunciation" is a clearer way of expressing the forms of breach in (i) because this involves verbal notification of unwillingness or inability to perform. The term "repudiation" (and "repudiatory breach") might be usefully confined to categories (ii) and (iii), because both concern non-verbal and actual default.

III.   UNFULFILLED DEPENDENT OBLIGATIONS: THE RIGHT TO WITHHOLD PERFORMANCE

5-019   As we shall see (Ch.15), the doctrine of "entire obligations" is to be distinguished from the question of breach, although these concepts can often overlap. Thus, if

---

[14]   J.W. Carter, *Carter's Breach of Contract*, 2nd edn (Oxford: Hart Publishing, 2019) at [1-14].

[15]   [1942] A.C. 356 at 378 HL; cf. J.W. Carter, *Carter's Breach of Contract* (Oxford, Hart Publishing, 2012), [7.03] and [7.07], preferring not to use "renunciation" and instead using "repudiation".

[16]   [2015] EWHC 718 (Comm); [2015] 1 All E.R. (Comm) 879 at [209]; the decision was affirmed in all respects at [2016] EWCA Civ 982; [2016] 2 Lloyd's Rep. 447 (Gross, Hamblen LJJ, Sir Terence Etherton MR).

[17]   (2000), *The Times,* 26 July; (2001) 3 L.G.L.R. 4 CA at [38].

party B's obligation is dependent on party A's performance but, *for whatever reason*, A fails to perform (and fails to achieve "substantial performance" of that obligation: on that concept see Ch.15), B is entitled to withhold performance. Normally B's capacity to withhold performance will take the form of B's right *to withhold payment* until there is complete performance by A. Usually, A's non-performance will involve breach, but sometimes his non-performance will be excused on the basis of "frustration" (Pt III of this work), that is, the result of extreme supervening events beyond his control (for example, para.15-009 concerning *Cutter v Powell*). In the event of frustration, A (and A's estate) will be excused: there will be no breach. For example, A might die before fully performing personal services. If so, B can withhold performance, but s.1(3) of the Law Reform (Frustrated Contracts) Act 1943 might enable A's estate to gain a "just sum" in respect of A's incomplete performance.

IV.   STRICT OR NON-STRICT OBLIGATIONS[18]

Breach of contract can involve failure to satisfy a strict obligation (for example, a seller's statutory obligations to deliver goods (or contracts for "digital content") which (i) correspond to their contractual description, or (ii) goods which are of satisfactory quality, or (iii) which are reasonably fit for their intended purpose.[19] However, some implied contractual obligations require only the exercise of reasonable care, or the meeting of the relevant professional level of diligence[20] (or exercise of best or reasonable endeavours, etc).[21]   **5-020**

The House of Lords affirmed in *Henderson v Merrett Syndicates Ltd*[22] that when a contractual duty of care overlaps with an essentially similar duty of care imposed by the tort of negligence, a case of "concurrent" obligations, a claimant can select whichever cause of action he prefers, or indeed plead both. (There has also been discussion of the "contract/tort interface" in US literature).[23]   **5-021**

The Court of Appeal in *Platform Funding Ltd v Bank of Scotland Plc*[24] acknowledged that, in a contract for professional services (doctors, lawyers, surveyors, vets, etc), the professional will normally merely owe a duty to exercise due care, but there can be exceptional instances of strict liability: (i) in accordance   **5-022**

---

18   J.W. Carter, *Carter's Breach of Contract*, 2nd edn (Oxford: Hart Publishing, 2019), [2-62]–[2-64]; for academic discussion, mostly from an US perspective, of the strict nature of many contractual obligations, see various papers within Michigan Law Review (symposium on "fault in American Contract Law") (2009) 107 Mich. L. Rev. 1431–1600.

19   Sale of Goods Act 1979 ss.13–15; Consumer Rights Act 2015 ss.9–32 (goods); Consumer Rights Act 2015 ss.33–47 (digital content agreements).

20   Generally, the Supply of Goods and Services Act 1982 s.13; Consumer Rights Act 2015 ss.48–57.

21   See discussion in N. Andrews, *Contract Law*, 2nd edn (Cambridge: Cambridge University Press, 2015) at 2.11. of the case law concerning procuring of planning permission; and see also the *Jet2.com Ltd v Blackpool Airport Ltd* [2012] EWCA Civ 417; [2012] 2 All E.R. (Comm) 1053, noted in Andrews at 4.08; on the express duty to supply a wholesale customer with gas in a reasonable and prudent manner, *Scottish Power UK Plc v BP Exploration Operating Co Ltd* [2015] EWHC 2638 (Comm); [2016] 1 All E.R. (Comm) 536 at [53] ff, per Leggatt J; decision affirmed, [2016] EWCA Civ 1043.

22   [1995] 2 A.C. 145 HL; on the topic of concurrent liability, H. Beale (ed), *Chitty on Contracts*, 34th edn (London: Sweet & Maxwell, 2021), para.3-010–3-064.

23   R. Kreitner, "Fault at the Contract/Tort Interface" (2009) 107 Mich. L. Rev. 1533.

24   [2008] EWCA Civ 930; [2009] Q.B. 426; J.W. Carter, *Carter's Breach of Contract*, 2nd edn (Oxford: Hart Publishing, 2019), paras 2.33–2.67.

with the specific terms of the agreement or on assurances given by the professional in the course of his performance, or (ii) based on the relevant context.[25]

5-023   The majority in the *Platform Funding* case (Moore-Bick and Rix LJJ) held that
a valuer's failure to inspect the relevant property was a breach of an implied strict
obligation to view the relevant property. His certificate, stating that he had inspected
the named property, constituted an express warranty (negligence had not been
pleaded).[26] But the dissenting judge, Sir Anthony Clarke MR (as he then was), said
there was no indication in this context that the certificate should trigger strict
liability.

5-024   Strict liability was imposed for bug bites suffered by a visitor to a Turkish baths
in *Silverman v Imperial London Hotels Ltd.* [27]

5-025   It is a matter of construction whether the contract contains language which is
inconsistent with the conclusion that an obligation (express or implied) is strict. It
is possible that instead of cutting back or diluting a presumptively strict obligation, and thus rendering it less than strict, instead the relevant qualification might
add a head of obligation and that the remainder of the contract will continue to
impose strict obligation. Thus, in *Scottish Power UK Plc v BP Exploration Operating Co Ltd*[28] Leggatt J held that the phrase "a [party] seeking in good faith to
perform its contractual obligations" imposed a two-fold obligation (i) that this party
should perform its obligations, and (ii) in so doing there was a super-added obligation to do so in good faith, that is, in a genuine manner. Leggatt J held that a gas
supplier's decision to close down a gas field and so stop (for a number of years) the
supply of gas to that customer was a breach of (i) and that it would be wrong to treat
element (ii) as eviscerating or diluting that basic obligation to maintain supply to
that customer.

5-026   Conversely, the Court of Appeal found no binding oral guarantee in the "unsuccessful vasectomy" case, *Thake v Maurice.*[29] And in *Easton v Hitchcock* a private
detective service was not liable for breach of confidentiality committed by *a former
employee*, even though the latter's revelation had wholly undermined the value of
detective work, and even though this defendant's advertising contained a promise
of complete "secrecy".[30]

5-027   *Evans v Kosmar Villa Operators* is an illustration of a contractual duty of care.[31]
The case concerned a tour operator's duty to take reasonable steps to guard its
customers and guests against personal injury, a duty arising both at Common Law
and under statute.[32] The Court of Appeal held that this duty did not require the
operator to protect a 17-year-old against the danger of injury caused by diving into
the shallow end of a swimming pool. The claimant was aware of the danger and the
defendant had taken adequate precautions.

5-028   Atkinson J in *Aerial Advertising Co v Batchelors Peas Ltd (Manchester)* held that

---

[25]   [2008] EWCA Civ 930; [2009] Q.B. 426 at [48] per Rix LJ.
[26]   [2008] EWCA Civ 930; [2009] Q.B. 426 at [63] (and see [53] per Rix LJ).
[27]   137 L.T. 57; [1927] All E.R. 712 at 714.
[28]   [2015] EWHC 2638 (Comm); [2016] 1 All E.R. (Comm) 536 at [55], [68], [79]–[81], [120], Leg-
        gatt J; decision affirmed, [2016] EWCA Civ 1043.
[29]   [1986] Q.B. 644 CA; on that case, N. Andrews, *Contract Law*, 2nd edn (Cambridge: Cambridge
        University Press, 2015), p.82.
[30]   [1912] 1 K.B. 535 (Divisional Ct).
[31]   [2007] EWCA Civ 1003; [2008] 1 W.L.R. 297.
[32]   Package Travel, Package Holidays and Package Tours Regulations 1992 (SI 1992/3288) reg.15.

performance of an aerial advertising campaign on behalf of a dried peas company[33] imported an implied term to use reasonable skill and care not to harm the company's interests, and certainly not to fly advertising planes on occasions which will bring its customer into hatred and contempt within the community at large. In breach of that term, the advertiser flew over an English town during the Armistice service just before 11.00 am on 11 November. This provoked public outrage. As a result, the advertising was a commercial disaster.

As the Court of Appeal noted in *Urban 1 (Blonk Street) Ltd v Ayres*, obligations to perform within a reasonable time, whether based on an express or implied term, are subject to a wide range of imponderable factors.[34]

    5-029

V. DELIBERATE BREACH

Lord Wilberforce in the *Suisse Atlantique* case made clear that deliberate breach of contract is not a special category of breach to be characterised as "fundamental breach"[35] (in any event, as noted at para.10-007, "there is no [separate] category of 'fundamental term'").

    5-030

However, (i) the fact that a breach is deliberate might be relevant in determining whether the guilty party has evinced an intention no longer to be bound by the contract ("a deliberate breach may give rise to a right for the innocent party to refuse further performance because it indicates the other party's attitude towards further performance"),[36] and (ii) an exclusion clause might not be construed to extend this far ("depending on what the party in breach 'deliberately' intended to do, it may be possible to say that the parties never contemplated that such a breach would be excused or limited").[37]

    5-031

As for proposition (ii), Gabriel Moss QC in *Internet Broadcasting Corp Ltd v MAR LLC*[38] held that there is a presumption that an exclusion clause, although literally wide enough to cover this, will not be construed to protect a person (including a company controlled by an identifiable person) from liability for loss of profit flowing from a personal and deliberate repudiation of the relevant contractual undertaking.

    5-032

As for the capacity to exclude or restrict liability even in respect of a deliberate

    5-033

---

33 [1938] 2 All E.R. 788 at 792.
34 [2013] EWCA Civ 816; [2014] 1 W.L.R. 756 at [49] per Sir Terence Etherton C (noting *Hick v Raymond & Reid* [1893] A.C. 22 at 32–33 HL per Lord Watson—there is no breach, notwithstanding protracted delay, so long as the delay is attributable to causes beyond a party's control and he has neither acted negligently nor unreasonably; and the fuller discussion by Maurice Kay LJ in *Peregrine Systems Ltd v Steria Ltd* [2005] EWCA Civ 239; [2005] Info T.L.R. 294 at [15], noting HH Judge Richard Seymour QC in *Astea (UK) Ltd v Time Group Ltd* [2003] EWHC 725 (TCC) at [144]).
35 *Suisse Atlantique Société d'Armement Maritime SA v NV Rotterdamsche* [1967] 1 A.C. 361 at 435 HL (also on "deliberateness", see 394E per Viscount Dilhorne; at 397–398, per Lord Reid; at 414, per Lord Hodson; at 429, per Lord Upjohn); R. Brownsword, in C. Mitchell and P. Mitchell (eds), *Landmark Cases in the Law of Contract* (Oxford: Hart Publishing, 2008), 299 ff; the statement by Lord Wilberforce in *Suisse Atlantique* was quoted in *Future Publishing Ltd v Edge Interactive Media Inc* [2011] EWHC 1489 (Ch); [2011] E.T.M.R. 50 at [62] per Proudman J.
36 *Suisse Atlantique Société d'Armement Maritime SA v NV Rotterdamsche* [1967] 1 A.C. 361 at 435 HL.
37 *Scottish Power UK Plc v BP Exploration Operating Co Ltd* [2015] EWHC 2638 (Comm); [2016] 1 All E.R. (Comm) 536 at [170], Leggatt J noted that it is a question of construction whether an exclusion clause applies to a case of deliberate breach; decision affirmed [2016] EWCA Civ 1043.
38 [2009] EWHC 844 (Ch); [2010] 1 All E.R. (Comm) 112 (see especially the distillation of principles at [33]).

breach, Leggatt J observed in *Scottish Power UK Plc v BP Exploration Operating Co Ltd*:[39]

"There is no rule of law that prevents the exclusion of liability arising from a deliberate act by a contracting party. It is always a matter of construction of the clause in question, and whether or to what extent the deliberateness of a breach is a relevant factor depends on the circumstances: see *Suisse Atlantique Société d'Armement Maritime v NV Rotterdamsche Kolen Centrale* [1967] 1 A.C. 361 at 435 (Lord Wilberforce); *Astrazeneca UK Ltd v Albemarle International Corp* [2011] EWHC 1574 (Comm), [288]–[301]."

5-034   Leggatt J in the *Scottish Power case* then addressed the question of damages arising from a deliberate breach:[40]

"The fact that a breach of contract is deliberate or that the party in breach makes a profit from it does not, save in very exceptional circumstances, affect the remedy available at common law. It is a basic principle that the object of an award of damages for breach of contract is to compensate the claimant for loss sustained as a result of the defendant's breach and not to deprive the defendant of any gain. Moreover, this principle applies and the measure of damages is the same irrespective of whether the breach was deliberate, careless or entirely innocent."

5-035   Furthermore, it is clear that a deliberate breach does not give rise to liability for exemplary damages in English contract law: indeed exemplary damages are not available at all for breach of contract.[41] (This topic has stimulated extensive discussion in the US).[42]

---

[39] [2015] EWHC 2638 (Comm); [2016] 1 All E.R. (Comm) 536 at [170] per Leggatt J; decision affirmed, [2016] EWCA Civ 1043.

[40] [2015] EWHC 2638 (Comm); [2016] 1 All E.R. (Comm) 536 at [170] per Leggatt J; decision affirmed, [2016] EWCA Civ 1043.

[41] *Addis v Gramophone Co Ltd* [1909] A.C. 488 HL; J. Edelman (ed.), *McGregor on Damages*, 21st edn (London: Sweet & Maxwell, 2021), 13-016; otherwise in Canada, *Royal Bank of Canada v Got* (2000) 17 D.L.R. (4th) 385 (Supreme Court of Canada); J. Edelman, "Exemplary Damages for Breach of Contract" (2001) 117 L.Q.R. 539; *Whiten v Pilot Insurance Co* [2002] SCC 18; [2002] 1 SCR 595 (Supreme Court of Canada); as for punitive damages in English tort law, *Kuddus v Chief Constable of Leicestershire* [2002] 2 A.C. 122 HL, and *A v Bottrill* [2003] 1 A.C. 449 PC; and for the position in deceit (exemplary damages available, at least in some instances of deceit; but not awarded in this case where the defendant was vicariously liable for another's deceit), *Parabola Investments Ltd v Browallia Cal Ltd* [2009] EWHC 901 (Comm) at [205] ff, per Flaux J (point not considered on appeal: [2010] EWCA Civ 486); as for the English courts' unwillingness to award punitive damages for breach of contract, S. Rowan, "Reflections on the Introduction of Punitive Damages for Breach of Contract" (2010) 30 O.J.L.S. 495–517 carefully examines this topic, and cites extensive literature at 496, fnn.3 and 4 (in alphabetical sequence): A.S. Burrows, *Remedies for Torts and Breach of Contract*, 4th edn (Oxford: Oxford University Press, 2019), pp.360–1; R. Cunnington, "Should Punitive Damages be Part of the Judicial Arsenal in Contract Cases?" (2006) 26 L.S. 369; J. Edelman, "Exemplary Damages for Breach of Contract" (2001) 117 L.Q.R. 539–45; Law Commission, *"Aggravated, Exemplary and Restitutionary Damages"* (L. Com. No.247, 1997); N. McBride, "'A Case for Awarding Punitive Damages in Response to Deliberate. Breaches of Contract" (1995) 24 Anglo-American L. Rev. 369–90; N. McBride, in P. Birks (ed), *Wrongs and Remedies in the Twenty-first Century* (Oxford: Oxford University Press, 1996), pp.175–202; E. McKendrick, in A. Burrows and E. Peel (eds), *Commercial Remedies: Current Issues and Problems* (Oxford: Oxford University Press, 2003), pp.93–107; S. Rowan, "Reflections on the Introduction of Punitive Damages for Breach of Contract" (2010) 30 O.J.L.S. 495–517; A. Tettenborn, "Punitive Damages – A View from England" (2004) 41 San Diego L. Rev. 1551–74 (see also Tettenborn's electronic publication, cited in S. Rowan (2010) 30 O.J.L.S. 495, 496, fn.4).

[42] O. Bar-Gill and O. Ben-Shahar, "An Information Theory of Willful Breach" (2009) 107 Mich. L. Rev. 1479; R. Cresswell, 1501.

In *Acre 1127 Ltd (formerly Castle Galleries) v De Montfort Fine Art Ltd*[43] **5-036**
Tomlinson LJ acknowledged that deliberate misconduct, or dishonesty, does not
ordinarily constitute a special form of breach or by itself render breach necessarily repudiatory. But he did note that in some contexts the position would be
otherwise:

> "the fact that a breach of contract is accompanied by dishonesty will not of itself convert
> that which is not repudiatory into repudiatory conduct, just as the fact that a breach of
> contract is deliberate will not of itself be relevant to the evaluation whether it is repudia-
> tory ... I would however accept that dishonesty may in this context be material, as Judge
> McGonigal held that it was in *Northern Foods Plc v Focal Foods Ltd* [2003] 2 Lloyd's
> Rep. 728 at 747. Ordinarily however dishonesty will be material only if it is of itself
> destructive of a necessary relationship of trust or if it is of itself indicative of an inten-
> tion no longer to be bound by the contract."

In the *Acre* case itself, De Montfort had faked an order from Castle, the other **5-037**
party to the contract. Although this was an inauspicious start to their relationship
(under which Castle was obliged to make quarterly orders for the supply of art by
De Montfort), the Court of Appeal held that it was not itself repudiatory:[44]

> "Performance of the contract ... did call for an element of trust between the parties but
> given the contemporary belief of the relevant parties as to the status of the first order
> [namely, the assumption that it was the product of dishonesty] it is in my view impos-
> sible to suggest that this foolish and dishonest conduct either destroyed that necessary ele-
> ment or indicated an intention on the part of De Montfort not to be bound by the terms
> of the contract."

VI. NOMINAL OR SUBSTANTIAL DAMAGES

Breach of contract always entitles the innocent party to nominal damages.[45] Such **5-038**
damages are a token sum intended to denote the unlawful nature of the defendant's
act or omission. The innocent party will only be entitled to "substantial damages"
if he can prove that he has suffered loss as a result of the breach (see, for example,
the *Multi Veste* case, on which see para.5-009).

VII. BREACHES WHICH JUSTIFY TERMINATION

Lord Porter said in *Heyman v Darwins Ltd*:[46] **5-039**

> "The three sets of circumstances giving rise to a discharge contract [for breach] are
> tabulated by Anson's Law of Contract [in the 1937 edn][47] as: (a) renunciation by a party
> of his liabilities ... (b) impossibility created by his own act; (c) total or partial failure of
> performance." (This classification was also adopted by Devlin J in *Universal Cargo Car-
> riers Corp v Citati* (1957)."[48]

As mentioned at para.5-011 above, the full list of Common Law grounds for

---

43 [2011] EWCA Civ 87 at [41] per Tomlinson LJ.
44 [2011] EWCA Civ 87 at [41] per Tomlinson LJ.
45 Putting aside failure to pay money, for which the action is one for debt, para.19-001.
46 [1942] A.C. 356 at 397 HL.
47 This passage is preserved in J. Beatson, A. Burrows and J. Cartwright, *Anson's Law of Contract*, 31st
edn (Oxford: Oxford University Press, 2020), p.510, fn.47.
48 [1957] 2 Q.B. 401 at 436–438 (appellate decisions at [1957] 1 W.L.R. 979 CA and [1958] 2 Q.B.
254 CA—does/do not disturb the judge's exposition of governing principles of breach); M. Mustill,

terminating a contract for breach comprises these:

(i)   the other party has shown (normally verbally, or by conduct) a clear unwillingness to satisfy his contract ("renunciation", express or implied); or

(ii)   performance has been rendered impossible by the default of the guilty party; or

(iii)   there has been a breach of an important term (a "condition"); or

(iv)   there has been breach of another term which can give rise to termination, depending on the seriousness of the breach (an "innominate term"); or

(v)   there has been a breach or set of breaches constituting repudiatory breach which goes to the root of the expected performance.

Furthermore, the contract might contain a termination for breach clause, specifying that the innocent party is entitled in certain circumstances to treat the contract as terminated for breach (on such clauses Ch.9).

5-040   In Singapore in *RDC Concrete Pte Ltd v Sato Kogyo (S) Pte Ltd* Phang JA analysed the right to terminate a contract for breach.[49] Although not every proposition in that long exegesis should be relied upon as necessarily a parallel statement of the English approach, the learned judge's inquiry is illuminating.

VIII.   "TERMINATION OR DISCHARGE FOR BREACH" AND "RESCISSION" (AB INITIO) FOR VITIATION

5-041   Termination or discharge for breach is to be distinguished from rescission for misrepresentation or for another "vitiating" factor, such as duress, undue influence, unconscionability, non-disclosure: Pt I para.2-001. Termination for breach brings to an end the parties' "primary" obligations. However, such termination does not nullify the whole contract (para.13-001). The guilty party's liability to pay compensation also remains. Exclusion and liquidated damages clauses, and arbitration or jurisdiction clauses also survive termination for breach. The nature of termination for breach is examined in detail in Ch.13.

"Anticipatory Breach: The Common Law at Work", Butterworths Lectures 1989–90 (London: Butterworths, 1990), p.69 ff (see also M. Mustill, "The Golden Victory—Some Reflections" (2008) 124 L.Q.R. 569–585).

[49] [2007] SGCA 39; [2007] 4 S.L.R. 413 at [90]–[114]; as for Phang JA's observations concerning "warranties", see the substantial quotation from this case at para.10-006 fnn.10 and 11.

CHAPTER 6

RENUNCIATION BY WORDS OR CONDUCT

I. RENUNCIATION: THE GENERAL CONCEPT

Renunciation—whether by (i) words, or (ii) implication from conduct—is the **6-001** communication of an intention that the renouncing party no longer wishes to be bound at all by the contract, or at least that he wishes to break free, in a material way, from the fetters of the contract. The other party must be notified, or at least receive clear evidence, of that renunciation.

As for (ii) (renunciation inferred from conduct, see preceding paragraph) the **6-002** circumstances might indicate that a party is intimating that he is walking away from the contract or intending to perform it on his own (deviating) terms. As Bowen LJ said in *Mersey Steel & Iron Co Ltd v Naylor Benzon & Co*:[1] "the test [is] whether the conduct of one party to the contract was really inconsistent with an intention to be bound any longer by the contract." Similarly, in *Federal Commerce & Navigation Co Ltd v Molena Alpha Inc ("The Nanfri")* (1979)[2] Lord Wilberforce cited Lord Cockburn CJ in *Freeth v Burr*: "an intimation of an intention to abandon and altogether to refuse performance of the contract" or "to evince an intention no longer to be bound by the contract"[3] Lord Coleridge's statement was cited by Earl of Selborne LC in the House of Lords in *Mersey Steel & Iron Co Ltd v Naylor Benzon & Co* (1884), the latter saying:[4]

"I am content to take the rule as stated by Lord Coleridge CJ in *Freeth v Burr* (1874) ... that you must look at the actual circumstances of the case in order to see whether the one party to the contract is relieved from its future performance by the conduct of the other; you must examine what that conduct is, so as to see whether it amounts to a renunciation, to an absolute refusal to perform the contract ... and whether the other party may accept it as a reason for not performing his part."

More generally on the two species of renunciation, the Court of Appeal in **6-003**

---

[1] *Mersey Steel & Iron Co Ltd v Naylor Benzon & Co* (1882) 9 Q.B.D. 648 at 670 CA. (Not disturbed on appeal: *Mersey Steel & Iron Co Ltd v Naylor Benzon & Co* (1884) 9 App. Cas. 434 HL.)
[2] [1979] A.C. 757 at 778–779 HL.
[3] (1873–74) L.R. 9 C.P. 208 at 213 per Lord Coleridge CJ (Court of Common Pleas); cited by the Earl of Selborne LC in *Mersey Steel & Iron Co Ltd v Naylor Benzon & Co* (1884) 9 App. Cas. 434 at 438–439 HL; Lord Salmon collected various formulations of the test in *Woodar Investment Development Ltd v Wimpey Construction UK Ltd* [1980] 1 W.L.R. 277 at 287–288 HL.
[4] (1884) 9 App. Cas. 434 at 438–439 HL.

Ampurius Nu Homes Holdings Ltd v Telford Homes (Creekside) Ltd adopted these textbook formulations (cited in the next two paragraphs).[5]

6-004   An explicit renunciation is defined as follows:[6]

"A renunciation of a contract occurs when one party by words or conduct evinces an intention not to perform, or expressly declares that he is or will be unable to perform, his obligations under the contract in some essential respect. The renunciation may occur before or at the time fixed for performance. An absolute refusal [will count] ... as will also a clear and unambiguous assertion by one party that he will be unable to perform when the time for performance should arrive."

6-005   An implicit renunciation is defined thus:[7]

"[This arises where] actions of the party in default are such as to lead a reasonable person to conclude that he no longer intends to be bound by its provisions. The renunciation is then evidenced by conduct. Also the party in default: '... may intend in fact to fulfil (the contract) but may be determined to do so only in a manner substantially inconsistent with his obligations'[8] ... If one party evinces an intention not to perform or declares his inability to perform some, but not all, of his obligations under the contract, then the right of the other party to treat himself as discharged depends on whether the non-performance of those obligations will amount to a breach of a condition of the contract or deprive him of substantially the whole benefit which it was the intention of the parties that he should obtain from the obligations of the parties under the contract then remaining unperformed."

6-006   In *Ross T Smyth & Co Ltd v TD Bailey, Son & Co* Lord Wright graphically referred to the need for words or conduct to communicate, in the relevant context, a "categorical refusal" to carry out the contract, or a "categorical refusal" to perform on radically new terms:[9]

"There was no categorical refusal on the part of the appellants, by words or by conduct, to perform the contract, or a categorical declaration that they would perform it only in the terms of the amended invoice."

6-007   On closer analysis, renunciation comprises three elements: (a) the express or implicit "message", (b) the content of the message, and (c) receipt. As for (a), the "message" can be (i) verbal—an expression of an intention or decision; (ii) or an inference drawn from the conduct or inaction. As for (b), the express or implied content of the "message" can be either (i) "I'm not going on", or (ii) "I'm only going on at my own pace or on my own terms, despite the fact that the contract provides otherwise". As for (c), the other party should discover the "message" and its contents. What counts is not merely that one party's intention can be inferred from his behaviour but that this inference has been furthermore registered, received, or absorbed by the other party. In *Woodar Investment Development Ltd v Wimpey Construction UK Ltd* (1980) Lord Scarman emphasised this need for a "message"

---

[5]   [2013] EWCA Civ 577; [2013] 4 All E.R. 377 at [70], citing (as the present edition now is) H. Beale (ed), *Chitty on Contracts*, 34th edn (London: Sweet & Maxwell, 2021), para.27-048.

[6]   [2013] EWCA Civ 577; [2013] 4 All E.R. 377 at [70], citing (as the present edition now is) H. Beale, *Chitty on Contracts*, 34th edn (London: Sweet & Maxwell, 2021), para. 27-048.

[7]   [2013] EWCA Civ 577; [2013] 4 All E.R. 377 at [70], citing (as the present edition now is) H. Beale (ed), *Chitty on Contracts*, 34th edn (London: Sweet & Maxwell, 2021), para.27-048.

[8]   This internal quotation is from *Ross T Smyth & Co Ltd v TD Bailey Son & Co* [1940] 3 All E.R. 60 at 72 HL per Lord Wright.

[9]   [1940] 3 All E.R. 60 at 71 HL.

to be "received":[10]

"The emphasis upon communication of the party's intention by his acts and conduct is a recurring theme in the abundant case law. Two well-known cases illustrative of the emphasis are *Mersey Steel & Iron Co Ltd v Naylor Benzon & Co*[11] and *Bradley v H Newsom, Sons and Co* (see in particular the speech of Lord Wrenbury)."[12]

A variation on this is the question whether a discussion or statement of inten-   **6-008**
tion by party B to a third party, which would be inconsistent with B's contract with A, might constitute a renunciation if the interchange between B and the third party is notified to party A (for example, B deciding to "copy in" A to this correspondence or discussion). This point was briefly considered by Lewison LJ in *Ampurius Nu Homes Holdings Ltd v Telford Homes (Creekside) Ltd* where he said:[13]

"the mere fact of a communication between [party B] and a third party but not acted upon (even though disclosed to [party A]) is too slender a foundation for a conclusion that [party B had] renounced the contract."

(The analogy of the discussion in the offer and acceptance cases might be considered;[14] furthermore, Lord Steyn in *"The Santa Clara"*[15] stated that an innocent party's termination for breach can be effectively communicated by an "unauthorised" party: but analogies are dangerous and these possible connections require further argument in future cases.)

The facts supporting the plea that there has been implicit renunciation can involve   **6-009**
actual repudiation (that is breach involving non-verbal serious default). And so there can be overlapping analysis, as *Yam Seng Pte Ltd v International Trade Corp Ltd* illustrates.[16] Similarly, cases[17] where there has been late payment under contracts requiring successive payments raise the same potential overlap: whether the facts support the inference that there has been a renunciation and/or a manifested repudiation. That determination will hinge on whether: (i) the payor has evinced an intention no longer to be bound by the contract; conversely, it might be evident that, despite late payment, the payor wishes the contract to continue (*Freeth* case[18] and *Mersey Steel* case[19]); (ii) the payor has made an unilateral attempt at radically re-

---

[10]   [1980] 1 W.L.R. 277 at 298 HL.
[11]   (1884) 9 App. Cas. 434 HL.
[12]   [1919] A.C. 16 at 57 HL.
[13]   [2013] EWCA Civ 577; [2013] 4 All E.R. 377 at [72].
[14]   N. Andrews, *Contract Law in Practice* (Oxford: Oxford University Press, 2021), paras 3.102–3.110 on indirect revocation, *Dickinson v Dodds* (1876) 2 Ch. D. 463 CA; N. Andrews, *Contract Rules: Decoding English Law* (Cambridge: Intersentia, 2016) at art.21; see also arts 20 and 22.
[15]   *Vitol SA v Norelf Ltd (The Santa Clara)* [1996] A.C. 800 at 811 HL, citing *Wood Factory Pty Ltd v Kiritos Pty Ltd* (1985) 2 N.S.W.L.R. 105 at 146 per McHugh JA; *Majik Markets Pty Ltd v S & M Motor Repairs Pty Ltd (No.1)* (1987) 10 N.S.W.L.R. 49 at 54 per Young J.
[16]   [2013] EWHC 111 (QB); [2013] 1 All E.R. (Comm) 1321 at [114] and [115].
[17]   *Withers v Reynolds* (1831) 2 B. & Ad. 882; 109 E.R. 1370; *Dymocks Franchise Systems (NSW) Pty Ltd v Todd* [2002] UKPC 50; [2002] 2 All E.R. (Comm) 849 at [870] per Lord Browne-Wilkinson; *Freeth v Burr* (1873–74) L.R. 9 C.P. 208 (Court of Common Pleas); *Mersey Steel & Iron Co Ltd v Naylor Benzon & Co* (1884) 9 App. Cas. 434 HL; *Decro-Wall International SA v Practitioners in Marketing* [1971] 1 W.L.R. 361 at 379–380 CA; *Shyam Jewellers Ltd v Cheeseman* [2001] EWCA Civ 1818; official transcript on Westlaw; *Valilas v Januzaj* [2014] EWCA Civ 436; [2015] 1 All E.R. (Comm) 1047 (Arden and Floyd LJJ, Underhill LJ dissenting).
[18]   *Freeth v Burr* (1873–74) L.R. 9 C.P. 208 (Court of Common Pleas).
[19]   *Mersey Steel & Iron Co Ltd v Naylor Benzon & Co* (1884) 9 App. Cas. 434 HL.

casting the payment obligation (*Withers* case[20]); (iii) late payment has been used as an instrument to try to procure a wider renegotiation (*Dymocks* case[21]); and compare the borderline *Valilas* case[22]); or (iv) the payee was entitled to infer that the payor would be unable to pay (not found in the *Decro-Wall* case[23] or the *Shyam Jewellers* case[24]).

6-010   Flaux J in *"The Pro Victor"*[25] noted Donaldson LJ's remarks on the nature of renunciation in *Chilean Nitrate Sales Corp v Marine Transportation Co Ltd (The Hermosa):*[26]

"(a)   ... renunciation is a drastic conclusion which should only be held to arise in clear cases of a refusal to perform contractual obligations...going to the root of the contract.

(b)   The refusal must not only be clear, but must be absolute ... [T]he declaration gives rise to a right of dissolution only if ... it is clear that it is not conditional upon his present appreciation of his obligations proving correct when the time for performance arrives.

(c)   What does or does not amount to a sufficient refusal is to be judged in the light of whether a reasonable person in the position of the party claiming to be freed from the contract would regard the refusal as being clear and absolute.

(d)   ... the conduct relied upon is to be considered as at the time of when it is treated as terminating the contract, in the light of the then existing circumstances ..."

6-011   Element (c), just cited, was endorsed by Etherton LJ in *Eminence Property Developments Ltd v Heaney.*[27]

6-012   In *"The Pro Victor"* Flaux J suggested, in dicta, that if party Y knows that X did not intend a renunciation, the objective approach will not be applied.[28] Liu has criticised this suggestion.[29] However, it is submitted that Flaux J's suggestion is attractive: Y should not be able to snap up a literal renunciation if Y realises that X had no such intention.

II.   PARTY'S DECLARATION THAT WILL NOT PERFORM

6-013   **Total abandonment test: no intention to be bound by contract**   When will contractual default be serious enough to provide the basis for inferring that a party

---

20   *Withers v Reynolds* (1831) 2 B. & Ad. 882; 109 E.R. 1370.

21   *Dymocks Franchise Systems (NSW) Pty Ltd v Todd* [2002] UKPC 50; [2002] 2 All E.R. (Comm) 849 at [870] per Lord Browne-Wilkinson; *Freeth v Burr* (1873–74) L.R. 9 C.P. 208 (Court of Common Pleas).

22   *Valilas v Januzaj* [2014] EWCA Civ 436; [2015] 1 All E.R. (Comm) 1047 (Arden and Floyd LJJ, Underhill LJ dissenting).

23   *Decro-Wall International SA v Practitioners in Marketing* [1971] 1 W.L.R. 361 at 379–380 CA.

24   *Shyam Jewellers Ltd v Cheeseman* [2001] EWCA Civ 1818; official transcript on Westlaw.

25   *SK Shipping (S) PTE Ltd v Petroexport Ltd* [2009] EWHC 2974 (Comm); [2010] 2 Lloyd's Rep. 158 at [85] per Flaux J.

26   *Chilean Nitrate Sales Corp v Marine Transportation Co Ltd (The Hermosa)* [1982] 1 Lloyd's Rep. 570 at 572–573 CA per Donaldson LJ (noting that (a) to (c) can be "gleaned" from *Woodar Investment Development Ltd v Wimpey Construction UK Ltd* [1980] 1 W.L.R. 277 HL; but proposition (d) was enunciated afresh in *The Hermosa*.

27   [2010] EWCA Civ 1168; [2011] 2 All E.R. (Comm) 223 at [61]–[64].

28   *SK Shipping (S) PTE Ltd v Petroexport Ltd* [2009] EWHC 2974 (Comm); [2010] 2 Lloyd's Rep. 158 at [89]–[98] (Flaux J).

29   Q. Liu, *Anticipatory Breach* (Oxford: Hart Publishing, 2011), p.76.

has implicitly renounced the contract? In *Freeth v Burr* Lord Coleridge CJ (in the Court of Common Pleas) formulated the following test:[30]

> "whether the acts or conduct of the [the allegedly renouncing party] do or do not amount to an intimation of an intention to abandon and altogether to refuse performance of the contract."

And he added: "the true question is whether the acts and conduct of the party evince an intention no longer to be bound by the contract".

Lord Coleridge CJ's statement in *Freeth v Burr*, just cited, has been approved in **6-014** numerous cases, notably the following: (i) by the House of Lords (Earl of Selborne LC and Lord Blackburn) in *Mersey Steel & Iron Co Ltd v Naylor Benzon & Co*[31] (and by a strong Court of Appeal, Jessel MR, Lindley, and Bowen LJJ,[32] also in the *Mersey Steel case*); (ii) by Lord Wilberforce in the House of Lords in *Federal Commerce & Navigation Co Ltd v Molena Alpha Inc ("The Nanfri")*;[33] and (iii) by Lords Salmon, Keith, and Scarman in the House of Lords in *Woodar Investment Development Ltd v Wimpey Construction UK Ltd*.[34]

Lord Salmon (in his dissenting speech) in *Woodar Investment Development Ltd* **6-015** *v Wimpey Construction UK Ltd* helpfully collected various judicial definitions of when a party's words or conduct will constitute a renunciation entitling the other to terminate the contract[35] (it is irrelevant that Lord Salmon dissented in this case in the application of these tests to the facts).[36] The next four paragraphs are quotations, therefore, from Lord Salmon's speech in the *Woodar* case.

> [Case 1 quoted from Lord Salmon in the *Woodar* case] "In *Freeth v Burr* (1874) L.R. 9 C.P. 208, 213 Lord Coleridge CJ said: '... where the question is whether the one party is set free by the action of the other, the real matter for consideration is whether the acts or conduct of the one do or do not amount to an intimation of an intention to abandon and altogether to refuse performance of the contract.'"
>
> [Case 2 quoted from Lord Salmon in the *Woodar* case] "In *Mersey Steel & Iron Co Ltd v Naylor Benzon & Co* (1884) 9 App. Cas. 434 Lord Selborne LC, said at 439: '... you must examine what that conduct is, so as to see whether it amounts to a renunciation, to an absolute refusal to perform the contract, such as would amount to a rescission if he had

---

30 (1873–74) L.R. 9 C.P. 208 at 213 per Lord Coleridge CJ (Court of Common Pleas).

31 (1884) 9 App. Cas. 434 HL at 442–444.

32 *Mersey Steel & Iron Co Ltd v Naylor Benzon & Co* (1882) 9 Q.B.D. 648 CA at 657, 665–6, 670, respectively; Jessel MR at 657 is especially luminous: "There is no absolute rule which can be laid down in express terms as to whether a breach of contract on the one side has exonerated the other from performance of his part of the contract. But I think the rule of law is properly stated in *Freeth v Burr* (1874) L.R. 9 C.P. 208 at 213 per Lord Coleridge CJ: 'I say this in order to explain the ground upon which I think the decisions in these cases must rest. There has been some conflict amongst them; but I think it may be taken that the fair result of them is as I have stated, namely, that the true question is whether the acts and conduct of the party evince an intention no longer to be bound by the contract.' That makes it a question of evidence; you must consider the nature of the breach, the circumstances under which the breach occurred, and then see whether that is the result of it. There may, indeed, be a case where one party says in so many words that he does not intend to go on with the contract, but generally you must infer the intention from the acts of the parties."

33 [1979] A.C. 757 HL at 778.

34 [1980] 1 W.L.R. 277 HL at 287, 294, 298, respectively.

35 [1980] 1 W.L.R. 277 HL at 287–288.

36 In New Zealand, renunciation (under the label "repudiation") is defined in Contractual Remedies Act 1979 (NZ) s.7(2) as follows: "a party to a contract may cancel it if, by words or conduct, another party repudiates the contract by making it clear that he does not intend to perform his obligations under it or, as the case may be, to complete such performance."

the power to rescind, and whether the other party may accept it as a reason for not performing his part'";

[Case 3 quoted from Lord Salmon in the *Woodar* case] "In *Spettabile Consorzio Veneziano di Armamento e Navigazione v Northumberland Shipbuilding Co Ltd* (1919) 121 LT 628 CA at 634–5, Atkin LJ said: 'A repudiation has been defined in different terms—by Lord Selborne as an absolute refusal to perform a contract; by Lord Esher as a total refusal to perform it; by Bowen LJ in *Johnston v Milling* (1886) 16 QBD 460 as a declaration of an intention not to carry out a contract when the time arrives, and by Lord Haldane in *Bradley v H Newsom Sons & Co* [1919] A.C. 16 as an intention to treat the obligation as altogether at an end. They all come to the same thing, and they all amount at any rate to this, that it must be shown that the party to the contract made quite plain his own intention not to perform the contract.'"

[Case 4 quoted from Lord Salmon in the *Woodar* case] "In *Heyman v Darwins Ltd* [1942] A.C. 356 at 378–379, Lord Wright said: 'the commonest application of the word repudiation is to what is often called the anticipatory breach of a contract where the party by words or conduct evinces an intention no longer to be bound and the other party accepts the repudiation and [terminates] the contract. In such a case, if the repudiation is wrongful and the [termination] is rightful, the contract is ended...but only as far as concerns future performance. It remains alive for the awarding of damages ... for the breach which constitutes the repudiation.'"

6-016   Clear statement that a party is calling off the contract: purportedly with justification: but in fact lacking justification: renunciation found The Privy Council in *Clausen v Canada Timber and Lands Ltd*[37] held that a party's renunciation of the contract, even though based on his mistaken interpretation of its terms, could be validly relied on by the other party as the basis for terminating the contract. This decision seems only to have gained currency in Canada, because it was not reported outside the Canadian system. The decision in *Clausen v Canada Timber and Lands Ltd* can be contrasted with: (i) *Vaswani v Italian Motors (Sales & Services) Ltd*,[38] where the Privy Council held that there was no renunciation or repudiatory breach by the vendor of a car when it proposed a contractually unjustified price increase before making the car available for collection; and with (ii) *Woodar Investment Development Ltd v Wimpey Construction UK Ltd*,[39] where a majority of the House of Lords held that there was no clear renunciation; and with (iii) those cases where a party relies on ground X for terminating the contract (as in the *Clausen* case, see the next paragraph) but (unlike the situation in the *Clausen* case) there is another basis, ground Y, which justifies termination so that, despite giving the wrong reason X, the relevant party can escape liability for breach by subsequently invoking ground Y.

---

[37]   [1923] 4 D.L.R. 751 PC, (Lords Sumner and Buckmaster, and Duff J); the Privy Council upheld the trial judge in British Columbia, and reversed the decision of the British Columbia Court of Appeal; the *Clausen* case is cited in S. Waddams, *The Law of Contracts*, 7th edn (Toronto: Sweet & Maxwell, 2017), para.625, and fn.159 also citing *Wile v Cook* (1986) 31 D.L.R. (4th) 205; [1986] 2 S.C.R. 137; *Guarantee Co of North America v Gordon Capital Corp* (1999) 178 D.L.R. (4th) 1; [1999] 3 S.C.R. 423 at 40; the *Clausen* case was cited by Mustill QC to Kerr J at first instance in *Federal Commerce & Navigation Co Ltd v Molena Alpha Inc ("The Nanfri")* [1978] Q.B. 927 at 945–946, who said that it had not been cited in the standard English textbooks, nor judicially considered; Mustill QC did not appear in the Court of Appeal and House of Lords appeals in this case, and his party's case was instead presented in those higher courts by Gordon Pollock and Peter Gross; and Kerr J's decision that there had not been repudiatory breach in this case (contrary to the arbitration award) was reversed by both the Court of Appeal and the House of Lords: see para.6-063.

[38]   [1996] 1 W.L.R. 270 PC.

[39]   [1980] 1 W.L.R. 277 HL at 287, 294, 298, respectively.

Clausen v Canada Timber and Lands Ltd[40] concerned these facts. Canada Timber **6-017** and Lands Ltd had agreed to sell timber from its land. The purchasers were a partnership, a group of loggers. The contract stipulated that the purchasers could not "assign this agreement...except upon the [prior] written agreement of the vendor". After the contract had run successfully for a while, the partnership dissolved. This did not have the effect of constituting a breach of the anti-assignment clause just mentioned. But the vendor mistakenly thought that such a breach had occurred. The vendor then wrote to the purchaser and purported to end the contract on this basis. The purchaser responded by declaring that this termination was inconsistent with the contract and, therefore, a renunciation. For that reason, the purchaser terminated the contract. Lord Sumner,[41] giving the advice of the Privy Council, agreed with the trial judge that the vendor's unjustified termination disclosed a clear intention to abandon the contract. Because the termination was unjustified, the purchaser was entitled to respond by terminating the contract and suing for damages. There was no indication on these facts that the vendor wanted to do anything other than end the contract. The purchaser could rely safely, therefore, on this renunciation. The case is thus consistent with the view that even a good faith (and unjustified) derogation from the terms of the contract can justify the other party's decision to terminate the contract.

III.   IMPLIED RENUNCIATION BY CONDUCT OR INACTION

Nature   The more usual form of "renunciation" is verbal notification of unwilling-   **6-018** ness or inability to perform, and this normally happens before the date for performance. But renunciation can be an inference drawn from conduct.[42] That possibility is explored in this section. Sir George Jessel MR in *Mersey Steel & Iron Co* even suggested that the "conduct" category might be more frequent than the "verbal" category, although this suggestion is debatable, indeed wrong.[43]

Types of conduct or inaction   There are various types of conduct or inaction   **6-019** which might be relied on to support the inference of renunciation. There might be: an absolute failure or refusal to act; or failure or refusal to act fully; or a failure or refusal to act other than on unjustified terms now proposed, or perhaps insisted upon, where these are inconsistent with the true agreement. It can thus involve indicating, that "I will not be doing this at all"; "I will not be doing this in full"; or "I will not be performing as originally agreed because I intend to carry out the contract in my way, even though this might be substantially inconsistent with the contract."

---

[40] [1923] 4 D.L.R. 751 PC.

[41] [1923] 4 D.L.R. 751 at 755–756.

[42] Q. Liu, *Anticipatory Breach* (Oxford: Hart Publishing, 2011), Chs 2–4. Liu contends that implied renunciation (which he styles "inferential renunciation") should provide an "unified" basis for anticipatory breach: that the test should be whether B's conduct, prior to the date of due performance, objectively and reasonably justifies A drawing the inference that B is definitely no longer perform at all, or at least that B will fail to perform in a fundamental way (this implication must be shown to a sufficiently high level of probability). However, this reconstruction of anticipatory breach has not been judicially adopted. The courts proceed on the basis of articulated renunciation, implicit renunciation, and inexcusable disablement.

[43] *Mersey Steel & Iron Co Ltd v Naylor Benzon & Co* (1882) 9 Q.B.D. 648 CA at 657: "There may, indeed, be a case where one party says in so many words that he does not intend to go on with the contract, but generally you must infer the intention from the acts of the parties." (Not disturbed on appeal: *Mersey Steel & Iron Co Ltd v Naylor Benzon & Co* (1884) 9 App. Cas. 434 HL.)

Objectively, in some contexts, silence might constitute renunciation. But the key to this is that silence is being considered in context. For this reason, it is submitted that the cases are really concerned with the combination of conduct and silence. Henshaw J in *Alegrow SA v Yayla Agro Gida San Ve Nak AS* (2020) noted[44] case law on this topic: the *Stocznia* case (2002)[45] and *"The Pro Victor"* (2009).[46]

6-020 **Application of test to facts** Particular circumstances will determine whether a party's breach discloses a wider intimation that he is walking away from the contract or intending to perform it on his own (deviating) terms. Bowen LJ explained this in the Court of Appeal in *Mersey Steel & Iron Co Ltd v Naylor Benzon & Co*:[47]

> "the test [is] whether the conduct of one party to the contract was really inconsistent with an intention to be bound any longer by the contract. Now in cases where the Court has to determine whether that principle of law applies, the facts may approach nearer to the line, or may be at a greater distance from it; and the difficulty is that the judges have had to draw inferences from the particular facts in order to determine whether the principle applies."

6-021 Bowen LJ continued:

> "Non-delivery of a single parcel would not be necessarily, of course, sufficient to intimate that the person who does not deliver intends no longer to be bound, but I am far from saying that non-delivery of a single parcel might not in particular contracts, and under particular circumstances, be sufficient. So as to non-payment. Non-payment of itself is certainly not necessarily evidence of an intention no longer to be bound by the contract, but I do not say there might not be circumstances under which the Court would be entitled to draw that inference from it."

6-022 There is a similar comment made by Salmon LJ in *Decro-Wall International SA v Practitioners in Marketing Ltd*.[48]

6-023 **Burden of proof** The promisee bears the burden of proof of showing that the other party's words or conduct indicate the latter's unwillingness or lack of readiness to perform.[49]

6-024 **Objective assessment** The question whether renunciation by conduct or inaction can be legitimately inferred by the promisee is an issue which the court must assess objectively. This involves application of the perspective of the reasonable person standing in the innocent party's shoes.[50] In *Woodar Investment Develop-*

---

44 [2020] EWHC 1845 (Comm) at [70], [71].
45 [2020] EWHC 1845 (Comm) at [70], citing *Stocznia Gdanska SA v Latvian Shipping Co (No.2)* [2002] EWCA Civ 889; [2002] 2 All E.R. (Comm) 768 at [95] and [96] per Rix LJ.
46 [2020] EWHC 1845 (Comm) at [72], citing *SK Shipping (S) PTE Ltd v Petroexport Ltd* [2009] EWHC 2974 (Comm); [2010] 2 Lloyd's Rep. 158 at [117] per Flaux J.
47 *Mersey Steel & Iron Co Ltd v Naylor Benzon & Co* (1882) 9 Q.B.D. 648 CA at 670. (Not disturbed on appeal: *Mersey Steel & Iron Co Ltd v Naylor Benzon & Co* (1884) 9 App. Cas. 434 HL).
48 [1971] 1 W.L.R. 361 CA at 369.
49 J.W. Carter, *Carter's Breach of Contract*, 2nd edn (Oxford: Hart Publishing, 2019) at [8-06] notes Australian authority, *Larratt v Bankers and Traders Insurance Co Ltd* (1941) 41 SR (NSW) 215 at 223 per Jordan CJ.
50 No objectively implicit renunciation was found in *H TV Ltd (formerly Can Associates TV Ltd) v ITV2 Ltd* [2015] EWHC 2840 (Comm) at [269] ff per Flaux J.

ment Ltd v Wimpey Construction UK Ltd (1980) Lord Keith approved a long-standing formulation of this approach:[51]

> "The matter is to be considered objectively: 'The claim being for wrongful repudiation of the contract it was necessary that the plaintiff's language should amount to a declaration of intention not to carry out the contract, or that it should be such that the defendant was justified in inferring from it such intention. We must construe the language used by the light of the contract and the circumstances of the case in order to see whether there was in this case any such renunciation of the contract'. (*Johnstone v Milling* (1886)[52] per Bowen LJ.)"

A good illustration of the process of objectively assessing whether conduct **6-025** indicates an implied renunciation is *Spar Shipping AS v Grand China Logistics Holding (Group) Co Ltd ("The Spar Draco")*,[53] where Popplewell J (the Court of Appeal agreeing) held that the long-standing pattern of delay in payment of hire under three charterparties had entitled the owner to terminate on the basis that the charterers' conduct constituted a renunciation. Another illustration is the *Flanagan case* where Henderson J concluded that a decision to put a partner on garden leave without authorisation by the relevant committee was objectively an act of renunciation.[54]

Whole context relevant   In *Woodar Investment Development Ltd v Wimpey* **6-026** *Construction UK Ltd* Lord Scarman (who, with Lords Wilberforce and Keith, formed the majority) emphasised that the allegedly renunciatory words (or implied renunciation by conduct) must not be taken out of context. Their impact on the other party must be assessed against the whole backcloth of their dealings. Lord Scarman said:[55]

> "the error of the majority of the Court of Appeal in the instant case was, notwithstanding some dicta to the contrary, to concentrate attention on one act, i.e. the notice of rescission with its accompanying letter. They failed to give the consideration which the law requires of all the acts and conduct of the defendants in their dealings with ... the plaintiff company. The law requires that there be assessed not only the party's conduct but also, 'objectively considered', its impact on the other party."

In the *Woodar* case, Lord Scarman continued:[56]   **6-027**

> "The error is neatly exposed in Goff LJ's[57] terse conclusion [in the Court of Appeal below—a decision reversed by the House of Lords, by a majority of 3 to 3]: 'In my judgment rescission is repudiation, and if it cannot be justified by the terms of the contract it is wrongful and a breach.' The learned Lord Justice was, with respect, concentrating too

---

51   [1980] 1 W.L.R. 277 HL at 287–288.
52   (1886) 16 Q.B.D. 460 at 474 per Bowen LJ.
53   [2015] EWHC 718 (Comm); [2015] 1 All E.R. (Comm) 879 at [223]; the decision was affirmed in all respects at [2016] EWCA Civ 982; [2016] 2 Lloyd's Rep. 447 (Gross, Hamblen LJJ, Sir Terence Etherton MR).
54   *Flanagan v Liontrust Investment Partners LLP* [2015] EWHC 2171 (Ch); [2015] Bus. L.R. 1172 per Henderson J at [185]–[198]; (although later in his judgment at [243], he decided that the doctrine of repudiation/renunciation does not apply to LLP agreements where there are more than two parties; latter aspect considered in *Roberts v Wilsons Solicitors LLP* [2016] I.C.R. 659; [2016] I.R.L.R. 586 EAT).
55   [1980] 1 W.L.R. 277 HL at 299.
56   [1980] 1 W.L.R. 277 HL at 299.
57   Sir Reginald Goff.

much attention on one act isolated from its surrounding circumstances and failing to pay proper regard to the impact of the party's conduct upon the other party."

6-028   **No reference to subsequent events**   When determining whether there has been a renunciation, the court will not consider evidence subsequent to the critical date. Instead attention is confined to information which was available at the time of the alleged renunciation. Thus the Court of Appeal emphasised in *Chilean Nitrate Sales Corp v Marine Transportation Co Ltd ("The Hermosa")* that this assessment must be carried out with regard to the circumstances prevailing *at the time of the decision to terminate* and not by reference to subsequent information.[58] Similarly, Peter Gibson LJ said in *Nottingham Building Society v Eurodynamics Systems Plc* (in this passage his Lordship is using "repudiation" to refer to verbal renunciation):[59]

> "[subsequently discovered] internal communings of the [allegedly renouncing party] are not relevant to the question whether there has been a repudiation [viz renunciation] by [that party], as the objective observer in the position of the [promisee] would not have seen any of these documents, and would have had to reach a conclusion on repudiation [viz renunciation] from what was revealed by the [contemporaneous] correspondence and at meetings with the [renouncing party]."

6-029   By contrast, in the case of the second species of anticipatory breach, namely anticipated inexcusable inability to perform, the court will assess the alleged inability of the relevant party to perform not just by reference to contemporaneous material but in the light of subsequent events as those matters have developed up to and including the trial (see para.7-052 ff).

6-030   **Is there an exception to the objective approach?**   In *"The Pro Victor"* Flaux J accepted the orthodox approach that the question whether there has been a renunciation normally involves an objective inquiry.[60] And the assessment is to be made by reference to all pieces of evidence rather than isolating particular phrases or fragments of communication.[61] In other words, Y can successfully allege that X has evinced an intention to renounce the contract if a reasonable person in Y's position would reasonably infer that this was X's intention, based on X's words and conduct, and having regard to the whole context of these impressions.[62] But will this always be so? Flaux J added, in an interesting dictum, that there might be a qualification on this objective approach where Y had special knowledge or a private

---

[58]   Proposition (d) in *Chilean Nitrate Sales Corp v Marine Transportation Co Ltd (The Hermosa)* [1982] 1 Lloyd's Rep. 570 CA at 572–573 per Donaldson LJ, giving the judgment of the Court of Appeal; passage cited in *SK Shipping (S) PTE Ltd v Petroexport Ltd* [2009] EWHC 2974 (Comm); [2010] 2 Lloyd's Rep. 158 at [85] and [86] per Flaux J.

[59]   *Nottingham Building Society v Eurodynamics Systems Plc* [1995] F.S.R. 605 CA at 612 per Peter Gibson LJ.

[60]   *SK Shipping (S) PTE Ltd v Petroexport Ltd* [2009] EWHC 2974 (Comm); [2010] 2 Lloyd's Rep. 158 per Flaux J at [86]–[87], citing *Chilean Nitrate Sales Corp v Marine Transportation Co Ltd (The Hermosa)* [1982] 1 Lloyd's Rep. 570 CA at 572–573 per Donaldson LJ.

[61]   *SK Shipping (S) PTE Ltd v Petroexport Ltd* [2009] EWHC 2974 (Comm); [2010] 2 Lloyd's Rep. 158 per Flaux J at [88].

[62]   Consistent with the approach to the question of offers: *Crest Nicholson (Londinium) Ltd v Akaria Investments Ltd* [2010] EWCA Civ 1331 at [25]: "In determining [whether there was] a proposal made by one party (A) which was capable of being accepted by the other (B)—the correct approach is to ask whether a person in the position of B (having the knowledge of the relevant circumstances which B had), acting reasonably, would understand that A was making a proposal to which he intended to be bound in the event of an unequivocal acceptance."

understanding which negatives that interpretation. If this is shown, Y's subjective and well-founded belief that in fact no renunciation was intended by X will trump the objective view.[63] This would be consistent with the well-established exception to objectivity developed in cases concerning offer and acceptance.[64] For example, Y might know that X's statement "I will definitely not perform this contract" is not in fact intended to be taken seriously. This is because X has accompanied his statement with a hand movement which X habitually uses to negative his utterances. This special feature is known to Y and only a few other confidants of X. In these circumstances, it would be unjust for Y to assert that X is bound by the objective meaning of his words and that the private signal negativing that meaning should not operate. However, Liu is highly critical of Flaux J's dictum, contending that it is inconsistent with authority and unattractive in principle and in practice.[65] It is submitted that the true position is that a party should only be able to rely on the objective analysis where he has actually perceived matters from that perspective. If, instead, the relevant party has understood or construed the other's words or conduct in a non-objective manner, and that interpretation or understanding is in fact correct, the objective principle falls away.

Summary of the cases   The reader should note that at para.6-040 ff these seven cases are examined in detail. What immediately follows is a synopsis of those leading decisions.   **6-031**

Case (i) in outline   *Freeth v Burr*[66] (see further para.6-040): Here a purchaser failed to pay for the first of two deliveries, which had been delayed, but it was clear that the purchaser was keen to receive complete delivery and so that party had not "evinced" an intention to renounce the whole contract.   **6-032**

Case (ii) in outline   *Mersey Steel & Iron Co Ltd v Naylor Benzon & Co*,[67] (see further para.6-043): In this case a purchaser's failure to pay for the first of five deliveries did not "evince" an intention to renounce the whole contract. Instead it   **6-033**

---

63   *SK Shipping (S) PTE Ltd v Petroexport Ltd* [2009] EWHC 2974 (Comm); [2010] 2 Lloyd's Rep. 158 at [89]–[98] per Flaux J; Flaux J at [92] and [93] noted the subjective analysis of Lord Shaw of Dunfermline in *Forslind v Bechely-Crundell* 1922 SC (HL) 173 at 191: "If, in short, A, a party to a contract, acts in such a fashion of ignoring or not complying with his obligations under it, B, the other party, is entitled to say: 'My rights under this contract are being completely ignored and my interests may suffer by non-performance by A of his obligations, and that to such a fundamental and essential extent that I declare he is treating me as if no contract exists which bound him'. The accent of the psychology is not upon the mind of the person who is defiant or heedless of his obligation, but as Lord Herschell put it, upon the mind of the person who is suffering from the defiance." Flaux J at [93] admitted that there were discordant voices in this 1922 decision: "This passage [from Lord Shaw's speech] in particular seems to support the proposition that the innocent party must have subjectively considered that the other party was renouncing the contract. However other passages from the speeches of their Lordships (specifically Viscount Haldane at 179 and Lord Dunedin at 190) seem to support the objective approach to renunciation." In Australia, although this precise issue raised in Flaux J's dictum—see above—was not considered, statements emphasise an objective approach, e.g. in *Laurinda Pty Ltd v Capalaba Park Shopping Centre Pty Ltd* (1989) 166 C.L.R. 623 at 658; [1989] HCA 23 per Deane and Dawson JJ.
64   N. Andrews, *Contract Law in Practice* (Oxford: Oxford University Press, 2021), paras 3.187–3.198 ff, considering in particular: *Hartog v Colin & Shields* [1939] 3 All E.R. 566 per Singleton J; *OT Africa Line Ltd v Vickers Plc* [1996] 1 Lloyd's Rep. 700 per Mance J; see also N. Andrews, *Contract Rules: Decoding English Law* (Cambridge: Intersentia, 2016), art.2 proposition (5).
65   Q. Liu, *Anticipatory Breach* (Oxford: Hart Publishing, 2011), p.76.
66   (1873–74) L.R. 9 C.P. 208 (Court of Common Pleas).
67   (1884) 9 App. Cas. 434 HL.

was plain that the purchaser was keen to obtain complete delivery. That party's failure to pay had been based on a mistake of law.

6-034 **Case (iii) in outline** *Decro-Wall International SA v Practitioners in Marketing Ltd*[68] (see further para.6-047). A party might repeatedly pay late, as in the *Decro-Wall* case. The UK sole concessionaire consistently paid late for successive supplies delivered by a French manufacturer. But, applying the tests already introduced, the Court of Appeal held that the payor had not "evinced" an intention to renounce the contract. The dilatory pattern had engendered annoyance, but not despair: the French supplier had suffered no anxiety concerning eventual payment, and it knew that the UK concessionaire would pay. Therefore, this repetitive breach did not disclose a renunciation (nor did it go to the root of the contract for the purpose of repudiation: see para.8-002). (The *Decro-Wall* case was distinguished in *Alan Auld Associates Ltd v Rick Pollard Associates*,[69] see case (vi) below)

6-035 **Case (iv) in outline** *Valilas v Januzaj* (see further 6-053)[70] Here a majority of the Court of Appeal (Floyd and Arden LJJ), applying the *Decro-Wall* case, just considered, and distinguishing *Alan Auld Associates Ltd v Rick Pollard Associates*, case (vi) below, held that a dentist's refusal to make payments on time to a fellow dentist's practice did not involve serious prejudice to the latter and that termination for breach was not justified. By contrast, the court held that a purchaser had gone too far in both case (v), *Withers v Reynolds*[71] (see para.6-058) and case (vi), *Alan Auld Associates Ltd v Rick Pollard Associates*.[72] However, Underhill LJ dissented in *Valilas v Januzaj*, suggesting that it was not enough that eventual payment was not in doubt. According to the dissenting judge, the decision to make late payment was a sufficiently serious departure from the contractual payment regime to justify termination either on the basis that it constituted a renunciation or because it was a repudiatory breach involving serious contractual default

6-036 **Case (v) in outline** *Withers v Reynolds* (see further on that case para.6-058):[73] The purchaser had insisted on paying not for the immediate delivery but only for the penultimate delivery. He thus postponed on each delivery his payment for that present delivery. That strategy, designed to keep the supplier "on his toes", was a radical re-structuring of the deal. It occurred without justification or consent. The court held that the seller was right to infer a renunciation.

6-037 **Cases (vi) and (vii) in outline** Case (vi) is *Alan Auld Associates Ltd v Rick Pollard Associates* (for details see para.6-061).[74] This case is a variation on this theme of persistent late payment. In that case the payor held back payment on 19 occasions for no good reason. The innocent party's protests were ignored. The Court of Appeal concluded that the payee had been entitled to despair and that the facts

---

[68] [1971] 1 W.L.R. 361 CA at 379–380.
[69] [2008] EWCA Civ 655; [2008] B.L.R. 419.
[70] [2014] EWCA Civ 436; [2015] 1 All E.R. (Comm) 1047.
[71] (1831) 2 B. & Ad. 882; 109 E.R. 1370.
[72] [2008] EWCA Civ 655; [2008] B.L.R. 419.
[73] (1831) 2 B. & Ad. 882; 109 E.R. 1370.
[74] [2008] EWCA Civ 655; [2008] B.L.R. 419.

disclosed a clear repudiation (although the court also cited[75] textbook discussion of renunciation).

As for case (vii), in *Spar Shipping AS v Grand China Logistics Holding (Group) Co Ltd ("The Spar Draco")* Popplewell J (the Court of Appeal agreeing) said that the charterer had twisted the deal and subverted a stipulated requirement for upfront payment into a stream of ex post facto payments. Case (vii) is further examined at para.6-074.   **6-038**

Case (viii)   *Al Giorgis Oil Trading Ltd v AG Shipping and Energy Pte Ltd* is   **6-039** similar to the Spar Shipping case (vii). In the *Al Giorgis* case Henshaw J concluded[76] that repeated dilatory payments by the charterer had evinced a renunciation. The owner was entitled, therefore, to terminate the contract. By contrast, in *Olympic Council of Asia v Novans Jets LLP*[77] a single disputed, or at any rate confusing, invoiced sum had become a point of protracted discussion. Moulder J concluded that the debtor's failure to pay punctually had not constituted renunciation.

Case (i) in greater detail   In *Freeth v Burr*[78] it was held that the buyer had not   **6-040** renounced the contract on these facts. The defendant contracted to sell to the plaintiffs 250 tons pig-iron at 56 shillings per ton. Half was to be delivered in two weeks, the other half in four weeks. Payment was to be within 14 days after delivery of each half. The market was rising. Delivery of the first 125 tons was not completed for nearly six months. The plaintiffs refused to pay for that delivery, claiming a right to set off the loss they had suffered from having to buy iron from an alternative supplier. But the plaintiffs insistently demanded that the defendant should deliver the second load. The defendant failed to do so, contending that the plaintiff's failure to pay for the first load constituted renunciation. There was no suggestion of inability on the part of the plaintiffs to pay, and the price of the first load was ultimately paid. The Court of Common Pleas held that mere refusal to pay for the first load did not indicate renunciation. Therefore, the plaintiffs were entitled to damages for the seller's failure to deliver the second load.

---

[75] [2008] EWCA Civ 655; [2008] B.L.R. 419 at [13], citing the discussion of renunciation now located at H. Beale (ed), *Chitty on Contracts*, 34th edn (London: Sweet & Maxwell, 2021), para.27-048.

[76] [2021] EWHC 2319 (Comm) at [37]–[40]. The salient facts, summarised at [40], are: "(i) Charterers had failed to pay hire from the outset, and this continued over the ensuing months ... (ii) At most, Charterers expressed a willingness to perform, but repeatedly proved unable or unwilling to do so. ... As recorded in Giorgis's solicitors' email of 7 January 2021, Charterers' solicitors had explained that Charterers had no money, were unable to make any further payment from their own funds, and were instead seeking to pressure third parties into making payments ... ((iii) Giorgis thus was not receiving, and had good reason to believe that they would not receive in the future, the regular, periodic payment of hire in advance for which the parties had bargained. (iv) As in [*Spar Shipping AS v Grand China Logistics Holding (Group) Co Ltd ('The Spar Draco')* [2016] EWCA Civ 982; [2016] 2 Lloyd's Rep. 447], Charterers' conduct in the present case deprived Giorgis of '*substantially the whole benefit*' of the Charterparty, and they were seeking to hold Giorgis to an arrangement '*radically different*' from that which had been agreed. Charterers had made clear that they could or would not perform the Charterparty in accordance with its terms. I consider that Charterers both were in repudiatory breach of the Charterparty and had renounced it."

[77] [2022] EWHC 88 (Comm) at [130]–[154]; at [152] the judgment indicates how the matter titled towards the debtor on the evidence: "[152] ... after the 'without prejudice' discussions failed Novans was no longer interested in engaging with OCA and this led it to serve the termination notice on 18 September 2019. By contrast as referred to above, in September 2019 the solicitors for OCA continued in correspondence to try and engage Novans, indicating that OCA was willing to pay the disputed funds into escrow whilst the issues were resolved through discussions and offering to defer the service of proceedings for seven days to explore settlement.

[78] (1873–74) L.R. 9 C.P. 208 (Court of Common Pleas).

6-041   In *Freeth v Burr* Lord Coleridge CJ explained:[79]

> "[Here] ... the mere non-payment for the first portion of the iron contracted for, unattended by any other act on the part of the purchasers, did not put an end to the contract so as to disentitle the purchasers to maintain an action for the non-delivery of the second portion, but only gave the seller a remedy by cross-action."

6-042   In a concurring judgment in *Freeth v Burr*,[80] Keating J said that the facts did not support the contention that the buyer was purporting to renounce the contract:

> "looking at all the circumstances of this case,—a rising market; a failure on the part of the defendant to deliver the iron according to the terms of the contract; a series of deliveries in small quantities long after the times for delivery provided for by the contract; and a refusal on the part of the plaintiffs to pay for the iron delivered, not only accompanied by remonstrances, but with a requisition to the seller to fix a day for the delivery of a certain quantity."

6-043   **Case (ii) in greater detail**   In *Mersey Steel & Iron Co Ltd v Naylor Benzon & Co* a large quantity of steel was ordered, delivery to be made in five instalments, for five months, beginning January 1881.[81] Payment was to be made within three days of each delivery. There was an incomplete delivery in January. The buyer did not pay for this delivery, having discovered that the sellers were insolvent. The buyer's solicitors wrongly advised that it was not possible to make a safe and effective payment to the sellers at this stage. Instead they advised that the buyers should wait until a liquidator had been appointed. However, the buyer made clear that it wished to keep the contract running and to take all the steel in due course. The sellers' liquidator contended that the buyer had committed (i) a repudiatory breach, and (ii) a renunciation of the contract. But the House of Lords, upholding the Court of Appeal,[82] rejected both contentions.

6-044   As for (i), the absence of a serious actual breach, Lord Blackburn said:[83]

> "[Counsel for the sellers] contended that whenever there was ... a breach of a material part of the contract ... it necessarily went to the root of the matter. I cannot agree with that at all ... There was a delay in fulfilling the obligation to pay the money, it may have been with or without good reason (if that would have made any difference), but it did not go to the root or essence of the contract."

6-045   Further, the Earl of Selborne LC said:[84]

> "I cannot ascribe to their conduct ... the character of a renunciation of the contract ... It

---

[79] (1873–74) L.R. 9 C.P. 208 at 214 per Lord Coleridge CJ.

[80] (1873–74) L.R. 9 C.P. 208 at 214–215 per Keating J.

[81] (1884) 9 App. Cas. 434 HL at 442–4.

[82] (1882) 9 Q.B.D. 648, where Sir George Jessel MR concluded at 658, and at 660: "I think the evidence is very strong, that the buyers were both ready and willing to pay if it had not been for the unlucky circumstance that induced them to refuse to pay under a mistake of law ... it seems to me that so far from their affording evidence of any desire on the part of the purchasers to put an end to the contract, it is clear that they wished the contract to go on, and the deliveries to continue. It is not suggested for a moment that this well-known firm were in any pecuniary difficulty, or wished to delay payment because it was not convenient to pay." The Court of Appeal had reversed the first instance decision of Lord Coleridge CJ in *Mersey Steel & Iron Co Ltd v Naylor Benzon & Co*; Coleridge CJ had given the leading judgment in *Freeth v Burr* (1873–74) L.R. 9 C.P. 208 (Court of Common Pleas).

[83] *Mersey Steel & Iron Co Ltd v Naylor Benzon & Co* (1884) 9 App. Cas. 434 at 444 HL.

[84] *Mersey Steel* case (1884) 9 App. Cas. 434 HL at 441–442.

is just the reverse; the purchasers were desirous of fulfilling the contract; they were advised that there was a difficulty in the way, and they expressed anxiety that that difficulty should be as soon as possible removed ..., [The buyers made clear that they were] prepared to accept all deliveries which the liquidator may make under the contract, and to pay everything due."

As for (b), absence of a renunciation, Lord Blackburn said:[85] **6-046**

"So far from the [buyers] saying that when the [steel] was brought in future they would not pay for it, they were always anxious to get it, and for a very good reason, that the price had risen high above the contract price. There was a statement that ... they were not willing to pay for the [steel] at present; and if that statement had been an absolute refusal to pay ... [that might have been] a refusal to go on with the contract in future ... But there is nothing of that kind here."

Case (iii) in greater detail In *Decro-Wall International SA v Practitioners in* **6-047**
Marketing Ltd[86] the Court of Appeal held that there had been no renunciation. In this case, there had been a string of late payments by a British concessionaire under an exclusive supply agreement. But the French supplier had not attempted to terminate the contract on this basis. Then they became fed up and purported to terminate for breach. The British concessionaire (the payor) challenged this, contending that there had been (i) no actual serious breach ("repudiation"), nor (ii) renunciation by conduct.

As for (i), the allegation of repudiation, the Court of Appeal held that there had **6-048**
been no serious breach: the innocent party's termination had not been justified because the payment date was not of the essence on these facts.

As for (ii) Buckley LJ (Salmon and Sachs LJJ agreeing) rejected the supplier's **6-049**
contention that this pattern of dilatory payment indicated an implicit renunciation. The supplier had at first displayed consistent tolerance, and its manager had testified that they had never despaired of receiving eventual payment. The supplier understood the payor's "cash flow problems".

Buckley LJ said that a renunciation will not necessarily arise whenever a party:[87] **6-050**

"manifests an intention not to perform in accordance with the contract some part of his unperformed obligations thereunder throughout the remainder of the subsistence of the contract ... however insubstantial the threatened departure from due performance of the contract may be."

He said "I cannot accept this contention": and added: "not every breach, even if its continuance is threatened throughout the contract or the remainder of its subsistence, will amount to a repudiation".

Buckley LJ distinguished *Millars' Karri and Jarrah Co v Weddel, Turner & Co*, **6-051**
where Bigham J had said:[88]

"if the breach is of such a kind or takes place in such circumstances as reasonably to lead to the inference that similar breaches will be committed in relation to subsequent deliveries, the whole contract may there and then be regarded as repudiated and may be rescinded."

---

[85] *Mersey Steel* case (1884) 9 App. Cas. 434 HL at 443.
[86] [1971] 1 W.L.R. 361 CA at 379–380.
[87] [1971] 1 W.L.R. 361 at 379.
[88] (1908) 14 Com. Cas. 25 at 29; (1908) 100 L.T. 128.

Buckley LJ in the *Decro-Wall* case explained that the breach in this 1908 case was "clearly one which went to the root of the contract, for the suppliers were proposing to deliver goods which were not in accordance with the contract ..."

6-052   Further, Salmon LJ in this case[89] admitted that it would be different if late payment under a continuing contract had been "such as reasonably to shatter the plaintiffs' confidence in the defendants' ability to pay". He said:

"in such circumstances, the consequences of the breach could properly have been regarded as most serious, indeed fundamental, and going to the root of the contract".

But he repeated the court's view that here:

"the plaintiffs never doubted that if they went on supplying the defendants with goods, the defendants would meet the bills. They would, however, in all probability, meet them some days late, as they had done throughout the whole course of the dealings between the parties."[90]

6-053   **Case (iv) in greater detail**   In *Valilas v Januzaj*[91] a majority of the Court of Appeal (Floyd and Arden LJJ) followed the *Decro-Wall* case and concluded that late payment did not, on the facts of the *Valilas* case, justify terminating the contract between two dentists who were collaborating in a shared practice. Floyd LJ said:[92]

"The effect of these past and threatened future breaches could not on any view be said to deprive the Defendant of 'substantially the whole benefit which it was the intention of the parties as expressed in the contract that he should obtain as the consideration for performing [his] undertakings', the test propounded by Diplock LJ in *Hongkong Fir Shipping Co Ltd v Kawasaki Kisen Kaisha Ltd* [1962] 2 Q.B. 26. Although he would be deprived of monthly payments, he would, as the judge held, obtain that to which he was entitled in the end. In the meantime he would no doubt be out of pocket, his cash-flow might be affected and he could, in theory at least, find himself paying interest on money borrowed to replace the Claimant's missed or reduced payments. The position is to be contrasted with one, clearly repudiatory, in which the Claimant refused to perform his side of the bargain altogether, by refusing to pay at all."

6-054   As for the contention (which formed the basis of Underhill LJ's dissent, see below) that the payor's unilateral decision to deviate from the contractual payment regime constituted a renunciation, Floyd LJ refused to accept that the threatened breach was here serious enough to justify termination by the innocent party. Floyd LJ said:[93]

"Whether a breach or threatened breach does give rise to a right to terminate involves a multi-factorial assessment involving the nature of the contract and the relationship it creates, the nature of the term, the kind and degree of the breach and the consequences of

---

[89] [1971] 1 W.L.R. 361 CA at 369.

[90] cf. in *Moschi v Lep Air Services Ltd* (also known as *Moschi v Rolloswin Investments Ltd* or *Lep Air Services v Rolloswin Investments*) [1973] A.C. 331 HL at 349 per Lord Diplock, a debtor's failure to pay instalments constituted repudiation, a serious actual breach, and this triggered the guarantor's liability to compensate the creditor for the full amount of the debtor's unpaid debt (Lord Diplock applying the *HongKong Fir* test [1962] 2 Q.B. 26 CA at 69–70, 72, enunciated by him in the 1962 case) said that the "cumulative effect of these failures was to deprive the creditor of substantially the whole benefit which it was the intention of the parties that he should obtain from the contract".

[91] [2014] EWCA Civ 436; [2015] 1 All E.R. (Comm) 1047.

[92] [2014] EWCA Civ 436; [2015] 1 All E.R. (Comm) 1047 at [43].

[93] [2014] EWCA Civ 436; [2015] 1 All E.R. (Comm) 1047 at [53].

the breach for the injured party: see the passage from the majority decision of the High Court of Australia in *Koompahtoo Local Aboriginal Land Council v Sanpine Pty Ltd* [2007] HCA 61 (2007) 82 AJLR 345 at [54] cited by Lewison LJ in *Telford Homes (Creekside) Ltd v Ampurius Nu Holdings* [2013] EWCA Civ 577 at [50]."

Floyd LJ noted that no concrete detriment had been shown by the innocent party beyond a short-term cash-flow disadvantage:[94]   **6-055**

"if the [innocent party] wished to establish that it involved serious consequences for him and his practice, the burden fell on him to establish it. It is clear that the judge considered that he had failed to do so."

Arden LJ agreed:[95]   **6-056**

"[the innocent party] was not deprived of substantially the whole of the benefit of the contract. The only likely loss was the loss of the use of the money in the meantime. True, [the guilty party] did not offer to pay him interest but it was unlikely to be a significant amount. Moreover, if [the innocent party] wanted interest, he could have taken out proceedings and sought summary judgment. He would then have received interest."

Finally, what of Underhill LJ's dissent in *Valilas v Januzaj*? His argument was that the declared unwillingness to pay at the agreed time involved an unilateral attempt at a reconstitution of the contract in a serious[96] manner, thus disclosing a renunciation.[97] It is submitted that Underhill LJ's underlying analysis is correct but perhaps his finding that the facts disclosed a serious enough deviation can be doubted. Thus, the real ground of separation between the majority and him was whether the late payment on these facts crossed the line between being merely a significant inconvenience to becoming (as the majority declined to find) a default having serious commercial impact. Underhill LJ encapsulated that point of difference in these clear terms:[98]   **6-057**

"the essential difference between us is that Floyd and Arden LJJ in the majority] attach less importance than I do to the fact that the [guilty party] deliberately declared that he would not, for an indefinite period, comply with the contract and more importance to the fact that the [innocent party] would be paid eventually and that there was no evidence that the delay would cause serious damage."

---

94 [2014] EWCA Civ 436; [2015] 1 All E.R. (Comm) 1047 at [56].
95 [2014] EWCA Civ 436; [2015] 1 All E.R. (Comm) 1047 at [52].
96 [2014] EWCA Civ 436; [2015] 1 All E.R. (Comm) 1047 at [33] ("a complete departure from the contractual arrangement. I would add that the sums involved were not trivial").
97 [2014] EWCA Civ 436; [2015] 1 All E.R. (Comm) 1047 at [33]: "It is well established that a declared intention by a party to fulfil a contract 'but in a manner substantially inconsistent with his obligations and not in any other way' is a repudiation: see per Lord Wright in *Ross T Smyth & Co Ltd v T D Bailey Son & Co* [1940] 3 All E.R. 60 at 72, quoted by Lord Wilberforce in *Federal Commerce & Navigation Co Ltd v Molena Alpha Inc ("The Nanfri")* [1979] A.C. 757 at 778–779. The judge may have been misled in this regard by his understanding that as a matter of law renunciation 'can only apply where the opposite party asserts total non-performance' (see [24] above), which led him to think that the Defendant was not entitled to terminate, because the Claimant was not refusing to attend the practice or to comply with other aspects of the 'suite of obligations' to which he referred. As appears from the passage from *"The Nanfri"* which I have set out, that is not the law: Lord Wilberforce was there at pains to point out that Diplock LJ's reference in *Hongkong Fir* to the victim of the breach being deprived of 'substantially the whole benefit' of the contract does not represent a statement of principle applicable in every case, and he endorsed also Buckley LJ's reference in *Decro-Wall* to the victim being deprived of 'a substantial part of the benefit to which he is entitled under the contract'."
98 [2014] EWCA Civ 436; [2015] 1 All E.R. (Comm) 1047 at [40].

6-058   **Case (v) in greater detail**   Renunciation by conduct was found in the early case of *Withers v Reynolds*.[99] The buyer went too far by insisting on paying systematically late (one delivery late), contrary to the terms of the supply agreement, and the court concluded that the seller was justified in stopping performance. Patteson J, the fourth judge in the *Withers* case, said:[100]

> "If the plaintiff had merely failed to pay for any particular load, that, of itself, might not have been an excuse to the defendant for delivering no more straw: but the plaintiff here expressly refuses to pay for the loads as delivered; the defendant, therefore, is not liable for ceasing to perform his part of the contract."

6-059   The *Withers* case was approved by Lord Blackburn in *Mersey Steel & Iron Co Ltd v Naylor Benzon & Co*,[101] and by Salmon LJ in *Decro-Wall International SA v Practitioners in Marketing Ltd* (1971).[102]

6-060   The *Withers* case also shows that renunciation by words or conduct might occur during performance, even though the performing party has not wholly refused to perform. Thus, once performance has begun, refusal to comply with the precise terms of the contract might indicate serious contractual difficulty. Such conduct might objectively and reasonably be perceived as "shattering the confidence" of the innocent party in the other's willingness or capacity to adhere to the contract. The innocent party might sometimes legitimately conclude that the party in breach has evinced an intention no longer to be bound by the relevant contractual regime: see para.6-058 for Patteson J's remarks in *Withers v Reynolds* and comments on that statement by Salmon LJ in case (iii) *Decro-Wall International SA v Practitioners in Marketing Ltd*[103] and by Lord Blackburn in case (ii) *Mersey Steel & Iron Co Ltd v Naylor Benzon & Co*.[104] The analogy is with the situation where prior to performance a party purports to demand that he should perform on terms other than those originally agreed, involving a serious or substantial departure from those terms, and the other party elects to terminate for renunciation: see discussion of the *Pitwood* case at para.6-075 ff.

6-061   **Case (vi) in greater detail (for case (vii), *"The Spar Draco"*, see para.6.070 below)**   In *Alan Auld Associates Ltd v Rick Pollard Associates*[105] the Court of Appeal held that the payee was entitled to terminate the contract following repeated late payments. On 19 occasions the innocent party's invoice was settled very late. The innocent party had been engaged to provide advisory work to a third party, the

---

[99]   (1831) 2 B. & Ad. 882; 109 E.R. 1370.

[100]   (1831) 2 B. & Ad. 882; 109 E.R. 1370 at 1372.

[101]   (1884) 9 App. Cas. 434 HL at 442–444: "in *Withers v Reynolds* [the buyer said in effect], 'You may bring your straw, but I will not pay you upon delivery as under the contract I ought to do. I will always keep one bundle of straw in hand so as to have a check upon you'"; Lord Blackburn continued: "that in effect amounts to saying, 'I will not perform the contract.'... The other party may say, 'You have given me distinct notice that you will not perform the contract. I will not wait until you have broken it, but I will treat you as having put an end to the contract.'"

[102]   [1971] 1 W.L.R. 361 CA at 368 per Salmon LJ: "[in *Withers v Reynolds*] the buyer refused to pay cash but insisted on credit for each instalment until the next was delivered. The court held that the seller was not obliged to go on with the contract on the terms which the buyer sought to dictate. This decision is explicable on the basis that the stipulation as to time of payment was intended by the parties to be of the essence of the contract; alternatively, that the buyer was seeking to alter the nature of the transaction by turning a cash into a credit transaction."

[103]   [1971] 1 W.L.R. 361 CA at 368.

[104]   (1884) 9 App. Cas. 434 HL at 442–444.

[105]   [2008] EWCA Civ 655; [2008] B.L.R. 419.

UK Atomic Energy Authority, but that third party's payment for the work was routed via the payor, who had won the contract to advise the third party. The Court of Appeal upheld the judge's decision that the pattern of late payment was not just persistent but cynical and serious enough to justify termination by the innocent party. Tuckey LJ said:[106]

> "The context in which the breaches in this case occurred is important. This was not a transaction in which the parties had a raft of mutual obligations to perform. [The innocent payee] was to do the work for the authority through the [payor] and the[payor] was to pay him for it. It was [the innocent payee's] only source of earned income. Although this was not a contract of employment, the analogy is a close one. The judge found that the term as to the time for payment lay at the heart of the agreement. The breaches of this term were *substantial, persistent and cynical*. Not one payment was made in time; most were made inordinately late ... These breaches occurred against a background of repeated complaints by [the innocent payee] and broken promises by the [payor]. [The innocent payee] was entitled to assume that he would be treated in the same way for the remainder of the project which still had a year or so to run. As [the innocent payee] said he was being used to fund the claimant's business. The judge suspected that this was because he was seen as a soft target. In these circumstances, I think the judge was perfectly entitled on the facts as she found them, to conclude that the claimant was in repudiatory breach of the agreement, which entitled [the innocent payee] to bring it to an end, as he did."

IV.   Proposed Performance Substantially Inconsistent with Agreed Terms

Clear indication of continuing unwillingness to adhere properly to the terms of the contract   In *Federal Commerce & Navigation Co Ltd v Molena Alpha Inc ("The Nanfri")*,[107] Lord Wilberforce cited this statement by Lord Wright in the House of Lords in *Ross T Smyth & Co v TD Bailey Son & Co*:[108]   6-062

> "I do not say that it is necessary to show that the party alleged to have repudiated should have an actual intention not to fulfil the contract. He may intend in fact to fulfil it, but may be determined to do so only in a manner substantially inconsistent with his obligations, and not in any other way."

Party threatening without justification to deviate from valid mode of performance   Serious Consequences: Renunciation Found: In *Federal Commerce & Navigation Co Ltd v Molena Alpha Inc ("The Nanfri")*[109] a shipowner refused to issue pre-paid bills of lading. But the shipowner had been acting on inaccurate legal advice because it had no right to refuse to do so. The result of this refusal would be calamitous for the charterer because that party would lose credibility with third-party cargo dealers in the relevant trade. Therefore, the charterer had no choice but to terminate the contract. Three members of the panel (Lords Wilberforce,[110] Scar-   6-063

---

[106] [2008] EWCA Civ 655; [2008] B.L.R. 419 at [20].
[107] [1979] A.C. 757 HL at 778–779.
[108] [1940] 3 All E.R. 60 HL at 72 (Lord Wright's statement was also quoted in *Future Publishing Ltd v Edge Interactive Media Inc* [2011] EWHC 1489 (Ch); [2011] E.T.M.R. 50 at [62] per Proudman J).
[109] [1979] A.C. 757 HL.
[110] Lords Wilberforce in [1979] A.C. 757 at 778, explicitly, Lord Scarman implicitly by agreeing with Lord Wilberforce's speech in general. Lord Wilberforce said: "the owners' instructions (communicated to the charterers) clearly constituted a threat of a breach, or an anticipatory breach of the contract".

man and Fraser)[111] treated the breach in this case as a "threatened" or "anticipatory" breach: that is, the owner's announcement, without contractual justification, of an *intention to act* inconsistently with the agreement, and in a manner which would have serious commercial consequences for the charterer. Only Viscount Dilhorne[112] held that the breach had been "actual", that is, the threat had been carried though sufficiently on these facts (the fifth judge, Lord Russell, was neutral on this point).[113] Thus the majority's analysis was that the shipowners had committed a renunciation: an indication by words or conduct that a party intended to abandon or to act inconsistently with the contract.

6-064   All the reasoned speeches in *Federal Commerce & Navigation Co Ltd v Molena Alpha Inc ("The Nanfri")*[114] emphasise the severity of the commercial consequences threatened by the owner (and commercial decisions of 2006[115] and 2008[116] re-emphasise the severe nature of these facts). Thus Lord Fraser said:[117]

> "[adopting] the formulation by Buckley LJ in [the *Decro-Wall* case, 1971] ...[118]: 'Will the consequences of the breach be such that it would be unfair to the injured party to hold him to the contract and leave him to his remedy in damages as and when a breach or breaches may occur? If this would be so, then a repudiation has taken place' ... I have no doubt that the breach here was repudiatory."

---

[111] Lord Fraser in [1979] A.C. 757 at 782: "True, the instructions were actually given to the masters and the charterers were so informed, but the issue of instructions was merely a preparatory step, useful in making the threat realistic and necessary to enable it to be carried out quickly. The instructions given by the owners to their own servants could be cancelled at any time and the umpire found that the charterers knew that if they paid the disputed deductions the instructions to the masters would be withdrawn. That is what happened; the threat to the charterers was enough and it did not have to be put into action".

[112] Only Viscount Dilhorne in [1979] A.C. 757 at 781, thought that there had been sufficient conduct for the owner's intimations to have crossed the line and become an "actual breach": "I think the giving by the owners of instructions to the masters to refuse to sign bills of lading marked 'freight pre-paid' and to insist that all bills of lading should be 'claused' was an actual and not anticipatory breach of contract as it amounted to a breach of clause 9 of the charterparty whereby it was agreed that the masters should be under the orders of the charterers. However it makes no difference whether the conduct of the owners amounted to an actual breach, or anticipatory breach for, as my noble and learned friend has so clearly demonstrated, their conduct was repudiatory."

[113] Lord Russell did not clearly state whether he regarded the breach as either (i) a threat not to adhere to the terms of the contract in a serious manner, or (ii) the issuing of an order to the relevant three ship-masters not to comply with the terms of the contract.

[114] [1979] A.C. 757 HL.

[115] *Dalkia Utilities Services Plc v Celtech International Ltd* [2006] EWHC 63 (Comm); [2006] 1 Lloyd's Rep. 599 at [148] per Christopher Clarke J: "in *'The Nanfri'* the repudiation consisted of an act—the instruction of the master not to sign pre-paid bills of lading—which had the immediate effect of substantially depriving the charterers of virtually the whole benefit of the charter since the issue of such bills was essential to the maintenance of the charterers' trade".

[116] *Gulf Agri Trade FZCO v Aston Agro Industrial AG* [2008] EWHC 1252 (Comm); [2009] 1 All E.R. (Comm) 991 at [43] per Aikens J (as he then was): "The charterers of three ships on time charter had made deductions from time charter hire which the shipowners regarded as unjustified. In retaliation the shipowners purported to revoke the authority of the charterers ... to sign bills of lading on behalf of the masters of the three vessels. Moreover, the shipowners ordered their masters to refuse to issue 'freight pre-paid' bills of lading if presented by the charterers. Their Lordships characterised these orders to the masters as acts which deprived the timecharterers of substantially the whole benefit of each of the three timecharters. Therefore, it was either an actual or an anticipatory repudiatory breach of the three charters."

[117] [1979] A.C. 757 HL at 783–784.

[118] [1971] 1 W.L.R. 361 CA at 380.

Lord Fraser continued: **6-065**

"The whole purpose of the contract from the charterers' point of view was that they should have the use of the ship for carrying on their trade from the Great Lakes, but if the owner's threat had been carried out it would have been ruinous to that trade. [As the arbitrators found] ... 'The charterers were likely to be blacklisted as grain carriers by Continental Grain, which is one of the world's largest shippers of grain ... [and] the charterers' reputation would be very seriously damaged ... [T]hey would probably have been unable to obtain business for the vessels from other major shippers of grain."

Privy Council decision that a party repudiates if he purports to pick and   **6-066**
choose which terms he will respect   The Privy Council in *Dymocks Franchise Systems (NSW) Pty Ltd v Todd* held that repudiation can occur if a party is only prepared to proceed with contractual performance if the terms of the contract are changed in its favour.[119] Lord Browne-Wilkinson said: "a party who intends to fulfil a contract but only in a way which is inconsistent with the terms of the contract is in repudiation of that contract".[120] He added: "a suspension of performance until the terms of the contract are changed is capable of being a repudiation."[121] In this case a party to a franchise agreement had refused to pay instalments outright to the other party. Lord Browne-Wilkinson explained:[122]

"this was not just a failure to pay one month's instalment ... [The payor insisted that fees should] be placed in the interest-paying credit account until the matter is satisfactorily resolved. What he is plainly proposing is an indefinite suspension of the actual payment of the fees until some alteration of the contract terms satisfactory to the [payor] has been agreed."

Lord Browne-Wilkinson added:[123]   **6-067**

"[the payor] submitted that the payment into an escrow account was not a repudiatory act because [he] intended to pay what was owing in due course. But a party is not entitled to insist that he is not repudiating because he proposes to perform part of the contract in a manner not permitted by the contract."

It had also become clear that the payee was unwilling to acquiesce in this   **6-068**
unilateral re-arrangement of payment. As Lord Browne-Wilkinson explained:[124]

"Nor can there be any doubt of the [payor] being aware of the consequences of non-payment. The letter from [the payee] spells out clearly [its] attitude: if you stop paying we will terminate your franchise agreement. [This made clear that] failure at any time thereafter to pay the franchise fees ... amounted in itself to a clear repudiation of the contract."

Need for serious deviation from the agreed terms   In *Valilas v Januzaj*[125] a   **6-069**
majority of the Court of Appeal (Floyd and Arden LJJ), held that a dentist's refusal to make payments on time to a fellow dentist's practice did not involve serious prejudice to the latter and that termination for breach was not justified. However, Underhill LJ dissented. He held that the guilty party's decision to make late pay-

---

119 [2002] UKPC 50; [2002] 2 All E.R. (Comm) 849 at [58].
120 [2002] UKPC 50; [2002] 2 All E.R. (Comm) 849 at [58].
121 [2002] UKPC 50; [2002] 2 All E.R. (Comm) 849 at [59].
122 [2002] UKPC 50; [2002] 2 All E.R. (Comm) 849 at [60].
123 [2002] UKPC 50; [2002] 2 All E.R. (Comm) 849 at [60].
124 [2002] UKPC 50; [2002] 2 All E.R. (Comm) 849 at [61].
125 [2014] EWCA Civ 436; [2015] 1 All E.R. (Comm) 1047.

ment was a sufficiently serious[126] departure from the contractual payment regime to justify termination either on the basis that it constituted a renunciation or because it was a repudiatory breach involving serious contractual default. The relevant passage requires close consideration:[127]

> "It is well established that a declared intention by a party to fulfil a contract 'but in a manner substantially inconsistent with his obligations and not in any other way' is a repudiation: see per Lord Wright in *Ross T Smyth & Co Ltd v T D Bailey Son & Co* [1940] 3 All E.R. 60 at 72, quoted by Lord Wilberforce in *Federal Commerce & Navigation Co Ltd v Molena Alpha Inc ('The Nanfri')* [1979] A.C. 757 at 778–9. The Judge may have been misled in this regard by his understanding that as a matter of law renunciation 'can only apply where the opposite party asserts total non-performance' (see 24 above), which led him to think that the Defendant was not entitled to terminate, because the Claimant was not refusing to attend the practice or to comply with other aspects of the 'suite of obligations' to which he referred. As appears from the passage from *'The Nanfri'* which I have set out, that is not the law: Lord Wilberforce was there at pains to point out that Diplock LJ's reference in *Hongkong Fir* to the victim of the breach being deprived of 'substantially the whole benefit' of the contract does not represent a statement of principle applicable in every case, and he endorsed also Buckley LJ's reference in *Decro-Wall* to the victim being deprived of 'a substantial part of the benefit to which he is entitled under the contract.'"

6-070 Although Underhill LJ's underlying analysis is correct, his finding in *Valilas v Januzaj* that the facts disclosed a serious enough deviation can be doubted (and the majority in that case held that no such serious deviation had occurred). Thus, the ground of separation between the majority and him was whether the late payment on these facts crossed the line between being merely a significant inconvenience to becoming (as the majority declined to find) a default having serious commercial impact. Underhill LJ encapsulated that point of difference in these clear terms:[128]

> "the essential difference between us is that Floyd and Arden LJJ in the majority] attach less importance than I do to the fact that the [guilty party] deliberately declared that he would not, for an indefinite period, comply with the contract and more importance to the fact that the [innocent party] would be paid eventually and that there was no evidence that the delay would cause serious damage."

6-071 In the majority in *Valilas v Januzaj*, Floyd LJ stated that not every deviation, even if deliberate, will justify termination. Instead the deviation must be not merely non-trivial but constitute a serious threatened breach. He said:[129]

> "It is of course in general correct that a declared intention by a party to perform a contract in a manner which is substantially inconsistent with his obligations may amount to a renunciation of it: see per Lord Wright in *Ross T Smyth & Co v TD Bailey, Son & Co* [1940] 3 All E.R. 60 at 72. However this is not a special rule applicable to deviations from contractual performance, making every such deviation give rise to a right in the opposite party to terminate. The breach involved must be analysed by the same standard to determine whether it has that consequence or not."

---

[126] [2014] EWCA Civ 436; [2015] 1 All E.R. (Comm) 1047 at [33]: "a complete departure from the contractual arrangement. I would add that the sums involved were not trivial".

[127] [2014] EWCA Civ 436; [2015] 1 All E.R. (Comm) 1047 at [33].

[128] [2014] EWCA Civ 436; [2015] 1 All E.R. (Comm) 1047 at [40].

[129] [2014] EWCA Civ 436; [2015] 1 All E.R. (Comm) 1047 at [52].

The Court of Appeal in *EMFC Loan Syndications LLP v Resort Group Plc*[130] did **6-072** not disagree with the trial judge's examination of the law concerning repudiation or renunciation by a party failing, or stating an unwillingness, to perform the contract on the terms which had been agreed:

"[86] The Judge correctly identified the relevant principles of law in relation to contractual repudiatory breach, affirmation and waiver [as follows]: '1. If one party evinces an intention not to perform or declares his inability to perform some but not all of his obligations under the contract, then the right of the other party to treat himself as discharged depends on whether the non-performance of those obligations will amount to a breach of the condition of the contract or deprive him of substantially the whole benefit which it was the intention of the parties that he should obtain from the obligations of the parties under the contract then remaining unperformed ...'"

But the facts in in *EMFC Loan Syndications LLP v Resort Group Plc* did not **6-073** involve a sufficiently serious deviation from the agreed arrangement, as explained in the following passage:[131]

"[92] ...it does not seem to me that: (i) either a refusal to work in conjunction with Investec; and/or (ii) a refusal to go to Cape Verde in February 2016, would have deprived TRG of substantially the whole benefit which it was the intention of the parties that it should obtain from the obligations of the parties under the Contract then remaining unperformed. Nor would it have amounted to an indication of an intention by EMFC to fulfil its obligations under the Contract but in a manner substantially inconsistent with those obligations..."

By contrast, an illustration of a court concluding that a pattern of deviation from **6-074** the contractual terms (combined with the prospect of repetition) indicated objectively an implied renunciation is *Spar Shipping AS v Grand China Logistics Holding (Group) Co Ltd ("The Spar Draco")* (this case was introduced as case (vii) at para.6-025 above). Here Popplewell J (the Court of Appeal agreeing) said that the charterer had twisted the deal and subverted a stipulated requirement for upfront payment into a stream of ex post facto payments:[132]

"If [contrary to the agreement] the charterer pays not in advance, but in arrears, even in full, he is performing a substantially different bargain from that which is contained in the charterparty ... Occasional and brief delays in payment will not be repudiatory, but where the hire is due semi monthly in advance, regular delays measured in weeks often will be, because in those circumstances performance is substantially different from what has been bargained for, which is a charterparty under which the owner is to meet his obligations from the hire which has already been provided...[In short in this situation of persistent late payment] the charterer is still treating the owner as obliged to perform when he is a month out of pocket for the expenses needed to perform throughout the period of the charter. However described, in substance the position is that throughout the whole of the charter the charterer is getting the services on credit, without paying interest, when the bargain is that owners should be funded in advance."

---

[130] [2021] EWCA Civ 844; [2022] 1 W.L.R. 717 at [86] and [87] (Carr LJ, with the agreement of Baker and Lewis LJJ).

[131] [2021] EWCA Civ 844; [2022] 1 W.L.R. 717 at [92] (Carr LJ, with the agreement of Baker and Lewis LJJ).

[132] [2015] EWHC 718 (Comm); [2015] 1 All E.R. (Comm) 879 at [214]; the decision was affirmed in all respects at [2016] EWCA Civ 982; [2016] 2 Lloyd's Rep. 447 (Gross, Hamblen LJJ, Sir Terence Etherton MR).

6-075   **Earlier Court of Appeal authority concerning a party's repudiatory attempt to pick and choose which terms he would respect**   A strong Court of Appeal in *Aktieselskabet Pitwood v J W Baird & Co Ltd*[133] (Bankes, Atkin, and Warrington LJJ) held that the seller had renounced the contract and that the buyer was entitled to terminate. It was a term that the goods (wooden pit-props) would be delivered "on the cranes" to the buyer in the port at West Hartlepool, as opposed to delivery at that port "on the quay", or "by lighters". The seller, Finnish merchants, by telegram through their agents, attempted to resile from this. They intimated that "they decline to agree to your stipulation in the contracts for crane discharge". Change of delivery would involve the buyer in some delay in gaining use of the goods, once they had arrived in the port. Delivery "at the cranes" would be commercially more convenient for the buyer. And so the buyer cancelled the contract (there were in fact two in the same form involving different vessels). The seller tried to insist on the contracts surviving.

6-076   Each of the Court of Appeal judges was convinced that a seller could not insist on a revision of the terms concerning "crane" delivery at this port (unanimously affirming Rowlatt J's reversal of the arbitration award).[134] Such a proposed change of the mode of delivery constituted renunciation. Therefore, the buyers had been entitled to terminate the contract.

6-077   All three judgments in the *Pitwood decision* (by Bankes,[135] Warrington[136] and Atkin LJJ)[137] strongly endorse the proposition that a party cannot insist that he will change the mode of performing the contract in some commercially significant way without running the peril that the other party might justifiably terminate the contract on the basis of renunciation. It did not matter that the buyer's motive in ending the

---

[133] (1926) 24 Ll. L. Rep. 282 CA.

[134] The arbitrator had (wrongly) held that there had been no breach justifying termination and he characterised the stipulation concerning discharge "at the cranes" as a mere collateral undertaking which produced liability only in damages. On a special case stated, Rowlatt J reversed this, and the Court of Appeal affirmed Rowlatt J's decision ((1925) 23 Lloyd's Rep. 247).

[135] (1926) 24 Ll. L. Rep. 282 CA at 284–285; noting that this was an anticipatory breach, he said: "the law does not recognise the position of a man who ... before the time comes for performance says: 'My good friend, I am quite prepared to perform all the terms except this one or that one or the other.' ... A man, having entered into his contract, must perform it as a whole or accept the position of having broken it ... He must take the contract for better or for worse; he must be prepared to perform it as a whole or be treated as a person who is repudiating the bargain".

[136] (1926) 24 Ll. L. Rep. 282 at 286: "The sellers were proposing to have a new contract not containing [the cranes discharge] provision, or in the alternative were refusing to carry out the existing contract. The buyers were not bound to modify the contract they had already made; and they were entitled ... quit clearly to insist upon their real contract or nothing; and as the sellers said they would not perform that contract the buyers were entitled to do as they did, to cancel those contracts".

[137] (1926) 24 Ll. L. Rep. 282 at 288: "It is said that it is not so because after all this is only a little breach, that the sellers in announcing that they were not going to perform their contract are entitled to pick out such small parts of the contract as do not really matter, and entitled to intimate that they are not going to perform their contract in its entirety." He continued: "If a man states he is not going to comply with the contractual stipulations, or any of them, and states so in advance, the other party is entitled to say: 'Very well, you are only going to perform something which I never agree: I am going to treat myself as no longer bound.'" He added "It seems to me quite irrelevant that the party affecting to repudiate the contract is dealing with a matter which he thinks relatively unimportant, or which may in fact be unimportant. The other party is entitled to say: 'I agreed to a contract with that term in it, and I am not going to be bound by a contract without that term'; otherwise the Courts would be reforming contracts for the parties and enforcing contracts to which the minds of the parties have never been directed".

contract was the "state of the market",[138] nor that a second dispute was "raging between these parties in reference to a cargo shipped on another vessel".[139]

The *Pitwood decision* languished unnoticed for half a century until it was dusted **6-078** off and presented by Mustill QC in argument[140] at first instance in *Federal Commerce & Navigation Co Ltd v Molena Alpha Inc ("The Nanfri")*. But Mustill QC's impressive research received an unconvincingly negative reception by Kerr J.[141] Furthermore, neither the Court of Appeal nor the House of Lords addressed this authority in their judgments, although it was cited to the House of Lords, and both appellate courts had sight of Kerr J's brief and negative examination of this authority.

Renunciation by proposing a deviation in contractual performance: the test of **6-079** **seriousness** It is submitted that an acceptable test is this: is the threatened or insisted unauthorised mode of performance a commercially significant deviation from the agreed mode of performance?[142] If so, the other party is entitled to terminate (for example, when a seller, unjustifiably on the facts, invokes a clause which on different facts would have entitled him, if there had been objective evidence of the buyer's "financial impairment", to require either advance payment in cash or some form of specified guarantee or security).[143] By contrast, termination is unjustified if the threatened, or insisted upon, alteration of terms is so trivial and trifling that it would be wholly unreasonable for that party to respond by terminating the contract.

Illustration of seriousness test Suppose a May Ball Committee hires a very large **6-080** marquee "for delivery and installation on 5 June, removal on 7 June, all to be done by the supplier" (curiously, in Cambridge, June is the month of May Balls). If the marquee supplier announces in April: "we will supply but you must put it up and take it down", without suggesting any appropriate discount in the hire payable, it would seem acceptable for the committee to cancel and find another supplier, because this would be a renunciation. But if the supplier states, "we will install and take down, but we will need three strong students to assist", this change (even if

---

138 (1926) 24 Ll. L. Rep. 282 CA at 284 per Bankes LJ.
139 (1926) 24 Ll. L. Rep. 282 at 284.
140 [1978] Q.B. 927 at 945–946 (Mustill QC did not appear in the Court of Appeal and House of Lords in this case, and his party's case was instead presented in those higher courts by Gordon Pollock and Peter Gross); and Kerr J's decision—that there had not been repudiatory breach in this case (contrary to the arbitration award)—was reversed by both the Court of Appeal and the House of Lords.
141 [1978] Q.B. 927 at 945–946.
142 Lord Wright in *Ross T Smyth & Co Ltd v TD Bailey Son & Co* [1940] 3 All E.R. 60 HL at 72, said: "I do not say that it is necessary to show that the party alleged to have repudiated should have an actual intention not to fulfil the contract. He may intend to fulfil it, but may be determined to do so only in a manner substantially inconsistent with his obligations, and not in any other way." This was adopted in New Zealand in *Starlight Enterprises Ltd v Lapco Enterprises Ltd* [1979] 2 N.Z.L.R. 744 NZCA, by Richardson J at 747–748, also noting that it chimed with the High Court of Australia's discussion in *DTR Nominees Pty Ltd v Mona Homes Pty Ltd* (1978) 52 A.L.J.R 360 at 364. Although concerned with actual breach (dilatory performance by a lessor of the obligation to deliver to the lessee a registrable lease), rather than anticipatory breach, Mason CJ's discussion in *Laurinda Pty Ltd v Capalaba Park Shopping Centre Pty Ltd* (1989) 166 C.L.R. 623 at 634–637, concludes with the test: whether the guilty party evinced an intention "only to perform the contract in a manner substantially inconsistent with its obligations": Deane and Dawson JJ at 659 referred to disavowal of the contract as a whole or "of a fundamental obligation under it".
143 *BV Oliehandel Jongkind v Coastal International Ltd* [1983] 2 Lloyd's Rep. 463 (Leggatt J) (because the seller had invoked this clause without justification, they had committed a repudiatory breach).

not put forward with a willingness to consider a discount) would be unlikely to constitute a sufficiently serious derogation from the original terms. It will be different if the marquee is to be supplied not to a Cambridge[144] college (where youthful muscle is plentiful, especially in some subjects), but to a couple soon to celebrate their diamond wedding in their (capacious) garden. In this situation, the supplier's request for help ("you must find three able-bodied people to assist in installing and in taking down") would entitle the couple to reply: "That was not what we agreed—all of our neighbours are as feeble as us—and we are cancelling".

6-081   **Seriousness test and the Pitwood and "The Nanfri" decisions**   It is submitted that a pre-performance threat, or forewarning, or insistent declaration, of a serious breach is enough.

6-082   The seriousness test, just explained, is consistent with both the *Pitwood decision* and *Federal Commerce & Navigation Co Ltd v Molena Alpha Inc ("The Nanfri")*.[145] Those cases can be reconciled by saying that in the earlier case the Court of Appeal was unwilling to trivialise the seller's threatened breach. And in *"The Nanfri"* the House of Lords emphasised (echoing the arbitrator's view on these facts) that the consequences of the threatened breach would have been commercially catastrophic or "ruinous".

6-083   It is pitching things too high to require that the change of performance should entail a commercial disaster (although in fact this was the level of threatened detriment, according to the arbitrators, Court of Appeal, and House of Lords on the facts of *"The Nanfri"*) need not be threatened.

6-084   There is much intermediate ground between threatening to shoot the other party with a pea-shooter ("I will turn up 10 seconds late to spite you") and threatening him with a pistol ("I will ruin your business"). Lord Denning in the Court of Appeal thought that *"The Nanfri"* threat was extreme, and that it could be located at the pistol end of the spectrum:[146]

> "That stroke by the owners was a pistol at the head of the charterers. If the owners carried out their threat—for that is what it was—it would mean disaster for the charterers."

He added:[147]

> "The owners fully realised the difficulties in which they put the charterers: and their very object was to bring irresistible pressure on the charterers to pay the hire without any deduction of disputed items. They were issuing a threat equivalent to 'Your money or your life'—that is to say "Pay up the hire in full without deductions or else we will play havoc with your trade."

V.   UNJUSTIFIED RENUNCIATION OCCURRING IN GOOD FAITH

6-085   **A party's mistaken but good faith statement that his non-performance is justified**   In general, where a party mistakenly believes that he is not required to perform, or that he is required to perform in a particular way, his statement that he will not perform, or that he will only perform in that particular way, will constitute

---

[144] Of course, All Souls College, Oxford, not having any students, would fall into the old couple category: but query whether All Souls would recognise the concept of a celebratory ball.

[145] [1979] A.C. 757 HL.

[146] [1978] Q.B. 927 CA at 970.

[147] [1978] Q.B. 927 CA at 970.

renunciation (similarly, if, instead of a renunciation, his good faith conduct is inconsistent with the continuation of the contract, a case of repudiatory breach). The law on this topic is evolving. But the following propositions summarise current judicial analysis of this thorny matter.

Proposition A: prima facie party X's good faith proposed serious non-compliance with the contract will constitute a renunciation if X was not in fact justified under the contract in resiling in this way: *Federal Commerce & Navigation Co Ltd v Molena Alpha Inc ("The Nanfri")*.[148]   **6-086**

Propositions B(i) to (iii): however, such good faith proposed serious non-compliance will not justify the other party in terminating the contract if:[149]   **6-087**

(i)   *obvious mistake*: it is obvious to party Y that X has made an erroneous step, in purported compliance with the contract and the true position is apparent to Y, and it is also obvious to Y that, once Y points out the error to the other side, X will quickly step back in line, and resume fidelity to the contract: *Eminence Property Developments Ltd v Heaney*;[150]

(ii)   *probable error*: X's proposed serious non-compliance might easily have been challenged by Y, so that X was asked to check and re-think, whereupon it would have been possible for X to make clear whether he was wishing to present to Y a "take-it-or-leave-it" ultimatum: *Vaswani v Italian Motors (Sales & Services) Ltd*;[151] or

(iii)   *contestable and genuine point of dispute presented in good faith* X and Y are agreed that the matter must be legally tested (by a court, arbitrator, or perhaps by some other mechanism) and that, if the relevant point is held against him, X will abide by the contract: *Woodar Investment Development Ltd v Wimpey Construction UK Ltd*.[152] Here the proposed default arises when there was adequate time and opportunity to test the contested point by reference to a neutral third party (such as a court or arbitrator); the law will allow a point to be referred for adjudication, but only if it is not a disingenuous attempt to stall and/or to resile, that is, provided the point has not been raised without an honest belief in its validity

As mentioned, approach (iii) presupposes that there is "time and space" to resolve this disputed matter. As the Court of Appeal observed in *James Shaffer Ltd v Findlay Durham & Brodie*,[153] modern practice has failed to maintain the speedy practice of the early twentieth century Commercial Court, when disputed ques-   **6-088**

---

[148] [1979] A.C. 757 HL.

[149] A similar tendency is discernible in New Zealand and Australian cases: *Starlight Enterprises Ltd v Lapco Enterprises Ltd* [1979] 2 N.Z.L.R. 744 NZCA, especially Richardson J at 747–748; applied in *Oxborough v North Harbour Builders Ltd* [2002] 1 N.Z.L.R. 145 NZCA at [13]; similarly, *The Edge Buying Group (Queenstown 2010) v Coca-Cola Amatil Ltd NZCA 145/02* (2002), noted M. Chetwin, "The Edge Buying Group (Queenstown 2000) Ltd v Coca-Cola Amatil (NZ) Ltd" (2003) N.Z.L.J. 117; High Court of Australia in *DTR Nominees Pty Ltd v Mona Homes Pty Ltd* (1978) 138 C.L.R. 423 at 432 (bona fide dispute as to the construction of a land transaction did not justify inferring that the mistaken party had evinced an intention not to perform the contract).

[150] [2010] EWCA Civ 1168; [2011] 2 All E.R. (Comm) 223 at [65].

[151] [1996] 1 W.L.R. 270 PC at 277 (Lord Woolf).

[152] [1980] 1 W.L.R. 277 HL at 282 per Lord Wilberforce, 297 per Lord Keith, 299 per Lord Scarman; for a similar case, *Alfred C Toepfer v Peter Cremer GmbH & Co* [1975] 1 Lloyd's Rep. 118 CA per Lord Denning MR at 125 left-hand column, and per Scarman LJ at 129 left-hand column; summarised by Aikens J in *Gulf Agri Trade FZCO v Aston Agro Industrial AG* [2008] EWHC 1252 (Comm); [2009] 1 All E.R. (Comm) 991; [2008] 2 Lloyd's Rep. 376; [2008] 1 C.L.C. 919 at [41].

[153] [1953] 1 W.L.R. 106 CA at 118 per Singleton LJ: "For more than 40 years the Commercial Court

tions of repudiation or renunciation were often taken to court within days of the relevant events. In the *James Shaffer* case, Singleton LJ also noted the speedy "referral" of a disputed renunciation in the *Spettabile case*.[154]

6-089 **Honest error concerning contractual rights is no defence to renunciation if time does not permit disputable point to be investigated at relative leisure or the actual breach takes immediate effect**   The innocent party will be entitled to terminate for breach, even though the defaulting party acts in good faith, if either (i) a threatened form of serious default occurs when there is no real opportunity to consult outside agencies to resolve the impasse, or (ii) the guilty party commits a serious default (including failure to perform) that takes effect immediately (situation (ii), involves repudiation).

6-090   Situation (i) involves renunciation. This occurred in *Federal Commerce & Navigation Co Ltd v Molena Alpha Inc ("The Nanfri")*.[155] In that case, the drastic nature of the breach and the inability of the parties to create a "window" within which to sort out this difference meant that the innocent party had no commercial choice other than to terminate the contract for repudiatory breach. It did not mat-

---

has been in existence, and very largely through Mathew J and Bray J it achieved a position under which the commercial world knew that it could resort to that court and get a point decided in a very short space of time, and if there was need for a journey to the Court of Appeal, that journey could be made speedily too. I think it is a matter for regret that the commercial world has ceased to make use of the commercial court to the extent to which it did. [In the present case, the James Shaffer decision] there was a dispute, or a disagreement, between the parties, as to the construction of a clause in this contract. Either party could have gone to the Commercial Court and have had that point determined at short notice. At that time there was only the disputed construction of the contract; the question whether there was a repudiation arose later. The commercial world was grateful in years gone by to those who arranged the working of the commercial court. I think myself the legal profession ought to pay more attention to it than it does now. If the point of construction had been decided in 1948, it might have been decided in half a day, and a great deal of what has taken place four years later would have been avoided, the costs of both sides would have been immeasurably less, and both parties would have been the richer."

[154] [1953] 1 W.L.R. 106 CA at 118 and 117–118 where Singleton LJ said: "in the *Spettabile case* (1919) 121 L.T. 628 CA ... the action which was before the court in that case was commenced on May 26, 1919, and the judgment of Bailhache J was given on June 6, 1919. At the commencement of his judgment Bailhache J said: 'In this case I am asked to exercise, I think, one of the most useful functions of the commercial court—namely, to say between parties to contracts whether those contracts are still binding upon them. That is a function of the court which saves parties in commercial transactions from a great deal of uncertainty and a great deal of money. It is a function which this court is always pleased to exercise when asked, and I desire to say that in cases of this kind the court is always ready to hear it at the shortest possible notice. In this particular instance the case came on for hearing before me yesterday, within some 10 or 12 days after the issue of the writ. The system would be perfect but for one thing that cannot be avoided—namely, the frailty of human judgment'." In the Court of Appeal in the *Spettabile* case, Atkin LJ said [(1919) 121 L.T. 628 at 635]: "The declaratory application or construction summons] is ... one of the most valuable contributions that the courts have made to the commercial life of this country. It has been developed very much in recent times, partly, no doubt, because the difficulties arise more acutely in modern times, when parties in commerce are given to binding themselves over long periods of time on stringent terms in contracts. No doubt questions of great difficulty arise between commercial men. And there are great uncertainties whether a contract between them will be performed or whether it will put them in the very gravest difficulty unless the dispute can be determined by the courts. The procedure before the court is now open to them, which is unchallenged, by which they can come to a court and in a very short time have those disputes resolved. That they can do without exposing themselves to the risk of having to take a definite course in repudiating a contract which, if it is wrong, may involve them in a very large sum of money." And Singleton LJ added in *James Shaffer Ltd v Findlay Durham & Brodie* [1953] 1 W.L.R. 106 CA at 118: "That was in 1919".

[155] [1979] A.C. 757 HL.

ter that the shipowner had in good faith misinterpreted its legal position. Here a shipowner, acting on incorrect legal advice, had refused to issue pre-paid bills of lading. The House of Lords unanimously held that the breach justified termination and that the owner's good faith was irrelevant: such good faith does not exonerate a party who has objectively committed a breach, whether by renunciation or repudiation, or other forms of actual default. There were three salient factors: (i) *clarity*: the repudiation was clear and emphatic; (ii) *danger*: the innocent charterer was placed in a very tight corner because it did not want to suffer damage to its commercial reputation amongst cargo dealers;[156] and (iii) *lack of time*: there was no time to spare, no commercial "window" within which to sort out this difference.

Lord Denning MR's comment in the *Federal Commerce case*, in the Court of Appeal[157] (affirmed by the House of Lords, also in the *Federal Commerce* case), was later adopted by Lord Woolf in the Privy Council in the *Vaswani v Italian Motors (Sales & Services) Ltd*.[158] In the *Vaswani* case, Lord Woolf, incorporating Lord Denning's remarks in the 1976 case, said:

6-091

> "Nor is conduct, if it is repudiatory, excused because it occurs in consequence of legal advice, as may be the case with the sellers' actions in this case. The position is correctly set out by Lord Denning MR in the *Federal Commerce case* (1978, CA),[159] in a passage of his judgment cited by Lord Scarman in *Woodar Investment Development Ltd v Wimpey Construction UK Ltd* (1980) HL.[160] [Lord Denning's statement] is in these terms: 'I have yet to learn that a party who breaks a contract can excuse himself by saying that he did it on the advice of his lawyers: or that he was under an honest misapprehension ... I would go by the principle ... that if the party's conduct—objectively considered in its impact on the other party—is such as to evince an intention no longer to be bound by his contractual obligations, then it is open to the other party to accept his repudiation and treat the contract as discharged from that time onwards'."

Possibility of retreat from disputed point: contract will then survive However, no renunciation occurs if the parties have understood that they will test the validity of party X's claim to have a right to cancel (etc) and that, if X's position proves to be invalid, the contract will live on. Here Y knows that X will remain faithful to the continuing contract if the disputed point goes against X. This qualification upon *Federal Commerce & Navigation Co Ltd v Molena Alpha Inc ("The Nanfri")* (see para.6-063 ff on this case) was added by the House of Lords in the *Woodar Investment Development Ltd v Wimpey Construction UK Ltd*,[161] where a bare majority

6-092

---

[156] This point was noted in *Dalkia Utilities Services Plc v Celtech International Ltd* [2006] EWHC 63 (Comm); [2006] 1 Lloyd's Rep. 599 at [148] per Christopher Clarke J; *Gulf Agri Trade FZCO v Aston Agro Industrial AG* [2008] EWHC 1252 (Comm); [2009] 1 All E.R. (Comm) 991 at [43] per Aikens J.

[157] *Federal Commerce & Navigation Co Ltd v Molena Alpha Inc ("The Nanfri")* [1978] Q.B. 927 CA at 979.

[158] [1996] 1 W.L.R. 270 PC at 277 (Lord Woolf).

[159] *Federal Commerce & Navigation Co Ltd v Molena Alpha Inc ("The Nanfri")* [1978] Q.B. 927 CA at 979.

[160] [1980] 1 W.L.R. 277 HL at 298.

[161] [1980] 1 W.L.R. 277 HL; for a similar case, *Alfred C Toepfer v Peter Cremer GmbH & Co* [1975] 2 Lloyd's Rep. 118 CA per Lord Denning MR at 125 left-hand column, and per Scarman LJ at 129 left-hand column; summarised by Aikens J in *Gulf Agri Trade FZCO v Aston Agro Industrial AG* [2008] EWHC 1252 (Comm); [2009] 1 All E.R. (Comm) 991; [2008] 2 Lloyd's Rep. 376 at [41].

(Lords Wilberforce, Keith and Scarman; dissenting, Lords Salmon and Russell) held that no renunciation had occurred on these facts.[162]

6-093   In the *Woodar* case[163] the claimant had agreed to sell land to the defendant, completion to occur after gaining planning permission. The defendant purchaser resiled from the deal, invoking in good faith, but mistakenly, a purported contractual right, contained in an obscure clause, to withdraw. A majority of the House of Lords (Lords Wilberforce, Keith and Scarman; dissenting, Lords Salmon and Russell) held that no renunciation had occurred on these facts, and that the defendant had not absolutely refused to perform. The majority considered that the parties understood that the defendant had not adopted a "take-it-leave-it stand": and the point had arisen in advance of the crucial date for completion. There was, it appears, time to have sorted out this problem. In this light, the *Woodar* case is an exception to the general proposition. The law should not be inverted so as to render a good faith infringement of a contract a non-breach.[164]

6-094   Commercial Court decisions of 2006[165] and 2008[166] have returned to the *Woodar* case, explaining the central findings of fact. Liu, in his book on *Anticipatory Breach*, also comments[167] that the majority's decision in the *Woodar* case, just summarised, rested on three main grounds: (i) "the purchasers acted bona fide upon their solicitors' advice"; (ii) the purchasers "did not intimate an intention to "abandon" or "repudiate" the contract": and (iii) the purchasers' "intention was qualified" by or " conditional" upon the outcome of ongoing court proceedings." Furthermore, Liu notes "almost unanimous criticism from commentators".[168] There is something troubling and odd about the *Woodar* decision. It is submitted that although the *Woodar* case does present a satisfactory category of mistaken but good faith default, which does not constitute renunciation or repudiation, that analysis subsists only

---

[162] Three members of the House of Lords in *Woodar Investment Development Ltd v Wimpey Construction UK Ltd* [1980] 1 W.L.R. 277 HL, Lords Wilberforce, Russell, and Scarman, had sat in the final appeal in *Federal Commerce & Navigation Co Ltd v Molena Alpha Inc ("The Nanfri")* [1979] A.C. 757 HL (see para.6-063 on this case).

[163] *Woodar Investment Development Ltd v Wimpey Construction UK Ltd* [1980] 1 W.L.R. 277 HL.

[164] cf. for such an inversion, *Golstein v Bishop* [2013] EWHC 881 (Ch); [2014] Ch. 131 (Nugee QC) at [161], treating the *Woodar* case as dominant and not citing the *Federal Commerce case* [1979] A.C. 757 HL. Similarly, *Scottish Power UK Plc v BP Exploration Operating Co Ltd* [2015] EWHC 2658 (Comm); [2016] 1 All E.R. (Comm) 536 at [55], [68], [79]–[81], [120] (Leggatt J); decision affirmed [2016] EWCA Civ 1043.

[165] *Dalkia Utilities Services Plc v Celtech International Ltd* [2006] EWHC 63 (Comm); [2006] 1 Lloyd's Rep. 599 at [145] per Christopher Clarke J.

[166] *Gulf Agri Trade FZCO v Aston Agro Industrial AG* [2008] EWHC 1252 (Comm); [2009] 1 All E.R. (Comm) 991 at [39] and [40], where Aikens J (as he then was) said that the three features of the *Woodar* case emphasised by Lord Wilberforce, in the majority in that case, were: "First, before Wimpey sent Woodar the notice there had been a meeting at which a representative of Woodar stated that if Wimpey attempted to [terminate the contract in reliance on their alleged contractual right to do so], Woodar would take Wimpey to court and the judge would have to decide whether the contract could be rescinded. Secondly ... Woodar's representative accepted that the notice would not be regarded as a hostile act. Thirdly, after the proceedings had been started by Woodar, [Woodar informed Wimpey], first, that Woodar must await the decision of the court on the issue of the validity of the notice and, secondly, that [Woodar] assumed that Wimpey would do so also. On the basis of those facts, Lord Wilberforce concluded that Wimpey had not manifested an intention to abandon or refuse further performance of the contract or to repudiate it".

[167] Q. Liu, *Anticipatory Breach* (Oxford: Hart Publishing, 2010), p.57.

[168] Q. Liu, *Anticipatory Breach* (Oxford: Hart Publishing, 2010), p.57, fn.250, citing A. Nicol and R. Rawlings, "Changing Attitudes to Anticipatory Breach and Third Party Beneficiaries" (1980) 43 M.L.R. 696; "Woodar v Wimpey" (case note) (1980) 96 L.Q.R. 321; J.W. Carter, "Regrettable Developments in the Law of Contract" [1980] C.L.J. 256.

as a matter of principle. With great respect, it seems probable that the decision was wrong on the facts. A majority of the House of Lords (Lords Wilberforce, Keith and Scarman; dissenting, Lords Salmon and Russell) held that no renunciation had occurred when one party decided to stall by raising a dubious point of construction of the contract which that party alleged have given him the right to withdraw. The decision is borderline. The majority approach in the House of Lords, in favour of the developer, Wimpey, seems uncommercially benevolent. The blunt fact was that the developer was keen to pull out of the contract and, to that end, seized on a bad point in the contractual wording. The point was tested before the High Court, which confirmed that the point taken was indeed a bad one. Three members of the House of Lords thought that this savoured of an honest wish to have an arguable point tested by a neutral adjudicator, and that the developer's conduct did not constitute implied renunciation or a repudiatory breach.[169] By contrast, the two dissentients (Lords Salmon and Russell) considered that the developer had been snatching at straws and had all along manifested a renunciatory stance. The decision is (manifestly) borderline. It would appear that the dissentients were (for good reason) not convinced that Wimpey had engaged in anything other than a disingenuous and desperate subterfuge to buy time and to escape a contract which they had come to regret (this characterisation of the facts, held by the dissentients in the House of Lords, had been the view adopted within the two lower courts, by Fox J in the High Court, and by Lawton and Reginald Goff LJJ, in the Court of Appeal, where Buckley LJ had dissented). It would appear that the majority of the House of Lords, therefore, disturbed a decision that had been rooted in a perception of the underlying facts, turning on an issue of good faith, motive, veracity. Such a reversal plainly runs counter to the doctrine of "concurrent findings of fact". This is an appellate practice which had been the basis for the dissents by Lords Wilberforce and Simon in *Barton v Armstrong*.[170] In that difficult case Lords Wilberforce and Simon had taken the view that the facts could not be revised on a second appeal: and that the findings of fact (at first instance and on appeal in New South Wales) demonstrated ("concurrent" findings at first instance and on first appeal) that in fact the threats

---

[169] As noted in *Flanagan v Liontrust Investment Partners LLP* [2015] EWHC 2171 (Ch); [2015] Bus. L.R. 1172 at [193]–[195] per Henderson J, the majority in *Woodar Investment Development Ltd v Wimpey Construction UK Ltd* [1980] 1 W.L.R. 277 HL took the view that Wimpey had not been dishonest in presenting their disputed point: Lord Wilberforce at 280G: "unless the invocation of that provision were totally abusive, or lacking in good faith, (neither of which is contended for), the fact that it has proved to be wrong in law cannot turn it into a repudiation"; and at 283D: "it would be a regrettable development of the law of contract to hold that a party who bona fide relies upon an express stipulation in a contract in order to rescind or terminate a contract should, by that fact alone, be treated as having repudiated his contractual obligations if he turns out to be mistaken as to his rights. Repudiation is a drastic conclusion which should only be held to arise in clear cases of a refusal, in a matter going to the root of the contract, to perform contractual obligations. To uphold the respondents' contentions in this case would represent an undesirable extension of the doctrine"; Lord Keith of Kinkel at 297B: "Where one party, honestly but erroneously, intimates to the other reliance upon a term of the contract which, if properly applicable, would entitle him lawfully to rescind the contract, in circumstances which do not and are not reasonably understood to infer that he will refuse to perform his obligations even if it should be established that he is not so entitled, legal proceedings to decide that issue being in contemplation, I do not consider it in accordance with ordinary concepts of justice that the other party should be allowed to treat such conduct as a repudiation"; and Lord Scarman, who "emphasised" (at 299E–H) the "honest belief" of Wimpey that the contract entitled it to serve the notice.

[170] [1976] A.C. 104 PC at 121–126 (decided in 1973).

had indeed been water off a duck's back and (ultimately, at the critical stage) had had no influence at all on the decision to contract.

6-095   **Harmonising Federal Commerce & Navigation Co Ltd v Molena Alpha Inc ("The Nanfri") and Woodar v Wimpey**   The task of reconciling the House of Lords decisions in *Federal Commerce & Navigation Co Ltd v Molena Alpha Inc ("The Nanfri")*[171] and *Woodar Investment Development Ltd v Wimpey Construction UK Ltd*[172] baffled some commentators. But more recent case law has declared that these House of Lords decisions can be harmonised.[173]

6-096   Thus, the Privy Council in the *Vaswani* case emphasised that the court will consider whether the addressee's reasonable interpretation of the other's words or conduct was that the contract was being abandoned forthwith and without more and was no longer open for performance.[174] The Privy Council proposed this test:[175]

> "if the [guilty party's] conduct … went beyond the assertion of a genuinely held view of the effect of the contract, the conduct could amount to a repudiation. This is the position if *the conduct is inconsistent with the continuance of the contract.* Then the bona fide motives of the party responsible do not prevent the conduct being repudiatory."

Another important statement is Lord Wright's comment in *Ross T Smyth and Co Ltd v TD Bailey, and Son and Co*:[176] a mere honest misapprehension, especially if open to correction, will not justify a charge of repudiation." That remark was

---

[171]   [1979] A.C. 757 HL.

[172]   [1980] 1 W.L.R. 277 HL; for a similar case, *Alfred C Toepfer v Peter Cremer GmbH & Co* [1975] 2 Lloyd's Rep. 118 CA per Lord Denning MR at 125 left-hand column, and per Scarman LJ at 129 left-hand column; summarised by Aikens J in *Gulf Agri Trade FZCO v Aston Agro Industrial AG* [2008] EWHC 1252 (Comm); [2009] 1 All E.R. (Comm) 991; [2008] 2 Lloyd's Rep. 376 at [41]. A renunciation is not found where there was opportunity for clarification and/or mistake, *Starlight Enterprises Ltd v Lapco Enterprises Ltd* [1979] 2 N.Z.L.R. 744 NZCA, especially Richardson J at 747–748; applied in *Oxborough v North Harbour Builders Ltd* [2002] 1 N.Z.L.R. 145 NZCA at [13], citing the *Woodar* case (1980 HL) (for a similar New Zealand decision, *The Edge Buying Group (Queenstown 2010) v Coca-Cola Amatil Ltd NZCA 145/02* (2002), noted M. Chetwin, "The Edge Buying Group (Queenstown 2000) Ltd v Coca-Cola Amatil (NZ) Ltd" (2003) N.Z.L.J. 117). And the High Court of Australia in *DTR Nominees Pty Ltd v Mona Homes Pty Ltd* (1978) 138 C.L.R. 423 at 432 (Stephen, Mason, and Jacobs JJ, Aickin J agreeing, Murphy J alone dissenting) held that a bona fide dispute as to the construction of a land transaction did not justify inferring that the mistaken party had evinced an intention not to perform the contract according to its terms or to repudiate it.

[173]   *Dalkia Utilities Services Plc v Celtech International Ltd* [2006] EWHC 63 (Comm); [2006] 1 Lloyd's Rep. 599 and *Gulf Agri Trade FZCO v Aston Agro Industrial AG* [2008] EWHC 1252 (Comm); [2009] 1 All E.R. (Comm) 991. See remarks at H. Beale (ed), *Chitty on Contracts*, 34th edn (London: Sweet & Maxwell, 2021), paras 27-050 and 24-051, noting also *Flanagan v Liontrust Investment Partners LLP* [2015] EWHC 2171 (Ch) (per Henderson J at [185]–[198], finding that an LLP had manifestly acted inconsistently with its obligations and this facts was registered by the innocent partner; although later in his judgment at [243], Henderson J decided that the doctrine of repudiation/renunciation does not apply to LLP agreements where there are more than two parties; latter aspect considered in *Roberts v Wilsons Solicitors LLP* [2016] I.C.R. 659; [2016] I.R.L.R. 586 EAT and *H TV Ltd (formerly Can Associates TV Ltd) v ITV2 Ltd* [2015] EWHC 2840 (Comm) at [269]–[275] per Flaux J (no objective intention to renounce contract and instead relevant party remaining reading, willing, and able to perform obligations).

[174]   [1996] 1 W.L.R. 270 at 276–277 PC (Lord Woolf); noted E. Peel, "Misinterpretation of Contractual Rights and Repudiation" [1996] L.M.C.L.Q. 309.

[175]   [1996] 1 W.L.R. 270 PC at 276–277 (counsel for the losing buyer was a future Attorney-General, Peter Goldsmith QC; and counsel for the seller was a future Supreme Court justice, Jonathan Sumption QC).

[176]   (1940) 67 Ll. L. Rep. 147 at 107.

[124]

adopted by Lord Keith in *Woodar Investment Development Ltd v Wimpey Construction UK Ltd*.[177]

In the *Vaswani* case (1996),[178] the sellers, Hong Kong luxury car-dealers, had **6-097** purported to increase the price payable for purchase of a Ferrari Testarossa sports car (from £179,500 to £218,800). In fact they had no contractual right to do this. But the Privy Council held that this did not amount to renunciation. The new figure had not been presented on a "take it or leave it" basis. The buyer could, and indeed should, have challenged the increase. And so the buyer had been snatching at an "exit sign". It did not exist. The buyer had wrongly terminated on this basis and run away from the deal. This meant that the seller was entitled to retain the deposit (£44,875) and to obtain compensation for any additional loss suffered.

Similarly, Christopher Clarke J said in *Dalkia Utilities Services Plc v Celtech* **6-098** *International Ltd*:[179]

"It seems to me that the *Woodar* case is distinguishable [from '*The Nanfri*']. On the facts of the [*Woodar* case] the majority felt able to conclude that, despite the unqualified terms of the notice, the circumstances in which it was given did not manifest an intention to refuse further performance. The time for performance had not arisen, Woodar needed to serve a notice in order to reserve its position, and the discussions between the parties had proceeded on the basis that the service of a notice was not to be regarded as a hostile act, and that the entitlement or otherwise of Woodar to serve the notice would be determined by the court, to which Woodar would apply, by whose decision both parties would abide."

The Court of Appeal in *Eminence Property Developments Ltd v Heaney*[180] also **6-099** considered that "*The Nanfri*" and *Woodar* cases are reconcilable. The Court of Appeal in this 2010 decision noted that the case law in this field is "highly fact sensitive".

In *Eminence Property Developments Ltd v Heaney*[181] the purchaser mistakenly **6-100** gave premature notice to terminate a contract for the purchase of flats. The Court of Appeal held that the innocent party had concocted in effect a storm in a tea-cup because it was obvious (i) that the purchaser had made a clerical error; (ii) and that it was not in the purchaser's commercial economic interest to pull out; and (iii) and if alerted to this error, the purchaser would have readily put right the error and stayed faithful to the contract.

In this case Etherton LJ,[182] after repeating the bald test for renunciation by **6-101**

---

177 [1980] 1 W.L.R. 277 at 295 HL.
178 [1996] 1 W.L.R. 270 PC at 276–277 (Lord Woolf); noted E. Peel, "Misinterpretation of Contractual Rights and Repudiation" [1996] L.M.C.L.Q. 309.
179 [2006] EWHC 63 (Comm); [2006] 1 Lloyd's Rep. 599 at [149]; similarly, Aikens J (as he then was) in *Gulf Agri Trade FZCO v Aston Agro Industrial AG* [2008] EWHC 1252 (Comm); [2009] 1 All E.R. (Comm) 991 said: "Ultimately, both cases hold that it is necessary to ask the question: what, objectively, is the intention of the party who has done something which is said to be a repudiation of the contract? Is it (objectively) that party's intention to abandon or repudiate the contract or not? This is a question of fact, to be determined by the fact finding tribunal from all the relevant evidence available".
180 [2010] EWCA Civ 1168; [2011] 2 All E.R. (Comm) 223.
181 [2010] EWCA Civ 1168; [2011] 2 All E.R. (Comm) 223 at [61]–[64], having considered (among other decisions) *Federal Commerce & Navigation Co Ltd v Molena Alpha Inc ("The Nanfri")* [1979] A.C. 757 HL; *Woodar v Wimpey* [1980] 1 W.L.R. 277 HL; *Vaswani v Italian Motors (Sales and Services) Ltd* [1996] 1 W.L.R. 270 PC at 277; and *Dalkia Utilities Services Plc v Celtech International Ltd* [2006] EWHC 63 (Comm); [2006] 1 Lloyd's Rep. 599 (Christopher Clarke J).
182 [2010] EWCA Civ 1168; [2011] 2 All E.R. (Comm) 223 at [61]–[64], having considered (among

conduct (which he called "repudiatory conduct"),[183] noted the "fact-sensitive" nature of the inquiry in this area:

"Whether or not there has been a repudiatory breach is highly fact sensitive. That is why comparison with other cases is of limited value ... although the test is simply stated, its application...case may not always be easy to apply, as is well illustrated by the division of view ... in the *Woodar* case itself."

6-102   The Court of Appeal has followed the *Eminence* decision in both *Oates v Hooper*[184] and *Samarenko v Dawn Hill House Ltd*.[185] In the *Samarenko* case, Lewison LJ summarised the *Eminence* case as follows:[186]

"The facts of the [*Eminence*] case are instructive. Sellers of property served notice to complete purportedly in accordance with the contract. In fact they miscalculated the length of notice required by the contract; and that mistake was obvious on the face of the notice. Not only was the mistake obvious but the buyer's solicitors realised that the mistake had been made. The sellers purported to terminate the contract on the date on which the notice to complete was expressed to expire; but it was in fact a few days premature. They did so because they made the same mistake again, which according to the judge at first instance was 'screamingly obvious'. A reasonable person in the position of the buyer would have realised that the mistake had been made. It was in those circumstances that this court held that purported reliance on the terms of the contract itself did not amount to a repudiation of the self-same contract."

6-103   **Summary of renunciation based on a mistaken assertion of contractual rights**   The Privy Council in *Vaswani v Italian Motors (Sales & Services) Ltd*[187] and the Court of Appeal in *Eminence Property Developments Ltd v Heaney*[188] have implicitly adopted considerations of fair dealing. A similar tendency is discernible in New Zealand[189] and Australian cases.[190] In both the *Vaswani* and *Eminence Property Developments* cases, the party who made (albeit in good faith) contractu-

---

other decisions): *Federal Commerce & Navigation Co Ltd v Molena Alpha Inc ("The Nanfri")* [1979] A.C. 757 HL; *Woodar Investment Development Ltd v Wimpey Construction UK Ltd* [1980] 1 W.L.R. 277 HL; *Vaswani v Italian Motors (Sales and Services) Ltd* [1996] 1 W.L.R. 270 PC; and *Dalkia Utilities Services Plc v Celtech International Ltd* [2006] EWHC 63 (Comm); [2006] 1 Lloyd's Rep. 599 (Christopher Clarke J).

183   [2010] EWCA Civ 1168; [2011] 2 All E.R. (Comm) 223 at [64], "the legal test is simply stated ... whether, looking at all the circumstances objectively, that is from the perspective of a reasonable person in the position of the innocent party, the contract breaker has clearly shown an intention to abandon and altogether refuse to perform the contact".

184   [2010] EWCA Civ 1346; [2010] 48 E.G. 85 (C.S.).

185   [2011] EWCA Civ 1445; [2013] Ch. 36.

186   [2011] EWCA Civ 1445; [2013] Ch. 36 at [44]; see also at [43] his citation of portions of Etherton LJ's judgment in *Eminence Property Developments Ltd v Heaney* [2010] EWCA Civ 1168; [2011] 2 All E.R. (Comm) 223.

187   [1996] 1 W.L.R. 270 PC.

188   [2010] EWCA Civ 1168; [2011] 2 All E.R. (Comm) 223.

189   A renunciation was not found where there was opportunity for clarification and/or mistake, *Starlight Enterprises Ltd v Lapco Enterprises Ltd* [1979] 2 N.Z.L.R. 744, NZCA, especially Richardson J at 747–748; applied in *Oxborough v North Harbour Builders Ltd* [2002] 1 N.Z.L.R. 145, NZCA at [13], citing *Woodar Investment Development Ltd v Wimpey Construction UK Ltd* [1980] 1 W.L.R. 277, HL; for a similar New Zealand decision, *The Edge Buying Group (Queenstown 2010) v Coca-Cola Amatil Ltd N.Z.C.A. 145/02* (2002), noted M. Chetwin, "The Edge Buying Group (Queenstown 2000) Ltd v Coca-Cola Amatil (NZ) Ltd" (2003) N.Z.L.J. 117.

190   *DTR Nominees Pty Ltd v Mona Homes Pty Ltd* (1978) 138 C.L.R. 423 at 432 H.Ct. Aust. (where Stephen, Mason, and Jacobs JJ, Aickin J agreeing, Murphy J alone dissenting, said that a bona fide

ally invalid pronouncements had not conveyed the message that the contract was being immediately abandoned.

These English (and Commonwealth) cases show that an innocent party cannot snatch at the opportunity to terminate the contract by reason of the other's breach where this would be unacceptably premature. Such a response will be too hasty if:[191] **6-104**

(i) *obviously unintended deviation from the contractual terms:* the opponent was clearly not committing himself to an irrevocable position but was instead labouring under a misapprehension, and it would have been easy for the innocent party to have dispelled that confusion, whereupon the guilty party would have been certain, or at least very likely, to have fallen into strict compliance with the contract (as in *Eminence Property Developments Ltd v Heaney*);[192]

(ii) *duty to invite clarification whether position adopted is "last word":* it would have been possible and reasonable to ask the opponent to have clarified whether he was taking a "stand" (no such clarification had been sought by the buyer in *Vaswani v Italian Motors (Sales & Services) Ltd*);[193] or

(iii) *opportunity for external verification of genuinely disputed issue:* a disputable point had been identified by the parties (it having been raised by one party in a genuine fashion, that is, not without an honest belief that the point might have substance or merit, rather than in bad faith as a pure stalling technique or as the means of exiting from the deal) and the parties realised that there was time to refer that point to a neutral third party for clarification (as in *Woodar Investment Development Ltd v Wimpey Construction UK Ltd*).[194] However, sometimes time will not be on the side of the parties so that situation (iii) will not be available. If this is the case, the innocent party can reasonably say: "I am not sure why you take that position, because that is not my reading of our arrangements; you have failed to convince me that you are in fact justified; we have no time to play with; and so I consider myself entitled to call off this transaction, holding you liable for this termination."

---

dispute as to the construction of a land transaction did not justify inferring that the mistaken party had evinced an intention not to perform the contract according to its terms or to repudiate it).

[191] For a careful survey of the *Woodar* and *Eminence Property* cases, see *Flanagan v Liontrust Investment Partners LLP* [2015] EWHC 2171 (Ch); [2015] Bus. L.R. 1172 at [185]–[195] per Henderson J.

[192] [2010] EWCA Civ 1168; [2011] 2 All E.R. (Comm) 223.

[193] [1996] 1 W.L.R. 270 PC.

[194] [1980] 1 W.L.R. 277 HL; for a similar case, *Alfred C Toepfer v Peter Cremer GmbH & Co* [1975] 2 Lloyd's Rep. 118 CA, per Lord Denning MR at 125 left-hand column, and per Scarman LJ at 129 left-hand column; summarised by Aikens J in *Gulf Agri Trade FZCO v Aston Agro Industrial AG* [2008] EWHC 1252 (Comm); [2009] 1 All E.R. (Comm) 991 at [41].

CHAPTER 7

ANTICIPATORY BREACH

I.   THE TWO CATEGORIES OF ANTICIPATORY BREACH[1]

Summary   Such a breach can take one of two forms:[2] (i) advance renunciation (for   **7-001**
example, an airline notifies passengers that it has cancelled a flight several weeks
in advance), or (ii) prevention of future performance, again when the date for
performance has not arrived (for example, instead of transferring at a future date,
as agreed, Blackacre, the promisor sells that land to a third party, thereby destroying the chance of transferring it to the promisee).[3]

In *Berkeley Community Villages Ltd v Pullen* (2007) Morgan J gave this suc-   **7-002**
cinct exegesis of these categories (numbered here for convenience):[4]

> (1) "The legal principles dealing with the concept of an anticipatory breach are clear and
> established. If, before the time arrives by which a party is bound to perform a contract,
> that party expresses an intention to break the contract, then he commits an anticipatory
> breach. (2) The doctrine of anticipatory breach is not confined to declarations of intended
> breach but also applies where the contracting party disables himself from performing an
> obligation which falls to be performed at a future date. (3) The doctrine of anticipatory
> breach applies even where the obligation to be performed at a future date is a contingent
> obligation: see *Frost v Knight* (1872) L.R. 7 Ex 111 and *Synge v Synge* [1894] 1 Q.B.
> 466."

---

[1]   Q. Liu, *Anticipatory Breach* (Oxford: Hart Publishing, 2011), especially Chs 2–4; M. Mustill,
      "Anticipatory Breach: The Common Law at Work", Butterworths Lectures 1989–90 (London: But-
      terworths, 1990); see also F. Dawson, "Metaphors and Anticipatory Breach of Contract" [1981]
      C.L.J. 83; G.H. Jones (with P. Schlechtriem), "Breach of Contract" in *International Encyclopaedia
      of Comparative Law*, Vol.VII (Contracts in General), (Tübingen: J.C.B. Mohr (Paul Siebeck), 1999),
      15-151 ff; J.C. Smith in E. Lomnicka and C.J.G. Morse (eds), *Contemporary Issues in Commercial
      Law: Essays in Honour of A.G. Guest* (London: Sweet & Maxwell, 1997), 175; S. Stoljar, "Some
      Problems of Anticipatory Breach" (1974) 9 Melbourne Univ. L. Rev. 355; E. Tabachnik, "Anticipa-
      tory Breach of Contract" [1972] C.L.P. 149; for a judicial survey of theories and literature, A. Phang
      Boon Leong JA in "The SPX Mumbai" [2015] SGCA 35; [2015] 5 S.L.R. 1; [2016] 1 Lloyd's Rep.
      157 at [42] ff Singapore CA; on the 19th century history of this topic, M. Lobban, in W. Cornish,
      The Oxford History of the Laws of England Vol.XII (1820–1914: Private Law) (Oxford: Oxford
      University Press, 2010), p.494 ff.
[2]   e.g. *Berkeley Community Villages Ltd v Pullen* [2007] EWHC 1330 (Ch); [2007] 3 E.G.L.R. 101;
      [2007] 24 E.G. 169 (C.S.); [2007] N.P.C. 71 at [79] per Morgan J (for quotations see next paragraph
      of this text).
[3]   Essentially the facts of *Lovelock v Franklyn* (1846) 8 Q.B. 871; 115 E.R. 916 (agreement to transfer
      land to claimant; defendant selling land to third party before due date; incapacitation; actionable
      breach); *Synge v Synge* [1894] 1 Q.B. 466 CA; *Omnium v Sutherland* [1919] 1 K.B. 618 CA;
      Berkeley Community Villages Ltd v Pullen [2007] EWHC 1330 (Ch); [2007] 3 E.G.L.R. 101; [2007]
      24 E.G. 169 (C.S.); [2007] N.P.C. 71; *Burntcopper Ltd v ITCA* [2014] EWHC 148 (Comm); [2014]
      2 All E.R. (Comm) 1055 at [29]–[34] per HH Judge Mackie QC.
[4]   [2007] EWHC 1330 (Ch); [2007] N.P.C. 71 at [79] per Morgan J.

7-003   Devlin J's judgment in *Universal Cargo Carriers Corp v Citati (No.1)* (1957)[5] provides another classic discussion of these two limbs. He began by quoting Lord Porter in the House of Lords in *Heyman v Darwins Ltd* (1942):[6]

> "The three sets of circumstances giving rise to a discharge contract [for breach] are tabulated by *Anson's Law of Contract* [in the 1937 edition][7] as: (1) renunciation by a party of his liabilities ... (2) impossibility created by his own act; (3) total or partial failure of performance."

It will be seen that (1) (nearly always) and (2) (nearly always) are forms of anticipatory breach, because they involve matters antedating the time for performance by the promisor. As Devlin J put the matter:[8]

> "The third of these is the ordinary case of actual breach, and the first two state the two modes of anticipatory breach [viz renunciation prior to the date of performance and anticipatory breach by self-disablement]. In order that the arguments which I have heard from either side can be rightly considered, it is necessary that I should develop rather more fully what is meant by each of these two modes."

7-004   Devlin J then developed the notion of anticipatory breach by renunciation:[9]

> "Since a man must be both ready and willing to perform, a profession by words or conduct of inability is by itself enough to constitute renunciation. But unwillingness and inability are often difficult to disentangle, and it is rarely necessary to make the attempt. Inability often lies at the root of unwillingness to perform. Willingness in this context does not mean cheerfulness; it means simply an intent to perform. To say: 'I would like to but I cannot' negatives intent just as much as 'I will not.' ... If a man says 'I cannot perform,' he renounces his contract by that statement, and the cause of the inability is immaterial."

7-005   Devlin J noted that anticipatory breach is consequent on the injured party's "anticipation" of an "inevitable" breach:[10]

> "The two forms of anticipatory breach have a common characteristic that is essential to the concept, namely, that the injured party is allowed to anticipate an inevitable breach. If a man renounces his right to perform and is held to his renunciation, the breach will be legally inevitable; if a man puts it out of his power to perform, the breach will be inevitable in fact - or practically inevitable, for the law never requires absolute certainty and does not take account of bare possibilities. So anticipatory breach means simply that a party is in breach from the moment that his actual breach becomes inevitable."

7-006   Explaining the nature of anticipated default founded upon inevitable inability to perform, Devlin J said:[11]

> "Since the reason for the rule is that a party is allowed to anticipate an inevitable event

---

5   [1957] 2 Q.B. 401 at 436–8. (Devlin J's exposition of governing principles of breach not disturbed on appeal in either [1957] 1 W.L.R. 979 CA or [1958] 2 Q.B. 254 CA). M. Mustill, "Anticipatory Breach: The Common Law at Work", Butterworths Lectures 1989–90 (London: Butterworths, 1990), p.69 ff; see also M. Mustill, "The Golden Victory—Some Reflections" (2008) 124 L.Q.R. 569–85.

6   [1942] A.C. 356 at 397 HL.

7   This passage is preserved in J. Beatson, A. Burrows, and J. Cartwright, *Anson's Law of Contract*, 31st edn (Oxford: Oxford University Press, 2020), 510 fn.47.

8   [1957] 2 Q.B. 401 at 436.

9   [1957] 2 Q.B. 401 at 437–8.

10   [1957] 2 Q.B. 401 at 438.

11   [1957] 2 Q.B. 401 at 438.

and is not obliged to wait till it happens, it must follow that the breach which he anticipates is of just the same character as the breach which would actually have occurred if he had waited ... If this is right, it seems to me to dispose in principle of [counsel's] submission that the disablement must be deliberate. If when the day comes for performance a party cannot perform, he is in breach, quite irrespective of how he became disabled. The inability which justifies the assumption of an anticipatory breach cannot be of any different character. Anticipatory breach was not devised as a whip to be used for the chastisement of deliberate contract-breakers, but from which the shiftless, the dilatory, or the unfortunate are to be spared. It is not confined to any particular class of breach, deliberate or blameworthy or otherwise; it covers all breaches that are bound to happen."

Faced by an advance renunciation or situation of inevitable default by the other side, it is clearly convenient for the promisee to be able to respond immediately by terminating the contract (releasing himself from unperformed primary obligations)[12] and claiming compensation. This will prevent waste. It will also spare the promisee from suffering a sterile and anxious period during which he would otherwise be forced to wait and see whether the other party might change his mind and recommit to performing after all.[13] As Lord Campbell CJ said in *Hochster v De La Tour* (1853):[14]   **7-007**

"Instead of remaining idle and laying out money in preparations which must be useless, [the claimant] is at liberty to seek service under another employer, which would go in mitigation of the damages to which he would otherwise be entitled for a breach of the contract."

II.   ANTICIPATORY BREACH BY RENUNCIATION

Before the date for performance, a party might indicate, whether explicitly or implicitly, that he does not intend to perform. The other party then generally has a choice (but for a qualification, see para.7-082 ff on the *White & Carter*[15] line of cases) whether to accept this, and terminate the contract, or to try and keep the contract alive. As mentioned, granting the promisee the option of terminating the contract and suing for compensation is efficient and fair.[16]   **7-008**

Maurice Kay LJ in *Tullett Prebon Plc v BGC Brokers LP* (2011)[17] suggested that "perhaps the clearest modern formulation [of anticipatory breach by renunciation] is that of Buckley LJ in *Gunton v Richmond BC* (1981)" and he then quoted the following passage from Buckley LJ's judgment in the *Gunton* case (1981):[18]   **7-009**

"The basis of the doctrine [of anticipatory breach] is that where a party to a contract before the date for performance has arrived evinces an intention not to perform his part of the contract, he has committed no breach until the date for performance arrives. Nevertheless the innocent party will be relieved of his obligations under the contract, if he so

---

[12] For a Singaporean case considering anticipatory breach where the innocent party has already performed his side of the bargain, *"The STX Mumbai"* [2015] SGCA 35; [2015] 5 S.L.R. 1; [2016] 1 Lloyd's Rep. 157 (noted Y. Goh and M. Yip, "Rationalising anticipatory breach in executed contracts" [2016] C.L.J. 18).

[13] e.g. Q. Liu, *Anticipatory Breach* (Oxford: Hart Publishing, 2010), pp.163–4.

[14] (1853) 2 E. & B. 678 at 690; 22 L.J. (QB) 455.

[15] [1962] A.C. 413 at 431 HL.

[16] e.g. Q. Liu, *Anticipatory Breach* (Oxford: Hart Publishing, 2010), pp.163–4 summarises the practical benefits of the anticipatory breach doctrine.

[17] [2011] EWCA Civ 131; [2011] I.R.L.R. 420 at [46] per Maurice Kay LJ.

[18] [1981] Ch. 448 CA at 467.

chooses, so as to render him free to arrange his affairs unhampered by the continued exist-ence of those obligations. It is for the innocent party to elect whether he wishes to be so relieved, which he does by accepting the repudiatory act of the guilty party as a repudia-tion of his, the guilty party's obligations under the contract. In those circumstances the innocent party may treat the guilty party as having committed an entire breach of the contract notwithstanding that the time for performance has not yet arrived."

7-010   Buckley LJ's lucid analysis in *Gunton v Richmond BC* (1981) continues:[19]

"Where the time for performance of part of the guilty party's obligations has arrived but some of those obligations remain executory, the position is the same as regards those obligations which remain executory as it is in respect of all the guilty party's obligations where none of them has yet become due for performance. If the guilty party has evinced an intention not to perform those obligations of his which remain executory, the in-nocent party may elect to treat himself as discharged from all obligations on his part to perform the contract any further. He does so by accepting the guilty party's repudiation of his outstanding obligations under the contract, in which case the innocent party may treat the guilty party as having committed an entire breach of all his outstanding obliga-tions under the contract notwithstanding that the time for performance of those obliga-tions, or some of them, may not yet have arrived."

7-011   Anticipatory breach by renunciation was recognised only in the mid-nineteenth century. There is a learned survey of this development in Lord Ackner's speech in *"The Simona"* (1989),[20] and another by an Australian judge in the *YP Barley* case (1927).[21] First, let us consider the seminal nineteenth century cases, *Hochster v De La Tour* (1853)[22] and *Frost v Knight* (1872).[23]

7-012   In *Hochster v De La Tour* (1853), the defendant engaged the claimant to act as courier on a projected foreign tour, starting on 1 June.[24] On 11 May, just over two weeks before the tour was to begin, the defendant renounced the engagement. It was held that the innocent party had a choice whether to accept the repudiation, or to keep the contract alive pending the date for due performance. There would be no "breach" if the innocent party decided not to accept the repudiation. In the present case, the claimant was entitled to seek damages immediately, once he had ac-cepted this renunciation. It was not necessary for him to wait to see whether the defendant might change his mind. This was advantageous on the facts because the claimant had decided, following the defendant's renunciation, to hire himself out straightaway to accompany a different client.

7-013   In *Frost v Knight* (1872),[25] the defendant had agreed to marry the claimant, once

19 [1981] Ch. 448 CA at 467–468.
20 *Fermometal SARL v Mediterranean Shipping Co SA ("The Simona")* [1989] A.C. 788 at 797–805 HL; Q. Liu,"Inferring Future Breach: Towards a Unifying Test of Anticipatory Breach of Contract" [2007] C.L.J. 573; *Berkeley Community Villages Ltd v Pullen* [2007] EWHC 1330 (Ch), Morgan J.
21 McArthur J in *YP Barley Producers Ltd v EVC Robertston Pty Ltd* [1927] V.L.R. 194 at 205–213.
22 (1853) 2 E. & B. 678; 22 L.J. (QB) 455.
23 (1872) L.R. 7 Ex. 111.
24 (1853) 2 E. & B. 678; 22 L.J. (QB) 455; P. Mitchell, in C. Mitchell and P. Mitchell (eds), *Landmark Cases in the Law of Contract* (Oxford: Hart Publishing, 2008), p.135; M. Mustill, "The Golden Vic-tory—Some Reflections" (2008) 124 L.Q.R. 569, 576–7; see also M. Mustill, "Anticipatory Breach: The Common Law at Work", *Butterworth Lectures 1989–90* (London: Butterworths, 1990).
25 (1872) L.R. 7 Ex. 111; M. Mustill, "The Golden Victory—Some Reflections" (2008) 124 L.Q.R. 569, 577, noting G. Frost, *Promises Broken: Courtship, Class and Gender in Victorian England* (Charlottesville: University of Virginia, 1995).

the defendant's father had died (engagement agreements are no longer actionable).[26] The defendant broke off the engagement before his father's death. Cockburn CJ said that this renunciation became a breach once the innocent party "treated the undertaking as broken". The guilty party's announcement only becomes wrongful if the other party decides that he will respond by calling off the contract. The innocent party can then demand compensation (an award of £200 was made). Cockburn CJ noted that the innocent party's power to terminate on these facts salvaged her from a very harsh situation:[27]

> "To hold that the aggrieved party must wait till the time fixed for marrying shall have arrived, or the event on which it is to depend shall have happened, would have the effect of aggravating the injury, by preventing the party from forming any other union, and by reason of advancing age rendering the probability of such a union constantly less."

Thus, the peculiarity of this form of default is that the guilty party's announce- **7-014** ment only becomes wrongful if the other party decides that he will respond by calling off the contract (but for the possibility, not yet clearly established, that there can be an actionable anticipatory breach even where the contract is not terminated, see para.7-076). The innocent party can then demand compensation. It should also be noted that the claimant's cause of action in *Frost v Knight* arose once she terminated the contract even though, at that point, it might be (i) that the defendant might have pre-deceased the father; (ii) that the defendant had not yet married a third party (although he had found one); and (iii) even if the defendant had married a third party, the defendant could still have satisfied his original promise if that spouse died, enabling the defendant to marry the claimant.

Similarly, in *Synge v Synge* (1894)[28] X and Y had entered into an ante-nuptial **7-015** agreement. X promised to create a life interest in land in favour of Y in X's will. During X's lifetime, X committed an anticipatory breach by selling the relevant land to Z. The Court of Appeal held that Y was entitled to compensation for the value of the lost life interest, although this would require proof of the chances of Y surviving her husband, and generally of her life expectancy (the duration of the life interest). Kay LJ, delivering the court's judgment, said:[29]

> "We have not before us the materials for assessing such damages. The amount must depend on the value of the possible life estate which [Y] Lady Synge would be entitled to if she survived her husband [X]. Their comparative ages would, of course, be a chief factor in such a calculation. There must be an inquiry as to the proper amount of damages."

The accurate soothsayer Renunciation does not occur if a party merely reports **7-016** inauspicious facts out of his control. Instead, as made clear by Popplewell J in *Geden Operations Ltd v Dry Bulk Handy Holdings Inc ("The Bulk Uruguay")* (2014),[30] anticipatory breach by renunciation occurs only if someone tells the other that he is unwilling to perform or implies that he is unwilling (the implication arising from conduct), that is, a party, by his conduct, has brought about a situation where it can be inferred (implicit renunciation) that he does not intend to proceed with the contract.

---

[26] Since 31 December 1970: Law Reform (Miscellaneous Provisions) Act 1970 s.1(1).
[27] (1872) L.R. 7 Ex. 111 at 116.
[28] [1894] 1 Q.B. 466 at 471 CA; on which, J.W. Carter, *Carter's Breach of Contract*, 2nd edn (Oxford: Hart Publishing, 2019), [7-81].
[29] [1894] 1 Q.B. 466 at 472.
[30] [2014] EWHC 885 (Comm) at [22] per Popplewell J.

7-017   And so the court will not find anticipatory breach if the cause of X's anxiety regarding Y's future performance is a contingency for which Y is not responsible: "Words or conduct which give rise to the uncertainty of future performance, the contingency of which rests upon conduct of a third party, will not necessarily evince an intention not to be bound."[31] In the *Geden* case (2014), party Y (the allegedly guilty party) had sub-chartered a ship to X. Y had chartered from Z, a third party. There was a chance that Z might in future decline to grant permission for the vessel to enter waters subject to the risk of piracy.[32] It was held (not disturbing an arbitral award) that Y was not in fact a guilty party and that he had not committed an anticipatory breach by renunciation on these facts. Admittedly, Y's future performance was overshadowed by the possibility of an adverse exercise by Z of his discretion, and naturally X, the sub-charterer, was anxious about this. But Y had not induced that anxiety, nor had Y assumed responsible for this contingency.

7-018   In the *Geden* case (2014), Popplewell J also cited the following passage, which contains a collection of situations where a person has committed an implicit renunciation by taking steps which prevent (or very likely will prevent) his eventual performance:[33]

> "In *Short v Stone* (1846) 8 Q.B. 358; 115 E.R. 911, it was held that if a man promises to marry a woman on a future day, and before that day marries another woman, he is instantly liable to an action; in *Ford v Tiley* (1827) 6 B. & C. 325; 108 E.R. 472, and *Lovelock v Franklyn* (1846) 8 Q.B. 871; 115 E.R. 916, it was held that if a man contracts to grant a lease on and from a future day for a certain term, and before that day he grants a lease to another for the same term, he may be immediately sued; in *Bowdell v Parsons* (1808), 10 East 359; 103 E.R. 811, it was held that if a man contracts to sell and deliver specific goods on a future day, and before that day he sells and delivers to another, he is immediately liable to the first purchaser. In each of the above cases it was not necessarily impossible for the defendant to perform the contract; for, prior to the day fixed, the first wife may have died, a surrender to the lease might have been obtained, and the defendant might have repurchased the goods; and in each case it seems better to say that the act of the defendant was tantamount to a refusal to perform his side of the contract which the plaintiff was entitled to accept as a breach in accordance with the principles above discussed; see *Hochster v De la Tour* (1853) 2 E. & B. 678, 688 at 688, per Lord Campbell; *Synge v Synge* [1894] 1 Q.B. 466 CA; *McIntyre v Belcher* (1853) 14 C.B. (N.S.) 654; *McIntyre v Belcher* (1853) 14 C. B. (N.S.) 654; 143 E. R. 602; *Ogdens Ltd v Nelson* [1905] A.C. 109."

7-019   **Anticipatory breach actionable if promisee elects to terminate the contract**   In the House of Lords in *Heyman v Darwins Ltd* (1942), Lord Wright said that "the breach is only complete and enforceable at the moment of rescission [viz termination for breach] so that breach and termination of the contract are simultaneous".[34] The same approach can be traced to Cockburn CJ's succinct statement in *Frost v Knight* (1872):[35] "... the promisee may ... treat the repudiation ... as a wrongful putting an end to the contract, and may at once bring his action as on a breach of it

---

[31]   [2014] EWHC 885 (Comm) at [21] per Popplewell J.

[32]   *Geden Operations Ltd v Dry Bulk Handy Holdings Inc ("The Bulk Uruguay")* [2014] EWHC 885 (Comm) at [20]–[22].

[33]   *Geden Operations Ltd v Dry Bulk Handy Holdings Inc ("The Bulk Uruguay")* [2014] EWHC 885 (Comm) at [19], citing *Smith's Leading Cases*, 13th edn (London: Sweet & Maxwell, 1929), pp.38–41; and this passage had been cited with approval in *Universal Cargo Carriers Corp v Citati (No.1)* [1957] 2 Q.B. 401 at 441 per Devlin J.

[34]   [1942] A.C. 350 at 382 HL.

[35]   (1872) L.R. 7 Ex. 111 at 112–113.

..." Cockburn CJ had earlier contrasted the situation where the "promise ... [treats] the notice of intention [viz the attempted renunciation] as inoperative ... and then [holds] the other party responsible for all the consequences of non-performance; but in that case he keeps the contract alive for the benefit of the other party as well as his own ..."

If the promisee elects to accept the renunciation and terminate the contract on the **7-020** basis of anticipatory breach, these consequences will flow: (i) the renunciation will have become a breach, and the innocent party's cause of action for that breach will have immediately arisen, including the capacity to sue for damages (see para.7-071 ff on damages for anticipatory breach); (ii) both parties will have been released from the contract, such release operating according to the prospective analysis of termination (accrued liabilities will remain actionable, and certain ancillary clauses will survive—for details see paras 13-013, 13-014). As Bowen LJ explained in *Johnstone v Milling* (1886):[36]

> "a promisee, who finds himself confronted with a declaration of intention by the promisor not to carry out the contract when, the time for performance arrives, may treat the contract as broken, and sue for the breach thereof ... [S]uch declaration only becomes a wrongful act if the promisee elects to treat it as such. If he does so elect, it becomes a breach of contract, and he can recover upon it as such."

Conversely, if the promisee elects not to terminate the contract, but instead af- **7-021** firms the contract, the traditional view is that the attempted renunciation will melt away.[37]

The correct analysis, therefore, is that when the innocent party's response to an **7-022** apprehended anticipatory breach is to terminate the contract for breach (which will be the usual context), the element which constitutes the other party's breach is the innocent party's decision, manifested by his termination of the contract, to treat the other party's renunciation or self-induced impossibility as a violation of the contract and thus a breach. This analysis is consistent with the general provision drafted by the Law Commission. This states that, in the face of an apprehended anticipatory breach, the innocent party's cause of action arises if he responds by "words or conduct showing an unequivocal intention to treat the other party as in breach".[38] At that point the innocent party should be recognised as having a cause of action for compensation, and in this situation the other party's breach (provided it was a

---

[36] *Johnstone v Milling* (1886) 16 Q.B.D. 460 CA at 472–3; cf. "An unaccepted repudiation is a thing writ in water and of no value to anybody: it confers no legal rights of any sort or kind", as Asquith LJ said in *Howard v Pickford Tool Co* [1951] 1 K.B. 417 CA at 421; and in the same case Sir Raymond Evershed MR said at 421 that it was "wholly nugatory"; in *Howard v Pickford Tool Co* the court refused to grant a declaration that there had been a renunciation by the employer, because the employee had responded by carrying on his duties without alteration. But the facts *might have disclosed* an actual breach, as distinct from a renunciation prior to performance; and so the court noted that the claimant employee might have had another cause of action for damages arising from the breach, but this had not been pleaded. Asquith LJ's statement concerns words or conduct which do not involve an actual breach, but are merely potentially a breach if the other party elects to terminate the contract in accordance with the doctrine of anticipatory breach.

[37] This proposition is undoubtedly the law; e.g. per Lord Wright in *Heyman v Darwins Ltd* [1942] A.C. 350 HL at 382: "it is true that the breach [his Lordship had just been discussing instances of anticipatory breach] is only complete and enforceable at the moment of rescission [viz termination for breach] so that breach and termination are simultaneous." The genesis of this proposition is explored by Q. Liu, *Anticipatory Breach* (Oxford: Hart Publishing, 2010), pp.22–25.

[38] H. McGregor QC, *Contract Code: Drawn up on behalf of the English Law Commission* (Milano: Giuffrè Publishing, 1993), p.73 at s.303(1) and (2).

clear renunciation or it was otherwise a sufficiently serious breach) will also provide the justification for terminating the contract.

7-023   However, one commentator has opposed this traditional analysis, preferring to contend that even when the contract is terminated for an anticipatory breach, the breach ante-dates the moment of termination. Liu in his book on *Anticipatory Breach* (2010) suggests[39] that "an anticipatory breach is best seen as a freestanding breach of contract whose constitution does not depend on…its victim's acceptance of the breach as such".[40] As for the well-known statement by Asquith LJ in *Howard v Pickford Tool Co Ltd* (1951)[41] that "an unaccepted repudiation is a thing writ in water and of no value to anybody: it confers no legal rights of any sort or kind", Liu says that this comment is concerned only with the proposition that termination of the contract for breach is not automatic and instead requires the innocent party's decision to treat the other's serious breach as entitling the innocent party to end the contract.[42] Liu contends that his analysis—that the claim for damages arises even before the contract is terminated—is supported by two English cases. First, Liu suggests[43] that Rix LJ's judgment in the *Manx Electricity* case (2003) distinguishes between the fact of a breach and the question whether it has become actionable, the latter depending on the innocent party's response to the breach.[44] However, that case in fact proceeds on orthodox grounds which assume that an anticipatory breach does not become actionable unless the innocent party chooses to render the proposed default actionable. Furthermore, the Court of Appeal did not decide clearly whether the relevant breaches in that case were actual repudiatory breaches or anticipatory breaches. Secondly, Liu cites[45] *Tilcon Ltd v Land & Real Estate Investments Ltd* (1987),[46] where Dillon LJ held that a repudiatory breach could furnish a sufficient cause of action, so as to be the subject of a valid pleading, even though the innocent party only subsequently decided to seek to amend his pleading so as to elect to terminate the contract for breach rather than to continue to seek payment of a debt, or continue to seek specific performance.[47] But this concerns the difference between a cause of action whereby a party attempts to enforce the other's primary obligations and the possible amendment of

[39]   Q. Liu, *Anticipatory Breach* (Oxford: Hart Publishing, 2010), p.28 ff; citing there at fn.111, among other literature, J.C. Smith, "Anticipatory Breach of Contract" in E. Lomnicka and C.G.J. Morse (eds), *Contemporary Issues in Commercial Law* (London: Sweet & Maxwell, 1997), p.180.

[40]   Q. Liu, *Anticipatory Breach* (Oxford: Hart Publishing, 2010), 30.

[41]   [1951] 1 K.B. 417CA at 421; in the same case Sir Raymond Evershed MR said that the unaccepted renunciation was "wholly nugatory".

[42]   Q. Liu, *Anticipatory Breach* (Oxford: Hart Publishing, 2010), p.30.

[43]   Q. Liu, *Anticipatory Breach* (Oxford: Hart Publishing, 2010), p.29.

[44]   Rix LJ in *Manx Electricity v JP Morgan Chase Bank* [2003] EWCA Civ 1324; [2003] B.L.R. 477 at [38] ff (and earlier Dillon LJ in *Tilcon Ltd v Land & Real Estate Investments Ltd* [1987] 1 W.L.R. 46 CA at 53).

[45]   Q. Liu, *Anticipatory Breach* (Oxford: Hart Publishing, 2010), pp.28–29.

[46]   *Tilcon Ltd v Land & Real Estate Investments Ltd* [1987] 1 W.L.R. 46 CA at 51–3.

[47]   *Tilcon Ltd v Land & Real Estate Investments Ltd* [1987] 1 W.L.R. 46 CA at 51–3, noting Lord Wilberforce's analysis in *Johnson v Agnew* [1980] A.C. 367HL at 394: "If … the vendor is entitled, after, and notwithstanding that an order for specific performance has been made, if the purchaser still does not complete the contract, to ask the court to permit him to accept the purchaser's repudiation and to declare the contract to be terminated why, if the court accedes to this, should there not follow the ordinary consequences, undoubtedly under the general law of contract, that on such acceptance and termination the vendor may recover damages for breach of contract?" In the *Tilcon* case at 53, Dillon LJ commented: "[*Johnson v Agnew*] was not directly concerned with points of pleading, which we are concerned with today, but it seems to me fundamental that their Lordships were recognising that the vendor's election to treat the contract as repudiated by what the purchaser had

that pleading whereupon the innocent party eventually chooses instead to seek compensation in respect of the other party's default. That distinction does not eliminate the so-called "breach-conversion" rule, since the latter rule is concerned with compensation for a breach and not with enforcement by specific performance of the promisor's primary obligation.

It is submitted that the better view is that anticipatory breach arises, where the **7-024** innocent party elects to terminate the contract, at the moment when the contract is terminated and not before. Liu's contention that breach arises before termination is not English law.

Termination for anticipatory breach requires proof of a serious default When **7-025** a party (party X) has declared an unwillingness to comply with a particular contractual obligation or it is apparent that he will be (inexcusably) unable to comply with that term, and the other party in response now proposes to terminate the contract on the basis of anticipatory breach, the correct approach is to assess whether, in the relevant context, party X's anticipated failure to comply with a term will be serious enough to justify immediate termination.

The proposition just formulated is consistent with Christopher Clarke J's ap- **7-026** proach in *PT Berlian Laju Tanker TBK v Nuse Shipping Ltd ("The Aktor")* (2008).[48] The main issue was whether a 90 per cent payment at venue X was enough, if taken in combination with a deposit paid at venue Y, or whether 100 per cent needed to be paid at venue X in addition to the separate payment obligation requiring the 10 per cent deposit to be paid at venue Y. The judge concluded that it was a condition of the contract that 100 per cent should be paid at venue X and that the payor's refusal to comply disclosed a renunciation, because that party had made clear (by a "settled intention only to make an invalid tender", see next but one paragraph) that it would not make the 100 per cent payment at venue X.

In greater detail, the facts of *PT Berlian Laju Tanker TBK v, Nuse Shipping Ltd* **7-027** *("The Aktor")* (2008) were as follows. The seller of a ship had agreed to receive a 10 per cent deposit at a Singapore bank. But the full price, 100 per cent payment, had to be paid at a Greek bank. The buyer had paid the 10 per cent deposit into a joint account held at a Singaporean bank. But this sum could be released only with the consent of both parties. The buyer insisted that it would only pay 90 per cent of the price at a Greek bank. The buyer contended that it would be enough that it would release the deposit in Singapore on the delivery day so that the value of that deposit could be credited outright to the seller and become part of the purchase money.[49] But the buyer lost on these points. Upholding the arbitrators' award, Christopher Clarke J held that: (1) It was a condition that full payment should be made in Greece. (2) And so the deposit needed to be paid as part of the 100 per cent tender of purchase money *at the relevant Greek bank*, or (if the 100 per cent payment were made at the Greek bank), the deposit would be returnable to the buyer. (3) The buyer had committed an anticipatory breach on these facts by making clear that it would not make the 100 per cent payment at the Greek bank. This breach

---

done did not have to be made before he issued his writ. He was entitled to elect in the course of the proceedings, at trial or even thereafter."

[48] [2008] EWHC 1330 (Comm); [2008] 2 All E.R. (Comm) 784; [2008] 2 Lloyd's Rep. 246.

[49] An earlier version of the parties' agreement had so provided; but Clarke J agreed with the arbitrators that this version had been superseded by another version and that there was no scope to rectify the later version by reference to the preceding version: the latter version was intended to supersede in all respects the earlier version.

entitled the seller to terminate the contract and hence to refuse to deliver the vessel. Christopher Clarke J said:[50]

"... Crediting the Sellers with some or all of the purchase price otherwise than at the place stipulated for payment would ... expose the Sellers to the risk involved in transferring the monies from the non-contractual place, where or from which the Buyers purported to make payment, to the place agreed. Monies that pass through the banking system may become unavailable to the payee because of claims to the money, or claims to freeze the money, by banks or others."

7-028 The learned judge emphasised the presence here of a "settled intention" not to adhere to an important term of the contract:[51]

"A defective tender may be cured by a subsequent tender made no later than the last day for performance. But, if the Buyers indicate a settled intention only to make an invalid tender i.e. to perform in a manner inconsistent with a condition of the contract, which, if persisted in, would entitle the Sellers to terminate, the Buyers are entitled to anticipate the breach and treat themselves as discharged."

He concluded:[52] "... the Buyers' obligation was to make payment in accordance with the contract. This they indicated that they were not prepared to do."

7-029 Liu in his book on *Anticipatory Breach* (2010)[53] notes that the courts have been reluctant to allow a prospective breach of an express condition to provide a trigger for accelerated termination. Instead the prospective breach must go to the root of the contract and substantially deprive the innocent party of the benefit of the contract (on these tests see para.8-001). In other words, threatened, or an apprehended future, breach of an express condition is not enough. Thus in *"The Afovos"* (1983), Lord Diplock said:[54]

"The doctrine of anticipatory breach is but a species of the genus repudiation and applies only to fundamental breach. If one party to a contract states ... in advance that he will not be able to perform a particular primary obligation ... when the time for performance arrives, the question whether the other party may elect to treat the statement as a repudiation depends upon whether the threatened non-performance would have the effect of depriving that other party of substantially the whole benefit which it was the intention of the parties that he should obtain from the primary obligations of the parties under the contract then remaining unperformed. If it would not have that effect there is no repudiation ... The non-performance threatened must itself satisfy the criteria of a fundamental breach."

7-030 Lord Diplock added:

"Similarly where a party to a contract, whether by failure to take timeous action or by any other default, has put it out of his power to perform a particular primary obligation, the right of the other party to elect to treat this as a repudiation of the contract by conduct depends upon whether the resulting non-performance would amount to a fundamental breach."

---

[50] [2008] EWHC 1330 (Comm); [2008] 2 All E.R. (Comm) 784; [2008] 2 Lloyd's Rep. 246 at [68].
[51] [2008] EWHC 1330 (Comm); [2008] 2 All E.R. (Comm) 784; [2008] 2 Lloyd's Rep. 246 at [69].
[52] [2008] EWHC 1330 (Comm); [2008] 2 All E.R. (Comm) 784; [2008] 2 Lloyd's Rep. 246 at [70].
[53] Q. Liu, *Anticipatory Breach* (Oxford: Hart Publishing, 2010), pp.79–85.
[54] Q. Liu, *Anticipatory Breach* (Oxford: Hart Publishing, 2010), p.81, examining *"The Afovos"* [1983] 1 W.L.R. 195HL at 203 per Lord Diplock.

III.   ANTICIPATORY BREACH BY SELF-DISABLEMENT[55]

Disablement at the "anticipatory" stage: impossibility by culpable self-inducement   This is the second form of anticipatory breach: where, in the absence of a renunciation, the guilty party incapacitates himself or prevents performance before the scheduled date. This incapacitation or prevention need not involve deliberate sabotaging of the contract. It is enough that the default involves breach of an express or implied term. But, as we shall see (para.7-036 ff), eventual default must be "practically inevitable".

7-031

An illustration is *Burntcopper Ltd v ITCA* (2014)[56] where the defendant's decision to sell its business to a third party destroyed the chance of the claimant being able to perform its services under the contract. This was a five-year agreement for the provision by the claimant of management services in annual trade shows organised by the defendant. The defendant committed breach involving self-induced frustration when it sold that business to another company, which had no use for the claimant. Judge Mackie QC held that the defendant was unable to exculpate itself on the basis of the following clause: "If for some unforeseen circumstances the trade show is cancelled or does not take place during the term of this contract, this contract will not be enforced for the year in question". The judge held that this clause would operate only if the event's cancellation occurred for reasons "unforeseeable" *by both parties*, but in fact the defendant had known in advance (and obviously at the time when it decided to sell the business) that it might or would sell to a third party.

7-032

This second category of anticipatory breach (where there is no accompanying renunciation) is sometimes described as "inevitable breach",[57] or "anticipatory breach through (inexcusable) impossibility",[58] or "impossibility created by [the defendant's] own act".[59] Popplewell J in *Geden Operations Ltd v Dry Bulk Handy Holdings Inc ("The Bulk Uruguay")* (2014) referred to the need for inevitable default:[60]

7-033

"self induced impossibility is narrowly confined to those cases where breach is rendered

---

55   Q. Liu, *Anticipatory Breach* (Oxford: Hart Publishing, 2010), p.60 ff; and especially p.74 ff (but caution is required because Liu's analysis arguably understates the level of cogent proof of inability required in the English cases).

56   [2014] EWHC 148 (Comm); [2014] 2 All E.R. (Comm) 1055 at [29]–[34] per HH Judge Mackie QC; and see the old case, *Lovelock v Franklin* (1846) 8 Q.B. 371; 115 E.R. 916 (agreement to transfer land to claimant; defendant selling land to third party before due date; incapacitation; actionable breach).

57   Patten J in *Simoco Digital UK Ltd v Thunderbird Industries Llc* [2004] EWHC 209 (Ch); [2004] 1 B.C.L.C. 541 at [23] and Popplewell J in *Geden Operations Ltd v Dry Bulk Handy Holdings Inc ("The Bulk Uruguay")* [2014] EWHC 885 (Comm) at [17] and [18], referred to the need for inevitable default; similarly, *Universal Cargo Carriers Corp v Citati (No 1)* [1957] 2 Q.B. 401 at 438 per Devlin J and *Cargo Ships El Yam Ltd v Invoeren Transport Onderneming Invotra NV* [1958] 1 Lloyd's Rep. 39 at 52 per Devlin J.

58   Aikens J in *Gulf Agri Trade FZCO v Aston Agro Industrial AG* [2008] EWHC 1252 (Comm); [2009] 1 All E.R. (Comm) 991; [2008] 2 Lloyd's Rep. 376; [2008] 1 C.L.C. 919 at [14].

59   *SK Shipping (S) PTE Ltd v Petroexport Ltd* [2009] EWHC 2974 (Comm) at [84] per Flaux J; for further comment, Flaux J, at [122] and [123], noting Devlin J's citation in *Universal Cargo Carriers Corp v Citati (No.1)* [1957] 2 Q.B. 401 at 436–7 of Lord Porter's adoption in *Heyman v Darwins Ltd* [1942] A.C. 356 HL at 397 of a formulation appearing in *Anson's Law of Contract*. This passage is preserved in J. Beatson, A. Burrows, and J. Cartwright, *Anson's Law of Contract*, 31st edn (Oxford: Oxford University Press, 2020), p.510, fn.47.

60   [2014] EWHC 885 (Comm) at [18] (see also [17]); similarly, Patten J in *Simoco Digital UK Ltd v Thunderbird Industries Llc* [2004] EWHC 209 (Ch); [2004] 1 B.C.L.C. 541 at [23].

inevitable. Save for possibilities which are so remote that in practice they can be ignored, what is required is inevitability. It is not sufficient if something is done which makes future performance unlikely, even very unlikely, still less that it renders performance uncertain."

He added:[61] "That is why renunciation is often a more favoured basis for invoking the doctrine of anticipatory breach".

7-034　　In *Universal Cargo Carriers Corp v Citati* (1957)[62] Devlin J noted Lord Sumner's 1923 formulation (in *British & Beningtons Ltd v North West Cachar Tea Co Ltd* (1923)[63] of this doctrine as requiring the innocent party to prove that the other had become "wholly and finally disabled" from performing as he had undertaken to do. And Devlin J in the *Citati* case said:[64]

"if a man puts it out of his power to perform, the breach will be inevitable in fact—or practically inevitable, for the law never requires absolute certainty and does not take account of bare possibilities. So anticipatory breach means simply that a party is in breach from the moment that his actual breach becomes inevitable."

7-035　　Devlin J also noted in *Universal Cargo Carriers Corp v Citati* (1957)[65] that termination on the ground of self-induced frustration involves the "serious risk" that the court might find that (contrary to the innocent party's pessimistic assessment) in fact the other party's inability to perform had not been shown to be inexorable or sufficiently probable because that party could yet have retrieved the situation. And so, to avoid this danger, the prudent course is to contend instead that the other party has *expressly renounced* the contract.

7-036　　**Burden and standard of proof**　　Unless it is indisputable that there has been self-induced frustration (see the *Burntcopper* case, at para.7-032, where the sale to the third party of the business was an indisputable fact), the onus of proving that a situation of impossibility had arisen lies with the party alleging that the other was guilty of self-disablement. The standard of proof is the balance of probabilities. It is necessary for the alleged victim to show convincingly that he was confronted by a clear case of the other party having become inevitably disabled (or virtually evitable or practically inevitable).

7-037　　An example of an unsuccessful attempt to invoke the doctrine of self-induced frustration is *Alfred Toepfer International GmbH v Itex Itagrani Export SA* (1993).[66] Here a seller prematurely calculated that the buyer would be unable to load a cargo

---

[61] [2014] EWHC 885 (Comm) at [18].

[62] [1957] 2 Q.B. 401 at 446–7.

[63] [1923] A.C. 48 at 72 HL.

[64] [1957] 2 Q.B. 401 at 436–8. (Devlin J's exposition of governing principles of breach not disturbed on appeal by either [1957] 1 W.L.R. 979 CA or [1958] 2 Q.B. 254 CA). M. Mustill, "Anticipatory Breach: The Common Law at Work", *Butterworths Lectures 1989–90* (London: Butterworths, 1990), p.69 ff; M. Mustill, "The Golden Victory—Some Reflections" (2008) 124 L.Q.R. 569–85.

[65] [1957] 2 Q.B. 401 at 436–8. (Not disturbed on appeal on this point: [1957] 1 W.L.R. 979 CA and [1958] 2 Q.B. 254 CA). M. Mustill, *Anticipatory Breach: Butterworths Lectures 1989–90* (London: Butterworths, 1990), p.69 ff; M. Mustill, "The Golden Victory—some reflections" (2008) 124 L.Q.R. 569, 580, fn.23, notes the galaxy of commercial talent employed in arguing this case.

[66] [1993] 1 Lloyd's Rep. 360, Saville J; similarly *Continental Contractors Ltd and Ernest Beck & Co Ltd v Medway Oil & Storage Co Ltd* (1926) 25 Lloyd's Rep. 288—suppliers of kerosene had not "wholly and finally disabled" themselves, even though they had encountered difficulties in procuring a supply (the *Toepfer* case and other authorities were considered by Proudman J in *Ridgewood Properties Group Ltd v Valero Energy Ltd* [2013] EWHC 98 (Ch); [2013] Ch. 525 at [30], [31], and [107], considering *Synge v Synge* [1894] 1 Q.B. 466; *Ogdens Ltd v Nelson* [1905] A.C. 109; *Fratelli*

in full. In fact, it was not at all certain that the buyer would have failed to do so. And so the seller was held to have repudiated. Saville J commented:[67] "[In] the present case there was only a chance that the buyers would be unable to perform".

Judicial exposition of anticipatory breach by disablement There are two lead- **7-038** ing expositions of this mode of anticipatory breach: Devlin J's in *Universal Cargo Carriers Corp v Citati* (1957)[68] and Kerr J's in *"The Angelia"* (1973),[69] and these will now be quoted.

(1) In *Universal Cargo Carriers Corp v Citati* (1957) Devlin J said:[70]

> "Of the two modes, renunciation has since the decision in *Hochster v De la Tour* (1853)[71] established itself as the favourite. The disadvantage of the other [infer-ence of self-incapacitation or disablement] is that the party who elects to treat impos-sibility as an anticipatory breach may be running a serious risk. Suppose, for example, that a man promises to marry a woman on a future date, or to execute a lease or to deliver goods; and that before the day arrives he marries another, or executes the lease in favour of another, or delivers the goods to a third party. The aggrieved party may sue at once. 'One reason alleged in support of such an action' Campbell CJ observed in *Hochster v De la Tour*,[72] 'is, that the defendant has, before the day, rendered it impossible for him to perform the contract at the day: but this does not necessarily follow; for, prior to the day fixed for doing the act, the first wife may have died, a surrender of the lease executed might be obtained, and the defend-ant might have repurchased the goods so as to be in a situation to sell and deliver them to the plaintiff.' But if the plaintiff treats the defendant's conduct as amount-ing to renunciation and justifies his [termination for breach] on that ground, the defendant could not avail himself of this defence."

In the *Citati* case (1957) Devlin J continued:[73] **7-039**

> "I said that it was after *Hochster v De la Tour*[74] that renunciation established itself as the favourite, because until then it was not certain that a man who said 'I will not perform' would be held to his word. In *Hochster v De la Tour* it was argued that he could change his mind, and that the fact that at one time he said he was not ready and willing did not necessarily mean that he would be unwilling when the time for performance came. *Hochster v De la Tour* established that a renunciation, when acted upon, became final. Thus, if a man proclaimed by words or conduct an inability to perform, the other party could safely act upon it without having to prove that when the time for performance came the inability was still effective. Since a man must be both ready and willing to perform, a profession by words or conduct of inability is by itself enough to constitute renunciation."

In the *Citati* case (1957) Devlin J further remarked on this species of anticipa- **7-040**

Sorrentino v Buerger [1915] 1 K.B. 307; *Omnium d'Enterprises v Sutherland* [1919] 1 K.B. 618 CA).

67 [1993] 1 Lloyd's Rep. 360, Saville J.
68 [1957] 2 Q.B. 401 at 437–8.
69 *Trade and Transport Inc v Iino Kaiun Kaisha Ltd ("The Angelia")* [1973] 1 W.L.R. 210 at 219; generally on this topic, Q. Liu, *Anticipatory Breach* (Oxford: Hart Publishing, 2011), pp.88–91.
70 [1957] 2 Q.B. 401 at 437–8 (passages cited with approval in *SK Shipping (S) PTE Ltd v Petroexport Ltd ("The Pro Victor")* [2009] EWHC 2974, Flaux J at [84]).
71 (1853) 2 E. & B. 678.
72 (1853) 2 E. & B. 678, 688.
73 [1957] 2 Q.B. 401 at 437.
74 (1853) 2 E. & B. 678 at 688.

tory breach:[75]

> "if the owner can establish that in the words of Lord Sumner [in *British & Beningtons Ltd v North West Cachar Tea Co Ltd* (1923)][76] the charterer had on July 18 'become wholly and finally disabled' from finding a cargo and loading it before delay frustrated the venture, he is entitled to succeed. Lord Sumner's words expressly refer to the time of breach as the date at which the inability must exist. But that does not mean, in my opinion, that the facts to be looked at in determining inability are only those which existed on July 18; the determination is to be made in the light of all the events—whether occurring before or after the critical date—put in evidence at the trial."

(2)   Kerr J in *"The Angelia"* (1973) provided another lucid exposition of this species of anticipatory breach:[77]

> "The anticipatory breach constituting a repudiation on which the owners relied was the alleged inability of the charterers to perform the charterparty by supplying a cargo for the vessel before the effluxion of a period of time sufficiently long to frustrate the charter. This type of repudiation was explained in the important decision of Devlin J in *Universal Cargo Carriers Corp v Citati* (1957)."[78]

7-041   Kerr J in *"The Angelia"* (1973) continued:[79]

> "... a party to a contract (who may for convenience be called the innocent party) may treat the other party as having committed an anticipatory breach amounting to a repudiation if the innocent party can establish that the other party had 'become wholly and finally disabled' from performing the contract by the time when such repudiation is claimed to have occurred. In order to amount to a repudiation the period of such inability of performance must be sufficiently long to frustrate the commercial purpose of the contract, and for the sake of brevity this period may conveniently be referred to as a 'frustrating time.'"

7-042   **The danger of jumping to the conclusion that the other party is bound to default**   As mentioned in Devlin J's exposition cited at para.7-039, to avoid the hazard of too readily and pessimistically inferring the other party's complete incapacitation, the prudent course is to contend instead (or in addition) that the other party has *expressly renounced* the contract, as occurred in *Hochster v De La Tour* (1853)[80] and *Frost v Knight* (1872).[81]

7-043   *"The Pro Victor"* (2009) is an example. Here a party succeeded in showing that there had been renunciation, although the same party could not show that the renouncing party would have been unable to perform. Therefore, the "anticipatory breach through (inexcusable) impossibility" ground was not simultaneously satisfied.[82]

7-044   Another example of the danger of too readily and unsafely inferring the other party's complete incapacitation is *Alfred Toepfer International GmbH v Itex Itagrani*

---

75   [1957] 2 Q.B. 401 at 446, 447.
76   [1923] A.C. 48 HL at 72.
77   *Trade and Transport Inc v Iino Kaiun Kaisha Ltd ("The Angelia")* [1973] 1 W.L.R. 210 at 219; generally, on this topic, Q. Liu, *Anticipatory Breach* (Oxford: Hart Publishing, 2011), pp.88–91.
78   [1957] 2 Q.B. 401.
79   [1973] 1 W.L.R. 210 at 219.
80   (1853) 2 E. & B. 678.
81   (1872) L.R. 7 Ex. 111.
82   *SK Shipping (S) PTE Ltd v Petroexport Ltd ("The Pro Victor")* [2009] EWHC 2974, per Flaux J at [122], and [123] on the impossibility ground.

Export SA (1993).[83] The seller prematurely calculated that the buyer would be unable to load a cargo in full. In fact, it was not at all certain that the buyer would have failed to do so. And so, the seller was held to have repudiated.

The underlined portions in the following passages further indicate the uphill task **7-045** of the party who invokes this head of anticipatory breach as his justification for terminating the contract. Saville J said in *Alfred Toepfer International GmbH v Itex Itagrani Export SA* (1993):[84]

> "The fact that that party has entered into inconsistent obligations does not in itself necessarily establish such inability, unless those obligations are of such a nature or have such an effect *that it can truly be said that the party in question has put it out of his power to perform his obligations.*"

Saville J added:[85] **7-046**

> "In the present case, however, the mere fact that the sub-buyers had contracted to load other goods on the vessel did not, in itself, establish that the buyers could not perform…it could not be said that the buyers had on the face of it … put it out of their power to perform … *there was only a chance that the buyers would be unable to perform.*"

Calibrating the likelihood of default   It is clear from the discussion by Saville **7-047** J in *Alfred Toepfer International GmbH v Itex Itagrani Export SA* (1993) that the relevant test is whether:[86] "on the balance of probabilities the party in question cannot perform his obligations". However, this should not be misinterpreted to mean that there is a merely probable chance that Y will not perform. Instead the question is whether it can be convincingly said by X that Y was definitely destined to fail to perform. Nothing short of a clear and convincing case of such prospective inability should suffice.

In establishing this, X should be able to draw upon all relevant evidence. The **7-048** evidential level of proof will be the civil standard, that is, a balance of probabilities test. But discharging that standard in this context, and satisfying the necessarily demanding criterion of a clear case of inability to perform, must be regarded as an uphill struggle for X. Otherwise the courts and arbitration tribunals would be flooded with ludicrous and embarrassing attempts by parties to exonerate themselves by presenting a watered down defence of "perceived and not unlikely future breach" by Y. Such an approach would be grotesque. It would render English law a laughing-stock in the wider commercial world. Commercial fidelity to contractual obligations would be seriously undermined. Bad and spurious claims and defences would be stimulated. Thus Saville J said in *Alfred Toepfer International GmbH v Itex Itagrani Export SA* (1993):[87]

> "*the mere fact that a third party is demonstrating an unwillingness to do something which the contracting party needs him to do to perform the contracting party's obligations means at best that the contracting party may not be able to perform, not that on the balance of probabilities he cannot perform.*"

Conversely, where the chance of the relevant contracting party being able to **7-049**

---

83   [1993] 1 Lloyd's Rep. 360, Saville J; and see cases cited at fn.65 above.
84   [1993] 1 Lloyd's Rep. 360 at 362.
85   [1993] 1 Lloyd's Rep. 360 at 362.
86   [1993] 1 Lloyd's Rep. 360 at 362.
87   [1993] 1 Lloyd's Rep. 360 at 362, col.2.

retrieve a very unpromising situation is very slim or highly speculative, it will be safe to infer that he will not in fact be able to perform. In this regard, Saville J in *Alfred Toepfer International GmbH v Itex Itagrani Export SA* (1993) cited *Omnium v Sutherland* (1919)[88] where the Court of Appeal held that a shipowner's decision to sell a vessel to a third party was enough to indicate that it would not be able to perform a charterparty. The chances of the owners being able to re-purchase or re-possess this vessel were too low to negative the sensible inference that performance had ceased to be practicable.

7-050   Popplewell J in *Geden Operations Ltd v Dry Bulk Handy Holdings Inc ("The Bulk Uruguay")* (2014) referred to the need for inevitable default:

> "self induced impossibility is narrowly confined to those cases where breach is rendered inevitable. Save for possibilities which are so remote that in practice they can be ignored, what is required is inevitability. It is not sufficient if something is done which makes future performance unlikely, even very unlikely, still less that it renders performance uncertain."

7-051   Devlin J in the *Citati* case (1957) adopted the criterion of default which is "inevitable in fact" or "practically inevitable":

> "if a man puts it out of his power to perform, the breach will be inevitable in fact—or practically inevitable, for the law never requires absolute certainty and does not take account of bare possibilities."[89]

7-052   **Hindsight relevant to assessment whether disablement existed**   In determining whether the other party was in fact fully disabled at the relevant time from achieving future performance, the party who has terminated on the basis of apprehended inability to perform is entitled to justify his decision not just by reference to information available to him at the time of his decision but by adducing evidence of subsequent clarification of the relevant events. Devlin J noted this last point in the *Citati* case (1957) when he said:[90] "the determination is to be made in the light of all the events—whether occurring before or after the critical date—put in evidence at the trial." Similarly, Kerr J explained in *"The Angelia"* (1973) that the innocent party for this purpose:[91] "is not restricted to reliance on facts then known to him or which had happened before the critical date, but is entitled to rely on all events to establish such impossibility whether occurring before or afterwards" (and he then cited the passage from Devlin J's judgment cited immediately above).

7-053   Hindsight might operate to the terminating party's benefit, where it vindicates or strengthens his prediction that future breach was bound to occur, but it might operate disadvantageously, when such subsequent information weakens or destroys the validity of the forecast.

7-054   The position just explained concerning the second species of anticipatory breach, namely anticipated inexcusable inability to perform, is to be contrasted with the renunciatory species of anticipatory breach, where the promisee is told by the other party that the latter does not intend to perform. The court will not consider evidence subsequent to the critical date in order to determine whether at that date there had

---

[88]   *Omnium v Sutherland* [1919] 1 K.B. 618 CA, cited by Saville J in *Alfred Toepfer International GmbH v Itex Itagrani Export SA* [1993] 1 Lloyd's Rep. 360 at 362, col.1.

[89]   *Universal Cargo Carriers Corp v Citati (No.1)* [1957] 2 Q.B. 401 at 438.

[90]   [1957] 2 Q.B. 401 at 446–7.

[91]   *Trade and Transport Inc v Iino Kaiun Kaisha Ltd ("The Angelia")* [1973] 1 W.L.R. 210 at 219.

been a renunciation. Instead the question must be posed by reference only to information currently available at the time of the alleged renunciation.[92]

Promisor's insolvency   Liu addresses the question whether a party's insolvency   **7-055**
has in all the circumstances indicated that a party cannot perform. The starting point is that insolvency per se does not disclose either disablement or renunciation.[93] This issue was also carefully considered by Andrew Phang Boon Leong JA in a case before the Singapore Court of Appeal, *"The SPX Mumbai"* (2015).[94] He held that insolvency might be a ground of anticipatory breach by inexcusable inability to perform if there is no real chance that the insolvent party's estate will elect to maintain the contract and satisfy their side of the bargain. The most obvious example, as on the facts of that case, if where the solvent party has already performed its part of the contract.[95] In this situation it would be unlikely that the insolvent party's estate would decide to honour its outstanding duties, notably its forthcoming obligation to pay for that which has already been done.

However, it is common for commercial contracts, including land transactions, to   **7-056**
contain an express clause permitting a party to terminate the contract, on giving notice, if the other party becomes insolvent. Such a clause, for example, was cited by Christopher Clarke J in *Dalkia Utilities Services Plc v Celtech International Ltd* (2006),[96] and another clause was cited by the Court of Appeal in *Force India Formula One Team Ltd v Etihad Airways PJSC* (2010).[97]

A variation on this theme is a clause entitling an anxious seller (where there is   **7-057**
objective evidence of the buyer's "financial impairment") to require either advance cash payment by the other party or some form of specified guarantee or security.[98]

---

[92] *Nottingham Building Society v Eurodynamics Systems Plc* [1995] F.S.R. 605 CA at 612 per Peter Gibson LJ.

[93] Q. Liu, *Anticipatory Breach* (Oxford: Hart Publishing, 2011), p.64.

[94] [2015] SGCA 35; [2015] 5 S.L.R. 1; [2016] 1 Lloyd's Rep. 157 at [79]–[89] (noted Y. Goh and M. Yip, "Rationalising anticipatory breach in executed contracts" [2016] C.L.J. 18).

[95] [2015] SGCA 35; [2015] 5 S.L.R. 1; [2016] 1 Lloyd's Rep. 157 at [87], distinguishing the English decisions in *Re Agra Ex p. Tondeur* (1867) L.R. 5 Eq. 160 at 165, Sir Page Wood VC and *Jennings' Trustee v King* [1952] 1 Ch. 899, Harman J, in both of which the court considered that the insolvent party's estate might decide that it would be beneficial to adopt the contract and fulfil the insolvent party's liabilities.

[96] *Dalkia Utilities Services Plc v Celtech International Ltd* [2006] EWHC 63 (Comm); [2006] 1 Lloyd's Rep. 599; [2006] 2 P. & C.R. 9 at [15]: "Under cl.14.1 either party could terminate the agreement forthwith by notice in writing if the other party ceased to trade or was wound up or entered into liquidation or compounded with its creditors or had a receiver, administrator, or similar officer appointed over all or a major part of its assets or undertaking, or any resolution was passed relating to any of the foregoing".

[97] [2010] EWCA Civ 1051; [2011] E.T.L.R. 10 at [14]: "Termination by the Sponsors: 21.3.1 The Sponsors may terminate this Agreement with immediate effect on the giving of written notice to [the Team] at any time on the happening of any of the following events by or in relation to the other party: ... an order is made or an effective resolution is passed for the liquidation, winding up or dissolution of [The Team] and such order or resolution is not cancelled within one month; [or] an encumbrancer takes possession or a receiver is appointed over all or any part of the assets or undertaking of [The Team]; [or] [The Team] becomes insolvent, enters into a voluntary arrangement with any of its creditors and is unable to pay its debts or admits in writing its inability to pay its debts as they fall due ..."

[98] *BV Oliehandel Jongkind v Coastal International Ltd* [1983] 2 Lloyd's Rep. 463, Leggatt J (although on the facts the seller had invoked this clause without justification and so had themselves committed a repudiatory breach).

7-058   **No dilution of the requirement that future default must be practically inevitable**   Liu in his book on *Anticipatory Breach* (2010) (for criticism see next paragraph) has proposed an unattractively wide and hazardous approach to the question of inferring what he calls "a reasonable inference" of "future breach".[99] He concludes his survey of the case law by suggesting that "a future breach is reasonably inferred only when it has a 51% or more chance of occurring".[100] In reaching this conclusion, Liu notes Mustill J's first instance suggestion (cited by Donaldson LJ in *Chilean Nitrate Sales Corp v Marine Transportation Co Ltd ("The Hermosa"* (1982))[101] that a "reasonable probability" of breach is required. He also notes Saville J's suggestion in *Alfred Toepfer International GmbH v Itex Itagrani Export SA* (1993)[102] (discussed at paras 7-044–7-048) that the test is whether "on the balance of probabilities" the other party has "put it out of [their] power" to perform. Finally, Liu notes that in *M&J Polymers Ltd v Imerys Minerals Ltd* (2008)[103] Burton J pitched the test at a low level: that it must be "more likely than not" that future breaches will occur. However, this last case belongs with the case law concerning the likelihood of serious breach recurring during performance of instalment contracts (on which para.8-042 ff), and in any event Burton J did not cite other case law. Liu also suggests that "any existing circumstances" can be used in so far as they are "indicative" of such a future breach.[104] These matters might include:[105] (i) "a prior actual breach, … irrespective of whether it gives rise to a right to terminate the contract": (ii) "… the words or conduct of a third party, such as a bank, supplier or sub-contractor": or (iii) "even … a general deterioration of the party's business", although he concedes that further supplementary evidence might be required in the last instance.

7-059   However, Liu's suggestion does not provide a satisfactory commercial approach to this question. It is true that the standard of proof in civil matters is a balance of probabilities. It is also true that a range of relevant material can be legitimately taken into account when assessing whether there is support for a party's contention that the other party stood in a position of inexcusable inability to perform in the future. If this is shown, the *Citati* case's (*Universal Cargo Carriers Corp v Citati* (1957))[106] second species of anticipatory breach will apply. However, Liu's discussion does not provide a satisfactory criterion for the central issue: what level of unlikelihood of such prospective inability is safe and reliable? The better approach, which is supported by English law (para.7-036 ff), is this: whether it can be convincingly said by party X that Y's default had become "practically inevitable". Nothing short of a clear and convincing case of such practically inevitable default should suffice.

---

[99]   Q. Liu, *Anticipatory Breach* (Oxford: Hart Publishing, 2011), p.76.

[100]   Q. Liu, *Anticipatory Breach* (Oxford: Hart Publishing, 2011), p.77.

[101]   *Chilean Nitrate Sales Corp v Marine Transportation Co Ltd ("The Hermosa")* [1982] 1 Lloyd's Rep. 570 CA at 580 per Donaldson LJ.

[102]   *Alfred Toepfer International GmbH v Itex Itagrani Export SA* [1993] 1 Lloyd's Rep. 360 at 362 per Saville J.

[103]   *M&J Polymers Ltd v Imerys Minerals Ltd* [2008] EWHC 344 (Comm); [2008] 1 All E.R. (Comm) 893; [2008] 1 Lloyd's Rep. 541; [2008] 1 C.L.C. 276 at [15] per Burton J.

[104]   Q. Liu, *Anticipatory Breach* (Oxford: Hart Publishing, 2011), p.75 ff.

[105]   Q. Liu, *Anticipatory Breach* (Oxford: Hart Publishing, 2011), p.75 ff.

[106]   [1957] 2 Q.B. 401 at 437–8 (passages cited with approval in *SK Shipping (S) PTE Ltd v Petroexport Ltd ("The Pro Victor")* [2009] EWHC 2974, Flaux J at [84]).

IV. Anticipatory Breach Applicable Even if the Innocent Party Has Already Performed Fully[107]

Andrew Phang Boon Leong JA in a case before the Singapore Court of Appeal, **7-060** *"The SPX Mumbai"* (2015),[108] has carefully reviewed the Common Law case law and literature on this point. He persuasively decided that the doctrine of anticipatory breach should apply even where the innocent party has already performed its side of the bargain. In that case the innocent party had supplied bunkers to a vessel and was apprehensive that the forthcoming duty to pay would not be honoured. Basing itself on the contention that an anticipatory breach had arisen by reason of inexcusable inability to pay, the innocent party arrested the ship. The Singapore Court of Appeal held that there was no rule of law that anticipatory breach could not arise when the innocent party had already fully performed. The innocent party, on appropriate facts, should be able to accelerate the moment of default and take steps which are legally founded on an immediate breach having occurred. Phang JA said:[109]

"... If it is the case that the defendant has evinced a clear intention that it will not perform its obligations under the contract, then we see little reason why this very fact might not itself form the basis for holding that, in principle and logic, an actual breach has, in substance, occurred—notwithstanding the fact that the time for the defendant's performance has yet to arrive under the contract ... Indeed, if this [rationalisation of] the doctrine of anticipatory breach is adopted, it follows, a fortiori, that it would not matter whether the contract was executed or executory. If there is a breach justifying the plaintiff in electing to treat the contract as discharged ... the doctrine of anticipatory breach could be applied, regardless of whether the contract is executed or executory."

Phang JA referred to English authorities (considered in the next two paragraphs **7-061** of this text):[110]

"... the leading English decision is *Moschi v Lep Air Services Ltd* [1973] A.C. 331, which permitted the operation of the doctrine of anticipatory breach in the situation where the contract was executed...This was also the case in the earlier English Court of Appeal decision of *Synge v Synge* [1894] Q.B. 466."

In *Moschi v Lep Air Services Ltd* (1973)[111] a debt, payable by instalments, had **7-062** arisen in favour of a creditor who had already performed services. The debt was guaranteed by the defendant and the creditor had, in consideration for the guarantee, removed its lien over the debtor's goods. When instalments were not paid, the creditor ended the whole contract and sued the guarantor for the total unpaid amount. The House of Lords upheld the claim. The decision thus assumes that the liability to pay the whole set of instalments had been triggered by the anticipatory breach committed by the debtor. Therefore, the doctrine of anticipatory breach can apply even where the innocent party's obligations had already been fully performed (the creditor's decision to release its lien, which act had provided consideration for the

---

107 J.W. Carter, *Carter's Breach of Contract*, 2nd edn (Oxford: Hart Publishing, 2019), [7-78]–[7-82].
108 [2015] SGCA 35; [2015] 5 S.L.R. 1; [2016] 1 Lloyd's Rep. 157 at [40]–[78] (noted Y. Goh and M. Yip, "Rationalising anticipatory breach in executed contracts" [2016] C.L.J. 18).
109 [2015] SGCA 35; [2015] 5 S.L.R. 1; [2016] 1 Lloyd's Rep. 157 at [51].
110 [2015] SGCA 35; [2015] 5 S.L.R. 1; [2016] 1 Lloyd's Rep. 157 at [54].
111 *Moschi v Lep Air Services Ltd (also known as Moschi v Rolloswin Investments Ltd or Lep Air Services v Rolloswin Investments)* [1973] A.C. 331 HL.

guarantee, and its earlier full performance of its services under the main transaction, as mentioned above).

7-063   In *Synge v Synge* (1894),[112] the earlier case mentioned by Phange JA in *"The SPX Mumbai"* (2015),[113] the same analysis was adopted (but again without elaboration). In *Synge v Synge* (1894)[114] X and Y had entered into an ante-nuptial agreement. X promised to create a life interest in land in favour of Y, his fiancée, in X's will. During X's lifetime, X committed an anticipatory breach when he sold the relevant land to Z. The Court of Appeal held that Y had an action for breach of contract, founded upon the doctrine of anticipatory breach. The claim would be for the value of the contemplated life interest in the property which (having been sold to the third party) could not now form the subject matter of a life interest. An inquiry as to damages was ordered so that a calculation could be made of the claimant's actual loss, taking into account the chances of Y surviving her husband, and generally of her life expectancy (the duration of the life interest). But the case is clearly one where Y had already provided consideration in full, by entering into marriage with X. As Kay LJ said:[115]

> "... the proposal of terms in this case was made as an inducement to the lady to marry, that she consented to the terms, and married the defendant on the faith that he would keep his word, and that accordingly there was a binding contract on the defendant's part to leave to his wife the house and land at Ardfield for her life. Then, secondly, what is the remedy? Marriage is a valuable consideration for such a contract of the highest order, and where, as here, the contract is in writing, so that there is no question upon the Statute of Frauds, in the language already quoted, a Court of Equity will take care that the party who marries on the faith of such a proposal 'is not disappointed, and will give effect to the proposal'."

V. NO RIGHT TO INSIST ON THE OTHER PARTY'S REASSURANCE THAT PERFORMANCE WILL OCCUR

7-064   Under English law, a party has no *right to demand and obtain* an assurance from the other side that the latter is still able and willing to carry on.[116] But there is "nothing to stop" a party from trying to elicit such reassurance, and the court will have regard to these communications when determining whether the contract was discharged by response to a renunciation or anticipatory breach founded on impossibility or even that the contract was terminated by mutual abandonment.[117]

7-065   By contrast to the absence of a right to demand assurance, mentioned in the opening sentence of the preceding paragraph, there are (unattractive) provisions on this in "soft law" materials (not binding in England). It is submitted that this type of provision is unattractive. Such a "reassurance" mechanism might well stir up a hornet's nest of accusation and counter-accusation. That danger outweighs the apparent gain that a party might obtain if it had a legally recognised right under

---

[112] [1894] 1 Q.B. 466 CA; on which, J.W. Carter, *Carter's Breach of Contract*, 2nd edn (Oxford: Hart Publishing, 2019), [7-81].

[113] [2015] SGCA 35; [2015] 5 S.L.R. 1; [2016] 1 Lloyd's Rep. 157.

[114] [1894] 1 Q.B. 466 CA.

[115] [1894] 1 Q.B. 466 CA at 469.

[116] J.W. Carter, "Suspending Contract Performance for Breach" in J. Beatson and D. Friedmann (eds), *Good Faith and Fault in Contract Law* (Oxford: Oxford University Press, 1995), pp.485, 487–8, citing authorities.

[117] *SK Shipping (S) PTE Ltd v Petroexport Ltd ("The Pro Victor")* [2009] EWHC 2974; [2010] 2 Lloyd's Rep. 158, Flaux J at [102]–[104].

general law to seek protection when he reasonably apprehends that the other party's major default is, if not inevitable, certainly a genuine source of anxiety. As mentioned, no such general Common Law right subsists in English law.

Article 8:105 (text cited at end of this paragraph) of the *Principles of European Contract Law* ("soft law", not binding on the English courts)[118] enables a party to seek "adequate assurance of due performance" and in the meantime "withhold performance of its own obligations"; and the party seeking reassurance will acquire the right to terminate if "this assurance is not provided within a reasonable time" and "if [that party] still reasonably believes that there will be a fundamental non-performance by the other party and gives notice of termination without delay." The full text of Art.8-105 of the *Principles of European Contract Law* reads:[119]

7-066

> "*Assurance of Performance* (1) A party which reasonably believes that there will be a fundamental non-performance by the other party may demand adequate assurance of due performance and meanwhile may withhold performance of its own obligations so long as such reasonable belief continues. (2) Where this assurance is not provided within a reasonable time, the party demanding it may terminate the contract if it still reasonably believes that there will be a fundamental non-performance by the other party and gives notice of termination without delay."

UNIDROIT's *Principles of International Commercial Contracts* (2016) (Art.7.3.4),[120] the US *Uniform Commercial Code* (s.2-609(1)),[121] the (US) *Contracts Restatement* 2d (1979) (s.251),[122] and the United Nations ("Vienna") Convention on International Sale of Goods (1980) (Art.71) contain similar provisions.

7-067

VI. INJUNCTION TO RESTRAIN ANTICIPATORY BREACH

It appears that the remedy of an injunction might be available in some cases to prevent a party committing an act which would constitute an anticipatory breach of the contract. The point did not arise directly for decision in *Berkeley Community Villages Ltd v Pullen* (2007),[123] but that case contains dicta which support this possibility. In this case P, a landowner, proposed to sell part of the land to a third party. That would deprive B, with whom P had entered into a development contract, of its right to commission. The proposed sale would involve a breach. P had conceded[124] that an injunction would be available if Morgan J found that the proposed sale would involve breach. The judge added dicta[125] (not necessary for his decision in view of this concession) that an injunction would have been available

7-068

---

[118] T. Naudé in H. MacQueen and R. Zimmermann (eds), *European Contract Law: Scots and South African Perspectives* (Edinburgh: Edinburgh University Press, 2006), Ch.11.

[119] T. Naudé in H. MacQueen and R. Zimmermann (eds), *European Contract Law: Scots and South African Perspectives* (Edinburgh: Edinburgh University Press, 2006), Ch.11.

[120] 4th edn (2016) text and comment, available at *http://www.unidroit.org/instruments/commercial-contracts/unidroit-principles-2016*. On the UNIDROIT principles, S. Vogenauer, *Commentary on the UNIDROIT Principles of International Commercial Contracts*, 2nd edn (Oxford: Oxford University Press, 2015), and E Broerdermann, *UNIDROIT Principles of International Commercial Contracts: An Article-by-Article Commentary* (Kluwer Law International, The Hague, 2018).

[121] G.H. Jones (with P. Schlechtriem) "Breach of Contract" in *International Encyclopaedia of Comparative Law* Vol.VII (Contracts in General) (Tübingen: J.C.B. Mohr (Paul Siebeck), 1999), 15-153.

[122] J.W. Carter, *Carter's Breach of Contract*, 2nd edn (Oxford: Hart Publishing, 2019), [7-32].

[123] [2007] EWHC 1330 (Ch); [2007] N.P.C. 71, Morgan J.

[124] [2007] EWHC 1330 (Ch); 2007 N.P.C. 71 at [142].

[125] [2007] EWHC 1330 (Ch); 2007 N.P.C. 71 at [79]–[83].

for anticipatory breach of an obligation (here, cl.10).[126] The injunction would prevent a party taking a step which would preclude him from complying in due course with that obligation even where that party's capacity to execute fully the relevant obligation is contingent on a third party's permission (such as planning permission).

Similarly, Lewison LJ in *Duval v 11-13 Randolph Crescent Ltd* (2018)[127] acknowledged that a *quia timet* injunction can be awarded to prevent a proposed breach in a similar context.

VII. DAMAGES FOR ANTICIPATORY BREACH

7-069   It is now clear that damages must reflect the prospective events which were *bound to occur, and did in fact occur, during the interval between breach and assessment of damages by the court.* The new approach was consolidated by the Supreme Court in *Bunge SA v Nidera BV* (2015)[128] in a case involving anticipatory breach of a contract for the sale of goods. That decision endorsed the majority analysis of the House of Lords in *Golden Strait Corp v Nippon Yusen Kubishika Kaisha ("The Golden Victory")*, a case concerning actual breach, as distinct from an anticipatory breach.[129] The upshot of these decisions is that damages for anticipatory or actual breach should reflect post-breach events if those events have in fact reduced or eliminated the claimant's loss.

7-070   The new approach involves a revision of the traditional starting-point which had been that damages are generally[130] assessed with regard to the subject-matter's market value at the time of breach,[131] notably in the cases of failure to accept or to

---

[126] "Clause 10. At the request of Berkeley ... Pullens shall enter into any planning agreement relating to the Property imposing covenants or planning obligations provided that the planning agreement: a) imposes no positive obligations on Pullens or (if it does) those positive obligations must be specified as not taking effect until the development is initiated and b) either contains a suitable indemnity from Berkeley or provides that Pullens shall be released from any liability thereunder on parting with all its interest in the Property or that part that is affected by that planning agreement."

[127] [2018] EWCA Civ 2298; [2019] Ch. 357 at [26] and [33]; affirmed [2020] UKSC 18; [2020] A.C. 845, but without discussion of the injunction point.

[128] [2015] UKSC 43; [2015] 3 All E.R. 1082; [2015] 2 All E.R. (Comm) 789; [2015] Bus. L.R. 987; [2015] 2 Lloyd's Rep. 469 at [21]–[23] per Lord Sumption, and at [83] per Lord Toulson; see also *Flame SA v Glory Wealth Shipping Pte Ltd ("The Glory Wealth")* [2013] EWHC 3153 (Comm); [2014] Q.B. 1080, Teare J (noted E. Peel (2015) 131 L.Q.R. 29) (Teare J at [18] and [85] suggesting that damages will not be awarded if the innocent party cannot show that he would have had the resources to complete its side of the bargain; but in the sequel to this decision, *Glory Wealth Shipping Pte Ltd v Flame SA* [2016] EWHC 293 (Comm); [2016] 2 All E.R. (Comm) 151; [2016] 1 Lloyd's Rep. 571 at [17]–[19] and [25]–[28] Teare J held that damages were payable to the claimant owners on these facts, even though, if there had been no breach, the owners would have disposed of their right to payment by directing payment to be made to third parties (as they had directed vis-à-vis earlier contracts). J.W. Carter and G. Tolhurst, "Contract damages following discharge for repudiation - revisiting later events" (2016) 132 L.Q.R. 1–6.

[129] [2007] UKHL 12; [2007] 2 A.C. 353; noted Lord Mustill, "The Golden Victory—Some Reflections" (2008) 124 L.Q.R. 569; J. Morgan, "Note of The Golden Victory, House of Lords" [2007] C.L.J. 263; C. Nicholls (2008) J.B.L. 91; B. Coote, "Breach, anticipatory breach, or the breach anticipated?" (2007) 123 L.Q.R. 503; Sir Bernard Rix, in M. Andenas and D. Fairgrieve (eds), *Tom Bingham and the Transformation of the Law: A Liber Amicorum* (Oxford: Oxford University Press, 2009), 679.

[130] cf. Lord Wilberforce in *Johnson v Agnew* [1980] 367 at 401 HL: "not an absolute rule ... the court has power to fix such other date as may be appropriate".

[131] S. Waddams, "The Date for the Assessment of Damages" (1981) 97 L.Q.R. 445–461.

deliver goods in contracts of sale.[132] This focus on establishing the market value of goods at the time of breach gave rise to the fallacious view[133] that damages "crystallise" at that date and that post-breach events are somehow irrelevant. For that reason, over many decades the courts grappled[134] with the question whether damages might be legitimately adjusted (in practice reduced) to reflect subsequent events or high probabilities. But, as mentioned, it is now clear, following the endorsement in *Bunge SA v Nidera BV* (2015)[135] of the House of Lords in *Golden Strait Corp v Nippon Yusen Kubishika Kaisha ("The Golden Victory")*,[136] that damages must reflect the prospective events which were *bound to occur during that interval* or *did in fact occur* during that interval. In short, the date of breach "rule" is not in fact a general rule governing assessment of damages for breach of contract but merely a criterion restricted to a particular issue: it provides the means of fixing the relevant market value in contracts for the sale of goods.

To take the more recent of these decisions first, in *Bunge SA v Nidera BV* (2015),[137] the defendant had agreed to sell a quantity of Russian wheat, delivery to occur between 23 and 30 August. On 5 August, the Russian Government announced a prohibition, to operate from 15 August, on the export of such cereal during the remainder of that calendar year. On 9 August, before the delivery "window" (23 to 30 August), the seller declared that it would not supply. The seller later conceded that it had repudiated by not waiting to see if the prohibition would be implemented. It was also established that the date for assessing the value of the cereal not delivered was the date when the seller's renunciation was accepted (11 August). That left the issue whether damages should reflect the now established fact (a matter occurring after the date of termination but prior to assessment of damages) that the Russian prohibition had been implemented. The Supreme Court held that damages should not be awarded with eyes closed to this now historic fact. Otherwise the buyer would receive contractual damages for a non-loss, that is, for failure to supply that which the prohibition would inevitably have prevented the seller from supplying even if the seller had not pulled the plug prematurely on the deal.

7-071

---

132 Respectively, Sale of Goods Act 1979 ss.50(3) and 51(3).
133 The fallacy is noted in A. Kramer, *The Law of Contract Damages* (Oxford: Hart Publishing, 2014), Ch.17, and A. Dyson and A. Kramer, "There is No 'Breach Date Rule'" (2014) 130 L.Q.R. 259–281.
134 e.g. *Maredelanto Compania Naviera SA v Bergbau-Handel GMBH ("The Mihalis Angelos")* [1971] 1 Q.B. 164 CA. (criticised, D.W. Greig, "Condition or Warranty?" (1973) 89 L.Q.R. 93, 100–104).
135 [2015] UKSC 43; [2015] 3 All E.R. 1082; [2015] 2 All E.R. (Comm) 789; [2015] Bus. L.R. 987; [2015] 2 Lloyd's Rep. 469 at [21]–[23] per Lord Sumption, and at [83] per Lord Toulson (noted, J.W. Carter and G. Tolhurst, "Contract damages following discharge for repudiation - revisiting later events" (2016) 132 L.Q.R. 1–6; see also *Flame SA v Glory Wealth Shipping Pte Ltd ("The Glory Wealth")* [2013] EWHC 3153 (Comm); [2014] Q.B. 1080, Teare J (noted E. Peel, "Desideratum or principle: the 'compensatory principle' revisited" (2015) 131 L.Q.R. 29).
136 [2007] UKHL 12; [2007] 2 A.C. 353; noted Lord Mustill, "The Golden Victory—some reflections" (2008) 124 L.Q.R. 569; J. Morgan, "A victory for 'justice' over commercial certainty" [2007] C.L.J. 263; C. Nicholls, "The 'available market' rule and period charters: Golden Strait Corp v Nippon Yusen Kubishika Kaisha (The Golden Victory)" (2008) J.B.L. 91; B. Coote, "Breach, anticipatory breach, or the breach anticipated?" (2007) 123 L.Q.R. 503; Sir B. Rix, in M. Andenas and D. Fairgrieve (eds), *Tom Bingham and the Transformation of the Law: A Liber Amicorum* (Oxford: Oxford University Press, 2009), p.679.
137 [2015] UKSC 43; [2015] 3 All E.R. 1082; [2015] 2 All E.R. (Comm) 789; [2015] Bus. L.R. 987; [2015] 2 Lloyd's Rep. 469.

7-072   Lord Sumption in *Bunge SA v Nidera BV* (2015)[138] distinguished between the breach date as a means of calculating the relevant market value of goods and the further requirement that damages should be attuned to events which have become clear fact:

> "[there are] two potential questions which are not always sufficiently distinguished in the case-law. The first question is: assuming that there is an available market, as at what date is the market price to be determined for the purpose of assessing damages? It is clear that once that date is determined, any subsequent change in the market price is irrelevant. Most of the case-law on the measure of damages for the repudiation of a contract of sale arises out of disputes about the relevant market price, and this is what judges speaking of the breach-date rule are usually referring to. The second question is: in what if any circumstances will it be relevant to take account of contingencies (other than a change in the market price) if subsequent events show that they would have reduced the value of performance, perhaps to nothing, even without the defaulter's renunciation? This may happen, for example, if the injured party would have been unable to perform it when the time for performance arrived, or if the defaulter would have been relieved of the obligation to perform by frustration or under the express terms."

7-073   The Supreme Court in *Bunge SA v Nidera BV* (2015)[139] approved the majority decision of the House of Lords in *"The Golden Victory"* (2007) where the same approach had been adopted (although not in the context of an anticipatory breach), namely that damages should be reduced to reflect post-breach events *if they are already known and they would have had the effect of diminishing the claimant's loss.*[140] *"The Golden Victory"* (2007) was summarised by Lord Sumption in the *Nidera* case as follows:[141]

> "a seven-year time charter had been brought to an end by the charterer's repudiation in the course of performance some four years before its contractual terms but only fourteen months before it would have been cancelled in any event under a war clause. At the time when the charterers' repudiation was accepted, war was far from inevitable. It was found to be no more than a possibility. The question was how long it should be assumed, in those circumstances, that the charterparty would have lasted if it had not been wrongfully

---

138 [2015] UKSC 43; [2015] 3 All E.R. 1082; [2015] 2 All E.R. (Comm) 789; [2015] Bus. L.R. 987; [2015] 2 Lloyd's Rep. 469 at [16].

139 [2015] UKSC 43; [2015] 3 All E.R. 1082; [2015] 2 All E.R. (Comm) 789; [2015] Bus. L.R. 987; [2015] 2 Lloyd's Rep. 469.

140 *Golden Strait Corp v Nippon Yusen Kubishika Kaisha ("The Golden Victory")* [2007] UKHL 12; [2007] 2 A.C. 353; noted Lord Mustill, "The Golden Victory—some reflections" (2008) 124 L.Q.R. 569; J. Morgan, "A victory for 'justice' over commercial certainty" [2007] C.L.J. 263; C. Nicholls, "The 'available market' rule and period charters: Golden Strait Corp v Nippon Yusen Kubishika Kaisha (The Golden" (2008) J.B.L. 91; B. Coote, "Breach, anticipatory breach, or the breach anticipated?" (2007) 123 L.Q.R. 503; M. Furmston, "Actual Damages, etc", in D. Saidov and R. Cunnington (eds), *Contract Damages: Domestic and International Perspectives* (Oxford: Hart Publishing, 2008), p.419 at p.424 ff; D. McLauchlan, *"Expectation Damages, etc"*, in D. Saidov and R. Cunnington (eds), Ch.15; J. Morgan, "A victory for 'justice' over commercial certainty" [2007] C.L.J. 263; G.H. Treitel, "Assessment of damages for wrongful repudiation" (2007) 123 L.Q.R. 9; B. Coote, "Breach, anticipatory breach, or the breach anticipated?" (2007) 123 L.Q.R. 503; C. Nicholls, "The 'available market' rule and period charters: Golden Strait Corp v Nippon Yusen Kubishika Kaisha (The Golden Victory)" (2008) J.B.L. 91; Sir Bernard Rix, "Lord Bingham's Contributions to Commercial Law", in M. Andenas and D. Fairgrieve (eds), *Tom Bingham and the Transformation of the Law: A Liber Amicorum* (Oxford University Press, 2009), pp.679–83; earlier, S. Waddams, "The Date for the Assessment of Damages" (1981) 97 L.Q.R. 445.

141 [2015] UKSC 43; [2015] 3 All E.R. 1082; [2015] 2 All E.R. (Comm) 789; [2015] Bus. L.R. 987; [2015] 2 Lloyd's Rep. 469 at [20].

terminated. The House held by a majority that the overriding principle (or 'lodestar') was the compensatory principle. Irrespective of the date as at which the market price was ascertained, it was necessary to take account of contingencies known at the date of the arbitrator's assessment to have occurred, if their effect was that the contract would have been lawfully terminated at or before its contractual term. It followed that damages were to be assessed on the assumption that the charter would have lasted for [only] another 14 months."

As mentioned, *"The Golden Victory"* (2007) did not involve an anticipatory **7-074** breach but instead a charterer's decision to withdraw from a hire which had already commenced. The facts in greater detail were as follows. On 10 July 1998, the shipowners chartered "The *Golden Victory*" to the charterers for seven years, one month more or less at the charterers' option. Clause 33 gave each party the right to cancel if war or hostilities were to break out between certain countries. On 14 December 2001, four years early, the charterers repudiated the agreement. On 17 December, the owners accepted the repudiation. They claimed damages and arbitration ensued. On 20 March 2003, war falling within cl.33 broke out. The central issue in *"The Golden Victory"* (2007) was whether damages should be awarded for four years of lost hire or for a shorter period of 14 months to reflect the fact that war with Iraq broke out in 2003 and the contract (cl.33) gave each party the right to cancel if war or hostilities were to break out between certain countries? The House of Lords, by a majority,[142] held (upholding the lower courts and the arbitral tribunal)[143] that such inevitable cancellation could not be swept under the forensic carpet. It was clear that the charterer would have cancelled the contract once war was declared between the US and Iraq in March 2003. From that point, the charterer would have been absolved from contractual liability to pay hire. Although, as the arbitrator found, at the time of breach, 17 December 2001, war was merely a possibility, damages should reflect the facts now known. It would be unjust for the award of damages not to reflect this hindsight, otherwise it would involve "overcompensation". And so compensation should be for 14 months and not four years: damages should run from the date of breach to the date of inevitable cancellation (20 March 2003) and not beyond to 2005. In *"The Golden Victory"* (see discussion above) Lords Bingham[144] and Walker dissented, the latter saying:[145]

"In this case an objective and well-informed observer, looking at the matter [at the time of the renunciation] would have thought ... that the prospect of the war clause option being exercised ... was a mere possibility carrying little or no weight in commercial terms."

Lord Mustill, writing extra-judicially in the *Law Quarterly Review*, supported the dissentients, suggesting that the cause of action based on anticipatory breach should be conceptualised as loss of the value of contractual rights, assessed as the market value of those rights at the time of discharge, with appropriate adjustment to reflect contingencies then also affecting the value of those rights.[146] But these criticisms are now chasing a lost cause because the Supreme Court in *Bunge SA v Nidera BV*

---

142 Lords Scott, Carswell and Brown (dissents by Lords Bingham and Walker).
143 Thus Langley J, the Court of Appeal, and a majority of the House of Lords upheld the arbitrator's award.
144 [2007] UKHL 12; [2007] 2 A.C. 353, notably at [22] and [23] (too long to cite here); in essence on the basis that the innocent party had lost a four-year charterparty which was marketable at the date of breach.
145 [2007] UKHL 12; [2007] 2 A.C. 353 at [46].
146 Lord Mustill, "The Golden Victory—some reflections" (2008) 124 L.Q.R. 569.

(2015)[147] has endorsed the majority decision in *"The Golden Victory"* and so the law is now wholly beyond doubt.

7-075   The result in *"The Golden Victory"* (see above) is difficult to reconcile with the outcome in *Classic Maritime v Limbungan Makmur Sdn Bhd*.[148] The *Classic Maritime* case was another example of an actual breach, as distinct from an anticipatory breach. The Court of Appeal, reversing the trial judge, held that substantial damages were available even though the relevant five instalments of performance had been rendered commercially and indeed physically impossible. This impossibility had been caused by a dam burst that had flooded the only available Brazilian mine during the period within which the five instalments were to be presented. (As for the alternative source in Brazil, the trial judge had investigated this closely and concluded that the charterer would not have succeeded in obtaining an alternative supply from another supplier at the alternative Brazilian port mentioned in the contract.) Clause 32, an exceptions clause, would have exonerated the charterer for failure to supply the five cargoes to the shipowner, but only if that party had been ready and willing to perform. But the trial judge, Teare J, had found that the charterer was not willing to perform. Although breach was established, and the exceptions clause had fallen away, Teare J had then gone on to award nominal damages. This nugatory award had been made on the basis that the breach was a technicality not resulting in any loss on these facts because the dam burst had physically destroyed any opportunity to perform. But the Court of Appeal in the *Classic Maritime* case reversed this and awarded damages for the gain that it had lost as a result of the charterer's failure to provide the five cargoes that it had undertaken to supply. The Court of Appeal held that Teare J's error was to have exculpated the party in breach by the back door at the stage of assessing damages, on the basis of the burst dam. In the Court of Appeal's opinion, the burst dam was irrelevant. The defendant charterer's decision not to perform in any event constituted the breach, and liability for this failure fell outside the exception clause (that clause operating only if the performer was ready and willing to perform, or engaged already in the performance). In his penetrating note on this case, Michael Bridge says that, although in breach, the charterer had not caused the shipowner any loss.[149] This is because it would not have been possible for the relevant five cargoes to have been found. The dam burst was the reason for that inability. And that inability to perform arose without the charterer needing to invoke the exceptions clause.

VIII.   CAN THERE BE AN ACTIONABLE ANTICIPATORY BREACH WITHOUT TERMINATION OF THE CONTRACT?

7-076   This question concerns the following gap: the breach occurs in anticipation of the due date for performance but in circumstances where the innocent party (i) either elects not to terminate the contract for breach or (ii) the relevant breach is not serious enough to justify termination for breach. Although it is not yet

---

[147] [2015] UKSC 43; [2015] 3 All E.R. 1082; [2015] 2 All E.R. (Comm) 789; [2015] Bus. L.R. 987; [2015] 2 Lloyd's Rep. 469 at [21]–[23] per Lord Sumption, and at [83] per Lord Toulson; noted J.W. Carter and G. Tolhurst, "Contract damages following discharge for repudiation - revisiting later events" (2016) 132 L.Q.R. 1–6; M. Yip and Y. Goh, "The compensatory principle: a golden victory for a new certainty" (2016) J.B.L. 335–345.

[148] [2019] EWCA Civ 1102; [2019] 2 All E.R. (Comm) 592; noted M. Bridge (2020) 136 L.Q.R. 1.

[149] M. Bridge (2020) 136 L.Q.R. 1.

established whether there can be an actionable breach in these circumstances, the Law Commission (see next paragraph) contemplated that a claim for damages could arise immediately upon acceptance of an anticipatory breach even where the innocent party (i) does not (because it does not wish to), or (ii) cannot (because the breach is insufficiently serious), elect to terminate for breach. The Law Commission's approach would be that in both situations (i) and (ii) a breach would occur and become actionable, thus giving rise to an immediate right to compensation, even though the contract is not terminated, provided the innocent party has responded by "words or conduct showing an unequivocal intention to treat the other party as in breach" (the approach taken by the Law Commission in its (proposed) Contract Code).[150] But Liu contends (see para.7-078) that no anticipatory breach can arise in situation (ii) and instead he takes the view that anticipatory breach is only available if the proposed breach is serious enough to justify termination.

The Law Commission in its (proposed) Contract Code presented this example of   **7-077** an anticipatory breach which should be actionable even though it does not give rise to a right of termination:[151]

> "Thus if a decorator, who has contracted with a householder to paint all the rooms in his new house and to return twelve months later to do any necessary touching up to them, announces upon the completion of the initial painting that he has no intention of returning to do the touching up, why should the householder have to wait a year before suing for damages for breach? Accordingly, even where a party's anticipated breach is not sufficiently substantial [to constitute a ground for termination], the Code ... [should allow] the other party to sue immediately while at the same time completing his own performance, if indeed he has not already completed it."

To the Law Commission's persuasive analysis Liu makes this unconvincing   **7-078** retort:

> "if the inferred [anticipatory] breach does not entitle the victim to terminate the contract, there would be no good reason to accelerate the right to damages for that breach. The victim is not prejudiced by being precluded from bringing a claim until the inferred breach actually materialises ... [Such early compensation] would not only subject the other party to a unilateral enlargement of its obligations ... but would also rest that party's liability upon an assumption that the future breach is likely to occur when it might still be put right."[152]

Furthermore, Liu contends that there can be no anticipatory breach in situation   **7-079** (ii) (where the relevant breach is not serious enough to justify termination for breach) because, in his view, all anticipatory breaches must satisfy the requirement of "fundamentality".[153] An anticipatory breach, in his opinion, must be "so serious as to deprive the victim of substantially all the benefit intended to be

---

[150] H. McGregor QC, *Contract Code: Drawn up on behalf of the English Law Commission* (Milano: Giuffrè, 1993), 73 at s.303(1) and (2).

[151] H. McGregor QC, *Contract Code: Drawn up on behalf of the English Law Commission* (Milano: Giuffrè Publishing 1993), pp.73–6; at 74–5, giving the example cited in the present text.

[152] Q. Liu, *Anticipatory Breach* (Oxford: Hart Publishing, 2010), pp.79–80.

[153] Q. Liu, *Anticipatory Breach* (Oxford: Hart Publishing, 2010), pp.79–85; see also his discussion at pp.71–3 of Lord Diplock in *Afovos Shipping v Pagnan ("The Afovos")* [1983] 1 W.L.R. 195 HL at 203 per Lord Diplock; and Liu's citation at 72 fn.339 of soft law approaches: Vienna Convention on International Sale of Goods Art.25 [although this is not addressed to anticipatory contexts]; Principles of European Contract Law Arts 8:103 [but 8.103(c) is equivocal and refers to deliberate breach] and 9:304 [concerned only with the right to terminate in respect of an anticipatory

acquired by it under the contract":[154] "the seriousness required for the inferred breach must be pitched at the level of a 'fundamental' breach ... Only then can future remedies be accelerated and the inferred breach be converted into an anticipatory breach".[155] Thus Liu refers consistently to a "serious breach",[156] which is "fundamental",[157] or a "repudiatory breach",[158] and one which is "serious enough to trigger a right of termination".[159] Liu then proceeds to conduct a detailed analysis of the requirement of "fundamentality" in cases of anticipatory breach.[160]

7-080　　However, the better view is that the Law Commission was right to make the suggestion that, on appropriate facts, anticipatory breach can be actionable even if termination for breach does not follow or is not possible (see the passage cited at para.7-077).[161]

7-081　　Another example of a need to recognise anticipatory breach, even if there is no consequent termination of the contract for breach, might be the following hypothetical situation. Suppose Cassandra, a singer, has been hired by Lumley (a) to perform as a soloist (the soloist role being "Ophelia") in Pt I of an oratorio and (b) to be the page-turner for the organist in Pt II of the same performance. Performance of (b) is possible because there is nothing for Cassandra to sing in Pt II of this oratorio. This is because the author of the *libretto* had killed off Ophelia at the end of Pt I. Now consider first that the singer makes a second booking which will require her to get into a taxi and drive off during the interval at the end of Pt I, and then miss Pt II. Lumley discovers this three days before the performance. The fact that Cassandra has made this second booking is an anticipatory breach of her obligation to act as a page-turner during the second half of the oratorio. It might be (1) that this entitles Lumley to terminate the contract for breach, or (2) it might be that this degree of default does not "go to the root" of the contract. But even if (1) applies, and Lumley does not terminate the entire performance contract, Lumley will be entitled to compensation for Cassandra's breach: that cause of action for damages will accrue even before Cassandra's actual non-performance of the page-turning obligation (for example, where Lumley's response to the anticipatory breach is to hire a replacement to act as page-turner; if so, Lumley should be immediately entitled to damages, and there should be no need for Lumley to dismiss Cassandra).[162] It does not matter whether Cassandra's anticipatory breach is characterised as "anticipatory breach by self-incapacitation" or "anticipatory breach by renunciation" (where Cassandra declares that she will satisfy her contract as far as Pt I of the oratorio is concerned but that she is unwilling to hang around to turn

---

fundamental breach]; and UNIDROIT's *Principles of International Commercial Contracts* Art.7.3.3, 4th edn (2016) text and comment, is available at *http://www.unidroit.org/instruments/commercial-contracts/unidroit-principles-2016* (concerned only with the right to terminate in respect of an anticipatory fundamental breach).

[154] Q. Liu, *Anticipatory Breach* (Oxford: Hart Publishing, 2010), p.37.
[155] Q. Liu, *Anticipatory Breach* (Oxford: Hart Publishing, 2010), p.37.
[156] Q. Liu, *Anticipatory Breach* (Oxford: Hart Publishing, 2010), pp.39 and 71–3.
[157] Q. Liu, *Anticipatory Breach* (Oxford: Hart Publishing, 2010), p.38.
[158] Q. Liu, *Anticipatory Breach* (Oxford: Hart Publishing, 2010), p.38.
[159] Q. Liu, *Anticipatory Breach* (Oxford: Hart Publishing, 2010), p.39.
[160] Q. Liu, *Anticipatory Breach* (Oxford: Hart Publishing, 2010), pp.79–85.
[161] H. McGregor QC, *Contract Code: Drawn up on behalf of the English Law Commission* (Milano: Giuffrè Publishing 1993), pp.73–6; the example cited in the present text occurs at pp.74–5.
[162] Lumley's decision to find a page-turner replacement and not to dismiss Cassandra would probably be consistent with Lumley's duty to mitigate his overall loss, and this would be consistent with the rationale that the anticipatory breach doctrine operates to avoid waste and prevent the innocent party suffering anxiety and avoidable prejudice.

pages during Pt II). The same analysis should apply in situation (2), that is, Lumley is informed that Cassandra's breach is insufficiently serious to justify termination of the contract.

IX.   ELECTION NOT TO ACCEPT AN ANTICIPATORY BREACH: WHITE & CARTER (1962)

A problematic aspect of contract law concerns the remedy for "debt" and the   **7-082**
principles of repudiatory breach (for further discussion of debt, see Pt IV Ch.19 ff
on remedies). An innocent party has an "election"—a choice—whether to "accept" the repudiation or to "affirm" the contract. This was the background to the
majority House of Lords' decision in *White & Carter v McGregor* (1962).[163] That
decision confirms that the innocent party might have the capacity to keep open the
contract (the right to "affirm the contract"), and complete his side of the bargain.
Such situations will be rare. This is because it is now apparent that there are two
restrictions upon the innocent party's opportunity to take advantage of this rule:[164]
(i) the claimant cannot succeed in suing for debt if his performance requires the
other party's co-operation[165] (in those circumstances the claimant will not be able
to generate an entitlement to claim for the debt, because that presupposes his capacity to perform as originally envisaged, and such performance is now obstructed by
removal of the other party's co-operation); and (ii) the innocent party's claim in debt

---

[163] [1962] A.C. 413 HL; J. Edelman (ed), *McGregor on Damages*, 21st edn (Sweet & Maxwell, London, 2021), para.9-024 ff; A.S. Burrows, *Remedies for Torts and Breach of Contract*, 4th edn (Oxford: Oxford University Press, 2019), pp.383–387; J. Carter, A. Phang and S.Y. Phang, "Performance Following Repudiation: Legal and Economic Interests" (1999) 15 J.C.L. 97; Q. Liu, *Anticipatory Breach* (Oxford: Hart Publishing, 2011), Ch.9; A. Tettenborn, *The Law of Damages*, 2nd edn (London: LexisNexis, 2010), p.5.65 ff; K. Scott, "Contract—Repudiation—Performance by Innocent Party" [1962] C.L.J. 12; P.M. Nienaber, "The Effect of Anticipatory Repudiation: Principle and Policy" [1962] C.L.J. 213; A.L. Goodhart, "Measure of Damages When a Contract is Repudiated" (1962) 78 L.Q.R. 263; M. Furmston, "The Case of the Insistent Performer" (1962) 25 M.L.R. 364; E. Tabachnik, "Anticipatory Breach of Contract: Current Legal Problems" (1972) C.L.P. 149; L.J. Priestley, "Conduct after Breach: The Position of the Party Not in Breach" (1991) 3 J.C.L. 218; for references to US and Canadian materials or case law, J. Beatson, A. Burrows, and J. Cartwright, *Anson's Law of Contract*, 31st edn (Oxford: Oxford University Press, 2020), p.577, fn.22; US law, which differs from English on this topic, was cited in *Clea Shipping Corp v Bulk Oil International ("The Alaskan Trader")* [1984] 1 All E.R. 129 at 137, per Lloyd J. For Canadian case law, S. Waddams, *The Law of Contracts*, 7th edn (Toronto: Sweet & Maxwell, 2017), ss.632 and 633, and S. Waddams, *The Law of Damages* (Toronto: Sweet & Maxwell, looseleaf, undated 2022), 15.410 ff, noting (amongst other decisions) *Asamera Oil Corp Ltd v Sea Oil & General Corp* (1978) 89 D.L.R. (3d) 1; [1979] S.C.R. 633.

[164] A.S. Burrows, *Remedies for Torts and Breach of Contract*, 4th edn (Oxford: Oxford University Press, 2019), pp.481–487.

[165] *Geys* case [2012] UKSC 63; [2013] 1 A.C. 523 at [114]–[116] per Lord Sumption; *Isabella Shipowner SA v Shagang Shipping Co Ltd ("The Aquafaith")* [2012] 2 All E.R. (Comm) 461; [2012] 2 Lloyd's Rep. 61 at [37], per Cooke J; *Barclays Bank Plc v Unicredit Bank AG* [2012] EWHC 3655 (Comm); [2013] 2 Lloyd's Rep. 1 at [105]; *Hounslow LBC v Twickenham Garden Developments Ltd* [1971] Ch. 233 at 253–4, Megarry J; *White & Carter v McGregor* [1962] A.C. 413 at 428, 430 HL; J. Edelman (ed), *McGregor on Damages*, 21st edn (Sweet & Maxwell, London, 2021), 9-025, 9-026, 9-035, 9-036, examining *Anglo-African Shipping Co v Mortner Ltd* [1962] 1 Lloyd's Rep. 81 at 94 col.2, Megaw J (agent transporting goods from New York to London, despite defendant's attempted cancellation). A. Dyson, "What do the White & Carter 'Limitations' Limit?", in G. Virgo and S. Worthington (eds), *Commercial Remedies: Resolving Controversies* (Cambridge: Cambridge University Press, 2017).

will also fail if he cannot show a "legitimate interest"[166] in pursuing his unwanted performance (although, see below at para.7-096 ff, the second restriction has yielded very few, indeed scarcely any, decisive applications in the case law). But when such an unusual opportunity exists (and neither the co-operation issue, point (i), nor the "legitimate interest" factor, point (ii), obstructs or bars the claim), the innocent party will be entitled to sue for the agreed price once he has done his agreed part under the contract.

7-083   In *White & Carter v McGregor* (1962)[167] the "pursuer" (a Scottish claimant) sought payment of the price agreed for its advertising services. The "defender" (a Scottish defendant) had ordered these services but immediately tried to cancel the contract. The pursuer was not bound to "accept", that is, acquiesce in, this proposed cancellation. Instead the pursuer could legitimately complete performance and successfully claim in debt for the agreed payment. An unusual feature of this situation was that the innocent party could complete his performance without any co-operation from the other party. In fact, the pursuer part-performed and the defender failed to pay the relevant instalment. An acceleration clause rendered the defendant liable for the whole set of instalments in the event of non-payment of one instalment.

7-084   The majority in *White & Carter v McGregor* (1962) (Lords Reid, Hodson and Tucker) upheld this acceleration clause and further held that the pursuer was entitled to claim the full amount of the debt. These judges held that an innocent party who elects not to terminate the contract, despite the other's attempted repudiation, is entitled to complete a "solo" performance (that is, without the other's co-operation or involvement). He can then validly claim the agreed price for the completed job or task. The majority held that, in general, it does not matter that the other party had declared that he no longer wanted or needed the relevant performance.

7-085   However, the two dissenting judges (Lords Morton and Keith) considered this claim for debt to be highly inefficient and unmeritorious. It would conflict with the economic goal of encouraging innocent parties to restrict their losses by taking "mitigating" steps. But the technical response to this dissenting argument is that the doctrine of "mitigation" is confined to claims for damages, and that the claimant is here asserting a right to a debt. Debt and damages are subject to different regimes.[168]

7-086   Cases subsequent to the *White & Carter decision* (1962) have established that there are two restrictions upon the innocent party's opportunity to take advantage of this rule:[169] (i) the claimant cannot succeed in suing for debt if his performance requires the other party's co-operation; and (ii) the claimant must show a "legitimate interest"[170] in pursuing his unwanted performance (but see para.7-096 on the paucity of cases applying factor (ii) decisively against a claimant).

7-087   **"Co-operation" qualification**   The leading discussion of this topic is *Isabella*

---

[166] Q. Liu, *Anticipatory Breach* (Oxford: Hart Publishing, 2011), pp.207–217.

[167] [1962] A.C. 413 HL.

[168] On the differences between debt and damages, see Millett LJ in *Jervis v Harris* [1996] Ch. 195 at 202–3 CA.

[169] A.S. Burrows, *Remedies for Torts and Breach of Contract*, 4th edn (Oxford: Oxford University Press, 2019), pp.381–387.

[170] Q. Liu, *Anticipatory Breach* (Oxford: Hart Publishing, 2011), pp.207–217.

Shipowner SA v Shagang Shipping Co Ltd ("The Aquafaith") (2012).[171] In that case Cooke J made clear that a time charterparty does not involve the charterer's co-operation. If the vessel is made available for the charterer, but the latter chooses not to issue orders to the master, the owner is entitled to claim hire: "In order to complete their side of the bargain, the owners do not need the charterers to do anything in order for them to earn the hire in question".[172] Hire is payable in advance and so the owner

> "can hold the ship available to the charterer without any need for the charterer to do anything in order to maintain [the owner's] claim for hire".

It is different, according to Cooke J's suggestion, if the hire takes the form of a *demise charterparty*, that is, a contract of hire where the charterer acquires a possessory interest in the subject matter during the term of the contract.[173] In such a case (according to Cooke J) the owner cannot hold the vessel available to the demise charterer, and instead the latter's cancellation will determine the fate of the contract. In *"The Aquafaith"*, Cooke J said:[174]

> "The very essence of the demise charter is that possession of the vessel is given to the demise charterer so that, as soon as possession is retaken [or resumed] by the owner [or if possession reverts to the owner], the latter can no longer be entitled to hire under the demise charter."

But, with respect, is not the demise charterparty an a fortiori instance of a legal relationship where the owner makes an item available for the other's use and, if the latter chooses not to use it, the owner can declare that physically it has performed all that it needs to do under the contract and that the charterer's unwillingness to use the ship is irrelevant (the element of "co-operation")? The fallacy underlying Cooke J's dictum on the demise charterparty point is to assume that the owner is interested in the achievement of the commercial purpose of the charterparty. Clearly the owner has no such interest, and his only involvement or interest in the transaction is to be paid (probably in advance) and to get the chartered item back, at the end of the relevant term, in good condition and on time.

In *Hounslow LBC v Twickenham Garden Developments Ltd* (1971), Megarry J **7-088** held that a builder could not perform once the owner of the site had ordered him to stop work. It would be going too far to require the owner to allow the builder access to the site.[175]

---

171 [2012] EWHC 1077 (Comm); [2012] 2 All E.R. (Comm) 461; [2012] 2 Lloyd's Rep. 61 at [37]; see also *Barclays Bank plc v Unicredit Bank AG* [2012] EWHC 3655 (Comm); [2012] EWHC 3655 (Comm); [2013] 2 Lloyd's Rep. 1; [2014] 1 B.C.L.C. 342 at [105] per Popplewell J (fees payable in respect of guarantees; guarantor not accepting beneficiary's attempted early cancellation).

172 [2012] EWHC 1077 (Comm); [2012] 2 All E.R. (Comm) 461; [2012] 2 Lloyd's Rep. 61 at [37].

173 See the exposition of the nature of a demise or bare-boat charterparty, in *Ark Shipping Co LLC v Silverburn Shipping (IoM) Ltd* [2019] EWCA Civ 1161; [2019] 2 Lloyd's Rep. 603 at [6] (on that case para.10.085).

174 [2012] EWHC 1077 (Comm); [2012] 2 All E.R. (Comm) 461 at [40].

175 [1971] Ch. 233 at 253–254; similarly, *Anglo-African Shipping Co v J. Mortner Ltd* [1962] 1 Lloyd's Rep. 81, 94 col. 2 (Megaw J) (agent transporting goods from New York to London, despite defendant's attempted cancellation); on this last case, J. Edelman (ed), *McGregor on Damages*, 21st edn (Sweet & Maxwell, London, 2021), 9-025, 9-026, 9-035, 9-036.

7-089   In *Ministry of Sound (Ireland) v World Online Ltd* (2003)[176] Nicholas Strauss QC (Deputy High Court judge) held that a packaging company had a prima facie valid claim for the last instalment under a two-year contract requiring it to give publicity to the defendant's CDs because the defendant could not factually obstruct the substance of the claimant's performance. He also found a "legitimate interest".

7-090   Lord Sumption in *Geys v Société Générale, London Branch* (2012)[177] acknowledged the co-operation restriction upon the innocent party's capacity to keep open the contract. However, the majority in that case did not accept Lord Sumption's suggestion[178] that the innocent party has no right of election unless the guilty party's obligations are specifically enforceable.[179]

7-091   **Innocent party lacking a "legitimate interest"**   This is the second restriction upon the operation of the rule in the *White & Carter case* (1962) (see para.7-087). Simon J in *"The Dynamic"* (2003) said that this second restriction applies only (i) in extreme cases, "where damages would be an adequate remedy and where an election to keep the contract alive would be unreasonable"; (ii) that the "burden is on the contract-breaker to show that the innocent party has no legitimate interest"; and (iii) it is not enough to show "that the benefit to the [innocent party] is small in comparison to the loss to the contract breaker"[180] (echoing Kerr J in 1974).[181]

7-092   And Cooke J in *Isabella Shipowner SA v Shagang Shipping Co Ltd ("The Aquafaith")* (2012)[182] formulated element (i) of this restriction as follows:

> "an innocent party will have no legitimate interest in maintaining the contract if damages are an adequate remedy and his insistence on maintaining the contract can be described as 'wholly unreasonable', 'extremely unreasonable' or, perhaps, in my words, 'perverse'."

In short, the decision to carry on despite the attempted renunciation must be (completely) "beyond the pale" of commercial reasonableness.[183]

7-093   As the Court of Appeal in *Reichman v Beveridge* (2006) noted,[184] explaining the genesis of this requirement, only Lord Reid in *White & Carter v McGregor* (1962)[185] had ventured this idea, "neither Lord Hudson nor Lord Tucker [the other members of the majority] alluded to such a possibility". For this reason, the Supreme Court could yet decide that the law should be wholly remoulded. In the *White & Carter case* (1962), Lord Reid said:

---

[176] [2003] EWHC 2178; [2003] 2 All E.R. (Comm) 823; on this decision, Q. Liu, *Anticipatory Breach* (Oxford: Hart Publishing, 2011), p.204 ff.

[177] [2012] UKSC 63; [2013] 1 A.C. 523 at [115] and [116] (Lord Sumption dissenting on a narrower issue, but not on this point of principle).

[178] [2012] UKSC 63; [2013] 1 A.C. 523 at [116].

[179] [2012] UKSC 63; [2013] 1 A.C. 523 at [89] per Lord Wilson, adopting K. Ewing's article, "Remedies for Breach of the Contract of Employment" [1993] C.L.J. 405, 410–411: "[Why should it be that] the contract is automatically terminated by the unilateral repudiation of either party, simply because it is not capable of specific performance. As such the argument is hopelessly circular".

[180] *Ocean Marine Navigation Ltd v Koch Carbon Inc ("The Dynamic")* [2003] EWHC 1936; [2003] 2 Lloyd's Rep. 693 at [23] per Simon J.

[181] *Gator Shipping Corp v Trans-Asiatic Oil Ltd SA and Occidental Shipping Establishment ("The Odenfeld")* [1978] 2 Lloyd's Rep. 357 at 374, Kerr J.

[182] [2012] EWHC 1077 (Comm); [2012] 2 All E.R. (Comm) 461; [2012] 2 Lloyd's Rep. 61 at [44].

[183] [2012] EWHC 1077 (Comm); [2012] 2 All E.R. (Comm) 461; [2012] 2 Lloyd's Rep. 61 at [49].

[184] [2006] EWCA Civ 1659; [2007] 1 P. & C.R. 20; [2007] L. & T.R. 18 at [14] (and at [15] summarising the case law).

[185] [1962] A.C. 413 at 431 HL.

"It may well be that, if it can be shown that a person has no legitimate interest, financial or otherwise, in performing the contract rather than claiming damages, he ought not to be allowed to saddle the other party with an additional burden with no benefit to himself ... and just as a party is not allowed to enforce a penalty, so he ought not to be allowed to penalise the other party by taking one course when another is equally advantageous to him."

As we shall see, only two reported cases at first instance have turned on proof   **7-094** that the creditor lacked a "legitimate interest" (*Clea Shipping Corp v Bulk Oil International ("The Alaskan Trader")* (1984),[186] case (6) below, and *MSC Mediterranean Shipping Co SA v Cottonex Anstalt* (2015)[187] (reversed on another point by the Court of Appeal)[188] case (7) below. But neither decision provides powerful support.

Performer enjoying a legitimate interest   Here we will consider five situations   **7-095** in which the legitimate interest factor was held not to have precluded the creditor from carrying on with performance, having elected not to terminate the contract, and then to charge the other side with liability in debt for completed performance.

(i)   *Time charterparty cases.* In "The Odenfeld" (1978),[189] Kerr J held that a shipowner did have a "legitimate interest" in maintaining the vessel on hire to the charterer until September 1976.[190] Simon J in *"The Dynamic"* (2003) decided a similar charterparty case in the same way.[191] Similarly, *Isabella Shipowner SA v Shagang Shipping Co Ltd ("The Aquafaith")* (2012) Cooke J held[192] (reversing the arbitrator)[193] that there was nothing exceptional or wholly unreasonable in an owner maintaining a time-chartered vessel at the other party's expense when the latter had tried to return it 94 days early. (But contrast case (6) below for a time charterparty kept alive by an owner, but where no legitimate interest was identified.)

(ii)   In *Barclays Bank Plc v Unicredit Bank AG* (2012) Popplewell J held that a bank was entitled to claim charges for providing a facility even when the commercial party had sought to cancel the arrangement.[194]

---

186 [1984] 1 All E.R. 129 at 136–7, Lloyd J.

187 [2015] EWHC 283 (Comm); [2015] 2 All E.R. (Comm) 614; [2015] 1 Lloyd's Rep. 359; [2015] 1 C.L.C. 143; J. Morgan, "Smuggling mitigation into White & Carter v McGregor: time to come clean?" [2015] L.M.C.L.Q. 575 at 584 ff (there are brief observations also in J. Morgan, "Resisting Judicial Review of Discretionary Contractual Powers" [2015] L.M.C.L.Q. 484–490); the Court of Appeal held that the agreement had been discharged by repudiation in circumstances where future performance had become impossible: [2016] EWCA 789.

188 [2016] EWCA Civ 789; [2017] 1 All E.R. (Comm) 483.

189 *Gator Shipping Corp v Trans-Asiatic Oil Ltd SA and Occidental Shipping Establishment ("The Odenfeld")* [1978] 2 Lloyd's Rep. 357 at 373, Kerr J.

190 [1978] 2 Lloyd's Rep. 357 at 374.

191 *Ocean Marine Navigation Ltd v Koch Carbon Inc ("The Dynamic")* [2003] EWHC 1936; [2003] 2 Lloyd's Rep. 693 at [23] per Simon J.

192 [2012] EWHC 1077 (Comm); [2012] 2 All E.R. (Comm) 461; [2012] 2 Lloyd's Rep. 61 at [56].

193 [2012] EWHC 1077 (Comm); [2012] 2 All E.R. (Comm) 461; [2012] 2 Lloyd's Rep. 61 at [51] and [52]: "a finding of no legitimate interest [on the present facts] is not simply a finding of fact with which this court cannot interfere. It is a conclusion based upon a misunderstanding of the test, a failure to take into account relevant factors and the taking into account of irrelevant matters".

194 *Barclays Bank Plc v Unicredit Bank AG* [2012] EWHC 3655 (Comm); [2012] EWHC 3655 (Comm); [2013] 2 Lloyd's Rep. 1; [2014] 1 B.C.L.C. 342 at [110] and [111].

(iii)   In *Ministry of Sound (Ireland) v World Online Ltd* (2003),[195] Nicholas Strauss QC, sitting as a Deputy High Court Judge, held that the claimant had a legitimate interest in continuing to provide publicity for the defendant[196] (the facts are analogous to the unwanted advertising in the *White & Carter* case).

(iv)   In *Reichman v Beveridge* (2006)[197] the Court of Appeal confirmed that a landlord is entitled to make periodic demands (an action in debt) in respect of rent accruing during the residue of a business tenancy. Most business tenancies will involve "quarterly" rent obligations (payment every three months). That case is analogous to the cases at (1) concerning hire from charterparties: *The Odenfeld"* (1978),[198] "The Dynamic" (2003),[199] and *Isabella Shipowner SA v Shagang Shipping Co Ltd ("The Aquafaith")* (2012).[200]

(v)   In *George Barker (Transport) Ltd v Eynon* the claimant carriers were owed money by the defendant, including under the current contract of carriage.[201] The claimant entered into an oral agreement with the defendant's receiver that they would be paid both arrears and the charge for completing the current contract, otherwise, the claimant would exercise a general lien and thus withhold the goods at the point of destination (selling, if necessary, the perishable goods—meat—at auction). The Court of Appeal upheld the lien analysis. Edmund-Davies LJ said[202] that the *White & Carter* doctrine entitled the carrier to refuse to accept any express or implied repudiation by the defendant. Instead the claimant had chosen to perform the carriage agreement. On these facts, performance was very advantageous to the claimant, because it enabled them to complete delivery and thus trigger the protection of the general lien. In turn this meant that, in the Court of Appeal's opinion, the defendant's receiver's undertaking to pay all arrears, etc, had to be honoured. In this manner the claimant meat supplier secured payment ahead of the defendant's other creditors.

7-096   **No legitimate interest cases**   There is very little on the other side of the "legitimate interest" ledger. There are two first instances decision (cases (vi) and (vii), neither of which is compelling, and dicta of the Court of Appeal (case (viii)) in a context where arguably performance would be barred by the need for the other side's co-operation.

7-097   (vi)   Lloyd J in *Clea Shipping Corp v Bulk Oil International ("The Alaskan Trader")* (1984),[203] upheld, but without enthusiasm, the arbitrator's decision that a shipowner was not entitled to keep a two year time-chartered vessel on hire, with full crew, for eight months and to charge this to the charterer (contrast cases (1) and (2) above). *"The Alaskan Trader"* was rationalised

---

[195] [2003] EWHC 2178; [2003] 2 All E.R. (Comm) 823.
[196] [2003] EWHC 2178; [2003] 2 All E.R. (Comm) 823 at [64]–[66].
[197] [2006] EWCA Civ 1659; [2007] 1 P. & C.R. 20; [2007] L. & T.R. 18.
[198] *Gator Shipping Corp v Trans-Asiatic Oil Ltd SA and Occidental Shipping Establishment ("The Odenfeld")* [1978] 2 Lloyd's Rep. 357 at 373, Kerr J.
[199] *Ocean Marine Navigation Ltd v Koch Carbon Inc ("The Dynamic")* [2003] EWHC 1936; [2003] 2 Lloyd's Rep. 693 at [23] per Simon J.
[200] [2012] EWHC 1077 (Comm); [2012] 2 All E.R. (Comm) 461; [2012] 2 Lloyd's Rep. 61 at [56].
[201] [1974] 1 W.L.R. 461, C.A.
[202] [1974] 1 W.L.R. 461 at 468, C.A.
[203] [1984] 1 All E.R. 129 at 136–7, Lloyd J.

by Cooke J in *Isabella Shipowner SA v Shagang Shipping Co Ltd ("The Aquafaith")* (2012) as resting on Lloyd J's recognition that an experienced arbitrator had applied the correct test and that the owner's bold claim in *"The Alaskan Trader"* to be entitled to keep a vessel on hire for eight dormant months was a "commercial absurdity".[204]

(vii)   Another reported case where the "legitimate interest" factor was success-   **7-098**
fully invoked at first instance by the guilty party is *MSC Mediterranean Shipping Co SA v Cottonex Anstalt* (2015).[205] However, the present point fell away when the case came before the Court of Appeal.[206] On appeal, it was held that this was not a case where the innocent party continued to enjoy the possibility of keeping the contract alive. And so the "legitimate interest" point disappeared. Instead the Court of Appeal held that the contract had been terminated in circumstances where continuing liability to pay demurrage had been extinguished.[207] However, Moore-Bick LJ in the Court of Appeal was sympathetic to the trial judge's conclusion that the "legitimate interest" factor, if relevant, might have succeeded on these facts, Moore-Bick LJ also suggested that the "legitimate interest" factor, whatever its precise scope and nature might be, was acknowledged as part of the law, commenting that:[208] "the existence of the broad principle towards which [Lord Reid] pointed has been accepted in a number of cases".

In greater detail, the issues in *MSC Mediterranean Shipping Co SA v Cottonex*   **7-099**
Anstalt (2015 and 2016) arose as follows. The carrier (owner of the containers) had provided the shipper (also referred to in the judgments as "the merchant") with 35 containers. Those were then used by the latter for shipment of raw cotton to Bangladesh. There was then a freak turn of events: buyers from the shipper, having paid for most of the cotton, decided not to collect the goods, because the value of cotton had fallen starkly. Because property in the goods had passed to the buyers, the shipper could not empty the containers and redeliver them to the owner. The situation had reached stalemate because, in the absence of a court order, the Bangladeshi customs authorities would not allow them to be removed, and the non-

---

[204] [2012] EWHC 1077 (Comm); [2012] 2 All E.R. (Comm) 461; [2012] 2 Lloyd's Rep. 61 at [44].

[205] [2015] EWHC 283 (Comm); [2015] 2 All E.R. (Comm) 614; [2015] 1 Lloyd's Rep. 359; [2015] 1 C.L.C. 143; J. Morgan, "Smuggling mitigation into White & Carter v McGregor: time to come clean?" [2015] L.M.C.L.Q. 575 at 584 ff (there are brief observations also in J. Morgan, "Resisting Judicial Review of Discretionary Contractual Powers" [2015] L.M.C.L.Q. 484–490).

[206] [2016] EWCA Civ 789; [2017] 1 All E.R. (Comm) 483.

[207] [2016] EWCA Civ 789; [2017] 1 All E.R. (Comm) 483 at [43] per Moore-Bick LJ: "If it had been open to the carrier to affirm the contract I should have agreed with the judge that it had no legitimate interest in continuing to insist on performance by the shipper of its remaining obligations under the contracts. The accrued demurrage already exceeded by a considerable amount the value of the containers. Replacement containers were readily available at Chittagong and the carrier had no interest in keeping the contract alive other than to earn demurrage pending their return. This is a classic case in which it would have been wholly unreasonable for the carrier to insist on further performance. The only reasonable course for it to take would have been to accept the shipper's failure to redeliver the containers as a repudiation of the contract. However, I do not think that the option of affirming the contracts remained open to the carrier once the adventure had become frustrated, because at that point further performance became impossible, just as it would if the shipper or those for whom it was responsible had caused the containers to be destroyed. With respect to the judge, therefore, I do not think that this is a case in which the White & Carter principle applies. As at 2nd February 2012 the shipper could no longer redeliver the containers and, having brought about that situation by its breach, had become liable in damages for their loss."

[208] [2016] EWCA Civ 789; [2017] 1 All E.R. (Comm) 483 at [40] per Moore-Bick LJ.

party buyers were not willing to co-operate in procuring such a court order. As long as the contract continued, the containers remained on hire and thus chargeable to the shipper. A demurrage clause (liquidated damages for the overrun period) quantified that charge at a daily rate (a rate which increased after specified periods of delay).[209] The shipper's breach was characterised as commercial delay (the relevant period varying between six and eight months, on these facts)[210] amounting to "frustration" attributable to the shipper's non-excused default (and so, rather confusingly, "frustration" was here mentioned in the broad sense that the contract had become so delayed so as to become an impossible and futile venture, rather than in the sense of a contract being terminated by operation of law for "frustration").[211] And so the Court of Appeal held that the contract had become discharged by the shipper's repudiation in circumstances where future performance of the contract had become impossible. Here there was no scope for the carrier to keep the contract alive. This meant that the liability to pay demurrage had ceased to apply at that time of discharge. The result was (i) the shipper had a liability to pay demurrage at the daily rate from the end of the "free period" until the date of discharge; and (ii) the shipper was also liable to pay for failure to redeliver the containers at the date of discharge, that being based on the market rate for the containers on that date. Tomlinson LJ explained:[212]

"[there are certain cases] where a contract has become repudiated because it is no longer capable of performance, as in the classic case of frustrating delay. That is the present case. Our conclusion is that as from 2 February 2012 the contract in its agreed form was not capable of performance—further performance in the changed circumstances brought about by the delay would be radically different from that agreed. The guilty party can no longer perform its obligations when the time comes. The time for performance of the obligations of the guilty party is long past. Redelivery of the containers at some future date would be an act radically different in kind from redelivery of the containers in accordance with the contractually agreed time-scale. In those circumstances, as it seems to me, the innocent party simply cannot treat the contract as subsisting because it is no longer capable of performance as agreed. There is no alternative to the conclusion that the contract has come to an end. The fact that the carrier continued to press for performance, in the shape both of redelivery of the containers and the payment of demurrage, is neither here nor there. Those were acts in vain, unrelated to an existing contract."

7-100   At first instance in *MSC Mediterranean Shipping Co SA v Cottonex Anstalt*, Leggatt J had also held[213] that the shipper's failure to hand back the containers to the carrier was a repudiation (although his date was held to be too early).[214] But, unlike the Court of Appeal (see above at paras 7-098, 7-099), Leggatt J had treated the contract as still alive, so that the demurrage clause continued to operate.

---

[209] US$10 per container per day for the first 10 days; US$18 per container per day for the next 10 days; and US$24 per container per day thereafter.

[210] [2016] EWCA Civ 789; [2017] 1 All E.R. (Comm) 483 at [26]–[28] per Moore-Bick LJ.

[211] [2016] EWCA Civ 789; [2017] 1 All E.R. (Comm) 483 at [25]–[28] per Moore-Bick LJ, applying at [25] *Universal Cargo Carriers Corp v Citati* [1957] 2 Q.B. 401 and *Nitrate Corp of Chile Ltd v Pansuiza Compania de Navegacion SA ("The Hermosa")* [1980] 1 Lloyd's Rep. 638.

[212] [2016] EWCA Civ 789; [2017] 1 All E.R. (Comm) 483 at [61]; and see Moore-Bick LJ at [25]–[28].

[213] [2015] EWHC 283 (Comm); [2015] 2 All E.R. (Comm) 614; [2015] 1 Lloyd's Rep. 359; [2015] 1 C.L.C. 143 at [87], [88], [122].

[214] [2016] EWCA Civ 789; [2017] 1 All E.R. (Comm) 483 at [27] and [28] per Moore-Bick LJ, identifying the crucial date of repudiatory breach as 2 February 2012, rather than, as found by Leggatt J, 27 September 2011.

However, he held that the carrier's decision to maintain the contract and to charge indefinitely under the demurrage clause was against good faith.[215] In the Court of Appeal the good faith argument was declared to be bad law.[216] Leggatt J at first instance added that the shipper's decision was also wholly unreasonable for the purpose of the "legitimate interest" criterion.[217] The result[218] was that demurrage was payable only until the date of repudiation. The Court of Appeal took the view that this was not a *White & Carter* situation because the effect of the repudiatory breach by delay on these facts was to render any post-breach survival of the contract an impossibility. The case discloses a rare phenomenon: a contract terminating by breach following repudiation without any requirement of acceptance by the innocent party. (The Court of Appeal also rejected the suggestion that a demurrage clause is a penalty if it contains no fixed "cut-off" point).[219]

(viii)   Dicta (but no binding decision) in *Attica Sea Carriers Corp v Ferrostaal*   **7-101**
Poseidon Bulk Reederei GmbH ("The Puerto Buitrago") (1976)[220] suggest that it would have been illegitimate, on the basis that it would have been disproportionate, for a shipowner at the end of a charter to have insisted on charging for repairs (US$2 million) exceeding the ship's value (US$1 million).[221] This discussion was defended by Cooke J in *Isabella Shipowner SA v Shagang Shipping Co Ltd ("The Aquafaith") (2012)* on the basis that

---

215   [2015] EWHC 283 (Comm); [2015] 2 All E.R (Comm) 614; [2015] 1 Lloyd's Rep. 359; [2015] 1 C.L.C. 143 at [97], [98].

216   [2016] EWCA Civ 789; [2017] 1 All E.R. (Comm) 483 at [45], per Moore-Bick LJ: "The judge drew support for his conclusion from what he described as an increasing recognition in the common law world of the need for good faith in contractual dealings. The recognition of a general duty of good faith would be a significant step in the development of our law of contract with potentially far-reaching consequences and I do not think it is necessary or desirable to resort to it in order to decide the outcome of the present case. It is interesting to note that in the case to which the judge referred as providing support for his view, *Bhasin v Hrynew* 2014 SCC 71; [2014] 3 S.C.R. 494, the Supreme Court of Canada recognised that in *Mid Essex Hospital Services NHS Trust v Compass Group UK and Ireland* [2013] EWCA Civ 200 this court had recently reiterated that English law does not recognise any general duty of good faith in matters of contract. It has, in the words of Bingham LJ in *Interfoto Picture Library Ltd v Stiletto Visual Programmes Ltd* [1989] Q.B. 433, 439, preferred to develop 'piecemeal solutions in response to demonstrated problems of unfairness', although it is well-recognised that broad concepts of fair dealing may be reflected in the court's response to questions of construction and the implication of terms. In my view the better course is for the law to develop along established lines rather than to encourage judges to look for what the judge in this case called some 'general organising principle' drawn from cases of disparate kinds. For example, I do not think that decisions on the exercise of options under contracts of different kinds, on which he also relied, shed any real light on the kind of problem that arises in this case. There is in my view a real danger that if a general principle of good faith were established it would be invoked as often to undermine as to support the terms in which the parties have reached agreement. The danger is not dissimilar to that posed by too liberal an approach to construction, against which the Supreme Court warned in *Arnold v Britton* [2015] UKSC 36; [2015] A.C. 1619."

217   [2015] EWHC 283 (Comm); [2015] 2 All E.R. (Comm) 614; [2015] 1 Lloyd's Rep. 359; [2015] 1 C.L.C. 143 at [117]–[121].

218   [2015] EWHC 283 (Comm); [2015] 2 All E.R. (Comm) 614; [2015] 1 Lloyd's Rep 359; [2015] 1 C.L.C. 143 at [122].

219   [2016] EWCA Civ 789; [2017] 1 All E.R. (Comm) 483 at [46] per Moore-Bick LJ: "it has never been suggested that a clause in a voyage charter providing for the payment of demurrage at a daily rate may be regarded as penal simply because it fixes no express limit on the period of the charterer's liability."

220   [1976] 1 Lloyd's Rep. 250 CA.

221   [1976] 1 Lloyd's Rep. 250 at 255.

it was a demise charterparty (requiring the charterer's co-operation)[222] and that, in any event, the owner's proposed repairs would be "an exercise in futility".[223]

Moore-Bick in *MSC Mediterranean Shipping Co SA v Cottonex Anstalt* (2016)[224] summarised the *Attica Sea Carriers case* as follows:

> "a vessel had been chartered by demise on terms which required the charterer to redeliver her at the end of the charter period in the same good order and condition as on delivery and to carry out at its own expense any repairs necessary in order to do so. In the event, the vessel needed extensive repairs which, if carried out, would have cost twice as much as her value when repaired. The charterer declined to carry out the repairs and the owner refused to accept redelivery until it had done so, claiming that hire continued to be payable for as long as the vessel remained in the possession of the charterer. [The Court of Appeal] held that carrying out the necessary repairs was not a pre-condition to effective redelivery, so that the charterer could redeliver the vessel in her unrepaired state, even though that involved a breach of contract. In the alternative, applying the ['legitimate interest'] principle ... all three members of the court held (albeit obiter) that, if that were wrong, the owner ought in all reason to have accepted the charterer's repudiation, since damages provided it with an adequate remedy. Accordingly, it could not recover hire."

7-102   **Reform?**   In *Ministry of Sound (Ireland) v World Online Ltd* (2003)[225] Nicholas Strauss QC, said: "The commercially just result would be to restrict the innocent party to its claim for damages. But I am far from convinced that, as a general rule, English contract law in this area is designed always to achieve the commercially just result". Might the UK Supreme Court decide to reverse the *White & Carter* doctrine?[226] Other systems have refused to follow the lead of English (and Scots) law in making this distinction in the reach of "mitigation" between debt and damages claims[227] (see, notably, Carter's examination of the position adopted in the US).[228]

7-103   If this question is re-opened at the highest level, before the Supreme Court, what factors will be relevant?

7-104   **Argument in favour of the White & Carter general rule**   The argument in favour of preserving the current law is that the mitigation doctrine can be technically confined, as a matter of positive law, to claims for compensatory damages. This is the formal position adopted by the majority in *White & Carter v McGregor*

---

[222] [2012] EWHC 1077 (Comm); [2012] 2 All E.R. (Comm) 461; [2012] 2 Lloyd's Rep. 61 at [40].

[223] [2012] EWHC 1077 (Comm); [2012] 2 All E.R. (Comm) 461; [2012] 2 Lloyd's Rep. 61 at [44].

[224] [2016] EWCA Civ 789; [2017] 1 All E.R. (Comm) 483 at [34].

[225] [2003] EWHC 2178 (Ch); [2003] 2 All E.R. (Comm) 823 at [61]; on this decision, Q. Liu, *Anticipatory Breach* (Oxford: Hart Publishing, 2011), p.204 ff.

[226] The author has considered the White & Carter "legitimate interest" criterion in some detail at Neil Andrews, *Contract Law in Practice* (Oxford: Oxford University Press, 2021), 27.50–27.68, including an "Evaluation"; L. McGregor in J. Smits, D. Haas, G. Hesen (eds), *Specific Performance in Contract Law: National and Other Perspectives* (Antwerp: Intersentia Publishing, 2008), pp.67, 89, noting *"Report on Remedies for Breach of Contract"* (Edinburgh: Scot Law Com No.174, 1999), Pt II.

[227] J. Beatson, A. Burrows, and J. Cartwright, *Anson's Law of Contract*, 31st edn (Oxford: Oxford University Press, 2020), p.577, fn.22, citing US and Canadian materials or case law.

[228] J.W. Carter, *Carter's Breach of Contract*, 2nd edn (Oxford: Hart Publishing, 2019), [11-53] ff.

(1962)[229] (Lords Reid, Hodson and Tucker). Moreover, the right to elect not to terminate the contract is in practice substantially fettered by the requirement that the performing party is seldom in a position to act without the other party's co-operation. The case law summarised at paras 7-089–7-092 confirms the vitality and commercial importance of this co-operation requirement. The "legitimate inter-est" factor, if preserved, will continue to operate in a tiny residuum of cases where, to adopt Cooke J's formulations in *Isabella Shipowner SA v Shagang Shipping Co Ltd ("The Aquafaith")* (2012) (para.7-092),[230] the creditor's conduct in generating extra financial liability is "wholly unreasonable", "extremely unreasonable" or "perverse" and thus (well) "beyond the pale" of commercial reasonableness.[231]

Arguments against the White & Carter general rule   It might be argued that   **7-105**
the mitigation principle should have a role to play even where the claim is to pay-ment of a debt, as distinct from a claim for compensatory damages.[232] If that first point is accepted, it might be further contended that the innocent party should normally be confined to a claim for compensation, and not be permitted stub-bornly to "hold out" for eventual complete payment of the agreed remuneration. This would reverse the approach currently adopted in English law. The next step would be to admit that there can be exceptional situations where the creditor's claim for debt should nevertheless succeed, in other words, that there is commercial merit in his decision not to have accepted the attempted renunciation and instead to have carried on performance.

The first possible exception, where the creditor's case would be commercially   **7-106**
meritorious, might be: (i) the claim for debt arises in a context where the paying party has assumed the commercial risk that he will not in fact need the relevant property or item for the full currency of the relevant term and so he has assumed an unqualified liability to pay once it is made available to him.

As for exception (i), see above, this factor will support the decision in the *Reich-*   **7-107**
man case (2006).[233] The Court of Appeal confirmed that a landlord should not be required to find a new business tenant, because landlords have no right to compensation in respect of future loss of rent, as Lloyd LJ noted[234] (although this last proposition has been contested by one commentator).[235] Indeed landlords often require guarantees from third parties to secure the tenant's continuing payment of rent. Landlords wish to ensure that leases continue to yield a flow of rent, should the tenant default.

It is possible that this might need to be qualified by a "safety-valve": namely, that   **7-108**
the length of the proposed or continuing performance has exceeded the point at which it is commercially acceptable for the performing party to continue to demand payment under the contract. As for this "safety-valve", compare the comment by Cooke J in *Isabella Shipowner SA v Shagang Shipping Co Ltd ("The Aquafaith")*

---

229 [1962] A.C. 413 HL.
230 [2012] EWHC 1077 (Comm); [2012] 2 All E.R. (Comm) 461; [2012] 2 Lloyd's Rep. 61 at [44].
231 [2012] EWHC 1077 (Comm); [2012] 2 All E.R. (Comm) 461; [2012] 2 Lloyd's Rep. 61 at [49].
232 J. Morgan, "Smuggling mitigation into White & Carter v McGregor: time to come clean?" [2015] L.M.C.L.Q. 575 presents this type of argument and develops it.
233 [2006] EWCA Civ 1659; [2007] 1 P. & C.R. 20; [2007] L. & T.R. 18.
234 [2006] EWCA Civ 1659; [2007] 1 P. & C.R. 20; [2007] L. & T.R. 18 at [18].
235 M. Pawlowski, "Tenant abandonment-damages for loss of future rent" (2010) 126 L.Q.R. 361–65, citing various authorities inconsistent with the proposition that a landlord cannot recover damages for loss of future rent.

(2012)[236] that Lloyd J's decision in *Clea Shipping Corp v Bulk Oil International ("The Alaskan Trader")* (1984)[237] was a response to the "commercial absurdity" of keeping a vessel on hire for eight dormant months.[238]

7-109   A second possible exception, where the creditor's case would be commercially meritorious, might be: (ii) the creditor can show that damages, assessed at the date of the attempted renunciation, would not have properly protected him in respect of an important commercial or other significant interest; but mere difficulty in assessing damages should not be sufficient, because compensation can be awarded despite difficulty in assessment; the relevant commercial or other significant interest should have been known to the guilty party, or reasonably obvious to him.

This factor will render it unlikely that a surveyor should be free to make a report on a property which the client is no longer interested in buying: his remedy should be in damages. Similarly, a management consultant should not ordinarily (see next sentence) be free to go to Hong Kong and make a report into a third party company if the commissioning party has decided to call off the engagement, the example given by Lord Reid in the *White & Carter case* (1962).[239] It is conceivable—although commercially unlikely—that a "first-time" management consultant might tell the other party: "this is my first and probably sole chance to prove myself to the market at large". But, even if this is said, and the other party makes no comment, it will be unlikely that the court will construe the other party as having assumed the risk that he must pay the fee come-what-may (even if the job turns out to be useless to that party and so he has decided to cancel it).

7-110   The better approach, in the author's opinion,[240] is that the *White & Carter* doctrine (namely, X's opportunity to charge the other party for performance despite earlier attempted cancellation by the other side) should be confined to (i) cases where the duty to make periodic payments has already arisen, at least in part, because property has already been hired out by X to the other; by contrast, X's opportunity to charge should not extend to (ii) situations where no duty to pay has yet been generated because the payment obligation will arise only if X furnishes performance (as on the facts of the *White & Carter* case itself). As for situation (i) (to which, it is submitted, the *White & Carter* doctrine should continue to apply), the main cases involve X's property being hired or let: either movable property (for example, a ship[241] has already been delivered and accepted[242] under a contract of hire in return for payment, or premises[243] have been let on payment of rent). From the owner's perspective, such a transaction is intended to provide an income stream

---

[236] [2012] EWHC 1077 (Comm); [2012] 2 All E.R. (Comm) 461; [2012] 2 Lloyd's Rep. 61 at [44].

[237] [1984] 1 All E.R. 129 at 136–7, Lloyd J.

[238] [2012] EWHC 1077 (Comm); [2012] 2 All E.R. (Comm) 461; [2012] 2 Lloyd's Rep. 61 at [44].

[239] [1962] A.C. 413 at 428–9, 442 HL, per Lord Reid (Lord Keith also quoting this example): "Then it was said that, even where the innocent party can complete the contract without such co-operation, it is against the public interest that he should be allowed to do so. An example was developed in argument. A company might engage an expert to go abroad and prepare an elaborate report and then repudiate the contract before anything was done. To allow such an expert then to waste thousands of pounds in preparing the report cannot be right if a much smaller sum of damages would give him full compensation for his loss. It would merely enable the expert to extort a settlement giving him far more than reasonable compensation".

[240] Neil Andrews, "Breach of Contract: A Plea for Clarity and Discipline" (2018) 134 L.Q.R. 117 at 124; Neil Andrews, *Contract Law in Practice* (Oxford: Oxford University Press, 2021), 27.50–27.68, including an "Evaluation".

[241] *Isabella Shipowner SA v Shagang Shipping Co Ltd ("The Aquafaith")* [2012] EWHC 1077 (Comm); [2012] 2 All E.R. (Comm) 461 (time charterparty). The standard arrangement is that X hires a ship to Y; but Y's inability to cancel should in principle extend to the situation where the hired subject-

of hire or rent, or an up-front "premium", to be paid by a party who has become committed to make such payments for the period of hire. That party cannot simply change his mind and return the subject matter. Although committed in this way, this party can often meet, or at least reduce, the financial burden which he has assumed by sub-letting or assigning the subject matter for the rest of the term. Situation (ii) (to which, it is submitted, the *White & Carter* doctrine should no longer extend) involves the innocent party taking positive steps (fresh performance or at least modifying[244]) to earn the right to a fee. Examples are: advertising[245] (or re-advertising),[246] publicising,[247] or arranging for the transport[248] of goods which have been bought by the claimant at the defendant's request.'

X. LIU'S UNITARY THEORY OF ANTICIPATORY BREACH

In his book, *Anticipatory Breach* (2010),[249] Liu contends that the notion of implied renunciation (which he styles "inferential renunciation") should provide an "unified" basis for anticipatory breach. In his view, the test should be whether party B's conduct, prior to the date of due performance, objectively and reasonably justifies party A drawing the inference that party B is "likely, on the balance of probabilities, to commit a fundamental breach when the time for [the relevant] performance arrives".[250] He writes:[251]

> "The 'inferential breach' analysis ... requires two steps to be taken. First, the party alleging an anticipatory breach must satisfy the court that a legal inference may be drawn that a future breach is likely to occur. Secondly, the party must also satisfy the court that the inferred breach is sufficiently serious to compel an acceleration of the legal remedies for it. For this purpose the inferred breach must be shown to be a 'fundamental' breach. Both of these tests must be met in order for an anticipatory breach to eventuate."

7-111

Critique of Liu's theory However, Liu's reconstruction of anticipatory breach has not been judicially adopted. The courts proceed on the basis of express renunciation (supplemented, where necessary, by implicit renunciation, that is,

7-112

---

242 matter is ship no.1 (or car, or lorry etc.), with the possibility of substitution of ship no.2 (car, lorry, etc.) during the period of hire.

242 *Karsales (Harrow) Ltd v Wallis* [1956] 1 W.L.R. 936, 944, CA; *National Cash Register Co Ltd v Stanley* [1921] 3 K.B. 292 at 296; *Wright v Melville* (1828) 3 Car. & P. 542; 172 E.R. 538 (Best CJ); *White & Carter Councils Ltd v McGregor* [1962] A.C. 413, 440–441, HL.

243 *Reichman v Beveridge* [2006] EWCA Civ 1659; [2007] 1 P. & C.R. 20.

244 In *White & Carter Councils Ltd v McGregor*, although a repeat order, new plates were prepared and positioned on the bins see [1962] A.C. 413 at 415 (facts summarised by reporter) and 426 (Lord Reid).

245 *Langford & Co Ltd v Dutch* 1952 S.C. 15; 1952 S.L.T. 72 (IH 1 Div), overruled by *White & Carter Councils Ltd v McGregor* [1962] A.C. 413.

246 [1962] A.C. 413.

247 *Ministry of Sound (Ireland) v World Online Ltd* [2003] EWHC 2178; [2003] 2 All E.R. (Comm) 823 (Nicholas Strauss QC).

248 *Anglo-African Shipping Co v J. Mortner Ltd* [1962] 1 Lloyd's Rep. 81 at 94, col. 2 (Megaw J); Q. Liu, "The *White & Carter* Principle: A Restatement" (2011) 74 M.L.R. 171, 191; J. Edelman (ed), *McGregor on Damages*, 21st edn (Sweet & Maxwell, London, 2021), 9-025, 9-026, 9-035, 9-036; S. Rowan, "The 'Legitimate Interest in Performance' in the Law on Penalties" [2019] C.L.J. 148, 169–170; S. Rowan, *Remedies for Breach of Contract: Comparative Analysis of the Protection of Performance* (Oxford: Oxford University Press, 2012), 23.

249 Q. Liu, *Anticipatory Breach* (Oxford: Hart Publishing, 2011), Chs 2–4.

250 Q. Liu, *Anticipatory Breach* (Oxford: Hart Publishing, 2011), pp.73, 74.

251 Q. Liu, *Anticipatory Breach* (Oxford: Hart Publishing, 2011), p.37.

renunciation by implication, or even by conduct), and inexcusable disablement. It is submitted that Liu's unitary theory, just summarised, unattractively welds together the practically important factual differences between the following three situations: (1) party B tells party A: "I know I am supposed to perform next week at the concert in Ruritania, as agreed, but I am telling you now that I have no intention of doing so" (explicit renunciation); (2) B tells X in A's presence: "next week I am going away on holiday to Greece and nothing will bring me back for the whole of that week" (implicit renunciation); and (3) the minimum time to gain a visa to enter Ruritania is 14 days, and such an application must be made by personal attendance at the Ruritanian Embassy in London, but seven days before B is required to travel to Ruritania to perform in a concert, as agreed with A, B has yet to apply to the Ruritanian Embassy for a visa (a case of disablement). The difference between (1) and (2) is between clear statements of unwillingness and implicit indications of unwillingness.

7-113   As demonstrated in this chapter, English courts currently distinguish (3) from (1) [and (2)]. This distinction is sound because (3) requires clear inability to perform: a likely failure to perform is not enough (para.7-036 ff). Thus, in situation (3) the claim that future performance is in fact impossible is one which requires proof to a very high level. The law prudently inclines in favour of the party whose future performance is in question. This is because life is full of examples of people pulling off a last-minute success. In the vernacular, this is described as a "narrow scrape", a "close-run thing", or escaping liability "by the skin of one's teeth". Conversely, the other party should not be encouraged to make gloomy prognostications: premature declarations of hopelessness where there is still a decent glimmer of hope.

7-114   By contrast, confronted by a case of explicit renunciation (situation (1)), the law respects a party's right to take this at face-value as a cancellation. This has been so since the break-through case of *Hochster v De la Tour* (1853).[252] If the cancellation is accepted, the innocent party should be able to obtain immediate compensation in respect of the lost contractual performance.

7-115   It would be odd, if one were to follow Liu, to collapse these three categories into a single test of "inferential breach" (see the summary of Liu's theory at para.7-118). This throws out two babies (situations (1) and (3) above) with the bathwater. And Liu's approach would introduce a seductive means of constructing an exit from a contract, based on a party's ostensible justified perception that "the other side was obviously not going to perform". In short, Liu's conceptual restructuring of anticipatory breach is unattractive. It is not consistent with the practicalities of this sphere. In practice, there will be profound disagreement between rival parties whether the alleged "victim" of anticipatory breach is truly a "victim" at all: or whether he is constructing a means of obtaining termination and damages based on the other party's apparently ominous lack of preparation or his lack of enthusiasm for a future task.

7-116   It is interesting to conclude by citing the definition of anticipatory breach proposed by the Law Commission in their draft codification of the law of contract

---

[252] (1853) 2 E. & B. 678; 22 L.J. (QB) 455; Q. Liu, *Anticipatory Breach* (Oxford: Hart Publishing, 2010), p.10 ff; P. Mitchell, in C. Mitchell and P. Mitchell (eds), *Landmark Cases in the Law of Contract* (Oxford: Hart Publishing, 2008), p.135; M. Mustill, "The Golden Victory—Some Reflections" (2008) 124 L.Q.R. 569, 576–7; see also M. Mustill, "Anticipatory Breach: The Common Law at Work", *Butterworth Lectures 1989–90* (London: Butterworths, 1990).

(s.303(1) and (2)). Although that Code was abandoned, there is much wisdom and illumination contained in its careful summaries of major principle.

On this topic, the draft Code states at s.303(1):[253]   **7-117**

"A party to a contract who, before the due time for performance of all or any of his contractual promises or other obligations, indicates a definite intention not to perform all or any separate and distinct part of them, or becomes unable to do so in circumstances not terminating the contract by frustration ..., commits a breach of contract if the other party elects to treat such intention or inability as an immediate breach: this type of breach is called an anticipated breach."

And on the question of election in this context, s.303(2) states: **7-118**

"Such election by the other party [the innocent party] (a) is precluded once the one who has declined or become unable to perform has, to the knowledge of the [innocent] party, reasserted his intention or regained his ability to perform; (b) is presumed where it would be unreasonable for [the innocent party] to continue with his own performance and so aggravate his loss; (c) otherwise requires words or conduct showing an unequivocal intention to treat the other party as in breach."

---

[253] *Contract Code: Drawn up on behalf of the English Law Commission* (Milano: Giuffre Publishing 1993), p.73.

CHAPTER 8

REPUDIATION BY ACTUAL BREACH

I. The General Concept of Repudiation

Summary   Repudiation involves an actual breach of contract by conduct (or **8-001** sometimes by omission) which is grave enough so as to go to the root of the contract. The hallowed[1] expression "goes to the root of the contract"[2] (or "goes to the whole root",[3] or "strike at the root or essence")[4] means that the breach is really serious. For example, the "going to the root" test was used in *Poussard v Spiers*[5] to justify an impresario's decision to find a non-temporary replacement, in order to keep a new opera from becoming an immediate commercial disaster. But there are various similar expressions of the test of sufficiently serious default. Thus, Lord Wright in *Ross T Smyth & Co Ltd v TD Bailey, Son & Co*[6] approached the question by asking whether the guilty party had conducted himself in a way which was "substantially inconsistent with his contractual obligations". A variation, adopting

---

[1] M.G. Bridge, *The Sale of Goods*, 4th edn (Oxford: Oxford University Press, 2019), paras 10.30 and 10.31, expresses a preference for this formulation.

[2] *Federal Commerce & Navigation Co v Molena Alpha Inc ("The Nanfri")* [1979] A.C. 757 at 778–779, 783, 784, 785, 786 HL; *Woodar Investment Development Ltd v Wimpey Construction UK Ltd* [1980] 1 W.L.R. 277 at 286–287, 298 HL; *Decro-Wall International SA v Practitioners in Marketing Ltd* [1971] 1 W.L.R. 361 at 374, 380 CA (where Sachs LJ traces the phrase to Lord Ellenborough CJ, in *Davidson v Gwynne* (1810) 12 East. 381 at 389; 104 E.R. 149 at 152 ("unless the ... breach ... goes to the whole root and consideration of it, the covenant broken is not to be considered as a condition precedent, but as a distinct covenant, for the breach of which the party injured may be compensated in damages"); Blackburn J used this criterion in *Bettini v Gye* (1876) 1 Q.B.D. 183 at 189; generally, J.W. Carter, *Carter's Breach of Contract*, 2nd edn (Oxford: Hart Publishing, 2019), Chs 8 and 9. Cf. Lewison LJ's sceptical comments in *Ampurius Nu Homes Holdings Ltd v Telford Homes (Creekside) Ltd* [2013] EWCA Civ 577; [2013] 4 All E.R. 377 at [50], concerning this metaphor, where he said: "the trouble with expressing important propositions of English law in metaphorical terms is that it is difficult to be sure what they mean. As the High Court of Australia majority judgment pointed out in *Koompahtoo Local Aboriginal Land Council v Sanpine Pty Ltd* [2007] HCA 61 (2007) 82 A.J.L.R. 345 at [54] to describe a breach as "going to the root of the contract" is: "a conclusory description that takes account of the nature of the contract and the relationship it creates, the nature of the term, the kind and degree of the breach, and the consequences of the breach for the other party".

[3] *Macandrew v Chapple* (1865–66) L.R. 1 C.P. 643 at 648 per Willes J: "a delay or deviation which, as it has been said, goes to the whole root of the matter, deprives the charterer of the whole benefit of the contract, or entirely frustrates the object of the charterer in chartering the ship, is an answer to an action for not loading a cargo; but that loss, delay, or deviation short of that gives an action for damages, but does not defeat the charter".

[4] *Federal Commerce & Navigation Co v Molena Alpha Inc ("The Nanfri")* [1979] A.C. 757 at 785 HL per Lord Russell.

[5] (1876) 1 Q.B.D. 410 at 415 per Blackburn J.

[6] [1940] 3 All E.R. 60 at 72 HL.

the innocent party's perspective, is Atkinson J's approach in *Aerial Advertising Co v Batchelors Peas Ltd (Manchester)*, where he posed the question whether the breach's impact had been so serious that it had become "commercially wholly unreasonable [for the innocent party] to carry on".[7] Commenting on this array of similar tests, Arden LJ said in *Valilas v Januzaj*:[8]

> "The common law adopts open-textured expressions for the principle used to identify the cases in which one contracting party ('the victim') can claim that the actions of the other contracting party justify the termination of the contract. I will use the formulation that asks whether the victim has been deprived of substantially the whole of the benefit of the contract. The expression 'going to the root of the contract' conveys the same point: the failure must be compared with the whole of the consideration of the contract and not just a part of it. There are other similar expressions. I do not myself criticise the vagueness of these expressions of the principle since I do not consider that any satisfactory fixed rule could be formulated in this field."

8-002   **Breach which "goes to the root" test**   In the context of actual breach, the courts have traditionally adopted the metaphor of breach which "goes to the root"[9] of the contract in order to identify a situation where the actual breach of contract is really serious. Besides the trawl undertaken by *Chitty on Contracts*,[10] these are leading modern instances of courts adopting the "goes to the root" test: (i) Lord Wright mentioned this test in *Ross T Smyth & Co Ltd v TD Bailey, Son & Co*;[11] (ii) Devlin J used this test in *Universal Cargo Carriers Corp v Citati (No.1)*;[12] (iii) all five Law

---

[7]   [1938] 2 All E.R. 788 at 794.

[8]   [2014] EWCA Civ 436; [2015] 1 All E.R. (Comm) 1047 at [59].

[9]   See fn.2 in this chapter for the history of the phrase.

[10]   H. Beale (ed), *Chitty on Contracts*, 34th edn (London: Sweet & Maxwell, 2021), para.27-015: "*In Bettini v Gye* (1876) 1 Q.B.D. 183 at 188 (citing Parke B in *Graves v Legg* (1854) 9 Exch. 709 at 716) Blackburn J stated that, in the absence of an express declaration of intention by the parties, the test was: '… whether the particular stipulation goes to the root of the matter, so that failure to perform it would render the performance of the rest of the contract a thing different in substance from what the defendant had stipulated for'." *Chitty* also cites at para.27-043, fn.175: *Davidson v Gwynne* (1810) 12 East 381 at 389; *Macandrew v Chapple* (1865–66) L.R. 1 C.P. 643 at 648; *Poussard v Spiers & Pond* (1876) 1 Q.B.D. 410 at 414; *Honck v Muller* (1881) 7 Q.B.D. 92 at 100; *Mersey Steel & Iron Co Ltd v Naylor Benzon & Co* (1884) 9 App. Cas. 434 at 443 HL; *Guy-Pell v Foster* [1930] 2 Ch. 169 at 187; *Heyman v Darwins Ltd* [1942] A.C. 356 at 397 HL; *Suisse Atlantique Societe d'Armement SA v NV Rotterdamsche Kolen Centrale* [1967] 1 A.C. 361 at 391 (Viscount Dilhorne, quoting Lord Atkin in an earlier case), 397, 399, 400, 401 and 403 (Lord Reid, also quoting Lord Denning and Donovan LJ)), 409 and 411 (Lord Hodson), 418, 422 and 423 (Lord Upjohn), 430 and 431 (Lord Wilberforce), HL; *Decro-Wall International SA v Practitioners in Marketing* [1971] 1 W.L.R. 361 CA at 374; *Cehave NV v Bremer Handels GmbH (The Hansa Nord)* [1976] Q.B. 44 CA at 60, 73; *Federal Commerce & Navigation Co Ltd v Molena Alpha Inc ("The Nanfri")* [1979] A.C. 757 HL at 779.

[11]   [1940] 3 All E.R. 60 HL at 73: "It must always be a question in such cases whether a refusal by word or conduct or failure to deliver more than certain instalments or quantities, and not the whole contract quantity, goes to the root of the contract so as to constitute a total repudiation".

[12]   [1957] 2 Q.B. 401 at 430: "When the delay becomes so prolonged that the breach assumes a character so grave as to go to the root of the contract, the aggrieved party is entitled to [terminate for breach]". In argument at 418, Devlin J noted that the same formulation had been used by Willes J in *Macandrew v Chapple* (1865–66) L.R. 1 C.P. 643 at 648 ("a delay or deviation which, as it has been said, goes to the whole root of the matter, deprives the charterer of the whole benefit of the contract, or entirely frustrates the object of the charterer in chartering the ship, is an answer to an action for not loading a cargo; but that loss, delay, or deviation short of that gives an action for damages, but does not defeat the charter") (Devlin J's exposition of governing principles of breach not disturbed on appeal in either [1957] 1 W.L.R. 979 CA or [1958] 2 Q.B. 254 CA). M. Mustill,

Lords used this phrase, drawing upon settled usage, in the *Suisse Atlantique* case;[13] (iv) Lords Wilberforce,[14] Fraser,[15] and Russell,[16] used this expression in *Federal Commerce & Navigation Co v Molena Alpha Inc ("The Nanfri")*; (v) Lord Wilberforce,[17] on this occasion joined by Lords Salmon[18] and Scarman,[19] again used this formulation in *Woodar Investment Development Ltd v Wimpey Construction UK Ltd*; and (vi) Buckley LJ[20] adopted this same language in *Decro-Wall International SA v Practitioners in Marketing Ltd*; and Sachs LJ's judgment contains a thesaurus;[21] (vii) the "goes to the root" formulation was also adopted by Foxton J[22] in *SK*

"Anticipatory Breach: The Common Law at Work", *Butterworths Lectures 1989–90* (London: Butterworths, 1990), p.69 ff (see also M. Mustill, "The Golden Victory—Some Reflections" (2008) 124 L.Q.R. 569–585).

[13] *Suisse Atlantique Société d'Armement Maritime SA v NV Rotterdamsche Kolen Centrale* [1967] 1 A.C. 361 at 391 (Viscount Dilhorne, quoting Lord Atkin in an earlier case), 397 and 399 and 400 and 401 and 403 (Lord Reid, also quoting Lord Denning and Donovan LJ)), 409 and 411 (Lord Hodson) 418 and 422 and 423 (Lord Upjohn) 430 and 431 (Lord Wilberforce) HL.

[14] [1979] A.C. 757 HL at 778–779.

[15] [1979] A.C. 757 at 783, 784.

[16] [1979] A.C. 757 at 785, 786.

[17] [1980] 1 W.L.R. 277 HL at 283: "Repudiation is a drastic conclusion which should only be held to arise in clear cases of a refusal, in a matter going to the root of the contract, to perform contractual obligations."

[18] [1980] 1 W.L.R. 277 HL at 286–287: "If this does not go to the root of the contract and evince an unequivocal intention no longer to be bound by it, and therefore amounts to a repudiation of the contract, I confess that I cannot imagine what would."

[19] [1980] 1 W.L.R. 277 HL at 298: "To be repudiatory, the breach, or threatened breach, must go to the root of the contract."

[20] [1971] 1 W.L.R. 361 CA at 380: "To constitute repudiation, the threatened breach must be such as to deprive the injured party of a substantial part of the benefit to which he is entitled under the contract. The measure of the necessary degree of substantiality has been expressed in a variety of ways in the cases. It has been said that the breach must be of an essential term, or of a fundamental term of the contract, or that it must go to the root of the contract. Various tests have been suggested". Citing: *Freeth v Burr* (1874) L.R. 9 C.P. 208 at 213, 214 per Lord Coleridge CJ and per Keating J; *Mersey Steel & Iron Co Ltd v Naylor, Benzon & Co* (1884) 9 App. Cas. 434 at 439, 443 per Lord Selborne LC and per Lord Blackburn; *HongKong Fir* case [1962] 2 Q.B. 26 CA at 66 per Diplock LJ.

[21] [1971] 1 W.L.R. 361 CA at 374: "For my part I prefer—perhaps at the risk of being dubbed old-fashioned—to adhere to the long-standing phraseology used by Lord Ellenborough CJ, in *Davidson v Wynne* (1810) 12 East. 381 at 389; 104 E.R. 149 at 153, much cited over the next 150 years by eminent judges including in 1884 Lord Blackburn in *Mersey Steel and Iron Co (Ltd) v Naylor, Benzon & Co* (1883–84) L.R. 9 App. Cas. 434 HL at 442–4, and adopted by Upjohn LJ in the *HongKong Fir* case [1962] 2 Q.B. 26 CA at 64, that to constitute repudiation a breach of contract must go to the root of that contract. (Since preparing this judgment our attention has been directed to the use of the same phrase by Lord Denning MR, in *'The Mihalis Angelos'* [1971] 1 Q.B. 164 CA at 193. That leaves the question whether a breach does thus go to the root as a matter of degree for the court to decide on the facts of the particular case … This constitutes the test even when there are recurring breaches—producing differing results according to the degree of non-compliance: cf. *Maple Flock Co Ltd v Universal Furniture Products (Wembley) Ltd* [1934] 1 K.B. 148 CA at 157 per Lord Hewart CJ. Notice that a breach is likely to occur or to recur cannot, of course, be treated as being a repudiation unless it would have that effect when it did occur or recur." (1810) 12 East 381, 389; 104 E.R. 149 at 153 per Lord Ellenborough CJ: "It is useless to go over the same subject again, which has been so often discussed of late. The sailing with the first convoy is not a condition precedent: the object of the contract was the performance of the voyage, and here it has been performed. The principle laid down in *Boone v Eyre* has been recognised in all the subsequent cases, that unless the non-performance alleged in breach of the contract goes to the whole root and consideration of it, the covenant broken is not to be considered as a condition precedent, but as a distinct covenant, for the breach of which the party injured may be compensated in damages'."

[22] [2020] EWHC 3448 (Comm) at [306], citing Arden LJ in *Valilas v Januzaj* [2014] EWCA Civ 436

Shipping Europe Ltd v Capital VLCC 3 Corp (The C Challenger), and his decision was not disturbed on appeal (the latter being focused on the issue of misrepresentation).[23]

8-003   However, Lord Wilberforce in *Federal Commerce & Navigation Co v Molena Alpha Inc ("The Nanfri")*[24] cited other formulations besides the "breach going to the root" test. The following paragraphs refer to all the suggested tests. There are seven tests. For convenience, these can be encapsulated here as: (i) the breach went to the root; (ii) the breach involved or results in radically different performance (in case of delay); (iii) performance was or is substantially inconsistent with contract; (iv) the facts indicate abandonment of contract or refusal to perform; (v) innocent party has been or is being deprived of substantially the whole contractually intended benefit; (vi) innocent party has been or is being deprived of a substantial part of the contractually intended benefit; (vii) the breach is serious enough that it would be unfair to confine innocent party to damages.

8-004   *Test (i): the "breach going to the root" test:* this has already been introduced.

8-005   *Test (ii); delay rendering the contract radically different from that originally undertaken:* where the breach takes the form of delay the Court of Appeal in *MSC Mediterranean Shipping Co SA v Cottonex Anstalt*[25] adopted the following test to determine whether the delay has become serious enough so as to justify termination:[26]

> "the test for determining whether the [guilty party's default by delay] amounted to a repudiation of the contract was in substance the same as it would be for frustration, namely, whether the delay was such as to render performance of the remaining obligations under the contract of carriage radically different from those which the parties had originally undertaken, or (where the delay was continuing) whether it would be regarded by a reasonable person in the position of the parties as being likely to last that long."

8-006   In *MSC Mediterranean Shipping Co SA v Cottonex Anstalt*[27] the Court of Appeal held that the hirer of ship containers had retained them, in breach of contract, for so long that there had come a point when the whole contract had been repudiated. Applying the test set out in the preceding paragraph, Moore-Bick LJ concluded:[28]

> "On 2nd February 2012 the [owner of the containers] offered to sell the containers to the [hiring party] in order to provide a solution to the problem. Negotiations ensued, albeit unsuccessfully. That, it seems to me, was the clearest indication that the commercial purpose of the adventure had by then become frustrated. Such a sale would have discharged the [hiring party's] obligation to redeliver the containers and with it the final obligations under the contracts of carriage which still remained to be performed. In my view the [hiring party] was in repudiation of the contract as from that date."

---

at [59] and [60], but the learned judge at [305] and [306] acknowledged that the criterion of depriving the innocent party of benefit of the whole of the benefit of the contract is another way of expressing the test (and Arden LJ in the *Valilas* case, [2014] EWCA Civ 436 at [59] and [60], conjoins these two formulations.

23   [2022] EWCA Civ 231; [2022] 2 All E.R. (Comm) 784.
24   [1979] A.C. 757 HL at 778–779.
25   [2016] EWCA Civ 789 at [25]–[28].
26   [2016] EWCA Civ 789 at [25], applying *Universal Cargo Carriers Corp v Citati* [1957] 2 Q.B. 401 and *Nitrate Corp of Chile Ltd v Pansuiza Compania de Navegacion SA ("The Hermosa")* [1980] 1 Lloyd's Rep. 638 at CA.
27   [2016] EWCA Civ 789 at [25]–[28].
28   [2016] EWCA Civ 789 at [28].

Test (iii): conduct "substantially inconsistent with his contractual obligations":   **8-007**
this test was suggested by Lord Wright in *Ross T Smyth & Co Ltd v TD Bailey, Son & Co*:[29]

> "I do not say that it is necessary to show that the party alleged to have repudiated should have an actual intention not to fulfil the contract. He may intend in fact to fulfil it, but may be determined to do so only in a manner substantially inconsistent with his obligations, and not in any other way."

Lord Wright's discussion in the *Ross T Smyth & Co Ltd* case seems to have been directed at the concept of renunciation, that is, a declared intention to deviate significantly and unacceptably from the contract. But it appears that Lord Wilberforce in *Federal Commerce & Navigation Co v Molena Alpha Inc ("The Nanfri")*[30] found Lord Wright's formulation in the *Ross T Smyth* case to be illuminating on the related question of repudiation by actual breach of the contractual terms. The "substantially inconsistent" test is an attractive way of reformulating the "breach which goes to the root" test. Tests (i) and (iii) can be viewed as alternative and complementary formulations. They are less demanding than test (v), which is unattractively severe (test (v) is: *whether the breach deprives the innocent party of* "of substantially the whole benefit which it was the intention of the parties that [the innocent party] should obtain from the further performance of" *the contract*).

Test (iv): conduct is repudiatory if it objectively indicates an intention to abandon   **8-008**
and altogether refuse to perform the contract: it will be seen immediately that this test creates confusion because the reference to intention and (verbal) refusal overlaps both in terms of raw fact and conceptually with renunciation (a separate category of serious breach, examined in Ch.6), in particular, implied renunciation by conduct (para.6-005). Nevertheless, and perhaps regrettably, Etherton LJ in *Eminence Property Developments Ltd v Heaney*[31] formulated this test to determine whether "conduct" is "repudiatory":

> "So far as concerns repudiatory conduct, the legal test is simply stated ... It is whether, looking at all the circumstances objectively, that is from the perspective of a reasonable person in the position of the innocent party, the contract breaker has clearly shown an intention to abandon and altogether refuse to perform the contract."

Etherton LJ added:[32] "whether or not there has been a repudiatory breach is   **8-009**
highly fact sensitive. That is why comparison with other cases is of limited value".

---

[29]   [1940] 3 All E.R. 60, 72, HL. Immediately before the passage cited in the text above, Lord Wright had said: "It must not be forgotten that repudiation of a contract is a serious matter, not to be lightly found or inferred. I cannot do better than quote the words of Lord Selborne in *Mersey Steel and Iron Co Ltd v Naylor, Benzon & Co* (1883–84) L.R. 9 App. Cas. 434 HL at 438, where he says that you must look at the 'actual circumstances of the case in order to see whether the one party to the contract is relieved from its future performance by the conduct of the other; you must examine what that conduct is, so as to see whether it amounts to a renunciation, to an absolute refusal to perform the contract, such as would amount to a rescission if he had the power to rescind, and whether the other may accept it as a reason for not performing his part ...' The facts of that case are significant. The appellants had failed to pay for an instalment, not because they were either unwilling or unable to pay, but in a mistaken view of the legal position. It was held that there was no repudiation".

[30]   [1979] A.C. 757 HL at 778–779. Lord Wright in *Ross T Smyth & Co Ltd v TD Bailey, Son & Co* [1940] 3 All E.R. 60 HL at 72.

[31]   [2010] EWCA Civ 1168; [2011] 2 All E.R. (Comm) 223 at [61].

[32]   [2010] EWCA Civ 1168; [2011] 2 All E.R. (Comm) 223 at [62].

And he commented:[33]

> "all the circumstances must be taken into account insofar as they bear on an objective assessment of the intention of the contract breaker. This means that motive, while irrelevant if relied upon solely to show the subjective intention of the contract breaker, may be relevant if it is something or it reflects something of which the innocent party was, or a reasonable person in his or her position would have been, aware and throws light on the way the alleged repudiatory act would be viewed by such a reasonable person."

8-010   Those remarks were considered by Maurice Kay LJ in *Tullett Prebon Plc v BGC Brokers LP*.[34] The facts were as follows. TB was under attack from BGC, which had lured TB's brokers and was offering them future contracts (those contracts had been agreed but had yet to commence). TB fought back by convening a meeting at which it attempted to keep the brokers on board. The trial judge, Jack J, concluded that BGC and others had engaged in a tortious conspiracy by unlawful means in order to harm TB. BGC sought to overturn this by contending that, in essence, the true fault lay with TB whose conduct of the meeting with its brokers involved a repudiatory breach of the implied term of trust and confidence. That argument failed both at first instance and on appeal. Maurice Kay LJ said that the judge, in determining whether TB had behaved in a repudiatory fashion, had been right to consider TB's motivation. Kay LJ concluded:[35]

> "The issue is repudiatory breach in circumstances where the objectively assessed intention of the alleged contract-breaker towards the employees is of paramount importance. I have no doubt that the Judge [Jack J] approached this issue correctly. He referred ... to the question whether the conduct of the Tullett hierarchy 'considered objectively was conduct likely to destroy or seriously damage the relationship of trust and confidence between Tullett and the brokers in question'. ... In order to address the issue of repudiatory breach in the circumstances of this case, it was necessary for him to include an objective assessment of the true intention of the Tullett hierarchy. In so doing, he reached the conclusion that that intention was not to attack but to strengthen the relationship. This was a permissible and, in my view, correct finding, reached after a careful consideration of all the circumstances which had to be taken into account 'insofar as they bear on an objective assessment of the intention of the [alleged] contract breaker' (Eminence)."[36]

8-011   *Test (v): whether the breach deprives the innocent party of "substantially the whole benefit which it was the intention of the parties ... that he should obtain":* This test was suggested by Diplock LJ in the *HongKong Fir* case, in the context of intermediate or innominate terms (on which Ch.12).[37] According to this test, breach will justify termination only if it deprives

> "the [innocent party] of substantially the whole benefit which it was the intention of the parties ... that the charterers should obtain from the further performance of their own contractual undertakings".

Arguably, this criterion is pitched too high, in favour of the guilty party, and (from

---

[33]   [2010] EWCA Civ 1168; [2011] 2 All E.R. (Comm) 223 at [63].
[34]   [2011] EWCA Civ 131; [2011] I.R.L.R. 420 at [22]–[29] per Maurice Kay LJ.
[35]   [2011] EWCA Civ 131; [2011] I.R.L.R. 420 at [27] per Maurice Kay LJ.
[36]   The internal quotation at the end of the cited passage is a reference to *Eminence Property Developments Ltd v Heaney* [2010] EWCA Civ 1168; [2011] 2 All E.R. (Comm) 223 at [63] per Etherton LJ.
[37]   *HongKong Fir Shipping Co Ltd v Kawasaki Kisen Kaisha Ltd* [1962] 2 Q.B. 26 at 72 per Diplock LJ.

the innocent party's perspective) is unacceptably severe, presenting too high a hurdle. But there is no doubt that this formulation enjoys judicial currency. For example, it was used by Lord Diplock in *"The Afovos"*,[38] by Etherton C in *Urban 1 (Blonk Street) Ltd v Ayres*,[39] in *Valilas v Januzaj* by both Floyd LJ[40] and Arden LJ,[41] and in the *C & S Associates UK* case by Males J.[42]

In *Urban 1 (Blonk Street) Ltd v Ayres*,[43] Etherton C, adopting Lord Wilberforce's presentation in *Federal Commerce & Navigation Co Ltd v Molena Alpha Inc ("The Nanfri")*, elided tests (iii) (iv) and (v) as follows:[44]   **8-012**

> "the contract-breaker will have repudiated the contract, or as it is sometimes put, renounced the contract, entitling the other party to terminate it, if the contract-breaker has demonstrated an intention never to carry out the contract or at any event, only to do so in a manner substantially inconsistent with his or her contractual obligations such as to deprive the other party of substantially the whole benefit which it was intended they should receive under the contract: *Federal Commerce & Navigation Co Ltd v Molena Alpha Inc ('The Nanfri')* [1979] A.C. 757 at 778–779 (Lord Wilberforce citing passages from several other cases)."

*Test (vi): whether the breach "deprive[s] the injured party of a substantial part   **8-013**
of the benefit to which he is entitled under the contract"*: this test was stated as follows in *Decro-Wall International SA v Practitioners in Marketing Ltd*[45] per Buckley LJ:

> "to constitute repudiation, the threatened breach must be such as to deprive the injured party of a substantial part of the benefit to which he is entitled under the contract".

It will be noted that, unlike test (v) already considered, test (vi) is satisfied even if the default concerns (only) a substantial "part" of the contemplated contractual benefit. Etherton C in *Urban 1 (Blonk Street) Ltd v Ayres*[46] noted Lewison LJ's observation in *Ampurius Nu Homes Holdings Ltd v Telford Homes (Creekside) Ltd* that there is a manifest discrepancy, therefore, between tests (v) and (vi), that is, (whether the deprivation is of the "whole" or "part" of the intended contractual benefit). The following remarks by Lewison LJ in *Ampurius Nu Homes Holdings Ltd v Telford Homes (Creekside) Ltd* show that the courts have not yet made a final election whether to adopt test (v) and (vi):[47]

> "[The earlier cases] adopt as the relevant test whether the breach has deprived the injured

---

38 [1983] 1 W.L.R. 195 HL at 203 per Lord Diplock.
39 [2013] EWCA Civ 816; [2014] 1 W.L.R. 756 at [48] (see also *Ampurius Nu Homes Holdings Ltd v Telford Homes (Creekside) Ltd* [2013] EWCA Civ 577; [2013] 4 All E.R. 377).
40 [2014] EWCA Civ 436; [2015] 1 All E.R. (Comm) 1047 at [43]–[48] (noting a range of tests).
41 [2014] EWCA Civ 436; [2015] 1 All E.R. (Comm) 1047 at [59]: "I will use the formulation that asks whether the victim has been deprived of substantially the whole of the benefit of the contract. The expression 'going to the root of the contract' conveys the same point: the failure must be compared with the whole of the consideration of the contract and not just a part of it. There are other similar expressions. I do not myself criticise the vagueness of these expressions of the principle since I do not consider that any satisfactory fixed rule could be formulated in this field."
42 *C & S Associates UK Ltd v Enterprise Insurance Co Plc* [2015] EWHC 3757 at [86].
43 [2013] EWCA Civ 816; [2014] 1 W.L.R. 756 at [44] (7) per Etherton C.
44 [2013] EWCA Civ 816; [2014] 1 W.L.R. 756 at [48] (see also *Ampurius Nu Homes Holdings Ltd v Telford Homes (Creekside) Ltd* [2013] EWCA Civ 577; [2013] 4 All E.R. 377).
45 [1971] 1 W.L.R. 361 CA at 380.
46 [2013] EWCA Civ 816; [2014] 1 W.L.R. 756 at [57].
47 *Ampurius Nu Homes Holdings Ltd v Telford Homes (Creekside) Ltd* [2013] EWCA Civ 577; [2013] 4 All E.R. 377 at [48].

party of 'substantially the whole benefit' of the contract; which is the same test as that applicable to frustration. This sets the bar high. Other cases adopt a view that is more favourable to the injured party. Thus in *Decro-Wall International SA v Practitioners in Marketing Ltd* [1971] 1 W.L.R. 361 ... Buckley LJ said: 'To constitute repudiation, the threatened breach must be such as to deprive the injured party of a substantial part of the benefit to which he is entitled under the contract'"

8-014   Lewison LJ added:[48]

"On the face of it therefore there is a tension between the test of deprivation of 'substantially the whole benefit' (Diplock LJ) and 'a substantial part of the benefit' (Buckley LJ). In *Federal Commerce & Navigation Co Ltd v Molena Alpha Inc ('The Nanfri')* [1979] A.C. 757 Lord Wilberforce ... said: 'The difference in expression between these two last formulations does not, in my opinion, reflect a divergence of principle, but arises from and is related to the particular contract under consideration: they represent, in other words, applications to different contracts, of the common principle that, to amount to repudiation a breach must go to the root of the contract'."

8-015   In *Rice v Great Yarmouth BC*[49] Hale LJ adopted the present criterion, that is test (vi), by posing the question whether, as a result of (on those facts) a set of breaches, the innocent party: "would thereby be deprived of a substantial part of that which it had contracted for" or failure to supply (adequately) "aspects of the contract" which are "so important" that failure is "sufficient in itself" to justify termination.

8-016   But once more the tendency to juxtapose or elide tests should be noted. For example, in the next quotation, the judge adopted the present test (test (vi)) and then presented the issue by reference to test (vii) (see para.8-017). Thus, in *Future Publishing Ltd v Edge Interactive Media Inc*[50] Proudman J said:

"The test for fundamental breach, approved by Lord Wilberforce in *Federal Commerce v Molena Alpha* [1979] A.C. 757 at 778–9 is that expounded by Buckley LJ in *Decro-Wall v Practitioners in Marketing* [1971] 1 W.L.R. 361 at 380: 'the breach must be such as to deprive the injured party of a substantial part of the benefit to which he is entitled under the contract? Will the consequences of the breach be such that it would be unfair to the injured party to hold him to the contract and leave him to his remedy in damages'."

8-017   *Test (vii) whether it would be "unfair" on the innocent party to confine him to damages, without the further option of termination:* this test was suggested by Buckley LJ in the *Decro-Wall* case:[51]

"Will the consequences of the breach be such that it would be unfair to the injured party to hold him to the contract and leave him to his remedy in damages ...?"

It is submitted that Buckley LJ's formulation in the *Decro-Wall* case is an unattractively nebulous test. And this approach should not be adopted, for these reasons: (i) the "Buckley LJ *Decro-Wall*" test would inject a large element of ex post facto subjective evaluation; and (ii) it would create great uncertainty; and (iii) because it manifests a bias in favour of non-termination, by suggesting that termination is

---

[48] *Ampurius Nu Homes Holdings Ltd v Telford Homes (Creekside) Ltd* [2013] EWCA Civ 577; [2013] 4 All E.R. 377 at [49].

[49] (2000) *Times*, 26 July; (2001) 3 L.G.L.R. 4 CA at [38]; distinguished in *Alan Auld Associates Ltd v Rick Pollard Associates* [2008] EWCA Civ 655; [2008] B.L.R. 419 at [17] and [20] as a case where there was a "raft of obligations" of different significance.

[50] [2011] EWHC 1489 (Ch); [2011] E.T.M.R. 50 at [60] per Proudman J.

[51] [1971] 1 W.L.R. 361 CA at 380.

a "super-response", this approach tends to undercut the legitimate expectations of the innocent party that the contract would be performed properly and not reconstituted at the whim of the guilty party, leaving the innocent party only with the opportunity to sue for damages.

Lord Wilberforce in *Federal Commerce & Navigation Co v Molena Alpha Inc* (*"The Nanfri"*)[52] did not refer to test (vii) and, impliedly, did not find it attractive. By contrast, Lord Fraser did adopt test (vii) in that case.[53] But it is submitted that Buckley LJ's test, test (vii), should not be allowed to "catch on". Indeed it should be excised.   **8-018**

Conclusion on the battle of the rival tests   It will be helpful to list the tests which have emerged: (i) the "breach going to the root" test; (ii) breach (notably, inexcusable delay) rendering the contract radically different from that originally undertaken; (iii) conduct "substantially inconsistent with his contractual obligation"; (iv) conduct is repudiatory if it objectively indicates an intention to abandon and altogether refuse to perform the contract; (v) whether the breach deprives the innocent party of "substantially the whole benefit which it was the intention of the parties that [the innocent party] should obtain from the further performance of" the contract; (vi) whether the breach "deprive[s] the injured party of a substantial part of the benefit to which he is entitled under the contract"; and (vii) whether it would be "unfair" on the innocent party to confine him to damages, without the further option of termination.   **8-019**

Tests (i) (*breach which "goes to the root" of the contract), test (ii) (delay rendering the contract radically different from that originally undertaken) and test (iii)* (*"substantially inconsistent with his contractual obligations"*) should prevail. Each of these three tests adopts essentially the same criterion, although in different language. They are attractive. The degree of seriousness must be such that the innocent party has a clear justification for quitting the contract. For this purpose, the level of default must be much greater than trivial, but need not be total, nor is it necessary that it should be almost total. The level is reliably conveyed by tests (i) to (iii).   **8-020**

Test (iv) (*conduct is repudiatory if it objectively indicates an intention to abandon and altogether refuse to perform the contract*) is confusing because it invites overlap, factual and conceptual, with renunciation and, in particular, implied renunciation by conduct (para.6-005). But renunciation is a separate category of serious breach, examined in Ch.6.   **8-021**

Test (v) (*whether the breach deprives the innocent party of "substantially the whole benefit which it was the intention of the parties...that he should obtain"*) is arguably too severe a formulation, although it is sometimes used by English judges,   **8-022**

---

[52]   [1979] A.C. 757 HL at 778–779: "The difference in expression between these two last formulations [viz. (iii) and (iv) cited in the preceding paragraph of the text] does not, in my opinion, reflect a divergence of principle, but arises from and is related to the particular contract under consideration: they represent, in other words, applications to different contracts, of the common principle that, to amount to repudiation a breach must go to the root of the contract."

[53]   [1979] A.C. 757 at 783: "I shall adopt the formulation by Buckley LJ in *Decro-Wall International SA v Practitioners in Marketing Ltd* (1971) as follows: 'Will the consequences of the breach be such that it would be unfair to the injured party to hold him to the contract and leave him to his remedy in damages as and when a breach or breaches may occur? If this would be so, then a repudiation has taken place'."

for example, by both Floyd LJ[54] and Arden LJ[55] in *Valilas v Januzaj* and Males J in the *C & S Associates UK* case.[56]

8-023   Test (vi) (*whether the breach "deprive[s] the injured party of a substantial part of the benefit to which he is entitled under the contract"*), although not as severe as test (v), is easily confused with it and offers scope for confusion, therefore.

8-024   As for test (vii) (*"unfair to the injured party to hold him to the contract"*), this test is too nebulous, and it is furthermore unattractively weighted against termination. It should not be adopted.

8-025   It follows that the most attractive approach is to adopt either test (i) or test (iii) and, in the case of delay, test (ii): (i) *the "breach going to the root" test*; or (ii) *conduct "substantially inconsistent with his contractual obligation"* (or (iii) *delay rendering the contract radically different from that originally undertaken*). Test (iii) is a specialised test peculiar to the problem of delay. Otherwise, and in the interest of economy, perhaps test (i) alone[57] should be adopted, suitably supplemented by reference to illustrative cases (for example, the discussion of repudiatory facts in the text at para.8-026 ff).

8-026   **The "high bar" of repudiatory breach**   Males J said in the *C & S Associates UK* case[58] that repudiation requires a high level of default, so as to go to the root of the contract, having regard to a range of factors (see the quotation in para.8-027):

> "There was no real dispute between the parties as to the principles to be applied, which can conveniently be taken from *Chitty on Contracts*, 32nd edn (2015), Vol.1 para.24-041 [now 34th edn (London: Sweet & Maxwell, 2021), para.27-043], citing among other cases *Ampurius Nu Homes Holdings Ltd v Telford Homes (Creekside) Ltd* [2013] EWCA Civ 577; [2013] 4 All E.R. 377 and *Valilas v Januzaj* [2014] EWCA Civ 436; [2015] 1 All E.R. (Comm) 1047: '... regard must be had to the nature and consequences of the breach in order to determine whether this right has arisen. The question whether a breach of an intermediate term is sufficiently serious to entitle the innocent party to treat himself as discharged is to be determined "by evaluating all the relevant circumstances". In conducting this inquiry, the court is not exercising a discretion, but is engaged in a fact-sensitive inquiry which involves "a multi-factorial assessment" and the use of various "open-textured expressions". The bar which must be cleared before there is an entitlement in the innocent party to treat himself as discharged is therefore a "high" one. A number of expressions have been used to describe the circumstances that warrant discharge, the most common being that the breach must 'go to the root of the contract'."

8-027   Males J added in the *C & S Associates UK* case:[59]

> "It was common ground also that in determining whether a breach is repudiatory the questions identified by Lewison LJ at [51] and [52] of his judgment in *the Ampurius Nu Homes Holdings Ltd v Telford Homes (Creekside) Ltd* [2013] EWCA Civ 577; [2013] 4 All E.R. 377 would be relevant: 'Whatever test one adopts, it seems to me that the starting point must be to consider what benefit the injured party was intended to obtain from performance of the contract ... The next thing to consider is the effect of the breach on the injured party. What financial loss has it caused? How much of the intended benefit

---

54   [2014] EWCA Civ 436; [2015] 1 All E.R. (Comm) 1047.
55   [2013] EWCA Civ 816; [2014] 1 W.L.R. 756 at [59].
56   *C & S Associates UK Ltd v Enterprise Insurance Co Plc* [2015] EWHC 3757 at [86].
57   As preferred by M.G. Bridge, *The Sale of Goods*, 4th edn (Oxford: Oxford University Press, 2017), 10.30, 10.31.
58   *C & S Associates UK Ltd v Enterprise Insurance Co Plc* [2015] EWHC 3757 at [78].
59   *C & S Associates UK Ltd v Enterprise Insurance Co Plc* [2015] EWHC 3757 at [79].

under the contract has the injured party already received? Can the injured party be adequately compensated by an award of damages? Is the breach likely to be repeated? Will the guilty party resume compliance with his obligations? Has the breach fundamentally changed the value of future performance of the guilty party's outstanding obligations?'"

Males J further commented:[60]   **8-028**

"For present purposes I must assume without deciding that it will be able to do so, and that the breaches which can be proved are serious and extensive. It seems to me that, if proved on a sufficient scale, the breaches alleged are undoubtedly capable of satisfying the criteria for a repudiatory breach identified above. Enterprise's case, put bluntly, is that far from receiving the services of a specialist claims handler exercising an appropriate level of skill and care, it turns out to have entrusted the handling of its third party motor claims to a company whose systems and procedures were fundamentally flawed and which repeatedly acted incompetently. If that proves to be so, it should not be difficult to conclude that the breaches had the effect of depriving Enterprise of substantially the whole benefit which it was intended to obtain from the contract and thus that they were sufficiently serious to entitle Enterprise to terminate the contract."

Repudiation found by reference to a range of factors In *Future Publishing Ltd*   **8-029**
v Edge Interactive Media Inc[61] the defendant companies, acting through Dr Langdell, had breached an agreement with the claimants that prevented the defendants from using a trademarked logo. Proudman J concluded that the breach was a repudiation, going to the root of the contract, taking into account three factors (although it should be noted that none is necessary and each is directed at the central determination whether breach goes to the root of the contract): (i) whether the breach involves non-compliance with one or more "critically important" obligations or terms; (ii) whether the breach was exacerbated by being deliberate (but it should be noted that there is no special category of general breach based on "deliberateness"; see para.5-030); and (iii) the wider and long-term impact on the claimant's commercial reputation if it remained associated with the defendant. Proudman J said:[62]

"the breaches are of critically important terms of the [contract]. They are breaches of the terms regulating the ongoing obligations of the parties. ... Where, as here, the parties have agreed terms which are to apply to both sides, the defendants' continuing refusal to comply with their side of the bargain is inconsistent with a right to insist on the contract continuing in force. Dr Langdell on behalf of the defendants has made it quite clear before and during this trial that they intend to continue to use their versions of the EDGE logo [in breach, as it was now decided, of the agreement]."

Proudman J added:[63]   **8-030**

"Secondly, the defendants' breaches were deliberately calculated to cause confusion. Thirdly, that confusion has necessarily caused substantial damage to the claimant's reputation."

Breach to be assessed in the context of the entire relationship In a continuing   **8-031**
or "relational" contract, it has been said that the test is not whether something bad,

---

60   *C & S Associates UK Ltd v Enterprise Insurance Co Plc* [2015] EWHC 3757 at [86].
61   [2011] EWHC 1489 (Ch); [2011] E.T.M.R. 50.
62   [2011] EWHC 1489 (Ch); [2011] E.T.M.R. 50 at [63] per Proudman J.
63   [2011] EWHC 1489 (Ch); [2011] E.T.M.R. 50 at [64] per Proudman J.

even something quite heinous, indeed even something dishonest and under-hand, has occurred, but whether the event or series of events, taking also into account the possibility or likelihood of recurrence, has destroyed or sufficiently damaged the parties commercial or working relationship. In *Bristol Groundschool v Intelligent Data Capture Ltd* Deputy High Court judge Richard Spearman QC held that no repudiatory breach had occurred when a party hacked into the other's computer during their contractual relationship. The event was now "historic" and did not destroy or wholly undermine their continuing commercial relationship:[64]

> "(xii) The conduct complained of was commercially unacceptable…(xiii) Nevertheless, I do not consider that the above breaches were repudiatory [because] … these breaches did not 'strike at the heart of the trust which is vital to any long-term commercial relationship'. There were a number of extenuating circumstances … [and] the financial damage caused to [the innocent party] was minimal, if not non-existent. Moreover, it was not necessary for the performance of the … Agreement for [the guilty party] to continue to have access to [the innocent party's] computer system … I do not consider that … [the guilty party] could not be trusted to perform the core creative, marketing and payment obligations in the contract. Those obligations did not depend upon good faith, but upon ordinary commercial considerations. (xiv) If one applies the tests and asks the questions adumbrated in … the judgment of Lewison LJ in *Ampurius Nu Homes Holdings Ltd v Telford Homes (Creekside) Ltd* [2013] EWCA Civ 577 at [39], [44], [51], [52]], it seems to me the answer [is that the guilty party's breach was not repudiatory on these facts]. (xv) That is, perhaps, especially so if the position is [considered] at the date of termination of the 2001 Agreement. By that time the conduct in question was largely historic (although the availability to [the guilty party] of the fruits of that conduct was continuing) and its only, or main, practical effect was to provide a safety net until [another part of the parties' deal] was ready."

8-032 **Gross misconduct justifying summary dismissal of an employee** In *Williams v Leeds United Football Club* Lewis J held that a senior club employee's emailing of offensive images to a female, junior employee, and to third parties, was a repudiatory breach.[65] The images were "obscene and pornographic".[66] That breach was discovered subsequent to the club's summary dismissal of the employee. The club was entitled to rely on this and was not, therefore, itself in breach.[67]

8-033 **Long-term relationship undermined by breach of the duty to maintain "honesty and integrity"** In *D&G Cars Ltd v Essex Police Authority*[68] a company breached its contract with a police authority by failing to "crush" a vehicle, as required by the contract, and instead unilaterally deciding to incorporate the vehicle into its own fleet. Dove J held that this was a breach of an implied term "to act with honesty and integrity".[69] He referred, in particular, to the need to maintain trust in a long-term contractual relationship:[70]

> "There may well be acts which breach the requirement of undertaking the contract with integrity which it would be difficult to characterise definitively as dishonest. Such acts would compromise the mutual trust and confidence between the parties in this long-term

---

64   [2014] EWHC 2145 (Ch) at [196].
65   [2015] EWHC 376 (QB); [2015] I.R.L.R. 383 at [50], [52], [53], [60], [61], [76], [77], [80], [83].
66   [2015] EWHC 376 (QB); [2015] I.R.L.R. 383 at [11] and [12].
67   [2015] EWHC 376 (QB); [2015] I.R.L.R. 383 at [80], [83].
68   [2015] EWHC 226 (QB).
69   [2015] EWHC 226 (QB) at [171], [173], [174] per Dove J.
70   [2015] EWHC 226 (QB) at [175] per Dove J.

relationship without necessarily amounting to the telling of lies, stealing or other definitive examples of dishonest behaviour. They would amount to behaviour which the parties would, had they been asked, have identified as obvious acts which were inconsistent with the maintenance of their intended long-term relationship of fair and open dealing and therefore would amount to a breach of their contract."

Dove J considered in *D&G Cars Ltd v Essex Police Authority*[71] the remarks concerning the nature of a "repudiatory breach" made by Etherton LJ in *Eminence Property Developments Ltd v Heaney*.[72] Dove J then concluded in the *D&G Cars Ltd* case that there had been a repudiatory breach:[73]

8-034

"Following the [company's managers'] discovery of what had occurred, the failure to adequately investigate or indeed explain what had happened reinforced rather than alleviated the legitimate concern of the [police] that what had happened betrayed their trust and confidence in the [company] and demonstrated a course of conduct which was wholly lacking in integrity even if not definitively dishonest. I am entirely satisfied that the reasonable person in the [police's] position, and in possession of the facts which the [police] had, would have done precisely what the [police] did and treat that which was discovered as a repudiatory breach and also grave misconduct so as to lead to the termination of the contract and the removal of the [company] from the tender process."

Reversal of arbitrators' decision concerning repudiation   In *Wuhan Ocean Economic & Technical Cooperation Co Ltd, Nantong Huigang Shipbuilding Co Ltd v Schiffahrts-Gesellschaft ("Hansa Murcia") MBH & Co KG*[74] Cooke J rejected the arbitrators' decision that there had been a repudiation, involving a breach which went to the root of the contract. The arbitrators' decision was palpably a misconstruction of the transaction and fell, therefore, to be corrected by the High Court under the power conferred by the Arbitration Act 1986 s.69. Cooke J explained:[75]

8-035

"The arbitrators erred in law. They set out the right test for repudiatory breach but they cannot have applied it if their earlier conclusion about the triggering effect of an arbitration, whenever commenced, as set out in paragraph 51 of their Reasons, is taken into account.[76] A correct application of the test for repudiatory breach in these circumstance would lead inevitably to one answer only and this is part of the second stage of reasoning to which Mustill J (as he then was) referred in 'The Chrysalis' (1983).[77] Furthermore, even if they did apply the right test, once they had decided as they did, correctly, in

---

71   [2015] EWHC 226 (QB) at [172] per Dove J.
72   [2010] EWCA Civ 1168; [2011] 2 All E.R. (Comm) 223 at [61]–[64].
73   [2015] EWHC 226 (QB) at [217] per Dove J.
74   [2012] EWHC 3104 (Comm); [2013] 1 All E.R. (Comm) 1277 at [53] and [54].
75   [2012] EWHC 3104 (Comm); [2013] 1 All E.R. (Comm) 1277 at [53] and [54].
76   The background to this is that Cooke J noted that the contract provided for automatic extension of a refund guarantee if arbitration proceedings were commenced; but this feature, although initially noted by the arbitral tribunal, was later overlooked at the crucial part of the award when the tribunal held that repudiation had occurred.
77   *Finelvet AG v Vinava Shipping Co Ltd ("The Chrysalis")* [1983] 1 W.L.R. 1469 at 1475; [1983] 1 Lloyd's Rep. 503 at 507 per Mustill J: "Starting therefore with the proposition that the court is concerned to decide, on the hearing of the appeal, whether the award can be shown to be wrong in law, how is this question to be tackled? In a case such as the present, the answer is to be found by dividing the arbitrator's process of reasoning into three stages: (1) The arbitrator ascertains the facts. This process includes the making of findings on any facts which are in dispute. (2) The arbitrator ascertains the law. This process comprises not only the identification of all material rules of statute and common law, but also the identification and interpretation of the relevant parts of the contract, and the identification of those facts which must be taken into account when the decision is reached.

paragraph 51, their conclusion is one that no reasonable arbitrators could reach. Their conclusion that the failure to extend the Refund Guarantee by 28th June 2010, 2 days before the expiry date of the existing guarantee, was a repudiatory breach, cannot be right as a matter of law." (On this type of challenge to an arbitral tribunal's decision, see also *White Rosebay Shipping SA v Hong Kong Chain Glory Shipping Ltd*, 2013)."[78]

II.   REPUDIATION OR RENUNCIATION BY REPETITIVE BREACH[79]

8-036   In continuing contracts, a party's *repeated breaches* might justify the other in terminating the contract even though there has been neither a breach of a "condition", nor a clear communication of unwillingness to honour the contract ("renunciation"). The court will assess whether the other side's default is grave enough, presently and prospectively, so as to strike at the root of the other party's contractual expectations. (On this topic see also the related question of repudiation or renunciation in respect of instalment contracts at para.8-042 ff.)

8-037   In *Force India Formula One Team Ltd v Etihad Airways PJSC*,[80] reversing the trial judge, the Court of Appeal held that a Formula One racing team's series of breaches of a sponsorship agreement had cumulatively involved repudiation. The sponsor's name was no longer explicitly associated with the racing team and there had been livery and logo changes. The innocent party, the sponsors, was entitled to terminate the contract and to claim damages. Rix LJ concluded that there had been "a series of repeated, or continuing, breaches which were sooner or later but ultimately repudiatory".[81]

8-038   The discussion in *Force India Formula One Team Ltd v Etihad Airways PJSC*[82] was noted by Foxton J in the following instructive passage in *SK Shipping Europe Plc v Capital VLCC 3 Corp* (The C Challenger):[83]

"[305] It is accepted that the terms of the Charterparty which are said to have been breached were innominate terms. However, it is clear that a series of non-repudiatory breaches may cumulatively amount to a renunciation or repudiation of a contract (see *Force India Formula One Team Ltd v Etihad Airways PJSC* [2011] ETMR 10, [87]). This

---

(3) In the light of the facts and the law so ascertained, the arbitrator reaches his decision. In some cases, stage (3) will be purely mechanical. Once the law is correctly ascertained, the decision follows inevitably from the application of it to the facts found. In other instances, however, stage (3) involves an element of judgment on the part of the arbitrator. There is no uniquely 'right' answer to be derived from marrying the facts and the law, merely a choice of answers, none of which can be described as wrong. [As for stage (2)] ... in some cases an error of law can be demonstrated by studying the way in which the arbitrator has stated the law in his reasons. It is, however, also possible to infer an error of law in those cases where a correct application of the law to the facts found would lead inevitably to one answer, whereas the arbitrator has arrived at another; and this can be so even if the arbitrator has stated the law in his reasons in a manner which appears to be correct, for the court is then driven to assume that he did not properly understand the principles which he had stated. Whether stage (3) can ever be the proper subject of an appeal, in those cases where the making of the decision does not follow automatically from the ascertainment of the facts and the law, is not a matter upon which it is necessary to express a view in the present case."

[78]   [2013] EWHC 1355 (Comm); [2013] 2 All E.R. (Comm) 449 at [35]–[41] per Teare J.
[79]   J.W. Carter, *Carter's Breach of Contract*, 2nd edn (Oxford: Hart Publishing, 2019), [8–17], citing authority that accumulated breaches must satisfy the criterion of requirement of "seriousness": Neil Andrews, *Contract Law in Practice* (Oxford: Oxford University Press, 2021) at 24.179–24.189.
[80]   [2010] EWCA Civ 1051; [2011] E.T.M.R. 10.
[81]   [2010] EWCA Civ 1051; [2011] E.T.M.R. 10 at [87].
[82]   [2010] EWCA Civ 1051; [2011] E.T.M.R. 10.
[83]   [2020] EWHC 3448 (Comm) at [305], (not disturbed on appeal: [2022] EWCA Civ 231; [2022] 2 All E.R. (Comm) 784).

is more likely to be the case when the breaches are linked in their effect, or when they reflect the pursuit by the defendant of an overriding strategy (as was the case in *Force India*). However, it is still necessary to establish that the cumulative effect of the various breaches, taken together, amounts to a repudiation..."

But the breaches fell short of justifying termination by the charterer (whose unjustified decision to terminate had become, therefore, a repudiatory breach). In determining that the owner's breaches did not cumulatively constitute repudiation, Foxton J said:[84]

> "[307] This was a two-year charterparty, with the Vessel delivered into the Charterer's service on 16 February 2017. The Charterer purported to terminate it after eight months. In my view, it cannot be said that the breaches I have found at [285], [288- 289] and [292] above, taken cumulatively, deprived the Charterer of substantially the whole benefit which it was intended to obtain under the Charterparty for the payment of hire, or "go to the root" of the Charterparty...The most significant breach – the over- consumption [of fuel]...was the subject of a contractual mechanism to reduce the hire payable...
>
> [309] This is not to under-estimate the Charterer's frustration with the Owner, or to deny that there were legitimate grounds for that frustration...But, however frustrating the Owner's conduct was in the conventional sense, it was not frustrating in a legal sense."

In *Rice v Great Yarmouth BC*[85] Hale LJ said that the test to determine repudiation for repetitive breaches is whether the innocent party: "would thereby be deprived of a substantial part of that which it had contracted for" or failure to supply (adequately) "aspects of the contract" which are "so important" that failure is "sufficient in itself" to justify termination. On the facts of the *Rice* case (see para.10-059) the Court of Appeal affirmed the trial judge's decision that the defendant contractor's successive failures to maintain the claimant's parks were not serious enough to satisfy this test. **8-039**

In *Alan Auld Associates Ltd v Rick Pollard Associates* the Court of Appeal concluded that a long series of late payments (19 dilatory responses) justified termination because the delay had been "substantial, persistent, and cynical" (for details of this case, see para.6-061 and on the same case paras 14-054–14-055).[86] But the third of those epithets is not necessary and merely a reflection of the facts in that particular case. **8-040**

It is submitted that, for the reasons stated at para.8-019 ff, a better formulation is whether the defendant has committed a series of *breaches which collectively* "go to the root" *of the contract* or which, taken together, are "substantially inconsistent with his contractual obligations". To indicate this calibration more precisely: the innocent party must have a clear justification for quitting the contract; the level of default must be much greater than trivial, but it need not be total, nor need it be almost total. **8-041**

---

[84] [2020] EWHC 3448 (Comm) at [307] and [309], (not disturbed on appeal: [2022] EWCA Civ 231; [2022] 2 All E.R. (Comm) 784).

[85] *Rice v Great Yarmouth BC The Times,* 26 July 2000; (2001) 3 L.G.L.R. 4 CA at [38] (distinguished in *Alan Auld Associates Ltd v Rick Pollard Associates* [2008] EWCA Civ 655; [2008] B.L.R. 419 at [17] and [20] as a case where there was a "raft of obligations" of different significance).

[86] [2008] EWCA Civ 655; [2008] B.L.R. 419 at [20] per Tuckey LJ.

III. REPUDIATION OR RENUNCIATION IN THE CONTEXT OF INSTALMENT CONTRACTS[87]

8-042   A contract might provide expressly, or by implication, that performance is to take place in stages or by instalments. The analysis here is that there is one contract, comprising all these instalments. The question is whether breach in respect of one (or more than one) instalment entitles the innocent party to terminate the whole contract. This will depend on whether the guilty party's breach discloses a renunciation of the whole contract, or whether his breach involves a repudiation of the whole contract. The relevant breach might occur at the time of appointed performance, or it might occur before that occasion, so that it becomes subject to the regime governing anticipatory breach (para.7-001 ff).

8-043   It is apparent from the cases that the courts in this context are primarily concerned to assess whether the relevant breach which has already occurred is serious and whether the facts support the innocent party's apprehension that there is a real commercial risk that breach of the same or similar gravity will recur. A one-off failure by a seller, even if serious enough to justify the buyer in rejecting the goods tendered in that particular instalment, will not necessarily justify termination of the whole supply contract. The courts will have regard both to the seller's capacity to reform its ways and to the importance and urgency of the buyer's need to be assured that future performance will comply with the contract.

8-044   The "renunciation" (announcement of intention not to comply with the contract) and "repudiation" (failure to comply with the contract in a way which goes to the root of expected performance) routes are illustrated by *Mersey Steel and Iron Co Ltd v Naylor, Benzon & Co*.[88] Here the House of Lords held that a buyer's default in payment of the first of five instalments did not entitle the seller to terminate the contract. The buyer's default did not involve a renunciation of the whole contract, nor did it involve a repudiation, in the sense of a serious breach going to the root of the contract.

8-045   The facts in *Mersey Steel and Iron Co Ltd v Naylor, Benzon & Co* were as follows. A large quantity of steel was ordered, delivery to be made in five instalments, for five months, beginning January 1881. Payment was to be made within three days of each delivery. There was an incomplete delivery in January. The buyer did not pay for this delivery, having discovered that the sellers were insolvent. The buyer's solicitors wrongly advised the buyer that it was not possible to make a safe and effective payment to the sellers at this stage but that it should wait until a liquidator had been appointed. However, the buyer made clear that it wished to keep the contract running, and that it wished to receive eventual supply of all the steel. The sellers' liquidator contended that the buyer was in breach by having withheld payment for the first instalment and that there had been a renunciation of the contract. But the House of Lords, upholding the Court of Appeal,[89] held that the

---

[87]   J.W. Carter, *Carter's Breach of Contract*, 2nd edn (Oxford: Hart Publishing, 2019), [8-30] ff; M. Bridge (ed), *Benjamin's Sale of Goods*, 11th edn (London: Sweet & Maxwell, 2021), Ch. 8, section 6 (delivery by instalments).

[88]   (1883–84) L.R. 9 App. Cas. 434 HL.

[89]   (1882) 9 Q.B.D. 648, where Sir George Jessel MR concluded at 658: "I think the evidence is very strong, that the buyers were both ready and willing to pay if it had not been for the unlucky circumstance that induced them to refuse to pay under a mistake of law"; adding at 660, "it seems to me that so far from their affording evidence of any desire on the part of the purchasers to put an

buyers had neither (i) committed a repudiatory breach on these facts nor (ii) renounced the contract.

Carter observes[90] that the *Mersey Steel & Iron* case was codified in Sale of Goods Act 1979 s.31(2) (previously the 1893 Act). Lord Hewart CJ in *Maple Flock Co Ltd v Universal Furniture Products (Wembley) Ltd*[91] also noted the influence of this case on the drafting of the (then) 1893 Act. Section 31(2) of the 1979 Act provides: **8-046**

> "Where there is a contract for the sale of goods to be delivered by stated instalments, which are to be separately paid for, and the seller makes defective deliveries in respect of one or more instalments, or the buyer neglects or refuses to take delivery of or pay for one or more instalments, it is a question in each case depending on the terms of the contract and the circumstances of the case whether the breach of contract is a repudiation of the whole contract or whether it is a severable breach giving rise to a claim for compensation but not to a right to treat the whole contract as repudiated."

However, that provision goes beyond the *Mersey Steel & Iron* case decision because the Act encompasses breaches by both sellers and buyers. The provision is not exhaustive, even in the context of sales of goods, because its literal terms do not cover cases where the seller makes no delivery at all of an instalment, or there is a provision that instalments are *not* to be paid for separately. In such circumstances the Common Law (on which s.31(2) is based) applies the same principles. **8-047**

In *Maple Flock Co Ltd v Universal Furniture Products (Wembley) Ltd*[92] the instalment contract was for supply of 100 tons of "rag flock", delivery by three loads a week, each load to consist of 60 bags or one and half tons. It was a term that the goods should comply with Government regulations which required the buyer to use rag flock which contained less than a specified amount of chlorine. At the time of purportedly justified termination by the buyer, there had been 20 good deliveries and one defective delivery: the first 15 deliveries had been perfect; but the 16th contained material which had a non-compliant level of chlorine; thereafter, four more deliveries had been made before the contract was terminated. These last four deliveries were also perfect. The trial judge had been impressed by the buyer's contention that any failure to comply with Government regulations might expose it to prosecution, and that even a remote risk of recurrence would justify termination. But the Court of Appeal thought that this was an alarmist and exaggerated perspective, and so it reversed the lower court. In the Court of Appeal, Lord Hewart CJ (giving the court's judgment, the other members were Lord Wright[93] and Slesser LJ) held that the seller's breach did not justify the buyer in terminating the supply contract. **8-048**

---

end to the contract, it is clear that they wished the contract to go on, and the deliveries to continue. It is not suggested for a moment that this well-known firm were in any pecuniary difficulty or wished to delay payment because it was not convenient to pay." The Court of Appeal had reversed the first instance decision of Lord Coleridge CJ in *Mersey Steel & Iron Co Ltd v Naylor Benzon & Co*; Coleridge CJ had given the leading judgment in *Freeth v Burr* (1873–74) L.R. 9 C.P. 208 (Court of Common Pleas).

[90] J.W. Carter, *Carter's Breach of Contract*, 2nd edn (Oxford: Hart Publishing, 2019), [8-33].

[91] [1934] 1 K.B. 148 CA at 153 per Lord Hewart CJ: "The language of the Act is substantially based on the language used by Lord Selborne LC in *Mersey Steel and Iron Co v Naylor, Benzon & Co* (1883–84) L.R. 9 App. Cas. 434, 438–439".

[92] [1934] 1 K.B. 148 CA at 156–157 per Lord Hewart CJ (on this case J.W. Carter, *Carter's Breach of Contract*, 2nd edn (Oxford: Hart Publishing, 2019), [8-39] and [8-40]; *Regent OHG Aisestadt v Franceasco of Jermyn Street Ltd* [1981] 3 All E.R. 327, Mustill J; Sale of Goods Act 1979 s.31(2).

[93] Lord Wright had been clearly selected to bolster the court because of his fairly recent decision at first instance in *Robert A Munro & Co v Meyer* [1930] 2 K.B. 312.

8-049   In the *Maple Flock Co Ltd* case Lord Hewart CJ formulated these criteria:[94]

> "First, the ratio quantitatively which the breach bears to the contract as a whole, and secondly, the degree of probability or improbability that such a breach will be repeated."

It was evident that (i) the isolated breach bore a small proportion to the total deliveries contemplated under this contact ("the delivery complained of amounts to no more than 1½ tons out of a contract for 100 tons").[95] The Court of Appeal in the *Maple Flock* case was also satisfied (ii) that there was no significant danger that the seller's breach would recur. On this point, Lord Hewart CJ said:[96]

> "the chance of the breach being repeated is practically negligible. We assume that the sample found defective fairly represents the bulk [of that particular delivery]; but bearing in mind the judge's finding that the breach was extraordinary and that the [seller's] business was carefully conducted, bearing in mind also that the [sellers] were warned, and bearing in mind that the delivery complained of was an isolated instance out of 20[97] satisfactory deliveries actually made both before and after the instalment objected to, we hold that it cannot reasonably be inferred that similar breaches would occur in regard to subsequent deliveries."

8-050   As for point (i), the ratio of breach point, in *Maple Flock Co Ltd v Universal Furniture Products (Wembley) Ltd* Lord Hewart CJ[98] cited the Divisional Court's decision in *Millers' Karri and Jarrah Co v Turner & Co*.[99] That case was a strong example of a very substantial proportion of the relevant goods being delivered by the seller in a defective state. The case was certainly not borderline. The contract in *Millers' Karri and Jarrah* was for 1100 pieces of timber. The first instalment of 750 pieces was rejected by the buyers. The arbitrator declared in his award:

> "the said shipment was, and is, so far from complying with the requirements of the said contract as to entitle the buyers to repudiate and to rescind the whole contract and to refuse to accept the said shipment and all further shipments under the said contract".

The Divisional Court upheld the award. Bigham J said:[100]

> "Thus, if the breach is of such a kind, or takes place in such circumstances as reasonably to lead to the inference that similar breaches will be committed in relation to subsequent deliveries, the whole contract may there and then be regarded as repudiated and may be rescinded. If, for instance, a buyer fails to pay for one delivery in such circumstances as to lead to the inference that he will not be able to pay for subsequent deliveries; or if a seller delivers goods differing from the requirements of the contract, and does so in such circumstances as to lead to the inference that he cannot, or will not, deliver any other kind

---

[94] [1934] 1 K.B. 148 CA at 157; in *M & J Polymers Ltd v Imerys Minerals Ltd* [2008] EWHC 344 (Comm); [2008] 1 All E.R. (Comm) 893; [2008] 1 Lloyd's Rep. 541 at [15], without reference to the *Maple Flock* case, Burton J formulated this test, in connection with alleged breach of an instalment contract by the supplier: "the [goods previously delivered] must be proved to have been, if and when further supplied, in serious breach of [the express clause concerning quality and fitness for purpose], and it must be shown that it is more likely than not that such serious breach would continue if further deliveries were made and accepted".

[95] [1934] 1 K.B. 148 CA at 157.

[96] [1934] 1 K.B. 148 CA at 157 per Lord Hewart CJ.

[97] The figure should be 19.

[98] [1934] 1 K.B. 148 CA at 156.

[99] (1908) 14 Com. Cas. 25; (1908) 100 L.T. 128 (Divisional Court).

[100] (1908) 14 Com. Cas. 25 at 29 (with whom Walton J agreed).

of goods in the future, the other contracting party will be under no obligation to wait to see what may happen; he can at once cancel the contract and rid himself of the difficulty."

In *Millers' Karri and Jarrah Co v Turner & Co* Bigham J applied the Sale of **8-051** Goods Act 1893 s.31(2) (now, in identical language, s.31(2) of the 1979 Act, cited in the text above). He held that the present facts justified an inference that the second instalment would also be similarly defective. The arbitrator, therefore, had been entitled to find for the buyer on these facts. In the same case Walton J noted[101] that a "repudiation" for the purpose of this provision does not require an intention to repudiate.

Lord Hewart CJ in *Maple Flock Co Ltd v Universal Furniture Products* **8-052** *(Wembley) Ltd*[102] also cited Wright J's decision in *Robert A Munro & Co v Meyer*.[103] That case concerned a contract for the sale of 1500 tons of bone meal. The sellers in this case were middlemen, who relied on their suppliers, the manufacturers, for correct delivery. Six hundred and eleven tons were delivered, but these were seriously adulterated with a foreign substance (cocoa husks). The source of the adulteration was the seller's suppliers, over whom the seller could not factually be expected to have complete control, although in law the seller would be strictly liable for the consequences of non-compliance attributable to this third party. Although not dangerous, this adulteration meant that the buyer could not sell the goods on (for use in animal feed) because they would not be consistent with usual market standards. Wright J held[104] that the buyer (if he had found out about this adulteration in time)[105] would have been entitled to say, in effect, "enough is enough; the risk of repetition is significant, and we are ending our contract". This is how Wright J expressed this point:[106]

> "in such a case as this, where there is a persistent breach, deliberate so far as the manufacturers are concerned, continuing for nearly one-half of the total contract quantity, the buyer, if he ascertains in time what the position is, ought to be entitled to say that he will not take the risk of having put upon him further deliveries of this character, and will not accept the position that he must always be watchful and analyse the goods that are delivered to see whether or not they answer to the contract ... [W]here the breach is substantial and so serious as the breach in this case and has continued so persistently, the buyer is entitled to say that he has the right to treat the whole contract as repudiated."

---

[101] (1908) 14 Com. Cas. 25 at 30–31.
[102] [1934] 1 K.B. 148 CA at 156–157.
[103] [1930] 2 K.B. 312, Wright J.
[104] 1930] 2 K.B. 312 at 331.
[105] The adulteration had occurred higher up the supply chain, and the immediate sellers in this case had not been guilty of any conscious default; of course, they were strictly liable for the breach in supply, because these goods did not comply with their description. The buyer had entered into a cancellation agreement at the time not realising that the goods had been defective. Wright J held that the buyers were entitled to damages ([1930] 2 K.B. 312 at 337). But he rejected the buyers' plea that the cancellation agreement had been vitiated by shared mistake in equity under the principle of *Cooper v Phibbs* (1867) L.R. 2 HL 149 at 170 per Lord Westbury. On this point Wright J said ([1930] 2 K.B. 312 at 335): "In all the circumstances I do not think I am justified in finding as a fact that the defendant would have elected to risk an arbitration and to claim that this contract was rescinded. I think it is practically certain that he would have attempted to compromise the matter by seeking a release on terms of compensation, and the actual compromise would have been not very, if at all, different from the terms of the agreement actually arrived at, because the agreement, as is pointed out in the letters, was very favourable to the defendant. I think there is no precedent for setting aside a contract in such circumstances, because I am unable to find that the making of the contract was conditioned by the mistake".
[106] [1930] 2 K.B. 312 at 331 per Wright J.

8-053   Wright J added:[107]

"the breach of contract in this case is very substantial, and I think it would be a very large assumption to assume that it could have been put right or that there was any guarantee as to what would happen in the future. It must be remembered that the goods had to be obtained from the Smithfield Company [the seller's suppliers], because they were the only people who manufactured goods which would be a compliance, as regards that part of the description, with the contract."

8-054   Lord Hewart CJ in *Maple Flock Co Ltd v Universal Furniture Products (Wembley) Ltd*[108] contrasted *Taylor v Oakes Roncoroni & Co*[109] where the Court of Appeal, upholding Greer J,[110] held that a buyer had not been entitled to terminate the whole contract. The case concerned two instalment contracts for the supply of large quantities of rabbit furs of specified quality. The buyer accepted some of these instalment deliveries. But the buyer then cancelled the rest. This was a repudiation. The buyers had been commercially induced to cancel because sub-purchasers in South America were no longer prepared to proceed, for financial reasons. Later the buyer discovered that the fur already accepted was defective because it did not match the contractual description. Greer J at first instance commented that this was a case where: "the goods delivered failed in an ... appreciable degree to come up to the standard required by the contract description".[111] This would have entitled the buyer to have rejected each instalment on delivery, because the term concerning description is a condition (the matter might now fall for consideration under Sale of Goods Act 1979 s.15A, para.10-096). But, as for future instalments, Greer J held that there was no clear case that "the [sellers] might not have been able to improve their further deliveries so as to make them a strict compliance with the contracts".[112] Therefore, for the purpose of the Sale of Goods Act (then 1893, now 1979) s.31(2), the breach in respect of the two instalments delivered "was not a repudiation of the whole contract".

8-055   A further argument was considered in this case: that, in the absence of insistence by the buyer, the sellers would have delivered goods of the same defective quality throughout the currency of the instalment contract. If so, the buyer would have received goods which it would be successively entitled to reject for breach of a condition (see above). The buyers contended that it should follow that it could retrospectively justify its repudiation. This would protect it from liability for damages to the seller for non-acceptance. The Court of Appeal in *Taylor v Oakes Roncoroni & Co* held that binding authority precluded this (*Braithwaite v Foreign Hardwood Co*).[113] But the House of Lords in "The Simona" declared that the *Braithwaite case* was wrong in principle.[114] It follows that the court on facts such

---

[107] [1930] 2 K.B. 312 at 332 per Wright J.
[108] [1934] 1 K.B. 148 CA at 157 (Bankes, Scrutton, and Atkin LJJ).
[109] (1922) 27 Com. Cas. 261 CA.
[110] (1922) 27 Com. Cas. 261 at 264–265, Greer J (affm.'d by CA).
[111] (1922) 27 Com. Cas. 261 at 264, Greer J (affm.'d by CA).
[112] (1922) 27 Com. Cas. 261 at 264–265, Greer J (affm.'d by CA).
[113] *Braithwaite v Foreign Hardwood Co.* [1905] 2 K.B. 543 CA.
[114] Lord Ackner in *Fermometal SARL v Mediterranean Shipping Co SA "The Simona"* [1989] A.C. 788 at 801–805 HL, held that the *Braithwaite* decision (*Braithwaite v Foreign Hardwood Co* [1905] 2 K.B. 543 CA) was wrong; and that the non-repudiating party is not absolved from tendering further performance under the contract if the repudiation is not accepted and the contract is kept alive; applied to the facts of *Taylor v Oakes, Roncoroni & Co* (1922) 27 Com. Cas. 261 CA, this would mean

as *Taylor v Oakes Roncoroni & Co*[115] would now be entitled to have regard to what would have occurred if the contract had been kept alive and the seller had tendered goods which (as shown by the evidence in this case) failed to match the contractual description.

In a New Zealand case, *Hammer and Barrow v Coca-Cola*,[116] Richmond J applied the English decisions the *Maple Flock* case[117] and in *Millers' Karri and Jarrah Co v Turner & Co*.[118] Using this guidance, he concluded that Coca-Cola had been entitled to reject defective goods supplied under an instalment contract for the supply of 200,000 yoyos, for use in a special advertising campaign. Eighty per cent of the first batch of 85,000 were defective (amongst other problems, the yoyos would not "run down the string freely").[119] The seller had been slow in indicating whether replacements could be produced or improvements in production achieved so that the whole contract would run smoothly.[120] The judge commented that **8-056**

> "the whole history of the matter was…extremely unsatisfactory and disquieting from the point of view of Coca-Cola … The yoyos were not articles which could be readily and speedily acquired elsewhere should [the seller] fail in future deliveries to produce articles in accordance with the contract."[121]

The judge concluded that these facts justified Coca-Cola terminating the whole supply contract "rather than submit to the risk of having put upon them further unsatisfactory deliveries".[122]

An unqualified refusal to pay for an instalment might amount to a repudiation of the whole contract.[123] **8-057**

In *Withers v Reynolds*[124] (further examined at paras 6-058–6-060) the court held that a purchaser had gone too far by insisting on paying for the penultimate delivery and thus serially postponing payment for the latest delivery. That strategy, designed to keep the supplier "on his toes", was a radical re-structuring of the deal. It lacked justification. The court inferred a renunciation. **8-058**

By contrast, in *Freeth v Burr*[125] (further examined at para.6-040) a purchaser failed to pay for the first of two deliveries, which had been delayed, but it was clear **8-059**

---

that if the buyer's repudiation was not accepted, and the seller made delivery of all the instalments, the seller's obligation to deliver goods matching the contractual description would have governed that contractual performance; and if those goods—as now shown in retrospect—would in fact have been tendered in breach of a condition, the buyer would be entitled to reject them upon the tender of each instalment. See also Q. Liu, *Anticipatory Breach* (Oxford: Hart Publishing, 2011), p.93 ff, noting at p.99 that the "central fallacy of the [Braithwaite decision] lies in its failure to recognize that the defendant in an action for breach of contract may rely upon the claimant's future breach as a complete defence either by way of establishing an anticipatory breach on the claimant's part or through the vehicle of the defence of anticipated breach". See also J.W. Carter, *Carter's Breach of Contract*, 2nd edn (Oxford: Hart Publishing, 2019), [9-29] ff.

[115] (1922) 27 Com. Cas. 261 CA.
[116] [1962] N.Z.L.R. 723 at 725–727 (Supreme Court at Christchurch).
[117] [1934] 1 K.B. 148 CA at 157.
[118] (1908) 14 Com. Cas. 25 at 29; (1908) 100 L.T. 128.
[119] [1962] N.Z.L.R. 723 at 726.
[120] [1962] N.Z.L.R. 723 at 726.
[121] [1962] N.Z.L.R. 723 at 726.
[122] [1962] N.Z.L.R. 723 at 727.
[123] *Withers v Reynolds* (1831) 2 B. & Ad. 882; 109 E.R. 1370; *Booth v Bowron* (1892) 8 T.L.R. 641.
[124] (1831) 2 B. & Ad. 882; 109 E.R. 1370.
[125] (1874) L.R. 9 C.P. 208 (Court of Common Pleas).

that the purchaser was keen to obtain complete delivery and so that party had not "evinced" an intention to renounce the whole contract.[126]

8-060   Similarly, in *Mersey Steel and Iron Co Ltd v Naylor, Benzon & Co*[127] (further examined at para.6-033) a purchaser's failure to pay for the first of five deliveries did not "evince" an intention to renounce the whole contract because it was plain that the buyer wished to obtain complete delivery and its failure to pay had been based on a mistake of law.

8-061   In *Decro-Wall International SA v Practitioners in Marketing Ltd*[128] (further examined at para.6-034) the Court of Appeal held that a party's pattern of late payments by an UK sole concessionaire for successive supplies by a French manufacturer had not "evinced" an intention by the payor to renounce the contract. The French supplier had suffered no anxiety whether the concessionaire would eventually pay. On the facts of the case, therefore, this repetitive breach did not go to the root of the contract for the purpose of repudiation nor did it disclose a renunciation. The Court of Appeal in the *Decro-Wall* case[129] emphasised that breach occurring within an instalment contract must be serious enough to justify termination and that not every breach, even if repeated, will necessarily do so.

8-062   The Court of Appeal in the *Decro-Wall* case made clear that Bigham J's dictum on the position of sellers in *Millers' Karri and Jarrah Co v Turner & Co*,[130] cited above at para.8-050, must not be taken out of context (the *Millers' Karri and Jarrah* case concerned defective supply). The Court of Appeal in the *Decro-Wall* case cautioned against a mechanical approach to the case of late payment. Salmon LJ saying:[131]

> "In that case the arbitrator had found that the first instalment of a contract intended to be performed in two instalments was so bad that the buyers were entitled to reject it and that the true inference from the facts was that the next instalment was likely to be just as bad. On those findings the court held, rightly, that there had been a fundamental breach or repudiation by the sellers which entitled the buyers to cancel the contract."

8-063   And Buckley LJ, also in the *Decro-Wall* case, made the following comment[132] on Bigham J's 1908[133] statement:

> "[this] must ... be read in relation to the facts of that case ... [where the breach] went to the root of the contract, for the suppliers were proposing to deliver goods which were not in accordance with the contract ... [B]ut not every breach, even if its continuance is threatened throughout the contract or the remainder of its subsistence, will amount to a repudiation. To constitute repudiation, the threatened breach must be such as to deprive the injured party of a substantial part of the benefit to which he is entitled under the contract."

8-064   In *Shyam Jewellers Ltd v Cheeseman*[134] Potter LJ helpfully discussed the problem arising from late payment by a party under an instalment contract. The court

---

[126] Q. Liu, *Anticipatory Breach* (Oxford: Hart Publishing, 2011), p.64 (unless that person's performance is of the essence of the contract).
[127] (1883–84) L.R. 9 App. Cas. 434 HL.
[128] [1971] 1 W.L.R. 361 CA at 379–380.
[129] [1971] 1 W.L.R. 361 CA.
[130] (1908) 14 Com. Cas. 25 at 29; (1908) 100 L.T. 128.
[131] [1971] 1 W.L.R. 361 CA at 369.
[132] [1971] 1 W.L.R. 361 CA at 379–380.
[133] (1908) 14 Com. Cas. 25 at 29; (1908) 100 L.T. 128.
[134] [2001] EWCA Civ 1818; official transcript on Westlaw.

distinguished between mere "foot-dragging" (which is insufficient) and, on the other hand, conduct indicating an inability to pay or a complete disregard for the stipulated timing of payments (as demonstrated by both *Alan Auld Associates Ltd v Rick Pollard Associates*, for details of this case, para.6-061 and paras 14-054–14-055, and *"The Spar Draco"*, on which para.6-074, a persistent pattern of late payment can disclose a repudiatory breach by repeated actual non-compliance, or implicit renunciation by the dilatory payor that is, an implied unwillingness to adhere to the contract in some serious manner).[135] To return to the *Shyam Jewellers* case, Cheeseman, who were shopfitters, had terminated a contract on the basis that Shyam had been slow in instalment payments in respect of Cheeseman's work. The Court of Appeal held that Cheeseman had "jumped the gun" and that, on the present facts, the pattern of Shyam's dilatory payments was such that did not justify such termination. Potter LJ said in the *Shyam* case:[136]

> "whilst accepting and respecting the remarks of Salmon LJ in the *Decro-Wall* case (1971) ... concerning breaches which shatter the confidence of the party not in breach, it is important to appreciate that, in making those remarks, Salmon LJ was, in the context of a case of delayed payments, emphasising the difference between mere foot-dragging in payment, where the party contractually obliged to make periodic payments regularly made them 'some days late as they had done throughout the whole course of the dealings between the parties', and a failure in payment of such a character as reasonably to give rise to a conclusion of inability to pay."

In the *Shyam Jewellers* case Potter LJ added:[137]   **8-065**

> "The principle which emerges from the authorities is that, in any given case, where a party is alleged to be in repudiatory breach by reason of a failure or delay in payment of an instalment or interim sum due under a contract, the 'potency' and legal effect of such breach falls to be judged in the light of the seriousness of the breach and its effect upon the continuing performance of the contract. This involves an examination of the circumstances of the breach itself as well as its implications for the future of the contract and any likelihood of repetition."

In the same case Potter LJ commented:[138]   **8-066**

> "It is also clear that, in assessing the nature and effects of the breach, the court is concerned to do so objectively. Thus it can only concern itself with the reasonable perceptions and reactions of the party asserting a repudiatory breach ... This will particularly be so where a party's actions are said to demonstrate a future inability to pay, bearing in mind the proper reluctance of the court to hold a party in anticipatory breach in the absence of clear evidence of that party's intention not to comply with its future contractual obligations."

Potter LJ concluded:[139]   **8-067**

> "I regret to say that I consider that the defendant 'jumped the gun' at a time of irritation and disillusion at the way he had been treated, and that, while sympathy may be due to his position, he nonetheless himself repudiated the contract by writing as he did on 19 February, indicating that the contract was at an end."

The Privy Council in *Dymocks Franchise Systems (NSW) Pty Ltd v Todd* (further   **8-068**

---

[135] [2008] EWCA Civ 655; [2008] B.L.R. 419 at [20] per Tuckey LJ.
[136] [2008] EWCA Civ 655; [2008] B.L.R. 419 at [57].
[137] [2008] EWCA Civ 655; [2008] B.L.R. 419 at [57].
[138] [2008] EWCA Civ 655; [2008] B.L.R. 419 at [58].
[139] [2008] EWCA Civ 655; [2008] B.L.R. 419 at [63].

examined at para.6-066) held that refusal to pay an instalment (and future instalments) under a franchise agreement constituted a repudiatory breach. There had been no justification for that party suspending such payments pending a renegotiation (at its insistence) of the terms of the contract.[140] Nor was that party's position rendered excusable merely because it had proposed to make such payments into an escrow account (an account controlled by a solicitor, or even by a neutral third party), pending adjustment of terms. The payee had made clear that these proposed steps would not be tolerated. The payor's persistence in this proposed unilateral reconfiguration of the contract led to the conclusion that it had renounced or repudiated the contract, even though its overall conduct did not indicate absolute refusal to proceed with the totality of its obligations. As Lord Browne-Wilkinson said:[141] "a party who intends to fulfil a contract but only in a way which is inconsistent with the terms of the contract is in repudiation of that contract".

IV. No Repudiation Where Good Reason Exists for Termination but the Wrong Reason (or No Reason) was Offered (The Boston Deep Sea Principle)

8-069   The basic proposition is that a party can justify a decision to terminate a contract if in fact he had at the relevant time justification for so doing. This applies where (i) he gave the wrong reason, or (ii) he gave no reason at all. But it should be noted that the justification must subsist at the time of the purported termination (even if the terminating party was unaware of it). This can be called conveniently the *Boston Deep Sea* principle: based on the leading case *Boston Deep Sea and Ice Co v Ansell* (1888); see further para.8-075 below).[142] In *Nakanishi Marine Co Ltd v Gora Shipping Ltd* (2012) Burton J doubted[143] that the *Boston Deep Sea* principle extends to the situation where a termination clause stipulates that default will justify termination under the clause only if the default relied upon is identified in the termination notice. The *Nakanishi* case was approved by Freedman J in *Lombard North Central Plc v European Skyjets Ltd* (2020).[144]

8-070   The Court of Appeal in the *Reinwood* case (2008) noted that this is a "general principle" which applies not just (as is usual) where the innocent party is unaware of the relevant justification at the time he inadvertently takes a false step, but also where he does know the true facts but falls into error or makes a miscalculation. The court noted:[145]

> "the general principle of contract law that if a party refuses to perform a contract, giving a reason which is wrong or inadequate, or giving no reason at all, or terminates a contract under a contractual provision to that effect, the refusal or termination may nevertheless be justified if there were at the time facts in existence which would have provided a good reason for the refusal: *Chitty on Contracts* [now 34th edn (2021) paragraph 27–067]. That principle is often used in relation to facts unknown to the party refusing at the time of its refusal, but there is no reason why it should not be used in relation to facts which were known to that party at that time. Waiver can apply to qualify that principle, but only in cases of, in effect, estoppel."

---

[140] [2002] UKPC 50; [2002] 2 All E.R. (Comm) 849 at 870 per Lord Browne-Wilkinson.
[141] [2002] UKPC 50; [2002] 2 All E.R. (Comm) 849 at 870 at [58].
[142] (1888) 39 Ch. D. 339 CA.
[143] [2012] EWHC 3383 (Comm) at [35](iii).
[144] [2020] EWHC 679 (QB) at [62] to [68].
[145] *Reinwood Ltd v L Brown & Sons Ltd* [2008] EWCA Civ 1090; [2008] 2 C.L.C. 422 at [51] per Lloyd LJ, the other judges agreeing.

As for the failure to give any reason at all, Lord Sumner said in *British and Ben-* **8-071**
ningtons Ltd v NorthWestern Cahar Tea Co Ltd, in the House of Lords, that a party
can lawfully terminate a contract without specifying *any* ground on which he
purports to do so, provided he in fact had contractual justification to do so at the
time when he decided to terminate.[146]

As for the proposition that the terminating party who gave a wrong reason can **8-072**
later invoke a different and truly supportive reason, that rule was affirmed in *Force
India Formula One Team Ltd v Etihad Airways PJSC* by the Court of Appeal in the
following terms:[147]

> "It is established law that, where one party to a contract has repudiated it, the other may
> validly accept that repudiation by bringing the contract to an end, even if he gives the
> wrong reason for doing so or no reason at all."

In *Force India Formula One Team Ltd v Etihad Airways PJSC* racing car spon- **8-073**
sors had purported to terminate the contract by invoking termination clauses. In fact,
these did not cover the relevant events. Nevertheless, the sponsors had made clear
that they wished to terminate the contract by reason of the other party's serious non-
compliance with the transaction. Termination for repudiatory breach at Common
Law remained available, even though the innocent party had chased down an inappropriate alley in trying to end the contract under the express machinery for
termination.

Similarly, in *Tele2 International Card Co SA v Post Office Ltd*[148] Aikens LJ noted: **8-074**

> "the principle that if a party terminates a contract for a bad reason but he subsequently
> discovers facts which would have constituted a good reason for terminating the contract,
> he is entitled to rely on those facts".

Aikens LJ cited[149] *Boston Deep Sea and Ice Co v Ansell*,[150] a case of dismissal **8-075**
which turned out to have been justified on a basis not known to the employer at
time. It had been subsequently discovered that the employee had earlier committed a breach of fiduciary duty. In this case, Bowen LJ said:[151]

> "I ... find it impossible to ... come to any other conclusion except that the managing direc-
> tor having been guilty of a fraud on his employers was rightly dismissed by them, and
> dismissed by them rightly even though they did not discover the fraud until after they had
> actually pronounced the sentence of dismissal."

---

[146] [1923] A.C. 48 HL at 71–72 per Lord Sumner: "I suppose all reasons and all defences in the action, partial or complete, would be open to [the party deciding to terminate]."
[147] [2010] EWCA Civ 1051; [2011] E.T.M.R. 10 at [116] citing *Stocznia Gdanska SA v Latvian Shipping Co (Repudiation)* [2002] EWCA Civ 889; [2002] 2 Lloyd's Rep. 436 at [32], and *Stocznia Gdynia SA v Gearbulk Holdings Ltd* [2009] EWCA Civ 75; [2010] Q.B. 37 at [153]; see also *Taylor v Oakes Roncoroni & Co* (1922) 127 LT 267 at 269 per Greer J and affm.'d by CA); *Tele2 International Card Co SA v Post Office Ltd* [2009] EWCA Civ 9 at [30], fn.17 (see text at para.8-073); Lord Sumner in *British and Benningtons Ltd v NorthWestern Cahar Tea Co Ltd* [1923] A.C. 48 at 71–72 (see text at paras 8-074 and 8-075); applied by Lord Denning MR in *Maredelanto Compania Naviera SA v Bergbau-Handel GMBH ("The Mihalis Angelos")* [1971] 1 Q.B. 164 CA at 193, 195. On this aspect of breach, J.W. Carter, *Carter's Breach of Contract*, 2nd edn (Oxford: Hart Publishing, 2019), [10-07]; Q. Liu, *Anticipatory Breach* (Oxford: Hart Publishing, 2011), pp.88–91.
[148] [2009] EWCA Civ 9 at [30], fn.17.
[149] [2009] EWCA Civ 9 at [30], fn.17.
[150] (1888) 39 Ch. D. 339 CA.
[151] (1888) 39 Ch. D. 339 at 364.

Then, Aikens LJ[152] noted Lord Sumner in *British and Benningtons Ltd v NorthWestern Cahar Tea Co Ltd*, who had said:[153]

"I do not think that ... [a party], who has repudiated a contract for a given reason which fails him, has, therefore, no other opportunity of defence either as to the whole or as to part, but must fail utterly. If he had repudiated, giving no reason at all, I suppose all reasons and all defences in the action, partial or complete, would be open to him. His motives certainly are immaterial, and I do not see why his reasons should be crucial."

8-076   Lord Sumner in *British and Benningtons Ltd v NorthWestern Cahar Tea Co Ltd* (1923) had added:[154]

"What he says is of course very material upon the question whether he means to repudiate at all, and, if so, how far, and how much, and on the question in what respects he waives the performance of conditions still performable in futuro or dispenses the opposite party from performing his own obligations any further; but I do not see how the fact, that the [innocent party has] wrongly said 'we treat this contract as being at an end, owing to your unreasonable delay in the performance of it' obliges them, when that reason fails, to pay in full, if at the very time of this repudiation, the [guilty party] had become wholly and finally disabled from performing essential terms of the contract altogether."

8-077   In *Williams v Leeds United Football Club* (also on this case, para.8-086) Lewis J held that an employer is entitled to rely on subsequent information (consistent with *Boston Deep Sea and Ice Co v Ansel*[155]), even if the employer had actively sought that material in order to relieve itself of a financial burden:[156]

"where, as here, there is a repudiatory breach of the contract of employment by the employee, and there has been no affirmation or waiver of the repudiatory breach, the employer is not prevented from relying on that breach as justifying summary dismissal because it had itself decided to breach its contractual obligations or was looking for a reason to justify dismissal or was motivated by its own financial interests. There is no basis for concluding that it is 'unfair' or 'unjust' to allow the Defendant to rely upon the Claimant's anticipatory conduct to resist a claim for wrongful dismissal in such circumstances."

8-078   Lewis J added:[157]

"That approach is also consistent with *Glencore Rotterdam BV v Lebanese Organisation for International Commerce* [1997] 4 All E.R. 514. There the Court of Appeal reaffirmed the basic rule in the law of contract that a person who terminates a contract, and subsequently discovers conduct which would have entitled him to terminate the contract, is entitled to rely upon that later conduct to resist a claim for damages for breach. That rule was subject to certain specified exceptions such as, for example, estoppel or waiver, where the facts 'justify a finding that there was an unequivocal representation made by one party, by conduct or otherwise, which was acted upon by the other' but 'Without such a representation, no such estoppel or waiver can arise, and there is no general rule that

---

[152] [2009] EWCA Civ 9 at [30], fn.17.
[153] [1923] A.C. 48 HL at 71–72; this authority was twice applied by Lord Denning MR in *Maredelanto Compania Naviera SA v Bergbau-Handel GMBH ("The Mihalis Angelos")* [1971] 1 Q.B. 164 CA at 193, 195.
[154] [1923] A.C. 48 HL at 71–72.
[155] (1888) 39 Ch. D. 339 CA.
[156] [2015] EWHC 376 (QB); [2015] I.R.L.R. 383 at [84].
[157] [2015] EWHC 376 (QB); [2015] I.R.L.R. 383 at [85].

what the court or tribunal may perceive as "unfairness or injustice" has the same effect'
see *Glencore* [1997] 4 All E.R. at 530j, to 531c."

In *Seadrill Management Services Ltd v OAO Gazprom ("The Ekha")*[158] Flaux J
doubted (and it is submitted the doubt is entirely sound and correct) whether the
proposition that a party can justify a decision to terminate a contract if in fact he
had at the relevant time justification for so doing will apply where the suggested
unknown breach had been a renunciation yet to be communicated at the relevant
time. Flaux J thought (again, entirely properly and based on correct principle) that
such a suggested "renunciation" was in fact inchoate because it would only become
complete once communicated to the relevant party (or at least, where the latter has
become aware of the relevant statement or renunciatory conduct):[159]

8-079

> "[a good argument to explain] why the Boston Deep Sea Fishing principle does not ap-
> ply to renunciation ... is that the cases where the principle has been applied are all cases
> where at the time of termination of the contract for a bad reason, there is, objectively
> speaking, albeit unknown to the innocent party at the time, a breach of contract which is
> repudiatory. When the innocent party finds out about that repudiatory breach, he can rely
> upon it as a good reason to justify the termination which would otherwise be wrongful.
> However, in the case of words and conduct which are said to be renunciatory, an es-
> sential ingredient of their amounting to repudiation of the contract is that they are com-
> municated to or otherwise known to the innocent party. If they are not, then by definition
> there cannot be a renunciation."

Exceptions to the operation of the Boston Deep Sea principle   There are three
exceptions to the main proposition that a party can justify a decision to terminate
a contract if in fact he had at the relevant time justification for so doing.

8-080

**Exception (1): Guilty party losing opportunity to avoid committing a
breach**   First, the Court of Appeal in *Glencore Grain Rotterdam BV v Lebanese
Organisation for International Commerce*[160] acknowledged the so-called *Heisler*
case exception: party A's failure to take the correct point is fatal if there was a
realistic prospect that party B could have put right this potential default within the
contractual deadline (or perhaps made up ground adequately where the default has
already occurred) if B had been accurately notified by A of the relevant problem[161]
(see paras 8-081 and 8-082). In essence, this exception rests on an objective
criterion of entrapment (whether intended or not): default could have been avoided
if the guilty party had received an accurate complaint about his contractual
performance.

8-081

Realistic prospect to avoid default   Males J in the *C & S Associates UK* case[162]
noted that, even where the *Heisler* rule does apply, "there must be at least a real
prospect as distinct from a merely theoretical or fanciful possibility of the necessary correction being made".[163]

8-082

---

[158] [2009] EWHC 1530 (Comm); [2010] 1 Lloyd's Rep. 543 at [265]–[267] per Flaux J (affm.'d [2010]
EWCA Civ 691; [2011] 1 All E.R. (Comm) 1077, although this point was not specifically addressed).

[159] [2009] EWHC 1530 (Comm); [2010] 1 Lloyd's Rep. 543 at [265] per Flaux J.

[160] [1997] 4 All E.R. 514; [1997] 2 Lloyd's Rep. 386 CA.

[161] [1997] 4 All E.R. 514 at 526 (noting *Heisler v Anglo-Dal Ltd* [1954] 1 W.L.R. 1273 CA at 1278).

[162] *C & S Associates UK Ltd v Enterprise Insurance Co Plc* [2015] EWHC 3757 at [96].

[163] *C & S Associates UK Ltd v Enterprise Insurance Co Plc* [2015] EWHC 3757 at [96].

8-083 **Opportunity to avoid default** In the same case, Males J[164] held that the *Heisler* case exception[165] applies only to anticipatory breaches and not to the situation (as in the *Glencore* case; see above) where the breach has already occurred at the time for performance so that history cannot be re-written:

> "it is clear that the Heisler qualification applies only to anticipatory breaches or, to the extent that this is different, to situations where if the point had been taken steps could have been taken to avoid the party being in breach altogether, either by giving it an opportunity to perform its obligation in time or by enabling it to perform in some other valid way".

8-084 **Exception (2): estoppel** Secondly, estoppel by representation (including representation by conduct) might render it unjust for party A, the innocent party, to invoke the true ground if party B has altered his position in a detrimental manner as a result of A's representation or conduct.[166] Evans LJ in the *Glencore Grain* case (whose judgment was approved by the other two judges) said:[167]

> "(1)   The *Panchaud Frères* case[168] is authority for the application of the common law rule of acceptance, now established in section 35 of the Sale of Goods Act 1979, in the comparatively limited circumstances of a case where a CIF buyer accepts documents but rejects or purports to reject the goods.
>
> (2)   The decision can equally be said to represent a form of 'estoppel by conduct', but there is no 'separate doctrine' derived from *Panchaud Frères* alone.
>
> (3)   Like all other forms of estoppel or waiver, the facts must justify a finding that there was an unequivocal representation made by one party, by conduct or otherwise, which was acted upon by the other
>
> (4)   When the facts do justify that finding, it is likely to be regarded as 'unfair and unjust' for the party which made the representation to a contrary effect to rely upon its contractual rights.
>
> (5)   Without such a representation, no estoppel or waiver can arise, and there is no general rule that what the court or tribunal may perceive as 'unfairness or injustice' has the same effect.
>
>   (Evans LJ's proposition (6), not cited here, is that the *Panchaud Frères* and subsequent cases illustrate the possible scope of an estoppel or waiver in circumstances such as these, but they do not reveal a further exception to the basic rule, that a party is entitled to rely upon his contractual rights. And Lewis J confirmed in *Williams v Leeds United Football Club* (2015) (see quotation in this note)[169] that, in the absence of waiver or estoppel, or acceptance by a buyer under a sale of goods, there is no general or residual exception to the innocent party's

---

[164] *C & S Associates UK Ltd v Enterprise Insurance Co Plc* [2015] EWHC 3757 at [93].

[165] Citing *Heisler v Anglo-Dal Ltd* [1954] 1 W.L.R. 1273 CA at 1278.

[166] [1997] 4 All E.R. 514 CA at 530–531, noting *Panchaud Frères SA v Etablissements General Grain Co* [1970] 1 Lloyd's Rep. 53 CA (the latter case contains loose dicta, especially by Winn LJ at 59).

[167] [1997] 4 All E.R. 514 CA at 530–531.

[168] *Panchaud Freres SA v Etablissements General Grain Co* [1970] 1 Lloyd's Rep. 53 CA; on this case, H. Beale (ed), *Chitty on Contracts*, 34th edn (London: Sweet & Maxwell, 2021), para.27-059.

[169] [2015] EWHC 376 (QB); [2015] I.R.L.R. 383 at [84]: "There is no basis for concluding that it is 'unfair' or 'unjust' to allow the Defendant to rely upon the Claimant's anticipatory conduct to resist a claim for wrongful dismissal in such circumstances". Adding at [86]: "That [restrictive] approach is also consistent with *Glencore Rotterdam BV v Lebanese Organisation for International Commerce* [1997] 4 All E.R. 514; [1997] 2 Lloyd's Rep. 386; [1997] C.L.C. 1274 CA. There the Court of Appeal re-affirmed the basic rule in the law of contract that a person who terminates a contract, and subsequently discovers conduct which would have entitled him to terminate the contract, is entitled to rely upon that later conduct to resist a claim for damages for breach. That rule was subject to certain specified exceptions such as, for example, estoppel or waiver, where the facts 'justify a

capacity to rely upon subsequent discovery of a justification for terminating the contract.)

(7)   Unfairness and injustice, however, will always be relevant where the court is required to exercise a discretionary power, e.g. where a party seeks leave to raise a fresh matter by way of amendment or at a late stage of the proceedings before it (see the example given by Lord Denning MR in *Panchaud Frères* at 57)."

Exception (3): payment in lieu of notice of dismissal   This third exception is confined to employment law. The Court of Appeal in *Cavanagh v William Evans Ltd*[170] held that an employer is bound to make payment of a sum agreed as payment in lieu of notice if the employer has chosen to exercise a contractual right to terminate a contract of employment on that basis. It does not matter that the employer subsequently discovers that the employee had committed breaches which would have justified termination for repudiation without notice and thus without such payment in lieu of notice.   **8-085**

But in *Williams v Leeds United Football Club*, (where a senior club employee's emailing of obscene images to a female, junior employee, and to third parties, was a repudiatory breach,[171] and that breach was discovered subsequent to the club's summary dismissal of the employee, Lewis J held that the club was entitled to rely on this and was not, therefore, itself in breach.[172] The *Cavanagh* exception (see para.8-085) was not applicable because in the *Leeds United* case there had been a summary dismissal without notice, whereas in the *Cavanagh* case there had been a dismissal with notice, but it had been agreed that there would be payment in lieu of notice.[173]   **8-086**

Limit on the Boston Deep Sea principle: innocent party unable to change basis of termination so as to claim loss of bargain damages   The *Boston Deep Sea* principle is, therefore, a shield, supplying a justification for what might be otherwise an unjustified termination, but not actively enabling the innocent party to make a positive claim superior than that earlier adumbrated or made. This emerges from the following judicial discussion. In *Phones 4U Ltd (in administration) v EE Ltd* Andrew Baker J noted[174] that the Court of Appeal in *Trademark Licensing Co Ltd v Leofelis SA*[175] had distinguished between (i) the innocent party's right to demonstrate that its mistaken termination was in fact justified (based on facts subsisting at the time but not properly understood by the innocent party, or facts not known to the innocent party) and (ii) the capacity of the innocent party to claim loss of bargain damages. On point (ii), Andrew Baker J said:[176]   **8-087**

"per Lloyd LJ at para 33 [in *Trademark Licensing Co Ltd v Leofelis SA*, passage quoted at para.8-087], the law did not allow the innocent party to assert, so as to found a loss of

---

finding that there was an unequivocal representation made by one party, by conduct or otherwise, which was acted upon by the other' but 'Without such a representation, no such estoppel or waiver can arise, and there is no general rule that what the court or tribunal may perceive as 'unfairness or injustice' has the same effect'."

170   [2012] EWCA Civ 697; [2013] 1 W.L.R. 238.
171   [2015] EWHC 376 (QB); [2015] I.R.L.R. 383 at [50], [52], [53], [60], [61], [76], [77], [80], [83].
172   [2015] EWHC 376 (QB); [2015] I.R.L.R. 383 at [80], [83].
173   [2015] EWHC 376 (QB); [2015] I.R.L.R. 383 at [76]–[80].
174   [2018] EWHC 49 (Comm); [2018] 2 All E.R. (Comm) 315 notably at [110], see also [76], [116] to [132].
175   [2012] EWCA Civ 985 (Lloyd, Pill, Lewison LJJ).
176   [2018] EWHC 49 (Comm); [2018] 2 All E.R. (Comm) 315 notably at [110].

bargain claim, that it did terminate upon the lawful basis that ex hypothesi had not in fact been relied on at the time; per Pill LJ [also in *Trademark Licensing Co Ltd v Leofelis SA* (2012)] at para 44, '… If the premature determination of the contract is for reasons other than those that subsequently emerge, a claim for post-termination loss cannot be sustained'."

8-088   In *Phones 4U Ltd (in administration) v EE Ltd* Andrew Baker J adopted[177] Lloyd LJ's analysis in *Trademark Licensing Co Ltd v Leofelis SA* of the essentially defensive operation of the *Boston Deep Sea* principle or rule:[178]

"The principle underlying the *Boston Deep Sea Fishing* case [*Boston Deep Sea and Ice Co v Ansell* (1888) 39 Ch D 339, 364, CA, per Bowen LJ] has never been put forward as being that the unknown but justified ground for accepting a repudiation is to be read into the letter or other communication by which the unjustified reason is asserted. I do not see that the principle can or should be understood as extending that far. It does not allow the innocent party to assert that it did accept repudiation on the correct (though unknown) ground; rather it allows that party to meet a claim that its conduct in terminating the contract, though apparently unjustified because done on the wrong ground, is to be taken as justified because it could have been done on the right ground, not because it was done on the right ground. It operates as a shield against a claim for damages on the basis of wrongful termination, not as a sword to claim damages (for the future) on the basis of justified termination."

Also on *Phones 4U Ltd (in administration) v EE Ltd* (2018) see Ch.9, notably at para.9-015.

8-089   Based on the authorities, Andrew Baker J said in *Phones 4U Ltd (in administration) v EE Ltd*[179] that he recognised:

"the correctness in principle of the proposition that if a termination letter communicates clearly a decision to terminate only under an express contractual right to terminate that *has arisen irrespective of any breach*, then it cannot be said that the contract was terminated for breach and so a claim for damages for loss of bargain at common law cannot run".

8-090   And so, in *Phones 4U Ltd (in administration) v EE Ltd*[180] Andrew Baker J held that a claim to loss of bargain damages requires that the contract was ended by reason of accepted renunciation or repudiation, etc, and that the innocent party had communicated an intention to terminate by reason of the other's breach.[181] If instead, as on the facts, the termination was made by reference to a right which does not presuppose breach (under a termination without proof of breach clause), the terminating party (although shielded by the *Boston Deep Sea* principle and thus not himself guilty of repudiation by terminating the contract) will be unable to make a positive claim for loss of bargain damages against the other. Andrew Baker J in *Phones 4U* explained[182] that the terminating party had thrown away its chance of claiming loss of bargain damages because its termination letter relied solely on the unilateral cancellation right. The claimant's invocation of that right, on these facts,

[177] [2018] EWHC 49 (Comm); [2018] 2 All E.R. (Comm) 315 at [110].
[178] [2012] EWCA Civ 985 at [33].
[179] [2018] EWHC 49 (Comm); [2018] 2 All E.R. (Comm) 315 at [121].
[180] [2018] EWHC 49 (Comm); [2018] 2 All E.R. (Comm) 315 at [121].
[181] Also noting that on the same point, the same analysis had been adopted by Tomlinson J in *Shell Egypt Manzala GmbH v Dana Gas Egypt Ltd* [2010] EWHC 465 (Comm) at [31] and [32].
[182] [2018] EWHC 49 (Comm); [2018] 2 All E.R. (Comm) 315 at [132].

carried no implication that termination was the consequence of breach. It was not possible to:[183] "re-characterise the events after the fact and claim that [the claimant] terminated for breach when that is simply not what it did. Nor can [that party] say that it treated Phones 4U's renunciation (as now alleged) as bringing the contract to an end when that, again, is just not what actually happened".

V. REPUDIATION BY UNJUSTIFIED CONTRACTUAL DEFAULT EVEN IF THIS OCCURS IN GOOD FAITH

A party's mistaken but good faith failure to comply with his contractual obliga- **8-091**
tions   This topic has been treated elsewhere because it overlaps with discussion of the parallel issue of a refusal to perform which occurs in good faith but without legal justification. This topic is examined in the chapter concerning renunciation: para.6-085 ff.

---

[183] [2018] EWHC 49 (Comm); [2018] 2 All E.R. (Comm) 315 at [132].

CHAPTER 9

TERMINATION CLAUSES[1]

I. SUMMARY

Types of termination clauses or powers   There are three possible types of   **9-001**
unilateral right to terminate, but only the third of these is exercisable in consequence
of breach: (i) an express right to cancel without showing the other party's breach
(a pure cancellation right not contingent on the other party's breach or default) (section II of this chapter, para.9-012); (ii) an express right to terminate in respect of
the other party's breach (section III of this chapter, para.9-016), including clauses
which define that right by reference to a "material" breach (section IV of this
chapter, also noting the concept of a "remediable" or "non-remediable" breach,
para.9-042); (iii) an implied right to cancel (upon giving reasonable notice) without
showing the other party's breach (section V of this chapter, para.9-066).

Need for clarity in exercise of the relevant termination power   In *Geys v*   **9-002**
Société Générale, London Branch Baroness Hale noted that a party needs to act in
an unequivocal manner when purporting to exercise a termination clause or other
unilateral notice clause,[2] but it should be noted that those remarks were made in the
context of notification of termination under a contract of employment. More generally, on the need to adhere to the mode or procedure specified in a termination
clause, see Carter's[3] and Treitel's[4] discussion, and see *Afovos Shipping Co SA v*
Pagnan ("The Afovos")[5] at para.9-035 ff and *Vivergo Fuels Ltd v Redhall Engineer-*
ing Solutions Ltd[6] at para.9-041. Some cases emphasise strongly an objective approach to the issue of notification, notably the *Vannin* case at para. 9-031, and see

---

[1]   Neil Andrews, *Contract Law in Practice* (Oxford: Oxford University Press, 2021), paras 24.125–
24.147; R. Hooley, "Express Termination Clauses", in G. Virgo and S. Worthington (eds), *Commercial Remedies: Resolving Controversies* (Cambridge: Cambridge University Press, 2017); K.
Lewison, *Interpretation of Contracts*, 7th edn (London: Sweet & Maxwell, 2020), paras 17.95–
17.124; G. McMeel, *The Construction of Contracts: Interpretation, Implication and Rectification*,
3rd edn (Oxford: Oxford University Press, 2017), para.23.02 ff; E. Peel, "The Termination Paradox"
[2013] L.M.C.L.Q. 519–543; J. Randall, "Express Termination Clauses" [2014] C.L.J. 113–141; J.E.
Stannard and D. Capper, *Termination for Breach of Contract*, 2nd edn (Oxford: Oxford University
Press, 2020), Ch.8; S. Whittaker, "Termination Clauses", in A.S. Burrows and E. Peel (eds), *Contract
Terms* (Oxford: Oxford University Press, 2007), Ch.13 (discussion of many related decisions
concerning "material breach" and similar contract drafting).
[2]   [2012] UKSC 63; [2013] 1 A.C. 523 at [52].
[3]   J.W. Carter, *Carter's Breach of Contract*, 2nd edn (Oxford: Hart Publishing, 2019), [10-12] ff.
[4]   G.H. Treitel (E. Peel, ed.), *The Law of Contract*, 15th edn (London: Sweet & Maxwell, 2020),
para.18-077.
[5]   [1983] 1 W.L.R. 195 HL.
[6]   [2013] EWHC 4030 (TCC) at [420]: "the following principles can be derived from *Mannai Investments Co Ltd v Eagle Star Assurance* [1997] A.C. 749 HL and *Architectural Installation Services*

also *Vivergo Fuels Ltd v Redhall Engineering Solutions Ltd* at para.9-041. (see the extensive quotation from the latter case which is set out at fn.6 of this chapter). There is one major trap revealed by the case law. As noted at para.9.014 ff below, Andrew Baker J's decision in *Phones 4U Ltd (in administration) v EE Ltd*[7] (confirming earlier analysis) shows that, where a party invokes a right to cancel under a termination power which is exercisable without the need to show default, that notification will not, without more, sufficiently indicate a decision to terminate at Common Law by reason of the other party's repudiatory breach, etc. And the result will be that loss of bargain damages will be unavailable. It is enough to warn the legal community that in the territory shared by factually overlapping termination clauses and Common Law rights to treat the contract as discharged for repudiatory breach, etc, there are unexploded mines. Entry on this land requires careful thought and composure.

Finally, as noted at para.8-069 ff, *Boston Deep Sea Fishing and Ice Co v Ansell* (1888)[8] made clear that a party can rely on a breach not known to it even though at the relevant date he had not expressly invoked that breach as justification for the decision to terminate the contract. But in *Nakanishi Marine Co Ltd v Gora Shipping Ltd* (2012) Burton J doubted[9] that this principle extends to the situation where a termination clause stipulates that default will justify termination under the clause only if the default relied upon is identified in the termination notice. The *Nakanishi* case was approved by Freedman J in *Lombard North Central Plc v European Skyjets Ltd* (2020).[10]

9-003　**Overlapping express and Common Law termination rights: a judicial survey**　In *Shell Egypt West Manzala GMBH v Dana Gas Egypt Ltd*[11] (which concerned, on its facts, a pure cancellation clause, that is, the relevant termination clause was exercisable without showing breach) Tomlinson J ranged broadly when seeking to summarise the principles governing termination of a contract where there is, or at least potentially there is, overlap or concurrence between the possibility of termination under an express contractual right of termination (whether a pure cancellation clause or a termination for breach clause) and termination for repudia-

---

Ltd v James Gibbons Windows Ltd (1989) 46 B.L.R. 91, HH Judge Bowsher QC. First that unilateral notices are to be construed in the same way as contractual documents and therefore it is necessary to construe them objectively against the background or 'the relevant objective contextual scene' known to both parties. Secondly the relevant meaning of the unilateral notices is the meaning that a reasonable recipient would have understood by the notices. The reasonable recipient 'would have had in the forefront of his mind the terms' of the relevant underlying contract. Thirdly, that the purpose of the notice is relevant to its construction and validity. Prima facie, if a notice unambiguously conveys the purpose, a court will ignore immaterial errors which would not have misled a reasonable recipient. Fourthly, the notice must be sufficiently clear and unambiguous to leave a reasonable recipient in no reasonable doubt as to how and when the notice is intended to operate. Fifthly, in the context of clause which require a default notice and then a termination notice, the two notices must be connected both in content and in time. Sixthly, in this case the notice must notify the default. However, I also consider that something is needed either indicating the seriousness of the situation or making some link to [underlying contractual right] so that the reasonable recipient would realise that it was [an official contractual] notice. Obviously, the background known to both parties may supply that."

7　[2018] EWHC 49 (Comm); [2018] 2 All E.R. (Comm) 315 at [132] per Andrew Baker J.
8　(1888) LR 39 Ch. D. 339 (CA).
9　[2012] EWHC 3383 (Comm) at [35](iii).
10　[2020] EWHC 679 (QB) at [62] to [68].
11　[2010] EWHC (Comm) 465 at [31] per Tomlinson J; noted Q. Liu, "The Puzzle of Unintended Acceptance of Repudiation" [2011] L.M.C.L.Q. 4–11.

tory, etc, breach at Common Law. In essence, Tomlinson J said, a distinction is to be drawn between:

- *Co-existent rights of termination:* situations where the termination is capable of being exercised simultaneously in respect of (i) the contractual scheme for termination (whether or not the express right is contingent on breach) and (ii) the Common Law right of termination for breach;
- *Expressly co-existent rights of termination:* a fortiori (i) and (ii) will co-exist if the contract expressly states that a party's right under (i) is "without prejudice" and hence additional to the ordinary Common Law right under (ii); for example, Ramsey J noted in *Vivergo Fuels Ltd v Redhall Engineering Solutions Ltd*:[12]

    "[the contractual right of termination for breach] is expressly stated to be without prejudice to 'any other rights and remedies which the Purchaser may possess' and does not accordingly preclude [the innocent party] from terminating at common law";

- *election between inconsistent rights to terminate:* the situation where the terminating party has an election as between (i) and (ii) because there is a disjuncture in the operation of these two modes of termination (referred to in the cases as "inconsistent" effects or consequences); and
- *absence of co-existent rights: a single exclusive express code:* this is the situation where (i) does not co-exist with (ii) because (i), that is, the special and express clause or set of provisions, is the exclusive or "self-contained" code applicable to the process of termination.

In the *Shell Egypt case* Tomlinson J surveyed these points as follows, drawing upon leading authorities (numbering of points as (1) to (5) has been added here).[13]   **9-004**

(1) "The invalid invocation of a right to terminate contractually on account of a   **9-005** breach of contract is capable of being effective to accept a repudiatory breach as terminating the contract if it unequivocally demonstrates an intention to treat the contractual obligations as at an end."[14] This denotes the process of objective construction of the terms and factual matrix of the termination notification.

(2) But Tomlinson J in the *Shell case* noted that the comment made at (1) was   **9-006** made in "a case where the contractual provision invoked was not a self-contained code, resort to which would necessarily exclude resort to the remedies generally available at law, but was rather 'built on the underpinnings of the common law remedies for breach of contract'—see per Rix LJ *Stocznia Gdanska SA v Latvian Shipping Co* (2002)".[15]

(3) On the facts of the *Shell case* Tomlinson J noted that although   **9-007**

    "[the termination clause] may not be a complete code [nevertheless] resort thereto is inconsistent with treating the contract as terminated by acceptance of a repudiatory breach, not least because the clause is not triggered by breach and provides that in the event of resort to it Centurion shall not be obliged to repay to Shell any amounts paid under [the contract]".

---

12 [2013] EWHC 4030 at [502].
13 [2010] EWHC (Comm) 465 at [31] per Tomlinson J.
14 See *Stocznia Gdanska SA v Latvian Shipping Co* [2002] 2 Ll. L. Rep 436.
15 [2002] EWCA Civ 889; [2002] 2 All E.R. (Comm) 768 at [72].

9-008   (4)   Tomlinson J then noted that it follows from proposition (3), just presented, that

> "if the Termination Letter is to be taken as an unequivocal communication by Shell of its decision to terminate the contract under [the contractual termination clause], [the termination letter] cannot also serve as effective to accept Centurion's repudiatory breach as terminating the contract".

Tomlinson J noted that points (3) and (4) are supported by the analysis of Christopher Clarke J in *Dalkia Utilities Services Plc v Celtech International Ltd*, who formulated this notion of unequivocal and fateful election in favour of the contractual scheme as follows:[16]

> "[if a notice] makes explicit reference to a particular contractual clause, and nothing else, this may, in context, show that the giver of the notice was not intending to accept the repudiation and was only relying on the contractual clause; for instance if the claim made under the notice of termination is inconsistent with, and not simply less than, that which arises on acceptance of a repudiation."

9-009   (5)   Finally, Tomlinson J noted that the preceding analysis was consistent with the following remarks of Moore-Bick LJ in *Stocznia Gdynia SA v Gearbulk Holdings Ltd*:[17]

> "If the contract and the general law provide the injured party with alternative rights which have different consequences, as was held to be the case in *Dalkia Utilities v Celtech*, he will necessarily have to elect between them and the precise terms in which he informs the other party of his decision will be significant, but where the contract provides a right to terminate which corresponds to a right under the general law (because the breach goes to the root of the contract or the parties have agreed that it should be treated as doing so) no election is necessary. In such cases it is sufficient for the injured party simply to make it clear that he is treating the contract as discharged ... If he gives a bad reason for doing so, his action is nonetheless effective if the circumstances support it. That, as I understand it, is what Rix LJ was saying in *Stocznia Gdanska SA v Latvian Shipping Co* (2002),[18] with which I respectfully agree."

9-010   Those principles were applied in *Shell Egypt West Manzala GMBH v Dana Gas Egypt Ltd*,[19] where Shell at the relevant time held the right at Common Law to terminate the contract by reason of the other party's repudiation (the other party was Centurion). Tomlinson J concluded that Shell had explicitly invoked the contractual machinery for termination in circumstances where they had objectively, in effect, abandoned their Common Law right to terminate for (serious) breach. As noted at para.9.014 ff below, Tomlinson J's decision was followed by Andrew Baker J in *Phones 4U Ltd (in administration) v EE Ltd*, where it was also held that reliance on a termination without breach clause had objectively indicated no intention to terminate for Common Law repudiatory breach, with the result that loss of bargain damages at Common Law were not available. Returning to the *Shell Egypt* case, Tomlinson J held that the express contractual scheme was inconsistent with the Common Law principles of termination. This was because the contractual scheme

---

[16]   [2006] 1 Ll. L Rep. 599 at 632–633 per Christopher Clarke J.
[17]   [2009] EWCA Civ 75; [2010] Q.B. 27 at [44] per Moore-Bick LJ (noted E. Peel, "Affirmation by Termination" (2009) 125 L.Q.R. 378–384).
[18]   [2002] EWCA Civ 889; [2002] 2 All E.R. (Comm) 768 at [32].
[19]   [2010] EWHC (Comm) 465 at [35] per Tomlinson J.

was capable of yielding a refund of expenditure, whereas the Common Law protection of an innocent party would necessarily provide instead the right to compensation for loss, which might not be the same monetary outcome as a refund. On the facts, Shell had wrongly concluded that the situation had produced for them a contractual right to a refund. Although it was obvious to the recipient of the notice (Centurion) that Shell had unaccountably made this mistaken supposition that Shell held a right to a refund, Tomlinson J rejected the contention that the reasonable recipient would have concluded that the entire notice was an error. The circumstances supported an objective inference that the innocent party was commercially desperate to exit from the contract in order to avoid imminent future financial commitment. Against that background, a notice indicating that the innocent party wished, in effect, to quit and cut its exposure made objective commercial sense. It followed that the invocation of the cancellation clause on these facts was an election that precluded resort by Shell to Common Law damages for loss of bargain. (As noted at para.9-014, the same election was held to have arisen in the *Phones 4U* case, with the same result: that damages for repudiatory damages had been taken off the table because of the maladroit decision to invoke a pure cancellation right.)

In the *Shell Egypt* case Tomlinson J expressed this conclusion as follows:[20]   **9-011**

"a reasonable recipient of the Termination Letter ... would regard it as plausible that [the innocent party] had simply decided to cut their losses and withdraw from the agreement on a basis which offered certainty that no further obligation would fall due for performance ... The letter as written plainly communicates an unequivocal election to terminate under Clause 3.1.8. In my judgment the obvious mistake contained in it does not, in context, derogate from that message, because it was a perfectly feasible commercial stance for [the innocent party] to adopt that they wished simply to withdraw from the Agreement without incurring any further obligation whether that enabled them to recover their initial payment or not. The imperative was clarity that [the innocent party] had no further obligation under the Agreement."

II.   EXPRESS RIGHT TO CANCEL WITHOUT BREACH

Nature of a pure unilateral cancellation clause: termination without need to   **9-012**
show breach   A contract might expressly permit a party to terminate a contract in specified circumstances without the need to show default, and thus without the need to show a Common Law right to terminate for breach (that is, in the absence of either renunciation or repudiation, or of breach of a condition, or serious breach of an intermediate term). Where a party terminates under a pure cancellation clause (termination without need to show default) that party might be entitled to obtain damages in respect of past breaches (because that cause of action, or set of causes of actions, have already accrued and are not affected by the termination). But the terminating party will have elected, or rather be treated to have elected, not to obtain damages for loss of the remaining period of the contract. That conclusion will apply *unless the facts disclose that there has been a repudiatory or renunciatory breach in respect of which the innocent party has demonstrated a wish to terminate the contract.*[21] As the Court of Appeal explained in the *Lombard* case, there had been no such repudiatory or renunciatory breach on the facts of the *Financings*

---

[20]   [2010] EWHC (Comm) 465 at [35] per Tomlinson J.
[21]   *Financings Ltd v Baldock* [1963] 2 Q.B. 104 at 110–111, 121 CA; Nicholls LJ in *Lombard North Central Plc v Butterworth* [1987] Q.B. 527 CA at 541–543, 546; noted G.H. Treitel, "Damages on

case.[22] This option to cancel analysis was noted as a feature of general law by Popplewell J (and upheld by the Court of Appeal) in *Spar Shipping AS v Grand China Logistics Holding (Group) Co Ltd ("The Spar Draco")*,[23] although the judge (and the Court of Appeal) found that termination for breach had occurred on the facts because the pattern of late payment was so serious that, assessed objectively, the relevant series of defaults disclosed a "renunciatory" intention. The shipowner was not precluded on the facts from relying on that renunciation. A clause might even stipulate that a contract will terminate automatically in specified circumstances, but, as Carter notes, the courts lean against enabling a party in default to take advantage of such a clause if it is to the other's detriment.[24]

9-013   **Reliance on pure cancellation right: no purported reliance on breach: terminating party inadvertently abandoning right to claim loss of bargain damages**   Where A terminates in reliance on a termination without breach clause, can A subsequently claim Common Law loss of bargain damages (on the basis of breach of condition, repudiation, renunciation)? The answer given in two first instance decisions is "no", the successful contention being that in such a situation the terminating party has not terminated the contract for breach, but has instead caused it to be terminated by exercise of a termination right which is not even dependent on proof of breach. First, Tomlinson J in *Shell Egypt Manzala GmbH v Dana Gas Egypt Ltd* held[25] that termination by invocation of a termination without breach clause precluded the terminating party from subsequently claiming loss of bargain damages founded on a Common Law repudiatory breach (the point turned on a concession made by Shell's counsel, whose unsuccessful argument was that the termination had been a patent error and thus ineffective, leaving intact the Common Law regime of rights).

9-014   Tomlinson J's decision in the *Shell Egypt* case, where Common Law loss of bargain damages consequent on repudiatory breach were declared to be unavailable, was followed by Andrew Baker J in *Phones 4U Ltd (in administration) v EE Ltd*.[26] This outcome, of great commercial significance, involves a trap: the innocent party by choosing to terminate a contract in reliance on a pure cancellation right (that is, a right to cancel which subsists without the need to show breach) cannot claim loss of bargain damages. This is because such compensation is only payable if the contract has been purportedly terminated for breach. Here, rather like a disorientated driver's wish to exit at the optimal point on a motorway, the contractual party needs to know which termination lever to pull. But the *Shell Egypt* and *Phones 4U* decisions establish that the innocent party, who pulls the pure

---

Rescission for Breach of Contract" [1987] L.M.C.L.Q. 143; W. Bojczuk, "When is a condition not a condition?" [1987] J.B.L. 353; B. Opeskin, "Damages for Breach of Contract Terminated under Express Terms" (1990) 106 L.Q.R. 293; similarly, in Australia, J.W. Carter, *Carter's Breach of Contract*, 2nd edn (Oxford: Hart Publishing, 2019), [13-07], noting *Shevill v Builders Licensing Board* (1982) 149 C.L.R. 620; 42 A.L.R. 305, H.Ct. Aust.

[22]   Nicholls LJ in *Lombard North Central Plc v Butterworth* [1987] Q.B. 527 at 541–542, noting Diplock LJ in *Financings Ltd v Baldock* [1963] 2 Q.B. 104 CA at 121.

[23]   [2015] EWHC 718 (Comm); [2015] 1 All E.R. (Comm) 879 at [92]–[207]; the decision was affirmed in all respects at [2016] EWCA Civ 982; [2016] 2 Lloyd's Rep. 447 (Gross, Hamblen LJJ, Sir Terence Etherton MR).

[24]   J.W. Carter, *Carter's Breach of Contract*, 2nd edn (Oxford: Hart Publishing, 2019) at [10-03].

[25]   [2010] EWHC 465 (Comm) at [31] and [32]; decision criticised by Q. Liu, "The Puzzle of Unintended Acceptance of Repudiation" [2011] L.M.C.L.Q. 4.

[26]   [2018] EWHC 49 (Comm); [2018] 2 All E.R. (Comm) 315 at [76], [116] to [132].

cancellation lever (termination without showing breach) cannot later seek to recharacterise the basis of termination as founded on discharge for Common Law repudiatory breach. As Andrew Baker J explained in the *Phones 4U* case:[27]

"EE's termination letter... communicated unequivocally that EE was terminating in exercise of, and only of, its right to do so under clause 14.1.2, a right independent of any breach. *Phones 4U* was not accused of breach. EE made clear it was not to be taken as waiving any breach that might exist, any rights in respect of which were reserved. But a right merely re-served is a right not exercised. EE can still sue upon any breach of contract committed by *Phones 4U* prior to termination. For any such breach, it may pursue all remedies that may be available to it bearing in mind that the contract was terminated under clause 14.1.2 and not for breach. But what EE cannot do is re-characterise the events after the fact and claim that it terminated for breach when that is simply not what it did. Nor can it say that it treated Phones 4U's renunciation (as now alleged) as bringing the contract to an end when that, again, is just not what actually happened."

It will be noted that Andrew Baker J was making a distinction between accrued **9-015** pre-termination causes of action for breach (which survive the termination) and the innocent party's claim for loss of bargain damages where that party has terminated without indicating any tincture of reliance upon the other party's breach, that is, by exercise of the pure cancellation rights (the right not being contingent on breach). The *Phones 4U* case is further explained at Ch.8 at paras 8-088–8-090 where it is noted that Andrew Baker J applied[28] Lloyd LJ's[29] analysis in *Trademark Licensing Co Ltd v Leofelis SA*. Lloyd LJ held that where party A gives reason Y (not based on breach) for termination, although party A will have a "shield" against liability for breach, namely party A's capacity to invoke as a basis for termination reason Z (the unknown fact that party B had been guilty of a repudiatory breach), party A's decision to terminate for reason Y precludes party A from obtaining loss of bargain damages on the basis of reason Z. In short, the doctrine in the *Boston Deep Sea Fishing* case[30]

"operates as a shield against a claim for damages on the basis of wrongful termination, not as a sword to claim damages (for the future) on the basis of justified."

(This quotation is taken from Lloyd LJ's judgment in *Trademark Licensing Co Ltd v Leofelis SA*, 2012.[31])

III.   EXPRESS RIGHT TO TERMINATE FOR BREACH

The Court of Appeal in *Stocznia Gdynia SA v Gearbulk Holdings Ltd* held that **9-016** an innocent party can exercise simultaneously an express power *to terminate for breach* and the Common Law right to terminate a contract because of the other party's repudiatory breach (Moore-Bick LJ giving the court's sole reasoned judgment).[32] The same court also held that an express and guaranteed right to recover pre-payments can co-exist with the background Common Law right to

---

27 [2018] EWHC 49 (Comm); [2018] 2 All E.R. (Comm) 315 at [132].
28 [2018] EWHC 49 (Comm); [2018] 2 All E.R. (Comm) 315 at [110].
29 [2012] EWCA Civ 985 at [33].
30 *Boston Deep Sea and Ice Co v Ansell* (1888) 39 Ch. D. 339, 364, CA, per Bowen LJ.
31 [2012] EWCA Civ 985 at [33].
32 [2009] EWCA Civ 75; [2010] Q.B. 27 (noted E. Peel, "Affirmation by Termination" (2009) 125 L.Q.R. 378–84).

terminate the contract by reason of repudiatory breach. The court concluded that the buyer's decision to invoke the *express* right to guaranteed repayment of purchase instalments was not incompatible with that innocent party's co-existing *common law* right to loss of bargain damages. The latter claim was consequent on the buyer's termination of the contract by reason of the seller's repudiatory breach.

9-017   The *Stocznia* case concerned contracts for the construction and sale of three ships. The seller failed to supply in time, and the buyer terminated all three contracts for repudiatory breach. The buyer exercised its express right to recover, under a guarantee facility, its pre-payments (see further below). But the parties went to arbitration on the disputed issue whether this transaction's clauses, providing both for termination (for serious breach) and repayment, had the effect of precluding a general Common Law claim for loss of bargain consequent upon termination for repudiatory breach. The seller contended that the contract's termination machinery (for breach) was the exclusive mode of terminating for breach; or, if this express machinery were an alternative mode of termination, available alongside Common Law termination principles, that the buyer had elected to invoke the express machinery alone, and so had lost any chance to obtain general Common Law compensation for loss of bargain. In *Stocznia Gdynia SA v Gearbulk Holdings Ltd* Moore-Bick LJ gave the following explanation for the proposition that the express right to terminate for serious default can co-exist with the (implicit) Common Law right to terminate for a repudiatory breach:[33]

> "[The parties had] agreed that there comes a point at which the delay or deficiency is so serious that it should entitle [the buyer] to terminate the contract…[T]he right to terminate the contract cannot sensibly be understood as anything other than embodying the parties' agreement that the buyer has the right to treat the contract as repudiated, with … the usual consequences."

9-018   Moore-Bick LJ continued:

> "[I]t is wrong to treat the right to terminate in accordance with the terms of the contract as different in substance from the right to treat the contract as discharged by reason of repudiation at common law. In those cases where the contract gives a right of termination they are in effect one and the same."

9-019   Moore-Bick LJ added:

> "The court is unlikely to be satisfied that a party to a contract has abandoned valuable rights arising by operation of law unless the terms of the contract make it sufficiently clear that that was intended. The more valuable the right, the clearer the language will need to be."

9-020   Moore-Bick LJ also explained that the buyer had become entitled to recover the pre-payments in restitution under the principle of total failure of consideration, once the contract of sale had been terminated before any delivery of the ships. The *express guaranteed right to repayment* was merely a specially protected consensual version of that right. And so the buyer's invocation of this guaranteed repayment did not preclude general compensatory rights for loss of bargain (namely for the difference between the contract price and the market value of the ship at the relevant

---

[33] [2009] EWCA Civ 75; [2010] Q.B. 27 at [20], [23]; distinguishing at [19], *Lockland Builders Ltd v Rickwood* (1995) 77 B.L.R. 42 CA, where the express termination for breach clause was construed as excluding the Common Law right to terminate for a repudiatory breach.

date). This can be explained, applying orthodox analysis of termination for breach, as follows. The innocent party's decision to end the contract by reason of the seller's repudiatory failure to build these ships on time involved: (i) termination of the contract's primary obligations (that is the duty, binding on both parties, to perform their respective obligations under the contract's main set of terms); (ii) survival of various ancillary provisions, such as exclusion clauses, arbitration clauses, and—on these facts—an express right to repayment of a pre-payment; (iii) the innocent party continued to enjoy a Common Law right to seek compensatory damages, including a claim for "loss of bargain": the cause of action underpinning (iii) is, of course, the innocent party's decision to terminate the contract by reason of the other party's repudiatory breach (or, on other facts, breach of a condition, or a very serious breach of an innominate term).

On these points, Moore-Bick LJ said in *Stocznia Gdynia SA v Gearbulk Hold-* **9-021**
ings Ltd:[34]

"the commercial context as well as the terms of the contract make it clear that the obligation to repay instalments of the price was intended to survive the termination of the contract, whether that occurred by reason of the exercise by [the buyer] of a right to terminate expressed in the contract itself or by its acceptance of a repudiatory breach on the part of the yard, each of which had the same consequences in law."

Moore-Bick LJ continued: **9-022**

"On discharge of a contract of this kind a buyer who has paid the whole or part of the price in advance is entitled, in the absence of any agreement to the contrary, to recover what he has paid by reason of a total failure of consideration. He therefore has a right to recover in restitution any payments he has made in respect of the price, a right which is quite distinct from any right he may have (if he is the injured party) to recover damages for the loss of his bargain ... There is no inherent inconsistency ... in recovering instalments of the price under [the guaranteed repayment clause] and recovering damages for loss of bargain at common law."

Moore-Bick LJ added: **9-023**

"Taking into account the contract as a whole I am left in no doubt that the parties intended [the guaranteed repayment clause] to provide a remedy additional to those that would ordinarily be available to [the buyer] on termination of the contract."

Underpinning this discussion is the presumption that a contract should not be **9-024** construed as an abandonment of remedies arising by operation of law. Clear words are required to demonstrate such an abandonment. *Lewison on the Interpretation of Contract* formulates this presumption as follows: "Clear words are necessary before the court will hold that a contract has taken away rights or remedies which one of the parties to it would have had at common law".[35]

This presumption was applied in *Seadrill Management Services Ltd v OAO* **9-025**
Gazprom[36] in the context of a complex contract for the hire of a drilling rig. Flaux J concluded that there had been no intention to exclude liability for negligent

---

[34] [2009] EWCA Civ 75; [2010] Q.B. 27 at [26]–[42]; explaining away, especially at [35], the apparently contradictory analysis in *United Dominions Trust (Commercial) Ltd v Ennis* [1968] 1 Q.B. 54 CA.
[35] K. Lewison, *Interpretation of Contracts*, 7th edn (London: Sweet & Maxwell, 2020), proposition at 12.144.
[36] [2009] EWHC 1530 (Comm); [2010] 1 Lloyd's Rep. 543 at [182]–[203].

performance of the contract. He said:

> "[there is a presumption] that clear words are necessary before a court will hold that a contract has taken away rights or remedies which one of the parties to it would have had at common law: ... *Gilbert-Ash (Northern) Ltd v Modern Engineering (Bristol) Ltd* [1974] A.C. 689 at 717–718 where Lord Diplock said: 'one starts with the presumption that neither party intends to abandon any remedies for its breach arising by operation of law, and clear express words must be used in order to rebut this presumption ... To rebut that presumption one must be able to find in the contract clear unequivocal words in which the parties have expressed their agreement that this remedy shall not be available in respect of breaches of that particular contract'."

9-026   Similarly, Males J in the *C & S* case held that a termination clause did not oust ordinary Common Law principles of repudiatory breach. And so, express provision for termination after the giving of specified notice and consequent on a "material" breach could co-exist with Common Law principles of termination for very serious breach (breach of a condition, renunciation, etc.). The key to Males J's reasoning is that termination for "material" breach operates in favour of the innocent party by increasing the opportunity for termination. This is because "material breach" can arise even where there would not be a breach "going to the root" for the purpose of Common Law repudiation (see para.9-050, *"Material Breach" Summarised*, where it is explained that "a 'material' breach is not trivial, but it must be 'substantial', although it need not be so serious as to justify termination applying the Common Law criterion for justified termination following breach"). Against that conceptual background, therefore, Males J made these observations on the relationship between the express provisions and the Common Law principles just mentioned:[37]

> "I do not accept that, in the case of those breaches which do satisfy those criteria, Enterprise has agreed not to exercise its common law right to treat the contract as discharged. Clause 15.2 provides an express contractual right to terminate, with the consequences set out in clause 16, *which is additional to the right to terminate for repudiation at common law*. Clear words would be required in order to conclude that termination for repudiation was excluded: cf. *Stocznia Gdynia SA v Gearbulk Holdings Ltd* [2009] EWCA Civ 75; [2010] Q.B. 27 at [23]. There are no such words here." (emphasis added)

9-027   Males J added:[38]

> "(1).   It is open to parties to agree that certain breaches or kinds of breach are not to be treated as repudiatory. Such clauses will be effective.
> (2).   Although every case will depend on the particular contract in issue, examples where clauses have been held to have this effect include (a) clauses which provide that specified conduct gives rise to a right of termination but only after service of a notice or a period of time, and (b) clauses which provide compensation for certain kinds of poor performance.
> (3).   Where a contract does provide that certain breaches or kinds of breach are not to be treated as repudiatory, that may provide guidance as to whether other kinds of breach qualify or are capable of qualifying as repudiatory. For example, breaches which are less serious are unlikely to do so.
> (4).   However, a clause such as clause 15.2 in the present case, providing for

---

[37] *C & S Associates UK Ltd v Enterprise Insurance Co Plc* [2015] EWHC 3757 at [101] per Males J.
[38] *C & S Associates UK Ltd v Enterprise Insurance Co Plc* [2015] EWHC 3757 at [107] per Males J; considering *BSkyB Ltd v HP Enterprise Services UK Ltd* [2010] EWHC 86 (TCC); [2010] B.L.R. 267 at [1362] ff per Ramsey J.

termination in the event of a material breach but only after the giving of a notice and a failure to remedy, will not by itself prevent a sufficiently serious breach from amounting to a repudiation of the contract justifying an immediate termination. *Such a clause will generally provide for a right to terminate which is in addition to a party's common law rights.*" (emphasis added)

Communication of decision to terminate for breach based both on the Common Law and on an express termination right A party might expressly terminate in a double-barrelled fashion (i) by relying on a termination for breach clause and (ii) by indicating, whether pellucidly or at least on construction (see para.9-029), that termination is also founded on Common Law repudiatory breach, etc. In *Gold Group Properties Ltd v BDW Trading Ltd (formerly known as Barratt Homes Ltd)*[39] Coulson J noted that:

9-028

"It is trite law that in order for a repudiatory breach to bring a contract to an end there must be a clear and unequivocal acceptance of that breach and that mere inactivity or acquiescence is generally not sufficient."

He then held that Gold's letter to Barratt, besides invoking a termination clause, also contained a clear decision to treat the contract as discharged for repudiatory breach:[40]

"the letter first of all relied upon the contractual right of termination, by referring to Clause 24 of the Agreement, and then, by reference to the letter of 2nd September, asserted that Barratt had no intention of performing the contract and that for that reason the Agreement 'has now terminated absolutely'."

The result was that:[41]

"this Agreement came to an end…both by virtue of the exercise of the right of termination pursuant to Clause 24 of the Agreement and by Gold's acceptance of Barratt's repudiatory breach. Such an outcome was explicitly recognised as being possible in certain circumstances in *Dalkia Utilities v Celtech* [2006] 1 Lloyd's Rep. 599 at [143], In short the exercise of the contractual right of termination was not an affirmation of the Agreement."

In *Parbulk II A/S v Heritage Maritime Ltd SA*[42] Eder J addressed "tentatively" and inconclusively (noting that the case had already turned on earlier points) the relationship between the Common Law principles of termination for breach and contractual machinery for notifying a party of default and terminating the contract under a consensual scheme. Eder J began by noting earlier judicial discussion:[43]

9-029

"the Owners sought to rely upon *Dalkia v Celtech International* [2006] 1 Lloyd's Rep. [Christopher Clarke J], specifically at [135]–[144] in support of the proposition that in an appropriate case a party with the benefit of a contractual right of termination need not elect between repudiation and contractual termination but can rely upon both. In other words in an appropriate case one letter can act both as a contractual termination and a common

---

39 [2010] EWHC 323 (TCC); [2010] B.L.R. 235 at [106].
40 [2010] EWHC 323 (TCC); [2010] B.L.R. 235 at [109].
41 [2010] EWHC 323 (TCC); [2010] B.L.R. 235 at [110].
42 [2011] EWHC 2917 (Comm); [2012] 2 All E.R. (Comm) 418 at [36] ff.
43 [2011] EWHC 2917 (Comm); [2012] 2 All E.R. (Comm) 418 at [36].

law acceptance of repudiation *if it is clear that the owner is by the letter bringing the primary contractual responsibilities to an end.*" (emphasis added and see [143] of the judgment)

9-030   Eder J held that the shipowner's notification in the present case did operate simultaneously as a Common Law termination and agreed notification:[44]

"On a fair construction, the termination notice did say enough to communicate reliance upon a repudiation at common law: 'In breach of your obligations under Charterparty, you have failed to pay hire ... we hereby withdraw the Vessel from your service and terminate the Charterparty with immediate effect'. This is not a case of exclusive reliance on a particular clause as the grounds for termination."

The further question in *Parbulk II A/S v Heritage Maritime Ltd SA* was quite intricate: whether the consequences of termination at Common Law and under the specific provisions of the contract were the same, or at least not "materially inconsistent". Eder J concluded[45] "tentatively" that there was no material inconsistency on the present facts.

9-031   **Communication of decision to terminate based on erroneous assumption that the default is covered by an express termination clause: terminating party objectively indicating termination for breach**   In *Vannin Capital PCC v RBOS Shareholders Action Group Ltd*, Joanna Smith QC, Deputy High Court Judge, applied an objective approach to the issue whether the innocent party had elected to treat the contract as discharged by reason of the repudiatory breach, etc.[46] In the *Vannin* case a party had purported to terminate two sets of agreement: one was thereupon validly terminated under a termination clause (that clause providing, essentially, that the terminating party's right to terminate would be triggered by the other party's default); but the agreement in the other set were not covered by a termination clause. As for the latter, the issue was whether the innocent party's purported reliance on a termination clause was effective to constitute acceptance of the Common Law right to accept repudiation (such a repudiatory breach had occurred with respect to that agreement). Adopting an objective perspective, the judge concluded[47] that the communication of an intention to terminate was effective on these facts to cover both sets of agreements; furthermore, objectively, the innocent party's communication constituted an election to terminate the second set of agreements by virtue of the other party's breach. It was here clear that the innocent party was responding to events by communicating a wish to end both sets of agreements and that the trigger for this response was the guilty party's breach. The fact that the innocent party had mistakenly linked this response to an assumption that both sets of agreement contained an identical termination for breach provision did not deprive this response of its character: a clear statement that the contract would be terminated (treated as discharged) by virtue of the other 's default. The default, on the facts, was repudiatory. Hence the termination was effective and valid.

---

[44]   [2011] EWHC 2917 (Comm); [2012] 2 All E.R. (Comm) 418 at [37].

[45]   [2011] EWHC 2917 (Comm); [2012] 2 All E.R. (Comm) 418 at [38] and [39].

[46]   [2018] EWHC 2821 (Ch) at [105]–[113] per Joanna Smith QC, Deputy High Court judge, citing *Vitol SA v Norelf Ltd ('The Santa Clara')* [1996] A.C. 800, 810H–811B per Lord Steyn; and *Shell Egypt West Manzala GmbH v Dana Gas Egypt Ltd* [2010] EWHC 465 (Comm) *at* [31] and [32] per Tomlinson J.

[47]   [2018] EWHC 2821 (Ch) at [106] and [111] per Joanna Smith QC.

Consequences of termination differing at Common Law and under the terms   9-032
of the contractual termination provision   This problem was examined in *Vivergo Fuels Ltd v Redhall Engineering Solutions Ltd*[48] by Ramsey J who adopted[49] the discussion by Moore-Bick LJ in *Stocznia Gdynia v Gearbulk Holdings*.[50] The salient portion of Moore-Bick LJ's statement is quoted here:[51]

> "If the contract and the general law provide the injured party with alternative rights which have different consequences, as was held to be the case in *Dalkia Utilities v Celtech*, he will necessarily have to elect between them and the precise terms in which he informs the other party of his decision will be significant, but where the contract provides a right to terminate which corresponds to a right under the general law (because the breach goes to the root of the contract or the parties have agreed that it should be treated as doing so) no election is necessary."

Applying this to the facts of *Vivergo Fuels Ltd v Redhall Engineering Solutions*   9-033
Ltd,[52] Ramsey J found a significant difference between the consequences of termination at Common Law and *under the particular arrangement of the contractual scheme in that case*. It followed that the innocent party would have to make an election whether to accept repudiation under Common Law principles or to give notice that termination would proceed under the specific contractual regime. If the contract were to be terminated by reason of Common Law repudiation, the innocent party would have to communicate acceptance of the other party's repudiation. In fact, an election did not arise in this case because Ramsey J held that there had been no such repudiation on these facts. The innocent party's sole complaint, therefore, was confined to "material breach" under the contractual scheme. Although there had been a "material breach" on these facts, it was held that the party in breach had rectified the position within the notice period. This left no further ground of complaint. And so, the complainant party's decision to exclude the construction company from the site was unjustified. This rendered that party—previously the innocent party vis-à-vis the "material breach"—the party ultimately in breach. That breach, unjustified exclusion of the other party from the site, was in fact repudiatory. The repudiation had been accepted and the contract terminated on that basis.

Common Law damages ousted by special contractual provision for compensa-   9-034
tion   In *Scottish Power UK Plc v BP Exploration Operating Co Ltd*[53] Leggatt J noted the presumption that

> "each party to the contract is to be entitled to all those remedies for its breach as arise by operation of law, so that sufficiently clear language is required to exclude or modify the availability of such remedies".

---

48   [2013] EWHC 4030 at [514]–[519].
49   [2013] EWHC 4030 at [514].
50   [2009] 1 Lloyd's Rep. 461 at [43] and [44].
51   [2009] 1 Lloyd's Rep. 461 at [44].
52   [2013] EWHC 4030 at [515]–[519].
53   [2015] EWHC 2638 (Comm); [2016] 1 All E.R. (Comm) 536 at [23] per Leggatt J (decision affirmed, [2016] EWCA Civ 1043 at [29] and [30] per Clarke LJ), citing *Gilbert-Ash Northern Ltd v Modern Engineering (Bristol) Ltd* [1974] A.C. 689 at 717 HL, per Lord Diplock; *Stocznia Gdanska SA v Latvian Shipping Co* [1998] 1 W.L.R. 574 HL at 585; *Stocznia Gdynia SA v Gearbulk Holdings Ltd* [2009] EWCA Civ 75; [2010] Q.B. 27 at [23].

But he held[54] that this presumption was rebutted in respect of a special clause which provided for compensation in the event of failure to supply ("underdelivery") nominated deliveries to the wholesale customer. That provision was construed as an "automatic" and "sole" source of compensation, so that the contract had ousted Common Law compensation arising from non-supply in those circumstances.[55]

9-035   *Afovos Shipping Co SA v Pagnan ("The Afovos")* demonstrates that termination cannot occur prematurely if the contract has specified the earliest point at which valid termination can occur.[56] The House of Lords held that the charterparty did not permit termination until notice had been validly given. Furthermore, withdrawal by the owner of the vessel could only occur once 48 hours had elapsed since such a valid notification (provided, of course, the charterers had not made full payment during that period). On the facts, valid notification could not occur before midnight on 14 June. The House of Lords held that shipowners had jumped the gun by purporting to terminate the charterparty by telex, received at 16.45 on 14 June (seven and a quarter hours too early). The contract did not permit termination until notice had been validly given.

9-036   In *Afovos Shipping Co SA v Pagnan ("The Afovos")*[57] the notice and payment clause (cl.5) stated:

> "Payment of said hire to be made in London, to the [nominated bank for the credit of the owners] … in cash in United States currency, semi-monthly in advance … otherwise failing the punctual and regular payment of the hire … the owners shall be at liberty to withdraw the vessel from the service of the charterers."

And this was qualified by a notice requirement, in cl.31 (a so-called "anti-technicality" clause), which read:

> "When hire is due and not received the owners, before exercising the option of withdrawing the vessel from the charterparty, will give charterers 48 hours notice, Saturdays, Sundays and holidays excluded and will not withdraw the vessel if the hire is paid within these 48 hours."

9-037   Lord Hailsham LC said in this case:[58]

> "Both the grammatical meaning of clause 31 and the policy considerations underlying the contract require that the moment of time at which the 48 hours' notice must be given did not arise until after the moment of time at which, apart from the clause, the right of withdrawal would have accrued … [A] premature notice would have the effect of allowing the shipowner to reduce the effective period of 48 hours' notice by anything up to 24 hours."

---

54   [2015] EWHC 2638 (Comm); [2016] 1 All E.R. (Comm) 536 at [171]–[175] per Leggatt J; decision affirmed, [2016] EWCA Civ 1043 at [29] and [30] per Clarke LJ.

55   [2015] EWHC 2638 (Comm); [2016] 1 All E.R. (Comm) 536 at [173] per Leggatt J ("But in circumstances where a breach of Article 7.1 causes loss by way of an underdelivery for which the *Buyer automatically receives compensation* pursuant to Article 16 in the form of Default Gas, that remedy is in my opinion intended to be *the sole remedy* available for the loss"); decision affirmed, [2016] EWCA Civ 1043.

56   [1983] 1 W.L.R. 195 HL.

57   [1983] 1 W.L.R. 195 HL at 197–198.

58   [1983] 1 W.L.R. 195 HL at 199.

IV. CLAUSES PERMITTING TERMINATION FOR "MATERIAL BREACH"

Concept of material breach "Material" breach is a concept used by draftsmen **9-038** in the practice of commercial agreements but this language does not form part of the terminology adopted by the Common Law system of principles governing breach. In short, the courts do not use the concept of "material breach", but contractual draftsmen frequently use this phrase.[59]

A breach will be "material" if it is "substantial" or "a serious matter"[60] (see **9-039** para.9-045 ff for quotations from the *Mid Essex* case). The case law shows that a "material" breach is not trivial, but it must be "substantial", although it need not be so serious as to justify termination applying the Common Law criterion for justified termination following breach.

Notice period and opportunity to comply with contractual require- **9-040** **ments** References to "material breach" in commercial contracts are often accompanied by a provision that the innocent party should allow the guilty party to have a chance to remedy the matter or pattern of non-compliance, that opportunity being normally restricted to a specified period. An example of such a term is to be found in the leading case, *Schuler v Wickman* (para.9-065).[61]

Effective unilateral notices In *Vivergo Fuels Ltd v Redhall Engineering Solu-* **9-041** *tions Ltd* Ramsey J held that the following principles[62] apply to determine the validity of unilateral notices: the notice will be construed objectively in accordance with ordinary principles governing interpretation of contractual documents; minor inadequacies are immaterial; the essential issue is whether the notice adequately conveys the relevant information concerning (i) the relevant default and/or the relevant next step to be taken by the notified party, and (ii) whether the notice makes the necessary link between the background contractual scheme and the event said to constitute grounds for issuing the notice.

Breach which is not "remediable"[63] In some situations it might be enough that **9-042** the default could be stopped, as for the future. But some breaches are not "remediable". As noted more fully in Ch.10 at paras 10.057 and 10-058, the Court

---

59 G. McMeel, *The Construction of Contracts: Interpretation, Implication and Rectification*, 3rd edn (Oxford: Oxford University Press, 2017), para.23.25.

60 *Mid Essex Hospital Services NHS Trust v Compass Group UK and Ireland Ltd* [2013] EWCA Civ 200; [2013] B.L.R. 265 at [126] per Jackson LJ, having considered at [124] and [125]: (i) *Dalkia Utilities Services Plc v Celltech International Ltd* [2006] EWHC 63 (Comm); [2006] 1 Lloyd's Rep. 599 at [102] per Christopher Clarke J ("neither trivial nor minimal" and "serious"); and (ii) *Fitzroy House Epsworth Street (No.1) Ltd v Financial Times Ltd* [2006] EWCA Civ 329; [2006] 1 W.L.R. 2207 at [35] (Sir Andrew Morritt C commenting that: "'substantial' and 'material', depending on the context, are interchangeable. The word 'reasonable' connotes a different test"). See also *C & S Associates UK Ltd v Enterprise Insurance Co Plc* [2015] EWHC 3757 at [97]–[107] per Males J, considering *BSkyB Ltd v HP Enterprise Services UK Ltd* [2010] EWHC 86 (TCC); [2010] B.L.R. 267 at [1362] ff per Ramsey J.

61 [1974] A.C. 235 at 248–249 HL (cl.11(a)(i)).

62 [2013] EWHC 4030 at [420] (this important but long passage is quoted in extenso earlier in this chapter at fn. 6).

63 *C & S Associates UK Ltd v Enterprise Insurance Co Plc* [2015] EWHC 3757 at [102] ff per Males J.

of Appeal in *Kason Kek-Gardner Ltd v Process Components Ltd* held[64] that the following clause gave the innocent party a right to terminate the contract irrespective of the gravity of the actual breach, because the clear intention underlying this clause was that the relevant breach (breach of a confidentiality obligation) would be both non-remediable and material:

> "Clause 11.2 Either party shall be entitled to terminate this Agreement immediately by written notice to the other in the event of: (a) any material breach by the other party of any of its obligations under this Agreement which, being a breach capable of remedy, is not remedied within 30 days of notice to the party in breach specifying the breach and requiring its remedy. (For this purpose…breach of the confidentiality obligations under clause 10 constitutes a non-remediable material breach)."

9-043   An earlier example of a "non-remediable" breach is *Force India Formula One Team Ltd v Etihad Airways PJSC*[65] where a Formula One racing team had breached its sponsorship agreement by restyling the team, excising reference to the contractual sponsors, and by changing the livery of the car or the logo of the team. A clause allowed the sponsors to terminate for breach if there had been "material" breaches which had not been remedied within a specified period. Here the Court of Appeal held that the harm could not be undone,[66] that is, as Rix LJ put it, the genie could not be put back into the bottle, nor could the clock be put back.[67] But in other situations it might be enough that the default could be stopped, as for the future, as noted by Lords Reid, Simon, and Kilbrandon in *Schuler v Wickman*.[68] In fact Lord Reid in *Schuler v Wickman*[69] suggested that this might be the more usual situation.

In *Force India Formula One Team Ltd v Etihad Airways PJSC* Rix LJ said:[70]

> "The [trial] judge [had wrongly] concluded that any breaches [as just summarised] were remediable, in the sense that Force India 'could have put matters right', either by changing the Team Name back to [include the sponsors' names] and/or by reverting to the previous livery and removing the Kingfisher logo."

9-044   In the same case Rix LJ continued:

> "However, in my judgment, these were not remediable breaches. The closest analogies are with the publication of confidential information or the publishing of advertising matter not containing a party's name: one releases information which should be kept confidential, the other broadcasts a product in an inappropriate way. Looking at the matter pragmatically and not technically, I think that a proper marketing campaign is, generally speaking, all of a piece. Where [in breach of contract the racing team] … had persistently marketed the team as 'Force India' to the Indian market and had publicised the car's new livery with deployment of the [new and unauthorised] logo … the marketing genie cannot be put back into the bottle. The breach is irremediable. This conclusion

---

[64] [2017] EWCA Civ 2132; [2018] 1 All E.R. (Comm) 381 at [58].

[65] [2010] EWCA Civ 1051; [2011] E.T.L.R. 10 at [100]–[109].

[66] [2010] EWCA Civ 1051; [2011] E.T.L.R. 10 at [108]: where per Rix LJ, "the breach or breaches are repeated, cumulative, continuing and repudiatory".

[67] [2010] EWCA Civ 1051; [2011] E.T.L.R. 10 at [108].

[68] [1974] A.C. 235 HL at 249–250, 265, 271 (as noted in *Force India Formula One Team Ltd v Etihad Airways PJSC* [2010] EWCA Civ 1051; [2011] E.T.L.R. 10 at [104]–[107]).

[69] [1974] A.C. 235 HL at 249–250.

[70] [2010] EWCA Civ 1051; [2011] E.T.L.R. 10 at [108].

is to my mind re-emphasised where the breach or breaches are repeated, cumulative, continuing and repudiatory."

Judicial consideration of "material breach" in the Mid Essex case[71]   In *Mid Essex Hospital Services NHS Trust v Compass Group UK and Ireland Ltd (Trading as Medirest)* a company, Compass (trading as "Medirest"), supplied cleaning and catering services to hospitals run by a NHS trust. The contract provided an elaborate mechanism for ensuring quality control. In essence, the NHS trust would make findings that there had been deficiencies in performance by Compass, according to a points system (notably, cl.5.8). Having made such findings the NHS trust possessed discretion under the contract to make deductions from payments to Compass. The NHS trust could terminate the contract if, within a six month period, Compass accumulated 1,400 deficiency points (cl.28.1). Conversely, Compass could terminate the contract if the NHS trust was guilty of a "material" breach (cl.28.4.1). The parties made a claim and counterclaim that the contract had been terminated by reason of the other party's breach. Reversing the judge, the Court of Appeal concluded that Compass had been in breach because its decision to terminate was not justified. Any historic failures by the NHS trust to operate the points system punctiliously did not any longer constitute a "material" breach by the NHS trust justifying termination by Compass. Instead Compass had accumulated over 1,400 points (which was not contested) and the NHS trust had justifiably terminated the contract under cl.28.1.

The following passages, drawn from Jackson LJ's judgment in the *Mid Essex* case, amplify the summary just given.[72]

9-045

9-046

(1)   *The issue:* Jackson LJ said:[73]

9-047

> "On 10th September 2009, when [Compass] served its notice of termination, there was only one continuing breach of contract which the Trust had failed to correct. This was the award of an excessive number of service failure points, contrary to clause 5.8 of the conditions. The question therefore arises as to whether this was a 'material' breach of contract within clause 28.4.1."

(2)   *First precedent on "material breach":* Jackson LJ continued:[74]

9-048

> "In *Dalkia Utilities Services Plc v Celltech International Ltd* [2006] EWHC 63 (Comm); [2006] 1 Lloyd's Rep. 599 the claimant agreed to provide electricity and steam to a large paper mill which the defendant was constructing. Clause 14 of the agreement provided that the claimant could terminate if the defendant was in material breach of its obligation to pay. The claimant successfully terminated pursuant to that provision. In commenting on the operation of that clause Christopher Clarke J observed at paragraph 102: 'The sums involved were neither trivial nor minimal. Celtech's continued failure to pay them was serious. In assessing the materiality of any breach it is relevant to consider not only of what

---

[71]   *Mid Essex Hospital Services NHS Trust v Compass Group UK and Ireland Ltd (Trading as Medirest)* [2013] EWCA Civ 200; [2013] B.L.R. 265.

[72]   *Mid Essex Hospital Services NHS Trust v Compass Group UK and Ireland Ltd (Trading as Medirest)* [2013] EWCA Civ 200; [2013] B.L.R. 265 at [123] per Jackson LJ.

[73]   *Mid Essex Hospital Services NHS Trust v Compass Group UK and Ireland Ltd (Trading as Medirest)* [2013] EWCA Civ 200; [2013] B.L.R. 265 at [124] per Jackson LJ.

[74]   *Mid Essex Hospital Services NHS Trust v Compass Group UK and Ireland Ltd (Trading as Medirest)* [2013] EWCA Civ 200; [2013] B.L.R. 265 at [125] per Jackson LJ.

the breach consists but also the circumstances in which the breach arises, including any explanation given or apparent as to why it has occurred'."

9-049   (3)   *Second precedent on "material breach":* Jackson LJ added[75]

"In *Fitzroy House Epsworth Street (No.1) Ltd v Financial Times Ltd* [2006] EWCA Civ 329; [2006] 1 W.L.R. 2207 a lease contained a break clause which the tenant could exercise if it had 'materially complied' with its obligations. The tenant was in breach of its repairing obligations in certain respects, but the Court of Appeal upheld a decision that the tenant was still entitled to exercise its right under the break clause. Sir Andrew Morritt C, with whom Jacob and Moore-Bick LJJ agreed, stated at paragraph 24 that the test for 'material compliance' was objective, not subjective. At paragraphs 35–36 the Chancellor elaborated on the meaning of 'material' as follows: '35. ... But I see no justification for attributing to the parties an intention that the insertion of the word "material" was intended to permit only breaches which were trivial or trifling. Those words are of uncertain meaning also and are not the words used by the parties. Nor is it, in my view, of any assistance to consider whether the word "material" permits more or different breaches than the commonly used alternatives "substantial" or "reasonable". The words "substantial" and "material", depending on the context, are interchangeable. The word "reasonable" connotes a different test'."

9-050   (4)   *"Material breach" summarised:* Jackson LJ continued:[76]

"I must consider what "material breach" means in the context of clause 28.4.1 of the conditions. In my view this phrase connotes a breach of contract which is more than trivial, but need not be repudiatory. Clause 28.4 has the drastic effect of allowing [Compass] to cancel a long term contract on one month's notice. Having regard to the context of this provision, I think that "material breach"; means a breach which is substantial. The breach must be a serious matter, rather than a matter of little consequence."

9-051   (5)   *The NHS trust's record of the Compass company's performance:* Jackson LJ commented:[77]

"Against this background, was the Trust's award of an excessive number of service failure points, contrary to clause 5.8 of the conditions, a 'material breach' within clause 28.4.1? In this regard four matters should be noted. First, all service failure points awarded up to March 2009 were time expired. This included the nine excessive assessments made in July and August 2008, which I have identified in Part [3 of his judgment] above. Secondly, in relation to the most recent six month period, it was not disputed that [Compass] had incurred more than 1,400 service failure points. Thus the Trust was entitled to terminate pursuant to clause 28.1. Thirdly, in so far as the Trust had awarded or purported to award points in excess of 1,400, these additional points had no contractual effect. Fourthly, the Trust had made it clear by 10th September that it would be reviewing its previous award of service failure points."

---

[75]   *Mid Essex Hospital Services NHS Trust v Compass Group UK and Ireland Ltd (Trading as Medirest)* [2013] EWCA Civ 200; [2013] B.L.R. 265 at [123]–[128] per Jackson LJ.

[76]   *Mid Essex Hospital Services NHS Trust v Compass Group UK and Ireland Ltd (Trading as Medirest)* [2013] EWCA Civ 200; [2013] B.L.R. 265 at [126] per Jackson LJ.

[77]   *Mid Essex Hospital Services NHS Trust v Compass Group UK and Ireland Ltd (Trading as Medirest)* [2013] EWCA Civ 200; [2013] B.L.R. 265 at [127] per Jackson LJ.

(6) *NHS Trust Not in "Material Breach":* Jackson LJ in the same case   **9-052**
concluded:[78]

> "having regard to all those circumstances, as at 10th September 2009 the Trust's
> breach of clause 5.8 in awarding an excessive number of service failure points
> 'did not amount to a "material breach" within clause 28.4.1. In the result,
> therefore, [Compass] was not entitled to terminate under clause 28.4 and its
> purported notice of termination was invalid'."

Debtor's default in payment of instalments constituting a "material"   **9-053**
breach   In *Dalkia Utilities Services Plc v Celtech International Ltd*[79] Christopher
Clarke J held that there had been a "material" breach by non-payment of certain
instalments under a power-supply agreement. He said:[80]

> "[the debtor] was in material breach of its obligation to pay the charges…The whole of
> three separate instalments of Charges was due and unpaid … Although the amounts due
> were a very small proportion of the total amount due over a 15 year period they were the
> amounts due in respect of a quarter of the current year and just over 8.5 per cent of the
> total charges unpaid, including interest, for the remainder of the initial period. The sums
> involved were neither trivial nor minimal. [The debtor's] continued failure to pay them
> was serious."

Christopher Clarke J continued:[81]   **9-054**

> "In assessing the materiality of any breach it is relevant to consider not only of what the
> breach consists but also the circumstances in which the breach arises, including any
> explanation given or apparent as to why it has occurred. The reason why payment was
> not forthcoming in the present case was not because of some mishap, mistake or
> misunderstanding. [The debtor] failed to pay because it did not then have the money to
> do so, in circumstances where the picture presented by [the debtor] to [the creditor] was
> that it was facing insolvency … The [debtor had also intimated] that, unless there was a
> renegotiation of the agreement, there was a real likelihood that [he] would not be able to
> continue paying in full in the future … It seems to me that a ['material' breach] clause of
> this kind, in this context, is designed to protect a [debtor] where the default is minimal
> or inconsequential or (even if it is not) is accidental or inadvertent, but otherwise to en-
> able [the creditor] to bring the period over which it is effectively extending credit to an
> end where there is a failure to keep up the payment schedule established by the contract."

Christopher Clarke J[82] collected statements in earlier cases. Interpretation of the   **9-055**
word "material" takes its colour from each clause and context. Nevertheless, discussion in the following four cases might assist (these decisions will be numbered (i)
to (iv) in the ensuing paragraphs; case (iv) is subsequent to the *Dalkia* case; the
other three cases, cases (i) to (iii), were examined in the *Dalkia* case).

---

[78] *Mid Essex Hospital Services NHS Trust v Compass Group UK and Ireland Ltd (Trading as Medir-est)* [2013] EWCA Civ 200; [2013] B.L.R. 265 at [128] per Jackson LJ.
[79] *Dalkia Utilities Services Plc v Celtech International Ltd* [2006] EWHC 63 (Comm); [2006] 1 Lloyd's Rep. 599.
[80] [2006] EWHC 63 (Comm); [2006] 1 Lloyd's Rep. 599 at [102].
[81] [2006] EWHC 63 (Comm); [2006] 1 Lloyd's Rep. 599 at [102].
[82] [2006] EWHC 63 (Comm); [2006] 1 Lloyd's Rep. 599 at [102].

9-056   **Additional case on "material" breach (i)**   Neuberger J held in *Glolite Ltd v Jasper Conran Ltd*[83] that an exclusive licensee had not committed a "material" and "irremediable" breach by infringing an "anti-copying" clause for a very short period and with a restricted geographical impact (as summarised by Christopher Clarke J in the *Dalkia* case[84]):

> "Neuberger J held that there had been neither a 'material' nor an 'irremediable' breach of a 10 or, if extended, 20 year agreement whereby the claimant was to enjoy an exclusive licence to manufacture products designed by Mr Conran. The breach complained of was the use by the claimant of the 'JC' logo without the prior consultation required by the agreement over at most a 10 day period (with only limited publicity) on Leyton Orient football club shirts, which were never made available to the public during that time."

9-057   Neuberger J also commented in *Glolite Ltd v Jasper Conran Ltd*:[85]

> "Whether a breach of an agreement is 'material' must depend upon all the facts of the particular case, including the terms and duration of the agreement in question, the nature of the breach, and the consequences of the breach ... When judging what the parties meant when they referred to a breach having to be 'material' and 'remediable' (sic) it seems to me that they must have had in mind, at least to some extent, the commercial consequences of the breach."

9-058   **Additional case on "material" breach (ii)**   In *National Power Plc v United Gas Co Ltd*[86] the relevant clause provided that the contract could be terminated:

> "if [a party] *shall be in material breach of any of its obligations hereunder and fails to commence to remedy the same within seven days after notice requiring such breach to be remedied*".

Colman J held that failure to provide information as to past non-performance of contractual obligations was a breach of an ancillary term and it involved little commercial detriment. The parties could not have intended that such a breach would have the draconian consequence of permitting the innocent party to terminate. The breach was not "material". Colman J (as summarised by Christopher Clarke in the *Dalkia* case) commented in the *National Power* case:[87]

> "'material' related to the magnitude of the commercial consequences of the breach for the innocent party were it to remain unremedied, and meant a breach which was: 'wholly or partly remediable and is or, if not remedied, is likely to become, serious'; for this purpose 'serious' should be understood to mean 'having a serious effect on the benefit which the innocent party would otherwise derive from performance of the contract in accordance with its terms'."

---

[83]   *The Times*, 28 January 1998, Neuberger J.
[84]   *Dalkia Utilities Services Plc v Celtech International Ltd* [2006] EWHC 63 (Comm); [2006] 1 Lloyd's Rep. 599 at [98].
[85]   *The Times*, 28 January 1998, Neuberger J.
[86]   *National Power Plc v United Gas Co Ltd* unreported 3 July 1998, Colman J.
[87]   *Dalkia Utilities Services Plc v Celtech International Ltd* [2006] EWHC 63 (Comm); [2006] 1 Lloyd's Rep. 599 at [99] (summarising and quoting from *National Power Plc v United Gas Co Ltd* unreported 3 July 1998 Colman J).

Additional case on "material" breach (iii)   The Court of Appeal in *Fortman*   **9-059**
Holdings Ltd v Modem Holdings Ltd[88] held that failure to pay (an isolated) one of
10 instalments on time constituted a "material" breach and this triggered (under the
express terms of the same clause) the duty to pay the principal sum at once. The
relevant clause stated:

> "the Principal Sum shall become immediately repayable [if, inter alia the debtor becomes]
> … in material or persistent breach of any obligation under these Notes and [fails] to
> remedy the same within fourteen days of it becoming aware of such breach".

The Court of Appeal held that "material or persistent" was a disjunctive use of "or".
Therefore, it was sufficient that the breach was "material" or that it was "persistent".
Here it was "material': namely a failure to pay one of the ten instalments on time,
and further failure to remedy this within 14 days. Judge LJ explained (with the
agreement of Pill LJ and Rimer J):[89]

> "While acknowledging the serious consequence of the breach—from [the debtor's]
> view—that an immediate liability to pay 10 per cent of the balance still unpaid would be
> triggered into a liability to pay the whole of it, the significance of the breach to [the credi-
> tor] was undeniable. It was non-payment of the whole of an agreed instalment, at a time
> when [the debtor] enjoyed an unrestricted right to the benefits of the sale agreement,
> without any contemporaneous purported justification … In my judgment, … the breach
> was material."

Additional case on "material" breach (iv)   Ramsey J held in *Vivergo Fuels Ltd*   **9-060**
v Redhall Engineering Solutions Ltd[90] that failure to provide a "programming"
report under a complex construction contract was a material breach. This case illustrates the fact-sensitive nature of the inquiry and the complexity that can arise
in making such an assessment.

When is a breach "remediable"?   The Court of Appeal in *Force India Formula*   **9-061**
One Team Ltd v Etihad Airways PJSC,[91] also considering the *Schuler case*, on which
see para.9-065) held that a racing team had committed "material" and "irremediable" breaches when it changed the racing car's logo and the team's name with the
result that the team ceased to be distinctively associated with its sponsor. Rix LJ
concluded[92] that where the team "persistently marketed" itself using the
unauthorised new name and logo "the marketing genie cannot be put back into the
bottle" and so "the breach is irremediable".

In this case, the owners of a Formula One racing team had breached their   **9-062**
sponsorship agreement (i) by restyling the team so as to excise reference to their
Abu Dhabi sponsors, (ii) by changing both the livery, and (iii) logo of the team. The
Court of Appeal held that these were serious breaches which constituted
repudiation. One of the contractual clauses allowed the sponsors to terminate for
breach if there had been "material" breaches which had not been remedied within
a specified period. The relevant clause provided:

> "Termination by the Sponsors: 21.3.1 The Sponsors may terminate this Agreement with

---

88 [2001] EWCA Civ 1235 (summarised in *Dalkia Utilities Services Plc v Celtech International Ltd*
   [2006] EWHC 63 (Comm); [2006] 1 Lloyd's Rep. 599 at [93]–[97]).
89 [2001] EWCA Civ 1235 at [21].
90 [2013] EWHC 4030 at [343]–[375].
91 [2010] EWCA Civ 1051; [2011] E.T.L.R. 10 at [100]–[109].
92 [2010] EWCA Civ 1051; [2011] E.T.L.R. 10 at [108].

immediate effect on the giving of written notice to [the Team] at any time on the happen-ing of any of the following events by or in relation to the other party: [The Team] has com-mitted any material breach of this Agreement which, if capable of remedy, has not been remedied within ten business days of receipt of written notice giving particulars of the breach and requiring its remedy ..."

9-063   But the Court of Appeal held that the facts of this case fell outside this termina-tion clause because the breaches committed were not "remediable" (on this point see further para.9-064). The sponsor's decision to terminate by reason of the team's breach fell to be considered, therefore, under general principle of Common Law breach doctrine, untrammelled by this specific clause. The Court of Appeal held that the breaches had been cumulatively serious enough to be "repudiatory" at Com-mon Law. Therefore, the sponsor had been justified in terminating the relevant rac-ing team's sponsorship agreement.

9-064   Rix LJ held that the breaches committed by the racing team were not "remediable": cumulating metaphors, he said that it would be neither possible for the genie to be put back into the bottle, nor for the clock to be put back:[93]

> "The [trial] judge [had wrongly] concluded that any breaches [as just summarised] were remediable, in the sense that Force India 'could have put matters right', either by chang-ing the Team Name back to [include the sponsors' names] and/or by reverting to the previ-ous livery and removing the Kingfisher logo ... However, in my judgement, these were not remediable breaches. The closest analogies are with the publication of confidential information or the publishing of advertising matter not containing a party's name: one releases information which should be kept confidential, the other broadcasts a product in an inappropriate way. Looking at the matter pragmatically and not technically, I think that a proper marketing campaign is, generally speaking, all of a piece."

9-065   **Earlier discussion of "remediable" breach**   The House of Lords in *Schuler (L) AG v Wickman Machine Tool Sales Ltd*[94] also considered the concept of a "remedi-able" breach (the facts of this case and its main reasoning are set out elsewhere, para.10-039 ff). The following passage by Lord Reid is an important discussion of "remediable" breaches:[95]

> "In order to explain the contention of the parties, I must now set out clause 11 of the agreement. '11. Duration of Agreement (a) ... Schuler ... may by notice in writing to the other determine this agreement forthwith if: (i) the other shall have committed a material breach of its obligations hereunder and shall have failed to remedy the same within 60 days of being required in writing so to do'. It appears to me that clause 11 (a) (i) is intended to apply to all material breaches of the agreement which are capable of being remedied. The question then is what is meant in this context by the word 'remedy'. It could mean obviate or nullify the effect of a breach so that any damage already done is in some way made good. Or it could mean cure so that matters are put right for the future. I think that the latter is the more natural meaning. The word is commonly used in con-nection with diseases or ailments and they would normally be said to be remedied if they were cured although no cure can remove the past effect or result of the disease before the cure took place, and in general it can only be in a rare case that any remedy of something that has gone wrong in the performance of a continuing positive obligation will, in addi-tion to putting it right for the future, remove or nullify damage already incurred before the remedy was applied. To restrict the meaning of remedy to cases where all damage past

---

93   [2010] EWCA Civ 1051; [2011] E.T.L.R. 10 at [108].
94   [1974] A.C. 235 HL.
95   [1974] A.C. 235 HL at 248–250.

and future can be put right would leave hardly any scope at all for this clause. On the other hand, there are cases where it would seem a misuse of language to say that a breach can be remedied. For example, a breach of clause 14 by disclosure of confidential information could not be said to be remedied by a promise not to do it again. So the question is whether a breach of Wickman's obligation under clause 7 (b) (i) is capable of being remedied within the meaning of this agreement. On the one hand, failure to make one particular visit might have irremediable consequences, e.g. a valuable order might have been lost when making that visit would have obtained it. *But looking at the position broadly I incline to the view that breaches of this obligation should be held to be capable of remedy within the meaning of clause 7. Each firm had to be visited more than 200 times. If one visit is missed I think that one would normally say that making arrangements to prevent a recurrence of that breach would remedy the breach.*" (emphasis added)

V. IMPLIED CANCELLATION RIGHTS

As the Court of Appeal confirmed in *Staffordshire Area Health Authority v South Staffordshire Waterworks Co*,[96] the courts will recognise that long-term contracts (unless there is an express or sufficiently clear contrary provision or indication) contain an implied term that either party can terminate the contract, without breach of contract, by giving the other reasonable notice. Thus, where a contract is of indefinite duration (as distinct from one restricted to a fixed term),[97] the courts will find an implied term that it is unilaterally terminable on reasonable notice, by either party.   **9-066**

Staffordshire Area Health Authority v South Staffordshire Waterworks Co concerned a hospital's water supply, the rate for which had been fixed since 1929 as follows: (i) the company would "at all times hereafter" supply to the hospital 5000 gallons per day free of cost; (ii) the hospital should "at all times hereafter" be at liberty to take from the mains any further quantity needed; and (iii) payment therefore would be [seven old pence] for each 1000 gallons so supplied. By 1978, the date of the appeal, it had ceased to be economic for the water company to supply at the 50-year-old rate (at seven old pence, that is, roughly three new pence for each 1,000 gallons consumed in excess of 5,000 gallons a day). The Court of Appeal held that the water company was entitled to terminate, on giving reasonable notice. This was the majority approach of Goff and Cumming-Bruce LJJ, the latter explaining:[98]   **9-067**

> "the words 'at all times hereafter' mean that the obligations granted and accepted by the agreement were only intended to persist during the continuance of the agreement; and the agreement, in my view, was determinable on reasonable notice at any time".

As for future supply, the Court of Appeal contemplated that the parties would reach a compromise on a new price.

The third judge, Lord Denning MR, (i) effectively agreed with the majority's   **9-068**

---

[96] [1978] 1 W.L.R. 1387 CA; on this topic, Neil Andrews, *Contract Law in Practice* (Oxford: Oxford University Press, 2021), Ch.23.

[97] Conversely, if the contract is of a fixed duration, there will be no implied term that a party can terminate it by giving reasonable notice: *Jani-King (GB) Ltd v Pula Enterprises Ltd* [2007] EWHC 2433 (QBD); [2008] 1 Lloyd's Rep. 305 per Coulson J at [60]–[66]. But if the agreement is "perpetual", Sales J in *BMS Computer Solutions Ltd v AB Agri Ltd* [2010] EWHC 464 (Ch) at [18], held (persuasively) that the relevant licence agreement was not ever-lasting, but merely an entitlement of no fixed duration.

[98] [1978] 1 W.L.R. 1387, 1406 CA.

reasoning, but also (ii) attempted to fashion a novel theory permitting release from contracts which have become economically very disadvantageous because of inflation. However, approach (ii) is a radical and indeed heretical view, and it was not accepted by the other judges.

9-069   What does not appear to have been examined is the supplementary, but logically prior, proposition that, although terminable in the manner just mentioned, in some situations there might be another implied term that an agreement of indefinite duration must last for a reasonable time before it can be terminated unilaterally. Such a contention cannot be dismissed as hopeless. But the courts might be reluctant to pronounce on the duration of a "reasonable time" for this purpose. And so, for the moment, it appears safe to assume that the courts will not prescribe a reasonable period of initial duration. The more likely development is that sometimes (and exceptionally) the court might find it safe and indeed necessary to recognise a minimum initial duration, based upon usage or longstanding practice in the relevant context.

CHAPTER 10

COMMON LAW RIGHT TO TERMINATE FOR BREACH OF CONDITION[1]

I. Overview of Termination for Breach of Promissory Terms

Classification of promissory terms The view taken in England and Wales is that there are three types of promissory obligation: conditions; innominate (or "intermediate") terms; and warranties.[2]   **10-001**

Breach of a condition entitles the other party to obtain damages and to terminate for breach of contract. Breach of an innominate term (Ch.12) also entitles the innocent party to claim damages; whether it also justifies termination of the contract depends on assessment of the breach's gravity on the particular facts. But breach of a warranty prima facie gives rise only to a duty to pay damages (for further comment on the nature of warranties see the next two paragraphs).   **10-002**

Commenting on warranties, *Chitty on Contracts* suggests[3] that the emergence of innominate terms has probably reduced this category to vanishing point, "save in the very exceptional circumstances where a term has been specifically so classified by statute".[4]

Carter[5] notes that the word "warranty" is ambiguous. Sometimes it is used in antithesis to "condition": if so "warranty" means a promissory obligation breach of which does not (automatically) justify termination. Sometimes "warranty" is used as a colourless or neutral word to denote a contractual undertaking or obligation[6] or to denote a verbal assurance (as in "collateral warranty")[7] or even as a   **10-003**

---

[1] The title of this chapter refers to "Common Law" rights to terminate for breach of a (promissory) condition, as distinct from express rights to terminate for breach of a contract (the latter topic is treated at Ch.9). Another clarification is required: a (promissory) condition can arise in various ways, including by virtue of a statutory regulation of the relevant type of transaction: para.10-037. Breach of a statutory condition involves exercise at Common Law of the power to terminate for breach.

[2] On the history of conditions, Jordan English, "The nature of 'promissory conditions'" (2021) 137 L.Q.R. 630–657; on the history of warranties and conditions, D.J. Ibbetson, *A Historical Introduction to the Law of Obligations* (Oxford: Oxford University Press, 1999), pp.83–87; G.H. Jones (with P. Schlecarkechtriem), "Breach of Contract" in *International Encyclopaedia of Comparative Law* Vol.VII (Contracts in General), (Tübingen: Mohr Siebeck and Dordrecht: 1999), 15–129 ff; M. Lobban, in W. Cornish, *The Oxford History of the Laws of England* Vol.XII (1820–1914: Private Law) (Oxford: Oxford University Press, 2010), p.485 ff.

[3] H. Beale (ed), *Chitty on Contracts*, 34th edn (London: Sweet & Maxwell, 2021), para.27-021.

[4] e.g. Sale of Goods Act 1979 (as amended) ss.11(3), 12(2) (4) (5) (5A), Supply of Goods (Implied Terms) Act 1973 (as amended) s.8(3).

[5] J.W. Carter, *Carter's Breach of Contract*, 2nd edn (Oxford: Hart Publishing, 2019), [4-16].

[6] J.W. Carter, *Carter's Breach of Contract*, 2nd edn (Oxford: Hart Publishing, 2019), [4-15] and [4-17].

[7] J.W. Carter, *Carter's Breach of Contract*, 2nd edn (Oxford: Hart Publishing, 2019), [4-18].

fundamental term justifying termination (this archaic usage is preserved in the field of insurance).[8]

10-004 **Warranty scepticism** However, Treitel notes the possible argument that even in the context of a sale of goods transaction, breach of a warranty might give rise to a right to reject, applying Common Law principles, where the breach on its facts gives rise to a substantial failure in performance.[9]

10-005 Similarly, in Singapore, in *RDC Concrete Pte Ltd v Sato Kogyo (S) Pte Ltd*, Phang JA suggested (see the next two notes for full quotation) that serious consequences flowing from breach of a "warranty" could justify termination for breach,[10] although he was then forced to wrestle with the paradox that this would mean that in substance there are only conditions and intermediate terms, warranties having ceased to be distinctive in their operation.[11] (See also at paras 12-037–12-039, an Australian judge's sceptical comments concerning this three-fold distinction; Kirby J in *Koompahtoo Local Aboriginal Land Council v Sanpine Pty Ltd* contending that there should be a simple dichotomy of conditions and non-conditions, the latter operating on a wait-and-see basis.)[12]

10-006 It becomes crucial, therefore, to determine whether a particular contractual obligation should be classified as a condition, innominate term, or a warranty. Often the categorisation, established by reference to the factors discussed at para.10-036 ff, is clear. However, sometimes this can become a perplexing question, and it can

---

8   J.W. Carter, *Carter's Breach of Contract*, 2nd edn (Oxford: Hart Publishing, 2019), [4-19].

9   G.H. Treitel, *The Law of Contract* (E. Peel ed.), 15th edn (London: Sweet & Maxwell, 2020), para.18-053.

10 [2007] S.G.C.A. 39; [2007] 4 S.L.R. 413 at [107] per Phang JA: "If, however, the term breached is a warranty, we are of the view that the innocent party is not thereby prevented from terminating the contract (as it would have been entitled so to do if the condition-warranty approach operated alone). Considerations of fairness demand, in our view, that the consequences of the breach should also be examined by the court, even if the term breached is only a warranty (as opposed to a condition). There would, of course, be no need for the court to examine the consequences of the breach if the term breached was a condition since, ex hypothesi, the breach of a condition would (as we have just stated) entitle the innocent party to terminate the contract in the first instance. Hence, it is only in a situation where the term breached would otherwise constitute a warranty that the court would, as a question of fairness, go further and examine the consequences of the breach as well. In the result, if the consequences of the breach are such as to deprive the innocent party of substantially the whole benefit that it was intended that the innocent party should obtain from the contract, then the innocent party would be entitled to terminate the contract, notwithstanding that it only constitutes a warranty. If, however, the consequences of the breach are only very trivial, then the innocent party would not be entitled to terminate the contract".

11 [2007] S.G.C.A. 39; [2007] 4 S.L.R. 413 at [108] per Phang JA: "It is true that the approach adopted in the preceding paragraph would, in effect, result in the concept of the warranty, as we know it, being effectively effaced since there would virtually never be a situation in which there would be a term, the breach of which would always result in only trivial consequences. In other words, if a term was not a condition under the condition-warranty approach, it would necessarily become an intermediate term, subject to the *Hongkong Fir* approach (see, in this regard, the perceptive observations by Robert Goff J (as he then was) in the English High Court decision of *'The Ymnos'* [1982] 2 Lloyd's Rep. 574 at 583). In other words, the traditional three-fold classification of contractual terms (comprising conditions, warranties and intermediate terms, respectively) would be a merely theoretical one only. However, the concept of the intermediate term was itself only fully developed many years after the condition-warranty approach (in *Hongkong Fir*). Further, and more importantly (from a practical perspective), it should also be observed that the spirit behind the concept of the warranty would still remain in appropriate fact situations inasmuch as the innocent party would not be entitled to terminate the contract if the consequences of the breach were found to be trivial (although it would, as we shall see, be entitled to damages that it could establish at law)".

12 [2007] HCA 61; (2007) 82 AL.J.R 345; (2008) 241 A.L.R. 88 H.Ct. Aust. at [74] ff.

divide judges at the highest level (notably *Schuler (L) AG v Wickman Machine Tool Sales Ltd*, discussed at para.10-039 ff). Designation of a term as a condition can be a particularly intricate inquiry. This topic will absorb many paragraphs at para.10-036 ff.

As Carter notes, once a term has judicially classified as a condition or innominate term it will be construed in the same manner unless the parties express a contrary intention.[13] He gives[14] as an example of that "default classification" the court's approach in *"The Hansa Nord"*,[15] on which see para.12-025 ff.

There is no[16] fourth category of "fundamental term".[17] As *Chitty on Contracts* **10-007** explains:[18]

> "it is neither necessary nor desirable to create a further category of contractual term-the 'fundamental breach' ... There is therefore strong ground for the view that English law does not recognize any category of 'fundamental term' distinct from conditions."

Even so, the expression "fundamental breach" recurs in modern judicial discus- **10-008** sion, for example, in Proudman J's judgment in *Future Publishing Ltd v Edge Interactive Media Inc*,[19] where the epithet "fundamental" is used repeatedly as a synonym for "repudiatory". And Lord Diplock used the term "fundamental breach" repeatedly in *"The Afovos"*, where he said:[20]

> "The doctrine of anticipatory breach is but a species of the genus repudiation and applies only to fundamental breach ... The non-performance threatened must itself satisfy the criteria of a fundamental breach ... Similarly where a party to a contract, whether by failure to take timeous action or by any other default, has put it out of his power to perform a particular primary obligation, the right of the other party to elect to treat this as a repudiation of the contract by conduct depends upon whether the resulting non-performance would amount to a fundamental breach."

Conditions precedent[21] A condition precedent is to be contrasted with a promis- **10-009** sory term, including a promissory condition. A (non-promissory) condition

---

[13] J.W. Carter, *Carter's Breach of Contract*, 2nd edn (Oxford: Hart Publishing, 2019), [6-05].

[14] J.W. Carter, *Carter's Breach of Contract*, 2nd edn (Oxford: Hart Publishing, 2019), [6-05].

[15] [1976] Q.B. 44 CA.

[16] Per contra, however, G.H. Treitel, *Some Landmarks of Twentieth Century Contract Law* (Oxford: Oxford University Press, 2002), Ch.3, pp.128-137 (contending that fundamental breach remains secreted in rules concerning deviation in shipping law and in the construction of exclusion clauses).

[17] *Suisse Atlantique Société d'Armement Maritime SA v NV Rotterdamsche* [1967] 1 A.C. 361 HL; *Photo Production Ltd v Securicor Transport Ltd* [1980] A.C. 827 HL; on the fundamental breach saga, see H. Beale (ed), *Chitty on Contracts*, 34th edn (London: Sweet & Maxwell, 2021), paras 17-023–17-027; 27-023–27-025.

[18] *Chitty on Contracts*, 34th edn (London: Sweet & Maxwell, 2021), para.27-025.

[19] *Future Publishing Ltd v Edge Interactive Media Inc* [2011] EWHC 1489 (Ch); [2011] E.T.M.R. 50 at [59], [60], [61], [62], [63], [66], [68] per Proudman J.

[20] Q. Liu, *Anticipatory Breach* (Oxford: Hart Publishing, 2010), p.81, examining *Afovos Shipping v Pagnan ("The Afovos")* [1983] 1 W.L.R. 195 HL at 203 per Lord Diplock.

[21] N. Andrews, *Contract Law*, 2nd edn (Cambridge University Press, 2015), 12.06(2); K. Lewison, *Interpretation of Contracts*, 7th edn (London: Sweet & Maxwell, 2021), paras 16-07–16-017; G. McMeel, *The Construction of Contracts: Interpretation, Implication and Rectification*, 3rd edn (Oxford: Oxford University Press, 2017), Ch.20; G.H. Treitel, "Conditions and Conditions Precedent" (1990) 106 L.Q.R. 185; *Scottish Power UK Plc v BP Exploration Operating Co Ltd* [2015] EWHC 2658 (Comm); [2016] 1 All E.R. (Comm) 536 at [194] ff, Leggatt J examined (inconclusive) case law concerning conditions precedent; decision affirmed, [2016] EWCA Civ 1043.

precedent is a contractual modality (it must be admitted that in some[22] nineteenth century case law, promissory obligations, if important, were sometimes denoted as "conditions precedent", but that usage seems now to have waned, even disappeared).

10-010   A non-promissory condition precedent can operate in one of three ways: to postpone the coming into effect of the whole contract; to render the mutual operation of the contract dependent on prior satisfaction by one party of an obligation; to suspend the operation of the obligations, but without rendering the whole contract inoperative. Thus, reflecting this trichotomy, *Chitty on Contracts*[23] distinguish between the following: (i) the parties enter an agreement expressly not binding on either party until a condition precedent has been fulfilled; (ii) one party assumes a binding unilateral obligation, but the other party is not bound by the agreement until the relevant condition is satisfied; and (iii) a mutually binding agreement is formed but subject to a condition precedent which suspends all or some of the obligations of the parties pending fulfilment of the condition precedent. And these three permutations will now be examined further.

10-011   An example of permutation (i) (whole contract not yet binding) is *Bentworth Finance Ltd v Lubert*.[24] Here a finance company was unable to claim instalments under a purported hire-purchase agreement from the defendant because the latter had not received the log-book for the vehicle. The Court of Appeal held that provision of the log-book was a suspensive condition, that is, a condition precedent. In its absence, no contractual rights had arisen in favour of the finance company. Furthermore, an indemnity agreement, made by a third party in favour of the finance company, was not enforceable, again because of the failure to provide a log-book.[25] Lord Denning MR said:[26]

> "[T]he contract did not come into operation. The provision of the log-book was a condition on which the very existence of the contract depended. It was, in technical language, a suspensive condition. Until the log-book was provided, there was no contract of hire-purchase at all. No instalments, therefore, fell due."

10-012   As for permutation (ii) (contract imposing a duty on one party to do something, pending which remainder of the contract is in suspense), in *UR Power GmbH v Kuok Oils and Grains Pte Ltd*[27] Gross J noted the distinction between a condition precedent, or "contingent condition", and a promissory condition binding on one party, and on the facts the present case concerned the latter. Thus Gross J held that the parties had intended that one of the parties had assumed a contractual obliga-

---

[22] e.g. Blackburn J said in *Bettini v Gye* (1876) 1 Q.B.D. 183 at 187: "Parties may think some matter, apparently of very little importance, essential; and if they sufficiently express an intention to make the literal fulfilment of such a thing a condition precedent, it will be one..." And Bowen LJ in *Bentsen v Taylor Sons & Co (No. 2)* [1893] 2 Q.B. 274 at 281, CA: "There is no way of deciding that question except by looking at the contract in the light of the surrounding circumstances, and then making up one's mind whether the intention of the parties, as gathered from the instrument itself, will best be carried out by treating the promise as a warranty sounding only in damages, or as a condition precedent by the failure to perform which the other party is relieved of his liability."

[23] 34th edn (London: Sweet & Maxwell, 2021), para.13-028.

[24] [1968] 1 Q.B. 680 CA.

[25] [1968] 1 Q.B. 680 CA at 685–686 (it appears that the finance company's failure under the indemnity contract was attributable to their fault in not providing the log-book, but the reasoning on this point is somewhat opaque).

[26] [1968] 1 Q.B. 680 CA at 685.

[27] [2009] EWHC 1940 (Comm); [2009] 2 Lloyd's Rep. 495 at [14]–[16], and [22].

tion to open a letter of credit:

> "[I]t is by no means untypical to find that such an obligation is treated as a promissory rather than a contingent condition precedent—so that failure to open the letter of credit constitutes a breach of contract, releasing the other party from further performance of the contract, rather than serving to prevent the contract from coming into existence."

As for permutation (iii) (agreement imposing mutual obligations, but held in suspense pending fulfilment of a condition precedent), an example would be where a ship is chartered to carry out research in Antarctica, but the parties make clear that the contract will not proceed unless a third party confirms that the vessel is suitable for such use. In the meantime, neither party can walk away because both are committed. But if the third party says "no, the ship is not suitable", the result is that "all bets are off", that is, the contract has dissolved. **10-013**

If, to vary the example just given, the period of hire is two years, and the vessel has already been to the Antarctic for one season, but the contract provides that it cannot return for a second season unless the third party confirms that it remains in a fit state for this demanding environment, this modality operates as a condition subsequent, its potential effect being to terminate a contract which has already been partly performed: see below. **10-014**

As noted in *Tullow Uganda Ltd v Heritage Oil and Gas*, the courts are reluctant to construe notification restrictions as strict conditions precedent to the liability of a potential indemnifier.[28] **10-015**

Conditions subsequent   Such a prescribed event has the effect of bringing the contract to an end, whether or not breach has occurred. An example is *Head v Tattersall*,[29] where a purchaser successfully invoked an express condition subsequent, entitling him to return a horse which did not correspond to its warranted description. **10-016**

Condition precedent or subsequent?   The question whether an "event" antedates or post-dates the purported contract can be problematic. The court might prefer one analysis if it provides greater scope to achieve justice in the relevant case. In *Graves v Graves* the court found an "implied condition subsequent"[30] which terminated an agreement, rather than a condition precedent which would suspend a contract before it had come into operation. As noted elsewhere,[31] the characterisation of the condition in the manner was a matter of fine judgement on these facts. **10-017**

Collateral agreements (and collateral warranties)   It is possible that the main contract can be qualified by a separate contract, this side agreement being "collateral" to the main contract. The consideration supporting the collateral agreement is normally the promisee's decision to enter into the main contract. When such a collateral contract or contractual warranty is found,[32] as *Chitty on Contracts* states, **10-018**

---

28 [2014] EWCA Civ 1048; [2014] 2 C.L.C. 61 at [33] (and generally [33] ff) per Beatson LJ.
29 (1871–72) L.R. 7 Ex. 7 (Kelly CB, Bramwell and Cleasby BB).
30 [2007] EWCA Civ 660; [2008] H.L.R. 10 at [38]–[41].
31 N. Andrews, *Contract Law* (Cambridge: Cambridge University Press, 2011), 10.11: discussion not repeated in 2nd edn (Cambridge: Cambridge University Press, 2015).
32 K.W. Wedderburn, "Collateral Contracts" [1959] C.L.J. 58; H. Beale (ed), *Chitty on Contracts*, 34th edn (London: Sweet & Maxwell, 2021), paras 15-018–15-021; F.A. Paterson, *Collateral Warranties Explained* (London: RIBA Publications, 1991); D.W. Greig, "Misrepresentation and Sales of Goods" (1971) 87 L.Q.R. 179.

"Breach of the collateral contract will give rise to an action for damages for its breach, but not as a general rule to a right to treat the main contract as repudiated".[33]

10-019   The test governing the finding of a collateral warranty remains strict (despite Lord Denning's suggestion in *Howard Marine v Ogden* that a more flexible approach should be adopted).[34] Thus, consistent with this traditionally strict approach, the Court of Appeal in *Business Environment Bow Lane Ltd v Deanwater Estates Ltd*[35] cited Lord Moulton's seminal comment in the *Heilbut, Symons* case:[36]

> "Such collateral contracts, the sole effect of which is to vary or add to the terms of the principal contract, are therefore viewed with suspicion by the law. They must be proved strictly. Not only the terms of such contracts but the existence of an animus contrahendi [an intention to make a contractual undertaking] on the part of all the parties to them must be clearly shown. Any laxity on these points would enable parties to escape from the full performance of the obligations of contracts unquestionably entered into by them and more especially would have the effect of lessening the authority of written contracts by making it possible to vary them by suggesting the existence of verbal collateral agreements relating to the same subject matter."

10-020   In determining whether a pre-contractual assurance gives rise to liability as an actionable collateral warranty, the courts will consider the following nine criteria.[37]

10-021   *Criterion (1): objective commitment by maker of statement:*   the court will conduct an objective assessment whether the representee was entitled reasonably to assume that the statement was being warranted, that is, guaranteed to be contractually binding.[38]

10-022   *Criterion (2): importance to representee emphasised:*   the court will consider whether the representee made plain that the matter was crucial to him.[39]

10-023   *Criterion (3): obvious importance:*   it will also be relevant to consider whether it was obvious from the circumstances that the matter was crucial to the representee. Thus, in *City & Westminster Properties (1934) Ltd v Mudd* the landlord assured a tenant, before a renewal to him of a tenancy, that he would be free to sleep in the demised business premises at night. This was contrary to the written terms of the lease. Harman J was convinced by the tenant's evidence that the matter covered by

---

[33]   H. Beale (ed), *Chitty on Contracts*, 34th edn (London: Sweet & Maxwell, 2021), para.15-020.

[34]   *Howard Marine and Dredging Co Ltd v A Ogden & Sons (Excavations) Ltd* [1978] Q.B. 574 CA at 590G.

[35]   [2007] EWCA Civ 622; [2007] L. & T.R. 26 at [23].

[36]   *Heilbut, Symons & Co v Buckleton* [1913] A.C. 30 HL at 47 (see also Lord Haldane at 37–39); citing *Chandelor v Lopes* (1603) Cro. Jac. 4; explained by Denning LJ in *Oscar Chess Ltd v Williams* [1957] 1 W.L.R. 370 CA; see also *Hopkins v Tanqueray* (1854) 15 C.B. (N.S.) 130.

[37]   cf. the string of factors successfully enumerated by counsel in *Howard Marine* case [1978] Q.B. 574 CA at 583: "Whether statement clear and definite; whether intended to be a guarantee; whether evidence of contractual intention; whether incorporated expressly into final contract; whether a matter of opinion or an estimate; whether contemporaneous with contract or weeks or months prior thereto; whether within the representor's knowledge and conversely whether the representee could be reasonably expected, or able, to ascertain it; whether inconsistent with written terms of final contract."

[38]   *Thake v Maurice* [1986] Q.B. 644 CA; reasonableness is also a factor in the tort of negligent misstatement, *Williams v Natural Life & Health Foods* [1998] 1 W.L.R. 830 HL at 837.

[39]   e.g. *Bannerman v White* (1861) 10 C.B. (N.S.) 844 (prospective buyer asking whether sulphur had been used in cultivation of hops; seller saying "no"; clear that purchaser would have walked away if the hops had been sulphurated; assurance having contractual effect).

this oral assurance had been a potential "deal-breaker". He held that the oral assurance should take effect as a collateral warranty. The effect of this warranty was that it was not possible for the landlord to forfeit the lease for breach of the covenant (contained in the formal written terms of the tenancy) not to reside there at night.[40]

Criterion (4): the court will consider the relative skill, knowledge and expertise of the parties:[41] In *Dick Bentley Productions v Harold Smith (Motors)*[42] the Court of Appeal held that a car-dealer's statement—that a car had merely covered 20,000 miles since a new engine had been fitted—was a contractual warranty. In fact, the car's true mileage since that engine had been fitted was 100,000. By contrast, in *Oscar Chess Ltd v Williams*[43] no warranty was established when a private vendor, basing himself on a log-book which had been forged by a third party, said in good faith that a car was a 1948 model, when in fact it was a 1939 model. In this case the buyer was an experienced car-dealer. **10-024**

Criterion (5): independent verification urged: the court will consider whether the representor asked the representee to verify the matter for himself.[44] **10-025**

Criterion (6): need for independent verification expressly negatived: conversely, it will be relevant to consider whether the representor assured the other that such verification was unnecessary.[45] **10-026**

Criterion (7) a representation of fact is more likely to have contractual effect than a forecast:[46]   in fact this is no more than a vague rule of thumb. Predictions can *sometimes* involve collateral warranties. For example, a forecast was held to involve a collateral warranty that the maker of it had reasonable grounds for believing the accuracy of his prediction in *Esso Petroleum Co Ltd v Mardon*.[47] The petrol company had made a statement concerning a filling station's likely level of customer demand (a "throughput" of 200,000 gallons). This forecast was treated as a collateral warranty that the oil company had reasonable grounds for making the prediction. But the statement was not regarded as a guarantee of that predicted level. A second and alternative basis of decision was that the petrol company had breached a tortious duty of care and that they were liable to compensate for their negligent misstatement. **10-027**

Criterion (8): timing: **10-028**

"the lapse of time between the statement and the making of the formal contract. The longer

---

[40] [1959] Ch. 129 at 145–146 per Harman J.
[41] *Harlingdon & Leinster Enterprises v Christopher Hull Fine Art* [1991] 1 Q.B. 564 CA (where the purchaser was an expert and placed no reliance on the seller's attribution of a work of art to a particular painter).
[42] [1965] 1 W.L.R. 623 CA.
[43] [1957] 1 W.L.R. 370 CA (Morris LJ dissenting).
[44] *Ecay v Godfrey* [1947] Lloyd's Rep. 286, Lord Goddard CJ (seller of second-hand boat making clear his belief that the purchaser would be having it surveyed first); cf. defendant encourages the plaintiff to rely on his assurance without further inquiry or verification (see next note) on *Schawel v Reade* [1913] 2 I.R. 64 HL.
[45] *Schawel v Reade* [1913] 2 I.R. 64 HL ("you need not look for anything; the horse is perfectly sound. If there were anything the matter with the horse, I should tell you").
[46] *Business Environment Bow Lane Ltd v Deanwater Estates Ltd* [2007] EWCA Civ 622; [2007] L. & T.R. 26 at [23].
[47] [1976] Q.B. 801 CA.

the interval, the greater the presumption must be that the parties did not intend the statement to have contractual effect in relation to a subsequent deal".[48]

10-029 *Criterion (9): subsequent negotiation superseding informal statement:*[49]

"whether the statement is followed by further negotiations and a written contract not containing any term corresponding to the statement. In such a case, it will be harder to infer that the statement was intended to have a contractual effect because the prima facie assumption will be that the written contract includes all the terms the parties wanted to be binding between them."

10-030 **Other case law concerning collateral warranties**   In *New York Laser Clinic Ltd v Naturastudios Ltd*,[50] Cavanagh J rightly rejected the bold but quite fallacious submission by claimant's counsel that the *Edwards v Skyways*[51] "intent to create legal relations presumption", applicable to business contexts, additionally renders a pre-contractual statement presumptively a collateral warranty, without the need for the claimant to satisfy an onus of proof by reference to established indicia.[52] The case contains a thorough survey of leading decisions on collateral warranties.[53] In the *New York Laser* case, Cavanagh J awarded damages for lost profits attributable to malfunctioning hair-removing lasers, the efficiency of which had been warranted.

10-031   An assertion that there has been a collateral warranty needs to be supported by evidence, because such an undertaking will not be conjured out of thin air. In *Fuji Seal Europe Ltd v Catalytic Combustion Corporation* Jackson J concluded that there was simply no evidence to support the assertion that a parent company had provided a collateral assurance relating to its subsidiary company:[54]

"Fuji could quite easily have asked for a parent company guarantee…. However, Fuji did not request this. Fuji, for its own business reasons, was content to rely upon its contract with a subsidiary company [CCE]."

Jackson J concluded that no collateral undertaking could be discerned:

"this situation is a far cry from that prevailing in Shanklin Pier.[55] It is not appropriate for this court to supplement the contractual arrangements which experienced and well-

---

[48]   *Business Environment Bow Lane Ltd v Deanwater Estates Ltd* [2007] EWCA Civ 622; [2007] L. & T.R. 26 at [23] (adopting Lightman J's statement in *Inntrepreneur Pub Co Ltd v East Crown Ltd* [2000] 2 Lloyd's Rep. 611 at 615); the court in *Business Environment* case also cited: *Henderson v Arthur* [1907] 1 K.B. 10 CA, *City & Westminster Properties (1934) Ltd v Mudd* [1959] 1 Ch. 129 (Harman J) and *Brikom Investments v Carr* [1979] 1 Q.B. 467 CA.

[49]   *Business Environment Bow Lane Ltd v Deanwater Estates Ltd* [2007] EWCA Civ 622; [2007] L. & T.R. 26 at [23].

[50]   [2019] EWHC 2892 (QB) at [64] and [65].

[51]   [1964] 1 W.L.R. 349 at 354–355, Megaw J.

[52]   [2019] EWHC 2892 (QB) at [64] and [65].

[53]   Cavanagh J noted the following cases on collateral warranties: *Brown v Sheen and Richmond Car Sales, Ltd* [1950] 1 All E.R. 1102 (Jones J), and *Shanklin Pier v Detel Products Ltd* [1951] 2 K.B. 854 (McNair J); *Andrews v Hopkinson* [1957] 1 Q.B. 229 (McNair J); *Yeoman Credit v Odgers Vospers Motor House Plymouth (Third Party)* [1962] 1 W.L.R. 215, CA; *Wells (Merstham) Ltd v Buckland Sand and Silica Ltd* [1965] 2 Q.B. 170 (Davies J); *Fuji Seal Europe Ltd v Catalytic Combustion Corp* [2005] EWHC 1659 (TCC); 102 Con. L.R. 47 at [149] to [158] per Jackson J.

[54]   [2005] EWHC 1659 (TCC); 102 Con. L.R. 47 at [149] to [158] per Jackson J.

[55]   *Shanklin Pier v Detel Products Ltd* [1951] 2 K.B. 854 (McNair J); *Andrews v Hopkinson* [1957] 1 Q.B. 229 (McNair J) (where an express collateral warranty had been given to a pier-owner by paint suppliers concerning the quality of paint to be used in a project; the paint was bought directly by

advised commercial parties choose to make. Fuji and CCC chose not to enter into any direct contract. In my judgment, no form of collateral warranty between [Fuji and CCC] can be read into or derived from the pre-contract documents."

In *MyBarrister Ltd v Hewetson*, Daniel Alexander QC, Deputy High Court Judge, **10-032** at a summary judgment hearing, held that the defendant's counterclaim contained an allegation that there was a collateral oral contract, namely an oral guarantee given by a company director.[56] The (alleged oral) guarantee was prima facie unenforceable under s.4 of the Statute of Frauds 1677. But the judge concluded that the claim could not be summarily dismissed and instead that trial would be necessary to investigate the claimant's plea, which was partly based on estoppel. The attempt to raise a binding collateral assurance on these facts was bold, in view of direct House of Lords authority[57] that ordinarily an estoppel could not be substantiated on such facts, but the attempt to raise a special estoppel could not be dismissed until witness evidence could be adduced at trial.

Supply of goods, digital content or services by traders to consumers: special **10-033** **provision in respect of terms imposed by the Consumer Rights Act 2015** It should be noted that, in the case of the supply of goods, digital content, or services by traders to consumers, the Consumer Rights Act 2015 does not use the terminology of "condition", but instead sets out the consequences of breach at s.19(3) (in the case of goods). Those possibilities include "the short-term right to reject" and "the final right to reject". Furthermore, the Consumer Rights Act 2015 s.19(1) excludes the Common Law right to "treat the contract as at an end" in respect of the seller's non-compliance with (statutory) terms imposed by the 2015 Act. Instead the buyer of goods in those circumstances is confined to the remedies in respect of breach contained in s.19(3), (4), and (6) (including include "the short-term right to reject" and "the final right to reject"). The salient provisions are (these requirements are amplified in the para.10-034):

- Consumer Rights Act 2015 s.9: goods to be of "satisfactory quality";
- 2015 Act s.10: goods to be "reasonably fit" for "any particular purpose" notified to the trader;
- 2015 Act s.11: goods to correspond to their "description"; and
- 2015 Act s.13: goods to "match" any sample (these requirements are amplified in the para.10-034).

Consumer Rights Act 2015 s.9 requires goods sold by a seller in the course of **10-034** business must be "of satisfactory quality" and that requirement is then elaborated. Section 10 of the 2015 Act requires goods sold to be "reasonably fit for" "any particular purpose for which the consumer is contracting for the goods" and that

---

the contractors, the pier-owner having so stipulated following the paint supplier's assurance just mentioned; a collateral contract was held to subsist between the paint supplier and the pier-owner that the paint would have the specified durability).

56 [2017] EWHC 2624 (Ch); [2018] Bus. L.R. 752 at [44]–[80], per Daniel Alexander QC, Deputy High Court Judge.

57 In *Actionstrength Ltd v International Glass Engineering In Gl En SpA* [2003] UKHL 17; [2003] 2 A.C. 541, the House of Lords held that failure to satisfy the requirement of writing contained in the Statute of Frauds 1677, s.4, cannot (except in special circumstances) be cured by estoppel; per Lord Bingham at [9], Lord Hoffmann at [26], Lord Walker at [52] and [53], and Lord Clyde at [35]. In the *MyBarrister* case (see preceding fn.) the special estoppel pleaded by the claimant involved an allegation that the defendant had given a special assurance that the oral guarantee would be legally respected by that party.

purpose is something which the consumer "makes known (expressly or by implication)" to the trader. Section 11 of the 2015 Act requires goods to match their description. Section 13(2)(a) of the 2015 Act requires goods to match any sample which is "seen or examined by the consumer before the contract is made", and imposes the further requirement (under s.13(2)(b) of the 2015 Act) that the goods must be "free from any defect that makes their quality unsatisfactory and that would not be apparent on a reasonable examination of the sample".

10-035   Similarly, in the case of "digital content contracts" the Consumer Rights Act 2015 also excludes (see s.42(8) of the 2015 Act) the Common Law power to terminate for breach of a statutory term. But in this context the buyer's remedies under the statute do not include a statutory right of rejection (s.42(2)–(7)). However, the Consumer Rights Act 2015 s.54(7)(f) preserves the Common Law right to terminate for breach of a statutory condition in respect of contracts for the supply of services to consumers. *Chitty on Contracts* notes[58] that the parties to a consumer purchase transaction can agree that a term will be treated as a condition or as a warranty, because Sale of Goods Act 1979 s.11(3) has not been disapplied from the 2015 Act.

II.   WHEN IS A TERM A (PROMISSORY) "CONDITION"?

10-036   A term is a condition (rather than an intermediate or innominate term, or a warranty), in any of the following five situations: (i) statute explicitly classifies the term in this way;[59] (ii) there is a binding judicial decision supporting this classification of a particular term as a "condition"; (iii) a term is described in the contract as a "condition" and upon construction it has that technical meaning; (iv) the parties have explicitly agreed that breach of that term, no matter what the factual consequences, will entitle the innocent party to terminate the contract for breach; or (v) as a matter of general construction of the contract, the clause must be understood as intended to operate as a condition. This classification was declared as "neat" by Waller LJ in *"The Seaflower"*,[60] who adopted the statement by *Chitty on Contracts*—although it should be noted that Chitty does not separate items (iii) and (iv) in this list.[61] Cavanagh J in *Duchy Farm Kennels Ltd v Steels* (2020) referred, by citation, to this analysis and other textbook discussion: on the *Duchy Farm* case itself see 12-007B.[62] These five situations (numbered (i) to (v) and referred to below as "Gateways to finding a condition") will now be explained in

---

58   H. Beale (ed), *Chitty on Contracts*, 34th edn (London: Sweet & Maxwell, 2021), para.46-056.
59   e.g. Sale of Goods Act 1979 (as amended) ss.12(5A), 13 (1A), 14(6), 15(3); in non-consumer cases, ss.13–15 must be read subject to the Sale of Goods Act 1979 s.15A, on which M. Bridge (ed), *Benjamin's Sale of Goods*, 11th edn (London: Sweet & Maxwell, 2021), para.12-024 ff; inserted by Sale and Supply of Goods Act 1994 s.4; M.G. Bridge, "The Sale and Supply of Goods Act 1994" [1995] J.B.L. 398; "Sale and Supply of Goods" [1987] L. Com. No.160.
60   *BS & N Ltd (BVI) v Micado Shipping Ltd (Malta) ("The Seaflower") (No.1)* [2001] 1 Lloyd's Rep. 341 at [42].
61   H. Beale (ed), *Chitty on Contracts*, 34th edn (London: Sweet & Maxwell, 2021), para.27-017; M. Bridge (ed), *Benjamin's Sale of Goods*, 11th edn (London: Sweet & Maxwell, 2021), para.10-037; J.E. Stannard and D. Capper, *Termination for Breach of Contract*, 2nd edn (Oxford: Oxford University Press, 2020), Ch.5.
62   [2020] EWHC 1208 (QB); [2020] I.R.L.R. 632 at [33], where Cavanagh J set out the principles by citing Judge Klein in *C21 London Estates v Maurice Macneill Iona Ltd* [2017] EWHC 998 (Ch) at [68], who said: "As Andrews, Clarke, Tettenborn, Virgo helpfully explain in *Contractual Duties: Performance, Breach, Termination and Remedies* [now 4th edn, Sweet & Maxwell, 2023, para.10-036], a contractual term is a condition in the following circumstances: 'A term is a condition (rather than an intermediate or innominate term, or a warranty), in any of the following five situations: (1)

detail. An even "neater" analysis is Michael Bridge's remark that a condition can arise "by statute, party choice, and commercial usage"[63] (the last compartment being the result of careful contextual construction combined with commercial sensitivity).[64]

Gateway (i) to finding a condition: statute explicitly classifies the term in this way[65]   Examples within the Sale of Goods Act 1979 are summarised at para.10-093. The Consumer Rights Act 2015 contains special provisions (not constituting "conditions") concerning contracts for the supply to consumers by traders of goods, digital content, or services (for example, and notably, Consumer Rights Act 2015 ss.9–18).

10-037

Gateway (ii) to finding a condition: there is a binding judicial decision supporting this classification of a particular term as a "condition"

(a) *Behn v Burness* (charterparty; owner's statement of the ship's present location; "the place of the ship at the date of the contract, where the ship is in foreign parts and is chartered to come to England, may be the only datum on which the charterer can found his calculations of the time of the ship's arriving at the port of load. A statement is more or less important in proportion as the object of the contract more or less depends upon it. For most charters,

10-038

---

statute explicitly classifies the term in this way; (2) there is a binding judicial decision supporting this classification of a particular term as a 'condition'; (3) a term is described in the contract as a 'condition' and upon construction it has that technical meaning; (4) the parties have explicitly agreed that breach of that term, no matter what the factual consequences, will entitle the innocent party to terminate the contract for breach; or (5) as a matter of general construction of the contract, the clause must be understood as intended to operate as a condition. This classification was declared as 'neat' by Waller LJ in *'The Seaflower'* [*BS&N Ltd (BVI) v Micado Shipping (Malta) (No 1)* [2001] 1 Lloyd's Rep. 341] who adopted the statement by *Chitty on Contracts*—although it should be noted that *Chitty* does not separate items (3) and (4) [see 34th edn (London: Sweet & Maxwell, 2021), para.27-017] in this list'". Judge Klein [2017] EWHC 998 (Ch) at [76] also cited *Carter's Breach of Contract* [now 2nd edn (Oxford: Hart Publishing, 2019), para.5-14] for the following factors: "(a) the form and structure of the term; whether entry into the contract was motivated by an understanding on the part of [the innocent party] that the term would be strictly complied with; (b) the relationship between the term in issue and the other terms of the contract; (c) the likely effects of any breach of the term; (d) the extent to which the [innocent party] will be adequately compensated by an award of damages for breach of the term; (e) whether construing the term as a condition will achieve a reasonable result; (f) the nature of the contract in which the term appears; (g) the nature of the subject matter of the contract; (h) the nature of the term and the obligation which it creates". And Judge Klein added at [72]: "I believe that all these factors are factors in the process which Lord Ackner approved in *'The Naxos'* [*Cie Commerciale Sucres et Denrees v C Czarnikow* [1990] 1 W.L.R. 1337 (HL)]". Judge Klein's decision was approved by the Court of Appeal in *Maurice MacNeill Iona Ltd (t/a Century 21 UK) v C21 London Estates Ltd* [2018] EWCA Civ 1823 (unreported).

63 M.G. Bridge, *The Sale of Goods*, 4th edn (Oxford: Oxford University Press, 2019), 10.36.

64 Notable examples being *Maredelanto Compania Naviera SA v Bergbau-Handel GMBH ("The Mihalis Angelos")* [1971] 1 Q.B. 164 CA (criticised, D.W. Greig, "Condition or Warranty?" (1973) 89 L.Q.R. 93, 100–104) and *Bunge v Tradax* [1981] 1 W.L.R. 711 HL at 715–716, noted F. Reynolds, "Discharge of Contract by Breach" (1981) 97 L.Q.R. 541; J. Carter, "Classification of Contractual Terms: The New Orthodoxy" [1981] C.L.J. 219).

65 e.g. Sale of Goods Act 1979 (as amended) ss.12(5A), 13(1A), 14(6) and 15(3); ss.13–15 must be read subject to s.15A; on which M. Bridge (ed), *Benjamin's Sale of Goods*, 11th edn (London: Sweet & Maxwell, 2021), para.12-024 ff; inserted by Sale and Supply of Goods Act 1994 s.4; M.G. Bridge, "The Sale and Supply of Goods Act 1994" [1995] J.B.L. 398; "Sale and Supply of Goods" [1987] L. Com. No.160.

considering winds, markets and dependent contracts, the time of a ship's arrival to load is an essential fact, for the interest of the charterer");[66]

(b)   *Bentsen v Taylor Sons & Co (No.2)* (statement that chartered ship "had sailed or was about to sail" from Mobile back to the UK was a condition; in fact vessel set sail nearly a month later);[67]

(c)   *"The Mihalis Angelos"* (owner's statement that vessel is "ready to load" is a condition; the statement must be made on reasonable grounds);[68]

(d)   *Bunge Corp v Tradax Export SA* (buyer's duty to give notice of vessel's readiness is a condition);[69] similarly, as held by Henshaw J in *A v B*,[70] the buyer's nomination of an "ETA" (estimated time of arrival) must be made on reasonable and honest grounds, otherwise the seller is at liberty to terminate for breach of a condition; however, an initial nomination which is invalid (because made unreasonably and not honestly) can be cured by a subsequent valid nomination of a substitute vessel within the relevant time-frame; furthermore, it is not a condition that the relevant nominated vessel should be the subject of a subsisting charterparty at the time of the nomination;

(e)   *Compagnie Commerciale Sucre et Denrees v C Czarnikow ("The Naxos")*

---

[66]   (1863) 3 B. & S. 751 at 759; 122 E.R. 281 at 284 (Erle CJ, Pollock CB, Williams and Keating JJ, and Channell B).

[67]   *Bentsen v Taylor Sons & Co (No.2)* [1893] 2 Q.B. 274 CA at 283 per Bowen LJ: "if that statement does not mean that the ship has actually sailed, it does mean that she is loaded, or may at all events for business purposes be treated as actually loaded; that she has got past the embarrassments and dangers attendant on loading, and that her sailing is the next thing to be looked for. And, with regard to … the phrase 'about to sail,' … it does not mean that the ship is to sail within a 'reasonable' or indefinite time, a statement which might lead to endless difficulties and expense, but that, if she has not already sailed, she is about to sail forthwith."

Although the defendant charterer succeeded in showing breach of a condition, entitlement to terminate had been waived by the defendant's subsequent letter and the defendant's remedy for breach was damages at 284.

[68]   [1971] 1 Q.B. 164 CA (criticised, D.W. Greig, "Condition or Warranty?" (1973) 89 L.Q.R. 93, 100–104).

[69]   [1981] 1 W.L.R. 711 HL, (noted F. Reynolds, "Discharge of Contract by Breach" (1981) 97 L.Q.R. 541; J. Carter, "Classification of Contractual Terms: The New Orthodoxy" [1981] C.L.J. 219).

[70]   [2021] EWHC 793 (Comm); [2021] Bus. L.R. 882 at [71] (Henshaw J): "[71] I conclude that the relevant principles are as follows: i) Where a contract of sale requires the buyer to nominate a vessel by a particular date (including by stipulating a notice period and a shipment period), then it is (subject to any contrary intention expressed in the contract) a condition of the contract that the buyer provide a valid nomination by the relevant deadline. That is a stipulation as to time in a mercantile contract in relation to which the parties should be taken to have intended time to be of the essence. ii) Accordingly, if by the latest date on which a valid nomination could be made the buyer has failed to provide one, then there is a breach of condition that will entitle the seller to treat the contract as being at an end. iii) A valid nomination is one made honestly and on reasonable grounds, and otherwise in accordance with the contract terms. iv) A valid nomination may be preceded by an initial nomination that is or becomes invalid, because either (a) it is 'non-contractual' in the sense of failing to provide the contractually stipulated notice period, or stating an ETA outside the contractual shipment window, (b) it is not made both honestly and on reasonable grounds, or (c) it becomes invalid due to subsequent events e.g. unforeseeable delays. v) The giving of the initial invalid nomination is not in itself a breach of condition: no breach of condition occurs provided that a valid and timely nomination is given in due course. vi) An initial invalid nomination made otherwise than honestly and in good faith (e.g. of a vessel which the buyer knows could not possibly meet the contractual lifting deadline) may evince an intention not to perform the contract, and thus entitle the seller to treat the contract as having been renounced by the buyer. vii) It is unnecessary to decide in the present case whether, and if so in what circumstances, a prior invalid nomination could amount to a breach of contract sounding in damages, no such claim having been advanced or arising on this appeal."

(seller's duty to have goods ready for delivery at any time within contract period is a condition);[71]

(f) *BS & N Ltd (BVI) v Micado Shipping Ltd (Malta) ("The Seaflower")* (shipowner's duty to obtain within 60 days third party oil company's approval of vessel chartered to claimant; duty is a condition);[72]

(g) *Barber v NWS Bank Plc* (a hire-purchase dealer had breached a condition that he would have title in a car which was sold conditionally to the claimant on hire-purchase);[73]

(h) *Samarenko v Dawn Hill House Ltd* (in a contract for the sale of land, a buyer's failure to pay a 10 per cent deposit on the stipulated day constituted breach of a condition);[74] and

(i) *PT Berlian Laju Tanker TBK v, Nuse Shipping Ltd ("The Aktor")* (payment of full price, to be made at a Greek bank, in purchase of a ship; condition that the whole sum be paid at the specified Greek bank, and not 90 per cent and 10 per cent in Singapore, where a deposit had been lodged by the payor).[75]

Gateway (iii) to finding a condition: a term is described in the contract as a "condition" and upon construction it has that technical meaning The House of Lords' decision in *Schuler (L) AG v Wickman Machine Tool Sales Ltd*[76] indicates that the courts will give effect to the word "condition", treating it as a promissory condition entitling the innocent party to terminate the contract, unless to give the word "condition" its technical meaning would be *incompatible with the internal structure of the various clauses within the contract.* Another part of the reasoning in this case is that the word "condition" should not be given its technical meaning would lead to *manifest absurdity or complete unreasonableness.* **10-039**

In essence, the House of Lords in *Schuler (L) AG v Wickman Machine Tool Sales Ltd* held that, on proper construction of the contract, the word "condition" (contained in cl.7(b)) might not have been intended to operate in a technical sense. Therefore, breach of the relevant obligation did not necessarily justify termination. The majority's decision turned on the need to harmonise different clauses within the contract. It was held that the innocent party could not invoke cl.7(b) (containing the word "condition") in order to bypass cl.11(a)(1), which provided that the innocent party must first serve notice on the other party requiring the latter to take remedial steps. The ensuing text contains detailed examination of *Schuler (L) AG v Wickman Machine Tool Sales Ltd* (there are general comments in *Tullow Uganda Ltd v Heritage Oil and Gas* on the *Schuler* case, and on the related topic of purported "conditions precedent").[77] **10-040**

---

[71] [1990] 1 W.L.R. 1337 HL; noted G.H. Treitel, "Time of Shipment in f.o.b. Contracts" (1991) L.M.C.L.Q. 147–154, noting at 152 and 154 that the decision is consistent with the need for (i) promotion of certainty, and (ii) the commercial importance of the term; and M.A. Clarke, "Time and Essence of Mercantile Contracts: The Law Loses its Way" [1991] C.L.J. 29.

[72] [2001] 1 Lloyd's Rep. 341 CA.

[73] [1996] 1 W.L.R. 641 CA at 646.

[74] [2011] EWCA Civ 1445; [2013] Ch. 36 per Lewison LJ at [24]–[27] per Etherton LJ at [52]–[54] and per Rix LJ at [60]–[64] (case noted J.W. Carter, " Deposits and 'time of the essence'" (2013) 129 L.Q.R. 149–152).

[75] [2008] EWHC 1330 (Comm); [2008] 2 All E.R. (Comm) 784, Christopher Clarke J.

[76] [1974] A.C. 235 HL.

[77] [2014] EWCA Civ 1048; [2014] 2 C.L.C. 61 at [33] (and generally [33] ff) per Beatson LJ; *Scottish Power UK Plc v BP Exploration Operating Co Ltd* [2015] EWHC 2658 (Comm); [2016] 1 All

10-041 **Main Facts of Schuler (L) AG v Wickman Machine Tool Sales Ltd**[78]   W agreed to act as a distribution agent for S, a German manufacturer. Clause 7(b) required W to send a representative at least once a week to six specified motor manufacturers. W had committed itself to making roughly 1400 visits over a four-and-a-half-year period to solicit orders for "panel pressers" (equipment used in the manufacture of vehicles). This clause was labelled a "condition". Another clause, 11(a)(1), allowed a party to terminate the contract in the event of a "material breach", provided the relevant breach had not been remedied within 60 days after the aggrieved party had given written notice. S sought to bypass this clause, and instead purported to terminate the contract on the basis of breaches of cl.7(b). S had waived[79] earlier defaults. But W consistently failed to make significant percentages of the stipulated visits.

10-042 **Arbitrator, High Court, and Court of Appeal, House of Lords**   In the *Schuler* case the arbitrator had held that the word "condition" had not been used in its technical sense and that it was necessary for Schuler to show a material breach by Wickmans. He found that there had been one period of material breach (before 13 January 1964), but that this had been waived. Later periods of default were held by him to have fallen short of material breach. Mocatta J reversed this, holding that the word "condition" had been used in a technical sense. The Court of Appeal by a majority (Lord Denning MR and Edmund-Davies LJ, Stephenson LJ dissenting) held that the word "condition" had not been used in a technical sense and that the waiver point should be upheld. This meant there had been no period of material breach. But the House of Lords held that "condition" had not been used in a technical sense, and agreed with the other aspects of the Court of Appeal's decision.

10-043   According to the majority in the House of Lords, the reference to a "condition" in cl.7 had to be linked (somewhat clumsily) with the reference elsewhere in the agreement (cl.11) to "material" breach. The principle that the whole contract must be considered when interpreting a particular clause, phrase, or word, is a cardinal feature of interpretation under English law: see, notably, the *Sigma*[80] and the

---

E.R. (Comm) 536 at [194] ff, Leggatt J examined (inconclusive) case law concerning conditions precedent; decision affirmed, [2016] EWCA Civ 1043.

[78]   During the Court of Appeal stage in *Schuler (L) AG v Wickman Machine Tool Sales Ltd* [1972] 1 W.L.R. 840 CA at 847–848, Lord Denning MR chronicled the facts as follows: "May 1, 1963, to January 13, 1964: The arbitrator found that during this period there were failures by Wickman Sales to visit the six firms as required by clause 7, and that these failures were a material breach of the obligation … [But the Court of Appeal held that there was a waiver by Schulers of their rights in respect of breaches antecedent to January 13, 1964.'] January 13, 1964, to July 13, 1964: From January 13, 1964, to June 29, 1964, … [out] of 144 weekly visits to the six firms, only 15 were missed. The arbitrator found that these failures were not a material breach … July 14, 1964, to October 27, 1964: Out of 96, only nine were missed. These were for good reasons, as, for instance, four because the works were shut down, and two because the firms went to visit Wickmans at their 'At Homes,' and so forth. The arbitrator found that these failures were not a material breach."

[79]   In the sense that no action had been taken at all: generally on the slippery terminology of "waiver" (H. Beale (ed), *Chitty on Contracts*, 34th edn (London: Sweet & Maxwell, 2021), paras 27-00–27-062) see, *Ross T Smyth & Co v TD Bailey Son & Co* [1940] 3 All E.R. 60 HL at 70 per Lord Wright, and Lord Hailsham's comments in *Banning v Wright* [1972] 1 W.L.R. 972 HL at 978–980; waiver of the right to terminate for breach of a condition was waived in, leaving intact the right to compensation for breach, *Bentsen v Taylor Sons & Co (No.2)* [1893] 2 Q.B. 274 CA at 284 per Bowen LJ.

[80]   *Re Sigma Finance Corp (in administrative receivership)* [2009] UKSC 2; [2010] 1 All E.R. 571.

Charter Reinsurance case[81] cases. The same approach is recognised in the (non-binding) codes: PECL, *Principles of European Contract Law* art.5:105 and UNIDROIT's *Principles of International Commercial Contracts* art.4.4.[82]

In the *Schuler case* Lord Reid hesitatingly concluded[83] that a spate of failed visits **10-044** could be (partly) "remedied" in the sense that the agent could "put his house in order" and reform its "system" of future visits (similarly, Lord Kilbrandon).[84] And so the 60-day notice period to remedy had to be complied with. The German company had not been justified in terminating the contract on these facts. (The Court of Appeal in *Force India Formula One Team Ltd v Etihad Airways PJSC*,[85] considered the concept of "remediable material" breaches, in the light of the *Schuler* case: see Remediable and Irremediable Material Breaches at para.9-042 ff).

Another (but perhaps not sufficient)[86] strand of reasoning in the *Schuler* case **10-045** concerned the hypothetical case of a "one-off"[87] unexcused missed visit. Lord Reid said: "The more unreasonable the result the more unlikely it is that the parties can have intended it".[88] But it is submitted that such a construction is justified only quite exceptionally, when it would lead to a *very or wholly* unreasonable result and the relevant word or phrase admits of more than one meaning. (For reference to this aspect of the *Schuler* case, see Sir Stanley Burnton's comment at 10-053 in *Personal Touch Financial Services Ltd v Simplysure Ltd, Usay Business Ltd* (2016).[89])

A harsh denial of termination? The Schuler case was not an example of trivial **10-046** **breach** The majority's *reductio ad absurdum* of the single unexcused missed visit certainly distorts the degree of default in the *Schuler* case itself. The amount of default was scarcely negligible (between 13 January and 27 October 1964, 18 out of 240 visits were missed for no good reason).

It is interesting to consider how the *Schuler case* would have been decided if cl.7 **10-047** had stood alone and cl.11 had not been added. Would the House of Lords have held in this situation that the word "condition" should be deprived of its technical meaning because a single unexcused visit should not be enough to justify termination? It is submitted that the proper construction would be that breach of the duty to make

---

[81] Lord Mustill in *Charter Reinsurance Co Ltd v Fagan* [1997] A.C. 313 HL at 384, quoted in *In Re Sigma Finance Corp (in administrative receivership)* [2009] UKSC 2; [2010] 1 All E.R. 571 at [9].

[82] 4th edn (2016), text and comment, available at *http://www.unidroit.org/instruments/commercial-contracts/unidroit-principles-2016*. On the UNIDROIT principles, S. Vogenauer, *Commentary on the UNIDROIT Principles of International Commercial Contracts*, 2nd edn (Oxford: Oxford University Press, 2015), and E Broerdermann, *UNIDROIT Principles of International Commercial Contracts: An Article-by-Article Commentary* (The Hague: Kluwer Law International, 2018).

[83] [1974] A.C. 235 HL at 252: "The contract is so obscure that I can have no confidence that this is its true meaning ...".

[84] [1974] A.C. 235 HL at 271.

[85] [2010] EWCA Civ 1051; [2011] E.T.L.R. 10 at [100]–[109].

[86] Lord Reid, [1974] A.C. 235 at 251, would have construed the word "condition" in cl.7 in its technical sense if cl.11 had not existed.

[87] In fact, the amount of default was scarcely negligible (between 13 January and 27 October 1964, 18 out of 240 visits were missed for no good reason; the degree of default had influenced Lord Wilberforce, who dissented: he said that the contract demanded "aggressive, insistent punctuality and efficiency": [1974] A.C. 235 HL at 263).

[88] [1974] A.C. 235 at 251 per Lord Reid (a useful "rule of thumb" per Lord Mustill in *Charter Reinsurance Co Ltd v Fagan* [1997] A.C. 313 HL at 387–388; e.g. applied in *Trafigura Beheer BV v Navigazione Montanari SpA* [2014] EWHC 129; [2014] 1 Lloyd's Rep. 550 at [9] per Andrew Smith J).

[89] [2016] EWCA Civ 461 at [28].

stipulated visits would constitute breach of a condition, justifying termination, provided there was a sufficient number of such missed visits, that is, provided the default was not so trivial as to be a wholly commercially unreasonable basis for termination (compare Sale of Goods Act 1979 s.15A, on which para.10-096 ff).

10-048   What if in the *Schuler case* there had been no visits made at all during the relevant period? In that event, to require compliance with the notice provision in cl.11 would be absurd. Instead total default would be repudiatory, that is (without turning to cl.7), the guilty party would have evinced an intention no longer to be bound by it.

10-049   **Lord Wilberforce's dissent in the Schuler case**   Lord Wilberforce in the *Schuler case* concluded that the word "condition" should be applied in its ordinary legal and technical sense: and it would justify termination for unexcused failure to make all agreed visits. In his view, the majority's approach relaxed the discipline of this commercial agreement, which he robustly described as demanding "aggressive, insistent punctuality and efficiency". He said:[90]

> "to call [cl.7(b)] arbitrary, capricious or fantastic, or to introduce as a test of its validity the ubiquitous reasonable man (I do not know whether he is English or German) is to assume, contrary to the evidence, that both parties to this contract adopted a standard of easygoing tolerance rather than one of aggressive, insistent punctuality and efficiency. This is not an assumption I am prepared to make, nor do I think myself entitled to impose the former standard upon the parties if their words indicate, as they plainly do, the latter. I note finally, that the result of treating the clause, so careful and specific in its requirements, as a term is, in effect, to deprive the appellants of any remedy in respect of admitted and by no means minimal breaches. The arbitrator's finding that these breaches were not 'material' was not, in my opinion, justified in law in the face of the parties' own characterisation of them in their document: indeed the fact that he was able to do so, and so leave [Schuler] without remedy, argues strongly that the legal basis of his finding—that clause 7(b) was merely a term—is unsound."

10-050   But Lord Wilberforce on this occasion was a solitary hawk, out-numbered in the Lords by a quartet of doves (in the lower courts, however, Lord Wilberforce's strict approach had been favoured by Mocatta J—on appeal from the arbitrator—and by Stephenson LJ, dissenting in the Court of Appeal).

10-051   **Renunciation inferred from repetitive breach: an overlooked route to termination**   It is also submitted that the German company on the *Schuler case* might have been entitled to terminate the present contract by contending that the repeated failures to make visits during the relevant period constituted an implied renunciation by conduct of the contract, and that the 60-day notice period should not clog the innocent party's Common Law right to terminate the contract on that basis for this analysis. It might have been necessary to consider (i) the ratio of the breach to the contract as a whole, and (ii) the likelihood-as it would seem to a reasonably situated person-of repetition of breach. Lord Hewart CJ in *Maple Flock Co Ltd v Universal Furniture Products (Wembley) Ltd* articulated these two factors, in the context of failure to make deliveries of goods in an agreed set of instalments.[91] In the *Schuler* case, the implied "renunciation" analysis would have avoided the need to pore over the meaning of "condition" in the relevant clause. However, the House of Lords' speeches did not address this matter.

---

[90] [1974] A.C. 235 at 263 HL.
[91] [1934] 1 K.B. 148 CA at 156–157 per Lord Hewart CJ; on which J.W. Carter, *Carter's Breach of*

Statutory regime concerning commercial agents   Finally, Whittaker has noted **10-052**
that facts similar to the *Schuler case* would now fall within the Commercial Agents
(Council Directive) Regulations 1993. And he suggests that the courts would now
"feel much less ready to 'read down' a term named by the parties as a 'condition'
[within that new statutory context]".[92]

Schuler case distinguished   In *Personal Touch Financial Services Ltd v* **10-053**
Simplysure Ltd, Usay Business Ltd[93] the Court of Appeal held that the word "condition" had been used in its technical promissory sense in the present case. An agent
of an insurance company was held to be in breach of the following clause (cl.7):
"It is a condition of the Agreement that the Appointed Representative be aware of
and abides by the rules of the regulator..." Sir Stanley Burnton, giving the court's
judgment, held that this was a condition:[94]

> "... the fact that a contractual provision is described as a condition of the agreement is
> not conclusive. Agreements often refer to all their terms as conditions, as in 'conditions
> of sale'. However, this was not such a case. The word 'condition' appears only once in
> the Agreement, in clause 7, and its use was emphasised by the introductory words, 'It is
> a condition of the agreement'. While its use is not conclusive, it must be given due weight
> when the agreement is construed. In *Schuler (L) Att.-Gen. v Wickman Machine Tool Sales
> Ltd* [1974] A.C. 235 Lord Reid said at 251: 'Schuler maintains that the use of the word
> "condition" is in itself enough to establish this intention [for the term to be a condition
> strictly so called]. No doubt some words used by lawyers do have a rigid inflexible
> meaning. But we must remember that we are seeking to discover intention as disclosed
> by the contract as a whole. Use of the word "condition" is an indication—even a strong
> indication—of such an intention but it is by no means conclusive.' [The insurance
> company] submit that the Judge [who had wrongly construed clause 7 as an intermediate
> term] failed to give any weight to the use in the Agreement of the words 'It is a condi-
> tion of the agreement'. I agree."

Sir Stanley Burnton added:[95]   **10-054**

> "Lord Reid continued in Schuler: 'The fact that a particular construction leads to a very
> unreasonable result must be a relevant consideration. The more unreasonable the result
> the more unlikely it is that the parties can have intended it, and if they do intend it the more
> necessary it is that they shall make that intention abundantly clear'."

Sir Stanley Burnton concluded:[96]   **10-055**

> "However, I do not think that construing clause 7 as a true condition leads to an unreason-
> able result. Its breach was liable to have serious consequences for [the insurance
> company]. Breach of the general prohibition is a criminal offence, and ... use of
> unauthorised personnel by [the agent] could render [the insurance company] criminally
> liable and would render it liable in damages to any client adversely affected, and could
> lead to a regulatory sanction. It was therefore commercially sensible for the parties to the
> Agreement to have included clause 7 as a true condition."

Contract, 2nd edn (Oxford: Hart Publishing, 2019), [8-39] and [8-40]; *Regent OHG Aisestadt v
Franceasco of Jermyn Street Ltd* [1981] 3 All E.R. 327, Mustill J; Sale of Goods Act 1979 s.31(2).
[92]   S. Whittaker, "Termination Clauses", in A. Burrows and E. Peel (eds), *Contract Terms* (Oxford:
Oxford University Press, 2007), Ch.13, pp.267–273.
[93]   [2016] EWCA Civ 461.
[94]   [2016] EWCA Civ 461 at [28].
[95]   [2016] EWCA Civ 461 at [28].
[96]   [2016] EWCA Civ 461 at [29].

10-056   In *Galtrade Ltd v BP Oil International Ltd*,[97] Adrian Beltrami QC held that the expressions "Guarantees" and "agreed specification" did not denote that the relevant terms denoted a "condition" and his decision was that the terms were innominate terms, and on the facts the breach had not been serious enough to justify termination by the buyer (on this aspect see para.12-029). The judge said:[98]

> "[72]… neither the Special Provisions nor the General Terms describes the obligations as conditions or specifies that there is an automatic right to reject if the specifications are not met. I agree that there is no such implication in the use of the word 'Guarantees' or 'agreed specification'. The Claimant makes the point that, equally, the obligations are not described as intermediate terms and nor is there a statement that there is no automatic right to reject. However, I consider that this absence tells against a construction of the obligations as conditions. Had commercial parties intended to strike such a balance, it may reasonably be expected that they would have said so."

10-057   **Gateway (iv) to finding a condition: the parties have explicitly agreed that breach of that term, no matter what the factual consequences, will entitle the innocent party to terminate the contract for breach**[99]   The *Schuler decision* shows that the word "condition" might sometimes be construed as a "term". Therefore, the safer course is for contractual draftsmen *to spell out the innocent party's unqualified right to terminate for any breach of the relevant obligation*. However, the Court of Appeal's decision in *Rice v Great Yarmouth BC* shows that very careful drafting is needed to achieve such an unqualified right to terminate the contract.[100] This decision shows that such a termination provision will not always be taken literally if this will lead to manifest absurdity ("fly in the face of commercial common-sense"). But before passing to that case it might be helpful more recent Court of Appeal authority (*Kason Kek-Gardner Ltd v Process Components Ltd*) which demonstrates the courts' willingness to give effect to a clearly expressed stipulation which entitles the innocent party to elect to treat the contract as discharged for breach of the relevant term, or relevant category of terms.

10-058   **Respect for freedom of control: parties controlling the language and express machinery governing termination for breach**   The Court of Appeal in *Kason Kek-Gardner Ltd v Process Components Ltd* held[101] that the following clause gave the innocent party a right to terminate the contract irrespective of the gravity of the actual breach, because the clear intention underlying this clause was that the relevant breach (breach of a confidentiality obligation) would be both non-remediable and material:

> "Clause 11.2 Either party shall be entitled to terminate this Agreement immediately by written notice to the other in the event of: (a) any material breach by the other party of any of its obligations under this Agreement which, being a breach capable of remedy, is not remedied within 30 days of notice to the party in breach specifying the breach and requiring its remedy. (For this purpose … breach of the confidentiality obligations under clause 10 constitutes a non-remediable material breach)."

See also Ch.9, paras 9-042 ff, on "non-remediable" or "remediable" breaches.

---

[97]   [2021] EWHC 1796 (Comm); [2021] 2 C.L.C. 408.
[98]   [2021] EWHC 1796 (Comm); [2021] 2 C.L.C. 408 at [72] and see [77] and [80].
[99]   *Lombard North Central Plc v Butterworth* [1987] Q.B. 527 CA.
[100]   26 July 2000, *The Times* CA; (2001) 3 L.G.L.R. 4 CA.
[101]   [2017] EWCA Civ 2132; [2019] 1 All E.R. (Comm) 381 at [58].

The Court of Appeal's treatment of this issue in *Kason Kek-Gardner Ltd v*   **10-059**
Process Components Ltd provides important guidance:[102]

> "[56]... the licence stated in terms that breach of the confidentiality obligations under
> clause 10 constituted a non-remediable material breach. Commission of a non-
> remediable material breach triggered the right of termination under clause 11.2....[57]
> ...[what] matters is what the parties have agreed about the circumstances in which the
> contract may be terminated. [58] ....this is not a blanket provision entitling the injured
> party to terminate on "any" breach of contract. In such a case the court may well read
> down the apparent width of the termination clause so as to confine it to repudiatory
> breaches (e.g. *Rice v Great Yarmouth BC 30 June 2000* (2001) 3 L.G.L.R. 4 and *Dominion
> Corporate Trustees Ltd v Debenhams Properties Ltd* [2010] EWHC 1193 (Ch)). In our
> case, however, clauses 10 and 5 are singled out for special treatment. Fourth, recent cases
> emphasise that where a contract provides expressly for rights of termination, it does not
> matter whether the events on which those rights are exercisable do or do not amount to
> repudiatory breaches (see, eg *Firodi Shipping Ltd v Griffin Shipping LLC* [2013] EWCA
> Civ 1567, [2014] 1 Lloyd's Rep. 471; *Newland Shipping and Forwarding Ltd v Toba
> Trading FZC* [2014] EWHC 661 (Comm)). For similar reasons I do not consider that we
> can derive any help from other cases which considered whether particular breaches were
> or were not "material" where the contract itself did not contain any similar deeming provi-
> sion; and the question whether a breach was "material" was left at large."

Rice case: a troubling authority   By contrast, and almost 20 years before, the   **10-060**
courts had displayed willingness to second-guess contractual language which
conferred (at least literally) a right to terminate for breach, at any rate where such
an unfettered and broad ground for termination would produce a "draconian"
regime and would "fly in the face of commercial common-sense" (see text below
for these comments by Hale LJ). *Rice v Great Yarmouth BC*[103] was a four-year
contract for the claimant to maintain the defendant's sports and parks facilities. The
written contract gave the defendant the right to terminate for "breach of any of
[Rice's] obligations under the Contract". The defendant terminated the contract
because of shortcomings in performance. The Court of Appeal held that "any"
should not be taken to mean "any at all", otherwise the parties would have created
a "draconian" contractual regime,[104] and that extreme interpretation would "fly in
the face of commercial sense". Instead "any" meant "any repudiatory" breach.[105]
And so termination would be justified only if there had been "repudiation" of the
overall contract by a pattern of breaches.[106] But the breaches had not been
cumulatively serious enough.

Appraisal of the Rice case   It is submitted that, as noted by Kitchin J in *Dominion*   **10-061**
Corporate Trustees Ltd v Debenhams Properties Ltd,[107] the *Rice* case (and its
precursor, *"The Antaios"*, on the latter case, para.10-067) should be understood to
turn on the wide range of breaches capable of being committed by the service

---

102 [2017] EWCA Civ 2132; [2019] 1 All E.R. (Comm) 381 at [56]–[58] per Lewison LJ (with the agree-
    ment of Kitchin and Floyd LJJ).
103 26 July 2000, The Times CA; (2001) 3 L.G.L.R. 4 CA.
104 *The Times*, 26 July 2000; (2001) 3 L.G.L.R. 4 CA at [22] per Hale LJ.
105 Adopting *Antaios Compania Naviera SA v Salen Rederierna AB ("The Antaios")* [1985] A.C. 191
    at 200–1 HL (clause entitling owner to terminate the charterparty for "any" breach did not cover
    minor breach, but only a repudiatory breach); on which *Multi-Link Leisure v North Lanarkshire*
    [2010] UKSC 47; [2011] 1 All E.R. 175 at [21] per Lord Hope.
106 *The Times*, 26 July 2000; (2001) 3 L.G.L.R. 4 CA at [17] per Hale LJ.
107 *Dominion Corporate Trustees Ltd v Debenhams Properties Ltd* [2010] EWHC 1193 (Ch); [2010]

provider on the facts of each case. But where the scope of the obligation is narrow and the wording is water-tight, effect must be given to the termination provision.

10-062   When considering the *Rice* case it is also important to recall Lord Mustill's comment in *Charter Reinsurance Co Ltd v Fagan* that it is illegitimate for courts or arbitrators to "force upon the words a meaning which they cannot fairly bear", since this would be "to substitute for the bargain actually made one which the court believes could better have been made".[108] It is also instructive to recall Blackburn J's statement in *Bettini v Gye* that:

> "Parties may think some matter, apparently of very little importance, essential; and if they sufficiently express an intention to make the literal fulfilment of such a thing [a promissory condition] it will be."[109]

That comment was among the expressions of fundamental principle cited by Mustill LJ in support of the following propositions in *Lombard North Central Plc v Butterworth*:[110]

> "That there exists a category of term, in respect of which any breach whether large or small entitles the promisee to treat himself as discharged, has never been doubted in modern times, and the fact that a term may be assigned to this category by express agreement has been taken for granted for at least a century [citing various authorities]."

10-063   Furthermore, Mustill LJ said in the *Lombard* case:[111]

> "a clause expressly assigning a particular obligation to the category of conditions is not a clause which purports to fix the damages for breach of the obligation, and is not subject to the law governing penalty clauses. I acknowledge, of course, that by promoting a term into the category where all breaches are ranked as breaches of condition, the parties indirectly bring about a situation where, for breaches which are relatively small, the injured party is enabled to recover damages as on the loss of the bargain, whereas without the stipulation his measure of recovery would be different. But I am unable to accept that this permits the court to strike down as a penalty the clause which brings about this promotion. To do so would be to reverse the current of more than 100 years' doctrine, which permits the parties to treat as a condition something which would not otherwise be so. I am not prepared to take this step."

10-064   The Singapore Court of Appeal in *Fu Yuan Foodstuff Manufacturer Pte Ltd v Methodist Welfare Services*[112] gave full effect to the following clause: "3.2 [The respondent] may terminate [the] Agreement without notice should the [appellant]

N.P.C. 63 at [32] per Kitchin J ("a multitude of obligations, many of which are of minor importance and which can be broken in many different ways").

[108] [1997] A.C. 313 at 388 HL.

[109] (1876) 1 Q.B.D. 183 at 187; cited J.W. Carter, *Carter's Breach of Contract*, 2nd edn (Oxford: Hart Publishing, 2019), [5-04].

[110] [1987] Q.B. 527 CA at 536.

[111] [1987] Q.B. 527 at 537 CA.

[112] [2009] S.G.C.A. 23; [2009] 3 S.L.R. 925 at [29]–[36] per Andrew Phang Boon Leong at [31] "Unlike the approach adopted in Rice, we gave full effect to the termination clause concerned (here, cl 3.2 read with cl 2.7.2) as it in fact reflected the parties' intentions. Indeed, if a termination clause is clearly drafted, its literal language ought to accurately reflect the intentions of the parties. This is precisely the situation here". And at [36]: "In the circumstances, therefore, there is no need (as was the situation in Rice) to 'read down' cl 3.2. The process of 'reading down' the scope of a termination clause is, of course, one of the legal mechanisms utilised by the courts in order to control termination clauses. Such an approach was, as we have seen, utilised in Rice. However, as we have explained above, there is no need to adopt this approach in the present appeal as, unlike the situa-

breach any item under Clauses 1.4, 2.3 and 2.7". The court was not persuaded that the English Court of Appeal's pro-breaching-party mode of construction in the *Rice* case was consistent with the principle of freedom of contract.

Commentators' criticisms of the Rice case   Chen-Wishart has criticised the   **10-065**
result in this case:

> "the decision is questionable; it renders the termination clause meaningless since [the innocent party] can already terminate for a repudiatory breach under general law": and "the courts' aversion to interpretations which lead to very unreasonable results is ... motivated by ... avoidance of harsh outcomes which defeat parties' reasonable expectations."[113]

Whittaker's analysis of the case[114] concludes with this criticism: **10-066**

> "its approach will encourage ever more elaborate attempts to set out a wide power of termination ('termination for any breach, whether material, trivial or otherwise of the obligations set out in clauses A, B, or C')."[115]

Furthermore, Burrows has queried whether a clause would be upheld if it states   **10-067**
that termination would be justified for "any breach, however trivial".[116] The answer must be: "yes" because, if the parties are commercial parties, the principle of freedom of contract requires the courts not to override such wording. Similarly, McKendrick has suggested that a clause would not be held ineffective to confer a right to terminate if it were worded as follows: "any breach (whether or not that breach is repudiatory)".[117] Finally, Bridge suggests that the result in the *Rice* case might have been more elegantly achieved by use of the concept of a fettered discretion whether to terminate, rather than by denying that the employing local authority had no rights to terminate, short of a high-level repudiatory default.[118]

"The Antaios":[119] precursor to the Rice case   The Court of Appeal's "purposive"   **10-068**
approach to the contractual phrase "any other breach" in the *Rice* case mirrored the approach adopted by the House of Lords in *Antaios Compania Naviera SA v Salen Rederierna AB ("The Antaios")*. In *"The Antaios"*, the House of Lords considered a clause in a charterparty which literally permitted the owner to terminate the charterparty for "any" breach committed by the charterer. Lord Diplock, giving the House of Lords' judgment on this point, held that this did not allow termination for

---

tion in Rice, the termination clause here was consistent with the commercial reality between the parties which centred on their desire to comply with the employment laws of Singapore. Indeed, each termination clause must be analysed by reference to the precise language utilised by the parties in the context in which they entered into the contract, bearing in mind the fact that the ultimate aim of the court is to give effect to the intentions of the parties as embodied within the wording of the termination clause in question."

[113] M. Chen-Wishart, *Contract Law*, 7th edn (Oxford: Oxford University Press, 2022), p.515 (s.12.2.3.3).

[114] S. Whittaker, "Termination Clauses", in A. Burrows and E. Peel (eds), *Contract Terms* (Oxford: Oxford University Press, 2007), Ch.13, pp.273-283; Whittaker's chapter contains valuable discussion of many related decisions concerning "material breach" and similar contract drafting.

[115] S. Whittaker, "Termination Clauses", in A. Burrows and E. Peel (eds), *Contract Terms* (Oxford: Oxford University Press, 2007), Ch.13, p.283.

[116] A.S. Burrows, *A Casebook on Contract*, 7th edn (Oxford: Hart Publishing, 2020), 379 (question 2, following presentation of the *Rice* case).

[117] E. McKendrick, *Text, Cases, and Materials*, 10th edn (Oxford: Oxford University Press, 2022), p.778.

[118] M. Bridge, "The Exercise of Contractual Discretion" (2019) 135 L.Q.R. 227 at 247.

[119] [1985] A.C. 191 HL.

a minor breach—inaccuracy in bills of lading submitted to the owner by the charterer. Instead the clause should be understood to apply only to a repudiatory breach.

In the following passages, Lord Diplock approved first the arbitrators' decision to construe the words "any other breach" as requiring a repudiatory breach objectively going to the root of the contract. Secondly, the House of Lords buttressed this by endorsing the need to construe the language of such a clause in a purposive fashion which reflects the entire structure of the contract and delivers a commercially acceptable result. Lord Diplock said (upholding the arbitrators' award):[120]

> "The arbitrators decided ... that 'any other breach of this charterparty' in the withdrawal clause means a repudiatory breach ... such as would entitle the shipowners to elect to treat the contract as wrongfully repudiated by the charterers, a category into which in the arbitrators' opinion the breaches complained of did not fall."

10-069   Lord Diplock then noted:

> "To the semantic analysis ... the arbitrators added an uncomplicated reason based simply upon business commonsense: '...the owners' construction is wholly unreasonable, totally uncommercial and in total contradiction to the whole purpose of the ... time charter form. The owners relied on what they said was 'the literal meaning of the words in the clause'. We would say that if necessary, in a situation such as this, a purposive construction should be given to the clause so as not to defeat the commercial purpose of the contract.'"

10-070   Lord Hope in the Supreme Court in *Multi-Link Leisure v North Lanarkshire*[121] made the following three points concerning *"The Antaios"*:

(i)   "Lord Diplock [in *'The Antaios'*] said that if detailed and syntactical analysis of words in a commercial contract is going to lead to a conclusion that flouts business common sense, it must yield to business common sense";

(ii)   Lord Hope in the *Multi-Link Leisure* (2010) case added: "see also *Investors' Compensation Scheme Ltd v West Bromwich Building Society* (1998)[122] where Lord Hoffmann included this as the fifth of his common sense principles."[123]

(iii)   Finally, Lord Hope in *Multi-Link Leisure v North Lanarkshire* (2010)

---

[120]   [1985] A.C. 191 HL at 200–201.
[121]   [2010] UKSC 47; [2011] 1 All E.R. 175 at [21].
[122]   [1998] 1 W.L.R. 896 at 913 HL (see passages cited in the next note).
[123]   As the UK Supreme Court in *Re Sigma Finance Corp (in administrative receivership)* [2009] UKSC 2; [2010] 1 All E.R. 571 at [10] noted, the following passages in Lord Hoffmann's leading speech in *Investors Compensation Scheme* [1998] 1 W.L.R. 896 HL at 913, are already canonical:

> "(i) Interpretation is the ascertainment of meaning which the document would convey to a reasonable person having all the background knowledge which would reasonably have been available to the parties in the situation in which they were at the time of the contract. (ii) The background [has been described] as the 'matrix of fact', but this phrase is, if anything, an understated description of what the background may include, subject to the requirement that it should have been reasonably available to the parties and to the exception to be mentioned next, it includes absolutely anything which would have affected the way in which the language of the document would have been understood by a reasonable man. (iii) The law excludes from the admissible background the previous negotiations of the parties and the declarations of subjective intent. The law makes this distinction for reasons of practical policy and, in this respect only, legal interpretation differs from the way we would interpret utterances in ordinary life. The boundaries of this

observed: "In *Mannai Investment Co Ltd v Eagle Star Life Assurance Co Ltd* (1997),[124] Lord Steyn ... said that words are to be interpreted in the way in which a reasonable commercial person would construe them, and that the standard of the reasonable commercial person is hostile to technical interpretations and undue emphasis on niceties of language."

De Minimis Default in Loan Repayment: Default Judgment Set Aside for Reconsideration on the Merits.   In *Lombard North Central Plc v European Skyjets Ltd* (2020)[125] Freedman J (setting aside a default judgment, despite a four year delay) said that there was an arguable case that the claimant lender could not show default on the part of the borrower, there having been a mere $179 dollar underpayment (the loan agreement contained an acceleration clause which the creditor alleged had been triggered by this default). The de minimis point was left open for eventual decision.[126]   **10-071**

Decisions giving effect to clear language and respecting the innocent party's right to terminate for breach   The Court of Appeal's rather cavalier re-drafting of the termination clause in the *Rice* case (examined at para.10-060 ff) can be contrasted with the admirably robust application in *BNP Paribas v Wockhardt EU Operations (Swiss) AG*[127] of a termination clause. In the latter case Christopher Clarke J was required to examine a sophisticated financial instrument. He concluded that the parties had intended that breach would necessarily entitle the innocent party to terminate the contract. Christopher Clarke J commented as follows on the *Rice case*:   **10-072**

"I do not ignore the fact that there are cases in which the Court has declined to accept that a provision that 'any' breach of contract shall give rise to a right to terminate extends to any breach whatever; and have restricted it to such breaches as are repudiatory: *'The Antaios'* [1985] A.C. 191 HL; *Rice v Great Yarmouth BC* [2001] 3 LGLR 4. But it is open to the parties to agree that any non-payment or non-delivery shall have that consequence and that, as it seems to me, is exactly what the draftsman of the [present agreement] has done, in a carefully drawn standard form intended for widespread commercial use."[128]

In *BNP Paribas v Wockhardt EU Operations (Swiss) AG* it was apparent that the parties had intended the relevant provision to have this effect, and there was no   **10-073**

---

exception are unclear. But this is not the occasion on which to explore them. (iv) The meaning which a document (or any other utterance) would convey to a reasonable man is not the same thing as the meaning of words. The meaning of words is a matter of dictionaries and grammars; the meaning of the document is what the parties using those words against the relevant background would reasonably have been understood to mean. The background may not merely enable the reasonable man to choose between the possible meanings of words which are ambiguous but even (as occasionally happens in ordinary life) to conclude that the parties must, for whatever reason, have used the wrong words or syntax. (v) The 'rule' that words should be given their 'natural and ordinary meaning' reflects the common sense proposition that we do not easily accept that people have made linguistic mistakes, particularly in formal documents. On the other hand, if one would nevertheless conclude from the background that something must have gone wrong with the language, the law does not require judges to attribute to the parties an intention which they plainly could not have had."

124 [1997] A.C. 749 HL at 771.
125 [2020] EWHC 679 (QB).
126 [2020] EWHC 679 (QB) at [44] and [45].
127 [2009] EWHC 3116 (Comm).
128 [2009] EWHC 3116 (Comm).

sound reason not to give it this clear and decisive effect. He also noted that the contract was "a carefully drawn standard form intended for widespread commercial use". Christopher Clarke J said:

"Whilst the parties have not used the expression 'condition' or 'repudiatory breach' they have specified that any failure to pay which continues after the first Local Business Day after notice of failure will entitle BNP to designate an Early Termination Date; and have gone on to provide that upon an effective designation no further payments or deliveries (the primary obligations under the contract) will be due."[129]

10-074   Christopher Clarke J continued:

"In providing for BNP's entitlement to terminate the ongoing primary obligations of the parties and the method of calculation of the sum to be paid in that event, the parties have ... spelt out the consequences which result from a breach of condition. It is unrealistic to suppose that, having done so, they are to be taken to have intended that a failure to pay should be regarded as a warranty or an innominate term."[130]

10-075   Christopher Clarke J added:

"I do not ignore the fact that there are cases in which the Court has declined to accept that a provision that 'any' breach of contract shall give rise to a right to terminate extends to any breach whatever; and have restricted it to such breaches as are repudiatory: 'The Antaios' [1985] A.C. 191, HL; Rice v Great Yarmouth BC [2001] 3 LGLR 4. But it is open to the parties to agree that any non-payment or non-delivery shall have that consequence and that, as it seems to me, is exactly what the draftsman of the [present agreement] has done, in a carefully drawn standard form intended for widespread commercial use."[131]

10-076   Similarly, in *Kuwait Rocks Co v AMN Bulkcarriers Inc ("The Astra")* Flaux J held that the following clause gave the owner a right to terminate the contract and to recover damages for breach:

"failing the punctual and regular payment of the hire, or bank guarantee ... the Owners shall be at liberty to withdraw the vessel from the service of the Charterers, without prejudice to any claim they (the Owners) may otherwise have".[132]

But this analysis was overruled in the *Spar Shipping* case which is considered in the next paragraph.

10-077   **Late payment of hire clause not rendering time of the essence**   In *Spar Shipping AS v Grand China Logistics Holding (Group) Co Ltd ("The Spar Draco")*[133] the Court of Appeal (upholding Popplewell J) held that the balance of authorities[134] supported the view that in a charterparty a duty to pay hire on time is not a condition but an intermediate term (overruling *Kuwait Rocks Co v AMN Bulkcarriers Inc ("The Astra")*, on which see para.10-076).

Clause 11 in *"The Spar Draco"* provided for payment by the charterer as follows:

---

[129] [2009] EWHC 3116 (Comm).
[130] [2009] EWHC 3116 (Comm).
[131] [2009] EWHC 3116 (Comm).
[132] *Kuwait Rocks Co v AMN Bulkcarriers Inc ("The Astra")* [2013] EWHC 865 (Comm); [2013] 2 Lloyd's Rep. 69, Flaux J; noted J. Shirley (2013) 130 L.Q.R. 185–188.
[133] [2016] EWCA Civ 982; [2016] 2 Lloyd's Rep. 447 (Gross, Hamblen LJJ, Sir Terence Etherton MR) (affirming [2015] EWHC 718 (Comm); [2015] 1 All E.R. (Comm) 879, Popplewell J).
[134] Collected at [2015] EWHC 718 (Comm); [2015] 1 All E.R. (Comm) 879 at [188].

"Failing the punctual and regular payment of the hire, or on any fundamental breach whatsoever of this Charter Party, the Owners shall be at liberty to withdraw the Vessel from the service of the Charterers without prejudice to any claims they (the Owners) may otherwise have on the Charterers."

And there was also a Grace Period provision:

"Where there is a failure to make punctual and regular payment of hire due to oversight, negligence, errors or omissions on the part of the Charterers or their bankers, the Charterers shall be given by the Owners 3 clear banking days ... written notice to rectify the failure, and when so rectified within those 3 days following the Owners' notice the payment shall stand as regular and punctual. Failure by the Charterers to pay the hire within 3 days of their receiving the Owners' notice as provided herein, shall entitle the Owners to withdraw as set forth in Sub-clause 11(a) above."

The Court of Appeal's conclusion in *Spar Shipping AS v Grand China Logistics* **10-078**
Holding (Group) Co Ltd ("The Spar Draco")[135] was that these provisions gave the owner the option to withdraw the vessel in the event of late payment, but they did not render punctual payment a condition. In other words, the Court of Appeal and Popplewell J in the *Spar Shipping* case applied the "option to cancel" without breach analysis adopted in *Financings Ltd v Baldock*.[136] And so exercise of the option to withdraw the vessel would entitle the owner to claim for hire not paid (past breaches and accrued sums) but would not render the charterer liable to pay damages in respect of the owner's prospective loss following termination of the contract.

However, the Court of Appeal (earlier, Popplewell J) in *Spar Shipping AS v* **10-079**
Grand China Logistics Holding (Group) Co Ltd ("The Spar Draco") then addressed the issue whether the charterer's conduct had manifested a renunciation of the contract entitling the innocent party to terminate for breach and obtain damages. Popplewell J at first instance defined renunciation in these terms:[137]

"Conduct is renunciatory if it evinces an intention to commit a repudiatory breach, that is to say if it would lead a reasonable person to the conclusion that the party does not intend to perform his future obligations where the failure to perform such obligations when they fell due would be repudiatory ... Evincing an intention to perform but in a manner which is substantially inconsistent with the contractual terms is evincing an intention not to perform: *Ross T Smyth & Co Ltd v T.D. Bailey, Son & Co* [1940] 3 All E.R. 60 at 72. Whether such conduct is renunciatory depends upon whether the threatened difference in performance is repudiatory."

On the distinction between actual breach constituting repudiation and a renuncia- **10-080**
tion, Popplewell J said in *Spar Shipping AS v Grand China Logistics Holding (Group) Co Ltd ("The Spar Draco")*:[138]

"conduct comprising a breach or breaches of obligations which have fallen due may be insufficient to be a repudiation but nevertheless be conduct which is a renunciation because it would lead the reasonable observer to conclude that there was an intention not to perform in the future, and the past and threatened future breaches taken together would

---

[135] [2016] EWCA Civ 982; [2016] 2 Lloyd's Rep. 446 (Gross, Hamblen LJJ, Sir Terence Etherton MR) (affirming [2015] EWHC 718 (Comm); [2015] 1 All E.R. (Comm) 879, Popplewell J).
[136] *Financings Ltd v Baldock* [1963] 2 Q.B. 104 CA at 110–111, 121.
[137] [2015] EWHC 718 (Comm); [2015] 1 All E.R. (Comm) 879 at [92]–[208]; affirmed [2016] EWCA Civ 982; [2016] 2 Lloyd's Rep. 447 (Gross, Hamblen LJJ, Sir Terence Etherton MR).
[138] [2015] EWHC 718 (Comm); [2015] 1 All E.R. (Comm) 879 at [209]; affirmed [2016] EWCA Civ 982; [2016] 2 Lloyd's Rep. 447 (Gross, Hamblen LJJ, Sir Terence Etherton MR).

be repudiatory. Such conduct is not infrequently referred to in the cases simply as a repudiation, but is more accurately described as a renunciation in the nomenclature I have adopted. The reason why a defaulting party commits an actual breach is generally irrelevant to whether it constitutes a breach, or whether the breach is a repudiation. But the reason may be highly relevant to what such breach would lead the reasonable observer to conclude about the defaulting party's intentions in relation to future performance, and therefore to the issue of renunciation. Often the question whether conduct is a renunciation falls to be judged by reference to the defaulting party's intention which is objectively evinced both by past breaches and by other words and conduct."

10-081   Popplewell J found (and the decision was affirmed by the Court of Appeal) on the facts of *Spar Shipping AS v Grand China Logistics Holding (Group) Co Ltd ("The Spar Draco")* that the charterer's long-standing and continuing pattern of late payment constituted a renunciation.[139] This entitled the owner to damages for the difference between the amounts received or recoverable in the market during the remainder of the time charter and the rate payable under the present contract:[140]

> "A failure to replace the lost bargain with a series of successive shorter time charters does not break the chain of causation any more than a choice to employ the vessel on the spot market. Neither reflects an ability to replace the lost bargain in specie. Provided the course taken by the owner is reasonable, his actual earnings from the subsequent employment of the vessel in either manner, or a combination of the two, or any other combination of reasonable methods of earning revenue from the vessel, are legally caused by the charterer's breach; and the amount by which actual earnings in such employment fall short of the hire which would have been earned under the broken charter is the measure of loss naturally arising out of the charterer's breach."

10-082   **Gateway (v) to finding a condition: general construction of the contract**[141]   If none of the preceding four tests renders the relevant obligation a "condition", the present "Gateway" provides "one last chance" that the court (or arbitral tribunal) might characterise the term as a "condition". The following test applies (taken from *Chitty on Contracts*,[142] and endorsed by Lords Wilberforce and Roskill in *Bunge Corp v Tradax Export SA*):[143]

> "the nature of the contract or the subject matter or the circumstances of the case might

---

139 [2015] EWHC 718 (Comm); [2015] 1 All E.R. (Comm) 879 at [211]–[215]; affirmed [2016] EWCA Civ 982; [2016] 2 Lloyd's Rep. 447 (Gross, Hamblen LJJ, Sir Terence Etherton MR).

140 [2015] EWHC 718 (Comm); [2015] 1 All E.R. (Comm) 879 at [223]; affirmed [2016] EWCA Civ 982; [2016] 2 Lloyd's Rep. 447 (Gross, Hamblen LJJ, Sir Terence Etherton MR).

141 Lord Wilberforce in *Bunge v Tradax* [1981] 1 W.L.R. 711 at 715–716 HL (noted F. Reynolds, "Discharge of Contract by Breach" (1981) 97 L.Q.R. 541; J. Carter, "Classification of Contractual Terms: The New Orthodoxy" [1981] C.L.J. 219) made clear that category (v) survives despite Diplock LJ's remarks *HongKong Fir Shipping Co Ltd v Kawasaki Kisen Kaisha Ltd* [1962] 2 Q.B. 1 CA at 69–70. Lord Wilberforce confirmed in the *Bunge* case that the courts can, in appropriate circumstances, find that a term is to operate as a condition, even though the contract has not explicitly stipulated for this. He rejected Diplock LJ's suggestion in the *Hongkong Fir* case that, unless the relevant clause has been classified by legislation or the parties' own provision as a condition, the innocent party is entitled to terminate for breach only if the consequences of breach have been very serious indeed. Diplock LJ's view is simply wrong and it is not English law. Instead the courts are prepared to classify a promissory term as a condition even though the contract does not so explicitly categorise the term in this way.

142 Passage now appearing at H.G. Beale (gen. ed.), *Chitty on Contracts*, 34th edn (London: Sweet & Maxwell, 2021), para.27-017.

143 *Bunge Corp New York v Tradax SA* [1981] 1 W.L.R. 711 HL at 715–716, 726 (also citing Lord Diplock in *Photo Production v Securicor Transport Ltd* [1980] A.C. 822 HL at 840).

support the conclusion that the parties must, by necessary implication, have intended that the innocent party would be discharged from further performance of his obligations in the event that the term was not fully and precisely complied with."

In 2021 the Court of Appeal in *EMFC Loan Syndications LLP v Resort Group Plc*[144] formulated the following summary of the legal test in this context: **10-083**

"[89] The question of whether a clause is a condition is a matter of construction. The court must look at the contract, in light of the surrounding circumstances, and decide whether the intention of the parties, as gathered from the instrument itself, will best be carried out by treating the particular promise as a warranty sounding only in damages or a condition in respect of which the failure to perform relieves the innocent party of further performance under the contract. Thus it is a question of identifying the intention of the parties on the true construction of the contract. Where, upon the true construction of the contract, the parties have not made the term a condition, it will be innominate if a breach may result in trivial, minor or very grave consequences. Unless it is clear that a term is intended to be a condition or (only) a warranty, it will be innominate. The courts should not be too ready to interpret contractual clauses as conditions. The modern approach is that a term is innominate unless a contrary intention is made clear. (See generally *Chitty on Contracts*, now 34th edn, (2021), para. 27-045, 27-046, and for example *Bunge Corpn, New York v Tradax Export SA, Panama* [1981] 1 WLR 711, 719 and 725; *Spar Shipping AS v Grand China Logistics Holding (Group) Co Ltd* [2017] Bus LR 663 at para 52.)"

Applying this test, the Court of Appeal in *EMFC Loan Syndications LLP v Resort Group Plc*[145] concluded that the clause in this case did not constitute a condition, for the following reasons: **10-084**

"[91] In my judgment, on a true construction of the Contract, clause 1.2 ['1.2 EMFC shall be working in conjunction with the Company's debt advisor, Investec Bank plc'] is not properly to be classified as a condition. My reasons are as follows:

(i)   Clause 1.2 appears in the opening 'Appointment' section of the Contract. It does not expressly impose any obligation on EMFC. Rather it reads as a record of the factual background: 'EMFC shall be working in conjunction with … Investec …' This is not clearly a contractual obligation of any sort (even without considering problems of lack of clarity and certainty considered further below);

(ii)   Even if clause 1.2 is to be read as amounting to a contractual obligation, it is not expressed to be a condition and appears as an innominate term. There is no contrary intention made clear anywhere in the Contract;

(iii)   Clause 1.2 does not appear in the list of conditions expressly identified in section 3 of the Contract;

(iv)   Clause 1.2 does not carry the clarity or certainty to be expected of a condition, given the consequences of breach. It is not at all clear what is meant by 'working in conjunction with' Investec. It would appear to encompass working directly together on a certain task or, for example, working entirely separately but in sequence;

(v)   Allied to this, given the breadth of clause 1.2, breach could have trivial, minor or very grave consequences. It could have no consequences. This is contra-indicative of a condition."

Earlier, in *Compagnie Commerciale Sucre et Denrees v C Czarnikow ("The*   **10-085**

---

[144]   [2021] EWCA Civ 844; [2022] 1 W.L.R. 717 at [89] (Carr LJ, with the agreement of Baker and Lewis LJJ).
[145]   [2021] EWCA Civ 844; [2022] 1 W.L.R. 717 at [91] (Carr LJ, with the agreement of Baker and Lewis LJJ).

Naxos"),[146] Lord Ackner (adopting Kerr LJ's analysis in *State Trading Corp of India Ltd v M Golodetz Ltd*)[147] noted "the classic judgment" of Bowen LJ in *Bentsen v Taylor Sons & Co (No.2)*:[148]

"There is no way of deciding that question except by looking at the contract in the light of the surrounding circumstances, and then making up one's mind whether the intention of the parties, as gathered from the instrument itself, will best be carried out by treating the promise as a warranty sounding only in damages, or as a condition precedent by the failure to perform which the other party is relieved of his liability."

10-086   Also in *Compagnie Commerciale Sucre et Denrees v C Czarnikow ("The Naxos")*,[149] Lord Ackner adopted Kerr LJ's comment in *State Trading Corp of India Ltd v M. Golodetz Ltd*)[150] that:

"At the end of the day, if there is no other more specific guide to the correct solution to a particular dispute, the court may have no alternative but to follow the general statement of Bowen LJ in *Bentsen v Taylor Sons & Co (No.2)* ... by making what is in effect a value judgement about the commercial significance of the term in question."

10-087   As noted at para.11-026, in *Pharmapac (UK) Ltd v HBS Healthcare Ltd* it was held that sales agreements for wholesale supply of face masks at the peak of the Covid pandemic, involved specified delivery dates which, as a matter of construction, rendered time of the essence (for other aspects of this case see paras 11-026, 14-042 and 14-067).[151]

10-088   By contrast, in *DD Classics Ltd v Chen*[152] (also on this case see paras 12-019, 14-068) Judge Keyser QC held that a date for payment in the contract of sale (a special motor car, worth €3.3 million) did not, when construed and considered in its commercial context, constitute a condition. The judge noted that in sales of goods there is no presumption that a specified date for payment renders time of the essence, citing at [43] this passage from *Chitty*:[153] "However, under the Sale of Goods Act 1979 s.10, unless a different intention appears from the terms of the contract, stipulations as to time of *payment* are not deemed to be of the essence of the contract of sale ". There were three factors which in fact operated to reinforce the presumption on the present facts. First, the wording[154] of the contract contained a distinction: although the clause concerning transfer of ownership (cl.4) had specifically referred to "time of the essence", by contrast the clause (cl.3) requiring payment on a specified day did not use the same wording. Secondly, the present of a right to withdraw

---

[146] [1990] 1 W.L.R. 1337 HL at 1347; noted G.H. Treitel, "Time of Shipment in f.o.b. Contracts" [1991] L.M.C.L.Q. 147–154 (noting at 152 and 154 that the decision is consistent with the need for (i) promotion of certainty, and (ii) the commercial importance of the term); and M. Clarke, "Time and Essence of Mercantile Contracts: The Law Loses its Way" [1991] C.L.J. 29.

[147] [1989] 2 Lloyd's Rep. 277 CA at 281–283.

[148] [1893] 2 Q.B. 274 CA at 281.

[149] [1990] 1 W.L.R. 1337 HL at 1347; noted G.H. Treitel, "Time of Shipment in f.o.b. Contracts" (1991) L.M.C.L.Q. 147–154 (observing at 152 and 154 that the decision is consistent with the need for (i) promotion of certainty, and (ii) the commercial importance of the term); and M. Clarke, "Time and Essence of Mercantile Contracts: The Law Loses its Way" [1991] C.L.J. 29.

[150] [1989] 2 Lloyd's Rep. 277 CA at 281–283.

[151] [2022] EWHC 23 (Comm) at [5] and [12] (Judge Cadwallader).

[152] [2022] EWHC 1357 (Comm) (Judge Keyser QC).

[153] Now, H.G. Beale (gen. ed.), *Chitty on Contracts* (34th edn, Sweet & Maxwell, London, 2021), para.24-052, cited by Judge Keyser QC, [2022] EWHC 1357 (Comm) at [43].

[154] [2022] EWHC 1357 (Comm) at [17], citing the text of the contract (Judge Keyser QC).

for late payment did not itself make the payment obligation a condition, the judge noting Court of Appeal authority on this last point.[155] Thirdly, there was insufficient material to displace that presumption, the judge commenting:[156]

> "[47] As the wording of the contract does not make clear that the time for payment here was a condition, one has to ask whether there are any circumstances of the contract or the nature of the subject matter which indicate that it must be construed as a condition. In that regard, nothing plausible has been identified in the circumstances of the contract. And, as I have already remarked, the subject matter of the contract is not such as to make its value highly time-sensitive, so that the time of the payment obligation will be construed to be of the essence. Rather, the case falls under the general commercial position that in a mercantile or commercial contract the time of payment will not be deemed to be of the essence. There is nothing to indicate the contrary."

Factors indicating a condition or an innominate term

Indicia suggested by commentators   And Chen-Wishart has suggested that the following rough guidance can be distilled from the modern case law. She suggests that a "condition" is likely to be found if it "involves a single performance with a clearly specified time and sequence of performance", or "it can only be breached in one way", or "is vital to the contract" or "necessary for commercial certainty", or damages would be difficult to assess. Conversely, she suggests that an innominate term is likely to arise if the term "can be breached in different ways with varying degrees of seriousness", or "performance is to take place over a long time and substantial performance may have been given" or "the obligation is loosely framed".[157] But such generalities are merely pointers. Carter[158] has suggested that the following factors (not an exhaustive list) will be relevant when determining whether the parties have impliedly agreed that a term is to be treated as a promissory condition: **10-089**

> "(a)   the form and structure of the term; whether entry into the contract was motivated by an understanding on the part of [the innocent party] that the term would be strictly complied with;
> (b)   the relationship between the term in issue and the other terms of the contract;
> (c)   the likely effects of any breach of the term;
> (d)   the extent to which the [innocent party] will be adequately compensated by an award of damages for breach of the term;
> (e)   whether construing the term as a condition will achieve a reasonable result;
> (f)   the nature of the contract in which the term appears;
> (g)   the nature of the subject matter of the contract;
> (h)   the nature of the term and the obligation which it creates."

---

[155] [2022] EWHC 1357 (Comm) at [46] (Judge Keyser QC): "I refer in particular to the judgment of Leggatt J in *Newland Shipping and Forwarding Ltd v Toba Trading FZC* [2014] EWHC 661 (Comm) at [49]–[54]. I refer also to the decision of the Court of Appeal in *Grand China Logistics Holding (Group) Co Ltd v Spar Shipping AS (Rev 1)* [2016] EWCA Civ 982 and, in particular, to the observation of Hamblen LJ at [93], in the context of a charterparty, that: '...the inclusion of an express right of withdrawal is an indication that payment of hire timeously is not a condition, since its inclusion would otherwise be unnecessary. On any view it does not make it clear that it is a condition.'...".

[156] [2022] EWHC 1357 (Comm) at [47] (Judge Keyser QC).

[157] M. Chen-Wishart, *Contract Law*, 7th edn (Oxford: Oxford University Press, 2022), p.515 (s.12.2.3.2(iii)).

[158] J.W. Carter, *Carter's Breach of Contract*, 2nd edn (Oxford: Hart Publishing, 2019), [5-14].

10-090   *Case law guidance*   There is an inevitable residuum of careful and contextual assessment to be made in particular situations when classifying a particular obligation. As Kerr LJ noted in *State Trading Corp of India Ltd v M Golodetz Ltd*, the court must form a "value judgement about the commercial significance of the term in question".[159] However, Kerr LJ's analysis in that case does yield more concrete guidance. He emphasised these points:[160] (i) it is not decisive[161] that a commercial contract prescribes a precise time for compliance; (ii) it might be that the relevant obligation is relatively minor and not central to the contract; (iii) there might be that there are internal points of construction tending against the conclusion that the obligation is a condition (in that case a similar obligation elsewhere in the contract was expressly described as *not being a condition*); (iv) the loss flowing from breach might not be great in comparison with other sums payable, and possible sources of loss capable of arising, under the same contract; (v) the relevant obligation might not be one which needs to be satisfied before the other contractual machinery can proceed; and (vi) it might be significant that the contract does not form part of a "string"[162] of transactions.

Ark Shipping Co LLC v Silverburn Shipping (IoM) Ltd[163] arguably indicates the following tendency: in the absence of express characterisation of a term as a condition, a term which, once breached, can give rise to a range of consequences is likely to be treated as an innominate term (even if capable of being breached only in one manner or in a narrow set of ways), unless there is textual or contextual evidence that it is intended to be, or commercially it would make good sense, or strongly desirable, that it should be a condition. In this case a term in a 15-year demise (or bareboat) charterparty requiring the charterer to maintain at all times the vessels' classification was held to be an innominate term (classification societies are independent maritime inspectors of vessels, effectively ensuing the maritime equivalent of a MOT certificate system). Gross LJ considered a large range of factors but concluded that there was nothing to render this obligation so significant that any breach would justify termination. The term stated that the charterers were required to "keep the Vessel with unexpired classification of the class indicated in

---

[159] [1989] 2 Lloyd's Rep. 277 CA at 283 col.2 per Kerr LJ.

[160] [1989] 2 Lloyd's Rep. 277 at 283 col.2 to 284.

[161] *Bunge Corp New York v Tradax SA* [1981] 1 W.L.R. 711 HL at 719 per Lord Lowry: "The treatment of time limits as conditions in mercantile contracts does not appear to me to be justifiable by any presumption of fact or rule of law, but rather to be a practical expedient founded on and dictated by the experience of businessmen". But Lord Wilberforce at 715–716 indicated that the court might lean in favour of the condition analysis if the clause is a time obligation (other than for payment of money) and it appears in a mercantile contract: "It remains true, as [Roskill LJ] has pointed out in *Cehave NV v Bremer Handelsgesellschaft mbH ('The Hansa Nord')* [1976] Q.B. 44 at 70–71, that the courts should not be too ready to interpret contractual clauses as conditions. And I have myself commended, and continue to commend, the greater flexibility in the law of contracts to which *Hongkong Fir* points the way (*Reardon Smith Line Ltd v Yngvar Hansen-Tangen* [1976] 1 W.L.R. 989 at 998). But I do not doubt that, in suitable cases, the courts should not be reluctant, if the intentions of the parties as shown by the contract so indicate, to hold that an obligation has the force of a condition, and that indeed they should usually do so in the case of time clauses in mercantile contracts." Roskill LJ said in *"The Hansa Nord"* [1976] Q.B. 44 CA at 70–71: "... a court should not be over ready, unless required by statute or authority so to do. to construe a term in a contract as a 'condition' any breach of which gives rise to a right to reject rather than as a term any breach of which sounds in damages".

[162] Contrasting *Bunge Corp New York v Tradax SA* [1981] 1 W.L.R. 711 HL (noted F. Reynolds, "Discharge of Contract by Breach" (1981) 97 L.Q.R. 541; J. Carter, "Classification of Contractual Terms: The New Orthodoxy" [1981] C.L.J. 219).

[163] [2019] EWCA Civ 1161; [2019] 2 Lloyd's Rep. 603.

Box 10 and with other required certificates in force at all times". The arbitrators had regarded this as an innominate term. Carr J had reversed and treated it as a condition.[164] But the Court of Appeal reinstated the arbitrators' award. With the agreement of McCombe and Leggatt LJJ, Gross LJ (who had given the main judgment in "*The Spar Draco*"; on that case para.10-077 ff) concluded that, both "textually and contextually",[165] the term was innominate and that[166] this avoided the "risk" of "trivial breaches having disproportionate consequences destructive of a long-term contractual relationship".

Nine main factors were considered by the Court of Appeal in the *Ark Shipping* **10-091**
case in reaching the conclusion that the term was innominate. In this battle of the warring factors, as we shall now see, the solitary "condition" argument lost i-viii to the "innominate term" arguments. Only point (iv) counted in favour of the condition argument. But even that point was directly nullified by point (viii) (the wide range of consequences of breach). The nine factors were:

(i)   the absence of express stipulation that it was a condition;[167]

(ii)   the clause did not require performance at a particular time (but rather maintenance of a complex set of documentary statuses);[168]

(iii)   there was no issue of interdependent performance;[169]

(iv)   admittedly, there was only one type of breach possible here, rather than a range, but this factor was outweighed by the others;[170]

(v)   the relevant clause was part of a set of repair and maintenance-related obligations, and these other obligations were not conditions;[171]

(vi)   there was a troubling widening of the category of documents, beyond the classification certificate, to "other required certificates in force at all times";[172]

(vii)   even the discrete obligation to maintain insurance was not a condition;[173]

(viii)   the consequences of breach would vary a lot: ranging across "trivial, minor or very grave consequences" (at [77] the underlying factual situation "peeped out", Gross LJ noting that the lapse in certification took place during a short period when the vessel, a tug, was in dry dock undergoing repair);[174]

(ix)   the advantages of certainty are outweighed here by the danger of "trivial breaches having disproportionate consequences".[175]

Another instructive decision is *PT Berlian Laju Tanker TBK v, Nuse Shipping Ltd* **10-092**
(*"The Aktor"*).[176] The seller of a ship had agreed to receive a 10 per cent deposit at a Singapore bank. But the full price, 100 per cent payment, had to be paid at a Greek bank. The buyer had paid the 10 per cent deposit into a joint account held at a

---

164 [2019] EWHC 376 (Comm); [2019] 1 Lloyd's Rep. 554.
165 *Ark Shipping case* [2019] EWCA Civ 1161; [2019] 2 Lloyd's Rep. 603 at [53] per Gross LJ.
166 *Ark Shipping case* [2019] EWCA Civ 1161; [2019] 2 Lloyd's Rep. 603 at [81] per Gross LJ.
167 [2019] EWCA Civ 1161; [2019] 2 Lloyd's Rep. 603 at [54].
168 [2019] EWCA Civ 1161; [2019] 2 Lloyd's Rep. 603 at [55].
169 [2019] EWCA Civ 1161; [2019] 2 Lloyd's Rep. 603 at [56].
170 [2019] EWCA Civ 1161; [2019] 2 Lloyd's Rep. 603 at [57].
171 [2019] EWCA Civ 1161; [2019] 2 Lloyd's Rep. 603 at [58]–[61].
172 [2019] EWCA Civ 1161; [2019] 2 Lloyd's Rep. 603 at [62]–[65].
173 [2019] EWCA Civ 1161; [2019] 2 Lloyd's Rep. 603 at [66]–[71].
174 [2019] EWCA Civ 1161; [2019] 2 Lloyd's Rep. 603 at [72]–[77].
175 [2019] EWCA Civ 1161; [2019] 2 Lloyd's Rep. 603 at [78] and [81].
176 [2008] EWHC 1330 (Comm); [2008] 2 All E.R. (Comm) 784; [2008] 2 Lloyd's Rep. 246.

Singaporean bank, which sum could be released only with the joint consent of the parties. The buyer insisted that it would only pay 90 per cent of the price at a Greek bank and that it would be enough that it agreed on delivery day to release the deposit in Singapore so that it became payable outright to the seller.[177] Upholding the arbitrators' award, Christopher Clarke J held that it was a condition that the payment should be made in Greece and that this payment should comprise 100 per cent of the price.

Christopher Clarke J began by noting that the buyers contended that the mode of payment was merely subject to a set of innominate terms: concluded:[178]

"The Buyers [resisting the view that the payment obligations were conditions] suggested that their payment obligations in respect of the price covered a number of matters: what the price was, when it should be paid, how it should be paid, and where it should be paid. Some breaches of those obligations, such as a refusal to pay the full amount would entitle the Sellers to terminate. Others would not. Here there was no question of the Buyers not paying in full, or not paying when the vessel was ready for delivery. The only issue was as to where the 10% should be paid. The obligation to pay 10% at NBG, Piraeus, if that was what the Buyers were bound to do, is an innominate term ... [and so] the Sellers would be entitled to recover any proved loss resulting from the 10% payment being made [in Singapore and not in Greece]. But [the Sellers] would not be entitled to throw up the whole contract."

10-093   But Christopher Clarke J rejected this, preferring the view that these obligations had real commercial significance and that they should be categorised as implied conditions:[179]

"... In *Bunge Corp v Tradax Export SA* [1981] 1 W.L.R. 711 Lord Roskill accepted that in a mercantile contract where a term has to be performed by one party as a condition precedent to the ability of the other party to perform another term, especially an essential term such as the nomination of a single loading port, the term as to time of performance of the former obligation would in general be treated as a condition. One of the reasons for this is the need for certainty in mercantile contracts; and the need for the parties to know where they stand at the time rather than wait upon events before their rights can be determined. In the present case payment of the purchase price and delivery of the vessel were concurrent conditions. That alone seems to me sufficient to render the obligation to tender payment in accordance with the provisions of the contract which specify how payment is to be made as a condition. Such a conclusion is supported by a consideration of the nature of payment."

10-094   Christopher Clarke J cogently observed:[180]

"The parties cannot have contemplated that the Sellers would be bound to make delivery of a valuable vessel without payment in full of the purchase price in accordance with the terms of the contract. Crediting the Sellers with some or all of the purchase price otherwise than at the place stipulated for payment would be likely to [delay satisfaction of any secured loan received by the seller as against the value of the vessel]; and would expose the Sellers to the risk involved in transferring the monies from the non-contractual place,

---

[177] An earlier version of the parties' agreement had so provided; but Clarke J agreed with the arbitrators that this version had been superseded by another version and that there was no scope to rectify the later version by reference to the preceding version: the latter version was intended to supersede in all respects the earlier version.

[178] [2008] EWHC 1330 (Comm); [2008] 2 All E.R. (Comm) 784; [2008] 2 Lloyd's Rep. 246 at [65].

[179] [2008] EWHC 1330 (Comm); [2008] 2 All E.R. (Comm) 784 at [66].

[180] [2008] EWHC 1330 (Comm); [2008] 2 All E.R. (Comm) 784 at [68].

where or from which the Buyers purported to make payment, to the place agreed. Monies that pass through the banking system may become unavailable to the payee because of claims to the money, or claims to freeze the money, by banks or others."

Christopher Clarke J concluded:[181]　　　　　　　　　　　　　　　　　**10-095**

"The arbitrators decided that paying 10% of the price by the release of the deposit in Singapore could not be said to satisfy the obligation that the purchase price 'be paid in full free of bank charges to Sellers nominated bank' ... [and] that the obligation to pay 100% of the purchase price at the Buyers' nominated bank in Piraeus was a condition of the contract; and that paying 10% of that price by releasing the deposit in Singapore would constitute a breach of that condition. I agree."

III.　STATUTORY CONTROL OF OVER-TECHNICAL REJECTION OF GOODS BY COMMERCIAL BUYERS

In the context of sales of goods (and goods and services transactions),[182] a 1994 **10-096** statutory amendment (Sale of Goods Act 1979 s.15A) is designed to counter over-technical termination by commercial[183] buyers based on sellers' breaches of implied conditions. Sale of Goods Act 1979 s.15A[184] allows the courts to hold that a buyer cannot reject goods even though the seller has breached an implied term contained in ss.13–15 (on which see para.10-098) of that statute (those provisions insert implied terms which are classified as conditions). This result is expressed as follows: "the breach is not to be treated as a breach of condition but may be treated as a breach of warranty". Section 15A(2) of the 1979 Act provides that s.15A does not apply if "a contrary intention appears in, or is to be implied from, the contract".[185] And so s.15A will not apply where the parties have expressly categorised the relevant term as a condition, or where the parties have expressly stated that termination is justified no matter how slight the defective performance might be.

The change followed a (controversial) recommendation by the Law Commis- **10-097** sion (1987).[186] Thus Treitel was unimpressed, commenting that "the section undermines the certainty which classification of the implied terms in question as conditions was intended to provide".[187] Michael Bridge is also critical.[188]

Sale of Goods Act 1979 s.13(1) concerns correspondence of goods with their **10-098** description, whether or not the sale is made by a seller in the course of business. Section 14(2) to (2F) of the 1979 Act imposes the requirement that goods sold by a seller in the course of business must be "of satisfactory quality". Section 14(3) of the 1979 Act imposes the requirement that goods sold by a seller in the course

---

[181] [2008] EWHC 1330 (Comm); [2008] 2 All E.R. (Comm) 784 at [70].

[182] Inserted by Sale and Supply of Goods Act 1994 s.4; parallel provisions appear in Supply of Goods and Services Act 1982 ss.5A, 10A.

[183] M.G. Bridge, "The Sale and Supply of Goods Act 1994" [1995] J.B.L. 398, 403: "The moral impera-tive that justifies the removal of rejection rights for non-consumers does not extend to consumer buy-ers, the given reason being that they need all the leverage they can obtain against sellers."

[184] For details, *Benjamin's Sale of Goods*, 11th edn (London: Sweet & Maxwell, 2021), 12.024 ff; M.G. Bridge, "The Sale and Supply of Goods Act 1994" [1995] J.B.L. 398; "Sale and Supply of Goods" [1987] L. Com. No.160.

[185] Sale of Goods Act 1979 s.15A(2).

[186] Amendment made in 1994, implementing "Sale and Supply of Goods" [1987] L. Com. No.160.

[187] G.H. Treitel (E. Peel, ed), *The Law of Contract*, 15th edn (London: Sweet & Maxwell, 2020), para.18-061.

[188] M.G. Bridge, *The Sale of Goods*, 4th edn (Oxford: Oxford University Press, 2019), 10.23 and 10.29.

of business are "reasonably fit for" any "particular purpose", and this applies if the buyer "expressly or by implication makes known to the seller any particular purpose for which the goods are being bought". Section 15(2) concerns correspondence to sample, and imposes the further requirement that the goods must be "free from any defect making their quality unsatisfactory" if this defect "would not be apparent on reasonable examination of the sample".

10-099   Under s.15A, a commercial buyer will be entitled only to damages, and will not be entitled also to terminate the contract, if (i) the breach is so "slight" that it would be "unreasonable" to reject the goods; (ii) both the parties are engaged in trade or business; and (iii) the contract neither expressly nor impliedly precludes this conclusion.[189] The seller bears the burden of proving (i).[190] The test stated at (i) is an objective inquiry: there is no need to prove subjective bad faith on the buyer's part. The same provision states that it will not apply if "a contrary intention appears in, or is to be implied from, the contract".[191] And so this set of provisions will not affect the situation where the parties have expressly categorised a term as a condition, thereby permitting termination, no matter how slight the breach, or where the parties have expressly stated that termination is justified no matter how slight the defective performance might be.

It should be noted that s.15A does not render the seller's obligation an intermediate term in the Common Law sense. Instead s.15A permits the commercial buyer to terminate unless the breach is "slight". If the breach is not slight, the second issue of reasonableness does not arise. By contrast, breach of an intermediate term justifies termination only if the innocent party is substantially deprived of the expected benefit (para.12-010 ff). Section 15A of the 1979 Act adopts a different emphasis, therefore. There is a parallel provision: s.30(2A) of the 1979 Act adopts a similar approach where goods delivered to a non-consumer are less than, or greater than, the quantity contracted for, but this quantitative deviation is "so slight that it would be unreasonable for" the buyer to reject the goods.

10-100   It appears that s.15A of the Sales of Goods Act 1979 has been applied in only one reported case. At first instance, in *Filobake Ltd v Rondo Ltd and Frampton International Ltd* it was held that there had been a trivial breach by the second defendant.[192] That defendant had supplied a samosa pastry producing machine, but the judge concluded that the relevant breach yielded only nominal damages and that termination for breach on these facts was unjustified, applying s.15A of the 1979 Act. The finding of breach was not disturbed on appeal, nor did the Court of Appeal reconsider the judge's suggested applicability of s.15A of the Sale of Goods Act 1979, in favour of the seller.[193]

10-101   **Sale of Goods Act 1979 s.15A, and two older cases**   Sale of Goods Act 1979 s.15A is intended to prevent over-technical resort by buyers of sellers' breaches of conditions. Two pre-s.15A cases should be considered.

10-102   First, in *Re Moore & Co and Landauer & Co*[194] the buyer was held to be entitled to reject goods (some of which were) sent in boxes of 24 rather than in boxes of

---

189   On this last factor, Sale of Goods Act 1979 s.15(A)(2).
190   Sale of Goods Act 1979 s.15A(3).
191   Sale of Goods Act 1979 s.15A(2).
192   [2004] EWHC 695 (TCC) at [121], per Deputy High Court judge, Richard Seymour QC.
193   [2005] EWCA Civ 563 at [3].
194   [1921] 2 K.B. 519 CA (D.W. Greig, "Condition or Warranty?" (1973) 89 L.Q.R. 93 at 97)); see also *Reardon Smith Line Ltd v Hansen Tangen* [1976] 1 W.L.R. 989 HL at 998 per Lord Wilberforce; R.

30, the contract having required boxing in quantities of 30. The assumption made here is that the contractual description of the goods' packaging would form part of the implied term concerning a sale by description under Sale of Goods Act 1979 s.13(1). In this case, Scrutton LJ (a celebrated authority on commercial law) said (Bankes and Atkin LJJ agreeing):

> "a man who has bought under a contract thirty tins to the case may have sold under the same description, and may be placed in considerable difficulty by having goods tendered to him which do not comply with the description under which he bought, or under which he has resold".

Such facts would now be subject to the two-fold test of s.15A: (i) was the breach of condition in fact so "slight" that (ii) it would be "unreasonable" for the buyer to reject. It seems highly probable that this test would now operate in favour of the seller in such a case.

However, deviations in "packaging" are one thing. What of deviations from the agreed substance of the goods? Treitel[195] wonders whether s.15A would change the result in *Arcos v Ronaasen* where the supply of timber of 9/16ths of an inch was held not to be equivalent to the contractually stipulated dimension of half an inch (8/16ths).[196] If, as Treitel suggests, a 1/16th discrepancy is not necessarily "slight", the commercial buyer would remain entitled to reject the goods.   **10-103**

In greater detail, the facts in *Arcos v Ronaasen*[197] were as follows. The buyer undertook to supply timber "half an inch" thick. But the timber had swollen, following exposure to damp. When delivered, the timber was 9/16ths of an inch thick. At trial and on successive appeals it was unanimously held that the seller was in breach of an implied condition that the goods would correspond to their "description" (under the Sale of Goods Act 1979 s.13(1)). Lord Atkin emphasised that the goods did not conform to the contractual description. That breach of a condition entitled the buyer to reject. Lord Atkin suggested that if the seller had wanted to bargain for a "margin of tolerance", it might have expressly stipulated for this. This was not, he added, a "microscopic" deviation from a contractual specification. It was irrelevant that the buyer's true motive in rejecting the goods was to escape a bargain. The price had become unattractive because the market price of timber had fallen between the date of contract and that of delivery. But the law does not scrutinise and weigh the buyer's motives.[198]   **10-104**

Finally, Lord Atkin added in the *Arcos* case that it was not a sound counter-argument for the seller to assert that the goods were fit for their intended purpose   **10-105**

Brownsword, "Retrieving Reasons, Retrieving Rationality: a New Look at the Right to Withdraw for Breach of Contract" (1992) 5 J.C.L. 83, 88 fn.26 says that there was no indication in this case that the buyer was seeking to escape for market-related reasons.

[195] G.H. Treitel (E. Peel, ed), *The Law of Contract*, 15th edn (London: Sweet & Maxwell, 2020), para.18-060.

[196] [1933] A.C. 470 HL; on this case, D. Campbell in D. Campbell, L. Mulcahy and S. Wheeler (eds), *Changing Concepts of Contract* (Basingstoke: Palgrave, 2013), Ch.7.

[197] [1933] A.C. 470 HL; R. Brownsword, "Retrieving Reasons, Retrieving Rationality: a New Look at the Right to Withdraw for Breach of Contract" (1992) 5 J.C.L. 83, 89–90, objects to the decision that it condones bad faith and opportunistic termination; and at 92 he expresses the central dilemma or tension as follows: "the challenge is to devise a legal regime in which the [innocent party's] option to withdraw operates as a security against breach but without becoming an excuse in post-breach situations for the innocent party to discharge itself from its contractual obligations whenever market conditions so favour".

[198] R. Brownsword, "Retrieving Reasons, Retrieving Rationality: A New Look at the Right to Withdraw for Breach of Contract" (1992) 5 J.C.L. 83.

(under of the Sale of Goods Act 1979 s.14(3)). It was true that the buyer might have used the wood for its intended purpose, which was for use in the construction of cement barrels. But he suggested that this was a bad point because a buyer might legitimately change his intentions and wish to use the goods for another purpose. If so, the fact that the goods did not correspond with their contractual description might render them unsuitable for that new purpose.

10-106 Section 60 and Sch.1 para.15 of the Consumer Rights Act 2015 have extended the Sale of Goods Act 1979 s.15A to consumer contracts. Section 15A of the 1979 Act was previously confined to contracts where the buyer was not a consumer. However, the change is in fact of no practical effect.[199] This is because s.15A can only operates with respect to terms which are statutory "conditions" and the Consumer Rights Act 2015 does not use that terminology or concept with respect to the terms inserted under the 2015 statute into consumer contracts.

IV. Time Stipulations in General

10-107 This topic is examined in Ch.11. That said, it is impossible to accommodate topics exclusively within individual chapters. And so, for cases within Ch.10 which concern allegations that time was of the essence, see para.10.075 ff on *"The Spar Draco"* and compare *Union Eagle Ltd v Golden Achievement Ltd*, in the next section of this chapter, where time was of the essence.

V. Relief Against Forfeiture of Proprietary or Possessory Interests[200]

10-108 **Summary** This doctrine protects borrowers or tenants suffering forfeiture following non-payment of mortgage debts or of rent. The Supreme Court in *Vauxhall Motors Ltd v Manchester Ship Canal Co Ltd* (2019) held[201] that the equitable doctrine extends to relief against forfeiture of a proprietary or possessory interest in land, no less than such interests in personalty. Here a licensee (a manufacturing company) had rights of drainage, whereby it was permitted to discharge water and effluent into the licensor's canal. Crucially, the arrangement had given the licensee possessory rights with respect to the drainage structure which it had constructed on

---

[199] G.H. Treitel (E. Peel, ed), *The Law of Contract*, 14th edn (London: Sweet & Maxwell, 2015), para.18-056.

[200] Robert Walker LJ in *On Demand Plc v Gerson Plc* [2001] 1 W.L.R. 155 CA at 163G-172 (reversed on another basis [2003] 1 A.C. 368 HL); L. Gullifer in A. Burrows and E. Peel (eds), *Commercial Remedies: Current Issues and Problems* (Oxford: Oxford University Press, 2003), p.191 at 212 ff; J.D. Heydon, M.J. Leeming and P.G. Turner (eds), *Meagher, Gummow and Lehane's Equity: Doctrines and Remedies*, 5th edn (Sydney: LexisNexis, 2014), Pt 4(7); J. McGhee (general ed), *Snell's Equity*, 34th edn (London: Sweet & Maxwell), Ch.13, Part 3 (Ben MacFarlane); the Supreme Court in *Vauxhall Motors Ltd v Manchester Ship Canal Co Ltd* [2019] UKSC 46; [2019] 3 W.L.R. 852 held that the doctrine extends to relief against forfeiture of a proprietary or possessory interest in land, no less than such interests in personalty; for a successful application for relief, in a commercial context, against the background of a fight to wrest control of a company from a defaulting debtor, the share interest being security for a large loan, and where Lords Neuberger and Sumption dissented in the Privy Council, *Çlukurova Finance International Ltd and another v Alfa Telecom Turkey Ltd (Nos 3 to 5)* [2013] UKPC 2; [2013] UKPC 20 (for comments on this case, S.M. Waddams, "Good Faith, Good Conscience, and the Taking of Unfair Advantage", in A. Dyson, J. Goudkamp, F. Wilmot-Smith (eds), *Defences in Contract* (Oxford: Hart Publishing, 2017), Ch.4 at pp.80–83).

[201] [2019] UKSC 46; [2020] A.C. 1161.

the licensor's land. Thus the doctrine covers all forms of property, but not money[202] unless held under trust.[203] The doctrine (therefore) does not extend to mere in personam rights (rights under licences;[204] or a "time charterparty").[205] Sometimes it is too late to seek relief because the relevant subject matter has already been sold to an innocent third party.[206]

The current doctrine is another possible fetter upon an innocent party's capacity to call off a deal on the basis of the other party's contractual default. The main contexts in which this jurisdiction operates are relief in favour of borrowers or tenants for non-payment of mortgage debts or of rent. This jurisdiction cannot be employed as a means of re-writing an unfavourable bargain.[207] Nor can it be applied when it is too late to seek relief because the subject matter of a lease has already been sold to a third party. In such a case, it will not be possible to restore the parties to the status quo.[208]   **10-109**

As mentioned, the jurisdiction is not confined to land, but can include chattels, and intangible property, such as shares or proprietary interests in intellectual property rights. It does not apply to mere in personam rights, that is, mere obligations, such as rights in another's property held by a mere *licensee*, incapable of being asserted against third parties, but creating merely a personal duty as between licensor and licensee.[209]   **10-110**

Equitable relief is confined to "proprietary or possessory interests". The House of Lords in the *Sport International* case drew a distinction between mere contractual rights (such as a licensee's right to intellectual property) and enjoyment of a "proprietary" or "possessory" interest.[210] Thus a licensee's rights under a trade mark agreement are neither possessory nor proprietary for this purpose.[211] Nor, as decided in *"The Scaptrade"*, is a "time charterparty" a proprietary or possessory interest.[212] Money does not[213] fall within this doctrine's scope, unless it takes the form of a proprietary interest, as under a trust, or a beneficial interest in a resulting or   **10-111**

---

[202] *UK Housing Alliance (North West) Ltd v Francis* [2010] EWCA Civ 117; [2010] 3 All E.R. 519 at [14] per Longmore LJ (loss of contingent right to a payment; noted by C. Conte, "The jurisdiction to relieve against penalties and forfeitures: time for a rethink" (2010) 126 L.Q.R. 529–534).

[203] *Nutting v Baldwin* [1995] 1 W.L.R. 201 at 209 per Rattee J.

[204] *Sport Internationals Bussum BV v Inter-Footwear Ltd* [1984] 1 W.L.R. 776 HL; considered in *Celestial Aviation 1 Ltd v Paramount Airways Private Ltd* [2010] EWHC 185 (Comm); 2010] 1 C.L.C. 15, Hamblen J; noted by L. Aitken, "Forfeiture and the 'operating lease'" (2010) 126 L.Q.R. 505–507; see also *UK Housing Alliance (North West) Ltd v Francis* [2010] EWCA Civ 117; [2010] 3 All E.R. 519 at [14]; noted by C. Conte, "The jurisdiction to relieve against penalties and forfeitures: time for a rethink" (2010) 126 L.Q.R. 529–534.

[205] *"The Scaptrade"* [1983] 2 A.C. 694 HL.

[206] [1983] 2 A.C. 694 HL.

[207] Robert Walker LJ in *On Demand case* [2001] 1 W.L.R. 155 CA at 163G-172 (reversed on another basis [2003] 1 A.C. 368 HL).

[208] Robert Walker LJ in *On Demand case* [2001] 1 W.L.R. 155 CA at 163G-172 (reversed on another basis [2003] 1 A.C. 368 HL).

[209] *Sport Internationals Bussum BV v Inter-Footwear Ltd* [1984] 1 W.L.R. 776 HL; considered in *Celestial Aviation 1 Ltd v Paramount Airways Private Ltd* [2010] EWHC 185 (Comm); [2010] 1 C.L.C.15, Hamblen J; noted L. Aitken, "Forfeiture and the 'operating lease'" (2010) 126 L.Q.R. 505–507; see also *UK Housing Alliance (North West) Ltd v Francis* [2010] EWCA Civ 117; [2010] 3 All E.R. 519 at [14]; noted C. Conte, "The jurisdiction to relieve against penalties and forfeitures: time for a rethink" (2010) 126 L.Q.R. 529–534.

[210] *Sport Internationals Bussum BV v Inter-Footwear Ltd* [1984] 1 W.L.R. 776 HL at 794.

[211] *Sport Internationals Bussum BV v Inter-Footwear Ltd* [1984] 1 W.L.R. 776 HL at 794.

[212] [1983] 2 A.C. 694 HL.

[213] *UK Housing Alliance (North West) Ltd v Francis* [2010] EWCA Civ 117; [2010] 3 All E.R. 519 at

constructive trust[214] (otherwise, forfeiture of money payments is subject to relief in the case of deposits or instalment payments, according to the doctrine in *Stockloser v Johnson*[215] although the point was not directly decided in that case).

10-112 The Privy Council in *Union Eagle Ltd v Golden Achievement Ltd* held that relief against forfeiture of a proprietary or possessory interest does not protect a purchaser of real property who has yet to go into possession of the relevant property.[216] Equity's intervention in this context would overcomplicate termination of transactions where timely payment has clearly been made "of the essence". Lord Hoffmann said that unacceptable uncertainty would arise:[217]

> "the right to [terminate the contract for breach], though it involves termination of the purchaser's equitable interest, [has as its] purpose [the need to] restore to the vendor his freedom to deal with his land as he pleases … [A] vendor should be able to know with reasonable certainty whether he may resell the land or not."

10-113 *Union Eagle Ltd v Golden Achievement Ltd* concerned the purchase of a flat in Hong Kong. The buyer tendered the price only 10 minutes late, but the vendor decided to terminate the contract and forfeit the deposit (the market price was rising). The buyer unsuccessfully contended that, even before attempting to pay, he had acquired a sufficient equitable title (or equitable right) to the property and that Equity would relieve against such forfeiture in the interests of fairness. This argument was based on the purchaser's acquisition of a constructive trust interest, that is, an inchoate equitable title to the property. That interest had arisen *before the buyer defaulted* by making late payment of the price. This equitable interest, according to the purchaser, had been forfeited summarily by the vendor's decision to seize upon the purchaser's 10-minute delay as a ground for terminating the contract and triggering forfeiture of the deposit. But the Privy Council rejected this analysis:[218] vendors must be free to walk away from the deal if the purchase money is paid late when punctual performance "is of the essence". This attractively robust decision contrasts with the pro-guilty-party case law concerning intermediate terms (Ch.12) and the decisions in the *Schuler* (para.10-039 ff) and *Rice* (para.10-060) cases.

---

[14] per Longmore LJ (loss of contingent right to a payment; noted C. Conte, "The jurisdiction to relieve against penalties and forfeitures: time for a rethink" (2010) 126 L.Q.R. 529–534).

[214] *Nutting v Baldwin* [1995] 1 W.L.R. 201 at 209 per Rattee J.

[215] [1954] 1 Q.B. 476 CA; in essence, Equity can relieve a party in breach against forfeiture of instalments already paid if the sum retained by the innocent party would be wholly disproportionate to the loss suffered by him as a result of the breach. Denning LJ ([1954] 1 Q.B. 476 at 490) enunciated two criteria: *the sum to be forfeited must be penal*; secondly, *its retention would be unconscionable*. These tests should be applied at the time of the claim, not at the earlier date of the transaction's formation. Denning and Somervell LJJ's suggestion is attractive. The sums to be forfeited are not deposits in the strict sense, and the courts should be willing to discover whether the innocent party's retention of the sums would operate punitively and unfairly. For discussion: C. Mitchell, P. Mitchell, S. Watterson (eds), *Goff & Jones: The Law of Unjust Enrichment*, 10th edn (London: Sweet & Maxwell, 2022), Ch.14, also noting *Stern v McArthur* (1988) 165 C.L.R. 489 H.Ct. Aust.(on which, *Union Eagle Ltd v Golden Achievement Ltd* [1997] A.C. 514 PC at 522); L. Gullifer in A.S. Burrows and E. Peel (eds), *Commercial Remedies: Current Issues and Problems* (Oxford: Oxford University Press, 2003), pp.191, 205–212; and J. Edelman, *McGregor on Damages*, 21st edn (London: Sweet & Maxwell, 2021), para.16-108 ff.

[216] [1997] A.C. 514 PC.

[217] [1997] A.C. 514 PC at 520.

[218] [1997] A.C. 514 PC at 520.

VI. THE MITIGATION DOCTRINE'S INDIRECT RESTRICTION ON TERMINATION FOR RENUNCIATION OR REPUDIATION

The main discussion of mitigation occurs elsewhere in this work (Pt IV para.24-044). But here it is necessary to note the connection that can sometimes occur between this doctrine and the operation of the rules concerning breach. If the court concludes (necessarily with hindsight) that the mitigation doctrine should restrict the innocent party's damages, cutting back the normal measure available when the contract has been justifiably terminated for breach, the indirect effect is that the innocent party's ostensible right to terminate is in fact fettered: for the court will have concluded that he should have remained on contractual terms with the guilty party, notwithstanding the latter's repudiation. In this way mitigation by the back door, determines whether termination was justified. As we shall see, this is an aspect of "breach law" which has yet to be fully harmonised with the rather broad-brush judicial application of the mitigation principle. **10-114**

The essence of the mitigation doctrine[219] is that a claimant must take reasonable steps to mitigate his loss, either by reducing or even by eliminating that loss. If mitigation efforts are successful, the defendant's liability is adjusted accordingly: and if there is a failure to mitigate, to that extent damages will also be reduced. Thus, in the *British Westinghouse* case Viscount Haldane LC said: "[this principle] imposes on a plaintiff the duty of taking all reasonable steps to mitigate the loss consequent on the breach and debars him from claiming any part of the damage which is due to his neglect to take such steps".[220] The mitigation doctrine concerns only claims for damages. Thus, it does not apply to actions for debt (Pt IV para.24-045). The defendant bears the burden of proving that there has been a failure to mitigate.[221] Faced by the other's renunciation or repudiation, a party can normally elect to terminate the contract. This is elementary. However, if the innocent party does decide to terminate the contract on that basis, the mitigation doctrine might affect his capacity to obtain damages. **10-115**

There have been problematic cases concerning sale of goods.[222] In *Payzu Ltd v Saunders* the Court of Appeal held that the buyer had not been justified in reject- **10-116**

---

[219] A.S. Burrows, *Remedies for Torts and Breach of Contract*, 4th edn (Oxford: Oxford University Press, 2019), 127–132; M. Bridge, "Mitigation of Damages in Contract and the Meaning of Avoidable Loss" (1989) 105 L.Q.R. 398; M. Bridge, "The Market Rule of Damages Assessment" in D. Saidov and R. Cunnington (eds), *Contract Damages: Domestic and International Perspectives* (Oxford: Hart Publishing, 2008), Ch.18; H. McGregor, "*The Role of Mitigation in the Assessment of Damages*", in D. Saidov and R. Cunnington (eds), Ch.14; for comparative sources, G. H. Treitel, *Remedies for Breach of Contract* (Oxford: Oxford University Press, 1988), [145] ff; *Principles of European Contract Law*, 9.505 and *UNIDROIT's Principles of International Commercial Contracts*, 4th edn (2016) art.7.4.8. Text and comment is available at *http://www.unidroit.org/instruments/commercial-contracts/unidroit-principles-2016* [Accessed 8 March 2022]. On the UNIDROIT principles, S. Vogenauer, *Commentary on the UNIDROIT Principles of International Commercial Contracts*, 2nd edn (Oxford: Oxford University Press, 2015) and E Broerdermann, *UNIDROIT Principles of International Commercial Contracts: An Article-by-Article Commentary* (The Hague: Kluwer Law International, 2018); and the (abortive) *Contract Code: Drawn up on behalf of the English Law Commission* (Milano: 1993), s.439.

[220] [1912] A.C. 673 at 689 HL; e.g. when a house-owner had not acted unreasonably in refusing to allow the builder to effect repairs, *Iggleden v Fairview New Homes (Shooters Hill) Ltd* [2007] EWHC 1573 (TCC), Coulson J.

[221] *Geest Plc v Lansiquot* [2002] UKPC 48; [2002] 1 W.L.R. 3111 PC; *Roper v Johnson* (1873) L.R. 8 C.P. 167, 178, 181–182.

[222] H. McGregor, "The Role of Mitigation in the Assessment of Damages", in D. Saidov and R. Cunnington (eds), *Contract Damages: Domestic and International Perspectives* (Oxford: Hart Publish-

ing the seller's revised payment terms and that instead the buyer should have accepted the seller's offer to continue to deal on his new and unjustified terms.[223]

10-117   The defendant had agreed to sell crêpe de chine (a fabric) in lots. The buyer agreed that he would pay for each delivery within one month of receipt, but not necessarily in cash. The buyer paid late for the first consignment. The seller wrongly inferred that the buyer was close to insolvency. And so the seller insisted on cash payment for future deliveries. But the buyer did not accept this revision. Instead the buyer chose to terminate the contract by reason of the seller's repudiation. The buyer sued for damages, namely the difference between the market and contract prices, the market having risen. The Court of Appeal held that the buyer should have accepted the seller's revised terms of business, that is, the new offer to continue the contractual deliveries, in return for cash payments. The buyer's decision not to continue relations was a failure to mitigate his loss. The decision is surprising because the court's application of the mitigation principle here denied the buyer the right to terminate. The seller had failed to adhere to the original terms of payment, and the difference between cash payment (as now insisted on, wrongly) and credit terms is of great commercial significance (for example, in another commercial sales contract, the sellers had sensed that the buyer might have become financially vulnerable, and so the sellers insisted that the buyer should pay in advance of delivery, but this new requirement was held to be unjustified and repudiatory).[224]

10-118   The Court of Appeal upheld the trial judge's decision (McCardie J), who had said:[225]

> "The question, therefore, is what a prudent person ought reasonably to do in order to mitigate his loss arising from a breach of contract. I feel no inclination to allow in a mercantile dispute an unhappy indulgence in far-fetched resentment or an undue sensitiveness to slights or unfortunately worded letters. Business often gives rise to certain asperities. But I agree that the plaintiffs in deciding whether to accept the defendant's offer were fully entitled to consider the terms in which the offer was made, its bona fides or otherwise, its relation to their own business methods and financial position, and all the circumstances of the case; and it must be remembered that an acceptance of the offer would not preclude an action for damages for the actual loss sustained."

10-119   McCardie J at first instance in *Payzu Ltd v Saunders*, had added:[226]

> "Many illustrations might be given of the extraordinary results which would follow if the plaintiffs were entitled to reject the defendant's offer and incur a substantial measure of loss which would have been avoided by their acceptance of the offer. The plaintiffs were in fact in a position to pay cash for the goods, but instead of accepting the defendant's offer, which was made perfectly bona fide, the plaintiffs permitted themselves to sustain a large measure of loss which as prudent and reasonable people they ought to have avoided."

10-120   In *Payzu Ltd v Saunders* in the Court of Appeal, Scrutton LJ tersely added:[227]

> "In certain cases of personal service it may be unreasonable to expect a plaintiff to

---

ing, 2008), Ch.14, p.335; M. Bridge, "Mitigation of Damages in Contract and the Meaning of Avoidable Loss" (1989) 105 L.Q.R. 398, 411 ff.
[223] [1919] 2 K.B. 581 CA.
[224] *BV Oliehandel Jongkind v Coastal International Ltd* [1983] 2 Lloyd's Rep. 463, Leggatt J.
[225] [1919] 2 K.B. 581 at 586; see also his statement in *Clayton Greene v de Courville* (1920) 36 T.L.R. 790.
[226] [1919] 2 K.B. 581 at 586.
[227] [1919] 2 K.B. 581 CA at 589.

consider an offer from the other party who has grossly injured him; but in commercial contracts it is generally reasonable to accept an offer from the party in default. However, it is always a question of fact. About the law there is no difficulty."

Therefore, the innocent party's compensation in the *Payzu* case was confined to **10-121** damages for business inconvenience and for the period of credit which the buyer would have lost by paying cash on delivery rather than when stipulated by the contract.

The Court of Appeal in *Strutt v Whitnell*[228] distinguished the *Payzu* case **10-122** (examined above). In the *Strutt* case the claimant had bought a house for £4,650. The defendants were in breach of a condition, because they had not given vacant possession (the house was occupied by a tenant enjoying Rent Act protection). The Court of Appeal upheld the award of £1,900 damages, for the difference in the value of the house with and without a sitting tenant. The defendants offered to buy back the property, although no price for the re-purchase had been agreed. The claimant, although a property developer, having no personal need of accommodation, refused to re-sell. It is likely that his motive was to see if property prices might rose. The defendants contended that the mitigation principle required the claimant to have agreed to the re-sale, thus eliminating the loss attributable to the sitting tenant. But the Court of Appeal held that a party who has bought defective goods or real property is not obliged to surrender them to the vendor, even if this is requested, so as to recover his full price, etc and thus eliminate the loss attributable to the relevant defect. By contrast, in the *Payzu* case, the buyer was held to have acted unreasonably (for the purpose of mitigating loss) by not proceeding with a series of purchases, as distinct from refusing to re-transfer defective property (as in the *Strutt* case). Sitting in the latter case, MacKenna J (who gave the third judgment in the Court of Appeal) said:[229]

> "... in the *Payzu* case the defendant in breach of contract had failed to deliver goods to the plaintiff at the contract price and on the contract conditions, but had offered him goods of the same kind at the same price but on less favourable (cash rather than credit) conditions. If the plaintiff had accepted them he would have suffered only a small loss because of the less favourable (cash rather than credit) conditions, which he could still have recovered by way of damages. But he refused the offer. In those circumstances it was held that he could not recover the difference between the market price and the contract price. He would not have suffered loss if he had accepted the defendant's offer which it was reasonable for him to do. There was no question in that case of the plaintiff being required to return goods which had already become his property or forfeit his right to substantial damages. That is the difference between the *Payzu* case [and the present one]."

Another problematic case is *"The Solholt"*.[230] Here mitigation reasoning was **10-123** pressed still further. Again, as seen in the *Payzu* case (see para.10-116), the indirect effect of the court's reliance on the mitigation principle is that a fetter is placed on the innocent party's ostensibly free capacity to terminate for repudiatory breach and obtain the usual measure of damages consequent on that termination.

In *"The Solholt"* the seller agreed to sell a vessel to the buyer for $5 million by **10-124**

---

228 [1975] 1 W.L.R. 870 CA (Cairns and Lawton LJJ, McKenna J).
229 [1975] 1 W.L.R. 870 CA at 875.
230 [1983] 1 Lloyd's Rep. 605 CA, noted E. Lomnicka, "Unreasonable termination and mitigation" (1983) 99 L.Q.R. 495–497; cf. *Sealace Shipping Co Ltd v Ocean Voice Ltd* [1996] 1 Lloyd's Rep. 120 CA at 125 (on which *Ruxley* case [1996] 1 A.C. 344HL at 371; latter case itself also example of damages claim disproportionate to innocent party's true loss).

31 August. However, the breached the contract by proposing to make delivery three days late, on 3 September. This was a repudiatory breach, on which basis the buyer justifiably terminated the contract. At the date of termination, the vessel's value had already increased 10 per cent to $5.5 million. The buyer tried to buy the vessel for $4.75 million, but the seller did not accept. The trial judge, Staughton J, found as a fact that the seller would have been prepared to sell under a renewed contract to the buyer for $5million and, furthermore, he held that it would have been reasonable for the buyer to have accepted that offer. Instead the seller sold the vessel to a third party for $5.8 million.[231] The Court of Appeal upheld Staughton J's decision that the buyer's failure to seek delivery under a revised contract at $5 million was an unreasonable failure to mitigate.

10-125   The decision in *"The Solholt"* goes further than the *Payzu* case (see above), because in that 1919 case the possibility of continuing relations had been expressly suggested by the vendor in breach (subject to cash payments), whereas no such suggestion had been made by the guilty vendor in *"The Solholt"* (no offer to sell the ship for a reduced price). On this last point, Bridge comments:[232]

> "In one respect, the decision in *'The Solholt'* goes beyond the *Payzu* case. On the facts, the trial judge believed that the buyer ought to have taken the initiative by offering to repurchase the ship at the original contract price. The buyer was aware that the ship was still available and evidence was accepted that the seller would have allowed the buyer to take the ship at the original price, yet there was no evidence at all of any overtures made by the seller to the buyer. Difficult as it is to criticise a decision based on an overall assessment of the facts, this seems quite extraordinary. Election of remedies and mitigation may indeed inhabit separate worlds, but requiring the buyer to take such an initiative, in principle as soon as it had discharged itself from the contract, makes little business sense."

10-126   Furthermore, *"The Solholt"* nullifies the buyer's ordinary right to compensation arising from his justified termination of the contract for repudiatory breach (late delivery). Bridge comments as follows on this aspect of the case:[233]

> "'*The Solholt*' must be regarded as wrongly decided. First of all, it makes the buyer's right of contractual discharge for late delivery utterly illusory. It is no answer to this to say that election of remedies and mitigation, as it bears on a subsequent claim for damages, are consecutive and distinct, for the application of the principle of mitigation rendered the buyer's election nugatory. It may be that the duty of timely delivery is sometimes treated too strictly and that, if goods are not traded in volatile market conditions—presumably the case for a 13-year-old ship like the one in '*The Solholt*'—a failure of consideration analysis[107] might more appropriately define the buyer's right of discharge. In '*The Solholt*' the presence of express provisions in the contract dealing with timely delivery created an opening for such an approach, but it was not taken. Discharge rights ought not to be undermined by covert means, though it should be added that nothing in the decision betrays judicial dissatisfaction with the strictness of time obligations in commercial sale of goods contracts."

10-127   Finally, Bridge rightly contends that the buyer should have been entitled to the

---

[231] As suggested by the trial judge, noted M. Bridge, "Mitigation of Damages in Contract and the Meaning of Avoidable Loss" (1989) 105 L.Q.R. 398, 418.

[232] M. Bridge, "Mitigation of Damages in Contract and the Meaning of Avoidable Loss" (1989) 105 L.Q.R. 398, 418.

[233] M. Bridge, "Mitigation of Damages in Contract and the Meaning of Avoidable Loss" (1989) 105 L.Q.R. 398, 420.

initial 10 per cent increase in the ship's value ($500,000)[234] as a "loss of bargain" which had already arisen. That claim should not have been nullified by the buyer's alleged "mitigation" failure. As for the additional $300,000 gain achieved by the sale to the third party, Bridge suggests that the seller should be entitled to keep this gain. This is because the buyer had already abandoned interest in this ship at the time this further increase in value occurred.

---

[234] M. Bridge, "Mitigation of Damages in Contract and the Meaning of Avoidable Loss" (1989) 105 L.Q.R. 398, 419.

CHAPTER 11

TIME STIPULATIONS

I. "TIME OF THE ESSENCE": A SUMMARY[1]

The main points will now be set out. **11-001**

(1) In *Lombard North Central Plc v Butterworth*, Mustill LJ said:[2] **11-002**

> "A stipulation [contained in the original terms of the relevant transaction] that time
> is of the essence, in relation to a particular contractual term, denotes that timely
> performance is a condition of the contract. The consequence is that delay in
> performance is treated as going to the root of the contract, without regard to the
> magnitude of the breach."

(2) The question of timely payment or performance is especially important in **11-003**
conveyancing transactions,[3] contracts of hire,[4] and commercial investment
instruments: *BNP Paribas v Wockhardt EU Operations (Swiss) AG*.[5]

(3) A time obligation might be (i) expressed to be strict, in the sense that the par- **11-004**
ties have spelt out that the obligation is a "condition" or that "time is of the
essence", or some similar expression. Alternatively, (ii) an ex facie neutral time
stipulation might be construed by the court as neither a mere warranty nor an
intermediate or innominate term but instead as a condition.

(4) These "express" and "construction" routes, just mentioned as (3)(i) and (ii), **11-005**

---

[1] K. Lewison, *Interpretation of Contracts*, 7th edn (London: Sweet & Maxwell, 2020), Ch.15; G.
McMeel, *The Construction of Contracts: Interpretation, Implication and Rectification*, 3rd edn
(Oxford: Oxford University Press, 2017), Ch.25; H. Beale (ed), *Chitty on Contracts*, 34th edn
(London: Sweet & Maxwell, 2021), paras 27-026–27-036; J. Stannard, *Delay in the Performance
of Contractual Obligations*, 2nd edn (Oxford: Oxford University Press, 2018); J.W. Carter, *Carter's
Breach of Contract*, 2nd edn (Oxford: Hart Publishing, 2019), Ch.5.
[2] *Lombard North Central Plc v Butterworth* [1987] Q.B. 527 CA at 535–6.
[3] The case law is extensive: see the authorities collected in *Urban 1 (Blonk Street) Ltd v Ayres* [2013]
EWCA Civ 816; [2014] 1 W.L.R. 756 at [44]; see also *Ampurius Nu Homes Holdings Ltd v Telford
Homes (Creekside) Ltd* [2013] EWCA Civ 577; [2013] 4 All E.R. 377.
[4] e.g. *Lombard North Central Plc v Butterworth* [1987] Q.B. 527 CA at 535–6; in a time charter a term
requiring punctual payment is not a condition unless it is very carefully made expressly a condition:
Spar Shipping AS v Grand China Logistics Holding (Group) Co Ltd ("The Spar Draco") [2016]
EWCA Civ 982; [2016] 2 Lloyd's Rep. 447 (Gross, Hamblen LJJ, Sir Terence Etherton MR)
(upholding [2015] EWHC 718 (Comm); [2015] 1 All E.R. (Comm) 879, Popplewell J, but overruling *Kuwait Rocks Co v AMN Bulkcarriers Inc ("The Astra")* [2013] EWHC 865 (Comm); [2013] 2
Lloyd's Rep. 69, Flaux J).
[5] [2009] EWHC 3116 (Comm) at [32].

were noted by Lord Simon of Glaisdale in *United Scientific Holdings Ltd v Burnley BC*, who approved this formulation:[6]

"Time will not be considered to be of the essence unless: (1) the parties expressly stipulate that conditions as to time must be strictly complied with; or (2) the nature of the subject matter of the contract or the surrounding circumstances show that time should be considered to be of the essence ..."

11-006 (5) In commercial arrangements, courts will give effect to strict time stipulations, whether or not couched expressly as "conditions", if the courts perceive that commercial certainty is important in that context.[7] But there is no presumption to this effect. Indeed, the Court of Appeal in *Spar Shipping AS v Grand China Logistics Holding (Group) Co Ltd ("The Spar Draco")* expressed the contrary starting-point, as far as payment obligations are concerned in the mercantile context.[8]

11-007 (6) But if the original terms of the contract do not expressly or by implication create a "condition", the next-best possibility is that the innocent party can notify the other party, who is already in breach, and make clear that performance must occur within a reasonable time. It is important to note that such a notice[9] does not (normally: for the qualification, see para.11-008) have the effect of rendering the time stipulation a condition.[10] Instead the notice operates as evidence of the date by which the promisee considers it reasonable to require the contract to be performed.[11] And thus the innocent party will need to show that the post-notification delay involves an element of serious default justifying termination, namely: (i) the failure to comply with the notice is held to be repudiatory[12] in the sense that it "goes to the root" of the contract;[13] (ii) the dilatory party's default discloses a renunciation, that is, an implicit "intima-

---

[6] *United Scientific Holdings Ltd v Burnley BC* [1978] A.C. 904 HL at 944, approving a passage in *Halsbury's Laws of England*.

[7] *Bunge Corp New York v Tradax SA* [1981] 1 W.L.R. 711 HL at 715–716, 726 (also citing Lord Diplock in *Photo Production Ltd v Securicor Transport Ltd* [1980] A.C. 822 HL at 840).

[8] [2016] EWCA Civ 982; [2016] 2 Lloyd's Rep. 447 (Gross, Hamblen LJJ, Sir Terence Etherton MR) at [35], [56], [100].

[9] *BNP Paribas v Wockhardt EU Operations (Swiss) AG* [2009] EWHC 3116 (Comm) at [40], per Christopher Clarke J noting *Re Olympia & York Canary Wharf Ltd (No.2)* [1993] B.C.C. 159, Morritt J; and Clarke J's own decision in *Dalkia Utilities Services Plc v Celtech International Ltd* [2006] EWHC 63 (Comm); [2006] 1 Lloyd's Rep. 599 at [131]; see also *Samarenko v Dawn Hill House Ltd* [2011] EWCA Civ 1445; [2013] Ch. 36 at [37] ff, per Lewison LJ (case noted J.W. Carter, 'Deposits and "time of the essence"' (2013) 129 L.Q.R. 149–152).

[10] *Urban 1 (Blonk Street) Ltd v Ayres* [2013] EWCA Civ 816; [2014] 1 W.L.R. 756 at [44] (proposition (6)) per Sir Terence Etherton C; *Behzadi v Shaftesbury Hotels Ltd* [1992] Ch. 1 CA at 24 per Purchas LJ.

[11] Lord Simon of Glaisdale in *United Scientific Holdings Ltd v Burnley BC* [1978] A.C. 904 at 946E–947A; *Behzadi v Shaftesbury Hotels Ltd* [1992] Ch. 1 CA at 24 per Purchas LJ; *Re Olympia & York Canary Wharf Ltd (No.2)* [1993] B.C.C. 159 at 173, Morritt J; *Astea (UK) Ltd v Time Group Ltd* [2003] EWHC 725 TCC at [147] ff.

[12] *Dominion Corporate Trustees Ltd v Debenhams Properties Ltd* [2010] EWHC 1193 (Ch); [2010] N.P.C. 63 at [55] per Kitchin J, for a payment default which was not repudiatory, etc.

[13] e.g. failure to pay a deposit in a real property contract by the agreed date, that date having been notified as crucial: *Samarenko v Dawn Hill House Ltd* [2011] EWCA Civ 1445; [2013] Ch. 36 at [37] ff, concluding at [47] per Lewison LJ (case noted J.W. Carter, "Deposits and 'time of the essence'" (2013) 129 L.Q.R. 149–152).

tion" to abandon the contract; or (iii) the default is a breach of an intermediate term which has gone to the root of the expected performance.[14]

Proposition (6) is subject to the qualification, noted by Barling J in *Cantt Pak Ltd* **11-008** *v Pak Southern China Property Investment Ltd* that the date for completion, although not initially of the essence, can become so if the contract in its original form states that notice can be given specifying a date which is to be treated as of the essence:[15]

> "The claimant's submission is that time was originally not of the essence for completion, and therefore a failure to complete on the contractual completion date would not enable the innocent party to treat the Contract as discharged by fundamental breach. [Standard Commercial Property Conditions (Second Edition)] enable one party unilaterally to make time of the essence by serving a notice to complete. Once made of the essence, a failure to complete on the date so fixed constitutes a fundamental breach, enabling the innocent party to rescind. Thus, a notice to complete makes time of the essence for both parties, and the validity of a notice to complete has to be assessed by reference to facts at the time of service; it is at that point that RWA to complete must exist in order for the notice to be effective in making time of the essence." (NB: the Standard Commercial Property Conditions (Second Edition) state: "8.1.1 Completion date is twenty working days after the date of the contract, but time is not of the essence of the contract unless a notice to complete has been served.")

Judicial summary of the leading principles Etherton C restated the leading **11-009** principles in *Urban 1 (Blonk Street) Ltd v Ayres*: (it will be seen that the portions of this long quotation, set out in para.11-010, and highlighted in italics at subparagraphs (6) and (7), are especially important).[16] The upshot of those particular passages is: (i) where a term is not *ab initio* a condition, the innocent party's decision to serve notice purporting to render time of the essence does not (normally: for the qualification, see para.11-008) upgrade the term into a condition (proposition (6) in the quotation in the next paragraph below); and (ii) instead failure to adhere to the deadline contained in the notice will need to be assessed to determine whether there has been a repudiatory breach going to the root of the contract, or whether there has been a renunciation, that is:

> "[where] the contract-breaker has demonstrated an intention never to carry out the contract or, at any event, only to do so in a manner substantially inconsistent with his or her contractual obligations such as to deprive the other party of substantially the whole benefit which it was intended they should receive under the contract." (proposition (7) in the quotation below)

Etherton C's statement of the leading principles in *Urban 1 (Blonk Street) Ltd v* **11-010** *Ayres* (2013) is as follows:[17]

> "I consider that the following principles under the current law, which are relevant to the present case, can be extracted from them.

---

[14] *Re Olympia & York Canary Wharf Ltd (No.2)* [1993] B.C.C. 159 at 165–173, especially at 173; *Ocular Sciences Ltd v Aspect Vision Care Ltd* [1997] R.P.C. 289 at 433 per Laddie J; *Astea (UK) Ltd v Time Group Ltd* [2003] EWHC 725 TCC at [151].

[15] [2018] EWHC 2564 (Ch) at [82].

[16] [2013] EWCA Civ 816; [2014] 1 W.L.R. 756 at [44] (see also *Ampurius Nu Homes Holdings Ltd v Telford Homes (Creekside) Ltd* [2013] EWCA Civ 577; [2013] 4 All E.R. 377).

[17] [2013] EWCA Civ 816; [2014] 1 W.L.R. 756 at [44].

(1) [Here his Lordship summarised the distinction between conditions, innominate terms and warranties.]

(2) Where a contract for the sale of land does not contain any specified date for completion, and subject to any contractual indication to the contrary, it is implied that completion will be within a reasonable time. There is no breach of contract until that time has arrived: the *Behzadi* case, [1992] Ch. 1 at 12G–13A, 23E.

(3) The moment that the contractual date for completion has passed, the contract-breaker who has delayed completing is liable in damages: *Raineri v Miles* [1981] A.C. 1050.

(4) Where the contractual date for completion has passed, the contract-breaker is still entitled to specific performance of the contract unless it would be inequitable to grant that relief: *Stickney v Keeble* [1915] A.C. 386 at 416, *Seton v Slade* (1802) 7 Ves. 265; 32 E.R. 108.

(5) It would be inequitable for there to be a grant of specific performance to the contract-breaker if the parties have expressly stated in the contract that the contract can be terminated forthwith on breach of the time provision or if it is to be implied from all the circumstances that they so intended: *Parkin v Thorold* (1852) 16 Beav. 59, 66; 51 E.R. 698. Accordingly, if, on the proper interpretation of the contract, the time provision is a condition in the technical sense I have mentioned, it is difficult to imagine that the court would grant the contract breaker specific performance. I respectfully agree, in this regard, with the doubt expressed by Rix LJ in *Samarenko v Dawn Hill House Ltd* [2013] Ch. 36 at [64][18] as to whether equity, as a distinct species of legal principles, now has anything to add in the context of contractual terms of fundamental importance.

(6) Service of a valid written notice to complete after the contractual completion date has passed has the effect of bringing to an end the possibility of equity's intervention by the grant of specific performance to the contract-breaker. A valid notice is one which calls on the contract-breaker to perform within a reasonable period, specifying exactly what it is that party must do and what consequences will follow (that is to say, exercise of the right to terminate if he or she fails to do so): *In re Olympia & York Canary Wharf Ltd (No.2)* [1993] BCC 159 at 169C–F citing *Behzadi v Shaftesbury Hotels Ltd* [1992] Ch. 1 at 12 letters B–E. *Statements in many of the cases and some textbooks that the service of a notice to complete makes time of the essence in equity are incorrect. Absent any relevant express provisions in the contract* (as are to be found in the Standard Commercial Property Conditions (Second Edition), for example [on this see the important qualification at para.11-008]), *it is contrary to all principle for one party to be able unilaterally to transform one type of contractual provision (namely, an innominate term or a warranty in the strict sense) into something different (a condition in the strict sense).* Equity's role, in this context, always has been to relieve a contract-breaker against the strict legal rights of the other party, not to enhance them: *Parkin v Thorold* (1852) 16 Beav. 59 at 71; 51 E.R. 698, *Behzadi's* case at 12 and 24.

---

[18] Rix LJ's cogent remarks are as follows: "the common law would always have regarded clause 2 in this case as a condition. In that case, I see no problem whatsoever in regarding the buyer's failure (indeed, its refusal) to pay the deposit within the time stipulated in the seller's notice as constituting a failure to meet that deadline and thus automatically amounting to a repudiatory breach of the condition. In such a case there is in my judgment no need to prove a repudiatory or renunciatory breach in the sense in which that concept is discussed in cases such as the *Hongkong Fir Shipping Co* case [1962] 2 Q.B. 26, *'The Nanfri'* [1979] A.C. 757, *Woodar Investment Development Ltd v Wimpey Construction UK Ltd* [1980] 1 W.L.R. 277, *Eminence Property Developments Ltd v Heaney* [2011] 2 All E.R. (Comm) 223 and others. The mere failure to meet the reasonably imposed deadline is sufficient proof of the repudiatory breach necessarily constituted by the failure to perform a condition in the time stipulated."

(7) *Accordingly, absent any relevant express terms in the contract, where a completion notice has been served and expired following breach of a time provision which is an innominate term, the question whether the other party can terminate the contract depends on that party's ordinary legal rights. This depends on two matters which, again, have often been confused in the case law. Firstly, the contract-breaker will have repudiated the contract, entitling the other party to terminate it, if and when the delay has been such as in all the circumstances to deprive the other party of substantially the whole benefit it was intended he or she should obtain from the contract, that is to say it has gone to the root of the contract.* The delay may or may not have reached that point at the time that the notice to complete has expired: *Peregrine Systems Ltd v Steria Ltd* [2005] Info T.L.R. 294 at [15]. *Secondly, the contract-breaker will have repudiated the contract, or as it is sometimes put, renounced the contract, entitling the other party to terminate it, if the contract-breaker has demonstrated an intention never to carry out the contract or, at any event, only to do so in a manner substantially inconsistent with his or her contractual obligations such as to deprive the other party of substantially the whole benefit which it was intended they should receive under the contract*: *Federal Commerce & Navigation Co Ltd v Molena Alpha Inc ('The Nanfri')* [1979] A.C. 757 at 778–779 (Lord Wilberforce citing passages from several other cases). *The failure to comply with the notice to complete may be some evidence of that, but an intention to renounce must be determined in the light of the evidence as a whole*: *Eminence Property Developments Ltd v Heaney* [2011] 2 All E.R. (Comm) 223 at [61]–[64]. I agree with Lewison LJ's further thoughts on this aspect when, in *Samarenko v Dawn Hill House Ltd* [2013] Ch. 36 at [42], he resiled from his earlier position in *Multi Veste 226 BV v NI Summer Row Unitholder BV* (2011).[19]

(8) Where, in the case of a time provision which is an intermediate term, a completion notice has not been served on the contract-breaker, an award of specific performance will be available to the contract-breaker until such time as the grant of that remedy would be inequitable. It is difficult to see in principle why that would be any different to the time when the breach due to the delay is such as to go to the root of the contract."

II. DETAILED EXAMINATION OF TIME STIPULATIONS

Where the parties have expressly stipulated in their contract that the time fixed **11-011** for performance must be exactly complied with, or (in other words) that time is to be "of the essence",[20] such a time stipulation will be treated as a "condition". In

---

[19] [2011] EWHC 2026 (Ch); 139 Con. L.R. 23 at [201] and [202] (in this earlier judgment at first instance, Lewison J had rather contortedly suggested that a notice making time of the essence could be conceptualised as rendering failure to satisfy the obligation by the relevant deadline as ipso facto a total failure to perform and thus a repudiation (or perhaps an implied renunciation). But in *Samarenko v Dawn Hill House Ltd* [2011] EWCA Civ 1445; [2013] Ch. 36 at [42], he recanted, preferring proof that the guilty party's continuing delay, in default of this deadline, has become a repudiation or renunciation: "If the case is one of a truly innominate term, in the sense of a term that can be broken in many different ways, some serious and others not, then it may be wrong to equate delay in performance (even after notice) with refusal to perform. Whether that is so or not may have to wait for another day. But where, as here, the case is one in which the term in question is one that would have been regarded by the common law as a condition of the contract, then it seems to me that failure to comply with a notice making time of the essence is tantamount to a refusal to perform that obligation."

[20] *United Scientific Holdings Ltd v Burnley BC* [1978] A.C. 904 HL at 943–944 per Lord Simon: "contractual stipulations as to time ... shall not be construed as essential, except where equity would

Lombard North Central Plc v Butterworth Mustill LJ said:[21]

"A stipulation that time is of the essence, in relation to a particular contractual term, denotes that timely performance is a condition of the contract. The consequence is that delay in performance is treated as going to the root of the contract, without regard to the magnitude of the breach ... A clause expressly assigning a particular obligation to the category of condition is not a clause which purports to fix the damages for breaches of the obligation, and is not subject to the law governing penalty clauses."[22]

11-012   When determining whether the original terms of the contract have the effect of rendering non-timely or non-punctual performance a matter capable without more of justifying termination, there is no need for the phrase "time of the essence" or the word "condition" to have been used. On ordinary principles of construction, the court will determine whether the relevant term requiring timely or punctual performance, such as payment, should be characterised expressly or by implication as essential and fundamental. The court will consider this question by reference to the whole contractual context. If the court decides that the clause does create an essential and fundamental obligation, the result will be that any breach will justify the innocent party in terminating the contract. In some circumstances, this construction will apply even though the parties have further incorporated (from the contract's inception) a notice procedure. The latter is not incompatible with the analysis that the duty to perform on time is to be treated as a condition.

11-013   All the points made in the preceding paragraph emerge from the discussion in *BNP Paribas v Wockhardt EU Operations (Swiss) AG*, where Christopher Clarke J, in the context of a sophisticated financial instrument, said[23]

"... Whilst the parties have not used the expression 'condition' or 'repudiatory breach' they have specified that any failure to pay which continues after the first Local Business Day after notice of failure will entitle BNP to designate an Early Termination Date; and have gone on to provide that upon an effective designation no further payments or deliveries (the primary obligations under the contract) will be due."

11-014   He added:[24]

"In providing for BNP's entitlement to terminate the ongoing primary obligations of the parties and the method of calculation of the sum to be paid in that event, the parties have, subject to one qualification, spelt out the consequences which result from a breach of

---

before 1875 have so construed them-i.e. only when the strict observance of the stipulated time for performance was a matter of express agreement or of necessary implication". Law of Property Act 1925 s.41 provides: "Stipulations in a contract, as to time or otherwise, which according to the rules of equity are not deemed to be or to have become of the essence of the contract, are also construed and have effect at law in accordance with the same rules."

21   [1987] Q.B. 527 CA at 535–536; noted G.H. Treitel, "Damages on Rescission for Breach of Contract" [1987] L.M.C.L.Q. 143; W. Bojczuk, "When is a condition not a condition?" [1987] J.B.L. 353; B. Opeskin, "Damages for Breach of Contract Terminated under Express Terms" (1990) 106 L.Q.R. 293.

22   A dramatic example, in the context of conveying land, is *Union Eagle Ltd v Golden Achievement Ltd* [1997] A.C. 514 PC, on which para.10-112 ff; noted J. Stevens, "Having Your Cake and Eating It? Union Eagle Ltd. v. Golden Achievement Ltd" (1998) 61 M.L.R. 255–62 (P sued D for specific performance; P had been 10 minutes late in tendering purchase price; specific performance denied; D entitled to forfeit P's deposit and terminate contract).

23   [2009] EWHC 3116 (Comm) at [32].

24   [2009] EWHC 3116 (Comm) at [33].

condition. It is unrealistic to suppose that, having done so, they are to be taken to have intended that a failure to pay should be regarded as a warranty or an innominate term."

There is no technical presumption of fact or rule of law that time is of the essence in mercantile contracts. As Lord Lowry commented in *Bunge Corp New York v Tradax SA*:[25] "The treatment of time limits as conditions in mercantile contracts does not appear ... to be justifiable by any presumption of fact or rule of law, but rather to be a practical expedient founded on and dictated by the experience of businessmen ..." Similarly, in *Spar Shipping AS v Grand China Logistics Holding (Group) Co Ltd ("The Spar Draco")*[26] Popplewell J (affirmed on appeal) said:[27] **11-015**

> "The principle that stipulations as to time of payment are not generally to be regarded as of the essence in commercial contracts unless a contrary intention appears from the contract or the surrounding circumstances has been judicially restated on a number of occasions: see for example per Christopher Clarke J, as he then was, in *Dalkia Utilities Services Plc v Celltech International Ltd* [2006] 1 Lloyd's Rep. 599 at [130]–[131]. It is reflected in the current edition of *Chitty on Contracts*, [now 34th edn, 2021 para.27-029] and *Halsbury's Laws* Vol.22 para.502."

Thus, a stipulation as to time in a "mercantile" contract may, on its true construction, be found to be merely an intermediate term. It should also be noted that under Sale of Goods Act 1979 s.10, unless a different intention appears from the terms of the contract, stipulations as to time of *payment* by the buyer of goods are not deemed to be of the essence. But where the court discerns, as a matter of construction, a shared intention that the time stipulation should operate as a condition, it will give effect to that interpretation of the parties' agreement. As Lord Wilberforce said in *Bunge Corp New York v Tradax SA*:[28] **11-016**

> "I do not doubt that, *in suitable cases*, the courts should not be reluctant, *if the intentions of the parties as shown by the contract so indicate*, to hold that an obligation has the force of a condition, and that indeed they should usually do so in the case of time clauses in mercantile contracts. To such cases the 'gravity of the breach' approach of the *HongKong Fir Shipping Co Ltd v Kawasaki Kisen Kaisha Ltd* (1962)[29] would be unsuitable." (emphasis added)

And *Chitty on Contracts* states: **11-017**

> "the mere fact that the contract can be labelled 'mercantile' or 'commercial' does not determine the issue...Whether a time limit is of the essence of contractual provision is a question of interpretation of the provision in the contract as a whole. The question is whether the time specified in the particular clause was (expressly or by necessary implica-

---

[25] [1981] 1 W.L.R. 711 at 719 HL (noted F. Reynolds, "Discharge of Contract by Breach" (1981) 97 L.Q.R. 541; J. Carter, "Classification of Contractual Terms: the New Orthodoxy" [1981] C.L.J. 219).

[26] [2015] EWHC 718 (Comm); [2015] 1 All E.R. (Comm) 879 at [171]; affirmed at [2016] EWCA Civ 982; [2016] 2 Lloyd's Rep. 447 (Gross, Hamblen LJJ, Sir Terence Etherton MR).

[27] [2015] EWHC 718 (Comm); [2015] 1 All E.R. (Comm) 879 at [171]; affirmed on this point, [2016] EWCA Civ 982; [2016] 2 Lloyd's Rep. 447 (Gross, Hamblen LJJ, Sir Terence Etherton MR) at [35], [56], [100].

[28] [1981] 1 W.L.R. 711 HL at 716. (noted F. Reynolds, "Discharge of Contract by Breach" (1981) 97 L.Q.R. 541; J. Carter, "Classification of Contractual Terms: the New Orthodoxy" [1981] C.L.J. 219).

[29] [1962] 2 Q.B. 26 CA at 72 per Diplock LJ.

tion) intended by the parties to be essential, e.g. because they needed to know precisely what were their respective obligations."[30]

11-018   In general, as Lord Ackner suggested in *Compagnie Commerciale Sucre et Denrees v C Czarnikow ("The Naxos")*,[31] the courts would prefer to promote commercial certainty. But this is nothing more than a pragmatic "rule of thumb" approach.

11-019   To sum up: there is no technical or rigid rule or even presumption that time stipulations in mercantile or commercial transactions will be construed as conditions.[32]

If, however, the court discerns a shared intention to impose a strict regime, the court should give effect to that. In some contexts, where decisions have to be made in a time-critical manner, it might be a relatively easy task to persuade the court that this construction is suitable or appropriate. For in such a situation, certainty is to be prized or might even be imperative. But the courts must approach these matters without any hard-and-fast preconceptions. Sweeping generalisations are not possible. Flexibility has been preserved. The inquiry is "fact-sensitive". Examples of situations where the construction has tipped in favour of a condition are provided in the ensuing paragraphs.

11-020   **Example (i): owner's "readiness to load" obligation**   In *"The Mihalis Angelos"* (1971) the Court of Appeal categorised as a condition an owner's statement in a voyage charterparty that the vessel was "expected ready to load under this charter about [a specified date]".[33] Megaw LJ attractively buttressed his decision on this point by making the following general argument in favour of a clear and predictable rule in this particular context:[34]

> "[Classifying this obligation as a condition] tends towards certainty in the law. One of the essential elements of law is some measure of uniformity. One of the important elements of the law is predictability. At any rate in commercial law, there are obvious and substantial advantages in having, where possible, a firm and definite rule for a particular class of legal relationship: for example, as here, the legal categorisation of a particular, definable type of contractual clause in common use."

11-021   Megaw LJ continued:

> "It is surely much better, both for shipowners and charterers (and, incidentally, for their advisers), when a contractual obligation of this nature is under consideration, and still more when they are faced with the necessity for an urgent decision as to the effects of a

---

30   H. Beale (ed), *Chitty on Contracts*, 34th edn (London: Sweet & Maxwell, 2021), para.27-029.

31   [1990] 1 W.L.R. 1337 HL at 1347; noted G.H. Treitel, "Time of Shipment in f.o.b. Contracts" (1991) L.M.C.L.Q. 147–154 (noting at 152 and 154 that the decision is consistent with the need for (i) promotion of certainty, and (ii) the commercial importance of the term); and M. Clarke, "Time and Essence of Mercantile Contracts: The Law Loses its Way" [1991] C.L.J. 29.

32   H. Beale (ed), *Chitty on Contract*, 34th edn (London: Sweet & Maxwell, 2021), para.27-029, citing extensive case law at fnn.92–97, notably, at fn.93, *Grand China Logistics Holding (Group) Co Ltd v Spar Shipping AS* [2016] EWCA Civ 982; [2016] 2 Lloyd's Rep. 447; on which, Neil Andrews, "Breach of Contract: A Plea for Clarity and Discipline" (2018) 134 L.Q.R. 117, 131-133.

33   [1971] 1 Q.B. 164 CA (Lord Denning MR, Edmund-Davies, and Megaw LJJ—reversing Mocatta J) (criticised, D.W. Greig, "Condition or Warranty?" (1973) 89 L.Q.R. 93, 100–104).

34   *Maredelanto Compania Naviera SA v Bergbau-Handel GMBH ("The Mihalis Angelos")* [1971] 1 Q.B. 164 CA at 205.

suspected breach of it, to be able to say categorically: 'If a breach is proved, then the charterer can put an end to the contract,' rather than that they should be left to ponder whether or not the courts would be likely, in the particular case, when the evidence has been heard, to decide that in the particular circumstances the breach was or was not such as 'to go to the root of the contract'."

Megaw LJ added: "Where justice does not require greater flexibility, there is everything to be said for, and nothing against, a degree of rigidity in legal principle." **11-022**

Example (ii): buyer's obligation to notify seller of intention to ship goods In **11-023** *Bunge Corp v Tradax Export SA* the House of Lords also treated as a condition a clause requiring the buyer to give at least 15 days' notice to the seller of the buyer's intention to ship the goods, whereupon the seller could decide which port to use for the shipment.[35] The transaction was part of a "string" of contracts for the transfer of these goods. Lord Lowry presented a rich list of pertinent factors, many of which (and cited here) are of general importance when deciding whether to ascribe to a commercial obligation the characteristic that it should be a "condition":

"(1)   There are enormous practical advantages in certainty, not least in regard to string contracts where today's buyer may be tomorrow's seller.

(2)   Most members of the string will have many ongoing contracts simultaneously and they must be able to do business with confidence in the legal results of their actions.

(3)   Decisions would be too difficult if the term were innominate, litigation would be rife and years might elapse before the results were known.

(4)   The difficulty of assessing damages is an indication in favour of [treating the obligation as a] condition …[36];

(5)   One can at least say that recent litigation has provided indications that the term is a condition. Parties to similar contracts should (failing a strong contraindication) be able to rely on this …[37];

(6)   To make 'total loss' the only test of a condition is contrary to authority and experience, when one recalls that terms as to the date of sailing, deviation from a voyage and the date of delivery are regarded as conditions, but that failure to comply with them does not always have serious consequences.

(7)   Nor need an implied condition pass the total loss test: see (6) above
         …

(11)   To accept the argument that conditions ought not to be implied 'because the parties themselves know how to describe a term' would logically condemn the entire doctrine of implied terms.

(12)   Arbitrators and courts might, if the term were innominate, give different answers concerning the effect of a breach in very similar transactions, and parties could never learn by experience what was likely to happen in a given situation. So-called string contracts are not made, or adjudicated on, in strings."

Example (iii): seller's duty to have goods ready for delivery at nominated **11-024** **port** In *Compagnie Commerciale Sucre et Denrees v C Czarnikow ("The Naxos")* the House of Lords held, as a matter of construction, that a condition had been

---

[35]   [1981] 1 W.L.R. 711 HL. (noted F. Reynolds, "Discharge of Contract by Breach" (1981) 97 L.Q.R. 541; J. Carter, "Classification of Contractual Terms: the New Orthodoxy" [1981] C.L.J. 219).

[36]   Citing *McDougall v Aeromarine of Emsworth Ltd* [1958] 1 W.L.R. 1126 at 1133.

[37]   Citing *Maredelanto Compania Naviera SA v Bergbau-Handel GMBH ("The Mihalis Angelos")* [1971] 1 Q.B. 164 CA at 199 per Megaw LJ (criticised, D.W. Greig, "Condition or Warranty?" (1973) 89 L.Q.R. 93, 100–104).

impliedly created when a clause required the sellers to have goods ready for delivery on the arrival of the vessel at port.[38]

11-025   **Example (iv): owner's duty to obtain third parties' approval of charterered vessel**   In *BS & N Ltd (BVI) v Micado Shipping Ltd (Malta) ("The Seaflower")* the Court of Appeal categorised as a condition a clause requiring the owners to obtain approval, within 60 days, from a specified oil company, Exxon, that the latter consented to use of the relevant vessel.[39] The court held that this was a condition, entitling the charterer to terminate the contract, once it became apparent that Exxon's approval had not been obtained within the 60-day period. This was so even though the clause did not contain an explicit right of cancellation, by contrast with other provisions of the charterparty (failure to maintain approval of four other oil companies, whose approval had already been given).

11-026   **Example (v): seller's duty to deliver Covid face masks on stipulated dates**   In *Pharmapac (UK) Ltd v HBS Healthcare Ltd*, it was held[40] (for other aspects of this case see paras 10-087, 14-042 and 14-067) that a set of sales between two merchants of face masks at the peak of the Covid pandemic, involved specified delivery dates where, as a matter of construction against the factual matrix, time was of the essence. The judge's lucid formulation of this issue reads as follows:[41]

"[5] The Claimant's case is that the Defendant's failure to deliver the instalments on 23 and 30 March and 6 and 30 April 2020 amounted to a repudiatory breach of the agreement, which entitled it to elect to treat the contract as discharged. The email agreement does not explicitly state that time is of the essence, or that delivery time is a condition of the agreement, or essential to it. There is no presumption of law that stipulations as to the time of delivery are of the essence of a contract: see *Chitty on Contracts* 34th ed., 46- 246. It is said that commercial (mercantile) contracts are frequently so construed, but it remains a matter of construction: see also section 10(2) of the Sale of Goods Act 1979. It follows that the agreement in question has to be construed as a whole and against the relevant background factual matrix: *Spar Shipping AS v Grand China Logistics (Group) Co Ltd* [2016] EWCA Civ 982. Unless the contract makes it clear that a particular stipulation was a condition or only a warranty, it is to be treated as an innominate term. It is true that the courts should not be too ready to interpret contractual clauses as conditions: ibid., per Gross LJ at [52]. Certainty is, however. a consideration of major importance when construing commercial contracts, both as a matter of legal principle and of commercial common sense, though it is a matter of striking the right balance: ibid. [58]-[59], [62]. So, for example, where the goods in question are perishable so that if late, they may be useless, or if the value of the goods is volatile, time is more likely to be found to be of the essence: see the discussion in *MSAS Global Logistics Ltd v Power Packaging Inc* [2003] EWHC 1393 (Ch). However, in *Bunge Corporation v Tradax Export SA* [1981] 1 W.L.R. 711, HL at 716 Lord Wilberforce said 'But I do not doubt that, in suitable cases, the courts

---

[38]   [1990] 1 W.L.R. 1337 HL; noted G.H. Treitel, "Time of Shipment in f.o.b. Contracts" (1991) L.M.C.L.Q. 147–154 (noting at 152 and 154 that the decision is consistent with the need for (i) promotion of certainty, and (ii) the commercial importance of the term); and M. Clarke, "Time and Essence of Mercantile Contracts: The Law Loses its Way" [1991] C.L.J. 29.

[39]   [2001] 1 Lloyd's Rep. 341 CA.

[40]   [2022] EWHC 23 (Comm) (Judge Cadwallader).

[41]   [2022] EWHC 23 (Comm) at [5] and [12] (Judge Cadwallader).

should not be reluctant, if the intentions of the parties as shown by the contract so indicate, to hold that an obligation has the force of a condition, and indeed they should usually do so in the case of time clauses in mercantile contracts.'

[12] Admittedly the deadline was not spelled out [so as explicitly to make time of the essence], nor explicitly as a deadline. The language identifies the delivery time, but does not state that it is essential. Moreover, the consequences of failing to deliver weekly were not specified. And the parties knew the Defendant [seller] was not in complete control of its supply chain. But against the background of the rapid start and the short and repeated delivery intervals, the developing pandemic, the high demand and volatile market, I conclude that time was of the essence. The point was not just to get the masks as soon as possible, but to be able to cancel the contract if they had not arrived in time."

In addition to the examples (i) to (v) just considered, the following are situa-   **11-027**
tions where time stipulations have been classified as conditions within the mercantile context:

- when a ship must be nominated: *Greenwich Marine Inc v Federal Commerce & Navigation Co Ltd ("The Mavro Vetranic")*;[42]
- when goods must be delivered under a contract of sale: *Hartley v Hymans*;[43] *Scandinavian Trading Co A/B v Zodiac Petroleum SA*;[44]
- when the loading port must be nominated: *Gill & Duffus SA v Société pour l'Exportation des Sucres*;[45]
- when the vessel must be provided: *Olearia Tirrena SpA v NV Algemeene Oliehandel*;[46]
- when, under an f.o.b. contract, goods must be shipped: *Bowes v Shand*;[47]
- when documents must be tendered: *Toepfer v Lenersan-Poortman NV*[48] and *Cerealmangimi Spa v Toepfer*;[49]
- when notice of appropriation must be given: *Reuter v Sala*[50] and *Bunge GmbH v Landboubelang GA* (1980);[51]
- when notice of shipment must be given: *Société Italo-Belge pour le Commerce etc v Palm and Vegetable Oils (Malaysia) Sdn Bhd*;[52] and
- when a letter of credit must be opened under a c.i.f. contract: as supported by various authorities.[53]

Hire is paid late under a time charter   In *Spar Shipping AS v Grand China*   **11-028**

---

42   [1985] 1 Lloyd's Rep. 580 (Staughton J).
43   [1920] 3 K.B. 475 at 484.
44   [1981] 1 Lloyd's Rep. 81.
45   [1986] 1 Lloyd's Rep. 322.
46   [1973] 2 Lloyd's Rep. 86.
47   (1877) 2 App. Cas. 455 HL.
48   [1980] 1 Lloyd's Rep. 143.
49   [1981] 1 Lloyd's Rep. 337.
50   (1879) 4 C.P.D. 239.
51   [1980] 1 Lloyd's Rep. 458.
52   [1981] 2 Lloyd's Rep. 695.
53   *Pavia & Co SpA v Thurmann Nielsen* [1952] 1 Lloyd's Rep. 153; *Ian Stach Ltd v Baker Bosley Ltd* [1958] 2 Q.B. 130 (Diplock J); *Nichimen Corp v Gatoil Overseas Inc* [1987] 2 Lloyd's Rep. 46; *Transpetrol Ltd v Transol Olieprodukten BV* [1989] 1 Lloyd's Rep. 309; see also *Michael I Warde v Feedex International Inc (No.2)* [1985] 2 Lloyd's Rep. 289 (nomination of bank); contrast *State Trading Corp of India Ltd v M Golodetz & Co Inc Ltd* [1989] 2 Lloyd's Rep. 277 (opening of counter-trade guarantee).

Logistics Holding (Group) Co Ltd ("The Spar Draco")[54] Popplewell J (his decision was affirmed on appeal) concluded that there is no automatic right to terminate for breach by late payment of hire in this context under Common Law principle. Instead the payee will be entitled to terminate for breach only if the contract creates an explicit condition, or the facts support a finding of implicit renunciation, as in fact found by the judge (and affirmed on appeal) in that case.

11-029 **Payment is late if the credit or funds are not immediately available for disposal by the intended payee** Payment will be late if it is not made so as to be in cash or a form equivalent to cash, that is, immediately available for disposal and, where desired, for deposit on an interest-yielding account. These points were confirmed in *A/S Awilco of Oslo v Fulvia Spar ("The Chikuma")*.[55] Here the House of Lords held that an owner was entitled to withdraw a chartered vessel because the charterer had not made an unconditional bank transfer of the sum by the relevant deadline. Instead the sum credited ($68,863.84, US) in favour of the owner would only be capable of being placed on deposit, and then attracting interest, three days later. The sum payable to gain the benefit of the right to immediate interest would be c $70 to 100 (US). Therefore, the owners contended it was not an outright and immediately effective payment equivalent to cash, and thus there had been a breach of cl.5, which stated that payment of the hire was "to be made ... in cash in United States currency, monthly in advance ... otherwise failing the punctual and regular payment of the hire ... the owners shall be at liberty to withdraw the vessel from the service of the charterers ...". The owner's argument prevailed. At first instance, Robert Goff J held that the owners were entitled to withdraw the vessel, and Lord Bridge, giving the House of Lords' decision,[56] agreed (overturning the Court of Appeal's decision to offer clemency[57] in favour of the payor). In the House of Lords, where the decision was in favour of the intended payee, the vessel's owner, Lord Bridge explained:[58]

> "The underlying concept is surely this, that when payment is made to a bank otherwise than literally in cash, i.e. in dollar bills or other legal tender (which no one expects), there is no 'payment in cash' within the meaning of clause 5 unless what the creditor receives is the equivalent of cash, or as good as cash."

And he added this remarkable statement in support of "bright-line" doctrine in the commercial field, when the parties enjoy relatively similar bargaining power:[59]

> "It has often been pointed out that shipowners and charterers bargain at arm's length.

---

[54] [2015] EWHC 718 (Comm); [2015] 1 All E.R. (Comm) 879 at [171]; [2016] EWCA Civ 982; [2016] 2 Lloyd's Rep. 447 (Gross, Hamblen LJJ, Sir Terence Etherton MR).

[55] [1981] 1 W.L.R. 314 HL.

[56] The other four members of the tribunal were: Lords Diplock, Simon of Glaisdale, Edmund-Davies, and Scarman.

[57] Lord Bridge [1981] 1 W.L.R. 314 at 320, noted the Court of Appeal's judgment as follows: "In the Court of Appeal it was calculated that the interest on the monthly instalment of hire from Thursday, January 22 to Monday, January 26 would have been U.S. $70 or $100. This calculation encouraged Lord Denning MR to say [1980] 2 Lloyd's Rep. 409, 412: 'It seems to me that that trifling bank charge, if it had been exacted, would not have affected the nature of the payment which had already been made. The credit was available to the owners, in their bank, as from midday on Thursday, 22 January. The owners had the full use of it. It was unconditional. The mere debiting of a trifling bank charge would not make it conditional'." But Lord Bridge and the House of Lords held that this was erroneous and that immediate and unconditional payment had not occurred on these facts.

[58] [1981] 1 W.L.R. 314 HL.

[59] [1981] 1 W.L.R. 314 HL at 320.

Neither class has such a preponderance of bargaining power as to be in a position to oppress the other. They should be in a position to look after themselves by contracting only on terms which are acceptable to them. Where, as here, they embody in their contracts common form clauses, it is, to my mind, of overriding importance that their meaning and legal effect should be certain and well understood. The ideal at which the courts should aim, in construing such clauses, is to produce a result, such that in any given situation both parties seeking legal advice as to their rights and obligations can expect the same clear and confident answer from their advisers and neither will be tempted to embark on long and expensive litigation in the belief that victory depends on winning the sympathy of the court. This ideal may never be fully attainable, but we shall certainly never even approximate to it unless we strive to follow clear and consistent principles and steadfastly refuse to be blown off course by the supposed merits of individual cases."

In the following three cases (listed as Cases (i) to (iii) below), time clauses were **11-030** not regarded as important enough to be construed as conditions in the relevant contexts.

Case (i): not a condition: date for redelivery by a charterer under a time **11-031** **charterparty** In *Torvald etc A/S v Arni Maritime Corp ("The Gregos")* the House of Lords made clear that there is no inflexible rule or even presumption that "neutral" time clauses in mercantile transactions will be regarded as conditions.[60] The House of Lords held that a clause specifying the date for redelivery under a time charterparty was not a condition, but an intermediate term, because a prospective short delay in redelivery would not justify the owner of the vessel in terminating the contract forthwith. However, on the facts the charterer was held to have acted so as to entitle the other party to terminate the contract.[61] The charterer had issued an order for the vessel to proceed to a new port, and this would involve a failure to meet the deadline for re-delivery of the ship. The charterer's persistence in maintaining this order was a renunciation, once it became plain that complying with it would certainly take the period of hire beyond the date for re-delivery.

Case (ii): not a condition: "laycan" period in a time charterparty In *Universal* **11-032** *Bulk Carriers Pte Ltd v Andre et Cie SA* the Court of Appeal held that an obligation to narrow a "laycan" period in a voyage charterparty was not important enough to constitute a condition.[62]

Case (iii): not a condition: failure to open a guarantee by a specified date In **11-033** *State Trading Corp of India Ltd v M Golodetz Ltd* the Court of Appeal held that failure to open a guarantee within seven days involved breach of an innominate term because it related to ancillary and future aspects of the transaction and did not impair the main performance by the parties.[63]

No relief against forfeiture of proposed land deal if purchaser pays late The **11-034** Privy Council in *Union Eagle Ltd v Golden Achievement Ltd* held that relief against forfeiture of a proprietary or possessory interest does not protect a purchaser of real

---

[60] [1981] 1 W.L.R. 314 HL at 321–322.
[61] [1981] 1 W.L.R. 314 HL at 1476.
[62] [2001] 2 Lloyd's Rep. 65 CA.
[63] [1989] 2 Lloyd's Rep. 277 CA.

property who has yet to go into possession of the relevant property.[64] And so that decision declares that Equity will not intervene to provide relief against forfeiture in favour of a purchaser of land who has failed to comply with an essential time stipulation. The interests of certainty preclude such a discretionary jurisdiction (on the equitable jurisdiction to relieve against forfeiture of a proprietary—land, goods, shares, or intellectual property—or possessory interest, see para.10-108 ff).

11-035 **Withdrawal or option to terminate clause** Even if a late payment does not give rise to a right to terminate for breach, the contract's express provisions might at least confer on the payee the right to end the contract other than by reason of breach (on such a cancellation without breach option, see *Financings Ltd v Baldock*[65] and *Spar Shipping AS v Grand China Logistics Holding (Group) Co Ltd ("The Spar Draco")*).[66]

11-036 Such a clause was considered in *Mardorf Peach & Co Ltd v Attica Sea Carriers Corp of Liberia ("The Laconia")*, where cl.5 provided:

> "Payment of said hire to be made … in cash … semi-monthly in advance … [F]ailing the punctual and regular payment of the hire, … or on any breach of this charterparty, the owners shall be at liberty to withdraw the vessel from the service of the charterers, without prejudice to any claim they (the owners) may otherwise have on the charterers."

11-037 The charterer failed to pay one instalment on time. The House of Lords upheld the owner's decision to withdraw the ship and terminate the contract. Lord Wilberforce said:[67]

> "I cannot find any difficulty or ambiguity in this clause. It must mean that once a punctual payment of any instalment has not been made, a right of withdrawal accrues to the owners. Conversely, it is incapable of meaning that a charterer who has failed to make a punctual payment, can (unless the owners have waived the default) avoid the consequences of his failure by later tendering an unpunctual payment."

11-038 In *Mardorf Peach & Co Ltd v Attica Sea Carriers Corp of Liberiu ("The Laconia")* Lord Wilberforce listed his conclusions as follows:[68]

> "1. Under the withdrawal clause [just cited] …, a right of withdrawal arises as soon as default is made in punctual payment of an instalment of hire. Whether or not this rule is subject to qualification in a case of punctual but insufficient payment as some authorities appear to hold, is not an issue which now arises and I express no opinion upon it.
> 2. The owners must within a reasonable time after the default give notice of withdrawal to the charterers. What is a reasonable time—essentially a matter for arbitrators to find—depends on the circumstances. In some, indeed many cases, it will be a short time—viz. the shortest time reasonably necessary to enable the shipowner to hear of the default and issue instructions. If, of course, the charterparty contains an express provision regarding notice to the charterers, that provision must be applied.
> 3. The owners may be held to have waived the default, inter alia, if when a late pay-

---

64 [1997] A.C. 514 PC.
65 *Financings Ltd v Baldock* [1963] 2 Q.B. 104 CA at 110–111, 121.
66 [2015] EWHC 718 (Comm); [2015] 1 All E.R. (Comm) 879 at [171]; affirmed, [2016] EWCA Civ 982; [2016] 2 Lloyd's Rep. 447 (Gross, Hamblen LJJ, Sir Terence Etherton MR).
67 [1981] 1 W.L.R. 314 HL at 867.
68 [1981] 1 W.L.R. 314 HL at 872.

ment is tendered, they choose to accept it as if it were timeous, or if they do not within a reasonable time give notice that they have rejected it."

In the same case, Lord Fraser said:[69]   **11-039**

"It is said that such a construction of withdrawal clauses in time charters in favour of the owners would be unduly harsh on the charterers, but I do not see why that should be so. If a charterer wishes to avoid the risk of having the ship withdrawn because of his accidental or inadvertent failure to pay the hire by the due date, he can include a stipulation for notice before withdrawal, as was done in the second 'anti-technicality clause' in *Oceanic Freighters Corp v MV Libyaville, Reederei und Schiffahrts GmbH* [1975] 1 Lloyd's Rep. 537, and by similar clauses in other forms of charterparty that were shown to us."

**Time provision not a condition, but innocent party serves notice for perfor-   11-040
mance upon dilatory party**   If the time stipulation is neither expressly, nor on construction, a condition, but party B has already been guilty of delay, party A may give notice requiring the contract to be performed within a reasonable time. In *BNP Paribas v Wockhardt EU Operations (Swiss) AG* Christopher Clarke J summarised the effect of such a notice as follows,[70] adopting the analysis of Morritt J in *Re Olympia & York Canary Wharf Ltd (No.2)* (1993),[71] and academic comment:[72]

"(a)   ... Whilst this is described as making time of the essence in reality the notice is the means of bringing to an end equity's interference with the contract ...[73];
(b)   Such a notice, which may be given in respect of any species of term, may not be served until the time for performance has expired; but it may be served as soon as that time arrives;
(c)   Such a notice must state clearly what the other party is required to do and the consequence if he fails, that is, that the contract may be terminated ...[74];
(d)   If the defaulting party fails to perform after service of such a notice, the failure is not automatically a repudiation of the contract, giving rise to a right to terminate. The breach must go to the root of the contract;
(e)   The notice operates as evidence of the date by which the promisee considers it reasonable to require the contract to be performed, failure to perform by which is evidence of an intention not to perform ..."[75]

The main points concerning such notices are: **11-041**

• *proposition (a):* notice can be served by party A on B once the latter party is in breach of an express clause time stipulation or of an implied term for performance within a reasonable time; party A need not wait, when deciding to issue a notice, for party B to commit further delay;[76]

---

69   [1981] 1 W.L.R. 314 HL at 883.
70   [2009] EWHC 3116 (Comm) at [40] Christopher Clarke J noted his decision in *Dalkia Utilities Services Plc v Celtech International Ltd* [2006] EWHC 63 (Comm); [2006] 1 Lloyd's Rep. 599 at [131].
71   [1993] B.C.C. 159, Morritt J.
72   J. Stannard, "In the contractual last chance saloon: Notices making time of the essence" (2004) 120 L.Q.R. 137.
73   Citing *Behzadi v Shaftesbury Hotel* [1992] Ch. 1 CA.
74   Citing *Afovos Shipping v Pagnan ("The Afovos")* [1982] 1 W.L.R. 848 HL at 854C.
75   Citing Lord Simon of Glaisdale in *United Scientific Holdings Ltd v Burnley BC* [1978] A.C. 904 at 946E–947A; *Astea (UK) Ltd v Time Group Ltd* [2003] EWHC 725 TCC at [147].
76   *Behzadi v Shaftesbury Hotels Ltd* [1992] Ch. 1 CA at 23, 24 per Purchas LJ: "[notice] cannot be

- *proposition (b):* the period of notice given must, however, be reasonable, according to all the circumstances of the case;[77]
- *proposition (c):* such a notice *does not elevate the obligation to the level of a condition*: the notice cannot have the effect of turning the non-essential term of the contract into a condition (subject to the qualification mentioned at 11-008); instead the notice operates as evidence of the date by which the promisee considers it reasonable to require the contract to be performed, failure to perform by which is evidence of an intention not to perform;[78] and
- *proposition (d):* where the innocent party cannot show that time was of the essence at the contract's inception, and instead he relies on subsequent notification, he must show that the post-notification delay involves an element of serious default justifying termination, namely:
  (i)   failure to comply with the notice is held to be repudiatory[79] in the sense that it "goes to the root" of the contract;[80]
  (ii) the same failure to comply constitutes breach of an intermediate term and, furthermore, applying the *HongKong Fir* test, the breach on the present facts has proved to be sufficiently serious to that the innocent party has the right to terminate for breach;[81] or
  (iii) the dilatory party's default discloses a renunciation, that is, an implicit "intimation" to abandon the contract.

11-042   As for the three possibilities of serious breach justifying termination, just mentioned, as (a), (b), and (c) in the preceding paragraph, no such serious delay was shown in *Urban 1 (Blonk Street) Ltd v Ayres*.[82] The defendants had agreed to buy a lease of a flat from the claimant vendor. The flat was still under construction. The parties did not make clear what was to happen if there were delay in finishing the work, which was set for December 2008. The Court of Appeal held that there was an implied intermediate (or innominate) term that the flat would be finished within a reasonable time. But here the delay of four weeks was described as "trivial" (a

---

served until after there has been a breach by the defaulting party either of the term fixing the date for compliance, or of the implied term where the contract is silent as to the date for performance". Further examined in *Re Olympia & York Canary Wharf Ltd (No.2)* [1993] B.C.C. 159.

[77]   *Behzadi v Shaftesbury Hotels Ltd* [1992] Ch. 1 CA.

[78]   *Urban 1 (Blonk Street) Ltd v Ayres* [2013] EWCA Civ 816; [2014] 1 W.L.R. 756 at [44] (proposition (6)) per Sir Terence Etherton C: "... it is contrary to all principle for one party to be able unilaterally to transform one type of contractual provision (namely, an innominate term or a warranty in the strict sense) into something different (a condition in the strict sense)". See also: Lord Simon of Glaisdale in *United Scientific Holdings Ltd v Burnley BC* [1978] A.C. 904 at 946E–947A; *Behzadi v Shaftesbury Hotels Ltd* [1992] Ch. 1 CA at 24 per Purchas LJ (quoted above); *Re Olympia & York Canary Wharf Ltd (No.2)* [1993] B.C.C. 159 at 173, Morritt J; *Astea (UK) Ltd v Time Group Ltd* [2003] EWHC 725 TCC at [147] ff per Deputy High Court Judge Richard Seymour QC.

[79]   *Dominion Corporate Trustees Ltd v Debenhams Properties Ltd* [2010] EWHC 1193 (Ch); [2010] N.P.C. 63 at [55] per Kitchin J, for a payment default which was not repudiatory, etc.

[80]   e.g. failure to pay a deposit in a real property contract by the agreed date, that date having been notified as crucial: *Samarenko v Dawn Hill House Ltd* [2011] EWCA Civ 1445; [2013] Ch. 36 at [37] ff, concluding at [47] per Lewison LJ (case noted J.W. Carter, "Deposits and 'Time of the Essence'" (2013) 129 L.Q.R. 149).

[81]   *Re Olympia & York Canary Wharf Ltd (No.2)* [1993] B.C.C. 159 at 165–73, especially at 173; *Ocular Sciences Ltd v Aspect Vision Care Ltd* [1997] R.P.C. 289 at 433 per Laddie J; *Astea (UK) Ltd v Time Group Ltd* [2003] EWHC 725 TCC at [151].

[82]   [2013] EWCA Civ 816; [2014] 1 W.L.R. 756 (see, notably, the statement of general principle at [44] per Etherton C).

lease of 125 years was to be granted),[83] and so there had been neither a sufficiently serious default nor did the facts independently disclose an implied renunciation.[84] The purchasers had acted, therefore, precipitately in calling off this contract. Damages were available; the deposit had been validly forfeited; but specific performance to compel the purchaser to accede to the transaction was no longer sought.

Proposition (d)(i) (see para.11-041: "failure to comply with the notice is held to be repudiatory in the sense that it "goes to the root" of the contract") was clearly expressed by Laddie J in *Ocular Sciences Ltd v Aspect Vision Care Ltd*:[85] **11-043**

> "The party giving the notice can only terminate where the failure of the other party to comply with the terms of the notice goes to the root of the contract so as to deprive that party of a substantial part of the benefit to which he was entitled under the terms of the contract. Failure to comply with the terms of the notice can therefore only be used as evidence of a repudiatory breach; it is not a repudiatory breach per se."

These were the salient facts in *Ocular Sciences Ltd v Aspect Vision Care Ltd*.[86] **11-044** Royalties were due to be paid by the claimant to the defendant on 15 January 1995. On 10 January, the claimant told the defendant that, because of the continuing litigation, the claimant was not willing to make a royalty payment which might prove to be irrecoverable after the litigation. The claimant suggested that the royalties be paid into an escrow account. In reply, on 12 January, the defendant said that it was not prepared to accept delayed payment and that any attempt to delay would be a breach of contract. They said: "we accept that time is not expressly made of the essence of the obligation to pay under the Patent Licence Agreement. Our clients therefore make time of the essence by this letter". The claimant was then given 14 days from 15 January to pay the royalties in full, and the defendant intimated that failure to do so would be treated as a repudiation which the defendant would accept. Despite this threat, the claimant paid the royalties into an escrow account. Laddie J rejected the argument that the giving of notice had rendered timely payment a condition, so that delay would justify terminating the contract for breach:[87]

> "it is vital to distinguish between the case where both parties agree that time is to be of the essence and the case where, following a breach of a non-essential term of the contract, the innocent party serves a notice on the other stating that time is to be of the essence. In the latter case, such a notice does not serve to make time of the essence as far as the obligations in the original contract are concerned, because one party cannot unilaterally vary the terms of a contract by turning what was previously a non-essential term of the contract into an essential term. The party giving the notice can only terminate where the failure of the other party to comply with the terms of the notice goes to the root of the contract so as to deprive that party of a substantial part of the benefit to which he was entitled under the terms of the contract. Failure to comply with the terms of the notice can therefore only be used as evidence of a repudiatory breach; it is not a repudiatory breach per se."

As for proposition (d)(ii) (see para.11-041) (serious breach of an intermediate **11-045** term), the question as to what degree of delay will produce a very serious breach

---

83 [2013] EWCA Civ 816; [2014] 1 W.L.R. 756 at [60] per Etherton C, and "trivial" at [69] per Floyd LJ.
84 [2013] EWCA Civ 816; [2014] 1 W.L.R. 756 at [48].
85 [1997] R.P.C. 289 at 433.
86 [1997] R.P.C. 289 at 432.
87 [1997] R.P.C. 289 at 432–3.

in this *HongKong Fir* sense will require examination of the particular circumstances. There has been some first instance discussion.[88]

11-046   As for proposition (d)(iii) (see para.11-041) ("the dilatory party's default discloses a renunciation, that is, an implicit "intimation" to abandon the contract"), Laddie J in *Ocular Sciences Ltd v Aspect Vision Care Ltd*[89] acknowledged this possibility, but on the fact he held that the contract was expressly irrevocable during its period of operation, and so could not be terminated by reason of the other party's default. Furthermore, the relevant conduct did not indicate a renunciatory intent. He presented these points as follows. First, Laddie J said:[90]

> "whatever may be the effect of a party unilaterally declaring time to be of the essence, it cannot be to give that party a right to terminate the agreement when the parties have made it clear that it should not be terminable. There is no doubt that the parties to the [patent licensing agreement] intended the licence to be granted under it to be irrevocable. Not only does the agreement say so in terms and use the expression 'perpetual' but there are no provisions relating to termination at all. Once again it should be borne in mind that the [patent licensing agreement] was brought into existence at the same time as all the other September 1992 agreements and the parties agreed that they should be read together. It is noticeable that the other agreements have termination provisions. This does not. In my view it is not open to the defendants unilaterally to make time of the essence so as to give rise to a right to terminate ... the parties expressly agreed that the licence was to be irrevocable."

11-047   Secondly, he said:[91]

> "The same conclusion can be arrived at in a different way. Whether a failure by a party to a contract to honour one or more of its terms amounts to repudiation is a question of fact. The court must make up its mind whether the party's intention was to abandon the contract. See *Woodar Investment Development Ltd v Wimpey Construction Ltd* [1980] 1 W.L.R. 277 HL. The payment of the royalties into an escrow account did not amount to an intimation on the part of the plaintiffs that they intended to abandon the [patent licensing agreement]. Therefore it did not amount to repudiation."

11-048   But the renunciatory route to the power to terminate by reason of delay was satisfied in *Spar Shipping AS v Grand China Logistics Holding (Group) Co Ltd ("The Spar Draco")*.[92] In that case the Court of Appeal upheld Popplewell J's decision that a long-standing pattern of delay in payment of hire under three charterparties had entitled the owner to terminate because the charterers' conduct constituted a renunciation.

III.   NOTIFICATION OF LATENESS: THE FINAL ANALYSIS

11-049   It is submitted that, even though there is no earlier right to terminate on the basis of breach by late payment or other dilatory performance (such a right would arise under a condition), but the innocent party, faced by delay, issues a notice prescrib-

---

[88] Deputy High Court Judge Richard Seymour QC commented in *Astea (UK) Ltd v Time Group Ltd* [2003] EWHC 725 TCC at [148] ff, considering *Universal Cargo Carriers Corp v Citati* [1957] 2 Q.B. 402 at 426 per Devlin J.
[89] [1997] R.P.C. 289 at 432–434.
[90] [1997] R.P.C. 289 at 433.
[91] [1997] R.P.C. 289 at 434.
[92] [2016] EWCA Civ 982; [2016] 2 Lloyd's Rep. 447 (Gross, Hamblen LJJ, Sir Terence Etherton MR) (affirming [2015] EWHC 718 (Comm); [2015] 1 All E.R. (Comm) 879 at [223]).

ing a deadline for performance, and when the relevant matter concerns an important aspect of the contract, the notified party's failure to meet this deadline will be an implicit renunciation of the contract, provided: (i) the notice was clear; (ii) it was not issued prematurely; (iii) termination of the contract will not be inconsistent with the original terms of the contract (for example, when a licence is declared to be irrevocable);[93] and (d) the notice period was reasonable.

Lord Simon of Glaisdale in the *United Scientific Holdings Ltd* case had sketched the basis for this, when he said:

11-050

"The notice operates as evidence that the promisee considers that a reasonable time for performance has elapsed by the date of the notice and as evidence of the date by which the promisee now considers it reasonable for the contractual obligation to be performed. The promisor is put upon notice of these matters. It is only in this sense that time is made of the essence of a contract in which it was previously non-essential. The promisee is really saying, 'Unless you perform by such-and-such a date, I shall treat your failure as a repudiation of the contract.' The court may still find that the notice stipulating a date for performance was given prematurely, and/or that the date fixed for performance was unreasonably soon in all the circumstances."[94]

The penultimate sentence in this quoted passage refers to "repudiation". The more attractive, and commercially more precise, manner of conceptualising this is to say that the notice provided it is neither premature nor unreasonably short in duration), sets a limit to the guilty party's continuing default. Such an injection of discipline and clarity must be preferable to the alternative approach: which would be to condone further delay unless that period becomes so prolonged that it deprives the innocent party of substantially the entire benefit of the bargain.[95] A bright-line

11-051

---

[93] cf. Laddie J in *Ocular Sciences Ltd v Aspect Vision Care Ltd* [1997] R.P.C. 289 at 433: "... it cannot be to give that party a right to terminate the agreement when the parties have made it clear that it should not be terminable. There is no doubt that the parties to the [agreement] intended the licence to be granted under it to be irrevocable. Not only does the agreement say so in terms and use the expression 'perpetual' but there are no provisions relating to termination at all ..."

This must be read in the light of *BMS Computer Solutions Ltd v AB Agri Ltd* [2010] EWHC 464 (Ch), where Sales J held that "perpetual" in a licence agreement did not mean "ever-lasting", but merely an entitlement of no fixed duration: see his cogent articulation of supporting reasons, [2010] EWHC 464 (Ch) at [18]. The courts can imply a right to terminate on reasonable notice if a contract does not specify a fixed duration. e.g. (as noted more fully at Ch.9, para.9-066 ff), in *Staffordshire AHA v South Staffordshire WW Co* [1978] 1 W.L.R. 1387 CA, Goff and Cumming-Bruce LJJ held that a 1929 agreement to supply 5000 gallons of water a day free of charge, thereafter at seven old pence per 1000 gallons "at all times hereafter", was neither a perpetual contract nor (as was evident) a contract of fixed duration. Since the contract was of indefinite duration, the Court of Appeal held that it was terminable by the giving of reasonable notice; but at 1397–1398, Lord Denning MR, in a minority opinion, reached the same conclusion by the heterodox route of finding frustration to be satisfied by inflation; T.A. Downes, "Nomination, Indexation, Excuse and Revalorisation: A Comparative Survey" (1985) 101 L.Q.R. 98, 104–108. Conversely, if the contract is of a fixed duration, there will be no implied term that a party can terminate it by giving reasonable notice: *Jani-King (GB) Ltd v Pula Enterprises Ltd* (2007) shows [2007] EWHC 2433 (QBD); [2008] 1 Lloyd's Rep. 305 per Coulson J at [60]–[66].

[94] *United Scientific Holdings Ltd v Burnley BC* [1978] A.C. 904 HL at 946.

[95] Deputy High Court Judge Richard Seymour QC in *Astea (UK) Ltd v Time Group Ltd* [2003] EWHC 725 TCC at [149] discussing the famous but deeply problematic *HongKong Fir* test [1962] 2 Q.B. 1 CA at 69–70 (see para.12-010 ff); on which Neil Andrews, "Breach of Contract: A Plea for Clarity and Discipline" (2018) 134 L.Q.R. 117.

doctrine is welcome here, as in other contexts where chronological exactitude is essential.[96]

---

[96] See discussion at para.10-112 ff of *Union Eagle Ltd v Golden Achievement Ltd* [1997] A.C. 514 PC.

CHAPTER 12

INTERMEDIATE OR INNOMINATE TERMS: "WAIT AND SEE" BECAUSE "IT ALL DEPENDS"

I. RECOGNITION OF THE INTERMEDIATE TERM IN THE HONGKONG FIR CASE (1962)

("Intermediate" and "innominate" are interchangeable, but the default term used **12-001** in this chapter will be "intermediate".) In *Hongkong Fir Shipping Co Ltd v Kawasaki Kisen Kaisha Ltd* (1962)[1] the concept of an intermediate term was recognised by the Court of Appeal. In this case Diplock LJ rejected the contention that the law recognises only a simple dichotomy of promissory term consisting of "conditions" and "warranties", the latter producing only liability in damages, and the former entitling the innocent party additionally to terminate the contract.[2] He accepted that some obligations can be breached only in a way which will necessarily have very serious consequences Conversely, other contractual obligations might never have serious consequences, and so they should be regarded as "warranties".[3] But, as he emphasised, this leaves a large category of obligations "of a more complex nature" where it will depend on the actual events following breach whether the innocent party can justify termination. (For discussion of the express characterisation of a breach as a "material breach", and of the distinction between "remediable" and "irremediable" "material breaches", see para.9-038 ff).

In *The Hongkong Fir* case (1962)[4] the Court of Appeal held that express terms **12-002** as to seaworthiness should not be treated as conditions. The court further held, agreeing with Salmon J at first instance, that termination was not justified for breach of intermediate terms on these facts. The case concerned a two-year charterparty. Clause 1 required the ship to be "in every way fitted for ordinary cargo service". Clause 3 stipulated that the owners should maintain the ship in a "thoroughly efficient state in hull and machinery during service". The vessel's condition and performance, as well as the deficiencies displayed by its crew, seem to have fallen well short of expected standards: the chief engineer was addicted to drink, the crew was insufficient, and there were several serious breakdowns in the machinery. The

---

[1] *Hongkong Fir Shipping Co Ltd v Kawasaki Kisen Kaisha Ltd* [1962] 2 Q.B. 1 CA; J.E. Stannard and D. Capper, *Termination for Breach of Contract*, 2nd edn (Oxford: Oxford University Press, 2020), Ch.6; D. Nolan, in C. Mitchell and P. Mitchell (eds), *Landmark Cases in the Law of Contract* (Oxford: Hart Publishing, 2008), p.269 ff; and for Lord Diplock's own account of this decision, "The Law of Contract in the Eighties" (1981) 15 U.Brit. Columbia L.R. 371; Lord Devlin, "The Treatment of Breach of Contract" [1966] C.L.J. 192; J.W. Carter, G.J. Tolhurst, E. Peden, "Developing the Intermediate Term Concept" (2006) 22 J.C.L. 268–286; for a general critique of the *HongKong* technique, Neil Andrews, "Breach of Contract: A Plea for Clarity and Discipline" (2018) 134 L.Q.R. 117.

[2] [1962] 2 Q.B. 1 CA at 69–70.

[3] [1962] 2 Q.B. 1 CA at 70.

[4] [1962] 2 Q.B. 1 CA.

charterer repudiated the agreement before the two years had elapsed. The owner alleged that there was no good reason for this. It was apparent that the charterer's motive in seeking to end the contract was that there had been a significant fall in the market rate for hire of such vessels, so that they were now locked into an uneconomic, or at least financially unattractive, contract.[5] The charterer was seeking to go elsewhere for a cheaper and better service.

12-003   The Court of Appeal in the *Hongkong Fir* case (1962) held that the express terms as to seaworthiness should not be treated as conditions, but instead as intermediate terms. Furthermore, termination was not justified on these facts. They noted that the "seaworthiness" obligations could be breached in a variety of ways, some of them serious, others relatively minor. Diplock LJ regarded the terms as intermediate. Upjohn LJ, adopting a similar approach;[6] agreed that, on the *facts which had occurred*, the only remedy was damages rather than termination of the contract.[7] The third judge, Sellers LJ, in fact classified the term as a "warranty",[8] but that characterisation cannot be accepted. This was a set of intermediate terms and the level of contractual default fell short of the level required to justify termination.

II.   CRITERIA FOR IDENTIFYING INTERMEDIATE TERMS

12-004   In Ch.10, during discussion of conditions, we noted the criteria for classifying a term as a condition or intermediate term, or occasionally as a pure warranty (if a warranty, incapable of giving rise to the right to terminate). As Hamblen LJ noted in *Spar Shipping AS v Grand China Logistics Holding (Group) Co Ltd ("The Spar Draco")*,[9] the intermediate term has become the "default term" in the sense that a promissory obligation will be categorised as such unless the obligation can be upgraded to a condition, applying the tests of (i) statutory characterisation as a condition; (ii) party designation of the term as having that quality; or (iii) (in the absence of (i) or (ii)) judicial determination that the term is a condition, based on either precedent or construction. Lists of factors suggested by commentators are presented at para.10.083. Attention was also given at para.10.084 ff, to judicial guidelines emerging from the following cases: *State Trading Corp of India Ltd v M Golodetz Ltd*[10] and *Ark Shipping Co LLC v Silverburn Shipping (IoM) Ltd*. For the sake of economy, that discussion will not be repeated here. It is enough to list the factors which were considered in those two cases.[11]

---

[5] [1962] 2 Q.B. 1 at 39 (Salmon J).
[6] [1962] 2 Q.B. 1 CA at 62.
[7] [1962] 2 Q.B. 1 CA at 64.
[8] [1962] 2 Q.B. 1 CA at 60.
[9] [2016] EWCA Civ 982; [2016] 2 Lloyd's Rep. 447 at [92]: "The modern English law approach to the classification of contractual terms is that a term is innominate unless it is clear that it is intended to be a condition or a warranty—see, for example, *Cehave N.V. v Bremer Handelgesellschaft ('The Hansa Nord')* [1976] Q.B. 44 at 70H–71B (Roskill LJ); *Bremer v Vanden* [1978] 2 Lloyd's Rep. 109 at 113, HL (Lord Wilberforce); *Bunge v Tradax* at 715H–716A (Lord Wilberforce) at 717G-H (Lord Scarman) and at 727E (Lord Roskill). As Lord Scarman stated at 717: 'Unless the contract makes it clear, either by express provision or by necessary implication arising from its nature, purpose, and circumstances…. that a particular stipulation is a condition or only a warranty, it is an innominate term, the remedy for a breach of which depends upon the nature, consequences, and effect of the breach.'"
[10] [1989] 2 Lloyd's Rep. 277 at 283 col.2 to 284 per Kerr LJ.
[11] [2019] EWCA Civ 1161; [2019] 2 Lloyd's Rep. 603.

First, in the *State Trading Corp of India* case, Kerr LJ referred to these factors:[12] **12-005**

(i)   it is not decisive[13] that a commercial contract prescribes a precise time for compliance;

(ii)   it might be that the relevant obligation is relatively minor and not central to the contract;

(iii)   there might be that there are internal points of construction tending against the conclusion that the obligation is a condition (in that case a similar obligation elsewhere in the contract was expressly described as *not being a condition*);

(iv)   the loss flowing from breach might not be great in comparison with other sums payable, and possible sources of loss capable of arising, under the same contract;

(v)   the relevant obligation might not be one which needs to be satisfied before the other contractual machinery can proceed; and

(vi)   it might be significant that the contract does not form part of a "string"[14] of transactions.

Next, the Court of Appeal in *Ark Shipping Co LLC v Silverburn Shipping (IoM)* **12-006**
Ltd considered these factors (reaching the conclusion that a term in a 15-year demise charterparty requiring the charterer to maintain at all times the vessels' classification was an intermediate term):

(i)   the absence of express stipulation that it was a condition;[15]

(ii)   the clause did not require performance at a particular time (but rather maintenance of a complex set of documentary statuses);[16]

(iii)   there was no issue of interdependent performance;[17]

(iv)   admittedly, there was only one type of breach possible here, rather than a range, but this factor was outweighed by the others;[18]

---

[12] [1989] 2 Lloyd's Rep. 277 at 283 col.2 to 284.

[13] *Bunge Corp New York v Tradax SA* [1981] 1 W.L.R. 711 HL at 719 per Lord Lowry: "The treatment of time limits as conditions in mercantile contracts does not appear to me to be justifiable by any presumption of fact or rule of law, but rather to be a practical expedient founded on and dictated by the experience of businessmen." But Lord Wilberforce at 715–716 indicated that the court might lean in favour of the condition analysis if the clause is a time obligation (other than for payment of money) and it appears in a mercantile contract: "It remains true, as [Roskill LJ] has pointed out in *Cehave NV v Bremer Handelsgesellschaft mbH ('The Hansa Nord')* [1976] Q.B. 44 at 70–71, that the courts should not be too ready to interpret contractual clauses as conditions. And I have myself commended, and continue to commend, the greater flexibility in the law of contracts to which *Hongkong Fir points the way (Reardon Smith Line Ltd v Yngvar Hansen-Tangen* [1976] 1 W.L.R. 989 at 998). But I do not doubt that, in suitable cases, the courts should not be reluctant, if the intentions of the parties as shown by the contract so indicate, to hold that an obligation has the force of a condition, and that indeed they should usually do so in the case of time clauses in mercantile contracts." Roskill LJ said in *"The Hansa Nord"* [1976] Q.B. 44 CA at 70–71: "a court should not be over ready, unless required by statute or authority so to do. to construe a term in a contract as a 'condition' any breach of which gives rise to a right to reject rather than as a term any breach of which sounds in damages".

[14] *Contrasting Bunge Corp New York v Tradax SA* [1981] 1 W.L.R. 711 HL (noted F. Reynolds, "Discharge of Contract by Breach" (1981) 97 L.Q.R. 541; J. Carter, "Classification of Contractual Terms: The New Orthodoxy" [1981] C.L.J. 219).

[15] [2019] EWCA Civ 1161; [2019] 2 Lloyd's Rep. 603 at [54].

[16] [2019] EWCA Civ 1161; [2019] 2 Lloyd's Rep. 603 at [55].

[17] [2019] EWCA Civ 1161; [2019] 2 Lloyd's Rep. 603 at [56].

[18] [2019] EWCA Civ 1161; [2019] 2 Lloyd's Rep. 603 at [57].

(v)   the relevant clause was part of a set of repair and maintenance-related obligations, and these other obligations were not conditions;[19]

(vi)   there was a troubling widening of the category of documents, beyond the classification certificate, to "other required certificates in force at all times;[20]

(vii)   even the discrete obligation to maintain insurance was not a condition;[21]

(viii) the consequences of breach would vary a lot: ranging across "trivial, minor or very grave consequences" (at [77] the underlying factual situation "peeped out", Gross LJ noting that the lapse in certification took place during a short period when the vessel, a tug, was in dry dock undergoing repair);[22]

(ix)   the advantages of certainty are outweighed here by the danger of "trivial breaches having disproportionate consequences".[23]

12-007   *Intermediate Term: Extension of Duration of a Guarantee.* In *Wuhan Ocean Economic & Technical Cooperation Co Ltd, Nantong Huigang Shipbuilding Co Ltd v Schiffahrts-Gesellschaft ("Hansa Murcia") MBH & Co KG* (2012)[24] Cooke J was asked to categorise an implied term that sellers of a ship would procure (within a reasonable time) extension of a guarantee in respect of a possible refund of monies by the seller to the purchaser. He held that this should be regarded as an intermediate term and not as a warranty. He noted:[25]

> "The Sellers relied on *Hong Kong Fir Shipping Co Ltd v Kawasaki Kisen Kaisha Ltd* [1962] 2 Q.B. 26 and *Woodar v Wimpey* [1980] 1 W.L.R. 277 for the proposition that, where a breach of a term could never deprive the other party of substantially the whole benefit of the contract or strike at its root, that term could only be a warranty."

Cooke J concluded:[26] "The term must be an innominate term because a breach could deprive the Buyers of substantially the whole benefit of the Contract, if they did not institute arbitration and thus extend the guarantee."

12-008   *Intermediate Term: Party's Assurance that Connected Third Party Would Pay.* In *Maurice MacNeill Iona Ltd v C21 London Estates Ltd* (2018)[27] MMI, which was the head franchisor of an estate agency brand, entered into successive franchise agreements for the running of estate agency businesses with the EREL company with respect to the Ilford district and with the C21 company with respect to the Chelsea area. Mr Noorkhan owned both EREL and C21. EREL had been slow to make payments to MMI under the Ilford contract, and so, before the Chelsea contract was granted, MMI insisted on a written side-letter whereby C21 guaranteed that EREL would meet its liabilities. The Court of Appeal held that the side-letter became incorporated as part of the Chelsea contract (notwithstanding that the standard terms of the contract contained an entire agreement clause). But the obligation on C21 within the side-letter did not create a promissory condition and instead

---

[19]   [2019] EWCA Civ 1161; [2019] 2 Lloyd's Rep. 603 at [58]–[61].
[20]   [2019] EWCA Civ 1161; [2019] 2 Lloyd's Rep. 603 at [62]–[65].
[21]   [2019] EWCA Civ 1161; [2019] 2 Lloyd's Rep. 603 at [66]–[71].
[22]   [2019] EWCA Civ 1161; [2019] 2 Lloyd's Rep. 603 at [72]–[77]).
[23]   [2019] EWCA Civ 1161; [2019] 2 Lloyd's Rep. 603 at [78] and [81].
[24]   [2012] EWHC 3104 (Comm); [2013] 1 All E.R. (Comm) 1277; [2013] 1 Lloyd's Rep. 273 at [32]–[39].
[25]   [2012] EWHC 3104 (Comm); [2013] 1 All E.R. (Comm) 1277; [2013] 1 Lloyd's Rep. 273 at [32].
[26]   [2012] EWHC 3104 (Comm); [2013] 1 All E.R. (Comm) 1277; [2013] 1 Lloyd's Rep. 273 at [39].
[27]   [2018] EWCA Civ 1823 (unreported).

operated as an intermediate term. It followed that non-payment by EREL occurring under the Ilford contract did not give rise to an automatic right for MMI to terminate the Chelsea contract. The nub of the decision appears in this passage, where Lewison LJ said:[28] "Under the standard terms of the franchise agreement (which applied to both Ilford and Chelsea) the failure to pay punctually is expressly designated a Curable Default. To hold that a failure to pay royalties under the Ilford agreement is a condition of the Chelsea agreement would be to bypass [that] contractual structure...Moreover, the consequences of [late or] non-payment of a trivial sum...cannot be said to have consequences so serious for [MMI] that there is any necessity for a breach of that obligation to be treated as a condition of a contract". The facts did not disclose a serious enough breach by C21 of an intermediate term to justify termination by MMI, nor a renunciation (because of the assurance given by C21 under the Chelsea contract, any Ilford non-payment by EREL became a concurrent default by C21 under the Chelsea contract. Contract). It followed that MMI had had no justification for terminating the Chelsea contract by reference to non-payment under the Ilford contract.

Intermediate Term: Confidentiality Clause: Settlement Agreement. Cavanagh **12-009** J held in *Duchy Farm Kennels Ltd v Steels* (2020)[29] that a "strictly confidential" clause in an employment settlement agreement did not constitute a condition, but merely an intermediate term. The former employee had breached the clause by divulging details to a third party. But the breach was not serious enough on the facts to entitle the employer to treat the settlement as discharged for breach. And hence the settlement sum, of £15,000, was still owed. Describing the clause as "ancillary", and not a promissory condition, Cavanagh J said:

> "[54]...this term [is] ancillary to the main part of the contract. Confidentiality was not at the core of the agreement...[55]...There may be cases where the allegations...and/or the [parties'] identity...are so sensitive that...confidentiality is the very essence of the benefit for the employer from the agreement. [If so, normally] the agreement will expressly stipulate that the term is a condition". Here the breach was not grave enough to entitle the employer to treat the settlement agreement as discharged for breach: "[68]...The breach was never likely to, and did not, result in any commercial embarrassment or other commercial problems for the [employer]. The risk that it would trigger expensive unmeritorious copy-cat claims was very remote, especially as the sum in issue was not very large...."

III.   DOES THIS BREACH OF THE INTERMEDIATE TERM ENTITLE THE INNOCENT PARTY TO TERMINATE

Level of default required: competing formulations   Diplock LJ[30] (but not **12-010** Upjohn LJ)[31] in the *Hongkong Fir* case (1962) suggested that the true test is to consider whether the breach's effect has been to "deprive the [innocent party] of substantially the whole benefit which it was the intention of the parties that he

---

28   [2018] EWCA Civ 1823 at [15]. Lewison LJ's discussion of promissory conditions in general at [12]–[16] is illuminating, but too long to cite fully here.
29   [2020] EWHC 1208 (QB); [2020] I.R.L.R. 632 (the case's illuminating but long exposition at [33], of the criteria for identifying a condition is cited at para.10-036).
30   [1962] 2 Q.B. 1 CA at 69–70.
31   [1962] 2 Q.B. 1 at 64

should obtain".[32] Judges continue to recant this formulation, including in the wider context of "repudiation".[33] In fact the terminology is not stable and a various of formulations have been adopted. Thus Lewison LJ in *Urban 1 (Blonk Street) Ltd v Ayres* (2013) said that the innocent party is entitled to terminate the contract for breach of an intermediate term only if the resulting harm:[34]

> "was such as to go to the root of the contract, that is to say it deprived the defendants of substantially the whole benefit which it was intended they should have under the contract; or ... the claimant showed that it had no intention of carrying out the contract or, at any event, only to do so in a manner substantially inconsistent with the claimant's contractual obligations such as to deprive the defendants of substantially the whole benefit which it was intended they should receive under the contract."

12-011   It is apparent from both Lewison LJ's analysis in *Urban 1 (Blonk Street) Ltd v Ayres* (2013)[35] and from Arden LJ's remarks in *Valilas v Januzaj* (2014)[36] that some judges regard the "going to the root" idea as a calibration of seriousness equivalent to the "substantial deprivation of the whole benefit" test:

> "The common law adopts open-textured expressions ... I will use the formulation that asks whether the victim has been deprived of substantially the whole of the benefit of the contract. The expression 'going to the root of the contract' conveys the same point ... There are other similar expressions." (The relevant passage is quoted in full at para.8-001.)

12-012   But it is suggested, with respect, that it is arguable that Diplock LJ's test imposes on the innocent party a very high threshold., requiring the innocent party to show that breach on the facts has deprived him "of substantially the whole benefit which it was the intention of the parties that he should obtain".[37] For many people, the "going to the root" notion (suggesting a truly but not catastrophically serious default) would be understood to operate as a less demanding criterion than breach which involves, as it were, almost total wipe-out of performance (the "substantial deprivation of the whole benefit" test). If so, the further issue arises: should it be enough that the breach is serious and "goes to the root"? There has been inconclusive re-examination of this issue.[38] It is interesting that Lord Denning MR in *"The Hansa Nord"* (1976) referred only to Upjohn LJ's "breach going to the root" formulation (made in the *Hongkong Fir* case (1962)),[39] and that Lord Denning made no refer-

---

[32]   Diplock LJ's criterion ([1962] 2 Q.B. 1 CA at 69–70) was applied, but the facts were held to fall short of this requirement, in *H TV Ltd (formerly Can Associates TV Ltd) v ITV2 Ltd* [2015] EWHC 2840 (Comm) at [277] and [278] per Flaux J.

[33]   e.g. *Flanagan v Liontrust Investment Partners LLP* [2015] EWHC 2171 (Ch); [2015] Bus. L.R. 1172; [2016] 1 B.C.L.C. 177 at [209] per Henderson J.

[34]   [2013] EWCA Civ 816; [2014] 1 W.L.R. 756 at [48] (see also *Ampurius Nu Homes Holdings Ltd v Telford Homes (Creekside) Ltd* [2013] EWCA Civ 577; [2013] 4 All E.R. 377).

[35]   [2013] EWCA Civ 816; [2014] 1 W.L.R. 756 at [48] (see also *Ampurius Nu Homes Holdings Ltd v Telford Homes (Creekside) Ltd* [2013] EWCA Civ 577; [2013] 4 All E.R. 377).

[36]   [2014] EWCA Civ 436; [2015] 1 All E.R. (Comm) 1047 at [59] (considered by Males J in *C & S Associates UK Ltd v Enterprise Insurance Co Plc* [2015] EWHC 3757 at [78] and [79]).

[37]   [1962] 2 Q.B. 1 CA at 69–70.

[38]   *Ampurius Nu Homes Holdings Ltd v Telford Homes (Creekside) Ltd* [2013] EWCA Civ 577; [2013] 4 All E.R. 377 at [38]–[50] per Lewison LJ (considered by Males J in *C & S Associates UK Ltd v Enterprise Insurance Co Plc* [2015] EWHC 3757 at [78] and [79]); *Urban 1 (Blonk Street) Ltd v Ayres* [2013] EWCA Civ 816; [2014] 1 W.L.R. 756 at [57] per Etherton C.

[39]   [1962] 2 Q.B. 1 CA at 64.

ence to Diplock LJ's (apparently) more exacting formulation (loss of "substantially the whole benefit") in the *Hongkong Fir* case.[40]

Judicial usage indicates that the courts are using these phrases in the knowledge **12-013** that they are mere short-hand for a wider inquiry into the seriousness of breach and the overall assessment whether termination is an appropriate response to the relevant default. For example, in the context of an intermediate term, Males J said in the *C & S Associates UK* case (2015)[41] that termination will be justified if there is a high level of default, so as to go to the root of the contract, having regard to a range of factors:

> "the court is not exercising a discretion, but is engaged in a fact-sensitive inquiry which involves 'a multi-factorial assessment' and the use of various 'open-textured expressions'. The bar which must be cleared before there is an entitlement in the innocent party to treat himself as discharged is therefore a 'high' one. A number of expressions have been used to describe the circumstances that warrant discharge, the most common being that the breach must 'go to the root of the contract'."

It is submitted that the UK Supreme Court might usefully re-open this question and that the test justifying termination of an intermediate term should be: "was the breach serious, as opposed to trivial or insignificant, in its impact?" An attractive lowering of the bar for termination for breach of an intermediate term is discernible in the leading Australian decision. The High Court of Australia in *Koompahtoo Local Aboriginal Land Council v Sanpine Pty Ltd* (2007)[42] said that the intermediate term doctrine permits termination for "serious and substantial breaches of contract". The same court appeared to treat the phrase "breach going to the root of the contract" and breach depriving the innocent party of "a substantial *part* of the contract" as synonymous.[43] It is submitted that it should be enough if the breach of an intermediate term produces very serious or substantial adverse consequences for the innocent party so that termination is a proportionate and reasonable response.

Factors relevant to the issue whether termination is appropriate for breach of **12-014** **an intermediate term** There has been one judicial statement of relevant factors and, as we shall see, some textbook lists. In *Ampurius Nu Homes Holdings Ltd v Telford Homes (Creekside) Ltd* (2013) Lewison LJ posed these questions:[44]

> "The next thing to consider is the effect of the breach on the injured party. What financial loss has it caused? How much of the intended benefit under the contract has the injured party already received? Can the injured party be adequately compensated by an award of damages? Is the breach likely to be repeated? Will the guilty party resume compliance with his obligations? Has the breach fundamentally changed the value of future performance of the guilty party's outstanding obligations?"

In *Seadrill Management Services Ltd v OAO Gazprom* Flaux J concluded that the **12-015** *HongKong Fir* test had not been satisfied and that the facts disclosed an instance of negligence in the performance of a contract for supply of a drilling rig which did

---

[40] [1976] Q.B. 44 CA at 60–1 (citing Upjohn LJ in *HongKong Fir Shipping Co Ltd v Kawasaki Kisen Kaisha Ltd* [1962] 2 Q.B. 1 CA at 64).

[41] *C & S Associates UK Ltd v Enterprise Insurance Co Plc* [2015] EWHC 3757 at [78].

[42] [2007] HCA 61; (2007) 82 A.L.J.R 345; (2008) 241 A.L.R. 88 at [52] H.Ct. Aust. (Gleeson CJ, Gummow, Heydon, Crennan JJ).

[43] [2007] HCA 61; (2007) 82 A.L.J.R. 345; (2008) 241 A.L.R. 88 at [54] and [71] H.Ct. Aust.

[44] [2013] EWCA Civ 577; [2013] 4 All E.R. 377 at [52].

not go to the root of the contract or deprive the hiring party of substantially the whole of the expected benefit.[45]

12-016   McKendrick compiles a list of factors which might be relevant to the assessment whether to declare that termination is justified in this context (numbering added here):[46]

> "(1) the benefit which it was intended that the innocent party would obtain from performance ... , (2) the losses suffered by the innocent party ... (3) the cost of making performance comply with the terms of the contract, (4) the value of the performance that has been received by the innocent party, (5) the willingness of the party in breach to make good the consequences of the breach, (6) the likelihood of a further breach by the party in breach, and (7) the adequacy of damages as a remedy to the innocent party. Given the range of factors ... and their generality, the balancing of these factors must, at the end of the day, depend to a large extent upon the facts of the individual case."

12-017   Similarly, Carter suggests that, when deciding whether breach of an intermediate term justifies termination in the particular case, the courts will take into account:[47]

> "(a)   any detriment caused, or likely to be caused, by the breach;
> (b)   any delay caused, or likely to be caused, by the breach;
> (c)   the value of any performance received by tendered to the [innocent party];
> (d)   the cost of making any performance, given or tendered by the party in breach, conform with the requirements of the contract;
> (e)   any offer by the party in breach to remedy the breach;
> (f)   whether the party in breach has previously breached the contract or is likely to breach it in the future; and
> (g)   whether the [innocent party] will be adequately compensated by an award of damages in respect of the breach."

12-018   Date for determining whether breach was serious enough to justify termination   The Court of Appeal in *Ampurius Nu Homes Holdings Ltd v Telford Homes (Creekside) Ltd* (2013) made clear that the relevant date is the time when the innocent party purports justifiably to terminate for repudiation (including, as on the facts of that case, breach of an intermediate terms, when the severity of the breach is to be assessed), and not the earlier date of actual breach.[48] This is because matters might have changed in the interval (however, short it might be) between breach and the decision to terminate. For example, as in the *Ampurius* case, the guilty party

---

[45]   [2009] EWHC 1530 (Comm); [2010] 1 Lloyd's Rep. 543; affm.'d [2010] EWCA Civ 691; [2011] 1 All E.R. (Comm) at [225]–[246].

[46]   E. McKendrick, *Text, Cases, and Materials*, 10th edn (Oxford: Oxford University Press, 2022), p.770; for a similar list, US *Restatement on Contracts* (2d) s.241, on which G.H. Jones (with P. Schlechtriem) "Breach of Contract" in *International Encyclopaedia of Comparative Law* Vol.VII (Contracts in General), (Tübingen: Mohr Siebeck Publishing, 1999), 15–131.

[47]   J.W. Carter, *Carter's Breach of Contract*, 2nd edn (Oxford: Hart Publishing, 2019), 6.57.

[48]   [2013] EWCA Civ 577; [2013] 4 All E.R. 377 at [43], citing Diplock LJ in *Hongkong Fir Shipping Co Ltd v Kawasaki Kisen Kaisha Ltd* [1962] 2 Q.B. 26 CA at 72 (the *Ampurius* case was considered in *Bristol Groundschool v Intelligent Data Capture Ltd* [2014] EWHC 2145 (Ch) at [178]–[196], on the latter case see text at para.8-031).

might have taken steps towards curing or mitigating his earlier default.[49] Lewison LJ said:[50]

> "There are three points which emerge from this [analysis of the statements in the *HongKong Fir* case and other cases]. First, the task of the court is to look at the position as at the date of purported termination of the contract even in a case of actual rather than anticipatory breach. Second, in looking at the position at that date, the court must take into account any steps taken by the guilty party to remedy accrued breaches of contract. Third, the court must also take account of likely future events, judged by reference to objective facts as at the date of purported termination."

DD Classics Ltd v Chen[51] illustrates the importance of the fact that the severity **12-019** of breach of an innominate term is to be assessed at the time when the innocent party purports justifiably to terminate for breach. The case is explained in detail elsewhere (paras 10-088, 14-068). In essence, the buyer had paid later than the stipulated date. The date had not been made time of the essence. The seller submitted that if the payment date involved an innominate term then the seller was justified on the facts in having terminated the contract for breach. But, as the judge explained in the following passage, there had been water under this bridge between breach and termination, and those events destroyed on these facts the seller's submission that termination was justified:[52]

> "[57]...the proposed analysis [is] completely hopeless. Whether one can terminate for breach of an intermediate or innominate term depends upon the seriousness of the breach having regard to the facts. In this case, by the time of the purported termination, the buyer had done everything it possibly could. It had authorised the transfer [of funds in payment of the car]. The transfer [of funds] had been made; if it had not reached the receiving account, that was a matter completely outside the control of the buyer and, indeed, had been outside its control for six days at the time of termination. In those circumstances, it is inconceivable that any court would hold that Mr Chen [the seller] was entitled to terminate the contract on account of breach of an innominate term."

Prospective matters contemplated at the date of termination On the ques- **12-020** tion of events which have not yet occurred (see the last sentence of the quotation from Lewison LJ, just cited: "the court must also take account of likely future events, judged by reference to objective facts as at the date of purported termination"), the court assesses matters prospectively by carrying out an (i) objective determination of future events based on (ii) events known and circumstances prevailing at the time when the decision to terminate was made by the innocent party.

Innocent party's degree of "risk-aversion" As for the degree of legitimate risk- **12-021** aversion, this is clearly dependent on the precise context. Carter[53] approves Lord Devlin's extra-judicial remark[54] that in the case of "airworthiness instead of seaworthiness" termination would be justified "if there were the slightest danger that

---

49 [2013] EWCA Civ 577; [2013] 4 All E.R. 377 at [44] and [63] per Lewison LJ (approved by Longmore LJ at [79]).
50 [2013] EWCA Civ 577; [2013] 4 All E.R. 377 at [44] per Lewison LJ.
51 [2022] EWHC 1357 (Comm) (Judge Keyser QC).
52 [2022] EWHC 1357 (Comm) at [57] (Judge Keyser QC).
53 J.W. Carter, *Carter's Breach of Contract*, 2nd edn (Oxford: Hart Publishing, 2019), [6-54].
54 [1966] C.L.J. 192, 198.

an aeroplane would not arrive safely at its destination". Similarly, returning to the case of seaworthiness, ecological concern for the possible devastation caused by a maritime disaster would justify termination of a charterparty if the relevant vessel is to be used for the transport of hazardous or polluting substances.

Of course, elongation of the period of "wait and see", and the imponderable issue of legitimately avoided risk, as mentioned in the preceding paragraphs, will add to the uncertainty of the *HongKong* approach (see further at paras 12-030–12-031 on the "pros and cons" of the intermediate term technique).

12-022 **Breach of intermediate term overlapping with a separate breach of a condition** Another problem might arise if a party terminates a contract on the basis that there has been a sufficiently serious breach of cl.1, which is construed as creating an intermediate term. Subsequently, it is discovered that the guilty party had committed some other default under the same contract, and that breach justifies termination on the basis of breach of a condition, perhaps contained in cl.2, or for a sufficiently serious breach of an intermediate term contained in cl.3. In that situation, general principle would seem to justify the innocent party gaining the right to terminate on this latter basis, even though this was not the reason given at the time: para.8-069.

12-023 **Intermediate obligation to comply with a notification requirement** The intermediate term device normally controls the issue whether the innocent party acquires, in addition to the basic damages claim, a right to terminate for breach. But it appears that the "wait-and-sea" device can be applied in the different context of assessing whether a party has become disqualified from relying on rights which would arise if he had acted punctiliously in giving notice under the relevant contractual regime of notification.[55] It was in this type of context that Leggatt J in *Scottish Power UK Plc v BP Exploration Operating Co Ltd* (2015)[56] Leggatt J examined the case law (notably the decision of the House of Lords in *Bremer Handels GmbH v Vanden-Avenne Izegem PVBA* (1978))[57] concerning the possibility that, even though damages are not in issue, an intermediate term might apply to certain duties of notification imposed under contract, with the result that the underlying right will be lost if the failure to notify has in fact caused very serious prejudice (and, conversely, the right will not be affected if the failure to comply is not serious in its impact on the facts of the case). But on the facts of the *Scottish Power case* (2015) Leggatt J held that failure to satisfy the relevant notification requirement did not constitute a condition precedent nor did it operate even potentially in a preclusive manner on the basis of an intermediate term.

12-024 **Application of the test requiring breach which goes to the root** In *Neath Port Talbot (Recycling) Ltd v James Heys and Sons Ltd*,[58] a contract required the claimant to collect from the local authority regular quantities of re-cycled waste. The claimant's failure to pay a particular invoice was held not to be serious enough to justify termination by the local authority, but that party's failure to collect waste

---

[55] For extensive analysis of this topic, J.W. Carter, G.J. Tolhurst, E. Peden, "Developing the Intermediate Term Concept" (2006) 22 J.C.L. 268, 276–286.

[56] [2015] EWHC 2638 (Comm); [2016] 1 All E.R. (Comm) 536; 162 Con. L.R. 195 at [194] ff, notably at [224], Leggatt J; decision affirmed, [2016] EWCA Civ 1043.

[57] [1978] 2 Lloyd's Rep. 109 HL.

[58] [2021] EWHC 3157 (Comm); 201 Con. L.R. 140 (Judge Keyser QC).

over a significant period did pass the test, so that in this latter respect the local authority had been justified in terminating the contract. On these two points, respectively, the judgment states:[59]

"[45]...the non-payment of the invoices for cardboard did not of itself entitle the claimant to terminate the ...In a commercial contract, time of payment is not generally of the essence of the contract. Here, it is true, there was short-payment followed by non-payment over a period of several months. The breach was serious. However, it did not affect the viability of the operations to which [the contract] was directed, namely the disposal of cardboard to approved final destinations, and it concerned only one of the four Lots with which the contract was concerned...

[55]...the defendant's breach of contract in respect of the removal of plastics in September and October 2018 did go to the root of the...and entitled the claimant to terminate the contract as it did. It is true that the breach went to only one of the Lots. However, the fundamental operational purpose of the contract was the removal of waste materials that had been received into the Site. The plastics were a very significant component of those materials. The breach was persistent and deliberate. The defendant had decided to stop the removal of plastics while it was uneconomic for it to remove them and instead to store them. This led not only to a build-up of baled plastics but, consequently, to a serious and unsanitary build-up of unbaled plastics on the Site. The defendant was, as I find, asked repeatedly to remove plastics and aware of the problems being caused on the Site, yet it took no action. It thereby evinced an intention not to perform the contract in accordance with its terms and committed a breach that went to the root of the contract. Although it is strictly unnecessary to refer to the matter, I note too that the defendant had at this time failed to pay a substantial debt in respect of cardboard; although that did not constitute a repudiation of the contract, it formed part of the context in which the breach in respect of plastics fell to be considered and tends to confirm that the defendant did not intend to treat itself as bound to perform the contract according to its terms."

IV. SALE OF GOODS TRANSACTIONS AND INTERMEDIATE TERMS

In *"The Hansa Nord"* (1976) the Court of Appeal held that an agreement falling within the scope of the Sale of Goods legislation (then the 1893 Act, now the 1979 Act) might contain an intermediate term even though the statute (in its classification of promissory terms) does not include that expression and instead refers to the simple dichotomy of conditions and warranties.[60] Carter notes that before this 1976 decision, "there was considerable academic support for the view that the [intermediate term device] could not be applied to contracts for the sale of goods" because of the antithetical and dichotomous language of "conditions" and "warranties" used to express *statutory* obligations under that Act.[61] In reaching this conclusion, Roskill LJ and Ormrod LJ noted that the sale of goods legislation (now s.62(2) of the 1979 Act) requires the "rules of the Common Law" to apply to sale of goods transactions.[62] One of these Common Law rules is the rule which was stated (or perhaps "rediscovered") in the *Hongkong Fir* case (1962) (para.12-001 ff): that a contractual obligation might be "intermediate" or "innominate": if so, the innocent party's capacity to terminate the contract will depend on the gravity or otherwise of breach, having regard to the actual consequences of that breach.

12-025

---

59 [2021] EWHC 3157 (Comm); 201 Con. L.R. 140 at [45] and [55] (Judge Keyser QC).
60 *"The Hansa Nord"* [1976] Q.B. 44 CA, noted A. Weir, "Contract—The Buyer's Right to Reject Defective Goods" [1976] C.L.J. 33.
61 J.W. Carter, *Carter's Breach of Contract*, 2nd edn (Oxford: Hart Publishing, 2019), [4-26], fn.151, citing comments by Reynolds, Montrose, Sutton, and Atiyah.
62 [1976] Q.B. 44 CA at 72, 83.

12-026   The contract in *"The Hansa Nord"* (1976) concerned supply of citrus pulp pellets from Florida (the pellets were a by-product of the Floridean orange-juice industry) to Rotterdam. These were to be used to manufacture cattle-feed. It was an *express term* that they should be delivered in good condition. The buyer rejected them when he discovered that some of the cargo was less than perfect (the market price had fallen so that this had become a bad bargain for the buyer). The seller then re-sold the goods at auction to X ("Mr Baas"). The buyer (who had just pulled out from the original deal) later bought these goods from the third party, X, for a much smaller sum[63] than he had originally agreed to pay the original vendor (£33,720 rather than £100,000). (The circumstances were suspicious: Carter notes that the Board of Appeal of the Grain and Feed Trade Association had estimated that commercial value of the goods at about £65,000).[64] It appears that the product had not deteriorated to the point that it could not be used lawfully and successfully to produce animal feed (and Lord Denning MR emphasised that the goods had been successfully used to produce animal feed and that the buyer had not shown any loss caused by the fact that the pellets had been less than perfect on arrival). The seller contended successfully that the buyer had not been entitled to reject the goods, and therefore the buyer should have been confined to a claim for damages. The price had already been paid before the goods arrived.

12-027   The result of the Court of Appeal's decision, therefore, was that the seller was entitled to retain the price, less a modest price allowance to reflect the fact that the pellets had been less than perfect:

> "the buyers were not entitled to reject the goods. They are, however, entitled to damages for the difference in value between the damaged goods and sound goods on arrival at Rotterdam. The case must be remitted to the board for this to be determined."[65]

12-028   In *"The Hansa Nord"* (1976) the Court of Appeal classified the present obligation as an intermediate term, rather than an express condition. It also held that there had been no breach of the (then applicable) statutory implied term that the goods must be of "merchantable quality" on the present facts.[66] So the court revoked the arbitrator's order for repayment of the price, and instead remitted the case for assessment of damages, based on the difference in the value of the goods supplied and of sound goods.

12-029   In *Galtrade Ltd v BP Oil International Ltd*,[67] Adrian Beltrami QC held that the specifications concerning fuel did not constitute conditions and that the discrepancies between the specifications and the product delivered fell short of constituting a breach which justified termination (on this case see also para.10-056). The deviation from the specified matters were not fundamental but could be compensated by

---

[63]   X, the go-between, seems not to have made any profit from the sale; and there is a suspicion that he had been interposed by the buyer to disguise the fact that the latter intended to reject the goods and then buy them back at a much lower price, knowing that the goods could still be used successfully to produce animal feed.

[64]   J.W. Carter, *Carter's Breach of Contract*, 2nd edn (Oxford: Hart Publishing, 2019), [6-72], fn.438.

[65]   *"The Hansa Nord"* [1976] Q.B. 44 CA at 63–4 per Lord Denning MR.

[66]   [1976] Q.B. 44 CA at 61–3, 77, 79, considering Sale of Goods Act 1893 s.14(2); now Sale of Goods Act 1979 s.14(2), which is concerned with the implied term that goods should be of "satisfactory quality", as amplified by s.14(2A)–(2F).

[67]   [2021] EWHC 1796 (Comm); [2021] 2 C.L.C. 408 at [86]–[98].

a reduction on the price:[68]

> "[95] ...the nature and extent of the deviations from specification could be assessed and a value placed on them. This was, perhaps, inevitable, given the agreement of the experts that [the relevant delivery] remained marketable, albeit at a reduced price. But once that premise has been established, it is difficult to avoid the conclusion that this is a case where the Claimant can properly be compensated for the financial effect of the breach rather than one where it has been deprived of the substantial benefit of its contract."

V.   The Pros and Cons of the Intermediate Term

The question whether breach of an intermediate term justifies termination requires assessment of the consequences of breach. If those consequences are really severe, the innocent party can justifiably terminate. Thus the doctrine of the intermediate term involves a more flexible approach. It is intended to work in favour of the guilty party because (unlike the operation of promissory "conditions") the intermediate term can shields the guilty party from the innocent party's over-zealous or punctilious demand for precise performance. In this way, the intermediate term approach is certainly an antidote to a ("draconian") regime of "zero-tolerance", where the innocent party can terminate a contract for technical and trivial breach, snapping at the slightest opportunity to end the contract.   **12-030**

But this antidote comes at a price. First, it introduces considerable uncertainty in the application of contractual terms both (i) at the stage when it must be determined whether a term is or is not an intermediate term, and (ii) at the subsequent stage when the court must assess whether breach on the facts of the case was so serious that it justifies the innocent party's decision to terminate the contract. These issues can divide both arbitral panels and judges. Obtaining a final answer might require protracted and expensive litigation, and the decision might be taken on more than one appeal. A second problem is that recognition of intermediate terms can induce sloppiness in performance of commercial contexts, because the guilty party will know that the contract cannot be terminated unless the breach is really bad, and instead the innocent party is confined to the less dramatic remedy of seeking compensatory damages.   **12-031**

VI.   Was the *Hongkong* Decision the Re-invention of the Wheel?

The jury is arguably still out on this question, although the more likely answer is that the Court of Appeal was merely articulating a legal approach or concept which was already embodied in the nineteenth century case law. Thus Lord Wilberforce in the *Schuler case* (1974)[69] and Lord Denning in *"The Hansa Nord"* (1976)[70] suggested that the category of intermediate terms had ante-dated the *HongKong* decision in 1962 and that it could be traced far back into the nineteenth century and well before the 1893 Sales of Goods Act (now the 1979 Act). According to these judicial historians, the existence of that third category of promissory term, intermediate between conditions and warranties, had become obscured by the binary structure of the sale of goods legislation. It has been suggested that the jurist responsible for this conceptual over-simplification was Sir Frederick Pollock. The   **12-032**

---

68   [2021] EWHC 1796 (Comm); [2021] 2 C.L.C. 408 at [95].
69   [1974] A.C. 235 HL at 262 F: "I do not think this was anything new ...".
70   *"The Hansa Nord"* [1976] 1 Q.B. 44 CA at 60.

finger was pointed at this celebrated commentator by Robert Goff QC and Brian Davenport during argument before the Court of Appeal in *"The Mihalis Angelos"*,[71] and this contention was adopted by Lord Denning MR in that case.[72] According to this view, Pollock introduced in the late nineteenth century the so-called condition/warranty exclusivity "heresy". The view that there were only two types of term explains the structure of the Sale of Goods Act 1893 (and its successor, the 1979 Act),[73] which refers only to conditions and warranties, and makes no reference to intermediate terms.

12-033   Although the fallacy of a simple condition/warranty dichotomy has now been exploded, it is important to be aware of this confusion. It must be admitted that, although the three-fold classification of promissory terms is no longer in doubt,

---

[71]   *Maredelanto Compania Naviera SA v Bergbau-Handel GMBH ("The Mihalis Angelos")* [1971] 1 Q.B. 164 at 187 (counsel):

"The *Hongkong Fir* case re-established the law as accepted in the mid-nineteenth century, viz., that the right to determine depends on whether the breach goes to the root of the contract: see *Freeman v Taylor* (1831) 8 Bing. 124 at 132, 138; *Glaholm v Hays* (1841) 2 Man. & G. 257 at 266; *Clipsham v Vertue* (1843) 5 Q.B. 265; *Ollive v Booker* (1847) 1 Exch. 416; *Tarrabochia v Hickie* (1856) 1 H. & N. 183, ... *Behn v Burness* 1 B. & S. 877 at 878, 881, 887 and (1863) 3 B & S 751, 757–760 ... [But in] the late nineteenth century, the heresy developed that all terms must be classified as either conditions or warranties (as those terms were understood in the years preceding The *Hongkong Fir* case). This heresy may have originated in the first edition of *Pollock on Formation of Contract* (1876), and was enshrined in the Sale of Goods Act, 1893: the analysis was accepted and followed in all subsequent textbooks and in many reported cases until The *Hongkong Fir* case (see, e.g. *Bentsen v Taylor Sons & Co* [1893] 2 Q.B. 274). In the latter case, Bowen LJ at 281–2 said: 'assuming the Court to be of opinion that the statement made amounts to a promise, or, in other words, a substantive part of the contract, it still remains to be decided by the Court, as a matter of construction, whether it is such a promise as amounts merely to a warranty, the breach of which would sound only in damages, or whether it is that kind of promise the performance of which is made a condition precedent to all further demands under the contract by the person who made the promise against the other party—a promise the failure to perform which gives to the opposite party the right to say that he will no longer be bound by the contract'."

[72]   *Maredelanto Compania Naviera SA v Bergbau-Handel GMBH ("The Mihalis Angelos")* [1971] 1 Q.B. 164 CA at 193 where Lord Denning MR said:

"Sir Frederick Pollock (*Formation of Contracts*) divided the terms of a contract into two categories: conditions and warranties. The difference between them was this: if the promisor broke a condition in any respect, however slight, it gave the other party a right to be quit of his future obligations and to sue for damages: unless he by his conduct waived the condition, in which case he was bound to perform his future obligations but could sue for the damage he suffered. If the promisor broke a warranty in any respect, however serious, the other party was not quit of his future obligations. He had to perform them. His only remedy was to sue for damages. This division was adopted by Sir Mackenzie Chalmers when he drafted the Sale of Goods Act, 1893, and by Parliament when it passed it. It was stated by Fletcher Moulton LJ in his celebrated dissenting judgment in *Wallis, Son & Wells v Pratt & Haynes* [1910] 2 K.B. 1003 at 1012, which was adopted in its entirety by the House of Lords in [1911] A.C. 394. It would be a mistake, however, to look upon that division as exhaustive. There are many terms of many contracts which cannot be fitted into either category. In such cases the courts, for nigh on 200 years, have not asked themselves: was the term a condition or warranty? But rather: was the breach such as to go to the root of the contract? If it was, then the other party is entitled, at his election, to treat himself as discharged from any further performance. That is made clear by the judgment of Lord Mansfield in *Boone v Eyre* (1777) 1 Hy. Bl. 273; and by the speech of Lord Blackburn in *Mersey Steel & Iron Co v Naylor, Benzon & Co* (1884) 9 App. Cas. 434 at 443–4; and the notes to *Cutter v Powell* (1795) 6 Term. Rep. 320 (*2 Smith's Leading Cases*, 13th edn (London: Sweet & Maxwell, 1929), pp.16–18). The case of *Hongkong Fir Shipping Co Ltd v Kawasaki Kisen Kaisha Ltd* [1962] 2 Q.B. 26 is a useful reminder of this large category."

[73]   J.W. Carter, *Carter's Breach of Contract*, 2nd edn (Oxford: Hart Publishing, 2019), [1-20].

earlier courts had not been consistent in their classification of promissory terms. The entire intellectual episode is learnedly surveyed by Lewison LJ in *Samarenko v Dawn Hill House Ltd* (2011):[74]

"... In order to understand the theory underlying the proposition that time may be 'made of the essence' of a contractual time limit it is necessary to go back a little into legal history. For many years, and certainly during the 19th century, it was accepted legal analysis to classify contractual obligations according to a binary categorisation. A contractual stipulation was either a condition (sometimes called a condition precedent) or a warranty. The difference is encapsulated in the well-known judgment of Bowen LJ in *Bentsen v Taylor, Sons & Co (No.2)* [1893] 2 Q.B. 274 at 281: 'There is no way of deciding that question except by looking at the contract in the light of the surrounding circumstances, and then making up one's mind whether the intention of the parties, as gathered from the instrument itself, will best be carried out by treating the promise as a warranty sounding only in damages, or as a condition precedent by the failure to perform which the other party is relieved of his liability'."

Lewison LJ added in the *Samarenko* case (2011):[75]   **12-034**

"The entrenchment of this binary classification in contractual analysis is borne out by the Sale of Goods Act 1893, which classified every term as either a condition or a warranty. It was not until the seminal judgment of Diplock LJ in *Hongkong Fir Shipping Co Ltd v Kawasaki Kisen Kaisha Ltd* [1962] 2 Q.B. 26 that it really dawned on [modern] English contract lawyers that there was a third category of term (now called either an intermediate or an innominate term) breach of which might or might not amount to a repudiation depending on the gravity of the consequences of the breach. This is an oversimplified historical perspective, as Lord Diplock explained in *United Scientific Holdings Ltd v Burnley Borough Council* [1978] A.C. 904 at 925–928, but it is sufficient for present purposes. The point is that even where the time for performance was regarded as a condition in courts of law, a court of equity would intervene to prevent one party from insisting on his strict legal rights. The practice began in cases of mortgage where the contractual arrangement was that the borrower lost the right to redeem if he did not repay the loan on time (usually 30 days). But equity would allow the borrower to redeem even after the expiry of the contractual deadline. This was later extended to contracts for the sale of land. As Lord Eldon LC explained in *Seton v Slade*; *Hunter v Seton* (1802) 7 Ves. 265 at 273 ..."

VII.   RECEPTION OF THE INTERMEDIATE TERM IN AUSTRALIA AND NEW ZEALAND

New Zealand   The concept of an intermediate term concept has been adopted in   **12-035**
New Zealand.[76]

Majority approval in Australia for the intermediate term   The High Court of   **12-036**
Australia in *Koompahtoo Local Aboriginal Land Council v Sanpine Pty Ltd* (2007)[77]
acknowledged the three-fold classification of conditions, intermediate terms, and
warranties, although Kirby J dissented on this aspect of taxonomy (paras 12-037–

---

74 [2011] EWCA Civ 1445; [2013] Ch. 36 at [28].
75 [2011] EWCA Civ 1445; [2013] Ch. 36 at [29].
76 *Holmes v Burgess* [1975] 2 N.Z.L.R. 311 at 318–20.
77 [2007] HCA 61; (2007) 82 A.L.J.R 345; (2008) 241 A.L.R. 88 H.Ct. Aust. (Gleeson CJ, Gummow, Heydon, Crennan JJ; Kirby J dissenting; noted K. Dharmanda and A. Papamatheos, "Termination and the third term: Discharge and repudiation" (2008) 124 L.Q.R. 373); for references to other Common Law jurisdictions on this topic, A. Phang, "Doctrine and Fairness in the Law of Contract" (2009) 29 L.S. 534, 546 ff.

12-039). The majority expressed approval of the approach in the *Hongkong Fir* case (England, 1962). They added that it had become "mainstream" doctrine in Australia.[78] The majority considered[79] that it imports flexibility and justice into the assessment whether termination for breach is justified. Secondly, they noted that it has the effect of restricting opportunity to terminate for breach to situations involving "serious and substantial breaches of contract". As for the criterion to determine whether breach of an intermediate term has justified termination, the majority appeared to treat the phrase "breach going to the root of the contract" and breach depriving the innocent party of "a substantial *part* of the contract" as synonymous.[80]

12-037 **Dissenting Australian opinion that terms should be classified as either essential (conditions) or inessential** However, in *Koompahtoo Local Aboriginal Land Council v Sanpine Pty Ltd* (2007) Kirby J,[81] in a minority opinion, preferred to adopt a dichotomy of "essential" obligations (viz., conditions) and inessential obligations (viz. covering the joint ground of intermediate terms and warranties, but without adopting that differentiation between those species of inessential terms). On Kirby J's model, the questions would become fewer:[82] (i) did D breach an essential obligation; if so the innocent party can terminate; and (ii) if D breached an inessential obligation, the innocent party is entitled to terminate only if the consequences of the breach were so serious that the innocent party suffered a "substantial loss of benefit" under the contract; and he acknowledged also that termination for breach would be justified if D has committed a renunciation of the contract. However, the disadvantage of Kirby J's approach is that it removes from the system of contractual classification the "inessential" term which in England is now classified as a "warranty". Such a term imposes a contractual obligation breach of which will never justify termination (even if the actual consequences of breach on the facts prove to be serious, so that—had it instead been an intermediate term— the innocent party would have been entitled to terminate). (See also Phang JA's reflections, in the Singapore Court of Appeal in *RDC Concrete Pte Ltd v Sato Kogyo (S) Pte Ltd* (2007)[83] on the nature of warranties).[84]

12-038 Perhaps Kirby J would have been prepared to acknowledge the parties' power *ex ante* to classify a term as a warranty in the sense that breach of that term will not justify termination. This would be consistent with the principle of freedom of contract. If so, a trichotomy of promissory terms seems inevitable, despite Kirby J's taxonomical contention that two categories are enough. But he does not consider this point.

12-039 The majority in this case did not address Kirby J's argument. Instead, as explained above, they saw virtue in the three-fold classification of conditions, intermediate terms, and warranties.

---

78 [2007] HCA 61; (2007) 82 A.L.J.R 345; (2008) 241 A.L.R. 88 H.Ct. Aust. (Gleeson CJ, Gummow, Heydon, Crennan JJ) at [50] fn.16 for references; noting also New Zealand adoption, at fn.16, citing *Holmes v Burgess* [1975] 2 N.Z.L.R. 311 at 318–20.
79 [2007] HCA 61; (2007) 82 A.L.J.R 345; (2008) 241 A.L.R. 88 H.Ct. Aust. (Gleeson CJ, Gummow, Heydon, Crennan JJ) at [52].
80 [2007] HCA 61; (2007) 82 A.L.J.R 345; (2008) 241 A.L.R. 88 H.Ct. Aust. at [54] and [71].
81 [2007] HCA 61; (2007) 82 A.L.J.R 345; (2008) 241 A.L.R. 88 H.Ct. Aust. at [74] ff.
82 [2007] HCA 61; (2007) 82 A.L.J.R 345; (2008) 241 A.L.R. 88 H.Ct. Aust. at [113]–[116].
83 [2007] SGCA 39; [2007] 4 S.L.R. 413 at [107] and [108] per Phang JA.
84 [2007] SGCA 39; [2007] 4 S.L.R. 413 at [107] and [108] per Phang JA.

CHAPTER 13

THE NATURE OF TERMINATION OR DISCHARGE FOR BREACH[1]

I. TERMINOLOGY

Termination or discharge for breach is to be distinguished from rescission for **13-001** misrepresentation or for another "vitiating" factor, such as duress, undue influence, unconscionability, or non-disclosure (Pt I, para.2-001 ff). Termination or discharge for breach brings to an end the parties' "primary" obligations. However, such termination or discharge does not nullify the whole contract. Accrued causes of action remain exigible (that is, breaches of contract or duties to pay, on either side, which ante-date the moment of termination or discharge). The guilty party's liability to pay compensation also remains. Exclusion and liquidated damages clauses, and arbitration or jurisdiction clauses also survive such termination. The process of termination or discharge is examined in Ch.14.

As just indicated, modern decisions distinguish two processes of terminating a **13-002** contract, depending on whether (i) the ground of termination is an initial impediment to the contract, the agreement being "vitiated", for example, for misrepresentation, duress, undue influence, unconscionability, or non-disclosure (notably in the case of insurance or re-insurance contracts); or whether (ii), by contrast, the contract's life is cut short, before complete performance, by supervening impossibility or frustration[2] (Pt III, para.18-001) or because an innocent party has chosen to terminate the contract, or treat it as discharged, for (serious) breach. As for (i), "rescission" involves the contract being dismantled with retroactive effect, with a mutual restoration of benefits (as explained in Chs 1-4). As for (ii), such termination or discharge brings the contract to an end from that point in time, but only prospectively. It does not annihilate the contract retrospectively. This is, therefore, prospective termination or termination in futuro.

In view of the modern analytical distinction between rescission for misrepresen- **13-003** tation (or some other preliminary ground of vitiation) and termination or discharge, the term "rescission" should be confined to the process of setting aside retrospectively a contract which is vitiated by reason of misrepresentation, or other grounds of initial invalidity. Most commentators recognise the need for terminological preci-

---

[1] J.W. Carter, *Carter's Breach of Contract*, 2nd edn (Oxford: Hart Publishing, 2019), Ch.12.
[2] In *Fibrosa Spolka Akcyjna v Fairbairn Lawson Combe Barbour Ltd* [1943] A.C. 32 HL at 67, Lord Wright said: "Impossibility of performance or frustration is only a particular type of circumstance in which a party who is disabled from performing his contract is entitled to say that the contract is terminated as to the future, and in which repayment of money paid on account of performance may be demanded". In this last phrase, Lord Wright was referring to the possibility of claiming repayment of money on the basis of total failure of consideration once (i) the contract is discharged for frustration or breach, and (ii) there has been a complete failure by the payee to performance in respect of the obligation corresponding to the payor's payment.

sion and have abandoned the old ambiguous language of "rescission for breach". However, as recently as 2003 Treitel adhered to the phrase "rescission for breach".[3] But this terminology has been abandoned by the current editor of Treitel.[4]

13-004   Lord Porter pointed out in *Heyman v Darwins Ltd*:[5]

"To say that the contract is rescinded [for breach] or has come to an end or has ceased to exist may in individual cases convey the truth with sufficient accuracy, but the fuller expression that the injured party is thereby absolved from future performance of his obligations under the contract is a more exact description of the position. Strictly speaking, to say that on acceptance of the renunciation of a contract the contract is rescinded is incorrect."

13-005   Lord Wilberforce explained in *Johnson v Agnew*:[6]

"although the [innocent party] is sometimes referred to in the above situation as 'rescinding' the contract, this so-called 'rescission' is quite different from rescission *ab initio*, such as may arise for example in cases of mistake, fraud or lack of consent".

His Lordship continued:

"In those cases [of rescission ab initio], the contract is treated in law as never having come into existence ... In the case of an accepted repudiatory breach, the contract has come into existence but has been put an end to or discharged."

He concluded:

"it is now quite clear, under the general law of contract, that acceptance of a repudiatory breach does not bring about 'rescission ab initio'."

13-006   In *Hurst v Bryk* Lord Millett said that "failure to distinguish between discharge for breach and rescission *ab initio* has led many courts astray and continues to do so".[7]

13-007   The Court of Appeal in *Howard-Jones v Tate*[8] noted an aberrant decision of the

---

3   In the last edition to be edited by Treitel—11th edn (London: Sweet & Maxwell, 2003), p.760 (but see fn.4); similarly, with elaboration, G.H. Treitel, *Some Landmarks of Twentieth Century Contract Law* (Oxford: Oxford University Press, 2002), pp.107–108.

4   E. Peel (ed) of G.H. Treitel, *The Law of Contract*, 15th edn (London: Sweet & Maxwell, 2020), Chs 17, 18, preferring the expression "termination for breach".

5   [1942] A.C. 356 HL at 399, and Dixon J in *McDonald v Denny Lascelles Ltd* (1933) 48 C.L.R. 457 at 476–477 H.Ct. Aust.

6   [1980] A.C. 367 HL at 392–393; citing Lord Porter in *Heyman v Darwins Ltd* [1942] A.C. 356 HL at 399; also citing Dixon J in *McDonald v Denny Lascelles Ltd* (1933) 48 C.L.R. 457 at 476–477 H.Ct. Aust.

7   [2002] 1 A.C. 185 HL at 194; but the actual decision, that partnerships can be dissolved under Common Law principles of repudiatory breach, has been held to be unsound: *Mullins v Laughton* [2002] EWHC 2761 (Ch); [2003] Ch. 250, Neuberger J, discussing the Partnership Act 1890; *Mullins* case followed in *Golstein v Bishop* [2013] EWHC 881 (Ch); [2014] Ch. 131 (C. Nugee QC) at [116] ff, affm.'d [2014] EWCA Civ 10; [2014] Ch. 455 at [9] and [10] per Briggs LJ; and the point was confirmed in *Flanagan v Liontrust Investment Partners LLP* [2015] EWHC 2171 (Ch); [2015] Bus. L.R. 1172; [2016] 1 B.C.L.C. 177 at [223] per Henderson J, observing that the *Golstein* case "went to the Court of Appeal, but on different grounds which involved no challenge to the judge's conclusion that the doctrine was inapplicable even in the case of a two-partner firm: see [2014] EWCA Civ 10; [2014] Ch. 455 at [9]–[10] per Briggs LJ who took the opportunity to add his personal view (without the benefit of adversarial argument) that [the position adopted by Nugee QC] was correct".

8   [2011] EWCA Civ 1330; [2012] 2 All E.R. 369.

Court of Appeal, *Gunatunga v DeAlwis*,[9] decided after *Johnson v Agnew*.[10] Lloyd LJ in the *Howard-Jones* case[11] suggested that the *Gunatunga* case had been decided per incuriam because *Johnson v Agnew* had not been cited and the analysis adopted in that 1996 case harked back to time when the terminology of "termination" or "discharge" and "rescission" had been muddled.

II.   Analytical Parallel with the Prospective Form of Discharge for Frustration

Frustration also causes the contract to end prospectively,[12] so that at Common **13-008** Law accrued obligations to pay or perform remain exigible (on the impact of the Law Reform (Frustrated Contracts) Act 1943, Ch.18. Here it is enough to note that termination or discharge for frustration operates automatically ("by operation of law") and is not dependent on any election by either party. Indeed, many instances of frustration occur without the parties' (or their successors) being aware that the Angel of Death has passed over their contract.

III.   Principles of European Contract Law and UNIDROIT's Principles of International Commercial Contracts

The "prospective" operation of termination or discharge for serious breach ac- **13-009** cords with the (non-binding) *Principles of European Contract Law* art.9:305(1), and UNIDROIT's *Principles of International Commercial Contracts* art.7.3.5.[13] And, in particular, both acknowledge (PECL art.9:305(1); UNIDROIT art.7.3.5(3)) specifically that "a provision for the settlement of disputes" survives that form of termination, as well as (as it is put vaguely) "any other term of the contract/ provision which is to operate even after termination".

IV.   Consequences of Termination or Discharge for Breach in English Law

Five things (presented in text at 13-011 to 13-028) follow from the fact that **13-010** termination or discharge operates only to terminate the contract in a prospective manner.

(1)   The innocent party retains the right to sue in respect of preceding breaches, that is, pre-termination defaults, in so far as these have not become statute-

---

9   (1996) 72 P. & C.R. 161 at 173 per Slade LJ.
10   [1980] A.C. 367 HL at 392–393; citing Lord Porter in *Heyman v Darwins Ltd* [1942] A.C. 356 HL at 399; also citing Dixon J in *McDonald v Denny Lascelles Ltd* (1933) 48 C.L.R. 457 at 476–477 H.Ct. Aust.
11   [2011] EWCA Civ 1330; [2012] 2 All E.R. 369 at [38]–[42].
12   In *Fibrosa Spolka Akcyjna v Fairbairn Lawson Combe Barbour Ltd* [1943] A.C. 32 at 67 HL, Lord Wright said: "Impossibility of performance or frustration is only a particular type of circumstance in which a party who is disabled from performing his contract is entitled to say that the contract is terminated as to the future."
13   4th edn (2016), text and comment available at *http://www.unidroit.org/instruments/commercial-contracts/unidroit-principles-2016* [Accessed 8 March 2022]. On the UNIDROIT principles, S. Vogenauer, *Commentary on the UNIDROIT Principles of International Commercial Contracts*, 2nd edn (Oxford: Oxford University Press, 2015), and E Broerdermann, *UNIDROIT Principles of International Commercial Contracts: An Article-by-Article* Commentary (The Hague: Kluwer Law International, 2018).

barred;[14] and the innocent party can also hold the guilty party liable in damages for the harmful consequences of that termination or discharge.

(2) Similarly, the innocent party can further hold the guilty party liable for any unpaid sums which have "accrued" before that date of termination. Thus termination or discharge does not disturb accrued obligations to pay agreed sums, for example, a partner's liability to make contributions to partnership expenses,[15] or a buyer's liability to pay accrued instalments under contract for construction of a ship,[16] or employers' duties to pay pensions, bonuses, or related benefits, and to exercise contractual discretion in a rational manner in the treatment of these benefits.[17] Similarly, *Hardy v Griffiths*[18] confirms that, following termination or discharge, the innocent party remains entitled to sue in debt or in a claim for damages in respect of an accrued right to receive a deposit, or in respect of the unpaid portion of deposit. The Supreme Court in *TAEL One Partners Ltd*[19] considered the notion of a liability "accruing" and Lord Reed said:

> "The word 'accrue' is generally used to describe the coming into being of a right or an obligation (as, for example, in *Aitken v South Hams District Council* [1995] 1 A.C. 262), so that the person in question then has an accrued right, or is subject to an accrued liability, as the case may be … The amount to which there is an entitlement may not be payable until a future date, but an entitlement may nevertheless have accrued."

13-011   Thus, in *Personal Touch Financial Services Ltd v Simplysure Ltd, Usay Business Ltd*[20] (see further on this case para.10-053) Sir Stanley Burnton, giving the court's judgment, held that an insurance company was not liable to pay commis-

---

[14]   *Photo Production Ltd v Securicor Transport Ltd* [1980] A.C. 827 HL at 849 per Lord Diplock; other leading authorities: *McDonald v Dennys Lascelles Ltd* (1933) 48 C.L.R. 457 at 476–477 H.Ct. Aust. per Dixon J; *Heyman v Darwins Ltd* [1942] A.C. 356 HL at 397 per Lord Porter; *Moschi v Lep Air Services Ltd* (also known as *Moschi v Rolloswin Investments Ltd or Lep Air Services v Rolloswin Investments)* [1973] A.C. 331 HL at 349–351 per Lord Diplock; *Johnson v Agnew* [1980] A.C. 367 HL at 396 per Lord Wilberforce; *Bank of Boston Connecticut v European Grain and Shipping Ltd* [1989] A.C. 1056 HL at 1098–1099 per Lord Brandon; *Stocznia Gdanska SA v Latvian Shipping Co* [1998] 1 W.L.R. 574 HL; *Hurst v Bryk* [2002] 1 A.C. 185 HL. On *Johnson v Agnew* [1980] A.C. 367 HL, see the study by C. Mitchell, in C. Mitchell and P. Mitchell (eds), *Landmark Cases in the Law of Contract* (Oxford: Hart Publishing, 2008), p.351 ff.

[15]   *Hurst v Bryk* [2002] 1 A.C. 185 HL, but, as noted by H. Beale (gen. ed.), *Chitty on Contracts*, 34th edn (London: Sweet & Maxwell, 2021), para.27-080, the suggestion that partnerships can be dissolved under Common Law principles of repudiatory breach is unsound, as Neuberger J held in *Mullins v Laughton* [2002] EWHC 2761 (Ch); [2003] Ch. 250.

[16]   *Stocznia Gdanska SA v Latvian SS Co* [1998] 1 W.L.R. 574 HL noted J. Beatson and G. Tolhurst, "Comment" [1998] C.L.J. 253, 256-257.

[17]   *Braganza v BP Shipping Ltd* [2015] UKSC 17; [2015] 1 W.L.R. 1661 at [54] per Lord Hodge (compare the doubt at [109], per Lord Neuberger on the survival of a duty of trust and confidence).

[18]   [2014] EWHC 3947 (Ch); [2015] Ch. 417, Deputy High Court judge Amanda Tipples QC at [107], [109], [117], following *Griffon Shipping LLC v Firodi Shipping Ltd ("The Griffon")* [2013] EWCA Civ 1567; [2014] 1 All E.R. (Comm) 593 and *Damon Cia Naviera SA v Hapag-Lloyd International SA ("The Blankenstein")* [1985] 1 W.L.R. 435 CA at 449, 457 (Robert Goff LJ dissented).

[19]   *TAEL One Partners Ltd v Morgan Stanley & Co International Plc* [2015] UKSC 12; [2015] 4 All E.R. 545 at [42] per Lord Reed (concerning Condition 11.9(a) of the Loan Market Association standard terms); for comment on the *TAEL* case, K. Rodgers and J. Ho, "TAEL One Partners: contractual interpretation as an iterative process" (2015) 5 J.B.L. 393 and Zhong Xing Tan, "Beyond the real and the paper deal: the quest for contextual coherence in contractual interpretation" (2016) 79 M.L.R. 623 at 642–643.

[20]   [2016] EWCA Civ 461.

sion to its agent in respect of *post-termination renewals of policies*, nor was there any implied term to support the agent's claim to such post-termination renewal commission (reversing the trial judge):[21]

"In the ordinary way, the executory obligations of the innocent party to a contract come to an end if the contract is terminated by the innocent party on the ground of the other party's repudiation, or breach of a true condition, of the contract. That consequence is of course subject to any clear term of the contract providing for the innocent party's obligation to continue after termination for repudiation."

Sir Stanley Burnton added:[22]   13-012

"the right to a renewal commission cannot accrue unless and until the policy is renewed. The right does not accrue when the policy is originally taken out. For post-termination renewals to result in a right to commission, it is necessary to find an implied term to that effect, and, moreover, a term that survives termination for repudiation."

Sir Stanley Burnton concluded:[23] In my judgment, there is no such implied term as the judge seems to have found.

(3) The prospective nature of termination or discharge operates equally in favour   13-013
of the guilty party. Thus, the innocent party's pre-termination unpaid sums or breaches giving rise to damages will remain relevant. Such sums will be set off against the guilty party's total liabilities to pay damages, etc. It is even possible that the innocent party's liabilities might exceed the guilty party's liabilities. If so, the guilty party, whose conduct caused the contract to be terminated for breach (and on the assumption that the guilty party became the defendant in an action brought by the innocent party), will recover this balance by way of a counterclaim against the claimant. For example, in *Acre 1127 Ltd (formerly Castle Galleries) v De Montfort Fine Art Ltd*[24] De Montfort was held to have repudiated a contract after roughly a year of its life, but before then De Montfort had been the victim of breach of contract by the other side (Castle Galleries). After the contract was terminated, by reason of De Montfort's repudiation, damages remained payable by Castle (the defendant) to De Montfort in respect of the pre-termination period:

"However I see no answer in principle to De Montfort's claim for loss of profit in respect of the second, third and fourth quarters, Castle's liability in respect of its failure to take goods during those quarters having already accrued due before De Montfort purported to terminate the contract on 18 April 2006."

(4) Furthermore, various ancillary obligations will continue to apply after termina-   13-014
tion or discharge of the contract, notably: exclusion clauses;[25] choice of law clauses;[26] jurisdiction clauses;[27] arbitration clauses;[28] mediation clauses;[29] a

---

[21] [2016] EWCA Civ 461 at [42].
[22] [2016] EWCA Civ 461 at [45].
[23] [2016] EWCA Civ 461 at [47].
[24] [2011] EWCA Civ 87 at [48] per Tomlinson LJ.
[25] *Photo Production Ltd v Securicor Transport Ltd* [1980] A.C. 827 HL.
[26] This follows a fortiori from *Mackender v Feldia AG* [1967] 2 Q.B. 590 CA (rescission for non-disclosure under an insurance contract does not wipe out a (i) jurisdiction, or (ii) a choice of law clause: especially, Diplock LJ at 603-4).
[27] See *Mackender v Feldia AG* [1967] 2 Q.B. 590 CA; note also the general reasoning of Lord

consensual time bar;[30] a stipulation for a retainer in an agency contract;[31] a software supplier's undertaking to provide continuing support and maintenance;[32] a clause allowing inspection of documents was held to have survived termination of an agency agreement for breach in the *Yasuda Fire* case;[33] finally, liquidated damages clauses (in so far as liability has already accrued thereunder, but such a clause will not apply to delay post-termination; as noted in *Triple Point Technology Inc v PTT Public Co Ltd* (2021), a liquidated damages clause which purports to continue to operate after termination of the contract cannot successfully operate after termination because there are no post-termination primary obligations).[34]

13-015 (5) More generally, following termination, rights acquired and consideration already paid under the contract will not be reversed and disentangled (unless, in the case of payments, there has been a total failure of consideration). For example, in *Future Publishing Ltd v Edge Interactive Media Inc*[35] Proudman J said:

Wilberforce in *Port Jackson Stevedoring Pty v Salmond & Spraggon (Australia) Pty ("The New York Star")* [1981] 1 W.L.R. 138 PC at 145; generally on such clauses, D. Joseph, *Jurisdiction and Arbitration Agreements and their Enforcement*, 3rd edn (London: Sweet & Maxwell, 2015).

[28] *Heyman v Darwins Ltd* [1942] A.C. 356 HL at 374; generally on such clauses, D. Joseph, *Jurisdiction and Arbitration Agreements and their Enforcement*, 3rd edn (London: Sweet & Maxwell, 2015); *Heyman v Darwins Ltd* [1942] A.C. 356 at 374, HL; K. Lewison, *Interpretation of Contracts*, 7th edn (London: Sweet & Maxwell, 2021), para.18.01–18.31; *Andrews on Civil Processes*, 2nd edn (Cambridge: Intersentia Publishing, 2019), Chs 32–34, and bibliography at p.1158; Neil Andrews, *Arbitration and Contract Law* (Dordrecht, Heidelberg, London, New York: Springer Publishing, 2016), Chs 2–4).

[29] *Cable & Wireless Plc v IBM United Kingdom Ltd* [2002] 2 All E.R. (Comm) 1041 (Colman J) (award of a stay pending compliance with a binding mediation clause); *Sulamerica Cia Nacional de Seguros SA v Enesa Engenharia SA* [2012] EWCA Civ 638, [2013] 1 W.L.R. 102 (mediation agreement which, on the facts, lacked certainty); for criticism of the certainty test adopted in that case, Neil Andrews, "Mediation Agreements: Time for a More Creative Approach by the English Courts"(2013) 18 *Revue de droit uniforme* 6-16 (also known as Uniform Law Review); K.P. Berger, "Law and Practice of Escalation Clauses" (2006) 22 *Arbitration International* 1–17.

[30] *Port Jackson Stevedoring Pty v Salmond & Spraggon (Australia) Pty ("The New York Star")* [1981] 1 W.L.R. 138 PC at 145 per Lord Wilberforce. *Senate Electrical Wholesalers Ltd v Alacatel Submarine Networks Ltd* [1999] 2 Lloyd's Rep. 243, CA; *Laminates Acquisition Co v BTR Australia* [2003] EWHC 2540 (Comm) (Cooke J); *Ocean Chemical Transport Inc v Exnor Craggs* [2000] 1 All E.R. (Comm) 519; [2000] 1 Lloyd's Rep. 446; *The Hut Group Ltd v Nobahar-Cookson* [2016] EWCA Civ 128; [2016] 1 C.L.C. 573; *Neon Shipping Inc v Foreign Economic & Technical Corp Co of China* [2016] EWHC 399 (Comm); [2017] 1 All E.R. (Comm) 964 (Burton J).

[31] *Duffen v FRA BO Spa (No.2)* [2000] 1 Lloyd's Rep. 180 (Judge Hallgarten QC, Central County Court, London).

[32] *Harbinger UK Ltd v GE Information Services Ltd* [2000] 1 All E.R. (Comm) 166: the case concerned a severable clause, which survived termination of the main contract; this clause provided that the company would maintain "in perpetuity" software supplied to the customer; the court noted that the commercial reality is that a customer would not everlastingly continue to use this soft-ware because technological advance would render it obsolete before very long; however, so long as the equipment did remain commercially useful, the supplier's obligation would endure.

[33] *Yasuda Fire & Marine Insurance Co of Europe Ltd v Orion Marine Insurance Underwriting Agency Ltd* [1995] Q.B. 174, Colman J.

[34] [2021] UKSC 29; [2021] A.C. 1148 at [87], [91], [92] per Lord Leggatt.

[35] *Future Publishing Ltd v Edge Interactive Media Inc* [2011] EWHC 1489 (Ch); [2011] E.T.M.R. 50 at [67] per Proudman J.

"assignment to the claimant of goodwill and registered trade mark rights ... payments ... of consideration under the agreements do not prevent termination. Each side is entitled to retain those benefits."

It should be noted also that in an instalment contract, party A might repudiate **13-016** only vis-à-vis a severable part of the contract, justifying termination by party B of that part, but not justifying termination of the whole contract. Mance LJ noted this possibility in *Friends Provident Life & Pensions Ltd v Sirius International Insurance Corp*:

"a failure under a contract for sale by instalments to make due delivery of one instalment within the contractually stipulated time may be accepted as *repudiatory of that instalment, but does not necessarily mean that the whole contract comes to an end*".[36](emphasis added)

Restrictive covenants within partnership or employment contracts Restric- **13-017** tive covenants (within partnership or employment agreements) do not survive in favour of the guilty party:[37] this is the rule in *General Billposting Co Ltd v Atkinson*.[38] This is a clear and settled[39] rule (see para.13-019 ff for the debate concerning its possible re-examination, if the point ever reaches the Supreme Court).

---

[36] [2005] EWCA Civ 601; [2005] 2 Lloyd's Rep. 517 at [31].
[37] S. Bloch and K. Brearley (eds), *Employment Covenants and Confidential Information*, 4th edn (London: Bloomsbury Professional Publishing, 2018); P Goulding (ed), *Employee Competition: Covenants, Confidentiality, and Garden Leave*, 3rd edn (Oxford: Oxford University Press, 2016); D. Cabrelli, "The Effect of Termination upon Post-Employment Obligations" in M. Freedland (ed), *The Contract of Employment* (Oxford: Oxford University Press, 2016), Ch.26; M. Freedland, "Repudiation of contract and breach of confidence: General Billposting v Atkinson revisited' (2003) 32 I.L.J. 48 at 52 (discussed in text below at para.13-028).
[38] *General Billposting Co Ltd v Atkinson* [1909] A.C. 118 HL; applied in *Argus Media Ltd v Halim* [2019] EWHC 42 (QB); [2019] I.R.L.R. 442 at [167], Freedman J; and *Group Lotus Plc v 1Malaysia Racing Team SDN BHD* [2011] EWHC 1366 (Ch); [2011] E.T.M.R. 62 at [364] to [371], Peter Smith J; *Brown v Neon Management Services Ltd* [2018] EWHC 2137 (QB); [2019] I.R.L.R. 30, where Choudbury J defends the rule (see discussion and quotation at paras 13-023–13-028).
For Commonwealth cases, F. Dawson, "Survival of restraint of trade clauses" (2013) 129 L.Q.R. 508–513; Dawson's suggestion is that there is no "rule" in the *General Billposting* case which categorically precludes a restrictive covenant from surviving in favour of the employer where the latter's breach has triggered termination by the employee, although there is a presumption to that effect; ultimately, he suggests, the matter should be one of interpretation of the contract.
[39] English courts adopt the view that there is a General Billposting "rule" and that it overrides even clear language inserted to preserve the covenant in the event of the covenantee being in breach: *Group Lotus Plc v 1Malaysia Racing Team SDN BHD* [2011] EWHC 1366 (Ch), [2011] E.T.M.R. 62 at [364]–[371] per Peter Smith J, noting at [367] and [368] that "a majority in *Rock Refrigeration Ltd v Jones* [1997] I.C.L.R. 938 CA (Simon Brown and Morritt LJJ) held that where a party repudiated a contract and the repudiation was accepted the latter was discharged in all further performance of the obligations under the contract. Thus in the case where the employer had repudiated the service contract the employee was no longer bound by his obligations and therefore there could be no enforceable covenants. This extends to an agreement where the draftsmen attempt to provide for the covenant to be enforceable howsoever the agreement is terminated": see Simon Brown LJ at 946C–D and Morritt LJ at 950D. Peter Smith J concluding in *Group Lotus Plc v 1Malaysia Racing Team SDN BHD* [2011] EWHC 1366 (Ch), [2011] E.T.M.R. 62 at [371]: "It seems to me that I am bound to follow the majority decision in Rock because it has not been overturned nor subject to any critical analysis. In so far as it has been considered in the Court of Appeal there has been no criticism of that majority decision. It follows therefore that had I decided that GL was in breach of the License Agreement it would not have been able to enforce [the relevant restrictive clause in this case]."

13-018   **Confidentiality clauses**   The position concerning confidentiality clauses is not set-tled (but see the ensuing paragraphs for general discussion). Thus, in an appeal from a summary judgment, the Court of Appeal in *Campbell v Frisbee* declared that the position regarding confidentiality clauses is developing, and the court decided to leave the matter open:[40]

> "We do not believe that the effect on duties of confidence assumed under contract when the contract in question is wrongfully repudiated is clearly established."

13-019   **Re-examination of the General Billposting rule?**   A "debate"[41] has been engendered by dicta in *Campbell v Frisbee*,[42] in which Lord Phillips MR expressed doubts about the *General Billposting* rule) see text above on that rule). Lord Phillips in that 2002 decision noted his earlier sceptical obiter comments in *Rock Refrigeration Ltd v Jones Rock Refrigeration Ltd v Jones*,[43] where he had (i) drawn attention to the general analysis in the *Photo Production* case[44] of the nature of discharge for breach and, against that background, of the (suggested) anomalous nature of the *General Billposting* rule; (ii) (also in the *Rock* case) Phillips LJ had contended (rather boldly) that there is no real harshness suffered by an employee if that 1909 rule were to be judicially reversed so that instead the employer could have his cake and eat it, that is, succeed in wrongfully terminating the contract and yet remain entitled to uphold the restrictive covenant against the employee.

13-020   In *Rock Refrigeration Ltd v Jones Rock Refrigeration Ltd v Jones*,[45] Phillips LJ developed his critical argument as follows:[46]

> "I do not accept that it is unreasonable for an employer to seek to impose restraints on his employee that will subsist, even should the employment come to an end as a consequence of a repudiation by the employer. On the contrary it seems to me commercially desirable that it should be possible to achieve this end, for the following reasons. Where an employer discloses to an employee confidential information, or otherwise puts the employee in a position to harm the employer's goodwill, it will usually be reasonable to impose negative restraints sufficient to protect those legitimate interests of the employer. Contracts of employment are now subject to complex statutory regulation, much of it designed to protect the employee. Cases of deliberate wrongful dismissal of employees, or repudiatory breach of the duties owed to them, are much less common than bona fide disputes as to whether or not there has been unfair or constructive dismissal. Employees who have been unfairly dismissed are entitled to statutory compensation. It does not seem to me necessarily fair or reasonable that an employer who is held liable to pay such compensation should also be at risk of losing the protection that is reasonably necessary to safeguard his confidential information or goodwill."

13-021   Phillips LJ continued:[47]

> "Can *General Billposting Co Ltd v Atkinson* be distinguished? In my judgment negative

---

[40] [2002] EWCA Civ 1374; [2003] I.C.R. 141 at [22]; for a comprehensive review of the principles governing the discretion whether to grant an interim injunction in favour of the former employer in this context, *Allfiled UK Ltd v Eltis* [2015] EWHC 1300 (Ch); [2016] F.S.R. 11 (Hildyard J).

[41] In *Geys v Société Générale* [2012] UKSC 63; [2013] 1 A.C. 523 at [68], Lord Wilson noted that this point is the subject of "debate'"(in fact this alludes to one judge's obiter doubts: see ensuing text).

[42] [2002] EWCA Civ 1374; [2003] I.C.R. 141 at [17].

[43] [1997] I.C.R. 938, 959–960, CA.

[44] *Photo Production Ltd v Securicor Transport Ltd* [1980] A.C. 827 HL.

[45] [1997] I.C.R. 938, 959–960, CA.

[46] [1997] I.C.R. 938, 959–960, CA.

[47] [1997] I.C.R. 938, 959–960, CA.

restraints agreed to apply after the termination of employment should not be equated with the primary obligations that are discharged when a contract of employment is terminated consequent upon repudiation. The consideration for such restraints is in reality not the obligation to give the appropriate notice of termination of the employee's services, but the granting of employment that affords access to confidential information and goodwill. Such restraints are not 'one of the purposes of the contract' (*Heyman v Darwins Ltd* [1942] A.C. 356)—they are ancillary to those purposes. But for the *General Billposting* case [1909] A.C. 118 I can see no principle of law which precludes the parties from validly agreeing to restraints that will subsist, even if the employment is brought to an end by repudiation. I think it at least arguable that, having regard to the subsequent development of this area of the law, not every restrictive covenant will be discharged upon a repudiatory termination of the employment. However, for the reasons which follow, it is not necessary to resolve this issue."

This takes us to point (ii) (as mentioned at para.13-019), that is, the second point **13-022** raised by Phillips LJ, as he then was, in the *Rock* case, noted above: his contention is that the employer should not be deprived of the protection of the restrictive covenant just because his conduct has led to wrongful dismissal. However, with respect, and against Lord Phillips' comment, it is submitted that the *Billposting* rule is a matter of elementary justice. It reflects the view that the employer's serious or repudiatory breach should disentitle that party from taking advantage of the constraint contained in the restrictive covenant. Moreover, the rule has stood for over a hundred years. It would be inappropriate for even the Supreme Court to cast aside this rule in the abstract interest of doctrinal symmetry or consistent conceptual analysis. The underlying merits of the attempt refutation presented by Lord Phillips are a matter for debate. This is quintessentially an area where the courts should desist from changing the law. Only Parliament can legitimately grasp this nettle.

The present author's suggestion is also consistent with the following judicial **13-023** comment. In *Brown v Neon Management Services Ltd*,[48] where Choudbury J poured cold water on the idea that the *General Billposting* rule is ripe for re-examination or reversal. In this case Choudbury J upheld a claim for damages made by former employees of the defendant company. The breaches comprised[49] failing to pay salary increases and discretionary bonuses that had been awarded to them, making the salary increases and bonuses conditional upon acceptance of detrimental new contractual terms and the removal of profit commission agreed at the time of their recruitment. The claimants succeeded in establishing that these breaches individually and cumulatively amounted to a repudiatory breach of contract entitling them to resign, which they did "on notice", and that further breaches occurred during that notice period. The case contains, therefore, a rich treatment of repudiatory breach in the employment context. Perhaps its more interesting feature is the following detailed rebuttal of the suggestion that the rule in the *General Billposting* case is ripe for reversal.

In *Brown v Neon Management Services Ltd*, Choudbury J said:[50] **13-024**

"As I have found that the contract of employment was repudiated by Neon and such repudiation having been accepted, the rule in *General Billposting Ltd v Atkinson* [1909] A.C. 118 (HL) ('the *General Billposting* Rule') would normally apply such that [post-termination restraints] fall away. However, Mr Solomon invites me to reject that rule. His

---

[48] *Brown v Neon Management Services Ltd* [2018] EWHC 2137 (QB); [2019] I.R.L.R. 30 at [170]–[173] (see quotation below).
[49] [2018] EWHC 2137 (QB); [2019] I.R.L.R. 30 at [2].
[50] *Brown v Neon Management Services Ltd* [2018] EWHC 2137 (QB); [2019] I.R.L.R. 30 at [170].

submissions in this regard may be summarised as follows:

(i)   There has been significant judicial comment to the effect that the *General Billposting* Rule should be revisited. In *Croesus Financial Services Ltd. v Bradshaw* [2013] EWHC 3685 (QB) at 88, Simler J (as she then was) said: '88 …The time may have come to revisit the [*General Billposting* Rule] but in light of my findings, this is not the appropriate case to do it.'

(ii)   In *Geys v Société Générale* [2013] 1 A.C. 523 at [141] Lord Sumption said: '[141] … In many contracts of employment, and perhaps in most modern ones, there is a large number of obligations which do not depend on the existence of the employment relationship. One example is the specific enforcement after a repudiation of express or implied covenant against competition, as in *Lumley v Wagner* (1852) 1 De GM & G 604. In appropriate cases, this may be subject to the proviso that the repudiation was not by the party in whose favour the covenant was included: see *General Billposting Co Ltd* [1909] A.C. 118…' And at [68], Lord Wilson said:"68 Contracts of employment often include provisions which are expressed to bind the parties following the termination of the contract: *Rhys-Harper v Relaxion Group Plc* [2003] I.C.R. 867, para 36 (Lord Nicholls of Birkenhead). For example, they may oblige the employee not to compete with the employer for a specified period nor to use information which he has obtained in confidence during the period of his employment. Or, as in the present case, they may oblige the employer, within a specified period following termination of the contract, to make to the employee a termination payment, to be calculated in accordance with terms specified in it, and may oblige the employee, in consideration of the payment, to enter into a termination agreement on terms also therein specified. Such provisions of the contract are, by their terms, enforceable following its termination. The enforceability of, for example, a restrictive covenant by the repudiator against the innocent party is now the subject of some debate: *Rock Refrigeration Ltd v Jones* [1997] I.C.R. 938. There is no problem about the enforceability of such provisions against the repudiator.

(iii)   Most significantly, in *Rock Refrigeration Ltd v Jones* [1997] I.C.R. 938, Phillips LJ (as he then was) at 958A–960B stated (albeit obiter) that the General Billposting Rule 'accords neither with current legal principle nor with the requirements of business efficacy' (at 958B). The Court gave the example of an employee who committed a repudiatory breach which was accepted by the employer, and comments that it would be 'absurd' to suggest that the employee would thereafter be released from his negative post-termination obligations (at 959C). The same applies to an employer in repudiatory breach (at 959D–G). Further, the Court stated that *General Billposting* could be legitimately distinguished (at 959G et seq)."

13-025   Choudbury J continued:[51]

"In my judgment, none of these judicial comments, all of which were obiter, provides a firm foundation for setting aside such a long-established rule as the *General Billposting* Rule, particularly where, as in this case, it is the repudiator who seeks to enforce the [post-termination restraints] against the innocent parties. The comment made by Simler J (as she then was) that the rule may need to be revisited was not based on any detailed analysis of the arguments on the issue. As for the comments of Lord Sumption and Lord Wilson in *Geys*, far from expressing a doubt as to the validity of the *General Billposting* Rule, they appear to approve the rule in so far as it applies to an attempt by the repudiator to

---

[51]   *Brown v Neon Management Services Ltd* [2018] EWHC 2137 (QB); [2019] I.R.L.R. 30 at [171].

enforce PTRs against the innocent party. That, as I have said, is this case. Those comments of the Supreme Court post-date, by some 20 years, the criticisms of the *General Billposting* Rule made by Phillips LJ in the Court of Appeal in *Rock Refrigeration.*"

Further, Choudbury J said:[52] **13-026**

"Perhaps of greater significance, given the terms of the Restrictive Covenant Agreement in this case, is Lord Sumption's comment in *Geys* that, 'Whether collateral obligations of this kind continue to bind after the termination of the contract... will normally depend on the construction of the contract...' (*Geys* case at [141])."

Choudbury J concluded:[53] "[These] authorities come nowhere close to setting **13-027**
aside the *General Billposting* Rule."

Professor Mark Freedland has proposed[54] a more nuanced approach to this issue. **13-028**
In this discussion, Mark Freedland first notes a different suggestion made by Linda Clarke. Clarke suggests that the equitable duty of confidentiality (on that topic see para.13-018) does survive termination, but not an express confidentiality clause. Instead Freedland proposes this change: that the issue whether, in the post-termination context, the restrictive covenant (or express confidentiality clause) survives or lapses (this being the current law) following wrongful dismissal by the employer, or other repudiatory breach, should be addressed:

"not according to the comprehensive all-or-nothing approach which was taken on the facts of [*General Billposting v Atkinson*], but instead by asking whether there had been such a total failure of consideration on the part of the employer, *for the particular obligation which it was now sought to enforce*, as to make it inappropriate to enforce that obligation. If the claim to damages survives that scrutiny, it should be subjected to the controls of contribution and mitigation." (Freedland's emphasis.)

Freedland's proposal would appear to require (both for the purpose of injunctive relief and damages) a calibration by the court of the gravity of the employer's breach and a comparison of the benefit to the employee (and consequent detriment to the employer) if the relevant covenant or clause ceases to apply post-termination. Such a balancing might be effected, Freedland suggests, under the court's discretionary power to grant or withhold an injunction. But query whether, under the current law, the courts would not simply approach the matter by leaning strongly in favour of the grant of an injunction.[55] But if such a balancing were to extend to the availability of damages this would render the award of compensation essentially discretionary. There are, admittedly, contexts in which damages are discretionary (see s.2(2) of the Misrepresentation Act 1967 and the discretionary award of damages in lieu of an injunction under s.50 of the Senior Courts Act 1981). But the modern tendency is not to expand the discretionary element in the availability of damages for breach of contract. As Lord Reed said in *Morris-Garner v One-Step Support Ltd*:[56]

---

52 *Brown v Neon Management Services Ltd* [2018] EWHC 2137 (QB); [2019] I.R.L.R. 30 at [172].
53 *Brown v Neon Management Services Ltd* [2018] EWHC 2137 (QB); [2019] I.R.L.R. 30 at [173].
54 M. Freedland, "Repudiation of contract and breach of confidence: General Billposting v Atkinson revisited" (2003) 32 I.L.J. 48 at 52.
55 See *Araci v Fallon* [2011] EWCA Civ 668; [2011] L.L.R. 440: not a restrictive covenant or employment case, but indicative of the long-standing tendency to award injunctions to uphold negative undertakings.
56 [2018] UKSC 20; [2019] A.C. 649 at [95], proposition (12).

"Common Law damages for breach of contract are not a matter of discretion. They are claimed as of right, and they are awarded or refused on the basis of legal principle."

V.   DISCHARGE OF CONTRACT BY CONSENSUAL ABANDONMENT

13-029   The parties can agree to terminate the contract, and this agreement can be manifested either expressly or impliedly (on the latter see next para). The consideration—element of mutual bargain—supporting this agreement to cancel will be the release of each party from his unperformed obligations under the contract. This species of discharge differs, therefore, from (i) termination by reason of one party's breach (which occurs without agreement), (ii) termination for frustration (which occurs by operation of law), (iii) termination in accordance with a right of cancellation (such a right is provided for ex ante: Ch.9), or (iv) termination under an express clause permitting termination or discharge (such a right is provided for ex ante: Ch.9).

13-030   The case law, it is submitted, supports the possibility of a court inferring objectively that the parties have impliedly terminated their agreement by consensus. This possibility is supported by Fox LJ in one Court of Appeal case, *André et Cie v Marine Transocean Ltd ("The Splendid Sun")*,[57] and is consistent with a decision of the Australian High Court.[58] Admittedly there are cautious and conservatively orthodox remarks by Robert Goff, both in the Court of Appeal, and in the House of Lords, in which he suggested that the law should be slow to infer such a consensus on the basis of mutual silence.[59] But, provided the courts proceed in a cautious manner, there should be scope for identifying implied consensual termination.[60] It is submitted that the courts should recognise, in the spirit of Fox LJ's analysis in *Andre et Cie v Marine Transocean Ltd ("The Splendid Sun")*,[61] that

---

[57]   Fox LJ's judgment in *André et Cie v Marine Transocean Ltd ("The Splendid Sun")* [1981] Q.B. 694, 714, CA, is clearest on the possibility of objective determination of an implied mutual abandonment.

[58]   *DTR Nominees Pty Ltd v Mona Homes Pty Ltd* (1978) 138 C.L.R. 423 at 434 (Stephen, Mason, Jacobs, Aickin JJ, Murphy J dissenting) (High Court of Australia) held that the parties had reached stalemate in a land transaction, each accusing the other of repudiation, and each regarded the contract as having ended; in these circumstances, the court held that the contract had indeed been terminated by implied mutual abandonment.

[59]   Robert Goff LJ said in *Allied Marine Transport Ltd v Vale do Rio Doce Navegacao SA ("The Leonidas D")* [1985] 1 W.L.R. 925, 940, CA, that there must be something more than mere inactivity on each side because silence can be equivocal and open to more than one interpretation; similarly, Lord Goff in *Food Corp of India v Antclizo Shipping Corp ("The Antclizo")* [1988] 1 W.L.R. 603 at 606, HL; having regard to *Paal Wilson & Co A/S v Partenreederei Hannah Blumental ("The Hannah Blumental")* [1983] 1 A.C. 854 HL, notably 915–916 (per Lord Diplock); for observations on implicit mutual abandonment, 914 (per Lord Brandon), 924–925 (per Lord Brightman).

[60]   Commenting on implied termination by consent, *Mustill & Boyd, Commercial Arbitration*, 2nd edn (London: Butterworths, 1989), 511, say (this being their summary of the cases considered above) that party O must have "so conducted himself as to entitle party A to assume that O was offering to enter into an agreement to abandon the reference. A will not be entitled to make this assumption unless the conduct of O leads unequivocally to this conclusion." They add: "inactivity on its own is equally consistent with O having forgotten the existence of the refence or having negligently failed to proceed with dispatch". Finally, they suggest that, "A must further show that he did in fact assume that O was offering to enter into an agreement to abandon the reference, and that by [A's] conduct, communicated to O, [A] accepted O's offer...[But] mere inaction on the part of A will not constitute acceptance."

[61]   Fox LJ's analysis in *André et Cie v Marine Transocean Ltd ("The Splendid Sun")* [1981] Q.B. 694 at 714, CA, is clearest on the possibility of objective determination of an implied mutual abandonment: "the lapse of time in this case, unaccompanied by any activity from the parties, is so

lapse of time can, but only in very clear circumstances, constitute a mutual form of implicit abandonment, that is, consensual termination, of a contract. For, just as contracts can sometimes be formed without identifiable offer and acceptance, so, by parity of analysis, consensual termination can arise by lapse of time (see, for qualification, the succeeding sentences). This submission should prevail, notwithstanding the elaborate emphasis on offer and acceptance noted by Lord Goff and Goff LJ, in respectively, *"The Antclizo"*[62] and *"The Leonidas D"*.[63] Offer and acceptance represent one way of discerning consensus, but it is an analysis which plainly does not monopolise the finding of consensus.

Consensual discharge might also involve a novation of the contract. Novation is **13-031** a substitution of a new agreement between the same parties: ("transaction") novation (first contract is replaced by a second between the same parties; or substitution of a new party: ("new party") novation; thus, a contract between A and B is replaced by a contract between A or B and C, a new party.[64]

---

great that the reasonable inference in January 1978 is that the owners had decided not to proceed with the arbitration and that the charterers had accepted that and were agreeable to it. If that is not so, I find it difficult to suppose that complete inactivity for any period, be it 10 or 20 years, would ever justify the conclusion that the claimants were not proceeding. The question is the impact of the events, or rather the absence of events, upon the charterers. I conclude that the proper inference from the facts is that, by January 1978, the parties had indicated an intention not to proceed with the reference and had put an end to the contract to refer...The reason why, as it seems to me, this contract came to an end was not because of breach or its consequences but because the inference is that both sides accepted that it should be terminated."

62 *Food Corp of India v Antclizo Shipping Corp ("The Antclizo")* [1988] 1 W.L.R. 603 at 606, HL.
63 *Allied Marine Transport Ltd v Vale do Rio Doce Navegacao SA ("The Leonidas D")* [1985] 1 W.L.R. 925 at 940, CA.
64 On these two forms of novation, see the remarks in by Lord Selborne LC in *Scarf v Jardine* (1882) L.R. 7 App. Cas. 345 HL at 351. On the issue whether a contract is extinguished and replaced by a new agreement, or merely varied, *Wadlow v Samuel* [2007] EWCA Civ 155 at [35]–[46], considering *Morris v Baron* [1918] A.C. 1 HL; *British and Benningtons Ltd v NW Cachar Tea Co Ltd* [1923] A.C. 48 HL; *United Dominions Corp (Jamaica) Ltd v Shoucair* [1969] 1 A.C. 340 PC; *Sookraj v Samaroo* [2004] UKPC 50 at [19]–[22] per Lord Scott.

CHAPTER 14

THE PROCESS OF TERMINATION OR DISCHARGE FOR BREACH

I. INNOCENT PARTY'S CHOICE

Breach entitling a party to terminate (para.5-011) does not automatically cause **14-001** the contract to be terminated. Instead the innocent party has a choice ("the right to elect"):[1] he can choose to terminate the contract ("accept the renunciation or repudiation") and sue for damages, or he can affirm the contract and sue for damages or, where appropriate, debt (Pt IV, para.24-048 and Pt II, para.7-084 ff).

The House of Lords in *Fercometal SARL v Mediterranean Shipping Co SA ("The* **14-002** *Simona")* confirmed the fundamental proposition that where a party's breach justifies the innocent party in terminating the contract the latter has a choice: he can accept the repudiation and thus terminate the contract and sue for damages, or he can affirm the contract and sue for damages.[2] This is known as "the right to elect". Similarly, the Privy Council in *Sookraj v Samaroo* acknowledged these "basic and well known principles":[3]

"a repudiation does not itself determine the contract. It gives a right to the innocent party, by accepting the repudiation, to determine the contract. If the innocent party does not accept the repudiation, the contract remains in existence for the benefit of both parties. The acceptance of a repudiation requires no particular form. But it must be unequivocal and it must be communicated to the party in breach."

In *Peyman v Lanjani*, the Court of Appeal confirmed that, just as a representee **14-003** must know of his right to rescind before he can be said to have elected not to rescind, so the innocent party must be aware of its *right to terminate for breach*.[4]

Once the election has been made, the law then requires firm adherence to the in- **14-004** nocent party's decision to affirm the contract or terminate it for breach (that is, treat it as discharged for breach). The innocent party's decision is an "election".

Judicial summary of the innocent party's election In *Delta Petroleum (Carib-* **14-005** *bean) Ltd v British Virgin Islands Electricity Corp*[5] the Privy Council held that the Court of Appeal of the East Caribbean had been wrong to apply the doctrine of election in the particular context of that case. After quoting three important passages

---

[1] On the subtleties of this analysis, J.W. Carter, "Discharge as the Basis for Termination for Breach of Contract" (2012) 128 L.Q.R. 283; J.E. Stannard and D. Capper, *Termination for Breach of Contract*, 2nd edn (Oxford: Oxford University Press, 2020), Ch.4.
[2] [1989] A.C. 788 HL; *Vitol SA v Norelf Ltd ("The Santa Clara")* [1996] A.C. 800 HL.
[3] [2004] UKPC 50 at [16] per Lord Scott.
[4] [1985] Ch, 457, CA at 487 per Stephenson LJ; at 494 per May LJ; at 500 per Slade LJ.
[5] [2020] UKPC 23; [2021] 1 W.L.R. 5741.

from earlier judgments, Lord Leggatt in the *Delta* case commented as follows on the nature of the election whether to affirm or to terminate the contract for breach:[6]

"The principle of waiver by election is not needed to explain why a decision to terminate a contract, once communicated, is final and irrevocable. A valid termination has the legal effect of discharging both parties (from then on) from their obligations under the contract. Those obligations could only be reinstated by making a new contract. But the principle is needed to explain why a party who communicates unequivocally an intention to continue with performance thereby loses the right to terminate the contract (in so far as the right was based on facts then in existence and known to the electing party). What is fundamental to the principle of waiver by election and crucial for present purposes is that it is only capable of applying where a choice must be made between two alternative and inconsistent (in the sense of mutually exclusive) courses of action, such that adopting one of them necessarily entails forsaking the other."

14-006   It will be seen that (a) the innocent party must decide whether to terminate or to affirm; (b) the decision to terminate is an exercise of the elective power, and is final and irrevocable; (c) likewise, the decision to affirm, and thus not to terminate with respect to that breach, is final and irrevocable, and this is the "flip-side" of point (b); (d) the decision, whether (b) or (c), must be either communicated or clearly inferred from the circumstances; (e) later events might recreate a new opportunity to elect whether to terminate for breach, but that new opportunity will necessarily arise from a fresh breach.

14-007   Also in *Delta Petroleum (Caribbean) Ltd v British Virgin Islands Electricity Corp*[7] Lord Leggatt noted the further possibility that the innocent party's position might be subject to estoppel by representation (operating to preclude the innocent party from electing to terminate for breach):

"[29] Where the principle of waiver by election does not apply, a different form of waiver may nevertheless arise by estoppel. If a party represents or promises unequivocally that it will not exercise a contractual right, the party will be estopped from afterwards exercising the right if and to the extent that the other party's reliance on the promise would make this inequitable: see eg 'The Kanchenjunga' [1990] 1 Lloyd's Rep. 391, 399 (HL)."

14-008   Earlier, summarising Lord Goff's restatement in *Motor Oil Hellas (Corinth) Refineries SA v Shipping Corp of India ('The Kanchenjunga')*,[8] Aikens LJ in *Tele2 International Card Co SA v Post Office Ltd* formulated these six propositions:[9]

"(1)   [where a right to terminate for breach exists] ... the innocent party is entitled to

---

6   [2020] UKPC 23; [2021] 1 W.L.R. 5741 at [18] to [20], respectively, *Kammins Ballrooms Co Ltd v Zenith Investments (Torquay) Ltd* [1971] A.C. 850, 883 (HL) per Lord Diplock; *Motor Oil Hellas (Corinth) Refineries SA v Shipping Corp of India ('The Kanchenjunga')* [1990] 1 Lloyd's Rep 391, 398 per Lord Goff; *Kosmar Villa Holidays Plc v Trustees of Syndicate 1243* [2008] EWCA Civ 147; [2008] Bus L.R. 931 at [38] per Rix LJ.

7   [2020] UKPC 23; [2021] 1 W.L.R. 5741 at [29].

8   *Motor Oil Hellas (Corinth) Refineries SA v Shipping Corp of India ("The Kanchenjunga")* [1990] 1 Lloyd's Rep. 391 HL at 399.

9   [2009] EWCA Civ 9 at [53]–[54]; Aikens LJ's exegesis was noted in these cases: *Obrascon Huarte Lain SA v Her Majesty's Att-Gen for Gibraltar* [2015] EWCA Civ 712; [2015] B.L.R. 521 at [120] per Jackson LJ ("in essence, a party makes an election when, with knowledge of the relevant facts, it acts in a manner which is consistent only with it having chosen one or other of two inconsistent courses of action"); and by Rix LJ in *Force India Formula One Team Ltd v Etihad Airways PJSC* [2010] EWCA Civ 1051; [2011] E.T.L.R. 10 at [112].

(2)   It is a prerequisite to the exercise of the election that the party concerned is aware of the facts giving rise to its right and the right itself.

(3)   The innocent party has to make a decision, because if it does not do so then '*the time may come when the law takes the decision out if [its] hands, either by holding [it] to have elected not to exercise the right which has become available to [it], or sometimes by holding [it] to have elected to exercise it*'. (emphasis added.)

(4)   Where, with knowledge of the relevant facts, the party that has the right to terminate the contract acts in a manner which is consistent only with it having chosen one or other of two alternative and inconsistent courses of action open to it (i.e. to terminate or affirm the contract), then it will be held to have made its election accordingly.

(5)   An election can be communicated to the other party by words or conduct. However, in cases where it is alleged that a party has elected not to exercise a right, such as a right to terminate a contract on the happening of defined events, it will only be held to have elected not to exercise that right if the party '*has so communicated [its] election to the other party in clear and unequivocal terms*'.

(6)   … a court has to make a finding one way or the other. Whether a party has elected to terminate or to affirm the contract is a question of fact: either a party has affirmed the contract or it has not. If the innocent party has not affirmed the contract, then the right to terminate will be exercisable still." (emphasis added)

Two elements: a decision or intention; secondly, communication or sufficient manifestation of the election   There must be (i) a decision or intention one way or the other, whether to terminate or to affirm the contract; and (ii) the decision or intention must be (a) communicated to the other party or (b) manifested, that is, the guilty party should discover this, or be deemed objectively to have done so. As for element (i), Lord Hope in *Geys v Société Générale, London Branch* said that "the requirement is for a real acceptance—a conscious intention to bring the contract to an end, or the doing of something that is inconsistent with its continuation".[10]   **14-009**

As for element (ii), the decision to terminate can be communicated or at least manifested expressly or impliedly. If the contention is that the innocent party has elected to continue the contract, although without explicit communication, that outcome can be readily inferred where the innocent party carries on the contract or otherwise acts in such a manner that, objectively, the proper implication is that this party has elected not to act on the opportunity to terminate the contract for the relevant renunciation, repudiation, or other serious breach.[11]   **14-010**

By contrast, the implicit species of notification will be less readily inferred where the contention is that the election has been to terminate the contract. This is because   **14-011**

---

[10] *Geys v Société Générale, London Branch* [2012] UKSC 63; [2013] 1 A.C. 523 at [17].

[11] *Alan Ramsay Sales & Marketing Ltd v Typhoo Tea Ltd* [2016] EWHC 486 (Comm); [2016] 4 W.L.R. 59 at [68] per Flaux J, proposition (3): "If the innocent party who is entitled to treat himself as discharged from the contract by the other party's breach, elects, with full knowledge, to treat the contract as continuing, he will be taken to have affirmed the contract. Affirmation can be express or implied. It will be implied if, with knowledge of the breach and of his right to choose whether to accept a repudiation or to affirm the contract, the innocent party does some unequivocal act from which it may be inferred that he intends to go on with the contract or that he will not exercise his right to treat the contract as repudiated…." At [83] Flaux J cited Moore-Bick J in *Yukong Line of Korea v Rendsburg Investments Corp of Liberia ("The Rialto")* [1996] 2 Lloyd's Rep. 604 at 607 proposition (8), that there must be "very clear evidence that the injured party has indeed chosen to go on with the contract"; but in the *Alan Ramsay* case Flaux J found such clear evidence of affirmation by conduct on the facts, [2016] EWHC 486 (Comm); [2016] 4 W.L.R. 59 at [84] ff.

an election to terminate the contract involves disturbance of the parties' legal and factual relationship. And so, in the absence of clear communication, the courts will scrutinise the facts carefully to determine whether the innocent party's decision to terminate has been both objectively manifested and that this "implied message" has come to the guilty party's notice, applying an objective appreciation of the facts. This process was summarised by Lord Steyn in *Vitol SA v Norelf Ltd ("The Santa Clara")*:

> "it is rightly conceded by counsel … that the aggrieved party need not personally, or by an agent, notify the repudiating party of his election to treat the contract as at an end. It is sufficient that the fact of the election comes to the repudiating party's attention".[12]

14-012 **Contrary suggestions from commentators** There are contrary suggestions in the literature. Burrows suggests that affirmation of the contract does not require communication or manifestation of the decision.[13] As suggested in the preceding discussion, the better view is that affirmation of the contract cannot be effected wholly *per silentium* but is instead a decision which can be more readily inferred from conduct than the converse election.

14-013 More radically, Carter[14] states that communication (or manifesting the decision) does not lie at the core of the election. But Carter's suggestion seems doubtful in the light of the cases discussed at 14-056–14-063 (especially *Vitol SA v Norelf Ltd ("The Santa Clara")*). The cases examined in those paragraphs indicate that conduct on the innocent party's side is effective to constitute a clear election only if it manifestly demonstrates to the guilty party that the latter's breach has been accepted as a ground for termination and the guilty party becomes aware of this. This issue was also noted by Kerr LJ in *State Trading Corp of India Ltd v M Golodetz Ltd*, who, having cited an Australian decision declaring that communication is not required, preferred the view that there should be either a successful communication of the innocent party's election to accept the repudiation or that such a decision should be "overtly evinced".[15]

---

[12] [1996] A.C. 800 HL at 811, per Lord Steyn; *Yukong Line of Korea v Rendsburg Investments Corp of Liberia ("The Rialto")* [1996] 2 Lloyd's Rep. 604 at 607 per Moore-Bick J, proposition (7).

[13] A. Burrows, *A Restatement of the English Law of Contract* (Oxford: Oxford University Press, 2016), s.19(6), p.112, Comment, says (acknowledging the contrary view of D. O'Sullivan, S. Elliott, R. Zakrzewski, *The Law of Rescission*, 2nd edn (Oxford: Oxford University Press, 2014), 23.57) [see now 3rd edn., 2023] that it is enough that the innocent party has with full knowledge of his right to terminate made the decision to keep the contract alive. But, with respect, it is suggested that the authorities support the view that a decision to affirm the contract becomes binding if it occurs in circumstances where it is "unequivocal" and supported by "very clear evidence". This is an objective determination. It necessarily imports the idea that the guilty party can safely infer that the innocent party has decided to continue with the contract.

[14] J.W. Carter, *Carter's Breach of Contract*, 2nd edn (Oxford: Hart Publishing, 2019), [10-18].

[15] [1989] 2 Lloyd's Rep. 277 CA at 286, col.2, noting *Holland v Wiltshire* (1954) 90 C.L.R. 409 H.Ct. Aust.; in this 1954 case at 416, Dixon CJ said that the innocent party's decision to sell to a third party was a clear enough election not to proceed with the relevant contract, and his decision occurred in the face of continuing unwillingness by the purchaser to proceed with the transaction; Taylor J's judgment at 424 makes the telling point that there had been extensive dealings between the parties and that this dispensed with any need for further notification by the innocent party to the defaulting purchaser; therefore, this case must be read as decided on its special facts and it does not dispense with the almost invariable need for communication or "overt" manifestation—perceived by the guilty party—of the innocent party's decision to terminate for breach.

Employment contracts no exception to the "elective" analysis of termination **14-014**
for breach The "elective", as distinct from "automatic", analysis applies to
employment contracts, as the Supreme Court confirmed in *Geys v Société Générale,
London Branch*,[16] and this might require further attention in the employment
context, as noted in *Sunrise Brokers LLP v Michael William Rodgers*.[17]

Termination by extreme delay an exception There is an exception to this "elec- **14-015**
tive" or non-automatic termination analysis in the context of insurance contracts.
In that context, the contract automatically terminates if a relevant term is breached.
And so an insurer is not bound to make an indemnity payment if the insured
transgresses or fails to satisfy an insurance warranty.[18] A further exception arises
as a result of *MSC Mediterranean Shipping Co SA v Cottonex Anstalt* (also on this
case paras 7-098–7-100).[19] A contract for hire of sea cargo containers required the
hiring party to redeliver the containers, emptied of their cargoes, at the end of the
period of hire. But the hiring party was not able to do so, although the contract had
not become frustrated by operation of law. The Court of Appeal held that the ensuing delay became repudiatory once it was plain that the contract's purpose had been
so severely subverted that was no longer "capable of performance as agreed". In
these circumstances, it is idle of the innocent party to pretend that he is capable of
keeping the contract alive, consistent with the general rule that repudiation leads
to termination only if the innocent party chooses to terminate. Instead this is a rare
situation where the occurrence of delay, accompanied by default, automatically
causes the contract to become terminated for breach. As Tomlinson LJ explained:[20]

> "from 2 February 2012 [when there had been significant delay and acknowledgement that
> the situation would not change] the contract in its agreed form was not capable of
> performance—further performance in the changed circumstances brought about by the
> delay would be radically different from that agreed. The guilty party can no longer perform
> its obligations when the time comes. The time for performance of the obligations of the
> guilty party is long past. Redelivery of the containers at some future date would be an act
> radically different in kind from redelivery of the containers in accordance with the
> contractually agreed time-scale. In those circumstances, as it seems to me, *the innocent
> party simply cannot treat the contract as subsisting because it is no longer capable of
> performance as agreed. There is no alternative to the conclusion that the contract has
> come to an end.* The fact that the carrier continued to press for performance, in the shape
> both of redelivery of the containers and the payment of demurrage, is neither here nor
> there. Those were acts in vain, unrelated to an existing contract." (emphasis added)

---

16 *Geys v Société Générale, London Branch* [2012] UKSC 63; [2013] 1 A.C. 523 (noted D. Cabrelli
   and R. Zahn, "The Elective and Automatic Theories of Termination in the Common Law of the
   Contract of Employment: Conundrum Resolved?" (2013) 76 M.L.R. 1106; and L. Aitken, "'Elective' or 'automatic' termination of a contract of employment" (2013) 129 L.Q.R. 335).
17 [2014] EWCA Civ 1373; [2015] I.C.R. 272 at [58] per Longmore LJ.
18 *Bank of Nova Scotia v Hellenic Mutual War Risk Assoc (Bermuda) Ltd ("The Good Luck")* [1992]
   1 A.C. 233 HL; G.H. Treitel, *Some Landmarks of Twentieth Century Contract Law* (Oxford: Oxford
   University Press, 2002), p.127.
19 [2016] EWCA Civ 789; [2017] 1 All E.R. (Comm) 483, notably at [41]–[43] per Moore-Bick LJ,
   and at [61] per Tomlinson LJ.
20 [2016] EWCA Civ 789; [2017] 1 All E.R. (Comm) 483 at [61]; and see Moore-Bick LJ at [25]–
   [28].

14-016 **Innocent party's occasional opportunity to keep contract alive and generate right to payment** A majority of the House of Lords in *White & Carter v McGregor*[21] held that the innocent party might sometimes have the capacity to keep open the contract (the right to "affirm the contract"), and complete his side of the bargain. He can then sue for the agreed price. Later cases have qualified this and prevented the innocent party from saddling the other party with unwanted performance. The topic of election in the case of anticipatory breach has been examined in Ch.7, para.7-082 ff, where this difficult case is assessed.

14-017 **Overlapping termination clause rights and Common Law rights: objective analysis** The rather intricate issue of the interplay between termination clauses and Common Law rights to treat the contract as terminated or discharged for breach is examined fully in Ch.9, notably at para.9.003 to 9-015 and 9-028 to 9-033. As noted at para.9-014, Andrew Baker J in *Phones 4U Ltd (in administration) v EE Ltd*[22] held that the innocent party's notification that he or she is terminating the contract in reliance on a pure cancellation right (that is, without the need to show breach) precludes that party from claiming loss of bargain damages. This is because such compensation is only payable if the contract has been purportedly terminated for breach. More generally, again as noted in the paragraphs mentioned in Ch.9, the courts adopt an objective perspective in order to determine whether an innocent party has terminated by reason of Common Law repudiatory breach, etc, or in exclusive reliance on express termination rights, or both. The objective inquiry is demonstrated by, in particular, these two decisions: *Vivergo Fuels Ltd v Redhall Engineering Solutions Ltd*[23] (Ramsey J) and *Shell Egypt Manzala GmbH v Dana Gas Egypt Ltd*[24] (Tomlinson J). The objective inquiry is whether the reasonable recipient of the purported termination would have understood that the notice rested upon the Common Law regime or the express termination regime, notably when those regimes in the particular case are inconsistent or incompatible.

14-018 **Burden of proof** The party (not necessarily the innocent party) who is seeking to demonstrate that the contract has been terminated has the burden of proving that the innocent party did in fact elect to terminate the contract for breach.[25] For an example of a case where there was both a claim and counter-claim, each saying that the other party had been in breach, but where it was at any rate clear that the contract had been terminated for breach by one of the parties, see discussion of the *Mid Essex* case[26] at para.9-045.

II. BINDING NATURE OF THE ELECTION

14-019 Lord Wilberforce said in *Johnson v Agnew*:[27]

---

21 [1962] A.C. 413 HL; as for the co-operation requirement, A. Dyson, "What do the *White & Carter* 'Limitations' Limit?", in G. Virgo and S. Worthington (eds), *Commercial Remedies: Resolving Controversies* (Cambridge: Cambridge University Press, 2016).
22 [2018] EWHC 49 (Comm); [2018] 2 All E.R. (Comm) 315 at [76], [116] to [132].
23 [2013] EWHC 4030 at [512]
24 [2010] EWHC 465 (Comm) at [35],
25 *Beazer Investments Lyd v Soares* [2004] EWCA Civ 482 at [25]–[27].
26 *Mid Essex Hospital Services NHS Trust v Compass Group UK and Ireland Ltd (Trading As Medirest)* [2013] EWCA Civ 200; [2013] B.L.R. 265.
27 Lord Wilberforce in *Johnson v Agnew* [1980] A.C. 367 HL at 398.

"Election, though the subject of much learning and refinement, is in the end a doctrine based on simple considerations of common sense and equity."

He added that once a decision to terminate has been communicated, it is too late to try to resurrect the contract:[28] "What is dead is dead."[29] Therefore, the innocent party cannot try to change his mind and revive the contract by a unilateral decision. Instead the contract can only be resurrected by the parties' joint decision.[30] Similarly, once the innocent party decides to affirm the contract, he cannot normally change his mind, at least where he has full knowledge[31] of the relevant facts and of his right to terminate. But the courts are prepared to conduct a careful examination of the innocent party's conduct in the relevant context in order to determine whether the post-repudiation events or response indicate affirmation of the contract or are instead consistent with a reasonable period of reflection on the appropriate response. An unequivocal affirmation is required. The innocent party was held not to have affirmed the contract and instead to have kept intact its right to terminate for breach in the following cases.

Case (i): Acre v Castle   It might be that the innocent party does not affirm the contract and instead its decision to terminate for breach is delayed. This was the position in *Acre 1127 Ltd (formerly Castle Galleries) v De Montfort Fine Art Ltd*[32] where the act of repudiation occurred on 18 April 2006 but was accepted by the innocent party only in October 2007.   **14-020**

Case (ii): Johnson v Agnew   The House of Lords in *Johnson v Agnew*[33] held that a party's decision to try to induce performance by obtaining specific performance does not close the door upon termination for breach if it turns out that the specific performance remedy cannot be implemented. This was the position on the facts of that case, where the innocent party, the vendor, lost title to the property following a third party lender's exercise of rights of sale under a mortgage. Because of the third party mortgagee's decision to sell the property, specific performance, which had been obtained, and was intended to compel the buyer to proceed, proved an abortive remedy. But the House of Lords made clear that the vendor retained his rights to terminate the contract and to seek compensation in respect of the buyer's repudiatory breach.   **14-021**

Case (iii): Yukong case   In *Yukong Line of Korea v Rendsburg Investments Corporation of Liberia ("The Rialto")*,[34] Moore-Bick J held that the innocent party   **14-022**

---

28   *Yukong Line of Korea v Rendsburg Investments Corp of Liberia ("The Rialto")* [1996] 2 Lloyd's Rep. 604 at 607, Moore-Bick J proposition (4).

29   Lord Wilberforce in *Johnson v Agnew* [1980] A.C. 367 HL at 398; *Yukong Line of Korea v Rendsburg Investments Corp of Liberia ("The Rialto")* [1996] 2 Lloyd's Rep. 604 at 607, Moore-Bick J proposition (4).

30   Q. Liu, *Anticipatory Breach* (Oxford: Hart Publishing, 2011), p.127, fn.637, citing J. Ewart, *Waiver Distributed* (Cambridge, MA: Harvard University Press, 1917), pp.83–84.

31   *Peyman v Lanjani* [1985] Ch. 457 CA; for an example of affirmation and waiver of the right to terminate, *Peregrine Systems Ltd v Steria Ltd* [2005] EWCA Civ 239; [2005] Info T.L.R. 294 at [16]–[23].

32   [2011] EWCA Civ 87 at [49] per Tomlinson LJ.

33   [1980] A.C. 367, HL.

34   [1996] 2 Lloyd's Rep. 604, Moore-Bick J.

had not disclosed an election to persevere with the contract. As Moore-Bick J commented:[35]

"The law does not require an injured party to snatch at a repudiation and he does not automatically lose his right to treat the contract as discharged merely by calling on the other to reconsider and recognise his obligations."

It was held that the owners (in fact this party, Yukong, had sub-chartered the vessel to Rendsburg) of a ship had not affirmed the contract. Instead this innocent party retained a right to terminate the contract in response to the other party's clear renunciation.

14-023   In the *Yukong* case[36] a renunciation occurred on 23 January 1996 when the charterers refused to perform. On 24 January, the owner protested that the charterers "are strongly requested to honour their obligations" (it was this telex which the charterers contended gave rise to an unequivocal affirmation of the contract).[37] On 25 January, the charterers repeated their unwillingness to perform. On 29 January the owner gave 12 days' notice of delivery of the ship. But on 1 February the owners recognised the futility of this chiding and accepted the repudiation of 23 January. The charterer contended that it was too late for the owner to do so. Moore-Bick J found for the owner, regarding the communications of 24 January and 29 January as protests rather than abandonment of the possibility of terminating the contract by reason of the renunciation on 23 January. Moore-Bick J explained:[38]

"it is impossible ... to find in [the 24 January telex] an unequivocal statement...that they will proceed with the contract and await performance in due course regardless of the position adopted by the charterers".

Similarly, the owner's protest of 29 January did not indicate:[39]

"that they would continue with the contract regardless of the charterers' attitude. Nor was it a step which was consistent only with the continuation of the contract".

But there was no suggestion on these facts that the charterer had relied on the 24 January and 29 January communications. Moore-Bick J said:[40]

"the Court should not adopt an unduly technical approach to deciding whether the injured party has affirmed the contract and should not be willing to hold that the contract has been affirmed without very clear evidence that the injured party has indeed chosen to go on with the contract notwithstanding the other party's repudiation."

14-024   Moore-Bick J added:[41]

"the Court should generally be slow to accept that the injured party has committed himself irrevocably to continuing with the contract in the knowledge that if, without finally committing himself, the injured party has made an unequivocal statement of some kind on which the party in repudiation has relied, the doctrine of estoppel is likely to prevent any injustice being done."

---

35   [1996] 2 Lloyd's Rep. 604.
36   [1996] 2 Lloyd's Rep. 604.
37   [1996] 2 Lloyd's Rep. 604 at 608, col.2.
38   [1996] 2 Lloyd's Rep. 604 at 609, col.1.
39   [1996] 2 Lloyd's Rep. 604 at 609, col.2.
40   [1996] 2 Lloyd's Rep. 604 at 608, col.1.
41   [1996] 2 Lloyd's Rep. 604 at 608, col.1.

Case (iv): Multi Veste case In *Multi Veste 226 BV v NI Summer Row Unitholder* **14-025**
BV[42] Lewison J held that the innocent party's calls for performance should not be
treated as affirmation of the contract. He cited the following remarks of Moore-
Bick J in the *Yukong* case:[43]

> "[It will often be the case that] the injured party's initial response to the renunciation of
> the contract has been to call on the other to change his mind, accept his obligations and
> perform the contract. That is often the most natural response and one which, in my view,
> the Court should do nothing to discourage. It would be highly unsatisfactory if, by
> responding in that way, the injured party were to put himself at risk of being held to have
> irrevocably affirmed the contract whatever the other's reaction might be, and in my judg-
> ment he does not do so. The law does not require an injured party to snatch at a repudia-
> tion and he does not automatically lose his right to treat the contract as discharged merely
> by calling on the other to reconsider his position and recognize his obligations."

Case (v): Flanagan v Liontrust In *Flanagan v Liontrust Investment Partners* **14-026**
LLP Henderson J concluded that a partner had not affirmed the contract by continuing to receive monthly payments from the partnership and not seeking to arrange
private medical care.[44] Henderson J said:[45]

> "I do not think it would be right to treat Mr Flanagan as having unequivocally elected to
> affirm the ... Agreement merely because he continued to accept monthly payments on ac-
> count of his fixed profit allocation until October 2013, and took no steps to arrange private
> medical insurance until after that date. It is true that Mr Flanagan took legal advice ... at
> an early stage, before sending his [termination] letter ... Privilege has not been waived
> ... but it is reasonable to infer that it must have included advice on the question of repudia-
> tion and the need not to take any steps that could constitute affirmation of the contract. I
> bear in mind that Mr Flanagan took no positive steps to procure the continuation of the
> monthly payments, and it is well established that 'mere inactivity after breach does not
> of itself amount to affirmation' [citing *Chitty*, now *Chitty on Contracts* 34th edn, (2021)
> para.27-056 text at fn.259]. Moreover, his continued acceptance of the payments was
> broadly consistent with his contention that he remained a member of the [partnership],
> even after termination of the ... Agreement, with default rights to share in profits which
> would entitle him to much larger sums than those which he received, albeit not by way
> of monthly payments on account."

Henderson J continued:[46] **14-027**

> "I also consider the present case to be a good example of 'a complex and medium term
> relationship' of the kind in respect of which Rix LJ recognised that 'it necessarily and
> legitimately takes time for the consequences to become clearer and for the innocent party
> to consider his position': [referring to *Force India Formula One Team Ltd v Etihad
> Airways PJSC* (2010)."[47]

That passage is cited in the text below at paras 14-039–14-041.

---

[42] [2011] EWHC 2026 (Ch); 139 Con. L.R. 23 at [203].
[43] *Yukong Line of Korea v Rendsburg Investments Corp of Liberia ("The Rialto")* [1996] 2 Lloyd's Rep.
604 at 608, col.1.
[44] *Flanagan v Liontrust Investment Partners LLP* [2015] EWHC 2171 (Ch); [2015] Bus. L.R. 1172
at [210]–[216], especially [216] (cited in full in the text below) (although later in his judgment at
[243], he decided that the doctrine of repudiation/renunciation does not apply to LLP agreements if
there are more than two parties).
[45] [2015] EWHC 2171 (Ch); [2015] Bus. L.R. 1172 at [216].
[46] [2015] EWHC 2171 (Ch); [2015] Bus. L.R. 1172 at [216].
[47] *Force India Formula One Team Ltd v Etihad Airways PJSC* [2010] EWCA Civ 1051; [2011]
E.T.L.R. 10 at [122].

14-028   Henderson J then said:[48]

> "I would therefore hold that Mr Flanagan had not lost the right to repudiate the contract before 8 February 2013, and that the position was not changed by his continuing receipt of monthly payments for a further nine months after that date."

14-029   **Case (vi): Garside v Black Horse**   Similarly, King J concluded in *Garside v Black Horse Ltd*[49] that a purchaser of a luxury car (an Aston Martin Vanquish S) (the car was in fact acquired under a hire purchase arrangement)[50] had not lost the right to terminate the contract by reason of a defect. For five months he had driven the car in the belief that his complaint (visual distortion caused by a defective rear window) would be met and the problem rectified. Against that background, no unequivocal act or pattern of conduct had occurred which might objectively indicate that he had affirmed the contract.[51] King J formulated the following test:[52]

> "It is common ground that such an affirmation can be made expressly or impliedly ... However ... analysis of the applicable legal principles emerging from the Court of Appeal decision in *Peyman v Lanjani* [1985] Ch. 457, contained in the judgment of the court in *Alpha Chauffeurs Ltd v City Gate Dealership and Lombard North Central Plc 2002*,[53] [indicates] that unless the party in breach can mount some sort of estoppel, the innocent party will not be treated as having elected to affirm the contract unless he has knowledge not only of the facts giving rise to his right to elect (knowledge of the facts amounting to the breach) but also of the right itself and even then he will not be treated as having elected to affirm the contract unless he has *unequivocally* (my emphasis) demonstrated to the other party that he intends to affirm."

14-030   **Case (vii): Atlas Residential Solutions v Greengate**   In *Atlas Residential Solutions Management UK Ltd v Greengate SARL*[54] Teare J held that there had been no affirmation of the contract by the innocent party. The claimant ran a property management company. The defendant was a property company. The claimant failed to replace a "key person" within six months, that period being prescribed by the contract. In response to that default, the defendant had validly exercised a termination clause and, contrary to the claimant's suggestion, it was held that the defendant's presence at a meeting[55] with the claimant, coupled with a relatively short period of delay,[56] had not constituted affirmation.[57]

III.   "NO THIRD CHOICE"

14-031   The innocent party does not have a "third" choice. As Lord Ackner explained in *Fermometal SARL v Mediterranean Shipping Co SA ("The Simona")*, the innocent party cannot:

---

[48]   [2015] EWHC 2171 (Ch); [2015] Bus. L.R. 1172 at [216].
[49]   [2010] EWHC 190 (QB).
[50]   This placed the buyer in a more favourable position because lapse of time would not by law be capable of barring his right to reject: [2010] EWHC 190 (QB) at [30].
[51]   [2010] EWHC 190 (QB) at [77]–[79].
[52]   [2010] EWHC 190 (QB) at [28].
[53]   13 May 2002, unreported, Deputy High Court judge Ronald Walker QC at [44] (reversed on a different point in [2002] EWCA Civ 207).
[54]   [2020] EWHC 366 (Comm) at [105]–[111].
[55]   [2020] EWHC 366 (Comm) at [109].
[56]   [2020] EWHC 366 (Comm) at [110].
[57]   [2020] EWHC 366 (Comm) at [106].

"affirm the contract and yet be absolved from tendering further performance unless and until [the repudiating party] gives reasonable notice that he is once again able and willing to perform".[58]

In other words, once the innocent party decides to continue with the contract, he too is "back on track" and must comply with his contractual obligations as they remain or arise. As Lord Ackner explained in *Fermometal SARL v Mediterranean Shipping Co SA ("The Simona"):*[59]

"There is no third choice, as a sort of via media, to affirm the contract and yet to be absolved from tendering further performance unless and until A gives reasonable notice that he is once again able and willing to perform."

The explanation for this is that: **14-032**

"such a [third] choice would negate the contract being kept alive for the benefit of both parties and would deny the party [party A] who [attempted to repudiate], the right to take advantage of any supervening circumstance which would justify him in declining to complete".[60]

This decision, in the words of Lord Mustill,[61] ended the debate engendered by "a notorious trio of cases"[62] which had "caused generations of contract lawyers to quail". The result of this clarification in *Fermometal SARL v Mediterranean Shipping Co SA ("The Simona")*[63] was that the charterers were held to have exercised validly (the second time) a cancellation right, even though they had on the first occasion jumped the gun by purporting to exercise that cancellation right prematurely. That had been a "boo-boo" which might have cost them dear: but they escaped disaster, the other party having decided not to accept this repudiation. exonerated on these facts. In essence, the charterer's earlier conduct had entitled the owner to terminate the contract for breach, but the owners had not exercised its right to treat the contract as discharged for breach and instead that party, the owner, had tendered performance. However, at that later point the owner's dilatory performance entitled the charterer to terminate by exercise of the express contractual cancellation power. For this reason, the conclusion was that the charterer was the innocent party. In greater detail, the facts of *Fermometal SARL v Mediterranean Shipping Co SA*

---

[58] *Fermometal SARL v Mediterranean Shipping Co SA ("The Simona")* [1989] A.C. 788 HL at 805 per Lord Ackner (criticised by G.H. Jones and W. Goodhart, *Specific Performance*, 2nd edn (London: Butterworths, 1996), pp.69–72, considering Australian case, *Foran v Wight* (1989) 168 C.L.R. 385 H.Ct. Aust. (on which, Q. Liu, *Anticipatory Breach* (Oxford: Hart Publishing, 2011), pp.107–112), and *Peter Turnbull & Co v Mundus Trading Co (Australasia)* (1954) 90 C.L.R. 235 H.Ct. Aust.) (on which see, Q. Liu, p.102); M. Mustill, "Anticipatory Breach: The Common Law at Work", *Butterworths Lectures 1989–90* (London: Butterworths, 1990), pp.65–68; *J.W. Carter in J. Beatson and D. Friedmann* (eds), Good Faith and Fault in Contract Law (Oxford: Oxford University Press, 1995), pp.485, 498, 502–504; also on "The Simona", Q. Liu, pp.104–105.

[59] [1989] A.C. 788 HL at 805.

[60] *Fermometal SARL v Mediterranean Shipping Co SA, "The Simona"* [1989] A.C. 788 HL at 805.

[61] M. Mustill, "Anticipatory Breach: The Common Law at Work", *Butterworths Lectures 1989–90* (London: Butterworths, 1990), p.65.

[62] *Braithwaite v Foreign Hardwood Co* [1905] 2 K.B. 543 CA; *Taylor v Oakes* (1922) 27 Com. Case. 261 CA at 268; *British & Beningtons v North West Cachar Co* [1923] A.C. 48 HL; Lord Ackner dealt with the first two decisions in *Fermometal SARL v Mediterranean Shipping Co SA ("The Simona")* [1989] A.C. 788 HL at 801–805; generally, Q. Liu, *Anticipatory Breach* (Oxford: Hart Publishing, 2011), Ch.5.

[63] *Fermometal SARL v Mediterranean Shipping Co SA ("The Simona")* [1989] A.C. 788 HL at 805.

(*"The Simona"*)[64] involved these eight points.

(1) The respondent charterers entered into a charterparty with the owners for carriage of steel from Durban to Bilbao by *The Simona*.

(2) (a) Clause 10 gave the charterers an option to cancel if the ship was not ready to load on or before 9 July 1982 (this was a charterer's cancellation clause: it did not impose an obligation on the owner to commence loading by 9 July, but instead it empowered the charterer to cancel if the vessel was not ready, on or before 9 July, for the loading of the charterer's cargo); but (b) it was conceded in this case that this option was only exercisable from 10 July onwards, and not earlier.

(3) The owners said that the loading dates would be 13–16 July.

(4) On 2 July, the charterers responded by prematurely (see point (2)(b)) purporting to terminate the agreement under cl.10. This was a repudiatory breach which, if it had been accepted, would have enabled the owners to terminate the contract and claim damages. Lord Ackner explained:[65]

> "It is common ground that the action of the charterers in giving the notice purporting to cancel the contract was premature. It constituted an anticipatory breach and repudiation of the charterparty, because the right of cancellation could not be validly exercised until the arrival of the cancellation date, some seven days hence. It is equally common ground that this repudiation was not accepted by the owners."

The charterer then arranged for its cargo to be loaded onto a different ship, *The Leo Tornado*, which was 'lined up' for that purpose and in fact confirmed as such on 8 July.

(5) But the charterer's repudiation was not accepted by the owners, and so the contract continued. Instead the owners told the charterers that the vessel would start loading on 8 July. (But the charterer did not trust the owner and so the charterer maintained its new fixture, *The Leo Tornado*.)

(6) On that date, the vessel arrived but she was not ready to load the steel. It followed that *The Simona* was not ready to load by the contractual deadline of the end of 9 July.

(7) In the light of the lack of readiness mentioned at (6), on 12 July the charterers rejected the owner's notice of readiness and the charterer terminated the contract in exercise of its cancellation option.

(8) The House of Lords held that the charterers had not lost their right to terminate under cl.10 because their earlier repudiatory breach had not been accepted by the owners, who had continued to perform. The decision in *"The Simona"* thus has the effect of enabling the charterer to terminate for breach even though the charterer at the time of the owner's failure to be ready to load the charterer was not itself ready willing and able to perform because it had loaded the relevant cargo onto a different ship (a point noted by Barling J in *Cantt Pak Ltd v Pak Southern China Property Investment Ltd*[66]). Lord Ackner summarised the position:[67]

---

64 [1989] A.C. 788 HL.
65 [1989] A.C. 788 HL at 796.
66 [2018] EWHC 2564 (Ch) at [114].
67 [1989] A.C. 788 HL at 801.

"the anticipatory breaches by the charterers not having been accepted by the owners as terminating the contract, the charterparty survived intact with the right of cancellation unaffected. The vessel was not ready to load by close of business on the cancelling date viz. 9 July and the charterers were therefore entitled to and did give what on the face of it was an effective notice of cancellation."

Lord Ackner also explained[68] that there was no factual basis for contending that the innocent party was estopped from terminating the contract; on the estoppel point in that case see paras 14-081 and 14-082.

Ready, willing and able   It should be noted that in *"The Simona"* the charterer's   **14-033** *termination of the contract had not been based on a Common Law right of termination for breach but upon a termination clause.* That decision does not directly, therefore, itself remove the requirement that a party must be ready willing and able to perform when it attempts to terminate the contract by reason of the other's repudiatory breach, etc (the "RWA" issue). As mentioned, at the time (on the second occasion) when the charterer chose validly to terminate the contract by invoking the express cancellation right, the charterer had already ceased to be able to perform, having hired already a substitute vessel and placed the relevant load on that vessel. Nevertheless, and independent of the present case, the RWA requirement is in retreat, at least in England.[69] Thus *Treitel*[70] and *Chitty*[71] cite case law for the proposition that a party can validly terminate, even though it turns out that he might not have been able to have performed his side of the contract: notably *British & Beningtons Ltd v North West Cachar Tea Co Ltd.*[72] In that 1923 case the buyer had been required in 1920 to deliver in London of three consignments of tea shipped from India. But the buyer had been unable to deliver in London, due to port congestion. The ships were rerouted to other British ports. Delay resulted. But this delay was not enough to justify the buyer's repudiation. And so, the House of Lords held that the buyer had unjustifiably repudiated. Lord Atkinson said:[73]

"the purchasers [in the present case], having on July 28, 1920, wrongfully repudiated their contract, the sellers were not, in order to recover damages for breach of this contract, bound to prove that they were ready and willing on that day to deliver the teas at London."

But Bridge is less confident that the RWA issue has been eliminated in such a context. He suggest that (in the context of an anticipatory breach) the real question is not whether the innocent party (once that party has elected to terminate) is released from a duty to make a futile "gesture" in preparing to make a proper tender of performance at the due date (that release is established and self-evident), but whether at the time of termination the innocent party had already ceased to be

---

68 [1989] A.C. 788 HL at 805–806.
69 For the vitality of the RWA factor in New Zealand, see F. Dawson, "Essential Terms and Condition Precedent" (2017) 133 L.Q.R. 183, noting *Kumar v Station Properties Ltd* [2015] NZSC 34; [2016] 1 N.Z.L.R. 99, where the New Zealand Supreme Court has denied that B is in breach if party A has failed to be RWA with respect to A's obligations (and earlier decisions, *Bahramitash v Kumar* [2005] NZSC 39; [2006] 1 N.Z.L.R. 577; *Property Ventures Investments Ltd v Regalwood Holdings Ltd* [2010] NZSC 47; [2010] 3 N.Z.L.R. 231 at [82]; *Ingram v Patcroft Properties Ltd* [2011] NZSC 49; [2011] 3 N.Z.L.R. 433).
70 E Peel (ed), *Treitel, The Law of Contract*, 15th edn (London: Sweet & Maxwell, 2020), 17-027.
71 H Beale (ed), *Chitty on Contracts*, 34th edn (London: Sweet & Maxwell, 2021), 27-072.
72 *British & Beningtons Ltd v North West Cachar Tea Co Ltd* [1923] A.C. 48 HL.
73 *British & Beningtons Ltd v North West Cachar Tea Co Ltd* [1923] A.C. 48 HL at 66 per Lord Atkinson.

RWA.[74]

14-034   There is also the issue of how damages are to be assessed, having regard to the big picture, that is, the fact that the innocent party can be shown not to have been able and willing to perform, or at least not able to do so. Although not dissenting from the result in the present case, the following remark in *British & Beningtons Ltd v North West Cachar Tea Co Ltd* indicates that Lord Sumner (presciently, see para.14-035) considered that the RWA factor might re-emerge as relevant when computing damages:[75]

> "I do not see how the fact, that the buyers [in the present case] have wrongly said "we treat this contract as being at an end, owing to your unreasonable delay in the performance of it" obliges them, when that reason fails, to pay in full, if, *at the very time of this repudiation*, the sellers *had become wholly and finally disabled from performing essential terms of the contract altogether. Braithwaite's Case says nothing, which affects the regular consequences, when it appears that at the time of breach the plaintiff is already completely disabled from doing his part at all.'* (emphasis added)

This statement was indeed prophetic because damages will be adjusted to reflect the broader context, as commentators note, based on judicial discussion.[76]

14-035   Contract terminated for breach: compensation reflecting subsequent events   If the promisee, party A, elects to terminate the contract and to seek compensation, the House of Lords in *Golden Strait Corp v Nippon Yusen Kubishika Kaisha ("The Golden Victory")*[77] held that damages for anticipatory breach should reflect post-breach events if those events have in fact reduced or eliminated the

---

[74]   MG Bridge, *The Sale of Goods* 4th edn (Oxford: Oxford University Press, 2019), 10.131, citing discussion by Francis Dawson, "Waiver of Conditions Precedent on a Repudiation" (1980) 96 L.Q.R. 239. The RWA issue is also examined by W. Goodhart and G.H. Jones, *Specific Performance*, 2nd edn (London: Butterworths, 1996), 68–72, where the authors assume that the RWA requirement has been struck off by *"The Simona"* (Goodhart and Jones also noting *Rightside Properties Ltd v Gray* [1975] Ch. 72, where Walton J held that the RWA requirement does not apply to a claim for damages consequent on the innocent party's election to terminate because of the other party's breach; Walton J's decision was considered by Barling J in *Cantt Pak Ltd v Pak Southern China Property Investment Ltd* [2018] EWHC 2564 (Ch) at [113]). See also on this issue paras 14-071–14-073.

[75]   *British & Beningtons Ltd v North West Cachar Tea Co Ltd* [1923] A.C. 48 HL at 71–72 per Lord Sumner.

[76]   Supporting the proposition that damages will need to be carefully considered in light of the fact, if proved, that the claimant would not have been able to perform in due course, had the contract not been terminated by the claimant by reason of the defendant's breach: (i) M.G. Bridge, *The Sale of Goods*, 4th edn (Oxford: Oxford University Press, 2019), paras 10.132, 10.133 (noting also discussion in *Berger & Co Inc v Gill & Duffus SA* [1984] A.C. 382 HL) (ii) E. Peel (ed), *Treitel, The Law of Contract*, 15th edn (London: Sweet & Maxwell, 2020), paras 17-029, 17-030 and (iii) *Chitty on Contracts*, 34th edn (London: Sweet & Maxwell, 2021), para.27-072, fn.372: Treitel and Chitty noting Teare J in *Flame SA v Glory Wealth Shipping Pte Ltd (The Glory Wealth)* [2013] EWHC 3153 (Comm); [2014] Q.B. 1080 at [18] and [85] (noted E Peel (2015) 131 L.Q.R. 29; and supported by D. McLauchlan, "Repudiatory Breach, Prospective Inability and 'The Golden Victory'" [2015] J.B.L. 530), in which Teare J suggested that damages will not be awarded if the innocent party cannot show that he would have had the resources to complete his side of the bargain; but, in the sequel, Teare J held that damages were payable to the claimant owners on these facts, even though, if there had been no breach, the owners would have disposed of their right to payment by directing payment to be made to third parties (as they had directed vis-à-vis earlier contracts): *Glory Wealth Shipping Pte Ltd v Flame SA* [2016] EWHC 293 (Comm); [2016] 1 C.L.C. 308 at [17]–[19] and [25]–[28].

[77]   [2007] UKHL 12; [2007] 2 A.C. 353; noted M. Mustill, "The Golden Victory—Some Reflections" (2008) 124 L.Q.R. 569; J. Morgan, "A Victory for 'Justice' over Commercial Certainty" [2007] 66 C.L.J. 263; C. Nicholls, "The 'available market' rule and period charters: Golden Strait Corp v Nippon Yusen Kubishika Kaisha" (2008) J.B.L. 91; B. Coote (2007) 123 L.Q.R. 503; Sir Bernard Rix,

claimant's loss. The Supreme Court in *Bunge SA v Nidera BV*[78] endorsed the majority analysis in that case. And so, the fact that A and B's contract would have been frustrated, if A had chosen not to terminate it by reason of B's breach, would be taken into account under this "compensation with full hindsight" regime. However, a problematic later case, which swims against the "compensation to reflect subsequent reality" tide is the Court of Appeal's decision to award loss of bargain damages against the charterer in *Classic Maritime v Limbungan Makmur Sdn Bhd*,[79] despite the apparent inability for the charterer to perform because of a dam burst which occurred subsequent to formation. The dam burst was not pleaded as a frustrating event, and the exceptions clause designed to protect the charterer was held to be inapplicable because the charterer had not been ready and willing to perform, irrespective of the dam burst. (Michael Bridge[80] suggests that the Court of Appeal decision was a misapplication of the law of damages, and that the claimant's actual loss was zero on these facts.)

Contract affirmed, despite repudiation etc, but contract subsequently   **14-036**
frustrated   A further consequence of the analysis examined here (that the contract is either on or off, and not in suspense to suit the innocent party) is that a frustrating event subsequent to the decision to *affirm the contract* can exonerate both parties, in accordance with the general principle governing the effects of frustration[81] (and see para.14-038 on *Avery v Bowden*[82]). There is a clear statement by Cockburn CJ in *Frost v Knight* of the "risk" taken by the promisee if he chooses not to terminate the contract by reason of the other's anticipatory breach but instead decides to keep the contract alive, awaiting performance and himself complying with his contractual obligations:[83]

"the promisee may...treat the notice of intention [viz the attempted renunciation] as inoperative ... and then hold the other party responsible for all the consequences of non-performance; but in that case he keeps the contract alive for the benefit of the other party as well as his own; he remains subject to all his own obligations and liabilities under it, and enables the other party not only to complete the contract, if so advised, notwithstanding his previous [unaccepted] repudiation of it, but also to take advantage of any supervening circumstances which would justify him in declining to complete it."

   "Lord Bingham's Contributions to Commercial Law", in M. Andenas and D. Fairgrieve (eds), *Tom Bingham and the Transformation of the Law: A Liber Amicorum* (Oxford: Oxford University Press, 2009), paras 14-071 to 14-073.

[78] [2015] UKSC 43; [2015] 3 All E.R. 1082 at [21]–[23] per Lord Sumption, and at [83] per Lord Toulson; see also *Flame SA v Glory Wealth Shipping Pte Ltd (The Glory Wealth)* [2013] EWHC 3153 (Comm); [2014] Q.B. 1080, Teare J (noted E. Peel, "Desideratum or principle: the 'compensatory principle' revisited" (2015) 131 L.Q.R. 29).

[79] [2019] EWCA Civ 1102; [2019] 2 All E.R. (Comm) 592 (reversing Teare J who had awarded merely nominal damages on these facts); Court of Appeal decision is noted by M. Bridge (2020) 136 L.Q.R. 1.

[80] M. Bridge (2020) 136 L.Q.R. 1.

[81] Frustration is concerned with drastic changes occurring *after the contract's* formation; the doctrine has the effect of terminating the contract by operation of law, that is, without either party needing actively to bring it to an end; as Lord Sumner said in the Privy Council in *Hirji Mulji v Cheong Yue Steamship Co Ltd* [1926] A.C. 497 PC at 505: "frustration brings the contract to an end forthwith, without more and automatically" (that is, without any need for the parties to be aware that it has occurred; the effect of such termination is that the parties are released from their *future* obligations under the contract; as for the position after this termination, the Law Reform (Frustrated Contracts) Act 1943 has ameliorated the Common Law consequences of frustration: see for details, Ch.18.

[82] (1855) 5 El. & Bl. 714; 119 E.R. 647; affm.'d (1856) 6 El. & Bl. 962; 119 E.R. 1122.

[83] (1872) L.R. 7 Ex 111 at 112–113.

14-037   This "subsequent frustration point", where the innocent party has elected to *affirm the contract*, is often stated in connection with *Avery v Bowden*.[84] As we shall see in para.14-038, that case in fact did not involve any initial attempted renunciation, but the case is nevertheless sound in its treatment of the present proposition of law.

14-038   In *Avery v Bowden*[85] a shipowner alleged that the defendant charterer had intimated that he would not be able to supply a cargo at Odessa and that the ship should leave. Four or five days later, the British and the Russians declared that they were at war. This rendered it illegal to trade in Odessa, because this was a Russian territory. In fact, the court held that no renunciation had occurred (and so, as Liu shows,[86] the "subsequent frustration" point arose in that case only indirectly, so that discussion of this point is merely dicta). Nevertheless, there is no doubt that where a contract survives a party's attempted anticipatory breach (the other party electing to affirm the contract), the contract might be terminated by subsequent frustration. Thus, in the *Avery* case, even if the charterer had renounced the contract (although in fact the court held that no such renunciation had occurred), and in response to that renunciation the shipowner had decided to keep the contract alive—so that the parties' obligation had remained fully operative during the "first phase"—the contract would have been frustrated by events subsequent to this first phase.

IV.   INNOCENT PARTY'S PAUSE FOR THOUGHT

14-039   Although the promisee must decide whether to terminate the contract or to sustain the contract, this does not prevent the courts from recognising the innocent party's need to pause for thought. Thus Rix LJ in the *Stocznia* case[87] held that *Fermometal SARL v Mediterranean Shipping Co SA ("The Simona")*[88]—discussed at para.14-028 ff—should not be taken too far. Rix LJ in the *Stocznia* case held that there is an obvious practical need to allow the innocent party a reasonable opportunity to assess briefly his option whether to affirm or to terminate, just as in international rugby the fourth official can be given a reasonable time to study camera footage to determine whether a disputed try should be awarded or not. But the time for assessment should not be prolonged. As Rix LJ said:[89] "If he does nothing for too long, there may come a time when the law will treat him as having affirmed."

14-040   The full text of this important statement in the *Stocznia* case reads as follows:[90]

> "there is of course a middle ground between acceptance of repudiation and affirmation of the contract, and that is the period when the innocent party is making up his mind what to do. If he does nothing for too long, there may come a time when the law will treat him as having affirmed. If he maintains the contract in being for the moment, while reserving his right to treat it as repudiated if his contract partner persists in his repudiation, then he has not yet elected. As long as the contract remains alive, the innocent party runs the risk

---

[84]   (1855) 5 El. & Bl. 714; 119 E.R. 647; affm.'d (1856) 6 El. & Bl. 962; 119 E.R. 1122.
[85]   (1855) 5 El. & Bl. 714; 119 E.R. 647; affm.'d (1856) 6 El. & Bl. 962; 119 E.R. 1122.
[86]   Q. Liu, *Anticipatory Breach* (Oxford: Hart Publishing, 2011), p.22, noting that both at first instance, before Lord Campbell CJ, and on appeal, it had been held that there had been no renunciation.
[87]   *Stocznia Gdanska SA v Latvian Shipping Co (No.3)* [2002] EWCA Civ 889; [2002] 2 All E.R. (Comm) 768 at [87].
[88]   [1989] A.C. 788 HL.
[89]   [2002] EWCA Civ 889; [2002] 2 All E.R. (Comm) 768 at [87].
[90]   [2002] EWCA Civ 889; [2002] 2 All E.R. (Comm) 768 at [87].

that a merely anticipatory repudiatory breach, a thing 'writ in water' until acceptance, can be overtaken by another event which prejudices the innocent party's rights under the contract—such as frustration or even his own breach. He also runs the risk, if that is the right word, that the party in repudiation will resume performance of the contract and thus end any continuing right in the innocent party to elect to accept the former repudiation as terminating the contract."

Rix LJ returned to this idea in *Force India Formula One Team Ltd v Etihad Airways PJSC*.[91] He held that, in accordance with this idea of the "middle ground between acceptance of a repudiation and affirmation of a contract", sponsors should be accorded (as was possible on those facts) a decent interval within which to assess whether to terminate the sponsorship agreement in response to the racing team's repudiation of some of its leading requirements. This "make your mind up" period was quite generous in the *Force India* case only because the relevant events had fallen within the long vacation of Formula One racing calendar, a fallow period (several months long) between racing seasons. Rix LJ explained that the operation of the "pause for thought" will depend on the context. As for the present context, he commented:[92] **14-041**

"Although delay may always be capable of being compromising, this contract, especially during the winter break between two racing seasons, did not present the typical case where mere delay may demonstrate a decision to affirm. Such cases typically occur where time is of the essence, for instance, in an extreme case where markets are always on the move such as in a share transaction, or more generally in a sales of goods case where a seller has to know whether or not his buyer is accepting the goods which have been delivered. In the present case, however, we are not faced with either an urgent situation of that kind, nor are we faced with some minor and remediable breach where the injured party only has to speak up for the matter to be remedied; or where firm protest is immediately necessary to prevent the party in breach from being misled."

Rix LJ added: **14-042**

"The present case concerns a complex and medium term relationship, which a takeover has destabilised, and where it necessarily and legitimately takes time for the consequences to become clearer and for the innocent party to consider his position. That is the middle ground between acceptance of a repudiation and affirmation of a contract which I discussed in the ... *Stocznia* case."[93]

Rix LJ concluded that there had been no affirmation of the contract by the innocent party:[94] **14-043**

"the sponsors were always in fact considering their position, and Force India knew or must have known that that was so. In the meantime Force India was prepared to press ahead with its new strategy, conscious of the difficulty created by that strategy, and indeed thriving on it. In my judgment there was no affirmation, waiver or acquiescence which prevented the sponsors from exercising their common law right to accept Force India's repudiation of the contract."

---

[91] [2010] EWCA Civ 1051; [2011] E.T.L.R. 10 at [122].
[92] [2010] EWCA Civ 1051; [2011] E.T.L.R. 10 at [122].
[93] Here referring to his earlier discussion in *Stocznia Gdanska SA v Latvian Shipping Co (No.3)* [2002] EWCA Civ 889; [2002] 2 All E.R. (Comm) 768 at [87].
[94] *Force India Formula One Team Ltd v Etihad Airways PJSC* [2010] EWCA Civ 1051; [2011] E.T.L.R. 10 at [122].

14-044   In *White Rosebay Shipping SA v Hong Kong Chain Glory Shipping Ltd*[95] Teare J said that the period during which the injured party can pause for thought must be a "reasonable" one.

In *Pharmapac (UK) Ltd v HBS Healthcare Ltd* (on which see also paras 10-087, 11-026 and 14-067), the judge commented as follows on the issue of a pause by the innocent party to decide whether to affirm the contract or to terminate for breach:[96]

> "[36] In considering whether at any point the Claimant elected to affirm the contract, one must bear in mind that a person entitled to make an election has a period of time to make up his mind what he is going to do. If he does nothing for too long, he may end up being treated as if he has affirmed; but if he maintains the contract in being for the moment, while reserving his right to treat it as repudiated if the repudiation is persisted in, he has not yet elected. *Force India Formula One Team Ltd v Etihad Airways PJSC* [2010] EWCA Civ 1051 is an example; and see the discussion at [112-113]. Moreover, waiver is based on encouraging the purchaser to think that he will be given time indefinitely and will not be cut off without further notice. Mere standing by is not enough, at all events unless it continues for an unreasonably long time: see *Buckland and Others v Farmar & Moody* [1979] 1 W.L.R. 221."

14-045   **Conclusion on the pause for reflection idea**   This notion of a period for reflection is commercially attractive, even though it is somewhat cloudy and might produce differences of opinion on particular facts. It is clear that English law has (at least at the level of Court of Appeal authority; see above for confirmation), adopted the concept of the "victim" having a (decent but not excessive) opportunity to "pause for reflection". The length of this period is entirely dependent on the context, some situations demanding swift decisiveness, others permitting a more leisurely approach. During that period the injured party can safely do nothing, without ipso facto being taken objectively to have committed himself to affirming the contract, that is, soldiering on with the contract and remaining committed to his obligations. And so, during this reasonable period the injured party is immune from the inference that his inactivity and silence constitute affirmation of the contract. Therefore, this flexible device of a pause for thought acts as a qualification upon the process of electing whether to affirm the contract (in other words, abandoning the right to terminate for breach) or terminate the contract for breach. (However, Liu finds this idea wholly unattractive and pours icy water on this development.[97])

V.   GUILTY PARTY NOTIFIED OR BECOMING AWARE OF INNOCENT PARTY'S ELECTION DECISION

14-046   The essence of the two-fold inquiry is (i) whether the innocent party has made a decision to terminate (whether there has been such a "decision" or "intention" will

---

[95] [2013] EWHC 1355 (Comm); [2013] 2 All E.R. (Comm) 449 at [21]–[26] per Teare J.

[96] [2022] EWHC 23 (Comm) at [36] (Judge Cadwallader) (on this case see also paras 10-087, 11-026)).

[97] Q. Liu, *Anticipatory Breach* (Oxford: Hart Publishing, 2011), p.132 ff; at p.135 commenting: "this 'third option' has a dubious status in law. It is in fact an ephemeral, undefined and thus unreal option … [and] its duration is left to be measured by a 'reasonable time' of which there appears to be no clearly discernible criterion … Moreover, the 'third option' seems to come alive only where the victim remains silent and inactive following the anticipatory breach. It is thus incapable of solving the problem that the victim tends to be unduly penalised under the orthodox test [of affirmation of the contract] for its efforts to rescue the contract."

be determined on an objective basis) and (ii) whether that decision has been adequately communicated or manifested, see para.14-058 ff, to the guilty party (that process also requiring an objective determination). The innocent party's decision whether to affirm or to terminate the contract requires no particular form. It can be manifested (element (i)), and then communicated (element (ii)), either expressly or impliedly.[98] The courts adopt an objective approach to determine whether the innocent party has successfully communicated a decision or an intention to terminate by acceptance of the guilty party's renunciation, repudiation, or other serious breach justifying termination

Determination whether the contract has been affirmed or determined involves　14-047
a fact-sensitive assessment　In *White Rosebay Shipping SA v Hong Kong Chain Glory Shipping Ltd*[99] Teare J held that the question whether the innocent party has elected to affirm the contract is a matter requiring appreciation of the facts and that there is no possibility of mechanically identifying a single, right answer. And so the court cannot second-guess an arbitral tribunal's decision on this point. It is enough that the arbitral tribunal has posed the issue correctly. (On this type of challenge to an arbitral tribunal's decision, see also *Wuhan Ocean Economic & Technical Cooperation Co Ltd, Nantong Huigang Shipbuilding Co Ltd v Schiffahrts-Gesellschaft ("Hansa Murcia") MBH & Co KG,*[100] considering Mustill J's fundamental analysis in *"The Chrysalis"* (1983) of the reasoning process in identifying the law and applying it accurately to the relevant facts.[101])

No objective evidence of an intention to terminate　By contrast, in *Melli Bank*　14-048
Plc v Holbud Ltd it was held that a bank customer's silence and inactivity did not disclose acceptance of an alleged repudiation,[102] but were instead consistent with the customer's decision not to avail itself of a credit facility and simply to allow the period within which that facility was available to expire.

Similarly, no termination or discharge for breach was held to have occurred in　14-049
Ridgewood Properties Group Ltd v Valero Energy Ltd.[103] Proudman J decided that the innocent party had not (i) elected to terminate the contract;[104] furthermore, (ii), in any event Proudman J went on to decide that the same party had not communicated acceptance of a repudiatory breach, nor could the guilty party be said to have inferred such acceptance on the basis of the innocent party's conduct.[105] The breach consisted of transfers of filling stations to third parties without reserving rights in favour of the claimant. The claimant held options to develop the sites. But the claimant's post-breach conduct did not disclose an intention to terminate for breach, no clear decision to terminate was established, and in fact the situation

---

[98]　*Vitol SA v Norelf Ltd ("The Santa Clara")* [1996] A.C. 800 HL at 810–811 per Lord Steyn; *Yukong Line of Korea v Rendsburg Investments Corp of Liberia ("The Rialto")* [1996] 2 Lloyd's Rep. 604, Moore-Bick J proposition (7).
[99]　[2013] EWHC 1355 (Comm); [2013] 2 All E.R. (Comm) 449 at [35]–[41] per Teare J.
[100]　[2012] EWHC 3104 (Comm); [2013] 1 All E.R. (Comm) 1277; [2013] 1 Lloyd's Rep. 273 at [53] and [54].
[101]　*Finelvet AG v Vinava Shipping Co Ltd ("The Chrysalis")* [1983] 1 W.L.R. 1469 at 1475; [1983] 1 Lloyd's Rep. 503 per Mustill J.
[102]　[2013] EWHC 1506 (Comm) at [27] per Robin Knowles QC.
[103]　[2013] EWHC 98 (Ch); [2013] Ch. 525.
[104]　*Ridgewood Properties Group Ltd v Valero Energy Ltd* [2013] EWHC 98 (Ch); [2013] Ch. 525 at [84].
[105]　[2013] EWHC 98 (Ch); [2013] Ch. 525 at [99]–[101].

objectively indicated instead that the claimant remained interested in pursuing the agreements.

14-050   **Mechanisms for communicating the innocent party's election decision (i): receipt of electronic message during normal office hours**   The House of Lords' decision in *Brinkibon v Stahag Stahl* (in the context of formation of contact) confirmed that notice of acceptance received in normal working hours by telex, email, fax or by hand delivery is deemed to be received straightaway, even if it is not immediately read.[106] A case which chimes precisely with the *Brinkibon* decision is *"The Brimnes"*.[107] That Court of Appeal decision is also relied on by the English courts as providing the analysis for communication in commercial dealings other than by means of postal offers, that is, communication by means of telexes, fax and email. Although both these cases involved the now defunct telex system, it is submitted that, transposed to the new electronic systems, the analysis adopted in these cases provides a workable rule. That rule can be formulated as follows: notification of an emailed communicated occurs at the moment of receipt by the addressee (including copied, or blind copied addressee(s)) if that receipt falls within the recipient's normal office hours. Otherwise notification occurs when the recipient's office re-opens for normal business.[108]

14-051   *"The Brimnes"* was summarised by Lord Kerr in *Gisda Cyf v Barratt*[109] as follows:

> "the owners of a ship sent a telex to the charterers at 5.45 pm on 2 April 1970 purporting to withdraw the vessel on the ground of late payment of the hire charge. The charterers' normal business hours ended at 6.00 pm. The telex was not seen until the morning of 3 April, although it had arrived in the charterers' office at 5.45 pm on 2 April. Brandon J found that the notice must be regarded as having been received by the charterers before 6.00 pm on 2 April. The Court of Appeal [agreed], Megaw LJ stating …:[110] 'if a notice arrives at the address of the person to be notified, at such a time and by such a means of communication that it would in the normal course of business come to the attention of that person on its arrival, that person cannot rely on some failure of himself or his servants to act in a normal businesslike manner in respect of taking cognisance of the communication so as to postpone the effective time of the notice until some later time when it in fact came to his attention.'"

14-052   **Mechanisms for communicating the innocent party's election decision (ii): receipt of electronic message outside normal office hours**   A sensible and clear rule has emerged: that electronic communication received by the addressee outside of that party's normal working hours will take effect when normal working hours next resume. This was the nub of Gatehouse J's decision (given in the context of termination of a contract) in *Schelde Delta Shipping BV v Astarte Shipping BV ("The Pamela")* (also known as *Mondial Shipping & Chartering BV v Astarte Shipping Ltd*).[111] This Commercial Court case shows that where written notice reaches the notified party outside that party's business hours, whether by telex, email, fax

---

[106] [1983] 2 A.C. 34 HL.
[107] [1975] Q.B. 929 CA.
[108] E. Haslam, "Email and Offer and Acceptance" (1996) N.L.J. 597..
[109] [2010] UKSC 41; [2010] I.C.R. 1475 at [15].
[110] [1975] Q.B. 929 CA at 966–967 per Megaw LJ; and Cairns LJ specifically said at 970, that the recipients on these facts had been culpable in not reading the telex ("some neglect of duty" by the recipient's staff).
[111] [1995] 2 Lloyd's Rep. 249; [1995] C.L.C. 1011, Gatehouse J.

or by hand delivery, communication occurs when business hours recommence on the next working day, at the location where the notified party is situated.

The *Mondial* case[112] concerned a shipowner's contractual right to withdraw a ves- **14-053**
sel for non-payment by the charterer. The issue was when the owner's notice of default, sent by telex, for non-payment had been received by the charterer. The owner's telex arrived Friday at 23.41, that is, not during the charterer's business hours. The charterer's office did not open again until Monday 9.00. In these circumstances, Gatehouse J held that the time of re-opening at the recipient's office was the moment of receipt of this notice:[113]

> "What matters is not when the notice is given/sent/despatched/issued by the owners but when its content reaches the mind of the charterer. If the telex is sent in ordinary business hours, the time of receipt is the same as the time of despatch because it is not open to the charterer to contend that it did not in fact then come to his attention (see *'The Brimnes'* [1975] Q.B. 929, CA. See the well-known passage in the speech of Lord Wilberforce in the *Brinkibon* case [1983] 2 A.C. 34 at 42 HL: [Where Lord Wilberforce said]: 'I would accept [the *Entores* rule 1955),[114] as a general rule. Where the condition of simultaneity is met, and where it appears to be within the mutual intention of the parties that contractual exchanges should take place in this way, I think it a sound rule, but not necessarily a universal rule ... The [telexed] message may not reach or be intended to reach the designated recipient immediately: messages may be sent out of office hours, or at night, with the intention, or upon the assumption, that they will be read at a later time ... and many other variations may occur. No universal rule can cover all such cases: they must be resolved by reference to the intentions of the parties, by sound business practice and in some cases by a judgment where the risks should lie."

Mechanisms for communicating the innocent party's election decision (iii): **14-054**
non-business addressees   It should be noted that the recipient in *"The Brimnes"*[115] was engaged in business and that the relevant communication was sent to that party's business address (using the now obsolete telex system). Different considerations would apply if the recipient were not engaged in business, especially if he or she received the relevant communication at home. On this point, although not necessary for its decision because the point turned on statutory employment law, the Supreme Court in *Gisda Cyf v Barratt*[116] noted the following remarks of Bean J in the Employment Appeal Tribunal in the *Gisda Cyf* case:

> "It is one thing to say that the owners or charterers of a ship, or similar large commercial concerns, must be taken to receive and read documents sent to them during normal business hours. It is quite another thing to say that the same principle of constructive knowledge should apply to individuals to whom a letter is sent at their home address. What of the person who lives alone and goes on holiday? What of the commercial traveller? What of the student who lives at university during term time and at the family home in the holidays? What of the individual fortunate enough to have a second home to which he or she goes at weekends? There is no principle equivalent to that enunciated in *'The Brimnes'* that an individual is expected to be at home to receive and open the post when it arrives or in the evening when he or she gets home, or that some arrangement must be

---

112 [1995] 2 Lloyd's Rep. 249; [1995] C.L.C. 1011, Gatehouse J.
113 [1995] 2 Lloyd's Rep. 249 at 252 (citing other judicial discussion).
114 *Entores Ltd v Miles Far East Corp* [1955] 2 Q.B. 327 CA at 332–334.
115 [1975] Q.B. 929 CA.
116 [2010] UKSC 41; [2010] I.C.R. 1475 at [16]: quoting Bean J (the latter's passage is cited below in the text).

made for someone else to open what may well be confidential correspondence in the recipient's absence."

14-055 **Mechanisms for communicating the innocent party's election decision (iv): postal communication** It is submitted that the offer and acceptance or formation rule, known as the English "postal rule",[117] does not, and should not, apply to the context of the termination or discharge of a contract by reason of repudiatory breach, etc. The innocent party is not creating a contract, but ending one. The postal rule gives the acceptor the benefit of knowing that a correctly addressed and stamped letter of acceptance, once posted, takes immediate effect, at that date and irrespective of whether it in fact reaches the offeror. But that analysis is inappropriate in the context of the election to terminate or affirm the contract. Instead, in that context, the guilty party needs to be told, and needs to know, whether the contract is off or still on. And so a posted letter from the innocent party will take effect only if received and only at the point when it is received, provided the receipt occurs during normal working hours, in accordance with the analysis explained above at paras 14-050–14-052.

14-056 **Decision to terminate adequately communicated** In *Alan Auld Associates Ltd v Rick Pollard Associates*[118] the innocent party and creditor Pollard was held to have adequately communicated by telephone his decision to end the contract. Pollard had worked for quite a while for Auld. But Auld had habitually been slow to settle Pollard's invoices. The Court of Appeal agreed that Auld's long series of late payments justified termination. Indeed, the delay was characterised as "substantial, persistent, and cynical" (for details of this case, para.6-037).

14-057 In the *Alan Auld* case Tuckey LJ explained as follows the critical discussion during which Pollard's election to terminate either by reason of repudiation or implicit renunciation hit home sufficiently:[119]

"By mid 2006 Dr Pollard [the innocent party] was understandably fed up with the way he was being treated. He did no work on the project in May 2006. On 7 June Dr Auld [the guilty party] phoned him to ask where [Pollard's] May invoice was … [Pollard] replied that he could not afford to invoice…the [guilty party] anymore, [in response to which Pollard received], as he noted in his diary, the 'usual platitudes'…[The trial judge] concluded that [Pollard's statement that he would no longer be invoicing Auld] must have meant that he would not continue to provide services to [Auld] and indeed that is how both parties proceeded following this telephone conversation. The judge said she was satisfied that 'he expressed those words to Dr Auld and that Dr Auld understood them to be a termination of the contract'."

14-058 **Decision to terminate manifested to guilty party by innocent party's positive conduct** Lord Steyn explained in *Vitol SA v Norelf Ltd ("The Santa Clara")*[120] that the court must consider whether the innocent party, in response to the other party's repudiation (renunciation, or other serious breach), has communicated an intention to terminate the contract or whether, in the absence of such a clear and explicit

---

[117] The postal rule is indubitably still applicable to formation of contract, but reported case law in England has dried up: H Beale (ed), *Chitty on Contracts*, 34th edn (London: Sweet & Maxwell, 2021), para.4-064–4-079.

[118] [2008] EWCA Civ 655; [2008] B.L.R. 419.

[119] [2008] EWCA Civ 655; [2008] B.L.R. 419 at [6] and [7].

[120] [1996] A.C. 800, HL.

communication, such an intention has been unequivocally manifested by conduct in circumstances where it can be inferred by the guilty party. *"The Santa Clara"* turned on positive conduct, rather than pure silence. Lord Steyn explained that conduct, which becomes manifest to the guilty party, might indicate that the innocent party has elected to terminate the contract. The claimant buyer had committed a repudiation when it prematurely concluded that the defendant seller would miss a deadline. The seller was held to have accepted this by conduct, namely by the sale of the subject matter to a third party. The repudiating party had become aware of the seller's conduct, and so the process of termination for breach had been completed. But Lord Steyn went further and suggested that occasionally even pure silence and the absence of positive conduct might provide solid enough evidence of how the innocent party has responded to the election whether to affirm or terminate the contract.

In greater detail, *Vitol SA v Norelf Ltd ("The Santa Clara")*[121] involved a contract for the sale of propane to the claimant. The defendant seller's vessel was required to berth and load by specified dates in order to carry the goods, once title had passed to the buyer. The seller was then required to tender a bill of lading and, 30 days later, the buyer was required to pay. On 8 March the buyer telexed the seller and said that, in its view, the loading would not be completed in time and that the seller would be treated as having repudiated the contract. The price was dipping and the buyer was attempting to get out of a bad bargain. The arbitrator held that the buyer had wrongly jumped the gun and that its telex was in fact an anticipatory breach. This was not challenged. But, on appeal from the arbitral tribunal, the issue was whether that breach had been accepted by the seller so as to terminate the contract. That point was considered by the Commercial Court, the Court of Appeal, and House of Lords. The seller had omitted to tender the bill of lading and had sold the cargo to a third party. Phillips J in the Commercial Court, upholding the award, treated the seller's conduct, which was known to the guilty party, as acceptance of the repudiation and hence as effective termination of the contract. The House of Lords agreed, reversing the Court of Appeal.

14-059

Lord Steyn said in *Vitol SA v Norelf Ltd ("The Santa Clara")*:[122]

14-060

"An act of acceptance of a repudiation requires no particular form: a communication does not have to be couched in the language of acceptance. It is sufficient that the communication or conduct clearly and unequivocally conveys to the repudiating party that that aggrieved party is treating the contract as at an end."

Lord Steyn added:[123]

14-061

"[The innocent party] need not personally, or by an agent, notify the repudiating party of his election to treat the contract as at an end. It is sufficient that the fact of the election comes to the repudiating party's attention, e.g. notification by an unauthorised broker or other intermediary may be sufficient."

---

[121] [1996] A.C. 800, HL.
[122] [1996] A.C. 800 HL at 810–811; Q. Liu, *Anticipatory Breach* (Oxford: Hart Publishing, 2011), pp.118–120.
[123] [1996] A.C. 800 HL at 811, citing *Wood Factory Pty Ltd v Kiritos Pty Ltd* (1985) 2 N.S.W.L.R. 105 at 146 per McHugh JA; *Majik Markets Pty Ltd v S & M Motor Repairs Pty Ltd (No.1)* (1987) 10 N.S.W.L.R. 49 at 54, per Young J.

14-062 **Decision to terminate inferred from omission to act in circumstances where positive conduct was expected** *Vitol SA v Norelf Ltd ("The Santa Clara")*[124] turned on positive conduct, rather than an omission to act or pure silence. But Lord Steyn in the following passages did contemplate that sometimes an omission to act might be pregnant with an implied message that the innocent party's inaction betokens a decision to terminate the contract for breach and, furthermore, that inference must have been objectively apparent to the other party, that is, to the party in repudiatory breach, etc. Thus Lord Steyn said:[125]

> "I am satisfied that a failure to perform may sometimes signify to a repudiating party an election by the aggrieved party to treat the contract as at an end. Postulate the case where an employer at the end of a day tells a contractor that he, the employer, is repudiating the contract and that the contractor need not return the next day. The contractor does not return the next day or at all. It seems to me that the contractor's failure to return may, in the absence of any other explanation, convey a decision to treat the contract as at an end. Another example may be an overseas sale providing for shipment on a named ship in a given month. The seller is obliged to obtain an export licence. The buyer repudiates the contract before loading starts. To the knowledge of the buyer the seller does not apply for an export licence with the result that the transaction cannot proceed. In such circumstances it may well be that an ordinary businessman, circumstanced as the parties were, would conclude that the seller was treating the contract as at an end."

14-063 Lord Steyn further commented:[126]

> "the passage from the judgment of Kerr LJ in *State Trading Corporation of India Ltd v M Golodetz* (1989),[127] if it was intended to enunciate a general and absolute rule [that non-performance by the innocent party is equivocal and so cannot constitute a decision to terminate the contract], goes too far. It will be recalled, however, that Kerr LJ spoke of a *continuing* failure [by the innocent party] to perform. One can readily accept that a continuing failure to perform, i.e. a breach commencing before the repudiation and continuing thereafter, would necessarily be equivocal. In my view too much has been made of the observation of Kerr LJ."

14-064 Finally, Lord Steyn said:[128]

> "[As for the submission] that a failure to perform a contractual obligation is necessarily and always equivocal I respectfully disagree. Sometimes in the practical world of businessmen an omission to act may be as pregnant with meaning as a positive declaration ... Thus in *Rust v Abbey Life Assurance Co Ltd* (1972)[129] the Court of Appeal held that a failure by a proposed insured to reject a proffered insurance policy for seven months justified on its own an inference of acceptance ... Similarly, in the different field of

---

[124] [1996] A.C. 800, HL.
[125] [1996] A.C. 800 HL at 811.
[126] [1996] A.C. 800 HL at 812.
[127] [1989] 2 Lloyd's Rep. 277 CA at 286.
[128] [1996] A.C. 800 HL at 812
[129] [1972] 2 Lloyd's Rep. 334 CA: this case is concerned with formation of contract; the defendant had acted *on the claimant's request* to open an investment bond and the claimant had earlier sent a cheque for this bond. But the claimant now sought return of her money. The first ground of decision was that the claimant had made an offer to the defendant which the latter had accepted by conduct. But a *second ground of decision* emerged. Even if the offer in fact emanated from the defendant, who had sent the relevant policy to the claimant, the claimant's substantial delay in acquiescing in receipt of that policy, and not seeking to cancel the apparent deal, was enough to indicate assent: generally on silence and acceptance, Neil Andrews, *Contract Law in Practice* (Oxford: Oxford University Press, 2021), 3.180–3.186. The *Rust* case makes sense: for if X starts the negotiations, and receives

repudiation, a failure to perform may sometimes be given a colour by special circumstances and may only be explicable to a reasonable person in the position of the repudiating party as an election to accept the repudiation."

It will be seen that Lord Steyn's statement in *"The Santa Clara"* is concerned **14-065** not only with the innocent party's mental decision to "call off the contract" but with the "conveying" of that decision to the other party. It is in this sense that Rix LJ's statement in *Force India Formula One Team Ltd v Etihad Airways PJSC* concerning the converse situation—an election to affirm the contract—should be understood. Rix LJ said:[130]

"a party may be taken to have elected to affirm where it acts in a manner which is consistent only with a decision to affirm or where it allows too much time to pass by without indicating any decision".

VI. INNOCENT PARTY WAIVING RIGHT TO TERMINATE OR LOSING RIGHT BECAUSE OF ESTOPPEL

A party can waive[131] a breach of condition (or other right to terminate for breach) **14-066** (for example, see the first of the three phases of default in the *Schuler* case, chronicled at para.10-042), or—in the case of sales of goods—a buyer can be treated under statutory rules as having "accepted" the goods.[132] Other examples of affirmation of the contract, that is, waiver of the right to terminate, are *Peregrine Systems Ltd v Steria Ltd*[133] and *Bentsen v Taylor Sons and Co (No.2)*.[134]

The Court of Appeal in *Bentsen v Taylor Sons & Co (No.2)*[135] held that a claim- **14-067** ant shipowner's statement that a particular ship "had sailed or was about to sail"

---

130 an offer or counter-offer from Y, on which X "sits" for a significant period, X's silence might be treated as consent; in this context, X cannot complain that he has been taken by surprise.

130 [2010] EWCA Civ 1051; [2011] E.T.L.R. 10 at [112].

131 H. Beale (ed), *Chitty on Contracts*, 34th edn (London: Sweet & Maxwell, 2021), para.27-060–27-062 (on the need for careful analysis). In *Ross T Smyth & Co Ltd v TD Bailey Son & Co* [1940] 3 All E.R. 60 HL at 70, Lord Wright said: "The word 'waiver' is a vague term used in many senses. It is always necessary to ascertain in what sense and with what restrictions it is used in any particular case. It is sometimes used in the sense of election as where a person decides between two mutually exclusive rights. Thus, in the old phrase, he claims in assumpsit and waives the tort. It is also used where a party expressly or impliedly gives up a right to enforce a condition or rely on a right to rescind a contract, or prevents performance, or announces that he will refuse performance, or loses an equitable right by laches. The use of so vague a term without further precision is to be deprecated." See also Lord Hailsham's comments in *Banning v Wright* [1972] 1 W.L.R. 972 HL at 978–980: (1) "the primary meaning of the word 'waiver' in legal parlance is the abandonment of a right in such a way that the other party is entitled to plead the abandonment by way of confession and avoidance if the right is thereafter asserted"; Lord Hailsham adding (2): "Waiver is the abandonment of a right … When a contract is broken the injured party in condoning the fault may be said either to waive the breach or to waive the term in relation to the breach. What in each case he waives is the right to rely on the term for the purpose of enforcing his remedy to the breach. I cannot construe 'waiver' as only applicable to the total abandonment of any term in the lease both as regards ascertained and past breaches, and as regards unascertained or future breaches."

132 For "acceptance" in the context of sales of goods, Sale of Goods Act 1979 ss.11(4), 35, 35A, 36; J. Beatson, A. Burrows and J. Cartwright, *Anson's Law of Contract*, 31st edn (Oxford: Oxford University Press, 2020), pp.156–157; but Sale of Goods Act 1979 s.11(4) is disapplied to consumer purchases by Consumer Rights Act 2015 Sch.1 para.10 (inserting a new s.11(4A), Sale of Goods Act 1979), and instead the regime under the Consumer Rights Act 2015 ss.19–22 applies.

133 [2005] EWCA Civ 239; [2005] Info T.L.R. 294 at [16]–[23].

134 [1893] 2 Q.B. 274, CA.

135 [1893] 2 Q.B. 274, CA.

from a particular port (Mobile, in the US) was a condition. The defendant shipowner erroneously made the statement just quoted, whereas in fact the ship eventually left the port 24 days later. However, waiver of the entitlement to terminate can occur. Here the charterer had elected not to terminate and had instead allowed the vessel to go from Mobile to Quebec. That constituted a waiver of the right to terminate for breach, relegating the charterer to a claim for damages if that it had sustained loss by reason of the delay in the vessel reaching Quebec. However, at Quebec the charterer failed to load a cargo, for which breach the charterer was liable for damages. The result, therefore, was that the owner had been in breach and then the charterer had been in breach, and there should be a set-off of those sums and judgment for the difference. The latter question, of quantification, was remitted by the Court of Appeal to arbitration. Lord Esher MR (and the other members of the court agreed) held that the right to terminate had been waived:[136]

> "The defendants [the charterer] had then a right to treat the contract as at an end, or they could, if they chose, treat it as still subsisting. But, if they intended to treat the contract as at an end, it was their duty so to exercise their right as not to lead the plaintiff to believe that he was still bound by the contract. Was the plaintiff [owner] led by the defendants to suppose that he was still bound? The defendants' letters, to my mind, clearly come to this: "You, the plaintiff, are bound to send the ship out to Quebec, and we shall load her there; but we shall do so under protest that is, we shall claim damages from you for breach of contract." No reasonable man can say that the plaintiff was not told by the defendants that he was still bound by the contract. The defendants cannot, therefore, now treat the contract as at an end; but they have a right to claim damages from the plaintiff, if they can prove that they have sustained any by reason of the delay in the sailing of the ship from Mobile."

14-068   A relatively straightforward example of the court concluding that an innocent party had elected (by conduct) not to terminate and instead to affirm the contract is *DD Classics Ltd v Chen*[137] The present point is technically a dictum because the judge had earlier held (on this point see paras 10-088, 12-019) that the buyer's late payment for a purchase of a car did not constitute breach of a condition. The buyer had failed to pay at the specified date, but payment was made later. It took some time for the money to pass through the banking system. In the interval between late payment and eventual receipt of the money the seller first made several communications in which he chased the buyer for payment and eventually the seller purported to terminate for breach of condition. Judge Keyser QC noted that the seller had elected to keep the contract "afoot":[138]

> "[53] [After the failure to pay on time, the innocent party] Mr Chen was treating the contract as afoot and, indeed, was encouraging and, to a degree, even facilitating performance up to and including the point when the [late] transfer of funds was made on 7 April. Moreover, he then continued to treat it as afoot by seeking confirmation from his own bank that moneys had been received. It was only on 13 April—after the communications that I have read out, after the payment made at his behest and with his encouragement on 7 April—that he purported to terminate the contract...."

Judge Keyser QC also explained that it was quite contrary to law for the innocent party to contend that no election to affirm the contract had occurred because he did not know of the technical operation of the doctrine of election. This hopeless argu-

---

136 [1893] 2 Q.B. 274, CA, 279–280.
137 [2022] EWHC 1357 (Comm) (Judge Keyser QC).
138 [2022] EWHC 1357 (Comm) at [53] (Judge Keyser QC).

ment was dismissed by the judge as follows:[139]

> "[55]…[the innocent party, the seller] Mr Chen well knew both what the contractual obligations were and what his rights were. If he says he had a right to terminate for a breach consisting of late payment, then he had what he always said he knew he had. The argument that he advances in his witness statement—namely, that he knew of the breach and he knew of his right to terminate but he did not know that if, he chose to keep the contract on foot rather than terminating, he could not thereafter change his mind—is a completely different argument. [His counsel] submitted that knowledge that, if one elects to affirm, one cannot thereafter change one's mind is required for a valid affirmation. He did not cite any authority for that proposition. I know of no authority to support it, and it is entirely ruinous of the whole operation of contracts in the event of repudiatory breach. The position is, in my view, straightforward. The innocent party has to know that he can choose to terminate the contract or choose not to terminate it. Once he makes his choice, that is that: if it were not, the concept of election would lose its practical significance and the party in breach could not know how the contract stood."

In *Parbulk II A/S v Heritage Maritime Ltd SA*[140] Eder J held (1) that there was **14-069** no principle that a demand for payment acted as a continuing affirmation of a contract. He then held that where there is a pattern of late payment, it is possible that fresh instances of late payment will provide grounds for termination, and an earlier waiver of late payment (in the sense that the innocent party chose not to terminate at that stage) will not operate prospectively. Furthermore, (2) the judge held that (a) if the innocent party has a ground for termination (by reason of the other party's default during period (i)), in respect of which the innocent party serves notice of default (consistent with an agreed notice period), no waiver of that right to terminate occurs if the innocent party goes on to serve an anticipatory notice of default in respect of (b) the next payment period (period (ii)). The judge's reasoning on point (2) seems to be that there can be no waiver capable of operating backwards in respect of the default during period (i)) at stage (2)(b) since the payor has yet to default in respect of period (ii).

VII. INNOCENT PARTY LOSING RIGHT TO TERMINATE BECAUSE OF ESTOPPEL

Lord Goff in *Motor Oil Hellas (Corinth) Refineries SA v Shipping Corp of India* **14-070** *("The Kanchenjunga")* acknowledged that it might sometimes happen that the innocent party will be estopped from terminating because his conduct has caused the other party to change his position.[141]

---

[139] [2022] EWHC 1357 (Comm) at [55] (Judge Keyser QC).
[140] [2011] EWHC 2917 (Comm); [2012] 2 All E.R. (Comm) 418 at [22]–[26].
[141] *Motor Oil Hellas (Corinth) Refineries SA v Shipping Corp of India ("The Kanchenjunga")* [1990] 1 Lloyd's Rep. 391 HL at 399 per Lord Goff; G.H. Jones (with P. Schlechtriem) "Breach of Contract" in *International Encyclopaedia of Comparative Law* Vol.VII (Contracts in General) (Tübingen: J.C.B. Mohr (Paul Siebeck), 1999), 15-134 and 15-135. No estoppel had arisen in this context on the facts of *Pharmapac (UK) Ltd v HBS Healthcare Ltd* [2022] EWHC 23 (Comm) at [41] (on which see also paras 10-087, 11-026 and 14-042), where Judge Cadwallader said: "[41] Nor did any of the communications to which I have referred amount, in my judgment, to representations capable of founding an estoppel. The Claimant's stance was to wait and see. Nor do I accept that if they had been representations, the Defendant placed any reliance or acted to its detriment upon them. Nor yet that there was any evidence upon which the Court could conclude that it would be inequitable for that or any other reason to allow the Claimant to rely on its strict legal rights. This allegation is hopeless, in my view. I should just add, however, that it was argued on behalf of the Claimant that one

14-071   In *Garside v Black Horse Ltd*[142] King J explained the essence of estoppel, as it applies in this context of the election to affirm the contract or to terminate the contract for breach:

> "The doctrine of estoppel is a different animal from that of affirmation. See *Chitty*, [now 34th edn (2021), para.27-060, 27-061]. [Estoppel] does not require in the innocent party knowledge as above, but rather a clear and unequivocal representation by words or conduct by the innocent party to the party in breach that he will not exercise his strict legal rights to treat the contract as repudiated, followed by a reliance by that party upon it in circumstances where it would be inequitable for the representor to go back on his representation. Estoppel in this sense, with its requirements of representation, reliance and detriment, has not been relied upon in this case."

14-072   In *Fermometal SARL v Mediterranean Shipping Co SA ("The Simona")* it was held that no estoppel had arisen so as to preclude the charterers from invoking the right to terminate by reason of late loading (for the facts and the result see para.14-028 to 14-037). Lord Ackner explained:[143]

> "If, in relation to this option to cancel, the owners had been able to establish that the charterers had represented that they no longer required the vessel to arrive on time because they had already [arranged to hire a different ship] and in reliance upon that representation, the owners had given notice of readiness only after the cancellation date, then the charterers would have been estopped from contending they were entitled to cancel the charterparty ...[But there] is a total lack of any material to show that the owners, because of the charterers' repudiatory conduct, viewed the cancellation clause as other than fully operative and therefore capable of being triggered by the vessel not being ready in time. The non-readiness of the vessel by the cancelling date was in no way induced by the charterers' conduct. It was the result of the owners' decision to load other cargo first."

14-073   Lord Ackner had earlier explained the nature of the estoppel argument as follows:[144]

> "Towards the conclusion of his able address, Mr. Boyd [counsel for the owners] ... submitted that the charterers' conduct had induced or caused the owners to abstain from having the ship ready prior to the cancellation date. Of course, it is always open to A, who has refused to accept B's repudiation of the contract, and thereby kept the contract alive, to contend that in relation to a particular right or obligation under the contract, B is estopped from contending that he, B, is entitled to exercise that right or that he, A, has remained bound by that obligation. If B represents to A that he no longer intends to exercise that right or requires that obligation to be fulfilled by A and A acts upon that representation, then clearly B cannot be heard thereafter to say that he is entitled to exercise that right or that A is in breach of contract by not fulfilling that obligation."

14-074   In *Cantt Pak Ltd v Pak Southern China Property Investment Ltd*,[145] Barling J provided a careful analysis and application of *"The Simona"* doctrine (para.14-

---

of the reasons why it would not be inequitable was that the Defendant, by Mr Patel, had effectively strung the Claimant along with its repeated assurances that the masks would be delivered before too long. It was made clear to me that it was no part of the Claimant's case Mr Patel had deliberately misled it, and my own conclusion is merely that in good faith he expressed more hope than subsequent events quite justified. I would not accept that this had any relevant bearing upon inequity."

[142] [2010] EWHC 190 (QB) at [29].
[143] [1989] A.C. 788 HL at 805–806.
[144] [1989] A.C. 788 HL at 805.
[145] *Cantt Pak Ltd v Pak Southern China Property Investment Ltd* [2018] EWHC 2564 (Ch).

028 to 14.039). In the *Cantt Pak* case the purchaser of commercial premises was held to have committed a repudiatory breach (failure to complete on the completion date, time having become of the essence). The vendor accepted this repudiation. Termination based on the buyer's breach occurred even though there had been an earlier serious breach by the vendor: the vendor's breach had been failure to clear the land so that he could give vacant possession; in a sense the vendor's breach was ongoing. The buyer's further argument based on estoppel failed on the facts: the vendor had made no representation to the defendant that it was, in effect, unnecessary for the defendant to continue to complete.[146] Barling J's judgment also contains valuable analysis of the Australian High Court's decision in *Foran v Wight*[147] (on which see also para.14-076 below).

Barling J's comments in *Cantt Pak Ltd v Pak Southern China Property Invest-*   **14-075**
ment Ltd are cited here:[148]

"[121] *Foran v Wight* (1989)[149] concerned a contract for the sale of land. The time for completion had been made of the essence and it was due to take place by 22 June 1983. It was a condition of the contract that before completion the vendor would obtain registration of a right of way. On 20 June the vendor notified the purchaser that it would not be able to do this by that date and could not complete on that date. By 20 June the purchaser had not been able to raise funds to purchase the property, and made no further attempt to do so. On 24 June the purchaser terminated the contract on the ground of the vendor's failure to complete. The purchaser then sought the return of its deposit. The majority of the court concluded that the purchaser was entitled to recover the deposit. However, the members took different approaches to the right of a party who was himself in breach of contract to accept a repudiation by the other party.

[122] One judge, Gaudron J, considered that *Fercometal* was correct, and that the vendor's notification of an inability to complete meant that the purchaser was not obliged to tender the purchase price and was entitled to accept the vendor's repudiatory breach without having to establish that it was itself ready willing and able to complete on the date for completion. Deane J considered that where both parties were in breach either of them could accept the other's repudiation and terminate the contract, recovering any deposit but not suing for damages. Brennan and Dawson JJ were of the view that where one party notified the other of its refusal or inability to perform its contractual obligations, and the other did not accept the repudiation until later, the latter must establish that when it received notification it was ready willing and able to fulfil its obligations. It was not, however, required to take further steps. These two members of the court were of the view that on the facts the purchaser was ready willing and able at the time of notification. Finally, Mason CJ, who dissented in the result, held that since the purchaser had not accepted the repudiation before the completion date, it was required to prove it was ready willing and able to complete on the completion date, which it had not done.

[123] *Foran* is of considerable interest for its exploration of the tricky issues involved. [Counsel for the purchaser in the present case] submitted that the majority of the members of the court were of the opinion that a party not ready willing and able ['RWA'] to perform its own obligations could not accept the other's unwillingness or inability to perform their obligations as a repudiatory breach. Whether or not that analysis of the decision is strictly accurate, the multiplicity of views expressed by the High Court of Australia render it very difficult to identify precisely what principles are to be derived from it. I share the view

---

146 *Cantt Pak Ltd v Pak Southern China Property Investment Ltd* [2018] EWHC 2564 (Ch) at [133]–[137].
147 *Foran v Wight* (1989) 168 C.L.R. 385, High Court of Australia, see text below.
148 *Cantt Pak Ltd v Pak Southern China Property Investment Ltd* [2018] EWHC 2564 (Ch) at [121]–[125].
149 *Foran v Wight* (1989) 168 C.L.R. 385, High Court of Australia.

of the learned authors of Jones & Goodhart [*Specific Performance*, 2nd edn (London: Butterworths, 1996), pp.68–72] who, when posing the question whether a party can accept a repudiation by the other party even when it is not itself ready willing and able to perform the contract, state that in the light of *Foran* so far as Australian law is concerned the answer is 'unclear'.

[124] However, the authors Goodhart and Jones [*Specific Performance*, 2nd edn (London: Butterworths, 1996), pp.68–72] are in no real doubt that English law provides a positive answer to that question [that is, a party can terminate for breach even though himself not ready willing and able to perform], based on [the leading decision in] *Fercometal*. The same authors [Goodhart and Jones, *Specific Performance*, 2nd edn (London: Butterworths, 1996), pp.68–72] point out that such a position is not optimal, in that it presents problems for a party who is [not yet] in breach himself and [who] wishes to keep the contract alive in the face of repudiation by the other side. In those circumstances [in order himself to avoid lapsing into repudiatory default] that innocent party may be driven to incur the expense and trouble of making a useless tender of performance in order not to provide the repudiator with an opportunity of himself terminating the contract by accepting the repudiatory non-performance of the "innocent" party. The authors suggest that hard cases might be mitigated by recourse to estoppel, or by restricting *Fercometal* to cases where specific performance is not an option [viz that the RWA requirement might be applied if the contract is specifically enforceable].

[125] However, I note that most, if not all, of the alternative approaches to this problem discussed by the authors have disadvantages of their own. In support of the *Fercometal* approach is the fact that it avoids…a 'Mexican stand-off', where a party who is in breach of an essential term of the contract cannot terminate it if the other party is also in breach, so that the contract is in limbo."

Such limbo would have arisen in the *Foran* case had not the High Court of Australia decided that the purchaser could validly terminate, notwithstanding the fact that the purchaser had not been RWA.

14-076   The High Court of Australia in *Peter Turnbull & Co Pty Ltd v Mundus Trading Co (Australasia) Pty Ltd*[150] suggested an important qualification (at any rate under Australian law) upon the general principle that the contract is either terminated or it is fully alive for both sides.[151] This qualification can be formulated as follows: where A's anticipatory breach is not accepted by B, A cannot escape liability for eventual actual breach by asserting that during the interval B had failed in some respect to comply precisely with the original terms of the contract, if the reason for B's failure so to do is directly and reasonably attributable to A's persistent failure to remain faithful to A's original commitment. The *Turnbull* case was considered by the High Court of Australia in *Foran v Wight*.[152] It might be that the same outcome (liability of A for eventual actual default) will be achieved under English law if the facts support the contention that A by conduct has represented to B that B's strict adherence to B's obligations is no longer required, on which B has relied, so that A has become estopped from invoking the fact that B might have committed a repudiatory breach subsequent to A's initial (but unaccepted) anticipatory breach. Otherwise, it would appear that (if B elects to keep the contract alive, and because there is, as Lord Ackner emphasised, "no third choice", no *via media*) the strict letter of Lord Ackner's analysis in *"The Simona"* (paras 14-028–14-039) will

---

[150] (1954) 90 C.L.R. 235 at 246–247 H.Ct. Aust.
[151] This qualification is encapsulated in *Foran v Wight* (1989) 168 C.L.R. 385 at 442 H.Ct. Aust. by Dawson J in the passage beginning, "I have said that there is a qualification …".
[152] *Foran v Wight* (1989) 168 C.L.R. 385 H.Ct. Aust. at 403–5 per Mason CJ, 419–421 per Brennan J, 433–434 per Deane J, 444–445 per Dawson J, 456 per Gaudron J (H.Ct. Aust.).

require B (defensively, strategically, and perhaps inefficiently) to remain faithful to his side of the bargain, so as to avoid the risk that B might present A with an opportunity to terminate the contract by reason of B's repudiatory default.

VIII. NEW OPPORTUNITY TO TERMINATE[153]

A party might gain a fresh right to elect to terminate the contract, because the **14-077** other party commits a fresh repudiation,[154] or because the guilty party's breach is continuous, such as a failure to pay money.[155] As Rix LJ said in the *Stocznia* case:[156]

> "If [the innocent party] maintains the contract in being for the moment, while reserving his right to treat it as repudiated if his contractual party persists in his repudiation, then he has not yet elected."

Jonathan Sumption QC (sitting as a deputy High Court judge) adopted this ap- **14-078** proach in *Safehaven Investments Ltd v Springbok Ltd*.[157] The contract was for the sale of lease for £1.7 million of a commercial property. Before completion, the purchaser purported to rescind on the basis of a misrepresentation by the vendor (letter of 16 March 1994). There was no basis for this plea of misrepresentation. And so the purchaser's attempted termination was a repudiatory act. The vendor urged the purchaser to proceed with the contract. Eventually on 20 April 1994, the vendor recognised that this would not work and so it purported to accept the earlier repudiation. Sumption QC held that (i) during the interval between 16 March and 20 April the vendor had affirmed the contract;[158] but (ii) that the vendor could validly terminate on 20 April because the facts disclosed a continuing breach by the purchaser.[159]

On point (i) the learned judge (later Lord Sumption) said:[160] **14-079**

---

[153] J.W. Carter, *Carter's Breach of Contract*, 2nd edn (Oxford: Hart Publishing, 2019), [11-57] ff.

[154] *Yukong Line of Korea v Rendsburg Investments Corp of Liberia ("The Rialto")* [1996] 2 Lloyd's Rep. 604 proposition (5).

[155] *Stocznia Gdanska SA v Latvian Shipping Co (No.3)* [2002] EWCA Civ 889; [2002] 2 All E.R. (Comm) 768 at [96]–[100]; see also *Safehaven Investments Ltd v Springbok Ltd* (1996) 71 P. & C.R. 59 (Ch), Jonathan Sumption QC (sitting as a deputy High Court judge). For observations on classification of breach as continuing or as complete but with continuing consequences', seen Julia Dias QC, in *Prakash Industries Limited v Peter Beck Und Partner* [2022] EWHC 754 (Comm) at [99]–[102]: "[99] ... especial care needs to be taken with the use of the term 'continuing breach'. On the one hand, it could mean a continuing wrong which gives rise to a continuing cause of action: see, for example, Chitty on Contracts (34th ed., Sweet & Maxwell) para.29-015. On the other, it could mean that the consequences of the breach continue even though the breach occurred at a single point in time and the cause of action accrued at that date. ... [101] In the present case, while the Subscription Agreement stipulated a date for the payment of interest, this was not a once-for-all affair in the sense that it was a terminal date for payment. ... A failure to pay interest is therefore a genuinely continuing breach which can in principle be remedied by the payment of all outstanding amounts. [102] By contrast, the Subscription Agreement provided that shares following a conversion were to be delivered by no later than the stipulated date. It is therefore difficult to see how a breach of that obligation can either continue or be remedied. The issuer is late and that is that. Only the consequences of the breach can be remedied by belated delivery of the shares." It would appear, therefore, that delivery of shares on a time-critical basis is a completed breach, but non-payment with the prospect of interest is a continuing breach.

[156] [2002] EWCA Civ 889; [2002] 2 All E.R. (Comm) 768 at [87].

[157] (1996) 71 P. & C.R. 59 (Ch).

[158] (1996) 71 P. & C.R. 59 (Ch) at 67–68.

[159] (1996) 71 P. & C.R. 59 (Ch) at 68–70.

[160] (1996) 71 P. & C.R. 59 (Ch) at 68.

"[Although the House of Lords in *Johnson v Agnew* (1980)[161] admitted that a party can seek specific performance and later, when that order is granted but not obeyed, it can terminate the contract for breach] it does not follow from this analysis that the innocent party may in all cases change his mind after affirming the contract. If, for example, after he had affirmed it, the repudiating party's conduct suggested that he proposed to perform after all, then that party's previous repudiation is spent. It had no further legal significance. If, on the other hand, the repudiating party persists in his refusal to perform, the innocent party may later treat the contract as being at an end. The correct analysis in this case is not that the innocent party is terminating on account of the original repudiation and going back on his election to affirm. It is that he is treating the contract as being at an end on account of the continuing repudiation reflected in the other party's behaviour after the affirmation."

14-080   On point (ii) Sumption QC said:[162]

"The question in the present case is whether on April 20, 1994, a reasonable person in the position of the vendor would have inferred from the overt acts of the purchaser that it was persisting in [its repudiation] on March 16."

He noted that the communications between the parties during this period objectively indicated that the purchaser did not wish to proceed on the original terms with the contract and was instead attempting to negotiate a lower price, and that it was continuing to insist that it was entitled to rescind the contract for misrepresentation.

14-081   Sumption QC's reasoning in *Safehaven Investments Ltd v Springbok Ltd* was approved by Rix LJ in the *Stocznia* case.[163] However, Liu finds the judge's reasoning on a "continuing" anticipatory breach muddled and unconvincing.[164] It is submitted that Sumption QC was correct and convincing in concluding that the purchaser on the facts of that case had continued to evince during this period a continuing unwillingness to proceed with the original contract.

14-082   In *Flanagan v Liontrust Investment Partners LLP*, Henderson J approved[165] the analysis in the *Safehaven* case and held that where a person repudiates once and then repeats the repudiation, the latter occasion creates a new opportunity for the innocent party to terminate the contract. The fact that the innocent party had earlier elected not to do so on the first occasion does not preclude the decision to end the contract on the second occasion.

---

[161] Discussed, (1996) 71 P. & C.R. 59 (Ch) at 68, by Sumption QC, noting [1980] A.C. 367 HL at 398, where Lord Wilberforce said: "a party who has chosen to seek specific performance may quite well thereafter, if specific performance fails to be realised, say, 'Very well then, the contract should be regarded as terminated'. It is quite consistent with the decision provisionally to keep alive to say 'Well this is no use—let us now end the contract's life'. A vendor who seeks (and gets) specific performance is merely electing for a course which may or may not lead to implementation of the contract—what he elects for is not eternal and unconditional affirmation, but a continuance of the contract under control of the court which control involves the power, in certain events, to terminate it."

[162] (1996) 71 P. & C.R. 59 (Ch Div) at 68.

[163] *Stocznia Gdanska SA v Latvian Shipping Co (No.3)* [2002] EWCA Civ 889; [2002] 2 All E.R. (Comm) 768 at [99], where Rix LJ preferred the view that an anticipatory breach might sometimes be characterised as continuing on a particular set of facts, so that an earlier failure by the victim to terminate the contract would not preclude a later termination for breach arising from a continuing anticipatory breach; and that the latter might occur even if the party in breach had remained silent in the interval. This last point seems loose and will require further consideration.

[164] Q. Liu, *Anticipatory Breach* (Oxford: Hart Publishing, 2011), pp.136–140.

[165] *Flanagan v Liontrust Investment Partners LLP* [2015] EWHC 2171 (Ch); [2015] Bus. L.R. 1172 at [217] per Henderson J (although later in his judgment at [243], he decided that the doctrine of repudiation/renunciation does not apply to LLP agreements if there are more than two parties).

As noted, the fact that breach is persistent or continuous will enlarge and keep **14-083** often the opportunity to terminate for breach, allowing the court to put aside the fact that there has been earlier inaction on the part of the innocent party, or that he has made calls for performance. For example, in *Future Publishing Ltd v Edge Interactive Media Inc* Proudman J said:[166]

"in August 2009 the claimant brought these proceedings for breach only. The claimant only purported to accept the defendants' repudiatory breaches by amendment to its pleading on 19th August 2010."

But Proudman J then explained:[167] **14-084**

"However this was a case in which the breaches were persisted in by the defendants. In those circumstances the fact that the claimant continued to press for performance should not preclude it from treating itself as discharged from its obligations under the contract. The claimant is not discharging on account of the original repudiation and trying to go back on an election to affirm. It is instead treating the contract as being at an end on account of the continuing repudiation reflected in the other party's behaviour: see *Chitty* [now 34th edn (2021), para.27-057] and cases therein cited."

In *White Rosebay Shipping SA v Hong Kong Chain Glory Shipping Ltd*[168] Teare **14-085** J also noted that, even where a party has affirmed the contract, the guilty party's renunciation might have continued (verbal declaration of unwillingness to perform; generally see Ch.6). However, that possibility of a continuing breach would require a positive finding of fact and cannot be deduced as a matter of law. It followed that the case needed to be remitted to the arbitral tribunal so that this point could be directly addressed and a decision made.

---

[166] [2011] EWHC 1489 (Ch); [2011] E.T.M.R. 50 at [68] per Proudman J.
[167] [2011] EWHC 1489 (Ch); [2011] E.T.M.R. 50 at [69] per Proudman J.
[168] [2013] EWHC 1355 (Comm); [2013] 2 All E.R. (Comm) 449 at [43]–[54] per Teare J.

CHAPTER 15

THE ENTIRE OBLIGATION RULE[1]

I. NATURE

Basic rules In contracts for services, or for goods and services, payment (whether **15-001**
in whole or in part) might be expressly or impliedly postponed until the job is
completed. The "entire obligation" rule will then prevent the contractor from
becoming entitled to payment until conclusion of the job. For example, in contracts
between householders and jobbing builders, the consumer normally postpones payment until the whole job is done (only a fool, although they exist, would pay a
builder or decorator by the hour or by the day: but nearly all litigants are fools,
because their lawyers are commonly paid by the six-minute "unit"). As Brian
Davenport QC observed in a *Law Commission Report* in 1983:

> "Experience has shown that it is all too common for such builders not to complete one
> job before moving on to the next".[2]

The entire obligation rule also reduces litigation, because it confers a self-help
defensive remedy (a shield) upon the innocent party. The latter is spared the
inconvenience, delay, expense and anxiety of seeking damages for the cost of curing a defective job in the courts.

Contractual obligations of an entire and non-entire nature A contract might **15-002**
comprise a range of obligations. For this reason, Treitel[3] has consistently drawn attention to the correct terminology of "entire obligations". Treitel gives this
example:[4]

> "A building contract may provide for payments as the work progresses, subject to a 'reten-
> tion fund' to be paid over on completion. There is then a series of severable obligations
> to complete each stage as well as an entire obligation to complete the whole."

In other words, the duty to make the bonus payment (held in the retention fund) is
dependent on complete performance of the whole, whereas the segmented pay-

---

[1] B. McFarlane and R. Stevens, "In Defence of Sumpter v Hedges" (2002) 118 L.Q.R. 569; G.H. Jones
(with P. Schlechtriem), "Breach of Contract" in *International Encyclopaedia of Comparative Law*
Vol.VII (Contracts in General) (Tübingen: J.C.B. Mohr (Paul Siebeck), 1999), 15-16—15-19, 15-
124—15-128.

[2] "Pecuniary Restitution on Breach of Contract" (1983) L. Com. No.121 36-37.

[3] G.H. Treitel (E. Peel (ed)), *The Law of Contract*, 15th edn (London: Sweet & Maxwell, 2020),
para.17-037.

[4] G.H. Treitel (E. Peel (ed)), *The Law of Contract*, 15th edn (London: Sweet & Maxwell, 2020),
para.17-037.

ments[5] are triggered by completion of each phase. Thus, Treitel argues that once an obligation is characterised as "entire", there is no scope for allowing substantial satisfaction of *that* obligation. He notes that not all the obligations expressly or impliedly undertaken by a party may be entire. Thus, the agreement might be "entire" in requiring the job to be "finished" but not entire as to the quality of the work or the time.

15-003 However, the courts tend to approach the issue in terms of "substantial performance of the contract", and do not "split" a duty to perform into particular obligations of "completion" "quality" and "timely execution".[6]

15-004 Approving Treitel's analytical approach, McFarlane and Stevens (2002) explain:[7]

> "Some cases and commentators refer not to entire and severable obligations, but rather to entire and severable contracts. However, Professor Treitel's insistence on using the terms to classify obligations rather than contracts is to be preferred. A contract may contain both entire and non-entire obligations. If a carrier performs the (entire) obligation to carry goods to the agreed destination he is entitled to be paid even though he is in breach of another obligation under the contract of carriage (e.g. to carry the goods with reasonable care) ... Similarly, under a contract for the sale of goods, the obligation as to quantity may be entire but the obligation as to quality may not be."

15-005 McFarlane and Stevens add:[8]

> "There is some judicial support for the view that there is an exception to the requirement of complete performance of an 'entire contract' where there has been 'substantial performance'. In *Hoenig v Isaacs* (1952)[9] the claimant contracted to redecorate and furnish the defendant's flat. The furnishings were defective. The claimant was entitled to be paid under the contract as he had substantially completed the work. It is submitted, however, that the leading textbook writers are correct to suggest that there is no room for the so-called doctrine of substantial performance. Obligations are entire, not contracts. The builder's obligation to complete the work was entire, his obligation to do so in a workman-like manner was not."

15-006 **Operation of the entire obligation rule**   In the typical case of a contract for work and materials, it will often be necessary for the job to be completed before payment is due. The notion of "completion" is pliable. If the job is to replace a floor with new tiling, then even 95 per cent of the job will not constitute "completion". But if the contractor fits all the tiles and, a day later, some of these have "lifted" because the job was done carelessly, it seems likely that the courts would regard this as "completion", but subject to a reduction for the cost of cure. There are borderline instances where it can be disputed whether the failure is in the quantity or quality of performance.

---

5   This is how the additional payments for each completed flat were structured in *Williams v Roffey & Nicholls (Contractors) Ltd* [1991] 1 Q.B. 1 CA; the Court of Appeal upheld Rupert Jackson QC's decision that there had been substantial performance of various flats under this re-negotiated rate of payment before the sub-contractor finally relinquished the overall job: [1991] 1 Q.B. 1 at 9–10 and 19 per Glidewell LJ, and [1991] 1 Q.B. 1 at 19 per Russell LJ.

6   e.g. *Bolton v Mahadeva* [1972] 1 W.L.R. 1010 CA at 1013 per Cairns LJ, "substantial performance of the contract"; for similar usage, see the references in B. McFarlane and R. Stevens, "In Defence of Sumpter v Hedges" (2002) 118 L.Q.R. 569, 571, fn.12.

7   B. McFarlane and R. Stevens, "In Defence of Sumpter v Hedges" (2002) 118 L.Q.R. 569 at 571.

8   "In Defence of Sumpter v. Hedges" (2002) 118 L.Q.R. 569 at 585–586.

9   [1952] 2 All E.R. 176 CA at 182.

Lord Cozens-Hardy MR in *H Dakin & Co Ltd v Lee* posed this example:[10] **15-007**

"to say that a builder cannot recover [the price or stage payment] merely because some item of the work has been done negligently or inefficiently or improperly is a proposition which I should not listen to unless compelled by a decision of the House of Lords. Take a contract for a lump sum to decorate a house; the contract provides that there shall be three coats of oil paint, but in one of the rooms only two coats of paint are put on. Can anybody seriously say that ... the builder could ... take the benefit of all the [work] without paying a penny?"

However, there will come a point at which unsatisfactory performance of an **15-008**
ostensibly "completed" job will be regarded as "no real job at all", so that the price will not be due. As we shall see (para.15-034), in *Bolton v Mahadeva*[11] a heating system was installed but it proved so defective, and indeed dangerous, that the Court of Appeal regarded it as an entirely bad job.[12] The contractor was not entitled to any payment. As Sachs LJ put it: "It is not merely that so very much of the work was shoddy, but it is the general ineffectiveness of it for its primary purpose that leads me to that conclusion".[13]

At Common Law it made no difference whether the failure to complete the entire **15-009**
contractual obligation involved breach or frustration. In *Cutter v Powell*[14] P hired C as a second mate for a voyage from Jamaica to Liverpool at a rate significantly higher than the local rate. Before the ship had reached Liverpool, C died and his widow sued for wages. The claim failed because payment required completion of the trip, and it did not matter whether C had jumped ship, been killed on board, or died of natural causes (although if he had been press-ganged by the King's officers into working on a naval ship, the seaman would have been entitled to a proportionate part).[15]

In *Cutter v Powell* Lord Kenyon said:[16] **15-010**

"Here the defendant expressly promised to pay the [sailor] thirty guineas, provided he proceeded, continued and did his duty as second mate in the ship from Jamaica to Liverpool ...; if there had been no contract between these parties, all that the [sailor] could have recovered on a quantum meruit for the voyage would have been eight pounds ... [The sailor] stipulated to receive the larger sum if the whole duty were performed, and nothing unless the whole of that duty were performed: it was a kind of insurance."

But the Law Reform (Frustrated Contracts) Act 1943 Pt III, para.18-001 ff now **15-011**

---

10 [1916] 1 K.B. 566 CA at 579.
11 [1972] 1 W.L.R. 1009 CA.
12 [1972] 1 W.L.R. 1010 CA.
13 [1972] 1 W.L.R. 1010 CA at 1015 per Sachs LJ.
14 *Cutter v Powell* (1795) 6 Term Rep. 320; 101 E.R. 573; M. Dockray, "Cutter v Power: A Trip Outside The Text" (2001) 117 L.Q.R. 664; similarly, in *Appleby v Myers* (1867) L.R. 2 C.P. 651, Blackburn J explained that the obligation to pay for the installation and maintenance of machinery in a factory required completion of the job, and that an accidental fire had precluded the performing party from suing for the price: "the plaintiffs, having contracted to do an entire work for a specific sum, can recover nothing unless the work be done". B. McFarlane and R. Stevens, "In Defence of Sumpter v Hedges" (2002) 118 L.Q.R. 569, 579 comment: "When the work was far advanced but incomplete the premises were destroyed by fire. Recovery for the value of the work was denied as the obligation to install the machinery was entire. *Appleby v Myers* seems correct in result as the defendant was not enriched by the work which was done. At the end of the day, the defendant had nothing and the work which was requested was never completed."
15 Mentioned by counsel in argument, citing Lord Holt in *Wiggins v Ingleton* (1706) 2 Lord Raym. 1211; 92 E.R. 300.
16 (1795) 6 Term. Rep. 320 at 324.

modifies the Common Law. The 1943 Act enables the court to award a "just sum" in respect of the "valuable benefit" conferred on the other party.[17]

15-012   Furthermore, sometimes a contract creates divisible obligations, that is, where "different parts of the consideration may be assigned to severable parts of the performance, for example, an agreement for payment pro rata".[18]

15-013   The entire obligation rule applies where party A's duty (normally to pay) is contingent on party B's prior and complete performance. The issue can arise, therefore, whether party A's obligation is dependent in this way. In *Donovan v Grainmarket Asset Management LLP*[19] the Court of Appeal considered this matter in the context of a joint venture agreement. The claimant, Donovan, had a relatively subsidiary role, being required to introduce investors. Most of the work under the joint venture was to be conducted by the defendant/appellant, Grainmarket. It was held, and the Court of Appeal upheld this decision, that this was not a situation where the claimant Donavan's right to take its agreed share of the success of the joint venture was dependent on complete performance. The position was analysed as follows:[20]

> "[52]…there is nothing in the express written terms of the agreement…to suggest that the right to a share of the performance fees was to be conditional on performance or substantial performance of either party's obligation. Nor was it suggested (and certainly there is no finding) that anything was ever agreed orally about this….
>
> [53] [Nor should such a term be implied here]. The agreement works well enough without it. Moreover, such a term would be likely to generate disputes about whether what might be relatively minor failings meant that a party had not substantially performed its obligations and had thereby lost its right to its share of the performance fees….
>
> [54] Rather, I would hold as a matter of construction of the agreement that, provided that the joint venture continued up to the time when a property was sold at a profit, a party's right to a share of the performance fees thus generated was unconditional. …
>
> [55] …If the joint venture continued to completion, the performance fees generated would be split in accordance with the parties' agreement. If it terminated because one of the parties repudiated its obligations before any right to a performance fee had accrued, that party would have no right to participate in those fees. If there was a breakdown in the parties' relationship but the agreement nevertheless continued, the right to performance fees would not be affected but any party who had caused loss as a result of failing to perform its obligations would be liable in damages."

II.   THE PATTERN OF THE CASES

15-014   The cases are considered in detail in the next section, but this section contains an overview.

15-015   It is arguable that the twentieth century cases show a disinclination to find that there has been a failure to satisfy an entire obligation in a contract involving materials and services or work: *H Dakin & Co Ltd v Lee*,[21] *Hoenig v Isaacs*,[22] and *Wil-*

---

[17]   The leading case is *BP Exploration Co (Libya) Ltd v Hunt (No.2)* [1979] 1 W.L.R. 783, Goff J: the appellate decisions [1981] 1 W.L.R. 232 CA and [1983] 2 A.C. 352 HL, do not affect Goff J's analysis of s.1(3) of the 1943 Act.

[18]   H. Beale (ed), *Chitty on Contracts*, 34th edn (London: Sweet & Maxwell, 2021), para.24-026.

[19]   [2021] EWCA Civ 686.

[20]   [2021] EWCA Civ 686 at [52]–[55] (Males LJ, with the agreement of Arnold and King LJJ).

[21]   [1916] 1 K.B. 566 CA (upholding Ridley and Sankey JJ, Divisional Court, but reversing the Official Referee).

liams v Roffey & Nicholls (Contractors) Ltd.[23] Denning LJ in the *Hoenig v Isaacs* case went further[24] and expressed a disinclination to construe a contract as entire just because the contract is structured so that the price is withheld until the "end" of the job.

But there are five reported cases going the other way, resulting in no liability to **15-016** pay for an extremely bad or job (each of these decisions will be introduced in the following paragraph, more detailed discussion ensuing in the next section).

(1) *Bolton v Mahadeva*[25] might be explained as a salutary exception to this trend, for there the work was quite seriously bad, indeed dangerous, and the contractor had shrugged his shoulders when asked to come and fix the defective work.

(2) There was a suggestion of a law firm "trying to pull a fast one" in *Pilbrow v Pearless de Rougemont & Co* by providing a non-legally qualified person to provide services when the client had specifically asked to a solicitor.[26]

(3) No one other than a self-interest undertaker could seriously dispute that the ghoulish failure in the *Vigers* case to satisfy a crucial element of the contemplated performance (the capacity to take the coffin into the church for the funeral service) justifiably disentitled that party from claiming its fee.[27]

(4) *Wiluszynski v Tower Hamlets LBC*[28] shows that an employee cannot claim wages or salary if his employer has made clear that his proposed or continuing partial or defective performance, if intentionally persisted in, will not qualify the employee for payment.

(5) Finally, *Systech International Ltd v PC Harrington Contractors Ltd*[29] decides that an adjudicator who fails to produce an enforceable decision (that decision having been declared a nullity for procedural reasons) is not entitled to claim his fee from the losing party.

III. CASES WHERE THE PERFORMING PARTY WAS HELD TO BE ENTITLED TO THE AGREED SUM

The so-called "substantial performance" doctrine might enable the performer to **15-017** claim the agreed sum even if performance has not been perfect. Then the innocent party's protection is confined to a cross-claim or deduction in respect of defective performance.[30] But the doctrine of substantial performance will not apply if the failure to perform is significant:[31] this depends on questions of proportionality, reasonableness and fairness.[32] The doctrine is traceable to the eighteenth century.[33]

---

22 [1952] 2 All E.R. 176 CA at 182.
23 [1991] 1 Q.B. 1 CA (at 9–10 and 19, Glidewell and Russell LJJ applied the *Hoenig* case, see above; but Purchas LJ did not address this point).
24 [1952] 2 All E.R. 176 CA at 180–181.
25 [1972] 1 W.L.R. 1009 CA.
26 [1993] 3 All E.R. 355; [1999] 2 Costs L.R. 109 CA.
27 *Vigers v Cook* [1919] 2 K.B. 475 Divisional Court and CA.
28 [1989] I.CR 493 CA at 503; G. Mead, "Restitution Within Contract?" (1991) 11 L.S. 172; B. McFarlane and R. Stevens, "In Defence of Sumpter v Hedges" (2002) 118 L.Q.R. 569 at 590–591.
29 [2012] EWCA Civ 1371; [2013] 2 All E.R. 69.
30 *Hoenig v Isaacs* [1952] 2 All E.R. 176 CA.
31 *Sumpter v Hedges* [1898] 1 Q.B. 673 CA.
32 As mentioned in *Bolton v Mahadeva* [1972] 1 W.L.R. 1010 CA.
33 *Boone v Eyre* (1779) 1 Hy. Bl. 273n (summarised in notes to *Cutter v Powell* (1795) 6 Term Rep.

The three leading[34] modern decisions are *Sumpter v Hedges*,[35] *Bolton v Mahadeva*,[36] and *Hoenig v Isaacs*,[37] but for completeness other cases will be noted.

15-018   Entitlement to payment was found in *H Dakin & Co Ltd v Lee*,[38] where the plaintiffs did repair work in the defendant's home. Some of this was defective. The decision is generous. As Pickford LJ explained:[39]

> "Here there was a contract to do a considerable amount of work to the defendant's house for the price of 264l. [There were defects in performance] According to a calculation made by the plaintiffs before they sent in their estimate the costs of these items were estimated, so far as the concreting went, at 60l, and as regards the other item at 70l, so that, although they were a substantial part of the work in the specification, they were not by any means the whole of the work which had to be done under it."

15-019   However, the duty to pay for the repair work was held to have arisen. The householder was confined to his right of set-off against the price. Pickford LJ said:[40]

> "There is nothing in all this that seems to me to amount to doing only a part of the work contracted for and abandoning the rest. What the plaintiffs have done is to perform the work which they had contracted to do, but they have done some part of it insufficiently and badly; and that does not disentitle them to be paid, but it does entitle the defendant to deduct such an amount as is sufficient to put that insufficiently done work into the condition in which it ought to have been according to the contract."

15-020   But the Court of Appeal in *Eshelby v Federated European Bank Ltd*[41] doubted the decision in *H Dakin & Co*. The court in the *Eshelby* case strongly hinted that they considered the 1916 decision was hard to reconcile with *Cutter v Powell*[42] and thus turned unconvincingly on the difference between not completing the job and completing the job but doing so imperfectly.

15-021   Another decision in favour of the defective performer is *Hoenig v Isaacs*.[43] The claimant had agreed to redecorate and furnish the defendant's flat for £750. The breach consisted of minor defects in performance but these could be rectified for £55. Adopting Cairns LJ's summary (in *Bolton v Mahadeva*) of the *Hoenig* case:

> "[the shortcomings were that] the door of a wardrobe required replacing, [and] that a bookshelf which was too short would have to be re-made, which would require alterations being made to a bookcase. [The] cost of remedying the defects was £55 18s 2d. That is on a £750 contract. The ground on which the Court of Appeal in that case held that the plaintiff was entitled to succeed, notwithstanding that there was not complete performance of the contract, was that there was substantial performance of the contract and that the

---

320; *Smith's Leading Cases*, 13th edn (London: Sweet & Maxwell, 1929); Lord Denning MR in *"The Hansa Nord"* [1976] 1 Q.B. 44 at 60 CA).

[34]   Other modern decisions: *Vigers v Cook* [1919] 2 K.B. 475 CA at 482, *Williams v Roffey & Nicholls (Contractors) Ltd* [1991] 1 Q.B. 1 CA at 8–10, 19, and *Pilbrow v Pearless de Rougemont & Co* [1993] 3 All E.R. 355 at 361 B, 360; [1999] 2 Costs L.R. 109 CA at 115-116.

[35]   [1898] 1 Q.B. 673 CA.

[36]   [1972] 1 W.L.R. 1010 CA.

[37]   [1952] 2 All E.R. 176 CA.

[38]   [1916] 1 K.B. 566 CA (upholding Ridley and Sankey JJ, Divisional Court, but reversing the Official Referee).

[39]   [1916] 1 K.B. 566 CA at 580–581.

[40]   [1916] 1 K.B. 566 CA at 581.

[41]   [1932] 1 K.B. 423 CA, Scrutton, Greer, and Slesser LJJ.

[42]   *Cutter v Powell* (1795) 6 Term Rep. 320; 101 E.R. 573; M. Dockray, "Cutter v. Power: A Trip Outside The Text" (2001) 117 L.Q.R. 664.

[43]   [1952] 2 All E.R. 176 CA.

defects in the work which there existed were not sufficient to amount to a substantial degree of non-performance."[44]

And so, the Court of Appeal in *Hoenig v Isaacs* held that the claimant had a good claim for the price, subject to a deduction under a cross-claim of £55 in respect of the defective performance. In short, the job had been done in *Hoenig* and the defects were relatively minor imperfections. Somervell LJ thought that the present facts were borderline.[45] Romer LJ was convinced, however, that the defects in the work were minor. Commenting on the *H Dakin & Co* case,[46] Romer LJ said in *Hoenig v Isaacs*:[47]

15-022

"if a man tells a contractor to build a ten foot wall for him in his garden and agrees to pay £x for it, it would not be right that he should be held liable for any part of the contract price if the contractor builds the wall to two feet and then renounces further performance of the contract, or builds the wall of a totally different material from that which was ordered, or builds it at the wrong end of the garden. The work contracted for has not been done and the corresponding obligation to pay consequently never arises."

Romer LJ added in *Hoenig v Isaacs*:[48]

15-023

"But when a man fully performs his contract in the sense that he supplies all that he agreed to supply but what he supplies is subject to defects of so minor a character that he can be said to have substantially performed his promise, it is, in my judgment, far more equitable to apply the *H Dakin & Co Ltd v Lee* principle than to deprive him wholly of his contractual rights."

In *Hoenig v Isaacs* Denning LJ reached the same result, but (unlike Somervell and Romer LJJ) he preferred to classify the case as not turning on postponement of the remainder of the price:[49]

15-024

"the first question is whether, on the true construction of the contract, entire performance was a condition precedent to payment. It was a lump sum contract, but that does not mean that entire performance was a condition precedent to payment. When a contract provides for a specific sum to be paid on completion of specified work, the courts lean against a construction of the contract which would deprive the contractor of any payment at all simply because there are some defects or omissions."[50]

Denning LJ continued:[51]

15-025

"The promise to complete the work is, therefore, construed as a term of the contract, but not as a condition. It is not every breach of that term which absolves the employer from his promise to pay the price, but only a breach which goes to the root of the contract, such as an abandonment of the work when it is only half done."

---

44 [1972] 1 W.L.R. 1009 CA at 1013 per Cairns LJ.
45 [1952] 2 All E.R. 176 CA at 179.
46 [1916] 1 K.B. 566 CA (upholding Ridley and Sankey JJ, Divisional Court, but reversing the Official Referee).
47 [1952] 2 All E.R. 176 CA at 182.
48 [1952] 2 All E.R. 176 CA at 182.
49 [1952] 2 All E.R. 176 CA at 180–181.
50 This aspect was followed in *Foxholes Nursing Home Ltd v Accora Ltd* [2013] EWHC 3712 (Ch) (unreported); similarly, for the argument that postponed payment should not, ipso facto, support the inference that the obligation is entire, B. McFarlane and R. Stevens, "In Defence of Sumpter v Hedges" (2002) 118 L.Q.R. 569, 594–599.
51 [1952] 2 All E.R. 176 CA at 180–181.

15-026   He added:[52]

"Unless the breach does go to the root of the matter, the employer cannot resist payment of the price. He must pay it and bring a cross-claim for the defects and omissions, or, alternatively, set them up in diminution of the price. The measure is the amount which the work is worth less by reason of the defects and omissions, and is usually calculated by the cost of making them good."

15-027   But Denning LJ further remarked that, even if he was wrong, and the contract was entire, there had been a waiver of the requirement that performance should be complete and precise:[53]

"Even if entire performance was a condition precedent, nevertheless ... the condition was waived. It is always open to a party to waive a condition which is inserted for his benefit. What amounts to a waiver depends on the circumstances ... [The innocent party] did not refuse to accept the work. On the contrary, he entered into possession of the flat and used the furniture as his own, including the defective items. That was a clear waiver of the condition precedent."

15-028   The Court of Appeal in *Williams v Roffey & Nicholls (Contractors) Ltd*,[54] applying the *Hoenig* case, found that there had been substantial performance in the *Williams* case. The question arose with respect to carpentry work done to a set of flats. The court considered each flat to be a severable unit of performance. It then posed the question whether the work done within each relevant flat was complete. Glidewell LJ[55] cited extensively portions of the three judgments in the *Hoenig* case (see the preceding paragraphs). He then said simply that the trial judge's decision in the *Williams* case, that the work had been completed in each of the relevant flats (a decision of Rupert Jackson QC) was supported by the *Hoenig* case. Russell LJ[56] in the *Williams* case adopted the same reasoning. Commentators[57] find the decision that the carpenters had achieved substantial performance inexplicably generous on these facts (the Court of Appeal accepted that £1800 should be deducted, in respect of defects, from the £4600 overall payment in respect of the bonus promise: contrast *Bolton v Mahadeva*, at para.15-034 and 15-035, where defective performance disqualified the performer from claiming the agreed sum.

IV.   SUBSTANTIAL PERFORMANCE: CASES WHERE THE PERFORMING PARTY WAS HELD NOT TO BE ENTITLED TO THE AGREED SUM

15-029   In *Sumpter v Hedges*[58] a builder was unable to obtain the contract price because he became insolvent before coming anywhere near completion. He had agreed to construct two houses for the defendant at a price of £565. He performed £333 worth of this, but was forced to abandon the job because of lack of funds. The innocent party had already paid £219 (made up of £119 cash and two horses worth £100). The Court of Appeal held that the innocent party was not liable to pay the rest of

---

52   [1952] 2 All E.R. 176 CA at 180–181.
53   [1952] 2 All E.R. 176 CA at 180–181.
54   [1991] 1 Q.B. 1 CA.
55   [1991] 1 Q.B. 1 CA at 9–10, per Glidewell LJ (the third judge, Purchas LJ, did not address this point).
56   [1991] 1 Q.B. 1 CA at 19, per Russell LJ; Purchas LJ did not address this point.
57   J. Adams and R. Brownsword, "Contract, Consideration and the Critical Path" (1991) 53 M.L.R. 536 at 538.
58   [1898] 1 Q.B. 673 CA.

the lump sum, because this obligation arose only on completion of the work. A claim for a quantum meruit (a restitutionary claim for the value of the services, and goods used) also failed because the builder's partial work (the partly finished building) had acceded to the defendant's land, and so the latter had not impliedly assumed a liability to pay a reasonable value for this partial performance (or become, to use the modern analysis, liable under restitutionary principles). But the defendant was liable to pay for loose materials left on site because he had freely decided to use these materials rather than returning them to a building merchant's yard and so "cashing them in" and then crediting them to the builder or to his trustee in bankruptcy. In short, these materials had not already acceded to his land (as where bricks and mortar now form a wall), but had been knowingly appropriated by the defendant.

In *Vigers v Cook*[59] undertakers failed to allow ventilation of a lead-lined coffin **15-030** containing an already badly decomposed body of a young army officer. The deceased's father had arranged for the plaintiff to carry out four related tasks: (i) to place the body in a coffin; (ii) to arrange for its custody pending the funeral; (iii) to convey the body to a church-yard and take the coffin into the church at Richmond for a funeral service; and (iv) finally to hand the body to the military so that they could complete the burial. The estimate for this work was £49. The undertaker at stage (ii) had closed the ventilation hole in the coffin the day before the funeral, following complaints of an offensive smell at the mortuary. The result was that the coffin could not be taken into the church for the funeral service at stage (iii) because the coffin was no longer secure. The county court judge held that, although element (iii) had not been achieved, the undertakers should receive a quantum meruit of £41 (it seems remarkable that the funeral directors were prepared to litigate at all on these grisly facts). But the Divisional Court held (and, as noted below at para.15-032, the Court of Appeal in due course agreed) that there was no entitlement to any payment on these facts (whether under the contract or on the basis of a quantum meruit). Lawrence and Lush LJJ concluding that this was an entire contract. Lawrence J said:[60]

> "The contract was to conduct the funeral in a reverent manner such as to conform with the sentiments of the family. It was an essential part of the funeral that the body should be taken into the church so that the service might be read in its presence. The various items of which the plaintiff's bill is made up are mere accidentals, and if he fails to carry out the essential part of his contract he fails to carry it out altogether. The case of *H Dakin & Co Ltd v Lee* (1916)[61] does not bear any comparison with the present case. There the default of the builder in carrying out the work was capable of being remedied by the expenditure of money, and he was held entitled to recover the contract price less so much as was required to make the defective work good. But it is impossible to apply that to a funeral. In my opinion the plaintiff's case fails, and there must be judgment for the defendant."

Lush J addressed the quantum meruit point, but held that the defendant had not **15-031** freely accepted any benefit on these facts:[62]

> "As the funeral was not decently conducted and as the plaintiff had made it impossible

---

[59] [1919] 2 K.B. 475 Divisional Court, and CA.

[60] [1919] 2 K.B. 475 at 479 Divisional Court.

[61] [1916] 1 K.B. 566 CA (upholding Ridley and Sankey JJ, Divisional Court, but reversing the Official Referee).

[62] [1919] 2 K.B. 475 at 480 Divisional Court.

to take the body into the church the defendant derived no benefit from what he did; and even if it could be said that he did derive a benefit it was one as to the acceptance of which he had no choice, and therefore there would be no grounds for inferring a fresh contract to pay a quantum meruit."

15-032   On appeal from the Divisional Court, the Court of Appeal in *Vigers v Cook* (Bankes, Scrutton, and Atkin LJJ) upheld the decision.[63] But Bankes LJ emphasised that the undertaker had failed to satisfy the onus of proof of showing that his failure to satisfy element (iii), that is, the capacity to take the coffin into the church, was attributable to events beyond his control and that, even if a correct ventilation system had been maintained, this impossibility would still have arisen. This shows that the obligation at phase (iii) of the performance was entire, *unless events rendered it impossible to perform and the performing party could not have altered this*. Bankes LJ (the other members of the Court of Appeal simply agreeing) formulated this point as follows:[64]

> "the contract ... included ... as an essential term the conveying of the body into the church for a part of the service, subject to this condition, that the body was in such a state as to permit of that being done. The body in this coffin was not in that state, but the onus was on the plaintiff to establish that it was not in that state owing to no default on his part. In my opinion he did not discharge that onus."

15-033   Bankes LJ continued:

> "although the plaintiff down to the time of the closing of the aperture [at stage (b), the day before the funeral] did nothing other than what a competent and careful undertaker would do, in the difficult circumstances which arose when he felt it necessary to close the aperture, he has not shown that it was owing to no fault on his part that one essential term of his contract was not fulfilled; and it being one entire contract, in my opinion he fails in proving that he is entitled to any portion of the one entire price which was payable for the entire contract."

15-034   In *Bolton v Mahadeva* the claimant had agreed to fit a heating and domestic hot water system for £560.[65] After the job was ostensibly "done", the defendant justifiably refused to pay, because the heating system produced 10 per cent less warmth than required and it emitted fumes.[66] The Court of Appeal held that the defendant's duty to pay the lump sum had not arisen on these facts. The level of defective performance was high. The court was convinced that the work was seriously shoddy, indeed dangerous. Furthermore, the contractor had wrongly refused to mend his botched job. Cairns LJ, who gave the main reasoned judgment, said:[67]

> "it is relevant to take into account both the nature of the defects and the proportion between the cost of rectifying them and the contract price. It would be wrong to say that the contractor is only entitled to payment if the defects are so trifling as to be covered by the de minimis rule."

15-035   Sachs LJ considered that the work had not merely been "shoddy": it had failed to achieve "its primary purpose" because the level of heating was inadequate and

---

[63] [1919] 2 K.B. 475 Divisional Court and CA.
[64] [1919] 2 K.B. 475 CA at 482–483.
[65] [1972] 1 W.L.R. 1009 CA.
[66] [1972] 1 W.L.R. 1009 CA at 1013F.
[67] [1972] 1 W.L.R. 1009 CA at 1013E.

the appliance emitted fumes.[68] He also noted that the present litigation had arisen only because the contractor had stubbornly refused to remedy these defects.[69]

Gareth Jones has suggested that "proportionality" should not be the only criterion, and that the questions of unfair prejudice to the guilty party and the factor of adequacy of damages to the innocent party should also be considered.[70]   **15-036**

In the context of contracts of employment, the Court of Appeal held in *Wiluszynski v Tower Hamlets LBC*[71] that where an employee fails to do his job properly, and the employer makes clear that this unauthorised lack of proper performance will not attract any payment, the employee cannot claim his wages for the relevant period, adopting analysis contained in the House of Lords decision in *Miles v Wakefield Metropolitan DC*.[72]   **15-037**

In *Wiluszynski v Tower Hamlets LBC* Nicholls LJ said:[73]   **15-038**

"If an employee states that for the indefinite future he will not be performing a material part of his contractual services, the employer is entitled in response, and in advance of the services being undertaken, to decline to accept the proffered partial performance. He can hold himself out as continuing to be ready and willing to carry out the contract of employment, and to accept from the employee work as agreed and to pay him for that work as agreed, while declining to accept or pay for part only of the agreed work."

In *Pilbrow v Pearless de Rougemont & Co*[74] Schiemann LJ, giving the Court of Appeal's judgment, held that a firm of solicitors was not entitled to payment if was asked to supply the services of a solicitor but instead it used a non-lawyer to assist the client. Here a prospective client had telephoned a firm of solicitors and asked to see a solicitor about a family matter. An appointment was made with a fee earner. But he was not a solicitor. The client was not informed of that advisor's true qualifications and status. The client paid £800 on account. But the firm sued for another £1,800. The Court of Appeal held (reversing the lower court's decision) that the client did not owe this extra amount (the client had not chosen to seek to recover the £800 already paid). The court regarded this as an example of non-performance of a contract to provide legal services through a qualified solicitor. Schiemann LJ's robust analysis deserves quotation:[75]   **15-039**

"I am satisfied in the present case that the Plaintiffs have failed to perform their contract

---

[68] [1972] 1 W.L.R. 1009 CA at 1015F.
[69] [1972] 1 W.L.R. 1009 CA at 1015H.
[70] G.H. Jones (with P. Schlechtriem), "Breach of Contract" in *International Encyclopaedia of Comparative Law* Vol.VII (Contracts in General) (Tübingen: Mohr Siebeck, 1999), pp.15–19, noting Australian criticism.
[71] [1989] I.C.R. 493 CA; G. Mead, "Restitution Within Contract?" (1991) 11 L.S. 172; B. McFarlane and R. Stevens "In Defence of Sumpter v Hedges" (2002) 118 L.Q.R. 569, 590–591.
[72] [1987] 1 A.C. 539 HL; in *Wiluszynski v Tower Hamlets LBC* [1989] I.C.R. 493 CA at 503-504, Nicholls LJ cited these statements in *Miles v Wakefield Metropolitan DC*: "I refer in particular to a passage in the speech of Lord Bridge of Harwich at 382: 'If an employee refuses to perform the full duties which can be required of him under his contract of service, the employer is entitled to refuse to accept any partial performance. The position then resulting, during any relevant period while these conditions obtain, is exactly as if the employee were refusing to work at all.' Likewise, Lord Brightman, at p. 383: 'If an employee offers partial performance, as he does in some types of industrial conflict falling short of a strike, the employer has a choice. He may decline to accept the partial performance that is offered, in which case the employee is entitled to no remuneration for his unwanted services, even if they are performed'."
[73] [1989] I.C.R. 493 at 503 CA.
[74] [1993] 3 All E.R. 355; [1999] 2 Costs L.R. 109 CA.
[75] [1993] 3 All E.R. 355 at 361B, 360; [1999] 2 Costs L.R. 109 CA at 115-116.

and the defendant is entitled to regard it as discharged by the Plaintiffs' breach. This case is not properly to be analysed as a case of defective performance of a contract for legal services with a term that these should be performed by a solicitor. I categorise it as one of non-performance of a contract to provide legal services by a solicitor. In my judgment a firm of solicitors which is asked for a solicitor and, without telling the client that the advisor is not a solicitor, provides an advisor who is not a solicitor should not be entitled to recover anything."

15-040 In *Systech International Ltd v PC Harrington Contractors Ltd*[76] an "adjudicator" (a neutral whose task is to make provisional decisions in the construction field, under a statutory scheme of dispute resolution) sued in respect of his invoice sent to the party against whom a decision had been made. However, the adjudicator's decision was declared unenforceable by a judge because the adjudicator had broken the rules of natural justice. The question before the Court of Appeal was whether the losing party was liable to pay the adjudicator's charges, despite the fact that his decision had misfired, having been declared a nullity. The main judgment was given by Lord Dyson MR. In the following passages, he explained that the contract between the parties and the adjudicator should be construed as requiring one of them to pay only if an enforceable decision is produced at the end of the process. He began by formulating the issue:[77]

"The question that arises ... is whether the contract was (a) an entire contract such that the bargained-for consideration was an enforceable decision or (b) a divisible contract for the performance of a series of 'ancillary and anterior functions' (to use the judge's phrase) culminating in the making of a decision. Another way of putting the question is to ask whether the adjudicator has performed any of the contractual functions in respect of which payment is due. That is a question of construction of the contract."

15-041 Lord Dyson then explained:[78] "the adjudicator had no discrete entitlement to his fees and expenses for the ancillary and anterior functions that he performed". And he concluded:[79]

"I return to the question: what was the bargained-for performance? In my view, it was an enforceable decision. There is nothing in the contract to indicate that the parties agreed that they would pay for an unenforceable decision or that they would pay for the services performed by the adjudicator which were preparatory to the making of an unenforceable decision. The purpose of the appointment was to produce an enforceable decision which, for the time being, would resolve the dispute. A decision which was unenforceable was of no value to the parties. They would have to start again on a fresh adjudication in order to achieve the enforceable decision which Mr Doherty had contracted to produce."

15-042 Although Lord Dyson MR suggested[80] that an arbitrator might not be subject to the same analysis, it is not clear whether in fact members of an arbitral tribunal which delivers an award which is later overturned by the court (under the Arbitra-

---

[76] [2012] EWCA Civ 1371; [2012] EWCA Civ 1371; considered by Akenhead J in *Kitt v Laundry Building Ltd* [2014] EWHC 4250 (TCC); [2015] B.L.R. 170, where, however, the adjudicator's decision was not a nullity and so his fee was payable; and in a Scottish case, the court indicated the possibility of repayment by an adjudicator's firm of fees paid in respect of a decision which later proved to be unenforceable because of procedural defects: *Stork Technical Services (RBG) Ltd v Ross's Executor* 2015 S.L.T. 160.

[77] [2012] EWCA Civ 1371; [2013] 2 All E.R. 69 at [17].

[78] [2012] EWCA Civ 1371; [2013] 2 All E.R. 69 at [31].

[79] [2012] EWCA Civ 1371; [2013] 2 All E.R. 69 at [32].

[80] [2012] EWCA Civ 1371; [2013] 2 All E.R. 69 at [36].

tion Act 1996 ss.67–69) might be treated as having failed to produce an enforceable award and thus not entitled to claim their fees from the "losing" party to the arbitration.

Finally, It should be noted that the Court of Appeal in *Cleveland Bridge UK Ltd*   **15-043**
v Multiplex Constructions (UK) Ltd[81] held that *Sumpter v Hedges* remained good law for the proposition that partial performance under a contract where entire performance is required as the trigger for payment does not generate a right to payment (either ex contractu or by virtue of unjust enrichment principles), unless the recipient has elected freely to take the value of the work performed.

V. ASSESSMENT

Some commentators consider that the entire obligation rule can operate harshly   **15-044**
where a party is indubitably in breach (the Law Reform (Frustrated Contracts) Act 1943, see Pt III, para.18-018 ff, deals with the problem of frustration) and he has conferred a large non-returnable benefit on the innocent party,[82] and the latter has not voluntarily accepted the benefit. For this reason, the Law Commission had proposed that supposed victims of the present doctrine should be given a statutory claim for the benefit of the work conferred in this situation.[83]

However, it is fortunate that Brian Davenport QC, as Law Commissioner, added   **15-045**
a note of dissent. He said: "Experience has shown that it is all too common for … builders not to complete one job … before moving on to the next … [The recommendations for 'reform' would] remove from the householder almost the only effective sanction he has. [because it would prevent him] from saying 'unless you come back I shan't pay you a penny'." These are cogent remarks, reflecting the practical hazards of dealing with various suppliers of "services". These comments are supportive of ordinary citizens and small businesses who lack practical access to justice before the courts. Against that background, Lord Hailsham LC sensibly decided to withhold legislative support for the proposal[84] (a decision rightly supported by McFarlane and Stevens[85]).

However, Burrows contended that Lord Hailsham should not have rejected the Law Commission's suggestion.[86]

It is submitted that legislation is not required. There are two main reasons why   **15-046**
a person is not entitled to restitutionary relief if he has partially or defectively performed services under a contract where the relevant obligation is "entire".

The first is that innocent party's duty to pay (or to render some other perfor-   **15-047**
mance) is clearly rendered conditional on complete satisfaction of the relevant

---

[81] [2010] EWCA Civ 139 at [131]–[138] (May LJ, Dyson and Stanley Burnton LJJ agreeing); noted, C. Mitchell, P. Mitchell, S. Watterson (eds), *Goff and Jones, Unjust Enrichment*; 10th edn (London: Sweet & Maxwell, 2022), para.3-32.

[82] This opinion is "almost uniform" amongst "leading unjust enrichment scholars", according to B. McFarlane and R. Stevens, "In Defence of Sumpter v Hedges" (2002) 118 L.Q.R. 569, fn.6 listing the extensive literature.

[83] "Law of Contract; Pecuniary Restitution on Breach of Contract" (London: 1983) L. Com. No.121; considered in detail by A. Burrows, "Law Commission Report on Pecuniary Restitution on Breach of Contract" (1984) 47 M.L.R. 76.

[84] "Law of Contract; Pecuniary Restitution on Breach of Contract" (London: 1983) L. Com. No.121, 36–37, Brian Davenport QC; for the final rejection, Law Commission, 19th Annual Report (1983–4), 2.11.

[85] B. McFarlane and R. Stevens "In Defence of Sumpter v Hedges" (2002) 118 L.Q.R. 569, 572–582.

[86] A. Burrows, "Law Commission Report on Pecuniary Restitution on Breach of Contract" (1984) 47 M.L.R. 76 and *The Law of Restitution*, 3rd edn (Oxford: Oxford University Press, 2010), 360.

obligation (whether that obligation concerns "finishing" or "nature" or "timing" or "quality"). To spell this out, the parties have agreed, at least impliedly, "unless you fully satisfy in this respect, I will not be obliged to pay you the whole sum, or any portion of it, under the contract, and nor will I be obliged under any other means to pay in respect of your incomplete or imperfect performance." The contract precludes payment, and this preclusion includes restitutionary awards.

15-048   The second reason is that the entire obligation device can be used as an instrument to induce complete or perfect performance. It is an "earnest" device, analogous to deposits. The courts have not lost sight of this valuable form of "self-help" protection. A clear example of this is *Bolton v Mahadeva* para.15-034 ff[87] (see also *Vigers v Cook* para.15-030–15.033,[88] *Wiluszynski v Tower Hamlets LBC* para.15-037–15.038,[89] and *Pilbrow v Pearless de Rougemont & Co* para.15-039[90]). Many of these dissatisfied parties will be consumers lacking appetite for small claims litigation.

---

[87] [1972] 1 W.L.R. 1009 CA.
[88] [1919] 2 K.B. 475 Divisional Court and CA.
[89] [1989] I.C.R. 493 CA at 503; G. Mead, "Restitution Within Contract?" (1991) 11 L.S. 172; B. McFarlane and R. Stevens, "In Defence of Sumpter v Hedges" (2002) 118 L.Q.R. 569, 590–591.
[90] [1993] 3 All E.R. 355; [1999] 2 Costs L.R. 109, CA.

PART III FRUSTRATION: DISCHARGE BY IMPOSSIBILITY, ILLEGALITY OR FRUSTRATION

By Professor Neil Andrews

CHAPTER 16

CORE FEATURES OF FRUSTRATION: LEGAL BASIS, RISK ALLOCATION AND "SELF-INDUCEMENT"

I.   NATURE AND LEGAL BASIS

Frustration[1] has been defined in numerous cases. Here three definitions have been **16-001**
selected. The first (1956) and second (1980) judicial summaries were declared by
a Commercial Court judge in 2018[2] to be "classic" statements, and the third (1945)
is added because it too is illuminating and attractive and has been neglected.

Lord Radcliffe in *Davis Contractors v Fareham* encapsulated the "radical dif-   **16-002**
ference" (also on this case, see paras 17-002 and 17-064)):[3]

> "Frustration occurs whenever the law recognises that without fault of either party, a
> contractual obligation has become incapable of being performed because the circum-
> stances in which performance is called for would render it a thing radically different from
> that which was undertaken by the contract. Non haec in foedera veni. It was not this that
> I promised to do."

Lord Simon said in *National Carriers Ltd v Panalpina (Northern) Ltd* that a mere   **16-003**
increase in the expense or onerousness of the contract cannot constitute frustration:[4]

> "Frustration of a contract takes place when there supervenes an event (without default of
> either party and for which the contract makes no sufficient provision) which so

---

[1]   For literature concerning force majeure clauses, see para.16.044, fn.45 below. Leading specialist
treatments of the frustration doctrine are: E. Peel, *Frustration and Force Majeure*, 4th edn (London:
Sweet & Maxwell, 2021) and Ben Symons, *Force Majeure and Frustration in Commercial
Contracts*, (London: Bloomsbury Professional, 2022). See also: H. Beale (ed), *Chitty on Contracts*,
34th edn (London: Sweet & Maxwell, 2021), Ch.26; J. Stannard, *Delay in the Performance of
Contractual Obligations* 2nd edn (Oxford: Oxford University Press, 2018), Ch.12 (frustrating delay).
An important analysis is M. Bridge, "Frustration and excused non-performance" (2021) 137 L.Q.R.
580-603; see also J. Beatson, "Increased Expense and Frustration", in F.D. Rose (ed), *Consensus ad
Idem: Essays in the Law of Contract in Honour of Guenter Treitel* (London: Sweet & Maxwell,
1996), 121; D. Ibbetson, "Absolute Liability in Contract: the Antecedents of *Paradine v Jayne*", in
F.D. Rose (ed), op cit, Ch. (for an earlier history); E. McKendrick, "Frustration, Restitution and Loss
Adjustment", in A.S. Burrows (ed), *Essays on Restitution* (Oxford: Oxford University Press, 1991),
147; E. McKendrick, "The Regulation of Long-Term Contracts in English Law", in J Beatson and
D Friedmann (eds), *Good Faith and Fault in Contract Law* (Oxford: Oxford University Press, 1995),
305 at 323 ff; See G. McMeel, "The Juridical Basis of Frustration Revisited" [2020] L.M.C.L.Q.
297; J. Morgan, *Great Debates in Contract Law*, 3rd edn (London: Palgrave Publishing, 2020), Ch.5;
A.W.B. Simpson, "Innovation in Nineteenth Century Contract Law'" (1975) 91 LQR 247 at 269–
273.
[2]   *Gemcorp Commodoties Trading SA v Zeefacto Oil & Gas Co* [2018] EWHC 3938 (Comm) at [13]
and [14] per Popplewell J.
[3]   [1956] A.C. 696 at 729, HL, per Lord Radcliffe.
[4]   [1981] A.C. 675, HL, per Lord Simon of Glaisdale.

significantly changes the nature (not merely the expense or onerousness) of the outstanding contractual rights and/or obligations from what the parties could reasonably have contemplated at the time of its execution that it would be unjust to hold them to the literal sense of its stipulations in the new circumstances; in such case the law declares both parties to be discharged from further performance.'"

16-004   In *Cricklewood Property and Investment Trust Ltd v Leighton's Investment Trust Ltd* Viscount Simon LC said:[5]

"Frustration may be defined as the premature determination of an agreement between parties, lawfully entered into and in course of operation at the time of its premature determination, owing to the occurrence of an intervening event or change of circumstances so fundamental as to be regarded by the law both as striking at the root of the agreement, and as entirely beyond what was contemplated by the parties when they entered into the agreement."

16-005   **The 'multifactorial' test**   The ingredients contained within the passages cited already have been arranged by Rix LJ in the *"The Sea Angel"*[6] (on this case see also paras 17-007, 17-065, 17-069, 17-089). His judgment contains the following "template" of issues, the so-called "multifactorial" test for frustration. Rix LJ's test confirms that frustration is exceptional and will arise only if the event, considered in all relevant circumstances, as it were, "ticks" the following six "boxes":[7] (i) the subsequent event is potentially frustrating (supervening illegality, physical destruction, frustrating delay, or very occasionally frustration of the venture);[8] (ii) there has been a complete undermining or destruction of the contract's foundation; (iii) the risk is not allocated to a party, expressly or impliedly (on the element of implied risk allocation, paras 16-012–16-021, and 17-008); (iv) nor was a party in default; (v) nor was a party making a choice;[9] finally, there is a "reality check": this last factor requires the court to consider whether a finding of frustration would be perceived by the commercial community as absurd or alarming. See Ch.17, notably at para.17-007 ff, for further comment on this test.

16-006   **Development of the doctrine**   The Common Law started from the strict view that,

---

5   [1945] A.C. 221 at 228, HL per Viscount Simon LC.
6   *Edwinton Commercial Corporation v Tsavliris Russ Ltd ("The Sea Angel")* [2007] EWCA Civ 547; [2007] 1 C.L.C. 876 at [132].
7   *Edwinton Commercial Corporation v Tsavliris Russ Ltd ("The Sea Angel")* [2007] EWCA Civ 547; [2007] 1 C.L.C. 876, notably at [110]–[112]; *"The Sea Angel"* was cited by Flaux J in *Bunge SA v Kyla Shipping Co Ltd (No.2)* [2012] EWHC 3522 (Comm); [2013] 1 Lloyd's Rep. 565 at [39]–[41]; *Bunge SA v Kyla Shipping Co Ltd (No.1)* [2013] EWCA Civ 734; [2013] 3 All E.R. 1006 at [7], per Longmore LJ; *Melli Bank Plc v Holbud Ltd* [2013] EWHC 1506 (Comm) at [15], per Robin Knowles QC; *Islamic Republic of Iran Shipping Lines v Steamship Mutual Underwriting Association (Bermuda) Ltd* [2010] EWHC 2661 (Comm); [2011] 2 All E.R. (Comm) 609 at [105], per Beatson J; *The Flying Music Co Ltd v Theater Entertainment SA* [2017] EWHC 3192 (QB) at [15]–[20], per Martin Griffiths QC, Deputy High Court Judge (the last case providing a succinct summary of the main authorities); a longer, magisterial and acute review of the modern doctrine and its various facets is provided by Marcus Smith J in *Canary Wharf (BP4) T1 Ltd v European Medicines Agency* [2019] EWHC 335 (Ch); 183 Con. L.R. 167 (which has not proceeded to appeal); see also the NZ Supreme Court's discussion in *Planet Kids Ltd v Auckland Council* [2013] NZSC 147; [2014] 1 N.Z.L.R. 149 at [60]–[62].
8   On the categories of frustration, see *Canary Wharf (BP4) T1 Ltd v European Medicines Agency* [2019] EWHC 335 (Ch); 183 Con LR 167, Marcus Smith J at [41].
9   On factors (iv) and (v), see Canary *Wharf (BP4) T1 Ltd v European Medicines Agency* [2019] EWHC 335 (Ch); 183 Con LR 167, Marcus Smith J at [43]–[46], and [201]–[207].

if a person chose to contract, that person must perform the contract "notwithstanding any accident by inevitable necessity, because he might have provided against it by his contract".[10] To a large degree personal responsibility remains the rule. Little justification can be found, concluded Trakman in the 1980s, "for courts of law to imply contract terms ... where the contracting parties themselves are able to provide for such excuses by commercial means".[11] Indeed, although no longer widely held today, a theory was once accepted that frustration might be justified on the basis of an implied term.

In the landmark case of *Taylor v Caldwell*, where the hall to be used had been destroyed by fire the day before the event, Blackburn J said: **16-007**

> "[In contracts] in which the performance depends on the continued existence of a given person or thing, a condition is implied that the impossibility of performance arising from the perishing of the person or thing shall excuse the performance."[12]

In this case Blackburn J broke new ground by recognising a general doctrine of frustration. The decision in that case was that where the subject matter of the contract physically ceases to exist or be available, frustration of the contract might arise, provided (i) neither party has been in default and (ii) the risk of relevant event has not been expressly or impliedly allocated to a party. Under an entertainment joint venture, the relevant music hall burned down, without either party having been at fault or having contractual responsibility for this outcome. The result of this contractual frustration was that the parties' prospective obligations terminated by operation of law. Blackburn J's innovation was to fashion a general doctrine, based on three pre-existing instances where a party is excused from performance: (i) a contracting party's death in a contract of personal services; (ii) destruction of specific goods after property has passed to the buyer; (iii) bailment where goods are destroyed without the bailee's fault. In effect Blackburn J joined up the dots, creating a new general doctrine which extended to physical annihilation of the contract's subject matter (on the facts of this case, destruction of the music hall), and which was capable of expansion over the ensuing decades.

The implied term theory, which had been introduced by Blackburn J in the case just summarised, took root, but it has now been removed. Lord Denning MR said in *"The Eugenia"* (1964):[13] **16-008**

> "the theory of an implied term has now been discarded...for the simple reason that it does not represent the truth. The parties would not have said: 'It is all over between us.' They would have differed about what was to happen. Each would have sought to insert reservations or qualifications of one kind or another."

And in *Davis Contractors v Fareham U.D.C.*, Lord Reid approved a fellow **16-009**

---

10 *Paradine v Jane* (1647) Al. 26 at 27; *82 E.R. 897.*
11 L.E. Trakman "Frustrated Contracts and Legal Fictions" (1983) 46 M.L.R. 39 at 55, after a review of decisions in which terms had been implied to excuse performance. In principle courts still expect parties to negotiate their own "excuses": e.g. *Lewis Emmanuel v Sammut* [1959] 2 Lloyd's Rep. 629 at 642 per Pearson J (c.i.f. contract); *Kawasaki Steel Corp v Sardoil SpA ("The Zuiho Maru")* [1977] 2 Lloyd's Rep. 552 at 554 per Kerr J (voyage charter).
12 *Taylor v Caldwell* (1863) 3 B. & S. 826 at 839.
13 [1964] 2 Q.B. 226 at 238, CA; for similar scepticism regarding the implied term theory of frustration, see the famous passage within Lord Radcliffe's speech in the *Davis Contractors* case [1956] A.C. 696 at 728, HL: "there is something of a logical difficulty in seeing how the parties could even impliedly have provided for something which ex hypothesi they neither expected nor foresaw".

Scot's reductio ad absurdum which was deployed to demolish the over-stretched device of an implied term in this context:[14]

> "I may be allowed to note an example of the artificiality of the theory of an implied term given by Lord Sands in *James Scott & Sons Ltd v Del Sel* 1922 SC 592, 597: 'A tiger has escaped from a travelling menagerie. The milkgirl fails to deliver the milk. Possibly the milkman may be exonerated from any breach of contract; but, even so, it would seem hardly reasonable to base that exoneration on the ground that "tiger days excepted" must be held as if written into the milk contract.'...It appears to me [Lord Reid] that frustration depends, at least in most cases, not on adding any implied term, but on the true construction of the terms which are in the contract read in light of the nature of the contract and of the relevant surrounding circumstances when the contract was made."

16-010   Lord Hailsham in *National Carriers Ltd v Panalpina (Northern) Ltd* reviewed an array of five theories, or conceptual bases, for frustration. These are (i) implied term (ii) total failure of consideration (iii) just solution (iv) foundation of the contract (v) construction of the contract's wording.[15] But the judicial preference is to adopt the fifth theory or juristic basis, namely the approach based on construction. Lord Hailsham concluded his survey as follows:

> "Another theory, of which the parent may have been Earl Loreburn in *FA Tamplin Steam-ship Co Ltd v Anglo-Mexican Petroleum Products Co Ltd* [1916] 2 A.C. 397 is that the doctrine is based on the answer to the question: 'What in fact is the true meaning of the contract?': see p.404. This is the 'construction theory'. In *Davis Contractors Ltd v Fareham U.D.C.* [1956] A.C. 696, 729 Lord Radcliffe put the matter thus, and it is the formulation I personally prefer: 'frustration occurs whenever the law recognises that without default of either party a contractual obligation has become incapable or being performed because the circumstances in which performance is called for would render it a thing radically different from that which was undertaken by the contract. Non haec in foedera veni. It was not this that I promised to do.'"

16-011   Similarly, also in *National Carriers Ltd v Panalpina (Northern) Ltd*, Lord Roskill commented:[16]

> "the doctrine has been described as a 'device' for doing justice between the parties when they themselves have failed either wholly or sufficiently to provide for the particular event or events which have happened. The doctrine is principally concerned with the incidence of risk - who must take the risk of the happening of a particular event especially when the parties have not made any or any sufficient provision for the happening of that event? When the doctrine is successfully invoked it is because in the event which has happened the law imposes a solution, casting the incidence of that risk on one party or the other as the circumstances of the particular case may require, having regard to the express provisions of the contract into which the parties have entered. The doctrine is no arbitrary dispensing power to be exercised at the subjective whim of the judge by whom the issue has to be determined. Frustration if it occurs operates automatically. Its operation does not depend on the action or inaction of the parties. It is to be invoked or not to be invoked by

---

[14]   [1956] A.C. 696 at 720–721, HL, per Lord Reid.
[15]   [1981] A.C. 675 at 687–688, HL, per Lord Hailsham LC.
[16]   *National Carriers Ltd v Panalpina Ltd* [1981] A.C. 675 at 712, HL, per Lord Roskill; in the same case Lord Hailsham at 688, and Lord Simon at 702, preferred the "construction theory", Lord Hailsham citing in support *Davis Contractors Ltd v Fareham UDC* [1956] A.C. 696 at 729 per Lord Radcliffe. The potential difficulty of the exercise is demonstrated by *Islamic Republic of Iran Shipping Lines v SS Mutual Underwriting Assoc (Bermuda) Ltd* [2010] EWHC 2661 (Comm); [2011] 1 Lloyd's Rep. 195.

reference only to the particular contract before the court and the facts of the particular case said to justify the invocation of the doctrine."

The doctrine had been described as a "device" by Lord Sumner in *Hirji Mulji v Cheong Yue Steamship Co Ltd*.[17]

II. RISK ALLOCATION

(On force majeure clauses, see para.16-044 ff below.) Before it can be finally decided whether indeed the contract has indeed been discharged, it must first be considered whether and to what extent the parties have provided for the possibility in the contract itself—by an express or implied assumption of the risk that the "frustrating" event will occur. Express assumption means that the terms of the contract deal expressly with the matter. Implied assumption means that the very fact that the parties have contracted as they have indicates that one or both of them must have intended to assume the risk of some problem or impediment affecting performance.   **16-012**

Express assumption   Express assumption turns on construction of the words used. The next paragraph examines three instances of express risk allocation precluding resort to the frustration doctrine. Sometimes the process of inferring risk assumption is not entirely transparent. And, because the contract can be opaque and disputable, cases are litigated.[18] The next paragraph examines three instances of express risk allocation precluding resort to the frustration doctrine.   **16-013**

Express risk allocation was found in *Gold Group Properties Ltd v BDW Trading Ltd (formerly Barratt Homes Ltd)*[19] Coulson J held that a significant drop in property prices was a risk for which there was already contractual provision, enabling the parties to negotiate a possible revision of the financial terms. Apart from the element of risk-allocation, it seems highly unlikely, if not simply inconceivable, in the light of the *Davis Contractors* case (paras 17-002 and 17-064)[20] that an economic or market "down-turn" could constitute a frustrating event. As the *Davis* case demonstrates, frustration does not arise merely because the supervening change of economic fortunes has the effect of reducing or eliminating the builder's profit, and the same should apply even if the contract becomes a loss-making venture. Similarly, express risk allocation was identified in *Dayah v Partners of Bushloe Street Surgery*[21] an agreement between different medical practices to pool expenses in the running of a shared medical facility was held not to have become frustrated when one of the contributing partnerships was struck off the list of authorised practices. Cavanagh J held that the agreement expressly anticipated this risk, so that there was no scope for the operation of the frustration doctrine. Thirdly, as explained in greater detail at paras 17-016 and 17-042, in *Bank*   **16-014**

---

17 [1926] A.C. 497 at 510, PC.
18 Thus, if what would otherwise be a frustrating event is covered by an obligation on a seller to maintain a level insurance, it may be inferred that the event is not frustrating: *Bunge SA v Kyla Shipping Co Ltd* [2012] EWHC 3522 (Comm); [2012] 2 C.L.C. 998 at [78], Flaux J; affirmed [2013] EWCA 734 (cost of repairing charterer vessel exceeding its market value; owner's duty to repair not frustrated; owner had undertaken to maintain insurance at level above the repair cost).
19 [2010] EWHC 323 (TCC); [2010] B.L.R. 235 at [67]–[84].
20 [1956] A.C. 696 HL.
21 [2020] EWHC 1375 (QB) at [78]–[81] (Cavanagh J).

of New York Mellon (International) Ltd v Cine-UK Ltd[22] Covid statutory restrictions had closed cinemas for many months, but the Court of Appeal held that this did not give tenants of those cinema sites a defence to a claim for rent for that period. To accede to the tenants' argument would involve overriding the restricted scope of each "cesser of rent" clause, which was restricted to physical damage to the property. That clause could not be re-written under the guise of the law of implied terms or "failure of basis".

16-015   **Implied assumption**   An example of an implied assumption of risk is that parties promising goods are assumed to ensure that any necessary (export) licences will be obtained,[23] and, where relevant, that their suppliers will indeed supply the goods.[24] Similarly, in the property market the Court of Appeal in *Amalgamated Investment and Property Ltd v John Walker & Sons Ltd* noted that:

> "the risk of property being listed as property of architectural or historical interest is a risk which inheres in the ownership of buildings … this is a risk of a kind which every purchaser should be regarded as knowing that he is subject to when he enters into his contract of purchase. It is a risk which I think every purchaser must carry".[25]

16-016   **Foreseeability and risk allocation**   The Court of Appeal's decision in *Ocean Tramp Tankers Corporation v V/O Sovfracht ("The Eugenia")*[26] is notable for discussion of risk allocation and the connection between that fundamental part of the "multi-factorial" test (on the "multi-factorial" test, see para.16-005 and, notably, para.17-007 ff) and the issue of foreseeability (on this case see also paras 16-017, 16-024, 17-059). The upshot of this analysis is that foreseeable events are less likely to be the cause of frustration; however, the real issue is not whether an event is foreseeable or foreseen, but whether the contract expressly or impliedly allocates the risk of the relevant event to one of the parties.

16-017   On the issue of foreseeability and risk allocation Lord Denning MR said in *"The Eugenia"* (on this case see also paras 16-016, 16-024, 17-059):[27]

> "It has frequently been said that the doctrine of frustration only applies when the new situation is 'unforeseen' or 'unexpected' or 'uncontemplated', as if that were an essential feature. But it is not so. The only thing that is essential is that the parties should have made no provision for it in their contract. The only relevance of it being 'unforeseen' is this: If the parties did not foresee anything of the kind happening, you can readily infer they have made no provision for it: whereas, if they did foresee it, you would expect them to make provision for it. But cases have occurred where the parties have foreseen the danger ahead, and yet made no provision for it in the contract. Such was the case in the Spanish Civil

---

22   [2022] EWCA Civ 1021; [2023] L. & T.R. 2 at [55], [138] and [139] (Flaux C, with the agreement of Snowden LJ and Sir Nicholas Patten), applying Carr LJ's summary of the rules governing terms implied in fact in *Yoo Design Services Ltd v Iliv Realty PTE Ltd* [2021] EWCA Civ 560 at [51]. The *Mellon* case is noted by A. Sahore [2022] C.LJ. 497-490.

23   H.J. Berman, "Force majeure and the denial of an export licence" (1960) 73 Harv. L. Rev 1128, 1141 ff. Cf. *Bangladesh Export Import Co Ltd v Sucden Kerry SA* [1995] 2 Lloyd's Rep. 1 CA.

24   *Lebeaupin v Richard Crispin & Co* [1920] 2 K.B. 714; E. Peel, *Frustration and Force Majeure*, 4th edn (London: Sweet & Maxwell, 2021), para.12.043.

25   *Amalgamated Investment and Property Ltd v John Walker & Sons Ltd* [1977] 1 W.L.R. 164 at 173, CA, per Buckley LJ.

26   [1964] 2 Q.B. 226, CA.

27   [1964] Q.B. 226 at 239, CA, per Lord Denning; also on foreseeability and the question of risk, see also the remarks in *Canary Wharf (BP4) T1 Ltd v European Medicines Agency* [2019] EWHC 335 (Ch); 183 Con. L.R. 167 at [211] ff, per Marcus Smith J.

War when a ship was let on charter to the republican government. The purpose was to evacuate refugees. The parties foresaw that she might be seized by the nationalists. But they made no provision for it in their contract. Yet, when she was seized, the contract was frustrated, see *WJ Tatem Ltd v Gamboa* [1939] 1 K.B. 132. So here the parties foresaw that the canal might become impassable: it was the very thing they feared. But they made no provision for it. So there is room for the doctrine to apply if it be a proper case for it."

Similarly, in *"The Sea Angel"*, Rix LJ said:[28]   **16-018**

"Even events which are not merely foreseen but made the subject of express contractual provision may lead to frustration: as occurs when an event such as a strike, or a restraint of prices, lasts for so long as to go beyond the risk assumed under the contract and to render performance radically different from that contracted for. However ... the less that an event, in its type and its impact, is foreseeable, the more likely it is to be a factor which, depending on other factors in the case, may lead on to frustration."

On this case see also paras 17-007–17-009, 17-065–17-069 and 17-089.

In practice, there tends to be a rather abstract and non-empirical discussion of   **16-019** foreseeability and attempts to assess the magnitude of a risk for the purpose of making a determination on risk allocation. This is despite the fact that insurers are constantly seeking to assess risk in order to rate it in the cover they sell. Behind insurers mathematicians and others have made significant advances in risk theory; they no longer have to "shoot in the dark".[29]

In the context of litigation disputes involving allegations of frustration, there are   **16-020** two hurdles. The first is to gain access to risk information.[30] The second is to decide whether the "contingency in question" was "*sufficiently* foreshadowed"[31] at the time of the contract for a court to decide that the contract was not subsequently discharged when the contingency occurred. Suspicion lingers that courts have to carry out this assessment as a matter of impression.

An American scholar has argued nonetheless for an "empirical method of   **16-021** measuring foreseeability".[32] This involves determining whether the probability of the event is outweighed by the transaction cost of negotiating a clause to deal with the contingency. If so, materialisation of the event discharges the contract. Thus when courts decide (that the contract is not discharged) on the basis that the promisor could (and by implication should) have insisted on an exculpatory clause to cover the situation, the courts are (intuitively) using just such a method. However, even assuming that this method is viable, it is apparent that judicial decisions remain based on impression, because of the absence of hard data.[33]

---

[28] [2007] EWCA Civ 547; [2007] 1 C.L.C. 876 at [127] per Rix LJ.

[29] e.g. actuaries on behalf of life insurers use sophisticated epidemiological models to predict the likely range of outcomes from an influenza pandemic or other catastrophes.

[30] M.A. Clarke, *Policies and Perceptions of Insurance Law in the Twenty-First Century* (Oxford: Oxford University Press, 2007), p.277 ff.

[31] The language of the Comment to the Uniform Commercial Code, (USA), para.2-615 (emphasis added).

[32] J. Elofson, "The Dilemma of Changed Circumstances in Contract Law" (1996) 30 Colum. J.L. & Soc. Probs. 1–39, 31 ff. He described (at 34) the test in the language of economists as one of "bounded rationality", a more nuanced view of the typical subjects of economic analysis. See R.B. Korobkin and T.S. Ulen, "Law and Behavioral Science: Removing the Rationality Assumption from Law and Economics", (2000) 88 Cal. L. Rev. 1051.

[33] Elofson acknowledged the difficulty: "The Dilemma of Changed Circumstances in Contract Law" (1996) 30 Colum. J.L. & Soc. Probs. 1 at p.39.

III. "SELF-INDUCEMENT" PRECLUDES FRUSTRATION

16-022   Frustration cannot arise if the relevant event was self-induced by one of the parties. That proposition sub-divides: (i) the party pleading frustration in fact brought it on itself as a result of his or her own culpable default, that is, contractual breach, or criminal wrongdoing or blameworthiness and criminal misconduct; or (ii) choice (as explained at para.16-029 ff, frustration is disapplied because the party invoking it in fact had room for manoeuvre and could have taken steps to avoid this outcome).

16-023   **Breach or culpable default**   Frustration operates only where the contract has become radically different as a result of a supervening event and that event must not be attributable to default by a party. And so the first (and self-evident) segment of the doctrine of "self-induced frustration" is that frustration does not occur if the supervening event is the result a party's (i) breach of contract or (ii) criminal wrongdoing or (iii) other blameworthy conduct. Each of these involves an element of default which is the antithesis of frustration.

16-024   As for (i), in *Ocean Tramp Tankers Corporation v V/O Sovfracht ("The Eugenia")* (on this case see also paras 16-015, 16-016, 17-059)[34] the charterer, in breach of contract, took the vessel into a war-zone, the Suez Canal. The ship was to proceed from the Black Sea to India. If the alternative route, via the Cape of Good Hope, had been taken, the journey would have taken longer, but the Court of Appeal held that the additional 38 days required for that longer voyage would not have constituted frustration. The charterer's unsuccessful argument was, in effect:

> "we know we were in the wrong place at the wrong time (the Suez canal, which had become a war-zone), but even if we had not made that error the contract would have been frustrated, because taking the vessel from Europe to India the long-way round, via the Cape of Good Hope, would have been an entirely different venture".

The charterer failed because (i) they had become stuck in the Suez Canal because of their own default (entering a war zone), (ii) the long-way round argument did not disclose an instance of frustration, because the extra days fell well short of constituting a radically different venture, applying the *Davis Contractors* test (see the quotation from Lord Radcliffe's speech, at para.16.002, and see paras 17-002 and 17-064)).

16-025   There are other instances of default constituting self-induced frustration. In addition to (i) breach of contract, just treated, frustration does not occur if the supervening event is the result a party's (ii) criminal wrongdoing or (iii) other blameworthy conduct. Each of these involves an element of default which is the antithesis of frustration.

16-026   As for (ii) and (iii), as noted more fully at paras 17-032 and 17-033, in *FC Shepherd (FC) & Co Ltd v Jerrom*[35] the Court of Appeal rejected an apprentice's counter-intuitive attempt to plead his own self-induced frustration to promote his overall legal strategy. His (unsuccessful) contention was that his contract of apprenticeship had not been frustrated by reason of his incarceration. Instead he argued that the contract had remained alive, and that if termination had been the result of the employer's decision to fire him. This submission was a tactical at-

---

[34]   [1964] 2 Q.B. 226, CA.
[35]   [1987] Q.B. 301, CA.

tempt by the apprentice to preserve the contract and to argue that the apprentice had been unfairly dismissed. The Court of Appeal held that the contract had been frustrated by virtue of his imprisonment.

Bingham LJ said in *"The Super Servant Two"*[36] that the concept of breach of a **16-027** duty by the defendant should not be placed into a legal "straitjacket" and that a party's fault will normally preclude frustration:

"A fine test of legal duty is inappropriate; what is needed is a pragmatic judgment whether a party seeking to rely on an event as discharging him from a contractual promise was himself responsible for the occurrence of that event."

There are dicta in the speeches of the House of Lords in *Joseph Constantine SS* **16-028** *Co v Imperial Smelting Corp Ltd*[37] concerning the hypothetical prima donna who catches a cold through neglect of her health, but this discussion was inconclusive. It is possible that, at least in some contexts, a party who has hired someone's services might contend that a contract for personal services should be treated as containing a term "implied in fact" that the performer will take reasonable steps, and avoid obvious risks, to keep open the possibility that he or she will be physically able to perform his contract. Breach of such an implied term will involve "self-induced frustration" and render him liable to pay damages. But the courts will be slow to recognise such an implied duty for three connected reasons: first, such a term might be regarded as by no means "obvious"; secondly, imposing such a term would be problematic because it might be perceived as unduly and unfairly fettering the performer's scope to conduct his or her leisure-time freed from legal constraint; thirdly, a hiring party who is jittery might be expected to discuss the matter explicitly with the relevant performer and seek to include an express term to cover this risk.

Choice precludes frustration   This is the second segment of the "self-induced **16-029** frustration" doctrine: preclusion of frustration because the alleged frustration involved, fatally, "choice" on the part of the party invoking the frustration doctrine.

Choice impinges as follows. Frustration will not arise if it remained physically **16-030** possible for a party to have performed his contract, but he chose not to do so, either (i) he failed, or chose not, to take steps which would have enabled him to keep the contract alive for performance (in the case of (i), such a failure or choice might arise even in the absence of breach of an express or implied term that such steps must be taken); or (ii) because he preferred to advance his own interests, or (iii) because (again without prioritising the other party's interests) he had already chosen to make arrangements with third parties which (in combination with the supervening event) preclude him from satisfying his contractual obligation to the other party, thereby taking the risk of a clear, or at least potential, "double-booking". Element (ii) is illustrated by the *Maritime National* case[38] and (iii) by *"The Super Servant Two"*.[39] These cases will be considered in turn below.

As for element (i), a plea of frustration failed in *Melli Bank Plc v Holbud Ltd*.[40] **16-031** A bank customer alleged that the only reason why a letter of credit facility had not

---

36   [1990] 1 Lloyd's Rep. at 10, CA.
37   [1942] A.C. 154 at 166–167, 179, 195, 202, HL (see also *"The Super Servant Two"* [1990] 1 Lloyd's Rep. 1 at 8, CA: "fault" is inconsistent with frustration).
38   [1935] A.C. 524, PC.
39   *J Lauritzen v Wijsmuller BV ("The Super Servant Two")* [1990] 1 Lloyd's Rep. 1.
40   [2013] EWHC 1506 (Comm) at [15]–[21], Robin Knowles QC, Deputy High Court Judge.

been used is that the UK Government had imposed restrictions on trading with designated Iranian entities or persons, including the claimant Iranian bank offering the credit facility. But the frustration plea failed because the bank customer had not bothered to apply for relaxation of this UK Government restriction. Such a licence would have been forthcoming. And so the judge upheld a claim for the fees for providing the letter of credit facility.[41]

16-032   As for element (ii), that is, following the supervening event, the party seeking to invoke the frustration doctrine has forfeited that possibility because he has preferred to advance his own interests, that was in essence the position in the leading case, *Maritime National Fish Ltd v Ocean Trawlers Ltd*.[42] The Privy Council held that a charterer could not invoke frustration because the facts disclosed an example of self-induced incapacity. The defendant ("the charterer") hired a trawler, the *St Cuthbert*, from the claimant ("the owner"). The charterer already had four other trawlers. As the parties foresaw, the trawlers could only operate under government licence. The charterer received only three licences, although he had applied for five. He then chose to use these licences against three of his vessels, electing not to license the *St Cuthbert*. When the owner sued him for the hire charges, the charterer unsuccessfully argued that the contract of hire had been frustrated by his inability to obtain sufficient licences. The Privy Council held that the charterer's decision to allocate the three licences to ships other than the present chartered vessel was an act of self-induced frustration.

16-033   As for element (iii), where the relevant party has made arrangements in its own interest which have led to the inability to perform, the Court of Appeal's decision in *J Lauritzen v Wijsmuller BV ("The Super Servant Two")*, provides convincing authority for this proposition.[43]

16-034   In that case, a charterparty provided that either giant barge *The Super Servant One* or *The Super Servant Two* could be supplied by the owner. The owner made his own self-interested decision to use "The Super Servant Two" for this customer and to allocate the other to another job. The obvious consequence is that there would be no "back-up" if something went awry and both the *Super Servants* became unavailable. In fact *The Super Servant Two* sank (or, rather, it became marooned, having become stuck in the bed of the River Zaire) and was unavailable. *The Super Servant One*, which would normally have been the "back-up", had been allocated to another customer.

16-035   In greater detail, the defendant had contracted to carry the claimant's drilling rig from Japan to Rotterdam on either of his two giant barges, *The Super Servant One* or *The Super Servant Two*. After the contract's formation, the defendant decided to allocate *The Super Servant Two* for this job, using *The Super Servant One* for another job with a third party (these giant barges seem to have been commercially interchangeable, possessing the same dimensions, etc). But, before the *The Super Servant Two* could be moved to work on the claimant's job, that vessel sank in the Zaire River.

16-036   The terms of the contract stated that the contract could be performed by use of either of two named vessels: the contract did not restrict performance to the vessel (*The Super Servant Two*) which, on these facts, in fact became unavailable. The fact

---

[41]   Also rejecting a further defence that the claimant had been in breach: even if the bank had committed a repudiatory breach by not having available funds—this fact was not in fact established—there had been no acceptance of that repudiation: [2013] EWHC 1506 (Comm) at [24]–[27].

[42]   [1935] A.C. 524, PC.

[43]   *J Lauritzen v Wijsmuller BV ("The Super Servant Two")* [1990] 1 Lloyd's Rep. 1.

that the contract could be performed using alternative vessels could work to the rig-owner's advantage (increasing the chances of a barge remaining available) and to the barge-owner's advantage (enabling him to avoid the other party's potentially problematic objection that only a single nominated vessel could be used for the job).

The Court of Appeal held that the physical unavailability of *The Super Servant* **16-037** *Two* (which had become stuck in the River Zaire) did not exonerate the defendant. The contract with the claimant had stipulated that either *The Super Servant One* or *The Super Servant Two* would be used. The defendant could not hide behind its own commercial decision to use *The Super Servant One* for the parallel contract with the third party. There was no reason why the claimant should suffer as a result of the defendant's commercial deployment of his remaining vessel. That deployment had been made to suit the defendant, and he had earned extra revenue from it.

The Court of Appeal's decision embraced these three points: (i) frustration by **16-038** physical unavailability of *The Super Servant Two* did not arise because it was W's choice not to make the alternative vessel *The Super Servant One* available; and (ii) frustration would further be precluded if it was W's fault which caused the relevant obstacle to performance; (iii) furthermore, a cancellation clause (cl.17.1) inserted by W, when construed against W as *proferens*, would only avail W if the sinking of *The Super Servant Two* was not due to W's negligence.

As for (i), the decision boils down to this: if Y hires out to X either *The Super* **16-039** *Servant One* or *The Super Servant Two*, the allocation being postponed to suit Y, so that it becomes a matter of unilateral decision by the owner which he in fact uses, then the supervening and excused unavailability of *The Super Servant Two* does not excuse Y from his duty to provide the other vessel, *The Super Servant One*, which is the back-up vessel. It is of no relevance to X that Y has double-booked *The Super Servant One*, the back-up vessel, having decided (whether prior to or after the contract with X) to use it to make money in a contract with a different customer.

The decision in *"The Super Servant Two"* is sound. As Bingham LJ observed, the **16-040** defendant's option to use *The Super Servant One* or *The Super Servant Two* had been inserted by the defendant *for its commercial convenience*.[44] Similarly, Dillon LJ noted that the defendant had extracted *extra revenue* from its *The Super Servant One* customers before finally allocating *The Super Servant Two* to the contract with the claimant.[45]

It would have been different if the contract had exclusively nominated *'The Super* **16-041** *Servant Two'*[46] assuming, of course, that its subsequent sinking was not attributable to the defendant's default. That would have sent the clear message:

"everything depends on the physical availability of *'The Super Servant Two'*; if it sinks etc, without my fault, you cannot sue me for non-supply".

As Dillon LJ mentioned in *"The Super Servant Two"*, the result in that case is **16-042** consistent with the Privy Council's decision in *Maritime National Fish Ltd v Ocean Trawlers Ltd*, where choice similarly precluded resort by a non-performing party to frustration as a round of excuse.[47]

A final aspect of *"The Super Servant Two"* is that the contract contained a cancel- **16-043**

---

[44] *J Lauritzen v Wijsmuller BV ("The Super Servant Two")* [1990] 1 Lloyd's Rep. 1 at 10.
[45] *J Lauritzen v Wijsmuller BV ("The Super Servant Two")* [1990] 1 Lloyd's Rep. 1 at 13, col.2, per Dillon LJ.
[46] *J Lauritzen v Wijsmuller BV ("The Super Servant Two")* [1990] 1 Lloyd's Rep. 1 at 9, col.2, per Bingham LJ.
[47] [1935] A.C. 524, PC.

lation clause (cl.17.1) (a force majeure clause giving a party the option to cancel): generally on force majeure clauses, para.16.044 ff). The present clause, read literally, would have enabled the defendant to escape liability by pointing to the sinking of *The Super Servant Two*, and then cancelling the contract vis-à-vis the remaining available vessel *The Super Servant One*. But the Court of Appeal held that this clause would not exonerate the defendant if there had been negligence on its part. Since the litigation was being conducted at this stage on preliminary points, the eventual result is not reported.

IV. FORCE MAJEURE CLAUSES

16-044 **Nature of force majeure clauses** Force majeure clauses,[48] sometimes called "hardship" clauses,[49] are frequently inserted into commercial or even consumer transactions. They are an explicit exercise in risk allocation. Such a clause has the effect of defining the relevant party or parties' primary obligations so that, if the relevant event occurs, there will be no breach and hence no contractual liability to pay compensation. Such a clause will normally broaden the relevant party's immunity from liability for default beyond the narrow set of excuses applicable as a result of the Common Law doctrine of frustration.

16-045 A force majeure clause will (i) operate to qualify an obligation so that upon the occurrence of a particular event no contractual default will arise (this is the invariable or minimum impact of the clause, if it has any application at all). But in addition such a clause might: (ii) have the effect of suspending the contract (see the *Tennants* case para.16-051 below); or (iii) allow a party to cancel the contract (as in "*The Super Servant Two*", cl.17.1, discussed below at paras 16-061, 16-062); or (iv) provide that the relevant event will produce automatic termination of the contract;

---

[48] As for force majeure clauses: M.G. Bridge (ed), *Benjamin's Sale of Goods*, 11th edn (London: Sweet & Maxwell, 2021), 8-074 ff; H. Beale (ed), *Chitty on Contracts*, 34th edn (London: Sweet & Maxwell, 2021), paras 26-059–26-088; K, Lewison, *Interpretation of Contracts*, 7th edn (London: Sweet & Maxwell, 2020), Ch.13; E. McKendrick (ed), *Force Majeure and Frustration of Contract*, 2nd edn (London: Lloyds of London, 1995), Chs. 1, 4, 5, 7–10, 13, 14, 17; E. McKendrick, "Force majeure Clauses: The Gap between Doctrine and Practice", in A.S. Burrows and E. Peel (eds), *Contract Terms* (Oxford: Oxford University Press, 2007), Ch.12; G. McMeel, *The Construction of Contracts: Interpretation, Implication and Rectification*, 3rd edn (Oxford: Oxford University Press, 2017), Ch.22 (on force majeure clauses); E. Peel (ed), Treitel, *The Law of Contract* 15th edn (London: Sweet & Maxwell, 2020), para.19-079; D. Robertson, "Force majeure Clauses" (2009) 25 J.C.L. 62; J. Stannard, *Delay in the Performance of Contractual Obligations*, 2nd edn (Oxford: Oxford University Press, 2018), 5.86 ff; Ben Symons, *Force Majeure and Frustration in Commercial Contracts*, (London: Bloomsbury Professional, 2022). See also H. Berman, "Force Majeure and the Denial of an Export License" (1960) 73 Harv. L. Rev 1128; E. Eriksen, "Terrorism and Force majeure in International Contracts" (2004) 16 Bond L. Rev. 176.

　For the converse situation, where the doctrine of frustration is excluded by express contractual provision: E. Peel, *Frustration and Force Majeure*, 4th edn (London: Sweet & Maxwell, 2021), Ch.12.

　For comment on the force majeure/exclusion clause division, M.G. Bridge (ed), *Benjamin's Sale of Goods*, 11th edn (London: Sweet & Maxwell, 2021), 8-074 (sentence 4); H. Beale (ed), *Chitty on Contracts*, 34th edn (London: Sweet & Maxwell, 2021), para.26-086; K. Lewison, *Interpretation of Contracts* 7th edn (London: Sweet & Maxwell, 2020), 13-07–13-14; G. McMeel, *The Construction of Contracts: Interpretation, Implication and Rectification*, 3rd edn (Oxford: Oxford University Press, 2017), 22-35 ff.

[49] e.g. E. McKendrick (ed), *Force Majeure and Frustration of Contract*, 2nd edn (London: Lloyd's of London, 1995), para.14.14. Also, called "intervener provisions" or as regards specific risks "price escalation" clauses. As regards "rise and fall" clauses see *Codelfa Construction Pty Ltd v State Rail Authority of NSW* [1982] HCA 24; (1982) 149 C.L.R. 337.

this takes effect as a consensual form of termination; it does not operate on the basis of Common Law frustration (on the automatic operation of that form of termination, para.18-001).[50]

Clause subject to reasonableness test in the Unfair Contract Terms Act 1977   **16-046** In *Target Rich International Ltd v Forex Capital Markets Ltd* (see also para.16-058) it was suggested in a *dictum* (the judge holding that no cause of action arose on these facts) that the reasonableness test within the Unfair Contract Terms Act 1977, notably s.3 of that statute, will apply to a force majeure clause.[51] Adrian Beltrami QC, the judge, also suggested that the relevant clause would have survived the reasonableness test, commenting:[52]

> "[133] ....There is no reason in principle why a force majeure clause engaged by an exceptional market event is inherently unreasonable...The reasonableness test must be assessed in the round, within the contract as a whole, rather than by reference to the specific benefit of individual clauses. In any event, as an Exceptional Market Event could adversely affect both FXCM and its clients, I do not accept the premise.
>
> [134] In all the circumstances, I am satisfied that a clause suspending obligations in the exceptional circumstances described satisfies the reasonableness test..."

Force majeure clause containing performance relief clause: party not elect-   **16-047** **ing to waive benefit of clause** In *Delta Petroleum (Caribbean) Ltd v British Virgin Islands Electricity Corp* (2020)[53] the issue was whether the doctrine of election applied. If so, the seller would have lost the protection of a "performance relief clause" ("PRC"). The seller had contracted to supply fuel to the buyer, which was the sole producer of electricity on the British Virgin Islands. The contract contained a force majeure clause, which included the following clause: "(2) If by reason of any causes referred to [above], either the availability...of crude oil or...the normal means of transport[ing it]...is delayed, hindered, interfered with, curtailed or prevented, then the Seller shall be at liberty to withhold, reduce or suspend the deliveries hereunder to such extent as the Seller may in its absolute discretion think fit and the Seller shall not be bound to purchase or otherwise make good shortages resulting from such causes." The seller's supplier, an oil refinery fairly nearby, closed its facility. And so, it was necessary for the seller to procure fuel from a more distant and expensive source. The seller nevertheless continued for a short period to supply the buyer without invoking the protection of the PRC. The Court of Appeal of the East Caribbean, upholding a BVI High Court decision, found that the seller had elected, in a technical sense, not to rely on the PRC and had thus lost the right to do so; and so the seller was ordered, by a final award of specific performance, to continue its supply. The Privy Council reversed this decision. It held (1) that an "election" is confined to a choice between inconsistent alterna-

---

50 As for modalities (iii) and (iv), see *Bremer Handelsgesellschaft mbH v Vanden Avenne-Izegem PVBA* [1978] 2 Lloyd's Rep. 109, HL, discussed in *Classic Maritime v Limbungan Makmur Sdn Bhd* [2019] EWCA Civ 1102; [2019] 2 All E.R. (Comm) 592 at [52] ff (latter case noted by M. Bridge (2020) 136 L.Q.R. 1). The clause in the *Classic Maritime* case was not a force majeure clause but an exceptions clause, the effect of which was that the party who failed to perform in specified circumstances, despite breach, was not liable to pay damages, but the clause only protected the party in default if he had been ready and willing to perform.

51 [2020] EWHC 1544 (Comm) at [133] (Adrian Beltrami QC).

52 [2020] EWHC 1544 (Comm) at [133] (Adrian Beltrami QC).

53 [2020] UKPC 23; [2021] 1 W.L.R. 5741.

tives, quoting passages from judgments by Lords Diplock,[54] Goff,[55] and Rix LJ[56] (Lord Leggatt in the *Delta* case also commenting on the need for an affirmation of a contract to be clear and unequivocal, on that topic see Ch.14).[57] But here the PRC gave a range of protective options to the seller (reduction, suspension, complete non-supply);[58] moreover, the true analysis was that the PRC did not result in the termination of the contract. The Privy Council held (2): reversal of the lower court's final judgment required the Privy Council, in exercise of its inherent appellate jurisdiction, to restore the parties to the position before the erroneous order of specific performance was made. During the period of specific performance the seller had been made to supply fuel below the appropriate price. And so, it should have received an extra payment. Now that the specific performance order had been rescinded, the seller was entitled to that extra payment, and to interest.

16-048   **Construction of a force majeure clause: express exception concerning the buyer's performance**   A clause might provide a potential shield for a party, but the same clause might specifiy that the shield will not apply in specified circumstances. This was the position in *Gemcorp Commodoties Trading SA v Zeefacto Oil & Gas Co.*[59] The case was a summary judgment application concerning a debt claim. The buyer pleaded unsuccessfully both frustration and a defence under a force majeure clause. Both defences were declared to have no real prospect of success. Judgment was awarded in favour of the claimant seller. The frustration

---

54   [2020] UKPC 23; [2021] 1 W.L.R. 5741 at [18]: *Kammins Ballrooms Co Ltd v Zenith Investments (Torquay) Ltd* [1971] A.C. 850, 883 (HL) per Lord Diplock: "[election can arise] in a situation where a person is entitled to alternative rights inconsistent with one another. If he has knowledge of the facts which give rise in law to these alternative rights and acts in a manner which is consistent only with his having chosen to rely on one of them, the law holds him to his choice even though he was unaware that this would be the legal consequence of what he did".

55   [2020] UKPC 23; [2021] 1 W.L.R. 5741 at [19]: *Motor Oil Hellas (Corinth) Refineries SA v Shipping Corpn of India ('The Kanchenjunga')* [1990] 1 Lloyd's Rep. 391, 398 per Lord Goff: "…where with knowledge of the relevant facts a party has acted in a manner which is consistent only with his having chosen one of the two alternative and inconsistent courses of action then open to him—for example, to determine a contract or alternatively to affirm it—he is held to have made his election accordingly … [An election] can be communicated to the other party by words or conduct; though, perhaps because a party who elects not to exercise a right which has become available to him is abandoning that right, he will only be held to have done so if he has so communicated his election to the other party in clear and unequivocal terms … Once an election is made, however, it is final and binding …"

56   [2020] UKPC 23, [2021] 1 W.L.R. 5741 at [20]: *Kosmar Villa Holidays Plc v Trustees of Syndicate 1243* [2008] EWCA Civ 147; [2008] Bus. L.R. 931 at [38] per Rix LJ: "[Election] generally requires knowledge of the facts giving rise to the choice on the part of the party electing, and knowledge of the choice having been made on the part of the other party…Thus the choice has either to be communicated unequivocally by the party electing to the other party or else the objective circumstances have to be such that the effluxion of time by itself constitutes that communication. Since the election is the choice of the party electing, it is his conduct which is decisive. Once made the election is final and irrevocable".

57   [2020] UKPC 23; [2021] 1 W.L.R. 5741 at [21] per Lord Leggatt: "…What is fundamental to the principle of waiver by election…is that it is only capable of applying where a choice must be made between two alternative and inconsistent (in the sense of mutually exclusive) courses of action, such that adopting one of them necessarily entails forsaking the other".

58   [2020] UKPC 23; [2021] 1 W.L.R. 5741 at [24]: "[The PRC] does not present the Seller with a binary, all-or-nothing choice between, on the one hand, putting an end prospectively to all the parties' obligations or, on the other hand, treating all those obligations as still binding. Rather, the Seller is 'at liberty to withhold, reduce or suspend the deliveries hereunder to such extent as the Seller may in its absolute discretion think fit'. This gives the Seller a range of options…".

59   [2018] EWHC 3938 (Comm).

point can be briefly noted here, before proceeding to the force majeure clause. Subsequent to formation of the contract, there had been a fall in the value of the relevant foreign exchange rates, to the buyer's detriment. But this did not count as frustration. Popplewell J held that the buyer's obligation to pay in US dollars had not been frustrated by the buyer's personal difficulty in converting its funds from one currency into dollars, following a post-formation change in the currency conversion rate. The risk of foreign fluctuation is borne by the payor.[60] This was a case of a more onerous performance and fell outside the recognised categories of frustration.[61] Popplewell J also rejected the buyer's (ingenious but desperate) argument that the "foundation"[62] of the payment obligation was that the buyer should personally remain able to fund the payment by converting receipts from sub-sales from one particular foreign currency into US dollars.

As for the force majeure clause, cl.14 (so far as relevant) stated: **16-049**

> "Neither seller nor buyer shall be liable in damages or otherwise for any failure or delay in performance of any obligation hereunder, other than the obligation to make payment, where such failure or delay is caused by force majeure, being any event, recurrence or circumstance reasonably beyond the control of the respective parties, including without prejudice to the generality of the foregoing,….restrictions imposed by any governmental authority."

Popplewell J noted[63] that it contained a "carve-out", namely the parenthetical   **16-050**
qualification, "other than the obligation to make payment". This had the effect that the clause expressly excluded from the scope of the clause the buyer's obligation to pay for goods supplied. Popplewell J, drawing upon the "carve-out" point, concluded:[64]

> "there is a positive support for the proposition that risk of fluctuations in exchange rates are assumed to be borne by the buyer in the force majeure clause *because it carves out from the scope of any exculpatory force majeure event, the obligation to make payment of the purchase price*. This is simply a case where performance of the contract on the part of the defendant has become about 30 per cent more expensive by reference to the means by which the defendant intended to perform its obligations. That is not a change in the nature of the payment obligation, let alone a significant one. At most, it is a change in the onerousness or expense of it." (emphasis added)

Suspension option when seller's performance "hindered", goods being in short   **16-051**
supply In *Tennants (Lancashire) Ltd v CS Wilson & Co Ltd*,[65] the House of Lords (Lord Finlay LC dissenting) held (reversing the Court of Appeal) that the seller's inability to satisfy all its subsisting contractual commitments, including its obligations towards the present buyer, was enough to fall within the scope of the force majeure clause. That clause had the effect of suspending obligations in the event that there was short supply in the market and that satisfaction of the seller's obliga-

---

[60] [2018] EWHC 3938 (Comm) at [17] per Popplewell J, citing *United International Pictures v Cine Bes Filmcilik AS* [2003] EWHC 798 (Comm) (Flaux QC, Deputy High Court judge).
[61] [2018] EWHC 3938 (Comm) at [18], quoted in full in the text below: "At most, it is a change in the onerousness or expense of it."
[62] [2018] EWHC 3938 (Comm) at [24]–[27].
[63] [2018] EWHC 3938 (Comm) at [4] and [12]; the argument was an attempt to adopt the analogy of *Krell v Henry* [1903] 2 K.B. 740, CA, para.17-077 ff.
[64] [2018] EWHC 3938 (Comm) at [18].
[65] [1917] A.C. 495, HL; E. Peel, *Frustration and Force Majeure*, 4th edn (London: Sweet & Maxwell, 2021), para.12-038.

tion had been "hindered". The main supplier of the relevant chemical was German, and the First World War had precluded supply from that German source (following the declaration of war with Germany, obtaining supplies from Germany would involve illegality, namely trading with the enemy). A limited supply existed from an English source, but insufficient to satisfy the supplier's needs under various contracts with different buyers, including the present. The supplier's other customers had not challenged the supplier's decision to suspend full performance of their contracts. But the present buyer was dissatisfied and contended that the supplier was in breach and that the force majeure clause did not apply.

16-052 **Lock down in India during COVID: seller of vessel not unable to transfer title: force majeure clause inapplicable** In *NKD Maritime Ltd v Bart Maritime (No. 2) Inc*[66] a vessel was to be delivered at a port in India, whereupon it would be scrapped by the buyer. The seller claimed that it had been prevented from performing because of Covid restrictions in India. Government officials had been required for a quite short period to concentrate on other tasks. This meant that there would be delay in those officials being free to board the ship and grant permission for the scrapping to proceed. Butcher J held that the seller's obligations to transfer title and to make delivery at, or near, the port had not been prevented. In case he was wrong on those points, he added, by way of *dicta*, remarks concerning the seller's contention that a force majeure clause operated on these facts. That clause (cl.10) stated (so far as material for this purpose):[67]

> "Should the Seller be unable to transfer title of the Vessel or should the Buyer be unable to accept transfer of the Vessel…due to outbreak of war between the nominated country of delivery and any other country, wreck, actual constructive or compromised total loss of the Vessel, restraint of governments, princes, rulers or people of any nation or the United Nations, act of God, then either the Buyer or the Seller may terminate this Agreement upon written or telegraphic notice from one party to the other without any liability upon either party and the Initial Payment referred to in Clause 1.b. hereof shall be released to the Buyer."

16-053 Butcher J held that the seller had been able to transfer title. In any event, the impact of the Indian Government's Covid restrictions had been relatively short.[68] The force majeure clause required "inability" to perform. The judge formulated the following test and concluded that the events here fell short of the level of impact which would be necessary for the force majeure clause to operate:[69]

> "[89] In my judgment, whether there is 'inability' to perform for the purposes of clause 10 by reason of a temporary restraint of governments (etc.) depends on whether the probable period of that restraint is such as materially to undermine the commercial adventure. In assessing this, similar considerations will be relevant as those which would be involved in the, admittedly analytically distinct, question of whether a contract is frustrated, and which are referred to in *Edwinton Commercial Corporation v Tsavliris Russ (Worldwide Salvage & Towage) Ltd (The 'Sea Angel')* [2007] EWCA 547; [2007] 2 Lloyd's Rep 517. …[91]…I do not consider that the delay that there had been by 14 April 2020, together with that which could then reasonably be anticipated as probable, constituted an 'inability' on the part of Bart to perform …for the purposes of clause 10. Nor, to the extent

---

[66] [2022] EWHC 1615 (Comm) (Butcher J).
[67] [2022] EWHC 1615 (Comm) at [3].
[68] [2022] EWHC 1615 (Comm) at [79]–[91] (Butcher J).
[69] [2022] EWHC 1615 (Comm) at [89]–[91] (Butcher J).

it is relevant, did the delay which would actually have occurred had the contract not been terminated [in breach of contract by the seller]. These delays did not materially undermine the commercial adventure."

Force majeure clause expressly or adequately referring to the risk of a   **16-054**
pandemic   In the Scottish case *Billy Graham Evangelistic Association v Scottish Event Campus Ltd* the force majeure clause explicitly referred to the risk of a pandemic, or (as in this case) "biological contamination", and so it took effect. Either party was allowed to terminate the contract for hiring an exhibition centre. There the clause referred to the risk of "biological contamination" and the "imposition [viz by government] of any embargo, sanction, or similar action", that is, resulting from the contamination.[70] Similarly, in *Dwyer (UK Franchising) Ltd v Fredbar Ltd*[71] it appears that the judge was prepared to treat the Covid pandemic as a "natural disaster", as mentioned in the force majeure clause.[72] However, the clause was wrongly disapplied by invoked a party in that case. That constituted a repudiatory breach. But the innocent party chose to affirm the contract.

Adverse economic or market change not a force majeure event   In *Tandrin*   **16-055**
Aviation Holdings Ltd v Aero Toy Store LLC[73] Hamblen J said:

"a change in economic or market circumstances, affecting the profitability of a contract or the ease with which the parties' obligations can be performed, is not regarded as being a force majeure event…see *'The Concadoro'* [1916] 2 A.C. 199; and likewise a rise in cost or expense - see *Brauer & C (GB) Ltd v James Clark (Brush Materials) Ltd* [1952] 2 All E.R. 497."

In the *Tandrin* case[74] a buyer of an executive jet tried to withdraw, relying on a   **16-056**
force majeure clause. The buyer had suffered from the 2008 financial crash and was now seeking to resile from the purchase of a $31.75 million executive jet. At issue was a deposit paid by the buyer representing 9.5 per cent of that purchase price. The first point of decision was that the force majeure clause operated only in favour of the seller with respect to the events specified, and not with respect to the buyer, so that the remaining discussion in the judgment comprises considered dicta, but from an authoritative and commercially renowned judge). Clause 7.17 provided as follows:

"*Force Majeure:* Neither party shall be liable to the other as a result of any failure of, or delay in the performance of, its obligations hereunder, for the period that such failure or delay is due to: Acts of God or the public enemy; war, insurrection or riots; fires; governmental actions; strikes or labor disputes; inability to obtain aircraft materials, accessories, equipment or parts from vendors; *or any other cause beyond Seller's reasonable control.* Upon the occurrence of any such event, the time required for performance by such party of its obligations arising under this Agreement, shall be extended by a period equal to the duration of such event." (emphasis added).

---

[70]   2021 S.L.T. (Sh Ct) 185 at [31] and [32] (Sheriff's Court).
[71]   *Dwyer (UK Franchising) Ltd v Fredbar Ltd* [2021] EWHC 1218 (Ch) at [261]–[274] (Judge Jones).
[72]   "[261] Clause 30.1 of the Agreement is entitled "Force Majeure" and reads: 'This Agreement will be suspended during any period that either of the parties is prevented or hindered from complying with their respective obligations under any part of this Agreement by any cause which the Franchisor designates as force majeure including strikes, disruption to the supply chain, political unrest, financial distress, terrorism, fuel shortages, war, civil disorder, and natural disasters.' [p1082]."
[73]   [2010] EWHC 40 (Comm); [2010] 2 Lloyd's Rep. 668 at [40]. On the *Tandrin* case, see E. Peel, *Frustration and Force Majeure*, 4th edn (London: Sweet & Maxwell, 2021), para.6-041.
[74]   [2010] EWHC 40 (Comm); [2010] 2 Lloyd's Rep. 668.

16-057   Even if potentially the buyer had been able to take shelter under this force majeure clause (which obviously the buyer could not because this part of the clause only protected the seller), it would not have been enough that there had been a severe economic depression, flowing from the financial crisis of 2008. Hamblen J said:[75]

> "Finally, to the extent that there may be some overlap between the operation of force majeure clauses and the doctrine of frustration, Lord Simon made clear in *National Carriers Ltd v Panalpina (Northern) Ltd* [1981] A.C. 675, 700, that an increase in the mere expense or onerousness of the contract cannot constitute frustration: 'Frustration of a contract takes place when there supervenes an event (without default of either party and for which the contract makes no sufficient provision) which so significantly changes the nature (not merely the expense or onerousness) of the outstanding contractual rights and/or obligations from what the parties could reasonably have contemplated at the time of its execution that it would be unjust to hold them to the literal sense of its stipulations in the new circumstances; in such case the law declares both parties to be discharged from further performance.'"

16-058   **"Exceptional Market Event": a force majeure event**   The unsuccessful claim for breach of contract in *Target Rich International Ltd v Forex Capital Markets Ltd* concerned the Swiss Flash Crash of 15 January 2015: namely, announcement that the value of the Swiss France would henceforth no longer be capped by reference to the value of the Euro. This event caused the claimant to suffer loss (the claimant held large amounts of Euros).[76] The claimant sued the defendant online trading platform for failing to implement stop loss orders (in accordance with subsisting emergency instructions), which would have closed down the relevant account so that the claimant's money would not be at risk during the period of volatility. But no potential breach of duty was found.[77] In any event, the judge held that a force majeure clause would have protected the defendant because it referred to an "Exceptional Market Event"[78] and this potentially covered these events (although the point is dictum). Furthermore, the judge indicated that the clause would not have been unreasonable under the Unfair Contract Terms Act 1977, because the clause, although excluding liability, was not unreasonable, all things considered (on this point see also para.16-046).

16-059   **Even drastic increase in cost of performance does not constitute inability to perform**   Similarly, in a discussion cited and considered by Hamblen J in the *Tandrin* case, Christopher Clarke J in *Thames Valley Power Ltd v Total Gas & Power Ltd*[79] rejected a gas supplier's contention that a force majeure clause operated so as to qualify its duty to make supply when, as had occurred, the cost to the supplier had become (extremely) financially unattractive. The relevant portions of the clause stated:

> "15.1 if either party is by reason of force majeure rendered unable wholly or in part to carry out any of its obligations under this agreement then upon notice in writing of such force majeure from the party affected to the other party as soon as possible after the occurrence of the cause relied on, the party affected shall be released from its obligations

---

75   [2010] EWHC 40 (Comm); [2010] 2 Lloyd's Rep. 668 at [50].
76   [2020] EWHC 1544 (Comm) (Adrian Beltrami QC).
77   [2020] EWHC 1544 (Comm) at [124]–[128].
78   [2020] EWHC 1544 (Comm) at [129], [131]–[134].
79   [2005] EWHC 2208 (Comm); (2006) 22 Const. L.J. 591–610; [2006] 1 Lloyd's Rep. 441 at [50].

and suspended from the exercise of its rights hereunder to the extent to which they are affected by the circumstances of force majeure and for the period during which those circumstances exist...

"15.2, in this standard condition "force majeure" means any event or circumstances beyond the control of the party concerned resulting in the failure by that party in the fulfilment of any of its obligations under this agreement and which notwithstanding the exercise by it of reasonable diligence and foresight it was or would have been unable to prevent or overcome. ...In assessing the circumstances of force majeure affecting the customer [NB: as distinct from the supplier], the price of gas under this agreement shall be excluded.

15.3, in the event of a circumstance of force majeure affecting the supplier's ability to supply gas hereunder, the supplier will, in so far as reasonably practicable, treat all its customers including the customer fairly and equally in determining the extent to which supplies are to be reduced, suspended or terminated."

Christopher Clarke J[80] gave these eight reasons for rejecting the supplier's resort **16-060** to the force majeure clause (total is the supplier and "TVPL" is the customer):

"[Reason 1] The force majeure event has to have caused Total to be unable to carry out its obligations under the GSA. ...The fact that it is much more expensive, even very greatly more expensive for [Total] to do so, does not mean that [Total] cannot do so.

[Reason 2] To interpret clause 15 as applicable in circumstances where performance is "commercially impractical" or Total is "commercially unable" to supply is to enforce a qualification highly uncertain in ambit and open ended in reach which is neither necessary nor obvious and which is inconsistent with the express terms of the GSA....

[Reason 3] The...last sentence of standard condition 15.2 [has the effect that the... customer cannot say that it is unable to pay the price because it is too high. It does not at all follow that the supplier is entitled to rely upon an increase in the market price in comparison to the contract price as a force majeure circumstance...

[Reason 4] This conclusion is consistent with a line of cases, both on force majeure clauses and on frustration...to the effect that the fact that a contract has become expensive to perform, even dramatically more expensive, is not a ground to relieve a party on the grounds of force majeure or frustration. I take as an example *Tennants Lancashire Ltd v Wilson CS & Co Ltd* [1917] A.C. 495 [on which para.16-051], a force majeure case where Lord Loreburn observed at p.510: 'The argument that a man can be excused from performance of his contract when it becomes "commercially impossible" seems to me to be a dangerous contention which ought not to be admitted unless the parties plainly contracted to that effect'. ...No case has been cited to me [Christopher Clarke J] in which a clause such as the present has been interpreted as relieving a party from its obligation to perform because the performance of the contract has become economically more burdensome. If a company as familiar with the effect of fluctuations as Total wished to secure that result, it would need to do so in much more explicit terms.

[Reason 5] This conclusion is also supported by a consideration of the factual matrix....TVPL were, in the absence of clear words to the contrary, entitled to expect that Total would supply them with gas against payment of the contract price throughout the 15 year term and would not be entitled to refuse to do so because the cost of so doing had increased even exponentially. That was Total's risk, particularly in the light of the price escalation clause which provided, within limits, for increases in the contract price in accordance with formulae based on indices. See *Publicker Industries Inc v Union Carbide Corporation* [1973] 17 UCC Reporter, Serv 989 where the existence of a contractual provision for limited increases in the price of ethanol resulting from a rise in the cost of ethylene 'impelled the conclusion that the parties intended that the risk of a substantial and unforeseen rise in its cost would be borne by the seller'.

[Reason 6] The letter of 5th July does not claim that Total has become unable to sup-

---

[80]   [2005] EWHC 2208 (Comm); (2006) 22 Const. L.J. 591; [2006] 1 Lloyd's Rep 441 at [50].

ply gas. It indicates that as a result of increasing prices and the price formula in the GSA, it will become "uneconomic" for large parts of the year to supply gas…At the same time it offers to supply gas at the market price. It thus indicates that Total can in fact continue to supply gas but at a loss or a lesser profit if it only receives the contract price.

[Reason 7] There is no evidence …that Total cannot supply gas for the remainder of the term. On the contrary, …if their argument on force majeure and remedies fails, Total have undertaken to continue to supply.

[Reason 8] [Total] also gives an estimate on a 'best guess basis' of Total's financial position in the future. [Its] evidence is to the effect that Total will lose about £9½ million up to the date of termination of the contract. The calculation assumes that the cap will be breached, i.e. the market price of gas will exceed the maximum that TVPL can be required to pay, in the second quarter of 2006 and never return under the cap until the end of the contract. Even on the assumption—which I do not accept—that a sufficiently dramatic increase in the price of gas could amount to a frustrating event even though Total could still supply gas, an increase in market price which took the market price to a height no greater than the cap [applicable to the buyer's price] could scarcely have that consequence."

Here the judge seems to be implying that a loss which exceeds the cap payable by the customer would fall within the ambit of risk borne by the supplier once that party had acceded to that price cap.

16-061 **Owner's cancellation option under charterparty exercisable only in absence of negligence** In *J Lauritzen v Wijsmuller BV ("The Super Servant Two")* (for the facts of this case and the discussion of self-induced frustration, para.16-033 ff), the relevant clause stated:[81]

"17.1. Wijsmuller has the right to cancel its performance under this Contract whether the loading has been completed or not, in the event of force majeur [sic], Acts of God, perils or danger and accidents of the sea, acts of war, warlike-operations, acts of public enemies, restraint of princes, rulers or people or seizure under legal process, quarantine restrictions, civil commotions, blockade, strikes, lockout, closure of the Suez or Panama Canal, congestion of harbours or any other circumstances whatsoever, causing extraordinary periods of delay and similar events and/or circumstances, abnormal increases in prices and wages, scarcity of fuel and similar events, which reasonably may impede, prevent or delay the performance of this contract."

16-062 The Court of Appeal said that this was not an exclusion clause. The right to cancellation given by this clause could not be relied upon where Wijsmuller (the owner of two giant barges used for the transporting of oil rigs) had been at fault or had not acted reasonably, whether that fault or failure occurred during or (as here) before the time for performance. In support of the conclusion summarized in the preceding sentence, Bingham LJ supplied many arguments, six of which have been selected here:[82]

"[Reason 4]: Wijsmuller's construction of clause 17, giving them a right to cancel the contract at any stage with financial impunity on occurrence of an event within the clause, even though the event is brought about by negligence on their part, would make this a very one-sided clause…

[Reason 5]: …The present clause is not…an exceptions clause….The clause is, however, one which confers on one party only a right exercisable in a very wide range of

---

[81] [1990] 1 Lloyd's Rep. 1, CA.
[82] Dillon LJ gave a concurring judgment.

circumstances to nullify the contractual bargain made between the parties at no cost to itself and regardless of the loss which the other party may sustain. To such a clause the broad approach indicated by Canada Steamship[83] is in my judgment appropriate.

[Reason 6] Clause 17.1 does not expressly provide that Wijsmuller may cancel even though the event in question is one which they could by the exercise of reasonable care have averted. There is an obvious contrast with the language of clause 16.1 where Wijsmuller...exempt themselves from liability for loss or damage to the [customer's] rig even though caused by their negligence.

[Reason 7] The language of clause 17.1 is, I think, wide enough to embrace events caused by Wijsmuller's negligence. But the general tenor of the clause, opening with a reference to force majeure and acts of God and including such events as acts of war, civil commotion, canal closure and harbour congestion, strongly points towards events beyond the direct or indirect control of Wijsmuller.

[Reason 8] Clause 17.1 is not deprived of a sensible application if read as excluding events brought about by the negligence of Wijsmuller their servants or agents. Almost all the events listed could only occur wholly independently of Wijsmuller and there is none which could only occur as the result of Wijsmuller's negligence ...

[Reason 12] [Counsel for Wijsmuller] also argued that if, contrary to his submission, negligence precluded reliance on clause 17.1 before the carriage began, then it had to be negligence on the part of Wijsmuller as opposed to its servants or agents. I do not accept this. There are undoubtedly instances in which actual fault or privity on the part of the shipowner must be shown if he is to be liable, and liability for the acts of servants or agents can of course be excluded by contract. In the ordinary way, however, English law treats a party, his servants and agents as one, and I would construe clause 17.1 as precluding reliance by Wijsmuller on any event which would not have occurred if they, their servants or agents had exercised reasonable care."

Events not within a party's "reasonable control": a comparatively high hurdle   The Court of Appeal held in *Elephant Corporation v Trafigura Beheer BV ("The Crudesky")*[84] that the force majeure clause in that case did not avail a party because the relevant event was not something beyond its "reasonable control". More generally, Longmore LJ said:[85]   **16-063**

"a force majeure clause must be construed in accordance with its own terms; it also need hardly be emphasised (a) that it is an exceptions clause and any ambiguity must be resolved against[86] the party seeking to rely on it and (b) that the concept of being "beyond [a corporate person's] control" sets a comparatively high hurdle since corporations usually do have a significant measure of control over their own business, see *Channel Island Ferries Ltd v Sealink UK Ltd* [1988] 1 Lloyd's Rep. 323 and *Mamidoil-Jetoil Greek Petroleum Co SA v Okta Crude Oil Refinery (No 3)* [2003] EWCA Civ 1031; [2003] 2 All E.R. (Comm) 640; [2003] 2 Lloyd's Rep. 635. All that said, it is necessary to look at the individual clauses."

Longmore LJ continued: **16-064**

"[26] ...Force majeure in connection with demurrage is specifically catered for by clause

---

[83]   Viz, construction *contra proferentem*, in accordance with *Canada Steamship Lines Ltd v The King* [1952] A.C. 192, PC; the recent case law on this topic has moved away from a mechanical application of the 1952 case's code of rules; see S. Tofaris, "Commercial Construction of Exemption Clauses" [2019] L.M.C.L.Q. 270.
[84]   [2013] EWCA Civ 905; [2013] 2 All E.R. (Comm) 992.
[85]   [2013] EWCA Civ 905; [2013] 2 All E.R. (Comm) 992 at [25].
[86]   On the modern case law concerning strict interpretation of exclusion clauses and similar terms, S. Tofaris, "Commercial Construction of Exemption Clauses" [2019] L.M.C.L.Q. 270.

21...[which contains] a specific list of causes of delay which can be relied on, the only relevant one of which is 'arrest or restraint of princes, rulers or peoples'. There is the further provision that the cause of the delay 'was not within the reasonable control of Charterers or Owners or their respective servants or agents'...

[27] ...I cannot agree with the judge that the delay occurring to the vessel was beyond Total's control. The question remains whether it was beyond their 'reasonable' control.

[28] My opinion is that the delay was not beyond Total's 'reasonable control' if one looks (as one should) at Total as one entity."

16-065   *Elephant Corporation v Trafigura Beheer BV ("The Crudesky")* concerned a ship's delay in leaving a Nigerian port. Trafigura, the charterer, was held liable for demurrage (agreed payment for delay) payable to GEC, the owner, as a result of the following events. The chartered ship was to be loaded with oil at Port Harcourt in Nigeria. The task of achieving this loading was delegated by Trafigura to an agent, Total, the operator of the loading facility. Loading required a permit from the Nigerian petroleum regulator, which was normally sought from the capital, Lagos. But Total took a short-cut and sought permission on the spot at the port. Problems arose and permission, although at first given, was revoked. Total tried to retrieve the situation by peremptorily removing a padlock from an appliance. It was then able to commence the flow of oil. This unilateral act caused outrage and a punitive response by the authorities. Extricating the ship not only required payment of a fine to the Nigerian authorities but involved delay. The Court of Appeal concluded, first, that Trafigura's force majeure clause did not exempt it from liability to pay demurrage because it was responsible for its agent's conduct. Secondly, the unlawful imposition of a fine by the Nigerian authorities did not break the chain of causation because it was not out of the ordinary for a governmental authority to react in a high-handed manner to violation of its regulations. This was sufficiently causally linked to the charterer's failure to have gained official permission.

16-066   **"Reasonable" endeavours to avoid or mitigate the effects of the force majeure event; multiple causes, including a non-force majeure event**   In *Seadrill Ghana Operations Ltd v Tullow Ghana Ltd*[87] Teare J concluded on the facts that a party had failed to satisfy the obligation to use all reasonable endeavours to remedy the situation (resulting from a foreign government's adverse decision, a "moratorium", concerning drilling operations), even if a force majeure "occurrence" had arisen (the decision primarily turns on the issue of causation,[88] there having been a non-force majeure event—a government decision not to allow wider exploitation of the relevant field—which the judge considered had the effect of nullifying the relevance

---

[87]   [2018] EWHC 1640; [2019] 1 All E.R. (Comm) 34 at [89], [93] and [96] (see also [28], [82]–[98]).

   "[89].... greater expense or a greater risk of an unprofitable outcome is not a matter which enables Tullow to say that it has exercised it reasonable endeavours. Were it sufficient for Tullow to show that drilling in Jubilee was not in its commercial interest Tullow would be able to avoid its obligation to provide drilling instructions on the grounds of expense or expected lack of profit-...Tullow could not rely upon such matters to excuse non-performance before a force majeure and, in my judgment, it cannot do so after a force majeure." And [93] "[a] party cannot ignore the commercial interests of the other party in the force majeure being avoided or circumvented". And [96]: "when drilling ...was prevented by the moratorium and Tullow was obliged to exercise its reasonable endeavours to avoid or circumvent the moratorium, Tullow was entitled to consider its own interests, and in particular, whether there was a business case for drilling at another well, but Tullow was also bound to consider the interests of Seadrill. It was not entitled to ignore the interest of Seadrill in receiving instructions ...to drill at a well not affected by the moratorium."

[88]   [2018] EWHC 1640; [2019] 1 All E.R. (Comm) 34 at [70]–[80], notably at [78] and [79]:

on these facts of the specified force majeure event, a "moratorium" on existing drilling). The relevant clause stated:[89]

> "Clause 27.5: In the event of force majeure occurrence, the party that is or may be delayed in performing the Contract shall notify the other party without delay giving the full particulars thereof and shall use all reasonable endeavours to remedy the situation without delay."

Force Majeure event "overcome" by payment in a different currency when contractually nominated currency no longer available   In *MUR Shipping BV v RTI Ltd* a majority of the Court of Appeal (Males and Newey LJJ, Arnold LJ dissenting) held that a force majeure clause did not operate to suspend a contract when an adequate non-contractual mode of payment had been offered.[90] The contractual currency had been contractually stipulated as US dollars, but euros (the currency used in most parts of the European Union) could have been paid instead, a finding made by the arbitrator. The agreement was a contract of affreightment. The charterer wished to make payment to the shipowner for a delivery of cargo to Ukraine. International sanctions prohibited receipt of payment in these circumstances in US dollars. But the arbitrator had held that, under the terms of the force majeure clause, an alternative form of payment, in euros, would have been an equivalent satisfaction of this payment obligation. That alternative currency would have enabled the parties to "overcome" the prohibition. The shipowner refused to accept payment in euros. **16-067**

In *MUR Shipping BV v RTI Ltd* Males LJ commented[91] that the charterer had insisted that it: "should make payment in euros which could be converted into dollars as soon as they were received by the owner's bank, and agreed to bear any additional costs or exchange rate losses in converting the euros into dollars. However, the owner rejected this proposal, insisting on its right to receive payment in dollars." The Court of Appeal held that this alternative currency would have "overcome by reasonable endeavours" (the phrase appearing in the force majeure clause) the **16-068**

"[78] Clause 27.1 contains a causation requirement in these terms: "if and to the extent that fulfilment has been delayed or temporarily prevented by an occurrence, as hereunder defined as Force Majeure". Tullow had intended to drill and complete wells in the Greater Jubilee Field from October 2016. That intention was not frustrated by a force majeure but by an event which was not a force majeure, namely, the failure of the Government to approve the Greater Jubilee Plan. Tullow's own intention with regard to drilling in the Greater Jubilee Field in October 2016 had also changed.

"[79] That approach is consistent with the approach of the Court of Appeal in *Intertradex v Lesieur* [1978] 2 Lloyd's Reports 509 where it was held that where two causes operated to prevent a seller from shipping goods a force majeure notice had to be given in respect of each of them. Where notice had only been given of one the seller could not rely upon the force majeure clause. That decision is regarded as one which establishes the proposition that a force majeure event must be sole cause of the failure to perform an obligation; see [in current edition] *Frustration and Force Majeure* by Edwin Peel, 4th edn, at paragraph 12-046. Ultimately, however, (and as Edwin Peel also accepts; see [in current edition] paragraph 12-046) the question is one of construction of the contract before the court. For the reasons I have given in the preceding paragraph I do not consider that clause 27.1 permits Tullow to rely upon it to excuse its failure to fulfil its obligations in October 2016."

89   [2018] EWHC 1640; [2019] 1 All E.R. (Comm) 34 at [282].
90   [2022] EWCA Civ 1406; [2023] 1 All E.R. (Comm) 501.
91   [2022] EWCA Civ 1406; [2023] 1 All E.R. (Comm) 501 at [2].

international sanction which prevented payment in dollars. Jacobs J,[92] on appeal under s.69 of the Arbitration Act 1996, from the LMAA arbitrators,[93] had been wrong to insist that "overcome" required an alternative mode of performance which was directly compliant with the contract. It is submitted that the majority decision of the Court of Appeal is attractive. On second appeal, in the Court of Appeal, Males LJ said:[94]

> "Terms such as 'state of affairs' and 'overcome' are broad and non-technical terms and clause 36 should be applied in a common sense way which achieves the purpose underlying the parties' obligations – in this case, concerned with payment obligations, that MUR [the shipowner] should receive the right quantity of US dollars in its bank account at the right time. I see no reason why a solution which ensured the achievement of this purpose should not be regarded as overcoming the state of affairs resulting from the imposition of sanctions. It is an ordinary and acceptable use of language to say that a problem or state of affairs is overcome if its adverse consequences are completely avoided."

16-069   In short, payment in euros achieved precisely the monetary satisfaction which would have been achieved by payment in US dollars. These were substitutable and precisely equivalent modes of satisfying the obligation to pay the relevant sum. But it is unclear what other types of non-contractual substituted forms of performance will be tolerated within this new principle. As Arnold LJ noted[95] in his dissent, it is uncertain whether where a contract requires loading or discharge of cargo at a nominated port the situation would fall within the present decision if the alternative presented itself and was achieved by loading or discharge at an alternative port, the relevant party bearing any costs incurred in arranging this alternative place of loading or discharge.

---

[92]   As noted at [2022] EWCA Civ 1406; [2023] 1 All E.R. (Comm) 501 at [32]: "Mr Justice Jacobs [on first appeal from the arbitrators] allowed the appeal and granted permission to appeal on this question to this court. His essential reason, expressed at [2022] EWHC 467 (Comm) at [98], was that the contract required payment in US dollars and that "a party is not required, by the exercise of reasonable endeavours, to accept non-contractual performance in order to circumvent the effect of a force majeure or similar clause", as shown by the decision of [the Court of Appeal] in *Bulman v Fenwick & Co* [1894] 1 QB 179.". And at [131] Jacobs J said: "Having considered the case-law in this area, I am ultimately persuaded that the exercise of reasonable endeavours did not require the Owners to sacrifice their contractual right to payment in US$, and with it their right to rely upon the force majeure clause. If there was a contractual right to payment in US$, and a contractual obligation to pay in that currency, then this was a right and obligation which formed part of the parties' bargain. The exercise of reasonable endeavours required endeavours towards the performance of that bargain; not towards the performance directed towards achieving a different result which formed no part of the parties' agreement. If reasonable endeavours did not require the acceptance of different contractual performance in *Bulman* and (by implication) *Vancouver Strikes*, I do not consider that it required such acceptance in the present case. I also accept Mr Eaton's submissions that if the loss of a contractual right turns purely on what is reasonable in a case, then the contractual right becomes tenuous, and the contract is then necessarily beset by uncertainty which is generally to be avoided in commercial transactions."

[93]   Mr Jeremy Russell QC, Mr Mark Hamsher and Ms Sarra Kay.

[94]   [2022] EWCA Civ 1406; [2023] 1 All E.R. (Comm) 501 at [56].

[95]   [2022] EWCA Civ 1406; [2023] 1 All E.R. (Comm) 501 at [74]: "Suppose the contract required carriage to port A which was strike-bound and the party invoking clause 36 was presented with an offer by the other party to divert the vessel to port B which would not in fact be detrimental to the party invoking the clause (say because the goods being carried were required at place C equidistant between port A and port B)? Is the party invoking the clause required to accept that offer? In my view the answer is no, because the party invoking the clause is entitled to insist on contractual performance by the other party. If the parties to the contract of affreightment intended clause 36.3(d) to extend to a requirement to accept non-contractual performance, clear express words were required and there are none."

Notification of force majeure   Leggatt J in *Scottish Power UK Plc v BP Explora-*   **16-070**
tion Operating Co Ltd examined the case law[96] (notably the decision of the House
of Lords in *Bremer Handels GmbH v Vanden-Avenne Izegem PVBA*[97]) concerning
the nature of such notification requirements. He considered the possibility that, even
though damages are not in issue, an intermediate term analysis (generally Ch.12)
might apply, so that the underlying protection might be lost if the failure to notify
has caused very serious prejudice. Conversely, the protection will not be forfeited
if the notification failure to comply is not serious in its impact on the facts of the
case. But on the facts of the *Scottish Power* case Leggatt J held that failure to satisfy
the relevant notification requirement did not constitute a condition precedent nor
did it operate even potentially in a preclusive manner on the basis of an intermediate term.

Automatic force majeure causes and exceptions clauses contrasted   In *Clas-*   **16-071**
sic Maritime v Limbungan Makmur Sdn Bhd[98] the Court of Appeal noted the distinction between an exceptions clause and a force majeure clause. The court held that
the clause in the present case did not constitute a force majeure clause. Instead it
provided a defence to liability to pay damages following breach. The clause in this
case was described aptly as a "ragbag".[99] It was construed as a set of exceptions
from liability to pay damages which operated only if the party prima facie in default
was in the throes of performance or at least ready and willing to perform. And so
the charterer could not invoke the protection of the clause if it was no longer ready
and willing to perform. The trial judge, Teare J, had found that the charterer was
not willing to perform. Clause 32 provided:

> "Exceptions. Neither the Vessel, her Master or Owners, nor the Charterers, Shippers or
> Receivers shall be Responsible for loss or damage to, or failure to supply, load, discharge
> or deliver the cargo *resulting From*: Act of God, act of war, ...accidents of navigation; *ac-*
> *cidents at the mine*...; always provided *that any such events directly affect the*
> *performance of either party under This Charter Party*. If any time is lost due to such
> events or causes such time shall not count as Laytime or demurrage (unless the Vessel is
> already on demurrage in which case only half time to count)." (emphasis added)

On the automatic force majeure/exceptions clause distinction, Males LJ said in   **16-072**
Classic Maritime v Limbungan Makmur Sdn Bhd:[100]

> "there is a distinction between a 'contractual frustration' clause (using that term in the
> sense explained) and an exceptions clause which relieves a party from responsibility for
> a breach...A critical distinction is that a 'contractual frustration' clause brings the contract
> (or the relevant part of the contract [for example] each shipment would be treated as a
> separate adventure) to an end forthwith and automatically once an event occurs, regard-
> less of the wishes of the parties, thereby relieving both parties from any further obliga-
> tion to perform under the contract or to accept the other's performance in the future. An
> exceptions clause, however, simply operates to relieve a party from the obligation to pay
> damages after a breach has occurred."

---

[96] [2015] EWHC 2658 (Comm); [2016] 1 All E.R. (Comm) 536 at [194] ff (affirmed [2016] EWCA
Civ 1043).
[97] [1978] 2 Lloyd's Rep. 109, HL.
[98] [2019] EWCA Civ 1102; [2019] 2 All E.R. (Comm) 592; noted M. Bridge (2020) 136 L.Q.R. 1.
[99] [2019] EWCA Civ 1102; [2019] 2 All E.R. (Comm) 592 at [44].
[100] [2019] EWCA Civ 1102; [2019] 2 All E.R. (Comm) 592 at [61].

16-073   Males LJ added:[101]

"Clause 32 [the exceptions clause in the present case] does not provide for any automatic cancellation of the contract (or of individual shipments) for the future and, accordingly, the reasoning of the House of Lords in *Bremer Handelsgesellschaft mbH v Vanden Avenne-Izegem PVBA* [1978] 2 Lloyd's Rep. 109 cannot apply to it. It was not a 'contractual frustration' clause."

16-074   In *Classic Maritime v Limbungan Makmur Sdn Bhd*[102] the result was that the charterer was liable for non-supply of cargoes (iron ore pellets to be shipped from one of two nominated Brazilian ports to Malaysia) under the contract of affreightment and the shipowner was entitled to damages in respect of its loss of freight, resulting in damages (agreed as a figure) of US $19,869,573 in respect of the five lost shipments. The Court of Appeal held that there had been breach; the exceptions clause did not apply because the defendant charterer had not in fact wished to perform; and damages would be awarded even though the cargoes could not have been procured from the intended mine (because of the dam burst) nor from the other available mine. In the Court of Appeal's opinion, the burst dam was irrelevant. The result is debatable. The defendant charterer's decision not to perform in any event constituted the breach and liability for this failure fell outside the exception clause (that clause operating only if the performer was ready and willing to perform, or engaged already in the performance). On this case, Michael Bridge says[103] that, although in breach, the charterer had not caused the shipowner any loss. This is because it would not have been possible for the relevant five cargoes to have been found. The dam burst was the reason for that inability. And that inability to perform arose without the charterer needing to invoke the exceptions clause.

V.   Economic Considerations

16-075   A range of economic theories has been advanced over the years to explain when and why contracts should be discharged for frustration.[104] One that has taken a certain hold in universities but not, it seems, in UK courts, is that advanced in the US by Richard Posner:[105]

---

[101] [2019] EWCA Civ 1102; [2019] 2 All E.R. (Comm) 592 at [62].

[102] [2019] EWCA Civ 1102; [2019] 2 All E.R. (Comm) 592; noted M. Bridge (2020) 136 L.Q.R. 1.

[103] M. Bridge (2020) 136 L.Q.R. 1.

[104] For a bibliography of other theories on when contracts should be discharged, see J. Elofson, "The dilemma of changed circumstances in contract law" (1996) 30 Colum. J.L. & Soc. Probs. 1, 2 fn.4. For related theories about contract law in general, see R.A. Hillman, *The Richness of Contract Law* (Dordrecht: Springer Publishing, 1998). H. Collins, *The Law of Contract*, 4th edn (Cambridge: Cambridge University Press, 2003) comments: "Economic analysis of law suggests a good reason why the courts should provide a set of default rules to govern contractual relations in the absence of express terms. Default rules save transaction costs by permitting the parties to avoid the cost of negotiating every detail of their arrangement."

[105] The seminal statement is found in R.A. Posner and A.M. Rosenfield, "Impossibility and Related Doctrines in Contract Law: An Economic Analysis" (1977) 6 Jo. of Legal Studies 83–118. This is an application of the "Coase Theorem" to the problem: R.H. Coase, "The Problem of Social Cost" (1960) 3 J.L. & Econ. 1. For an account of subsequent developments in such theory—"bounded rationality" and "institutional" economics—see D. Robertson, "Force majeure clauses" (2009) 25 J.C.L. 62.

"In every discharge case the basic problem is the same: to decide who should bear the loss resulting from an event that has rendered performance by one party uneconomical."[106]

In this connection, one of the purposes of contract law: **16-076**

"[I]s to reduce the cost of contract negotiation by supplying contract terms that the parties would probably have adopted explicitly had they negotiated over them."[107]

This serves to legitimise "implication" of outcomes of this kind,[108] especially in   **16-077**
contracts concluded by consumers and SMEs.[109] Subject to the impact of administration costs:

"[D]ischarge should be allowed where the promisee is the superior risk bearer; if the promisor is the superior risk bearer, non-performance should be treated as a breach of contract ... A party can be a superior risk bearer for one of two reasons. First, he may be in a better position to prevent the risk form materializing."[110]

Although downgrading the importance of prevention in this context, it is   **16-078**
conceded that this "resembles the economic criterion for assigning liability in tort cases" and that prevention is:

"[A]n important criterion in many contract settings, too, but not in this one. Discharge would be inefficient (sic) in any case where the promisor could prevent the risk from materializing at a lower cost than the expected cost of the risky event. In such a case efficiency would require that the promisor bear the loss resulting from the occurrence of the event, and hence that occurrence should be treated as precipitating a breach of contract."[111]

Indeed many would say: the promisor "could prevent the risk from material-   **16-079**
izing at a lower cost" simply by not contracting at all. Prima facie, the person who chooses to make a promise bears the risk of being unable to perform it. However, prevention, the Posner argument continues, "is only one way of dealing with risk; the other is insurance",[112] and, being risk averse, this clearly is what many people prefer.[113] "The factors relevant to determining which party to the contract is the

---

[106] R.A. Posner and A.M. Rosenfield, "Impossibility and Related Doctrines in Contract Law: An Economic Analysis" (1977) 6 Jo. of Legal Studies 83 at 86, 90.
[107] R.A. Posner and A.M. Rosenfield (1977) 6 Jo. of Legal Studies 83 at 88, with reference to the ideas of Jeremy Bentham.
[108] R.A. Posner and A.M. Rosenfield (1977) 6 Jo. of Legal Studies 83 at 89: "If the purpose of the law of contracts is to effectuate the desire of the contracting parties, then the proper criterion for evaluating the rules of contract law is surely that of economic efficiency."
[109] R.A. Posner and A.M. Rosenfield (1977) 6 Jo. of Legal Studies 83 at 89: "the role of contract law in supplying contract terms, like the role of the standard form of contract, is less important the larger the stakes in the contract and hence the smaller the ratio of the costs of transacting to the value of the exchange. The larger the stakes, the more it will pay the parties to negotiate terms finely adapted."
[110] R.A. Posner and A.M. Rosenfield (1977) 6 Jo. of Legal Studies 83 at 90.
[111] R.A. Posner and A.M. Rosenfield (1977) 6 Jo. of Legal Studies 83 at 90.
[112] R.A. Posner and A.M. Rosenfield (1977) 6 Jo. of Legal Studies 83 at 90.
[113] R.A. Posner and A.M. Rosenfield (1977) 6 Jo. of Legal Studies 83 at 91: "Compare a 100 per cent chance of having to pay $10 with a one percent chance of having to pay $1000. The expected cost is the same in both cases, yet ... Many people would be willing to pay a substantial sum to avoid the uncertain alternative—for example, $15 to avoid [the above]. Such people are risk averse. The prevalence of insurance is powerful evidence that risk aversion is extremely common, for insurance is simply trading an uncertain for a certain cost". Insurance "is a particularly important method of cost avoidance in the impossibility context because the risks ... are generally not preventable by the party charged with non-performance."

cheaper insurer" say Posner and Rosenfield "are (1) risk appraisal costs and (2) transaction costs",[114] it being conceded that the first are really part of the second.

16-080   Against all this, some have argued that a purely economic assessment is too narrow a view of personal well-being.[115] Others, while accepting the significance of the exercise, have pointed out that it may be difficult to identify the party better placed to bear the risk.[116] The exercise assumes that parties behave rationally and that where, for example, a sensible party would buy (fire) insurance, that party will buy it.[117] Posner himself later conceded the point.[118] In the UK it has been shown that most courts today are wary of such exercises,[119] in part because the necessary information is not available to them.[120] Courts depend on the submissions of counsel. Counsel are unlikely to incur the cost of research into disciplines such as economics, generally or in the context of the particular case, unless encouraged by the court. Be that as it may, Posner's work merits more judicial attention than it has received in the UK.

---

[114] R.A. Posner and A.M. Rosenfield (1977) 6 Jo. of Legal Studies 83 at 92–93, present a case study: A, maker of printing machinery (PM) promises B to sell and install PM on B's premises—customised PM of little resale value. Before installation there is a fire at B's premises, B goes out of business. A sues for the price of the PM, but B (non negligent) argues B discharged. Appraisal: "while B was in a better position to determine the probability that a fire would occur, A was in a better position to determine the magnitude of the relevant loss (the loss of resources that went into the making of the machine) if the fire did occur." Insurability: "Depending on the volume of A's production and on A's prior experience with contingencies" such as this, "A may be able to eliminate the risk … simply by charging a higher price—in effect, an insurance premium—to all of its customers; A may in short be able to self-insure. B is less likely to be able to do so: the magnitude of its potential liability to A in the event of a default may greatly exceed any amount it could hope to pass on to its customers in the form of higher prices. As for market insurance, it seems unlikely that D could obtain for a reasonable price a fire insurance policy" for damage to premises and perhaps business loss and "also against its contractual liability to A which… depends on the stage of production at which the fire occurs, a matter within the private knowledge of A". Thus, A being best risk bearer, B is discharged.

[115] e.g., J. Gordley, "The Moral Foundations of Private Law" (2002) 47 Am. Jo. of Jurisprudence 1.

[116] e.g. J. Elofson, "The Dilemma of Changed Circumstances in Contract Law" (1996) 30 Colum. Jo. of L. & Soc. Probs. 1, 8 ff, who contends inter alia that the theory "depends on unwarranted assumptions".

[117] See, e.g. A. Leff, "Economic Analysis of Law: Some Realism about Nominalism" (1974) 60 Va. L.R. 451 at 456 ff; J. Elofson, "The Dilemma of Changed Circumstances in Contract Law" (1996) 30 Colum. J.L. & Soc. Probs. 1 at 24; the "inherent limits in economic analysis of contract law" were also stressed by S. Waddams in "The Economics of Contract Law" (2007) 45 C.B.L.R. 305 at 310 ff.

[118] R.A. Posner, *The Problems of Jurisprudence* (Cambridge, MA: Harvard University Press, 1993), p.365.

[119] Or of anything that savours of social engineering: J. Shand "Unblinkering the Unruly Horse: Public Policy in the Law of Contract" [1972A] C.L.J. 144 at 154; P. Devlin, *The Enforcement of Morals* (Oxford University Press, 1965), p.56. *Charlton v Fisher* [2001] EWCA Civ 112; [2002] Q.B. 578. Commentators in the US have criticised leading cases in England, such as *Tsakiroglou & Co Ltd v Noblee Thorl Gmbh* [1962] A.C. 93 (see para.17-045), for not taking account of economics, e.g. J.H. Schlegel, "Of Nuts, and Ships, and Sealing Wax, Suez, and Frustrating Things" (1969) 23 Rutgers L. Rev 419 at 448. However, English courts have been apparently unmoved.

[120] M.A. Clarke, *Policies and Perceptions of Insurance Law in the Twenty-First Century* (Oxford: Oxford University Press, 2007), p.278 ff.

CHAPTER 17

CATEGORIES OF FRUSTRATION

I. Introduction

This chapter examines the main features of frustration.[1] The law started from the **17-001** rule of "absolute contracts", that when a "party by his own contract creates a duty or charge upon himself, he is bound to make it good" unless that would be contrary to law "notwithstanding any accident by inevitable necessity, because he might have provided against it by his contract".[2] This remains the starting point of analysis today; cases in which a contract is frustrated are the exception, to be proved by the party alleging frustration, often a defendant in a dispute.[3] Generally, frustration occurs, according to Lord Radcliffe in *Davis Contractors Ltd v Fareham U.D.C.* (see also paras 16-002 and 17-064), the leading case, whenever:

> "[W]ithout default of either party a contractual obligation has become incapable of being performed because the circumstances in which performance is called for would make it a thing radically different from that which was undertaken by the contract."[4]

[1] Leading specialist treatments of the frustration doctrine are: E. Peel, *Frustration and Force Majeure*, 4th edn (London: Sweet & Maxwell, 2021), and Ben Symons, *Force Majeure and Frustration in Commercial Contracts*, (London: Bloomsbury Professional, 2022). See also: H. Beale (ed), *Chitty on Contracts*, 34th edn (London: Sweet & Maxwell, 2021), Ch.26; J. Stannard, *Delay in the Performance of Contractual Obligations*, 2nd edn (Oxford: Oxford University Press, 2018), Ch.12 (frustrating delay). An important analysis is M. Bridge, "Frustration and excused non-performance" (2021) 137 L.Q.R. 580-603; see also J. Beatson, "Increased Expense and Frustration", in F.D. Rose (ed), *Consensus ad Idem: Essays in the Law of Contract in Honour of Guenter Treitel* (London: Sweet & Maxwell, 1996), 121; D. Ibbetson, "Absolute Liability in Contract: the Antecedents of *Paradine v Jayne*", in F.D. Rose (ed), op cit, Ch. (for an earlier history); E. McKendrick, "Frustration, Restitution and Loss Adjustment", in A.S. Burrows (ed), *Essays on Restitution* (Oxford: Oxford University Press, 1991), 147; E. McKendrick, "The Regulation of Long-Term Contracts in English Law", in J Beatson and D Friedmann (eds), *Good Faith and Fault in Contract Law* (Oxford: Oxford University Press, 1995), 305 at 323 ff; See G. McMeel, "The Juridical Basis of Frustration Revisited" [2020] L.M.C.L.Q. 297; J. Morgan, *Great Debates in Contract Law*, 3rd edn (London: Palgrave Publishing, 2020), Ch.5.

[2] *Paradine v Jane* (1647) Al. 26; (1647) 82 E.R. 519; for microscopic scholarly examination of this case, D. Ibbetson, "Absolute Liability in Contract: the Antecedents of Paradine v Jayne", in F.D. Rose (ed), *Consensus ad Idem: Essays in the Law of Contract in Honour of Guenter Treitel* (London: Sweet & Maxwell, 1996), Ch.1.

[3] Except where the impediment is that performance has become illegal (see para.17-050) where, if the illegality becomes apparent, the court must take it into account anyway.

[4] *Davis Contractors Ltd v Fareham U.D.C.* [1956] A.C. 696 at 729, HL. See also *National Carriers Ltd v Panalpina (Northern) Ltd* [1981] A.C. 675 at 700, HL per Lord Simon. Neil Andrews, *Contract Rules—Decoding English Law* (Cambridge: Intersentia Publishing, 2016), art.125. Leading specialist treatments of the frustration doctrine are: E. Peel, *Frustration and Force Majeure*, 4th edn

17-002   The decision of the House of Lords in *Davis Contractors v Fareham U.D.C.*[5] remains the seminal authority governing the scope of the doctrine of frustration. This is because it crystallised the "radical difference"[6] general criterion of frustration and, furthermore, the case demonstrated that commercial hardship does not constitute frustration (see also para.17-064). Thus, frustration does not arise if a contract becomes more difficult or expensive to perform. It is not enough that a party's profit margin is reduced or even that the deal becomes an economic disaster for this party. No radical frustrating difference had arisen on the facts of that building contract case merely because a skilled labour shortage had caused a 14-month delay and 25 per cent increased expense in the completion of the work. In this case Lord Radcliffe said:[7]

> "frustration occurs whenever the law recognises that without default of either party a contractual obligation has become incapable of being performed because the circumstances in which performance is called for would render it a thing radically different from that which was undertaken by the contract".

As mentioned at para.16-001 ff, this is one of the classic judicial definitions of the frustration doctrine.

17-003   The fact that hardship or economic difficulty is not a ground for release from, or relaxation of, contractual obligations is arguably the starting point. In *Tandrin Aviation Holdings Ltd v Aero Toy Store LLC*[8] Hamblen J said:

> "Lord Simon made clear in *National Carriers Ltd v Panalpina (Northern) Ltd* [1981] A.C. 675, 700, that an increase in the mere expense or onerousness of the contract cannot constitute frustration: 'Frustration of a contract takes place when there supervenes an event (without default of either party and for which the contract makes no sufficient provision) which so significantly changes the nature (not merely the expense or onerousness) of the outstanding contractual rights and/or obligations from what the parties could reasonably have contemplated at the time of its execution that it would be unjust to hold them to the literal sense of its stipulations in the new circumstances; in such case the law declares both parties to be discharged from further performance.'"

17-004   A similar endorsement of this "starting-point" is Popplewell J's comment in *Gemcorp Commodoties Trading SA v Zeefacto Oil & Gas Co.*[9] Here the buyer boldly but unsuccessfully contended that adverse currency movement, subsequent to formation of the contract, constituted frustration. But Popplewell J held that this was merely a case of a more onerous performance and fell outside the recognised categories of frustration:[10]

> "This is simply a case where performance of the contract on the part of the defendant has become about 30 per cent more expensive by reference to the means by which the defendant intended to perform its obligations. That is not a change in the nature of the payment

---

(London: Sweet & Maxwell, 2021) and Ben Symons, *Force Majeure and Frustration in Commercial Contracts*, (London: Bloomsbury Professional, 2022).

5   [1956] A.C. 696, HL.
6   On the radical difference criterion, see remarks in *Canary Wharf (BP4) T1 Ltd v European Medicines Agency* [2019] EWHC 335 (Ch); 183 Con. L.R. 167 at [26] sub-para.[5], [27], and [235] per Marcus Smith J.
7   [1956] A.C. 696 at 729, HL.
8   [2010] EWHC 40 (Comm); [2010] 2 Lloyd's Rep. 668 at [50].
9   [2018] EWHC 3938 (Comm).
10   [2018] EWHC 3938 (Comm) at [18] per Popplewell J.

obligation, let alone a significant one. At most, it is a change in the onerousness or expense of it."

Generally, any unexpected cost in performance is a risk assumed by the obligor. **17-005** In particular, currency fluctuations, even devaluation, are a commercial risk assumed by traders and not a ground of termination in the relevant trade.[11] In the context of global trade, in *Tsakiroglou & Co Ltd v Noblee Thorl GmbH*[12] Viscount Simonds observed that freight "charges may go up or down" and that, if "the parties do not specifically protect themselves against change, the loss must lie where it falls". In the Suez string of cases, as in the *Tsakiroglou* decision, the extra cost of routing goods around the Cape of Good Hope rather than more directly and expeditiously through the Suez Canal is barely mentioned.

Some decisions in the early twentieth century show that large increases in the **17-006** costs impacting sellers of goods do not discharge contracts of sale.[13] The risk is allocated under the contract. In *British Movietonews Ltd v London and District Cinemas Ltd* Viscount Simon said:[14]

> "[A] wholly abnormal rise or fall in prices, a sudden depreciation of currency, an unexpected obstacle to execution or the like. Yet this does not in itself affect the bargain they have made. If ... a consideration of the terms of the contract, in the light of the circumstances existing when it was made, shows that they never agreed to be bound in a fundamentally different situation which has now un expectedly emerged, the contract ceases to bind at that point—not because the court in its discretion thinks it just and reasonable to qualify the terms of the contract, but because *on its true construction* it does not apply in that situation."

Multi-factorial test

As to whether a particular contract should be discharged today, in 2007 Rix LJ **17-007** quoted that statement,[15] and said that, although the doctrine of frustration still needed overall tests like that of Lord Radcliffe in the *Davis Contractors* case (paras

---

[11] See, e.g. *British Movietonews Ltd v London and District Cinemas Ltd* [1952] A.C. 166 at 185; *National Carriers Ltd v Panalpina Ltd* [1981] 1 A.C. 675 at 712; and more recently *Tandrin Aviation Holdings Ltd v Aero Toy Store LLC* [2010] EWHC 40 (Comm); [2010] Lloyd's Rep. 668 at [49] ff. per Hamblen J. In most cases, however, this general rule may be countered by particular indications of party intention.

[12] *Tsakiroglou & Co Ltd v Noblee Thorl GmbH* [1962] A.C. 93 at 113, HL.

[13] *Instone & Co Ltd v Speeding Marshall & Co Ltd* (1916) 33 T.L.R. 202; *Blythe & Co v Richards, Turpin & Co* (1916) 85 L.J.K.B. 1425; and *Hutton & Co Ltd v Chadwick Taylor & Co Ltd* (1918) 34 T.L.R. 230. Cf. the view that where alternative modes of performance are provided for, but the primary mode becomes impossible and the other involves "prohibitive" cost, the contract is discharged: E. Peel, *Frustration and Force Majeure*, 4th edn (London: Sweet & Maxwell, 2021), para.6-026 with reference to *Edward Grey & Co v Tolme & Runge* (1915) 31 T.L.R. 551 at 553. Cf. also, under American law, the Restatement 2d. (U.S.A.), which states (para.261 Comment d) that an increase "well beyond the normal range" might discharge contracts. The most controversial instance is *The Alcoa case, Aluminium Corp of America v Essex Group Inc* 499 F. Supp. 53 (1980), on which E. Peel, *Frustration and Force Majeure*, 4th edn (London: Sweet & Maxwell, 2021), para.6-023, in which there was a flexible pricing formula for aluminium but costs (of electricity for the smelting process) increased more steeply than expected and the smelting company was entitled to relief.

[14] *British Movietonews Ltd v London and District Cinemas Ltd* [1952] A.C. 166, HL at 185 (emphasis added).

[15] *Edwinton Commercial Corp v Tsavliris Russ Ltd ("The Sea Angel")* [2007] EWCA Civ 547; [2007] 1 C.L.C. 876 at [84].

16-002, 17-002), the *application* of the doctrine "requires a multi-factorial approach" (see also para.16-005), and the factors include "the terms of the contract itself, the parties' knowledge, expectations and assumptions and contemplations, in particular as to risk".[16] Rix LJ's test in *"The Sea Angel"'* (on this case see also paras, 17-065–17-069 and 17-089) confirms that frustration is exceptional and will arise only if the event, considered in all relevant circumstances, as it were, "ticks" the following six "boxes":[17]

(1) The subsequent event is potentially frustrating (supervening illegality, physical destruction, frustrating delay, or very occasionally frustration of the venture);[18]

(2) there has been a complete undermining or destruction of the contract's foundation;

(3) the risk is not allocated to a party, expressly or impliedly (on the element of implied risk allocation, paras16-005 and 16-012-16-021);

(4) nor was a party in default;

(5) nor was a party making a choice;[19]

(6) finally, there is a "reality check": although unhelpfully, indeed dangerously couched in terms of "justice", the essence of this last factor is that the court (or arbitral tribunal) must consider whether a finding of frustration would be perceived by the relevant commercial community as absurd or alarming; commenting on factor (6), Rix LJ explained:[20]

> "[As for 'justice'], …[this] is not an additional test, but it is a relevant factor which underlies all and provides the ultimate rationale of the doctrine. If one uses this factor as a reality check, its answer should conform with a proper assessment of the issue of frustration. If it does not appear to do so, it is probably a good indication of the need to think again."[21]

17-008 Indeed, as Rix LJ emphasised, factor (6), the so-called "justice" element, is re-

---

[16] [2007] EWCA Civ 547; [2007] 1 C.L.C. 876 at [110]–[111]. See also *Islamic Republic of Iran Shipping Lines v Steamship Mutual Assoc (Bermuda) Ltd* [2010] EWHC 2661 (Comm); [2011] 2 All E.R. (Comm) 609 at [105]–[106] per Beatson J.

[17] *Edwinton Commercial Corp v Tsavliris Russ Ltd ("The Sea Angel")* [2007] EWCA Civ 547; [2007] 1 C.L.C. 876 notably at [110]–[112]; *"The Sea Angel"* was cited by Flaux J in *Bunge SA v Kyla Shipping Co Ltd (No. 2)* [2012] EWHC 3522 (Comm); [2013] 1 Lloyd's Rep. 565 at [39]–[41]; *Bunge SA v Kyla Shipping Co Ltd (No. 1)* [2013] EWCA Civ 734; [2013] 3 All E.R. 1006 at [7], per Longmore LJ; *Melli Bank Plc v Holbud Ltd* [2013] EWHC 1506 (Comm) at [15], per Robin Knowles QC; *Islamic Republic of Iran Shipping Lines v Steamship Mutual Underwriting Association (Bermuda) Ltd* [2010] EWHC 2661 (Comm); [2011] 2 All E.R. (Comm) 609 at [105], per Beatson J; *The Flying Music Co Ltd v Theater Entertainment SA* [2017] EWHC 3192 (QB) at [15]–[20], per Martin Griffiths QC, Deputy High Court Judge (the last case providing a succinct summary of the main authorities); a longer, magisterial and acute review of the modern doctrine and its various facets is provided by Marcus Smith J in *Canary Wharf (BP4) T1 Ltd v European Medicines Agency* [2019] EWHC 335 (Ch); 183 Con. L.R. 167 (which has not proceeded to appeal); see also the NZ Supreme Court's discussion in *Planet Kids Ltd v Auckland Council* [2013] NZSC 147; [2014] 1 N.Z.L.R. 149 at [60]–[62].

[18] On the categories of frustration, see *Canary Wharf (BP4) T1 Ltd v European Medicines Agency* [2019] EWHC 335 (Ch); 183 Con. L.R. 167 at [41], per Marcus Smith J.

[19] On factors 4 and 5, see *Canary Wharf (BP4) T1 Ltd v European Medicines Agency* [2019] EWHC 335 (Ch); 183 Con. L.R. 16 at [43]–[46], and [201]–[207], per Marcus Smith J.

[20] *Edwinton Commercial Corp v Tsavliris Russ Ltd ("The Sea Angel")* [2007] EWCA Civ 547; [2007] 1 C.L.C. 876 at [132].

[21] There is no parallel safety-valve factor within the sibling doctrine of shared fundamental mistake;

ally a misnomer[22] because the court has no broad absolving power.[23] Instead this final and residual criterion involves the court posing the following final-stage question: would release of both parties from their obligations on these facts be consistent with commercial and practical expectations of the limits of binding promises, taking into account the fact that neither party being in default, or having made a choice, and the relevant risk not having been allocated expressly or impliedly to each other? It is submitted, with respect, that references to "justice"[24] in an abstract sense, even as one facet of the "multifactorial" test, are unhelpful and perilous and the true issue is whether the application of the frustration doctrine would be perceived by the relevant commercial community as absurd or alarming.[25]

Consistent with the author's submission in the preceding paragraph, Julia Dias **17-009** Q.C. in *Wilmington Trust SP Services (Dublin) Ltd v Spicejet Ltd*[26] noted that the final factor of "justice" is a final check or safety-valve mechanism, appliable only if the court is minded to find frustration by application of the other aspects of the multifactorial test. Julia Dias Q.C. said:[27]

---

furthermore, as quoted by Rix LJ, *Edwinton Commercial Corp v Tsavliris Russ Ltd ("The Sea Angel")* [2007] EWCA Civ 547; [2007] 1 C.L.C. 876 at [114], Dillon LJ in *Notcutt v Universal Equipment Co (London)* [1986] 1 W.L.R. 641 at 647, CA, said: "I do not for my part see that these references to justice or injustice introduce any further factor. If the unexpected event produces an ultimate situation which, as a matter of construction, is not within the scope of the contract or would render performance impossible or something radically different from that which was undertaken by the contract, then it is unjust that the contracting party should be held to be still bound by the contract in those altered circumstances."

[22] [2007] EWCA Civ 547; [2007] 1 C.L.C. 876 at [111]–[116], [132].
[23] [2007] EWCA Civ 547; [2007] 1 C.L.C. 876 at [113]–[116], [132].
[24] e.g. *J Lauritzen A/S v Wijsmuller BV ("The Super Servant Two")* [1990] 1 Lloyd's Rep. 1, 8, CA, where Bingham LJ said: "The doctrine of frustration was evolved to mitigate the rigour of the common law's insistence on literal performance of absolute promises (*Hirji Mulji v Cheong Yue Steamship Co Ltd* [1926] A.C. 497 at 510; *Denny Mott & Dickson Ltd v James B Fraser & Co Ltd* [1944] A.C. 265 at 275; *Joseph Constantine Steamship Line Ltd v Imperial Smelting Corp Ltd* [1942] A.C. 154 at 171). *The object of the doctrine was to give effect to the demands of justice, to achieve a just and reasonable result, to do what is reasonable and fair, as an expedient to escape from injustice where such would result from enforcement of a contract in its literal terms after a significant change in circumstances* (*Hirji Mulji*, supra at 510; *Joseph Constantine Steamship Line Ltd* (supra) at 183, 193; *National Carriers Ltd v Panalpina (Northern) Ltd* [1981] A.C. 675 at 701.' (emphasis added here). These are dangerous and open-textured generalisations which, in the wrong hands, could torpedo too many transactions. Perhaps the high-water mark of dangerous emphasis upon vague notions of justice and reasonableness is the long passage in Lord Wright's speech in *Joseph Constantine SS Line Ltd v Imperial Smelting Corp Ltd* [1942] A.C. 154, HL, 183-186, where the following four phrases occur: (1) "The doctrine of frustration is intended to achieve a just and reasonable result" (183); (2) "the courts set themselves to avoid these results wherever justice seemed to require. The doctrine of frustration is thus, in Lord Sumner's words (*Hirji Mulji v Cheong Yue Steamship Co* [1926] A.C. 497 at 510, PC), 'a device by which the rules as to absolute contracts are reconciled with a special exception which justice demands.'" (184); (3) "It is a question of the construction of the particular contract, whether the obligation is absolute or whether it is qualified. It is thus seen that the court is not claiming to exercise a dispensing power, or to modify or alter contracts." (185); (4) "the court is exercising its powers, when it decides that a contract is frustrated, in order to achieve a result which is just and reasonable" (186).
[25] In that spirit Flaux J double-checked his conclusion in *Bunge SA v Kyla Shipping Co Ltd* [2012] EWHC 3522 (Comm); [2012] 2 C.L.C. 998 at [82]; affirmed [2013] EWCA 734 (cost of repairing charterer vessel exceeding its market value; owner's duty to repair not frustrated; owner had undertaken to maintain insurance at level above the repair cost).
[26] [2021] EWHC 1117 (Comm).
[27] [2021] EWHC 1117 (Comm) at [67].

"[67]…as I read [Rix LJ's] comments[28], the interests of justice only come into play if the court is otherwise minded to hold that a contract has been frustrated. In other words, it is required to pause before reversing the contractual allocation of risk. I do not understand him to be saying that the court effectively has a discretion to invoke the doctrine even if it is not satisfied that the threshold test of "radical difference" has been met. Since in my view that test has not presently been met, I do not consider that the interests of justice arise for separate consideration."

The event must be truly a supervening one

17-010   In *The Flying Music Co Ltd v Theater Entertainment SA* (2017) it was held that inability to give a high proportion of the scheduled performances on a music tour in Greek cities, as a result of civil unrest, could not be treated as a supervening event. Instead it was a continuation, and perhaps an aggravation, of a known problem subsisting at the time of formation:[29]

"Even if the prolongation of trouble was unexpected, as [the defendant] says it was to her, it was clearly a possibility, and it was for the parties to make their bargain accordingly."

17-011   In *The Flying Music Co Ltd v Theater Entertainment SA* the judge added:[30]

"I am not persuaded on the evidence that the Contract was frustrated …There was already unrest. How long it would last was uncertain. Ticket sales had already begun, and they were low. There were already road closures. There were already demonstrations. There was already violence. The Troika had already arrived. Thessaloniki and Athens had already erupted. The parties both knew enough about the risks that this posed to the success of the production for it to be wrong, now, with the benefit of hindsight, to reallocate those risks by releasing the Theater Entertainment from its Contract obligations."

17-012   A short-term impediment or reason for stoppage might have no overall effect on the contract. Context is crucial. In *Minnevitch v Café de Paris (Londres) Ltd*[31] the defendant was held to be justified in refusing to permit the plaintiff cabaret performers to perform on the day of the King's death (George V) and the next day, but not thereafter. The contract was for just seven days and contained a "no play no pay" clause.[32] As regards the possibility of discharge, the question is the general one whether the impediment defeats the purpose of the contract.[33] In this 1936 case the answer was "no".

---

[28]   *Edwinton Commercial Corp v Tsavliris Russ (Worldwide Salvage & Towage) Ltd (The Sea Angel)* [2007] EWCA Civ 547; [2007] 1 C.L.C. 876 at [111]–[116], [132]; the judge does not refer to paras [113]–[116] and [132], but only to [112], but nothing hinges on this.

[29]   [2017] EWHC 3192 (QB) at [67], per Martin Griffiths QC, Deputy High Court Judge; his discussion contains a succinct summary of the main authorities regarding frustration.

[30]   [2017] EWHC 3192 (QB) at [68], per Martin Griffiths QC, Deputy High Court Judge.

[31]   *Minnevitch v Café de Paris (Londres) Ltd* [1936] 1 All E.R. 884; on which, E. Peel (ed), Treitel, The Law of Contract, 15th edn (London: Sweet & Maxwell, 2020), para.17-059.

[32]   G.H. Treitel, *Remedies for Breach of Contract, A Comparative Account* (Oxford: Oxford University Press, 1988), para.5-058.

[33]   E. Peel (ed), *Treitel, The Law of Contract*, 15th edn (London: Sweet & Maxwell, 2020), para.19–052. Cf. *Howell v Coupland* (1876) 1 Q.B.D. 258, CA, where, without fault, a farmer was unable to deliver more than 80 of the promised 200 tons of a designated crop of potatoes, he was excused; but the case is not clear, see E. Peel, *Frustration and Force Majeure*, 4th edn (London: Sweet & Maxwell, 2021), para.4-075 to 4-078.

II.   LEGAL IMPOSSIBILITY: SUPERVENING ILLEGALITY

The contract will be frustrated if, subsequent to the contract's formation, **17-013** performance of the contract for either party becomes illegal: *Fibrosa Spolka Akcyjna v Fairbairn Lawson Combe Barbour Ltd*[34] and *Gamerco SA v ICM/Fair Warning (Agency) Ltd*[35] (on the latter case see para.18-012 ff). The supervening illegality might be a statutory change (including a change in the operation of a statutory regime), or a non-statutory legal change, or implementation of a subsisting source of prohibition, or withdrawal or serious modification of a legal permission. It is not possible to contract out of supervening illegality if to do so would be contrary to public policy. This was made clear in *Ertel Bieber & Co v Rio Tinto Co Ltd*.[36] In the *Fibrosa* case[37] a contract for the supply by a British company of machinery to a port in Poland was frustrated when the German forces took control of Poland. In this situation, the contract became one requiring the supplier to trade with the enemy. That is a clear-cut instance of illegality.

In the "Brexit" case (the UK's secession from the European Union), *Canary* **17-014** *Wharf (BP4) T1 Ltd v European Medicines Agency*, Marcus Smith J held[38] that a lease of London premises had not been frustrated (whether on the ground of illegality or frustration of the venture) by the UK's decision to leave, or by the eventual political and legal departure from the European Union in 2020.

In *Islamic Republic of Iran Shipping Lines v Steamship Mutual Underwriting Association (Bermuda) Ltd*, Beatson J held that partial supervening illegality did not **17-015** have the effect of frustrating a contract of marine insurance, because its essence had not been radically altered.[39]

Temporary illegality affecting use of cinemas was held not to exonerate tenants **17-016** from their liability to pay rent in *Bank of New York Mellon (International) Ltd v Cine-UK Ltd*.[40] Covid statutory restrictions had closed cinemas for many months. The tenant suggested that this extraordinary statutory restriction provided it with a defence to a claim for rent for that period, but the cesser of rent clause in these leases was restricted to physical damage to the property. The Court of Appeal concluded that there was no basis for re-writing that clause under the guise of the law of implied terms. Flaux C said:

> "[138] …the business efficacy test…will only be satisfied where, without the implied term, the contract would lack commercial or practical coherence. That simply cannot be said of the leases in the Hengrove and Trocadero cases. They both work perfectly well without the implied terms. Both leases allocate the risk that the premises cannot be used for their intended purpose to the tenant, so that the tenant is obliged to continue to pay

---

[34]   [1943] A.C. 32, HL.

[35]   [1995] 1 W.L.R. 1226, per Garland J.

[36]   [1918] A.C. 260 at 273, HL.

[37]   [1943] A.C. 32 at 39–40, HL.

[38]   [2019] EWHC 335 (Ch); 183 Con. L.R. 167 at [96], [160] sub-para.(2), [187], [190], where Marcus Smith J, held that a lease of London premises had not been frustrated (whether on the ground of illegality or frustration of the venture) by the United Kingdom's decision to leave the European Union, or by the eventual political and legal departure from the EU in 2020.

[39]   [2010] EWHC 2661 (Comm); [2011] 2 All E.R. (Comm) 609 notably at [115], [116], [121], and [126]–[128].

[40]   [2022] EWCA Civ 1021; [2023] L. & T.R. 2 at [55], [138] and [139] (Flaux C, with the agreement of Snowden LJ and Sir Nicholas Patten), applying Carr LJ's summary of the rules governing terms implied in fact, in *Yoo Design Services Ltd v Iliv Realty PTE Ltd* [2021] EWCA Civ 560 at [51]. The *Mellon* case is noted by A. Sahore [2022] C.L.J. 497–490.

rent where the cesser of rent provisions are not applicable (...[as] on the present facts) and there is nothing unworkable or incoherent about that allocation of risk.

[139] The obviousness test is equally inapplicable. The term which it is sought to imply has to be precisely expressed and must be so obvious to go without saying. If the officious bystander had asked the question whether the parties intended that, if the premises could not be used lawfully because of restrictions such as the Coronavirus restrictions, the obligation to pay rent would be suspended, far from a testy 'of course' from both parties, it seems to me the landlord in each case would have said 'of course not, the rent is payable throughout unless physical damage to or destruction of the premises has rendered them unfit for occupation or use'..."

The court also held[41] that partial failure of consideration (that is, partial "failure of basis") did not apply in this particular context because the facts did not involve failure of basis: the lease granted exclusive possession and the qualifications upon payment of rent were prescribed under the lease's express terms.

17-017   A contract governed by English law will be affected by foreign illegality only where the contract cannot be performed without necessarily infringing the relevant foreign law. Cockerill J examined this proposition in *Banco San Juan International Inc v Petroleos de Venezuela SA*.[42] It was held that the defendant payor could not seek shelter beneath this proposition on the facts because it had failed to seek relief from the relevant foreign legal restriction.[43] The following passages usefully summarise the position:[44]

"[76] In general, illegality under foreign law does not frustrate or otherwise relieve a party from performance of an English law contract: see e.g. *Canary Wharf (BP4) T1 Ltd v European Medicines Agency* [2019] EWHC 335 (Ch) at [187] per Marcus Smith J. 'the validity and enforceability of a contract governed by English law is not as a general rule affected by the question whether the contract would be regarded as valid or whether its performance would be lawful according to the law of another country.'

[77] The rule in *Ralli Bros. v Compania Naviera Sota y Aznar* [1920] 2 K.B. 287 operates as a limited exception to this general rule. It provides that an obligation under an English law contract is invalid and unenforceable, or suspended in the case of a payment obligation, insofar as the contract requires performance in a place where it is unlawful under the law of that required place of performance. (The rule in *Foster v Driscoll* [1929] 1 K.B. 470, 521,[45] which offers another exception, is agreed not to be relevant here)."

III.   PHYSICAL IMPOSSIBILITY

Destruction of property which was essential to the contract

17-018   Impossibility was the basis of one of the first exceptions to the rule of "absolute contracts" at common law, one later endorsed by statute.[46] The exception can be traced back to *Taylor v Caldwell*, where a contract to hire out a music hall and

---

41   [2022] EWCA Civ 1021; [2023] L. & T.R. 2 at [147], [158].
42   [2020] EWHC 2937 (Comm); [2021] 2 All E.R. (Comm) 590 at [75]–[83].
43   [2020] EWHC 2937 (Comm); [2021] 2 All E.R. (Comm) 590 at [104].
44   [2020] EWHC 2937 (Comm); [2021] 2 All E.R. (Comm) 590 at [75]–[83]; see also *Magdeev v Tsvetkov* [2020] EWHC 887 (Comm) (Cockerill J) and *Ridley v Dubai Islamic Bank PJSC* [2022] EWHC 1912 (Comm) at [63]–[69] (Lionel Persey Q.C.); and on these cases, H. Beale (ed), *Chitty on Contracts*, 34th edn (London: Sweet & Maxwell, 2021), paras 18-076, 18-076A and 26-027.
45   On which H. Beale (ed), *Chitty on Contracts*, 34th edn (London: Sweet & Maxwell, 2021), para.18-075A and see *Haddad v Rostamani* [2021] EWHC 1892 (Ch).
46   Sale of Goods Act 1979 s.6 provides that where there is a contract for the sale of specific goods and

gardens for an entertainment on a certain date was discharged because the hall had been destroyed by fire the day before.[47] The judge, Blackburn J, said that in contracts in which the performance:

"[D]epends on the continued existence of a given person or thing, a condition is implied that the impossibility of performance arising from the perishing of the person or thing shall excuse the performance."[48]

In each case courts ask: **17-019**

"[F]irst, what, having regard to all the circumstances, was the foundation of the contract? Secondly, was the performance of the contract prevented? Thirdly, was the event which prevented the performance of the contract of such a character that it cannot reasonably be said to have been in the contemplation of the parties at the date of the contract?"[49]

If so both parties are discharged. In *Taylor v Caldwell* the contract was discharged **17-020** on grounds of impossibility, even though the gardens around the hall were still available, in which the owners had agreed to put on side-shows. Why? Some would say that that conclusion was reached as a matter of impression. However, it was clear that to postpone the entertainment was theoretically possible as "an entertainment" but not as "this entertainment", the one contracted for, a question of construction. Thus, the main purpose of the contract could not be achieved.

An earlier case, *Appleby v Myers*,[50] concerned a contract to install machinery (a **17-021** steam engine) in the defendant's factory and to keep it in repair for two years. After part of the work had been done, the factory with all the machinery and materials in it was destroyed by an accidental fire. The work might have been completed if and when a new factory was built but nonetheless the Court of Exchequer Chamber was in no doubt that, absent any agreement about who should bear the risk of the event, both parties were excused from further performance of the contract. Blackburn J, giving the judgment of the court,[51] said that the "whole question depends upon the true construction of the contract". He continued:

"[T]he work which the plaintiffs agreed to perform could not be performed unless the defendant's premises continued in a fit state to enable the plaintiffs to perform the work on them."

However, the court:

"[did not] agree with them in thinking that there was an absolute promise or warranty by the defendant that the premises should at all events continue so fit. We think that where, as in the present case, the premises are destroyed without fault on either side, it is a

---

"goods without the knowledge of the seller have perished at the time when the contract is made, the contract is void". Section 7 provides that where "there is an agreement to sell specific goods and subsequently the goods, without any fault on the part of the seller or buyer, perish before the risk passes to the buyer, the agreement is avoided".

[47] (1863) 3 B. & S. 826; 122 E.R. 309.
[48] (1863) 3 B. & S. 826; 122 E.R. 309 at 839 per Blackburn J; see also E. Peel, *Frustration and Force Majeure*, 4th edn (London: Sweet & Maxwell, 2021), paras 2-030, 2-031, 4-022 and 4-023; Neil Andrews, *Contract Rules—Decoding English Law* (Cambridge: Intersentia Publishing, 2016), art.128.
[49] Vaughan Williams LJ (with whom Romer and Stirling LJJ agreed briefly) in *Krell v Henry* [1903] 2 K.B. 740 at 751;, having first referred to *Taylor v Caldwell*.
[50] (1866) L.R. 1 C.P. 615; (1867) L.R. 2 C.P. 651.
[51] (1866) L.R. 1 C.P. 615; (1867) L.R. 2 C.P. 651 at 658–659.

misfortune equally affecting both parties; excusing both from further performance of the contract, but giving a cause of action to neither."

17-022 As regards destruction of goods and contracts to sell goods, the rule depends on whether the goods are specific[52]—frustration if so. But if the goods are not specific ("unascertained" goods), the contract is not frustrated.[53] And so the seller must find similar goods.[54]

Commercial destruction

17-023 Goods may be destroyed not only by fire but also by water, as in *Asfar v Blundell*: dates (that is, fruits eaten mostly in the UK at Christmas) were (good) dates when shipped. Later they still looked like dates, but they had become bad even evil dates, and retained considerable value for distillation into spirit, but had been so impregnated with sewage (the frustrating event) and were in such a condition of fermentation, that they were, the court decided, no longer saleable as dates.[55]

17-024 In *Joseph Constantine SS Line Ltd v Imperial Smelting Corp Ltd*[56] a vessel, the *S.S. Kingswood*, suffered an explosion in an auxiliary boiler, while she was waiting for a berth. She remained afloat, but had been severely damaged. The consequent delay in rectifying the ship was such that the commercial object of the venture was "frustrated". Viscount Maugham observed that in such a case the "doctrine of frustration is only a special case of the discharge of contract by impossibility".[57] To get the vessel repaired and ready to load within the necessary time was impossible. The case might be better rationalised as an instance not of impossibility but as one of frustration of the commercial purpose by delay (see para.17-059 ff).

17-025 A contract may also be discharged where something essential has been not destroyed but has become unavailable, for example detained by hostilities or requisitioned by government in time of national need. Thus in *Bank Line Ltd v Arthur Capel & Co* a 12-month coal charter could not be performed because the relevant vessel had been requisitioned by the British Government, and frustration was declared by the court.[58]

17-026 But courts should not be too quick to treat non-destructive physical mishaps as frustrating events. For example, in *Nickoll & Knight v Ashton, Edridge & Co*,[59] the majority of the Court of Appeal surprisingly held that where a stipulated vessel had

---

[52] Goods identified and agreed upon at the time of the contract.

[53] E. Peel (ed), *Treitel, The Law of Contract* 15th edn (London: Sweet & Maxwell, 2020), para.19-014 which discusses possibilities. In the US, Posner (R.A. Posner, "Impossibility and Related Doctrines in Contract Law" (1977) 6 J. of Legal Studies 83 at 108 ff) refers to the Unform Commercial Code (US.) as having not much changed the common law, and to s.2-319 from which it appears that in 1977 at least the position in the US was similar to that in England.

[54] E. Peel, *Frustration and Force Majeure*, 4th edn (London: Sweet & Maxwell, 2021), Ch.3, pt.V ('Discharge and the Passing of Risk').

[55] [1896] 1 Q.B. 123 CA; thus, there was a total loss of the dates and shippers were discharged from their obligation to pay freight. Of the contrary argument, Lord Esher MR said, [1896] 1 Q.B. 123 at 127, that the "ingenuity of the argument might commend itself to a body of chemists, but not to business men".

[56] *Joseph Constantine SS Line Ltd v Imperial Smelting Corp Ltd* [1942] A.C. 154, HL.

[57] [1942] A.C. 154 at 168, HL.

[58] *Bank Line Ltd v Arthur Capel & Co* [1919] A.C. 435, HL, where, during the First World War, a 12-month coal charter could not be performed because the relevant vessel had been requisitioned by the British Government.

[59] [1901] 2 K.B. 126, CA.

not perished, but had been unavailable due to temporary running aground, the contract for sale of a cargo of cotton, for the supply of which the vessel was intended, was frustrated (the ship was proceeding to the port where the cargo would be loaded by the seller): A.L. Smith MR, Romer LJ: dissenting, Vaughan Williams LJ. This was a contract for the sale of cotton seed, the cargo to be delivered in Alexandria to the claimant buyer in January 1900 on the ship *The Orlando*. It was held that the contract was frustrated when that ship, for the relevant month, became stranded on a rock in the Baltic. This was a maritime casualty not attributable to either party's fault. And the majority considered that this risk was not borne by either party. The majority decision is unpersuasive both because (i) the time restriction and (ii) the vessel's identity should not have been regarded as commercially critical.

The dissentient in this case, Vaughan Williams LJ,[60] would have awarded damages to the claimant buyer for failure to deliver. He considered that the subsequent event had not absolutely undermined the contract, and the question of timing was a matter which could have been waived without destroying the essence of the contract. The dissenting judge had clearly cottoned on to the injustice of allowing the seller to wriggle free from contractual liability on the basis of a specification of the vessel, and a time provision, which the buyer would have been happy to waive, and which scarcely formed the kernel of the contract.

17-027

Personal destruction: death, incarceration and incapacity

A contract for the performance of personal services[61] by an individual who is party to the contract will be frustrated if, before completion, without his default, he or she dies, or is incapacitated by illness, or is otherwise physically unable to perform, including having become incarcerated, or becomes mentally incapable of acting. Whether less obvious degrees of infirmity, etc, create frustration is intensely "fact-dependent".[62]

17-028

In *Stubbs v The Holywell Railway Co* the death of the engineer especially employed to complete construction work on a specified railway "dissolved the contract".[63]

17-029

By contrast, in *Phillips v Alhambra Palace Co* a contract between the claimant performers and a three-person partnership, for performance at a theatre, was not frustrated when one of the three partners died. Lord Alverstone CJ said:[64]

17-030

"If in any particular case the contract is one which has relation to the personal conduct of the contracting party, then the death of that party puts an end to the contract; if, on the other hand, it has no such relation, the death of the contracting party has not that effect. In the present case I have come to the conclusion that the plaintiffs did not rely on the personnel of the partners, who were unknown to them. And under those circumstances I am of opinion that the liability contracted by the three partners can after the death of one of them be enforced against the two survivors."

---

[60] [1901] 2 K.B. 126 at 136–138, CA, per Vaughan Williams LJ.

[61] [1901] 1 Q.B. 59 (Queen's Bench Division, Lord Alverstone CJ and Kennedy J).

[62] E. Peel, *Frustration and Force Majeure*, 4th edn (London: Sweet & Maxwell, 2021), para.2-017–2-022 at 2-022 explaining the difficult finding in *Hall v Wright* (1858) El. Bl. & El. 765 at 793–794; 120 E.R. 695; D. Cabrelli, "Duration, Lawful Termination, and Frustration of the Employment Contract" in M. Freedland (ed), *The Contract of Employment* (Oxford: Oxford University Press, 2016), Ch.24.

[63] *Stubbs v The Holywell Railway Co* (1866-67) L.R. 2 Ex. 311 at 313 per Kelly CB.

[64] [1901] 1 Q.B. 58, 63–64.

17-031 In *Robinson v Davison* a contract by an eminent concert pianist to play at a particular concert on a particular day was discharged by her illness.[65] It was not impossible for her to play the piano but, had she done so, either it would have been a bad performance or bad for her health.[66] Noting that the contract contained no express term about incapacity, Bramwell B concluded that "the contract must in my judgment be taken to have been conditional and not absolute".[67] Similarly, in *Notcutt v Universal Equipment Co (London)*, a contract of employment was frustrated (at the latest) when the employee was medically diagnosed as no longer employable because of a recent heart attack.[68] The effect was that the contract had become discharged from that point onwards by operation of law, and the employer's giving of notice was otiose and irrelevant.

17-032 It was held in *Morgan v Manser* that a comedian's promise in 1938 to be available for performances over a period was discharged by the promisor's call-up (conscription having been introduced at the start of the Second World War) to the British Army in 1940.[69] But the comedian did not have to perform when he was released from the army in 1946 for his promise (and contract) had been discharged by his call-up (and perhaps he was no longer funny).

17-033 A sufficient period of imprisonment, or similar incarceration, will frustrate a contract or employment, or other undertaking requiring provision of personal services. In *Horlock v Beal* the House of Lords held that a contract of service had been frustrated when the ship on which the employees were serving was detained by Germans, at the outbreak of the First World War, and the men were later imprisoned by the enemy.[70] Lords Atkinson, Shaw, and Wrenbury considered that the moment of frustration was the detention of the ship. Earl Loreburn was prepared to wait until November, a few months later, when the men were taken from the ship (which had been under arrest) and removed to imprisonment. Lord Parmour dissented, taking the view these events outside the scope of the frustration rule. And in *Harrington v Kent County Council* a sentence of 12 months' imprisonment imposed on a schoolmaster convicted of indecency was held to have frustrated his contract of employment.[71]

17-034 However, in *FC Shepherd (FC) & Co Ltd v Jerrom*[72] the Court of Appeal rejected an apprentice's contention that frustration had not terminated his contract by reason of his having been sentenced to a period of imprisonment. This was a tactical attempt to argue that the apprentice had been unfairly dismissed, rather than that the contract had been frustrated. The apprentice's submission was unsuccessful because it would involve his own reliance on his own admitted "self-induced frustration", that is, he would be seeking to put forward his own criminal conduct as the means of defeating termination for frustration, and so his strategy was devoid of merit. In

---

[65] *Robinson v Davison* (1871) L.R. 6 Ex. 269: the contract was to play and also to find a "vocalist" to perform with her; all agreed that the contract was discharged; this rule was applied to the mental illness of a (pop music) drummer in *Condor v The Barron Knights Ltd* [1966] 1 W.L.R. 87; E. Peel, *Frustration and Force Majeure*, 4th edn (London: Sweet & Maxwell, 2021), para.4-028. As regards the incapacity of corporations see the Companies Act 2006 and Treitel, ibid, para.4-033 ff.

[66] *Condor v The Barron Knights Ltd* [1966] 1 W.L.R. 87 (on the facts of this case see fn.66 below).

[67] *Robinson v Davidson* (1871) L.R. 6 Ex. 269 at 278. The illness may only have lasted for a few days: e.g. *Poussard v Spiers* (1876) 1 Q.B.D. 410.

[68] [1986] 1 W.L.R. 641, CA.

[69] *Morgan v Manser* [1948] 1 K.B. 184. Cf. *Nordman v Rayner & Sturgess* (1916) 33 T.L.R. 87.

[70] [1916] 1 A.C. 486, HL.

[71] [1980] I.R.L.R. 353.

[72] [1987] Q.B. 301, CA.

FC Shepherd (FC) & Co Ltd v Jerrom, as Lawton LJ explained, Jerrom's four-year apprenticeship had begun in June 1980.[73] Thereafter he became involved in an organised out-of-work "punch up" with a rival gang. In June 1981 he was convicted of assault and affray, was likely to serve 39 weeks of incarceration in a Borstal (a youth prison).

In *FC Shepherd (FC) & Co Ltd v Jerrom* Mustill LJ concluded that frustration   **17-035**
had occurred on these facts:[74]

> "Here there was a contract for a period of four years...By the time his sentence was imposed there remained rather more than half this period still to run. The sentence was indeterminate...His training would inevitably suffer really substantial disruption, as would the timetable of the employers, who had planned to train him up to replace one of their full-time plumbers who was due to retire. If this were a commercial contract, of the type from which many of the reported decisions on frustration have sprung, it would be debatable whether an interruption of this duration would be enough to frustrate the object of the adventure. But an apprenticeship is a long way from a charterparty, and I conclude that in the special circumstances of this case the likely interruption was sufficient to discharge the employers from any further obligation, from the moment when the sentence of Borstal training was imposed."

In *Higgins & Co Lawyers Ltd v Evans*[75] Saini J upheld a solicitor firm's claim,   **17-036**
deciding (amongst other things) that the clause validly imposed liability to pay the lawyers for their work in the event of the client's death, the contract providing expressly that the contract was terminated on death. In other words, no issue of frustration arose. Instead the contract's express provision concerning the impact of the client's death prevailed.

A person's supervening mental capacity might cause the contract to become   **17-037**
frustrated.[76] For example, a professor whose madness progresses from sporadic and partial to permanent and total will (probably) be incapable of teaching and this will cause the contract to be frustrated, unless the particular office carries no teaching responsibility and is solely research-based. Even then it will be a question of fact whether the form of insanity impedes or prevents satisfactory research activity.

But in *Blankley v Central Manchester Children's University Hospitals NHS*   **17-038**
Trust[77] the Court of Appeal held that a conditional fee agreement[78] is not frustrated if the client had become incapable of giving personal instructions because, since commencement of the lawyer–client relationship, the client had ceased to have

---

73   [1987] Q.B. 301 at 312–313, CA, per Lawton LJ.
74   [2987] Q.B. 301 at 329, CA.
75   [2019] EWHC 2809 (QB); [2020] 1 W.L.R. 2809.
76   *Condor v The Barron Knights Ltd* [1966] 1 W.L.R. 87, 91: a 16-year-old drummer, required to work seven days a week, for a band, collapsed in a manner which seems to have straddled physical and mental breakdown (he had been living in a caravan; the winter of 1961–1962 was severed, and he had become malnourished); he was taken to a mental hospital for a short time; his manager was told by the medical authorities that the drummer could henceforth work only for a maximum of four nights a week; the band decided that could not keep him on such new terms. Thompson J held that the contract had become frustrated and had terminated by operation of law, and thus there had been no wrongful dismissal: "on February 1, 1963, the situation was that the plaintiff was not fit to perform his part of the contract and at that date there was no reasonable likelihood that he would in the near future become so able. [And so] by reason of the impact upon his health and well-being of his life, far too strenuous and exhausting for a boy of 16, talented though he was and ambitious though he was, the impact was such...that [the pressure and hard work] had in a business sense made it impossible for him to continue to perform or for the defendants have him perform the terms of the [seven day a week] contract as a member of their group."
77   [2015] EWCA Civ 18; [2015] 1 W.L.R. 4307 at [38].

mental capacity. Even after the client's mental collapse, a representative of the client might still have given instructions to the lawyer.

Contemplated route now impossible

17-039   If a contract specifies the mode of contract performance, such as the ship on which goods are to be consigned,[79] or the route that the ship is to take, and the specified mode becomes impossible,[80] performance in accordance with the terms of the contract will have ceased to be possible. The contract *might* be discharged—but only if the specified mode is fundamental to the particular contract. The fact that "some minor aspect of performance" such as delivery in Portugal for weighing rather than a neighbouring country "becomes impossible does not necessarily frustrate the contract".[81]

Partial frustration: severable units

17-040   Some contracts comprise severable parts, and frustration of one or more parts leaves the remaining in operation.[82] So, in the soya bean meal cases, where the US export restrictions applied to, say, 60 per cent of the soya bean meal sold under a given contract, the prohibition did not affect the seller's liability to deliver the 40 per cent which could lawfully be delivered. The outcome was similar in the case before the court.[83]

17-041   In the *Iran Shipping Lines* case[84] Beatson J used the soya bean meal cases as illustrations of the principle that the liability to perform the part of a contract which is still lawful may remain even though other parts of the contract have been prohibited. This will be so where:

"the part which remains lawful would make as much commercial sense as performance of the whole, and in which performance of the part which remains lawful is in no way dependent on the other part, the performance of which has been prohibited."[85]

17-042   Partial frustration (pleaded on the basis of an alleged implied term, or on the basis of failure of basis) was held not to apply on the facts of *Bank of New York Mellon*

---

[78]   On which *Andrews on Civil Processes*, 2nd edn (Cambridge: Intersentia Publishing, 2019), para.20-11 ff.

[79]   *Nickoll & Knight v Ashton Edridge & Co* [1901] 2 K.B. 126 CA.

[80]   In *Re L Sutro* [1917] 2 K.B. 348 CA: since the contract of *sale* clearly contemplated carriage by sea from the loading port to the ultimate port of discharge it could not be performed by carriage partly by sea and partly by rail, though the arbitrators had found that that method of transport had become a usage in the trade. However, the decision was doubted in *Tsakiroglou & Co Ltd v Noblee Thorl GmbH* [1962] A.C. 93, HL at 113 by Viscount Simonds at 127 by Lord Hodson at 133 by Lord Guest.

[81]   *Congimex SARL v Tradax Export SA* [1983] 1 Lloyd's Rep. 250 at 253 per Donaldson LJ concerning a contract of sale c.i.f.

[82]   E. Peel, *Frustration and Force Majeure*, 4th edn (London: Sweet & Maxwell, 2021), 5-06 to 5-08.

[83]   [2010] EWHC 2661 (Comm); [2011] 2 All E.R. (Comm) 609; [2011] Lloyd's Rep. IR 145 at [126]; and see, ibid at [128].

[84]   *Islamic Republic of Iran Shipping Lines v Steamship Mutual Assn (Bermuda) Ltd* [2010] EWHC 2661 (Comm); [2011] 2 All E.R. (Comm) 609.

[85]   [2010] EWHC 2661 (Comm); [2011] 2 All E.R. (Comm) 609 at [123] while recognising that the soya bean meal cases "turned on the operation of express provisions in the contract dealing with prohibitions of export or force majeure": the *Islamic Insurance* case is considered at E. Peel, *Frustration and Force Majeure*, 4th edn (London: Sweet & Maxwell, 2021), para.8-050.

(International) Ltd v Cine-UK Ltd[86] (see para.17-016). Tenants unsuccessfully contended that Covid statutory restrictions, which had closed cinemas for many months, provided a defence to a claim for rent for that period, The suggested defence could not be reconciled with the restricted scope of each "cesser of rent" clause, which was restricted to physical damage to the property. It was not legitimate to re-write that clause under the guise of the law of implied terms or "failure of basis".

Suez crisis 1956

Many disputes arose out of the closure of the Suez Canal in November 1956. In the twentieth century, shipping from Europe to India and beyond contemplated passage through the Suez Canal. But the general c.i.f. practice of that era was not to specify a route at the time of contract but to follow the route usual at the time of due performance. When the canal was blocked in 1956, such contracts could only be performed via the Cape of Good Hope, that is, via the coast of South Africa. This route was relatively long and twice the cost but the practice was held to be applicable by the House of Lords in *Tsakiroglou*.[87] Further, if the Suez route had been specified, the blocking of the Canal would only have discharged the contract "if the route was of fundamental importance", which was not so in the instant case.[88] In other circumstances, said Lord Reid,[89] the nature of the voyage might have affected the buyers: **17-043**

> "There might be cases where damage to the goods was a likely result of the longer voyage which twice crossed the Equator, or perhaps the buyer could be prejudiced by the fact that the normal duration of the voyage via Suez was about three weeks whereas the normal duration via the Cape was about seven weeks. But there is no suggestion in the case that the longer voyage could damage the groundnuts or that the delay could have caused loss to *these* buyers of which they could complain."

Time in this case was plainly elastic. Not only did the sellers have the option of choosing any date within a two-month period for shipment, but also there was a wide margin within which there might be variations of the speed capacity of the vessel selected. There was no stipulated date for arrival at Hamburg; no suggestion that the Cape route would be prejudicial to the condition of the goods or would involve their being specially packed; nor does there seem to have been any seasonal market to be considered.   **17-044**

Indeed Viscount Simonds recalled the traditional view, that: **17-045**

---

[86] [2022] EWCA Civ 1021; [2023] L. & T.R. 2 at [55], [138] and [139] (Flaux C, with the agreement of Snowden LJ and Sir Nicholas Patten), applying Carr LJ's summary of the rules governing terms implied in fact, in *Yoo Design Services Ltd v Iliv Realty PTE Ltd* [2021] EWCA Civ 560 at [51]. The *Mellon* case is noted by A. Sahore [2022] C.LJ. 497–490.

[87] *Tsakiroglou & Co Ltd v Noblee Thorl Gmbh* [1962] A.C. 93, HL: shipment from Port Sudan east of the Suez Canal to Hamburg in Germany; see also *Ocean Tramp Tankers Corp v V/O Sovfracht ("The Eugenia")* [1964] 2 Q.B. 226, CA (the latter case was a time charter for a voyage to India via the Black Sea from Genoa; the difference over the whole voyage of a Cape of Good Hope route was not so radical as to produce frustration; a voyage via the Cape would have taken 138 days as against 108 days via Suez; the actual voyage round the Cape made no great difference except that it took a good deal longer and was more expensive for the charterers.

[88] E. Peel, *Frustration and Force Majeure*, 4th edn (London: Sweet & Maxwell, 2021), para.4-103–4-114.

[89] *Tsakiroglou & Co Ltd v Noblee Thorl GmbH* [1962] A.C. 93 at 118, HL per Lord Reid; 115 per Viscount Simonds.

"it does not automatically follow that, because one term of a contract, for example, that the goods shall be carried by a particular route, becomes impossible of performance, the whole contract is thereby abrogated".[90]

As Lord Radcliffe pointed out, having ascertained "the commercial nature or purpose of the adventure", the court had to identify:

"the essential terms which, so far as not expressed, must be implied in order to make the contract efficacious as a business instrument".[91]

17-046   What occurred in Egypt in 1956 was a small armed conflict which affected the contemplated mode of performance.[92] Contrast the Second World War, which gave rise to the litigation in the *Fibrosa* case.[93] In this case the defendants, Leeds manufacturers of textile machinery, agreed in July 1939, to manufacture for the plaintiffs two machines, delivery c.i.f. Gdynia (Poland). A prepayment was made in July, the balance being payable in due course against shipping documents. On 1 September 1939 Germany invaded Poland. The Court of Appeal held that, having regard to the Trading with the Enemy Act 1939, performance of the contract by delivery in Gdynia would have been unlawful. And so the contract had been frustrated (the House of Lords did not disturb this finding of frustration, but the House of Lords instead reversed the Court of Appeal's decision on the failure of consideration issue, see para.18-003 ff).[94]

17-047   In the Court of Appeal, MacKinnon LJ considered the plaintiffs' contention that, although the defendants could not perform the contract according to the agreed terms, they could nonetheless effect delivery of the machines to the plaintiffs in a different manner, either by shipment to Riga (Latvia), or delivery in Leeds (Yorkshire, England).

17-048   Rejecting the contention, MacKinnon LJ said that this was "a quite impossible proposition ... so completely unfounded that it is not worth discussion at any length".[95] He added:

"[T]he rigour of the obligations of such a contract is well settled. If a man sells c.i.f. June shipment, and he tenders a bill of lading dated in July, the buyer can treat the contract as broken, and it is in vain for the seller to say that the goods are just as good as they would be if shipped a week earlier. Conversely, if an embargo or prohibition prevented shipment abroad, the buyer could not possibly say: 'You can buy these goods in this country, and deliver them to me here', and, 'if you do not, I can claim damages'."

17-049   As to risk, in a leading case a court in the US considered it more reasonable to

---

90   *Tsakiroglou & Co Ltd v Noblee Thorl GmbH* [1962] A.C. 93 at 112.
91   *Tsakiroglou & Co Ltd v Noblee Thorl GmbH* [1962] A.C. 93 at 122, HL.
92   E. Peel, *Frustration and Force Majeure*, 4th edn (London: Sweet & Maxwell, 2021), paras 4-103–4-114; but nonetheless one which "gave rise to voluminous litigation": R.A. Posner, "Impossibility and Related Doctrines in Contract Law" (1977) 6 Jo. of Legal Studies 83, 103.
93   *Fibrosa Spolka Akcyjna v Fairbairn Lawson Combe Barbour Ltd* [1942] 1 K.B. 12; reversed on other grounds, viz., whether the buyers could recover the prepayment: [1943] A.C. 32; Neil Andrews, *Contract Rules—Decoding English Law* (Cambridge: Intersentia Publishing, 2016), art.196.
94   Notwithstanding cl.7 of the conditions of sale, since that clause must be construed as providing for an extension of time only when war had produced a minor delay and the war in this case was not of that character.
95   [1942] 1 K.B. 12 at 27 (the Court of Appeal decision concerning supervening illegality and frustration was not disturbed on appeal; but the refusal to recognise total failure of consideration in this context was reversed, *Chandler v Webster* [1904] 1 K.B. 493, CA, being overruled by the HL in the *Fibrosa* case at [1943] A.C. 32).

expect affected shipowners "to insure against the hazards of war. They are in the best position to calculate the cost of performance by alternative routes".[96] Posner comments that the shipowner

"is the superior risk bearer because he is better able to estimate the magnitude of the loss (a function of delay, and of the value and nature of the cargo …) and the probability of the unexpected event".

Total failure of supply

The parties to an executory contract are sometimes faced with a turn of events which they did not anticipate at all such as: **17-050**

"[A] wholly abnormal rise or fall in prices, a sudden depreciation of currency, an unexpected obstacle to execution, or the like. Yet this does not in itself affect the bargain they have made."[97]

Nor did it affect the bargain in the case in which this was said, where a wartime government restricted the supply of film material needed to make newsreels. As regards goods, in *The "Mary Nour"* Moore-Bick LJ said:[98]

"[it is] clear that, in the absence of some exceptional supervening event, such a contract will not be frustrated simply by a failure on the part of the ultimate supplier to make goods available for delivery. [The seller] takes the risk of his supplier's failure to perform."

The same rule may apply even where the supplier is the sole supplier. A leading case is *Intertradex SA v Lesieur-To(urteaux SARL Intertradex*,[99] where delivery c.i.f. of Mali processed groundnuts was prevented by manufacturing and transport interruptions in Mali (the capital of the Maldives, in the Indian Ocean). Lord Denning MR[100] pointed out that such "events are commonplace in the world of affairs". So, "if a party desires to avoid such consequences, he must insert a stipulation to excuse him. He cannot avoid them by a plea of frustration". Such risks are for the CIF seller; however, such contracts can also be performed in theory by the seller's obtaining goods afloat, i.e. processed groundnuts which had left Mali before the **17-051**

---

[96] *Transatlantic Financing Corp v United States* 363 F 2d. 312 at 319 (DC Cir., 1966), discussed by R.A. Posner, "Impossibility and Related Doctrines in Contract Law" (1977) 6 Jo. of Legal Studies 83, 103-104.

[97] *British Movietonews Ltd v London and District Cinemas Ltd* [1952] A.C. 166 HL at 185 per Viscount Simon, with whom Lord Simonds (at 186) Lord Morton (at 188) and Lord Tucker (at 188) agreed.

[98] *CTI Group Inc v Transclear SA (The "Mary Nour")* [2008] EWCA Civ 856, [2008] 2 Lloyd's Rep. 526 at [23], per Moore-Bick LJ; see also *Blackburn Bobbin Co Ltd v TW Allen & Sons Ltd* [1918] 2 K.B. 467 CA.

[99] [1978] 2 Lloyd's Rep. 509 CA. A leading judgment of an earlier generation is that of Pearson J in *Lewis Emmanuel v Sammut* [1959] 2 Lloyd's Rep. 629 at 640; he referred to *Blackburn Bobbin Co Ltd v TW Allen & Sons Ltd* [1918] 2 K.B. 467 CA, to *Ashmore & Son v CS Cox & Co* [1899] 1 Q.B. 436 and to *WT Sargant & Sons v Eric Paterson & Co* (1923) 15 Lloyd's Rep. 20; (1923) 129 L.T. 471. Having discussed these cases Pearson J said (at 640): "it may well be that, in view of the nature of these contracts, it would be more difficult to find a frustrating event than it would in the case of some other contracts for specifically ascertained goods and so on. But, to my mind, exactly the same principle of frustration applies; it is only that there may be greater difficulty in showing it in cases of that character."

[100] [1978] 2 Lloyd's Rep. 509 at 514 per Lord Denning, 515 per Goff LJ, and 518 per Cumming-Bruce LJ. Cf. *In Re Badische Co Ltd* [1921] 2 Ch. 331 at 379, (Russell J), on that case E. Peel, *Frustration and Force Majeure*, 4th edn (London: Sweet & Maxwell, 2021), para.4-083.

interruptions took effect. Why, asked Pickford LJ in the *Blackburn Bobbin* case:[101]

"should a purchaser of goods, not specific goods, be deemed to concern himself with the way in which the seller is going to fulfil his contract by providing the goods he has agreed to sell?"

17-052   But the contract might be frustrated if the contract specifies a source. *Howell v Coupland*[102] concerned a contract to sell 200 tons of "regent" potatoes grown on (specified) land in Lincolnshire belonging to the defendant. The land usually produced far more than 200 tons. But disease attacked the crop. The result was that the defendant could deliver only 80 tons. It was held that the contract had been discharged because it had become impossible for the seller to perform the contract, which Lord Coleridge CJ construed as dependent on that quantity of potatoes being produced:[103]

"[B]y the simple and obvious construction of the agreement both parties understood and agreed, that there should be a condition implied that before the time for the performance of the contract the potatoes should be, or should have been, in existence, and should still be existing when the time came for the performance."[104]

17-053   The leading case on supply contracts is *"The Mary Nour"*,[105] where the Court of Appeal held that the contract had not been frustrated.[106] A f.o.b. contract for cement was not performed because the sellers' suppliers could not obtain the cement.[107] Moore-Bick LJ observed[108] that at one end of the scale there are cases:

"[I]n which the question is essentially one of fact and degree, calling for the evaluation of a range of factors which a commercial tribunal is particularly well equipped to undertake. At the other there are cases which call for the application of established principles to a clearly defined event rendering performance impossible. Such cases give rise to a clear-cut issue of law."

---

[101] *Blackburn Bobbin Co Ltd v TW Allen & Sons Ltd* [1918] 2 K.B. 467 CA.

[102] (1876) L.R. 1 Q.B.D. 258. Likewise a sale of "New South Wales wheat" where the crop failed without fault on the part of the seller: *Gelling v Crispin* (1917) 23 C.L.R. 443.

[103] (1876) L.R. 1 Q.B.D. 258 at 261 per Lord Coleridge CJ, with whom at 262, James and Mellish LJJ agreed, applying *Taylor v Caldwell* (1863) 3 B. & S. 826 and *Appleby v Myers* (1867) L.R. 2 C.P. 651.

[104] (1876) L.R. 1 Q.B.D. 258 at 261 per Lord Coleridge CJ, who added: "It was not an absolute contract of delivery under all circumstances, but a contract to deliver so many potatoes, of a particular kind, grown on a specific place, if deliverable from that place." At 262, Mellish LJ said: "No doubt there is a distinction in the present case, that the potatoes, the things contracted for, were not in existence at the time the contract was entered into. But can that make any real difference in principle?"

[105] *CTI Group Inc v Transclear SA ("The Mary Nour")* [2008] EWCA Civ 856; [2009] 2 All E.R. (Comm) 25.

[106] The failure of a source mutually contemplated but unmentioned in the contract leading to contract frustration, apparently contrary to the *Blackburn Bobbin* case (above), has been said to be supported by *Re Badische Co Ltd* [1921] 2 Ch.331; but, as has been pointed out, E. Peel (ed), *Treitel, The Law of Contract* 15th edn (London: Sweet & Maxwell, 2020), para.19-028 and E. Peel, *Frustration and Force Majeure*, 4th edn (London: Sweet & Maxwell, 2021), para.4-083, that case is one of illegal performance, and hence distinguishable.

[107] In fact the buyers attempted to break a cartel in Mexico: *CTI Group Inc v Transclear SA ("The Mary Nour")* [2008] EWCA Civ 856; [2009] 2 All E.R. (Comm) 25 at [12] per Moore-Bick LJ, who said "it is important, in my view, to recognise that the root cause of the sellers' inability to deliver the goods they had contracted to sell was the abuse by Cemex of its commercial position combined with the willingness of suppliers to acquiesce in its demands".

[108] With whom the other members of the CA concurred *CTI Group Inc v Transclear SA ("The Mary Nour")* [2008] EWCA Civ 856; [2009] 2 All E.R. (Comm) 25 at [29] and [30].

The case before them was towards the latter end of the scale, "requiring little **17-054** more than the application of established principles to the particular facts of the case".[109] Moore-Bick LJ reaffirmed that mostly frustration depends:

"[O]n the true construction of the terms which are in the contract read in light of the nature of the contract and of the relevant surrounding circumstances when the contract was made."

There is no need to consider how "reasonable men in their shoes would have dealt with the new situation if they had foreseen it".[110]

Moore-Bick LJ then approved[111] various cases raising supply problems, includ- **17-055** ing, first, *Blackburn Bobbin Co Ltd v TW Allen & Sons Ltd*[112] where "the seller took the risk of being able to obtain the goods needed to perform his contract"; and, secondly, Moore-Bick LJ referred to *Intertradex v Lesieur-Tourteaux SARL*,[113] as authority for the proposition that, "in the absence of a term to the contrary, the seller takes the risk of disruption resulting from commonplace occurrences" such as "breakdown of the machinery at the supplier's factory". Moore-Bick LJ concluded that the previous cases:

"make it clear that, in the absence of some exceptional supervening event, such a contract will not be frustrated simply by a failure on the part of the ultimate supplier to make goods available for delivery. The reason for that is not far to seek: it is implicit in a contract of this kind that the seller will either supply the goods himself or (more likely) will make arrangements, directly or indirectly, for the goods to be supplied by others. In other words, he undertakes a personal obligation to procure the delivery of contractual goods and thereby takes the risk of his supplier's failure to perform."[114]

Contemplated mode impossible: partial failure of supply

If a seller can obtain part of what has been promised but no more, usually the **17-056** position is no different, and thus the seller becomes liable for default. Here the position is straightforward: where a seller delivers to a buyer "a quantity of goods less than he contracted to sell, the buyer may reject them".[115] Nor does the position differ where a seller has multiple purchasers but not enough to go around. If a seller has enough for buyers A and B, but not C as well, and supplies only A and B, the seller is liable for failure to perform the contract with C.

Huan Gunn & Co Ltd v R Jumabhoy & Sons[116] concerned a contract between **17-057** merchants in Singapore. Party J contracted to sell to HG 50 tons of second-grade Zanzibar cloves, December shipment, "subject to force majeure and shipment". J did have enough cloves to fulfil the contract with HG, but not sufficient to meet all

---

109 [2008] EWCA Civ 856; [2009] 2 All E.R. (Comm) 25 at [11], with reference to *Pioneer Shipping Ltd v BTP Tioxide Ltd ("The Nema") (No.2)* [1982] A.C. 724.
110 [2008] EWCA Civ 856; [2009] 2 All E.R. (Comm) 25 at [13]. Cf. the observations of Rix LJ in *"The Sea Angel"* [2007] EWCA Civ 547; [2007] 1 C.L.C. 876 at [111].
111 [2008] EWCA Civ 856; [2009] 2 All E.R. (Comm) 25 at [16] ff.
112 [1918] 2 K.B. 467.
113 [1978] 2 Lloyd's Rep. 509, CA.
114 [2008] EWCA Civ 856; [2009] 2 All E.R. (Comm) 25 at [23], noting *Co-operative Suisse des Cereales et Matieres Fourrageres v La Plata Cereal Co SA* (1946) 80 Lloyd's Rep. 530 and *Lewis Emanuel & Son Ltd v Sammut* [1959] 2 Lloyd's Rep. 629.
115 Sale of Goods Act 1979 s.30(1) which continues: "but if the buyer accepts the goods so delivered he must pay for them at the contract rate".
116 [1960] A.C. 684, PC.

their commitments to other buyers. J allocated the cloves among the latter, and purported to cancel their contract with HG on the basis that their contract was made "subject to shipment". The Privy Council held that, as a matter of construction,[117] the wording did not excuse J. That party could not be allowed to excuse their non-performance by reference to their other commitments. Accordingly, J were liable to HG in damages. The contract "was simply a contract for the sale by the respondents of cloves of the quantity and description set out in the contract". J had failed to fulfil their obligations.[118] Theirs was the risk of supply failure. As Lord Morris explained:

> "[J were in the market as] importers and stockists and their necessity was to secure that they arranged for sufficient goods to be shipped to themselves in Singapore, so that they could then meet all their obligations in Singapore."[119]

J's shipping arrangements were of no concern of HG. Furthermore, the contract contained no stipulation relating to the problem of other customer orders.[120]

17-058 Where a contract of sale specifies a source and that source fails, the contract can be frustrated.[121] Where the contract does not specify a source, the contract is not normally frustrated by failure of the source which the seller happened to have in mind.[122] Here the seller takes the risk of unavailability.[123]

17-059 There is little direct authority on the issue of a contract which does not specify the source, but where a failure occurs of the source which both parties had in mind but had not specified, perhaps because it was so obviously the unique source.[124] Nowadays courts will admit extrinsic evidence of factual matrix, which might enable the court to receive evidence of usual practice.[125]

17-060 Where the source is obvious but the "failure" (the problem) is that there is "not

---

[117] *Hong Guan & Co Ltd v R Jumabhoy & Sons* [1960] A.C. 684, PC at 700 per Lord Morris, who approved *Pool Shipping Co Ltd v London Coal Co of Gibraltar Ltd* (1939) 63 Lloyd's Rep. 268; the latter was a test action concerning the supply of coal for ships, in which Branson J upheld as effective to discharge the contract the following clause: "In the event of any cause or circumstance beyond the control of the sellers and/or suppliers of whatsoever description and wheresoever occurring...which prevents the supply, shipment, carriage or delivery of all or any one or more of the descriptions of coal herein contracted for ... sellers or suppliers shall be entitled to relief from all obligations under this contract during the continuance of any such causes or circumstances...".

[118] See [1960] A.C. 684 at 702 per Lord Morris.

[119] See [1960] A.C. 684 at 702 per Lord Morris.

[120] See [1960] A.C. 684 at 702 per Lord Morris.

[121] e.g. a particular crop of potatoes: *Howell v Coupland* (1876) 1 Q.B.D 258; or of wheat: *Ockerby & Co Ltd v Murdock* (1916) 22 C.L.R. 420; E. Peel, *Frustration and Force Majeure*, 4th edn (London: Sweet & Maxwell, 2021), Ch.4, Pt V(2).

[122] *Blackburn Bobbin Co Ltd v Allen Ltd* [1918] 2 K.B. 467: "Finland birch timber"; *Gelling v Crispin* (1917) 23 C.L.R. 443: "New South Wales wheat" which could have been bought elsewhere; except where there has been a "string" of such sales c.i.f.: *Bremer Handels GmbH v Vanden Avenne-Izigem PVBA* [1978] 2 Lloyd's Rep. 109 at 115, 125, HL; or the point is regulated by "force majeure" clauses: see para.16-044 ff.

[123] *Intertradex SA v Lesieur Torteaux SARL* [1978] 2 Lloyd's Rep. 509 CA: Mali groundnuts, which in fact could not have been bought elsewhere.

[124] E. Peel, *Frustration and Force Majeure*, 4th edn (London: Sweet & Maxwell, 2021), para.4-080; E. Peel (ed), *Treitel, The Law of Contract*, 15th edn (London: Sweet & Maxwell, 2020), para.19-027.

[125] *Investors Compensation Scheme Ltd v West Bromwich BS* [1998] 1 W.L.R. 896 at 912, HL, per Lord Hoffmann; *BCCI v Ali* [2001] UKHL 8; [2002] 1 A.C. 251; in the context of standard forms of contract, Lord Bingham said in *Dairy Containers v Tasman Orient Line* [2004] UKPC 22; [2004] 2 Lloyd's Rep. 647 at [12]: "There may reasonably be attributed to the parties to a contract such as this such general commercial knowledge as a party to such a transaction would ordinarily be

enough to go round" and the seller must choose which customer gets all (or most) of it, arguably the failure is one of "self-induced frustration" on the part of the seller and not a case of impossibility leading to contract termination.[126] Alternatively, the outcome might be pro rata distribution, but this involves effectively rewriting the contract, which the courts cannot do (of course, a pro rata solution might be available if a force majeure clause so permits or requires).[127]

Money is a commodity that is deemed unlimited, and so a buyer's post-formation inability to pay (that is, to effect a positive and successful and complete credit in favour of the seller or of a third party nominated by the seller) will not count as frustration: payment is always possible.[128] In other words, if a buyer's supply of money fails, that is the buyer's "problem" and no excuse for the buyer's non-performance. This proposition is affirmed and applied in the *Gemcorp* case (2018),[129] in which a buyer unsuccessfully (optimistically and audaciously) pleaded as a defence to non-payment both frustration and a force majeure clause. Neither defence succeeded and the case is conveniently examined in one place at para.16-046 ff. **17-061**

IV. FRUSTRATING DELAY

Delay, provided it is not attributable to the relevant party's default, might cause the relevant contract to be frustrated but only if (i) the delay was so great that the parties' assumptions at the time of formation have been radically altered and (ii) the risk of such an alteration is not allocated to one of the parties. There was no frustrating delay on the facts of *Davis Contractors Ltd v Fareham U.D.C.* (see also para.17-064),[130] nor in *"The Sea Angel"* (on this case see also paras 17-007–17-009, 17-065–17-069, 17-089),[131] nor in *Ocean Tramp Tankers Corporation v V/O Sovfracht ("The Eugenia")* (on this case see also paras 16-015, 16-016, 16-024).[132] **17-062**

Much depends on the degree of impediment posed by the unexpected event, and as regards delay, the degree of delay, its duration. The likely duration of the impediment is an issue whether contract performance is due shortly or has already begun.[133] **17-063**

---

expected to have, but with a printed form of contract, negotiable by one holder to another, no inference may be drawn as to the knowledge or intention of any particular party. The contract should be given the meaning it would convey to a reasonable person having all the background knowledge which is reasonably available to the person or class of persons to whom the document is addressed." See generally, M. Clarke, *The Law of Insurance Contracts* (London: Informa Publishing, 2016), 15-3B.

126 On self-induced frustration involving "choice", para.16-029 ff.

127 E. Peel (ed), *Treitel, The Law of Contract* 15th edn (London: Sweet & Maxwell, 2020), para.19-030 (sub-paragraph commencing "A fourth view..."). See also "supplier of choice" arrangements, considered in *Jayam NV v Diamond Trading Co Ltd* [2007] EWCA Civ 1360. Force majeure clauses are discussed at para.16-044 ff.

128 E. Peel, *Frustration and Force Majeure*, 4th edn (London: Sweet & Maxwell, 2021), para.4-088, citing *Universal Corp v Five Ways Properties* [1979] 1 All E.R. 552.

129 *Gemcorp Commodoties Trading SA v Zeefacto Oil & Gas Co* [2018] EWHC 3938 (Comm).

130 [1956] A.C. 696, HL.

131 *Edwinton Commercial Corp v Tsavliris Russ Ltd ("The Sea Angel")* [2007] EWCA Civ 547; [2007] 1 C.L.C. 876.

132 [1964] 2 Q.B. 226, CA.

133 J.E. Stannard, *Delay in the Performance of Contractual Obligations*, 2nd edn (Oxford: Oxford University Press, 2018), para.12-074 ff.

17-064   In *National Carriers Ltd v Panalpina Ltd*[134] a warehouse lease for 10 years was not frustrated (after roughly five and a half years) by closure of the sole access road for 20 months (the House of Lords made clear in that case, however, that in principle a lease can be frustrated).

17-065   Similarly, in *Cricklewood Property and Investment Trust Ltd v Leighton's Investment Trust Ltd*,[135] (temporary) wartime restrictions on building were held not to have frustrated a 99-year building lease, which began in 1936. There would be plenty of time for the project after the war (the House of Lords gave judgment on 25 January 1945, and the war ended in Europe on 8 May 1945, and in the Pacific on 2 September 1945 (Japan having surrendered in mid-August). The lease required the tenant to pay rent on relevant sites after planning permission had been obtained; but the duty on the tenant to build would be suspended if there were restrictions imposed by Government; the duty to pay rent was independent of the construction of shops and dwellings on the various sites. On such facts the House of Lords concluded that even if frustration could apply to a lease, the duty to pay rent was unaffected by the wartime restrictions on building works.

17-066   The relevant time for decision is when the unexpected event occurs.[136] The question has been formulated as follows: "what estimate would a reasonable man of business take of the probable length" of the event;[137] or was the party affected still bound to perform or not, although in practice the parties will "wait and see", not to the "bitter end" but "long enough to make a reasonable prognosis".[138] In this process an important factor is the ratio of delay to the duration of promised performance, referred to as the "deprivation/unexpiration principle",[139] something important in both the *Panalpina* and *Cricklewood* cases (see preceding paragraphs).[140]

17-067   In *Davis Contractors v Fareham U.D.C.* (on this case see also paras 16-002 and 17-002)[141] no radical frustrating difference had arisen on the facts of that building contract case merely because a skilled labour shortage had caused a 14-month delay and 25 per cent increased expense in the completion of the work. Lord Reid was clear that delay on these facts fell well short of constituting a frustrating event.[142] So too Lord Radcliffe was emphatic that no frustration arose on these facts:[143]

> "Two things...prevent the application of ...frustration to this case. One is that the cause of the delay was not any new state of things which the parties could not reasonably be thought to have foreseen. On the contrary, the possibility of enough labour and materials not being available was before their eyes and could have been the subject of special

[134] *National Carriers Ltd v Panalpina Ltd* [1981] A.C. 675.

[135] *Cricklewood Property and Investment Trust Ltd v Leighton's Investment Trust Ltd* [1945] A.C. 221.

[136] *Bank Line Ltd v Arthur Capel & Co* [1919] A.C. 435; J.E. Stannard, *Delay in the Performance of Contractual Obligations*, 2nd edn (Oxford: Oxford University Press, 2018), para.12.26 ff.

[137] *Anglo-Northern Trading Co Ltd v Emlyn Jones* [1917] 2 K.B. 78 at 85 per Bailhache J in respect of the withdrawal of a ship from service.

[138] *Pioneer Shipping Ltd v BTP Tioxide Ltd ("The Nema")* [1982] A.C. 724 at 752 per Lord Roskill; J.E. Stannard, *Delay in the Performance of Contractual Obligations*, 2nd edn (Oxford: Oxford University Press, 2018), para.12.29.

[139] Criticised by Dunn LJ in *International Sea Tankers Inc v Hemisphere Shipping Co Ltd ("The Wenjiang")* [1982] 1 Lloyd's Rep. 128, CA at 131.

[140] In this connection see also the *Hong Kong Fir case* [1962] 2 Q.B. 26 CA; and *International Sea Tankers Inc v Hemisphere Shipping Co Ltd ("The Wenjiang" (No. 2))* [1983] 1 Lloyd's Rep. 400 at 408 per Bingham J.

[141] [1956] A.C. 696, HL.

[142] [1956] A.C. 696 at 724, HL.

[143] [1956] A.C. 696 at 731. HL.

contractual stipulation. It was not made so. The other thing is that…the tender must necessarily take into account the margin of profit that [the contractor] hopes to obtain upon his adventure and in that any appropriate allowance for the obvious risks of delay. To my mind, it is useless to pretend that the contractor is not at risk if delay does occur, even serious delay, and I think it a misuse of legal terms to call in frustration to get him out of his unfortunate predicament."

No frustration arose on the facts of *"The Sea Angel"* (on this case see also paras **17-068** 17-007–17-009 and 17-089).[144] The vessel had been hired for up to 20 days to assist in a salvage operation. Foreign official obstruction prevented the return of a salvage vessel for 108 days. Instead it was stuck for this period in a foreign port. This was a risk borne by the hirer. It is no real surprise that a salvage operation involving a vessel which is causing pollution has engendered some over-reaction on the part of national officials to the spillage and cleansing arrangements. Thus, the vessel had been prevented by the Pakistani port authority from leaving its port until payment had been made for the loss caused by pollution (oil leaking from a tanker which the salvage vessel had been hired to rescue). Extricating the salvage vessel from this situation prolonged the transaction by over three months (as mentioned, the anticipated length of the salvage hire was merely 20 days). The Court of Appeal (upholding Gross J at first instance) held that the charterparty had not been frustrated. This was because delay, even if, as here, significant, fell within the scope of the risk borne by the charterer. That party was, therefore, liable to pay hire at the agreed daily rate during the entire period when the vessel had been on hire, that is, before its return to the owners.

In greater detail, *The Sea Angel*[145] was hired on 26 August 2003. It was to be **17-069** returned on 15 September 2003. On 9 September, after it had been used in a pollution clear-up, the hirer, Tsavliris, gave a three-day definite notice of redelivery at Fujairah, the contractual redelivery port, which could be reached by a three days' voyage. But this planned return was prevented by the fact that the vessel was detained at Karachi for some 108 days.[146] The vessel could not leave Karachi until 26 December and was not redelivered until 1 January, 2004. The port authority had refused to issue the necessary "no demand certificate", a certificate that no outstanding port dues were required and a prerequisite to port clearance. Tsavliris paid no hire for *"The Sea Angel"* after 18 September. But the Court of Appeal held that further hire was owed. It held that the venture had not been frustrated. This type of official detention was a risk intrinsic to such a salvage operation. The risk could be imputed to the hirer. In short, this was a case where the contract had become more expensive for the hirer. But this did not constitute frustration.

In *"The Sea Angel"* Rix LJ referred to situations where the period of interrup- **17-070** tion attributable to delay is not immediately and manifestly sufficient to constitute frustration and instead a mature assessment must be made after the relevant event has already started to impinge:[147]

"this is not a case like (1) *Anglo-Northern Trading Co Ltd v Emlyn Jones & Williams*

---

[144] *Edwinton Commercial Corp v Tsavliris Russ Ltd ("The Sea Angel")* [2007] EWCA Civ 547; [2007] 1 C.L.C. 876.

[145] *Edwinton Commercial Corp v Tsavliris Russ Ltd ("The Sea Angel")* [2007] EWCA Civ 547; [2007] 1 C.L.C. 876.

[146] *Edwinton Commercial Corp v Tsavliris Russ Ltd ("The Sea Angel")* [2007] EWCA Civ 547; [2007] 1 C.L.C. 876 at [9]

[147] *Edwinton Commercial Corp v Tsavliris Russ Ltd ("The Sea Angel")* [2007] EWCA Civ 547; [2007] 1 C.L.C. 876 at [120].

[1917] 2 K.B. 78, affirmed *Countess of Warwick Steamship Co v Le Nickel Societe Anonyme* [1918] 1 K.B. 372 and (2) *Tatem v Gamboa* [1939] 1 K.B. 132, where the charters were frustrated then and there by the supervening event. Ours is one of those 'wait and see' situations discussed in other authorities. In such situations, it is a matter for assessment, on all the circumstances of the case, whether by a particular date the tribunal of fact, putting itself in the position of the parties, and viewing the matter in the role of reasonable and well-informed men, concludes that those parties would or properly speaking should have formed the view that, in all fairness and consistently with the demands of justice, their contract, as something whose performance in the new circumstances, past and prospective, had become 'radically different', had ceased to bind."

17-071   Case (1) and related decisions were considered by Rix LJ,[148] but his discussion is too long to quote verbatim here.

17-072   On case (2), Rix LJ commented:[149]

> "*Tatem v Gamboa* [1939] 1 K.B. 132...concerned a 30 day charter of a vessel by the Republicans during the Spanish Civil War. After a fortnight the vessel was seized by a Nationalist ship and detained for just under two months, whereupon she was redelivered to her owner. The charterers claimed that the charter had been frustrated from the moment of seizure, and Goddard J agreed. He was prepared to assume that the parties contemplated that the vessel might be seized and detained, but not for the length of time in question (at 135/6). He said (at 137/8): 'It is true that in many of the cases there is found the expression "unforeseen circumstances", and it is argued that "unforeseen circumstances" must mean circumstances that could not have been foreseen. But it makes very little difference whether the circumstances are foreseen or not. If the foundation of the contract goes, it goes whether or not the parties have made a provision for it.'"

Delay and the commercial purpose

17-073   Delay in fact produced the first case of "frustration of the commercial venture". In *Jackson v Union Marine Ins Co*[150] a ship was chartered for a voyage from Liverpool, where she then was, to Newport, to load rails, and proceed to deliver them in San Francisco. Having left Liverpool, the ship failed to make Newport (in South Wales) (having grounded in Carnarvon Bay en route from Liverpool to Newport). Only eight months later was the repaired and fit to complete the voyage. The claimant ship owner's action to enforce freight *insurance* eventually succeeded in the Court of Exchequer Chamber on the premise that the claimant had lost the freight because the voyage charter had been frustrated. This was because in the court below the jury had found that "the voyage the parties contemplated had become impossible"; a voyage

---

[148] *Edwinton Commercial Corp v Tsavliris Russ Ltd ("The Sea Angel")* [2007] EWCA Civ 547; [2007] 1 C.L.C. 876 at [89]–[95]; the authorities considered by Rix LJ are: *Bank Line Ltd v Arthur Capel & Co* [1919] A.C. 435, HL; *Pioneer Shipping Ltd v BTP Tioxide Ltd ("The Nema")* [1982] A.C. 724, HL.

[149] *Edwinton Commercial Corp v Tsavliris Russ Ltd ("The Sea Angel")* [2007] EWCA Civ 547; [2007] 1 C.L.C. 876 at [96].

[150] *Jackson v Union Marine Ins Co* (1874) L.R. 10 C.P. 125 CA; described as the "foundation case" of the doctrine of the frustration of purpose in M. Mustill, *Butterworth Lectures 1989-90* (London: Butterworths, 1990), 56.

"after the ship was sufficiently repaired would have been a different voyage, not, indeed different as to the ports of loading and discharge, but different as a different venture".[151]

The court did not specify why the ship had to be in San Francisco in good time, but it was apparent that the charterparty was to carry rails from Newport, in Wales, to California, and it was necessarily the case that the ship should arrive in good time in Newport to accomplish its voyage to the west coast of the US. Instead of this it foundered on its way from Liverpool to Newport and the delay was seven months for it was ready for such a voyage. Men of commerce:

"[M]ust not be asked to wait till the end of a long delay ... ; they must be entitled to act on reasonable probabilities at the time when they are called upon to make up their minds."[152]

Thus, such contracts may be frustrated—prospectively.

Sometimes prolonged delay, the end of which cannot be foreseen, and which is **17-074** attributable to international events or shifts, can cause a contract to be frustrated. *"The Playa Larga"* concerned a contract to sell Cuban sugar to Chile. The contract was formed in February 1973 when the governments of the two countries were in a state of amity, both then being Marxist regimes.[153] The contract was to be performed by a series of shipments ending in October 1973. On 11 September, a coup in Chile replaced the government there (the Marxist regime being replaced by a right-wing party). On 27 September, the Cuban Government passed legislation making (further) deliveries by the Cuban sugar dealer unlawful. The issue which came before the English courts, following earlier arbitration, concerned performance of the contract between the two dates in September.[154] The decision of the Court of Appeal covered, inter alia, non-shipment of sugar and whether the contract was frustrated on 13 September (viz even before illegality had supervened as a discharging factor). Although at that date performance was neither impossible nor illegal, the arbitrators had found that it was reasonably plain by that date:

"[T]hat there was no possibility of the contract being further implemented on either side in view of the antagonism which then existed and was likely in the foreseeable future to continue to exist between the Cuba Government and the new government in Chile."

This finding was accepted by Mustill J and the Court of Appeal.[155] Treitel and Peel interpret the case as an unusual instance of political impracticability.[156]

---

[151] See *Jackson v Union Marine Ins Co* (1874) L.R. 10 C.P. 125 at 141 per Bramwell B delivering the judgment of the majority of the court.

[152] *Embiricos v Sydney Reid & Co* [1914] 3 K.B. 45 at 54 per Scrutton J.

[153] *Empresa Exportadora de Azucar v Industria Azucarera Nacional SA ("The Playa Larga" and "The Marble Island")* [1983] 2 Lloyd's Rep. 171; [1983] Com. L.R. 58 CA; on the political background, Ackner LJ at 188; an appeal and cross-appeal against the (lengthy and unreported) judgment of Mustill J (Lexis SJ/160/78) were dismissed.

[154] It focused inter alia on non-delivery by *"The Playa Larga"*, which was in the (Chilean) port of Valparaiso on 11 September but escaped back to Cuba.

[155] Ackner LJ, giving the judgment of the court at [1983] 2 Lloyd's Rep. 171 at 187 ff.

[156] E. Peel, *Frustration and Force Majeure*, 4th edn (London: Sweet & Maxwell, 2021), paras 6-048, 8-071; E. Peel (ed), *Treitel, The Law of Contract* 15th edn (London: Sweet & Maxwell, 2020), para.19-039.

V. FRUSTRATION OF THE VENTURE: PERFORMANCE NOT "POINTLESS"

17-075   We should start negatively: no frustration occurs just because the bargain has gone sour or proved disadvantageous, or caused great disappointment. Hardship or greater onerousness does not constitute frustration: that is a fundamental, and hence trite, proposition of English law (see paras 17-002–17-006 above)

17-076   But now for the positive but quite exceptional possibility: frustration can arise, but very rarely does, where the performance contracted for is possible, both physically and legally, but has become "pointless",[157] either because an event on which it centered has been cancelled or postponed, or because the underlying commercial purpose cannot be achieved.

17-077   The classic (and rather isolated) case of pure "frustration", that is simple "pointlessness" brought about because the contract's main focus has aborted, due to supervening events, without either illegality or physical destruction or mishap,[158] is *Krell v Henry*. This case concerned payment for a day-time licence to use a residential address on 56A Pall Mall, central London on 26 and 27 June 1902, from which to view the coronation procession (26 June) and next day "the Royal Progress", for £75, of which £25 was paid upfront, the remainder to be paid on 24 June. The result in the case was that the balance was no longer payable, as a result of frustration, but the £25 was "abandoned" as a counterclaim by the property owner, Krell.[159] The sibling case which (like many siblings) went in the opposite direction is *Herne Bay Steamboat Co v Hutton*, where a boat had been hired for two days to enable the charterer's paying passengers to receive entertainment on board and to see the King's inspection of the Royal Navy fleet at anchor. The King in fact missed the occasion. No frustration occurred in this commercial charterparty case.

17-078   These cases came before the Court of Appeal more or less contemporaneously: *Herne Bay Steamboat Co v Hutton* (appeal heard 6 August 1903) and *Krell v Henry* (appeal held 11 August). They are plainly reconcilable.[160] In the coronation frustration cases, the hearings before the Court of Appeal overlapped, *Krell v Henry* having been argued on 13–15 July, but judgment was not given until 11 August, and the *Herne Bay* case having been heard and judgment given on 6 August. One might infer that the *Herne Bay* case was regarded as straightforward, having been disposed of quickly, whereas *Krell v Henry* required the Court of Appeal to pause for almost a month after the close of argument in order to feel comfortable with its reasoning.

17-079   In greater detail, in *Krell v Henry*[161] a licence to use rooms as a vantage-point from which to see the coronation procession was held to have become frustrated

---

[157] Ackner LJ in *"The Playa Larga"* [1983] 2 Lloyd's Rep. 171; [1983] Com. L.R. 58 at 187, with reference to *Krell* (below).

[158] Of course the King had suffered a mishap, for which he needed emergency surgery: appendicitis. A more interesting case would have been if the King decided to abdicate, as occurred, somewhat unforeseeably in 1938, when the King's grandson, Edward VIII, elected to marry Mrs Simpson, and thus to forfeit the throne, under the then prevailing constitutional mores.

[159] E. Peel, *Frustration and Force Majeure*, 4th edn (London: Sweet & Maxwell, 2021), paras 7-006–7-019.

[160] The identical composition of the Court of Appeal in these two cases, decided within a week of each other, is noted by Newey J in *North Shore Ventures Ltd v Anstead Holdings Inc* [2010] EWHC 1485 (Ch); [2011] 1 All E.R. (Comm) 81 at [309], and the cases are reconciled at [308]–[312] (reversed on a different point; [2011] EWCA Civ 230; [2012] Ch 31). Also reconciling the cases, see E. Peel, *Frustration and Force Majeure*, 4th edn (London: Sweet & Maxwell, 2021), para.7-019. It is remarkable that none of the judges in *Krell v Henry* (1903) referred to the *Herne Bay* case.

[161] In *Krell v Henry* [1903] 2 K.B. 740, CA, the event was the procession; admittedly, there was no mention of that in the contract but the rooms were advertised by Krell's agent as being for hire to view

because the King's coronation had to be postponed, as a result of his appendicitis.[162] The decision to declare frustration on these facts (and thus to cancel the debt and, if payment has been made, to allow repayment; on the latter point see 18-008 ff) was a satisfactory and indeed self-evident result. Any doctrinal sceptics tempted to protest against this result should put themselves in the position of an ordinary citizen who has paid, or agreed to pay, a significant sum for no possible benefit other than to view a one-off event which is expected to take place on the relevant hiring date(s).

Thus, three decades later, in 1932, Lord Atkin[163] explained the *Krell v Henry* **17-080** contract as not simply for the (hire of) "rooms" but for "rooms to view the Coronation processions". It is true that the written contract made no reference to processions. But not everything needs to be spelt out in order to be recognised by the courts as contractually crucial ("deal-breaker" assumptions). Consistent with the obvious focus of the *Krell v Henry* licence on the (anticipated) coronation procession, the *Krell* contract was for the day-time only. This was not an Edwardian "AirBnB". The key to the decision was that the customer was not engaged in trade, capable of bearing the risk of successful and less successful "ventures", and the implicit assumption, as it were the foundation of the contract, was clearly "'procession' or no-deal".[164] Admittedly, *Krell v Henry* has not been successfully invoked in later cases.[165] That might be because it is unusual for a risk not to be at least impliedly allocated to one or other of the parties (on the element of implied risk al-

---

the procession; in *Herne Bay Steamboat Co v Hutton* [1903] 2 K.B. 683 CA the event was the Royal review of the fleet; and the contract stated that the boat was chartered for the purpose of seeing the royal review of the fleet, but the Court of Appeal held that this was surplusage and that the contractual foundation had not become a hiring for that specific purpose: Stirling LJ said, [1903] 2 K.B. 683, 691-693: "this venture was the venture of the defendant alone, and that although the plaintiffs assisted him by selling tickets and posting notices of what was proposed to be done, yet the risk was entirely that of the defendant. ...[T]he reference in the contract to the naval review is easily explained; it was inserted in order to define more exactly the nature of the voyage, and I am unable to treat it as being such a reference as to constitute the naval review the foundation of the contract so as to entitle either party to the benefit of the doctrine in *Taylor v Caldwell*. I come to this conclusion the more readily because the object of the voyage is not limited to the naval review, but also extends to a cruise round the fleet. The fleet was there, and passengers might have been found willing to go round it. It is true that in the event which happened the object of the voyage became limited, but, in my opinion, that was the risk of the defendant whose venture the taking the passengers was. For these reasons I am unable to agree with the learned judge in holding that in the contemplation of the parties the taking place of the review was the basis for the performance of the contract, and I think that the defendant is not discharged from its performance."

162 A flat in Pall Mall for the two days of coronation processions, advertised to be available by a note in the windows of the flat.

163 In *Bell v Lever Bros Ltd* [1932] A.C. 161 HL at 226; this view of the coronation cases was also accepted in *Great Peace Shipping v Tsavliris ("The Great Peace")* [2002] EWCA Civ 1407; [2003] Q.B. 679 at [66] by Lord Phillips MR, who delivered the judgment of the court.

164 Nor had he or Mr Henry taken insurance against the possibility of cancellation—unlike persons who had erected stands to enable the paying public to watch the procession. Nor had Colonel Brymer MP, who owned the flat rented to watch the procession in the "mistake" case of *Griffith v Brymer* (1903) 19 T.L.R. 434; contract void for mistake. R.A. Posner, "Impossibility and Related Doctrines in Contract Law" (1977) 6 J. of Legal Studies 83, 110, dismisses these cases as ones in which it was not apparent who was the superior risk bearer. In this connection see E. Peel, *Frustration and Force Majeure*, 4th edn (London: Sweet & Maxwell, 2021), paras 7-015 and 7-016 who discusses and dismisses both an "insurance argument" and a "postponement" argument advanced by Posner J in *Northern Indiana Public Service Co v Carbon County Coal Co* 799 F 2d. 265 (1986).

165 E. Peel (ed), *Treitel, The Law of Contract* 15th edn (London: Sweet & Maxwell, 2020), 19-044; thus in *Leiston Gas Co v Leiston-cum-Sizewell UDC* [1916] 2 K.B. 428, no frustration had occurred of a contract for street lamps when wartime black-out regulations prohibited them; the maintenance

location, paras 16-005 and 16-012–16-021, and 17-008). Although the decision has not produced a line of positive applications, it might be that there are various situations where *Krell v Henry* might apply by analogy and the circumstances make plain that the party paying should enjoy a refund because the contract was based on a specific event occurring, and that event has been called off, or its date has been shifted. Common-sense often determines the result, without the intervention of the Court of Appeal.

17-081   To conclude on *Krell v Henry*,[166] this "solitary beacon" of a case shows that a contract can be frustrated even though it has not become illegal to perform and even though the contracting parties survive and are physically capable and the physical subject matter of the contract also remains intact. Exceptionally, the abstract platform of the contract can disappear, rendering physical performance a hollow and futile activity. This exceptionally rare situation is known as "frustration of the venture".[167] But total solar eclipses are more common. Frustration of the venture has seldom been successfully argued in a reported case.[168] Certainly, as the *Herne Bay Steam Boat* case shows, such an abstract "frustration of the venture" will not occur if the relevant risk is borne by one of the parties. The *Herne Bay* case is, therefore, the default position, and to that we now turn.

17-082   The *Herne Bay* case was a short charterparty of a pleasure boat. The contract was for two days "for the purpose of viewing the naval review" at Spithead by the King "and for a day's cruise round the fleet".[169] The King's "no show" at Spithead (attributable to his emergency operation for appendicitis, the same event which caused the coronation in London to be postponed) did not render this commercial contract frustrated by operation of law. The charterer, Hutton, had intended to attract 10 paying passengers on successive days to receive entertainment on board and to see the King's inspection of the Royal Navy fleet at anchor at Spithead. These events were to take place after the coronation of the King. When the coronation was postponed, the defendant refused to pay for the hire of the vessel. The Court of Appeal held that there had been no frustration of the contract. The King's inability to enhance this occasion did not render the whole venture pointless. The fleet remained at anchor and was a great spectacle. In any event, this commercial disappointment was a risk borne by the charterer rather than the vessel owner. The King's presence did not form part of the underlying purpose of the contract of hire. His absence was not a complete game-changer as between these parties. And so, the charterer owed the unpaid hire (subject to a deduction in respect of the money made by the vessel's owner who used the boat for a different voyage when the claimant cancelled). The

---

obligation surviving and being non-trivial; similarly, in *Amalgamated Investment & Property Co Ltd v John Walker & Sons Ltd* [1977] 1 W.L.R. 164, CA, a contract to buy property for redevelopment not frustrated when the property was listed as being of special architectural interest.

[166] [1903] 2 K.B. 740, CA.

[167] On this category see comments in *Canary Wharf (BP4) T1 Ltd v European Medicines Agency* [2019] EWHC 335 (Ch); 183 Con. L.R. 167 at [35]–[38], per Marcus Smith J; ibid, on *Krell v Henry* (1903) at [38] sub-para.(4); also concluding that there had been no frustration of the venture or common purpose in the *Canary Wharf* case, ibid at [244], [245], [258].

[168] Lord Wright in the *Maritime National Fish* case [1935] A.C. 524 at 529, PC, noted the exceptional nature of *Krell v Henry* (1903).

[169] *Herne Bay Steamboat Co v Hutton* [1903] 2 K.B. 683, CA; E. Peel (ed), *Treitel, The Law of Contract* 15th edn (London: Sweet & Maxwell, 2020), para.19-043. The boat usually sailed between Herne Bay and Gravesend.

result was that the owner recovered the outstanding payment,[170] less money which the owner had earned from using the boat for cruises on the Thames during the relevant two days, following Hutton's renunciation. That money had to be deducted on the basis of mitigation of loss (the claim being for damages[171] for loss of revenue).

A moment's reflection on the contrasting nature of the payors in these respec- **17-083** tive contracts reveals that, from a commercial perspective, they were chalk and cheese, one a consumer and the other a "merchant venturer" attempting to make profit. Admittedly, in both cases an underlying feature was that the relevant property was being hired in connection with the coronation of the King. But in *Krell v Henry*, the risk of disappointment and/or loss arising from postponement was held not to have been allocated to the customer, whereas in the other case, *Herne Bay Steamboat Co v Hutton*, the risk was borne by a commercial charterer. It is submitted that *Krell v Henry* would have been decided in the same way as *Herne Bay* only if the payor had been engaged in business and was seeking the opportunity to make a financial gain by sub-licensing the premises to members of the public or for the purpose of corporate entertainment.

Perhaps the key to the court's thinking lies in the hypothetical case mentioned **17-084** in both decisions: the cab to the Epsom Derby, a hypothetical situation chosen to focus attention on the requirement that this branch of frustration requires frustration presupposes frustration of the *common* objective of the contractual venture.[172] The cabman hypothesis was introduced as follows. In *Krell v Henry* Vaughan Williams LJ referred to the argument that "if a cabman were engaged to take someone to Epsom on Derby Day at a suitably enhanced price" and the Derby were cancelled, "both parties to the contract would be discharged". But he rejected this argument, saying "I do not think that in the cab case the happening of the race would be the foundation of the contract."[173] He said that no "doubt the purpose of the engager would be to go and see the Derby" and whether the race were held or not he could have said to the driver "you have nothing to do with the purpose for which I hire the cab".[174] From the perspective of risk-allocation it is clear that in *Herne Bay Steam Boat Co v Hutton* (as Stirling LJ said in that very case, the "venture was the venture of [Hutton] alone, ... the risk was entirely that of

---

170 The amount of hire was £250, of which £50 was paid upfront; that left a balance of £200; there was a counterclaim to recover the £50 on the basis of total failure of consideration; the owner made a profit of £90 on their running of the ship during the two days in question, so that at the trial they reduced the amount of their claim to £110: [1903] 2 K.B. 683, 685.

171 [1903] 2 K.B. 683, 688, per Vaughan Williams LJ characterising the claim as one for damages.

172 e.g. Stirling LJ, *Herne Bay Steamboat Co v Hutton* [1903] 2 K.B. 683 at 691–692: Hutton (the charterer) "formed the idea of making a profit by the conveyance of passengers" on the two days but it is "clear that this venture was the venture of [Hutton] alone, and that although the [shipowner] assisted him by selling tickets ... yet, the risk was entirely that of [Hutton]." Romer LJ, ibid, 690, expressed the perspective of the owner: I am concerned with the ship only "as a passenger or cargo carrying machine, and I enter into the contract simply in that capacity; it is for the hirer to concern himself about the objects". It was "not ... in any sense a joint speculation". The importance of the common purpose in this context was also stressed in *Hirji Mulji v Cheong Yue SS Co Ltd* [1926] A.C. 497 at 507, PC; *North Shore Ventures Ltd v Amstead Holdings Inc* [2010] EWHC 1485 (Ch); [2010] 2 Lloyd's Rep. 265 at [314]; and in Australia in *Scanlan's New Neon Ltd v Tooheys Ltd* (1943) 67 C.L.R. 169 at 224 at 231 (HCA).

173 *Krell v Henry* [1903] 2 K.B. 740 at 750, CA, per Vaughan Williams LJ.

174 *Krell v Henry* [1903] 2 K.B. 740 at 750, CA, per Vaughan Williams LJ. Note also that Vaughan Williams LJ said (at 751) that in the cab case any other cab would have done as well, whereas in *Krell* itself "the rooms were offered and taken, by reason their peculiar suitability from the position of the rooms for a view of the coronation procession".

[Hutton]".[175] Vaughan Williams LJ in *Herne Bay* rejected the argument that "the happening of the naval review was contemplated by both parties as the basis and foundation" of the contract.[176]

17-085 In *Islamic Republic of Iran Shipping Lines v Steamship Mutual Underwriting Association (Bermuda) Ltd* an argument based on alleged "frustration of the venture" was presented. But Beatson J held[177] that partial supervening illegality did not have the effect of frustrating a contract of marine insurance, because the contract's essence had not been radically altered.

17-086 Beatson J commented:[178]

> "[The Court of Appeal's decision in] *Leiston Gas Co v Leiston-cum-Sizewell UDC* [1916] 2 K.B. 428...[was] doubted in *Denny-Mott*'s case by Viscount Simon LC and Lord Wright: see [1944] A.C. at 271 and 280, HL. The *Leiston Gas* case concerned the impact of wartime blackout regulations on a five-year contract to provide gas street lamps, to maintain them, and to light and extinguish them at set times. Four years later the lighting of street lamps was prohibited by the regulations. It was held that the contract was not frustrated because the contract also provided for supply and maintenance of the plant and those parts of the contract remained lawful. [As for]...the doubt expressed in *Denny-Mott*'s case by Viscount Simon and Lord Wright about the result...[the explanation] may possibly be because they considered that lighting the district was in fact the main purpose of a street-lighting contract. In any event, the House of Lords did not overrule the decision and it is not questioned by Sir Guenter Treitel in *Frustration and Force Majeure* [(3rd edn, Sweet & Maxwell, London, 2014), see 7–017 et seq and 8–31; now Edwin Peel, 4th edn, 7-023 and 7-024, and 8-046]. Sir Guenter notes that in none of the English cases in which the effect of blackout regulations on street-lighting contracts was considered was the contract held to be frustrated. In *Egham and Staines Electricity Co v Egham U.D.C.* [1944] 1 All E.R. 107 the House of Lords (including three members of the Appellate Committee in the *Denny-Mott* case) held that, as a result of the blackout regulations, the local authority was excused from making further payments under a street-lighting contract. This, however, was because of an express term of the contract and not because the contract was frustrated."

17-087 The risk point reappears in the very different modern context of international trade in *Congimex Sarl v Tradax Export SA*.[179] This decision concerned four contracts subject to GAFTA 100 terms, whereby S sold 16,500 tons of soya bean meal to B c.i.f. Lisbon free out for shipment in four instalments. B was unable to obtain a licence from the state licensing authority in respect of the final instalment. One ground for the decision rejecting B's argument for frustration was that the

> "frustrated expectations and intentions of *one* party to a contract do not necessarily or indeed usually lead to the frustration of that contract".[180]

The seller under a c.i.f. contract has performed its side of the bargain fully by suc-

---

175 *Herne Bay Steamboat Co v Hutton* [1903] 2 K.B. 683, CA, 692 per Stirling LJ. See also in this sense Romer LJ, ibid at 690. Also, there is a hint of focus on risk in the brief judgment of Romer LJ in *Krell v Henry* [1903] 2 K.B. 740 at 755, CA.

176 *Herne Bay Steamboat Co v Hutton* [1903] 2 K.B. 683 at 689, CA, per Vaughan Williams LJ.

177 [2010] EWHC 2661 (Comm); [2011] 2 All E.R. (Comm) 609, notably at [115], [116], [121], and [126]–[128].

178 [2010] EWHC 2661 (Comm); [2011] 2 All E.R. (Comm) 609 at [117].

179 [1983] 1 Lloyd's Rep. 250, CA; E. Peel, *Frustration and Force Majeure*, 4th edn (London: Sweet & Maxwell, 2021), para.7-040.

180 [1983] 1 Lloyd's Rep. 250 at 253, CA, per Sir John Donaldson MR.

cessfully shipping the goods to their destination and providing the relevant documents to the buyer. The absence of an import licence is no concern to the seller.

VI. Long-term Contracts

Contracts of indefinite duration   "Long term contracts of indefinite duration" form a residual but important category.[181] Sixty years before the litigation, in 1919, in the *Staffordshire Water* case[182] (on that case see also para.9-066 ff) a waterworks company had agreed "at all times here-after" to supply water to a hospital at fixed prices. By 1975 the cost (per unit) to the supplier had reached more than 18 times the price fixed. The notice of termination by the company to the hospital was held to be effective by the Court of Appeal. The majority said that this was because the words "at all times hereafter" were not to be taken literally and in isolation but were subject to an implied term in favour of termination by reasonable notice.[183] Lord Denning MR, however, concluded that the agreement was no longer binding because the situation had "changed so radically since the contract was made" that it had been frustrated.[184] Certainly, it is hard to interpret the contract of 1919 as one intended to bind parties regardless of changes in the value of money, as well as labour costs and hospital water requirements that would and did occur in the subsequent half century. Could it really be said that the supplier had assumed the inevitable risk? Generally, an affirmative answer can be given to such questions only where the contract is for a fixed term of moderate length.[185] Thus the safer view of the case is that of the court majority, a case of construction.   **17-088**

Leases   If one of the parties is to occupy premises on the land in question, the lease may well be frustrated and relatively quickly by an event preventing occupation.[186] Again, if the unexpected event is the destruction of the property leased frustration is immediate. Where: **17-089**

> "[S]ea-erosion has undermined a cliff causing property on the top of the cliff to be totally lost for occupation: obviously occupation of a dwelling house is something significantly different in nature from its aqualung contemplation after it has suffered a sea-change."[187]

And frustration of the lease occurs.[188]

Such cases apart, for a time it was unclear whether a lease could ever be frustrated. At one time the answer was "never" on the basis that tenants received   **17-090**

---

[181] E. Peel, *Frustration and Force Majeure*, 4th edn (London: Sweet & Maxwell, 2021), para.6-044.

[182] *Staffordshire Area Health Authority v South Staffordshire Waterworks Co* [1978] 1 W.L.R. 1387, CA; generally on this topic, Neil Andrews, *Contract Law in Practice* (Oxford: Oxford University Press, 2021), Ch.23.

[183] The ground of decision favoured by E. Peel, *Frustration and Force Majeure*, 4th edn (London: Sweet & Maxwell, 2021), para.6-044 as being better reconcilable with other English precedent. It is consistent with the position adopted in the US, in the UCC s.2-309.

[184] [1978] 1 W.L.R. 1387 at 1398 per Lord Denning MR.

[185] But concerning which public authority should bear the increased cost of maintaining cemeteries, cf. *Watford B.C. v Watford R.D.C.* (1988) 86 L.G.R. 524 (agreement for public authorities to share cost of maintaining cemeteries under the Burial Acts), discussed by E. Peel, *Frustration and Force Majeure*, 4th edn (London: Sweet & Maxwell, 2021), para.6-047.

[186] e.g., *Wong Lai Ying v Chinachem Investment Co* (1979) 13 B.L.R. 81 PC; see also *E Johnson & Co (Barbados) Ltd v NSR Ltd* [1997] A.C. 400 PC.

[187] *National Carriers Ltd v Panalpina (Northern) Ltd* [1981] A.C. 675 at 701, per Lord Simon.

[188] cf. where destruction is the result of enemy action: *Redmond v Dainton* [1920] 2 K.B. 256; and *Denman v Brise* [1949] 1 K.B. 22.

and retained property rights which were unaffected by anything occurring later. That view was finally and firmly rejected by the House of Lords in *National Carriers Ltd v Panalpina (Northern) Ltd*.[189] But frustration of leases will seldom occur. For example, referring to the present facts in that case, Lord Wilberforce said that no doubt the appellant's business will have been "severely dislocated " but "this does not approach the gravity of a frustrating event".[190] So, leases are but rarely frustrated but, if so, how soon a lease is frustrated depends on the purpose of the lease.

17-091   If the purpose of the lease is development (buildings of some kind) there is usually an element of speculation. The risk of the unexpected is usually on the speculator, the developer where a building exists but the land owner where the land is vacant,[191] subject always to particular contract terms.[192] If the purpose is occupation and the lease is short, however, the unexpected may well frustrate it.[193] If such a lease is long, frustration is most unlikely as it can be assumed that the parties realise that "anything might happen"[194] and that, if it does, it is likely that the interruption will be of relatively short duration.[195]

17-092   As noted at para.17-016, the Court of Appeal held in *Bank of New York Mellon (International) Ltd v Cine-UK Ltd*[196] that a tenant could not found a defence to its duty to pay rent on the basis of an implied term of "failure of basis" because the terms of the lease were inconsistent with that suggestion.

17-093   A plea of frustration was directly raised in the following case, but it was rejected. Foxton J held in *Salam Air SAOC v Latam Airlines Groups SA* that six-year leases of three aircraft had not been frustrated by a statute in Oman which temporarily prevented the lessee during the Covid pandemic from flying to or from Omani airports. The lease's terms rendered the lessee's obligation to pay rent close to absolute, as the judge emphasised. Foxton J said:[197]

> "[51]…the Aircraft Leases were drafted to make it clear that Salam Air's obligation to pay rent continued in almost any conceivable circumstances (what is sometimes referred to as a 'hell or highwater' basis: e.g. *Bitumen Invest AS v Richmond Mercantile Ltd FZC* [2016] EWHC 2957 (Comm), [8]). Thus the obligation to pay rent was expressed to be 'absolute and unconditional irrespective of any contingency whatsoever' including 'the

---

[189] *National Carriers Ltd v Panalpina (Northern) Ltd* [1981] A.C. 675, HL; E. Peel, *Frustration and Force Majeure*, 4th edn (London: Sweet & Maxwell, 2021), Ch.11.

[190] [1981] A.C. 675 at 697–698 per Lord Wilberforce at 707 per Lord Simon.

[191] And in the case of a contract to purchase such land, the risk is for the purchaser: *Amalgamated Investment & Property Co Ltd v John Walker & Sons Ltd* [1977] 1 W.L.R. 164 CA: contract to buy property for redevelopment not frustrated when the property was listed as being of special architectural interest.

[192] e.g. the view taken by Lord Roskill in *Panalpina* (at [26]) of *Matthey v Curling* [1922] 2 A.C. 180, "a singularly harsh decision from the tenant's point of view": lessee held bound to pay rent where dispossessed by military authority.

[193] e.g. *Tay Salmon Fisheries Co v Speedie* [1929] SC 593; in principle, the same should be true in England but no case of frustration has been reported, perhaps because leases usually provide for the possibility: J. Beatson, A. Burrows and J. Cartwright, *Anson's Law of Contract*, 31st edn (Oxford: Oxford University Press, 2020), p.492.

[194] *Cricklewood Property and Investment Trust Ltd v Leighton's Investment Trust Ltd* [1945] A.C. 221 at 229 per Viscount Simon.

[195] e.g. wartime restriction on building, as in *Cricklewood Property and Investment Trust Ltd v Leighton's Investment Trust Ltd* [1945] A.C. 221.

[196] [2022] EWCA Civ 1021; [2023] L. & T.R. 2 at [55], [138] and [139] (Flaux C, with the agreement of Snowden LJ and Sir Nicholas Patten), applying Carr LJ's summary of the rules governing terms implied in fact, in *Yoo Design Services Ltd v Iliv Realty PTE Ltd* [2021] EWCA Civ 560 at [51].

[197] [2020] EWHC 2414 (Comm); [2021] 1 C.L.C. 795 at [51]; case noted J. Morgan, "Frustration and the pandemic" (2021) 137 L.Q.R. 2021, 563–568.

ineligibility of the aircraft for particular use or trade' (Clause 8.2), and even if the Aircraft became a Total Constructive Loss (clause 21.3) or was requisitioned (clause 22). The Aircraft Lease expressly placed on Salam Air 'the full risk of any ... occurrence of whatever kind which shall deprive [Salam Air] of the use, possession and enjoyment thereof'.... These clauses are...fundamentally inconsistent with any suggestion that regulations in Oman which (for so long as they remained in force) prevent Salam Air from using the Aircraft to earn revenue through passenger flights with an Omani terminus...had the effect of terminating the Aircraft Leases and freeing Salam Air of its obligation to pay rent."

Similarly, Julia Dias Q.C. held in *Wilmington Trust SP Services (Dublin) Ltd v Spicejet Ltd*[198] that there had been no frustration of a set of aircraft leases. The relevant aircraft had been grounded by the Indian Government following crashes in other parts of the world of the same type of aircraft. Design faults were in issue, therefore. But the terms of the leases were so starkly formulated in favour of the lessor that there was no scope for a finding of frustration on the present facts, although the judge did not rule out that more extreme facts might edge close to frustration, The judge said:[199] **17-094**

"[64]...these were ten-year dry leases under which the Defendant assumed the entire commercial risk of operating the aircraft. ...[If, as here] the Defendant was not absolved from paying rent by the total loss of the aircraft, it is difficult to see how a temporary prohibition on use could put it in a better position. If the ban imposed [on use of these aircraft] were permanent, that might be a different matter but it has never been suggested that the ban is other than temporary even if it is currently indefinite with no sign of imminent removal....

[65] I am far from saying that these leases can never be frustrated. It may be (I express no view one way or the other) that if there is still no sign of the ban being lifted in, say, three years' time, that might amount to frustration. But in the context of a ten-year lease, I find it very difficult to say that a suspension of use for roughly 10% of the term of the lease amounts to a change of circumstances which renders performance of the lease 'radically different' rather than simply more onerous. I am therefore quite satisfied that, whatever the position may be in the future, the leases have not yet been frustrated as at today's date."

Similarly, Judge Robin Vos held in *London Trocadero (2015) LLP v Picturehouse Cinemas Ltd*[200] that the closure of cinemas during the lock down period (March to July 2020) of the Covid pandemic was not a defence to a claim for payment of rent.[201] No implied term of fact could be discovered to suspend or release the duty **17-095**

---

[198] [2021] EWHC 1117 (Comm).
[199] [2021] EWHC 1117 (Comm) at [64], [65].
[200] [2021] EWHC 2591 (Ch); [2022] 2 P. & C.R. 19.
[201] [2021] EWHC 2591 (Ch); [2022] 2 P. & C.R. 19 at [72], [78]: "[72]... the requirement for the Tenant to pay rent even though the premises could not be used for the intended purpose as a result of unforeseen, extraneous events does not deprive the leases of business efficacy or mean that they lack commercial or practical coherence. Clearly, without the implied terms, the risk is shouldered by the Tenant. However, there is no good commercial reason why the loss should necessarily be borne by the Landlord....[78] ...In circumstances where the Landlord expressly gives no warranty that the premises can lawfully be used as a cinema, and even taking account of the fact that that there is a covenant not to use the premises for any other purpose, it simply cannot be said that it is obvious that the Tenant should be excused from paying rent for any period when it cannot be so used."

to pay rent. The lease referred specifically to physical destruction or damage but did not extend its protection towards the tenant to the present facts.[202]

17-096 **Charterparties** Charterparties can be (but not necessarily) a species of long-term contract. This is an important commercial category which has produced a mass of litigation in London and doctrinal development,[203] such as the "multi-factorial" approach adopted in *"The Sea Angel"* (para.17-007 ff). The application of the doctrine of frustration:

> "[R]equires a multi-factorial approach. Among the factors which have to be considered are the terms of the contract itself, its matrix or context, the parties' knowledge, expectations, assumptions and contemplations, in particular as to risk, as at the time of contract, at any rate so far as these can be ascribed mutually and objectively, and then the nature of the supervening event, and the parties' reasonable and objectively ascertainable calculations as to the possibilities of future performance."[204]

And this was true of charter parties such as that before the court, a time charter where the ship had been arrested in Karachi.

17-097 Other factors include the importance to be given to construction and contract wording. In the *Golden Fleece* case,[205] for example, Longmore LJ referred to the standard Shelltime 4 time charterparty which, as he said, had "been used in the trade for many years" and continued with the comment that in such circumstances

> "facts peculiar to the background of the making of the particular charters are not likely to carry much weight against the actual words used [in the charter]".

---

[202] [2021] EWHC 2591 (Ch); [2022] 2 P. & C.R. 19 at [79]: "...clause 5.2 [suspended the payment of rent or service charge where the premises are unfit for use as a result of being [physically] damaged or destroyed by any of the Insured Risks].... [The] fact that the parties have thought about the suspension of rent and service charge and made express provision for it in certain circumstances in my view inevitably leads to the conclusion that it is not obvious that a further term should be implied providing for a suspension of rent or service charges in other circumstances. It certainly cannot be said that, had the parties foreseen the possibility of a pandemic, the proposed implied terms represent the only contractual solution or the one which would, without doubt, have been preferred."

[203] cf. J.E. Stannard, *Delay in the Performance of Contractual Obligations*, 2nd edn (Oxford University Press, 2018), para.12.92 to 12-97, observing that "arguments based on frustrating delay are more likely to succeed in this context than they are elsewhere" inter alia because they are more likely to be raised because of the large sums of money involved, of which the most recent instances at the time were the arbitrations over the ships trapped in Shatt-el-Arab waterway by the war between Iraq and Iran.

[204] [2007] EWCA Civ 547 at [111]. What appears to be temporary may turn out otherwise; an early instance is *Countess of Warwick SS Co v Le Nickel SA* [1918] 1 K.B. 372: one-year time charter frustrated by requisition after six months; this may also be true of the effect of strikes: *Pioneer Shipping Ltd v BTP Tioxide Ltd ("The Nema")* [1982] A.C. 724 [1982] A.C. 724.

[205] *Golden Fleece Maritime Inc v St Shipping and Transport Inc ("The Elli")* [2008] EWCA Civ 584; [2009] 1 All E.R. (Comm) 908; at [15]–[16].

CHAPTER 18

THE AFTERMATH OF FRUSTRATION

I. Overview

As Lord Sumner said in *Hirji Mulji v Cheong Yue Steamship Co Ltd* (a Privy **18-001**
Council decision on appeal from Hong Kong), frustration "brings the contract to
an end forthwith, without more and automatically" (that is, without any need for
the parties to be aware that it has occurred).[1] It releases the parties from their
unperformed primary obligations. The *Hirji Mulji* case directly concerned the issue whether an arbitration clause "survives" frustration of the main contract. On that
point it is now overtaken by the rise of the "separability"[2] doctrine, on which see
s.7 of the Arbitration Act 1996. The case is famously illuminating on the Common
Law operation of frustration, and in that respect the decision continues to form the
bed-rock of the impact at Common Law of frustration, where the entire contract is
terminated on that basis.

For most (but not all, see para.18-028 for more details on the Act's scope)[3] types **18-002**
of contract, the Law Reform (Frustrated Contracts) Act 1943 has ameliorated the
following three Common Law consequences of frustration.

(1) At Common Law, money paid before the contract is frustrated can be **18-003**
recovered only if there is a total failure of consideration (s.1(2) of the 1943
Act changed this, in the context of frustration). In the *Fibrosa* case,[4] the
House of Lords reversed the Court of Appeal's fallacious decision in
Chandler v Webster,[5] which had held that there can be no total failure of
consideration unless a contract is rescinded *ab initio*. Instead, as the House
of Lords clarified, money is repayable if the payor has received not one jot
of performance by the payee under the contract.

(2) At Common Law, accrued debt obligations (that is, contractual payment

---

1   [1926] A.C. 497 PC at 505 per Lord Sumner.
2   *Premium Nafta Products Ltd v Fili Shipping Co Ltd* [2007] UKHL 40; [2007] 4 All E.R. 951 at [10]
    (Lord Hoffmann) (otherwise known as the *Fiona Trust* case; *Andrews on Civil Processes*, 2nd edn
    (Cambridge, Intersentia Publishing, 2019), 32.64–32.76; *Enka Insaat ve Sanayi AS v 000 Insur-
    ance Company Chubb* [2020] UKSC 38; [2020] 1 W.L.R. 4117 at [60] to [64] (Lords Hamblen and
    Leggatt).
3   Law Reform (Frustrated Contracts) Act 1943 s. 5(2) creates exceptions in the case of voyage
    charterparties, contracts for the carriage of goods by sea, insurance agreements, and contracts for
    the sale of specific goods; cf. *Islamic Republic of Iran Shipping Lines v Steamship Mutual
    Underwriting Association (Bermuda) Ltd* [2010] EWHC 2661 (Comm); [2011] 1 Lloyd's Rep. 195;
    (the insurance contract had not been frustrated; if it been, the premium would not be recoverable
    unless there had been total failure of consideration—on this see fn.3).
4   *Fibrosa Spolka Akcyjna v Fairbairn Lawson Combe Barbour Ltd* [1943] A.C. 32 at 45–48, HL.
5   [1904] 1 K.B. 493 at 499–501, CA, per Lord Collins MR.

obligations which had arisen prior to termination) remained enforceable. Section 1(2) of the 1943 Act changed this, in the context of frustration.

(3) At Common Law, there was no scope to award recompense for partially completed work (this is because of the doctrine of entire obligations: payment is owed for contractual performance only if that performance, or a severable part of it, is completed or substantially performed before the contract's frustration; generally on the Common Law doctrine of entire obligations and substantial performance, Ch.15). But s. 1(3) of the 1943 Act changed this in the context of frustration.

18-004 **Summary of s.1(2) and (3)** Section 1(2) of the 1943 Act permits the court or arbitrator to engage in qualified loss adjustment. The device used is that of a "kitty" consisting of sums paid or payable before the time of contractual termination: (i) prima facie that sum is repayable or the sum payable need not be paid; but (ii) this is qualified by the court's discretion to allow the "kitty" holder to keep or recover in respect of his expenses. As for (ii), *Gamerco SA v ICM/Fair Warning (Agency) Ltd*[6] emphasises that there are no rules, legal or even matters of thumb, nor even any presumption governing how that kitty is to be distributed under the Act. This provision, and the discretion which it confers, has been received, therefore (admittedly in this isolated reported decision) as dogma-free and context-dependent.

18-005 Section 1(3) can be rationalised as the award of a restitutionary valuation of the benefit of non-monetary contractual performance, subject to discretionary loss adjustment (award of a just sum not to exceed the valuable benefit received).

18-006 Although s.1(2) can be loosely explained as reflecting the commercial implication that money paid or payable is available to protect the payee, s.1(3) rests on no such parallel implication. The truth is, therefore, that s.1(3) is a hybrid device, allowing qualified restitution for non-monetary benefits.

18-007 In *BP Exploration Co (Libya) Ltd v Hunt (No.2)*, Robert Goff J summarised the effect of s.1(2) and (3) of the 1943 Act:[7]

"The [Act] is not designed to do certain things: (i) It is not designed to apportion the loss between the parties ,,, (ii) It is not concerned to put the parties in the position in which they would have been if the contract had been performed. (iii) It is not concerned to restore the parties to the position they were in before the contract was made."

II. MONEY PAID OR MONEY OWING PRIOR TO FRUSTRATION

18-008 Section 1(2) of the 1943 Act states:[8]

"All sums paid or payable to any party in pursuance of the contract before the time when the parties were so discharged (in this Act referred to as 'the time of discharge') shall, in the case of sums so paid, be recoverable from him as money received by him for the use of the party by whom the sums were paid, and, in the case of sums so payable, cease to be so payable: Provided that, if the party to whom the sums were so paid or payable incurred expenses before the time of discharge in, or for the purpose of, the performance of the contract, the court may, if it considers it just to do so having regard to all the circumstances of the case, allow him to retain or, as the case may be, recover the whole

6 [1995] 1 W.L.R. 1226, Garland J.
7 The main discussion by Robert Goff J is at [1979] 1 W.L.R. 783 at 799; subsidiary aspects are examined in successive appeals, [1981] 1 W.L.R. 232, CA; [1982] 2 A.C. 352, HL.
8 E. Peel, *Frustration and Force Majeure*, 4th edn (London: Sweet & Maxwell, 2021), paras 15-064–15-069.

or any part of the sums so paid or payable, not being an amount in excess of the expenses so incurred."

The effect of s.1(2) is that a party can reclaim money paid before the frustrating **18-009** event, even if there has been some partial performance by the recipient. This reverses the *Fibrosa* case in this context.[9] But this refund is subject to the recipient's counter-claim for an allowance for his expenditure: see the second part of s.1(2), after the words "Provided that ..." above. The allowance referred to therein is at the court's discretion (para.18.012 ff.).

Another aspect of s.1(2) is that it reverses the Common Law by prima facie **18-010** cancelling an outstanding liability to pay if this duty has arisen (liability has "accrued") before the contract was frustrated. But this provisional cancellation can be reversed, in whole or in part, if, in exercise of the court's discretion (para.18-012 ff), it is decided that the intended payee should be paid such unpaid sums to cover the payee's expenditure.

The upshot of s.1(2) is that in general the payee must repay money paid and **18-011** forget money payable but not yet paid unless he can persuade the court that (i) the paid and (ii) payable but unpaid sums should be used as a "kitty" out of which it would be fair to reimburse his expenses, in full or at least in part. The "kitty" (comprising (i) and (ii)) is the maximum fund available under s.1(2) for this purpose.

Thus, under s.1(2) of the 1943 Act, the court receives a twofold discretion: to **18-012** order repayment; and to reverse cancellation of debts already accrued. In *Gamerco SA v ICM/Fair Warning (Agency) Ltd*, Garland J held that the court has a free hand when exercising these discretions.[10] He rejected two rigid approaches: to split the payee's reliance on an equal basis between him and the payor; or to allow the payee always to retain the money to the extent of his reliance.

In the *Gamerco* case, the claimant company had hired the defendant rock band **18-013** to perform at a concert in a Madrid stadium. The contract was subject to English law. After the contract's formation, the Spanish authorities condemned the proposed venue as unsafe. This prohibition was, therefore, a supervening event. As a result, the contract had been frustrated. The claimant had made a large prepayment to the band.

Garland J held that (i) the payee has the onus of establishing that there should **18-014** be some "discretionary retention";[11] but, in this case, the defendant had not adduced clear evidence of its expenditure in preparation for the concert;[12] and (ii) the court's discretion is wholly unfettered; there are thus no fixed rules, nor even rules of thumb, such as a presumption of "total retention" of sums paid or payable, or a presumption that the losses suffered by both parties should be cumulated and then split equally, by adjustment of the award under this subsection.[13] On the facts of this case Garland J held (iii) that the claimant should recover the whole prepayment, and he noted that the payor's wasted expenditure certainly exceeded the amount of that recovery.

Garland J's major point of decision was that the court's discretion is not subject **18-015** to fixed rules, nor even rules of thumb, such as a presumption of "total retention"

---

9   [1943] A.C. 32, HL.
10 [1995] 1 W.L.R. 1226.
11 [1995] 1 W.L.R. 1226 at 1235 G.
12 [1995] 1 W.L.R. 1226 at 1237 F.
13 [1995] 1 W.L.R. 1226 at 1236–1237.

of sums paid or payable, or a presumption that the losses suffered by both parties should be cumulated and then split equally, by adjustment of the award under this subsection.[14] Instead Garland J held that the court has a (virtually) unfettered discretion under s.1(2) of the 1943 Act when determining whether a payee should be allowed to retain all, some, or none of a pre-frustration payment in respect of the payee's expenses. This discretion is subject only to the constraints that, first, the court has not acted irrationally nor, secondly, has it taken into account irrelevant considerations. Subject to this, the adjudicator has a free hand whether to order complete or partial repayment to the payor. He also held that the payee has the onus of establishing that there should be some "discretionary retention".[15] But, in this case, the defendant had not adduced clear evidence of its expenditure in preparation for the concert.

18-016   Applying this test, Garland J held on the present facts that the appropriate response was that the court should order the rock band to repay in full the promoter's pre-payment.

18-017   It is possible, reading between the lines of the judgment, that the scale of the promoter's loss ($450,000), irrespective of the payment ($412,500) made to the band, was so great that the judge considered the fairer approach was to require the band to return the whole of the $412,500 to the promoter. This meant that the band's own loss, which was relatively small ($50,000), should be wholly borne by the band.

18-018   On the discretion whether to allow the defendant payee to retain any of the sums paid (or to recover sums payable or not yet paid), Garland J said, adopting the view that the court has a complete and unfettered discretion, and rejecting both the rival approaches (total retention and equal division, see below):[16]

> "Various views have been advanced as to how the court should exercise its discretion and these can be categorised as follows.
>
> (1) Total retention. This view was advanced by the Law Revision Committee in 1939 (Cmd 6009) on the questionable ground 'that it is reasonable to assume that in stipulating for prepayment the payee intended to protect himself from loss under the contract.' As *Chitty on Contracts* [now 34th edn (London: Sweet & Maxwell, 2021), 26-111 n 488,] comments: 'He [the payee] probably [instead] intends to protect himself against the possibility of the other party's insolvency or default in payment.' To this, one can add: 'and secure his own cash flow...'
>
> (2) Equal division. This was discussed by Professor Treitel in *Frustration and Force Majeure* [Garland J then referred to an earlier edition]. ...[The objection to this is that the parties' respective] losses may, as in the present case, be very unequal. Professor Treitel therefore favours the third view [see below].
>
> (3) *Broad discretion. It is self-evident that any rigid rule is liable to produce injustice. The words [in section 1(2)], 'if it considers it just to do so having regard to all the circumstances of the case,' clearly confer a very broad discretion. Obviously the court must not take into account anything which is not 'a circumstance of the case' or fail to take into account anything that is and then exercise its discretion rationally. I see no indication in the Act, the authorities or the relevant literature that the court is obliged to incline towards either total retention or equal division. Its task is to do justice in a situation which the parties had neither contemplated nor provided for, and to mitigate the possible harshness of allowing all loss to lie where it has fallen.*
>
> *I have not found my task easy. As I have made clear, I would have welcomed as-*

---

[14]   [1995] 1 W.L.R. 1226 at 1236–1237.
[15]   [1995] 1 W.L.R. 1226 at 1235 G.
[16]   [1995] 1 W.L.R. 1226 at 1236–1237

sistance on the true measure of the defendants' loss and the proper treatment of overhead and non-specific expenditure. Because the defendants have plainly suffered some loss, I have made a robust assumption. In all the circumstances, and having particular regard to the plaintiffs' loss, I consider that justice is done by making no deduction under the proviso." (Emphasis added.)

III. SERVICES PERFORMED OR GOODS DELIVERED PRIOR TO FRUSTRATION

What of performance other than by payment of money (use of goods or performance of services)? Section 1(3) of the 1943 Act provides:[17] **18-019**

"Where any party to the contract has, by reason of anything done by any other party thereto in, or for the purpose of, the performance of the contract, obtained a valuable benefit (other than a payment of money to which the last foregoing subsection applies) before the time of discharge, there shall be recoverable from him by the said other party such sum (if any), not exceeding the value of the said benefit to the party obtaining it, as the court considers just, having regard to all the circumstances of the case and, in particular—

(a) the amount of any expenses incurred before the time of discharge by the benefited party in, or for the purpose of, the performance of the contract, including any sums paid or payable by him to any other party in pursuance of the contract and retained or recoverable by that party under the last foregoing subsection, and

(b) the effect, in relation to the said benefit, of the circumstances giving rise to the frustration of the contract."

There are two stages in the application of s.1(3): (i) quantifying the valuable **18-020** benefit obtained prior to the date of frustration; (ii) assessing the just sum payable to the performing party, that sum not to exceed the amount established at stage (i). At stage (ii) the court will take into account the impact of the frustrating event upon the relevant benefit.

The only reported English case on s.1(3) of the 1943 Act is *BP Exploration Co* **18-021** *(Libya) Ltd v Hunt (No.2)*,[18] which (no less than for the trial judge) is a factual nightmare for students and advisors.

The claimant, British Petroleum, had entered into a complicated joint venture **18-022** with the defendant, Hunt. The parties had agreed to develop and exploit an oil field in Libya. Hunt owned the oil concession. The terms of this contract gave BP a right to "reimbursement oil". Once reimbursed for its expenditure in developing the oil field, the oil revenue would be divided equally between the two parties. BP

---

[17] A.S. Burrows, *The Law of Restitution*, 3rd edn (Oxford University Press, 2010), 366–371; C. Mitchell, P. Mitchell and S. Watterson (eds), *Goff and Jones, Unjust Enrichment* 10th edn (London: Sweet & Maxwell, 2022), 15.28–15.50; J.L. Harrison, "A Case for Loss Sharing" (1983) 56 S. Cal. L. Rev. 573; A.M. Haycroft and D.M. Waksman, "Frustration and Restitution" (1984) J.B.L. 207; A. Kull, "Mistake, Frustration and the Windfall principle of Contract Remedies" (1991) 43 Hastings L.J. 1; E. McKendrick, "Frustration, Restitution and Loss Adjustment", in A.S. Burrows (ed), *Essays on Restitution* (Oxford: Oxford University Press, 1991), 147; E. McKendrick (ed), *Force Majeure and Frustration of Contract*, 2nd edn (London: Lloyd's of London Press, 1995), Ch.11; J. Morgan, *Great Debates in Contract Law*, 3rd edn (London: Palgrave Publishing, 2020), 198–208; A. Stewart and J.W. Carter, "Frustrated Contracts and Statutory Adjustment: the Case for a Reappraisal" [1992] C.L.J. 66; E. Peel, *Frustration and Force Majeure*, 4th edn (London: Sweet & Maxwell, 2021), paras 15-074–15-081; G. Virgo, *Principles of the Law of Restitution*, 3rd edn (Oxford: Oxford University Press, 2015), 360–367.

[18] The main discussion by Robert Goff J is at [1979] 1 W.L.R. 783; subsidiary aspects are examined in successive appeals, [1981] 1 W.L.R. 232, CA; [1982] 2 A.C. 352, HL.

expended large sums on the project. As a result, the parties succeeded in extracting oil. The contract had operated successfully for almost five years when the Libyan government decided to expropriate the oil field. Robert Goff J held that, in principle, the valuable benefit obtained by Hunt on these facts was not the oil but the enhancement of the value of the oil rights. So the judge assessed the benefit by reference to the amount of oil received by Hunt and the amount of the Libyan government's compensation for the expropriation. The total was approximately $85 million. He then awarded a "just sum" of approximately $11 million, which took account of: (i) the fact that the field had been expropriated; (i) the parties' pre-existing receipts under the contract; and (iii) Hunt's recovery of modest compensation from the Libyan government.

18-023   Perhaps a more illuminating approach to s.1(3) is to take the following hypothetical case. Suppose A agrees with B to build a factory for £2 million. Halfway through the job, the factory is destroyed in a fire caused by vandals. At that point, A had spent £1.25 million. No money was yet owed by B to A. Goff J suggested in the following dictum in *BP v Hunt (No.2)* that the valuable benefit under s.1(3) in this context would be the scrap value of A's ruined work.[19] However, this dictum involves a misconstruction of this provision, as Treitel contends[20] (Treitel noting that s.1(3) requires the court to identify a "valuable benefit" obtained "before" the contract's termination; the relevant "valuable benefit", therefore, would be the value of the building *before* the conflagration). Instead, as Treitel observes, the structure of s.1(3) requires the court to assess a "just sum"; and in making this assessment it must take into account all the factors, including, as directed by s.1(3)(b), the impact on the valuable benefit of the events giving rise to the frustration. On the present imaginary[21] facts, the fire destroyed the building. On this basis, it seems likely that the court would fix the valuable benefit at either £1 million or £1.25 million. It might then split this loss between A and B. But the court has a complete discretion whether to give A full protection, zero protection or a partial award. The court cannot award more than the valuable benefit.

18-024   This discussion of the building which burns down concerns a situation where Goff J's analysis requires identification of an "end product", a term not in fact used in s.1(3). However, Goff J added that the end-product analysis will not apply to services consisting of the surveying of land or the transport of goods:[22]

> "[I]n some cases the services will have no end product; for example, where the services consist of doing such work as surveying, or transporting goods. In each case, it is necessary to ask the question: what benefit has the defendant obtained by reason of the plaintiff's contractual performance?"

18-025   But this judgment, however elaborate, is merely one judge's approach to the application of this open-textured provision. And so, Goff J's analysis, although the first (and thus far the only first instance) judicial word on this topic, might not be the

19   [1979] 1 W.L.R. 783, 801–802.
20   E. Peel (ed), *Treitel, The Law of Contract* 15th edn (London: Sweet & Maxwell, 2020), 19-110 (discussing the facts of (1867) L.R. 2 C.P. 651).
21   The nineteenth-century case, *Appleby v Myers* (1867) L.R. 2 C.P. 651, involved very similar facts (a factory consumed by fire, causing destruction of, among other things, machinery installed by one of the parties), although, of course, this case antedated the 1943 Act.
22   [1979] 1 W.L.R. 783 at 801–802.

last. This point was made rather bluntly by Lawton LJ in the Court of Appeal:[23]

"[Section 1(3)] gives no help as to how, or upon what principles, the court is to make its assessment or as to what factors it is to take into account. The responsibility lies with the judge: he has to fix a sum which he, not an appellate court, considers just. This word connotes the mental processes going to forming an opinion. What is just is what the trial judge thinks is just. That being so, an appellate court is not entitled to interfere with his decision unless it is so plainly wrong that it cannot be just. The concept of what is just is not an absolute one. Opinions among right thinking people may, and probably will, differ as to what is just in a particular case. No one person enjoys the faculty of infallibility as to what is just. It is with these considerations in mind that we approach this case."

Lawton LJ added:[24]   **18-026**

"[Counsel for] the plaintiffs, accepted that there could be more than one way of assessing a just sum. He pointed out that there was nothing in the Act to indicate that its purpose was to enable the judge to apportion losses or profits, or to put the parties in the positions which they would have been in if the contract had been fully performed or if it had never been made. This we accept. He submitted that the concept behind the Act was to prevent unjust enrichment. This is what the judge had thought. We get no help from the use of words which are not in the statute…This court would not be justified in setting aside the judge's way of assessment merely because we thought that there were better ways. Mr Rokison tried to show that the judge's way was wrong and palpably wrong…It cannot be said that the judge went wrong, and certainly not palpably wrong, in assessing a just sum by reference to the concept of reimbursing the plaintiffs."

Section 1(5) of the 1943 Act provides that, if an express term of the contract **18-027** required B (or A) to insure against a risk, that term must be taken into account for the purpose of determining whether any sum should be recovered or retained under s.1(2) and (3). But, if either A or B had in fact decided to take out insurance, even though he had not been expressly bound to do so under the A/B contract, the court cannot take the fact of insurance into account. The rationale of this distinction is that a contractual allocation of risk can be inferred (and then taken into account under the Act) only if one party was contractually obliged to take out insurance.

Scope of the Act   The Act applies all contracts except those excluded from the **18-028** operation of the Act by s.2(5). The Act does not apply

"(a) to any charter party, except a time charterparty or a charterparty by way of demise, or to any contract (other than a charterparty) for the carriage of goods by sea".

This provision reflects the importance and autonomy of such contracts at the time of the Act,[25] and the same factor, albeit with less force, applies today. No exception is made for other contracts of carriage, such as carriage by road or by air, the significance of which is evidently greater now than it was in 1943 but which may

---

23   [1981] 1 W.L.R. 232 at 238, CA.
24   [1981] 1 W.L.R. 232 at 242–243, CA; it is clear that Lord Goff was unimpressed by Lawton LJ's remark in the Court of Appeal: Lord Goff, "The Search for Principle" (Maccabaean Lecture, 1983), reprinted in William Swadling and Gareth Jones (eds), *The Search for Principle: Essays in Honour of Lord Goff of Chieveley* (Oxford: Oxford University Press, 1999), 313 at 324.
25   In particular to preserve the rule that freight due before frustration remains due (*Byrne v Schiller* (1871) L.R. 6 Ex. 319); G.L. Williams, *The Law Reform (Frustrated Contracts) Act 1943* (London: Stevens & Sons, 1944), p.72 ff.

well lack the element of duration found in charterparties of ships.

18-029   The Act does not apply (b) to contracts of insurance,[26] largely to maintain an old and established rule about the non-apportionment of premiums once the risk insured has started to run.[27]

18-030   The Act does not apply (c) to any contract to which the Sale of Goods Act 1979 s.7 applies,[28]

> "or to any other contract for the sale, or for the sale and delivery, of specific goods, where the contract is frustrated by reason of the fact that the goods have perished".[29]

18-031   It is remarkable that only two cases on the Act have been reported.[30] In each relatively large sums of money were at stake. In practice, it seems that disputes arising from frustrated contract are resolved by other means, such as arbitration. An alternative explanation is that the Act applies to contracts that have been frustrated, and the doctrine of frustration is "not lightly to be invoked to relieve contracting parties of the normal consequences of imprudent bargains".[31]

---

[26]   The subsection continues "save as is provided by subsection (5) of the foregoing section", a reference to the calculation of the "just sum".

[27]   *Tyrie v Fletcher* (1777) 2 Cowp. 666 at 668 per Lord Mansfield.

[28]   This section avoids contracts for the sale of specific goods which perish before the risk has passed to the buyer, an exception "to be regretted" according to G.L. Williams, *The Law Reform (Frustrated Contracts) Act 1943* (London: Stevens & Sons, 1944), p.81.

[29]   For the "entirely capricious distinctions" which may be produced by s.2(5)(c) and for which the purpose is not apparent, E. Peel (ed), Treitel, *The Law of Contract* 15th edn (London: Sweet & Maxwell, 2020), 19-122

[30]   *BP (Exploration) Libya Ltd v Hunt* [1983] 2 A.C. 352 and *Gamerco SA v ICM/Fair Warning (Agency) Ltd* [1995] 1 W.L.R. 1226. The scope of the Act was a marginal issue in *DVD Bk v Shere Shipping* [2013] EWHC 2321 (Ch) but did not have to be applied.

[31]   *Pioneer Shipping Ltd v BTP Tioxide Ltd "The Nema"* [1982] A.C. 724 at 752 per Lord Roskill. This attitude persisted through the 2008 economic crisis; e.g. *Gold Group Properties v BDW Trading Ltd* [2010] EWHC 323 (TCC); [2010] B.L.R. 235.

PART IV REMEDIES

By Professor Andrew Tettenborn

CHAPTER 19

CLAIMS IN DEBT

I. THE NATURE OF DEBT

The action of debt

Although the action of debt most commonly arises in the context of contractual **19-001**
liability, it is a general cause of action applicable to any "sums of money subject
to an obligation, however arising, to repay them".[1] It is thus not limited to contract.[2]

In the context of contract, an action of debt can take one of two forms. First, and **19-002**
most importantly, it can take the form of an action for a sum of money due to the
claimant under an express or implied promise by the defendant to pay it. Its most
obvious manifestation in this context is a claim for the price of goods or services
supplied. But it can equally be a claim for rent under a subsisting lease of land[3] or
chattels;[4] for money due on the happening of some event, as where a buyer of land
promises to pay a sum as and when planning permission is obtained, or an employer
agrees to make a payment to a dismissed employee in lieu of notice;[5] or for that mat-

---

[1] See Longstaff J in *R (Kemp) v Denbighshire Local Health Board* [2006] EWHC 181 (Admin); [2007]
1 W.L.R. 639 at [86]; also McPherson J in *Rothwells Ltd v Nommack (No. 100) Pty Ltd* [1990] 2
Qd. R. 85; (1988) 13 A.C.L.R. 421 at 422 ("a liquidated sum in money presently due, owing and
payable by one person, called the debtor, to another person called the creditor").

[2] For example, a duty to pay a sum by way of restitution of unjust enrichment is a "debt" (*Chitty on
Contracts*, 34th ed, London, Sweet & Maxwell, 2022, para.32-17): see Rimer J's discussion in *Hope
v Premierpace (Europe) Ltd* [1999] BPIR 695 and also the Irish *McGrath v O'Driscoll* [2006] IEHC
195; [2007] 1 I.L.R.M. 203; also cf. *Woolwich Equitable Building Society v Inland Revenue Comrs*
[1993] A.C. 70 (where the point was accepted). So is a tax liability (*Comr of Stamps (WA) v West
Australian Trustee, Executor & Agency Co Ltd* (1925) 36 C.L.R. 98; *Re McGreavy* [1950] Ch. 269),
and the liability arising from a foreign judgment (see *Godard v Gray* (1870–71) L.R. 6 Q.B. 139 at
147 (Blackburn J) and *Rubin v Eurofinance SA* [2012] UKSC 46; [2013] B.C.C. 1 at [9] (Lord
Collins)). So too with an interim costs award: *King v Bar Mutual Indemnity Fund* [2023] EWHC
1408 (Ch).

[3] See e.g. *Reichman v Beveridge* [2006] EWCA Civ 1659; [2007] 1 P. & C.R. 20 (right to rent subsisting as a debt, not damages, and hence no duty to mitigate loss unless and until lease surrendered or
terminated).

[4] E.g. *ILFC UK Ltd v Olympus Airways SA* [2020] EWHC 221 (Comm) at [23] (lease of aircraft: while
lease subsisted, claim in debt for rent, then after termination for damages for loss of income stream).

[5] See *Abrahams v Performing Rights Society Ltd* [1995] I.C.R. 1028 and more recently *Geys v Societe
Generale* [2012] UKSC 63; [2013] 1 A.C. 523 and *Mackenzie v AA Ltd (formerly AA Plc)* [2022]
EWCA Civ 901; [2022] I.C.R. 1362. So also with a stakeholder looking after monies pending some
event: see *Various North Point Pall Mall Purchasers v 174 Law Solicitors Ltd* [2022] EWHC 4 (Ch)
at [37]–[38] (though note *Hastingwood Property Ltd v Saunders Bearman Anselm* [1991] Ch. 114,
123-124, where it was said that the cause of action might also be money had and received).

ter an abstract payment undertaking or similar claim, as where a bank issues a bond payable on demand or letter of credit.[6]

19-003   The second form an action in debt can take is that of a restitutionary claim arising in connection with a contract. Examples include claims for the repayment of money paid for a consideration that totally fails,[7] and the right to sue for a *quantum meruit* or *quantum valebat* in the case of a contract either ineffective or which is terminated for breach[8] or (it is suggested) for some other reason.[9] In a suitable claim both types of claim may co-exist: Thus a claim for the value of services rendered under a contract without agreement as to price may as often as not be expressed either as a claim for a *quantum meruit* or as a claim to enforce an implicit contractual obligation to pay a reasonable price.[10]

19-004   There seems no doubt that an action in debt may co-exist with, and cover much the same ground as, other kinds of claims that can arise out of a contract, such as a claim for damages. For example, where a contract is repudiated after services have been rendered under it but before payment has become due for them, the innocent party has a choice whether to claim in debt for a *quantum meruit* or in damages for loss suffered.[11] Again, where A is contractually liable to account to B for sums received on B's behalf, B's claim may on occasion be characterised as a claim for damages.[12] Nevertheless, an action in debt remains a distinct cause of action;[13] and it is worth spending a little time outlining the differences.[14]

---

[6]   See *Standard Chartered Bank v Dorchester LNG (2) Ltd* [2014] EWCA Civ 1382; [2016] Q.B. 1; and generally R. Goode, "Abstract Payment Undertakings" in P. Cane & J. Stapleton (eds), *Essays for Patrick Atiyah* (Oxford: Oxford University Press, 1991).

[7]   Accepted, for the sake of argument, by Nugee J in *Howell v Lerwick Commercial Mortgage Corp Ltd* [2015] EWHC 1177 (Ch); [2015] 1 W.L.R. 3554 at [20]; see too the same judge in *Glenn v Watson* [2018] EWHC 2016 (Ch) at [539].

[8]   *Segur v Franklin* (1934) 34 SR (NSW) 67 at 72 (Jordan CJ); *Mann v Paterson Constructions Pty Ltd* [2019] HCA 32 at [70] ff (Gageler J) and [198] (Nettle, Gordon & Edelman JJ).

[9]   For example, an express termination clause or frustration.

[10]   See e.g. *Dŵr Cymru (Welsh Water) Cyf v Carmarthenshire CC* [2004] EWHC 2991 (TCC) at [40]–[41] (Jackson J); *Phillips & Co (a firm) v Bath Housing Co-operative Ltd* [2012] EWCA Civ 1591; [2013] 1 W.L.R. 1479 at [16]–[19]. It is nevertheless true that in the context of claims for the reasonable value of services rendered under a contract, the terms of the contract and the intention of the parties will be of crucial importance in quantifying the claim, and the claimant will not be allowed to be in a better position suing in restitution that he would have been in had the contract been performed. See *Benedetti v Sawiris* [2013] UKSC 50; [2014] A.C. 938 at [9] (Lord Clarke) and *Mann v Paterson Constructions Pty Ltd* [2019] HCA 32; [2019] 267 C.L.R. 560.

[11]   See cases such as *Planché v Colburn* (1831) 8 Bing 14 as explained in *Mann v Paterson Constructions Pty Ltd* [2019] HCA 32.

[12]   So held in *Equitas Ltd & Anor v Walsham Bros & Co Ltd* [2013] EWHC 3264 (Comm); [2014] P.N.L.R. 8; also *Various North Point Pall Mall Purchasers v 174 Law Solicitors Ltd* [2022] EWHC 4 (Ch) at [71]–[72] (although a stakeholder's liability to return the stake sounded in debt, also a claim for damages when stake released in breach of contract).

[13]   Thus even if a contract is for some reason unenforceable, this is no *necessary* ground for refusing an action for the reasonable value of services rendered under it, provided that allowing such a claim would not undermine the policy of the law: see e.g. *Scott v Pattison* [1923] 2 K.B. 723 and the Australian decision in *Pavey & Matthews Pty. Ltd. v Paul* (1987) 162 C.L.R. 221.

[14]   A. Burrows, *Remedies for Torts and Breach of Contract*, 4th edn (Oxford: Oxford University Press, 2019), Ch.1.

Primary and secondary liability

As stated elsewhere,[15] the duties arising from a contract can be fairly neatly **19-005** divided into "primary" duties, contained in the terms of the contract itself, and "secondary" obligations, which are not. The liabilities enforced by actions for damages, for example, fall clearly in the second category. A duty to pay compensation for a breach of contract arises only on non-performance: and in enforcing it the court is not causing any express or implied promise by the contract-breaker to be performed, but rather seeking as best it can to repair the effects of the breach.[16] The action of debt, by contrast, exists to enforce the first category of obligation: the result of the court's order is that the defendant is bound to do exactly what the contract required. As will appear below, this has a number of consequences.

The significance of the distinction between debt and other claims

The difference between debt and other claims arising under a contract is far from **19-006** a mere academic issue.[17] A number of important practical consequences follow from it. The most important results of a decision to classify a claim as one in debt are summarised below:

(1) Unlike a claim in damages, in a simple debt claim no issue arises of proof of loss.[18] Suppose, for example, A agrees to build a ship for B and B agrees to pay the first instalment of the price when the keel is laid. If B repudiates after the instalment is due, A can claim it, without having to show that he has suffered loss, or that he cannot dispose of the half-built vessel elsewhere.[19]

(2) Since loss is out of account, it equally follows that there can be no question of a claimant's duty to mitigate: one cannot be bound to mitigate a loss that one is not claiming in respect of. The point is comprehensively illustrated by the House of Lords' decision in *White & Carter (Councils) Ltd v McGregor*.[20] There, claimants sued for their agreed fee for advertising the defenders' business. A plea by the defenders that they had countermanded the order before anything had been done, and hence that the claimants had been bound to mitigate by claiming damages (which no doubt would have amounted to a good deal less) was roundly dismissed by majority of the House of Lords. The action, it was pointed out, was one to recover a debt; this being so, loss or lack of it was out of account. To take another illustration, where an employee's contract provides for a payment of salary in lieu of notice, he is under no duty to mitigate by trying to look for another job

---

during the notional notice period, despite the fact that he would have been so bound had he sued for damages for wrongful dismissal.[21] And other cases have made the same point in other contexts.[22]

(3)   Matters which would allow a defendant to resist a suit for damages may well not have the same effect as regards a debt claim. For example, where an employee is dismissed for an inadequate reason it is always open to the employer to argue in response to a claim for damages that the employee had in fact, unknown to it, been guilty of a repudiatory breach justifying dismissal;[23] but if there is an agreement to pay salary in lieu of notice, the stipulated salary remains exigible once notice is given despite the existence of independent reasons which might have justified dismissal with no payment at all.[24]

(4)   Claims in debt are freely assignable.[25] Damages claims (and, it is suggested, claims in unjustified enrichment) may be assigned on principle, but nevertheless only subject to much more restrictive conditions. Effectively, assignment is effective only where the assignee can demonstrate that he has a bona fide and legitimate commercial interest in taking the assignment.[26]

(5)   Contribution between persons liable to a common claim in unliquidated damages is governed exclusively by the Civil Liability (Contribution) Act 1978; between those liable in debt, by the rules of common law and equity.[27]

(6)   Set-off is much less readily available in respect of liabilities to pay damages than in respect of mutual debts.[28]

(7)   Where an individual defendant is insolvent, a creditor may institute bankruptcy proceedings in respect of a debt, but he may not do so for a li-

---

[21]   See *Abrahams v Performing Rights Society Ltd* [1995] I.C.R. 1028.

[22]   E.g. leases (*Reichman v Beveridge* [2006] EWCA Civ 1659; [2007] 1 P. & C.R. 20). See also *Codemasters Software Co Ltd v Automobile Club de l'Ouost (No.2)* [2009] EWHC 3194 (Ch); [2010] F.S.R. 348 at [29]–[35].

[23]   *Boston Deep Sea Fishing & Ice Co v Ansell* (1888) 39 Ch D 339; *Cyril Leonard & Co v Simo Securities Trust Ltd* [1972] 1 W.L.R. 80.

[24]   *Cavenagh v William Evans Ltd* [2012] EWCA Civ 697; [2013] 1 W.L.R. 238.

[25]   See e.g. *Fitzroy v Cave* [1905] 1 K.B. 564; *Norglen Ltd v Reeds Rains Prudential Ltd* [1999] 2 A.C. 1; *Camdex International Ltd v Bank of Zambia* [1998] Q.B. 22; *Ndole Assets Ltd v Designer M & E Services UK Ltd* [2017] EWHC 1148 (TCC), [2017] 1 W.L.R. 4367 at [61]–[62] (Coulson J); M. Smith, *The Law of Assignment*, 2nd ed (Oxford: Oxford University Press, 2013), paras 23-39—23-46.

[26]   See in particular *Trendtex Ltd v Crédit Suisse* [1982] A.C. 679 and *Massai Aviation Services Ltd v Att-Gen of the Bahamas* [2007] UKPC 12; also generally A. Tettenborn, "Assignment of Rights to Compensation" [2007] L.M.C.L.Q. 392. For a case of a blatant assignment with no such legitimate interest, see *Simpson v Norfolk & Norwich University Hospital, NHS Trust* [2011] EWCA Civ 1149; [2012] Q.B. 640.

[27]   *Hampton v Minns* [2002] 1 W.L.R. 1; also *RSA Insurance Plc v Assicurazioni Generali SpA* [2018] EWHC 1237 (QB) (contribution between liability insurers governed by 1978 Act because liabilities lay in damages). The point can matter because there is a short two year limitation for statutory claims to contribution but not for other contribution claims: see s.10 of the Limitation Act 1980. It was this matter that was in issue in *RSA*.

[28]   The reason being that both statutory and equitable set-off are available in debt claims, whereas only equitable set-off applies to unliquidated damages claims. See generally R. Derham, *Derham on the Law of Set-off*, 4th edn (Oxford: Oxford University Press, 2010), Ch.2. For an early example of a case where this mattered, see *Luckie v Bushby* (1853) 13 C.B. 864 (no statutory set-off against liability of insurer, the latter being an unliquidated claim).

ability in damages unless and until he has obtained judgment on his claim and thus transmuted it into a debt.[29]

(8) Where a debt is paid late, the creditor may, quite apart from his right to statutory pre-judgment interest,[30] claim damages at large for any loss he has suffered as a result of being kept out of his money, on the simple basis that the debtor who pays late commits a breach of contract.[31] In addition, if the debt is a trade or governmental debt, there may also be a statutory right to generous interest under the provisions of the Late Payment of Commercial Debts Act 1998.[32] Damages, by contrast, are treated in an entirely different way. The duty to pay damages not being a primary duty arising under the terms of the contract, it follows that there can be no liability in breach of contract for delay in paying them.[33] For late payment of damages, the only remedy is a statutory claim for pre-judgment interest, which is often far less advantageous to the claimant.

II.   The Right to Sue for a Debt

When an action in debt can be brought—general

Unlike an action for damages, the availability of an action for debt[34] based on a **19-007** contractual right to payment depends entirely on the express or implied terms of the contract. A sum payable on demand may be sued for as soon as demand is made and the defendant has had a reasonable chance of making the mechanical arrangements to pay;[35] if money is expressed to be payable on the occurrence of a given event, or on a particular date, the right to sue for it arises on that date or as soon as

---

[29] Insolvency Act 1986 s.267 (strictly speaking referring to a "debt for a liquidated sum"). Company insolvency proceedings, by contrast, may be based on almost any liability: see Insolvency Rules 1986 (SI 1986/1925) r.13.12.

[30] Under s.35A of the Senior Courts Act 1981 or s.69 of the County Courts Act 1980, as the case may be.

[31] See the important decision in *Sempra Metals Ltd (formerly Metallgesellschaft Ltd) v Inland Revenue Commissioners* [2007] UKHL 34; [2008] 1 A.C. 561; also *Sagicor Bank Jamaica Ltd v Seaton* [2022] UKPC 48; [2023] 2 All E.R. 81.

[32] See s.1. The right can be ousted by contract, but only subject to certain restrictions (ss.8–9). Furthermore the Act does not apply at all in the case of contracts governed by English law only by choice of the parties: s.12(1). The Act, although based on an EU Directive (the Late Payment Directive, 2011/7/EU), remains in force despite Brexit.

[33] "There is no such thing as a cause of action in damages for late payment of damages. The only remedy which the law affords for delay in paying damages is the discretionary award of interest pursuant to statute." (Lord Brandon in *President of India v Lips Maritime Corp* [1988] A.C. 395 at 425). See too *Sprung v Royal Insurance (UK) Ltd* [1997] C.L.C. 70 (no extra compensation for late settlement of claim by insurer, on the basis that the insurer's claim sounds in damages and not in debt: since reversed, in the specific case of insurance, by the Insurance Act 2015 s.13A). So too s.29 of the Limitation Act 1980 does not apply to an insurance claim sounding claim in damages: *Bann Carraig Ltd v Great Lakes Reinsurance (UK) Plc* [2021] NIQB 63 (decided under the equivalent NI legislation).

[34] Note, however, that a debt itself may come into existence before it is payable or able to be sued on (a phenomenon sometimes referred to by use of the Latin tag *debitum in praesenti, solvendum in futuro*). This may be important for the purposes, for instance, of assignment (e.g. *Earle (G.T.) Ltd v Hemsworth RDC* (1928) 44 T.L.R. 605) or insolvency (e.g. *O'Driscoll v Manchester Insurance Committee* [1915] 3 K.B. 499, esp at 516–517 (Bankes LJ)).

[35] For detailed discussion of this, see *Cripps (Pharmaceuticals) Ltd v Wickenden* [1973] 2 All E.R. 606 and *Bank of Baroda v Panessar* [1987] Ch. 335.

the event occurs.[36] So where a contract to supply goods provides unconditionally for payment at a given time, this sum can be sued for entirely independently of whether there has been delivery or a transfer of ownership;[37] and the same thing may well go for a promised weekly or monthly payment in exchange for which goods or services are to be periodically provided.[38] Similarly it is possible, though very unlikely, for a buyer of real estate to agree to pay the price independently of whether he gets the land.[39] Again, where a contract requires payment on a given date of a deposit[40] or other irrecoverable advance payment,[41] there is no doubt that this can be sued for even if the contract has otherwise been cancelled, and independently of any loss suffered by the person suing for it.[42]

19-008   It follows that, where under the terms of a contract a sum of money becomes payable at a given point in time, the payee's right cannot be taken away by a prior wrongful repudiation of that contract by the other party, unless the repudiation is accepted. So an employee's right to a seniority-based severance payment remains unaffected even if the employer purports at an earlier time to dismiss the employee immediately without giving the requisite period of notice.[43] Conversely, once such a right has arisen, it is not taken away by a subsequent repudiation of the contract, even if it is accepted. One example is the case of a deposit, referred to above: if a contract of sale stipulates for payment of a deposit, this remains payable even if the contract is brought to an end following repudiation by the buyer.[44] Hence in *Hyundai Heavy Industries Co Ltd v Papadopoulos*[45] where shipbuilders stipulated for various stage payments to become payable at particular points in the process of construction, these stage payments remained payable by the buyers and hence by their guarantors, despite the subsequent cancellation of the contract as a result of non-payment of later instalments by the buyers. Only if the contract has been terminated before the due date for payment, whether by frustration, accepted

---

[36]   There is generally no need for notice to the debtor: *Bradford Old Bank Ltd v Sutcliffe* [1918] 2 K.B. 833 at 848 (Scrutton LJ).

[37]   In certain cases—notably, where the price is payable "on a day certain irrespective of delivery"— this is statutory: see Sale of Goods Act 1979 s.49(2). But even where the statute does not apply, either because the contract is not one for the sale of goods or because the criterion of a "day certain irrespective of delivery" is not satisfied, the same result follows as a matter of the general law. See *PST Energy 7 Shipping LLC v OW Bunker Malta Ltd* [2016] UKSC 23; [2016] A.C. 1034 at [40]– [58]. However, this is subject to the implicit qualification that the claimant is not clearly unable to perform the contract: *Otis Vehicle Rentals Ltd (formerly Brandrick Hire (Birmingham) Ltd) v Ciceley Commercials Ltd (Damages)* [2002] EWCA Civ 1064.

[38]   Compare the Australian decision in *Chinatex (Australia) Pty Ltd v Bindaree Beef Pty Ltd* [2018] NSWCA 126 at [57]–[64].

[39]   As in the antique but very important decision in *Pordage v Cole* (1669) 1 Wms. Saund. 319. Normally, however, the inference is that conveyance is necessary: *Heard v Wadham* (1801) 1 East 619.

[40]   *Hardy v Griffiths* [2014] EWHC 3947 (Ch); [2015] Ch. 417; also *Firodi Shipping Ltd v Griffon Shipping LLC* [2013] EWCA Civ 1567; [2014] 1 C.L.C. 1.

[41]   E.g. *Unaoil Ltd v Leighton Offshore Pte Ltd* [2014] EWHC 2965 (Comm); (2014) 156 Con. L.R. 24 (non-refundable advance payment to pipeline sub-contractor).

[42]   See the cases referred to in the previous two notes.

[43]   *Geys v Société Générale, London Branch* [2012] UKSC 63; [2013] 1 A.C. 523.

[44]   *Hardy v Griffiths* [2014] EWHC 3947 (Ch); [2015] Ch. 417; *Firodi Shipping Ltd v Griffon Shipping LLC* [2013] EWCA Civ 1567; [2014] 1 C.L.C. 1.

[45]   [1980] 1 W.L.R. 1129; also *Stocznia Gdanska SA v Latvian Shipping Co* [1998] 1 W.L.R. 574. See too *Brooks v Beirnstein* [1909] 1 K.B. 98 and *Chatterton v Maclean* [1951] 1 All E.R. 761 (hire and hire purchase respectively: accepted repudiation does not take away right to accrued hire).

repudiation or any other means, do sums payable under it cease to be payable;[46] and even there, it may well be open to the parties to stipulate that an obligation to pay will nevertheless remain enforceable.[47] A fortiori, the fact that a party is in breach of his obligations under a contract will presumptively not deprive him of his right to claim a debt payable under it once the right has accrued.[48]

Conditional obligations to pay

A sum may be payable on principle under a contract, but the claimant's right to sue the defendant for it may be subject to some further condition. For example, goods may have been delivered or services rendered subject to a stipulation that the recipient need not pay until they have been certified as satisfactory; or a contracting party may be entitled to a particular payment only if he has observed a given stipulation in the contract. As a general rule such provisions mean exactly what they say: so long as the condition remains unsatisfied, the debtor cannot be sued.[49] But there is one important exception. A contractor is normally bound implicitly not deliberately to prevent the fulfilment of the contract;[50] and if the only reason the condition fails is the defendant's breach of this or some other contractual obligation,[51] then the latter is barred from invoking it as a defence. This seems the best interpretation of the sale of goods case of *Mackay v Dick*.[52] Sellers delivered a mechanical digger to buyers under an arrangement that the latter could change their mind if the machine failed a test of effectiveness. The buyers having prevented any such test being carried out, the House of Lords held them liable to pay the price. Similarly, where buyers' obligation to pay for goods once delivered was conditional on customs clearance, they were held liable to pay where owing to their breach of contract no such clearance could take place.[53] And an agreement to pay for services was similarly treated by the Court of Appeal in *Frederick Leyland & Co Ltd v*

19-009

---

[46] See e.g. *The Lorna I* [1983] 1 Lloyd's Rep. 373 (advance freight: contract frustrated by sinking of vessel).

[47] See *Geys v Société Générale, London Branch* [2012] UKSC 63; [2013] 1 A.C. 523 at [68] (Lord Wilson); also the comments in *Rock Refrigeration Ltd v Jones* [1997] I.C.R. 938 at 947 (Simon Brown LJ) and 958–960 (Phillips LJ). These comments concerned covenants against non-competition, but there is no reason to limit them to that context or to disapply them to other promises, for example to pay money.

[48] *Donovan v Grainmarket Asset Management LLP* [2020] EWHC 17 (Comm) esp at [197]–[200] (performance fees payable under joint venture agreement). Note, however, that it may have the converse effect of precluding a claim for unjust enrichment in respect of the same performance: see the Australian decision in *Mann v Paterson Constructions Pty Ltd* [2019] HCA 32; [2019] 267 C.L.R. 560 at [25]–[27] (Kiefel CJ, Bell and Keane JJ) and [176] (Nettle, Gordon and Edelman JJ).

[49] For a straightforward example, see *Euro London Appointments Ltd v Claessens International Ltd* [2006] EWCA Civ 385; [2006] 2 Lloyd's Rep. 436 (right to refund of fees from employment agency where employee resigned conditional on prompt payment of those fees: no right where fees paid late).

[50] See Lord Blackburn in *Mackay v Dick* (1881) 6 App. Cas. 251 at 263; also *Merton LBC v Stanley Hugh Leach Ltd* (1986) 32 B.L.R. 51 and *CEL Group Ltd v Nedlloyd Lines UK Ltd* [2004] 1 Lloyd's Rep. 381.

[51] There must be a wrong: the mere fact that the defendant for self-serving reasons chooses to act in such a way as to prevent the fulfilment of the condition, but without committing a breach of contract, will not do. See *Thompson v ASDA-MFI Group Plc* [1988] Ch. 241 (director's perk dependent on employer being subsidiary of holding company: holding company able to rely on condition despite fact that it had voluntarily sold the subsidiary); also *The Antclizo* [1992] 1 Lloyd's Rep. 558 at 567–568 (Parker LJ).

[52] (1880-81) L.R. 6 App. Cas. 251.

[53] *Tiberghien Draperie SaRL v Greenberg & Sons (Mantles) Ltd* [1953] 2 Lloyd's Rep. 739. See too

Compañía Panameña Europea Navegación Lda.[54] The limited nature of this exception must, however, be noted. It only applies where the right to payment has actually accrued: if the defendant's breach of contract prevents it accruing at all, as where a buyer simply refuses to accept goods in the first place, the only remedy is damages.[55]

When an action of debt can be brought—payment for services and assets

19-010 **(i) Payment for services** In the absence of contrary provision, the right to sue in debt for the price of services rendered arises when, and only when, performance has been rendered in full.[56] If any substantial part remains to be provided, there can be no action for the price, even subject to a set-off for that which is missing. Thus in *Cutter v Powell*,[57] a sailor who agreed for £30 to serve for a voyage from Jamaica to Liverpool died en route. His widow recovered nothing: he simply had not provided that for which the shipowner had agreed to pay him. In similar vein, a construction contractor who abandons work half-done[58] or is prevented by external causes from completing it[59] is in a similar position.[60] And more recently, it has been stated that for the same reason employees who refuse to do a substantial part of their job forfeit the right to be paid their salary save to the extent that the employer specifically accepts what is done.[61] Moreover, this rule continues to apply even if the only reason why performance has not been rendered is the defendant's own breach in preventing it, as where a builder is wrongfully dismissed before he has had a chance to complete the work he has contracted to do.[62]

19-011 Nevertheless, the requirement for complete performance is not quite as demand-

---

General Trading Co (Holdings) Ltd v Richmond Corp'n Ltd [2008] EWHC 1479 (Comm); [2008] 2 Lloyd's Rep. 475; also Oricon Waren-Handelsgeschellshaft mbH v Intergraan NV [1967] 2 Lloyd's Rep. 82.

[54] (1943) 76 Ll. L. Rep. 113 (ship repairs to be certified by owners' surveyor). See too *Ministry of Sound (Ireland) Ltd v World Online Ltd* [2003] EWHC 2178 (Ch); [2003] 2 All E.R. (Comm) 823 (agreement whereby W paid periodic sums and M promoted W's internet business and distributed W's CDs: M entitled to payment despite W's breach of contract in failing to provide disks).

[55] See *Colley v Overseas Exporters Ltd* [1921] 3 K.B. 302, where *Mackay* was distinguished on precisely this ground; also *Ministry of Sound (Ireland) Ltd v World Online Ltd* [2003] EWHC 2178 (Ch); [2003] 2 All E.R. (Comm) 823 at [33]. So also with land, as pointed out by the High Court of Australia in *Sunbird Plaza Pty Ltd v Maloney* (1989) 166 C.L.R. 245. Also see para.19-020, below.

[56] *Cutter v Powell* (1795) 6 Term. Rep. 320, below. See too *O'Driscoll v Manchester Insurance Committee* [1915] 3 K.B. 499, esp at 517 (Bankes LJ): *Bolton v Mahadeva* [1972] 1 W.L.R. 1009, esp at 1011–1013 (Cairne LJ); *Miles v Wakefield MBC* [1987] A.C. 539, esp at 552, 561 (Lords Brightman and Templeman); *Chitty on Contracts*, 33rd edn (London: Sweet & Maxwell, 2019), para.21-031.

[57] (1795) 6 Term. Rep. 320. The plaintiff also failed in a claim pro rata for work actually done, though that part of the decision has now been reversed by statute: see the Apportionment Act 1870 s.2.

[58] E.g. *Shelbourne & Co v Back & Manson* (1926) 24 Ll. L. Rep. 144; *Ibmac v Marshall (Homes) Ltd* (1968) 208 E.G. 851. See too *Sumpter v Hedges* [1898] 1 Q.B. 673 (strictly speaking a decision that there was no right to pro rata payment: but a fortiori there could be no right to the contract price); and the similar solicitors' case of *Gill v Heer Manak Solicitors* [2018] EWHC 2881 (QB); [2019] P.N.L.R. 10.

[59] *Appleby v Myers* (1866-67) L.R. 2 C.P. 651; see esp 661 (Blackburn J).

[60] He may of course have a restitutionary claim in *quantum meruit*.

[61] *Miles v Wakefield Metropolitan District Council* [1987] A.C. 539 at 553, 561 (Lords Brightman and Templeman). For obvious reasons, this rule is of enormous significance in the law of industrial relations.

[62] *Planché v Coburn* (1831) 8 Bing. 14; *National Cash Register Co Ltd v Stanley* [1921] 3 K.B. 292.

ing as it looks. Despite older authority to the contrary,[63] it is now clear that what is required is substantial performance, rather than literal, absolute completion. Relatively minor omissions may be condoned. This has indeed been long accepted in respect of utterly trivial matters: a decorator who agrees to decorate an entire house with three coats of paint, for example, does not forfeit his right to be paid merely because he forgets to apply one coat in one room.[64] But the exception is not limited to such cases;[65] provided an omission is comparatively unimportant and does not amount to a repudiation or otherwise go to the root of the contract, the claimant may recover the price subject only to the defendant's right to counterclaim. So in the leading decision in *Hoenig v Isaacs*,[66] failure in the course of decorating a flat to provide certain stipulated bookcase fitments was held not to prejudice a claim for the price of the work subject to a counterclaim for any loss caused. "Unless the breach does go to the root of the matter," said Denning LJ, "the employer cannot resist payment of the price."[67] This breach did not, and he could not.

We saw above that a claimant who fails to perform in full cannot recover the **19-012** price. The converse also applies: once performance has been rendered in full, then as a general rule the defendant has no answer to an action for the price, whatever the other circumstances. Hence in the important case of *White & Carter (Councils) Ltd v McGregor*[68] it was held that advertising agents had a claim for services rendered, despite the fact that to their knowledge their performance had been unwanted because the defendant clients had made it quite clear that they had changed their minds.

On a similar basis, the mere fact that work has been done incompetently or **19-013** defectively will not prevent a claim for payment succeeding if the work has in fact been finished[69] (though there is obviously likely to be a set-off available to the defendant[70]). *Dakin & Co Ltd v Lee*[71] in 1916, the leading decision on the point, illustrates the issue very neatly. In that case jobbing builders underpinned a house, but in so doing used less than the stipulated depth of cement. The Court of Appeal unhesitatingly allowed them to sue for the price of their services notwithstanding. As Pickford LJ put it:

"What the plaintiffs have done is to perform the work which they had contracted to do,

---

As Lloyd J pithily put it in *The Alaskan Trader (No.2)* [1983] 2 Lloyd's Rep. 645 at 649: "You cannot claim remuneration under a contract if you have not earned it; if you are prevented from earning it, your only remedy is in damages."

63 See e.g. *Ellis v Hamlen* (1810) 3 Taunt. 52 (disapproved in *Dakin & Co Ltd v Lee* [1916] 1 K.B. 566).

64 An example given in *Dakin & Co Ltd v Lee* [1916] 1 K.B. 566 at 579 (Cozens-Hardy MR); see too *Bolton v Mahadeva* [1972] 1 W.L.R. 1009 at 1011 (Cairns LJ). In *Dakin v Lee* itself, a failure to bolt certain joists together was accordingly held insufficient to disentitle a builder to payment.

65 "It would be wrong to say that the contractor is only entitled to payment if the defects are so trifling as to be covered by the de minimis rule": Cairns LJ in *Bolton v Mahadeva* [1972] 1 W.L.R. 1009 at 1013. See too *Mondel v Steel* (1841) 8 M & W 858 at 870 (Parke B).

66 [1952] 2 All E.R. 176. See too *Forrest v Scottish County Investment Co*, 1916 S.C. (HL) 28 (slight deviation from plans does not disentitle builder to claim price of work).

67 [1952] 2 All E.R. 181.

68 [1962] A.C. 413. See above, para.7-082 ff.

69 See the old cases of *Broom v Davis* (1794) 7 East 480 and *Cutler v Close* (1832) 5 C & P 337. The rule in *Dakin v Oxley* (1864) 15 C.B. (N.S.) 646, that freight is deemed earned even if the goods are delivered damaged, is another manifestation of the same principle.

70 See e.g. *Sim v Rotherham MBC* [1987] Ch. 216 (teacher refusing to do small part of work: employer can dock pay by way of set-off for damages).

71 [1916] 1 K.B. 566. See too *Hoenig v Isaacs* [1952] 2 All E.R. 176.

but they have done some part of it insufficiently and badly; and that does not disentitle them to be paid.[72] "

19-014 Nevertheless, it should be noted that some defects in performance are so serious that they can be regarded as a failure substantially to complete work at all. So lawyers who provide the services of an unqualified clerk rather than those of a solicitor as promised are regarded as not having provided the necessary contractual performance at all, and therefore cannot recover their fees, however competently the clerk may in fact have served the client.[73] And very serious incompetence itself may occasionally have the same effect. A case in point is *Bolton v Mahadeva*,[74] where grave and dangerous defects in a central heating system costing £560 cost some £175 to rectify: there Cairns LJ, considering "both the nature of the defects and the proportion between the cost of rectifying them and the contract price",[75] distinguished *Dakin v Lee* and dismissed the installer's claim for the price. Similarly, in the grisly case of *Vigers v Cook*[76] decided some years earlier, an undertaker failed in his action for fees when he put a cadaver in an unventilated coffin which ruptured, producing foul-smelling effluvia that effectively prevented the coffin's introduction into the church at all. As Lush J put it, justifying his decision, "the work done by the plaintiff was entirely different from what was contracted for".[77]

19-015 So far we have been assuming that under the terms of a contract services the ordinary rule applies and are to be paid for as and when rendered. This is, however, not necessarily the case: the parties may have stipulated for prepayment of part or all of the price. Where this is so, clearly the rules above cannot apply, and an action for the price must lie as soon as the date for payment has arrived. As Lord Alverstone CJ put it in 1908:

> "where an agreement provides for the payment of a sum of money, and does not make the performance of the thing which is the consideration for the payment a condition precedent to or concurrent with the payment, an action may be maintained for the recovery of the sum of money without such performance".[78]

But this is subject to two exceptions. First, where the provider has previously repudiated the contract and the recipient has accepted that repudiation, then the obligation to pay in advance will equally have disappeared. And secondly, it is suggested that there will be no duty to pay where it is clear, whether from the buyer's own statement or from other circumstances such as the buyer's insolvency, that the contract will not be performed. To put another way, the duty to pay the price of services is subject to an implicit condition that the claimant be willing and able to perform them.[79]

19-016 One final point needs to be made concerning the right to be paid for services. The

---

[72] [1916] 1 K.B. 582. See too Lord Cozens-Hardy at 579.

[73] See *Pearless de Rougemont & Co v Pilbrow* [1999] 3 All E.R. 355.

[74] [1972] 1 W.L.R. 1009.

[75] [1972] 1 W.L.R. 1013.

[76] [1919] 2 K.B. 475

[77] [1919] 2 K.B. 480.

[78] *Workman, Clark & Co Ltd v Lloyd Brazileño* [1908] 1 K.B. 968 at 976–977. Compare too *Pordage v Cole* (1668) 1 Wms Saunders 319 and *Mattock v Kinglake* (1839) 10 A & E 50 (cases concerning prepayment for real property); also s.49(2) of the Sale of Goods Act 1979.

[79] Compare the sales cases of *Maclean v Dunn* (1828) 4 Bing. 722 (decided at common law), and *Otis Vehicle Rentals Ltd (formerly Brandrick Hire (Birmingham) Ltd) v Ciceley Commercials Ltd (Dam-*

rules described above are default rules, and must give way to any express or implied contrary stipulation. In particular, it may be that the terms of a contract import an intention that, exceptionally, a particular risk associated with non-performance should be placed on the recipient of the services. If this is so then, in so far as the reason for failure to complete performance is the occurrence of that risk, there is no bar to claiming payment. This arises particularly in the case of carriage contracts that provide for a lump sum or charter freight. Such contracts are normally regarded as placing the risk of loss in transit on the shipper; hence the courts have consistently held that if goods are lost at sea freight is nevertheless payable.[80]

(ii) Payment for assets sold As regards sale of goods and other assets, the reasoning is much the same as with services; unless the duty to pay is independent of the seller's duty to transfer the assets—a fact not readily inferred—performance is essential to a claim for the price.[81] But a number of specialised rules have grown up. For these purposes, a contract of sale of goods seems prima facie to be regarded as fully performed by the seller once the ownership in the goods has passed to the buyer.[82] Thus s.49(1) of the Sale of Goods Act 1979[83] provides that once this has happened, the seller can recover the price even though the goods may not have been delivered and indeed even though the buyer has no intention of accepting them.[84] Hence a seller remaining in possession of goods after property has passed can simply demand the price and tell the buyer that the goods are at his risk and disposal, however intransigent the buyer and however reasonable it might be for the seller to try to resell.[85] Admittedly, this leaves a theoretical problem where it is clear that the seller at the time of the action either cannot or will not deliver the goods at all. In such a case, it is suggested that the buyer can resist liability either on the basis of s.28 of the Act, which makes the right to the price also conditional on readiness and willingness to deliver,[86] or on the principle of circuity of action, since if forced to pay for something which ex hypothesi he will not get, the buyer will in any case be able to recover his money on the basis of failure of consideration.[87] Two qualifications to the above rule must be noted, however, both concerned with defective deliveries.

19-017

---

ages) [2002] EWCA Civ 1064 (decided under s.49(2) of the Sale of Goods Act 1979). Another way to reach the same result is circuity of action: the buyer is under no duty to pay money which he will later and inevitably have the right to recover as money paid for a failed consideration.

[80] See e.g. *Robinson v Knights* (1872-73) L.R. 8 C.P. 465; *Merchant Shipping Co v Armitage* (1873) L.R. 9 Q.B. 99; *The Tarva* [1973] 2 Lloyd's Rep. 385. In *New Line SS Co Ltd v Bryson & Co*, 1910 S.C. 409 the rule was accepted, but disapplied on the facts.

[81] E.g. *Colley v Overseas Exporters Ltd* [1921] 3 K.B. 302 (goods); *Heard v Wadham* (1801) 1 East 619 (land); *Doherty v Fannigan Holdings Ltd* [2018] EWCA Civ 1615; [2018] 2 B.C.L.C. 623 (other assets).

[82] A somewhat curious idea, since one would have thought a buyer was at least as interested in physically getting hold of the goods as in owning them. But this seems to be dealt with by s.28 of the Act: see below.

[83] Following the common law on this point: e.g. *Martindale v Smith* (1841) 1 Q.B. 389 at 395 (Lord Denman CJ).

[84] The seller may alternatively claim damages; and if he resells the goods under s.48 this is his only remedy: *Ward (RV) v Bignall* [1967] 1 Q.B. 534.

[85] This is an unbusinesslike solution, which for that reason is heavily qualified in the US: see UCC, para.2-709(1)(b), requiring the seller to make reasonable efforts to resell and denying him the right to recover the price if he has not done so.

[86] See *Otis Vehicle Rentals Ltd v Ciceley Commercials Ltd* [2002] EWCA Civ 1064, esp at [16] (Potter LJ); also the earlier *Maclean v Dunn* (1828) 6 LJCP (OS) 184.

[87] A point assumed, though on the facts it did not apply, in the shipbuilding case of *Hyundai Heavy*

19-018   First, while the buyer must pay the price of defective goods if he accepts them,[88] a buyer who rightfully rejects[89] ceases to be liable to pay the price even if title had previously passed to him.[90] This commercially vital result can, if necessary, be justified theoretically on the basis that a rightful rejection causes property to be regarded as having remained in the seller throughout,[91] and hence that the foundation for the seller's right to sue for the price has retrospectively disappeared.

19-019   Secondly, where the wrong quantity of goods is delivered, the Sale of Goods Act 1979 (or, in consumer sales, the Consumer Rights Act 2015) similarly settles the matter of liability for the price by reference to whether the buyer has accepted the goods.[92] If the buyer does accept a short delivery, he need only pay pro rata;[93] from which it seems to follow that, however small the discrepancy, he cannot be forced to pay the actual contract price. An analogous rule applies to excessive delivery. If the buyer accepts the contractual quantity only, as he is entitled to do,[94] he is liable for the price in the normal way; if he accepts the whole he must pay pro rata for the excess.[95]

19-020   Just as a seller can presumptively claim the price once ownership has passed, conversely he cannot do so if this has not occurred. In such a case his only action is for damages for non-acceptance.[96] Moreover, as with services, this remains true even if the only reason for non-performance is the buyer's own breach of contract, despite the fact that this allows the buyer to escape his obligations by his own wrong.[97] Thus in *Stein, Forbes & Co v County Tailoring Co*,[98] where c.i.f. buyers of sheepskins wrongfully failed to take up the documents and thus obtain ownership of the goods, the sellers were limited to a claim in damages; and similarly in *Colley v Overseas Exporters*[99] the same thing happened in a contract f.o.b. where property was to pass when the goods passed the ship's rail, but the buyers failed to provide a ship.

19-021   There is, however, one exception to this principle made necessary by the doctrine

---

> *Industries Co Ltd v Papadopoulos* [1980] 1 W.L.R. 1129 (where the contract was held to be one for services as well as sale of goods).

88   This is the result of the Sale of Goods Act 1979, ss.11 and 53(1)(a). It remains true even if the goods are seriously defective; hence a "no set-off" clause is effective in such a case. See *Readie Construction Ltd v Geo Quarries Ltd* [2021] EWHC 3030 (QB).

89   E.g. because of the seller's breach of some contractual stipulation, or because the goods are defective within ss.13-15 of the 1979 Act (or, in the case of a consumer sale, the equivalent obligations under the Consumer Rights Act 2015). Obviously, this is limited to rightful rejection: a buyer cannot retrospectively take away the seller's right to the price by a purported but wrongful later rejection of the goods.

90   And, if he is paid, can recover the price.

91   See *Head v Tattersall* (1871-72) L.R. 7 Ex. 7 (where goods rejected, property and hence risk deemed always to have been in seller). Although decided at common law, it is submitted that this case remains good law under the 1979 Act (and, in the case of consumer sales, under the Consumer Rights Act 2015).

92   The buyer may always reject in consumer cases: Consumer Rights Act 2015 s.25. In commercial cases he may do so under the Sale of Goods Act 1979 ss.30(1) and 30(2), save where the discrepancy is so small that it is unreasonable to do so (s.30(2A)). See M. Bridge (ed), *Benjamin's Sale of Goods*, 11th edn (London: Sweet & Maxwell, 2020), paras 8-041–8-044.

93   1979 Act s.30(1); 2015 Act s.25(1).

94   1979 Act s.30(2); 2015 Act s.25(2).

95   1979 Act s.30(3); 2015 Act s.25(3).

96   *Ward (RV) Ltd v Bignall* [1967] 1 Q.B. 534.

97   Any doubts on this score were dispelled by McCardie J in *Colley v Overseas Exporters Ltd* [1921] 3 K.B. 302.

98   (1916) 86 L.J.K.B. 448

99   [1921] 3 K.B. 302

of risk. This applies if risk passes before property is transferred. If goods are merely damaged after the risk has passed, then the normal rule applies: if the buyer does not accept them, he is liable in damages, but (it seems) not for the price. But if the goods are actually destroyed, then it seems the seller can recover the price despite the fact that ex hypothesi there can never now be a transfer of ownership.[100]

As with services, there have to be special rules for contracts requiring prepay- **19-022** ment for goods to be supplied in the future. Where a sale contract requires the advance payment to be made at a particular time, then exceptionally s.49(2) of the Sale of Goods Act 1979 provides that the seller can sue for payment as soon as that time has arrived, even though delivery has not been made and title has not passed.[101]

Strictly speaking, s.49(2) only applies to the situation where the price is pay- **19-023** able on a "day certain" before the passing of property: from which it follows that it is inapt to cover cases where the time of payment is moveable and depends on outside contingencies (straightforward examples being progress payments on large items as construction progresses, or provisions for payment for goods on shipment, arrival or presentation of documents).[102] Nevertheless, it is now clear that s.49(2) is not an exhaustive description of the cases where the seller can claim the price notwithstanding that property has not passed. One example is provisions for payment against documents, or for goods on shipment or arrival, all of which are accepted to be enforceable despite being outside s.49. Another, mentioned above, is where goods are lost after risk, but not property, has passed to the buyer.[103] Furthermore, it has been held that s.49(2) is not exhaustive of the seller's rights, and does not preclude parties agreeing to make the price payable on the basis of other events if they so wish.[104]

Nevertheless, it should be noted that any right in the seller to prepayment has **19-024** been held to be subject to one implicit qualification. This is that the seller must, at

---

[100] There are surprisingly few statements of this principle. But see the pre-sale of Goods Act cases of *Castle v Playford* (1871–72) L.R. 7 Ex. 98; *Martineau v Kitching* (1872) L.R. 7 Q.B. 436 at 455 (Blackburn J); and also *PST Energy 7 Shipping LLC v OW Bunker Malta Ltd* [2016] UKSC 23; [2016] A.C. 1034 at [50]–[57] (Mance J). Generally see L. Sealy, "Risk in the Law of Sale" [1972B] C.L.J. 225 at 234. The UCC makes the point explicit: see art.2-709(1)(a) (right to sue for price of "conforming goods lost or damaged within a commercially reasonable time after risk of their loss has passed to the buyer"). Note that in the case of consumer sales risk cannot pass before delivery: Consumer Rights Act 2015 s.29(2).

[101] A section based on the common law decision in *Dunlop and Others v Grote and Another* (1845) 2 Car. & K. 153. It applies equally where the goods supplied are defective, though not (it seems) where it is clear that anything delivered is or will be entirely different from what has been ordered. See *Readie Construction Ltd v Geo Quarries Ltd* [2021] EWHC 3030 (QB).

[102] See notably *Stein Forbes & Co v County Tailoring Co* (1916) 86 L.J.K.B. 448 (payment on presentation of documents); *Harrison v Holland & Hannen Ltd* [1921] WN 235 (ditto); *Tradax Internacional SA v Goldschmidt SA* [1977] 2 Lloyd's Rep. 604 (ditto); *Colley v Overseas Exporters Ltd* [1921] 3 K.B. 302 at 306 (payment on shipment); also *Shell-Mex Ltd v Elton Co-operative Dyeing Co Ltd* (1928) 34 Com. Cas. 39 at 43 (Wright J). *Contra*, however, *Workman, Clark & Co Ltd v Lloyd Brazileño* [1908] 1 K.B. 968 at 977 (progress payment in shipbuilding contract is within s.49(2)).

[103] Above, para.19-021.

[104] *PST Energy 7 Shipping LLC v O W Bunker Malta Ltd* [2016] UKSC 23; [2016] A.C. 1034 at [40]–[58] (Lord Mance), overruling *FG Wilson (Engineering) Ltd v John Holt & Co (Liverpool) Ltd* [2013] EWCA Civ 1232; [2014] 1 W.L.R. 2365 in so far as it held the contrary. See also earlier suggestions to this effect in *Polenghi v Dried Milk Co* (1904) 10 Com. Cas. 42 and suggestions by Latham CJ and Williams J in *Minister for Supply v Servicemen's Co-op Manufacturers Ltd* (1951) 82 C.L.R. 621 at 636, 642. It is worth noting that the art.58 of the CISG takes this approach in a beautifully simple statement: "If the buyer is not bound to pay the price at any other specific time, he must pay it when the seller places either the goods or documents controlling their disposition at the buyer's disposal".

the time he sues for the price, be potentially able and willing to perform.[105] If it is clear then that he will not deliver at all, or that he cannot (for instance because he is insolvent, or because he has already sold the goods elsewhere), then s.49(2) does not apply.[106] A fortiori, it is submitted that the result will be the same where the reason for non-delivery is that the sale contract itself has been cancelled by one party on the basis of the other's breach,[107] unless the claim is for a proportion of the price characterised as a deposit[108] or, properly construed, the contract provides that the buyer is to have the right to be paid in any case, as in the case of a hire or hire purchase contract,[109] or a shipbuilding contract with stage payments intended to reflect the builder's expenditure from time to time whether or not he delivers the ship.[110]

III. DEBT OR DAMAGES: BORDERLINE CASES

19-025   In most situations, the distinction between claims in debt and damages is an obvious one that creates no problems. A promise to pay money, whether conditional or otherwise, gives rise to a debt.[111] On the other hand, breach of a promise to do something other than pay money creates a damages liability; as does a promise that something is, or will be, the case, or a promise to procure a given outcome.[112] Thus there is no doubt that an action on a warranty sounds in damages only. A warrantor, in other words, promises that a particular state of affairs exists; he does not promise to pay money, conditional on the warranty being broken. In a few cases on the borderline, however, difficulties may arise: in particular, certain claims that may look like debt claims are classified somewhat counter-intuitively as sounding in damages.

---

[105] This arguably follows in any case from s.28, which makes the duty to pay the price dependent on the seller being ready and willing to deliver. Compare *Readie Construction Ltd v Geo Quarries Ltd* [2021] EWHC 3030 (QB).

[106] *Otis Vehicle Rentals Ltd v Ciceley Commercials Ltd* [2002] EWCA Civ 1064 (where the seller had already disposed of the goods). See too *Ward (R.V.) v Bignall* [1967] 1 Q.B. 534 and the early common law case of *Maclean v Dunn* (1828) 4 Bing. 722.

[107] This is implicit in *Dies v British & International Mining & Finance Corp Ltd* [1939] 1 K.B. 724, where it is held that in such circumstances moneys, having paid, can be recovered by the buyer (on which see *Hyundai Heavy Industries Co Ltd v Papadopoulos* [1980] 1 W.L.R. 1129 at 1133–1134 (Lord Dilhorne), 1142–1143 (Lord Edmund-Davies), 1147–1148 (Lord Fraser). Cf. *McDonald v Dennys Lascelles Ltd* (1933) 48 C.L.R. 457 (no suit for instalment of payment for land after contract of sale rescinded).

[108] As in *The Blankenstein* [1985] 1 W.L.R. 435.

[109] *Brooks v Beirnstein* [1909] 1 K.B. 98; also *Chatterton v Maclean* [1951] 1 All E.R. 761

[110] *Hyundai Shipbuilding & Heavy Industries Co Ltd v Papadopoulos* [1980] 1 W.L.R. 1129 (criticised in J. Carter & G. Tolhurst, "Recovery of Contract Debts Following Termination for Breach" (2009) 25 JCL 191).

[111] Money for these purposes means, it is suggested, sterling or foreign currency, whether national or regional (as in the case of the Euro or the Central African franc). It is probably limited to fiat money, so as not to include (for instance) cryptocurrency such as Ethereum or Bitcoin: cf. D. Fox and S. Green, *Cryptocurrencies in Public and Private Law* (OUP, 2019), paras 2.10, 2.42–2.43. An obligation to transfer an amount of the latter would therefore sound in damages and not debt.

[112] For an example near the line, see *Moss Empires Ltd v Olympia (Liverpool) Ltd* [1939] A.C. 544 (statute limiting recoverability of *damages* for breach of a tenant's repairing covenant inapplicable to a promise by the tenant to spend a given sum annually on repairs and if not to pay any shortfall to the landlord: this was debt, not damages). See too *Jervis v Harris* [1996] Ch. 195.

Liquidated damages

It is very common practice for a contract, instead of leaving it up to the parties **19-026** to prove loss in the case of breach, to provide a "liquidated damages" clause.[113] Examples are stipulated payments for non-delivery of commodities or late completion of construction work, and demurrage clauses in voyage charterparties. A cursory glance might suggest that a clause of this sort created a simple conditional debt:[114] that is, a liability to pay the sum concerned, subject to the condition that it was exigible from a defendant only in the event of a relevant breach. Such a view seems plausible, if only because ex hypothesi one of the hallmarks of a damages claim, the need to prove loss, cannot apply to it. In fact, however, the law looks to the substance rather than the form and, despite their outward appearance, clauses of this sort are generally treated as giving rise to damages liabilities.[115] The point was neatly illustrated in the 1988 House of Lords decision in *President of India v Lips Maritime Corp.*[116] Shipowners received demurrage payments—that is, liquidated damages for delay in unloading—under a voyage charterparty, but they were paid late by the charterers. The payments were denominated in sterling, and because sterling was devalued during the interval the owners suffered sizeable exchange losses. The House of Lords held these losses irrecoverable from the charterers, on the basis that there could be no cause of action at common law for late payment of damages, and that demurrage payments, while liquidated in form, were damage payments nonetheless, and hence subject to the rule.

Indemnities

Suppose A gives B a contractual indemnity against the possibility that B may suf- **19-027** fer loss in a given transaction, or against some potential liability of B vis-à-vis a third party C. A's obligation could be analysed in two ways: first, as a promise to pay B a sum of money, the sum payable to be quantified by the amount of B's loss or liability; or secondly, as a guarantee that B will not suffer loss, engendering a (secondary) duty to pay damages to compensate him if and to the extent that he does. Both are superficially plausible analyses. It is submitted that the fundamental issue as to which applies is one of interpretation; a promise to ensure that an obligation is performed sounds in damages, while a promise to provide a sum of money to the beneficiary of the indemnity in certain events sounds in debt.[117]

An express promise to "hold harmless" a beneficiary in respect of losses suf- **19-028** fered as a result of entering into a given transaction with a third party is some

---

[113] Below, Ch.25.
[114] See *Cavendish Square Holding BV v Makdessi* [2015] UKSC 67; [2015] 3 W.L.R. 1373 at [4] (Lords Neuberger and Sumption). It may of course be open to attack as a penalty: see below, Ch.00. But that does not affect the point here.
[115] See, for example, Lord Salvesen in *Moor Line Ltd v Distillers Co Ltd* 1912 S.C. 514 at 520 on the subject of demurrage: "[T]the more correct view is that demurrage is 'agreed damages to be paid for delay of the ship in loading or unloading beyond an agreed period.' In other words, the distinction between 'demurrage' and damages for detention is that the one is liquidated damages and the other unliquidated. A claim under either head is a claim in respect of detention, and is in the nature of a claim of damages"; also *K Line Pte Ltd v Priminds Shipping (HK) Co Ltd* [2021] EWCA Civ 1712; [2022] 3 All E.R. 396 at [21]–[22] (Males LJ).
[116] [1988] A.C. 395
[117] *RSA Insurance Plc v Assicurazioni Generali SpA* [2018] EWHC 1237 (QB) at [89] (stating "no absolute rule").

indication of a liability sounding in unliquidated damages.[118] Lord Goff made this point in a lapidary way in 1991:

> "A promise of indemnity is simply a promise to hold the indemnified person harmless against a specified loss or expense. On this basis, no debt can arise before the loss is suffered or the expense incurred; however, once the loss is suffered or the expense incurred, the indemnifier is in breach of contract for having failed to hold the indemnified person harmless against the relevant loss or expense.[119] "

It used to be thought, indeed (and a previous edition of this work expressed the view[120]) that this was the presumptive position in the absence of a clear indication either way. But the modern tendency, it is suggested, is to regard indemnities as sounding in debt rather than damages.[121] This presumption is clear where clear means are given for calculating the sums for which the indemnifier is liable; for example, where an indemnifier agrees to pay a finance lessor all a defaulting lessee's arrears of rent less the goods' proceeds and accelerated payment discount,[122] or to "indemnify, defend and hold harmless" a beneficiary against "any and all claims, causes of action, suits, damages or demands" arising out of a given transaction.[123] But it goes further. In *ABN AMRO Commercial Finance Plc v McGinn*[124] an agreement to "indemnify you against all loss you may suffer in consequence of" a breach of certain contractual obligations was similarly construed; and in *ENE Kos 1 Ltd v Petroleo Brasileiro SA (No.2)*[125] Lord Sumption said that a standard indemnity in a charter against the consequences of obeying charterers' instructions was not an action in damages.

Insurance

19-029   Whatever the principles relating to indemnities generally, the liability of an indemnity insurer to indemnify his insured is subject to its own special rules. Although it might be thought that an underwriter simply promised to pay the

---

[118] *Durley House Ltd v Ferndale Hotels Plc* [2014] EWHC 2608 (Ch) at [108].

[119] *Firma C-Trade SA v Newcastle Protection & Indemnity Assn* [1991] 2 A.C. 1 at 35–36; also *Golstein v Bishop* [2016] EWHC 2187 (Ch) at [33]–[34] (Warren J). See too Bowen LJ in the much earlier *Birmingham & District Land Co v London & North Western Ry Co* (1886) 34 Ch. D. 261 at 274–275. Cf. *Muhammad Issa El Sheikh Ahmad v Ali* [1947]1 A.C. 414 at 426 (promise of an indemnity held by the Privy Council not to be a "promise to pay money" within Palestinian legislation).

[120] See the second edition, para.19 26. The same view continues occasionally to be expressed today: e.g. *AXA SA v Genworth Financial International Holdings Inc* [2019] EWHC 3376 (Comm) at [117] (Bryan J).

[121] R. Zakrzewski, "The Nature of a Claim on an Indemnity" (2006) 22 JCL 54. It is worth noting that in *Firma C Trade SA v Newcastle Protection & Indemnity Assn* [1991] 2 A.C. 1, noted above, what was involved was an insurance contract, in the shape of a P&I Club's contract to indemnify a shipowner. As appears below, indemnity insurance is subject to special rules.

[122] *Royscot Commercial Leasing Ltd v Ismail* unreported 29 April 1993, CA.

[123] *Codemasters Software Co Ltd v Automobile Club de l'Ouest (No.2)* [2009] EWHC 3194 (Ch); [2010] F.S.R. 13 esp at [29]–[35]. See too *Pullman Foods Ltd v Welsh Ministers* [2020] EWHC 2521 (TCC) at [183]–[201], holding on broadly similar wording that an action in debt was appropriate and a duty to mitigate was therefore not.

[124] [2014] EWHC 1674 (Comm); [2014] 2 C.L.C. 184

[125] [2012] UKSC 17; [2012] 2 A.C. 164 at [7]; and compare *The Island Archon* [1994] 2 Lloyd's Rep. 227 at 234 (stressing the availability of an indemnity against all losses caused by a given event even in the absence of a breach of contract).

amount of the loss if a given event occurred, it has long been clear[126] that in fact his promise is technically treated as a promise that the insured event will not occur, giving rise to a claim for unliquidated damages if it does eventuate.[127] So in the early case of *Luckie v Bushby*,[128] an insurance claim was assessed as a claim for unliquidated damages rather than an action of debt for the purpose of set-off; and in 2021 it was held that the standard measure of indemnity in a policy on buildings was the same as what would have been an award of damages against a wrongdoer.[129] Again, in *Post Office v Norwich Union Fire Insurance Society Ltd*[130] it was confirmed on a similar basis that there could be no action on a liability insurance policy until a loss in the form of a judgment or admission of liability was established. Similar results have been reached in the limitation[131] and contribution[132] contexts. And in *The Italia Express*[133] Hirst J held, consistently with this reasoning, that insurance payments were subject to the rule that there could be no liability in damages for late payment of damages, a conclusion later approved in the Court of Appeal[134] and it seems by Lord Mance in the Supreme Court.[135]

Suretyship

Contracts of suretyship are less straightforward than insurance contracts, in that **19-030** according to their precise terms they may fall to be construed either as simple promises to pay the principal debt if the principal debtor does not, or alternatively

---

[126] See *Grant v Royal Exchange Assurance Co* (1816) 5 M & S 439.

[127] "All actions against insurers under indemnity policies sound in unliquidated damages rather than debt." (Donaldson J in *Forney v Dominion Insurance Co Ltd* [1969] 1 W.L.R. 928 at 936). See too *William Pickersgill & Sons Ltd v London & Provincial Marine Insurance Co Ltd* [1912] 3 K.B. 614 at 621 (Hamilton J); *Endurance Corporate Capital Ltd v Sartex Quilts & Textiles Ltd* [2020] EWCA Civ 308; [2020] 1 C.L.C. 374 at [35]. A neat illustration is the Northern Ireland case of *Bann Carraig Ltd v Great Lakes Reinsurance (UK) Plc* [2021] NIQB 63, holding at [20]–[22] that the Limitation (Northern Ireland) Order 1989 art.65(1) (equivalent to s.29 of the Limitation Act 1980), extending the limitation period where a debt was later acknowledged, did not apply to an indemnity insurance claim, since the latter lay in damages not debt.

[128] (1853) 13 CB 864.

[129] *Endurance Corporate Capital Ltd v Sartex Quilts and Textiles Ltd* [2020] EWCA Civ 308; [2020] 1 C.L.C. 374 at [35].

[130] [1967] 2 Q.B. 363 (a case on the extent of rights transferred under the Third Parties (Rights against Insurers) Act 1930).

[131] E.g. *Chandris v Argo Insurance Co Ltd* [1963] 2 Lloyd's Rep. 65, approved in *Castle Insurance Co Ltd v Hong Kong Islands Shipping Co Ltd* [1984] A.C. 226.

[132] See *International Energy Group Ltd v Zurich Insurance Plc UK* [2015] UKSC 33; [2016] A.C. 509 at [89], [181]; *RSA Insurance Plc v Assicurazioni Generali SpA* [2018] EWHC 1237 (QB); [2019] 1 All E.R. (Comm) 115 at [114] (applicability of the Civil Liability (Contribution) Act 1978 on the basis that both underwriters liable for "damage").

[133] [1992] 2 Lloyd's Rep. 281. And similarly with the right to prejudgment interest: *Edmunds v Lloyd Italico SpA* [1986] 1 Lloyd's Rep. 326.

[134] See *Sprung v Royal Insurance (UK) Ltd* [1999] Lloyd's Rep. IR 111; also more recently *RSA Insurance Plc v Assicurazioni Generali SpA* [2018] EWHC 1237 (QB) at [114] (after extended discussion, contribution between liability insurers governed by 1978 Act because liabilities lay in damages); and see too *Globe Church Inc v Allianz Australia Insurance Ltd* [2019] NSWCA 27 at [208]–[212]. The actual decisions in *The Italia Express* and *Sprung v Royal Assurance* are reversed as from May 2017 by s.13A of the Insurance Act 2015, which gives a statutory cause of action for late payment of insurance claims: but this does not alter the point in the text.

[135] *International Energy Group Ltd v Zurich Insurance Plc* [2015] UKSC 33; [2016] A.C. 509 at [89] (where the matter in issue was set-off).

as contracts to indemnify the creditor against non-payment.[136] This distinction gives rise to important differences. A claim under the former head is classed as a claim in debt. It is therefore not dependent on proof of loss,[137] but has the disadvantage that it is caught by the Statute of Frauds 1677, and in addition stands or falls with the validity of the principal debt.[138] On the other hand, a true indemnity is not caught by either rule: it is not a promise to pay the debt but rather a guarantee of the principal creditor against loss arising from non-payment.[139]

19-031   Which side of the line a guarantee falls, and whether it engenders a liability in debt or damages, is a matter of construction. A simple promise without more to pay another's debt[140] and a straightforward performance bond payable on demand[141] create a mere liability in debt. By contrast, a contract expressed as one to indemnify the creditor in respect of loss,[142] an undertaking that a debt will be paid,[143] and the old-fashioned conditional bond defeasible if the principal debtor "shall duly perform and observe" given covenants,[144] are regarded as giving rise to a liability in damages. There is indeed high authority that a surety's obligation in respect of a debt is prima facie to be categorised as a duty to see that the debt is paid, and hence as giving rise to a claim for unliquidated damages.[145] However, it must be stressed that in the last resort the matter is simply one of construing the defendant's undertaking according to its terms.[146] A carefully drafted term that a guarantor must pay immediately on demand, without any requirement to claim first against the principal debtor, and that his obligations are those of principal, not surety, is likely to give rise to a liability in debt.[147] It may even be that a suitably drafted guarantee

---

[136] See *Moschi v Lep Air Services Ltd* [1973] A.C. 331 at 344–345 (Lord Reid), 348 (Lord Diplock).

[137] On which see *Trafalgar House Ltd v General Surety Co Ltd* [1996] A.C. 199 (where however the instrument was held to be an indemnity).

[138] E.g. *Coutts & Co v Browne-Lecky* [1947] K.B. 104. The result in that particular case no longer applies since the enactment of the Minor's Contract Act 1987 s.2 but the general point remains good.

[139] See e.g. *Lakeman v Mountstephen* (1874) L.R. 7 HL 17 (Statute of Frauds); *Yeoman Credit Ltd v Latter* [1961] 1 W.L.R. 828 (invalidity of principal debt).

[140] *Coutts & Co v Browne-Lecky* [1947] K.B. 104 (promise to pay minor's hire purchase debt unenforceable). (The actual decision is reversed by s.2 of the Minors' Contracts Act 1987: but the point of principle remains.) See too *Hampton v Minns* [2002] 1 W.L.R. 1 (simple promise to pay debt to bank).

[141] *Gold Coast Ltd v Caja de Ahorros del Mediterraneo* [2002] EWCA Civ 1806; [2002] 1 Lloyd's Rep. 617. See too *Esal (Commodities) Ltd v Oriental Credit Ltd* [1985] 2 Lloyd's Rep. 546 at 549 (Ackner LJ); *IIG Capital LLC v Van Der Merwe* [2008] EWCA Civ 542; [2008] 2 Lloyd's Rep. 187.

[142] *Yeoman Credit Ltd v Latter* [1961] 1 W.L.R. 828.

[143] *Lakeman v Mountstephen* (1874) L.R. 7 HL 17 (Statute of Frauds inapplicable); see too *Moschi v Lep Air Services Ltd* [1973] A.C. 331 (guarantor "has personally guaranteed the performance" of principal debtor; no defence that principal contract terminated); and more recently *Golstein v Bishop* [2016] EWHC 2187 (Ch) at [23]–[34] (Warren J).

[144] See *Trafalgar House Ltd v General Surety Co Ltd* [1996] A.C. 199 (need for proof of damage in guarantee of performance). See too the earlier *Trade Indemnity Co Ltd v Workington Harbour Board* [1937] A.C. 1.

[145] See *Moschi v Lep Air Services Ltd* [1973] A.C. 331 at 345 (Lord Reid); *IIG Capital LLC v Van Der Merwe* [2008] EWCA Civ 542; [2008] 2 Lloyd's Rep. 187 at [30] (Waller LJ). See too *Black & Veatch Corp v Kazstroyservice Global BV* [2021] EWHC 2104 (QB) at [33].

[146] *Gold Coast Ltd v Caja de Ahorros del Mediterraneo* [2002] EWCA Civ 1806; [2002] 1 Lloyd's Rep. 617 at [15] (Tuckey LJ); *IIG Capital LLC v Van Der Merwe* [2008] EWCA Civ 542; [2008] 2 Lloyd's Rep. 187 at [7] (Waller LJ).

[147] *McGuinness v Norwich & Peterborough Building Society* [2010] EWHC 2989 (Ch), [2011] 1 W.L.R. 613; see too the earlier *Hampton v Minns* [2002] 1 W.L.R. 1.

can partake of both natures at the same time, with some stipulations sounding in debt and others in damages.[148]

Whichever side of the line the surety's own liability falls, it seems that any claim against the principal debtor is likely to be regarded as sounding in debt.[149]   **19-032**

Bills of exchange

The duty of a party signing a bill of exchange may look like a simple duty to pay money enforceable at the suit of the holder. In fact, however, it has always been regarded as a liability in damages. This was so at common law,[150] and now by s.57 of the Bills of Exchange Act 1882 the liability of a party to a bill of exchange who fails to pay it "shall be deemed to be liquidated damages".[151] This is perhaps understandable where the claim is against a person secondarily liable on a bill, such as a drawer or endorser, who both engage "that, on due presentment, it shall be accepted and paid".[152] But it has been held[153] that the same rule applies to the acceptor's liability, even though he "engages that he will pay it according to the tenor of his acceptance".[154]   **19-033**

Letters of credit   For many years it seems to have been assumed that where an issuing or confirming bank failed to honour a letter of credit providing for payment of a fixed sum, the beneficiary's cause of action against it was like a claim under a bill of exchange: that is, strictly a claim for damages rather than a claim in debt.[155] But the authorities were not all one way,[156] and in *Standard Chartered Bank v Dorchester LNG (2) Ltd*[157] the Court of Appeal settled the matter. The issue was whether, if a bill of lading was tendered under a letter of credit but payment was wrongly refused, a later payment by the bank under the threat of legal proceedings amounted to payment of the price of the bill of lading so as to vest the latter in the bank. The court held that this was so, and that the nature of a claim under a letter   **19-034**

---

[148] See the comments of Briggs J in *McGuinness v Norwich & Peterborough Building Society* [2010] EWHC 2989 (Ch.); [2011] 1 W.L.R. 613, above at [20].

[149] See the Irish decisions in *Borland v Curry* (1879) 4 L.R. Ir. 273 (Ir. CA) and *McGrath v O'Driscoll* [2006] IEHC 195; [2007] 1 I.L.R.M. 203.

[150] See *Browne v London* (1670) 1 Mod 285 (debt will not lie where endorsee sues acceptor: necessity of action on the case).

[151] See *Ledeboter NV v Hibbert* [1947] K.B. 964; *Standard Chartered Bank v Dorchester LNG (2) Ltd* [2014] EWCA Civ 1382; [2016] Q.B. 1 at [40] (Moore-Bick LJ); also the Senior Courts Act 1981 s.35A(8), and County Courts Act 1984 s.69(7), also referring to "damages" for dishonour of a bill of exchange. For the measure of damages, see s.57(1); A.G. Guest, *Chalmers on Bills of Exchange and Cheques*, 18th edn (London: Sweet & Maxwell, 2016), para.7-043.

[152] See ss.55(1)(a) and 55(2)(a).

[153] See *Ledeboter NV v Hibbert* [1947] K.B. 964 at 967 (Morris J); *Barclays Bank International Ltd v Levin Brothers (Bradford) Ltd* [1977] Q.B. 270 at 282–283 (Mocatta J).

[154] See s.54(1).

[155] See e.g. *Stein v Hambro's Bank of Northern Commerce* (1921) 9 Ll L Rep 433 at 434 (Rowlatt J); *Dexters Ltd v Schenker & Co* (1923) 14 Ll L Rep 586 at 588 (Greer LJ); and generally *Trendtex Trading Corp v Crédit Suisse* [1982] A.C. 679 (in which the point was it seems assumed, the discussion being simply on the assignability in principle of a cause of action in damages). The cases are collected in *Standard Chartered Bank v Dorchester LNG (2) Ltd* [2014] EWCA Civ 1382; [2016] Q.B. 1 at [41]–[45].

[156] For example, *Power Curber International Ltd v National Bank of Kuwait SAK* [1981] 1 W.L.R. 1233 clearly proceeded on the assumption that the claim lay in debt, the argument turning on what the lex situs of a debt was under private international law.

[157] [2014] EWCA Civ 1382; [2016] Q.B. 1. See too *Taurus Petroleum Ltd v State Oil Marketing Co of the Ministry of Oil, Iraq* [2017] UKSC 64; [2018] A.C. 690, where this was assumed.

of credit was indeed a claim in debt, with all the consequences that followed from that. This does not mean, however, that non-payment of a letter of credit cannot also be characterised as a breach of contract sounding in damages if the claimant so chooses: for example, if a claimant suffers loss of business as a result of wrongful dishonour by the bank.[158]

IV. LIMITS TO THE ACTION OF DEBT

19-035   Since the action of debt is based on an express or implied promise to pay money, prima facie the question if it can be brought and, if so, when, is simply a matter of contractual interpretation. If the debt is payable at the time suit is brought, then the claimant's right to bring the action is virtually unqualified. In particular, the fact that he is acting unreasonably in seeking to enforce the debt, or that by doing so he will obtain an unjustified windfall, is irrelevant.[159] Nevertheless, there are two important limitations to this principle that need to be noted.

Contractual penalties

19-036   The first qualification arises where a promise to pay a sum of money takes the form of a liquidated damages clause—that is, a promise to pay conditioned on a breach of contract by the promisor. In this case, the rules as to penalties, either at common law or under the Consumer Rights Act,[160] will apply. These rules are dealt with in detail in Ch.25, below.

"Legitimate interest" and limitations on the right to claim payment

19-037   In *White & Carter (Councils) Ltd v McGregor*,[161] it will be remembered, the House of Lords rejected the idea that a creditor had to act reasonably in enforcing his right to sue in debt. Thus where a three-year advertising contract was wrongfully repudiated before performance had even begun, it was held by a majority[162] that the advertiser was nevertheless within his rights in performing it against the client's will and suing for the price of performance.[163] The fact that a reasonable person in his position might have acted differently, or sought to mitigate the effects of the breach by merely suing for damages, was beside the point.[164] The case was then,[165] and remains, controversial,[166] if only because the result seems counter-intuitive and because it seems to condone the wasteful expenditure of resources and

---

[158] See e.g. *Urquhart Lindsay & Co Ltd v Eastern Bank Ltd* [1922] 1 K.B. 318; *Fortis Bank SA v Indian Overseas Bank (No.2)* [2011] 2 Lloyd's Rep. 190.

[159] See e.g. *White & Carter (Councils) Ltd v McGregor* [1962] A.C. 413 and *Abrahams v Performing Rights Society Ltd* [1995] I.C.R. 1028 (see para.7-082 ff above).

[160] Notably Sch.2, Pt 1, para.5.

[161] [1962] A.C. 413.

[162] Lords Morton and Keith dissenting.

[163] Overruling a previous Scots decision which on virtually identical facts had denied recovery: see *Langford & Co. Ltd v Dutch*, 1952 S.C. 15.

[164] "It might be, but it never has been, the law that a person is only entitled to enforce his contractual rights in a reasonable way, and that a court will not support an attempt to enforce them in an unreasonable way" (Lord Reid at [1962] A.C. 413 at 430). See too Lord Hodson at 445.

[165] See the attack on its grasp of history in P. Nenaber, "Anticipatory Repudiation: Principle and Policy" [1962] C.L.J. 213.

[166] The Supreme Court of Canada has viewed it with hostility: *Asamera Oil Corp v Sea Oil Corp* [1979] 1 SCR 633. It also does not represent the law in most US jurisdictions: see e.g. the leading North

money on services that no-one wants.[167] Moreover, in at least two subsequent cases courts have expressed thinly-veiled disapproval of it.[168] Nevertheless, for the moment it still represents the law.[169]

The principle in *White & Carter*, that a claimant can claim the price of **19-038** performance even where the defendant refuses to accept it, is nonetheless not entirely unqualified. For one thing, in cases where payment is dependent on performance[170] it can only logically apply where the claimant can provide that performance willy-nilly the defendant.[171] This is in practice uncommon. Most employees, for instance, cannot fulfil their contracts of employment if locked out or otherwise excluded: from which it follows that any cause of action for wrongful dismissal is likely to be for damages alone.[172] Again, most contracts of sale are fulfilled by physical delivery to, and acceptance by, the buyer: since there can in the nature of things be no delivery to a recalcitrant defendant who simply refuses to take the goods, it follows that in the case of stubborn non-acceptance there cannot be a claim for the price, but only for damages.[173]

More importantly, however, Lord Reid in *White & Carter* pointedly made this **19-039** remark:

"It may well be that, if it can be shown that a person has no legitimate interest, financial or otherwise, in performing the contract rather than claiming damages, he ought not to be allowed to saddle the other party with an additional burden with no benefit to himself. If a party has no interest to enforce a stipulation, he cannot in general enforce it: so it might be said that, if a party has no interest to insist on a particular remedy, he ought not to be allowed to insist on it."[174]

To illustrate, his lordship gave the example of a consultant engaged to go abroad **19-040**

Carolina case of *Rockingham County v Luten Bridge Co* 35 F.2d 301 (1929). It is not well received in Q. Liu, "The White & Carter principle: a restatement" (2011) 74 M.L.R. 171.

[167] A point made, e.g. in P. Nenaber, "Anticipatory Repudiation: Principle and Policy" [1962] C.L.J. 213.

[168] In *Hounslow London Borough Council v Twickenham Garden Developments Ltd* [1971] Ch. 233 at 251 Megarry J regarded the case as "striking" and thought it should not be followed in "any case not fairly within the contemplation of their Lordships"; and in *The Puerto Buitrago* [1976] 1 Lloyd's Rep. 250, 255 Lord Denning MR, forthrightly as usual, only wished to apply it in a case "on all fours".

[169] Thus it was followed, with no serious signs of disapproval, by the Inner House of the Court of Session in *AMA (New Town) Ltd v Law* [2013] CSIH 61; 2013 S.C. 608.

[170] Which it normally is, but not always. For a case where it was not, see *Ministry of Sound (Ireland) Ltd v World Online Ltd* [2003] EWHC 2178 (Ch); [2003] 2 All E.R. (Comm) 823 (agreement for W to pay M periodic sums and M to W's internet business and distribute W's CDs: M entitled to payment despite W's breach of contract in failing to provide disks, since on a proper interpretation right to payment not dependent on their distribution).

[171] *White & Carter (Councils) Ltd v McGregor* [1962] A.C. 413 at 428 (Lord Reid). This criterion, perhaps surprisingly, was held fulfilled in the case of a contract for the sale of land in the later Scots decision of *AMA (New Town) Ltd v Law* [2013] CSIH 61; 2013 S.C. 608. Note, however, that a contract that can physically be performed, but only by trespassing on the defendant's property, is not for these purposes one that can be effectively performed against the defendant's will: see *Hounslow London Borough Council v Twickenham Garden Developments Ltd* [1971] Ch. 233 at 253–254 (Megarry J) and *Finelli v Dee* (1968) 67 D.L.R. (2d) 393.

[172] See *The Puerto Buitrago* [1976] 1 Lloyd's Rep. 250 at 255 (Lord Denning MR).

[173] See *The Alaskan Trader (No.2)* [1983] 2 Lloyd's Rep. 645 at 648 (Lloyd J). Though even here there are exceptions. Cf. *Anglo-African Shipping Co of New York, Inc v J. Mortner Ltd* [1962] 1 Lloyd's Rep. 81 (appealed on other grounds, [1962] 1 Lloyd's Rep. 610) (goods could be shipped to f.a.s. buyers despite purported countermand of order: *White & Carter* applied to allow confirming house to claim price).

[174] See [1962] A.C. 413 at 431.

and prepare a complex and expensive report, and suggested that were the order to be countermanded before he had begun to perform, the consultant would not be entitled to go ahead nevertheless and claim his fee on return. It is true that of the judges who decided *White & Carter* only Lord Reid adverted to this point. Nevertheless, a series of subsequent decisions accepted the existence of some limitation of the claimant's rights based on the "legitimate interest" principle;[175] and in 2015 Lords Neuberger and Sumption in the Supreme Court referred to it as an aspect of

> "broader social and economic considerations, one of which is that the law will not generally make a remedy available to a party, the adverse impact of which on the defaulter significantly exceeds any legitimate interest of the innocent party".[176]

19-041   Unfortunately, Lord Reid did not expatiate on what "legitimate interest" was present in *White & Carter* but not in the case of the consultant.[177] But two things are worth noting. First, the disproportion between the expense of performance and any benefit to the defendant was small in *White & Carter*.[178] And secondly, the pursuers presumably had some legitimate interest in obtaining the wherewithal to pay their staff. Moreover, it is not difficult to think of other factors that might well justify a claimant in performing: for instance, the fact that he had himself entered into commitments with third parties.[179] But if factors such as these are not present, it is suggested that a court will be more amenable to a plea of "no legitimate interest".

19-042   Nevertheless, it must be admitted that the practical application of the rule has been and still remains somewhat uncertain.[180] Claims have been allowed without much question in cases where there has clearly been a tangible advantage for the claimant in performing: for example, where a confirming house, having made all necessary arrangements with third parties, shipped goods despite a purported

---

[175] Any doubts on this score must now be regarded as settled since its consistent acceptance in *The Odenfeld* [1978] 2 Lloyd's Rep. 357, *The Alaskan Trader (No.2)* [1983] 2 Lloyd's Rep. 645, and *The Dynamic* [2003] EWHC 1936 (Comm); [2003] 2 Lloyd's Rep. 693. See generally Q.Liu, "The White & Carter Principle: A Restatement" (2011) 74 MLR 171 and D.Winterton, "Reconsidering White & Carter v McGregor" [2013] L.M.C.L.Q. 5.

[176] *Cavendish Square Holding BV v Makdessi* [2015] UKSC 67; [2015] 3 W.L.R. 1373 at [29]. In saying this their lordships were drawing a broad analogy between the rule and the supervisory jurisdiction exercised by the courts over penalty clauses.

[177] Legatt J in *MSC Mediterranean Shipping Co SA v Cottonex Anstalt* [2015] EWHC 283 (Comm); [2015] 1 C.L.C. 143 at [97] suggested that the proper criterion was one of good faith, analogous to the rule that an apparently unfettered discretion in a contracting party could not be exercised arbitrarily, capriciously or irrationally. With respect, this seems tendentious.

[178] Since the defenders presumably got some benefit from performance, even if it was a benefit they said they did not want. Furthermore, the expense of performance was minimal, since a perusal of the facts shows that the contract was a renewal and hence the advertising (small plates on litterbins) was already there. But note that the presence of a disproportion is not necessarily enough to oust the claimant's right: *The Dynamic* [2003] EWHC 1936 (Comm); [2003] 2 Lloyd's Rep. 693 at [23] (Simon J).

[179] Cf. *Anglo-African Shipping Co of New York, Inc v J. Mortner Ltd* [1962] 1 Lloyd's Rep. 81 (appealed on other grounds, [1962] 1 Lloyd's Rep. 610), where this factor was present, and was regarded as a strong argument in favour of the plaintiffs.

[180] As Leggatt J drily put it in *MSC Mediterranean Shipping Co SA v Cottonex Anstalt* [2015] EWHC 283 (Comm); [2015] 1 C.L.C. 143 at [94], the principle is "of very uncertain scope".

countermand by the buyer;[181] where carriers insisted on carrying goods to the contractual destination in order to cement their lien for carriage charges against an insolvent client;[182] and where a lessor faced with a non-paying tenant chose to sue the tenant for rent accruing due rather than terminating the lease.[183] By contrast, practicalities may dictate an obligation to accept the repudiation. One is where the loss of an asset of relatively small value could otherwise engender a claim to a never-ending and wholly disproportionate income stream for the innocent party. Thus in *MSC Mediterranean Shipping Co SA v Cottonex Anstalt*[184] shippers of goods agreed to unload 35 of the carrier's containers within a fixed period and then to pay daily "demurrage" on them until their return. By 2015 the containers had been immobilised for something over three years in a Bangladesh port by a combination of Bangladeshi bureaucracy and an insolvent buyer, with no end in sight, and the carriers' claim had mounted to something over $1 million, about ten times their capital value. The Court of Appeal had no doubt that, once it became clear that the containers were unlikely ever to be redelivered, any legitimate interest in maintaining the contract disappeared; he accordingly cut off the demurrage claim at that point.

Elsewhere, the approach has varied. One not uncommon situation arises in shipping law, where owners faced with a time charterer's repudiation have sought simply to carry on claiming monthly hire without going to the trouble of reletting the vessel or pleading and proving a claim for damages.[185] In cases such as this, it now seems that presumptively, at least where no more than a few months are in account, the claim for hire should succeed. So in *The Aquafaith*[186] charterers under a five-year charter wrongfully redelivered the vessel three months early, whereupon the owners invoiced them for three months' hire; in doing so, they made it clear that the ship was ready to obey any orders given, even though the charterers declined to provide any. Cooke J overturned an arbitrator's decision that this was an act done without legitimate interest, and allowed the claim. Only, he said, where insistence on maintaining the contract could be described as "wholly unreasonable", "extremely unreasonable" or perhaps "perverse", could the owner be bound to accept the repudiation: furthermore, he was unwilling to encourage efforts by a contract-breaker to burden the innocent party with the trouble of trying to trade a vessel in a difficult market in order to minimise loss, together with the loss of as-

19-043

---

181 *Anglo-African Shipping Co of New York, Inc v J. Mortner Ltd* [1962] 1 Lloyd's Rep. 81 (appealed on other grounds, [1962] 1 Lloyd's Rep. 610).

182 *George Barker (Transport) Ltd v Eynon* [1974] 1 W.L.R. 462.

183 *Reichman v Beveridge* [2006] EWCA Civ 1659; [2007] 1 P. & C.R. 20; on which, see generally M.Pawlowski, "Landlord's choice of remedies on tenant abandonment – time for a rethink?" [2019] Conv 355.

184 [2016] EWCA Civ 789.

185 Claim allowed: *The Odenfeld* [1978] 2 Lloyd's Rep. 357 and *The Aquafaith* [2012] EWHC 1077 (Comm); [2012] 1 C.L.C. 899. Claim dismissed: *The Alaskan Trader (No.2)* [1983] 2 Lloyd's Rep. 645 and *The Puerto Buitrago* [1976] 1 Lloyd's Rep. 250. In practice a finding by a first instance judge or arbitrator one way or the other is unlikely to be upset (see *The Alaskan Trader (No.2)* [1983] 2 Lloyd's Rep. 645 at 651), unless it involves a misunderstanding of the correct test, a failure to take into account relevant factors or the regarding of irrelevant matters (see *The Aquafaith* [2012] EWHC 1077 (Comm); [2012] 1 C.L.C. 899 at [51]).

186 [2012] EWHC 1077 (Comm); [2012] 1 C.L.C. 899. See J. Carter, "White and Carter v McGregor— how unreasonable?" (2012) 128 L.Q.R. 490.

sured cash-flow that that entailed.[187] On the other hand, he seemingly accepted that that things might be different where there was no advantage to anyone in the continued performance of the charter, for instance where the vessel was laid up damaged and effectively irreparable,[188] and possibly also that a claim for continued hire might not be available for very substantial period.[189]

---

[187] [2012] EWHC 1077 (Comm); [2012] 1 C.L.C. 899 at [44]–[48]. See too *The Dynamic* [2003] EWHC 1936 (Comm); [2003] 2 Lloyd's Rep. 693 at [23] (Simon J).

[188] As in *The Puerto Buitrago* [1976] 1 Lloyd's Rep. 250, above.

[189] For example, eight months out of two years in *The Alaskan Trader (No.2)* [19 83] 2 Lloyd's Rep. 645, above.

CHAPTER 20

DAMAGES FOR BREACH OF CONTRACT—INTRODUCTION[1]

I. DEFINITIONS

After debt, the remedy of damages for breach is the most significant money 20-001
response available to an unsatisfied contracting party. The concept of damages, as
we will see, is a wide one. Nevertheless, it is not unlimited, and some definition is
needed. For the purposes of the coverage in this book, an award of damages will
be broadly defined as (i) a remedy at common law, (ii) awarded by a court or arbitrator, (iii) which arises from the defendant's breach of a contractual obligation owed
to the claimant, and (iv) which exists in order to compensate the claimant for that
breach or otherwise mark the fact that his contractual rights have been infringed.[2]

A number of elements of this definition are important, and worth going into in a 20-002
little more detail.

A remedy at common law

The action for damages for breach of contract proper is a common law remedy: 20-003
there is no such thing as equitable damages for breach of contract (though there may
be a statutory award of damages in lieu of an injunction or specific performance
under s.50 of the Senior Courts Act 1981).[3] Nevertheless it needs to be noted that
contractual obligations are frequently accompanied by parallel and fairly similar
obligations existing in equity. It follows that, even though there is no such thing as
equitable damages for breach of contract, the disappointment of contractual obligations will often be capable of giving rise to equitable remedies at the suit of the
beneficiary. For example, an employee revealing his employer's trade secrets commits not only breach of contract but the equitable wrong of breach of confidence

---

[1] Apart from *McGregor on Damages*, 21st edn (London: Sweet & Maxwell, 2022), Chs 24–36, see
A. Kramer, *The Law of Contract Damages* (Oxford: Hart, 2014).

[2] Cf. the definition in the *New Oxford Companion to Law* (Oxford: Oxford University Press, 2008),
p.295: "a monetary remedy awarded by the court to a successful claimant ... for a breach of contract
... ... in an amount determined by the court, normally as an assessment of the claimant's losses."
A. Burrows, *Remedies for Torts, Breach of Contract, and Equitable Wrongs*, 4th edn (Oxford: Oxford
University Press, 2019) at p 35 ("a sum of money assessed by the court is required to be paid by
the defendant to the claimant"). And see too D. Harris, D. Campbell & R. Halson, *Remedies in
Contract and Tort*, 2nd edn (London: Butterworths, 2002), p.73 ("a compensatory substitute for [the
defendant's] promised performance").

[3] Known as "damages under Lord Cairns' Act", after the statute (the Chancery Amendment Act 1858)
that first introduced them and was the predecessor to s.50 of the Senior Courts Act 1981.

as well;[4] similarly, a breach of contract by a solicitor or someone else may also amount to a breach of fiduciary duty,[5] provided it is a deliberate disregard of his duty to safeguard the client's interests,[6] or even to a breach of trust.[7]

20-004   In the light of this consideration, and the fact that since the Judicature Acts some 145 years ago all courts have been able to award all remedies, it could be argued that it is inappropriate today to keep alive the historical distinction between common-law and equitable liability and discuss the former in isolation. It is also notable that, whether or not formally part of the law of contract, many equitable remedies serve the function of compensating what are essentially breaches of promises,[8] and indeed there is some evidence that the rules relating to their computation, if not identical, are converging.[9]

20-005   However, there still remain good reasons for dealing with contract damages separately. The courts remain chary of referring to equitable forms of compensation as "damages":[10] moreover, despite some approximation the remedies available, and the principles on which they are awarded, continue to be rather different from the situation obtaining at common law.[11] For these reasons, we will leave equitable liability aside.

Common law and equity: damages under Lord Cairns' Act in lieu of specific performance or injunction[12]

20-006   But there will be one exception to the exclusion of equitable liability. Damages under Lord Cairns' Act in lieu of an injunction or specific performance,[13] while

---

[4]   On the relation between these two, see *Campbell v Frisbee* [2002] EWCA Civ 1374; [2003] I.C.R. 141 at [22] (Lord Phillips).

[5]   See, for example, *Bristol & West Building Society v May May & Merrimans (No.1)* [1996] 2 All E.R. 801; [1996] P.N.L.R. 138 (deliberate failure by mortgage lenders' solicitors to disclose information). The matter is discussed at length by Millett LJ in *Bristol & West Building Society v Mothew (t/a Stapley & Co)* [1998] Ch. 1 at 15 ff.

[6]   Deliberate action of some kind is essential for this head of liability, mere negligence being insufficient: *Bristol & West Building Society v Mothew (t/a Stapley & Co)* [1998] Ch. 1, above.

[7]   As in cases such as *Target Holdings Ltd v Redferns* [1996] A.C. 421 and *AIB Group (UK) Plc v Mark Redler & Co* [2014] UKSC 58; [2015] A.C. 1503 (wrongful paying away of mortgage money held in escrow); and also *Lloyds TSB Bank Plc v Markandan & Uddin (A Firm)* [2012] EWCA Civ 65; [2012] 2 All E.R. 884 and *P&P Property Ltd v Owen White & Catlin LLP* [2018] EWCA Civ 1082; [2019] Ch. 273.

[8]   On which, see e.g. E. Davidson, The Equitable Remedy of Compensation (1982) 13 M.U.L.R. 349; P. Birks & F. Rose (eds), *Restitution in Equity*, 173 ff (C.Rickett).

[9]   Cf. *Bristol & West Building Society v Mothew* [1998] Ch. 1 at 17, per Millett LJ; *AIB Group (UK) Plc v Mark Redler & Co* [2014] UKSC 58; [2015] A.C. 1503 at [71] per Lord Toulson; and also A. Burrows, "We do This at Common Law but That in Equity" (2002) 22 OJLS 1 at 7 ff.

[10]   But even this usage may be changing. Where compensation was claimed for breach of fiduciary duty by an agent under an insurance "fronting" agreement, Waller LJ (with the agreement of Clarke LJ) said that the "reality of the claim is that it is one for damages": *Companhia de Seguros Imperio v Heath (REBX) Ltd* [2001] Lloyd's Rep. IR 109 at 116.

[11]   See, e.g. Lord Browne-Wilkinson in *Target Holdings Ltd v Redfern* [1996] A.C. 421 at 434 ("the common law rules of remoteness of damage and causation do not apply"); also Mummery LJ's comments in *Swindle v Harrison* [1997] 4 All E.R. 705 at 733–734.

[12]   J.A. Jolowicz, "Damages in Equity. A Study of Lord Cairns' Act" [1975] C.L.J. 224.

[13]   The term "damages under Lord Cairns' Act" remains embedded in legal usage. In actual fact the relevant legislation, s.2 of the Chancery Amendment Act 1858 (the official name for Lord Cairns' Act), was repealed by the Statute Law Revision and Civil Procedure Act 1883. But this repeal was explicitly made subject to a curious proviso that it should not affect any jurisdiction created by the

technically regarded as equitable,[14] and hence subject to equitable discretion,[15] are so ingrained in the fabric of common law damages that it would be inappropriate to segregate them. They will therefore be dealt with as and when they arise in connection with the discussion of contract damages.

In most contract cases the availability of damages under Lord Cairns' Act is not enormously important in practice. In particular, where such damages parallel those available at common law it is now clear that on principle no different *measure* of recovery is applicable.[16] However, the existence of a separate jurisdiction to award them remains important in a few cases. One example is where a court wishes to award damages in reference to a breach of contract which has not yet technically taken place[17] or for future breaches of a continuing covenant,[18] since in neither of these cases are damages available at common law at all. Another case arises where a remedy is needed for a single act or omission amounting to a breach of contract as regards a number of separate claimants, for example a failure to keep in repair the common parts of an apartment building. Here the award can be more precisely tailored to the necessities: for instance by taking the form of the setting up of a fund to remedy the breach at the defendant's expense.[19]

20-007

A remedy dependent on a breach of contract

Damages presuppose a wrong: they are by their nature a pecuniary response to a defendant's infringement of the claimant's rights. In the context of contracts, this means that the availability of a damages award against a defendant depends on a breach by him of some contractual obligation owed to the claimant. This is what distinguishes damages awards from a number of other types of claim, notably claims for agreed sums and actions based on unjustified enrichment, which do not depend on a showing of any breach at all.

20-008

(i) Damages and claims for agreed sums Chapter 19 described in detail the   20-009

---

14   1858 Act which it suppressed (on which see *Leeds Industrial Co-Operative Society Ltd v Slack* [1924] A.C. 851 at 861–863 (Viscount Finlay)). The provision for an explicit statutory power to grant such damages was resurrected nearly a century later in s.50 of the Senior Courts Act 1981, which remains in force today. See P. McDermott, "Survival of jurisdiction under the Chancery Amendment Act 1858 (Lord Cairns' Act)" (1987) 6 C.J.Q. 348.

14   Since the power to grant them was given to the Court of Chancery under s.2 of the Chancery Amendment Act 1858. However, it is worth noting that the current statutory power to award them, s.50 of the Senior Courts Act 1981, makes no mention of equity.

15   Hence there are apparently no fixed rules as to their measure, despite the fact that they generally track common-law damages in cases of parallel liability: see Lord Reed in *One Step (Support) Ltd v Morris-Garner* [2018] UKSC 20; [2019] A.C. 649 at [63].

16   See the discussion in *Johnson v Agnew* [1980] A.C. 367; also *Jaggard v Sawyer* [1995] 1 W.L.R. 269 at 290–291 (Millett LJ); *Att-Gen v Blake* [2001] 1 A.C. 268 at 281 (Lord Nicholls). Where there is a past breach but the possibility of a future loss, an indemnity may well be appropriate: e.g. *Dana UK Axle Ltd v Freudenberg FST GmbH* [2021] EWHC 1751 (TCC).

17   E.g. *Oakacre Ltd v Claire Cleaners (Holdings) Ltd* [1982] Ch 197 (sale of land: damages in lieu of specific performance before time fixed for completion).

18   *Jaggard v Sawyer* [1995] 1 W.L.R. 269, esp at 290–291 (Millett LJ); *Meretz Investments NV v ACP Ltd* [2006] EWHC 74 (Ch) [2007] Ch. 197 at [251] (Lewison J). Another example is where a person claiming as assignee or subrogee sues in breach of a jurisdiction agreement entered into by the original contractor: *Argos Pereira Espana SL v Athenian Marine Ltd* [2021] EWHC 554 (Comm); [2022] 1 All E.R. (Comm) 345.

19   *Hunt v Optima (Cambridge) Ltd* [2013] EWHC 681 (TCC) at [242] (Akenhead J). The point was not argued on appeal at [2014] EWCA Civ 714; [2015] 1 W.L.R. 1346.

nature of the action for an agreed sum, and in so doing the differences between it and the action for damages. This will not be repeated here: but to recapitulate, the essential distinctions are as follows.

20-010   First, the aim of such an action is not to sanction or mark a breach of contract, but to enforce in specie a promise to pay a sum of money.[20]

20-011   Secondly, unlike the situation with actions for damages, no legal difficulties can arise over the quantification of an award of an agreed sum. The only possible amount of any such award is the amount which, on a proper interpretation of the contract, is due.[21]

20-012   Thirdly, it follows from the above that a number of matters which would be relevant to the computation of a claim for damages can be ignored. Thus issues such as whether a given loss has been suffered at all (or could have been avoided), or whether any loss suffered by the claimant is unforeseeable or too remote, are out of account.[22]

20-013   **(ii)   Damages and obligations based on unjust enrichment**   At common law the non-fulfilment of a contractual expectation may give birth not only to a claim for damages, but also to all sorts of other money liabilities, such as claims for the return of money paid by mistake; for money paid for a consideration that has failed; and for the reasonable value of goods supplied or services rendered other than under contract. What is important to note is that, while these claims often accompany a breach of contract by a defendant, none of them actually requires it.[23] Thus a buyer who does not get goods or services he has paid for recovers his money not only if the seller is in breach, but even if he is not: a straightforward example being the case where the seller's non-performance is excused by an exception clause or some other factor.[24] Again, a person who partly performs is not prevented from recovering a reasonable sum merely because the contract is unenforceable, or has been terminated by subsequent events, and thus the defendant could not be sued for breach of it.[25] Instead, what all these claims have in common is that they exist to reverse some enrichment gained by the defendant which is not justified by the terms of a contract or otherwise.

20-014   The significance of this distinction between damages and restitution lies largely

---

[20]   For a helpful discussion, see *Standard Chartered Bank v Dorchester LNG (2) Ltd, The Erin Schulte* [2014] EWCA Civ 1382; [2016] Q.B. 1 at [37]–[52] (Moore-Bick LJ).

[21]   Of course an action for an agreed sum can be combined with an action for damages, as where a claim is made for interest as damages at common law under the rule in *Sempra Metals Ltd v Inland Revenue Commissioners* [2007] UKHL 34; [2008] 1 A.C. 561; and in this case the damages portion will be subject to all the damages rules. But this does not affect the point in the text. If a claim for an agreed sum is brought as a claim in damages for non-payment (as seems possible), then the damages rules apply: see *Barber (t/a Barber & Co Solicitors) v Medico Services Ltd* [2020] EWHC 810 (QB) (claim for non-payment of agency fees: deduction to extent that third parties did not claim payment from agency).

[22]   See e.g. *White & Carter (Councils) Ltd v McGregor* [1962] A.C. 413 and *Abrahams v Performing Rights Society Ltd* [1995] I.C.R. 1028, esp. at 1041 (no duty to mitigate); and *Firodi Shipping Ltd v Griffon Shipping LLC* [2013] EWCA Civ 1567; [2014] 1 C.L.C. 1 (successful action by seller against defaulting buyer for whole of unpaid deposit, even though loss much smaller).

[23]   P. Birks, *An Introduction to the Law of Restitution* (Oxford: Clarendon Press, 1989), p.39 ff, though now somewhat dated, makes the point well.

[24]   E.g. *Newland Shipping and Forwarding Ltd v Toba Trading FZC* [2014] EWHC 661 (Comm) and *BP Oil International Ltd v Vega Petroleum Ltd* [2021] EWHC 1364 (Comm) at [219]–[222] (contract repudiated by claimant and hence not enforceable by it); cf. *Goss v Chilcott* [1996] A.C. 788 (alteration of contract by third party made it unenforceable against defendant).

[25]   *Scott v Pattison* [1923] 2 K.B. 723.

in the measure of recovery (though this is by no means the only difference[26]). Damages look to the position of the claimant, and seek to put him in the position he would have occupied had he received his contractual entitlement: by contrast, in unjust enrichment what matters is the enrichment of the defendant, and the claimant's position is generally irrelevant. The point comes out neatly from the decision in *Wilkinson v Lloyd*.[27] A buyer paid in advance for shares that he never got, but in the event made a bad bargain (by agreeing to pay more than the shares were worth). Damages would have amounted to the value of the shares, which was less than the price paid. But by suing for restitution the buyer nevertheless recovered all his money, on the basis that no consideration had moved from the seller. Similarly, it has been held that a buyer of goods from a seller without title is generally entitled to restitution for what he has paid without reference to any free use which he may have obtained in the meantime, even though had he sued for damages he would have had to give credit for it.[28]

There is, however, one qualification to this. Although according to the existing **20-015** English authorities there can be no award of overtly punitive damages for breach of contract,[29] in a few cases damages may be awarded not to compensate the claimant for his loss, but specifically in order to deprive a contract-breaker of the profits he has made from the breach. These are dealt with in Ch.26, below.

A remedial (secondary) liability

A contractor's promise is a promise to keep his contract, no more and no less. **20-016** Although he may be liable in damages if he does not, it is not true as a matter of English law to say that he promises to pay those damages in the event of non-performance. It follows that an order by a court to pay damages following a breach is not the same thing as directly enforcing an obligation contained in the original contract. It is an attempt to remedy the effects of its breach, which is something different. In England, this important distinction is normally expressed by referring to the duty to perform a contract as a primary obligation and the liability to pay damages for breach of it as a secondary one, arising as a matter of law once the primary contractual obligation is broken. Lord Diplock analysed the position thus

---

[26] For example, the distinction may matter crucially where a defendant wishes to reduce any recovery by alleging contributory negligence by the claimant, or to exercise rights to contribution under the Civil Liability (Contribution) Act 1978. There may also be interstitial differences in limitation periods. Thus for tort purposes time runs from the time the tort was committed (or, with torts not actionable per se, when loss is suffered); whereas for restitution claims the clock starts when the enrichment is received: *Kleinwort Benson v South Tyneside MBC* [1994] 4 All E.R. 974 at 978, and G. Virgo, *The Principles of the Law of Restitution*, 3rd edn (Oxford: Oxford University Press 2015), Ch.29. And the distinction may be vital in private international law: see, e.g. *Macmillan Inc v Bishopsgate Investment Trust Plc (No.3)* [1996] 1 W.L.R. 387.

[27] (1845) 7 Q.B. 27. Cf. too *Knowles v Bovill* (1870) 22 L.T. 70.

[28] *Rowland v Divall* [1923] 2 K.B. 500.

[29] In *Travelers Casualty & Surety Co of Europe Ltd v Sun Life Assurance Co of Canada (UK) Ltd* [2004] EWHC 1704 (Comm); [2004] Lloyd's Rep. I.R. 846 it was suggested at [76] that, despite the general loosening of the requirements for punitive damages generally *in Kuddus v Chief Constable of Leicestershire* [2002] 2 A.C. 122, only the House of Lords (now the Supreme Court) could introduce them in contract. See too *Aarons v Brocket Hall (Jersey) Ltd* [2018] EWHC 222 (QB) at [7]. Earlier authority was solidly against: see e.g. *Addis v Gramophone Co Ltd* [1909] A.C. 488 and *Perera v Vandiyar* [1953] 1 W.L.R. 672. See generally J. Edelman, "Exemplary Damages for Breach of Contract" (2001) 117 L.Q.R. 539.

in *Moschi v Lep Air Services Ltd*:[30]

"Generally speaking, the rescission of the contract puts an end to the primary obligations of the party not in default to perform any of his contractual promises which he has not already performed by the time of the rescission. It deprives him of any right as against the other party to continue to perform them ... The primary obligations of the party in default to perform any of the promises made by him and remaining unperformed likewise come to an end as does his right to continue to perform them. But for his primary obligations there is substituted by operation of law a secondary obligation to pay to the other party a sum of money to compensate him for the loss he has sustained as a result of the failure to perform the primary obligations."

20-017   Thus in *Moschi's* case itself, A, who was owed a large sum of money by B, agreed to forbear from suing provided B paid £6,000 per week. C guaranteed that B would perform this latter obligation. B failed to pay, whereupon A rescinded the agreement not to sue and sued C on his guarantee. The House of Lords were quite clear that, on principle, a guarantee of a debt was a guarantee of the debt alone and presumptively did not extend to a liability in damages once the original obligation had disappeared.[31] It is true that on the facts it was actually held that C was liable to A, despite the fact that any duty to pay the instalments had ceased to exist owing to A's rescission. But this was only because C's guarantee, like most guarantees,[32] fell to be construed as covering not only the actual instalments of £6,000 per week but any damages owing by B to A as a result of their non-payment. Had C's obligation been limited to the actual instalments, he would have escaped.

20-018   Another illustration of the same principle comes in the rule concerning late payment. The late performance of a contractual obligation is a breach of contract and, as such, invariably attracts substantial damages in so far as loss is proved and is not too remote. Obligations to pay money are no different: from which it follows that in the event of such late payment, in so far as the payee can prove loss of interest or other loss, he can recover it.[33] But late payment of damages is different: it is not a breach of contract and hence can attract no damages.[34] It can be visited only by an award of interest under s.35A of the Senior Courts Act 1981 and equivalent provisions.

---

[30] [1973] A.C. 331 at 350. See too *Photo Production Ltd v Securicor Transport Ltd* [1980] A.C. 827 at 845 (Lord Wilberforce); *Law Debenture Trust Corp v Ural Caspian Oil Corp Ltd* [1995] Ch. 152 at 165 (Bingham MR), 171–172 (Saville LJ); *Barber (t/a Barber & Co Solicitors) v Medico Services Ltd* [2020] EWHC 810 (QB) at [42] (Tipples J); also the Irish decision in *Ulster Bank DAC v McDonagh* [2022] IECA 87 at [67].

[31] See the instructive Australian decision in *Sunbird Plaza Pty Ltd v Maloney* (1989) 166 C.L.R. 245 (guarantee that buyer would pay price of land inapplicable to liability in damages for refusing conveyance).

[32] See, e.g. *Chatterton v Maclean* [1951] 1 All E.R. 761.

[33] *Sempra Metals Ltd (formerly Metallgesellschaft Ltd) v Inland Revenue Commissioners* [2007] UKHL 34; [2008] 1 A.C. 561 at [16]–[17], [74], [89], [92]–[100], [132], [151], [165], [215]–[217]. See also the clarification of the present status of *Sempra* in *Sagicor Bank Jamaica Ltd v Seaton* [2022] UKPC 48; [2023] 2 All E.R. 81, making it clear that while late payment of a debt can give rise to a damages claim, the loss alleged must be proved and will not be inferred simply from the fact that money has a time value.

[34] *President of India v Lips Maritime Corp* [1988] A.C. 395.

II. THE AIMS OF DAMAGES FOR BREACH OF CONTRACT

In tort, despite such statements as that "damages are, in their fundamental nature, **20-019**
compensatory",[35] or that they exist to put the victim "in the same position as he
would have been in if he had not sustained the wrong",[36] there is little doubt that
they serve many other purposes as well. These include punishment;[37] deterrence;[38]
the expression of curial disapproval of the defendant's conduct;[39] the reversal of
unjust enrichment; and, for that matter, the simple symbolic establishment that the
claimant's rights have been infringed in the first place.[40]

The accepted aims of contract damages, by contrast, are slightly more narrow.[41] **20-020**
Thus, even though punitive damages are very well established in tort and their ambit
there is likely to grow,[42] the trend of present authority in England is fairly strongly
against overtly punitive awards for breach of contract[43] (though this is not necessarily the case elsewhere in the Commonwealth[44]). Again, in contrast to at least
some torts, a contract-breaker's motives, and his good faith (or lack of it), are generally irrelevant to the computation of his liability;[45] from which it follows that matters such as the court's desire to express disapproval of the defendant's conduct are
out of account.

Nevertheless, contract damages are not necessarily limited to strict compensa- **20-021**

---

[35] *Whitfield v de Laurent & Co Ltd* (1920) 29 C.L.R. 71 at 77, per Knox J.

[36] *Livingstone v Rawyards Coal Co* (1880) 5 App. Cas. 25 at 39 (Lord Blackburn).

[37] As in the case of punitive damages.

[38] As with punitive damages, and possibly also disgorgement damages under *Att-Gen v Blake* [2001] 1 A.C. 268.

[39] As with punitive damages against public authorities.

[40] See, e.g. Lord Griffiths in *Murray v Ministry of Defence* [1988] 1 W.L.R. 692 at 703: "The law at-taches supreme importance to the liberty of the individual and if he suffers a wrongful interference with that liberty it should remain actionable even without proof of special damage."

[41] A. Tettenborn & D. Wilby, *The Law of Damages*, 2nd edn (London: Butterworths, 2003), §1.34 ff. For discussion of the aims of damages more generally, see A. Burrows, *Remedies for Torts and Breach of Contract*, 4th edn (Oxford University Press 2019), Chs 1 and 3; *McGregor on Damages*, 21st edn (London: Sweet & Maxwell, 2022), Ch.1, Pt 1A.

[42] Particularly since the decision in *Kuddus v Chief Constable of Leicestershire* [2001] UKHL 29; [2002] 2 A.C. 122.

[43] In *Perera v Vandiyar* [1953] 1 W.L.R. 672 the Court of Appeal flatly denied their availability in contract. Despite their limited liberalisation in the tort context in *Kuddus v Chief Constable of Leicestershire* [2001] UKHL 29; [2002] 2 A.C. 122, referred to above, it seems that any serious further development is to be left to the House of Lords: see *Travelers Casualty & Surety Co of Europe Ltd v Sun Life Assurance Co of Canada (UK) Ltd* [2004] EWHC 1704 (Comm); [2004] Lloyd's Rep. I.R. 846 at [76] and *Aarons v Brocket Hall (Jersey) Ltd* [2018] EWHC 222 (QB) at [7]. Australian authority is equally against the availability of such damages in contract (see *Hospital-ity Group Pty Ltd v Australian Rugby Union Ltd* (2001) 110 FCR 157; cf *Mann v Paterson Construc-tion Pty Ltd* [2019] HCA 32; [2020] B.L.R. 156 at [37]), as is Singapore (*PH Hydraulics & Engineer-ing Pte Ltd v Airtrust (Hong Kong) Ltd* [2017] SCGA 26; [2017] 2 S.L.R. 129).

[44] Thus punitive damages for breach of contract can apparently be had in limited circumstances in Canada, especially in the insurance context (see *Whiten v Pilot Insurance Co Ltd* (2002) 209 D.L.R. (4th) 257) and occasionally elsewhere (e.g. *Royal Bank of Canada v Got & Associates Electric Ltd* (2000) 178 D.L.R. (4th) 385 (abusive cutting off of credit, referred to in J. Edelman, "Exemplary Damages for Breach of Contract" (2001) 117 L.Q.R. 539).

[45] "The damages awarded [for breach of contract] cannot therefore be affected by whether the breach was deliberate or self-interested."—Lord Reed in *One Step (Support) Ltd v Morris-Garner* [2018] UKSC 20; [2019] A.C. 649 at [35]. Cf. France, where a distinction may be drawn between good faith and bad faith breaches, for instance in connection with remoteness: *Code Civil*, Art.1231-3.

tion, despite numerous traditional suggestions to the contrary.[46] Although in most cases the court's overriding aim in awarding them is to put the victim of breach "so far as money can do it ... in the same situation ... as if the contract had been performed",[47] such damages may equally well serve other ends, such as the reversal of unjust enrichment, and, occasionally, deterrence.

The protection of the value of claimant's right to performance

20-022 The purpose of compensating the claimant for the fact that he has not received the performance promised to him is undoubtedly the most important. This is on occasion expressed in terms of a duty in the defendant to compensate for losses incurred by the claimant as a result of his breach of contract, provided those losses were neither avoidable nor otherwise too remote. Lord Haldane used such a formulation in 1912,[48] much followed since.[49] On the other hand, the concept of a "loss" is not always entirely straightforward and, strictly speaking, it is probably more accurate to say that damages exist to make good the claimant, as far as money can do it, for his failure to receive the performance he was entitled to. Thus there may be a more than nominal award aimed at marking the fact that the claimant has not received that which he contracted for;[50] and a contractor is not barred from claiming for loss of a profitable contract by the fact that payment would have been made to a third party,[51] despite the fact that in both cases it could be argued that on a balance sheet view the claimant is ultimately no worse off as a result of the non-performance. Again, a seller of oil for a good deal more than the market price can recover the difference from a defaulting buyer despite the fact that he has unwound the transaction with his own seller and, in strictly balance sheet terms, has lost nothing.[52]

20-023 The best expression, it is suggested, remains that of Parke B in *Robinson v Harman*,[53] oft-quoted[54] and indeed applicable in tort as much as in contract:[55]

---

[46] "In the ordinary way, damages bear no resemblance to a criminal penalty. The damages awarded to a plaintiff will be such as will compensate him for the loss he has suffered as a result of the wrong, so far as money can. The court looks to the plaintiff's loss, not to the quality of the defendant's conduct": Lord Bingham CJ in *AB v South West Water Services Ltd* [1993] Q.B. 507 at 528. For other similar statements, see *Dunhill v Walrock* (1951) 95 Sol. Jo. 451; *Johnson v Agnew* [1980] A.C. 367 at 400 (Lord Wilberforce); *Ruxley Electronics & Engineering Ltd v Forsyth* [1996] A.C. 344 at 353, 365.

[47] *Robinson v Harman* (1848) 1 Exch 850 at 855 (Parke B). Similarly: *Wertheim v Chicoutimi Pulp Co Ltd* [1911] A.C. 301, 307; *British Westinghouse Co v Underground Electric Railways of London Ltd* [1912] A.C. 673 at 689; *Monarch SS Co v Karlshjamns Oljefabriker* [1949] A.C. 196 at 220; *Sunley & Co Ltd v Cunard White Star Ltd* [1940] 1 K.B. 740 at 745; *Ruxley Electronics & Engineering Ltd v Forsyth* [1996] A.C. 344 at 353, 365 (Lords Bridge and Lloyd).

[48] "The fundamental basis is thus compensation for pecuniary loss naturally flowing from the breach; but this first principle is qualified by a second, which imposes on a plaintiff the duty of taking all reasonable steps to mitigate the loss consequent on the breach": *British Westinghouse Electric Co Ltd v Underground Electric Rys Co of London* [1912] A.C. 673 at 689 (Lord Haldane).

[49] E.g. *Payzu Ltd v Saunders* [1919] 2 K.B. 581 at 586 (McCardie J); *Pilkington v Wood* [1953] Ch. 770 at 776 (Harman J); *Pagnan & Fratelli v Corbisa Industrial Agropacuaria Ltd* [1969] 2 Lloyd's Rep. 129 at 148 (Roskill J); *Ruxley Electronics & Construction Ltd v Forsyth* [1996] A.C. 344 at 355, 365 (Lords Jauncey and Lloyd).

[50] *Ruxley Electronics & Construction Ltd v Forsyth* [1996] A.C. 344.

[51] *Glory Wealth Shipping Pte Ltd v Flame SA (No 2)* [2016] EWHC 293 (Comm).

[52] *Glencore Energy UK Ltd v Cirrus Oil Services Ltd* [2014] EWHC 87 (Comm); [2014] 2 Lloyd's Rep. 1.

[53] (1848) 1 Ex 850 at 855. The case concerned breach of an agreement to grant a lease; the claimant

"The rule of the common law is, that where a party sustains loss by reason of a breach of contract, he is, so far as money can do it, to be placed in the same situation, with respect to damages, as if the contract had been performed."[56]

To say that damages protect the claimant's right to performance is, however, the **20-024** beginning rather than the end of the classification exercise. Protection of that right may take various forms. For many years, as a result of a seminal American article in 1937,[57] the fashion was to analyse damages in terms of the "expectation", "reliance" and "restitution" interests. These corresponded broadly to the profits that would have been made by the claimant; to any amount by which he was out of pocket as a result of relying on the contract being kept; and the amount of anything received by the defendant without anything having been received in exchange. On the other hand, as will appear below,[58] this analysis is somewhat over-simplified. The "restitution interest" is not really anything to do with damages at all: and furthermore, the remaining heads of "expectation" and "reliance" cannot convincingly accommodate all compensatory awards.[59] Hence in this book a slightly different division will be adopted. Broadly, consequential damages will be divided threefold, into compensation for (i) the value of benefits not received, (ii) any expenditure wasted as a result of the non-performance, and (iii) any consequential other consequential losses resulting from the breach.[60]

Deterrence

It is true that the idea of deterrence plays a very subsidiary part in contract **20-025** damages. As stated above, punitive damages are not, it seems, available.[61] And added to this there is a respectable economic argument that, in at least some cases, breaches of contract should be condoned or even encouraged. The assumption is that, provided the victim is fully compensated for any losses resulting from the breach, and that any externalities are adequately dealt with, any extra profit made by the breaching party over and above that loss means that the breach is "efficient" and gives rise to a net gain to the parties as a whole. This assumption is easiest to grasp in the case of sales of relatively undifferentiated commodities. Take a seller who has agreed to sell a parcel of oil or soya beans to A for £x but who now

---

recovered the entire gain foregone, despite an argument by the defendant that damages should be limited under the now-abrogated rule in *Flureau v Thornhill* (1775) 2 Wm Bl 1078.

[54] E.g. *Lock v Furze* (1866) L.R. 1 C.P. 441 at 450–451; *Wertheim (Sally) v Chicoutimi Pulp Co Ltd* [1911] A.C. 301 at 307; *Watts v Mitsui & Co Ltd* [1917] A.C. 227 at 241; *Banco de Portugal v Waterlow Ltd* [1932] A.C. 452 at 474; *Koufos v C. Czarnikow Ltd* [1969] 1 A.C. 350 at 414; *Johnson v Agnew* [1980] A.C. 367 at 400; *Commonwealth v Amann Aviation Ltd* (1991) 174 C.L.R. 64 at 80, 98, 117, 134, 148, 161.

[55] See Lord Blackburn in *Livingstone v Rawyards Coal Co* (1880) 5 App. Cas. 25 at 39 ("that sum of money which will put the party who has been injured, or who has suffered, in the same position as he would have been in if he had not sustained the wrong for which he is now getting his compensation or reparation").

[56] (1848) 1 Ex 850 at 855.

[57] L. Fuller & R. Perdue, "The Reliance Interest in Contract Damages", 46 Yale LJ 52 (1937) (on which the most valuable commentary is R. Craswell, "Against Fuller and Perdue", 67 U. Chi. L. Rev. 99 (2000)).

[58] See para.21-038 ff, below.

[59] A point briefly explained in A. Tettenborn, "Consequential damages in contract–the poor relation?" 42 Loyola L.Rev. 177, 178 (2008).

[60] Para.21-038 ff, below.

[61] Para.20-020, above.

wishes to sell it to B for £(x+y). If the seller is willing and able to pay A any loss he has suffered through having to buy in more expensively from someone else, then there is every reason for the sale to B to take place: the seller, A and B all get what they want and none of them ends up dissatisfied. Conversely, if the damages available to A against the seller are increased so as to motivate the latter to sell to A, then this will not be the case.[62]

20-026 Nevertheless, despite these arguments deterrence remains a defensible rationale. It is arguably undesirable for the law to accept a neutral stance as regards, and hence to take no steps to discourage, at least some deliberate breaches of promise. This is an argument that is particularly strong in the case of promises aimed at protecting individualistic or aesthetic interests where the quantification of any loss flowing from breach is likely to be very awkward. Furthermore, for all its initial beguiling simplicity, the argument from efficient breach has its limits, since the assumptions that it is based on are often implausible. Few breaches, if any, do in practice leave the victim fully compensated. Nor are many breaches entirely without uncompensated external effects on third parties.

20-027 No doubt as a result of these and similar arguments, there are indications that considerations of deterrence are not entirely absent from the law on damages for breach of contract. This can be seen in at least three cases.

20-028 First, in 2001 the House of Lords decided in *Att Gen v Blake*[63] that, in exceptional cases where ordinary remedies based on loss might be inadequate or nugatory, a defendant might be liable to disgorge profits made in breach of contract. Hence where an ex-employee of MI6 broke his contract of employment by publishing his memoirs at large gain to himself but no obvious loss to the Crown, he was held liable to account for that gain. Although the precise ground of the decision is not clear, the House clearly had at least one eye on the possibility that it might be desirable to deter breaches of this sort.[64]

20-029 Secondly, where it is not immediately obvious how to compute the claimant's loss resulting from a breach of contract, courts may reckon it in a way that at least makes it difficult for a defendant in clear breach to escape with impunity. For example, where a landowner contracts not to use his land in a particular way, or a licensee of intellectual property agrees to limits on his power of exploitation, damages can be set at a "licence fee" or "buy-out" sum, which is aimed at least partly at ensuring that the defendant should not be allowed to nullify a bargain properly made.[65] As Brightman J said in *Wrotham Park Estate Co Ltd v Parkside Homes Ltd*, the leading case awarding "buy-out" damages in this context for breach of a restrictive covenant causing no immediate loss,

> "is it just that the plaintiffs should receive no compensation and that the defendants should be left in undisturbed possession of the fruits of their wrongdoing? Common sense would seem to demand a negative answer to this question."[66]

---

[62] R. Posner, *Economic Analysis of Law*, 6th edn (New York: Aspen Publishers, 2003), para.4.9.

[63] [2001] 1 A.C. 268. This case is dealt with in detail in Ch.26 below.

[64] [2001] 1 A.C. 268 at 288 (Lord Nicholls, quoting *Snepp v United States* 444 US 507 (1980) and referring specifically to the need for deterrence).

[65] See *Wrotham Park Estate Co Ltd v Parkside Homes Ltd* [1974] 1 W.L.R. 798 and *Experience Hendrix LLC v PPX Enterprises Inc* [2003] EWCA Civ 323; [2003] FSR 46; discussed below, Ch.26.

[66] [1974] 1 W.L.R. 798 at 812. See too *WWF World Wide Fund for Nature v World Wrestling Federation Entertainment Inc* [2007] EWCA Civ 286; [2008] 1 W.L.R. 445 at [27] (Chadwick LJ); *Giedo*

Thirdly, the law of agreed damages[67] now condones a degree of deterrence. Having for some years flirted with the idea that an agreed damages clause would not be enforced if its sole, or predominant, aim was to discourage non-performance rather than compensate for the actual effects of breach,[68] in *Makdessi v Cavendish Square Holdings BV*[69] in 2015 the Supreme Court avowedly took a new turn, and decided that provided such a clause protected a claimant's legitimate interests it could be valid, despite an overtly penal element.[70]

20-030

Marking of the claimant's rights

On occasion, as in tort,[71] an award is made in a breach of contract case that is difficult to regard as related to any quantifiable loss suffered by the victim, rather than simply an attempt to recognise, however crudely, that the claimant's rights have been infringed. An example of a case of this sort is the difficult decision in *Ruxley Electronics & Construction Ltd v Forsyth*,[72] where contractors built a domestic swimming pool a few inches too shallow. While this was a breach of contract, it was one with no appreciable effects on the pool's usability or value. Having smartly refused to allow as damages the vast cost of digging out the entire pool with a view to deepening it so as to conform with the contract, the House of Lords equally declined to give merely nominal damages, preferring instead to reinstate the original judge's somewhat impressionistic award of £2,500. Nevertheless they preferred to formulate its basis rather differently. Although that award had ostensibly been for a somewhat implausible "loss of amenity", their Lordships preferred to characterise it more abstractly: the sum could be justified as making up for the loss of a "a personal, subjective and non-monetary" benefit,[73] or as a "modest sum, not based on difference in value, but solely to compensate the buyer for his disappointed expectations".[74]

20-031

The reversal of unjust enrichment

In tort, it is well-established that on occasion damages may in effect be awarded on the basis of the gain made by the defendant from his wrong (the award of dam-

20-032

Van Der Garde v Force India Formula One Team Ltd [2010] EWHC 2373 (QB) at [510] ff (Stadlen J).

[67] Below, Ch.25.

[68] See para.25-030 ff below.

[69] [2015] UKSC 67; [2016] A.C. 1172.

[70] Thus in *Makdessi* itself, one of the conjoined appeals was *Parkingeye Ltd v Beavis*: here an admittedly penal charge of £85 for overstaying in a car park was upheld.

[71] See, in particular, *Rees v Darlington Memorial Hospital NHS Trust* [2003] UKHL 52; [2004] 1 A.C. 309 (fixed award to victim of failed sterilisation to mark infringement of rights, even though real loss, the cost of rearing the unwanted child, was an inadmissible head of claim); notably at [8] (Lord Bingham), [17] (Lord Nicholls), [125] (Lord Millett).

[72] [1996] A.C. 344. On this aspect of the case see D. Pearce & R. Halson, "Damages for breach of contract: compensation, restitution and vindication" (2008) 28 OJLS 73, esp at 93 ff.

[73] [1996] A.C. 344 at 360–361 (Lord Mustill).

[74] [1996] A.C. 344 at 374 (Lord Lloyd). See too Lord Scott in the later *Farley v Skinner* [2001] UKHL 49; [2002] 2 A.C. 732 at [86].

ages for mesne profits[75] or wayleave values[76] in trespass, and for use value in conversion,[77] are straightforward examples).

20-033   This tendency is less pronounced in contract damages. Nevertheless, it is not entirely absent. The power referred to above, to award damages on a licence fee or "buy-out" basis, can possibly be explained in this way.[78] Though this can best be defended (and indeed will be below) as a form of compensatory damages,[79] it is also arguable that unjust enrichment reasoning plays a part. Put shortly, by making a defendant who breaks his contract pay such sum as might reasonably have been demanded for the release of his duty, the law is on this argument making him pay over the profit he has made by not paying for the right.[80] Another arguable example is the decision of the House of Lords in *Att Gen v Blake*,[81] also mentioned above. The compulsion on the defendant in that case to pay over his profits can be seen as referable to the idea that those profits were gains from wrongdoing and thus represented an unjustified enrichment in his hands.

III.   DAMAGES FOR BREACH: THE MEASURES OF AWARD

20-034   From what has been said above, it is apparent that awards of damages for breach of contract can take a number of different forms. For the purposes of this part, however, some broad categorisation will have to be chosen. Essentially, there are four kinds of award of damages in a breach of contract case (assuming, as suggested above, that punitive damages are unavailable): nominal damages, damages to compensate for financial loss, damages representing non-financial harms, and gain-based damages.

Nominal damages

20-035   First, there are damages which reflect the fact that there has been a breach of contract, but nothing else. Since breach of contract is a wrong actionable per se, it follows that a claimant who proves a breach is entitled to at least some damages. If he cannot prove a compensable loss or some other reason for recovering a substantial sum (such as an entitlement to gain-based damages), he will receive a nominal[82] award. Awards of this sort serve little function apart from making it clear

---

[75]   E.g. *Ministry of Defence v Ashman* [1993] 2 E.G.L.R. 102. See Cooke (1994) 110 L.Q.R. 420. See too *Inverugie Investments Ltd v Hackett* [1995] 1 W.L.R. 713.

[76]   *Martin v Porter* (1839) 5 M. & W. 351. See too *Jegon v Vivian* (1871) L.R. 6 Ch. App. 742; *Phillips v Homfray (No.3)* [1892] 1 Ch. 465 at 770, CA; and *Whitwam v Westminster Brymbo Coal Co* [1892] 2 Ch. 538.

[77]   E.g. *Strand Electric Co Ltd v Brisford Entertainments Ltd* [1952] 2 Q.B. 246. See too *Watson Laidlaw & Co Ltd v Pott Cassels & Williamson* (1914) 31 R.P.C. 104 at 119 (Lord Shaw). The matter is dealt with in detail below: see Ch.00.

[78]   E.g. R. Cunningham and D. Saidov (eds), *Contract Damages: Domestic and International Perspectives* (Oxford: Hart, 2008), Chs 7 and 9 (by A. Burrows and R. Cunnington respectively).

[79]   Para.26-016 ff, below; and see *One Step (Support) Ltd v Morris-Garner* [2018] UKSC 20; [2019] A.C. 649, esp at [91], [127].

[80]   See e.g. *Att-Gen v Blake* [2001] 1 A.C. 268 at 283–284 (Lord Nicholls). But note the rejection of this explanation by Lord Sumption in *One Step (Support) Ltd v Morris-Garner* [2018] UKSC 20; [2019] A.C. 649 at [114].

[81]   [2001] 1 A.C. 268.

[82]   Traditionally between £2 and £10.

that the claimant's rights have been infringed[83]—indeed, they could equally well be replaced by a duty in the court simply to declare that there has been a breach, and leave it at that.[84]

Nominal damages raise no issues of great importance in the law of contract[85] and will not be dealt with at any length. Where a claimant proves a breach but no recoverable loss, the court has effectively no choice but to make a nominal award. An early, and usefully illustrative, instance is *Marzetti v Williams*[86] in 1830, a straightforward case of a bank wrongfully dishonouring a customer's cheque. Even though on the evidence the customer was put to no loss, the court upheld a verdict for nominal damages. As Parke J put it, "wherever there is a breach of contract or any injury to the right arising out of that contract, nominal damages are recoverable". Subsequent cases have included situations where a buyer of goods failed to obtain them but then took steps which had the effect of wiping out any resulting loss,[87] or where he suffered a loss but could have reduced it to zero by suitable mitigation;[88] where ship charterers wrongfully threw up the charter before performance was due but could, and would, have rightfully cancelled it at a later stage anyway when the vessel was not forthcoming;[89] or where there was a clear case of professional negligence vis-à-vis a contractual client, but no recoverable loss resulting from it.[90]

20-036

Damages compensating pecuniary loss

Secondly, there are damages which aim to compensate for pecuniary, or at least asset-based losses resulting from breach of contract. These form the subject of Ch.21, below.

20-037

---

[83] As Lord Halsbury put it in the context of tort (where such damages are available for some, though not all, wrongs), nominal damages are available for the "infraction of a legal right which, though it gives you no right to any real damages at all, yet gives you a right to the verdict or judgment because your legal right has been infringed." See *The Mediana* [1900] A.C. 113 at 116.

[84] This point is not new. It was well made in A. Burrows, *Remedies for Torts and Breach of Contract*, 4th edn (Oxford: Oxford University Press, 2019), Ch.25.

[85] It was once thought that a claimant who got nominal damages ought generally to get his costs on the basis that he had obtained at least some remedy against the defendant. But this heresy is long exploded, and it is now clear that, whether or not a nominal award is made, the issue is simply whether the claimant has, in a broad sense, won. Cf. Devlin J in *Anglo-Cyprus Agencies Ltd v Paphos Industries Ltd* [1951] 1 All E.R. 873 at 874: "[I]t is necessary to decide whether the plaintiff really has been successful, and I do not think that a plaintiff who recovers nominal damages ought necessarily to be regarded in the ordinary sense of the word as a 'successful' plaintiff. In certain cases he may be, e.g., where part of the object of the action is to establish a legal right ... but it is necessary to examine the facts of each particular case." See too *Alltrans Express Ltd v CVA Holdings Ltd* [1984] 1 All E.R. 685.

[86] (1830) 1 B. & Ad. 415.

[87] *Pagnan (R) & Fratelli v Corbisa Industrial Agropacuaria SA* [1970] 1 W.L.R. 1306.

[88] *Melachrino v Nickoll & Knight* [1920] 1 K.B. 693.

[89] *The Mihalis Angelos* [1971] 1 Q.B. 164.

[90] *Mappouras v Waldrons* [2002] EWCA Civ 842 at [9] (Kay LJ) (negligence, but no resulting loss, shown in contractual action against solicitors: technically wrong to dismiss action rather than give nominal damages).

Damages in respect of non-pecuniary harms

20-038   Thirdly, there are awards aimed at making good non-pecuniary losses such as disappointment, distress, inconvenience and the like. These are dealt with in Ch.22, below.

Gain-based damages

20-039   Lastly, there are awards which are, to a greater or lesser extent, "gain-based". Coverage of these will be found in Ch.26.

CHAPTER 21

DAMAGES: FINANCIAL LOSS

I. IN GENERAL

The most straightforward, and practically the most important, instance of **21-001**
compensatory damages for breach of contract concerns damages for financial loss.
For the purposes of this chapter this means compensation for loss or damage which
can more or less be reduced to money terms. More negatively, it can be defined as
the making good of losses which are not in their nature imponderable, such as disappointment, distress or annoyance, which (as will appear below) are subject under
English law[1] to considerably different rules. In practice the large majority of breach
of contract claims come within this category. In particular it includes all claims for
lost profits, for other kinds of financial or asset losses (for example, loss of or damage to tangible property or securities), and indeed for any kind of harm which is essentially commercial or will or might appear in a claimant's balance sheet.

The recoverability of financial loss

On principle, English law takes the view that the victim of a breach of contract **21-002**
can always recover such financial loss as he can prove results from it. Put
compendiously, a person can sue as a matter of course to the extent that he "is
financially worse off by reason of the breach of duty than he would otherwise have
been";[2] or (as another judge put it in 1982) if he suffers

"any detriment, liability or loss capable of assessment in money terms ... [including] ...
liabilities which may arise on a contingency, particularly a contingency over which the
plaintiff has no control; things like loss of earning capacity, loss of a chance or bargain,
loss of profit, losses incurred from onerous provisions or covenants in leases".[3]

The general recoverability of financial losses in breach of contract cases is subject **21-003**
to a few exceptions. For example, the rule against the recovery of reflective loss bars
recovery by a shareholder in a company for breach of contract in so far as his
damnification reflects a diminution of the assets of the company for which the
company itself could have sued. In such a case the right of suit is reserved to the

---

[1] As against (say) French law, which regards *dommage moral* as simply a form of damage like any
other and as giving rise to liability on a similar basis. See para.22-002 below.
[2] *Nykredit Mortgage Bank Plc v Edward Erdman Ltd (No.2)* [1997] 1 W.L.R. 1627 at 1639 (Lord
Hoffmann).
[3] *Forster v Outred & Co* [1982] 1 W.L.R. 86 at 94 (Stephenson LJ). The case actually concerned the
effect of the Limitation Act 1939 but the definition is as good as any.

company itself.[4] On occasion also, considerations of policy may intervene. Thus just as in the case of a failed sterilisation or contraception there can be no recovery in tort for the cost of raising a healthy child,[5] there can equally be no claim for breach of contract in respect of such losses.[6] But these exceptions are narrowly drawn, and the statement in para.21-002 remains largely true.

Claimant prima facie must prove loss

21-004   Presumptively, the burden of proof is on the claimant to prove the existence and amount of any financial loss for which he seeks to recover,[7] and to do so with some degree of specificity.[8] If he cannot, he is limited to nominal damages. So a university professor dismissed without proper notice but paid a full professorial salary during the notice period recovered only nominal damages;[9] while a client whose solicitors' negligence deprived him of his house was held to have failed to prove any loss when it transpired that the house was subject to negative equity and hence of no value to him in any case.[10] Similarly, a shipowner faced with the repudiation of a lucrative time charter fails to show loss in so far as the charterer could lawfully have cancelled it later;[11] and a buyer of commodities can recover no substantial damages from a seller guilty of anticipatory repudiation in so far as the latter could in any case have relied on a force majeure clause to excuse non-delivery when the relevant time arrived.[12] Again, while a victim of late payment can claim interest as damages for breach of contract, in order to recover he must allege and prove the amount of any expense incurred or income foregone.[13] The requirement for proof of loss, it should be added, remains even if the claimant is insolvent: hence no claim

---

[4]   See e.g. *Johnson v Gore Wood* [2002] 2 A.C. 1; *Sevilleja Garcia v Marex Financial Ltd* [2020] UKSC 31; [2021] A.C. 39 and A.Tettenborn, "Less law is good law? The taming of reflective loss" (2021) 137 L.Q.R. 16.

[5]   See *McFarlane v Tayside Health Board* [2000] 2 A.C. 59 and *Rees v Darlington Memorial Hospital NHS Trust* [2003] UKHL 52; [2004] 1 A.C. 309 (though the latter case allows an arbitrary sum in damages in lieu, to reflect the loss of reproductive autonomy).

[6]   See *ARB v IVF Hammersmith Ltd* [2018] EWCA Civ 2803; [2019] 2 W.L.R. 1094.

[7]   "[T]o entitle a plaintiff to recover damages in an action upon a contract, he must shew a breach and that he has sustained damage by reason of that breach": *Roper v Johnson* (1872-73) L.R. 8 C.P. 167 at 179 (Brett J). See too *Charter v Sullivan* [1957] 2 Q.B. 117 at 132 (Jenkins LJ); *Sony Computer Entertainment UK Ltd v Cinram Logistics UK Ltd* [2008] EWCA Civ 955; [2008] 2 C.L.C. 441 at [37] (Rix LJ). Lord Nicholls put the point as laconically as possible in *Sempra Metals Ltd v Inland Revenue Comrs* [2007] UKHL 34; [2008] 1 A.C. 561 at [96]. "Loss," he said, "must be proved."

[8]   Compare the Supreme Court of Texas in *Texas Instruments v Teletron Energy Management* 877 SW 2d 276 at 279-280 (1994): "Profits which are largely speculative, as from an activity dependent on uncertain or changing market conditions, or on chancy business opportunities, or on promotion of untested products or entry into unknown or unviable markets, or on the success of a new and unproven enterprise, cannot be recovered. Factors like these and others which make a business venture risky in prospect preclude recovery of lost profits in retrospect."

[9]   *Wray v West Indies University* [2007] UKPC 14.

[10] *Aylwen v Taylor Joynson Garrett* [2001] EWCA Civ 1171; [2001] P.N.L.R. 903.

[11] See *The Mihalis Angelos* [1971] 1 Q.B. 164, and also *The Golden Victory* [2007] UKHL 12; [2007] 2 A.C. 353.

[12] *Novasen SA v Alimenta SA* [2013] EWHC 345 (Comm); [2013] 1 Lloyd's Rep. 648; also *Bunge SA v Nidera BV (formerly Nidera Handelscompagnie BV)* [2015] UKSC 43; [2015] 3 All E.R. 1082. The latter case was decided under an express clause providing for the measure of damages, but it was made clear that the same result would have applied at Common Law.

[13] *Sempra Metals Ltd (formerly Metallgesellschaft Ltd) v Inland Revenue Commissioners* [2007] UKHL 34; [2008] 1 A.C. 561 at [17] (Lord Hope), [94]–[96] (Lord Nicholls), [216] (Lord Mance); *Sagicor Bank Jamaica Ltd v Seaton* [2022] UKPC 48; [2023] 2 All E.R. 81. He can, however, claim statutory prejudgment interest under s.35A of the Senior Courts Act 1981.

lies at an insolvent company's suit for substantial damages where the only result of a breach of contract was the diversion of funds from the general body of creditors to other creditors.[14]

On the other hand, the rule requiring proof of actual loss is not quite as absolute **21-005** or stark as it looks. To begin with, in a few isolated cases of breach of contract, financial loss may exceptionally be presumed without strict proof. So, for example, when a bank wrongfully refuses to pay its customer's cheque, an award to the customer of general damages for lost creditworthiness is standard practice; the customer is not put to proof of specific refusals to grant him credit or accept his drafts.[15] Moreover, in suitable cases courts may simply infer a loss from suggestive facts that have been established, and then impose at least an evidential burden on a defendant to rebut that inference. A neat instance is *Sony Computer Entertainment UK Ltd v Cinram Logistics UK Ltd.*[16] Carriers lost electronic memory cards belonging to the claimants that were made for pennies but sold for pounds. The Court of Appeal upheld a judgment for the retail value of the cards, despite an argument that the claimants had not actually proved any damage (such as loss of sales) beyond the paltry cost of reproducing the lost items. Rix LJ said:

"Of course, the legal burden rests on a claimant to prove his loss: but the evidential burden shifts, and on these facts rested, as I think, on [the defendants]."[17]

Since the defendants had raised no evidence limiting the claimant's loss to the cost of replacement, the claimants were entitled to recover in full.

Lastly, there is a well-established practice whereby courts may in cases of doubt **21-006** be prepared to incline against the breaching party and "give the claimant a fair wind in establishing what he has lost",[18] though Leggatt J has observed that this this principle needs to be kept in check: it should not be over-extended so as to morph the fair wind into a "free ride."[19]

---

[14] *Stanford International Bank Ltd (In Liquidation) v HSBC Plc* [2022] UKSC 34; [2023] 2 W.L.R. 79; [2023] P.N.L.R. 10 (claim by liquidator against bank for making payments allegedly in breach of mandate that had the effect of preferring some creditors and depriving the liquidator of funds). Such imbalances may sometimes be open to adjustment under the insolvency legislation (for example, s.239 of the Insolvency Act 1986): but that is beyond the scope of this book.

[15] See generally *Kpohraror v Woolwich Building Society* [1996] 4 All E.R. 119 (extending a rule previously limited to business customers: cf. *Gibbons v Westminster Bank Ltd* [1939] 2 K.B. 882): and see R. Hooley, "Remedies for Wrongful Dishonour of a Cheque" [1996] CLJ 189). No doubt the same would apply to wrongful failure to give effect to a debit or credit card, or (subject to the terms of the bank's contract with its customer) a duly mandated BACS transfer. Similarly, too, with a bank that fails to perform an express promise to supervise a customer's financial affairs, causing money matters to become confused and debts to go unpaid: see *Wilson v United Counties Bank Ltd* [1920] A.C. 102 at 112 (Lord Birkenhead).

[16] [2008] EWCA Civ 955; [2008] 2 C.L.C. 441.

[17] [2008] EWCA Civ 955; [2008] 2 C.L.C. 441 at [37].

[18] The origin of this principle lies in the antique tort case of *Armory v Delamirie* (1722) 1 Strange 505. More up-to-date contractual instances include *Browning v Brachers (A Firm) (Damages)* [2005] EWCA Civ 753; [2005] P.N.L.R. 44 at [79] (Jonathan Parker LJ); *Marathon Asset Management LLP v Seddon* [2017] EWHC 300 (Comm) at [164] (Leggatt J); [2017] 2 C.L.C. 182; and *Medsted Associates Ltd v Canaccord Genuity Wealth (International) Ltd* [2020] EWHC 2952 (Comm) at [85].

[19] *Marathon Asset Management LLP v Seddon* [2017] EWHC 300 (Comm) at [165]; [2017] 2 C.L.C. 182.

II.   THE BASIC MEASURE OF RECOVERY: REPLICATING THE CLAIMANT'S NET POSITION AS IF CONTRACT PERFORMED

21-007   When computing the measure of damages for financial loss, the fundamental principle is not in doubt. It is to provide compensation for all losses incurred by the innocent party which flow from the breach, subject to such issues as remoteness.[20] Thus the traditional starting-point is the formulation of Parke B in *Robinson v Harman*:[21]

> "The rule of the Common Law is, that where a party sustains loss by reason of a breach of contract, he is, so far as money can do it, to be placed in the same situation, with respect to damages, as if the contract had been performed."[22]

This is a proposition that has been repeated, or at least paraphrased, countless times since then.[23] The court's primary duty, in other words, is to compare the claimant's present position with the position he would have been in had the defendant performed as required, and to compensate the claimant accordingly.

21-008   Three sub-principles immediately follow from what has just been said. One is that it can be vital, when reckoning damages, to see precisely what was promised by the defendant, and to limit damages to the consequences of its not being provided. The second is the "net loss rule". In awarding contract damages courts are generally concerned with the effects as a whole of the breach: thus they see their task as calculating the overall net damage to the claimant, with any countervailing gains or savings being available to offset gross losses. The third, the "no duplication rule", emphasises that care must be taken to avoid compensating the same loss twice, or in two different forms. Each of these rules now engenders some little complexity, and for that reason each deserves a brief special treatment.

What did the defendant promise?

21-009   The limits of a defendant's promise can be very important. Imagine, for example, that a surveyor is asked by a purchaser to value a house priced at £1 million. In breach of contract he negligently values it at £1.2 million, whereas its true value is £0.8 million; the client then buys it for £0.9 million. The client's damages are the £0.1 million by which he is out of pocket, not £0.3 million. The surveyor did not

---

[20]   See *British Westinghouse Electric Co Ltd v Underground Electric Rys Co of London* [1912] A.C. 673 at 689 (Lord Haldane).

[21]   (1848) 1 Ex 850. The principle, though not its articulation, goes back earlier: e.g. *Cud v Rutter* (1719) 1 P Wms 570. The history is described in G. Washington, "Damages in Contract at Common Law" (1932) 48 L.Q.R. 90.

[22]   (1848) 1 Ex 850 at 855. See too Lord Blackburn in the tort case of *Livingstone v Rawyards Coal Co* (1880) 5 App. Cas. 25 at 39 ("Where any injury is to be compensated by damages, in settling the sum of money to be given for reparation of damages you should as nearly as possible get at that sum of money which will put the party who has been injured, or who has suffered, in the same position as he would have been in if he had not sustained the wrong").

[23]   A representative sample: *Wertheim (Sally) v Chicoutimi Pulp Co Ltd* [1911] A.C. 301 at 307 (Lord Atkinson); *Watts v Mitsui & Co Ltd* [1917] A.C. 227 at 241 (Lord Dunedin); *Banco de Portugal v Waterlow Ltd* [1932] A.C. 452 at 474 (Viscount Sankey); *Koufos v C Czarnikow Ltd* [1969] 1 A.C. 350 at 414; *Johnson v Agnew* [1980] A.C. 367 at 400 (Lord Wilberforce); *Pennant Hills Restaurants Pty Ltd v Barrell Insurances Pty Ltd* (1981) 145 C.L.R. 625 at 637 (Gibbs J); *Ruxley Electronics & Construction Ltd v Forsyth* [1996] A.C. 344 at 365 (Lord Lloyd); *Golden Strait Corp v Nippon Yusen Kubishika Kaisha* [2007] UKHL 12; [2007] 2 A.C. 353 at [29] (Lord Scott); *Bunge SA v Nidera BV* [2015] UKSC 43; [2015] 2 Lloyd's Rep. 469 at [14] (Lord Sumption).

promise that the house was worth £1.3 million, but merely that his valuation would be careful. Had he kept his promise he would have produced a valuation of £0.8 million and the client would have looked elsewhere; and this is the position to which the client must be restored.[24]

While this is clear with negligent professional advice, it can cause problems with **21-010** vendors' warranties, especially in the common case of warranties as to the accuracy of a company's accounts. Suppose a company vendor supplies accounts, whose accuracy he warrants, saying that the company is worth £10 million, whereas in fact it is worth only £7 million; the buyer purchases the business for £9 million. Has the seller warranted (i) that the company is actually worth what the accounts say, or (ii) simply that the accounts reflect the factual value of the company, warts and all? In the former case damages will be £3 million; in the latter £2 million.[25] The answer to the question depends on the interpretation of the contract in every case,[26] but the tendency is to interpret the warranty in the former way.[27] Similarly, agreements to deal only through an agency can cause difficulty. Do they amount to agreements by the principal not to carry out deals not notified to the agent, or to notify to the agent all deals the principal in fact does (since in the event of breach the latter yields a higher measure of damages)?[28]

The net loss rule

In awarding damages for breach of contract, as in tort,[29] the court is seeking to **21-011** make good the claimant's net loss, and only his net loss, resulting from the defendant's wrong.[30] It follows that, on principle and subject to a number of exceptions, all matters that go to reduce the actual damage suffered must be brought into account. After all, compensation is, as Nourse LJ briskly put it in 1996, "a reward for real, not hypothetical, loss".[31]

By way of straightforward examples, it has been held that a seller of goods su- **21-012** ing for the difference between price and value following wrongful rejection must

---

24 See e.g. *Phillips v Ward* [1956] 1 W.L.R. 471; *Ford v White* [1964] 1 W.L.R. 885; cf *Swingcastle Ltd v Alastair Gibson (A Firm)* [1991] 2 A.C. 223. This is sometimes stated to be a difference between the measure of damages in contract and tort (e.g. G.Treitel, "Damages for Deceit" (1969) 32 M.L.R. 556 at 558–559 and *Wemyss v Karim* [2016] EWCA Civ 27 at [23]–[25]. But this is not entirely accurate; as appears above, in cases of negligent advice or misrepresentation, it matters not whether the basis of claim is contractual or tortious.

25 Since in the latter case, had the accounts reflected the company's true value, the buyer would presumably have walked away, so that his loss is simply the amount he is out of pocket.

26 Compare Lord *Hoffmann in Lion Nathan Ltd v CC Bottlers Ltd* [1996] 1 W.L.R. 1438 at 1441.

27 See *Ageas (UK) Ltd v Kwik-Fit (GB) Ltd* [2014] Bus. L.R. 1338; *The Hut Group Ltd v Nobahar-Cookson* [2014] EWHC 3842 (QB); and also *Oversea-Chinese Banking Corp Ltd v Ing Bank NV* [2019] EWHC 676 (Comm).

28 In *Medsted Associates Ltd v Canaccord Genuity Wealth (International) Ltd* [2020] EWHC 2952 (Comm) the court plumped for the latter.

29 Statements of the position in tort are legion. Two good examples are *Hodgson v Trapp* [1989] 1 A.C. 807 at 819 (Lord Bridge); and *Dimond v Lovell* [2002] 1 A.C. 384 at 398-400 (Lord Hoffmann).

30 See *British Westinghouse Electric & Manufacturing Co Ltd v Underground Electric Railways Co of London Ltd (No.2)* [1912] A.C. 673 at 689 (Lord Haldane) and *Stanford International Bank Ltd (In Liquidation) v HSBC Plc* [2022] UKSC 34; [2023] P.N.L.R. 10 at [55]. Other statements: *R Pagnan & Fratelli v Corbisa Industrial Agropacuaria Ltd* [1970] 1 W.L.R. 1306 at 1316 (Salmon LJ); *Omak Maritime Ltd v Mamola Challenger Shipping Co Ltd* [2010] EWHC 2026 (Comm); [2010] 2 C.L.C. 194 at [15] (Teare J); *Palmali Shipping SA v Litasco SA* [2020] EWHC 2581 (Comm) at [30] (Foxton J).

31 *Kennedy v Van Emden* [1996] P.N.L.R. 409 at 414.

give credit for a handsome profit made by selling elsewhere the goods thus released;[32] that damages against a bank for wrongfully transferring monies must give credit for the fact that the funds transferred went to pay off a valid obligation of the account holder;[33] that a person suing for misadvice over investments must give credit for ex gratia compensation received from the company administering the investment;[34] that where landlords sue their solicitors for negligently causing a tenant to leave with a right to handsome compensation, they must nevertheless give credit for the large benefit of vacant possession thus obtained;[35] and that an employee suing for wrongful dismissal must give credit for savings caused by the dismissal, such as unincurred commuting costs, and the tax he will now not have to pay on the earnings foregone.[36] In a more recent example, a lessor's breach of contract in choking off traffic past a lessee's subway station sales booth caused large losses of profits at that booth. The lessor was nevertheless able to reduce its liability by pointing out that the lessee had had two booths at the station, and that much of the lost traffic had in fact simply been diverted past the second one, increasing its takings substantially.[37] A financier which lost money as a result of lending against negligently overvalued real estate had to give credit for the fact that it was merely refinancing an earlier doubtful loan it had itself made, and which had as a result of the refinancing been paid off in full.[38] In similar vein, the victim of anticipatory breach of contract seeking to recover wasted expenditure must allow for, and deduct, the savings he will now make through not having to perform;[39] and a vendor of land, if suing for damages for failure to accept the conveyance, must deduct the amount of any deposit forfeited by the buyer.[40]

The net loss rule: Compensation received elsewhere

21-013 A claimant may well be in a position to recover compensation for a given loss from several possible defendants. In such a case he may sue any of them for the full amount: but he cannot be compensated twice over for his damage. It follows that

---

[32] *Hill v Showell* (1918) 87 L.J.Q.B. (HL) 1106. This is akin to the principle in *Charter v Sullivan* [1957] 2 Q.B. 117, that if a seller can sell all the goods of a given kind that he can get hold of, a buyer who repudiates a particular transaction has deprived him of neither sales nor profits and hence is normally liable only for nominal damages.

[33] *Stanford International Bank Ltd (In Liquidation) v HSBC Plc* [2022] UKSC 34; [2023] P.N.L.R. 10.

[34] *Rubenstein v HSBC Bank Plc* [2012] EWCA Civ 1184; [2012] 2 C.L.C. 747. See too *Hamilton v Osborne* (2009) 83 OLR (3d) 157; [2009] ONCA 684 (claim against tradesman: compensation from trade association in account).

[35] *Nadreph v Willmett & Co* [1978] 1 W.L.R. 1537.

[36] Thus, for example, damages reflecting loss of taxable income are understandably awarded net of the tax saved: *Beech v Reed Corrugated Cases Ltd* [1956] 1 W.L.R. 807. See also *Nabi v British Leyland (UK) Ltd* [1980] 1 W.L.R. 529 (action in contract for disabling personal injury: unemployment benefit to be deducted). In *Palmali Shipping SA v Litasco SA* [2020] EWHC 2581 (Comm) at [37] Foxton J suggested, with good reason, that while a liability avoided should be deducted from any damages this should not be so where the liability would have been released in any event.

[37] *Platt v London Underground Ltd* [2001] 2 E.G.L.R. 121. But elsewhere such gains may be regarded as too remote: cf. *Jebsen v East & West India Dock Co* (1875) L.R. 10 C.P. 300 (passenger fares lost through late return of ship: no reduction in damages merely because many of the passengers later booked passages on other ships in same ownership).

[38] *Tiuta International Ltd (In Liquidation) v De Villiers Surveyors Ltd* [2017] UKSC 77; [2018] P.N.L.R. 12

[39] *Omak Maritime Ltd v Mamola Challenger Shipping Co Ltd* [2010] EWHC 2026 (Comm); [2010] 2 C.L.C. 194.

[40] *Ng v Ashley King (Developments) Ltd* [2010] EWHC 456 (Ch); [2011] Ch. 115.

in so far as a claimant has already received money from a third party to compensate for a loss,[41] credit must be given for the amount received.[42] It should be noted, however, that for the purpose of calculating the credit due to the defendant in such a situation the amount of the third party receipt falls to be deducted from the amount of the loss, and not from the amount recoverable from the defendant (which may well be less). Suppose, for example, that a claimant suffers a loss of £1 million due to a defendant's breach of contract, but that for some reason (such as remoteness) he can sue for only £800,000 of that. If he has already received £300,000 from a third party in compensation, he will recover £700,000 and will not be limited to £500,000.[43]

The net loss rule: Extraneous factors reducing loss

Loss suffered may be reduced by entirely extraneous matters; and if it is, then **21-014** (as in tort[44]) this reduction must prima facie be reflected in any damages. In a series of professional negligence cases, for example, events occurring between the transaction the subject of the claim and the time of judgment have been taken into account in reduction of the client's recovery. So in *Gregory v Shepherds*[45] solicitors negligently caused their client to buy a property encumbered by an unexpected mortgage: but afterwards, as it happened, the mortgage was discharged at no cost to the buyers. The buyers had, it was held, to give credit for this later development. Again, the point was illustrated more recently in a different context in *Golden Strait Corp v Nippon Yusen Kubishika Kaisha*.[46] Charterers repudiated a time charter at a very high rate when it had still four years to run, potentially exposing themselves to an enormous damages claim. But a few months later an unexpected event occurred that would, under the terms of the erstwhile charter, have permitted them to throw it up as of right. A majority of the House of Lords held that this factor had to be in account in reduction of the damages.

But such events will only have this effect if they are not too remote from the **21-015** breach. An example of a situation that did not satisfy this criterion was the professional negligence decision in *Needler Financial Services Ltd v Taber*.[47] Owing to bad advice from financial consultants, a client took out an extremely unsuitable and (as it turned out) ruinously expensive personal pension with a mutual provider. He

---

41 If he could have received a sum from a third party but has not done so, the matter is different and no deduction falls to be made: see *Peters v East Midlands SHA* [2009] EWCA Civ 145; [2010] Q.B. 48 and below, para.24-073 ff.

42 See for instance *Rubenstein v HSBC Bank Plc* [2012] EWCA Civ 1184; [2012] 2 C.L.C. 747 (bad investment advice: deduction of ex gratia payment received under rubric of "treating customers fairly" from company administering scheme in which claimant advised to invest).

43 See *Banco de Portugal v Waterlow & Sons Ltd* [1932] A.C. 452 at 473, 493, 512; and the tort cases of *The Morgengry* [1900] P 1 and *Banque Keyser Ullmann SA v Skandia (UK) Insurance Co (No.2)* [1988] 2 All E.R. 880 at 883 (Steyn J).

44 See in particular the discussion of principle in *Dimond v Lovell* [2000] 1 A.C. 384 at 398-401 (Lord Hoffmann).

45 [2000] P.N.L.R. 769. See too *Devine v Jefferys* [2001] P.N.L.R. 407 (claimant overpaid for house but later got into negative equity and was allowed to surrender it to lender: loss, and hence claim, thus reduced to nil); *McKinnon v E-Surv Ltd* [2003] EWHC 475 (Ch); [2003] Lloyd's Rep. PN 174 (surveyors failing to notice subsidence, but premises later stabilised: damages reduced); also *Kennedy v Van Emden* [1996] P.N.L.R. 409. As Nourse LJ put it in the latter case at p.414, "Compensation is a reward for real, not hypothetical, loss."

46 [2007] UKHL 12; [2007] 2 A.C. 353.

47 [2002] 3 All E.R. 501. See too the similar result in *Primavera v Allied Dunbar Assurance Plc* [2002] EWCA Civ 1327; [2003] P.N.L.R. 12 (misadvice over tax treatment of pension investment causes

not only successfully recovered for loss of sufficient pension provision, but significantly did not have to give credit for the fact that when the pension provider was demutualised some time later, he received free shares in it of considerable value. The reason was that the connection between the two events was in the circumstances too tenuous. Again, in another professional negligence case, *Gardner v Marsh & Parsons*,[48] surveyors in breach of contract with their client negligently missed structural defects in a leasehold flat, with the result that the client paid considerably more than the flat was worth. The buyer obtained damages from them based on this difference in value, even though the landlord later rectified them under the terms of the lease: the later rectification, said Hirst LJ, was not "part of a continuous transaction of which the purchase of the lease ... was the inception".[49]

The net loss rule: Effect of the claimant's own acts

21-016   The net loss rule applies in particular to the claimant's own acts calculated to reduce his loss.[50] As Longmore LJ put it,

> "If a claimant adopts by way of mitigation a measure which arises out of the consequences of the breach and is in the ordinary course of business and such measure benefits the claimant, that benefit is normally to be brought into account in assessing the claimant's loss unless the measure is wholly independent of the relationship of the claimant and the defendant."[51]

The leading decision here is that of the House of Lords in *British Westinghouse Electric Co Ltd v Underground Electric Railways of London Ltd*.[52] Buyers of electrical plant found that it did not work satisfactorily, and that this was due to the sellers' breach of contract. With a shrewd business sense, they took the opportunity to buy in replacement machinery which was even more up-to-date and economical than that which the seller would have provided had it kept its contract. They then sued for loss of profits. It was held that, although the buyers had been under no obligation to buy in this newer machinery at all, and could simply have claimed loss of profits with reference to the old, their claim now had to be reduced to reflect the increased profitability of the replacement goods. More recently, similar reasoning was applied where an airline, having been let down by its supplier of passenger

---

loss to client in regularising position: recovery in full, with no credit for rise in capital value of underlying investments).

[48] [1997] 1 W.L.R. 489. This case is, however, near the line of acceptability. It is heavily criticised in M. Thompson & D. Allen, "Surveyor's negligence and collateral benefits" [1998] Conv 303. It also encounters some scepticism in the later *Murfin v Campbell* [2011] EWHC 1475 (Ch); [2011] P.N.L.R. 28 at [17]; and in *Bacciottini v Gotelee & Goldsmith (A Firm)* [2016] EWCA Civ 170; [2016] P.N.L.R. 22 at [65], Davis LJ said that he regarded Peter Gibson's dissenting judgment in Gardner as "most powerful".

[49] [1997] 1 W.L.R. 489 at 503. Note, however, that this case is near the line: see previous note.

[50] *British Westinghouse Electric & Manufacturing Co Ltd v Underground Electric Railways Co of London Ltd* [1912] A.C. 673 at 689 (Lord Haldane); *Gardner v Marsh & Parsons* [1997] 1 W.L.R. 489 at 506 (Peter Gibson LJ).

[51] *Fulton Shipping Inc of Panama v Globalia Business Travel SAU* [2015] EWCA Civ 1299; [2016] 1 Lloyd's Rep. 383 at [23]. The statement of principle is unaffected by the Supreme Court's decision reversing that of the Court of Appeal at [2017] UKSC 43; [2017] 1 W.L.R. 2581.

[52] [1912] A.C. 673. See too, more recently, *LSREF III Wight Ltd v Gateley LLP* [2016] EWCA Civ 359; [2016] P.N.L.R. 21 (solicitors' negligence led to lease offered as security being almost useless for that purpose: lender's successor later made canny transaction with lessor greatly increasing value of lease as security: gain in account).

seats, bought in replacement seating which cost considerably more, but was much lighter and thus enabled the airline to save a small fortune in fuel costs.[53]

Another instance of the same idea is *Laverack v Woods of Colchester Ltd*.[54] A **21-017** senior employee, when wrongfully dismissed, took a new job that paid less but which gave him the opportunity to buy a sizeable equity stake in his new employer which in due course appreciated handsomely. The Court of Appeal decided that credit had to be given for this gain. More recently the same principle was applied in the shipping context in *The Elbrus*.[55] Charterers' early repudiation of a fixture proved a blessing in disguise to shipowners, who were enabled to employ the vessel much more profitably not only during the remainder of the original charter but for a considerable time after that. Teare J, on an appeal from arbitrators, had no doubt that the whole of this extra profit should be in account in reckoning damages against the original charterer.

The principle is similarly demonstrated in the case of sales of commodities. Even **21-018** if the standard measure of damages for non-delivery is the difference between price and value,[56] steps taken with the effect of reducing loss to some lower figure may still be in account. So where buyers rightfully rejected a cargo of maize on technical grounds at a time when its market value was some $2 a ton above the contract price, but then utilised the seller's awkward position to buy in the very same maize at a much lower price, the Court of Appeal had no doubt that the profit they thereby made had to be deducted from their subsequent claim for damages, which would otherwise have been a simple claim for $2 a ton.[57] And where sellers failed to deliver oil to buyers who had hedged their exposure to the market, they were held entitled to pray in aid the fact that the buyers had immediately closed out their hedge and thus reduced their loss to a lower figure than the difference between price and value at the time for delivery.[58]

In this connection, moreover, it is irrelevant that the measures taken by the claim- **21-019** ant went beyond those which were reasonably required under the doctrine of mitigation of loss.[59] Even if the claimant could on principle have claimed his entire loss had he done nothing, the defendant remains entitled to appropriate for his own benefit the claimant's supererogatory actions and apply them in reduction of his liability.[60]

However, as is the case with extraneous events,[61] in order to trigger a reduction **21-020** under the net loss rule, the effects of the claimant's act must be not only caused by

---

[53] *Thai Airways International Public Co Ltd v KI Holdings Co Ltd (formerly Koito Industries Ltd)* [2015] EWHC 1250 (Comm); [2015] 1 C.L.C. 765.

[54] [1967] 1 Q.B. 278. See too *Cerberus Software Ltd v Rowley* [2001] EWCA Civ 78; [2001] I.R.L.R. 160 (wrongful dismissal: credit to be given when claimant took another job that paid considerably more).

[55] [2009] EWHC 3394 (Comm), [2010] 1 C.L.C. 1.

[56] Because of the Sale of Goods Act 1979 s.51(3).

[57] *Pagnan & Fratelli v Corbisa Industrial Agropacuaria Lda* [1970] 1 W.L.R. 1306.

[58] *Glencore Energy UK Ltd v Transworld Oil Ltd* [2010] EWHC 141 (Comm), [2010] 1 C.L.C. 284

[59] On which, see Ch.24 below.

[60] "[W]hen in the course of his business [the plaintiff] has taken action arising out of the transaction, which action has diminished his loss, the effect in actual diminution of the loss he has suffered may be taken into account even though there was no duty on him to act": Lord Haldane in *British Westinghouse Electric & Manufacturing Co Ltd v Underground Electric Railways Co of London Ltd* [1912] A.C. 673 at 689; see too *Gardner v Marsh & Parsons* [1997] 1 W.L.R. 489 at 506 (Peter Gibson LJ).

[61] Above, para.21-014

the defendant's breach of contract but fairly closely connected with it.[62] As Peter Gibson LJ put it in 1996, such happenings may be ignored

> "unless such conduct flows inexorably from the original transaction, and can properly be seen as part of a continuous course of dealing with the situation in which the plaintiff originally found himself".[63]

A straightforward example of a case where no such close connection existed is *Hussey v Eels*.[64] A buyer was misled into buying a seriously defective property: but instead of leaving matters there, he enterprisingly chose to demolish the whole building and redevelop the site. The result was a large profit. The profit, not being regarded as part of a continuous transaction with the original purchase, was not deducted from his claim for damages against the seller for misrepresentation.[65] On a similar basis, if a building owner has a claim against a builder for shoddy construction work, this claim is not eliminated merely because he may subsequently have sold the building at full value to a third party.[66] Again, in *Laverack v Woods of Colchester Ltd*,[67] referred to above, the claimant on his wrongful dismissal by the defendant employer also took the opportunity, previously denied to him under his terms of employment, to invest in a competing business. In the event the investment proved highly successful: nevertheless, it was held too remote from the original breach to be deductible from any damages.

21-021 In deciding whether a particular gain is sufficiently connected with the defendant's breach of contract to fall to be deducted from damages, the fact that the gain comes from some speculation undertaken by the claimant at his own risk is a strong indication that it is not. The reasoning is that the claimant, having risked an uncompensable loss, should not be deprived of the benefit of success. *Hussey v Eels*, referred to in para.21-020, is one instance.[68] Another straightforward example is where a buyer is sued for non-acceptance of an asset: he is generally liable for the difference between price and value, even if the asset has since appreciated in the hands of the seller. It was the seller's choice to retain it and, as such, any benefit should enure to the seller. The classic illustration is *Jamal v Moolla Dawood, Sons & Co*,[69] where a buyer of securities was sued for wrongful rejection and unsuccessfully sought to pray in aid their subsequent appreciation. As Lord Wrenbury put it:

> "If the seller retains the shares after the breach, the speculation as to the way the market

---

[62] A rule also applicable in tort: e.g. *Jewelowski v Propp* [1944] K.B. 510 and *Great Future International Ltd v Sealand Housing Corp* [2002] EWHC 2454 (Ch).

[63] See *Gardner v Marsh & Parsons* [1997] 1 W.L.R. 489 at 503.

[64] [1990] 2 Q.B. 227 (for a cautious comment see A. Oakley, "The Effect on the Availability of Damages for Misrepresentation of a Profitable Resale" [1990] C.L.J. 394). See too *Newton Abbot Development Co Ltd v Stockman Bros* (1931) 47 T.L.R. 616 (redevelopment profits following bad building work).

[65] See [1990] 2 Q.B. 227 at 241 (Mustill LJ).

[66] *Newton Abbot Development Co Ltd v Stockman Bros* (1931) 47 T.L.R. 616; *Linden Gardens Trust Ltd v Lenesta Sludge Disposals Ltd* [1994] 1 A.C. 85. As Lord Griffiths pithily put it in the latter case, "who actually pays for the repairs is no concern of the defendant who broke the contract" (see [1994] 1 A.C. 85 at 97).

[67] [1967] 1 Q.B. 278.

[68] See too the spectacular New Zealand decision in *Turner v Superannuation & Mutual Savings Ltd* [1987] 1 N.Z.L.R. 218. A buyer agreed to buy commercial premises for $1.1 million, some $400,000 more than they were worth, whereupon the seller bought other premises for $375,000. The buyer, having repudiated, was held liable for the full $400,000, despite the fact that the two buildings had by the time of judgment appreciated in the seller's hands to a total of $7 million.

[69] [1916] 1 A.C. 175

will subsequently go is the speculation of the seller, not of the buyer; the seller cannot recover from the buyer the loss below the market price at the date of the breach if the market falls, nor is he liable to the purchaser for the profit if the market rises."[70]

In other words, it seems that a claimant who chooses not to mitigate his loss should not be deprived of his right to claim damages reckoned on the basis that he has done so. It is submitted that this or similar reasoning underlies the otherwise difficult decision in *Fulton Shipping Inc of Panama v Globalia Business Travel SAU*.[71] There, following early termination of a time charter by the charterer, the owner immediately sold the vessel rather advantageously; had the charter run its course and the vessel been sold at the end of it, an intervening slump in the market would have drastically reduced the price. The Supreme Court held the owner entitled to its loss of charter hire without any deduction reflecting the increased price obtained on sale. Although the grounds for the decision were not of the clearest, the best explanation appears to be that, as Lord Clarke said, the owners' act was not an act in mitigation, and indeed had no necessary connection at all with the termination of the charterparty which deprived it of the charter hire it would otherwise have received.[72]

21-022

The net loss rule: General exceptions

Apart from the case where a gain is only tenuously connected with the claimant's loss, the "net loss" principle is subject to a number of further general exceptions. To begin with, matters that would be disregarded under the "collateral benefit rule" in tort[73] will, it seems, equally be ignored in a breach of contract claim. So contract defendants, like tortfeasors,[74] are not entitled to reduce their liability by reference to the fact that the claimant was insured against the very loss that eventuated.[75] Similarly, just as a tort claimant disabled from working can recover lost earnings without reference to any disablement pension,[76] the same has been held to go for the victim of wrongful dismissal, whose claim lies in contract.[77] And so too with charitable or benevolent payments: these do not reduce damages for breach of contract[78] any more than they go to relieve tortfeasors of responsibility.[79] On the other hand, these exceptions are narrowly construed and limited to cases where the

21-023

---

[70] [1916] 1 A.C. 175 at 180. *Hussey v Eels* [1990] 2 Q.B. 227, referred to above, involves similar reasoning: see in particular Mustill LJ at 241.

[71] [2017] UKSC 43; [2017] 1 W.L.R. 2581

[72] See [2017] UKSC 43; [2017] 1 W.L.R. 2581 at [32]–[34]. The case is well analysed at D. McLauchlan and A. Summers, "Mitigation and Causation of Benefits" [2018] L.M.C.L.Q. 171.

[73] See *McGregor on Damages*, 21st edn (London: Sweet & Maxwell, 2022), para.40-225 ff.

[74] See *Bradburn v Great Western Rly Co* (1874) L.R. 1 Ex. 1.

[75] E.g. *Bristol & West Building Society v May, May & Merrimans (No.2)* [1998] 1 W.L.R. 336 and *Portman Building Society v Bevan Ashford* [2000] P.N.L.R. 336 (contract claim by lenders against negligent valuers for shortfall: recovery under mortgage indemnity policy irrelevant); *Brown v KMR Services Ltd* [1994] 4 All E.R. 385 (recovery by Lloyds underwriters from negligent agents unaffected by claim on stop-loss policies). See too *Naumann v Ford* (1985) *Times*, 13 March; also *Quilter v Hodson Developments Ltd* [2016] EWCA Civ 1125 at [39] (defective house: benefit of NHBC guarantee ignored).

[76] *Parry v Cleaver* [1970] A.C. 1.

[77] *Hopkins v Norcross Ltd* [1994] ICR 11.

[78] *Hamilton-Jones v David & Snape (a firm)* [2003] EWHC 3147 (Ch); [2004] 1 W.L.R. 924, esp at [70] ff (large travel expenses incurred by client owing to solicitors' negligence: recoverable even though in fact reimbursed by client's mother).

[79] See *Redpath v Belfast & Co Down Ry Co* [1947] NI 167; *Liffen v Watson* [1940] 1 K.B. 556.

gain is a matter of charity or (as in the case of insurance) the product of the claimant's own thrift. Thus where an investment company X made a loan to a borrower on the basis of bad advice and that loan was later refinanced personally by the controller of X, the Supreme Court had no doubt that the refinancing, which fell within none of these categories, had had the effect of eliminating any loss otherwise suffered by X.[80]

21-024   Secondly, the courts are generally unwilling to allow defendants to pray in aid contractual arrangements between a claimant and a third party which mean that the real risk of loss is borne by the latter rather than the claimant himself. So a lender can claim for misvaluation leading to the loss of the monies lent, even though the actual monies were provided, and the entire risk taken, by the lender's holding company;[81] and on a similar basis a lender can recover in full even if the loan was a syndicated one and thus this particular claimant only suffered a small proportion of the loss.[82] A fortiori, it is no defence to an action for breach of contract that the claimant who has suffered loss is actually suing for the benefit of, and indeed at the risk and expense of, another commercial party.[83]

21-025   Thirdly, it seems that in the sale of goods context, contractual arrangements between the claimant and a third party may be ignored more generally where the claimant is suing for simple "value less price" damages. So over a century ago in *Williams Bros Ltd v Agius Ltd*[84] it was held that just as a disappointed buyer could not increase his damages by pointing to an unusually profitable sub-sale,[85] damages would not be reduced merely because had the contract been performed he would have resold the goods at below market value.[86]

21-026   Fourthly, as in tort,[87] courts are often unwilling to make any deduction for benefits which are in a sense forced on the claimant, at least if they cannot be read-

---

[80] *Swynson Ltd v Lowick Rose LLP* [2017] UKSC 32; [2018] A.C. 313

[81] *Legal & General Mortgage Services Ltd v Underwoods* [1997] P.N.L.R. 567.

[82] *Interallianz Finanz AG v Independent Insurance Co Ltd* [1997] N.P.C. 89; *VTB Capital Plc v Nutritek International Corp* [2011] EWHC 3107 (Ch) [2012] EWCA Civ 808; [2012] 2 Lloyd's Rep. 313; *Titan Europe 2006-3 Plc v Colliers International UK Plc (In Liquidation)* [2015] EWCA Civ 1083; [2016] P.N.L.R. 7; also *Anthracite Rated Investments (Jersey) Ltd v Lehman Brothers Finance SA* [2011] EWHC 1822 (Ch); [2011] 2 Lloyd's Rep. 538 at [112]–[122]. So too no deduction falls to be made where loss suffered by a company is made good by an injection of cash on the part of the controlling shareholder: *Swynson Ltd v Lowick Rose LLP (In Liquidation)* [2015] EWCA Civ 629; [2016] 1 W.L.R. 1045.The application of the principle is criticised in N. Goh, "Syndicated Loans, Recovery of Third party Loss and the Res Inter Alios Acta Principle" [2016] L.M.C.L.Q. 368.

[83] *Mobil North Sea Ltd v PJ Pipe & Valve Co Ltd* [2001] EWCA Civ 741; [2001] 2 All E.R. (Comm) 289 (claimant, in settlement of litigation by third party, agrees that proceeds of claim to go to third party: held, irrelevant to damages claim). This has similarities with the rule discounting the benefit of insurance coverage: see above, para.21-023.

[84] [1914] A.C. 510. See too the earlier *Rodocanachi v Milburn Bros* (1886) 18 Q.B.D. 67; and *Mouat v Betts Motors* [1959] A.C. 71 (rule applies even if buyer would have had to sell actual goods at less than market price).

[85] *Williams v Reynolds* (1865) 6 B. & S. 495. Nor are the courts readily inclined to allow buyers of straightforwardly marketable commodities to claim on other bases, such as the cost to them of unwinding a hedging transaction: *Vitol SA v Beta Renowable Group SA* [2017] 2 Lloyd's Rep. 338.

[86] Note, however, that this is a controversial result. It is against the preponderance of US authority (typical of which is *H-W-H Cattle Co v Schroeder* 767 F.2d 437 (1985)). See too some possible scepticism where subsale specifically contemplated: *Louis Dreyfus Trading Ltd v Reliance Trading Ltd* [2004] EWHC 525 (Comm), [2004] 2 Lloyd's Rep. 243 at [24] (Andrew Smith J).

[87] See, for example, the shipping collision cases of *The Pactolus* (1856) Sw. 173 and *The Bernina (No.3)* (1886) 6 Asp. M.C. 65. But there are signs that this may be changing: compare the recent Canadian tort case of *Laichkwiltach Enterprises v Pacific Faith* (2009) 89 B.C.L.R. (4th) 322.

ily turned into cash.[88] The point is well illustrated by *Harbutt's 'Plasticine' Ltd v Wayne Tank & Pump Co Ltd*.[89] Following the destruction of a nineteenth-century factory caused by the defendants' breach of contract, the owners replaced it (as required by good practice and indeed the planning laws) with a contemporary building which was both more commodious and more valuable. The Court of Appeal declined to deduct this forced betterment from the damages. Similarly, it is not the practice to make any "new for old" deduction where defective goods have to be repaired with new parts,[90] or where unsatisfactory computers have to be replaced with models that, owing to swift technological progress, are vastly better.[91]

The net loss rule: The effect of tax

The treatment of damages for breach of contract in terms of tax is important, and needs a brief treatment of its own. The difficulty arises from the fact that damages for breach of contract may or may not be taxable in the hands of the recipient. Prima facie they are, like any receipt not covered by a specific tax charge, tax-free. Nevertheless, in particular cases they may count as taxable income[92] or capital gains[93] when recovered by an individual, or as assessable corporate profits in the case of a business.[94] Conversely, it also has to be remembered that the gains that the damages went to replace may or may not have been taxable themselves in the recipient's hands.   **21-027**

Where tax-free damages reflect taxable income or gains, the position is clear: the net loss rule requires that the would-be tax be deducted. This was first established in the case of tort claims for personal injury in the leading case of *British Transport Commission v Gourley*:[95] but it is now clear that it applies to actions for breach of contract as well, whether the claim is specialised, as in the case of wrongful dismissal,[96] or simply one for breach of an ordinary commercial agreement.[97] In computing the deduction, the claimant's position is looked at as a whole. Thus it is the claimant's marginal rate of tax that matters,[98] the claimant for his part being   **21-028**

---

88 For which a justification might be that their deduction would unfairly disturb the claimant's cash-flow. For where no such issue arose, see the tort case of *Voaden v Champion* [2002] EWCA Civ 89; [2002] C.L.C. 666 ("new for old" deduction for item in respect of which claimant would have had to set aside replacement monies anyway).

89 [1970] 1 Q.B. 447. The same goes for promises to restore damaged property: see *Haysman v Mrs Rogers Films Ltd* [2008] EWHC 2494 (QB) (promise to restore driveway damaged during filming: no deduction for fact that restored driveway would be newer and better than old one).

90 *Bacon v Cooper (Metals) Ltd* [1982] 1 All E.R. 397.

91 *Pegler Ltd v Wang (UK) Ltd* (1999) 70 Const L.R. 68

92 As in the case of damages for wrongful dismissal (see s.401 ff of the Income Tax (Earnings and Pensions) Act 2003). See too *Riches v Westminster Bank Ltd* [1947] A.C. 390 (interest by way of damages).

93 For example, a breach of contract claim against a gallery for loss of a valuable picture might well amount to a disposal of the picture sufficient to trigger a capital gains tax liability in the owner.

94 See generally Diplock LJ in *London & Thames Haven Oil Wharves Ltd v Attwooll (Inspector of Taxes)* [1967] Ch. 772 at 815 (concerning the tax status of damages recovered for breach of a contract of sale).

95 [1956] A.C. 185.

96 *Parsons v BNM Laboratories Ltd* [1964] 1 Q.B. 95; see too *Shove v Downs Surgical Plc* [1984] 1 All E.R. 7.

97 E.g. *Julien Praet et Cie SA v Poland Ltd* [1962] 1 Lloyd's Rep. 566 (insurance agency).

98 See the wrongful dismissal case of *Lyndale Fashion Manufacturers Ltd v Rich* [1973] 1 All E.R. 33.

entitled to bring into the equation any measures he might have taken to minimise his liability.[99]

21-029   The situation where taxable damages replace taxable gains is more complex. In the case of wrongful dismissal, where the tax treatment of severance payments is less than straightforward,[100] the courts take the logical view and hold that tax is in account on both sides of the equation,[101] with the claimant being entitled to such sum as, after deduction of whatever tax is payable on the damages, will yield the after-tax income it replaced.[102]

21-030   Elsewhere, however, the tradition has been more rough-and-ready. In effect, courts awarding damages for breach or ordinary commercial contracts have tended to proceed on the assumption that the tax on the damages exactly mirrors the hypothetical tax on the income those damages replace, with the convenient result that the one cancels out the other and hence the issue can be ignored. A typical instance was *Diamond v Campbell-Jones*.[103] A professional property developer, amenable to income tax on his business profits, recovered damages from a default-ing seller. Buckley J simply awarded the gross profit with no deduction:

> "If the damages would be taxable in the hands of the plaintiff, in order to give him the degree of indemnity to which he is entitled, I must, I think, award him a gross sum in dam-ages equal to the gross amount of the profit which he would be likely to have made had there been no breach of contract."[104]

21-031   In *Diamond v Campbell-Jones*[105] the balance was indeed probably fairly near. But, largely with a view to saving time and trouble,[106] the courts made it clear that (perhaps subject to revision in truly exceptional circumstances[107]) they were will-ing to ignore even fairly patent differences. Thus in *Julien Praet et Cie SA v Poland Ltd*,[108] where damages taxable in England replaced Belgian income which indubitably would have borne higher tax there, Mocatta J still refused to make any *Gourley*-style adjustment. Furthermore, a good deal later Potter J did the same thing

---

99   See *Beach v Reed Corrugated Cases Ltd* [1956] 1 W.L.R. 807 at 814–816 (Pilcher J), another wrong-ful dismissal case. No doubt the same would apply to a corporate claimant that would have taken more complex steps to minimise its liability.

100   Effectively damages are tax-free up to £30,000 but taxable thereafter: Income Tax (Earnings and Pen-sions) Act 2003 s.403.

101   *Parsons v BNM Laboratories Ltd* [1964] 1 Q.B. 95.

102   *Shove v Downs Surgical Plc* [1984] 1 All E.R. 7; see also *Stewart v Glentaggart Ltd* 1963 SC 300.

103   [1961] Ch. 22. See too the earlier *Morahan v Archer* [1957] NI 61.

104   See [1961] Ch. 22 at 27.

105   [1961] Ch. 22.

106   "[B]oth the lost profits and the damages to be awarded have the character of taxable subject-matter, and rough justice is done and a great expenditure of time and costs is saved by ignoring the tax on both sides so that in effect the tax on the lost earnings is set off against and cancelled out by the tax on the damages. The actual amounts of the tax (if any) to be paid on the one side and the other would depend on the special circumstances of the particular case and might differ widely, but no attempt is made to ascertain the actual difference and adjust the damages accordingly." (Pearson LJ in *Parsons v BNM Laboratories Ltd* [1964] 1 Q.B. 95 at 134–135). See too *Julien Praet et Cie SA v Poland Ltd* [1962] 1 Lloyd's Rep. 566 at 595 (Mocatta J).

107   *Parsons v BNM Laboratories Ltd* [1964] 1 Q.B. 95 at 139 (Pearson LJ). Cf. *Gill v Australian Wheat Board* [1980] 2 N.S.W.L.R. 795, where the tax liability on the damages awarded was much larger than that on the income they replaced. This was taken as an exceptional circumstance within Pearson LJ's dictum, and the award adjusted upwards accordingly.

108   [1962] 1 Lloyd's Rep. 566.

in *Deeny v Gooda Walker Ltd*,[109] where in compensating Lloyds underwriters for profits lost by underwriters' negligence, he refused to make any adjustment to reflect the labyrinthine tax structures of the insurance business.

Nevertheless, despite the suggestion in these cases that in the commercial context **21-032** the principle of taking tax into account is effectively a dead letter,[110] the decisions are not all one way. In at least two cases the Technology and Construction Court has adjusted damages to take account of differential treatment of profits and damages.[111] The matter thus remains uncertain, though it may well be that these latter decisions represent the trend of future developments.

It is thought that what goes for income and corporation tax will also go for VAT: **21-033** that is, where the damages and the income they replace would both have been chargeable to VAT, then courts will proceed on the assumption that one will cancel the other and award damages on an ex-VAT basis.[112]

The rule against duplication of loss

In many cases, the victim of a breach will frequently be able to frame a claim **21-034** for damages in a number of alternative ways. Nevertheless, there remains an overriding principle that recovery will be denied in so far as it would result in double-counting, or the same loss being compensated twice over. Suppose, for example, that a claimant pays £1,000 for an asset guaranteed to produce an income of £1,200 during the course of its life. In fact, the asset produces no income and is worthless. In an action for breach of contract, there is no doubt that the buyer can recover £1,200 representing the lost income. Alternatively, he can just as permissibly quantify his loss as £1,000, representing the price paid for, and ultimately wasted on, a valueless asset. But he cannot claim both sums, since if this was permitted it would leave him better off than if there had been no breach at all.[113]

The decision in *Nahome v Last Cawthra Feather*[114] illustrates the issue in **21-035** practice. Solicitors acting for commercial lessees negligently failed to take the proper steps to exercise a right to renew their lease under the Landlord and Tenant Act 1954. The clients in due course claimed both the capital value of the lease lost, and also the profit lost as a result of being evicted. But the court correctly struck

---

[109] [1995] S.T.C. 439 (upheld by the HL without discussion of the point at [1996] 1 All E.R. 933). See too *Daniels v Anderson* (1995) 16 ACSR 607.

[110] Indeed, Ouseley J effectively let this cat out of the bag in *Finley v Connell Associates* [2002] Lloyd's Rep. PN 62 when he said bluntly that as a normal rule tax was ignored in the computation of damages.

[111] See *Amstrad Plc v Seagate Technology Inc* 86 B.L.R. 34; also *BSkyB Ltd v HP Enterprise Services UK Ltd* [2010] EWHC 862 (TCC); 131 Con. L.R. 42; welcomed in *McGregor on Damages*, 21st edn (London: Sweet & Maxwell, 2022), para.18–19.

[112] Compare *Scout Association Trust Corp v Secretary of State for the Environment* [2005] EWCA Civ 980; [2005] S.T.C. 1808 (a compulsory purchase case, but still in point).

[113] More precisely, had there been no breach he would have made a net gain of £200 (£1,200 – £1,000), whereas to give him damages of £2,200 would leave him with a net gain of £1,200. For useful exposition of the principle, see the judgments in *JP Morgan Chase Bank v Springwell Navigation Corp* [2006] EWCA Civ 161; [2006] P.N.L.R. 28 at [10], [14], [19].

[114] [2010] EWHC 76 (Ch); [2010] P.N.L.R. 19. See too the similar reasoning in *Riyad Bank v Ahli United Bank (UK) Plc* [2005] EWHC 279 (Comm); [2005] 2 Lloyd's Rep. 409 (bad investment advice to investment company: no claim for both diminution in value of assets and excessive distributions to investors); and in *Primavera v Allied Dunbar Assurance Plc* [2002] EWCA Civ 1327; [2003] P.N.L.R. 12 (claimant deprived of capital sum necessary to pay off loan: no award of both pre-judgment interest on capital sum and also costs of servicing loan, since this would amount to double-dipping).

out the latter claim as essentially duplicative of the former: the capital value was simply another way of expressing the value of the profit to be gained from the use of the premises. Similarly, in the earlier (and better known) *Cullinane v British "Rema" Manufacturing Co Ltd*[115] the Court of Appeal declined to allow the buyer of useless machinery to recover both the capital cost lost and also the profit that the machine should have made but would not. Although double recovery was not the ostensible ground of the decision,[116] it is suggested that it is best explained on the basis of it.[117]

21-036   The double recovery principle may also apply in a more indirect way, as demonstrated in *Corbett v Bond Pearce (A Firm)*.[118] Solicitors negligently prepared an invalid will; the would-be beneficiaries under that will duly recovered their lost entitlement in a direct tort suit against the solicitors.[119] The estate's subsequent claim for the costs incurred in probate proceedings failed in the Court of Appeal, partly because the costs would otherwise have been deducted from the sums due to the beneficiaries, and that therefore allowing the action would indirectly lead to impermissible double recovery by the latter.

III.   WAYS OF EXPRESSING THE LOSS RESULTING FROM NON-PERFORMANCE: THE CONCEPTS OF EXPECTATION, RELIANCE AND CONSEQUENTIAL DAMAGE

21-037   There is a venerable academic tradition[120] of dividing the compensatory damages available in a breach of contract case into three heads, reflecting what are known as the claimant's expectation, reliance and restitution interests. In summary, suppose a seller of goods wrongfully fails to supply them. The buyer's expectation interest is typified by his claim for potential lost profit (i.e. the market value of the goods, less their contract price); his reliance interest by his claim for expenditure thrown away in a fruitless attempt to collect the non-existent goods; and the restitution interest by his right to recover any prepayment for which he has received nothing in return. Nevertheless, for all its respectability and the occasional judicial invocation of its terms by English judges,[121] this scheme is not entirely satisfactory. For one thing, it fails to take proper account of consequential

---

[115] [1954] 1 Q.B. 292.

[116] Which at least in the main, was that claims for lost profits and capital loss were alternative and inconsistent forms of claim between which a claimant had to elect (see Evershed MR at [1954] 1 Q.B. 292 at 303). It will be suggested below (para.21-055 ff) that this is a misguided view.

[117] As may indeed have been at the back of Evershed MR's mind: compare his comment at [1954] 1 Q.B. 292 at 302 that "a claim for loss of profits could only be founded upon the footing that the capital expenditure had been incurred".

[118] [2001] EWCA Civ 531; [2001] P.N.L.R. 31.

[119] Under the principle in the tort case of *White v Jones* [1995] 2 A.C. 207.

[120] It originates in an immensely (perhaps excessively) influential pre-war American law review article: see L. Fuller and W. Perdue, "The Reliance Interest in Contract Damages", 46 Yale L.J. 52 (1936) at 54. That article went on to suggest that the expectation interest had previously been exaggerated in importance vis-à-vis the other two.

[121] Examples of this invocation include *Shipping Corp of India v NSB* [1991] 1 Lloyd's Rep. 77 at 80–81 (Steyn J); *Surrey CC v Bredero Homes Ltd* [1993] 1 W.L.R. 1361 at 1369 (Steyn LJ); *Darlington BC v Wiltshier Developments Ltd* [1995] 1 W.L.R. 68 at 80 (Steyn LJ); *Regalian Plc v London Docklands Development Corp* [1995] 1 W.L.R. 212 at 222 (Rattee J); and *White v Jones* [1995] 2 A.C. 207 at 265–269 (Lord Goff).

losses, which cannot plausibly fit into any of its categories.[122] Furthermore, the restitution interest seems logically superfluous. A buyer's claim to get back money paid for nothing, in so far as it is based on loss, is simply an aspect of reliance loss: and in so far as bottomed on a failure of consideration, it is not a claim for loss at all and hence lies outside the field of damages in any case.[123] For this reason, this book, while accepting that damages do vary in the interest protected, will use a slightly different categorisation: namely, expectation, reliance and consequential losses.

The modern categories of damage: Expectation, reliance and consequential losses

It is convenient to classify damages for financial loss resulting from a breach of contract into three rough categories, depending on the kind of damage that they aim to make whole. This is because, although they all reflect the same fundamental principle (i.e. that the claimant is entitled to that sum which will put him in the position he would have occupied had he received the performance to which he was entitled[124]), the issues they raise can differ, and indeed on occasion the detailed rules of quantification may not be the same.[125]   **21-038**

The first category is "expectation losses": that is, damages aimed at making good any direct gains the claimant would have made had the contract been kept. Secondly, there are "reliance losses": compensation predicated, not on a gain foregone because the contract was broken, but on the claimant having spent money in reliance on its being kept, and hence to that extent being worse off as a result of the breach. And thirdly, there are claims based on consequential losses: that is, on other losses not falling in either of these categories, but which nevertheless follow on from the breach. For example, if machinery is not delivered on time, the industrialist's claim for profits lost as a result of the non-delivery is a consequential claim. Each of these will now be dealt with in more detail.   **21-039**

Expectation losses

Expectation damages exist to compensate for the value of some benefit the claimant would have got under a contract had it been properly performed. A straightforward example is damages for breach of an executory contract for the sale of goods or other assets. Here the buyer presumptively recovers the amount, if any, by which   **21-040**

---

[122] On which see A. Tettenborn, "Consequential Damages in Contract—The Poor Relation?" 42 Loyola of Los Angeles L.Rev. 117 (2009).

[123] Illustrated by the fact that matters reducing the amount of claimant's loss are irrelevant in such cases: for instance, benefits received under the contract (*Rowland v Divall* [1923] 2 K.B. 500) or the fact that the claimant made a losing bargain in the first place (*Wilkinson v Lloyd* (1845) 7 Q.B. 27).

[124] "[T]he expressions 'expectation damages', 'damages for loss of profits', 'reliance damages' and 'damages for wasted expenditure' are simply manifestations of the central principle enunciated in *Robinson v Harman* rather than discrete and truly alternative measures of damages which a party not in breach may elect to claim": Mason CJ and Dawson J in *Commonwealth of Australia v Amann Aviation Pty Ltd* (1991) 66 A.L.J.R. 123 at 182.

[125] In particular, there may be differences in the rules as to remoteness, and in the ability of the defendant to reduce or eliminate his liability by showing that the claimant has not suffered any substantial loss at all. See below, generally A. Tettenborn, "Consequential Damages in Contract-The Poor Relation?" 42 Loyola of Los Angeles L.Rev.117 (2009).

the market value of the asset exceeds the price[126] (and the seller the converse difference where it is the buyer who breaches[127]). A similar rule applies to services, though such cases do not seem to arise commonly,[128] except in specialised contexts such as time charters.[129] No doubt for this reason, such damages are sometimes known as "loss of bargain" damages. But the idea of expectation loss goes a good deal further than this. Even where there is no available market the court must, in the event of non-performance, do its best to value the gain the claimant has been deprived of.[130] Again, many claims for breach of warranty are essentially claims for expectation loss, as where the seller of a business warrants that its profits will reach a certain level in the course of the next year, or a seller of shares guarantees their market value at some time in the future. Again, the same goes for the situation where the claimant seeks to recover the cost of paying a third party to do what the defendant ought to have done, for instance, contracted building works that have not been carried out.[131]

21-041   In most cases a claimant, whatever kind of loss he is seeking to recover, will in the nature of things have relied on the relevant term of the contract being observed. Nevertheless, this is not a requirement for recovery of expectation damages. On the contrary: the claimant need not show he even knew of the term involved, or

---

[126] Goods: see Sale of Goods Act 1979 s.51(3) (reproducing the Common Law position). Other assets are governed by the Common Law: *Golden Strait Corp v Nippon Yusen Kubishika Kaisha* [2007] UKHL 12; [2007] 2 A.C. 353 at [79] (Lord Brown). See, e.g., *Bear Stearns Bank Plc v Forum Global Equity Ltd* [2007] EWHC 1576 (Comm) at [197] (securities) and *Deutsche Bank AG v Total Global Steel Ltd* [2012] EWHC 1201 (Comm); [2012] Env. L.R. D7 (EU emissions allowances). Such awards are compensation for the loss of an abstract gain. The fact that no actual cash loss was suffered is irrelevant: see the Australian decision in *Clark v Macourt* [2013] HCA 56; (2013) 304 A.L.R. 220 (high-priced business assets in fact useless: buyer recovers value, even though costs in fact all recouped from customers).

[127] Goods: Sale of Goods Act 1979 s.50(3). Other assets not covered by the Sale of Goods Act 1979: *Jamal v Moolla Dawood, Sons & Co* [1916] 1 A.C, 175 (securities) and, more recently, *Deutsche Bank AG v Total Global Steel Ltd* [2012] EWHC 1201 (Comm) (tradeable EU pollution permits)). As with awards to a disappointed buyer, awards of this sort are made in respect of the loss of an abstract gain. See *Glencore Energy UK Ltd v Cirrus Oil Services Ltd* [2014] EWHC 87 (Comm); [2014] 2 Lloyd's Rep. 1 (not within description in contract of awards for loss of profits) and *Glory Wealth Shipping Pte Ltd v Flame SA* [2016] EWHC 293 (Comm); [2016] 1 Lloyd's Rep. 571 (irrelevant that payment for goods not accepted would have been made to a third party).

[128] One such, however, was *Western Web Offset Printers Ltd v Independent Media Ltd* Times, October 10, 1995 (failure to accept printing services: claim by printer for price, less value of services refused). Another case where the issue incidentally arose was *Neath Port Talbot (Recycling) Ltd v James Heys and Sons Ltd* [2021] EWHC 3157 (Comm); 201 Con. L.R. 140 (contract to remove waste). See too *Anthracite Rated Investments (Jersey) Ltd v Lehman Brothers Finance SA (In Liquidation)* [2011] EWHC 1822 (Ch); [2011] 2 Lloyd's Rep. 538 at [119]–[129] (Briggs J).

[129] "[T]there is, I consider, a normal measure of recovery in cases of premature wrongful repudiation of a time charter by the owners, and that normal measure is that, if there is at the time of the termination of the charter-party an available market for the chartering of a substitute vessel, the damages will generally be assessed on the basis of the difference between the contract rate for the balance of the charter-party period and the market rate for the chartering in of a substitute vessel for that period": Robert Goff J in *The Elena D'Amico* [1980] 1 Lloyd's Rep. 75 at 87. See too *The Great Creation* [2014] EWHC 3978 (Comm); [2015] 1 C.L.C. 16 at [16] (Cooke J).

[130] See e.g. the sale cases of *The Ile aux Moines* [1974] 2 Lloyd's Rep. 502 (unusual ship) and *Hughes v Pendragon Sabre Ltd* [2016] EWCA Civ 18; [2016] 1 Lloyd's Rep. 311 (virtually unobtainable Porsche). So too in other situations: see for example, the charter case of *Glory Wealth Shipping Pte Ltd v Korea Line Corp (The Wren)* [2011] EWHC 1819 (Comm); [2011] 2 Lloyd's Rep. 370

[131] As in cases such as *Radford v De Froberville* [1977] 1 W.L.R. 1262.

otherwise acted (or failed to act) in reliance on performance being forthcoming.[132] All that he needs to show is that the term was broken. So, for example, there is no reason why the buyer of a car should not be entitled to enforce a promise as to (say) the longevity of the exhaust system, even though the promise was buried deep in an unread warranty agreement and he did not know of its existence until a problem occurred that was covered by it.

It is sometimes said that the availability of expectation damages, with their **21-042** concentration on the position "as if the contract had been performed," is what marks off damages in contract from those in tort, which look to the position as if no tort had been committed.[133] At first sight this seems plausible. This is especially the case with damages for inaccurate representations, where as a rule the hypothetical position had the statement been true is relevant in contract (that is, in so far as the claimant proves that the statement was a warranty and sues on that basis), but not otherwise. Imagine that A owns an asset worth £900, which he persuades B to buy for £1,000 by saying (incorrectly) that it has some quality making it worth £1,200. If B can prove a contractual warranty, he recovers £300, the difference between the value of the asset he now has (£900) and his hypothetical position had the statement been true (in which case he would have had something worth £1,200). In contrast, by suing in tort for negligent misrepresentation or deceit he gets £100 only, on the basis that there been no tort he would not have bought it at all and hence would still have his original £1,000.[134] In fact, however, the dichotomy is a false one. In both cases the claimant recovers by reference to his would-be position if the wrong—breach of contract or tort as the case may be—had not been committed. The only reason for the apparent difference is that most contractual duties are positive, whereas most tortious ones are negative. Thus there are cases of breach of contract where the would-be position had the statement been true is irrelevant:[135] there are equally cases in tort where a defendant is held to what would normally be referred to as expectation damages.[136]

Reliance losses[137]

Expectation damages deal with claims for what would have been a direct gain **21-043** to the claimant from performance of the contract. Reliance damages, by contrast, compensate for losses suffered in a more indirect way, as a result of relying on the

---

[132] "If a party wishes to claim relief in respect of a breach of a term of a contract ... he need prove no actual reliance"—per Slade LJ in *Harlingdon and Leinster Enterprises Ltd v Christopher Hull Fine Art Ltd* [1991] 1 Q.B. 564 at 584. See too Stuart-Smith LJ at 579. This means, for example, that a buyer of goods can invoke the terms of a warranty even though he never reads it at the time of contracting and only finds out about it later.

[133] For straightforward instances, see Ackner J in *André & Cie SA v Ets Michel Blanc & Fils* [1977] 2 Lloyd's Rep. 166 at 181, and Lord Reed in *Morris-Garner v One Step (Support) Ltd* [2018] UKSC 20; [2019] A.C. 649 at [31].

[134] See e.g. *McConnell v Wright* [1903] 1 Ch. 546 at 554 (Collins MR); *Doyle v Olby (Ironmongers) Ltd* [1969] 2 Q.B. 158 at 166 (Lord Denning MR) (both deceit cases).

[135] Notably cases of negligent valuations: e.g. *Philips v Ward* [1956] 1 W.L.R. 471 and *Perry v Sydney Phillips* [1982] 1 W.L.R. 1297.

[136] *White v Jones* [1995] 2 A.C. 207 is as good an instance as any.

[137] See generally L. Fuller and W. Perdue, "The Reliance Interest in Contract Damages", 46 Yale LJ 52 (1936–7); P. Jaffey, "A New Version of the Reliance Theory" [1998] NILQ 107. A more sceptical view comes in M. Kelly, "The Phantom Reliance Interest in Contract Damages" [1992] Wis L.Rev. 1755, and D. McLaughlan, "The redundant reliance interest in contract damages" (2011) 127 L.Q.R. 23.

contract being kept and then being disappointed in that reliance. Straightforward examples are where an industrialist has invested money (which is now wasted) in buying machinery which in the event does not work;[138] where a lessee pays a premium for a lease and is then wrongfully evicted during the term;[139] or where a professional in breach of contract gives careless advice and a client loses money by relying on it.[140]

21-044   It follows from this, of course, that in order to recover such damages, a showing of reliance is crucial. In so far as the claimant cannot demonstrate that he has changed his position on the basis of the prospect of performance, he must fail. Take, for example, a client who suffers loss after receiving negligent advice from his solicitor. He will nevertheless fail if it is apparent that he would have acted in the same way even if properly advised.[141]

21-045   It is a feature of most claims for reliance loss that the claimant is complaining of being out-of-pocket as a result of the breach: that is, worse off than he was before the contract was concluded (a factor which has caused some commentators to regard such claimants as inherently more deserving than those seeking expectation recovery[142]). Nevertheless, this is not always the case; and the principle of reliance recovery can equally well encompass claims for profits foregone or other opportunity costs. Thus in *Swingcastle Ltd v Alastair Gibson*,[143] a case of negligent misvaluation of mortgage security for a lender, the lender recovered not only the capital lost but also the interest which that capital would have earned if invested successfully elsewhere (which it would have been but for the defendants' negligence). In *Swingcastle* it is true that the claimant, having lost a large portion of its capital, was worse off overall than if it had never contracted; but there is no reason why this should be necessary. If an investor is negligently advised to buy securities whose value remains static rather than others which appreciate, it is submitted that he will recover, as reliance loss, the appreciation he has been deprived of.[144]

21-046   It equally follows from this that one must regard as extremely doubtful suggestions that whereas expectation damages look to the claimant's hypothetical position had the contract been performed, reliance damages aim to replicate the claimant's situation had he never contracted at all.[145] On the contrary: reliance damages, while they typically involve different fact situations from expectation damages, are like the latter in that their object is—as with all contract damages—to

---

[138] E.g. *Cullinane v British "Rema" Manufacturing Co Ltd* [1954] 2 Q.B. 292.

[139] As in *C&P Haulage Ltd v Middleton* [1983] 1 W.L.R. 1461 and *Grange v Quinn* [2013] EWCA Civ 24; [2013] 1 P. & C.R. 18.

[140] Or, more accurately, relying on the professional to perform his contractual obligation to give careful advice.

[141] *Sykes v Midland Bank Executor & Trustee Co Ltd* [1971] 1 Q.B. 113

[142] This is the thrust of much of L. Fuller and W. Perdue, "The Reliance Interest in Contract Damages", 46 Yale LJ 52 (1936–7), and of P. Atiyah, *Essays on Contract*, 124 ff.

[143] [1991] 2 A.C. 223. Cf. *East v Maurer* [1991] 1 W.L.R. 461, applying a similar rule in tort. Similarly with investment advisers: where their negligence causes a client to lay out funds and lose them, the client may recover for the profits they would have made from later investing those same funds had they still had them available (*JP Morgan Chase Bank v Springwell Navigation Corp* [2006] EWCA Civ 161; [2006] P.N.L.R. 28). But such profits must be proved, and will not be presumed: compare the deceit case of *Mortgage Express v Countrywide Surveyors Ltd* [2016] EWHC 1830 (Ch); [2016] P.N.L.R. 35.

[144] Compare the deceit case of *Clef Aquitaine SarL v Laporte Minerals (Barrow) Ltd* [2001] Q.B. 488, where (effectively) this happened.

[145] L. Fuller and W. Perdue, "The Reliance Interest in Contract Damages", 46 YLJ 52 at 54 (1936). This

replicate the claimant's position had there been proper performance.[146] The relevant question in all cases is thus whether the claimant would have suffered the loss he did if the contract had been fulfilled.

Reliance losses can effectively be divided into two types. The first is where the claimant incurs expenditure which he would not have undertaken at all had the defendant performed his contractual obligations and which is now wasted. Most cases where a party claims contractual damages for professional negligence or negligent misinformation fall in this category. For instance, where a lender advances money on the basis of a negligent property valuation and subsequently loses part or all of it, his claim is essentially that if he had been properly advised he would not have made the bad loan he did: again, where solicitors' incompetence causes a client to lease premises useless for his business, the client can recover the costs associated with taking over the lease.[147]   **21-047**

The second, and more common, type of reliance loss involves a slightly differ-   **21-048**
ent situation. Here the claimant's argument is not that he made the expenditure in reliance on the contract, but that the breach of the contract has caused existing expenditure of his to be wasted.[148] The simplest case is that of the buyer who pays for something he does not get: that price, which would otherwise have borne fruit, is now wasted and for that reason is recoverable from the seller.[149] The situation is exemplified by cases such as *CCC Films (London) Ltd v Impact Quadrant Ltd*.[150] The plaintiffs paid the defendants $12,000 for a licence to distribute certain films: when the defendants failed to provide copies of the movies concerned, the plaintiffs successfully sued to get back their $12,000. But there are many other cases of sunk costs associated with performance. So in the well-known Australian decision in *McRae v Commonwealth Disposals Commission*[151] an enterprising scrap merchant to whom the Australian government had inadvertently sold a non-existent marine wreck recovered from them the cost of fruitlessly looking for it. Again, in *Mason*

---

is regarded as almost axiomatic in much American writing, though not without criticism (e.g. M. Kelly, "The Phantom Reliance Interest in Contract Damages" (1992) Wis. L.R. 1755).

[146] "I consider that the weight of authority strongly suggests that reliance losses are a species of expectation losses and that they are neither … 'fundamentally different' nor awarded on a different juridical basis of claim". Teare J in *Omak Maritime Ltd v Mamola Challenger Shipping Co Ltd* [2010] EWHC 2026 (Comm); [2010] 2 C.L.C. 194 at [42]. See too a similar remark by Leggatt J in *Yam Seng Pte Ltd v International Trade Corp Ltd* [2013] EWHC 111 (QB); [2013] 1 C.L.C. 662 at [187]. Gaudron J had earlier said much the same in the High Court of Australia: see *Commonwealth v Amann Aviation Pty Ltd* (1991) 174 C.L.R. 64 at 154.

[147] *Hayes v James & Charles Dodd* [1990] 2 All E.R. 815; see R. Halson, "Contract damages, Expectation, Reliance and Mental Distress" [1991] C.L.J. 31.

[148] "[W]asted expenditure can be recovered when it is *wasted by reason of the defendant's breach of contract*." Lord Denning MR in *Anglia Television Ltd v Reed* [1972] 1 Q.B. 60 at 64 (italics supplied). See too *McRae v Commonwealth Disposals Commission* (1951) 84 C.L.R. 377 at 413–414 (Dixon and Fullagar JJ).

[149] It may also be recoverable, at the claimant's option, as money paid on a total failure of consideration, assuming there has been such a total failure: but that does not alter the point in the text. Any lingering belief that the claimant might not have a free choice between these remedies, or that the unavailability of the restitutionary claim might also bar the damages claim, was finally dispelled by Henshaw J in a lapidary passage in *Havila Kystruten AS v Abarca Companhia De Seguros SA* [2022] EWHC 3196 (Comm) at [321] ff. (See too Butcher J in *Cardiorentis AG v Iqvia Ltd* [2022] EWHC 250 (Comm) at [452].).

[150] [1985] Q.B. 16. Another example is the unreported *Cullinane v National Westminster Bank Ltd* (12 July 1985) (payment to bank for accountant's report for plaintiff's benefit: bank obtains report for its own sole benefit: plaintiff entitled to damages measured by amount of payment).

[151] (1951) 84 C.L.R. 377 (esp 411 (Dixon and Fullagar JJ)). A simpler example is collection costs of goods which a seller fails to deliver, as in the very early Queensland decision in *Pollock v McKenzie*

v Burningham[152] a buyer of a typewriter spent money overhauling it, only later to be told that her seller had had no title and forced to return the typewriter, improvements and all, to the true owner. She recovered the wasted cost of the overhaul. Other examples might be where a buyer sends a lorry to collect goods which, owing to breach by the seller, are not there to collect; where a buyer of land spends money improving it, only to find that the seller has no title to it;[153] a timber company incurs the cost of cutting timber, but the haulier he engages fails to truck it away;[154] or an employer flies an employee out to work in an exotic location, whereupon the employee refuses to work and demands to be brought home again.[155]

21-049   The characterisation of these latter cases as cases of expenditure caused to be wasted, rather than of simple reliance, has the advantage of clarifying certain other points. To begin with, it deals with the otherwise difficult argument that in so far as a claimant is being allowed to recover expenditure that would have been incurred even if the contract had not been broken, he is being put in a better position than if it had been kept.[156] It is only by characterising his claim as one for causing the expenditure to be wasted, and hence creating a dead loss to the claimant, that we can get over this problem of causation.[157] And secondly, the "wasted cost" analysis justifies two further rules referred to below, namely (i) the fact that it is apparently open to a defendant to reduce or eliminate his liability in so far as the expenditure is not in fact wasted; and (ii) there is no bar on the recovery of pre-contract expenditures.

Reliance losses: Expenditure wasted in any event

21-050   A claimant arguing that the defendant's breach has caused expenditure to be wasted must, of course, prove it. It is submitted that this is the best explanation for the otherwise difficult decision in *C & P Haulage Ltd v Middleton*.[158] The plaintiff, who had taken a licence of commercial premises for a period of six months, spent money in improving them. Under the terms of the licence, such improvements were to vest in the landlord. Very shortly before the end of the term the landlord wrongfully evicted the plaintiff. The latter's claim to recover his expenditure as damages for breach of contract failed. Although the decision was put on another basis,[159] the best explanation is that the expenditure had not in the circumstances been wasted.

(1866) 1 QSCR (breach of contract to sell cattle: recovery by buyer of costs of wasted journey to collect them).

[152] [1949] 2 K.B. 545

[153] E.g. *Bunny v Hopkinson* (1859) 27 Beav. 565; also *Rolph v Crouch* (1867) L.R. 3 Ex. 44; and *Lloyd v Stanbury* [1971] 1 W.L.R. 535 (where, however, the claim failed on remoteness grounds). See too *Clark v Macourt* [2013] HCA 56; (2013) 304 A.L.R. 220 (high-priced business assets in fact useless: buyer recovers value, even though costs in fact all recouped from customers).

[154] As in the Canadian *Bowlay Logging Ltd v Domtar Ltd* (1982) 135 D.L.R. (3d) 179 (though the claim there largely failed for other reasons).

[155] *Technicare Private Ltd v Heathcote* (unreported 25 October 1990).

[156] Hence the rule that, if a house purchaser obtains damages for loss of bargain, he cannot also recover wasted conveyancing costs: he would have had to incur them to get the bargain in any case (see *Re Daniel* [1917] 2 Ch. 405).

[157] See A. Burrows, *Remedies for Torts and Breach of Contract*, 3rd edn (Oxford: Oxford University Press 2004), pp.71-72; G.H. Treitel, "Damages for Breach of Contract in the High Court of Australia" (1992) 108 L.Q.R. 226.

[158] [1983] 1 W.L.R. 1461

[159] Namely, that since all improvements belonged to the landlord anyway, to award the expense as damages would put the licensee in a better position than he would have occupied had the contract been kept. This, with respect, is difficult to see.

The plaintiff had had most of the occupation for which he had stipulated, and which presumably he regarded as a suitable return for his improvements.[160] Had the landlord repudiated the contract at the beginning of the period and thus deprived the plaintiff of effectively any return for his expenditure, it is suggested that the result would have been different.[161]

Reliance losses: Pre-contract expenditure

Can a claimant recover reliance damages for breach of contract that reflect **21-051** expenditure made before the contract had even been concluded? The point is an important one in practice, since businessmen do not necessarily have the leisure to wait scrupulously until a contract has been signed before incurring costs in preparing to perform it.

Older authority fairly consistently denied liability here, essentially on causation **21-052** grounds (since ex hypothesi the money in issue would have been spent even if there had been no breach and, indeed, even if there had been never been a contract at all[162]). More recently, however, this bar has been lifted. And rightly so: although ex hypothesi the breach of a contract not in existence at the time of the incurring of expenditure cannot be said to have caused that expenditure to be *made*, there is no reason at all why breach of that contract cannot cause expenditure already made to be *wasted*.

A straightforward instance is *Lloyd v Stanbury*.[163] The seller of a house failed to **21-053** make title; and as a result was held liable for the purchaser's wasted conveyancing costs, even though some of these had been incurred before contracts had been exchanged.[164] This result was duly upheld shortly afterwards by the Court of Appeal in *Anglia Television Ltd v Reed*.[165] An actor agreed to appear in a television series, before realising that he was double-booked and repudiating the contract four days later. As a result of the non-availability of the actor the series had to be aborted. The television company sued the actor for its wasted expenditure of £2,750, including nearly £2,000 spent before the contract had been signed. Their action succeeded. The defendant must have realised, said Lord Denning MR, that if he broke his contract all the plaintiffs' expenditure would be wasted, and this was sufficient to make him liable to make good this loss. On the other hand, it is suggested that the claimant must actually prove that his expenditure has been wasted. There can be little doubt that if the claimants in the *Anglia Television* case had managed to find another actor and thus make use of their expenditure, their claim against the defendant must have failed.

---

[160] Compare Fox LJ's comment: "While it is true that the expenditure could in a sense be said to be wasted in consequence of the breach of contract, it was equally likely to be wasted if there had been no breach": see [1983] 1 W.L.R. 1461 at 1468.

[161] As was indeed decided some 30 years later, in *Grange v Quinn* [2013] EWCA Civ 24; [2013] 1 P. & C.R. 18.

[162] See, for example, *Hodges v Litchfield (Earl)* (1835) 1 Bing. N.C. 492 at 498 (Tindal CJ); *Perestrello v United Paint Co Ltd* (1969) 113 Sol Jo 324; and also the argument in A. Ogus, "Damages for Pre-Contract Expenditure" (1972) 35 M.L.R. 423.

[163] [1971] 1 W.L.R. 535

[164] See [1971] 1 W.L.R. 535 at 544. A similar result had been reached earlier in *Wallington v Townsend* [1939] Ch. 588, though no-one in that case seems to have regarded the point as important.

[165] [1972] 1 Q.B. 60.

Consequential losses

21-054   Expectation damages compensate the claimant for the loss of the immediate advantage that performance would otherwise have provided for him; reliance damages make good the loss of expenditure that would not have been wasted but for the breach. But a breach of contract, like any wrong, can have further long-tail effects in terms of losses (or loss of profits) naturally resulting from it, which do not fall under either of these heads. To put the claimant in the position he would have occupied had there been no breach these losses must be made good, and hence there has never been any doubt that consequential damages form a valid head of claim. The instances are too numerous and varied to list. But common examples include loss of lucrative markets[166] or prospective profits,[167] personal injury,[168] damage to property,[169] loss of use of property,[170] liability to third parties[171] or to charges levied by public authorities.[172] Similarly, most professional negligence claims, such as those against dilatory lawyers for the loss of a cause of action, or against incompetent insurance brokers for the consequences of losses being uninsured.

Expectation, reliance and consequential claims: Can they be combined?

21-055   Some older authorities went one stage further than distinguishing between the various heads of damage referred to above. In particular they seem to have regarded them—at least in the case of expectation and reliance damages—as mutually exclusive remedies, such that although a claimant could select whichever was most advantageous to him,[173] this right was balanced by a requirement to elect formally between them.[174] It is submitted, however, that this view is misconceived. Since all these heads recognise the single aim of restoring the claimant to his position had

---

[166] *Koufos v C Czarnikow Ltd* [1969] 1 A.C. 350 (result of late delivery of sugar by carrier).

[167] E.g. *Simpson v London & North-Western Ry Co* (1876) 1 Q.B.D. 274 (carrier's default: loss of trade fair profits).

[168] E.g. *Frost v Aylesbury Dairy Ltd* [1905] 1 K.B. 608 (illness from diseased milk).

[169] *Mullet v Mason* (1866) L.R. 1 C.P. 559 (sheep dead from quack medicine); *The Moorcock* (1889) 14 PD 64 (ship holed by underwater obstruction in dock). On the computation of compensation for damage to property caused by a breach of contract, see *Waterdance Ltd v Kingston Marine Services Ltd* [2014] EWHC 224 (TCC); [2014] B.L.R. 141, and compare the tort case of *Coles v Hetherton* [2013] EWCA Civ 1704; [2015] 1 W.L.R. 160.

[170] As where building works overrun, leaving the building owner paying rent and rates on unusable premises: see the Australian decision in *Leeda Projects Pty Ltd v Zeng* [2020] VSCA 192; (2020) 61 V.R. 384.

[171] The most straightforward example being the liability of a buyer of bad goods to compensate a subbuyer: e.g. *Hammond & Co v Bussey* (1887) 20 Q.B.D. 79; *Biggin v Permanite Ltd* [1951] 2 K.B. 314 and more recently *McAlpine Grant ILCO Ltd v AFR Refrigeration Ltd* [2020] EWHC 106 (QB) and *Dana UK Axle Ltd v Freudenberg FST GmbH* [2021] EWHC 1751 (TCC); [2021] T.C.L.R. 6. For a variant see *The Selda* [1998] 1 Lloyd's Rep. 416 (buyer wrongfully refusing liable goods to indemnify seller for his liability to the carrier who would have transported the goods).

[172] E.g. *Smith v Johnson* (1899) 15 T.L.R. 179 (substandard mortar supplied: buyer who used it for building forced by local authority to bear cost of demolition); *The Ardennes* [1951] 1 K.B. 55 (late delivery by carrier: increased import duty charged to buyer as a result).

[173] See, for instance, *CCC Films (London) Ltd v Impact Quadrant Films Ltd* [1985] Q.B. 16 at 32, where Hutchison J referred to the claimant's "unfettered choice"; also *Anglia Television Ltd v Reed* [1972] 1 Q.B. 60 at 64 (Lord Denning MR); *Cullinane v British "Rema" Manufacturing Co Ltd* [1954] 2 Q.B. 292 at 303 (Evershed MR); and *Commonwealth of Australia v Amann Aviation Pty Ltd* (1991) 174 C.L.R. 64.

[174] "[A plaintiff] can either claim for his loss of profits; or for his wasted expenditure. But he must elect

the contract been fulfilled, it follows that (subject to the obvious qualification that a claimant cannot have double recovery) there is no reason to require any election, or to hold that two or more of these heads cannot be combined.

Thus there is no necessary bar to cumulating reliance and expectation losses.[175] **21-056** So in an old Australian case where a state government reneged on a contract to buy maps to be made by the claimant, a direction was held good that the claimant should recover not only any expenditure irrevocably thrown away, but also his would-be profit on the maps had they been accepted and paid for;[176] and in a later decision concerning the supply of an ineffective machine, it was held that damages could legitimately be reckoned as the cost of the machine plus the net profits to be made from it after taking into account that cost.[177] To take another instance, suppose that a seller, having agreed to sell goods worth £12,500 for £10,000 and received a £1,000 deposit, breaks his contract. There is no reason why the buyer should not recover £3,500, representing both the prepayment and the price-value differential; and, it is suggested, the same will apply if the buyer has wasted £500 in attempting to collect the goods and will have to spend the same sum again. The point is neatly illustrated, although in a slightly different context, by *JP Morgan Chase Bank v Springwell Navigation Corp*.[178] Investment advisers' incompetence caused large sums to be irretrievably lost to their client. The Court of Appeal, in a careful judgment, saw no difficulty in allowing the client to recover both the vanished capital and the gains that would have been made had they received the advice they were entitled to. There was, as Wall LJ said, simply "no inconsistency" between these claims.[179]

Again, the same applies to consequential damages. These were rightly combined **21-057** with reliance loss in the old case of *Bostock & Co Ltd v Nicholson & Sons Ltd*,[180] where specialised sugar manufacturers bought contaminated ingredients. They recovered both the amount paid and the value of their own product destroyed. More recently, in the land case of *Lloyd v Stanbury*[181] the vendor of a house who turned out to have no title to it was held liable not only for the buyer's wasted conveyancing costs, but also for his consequential damages, in the form of loss of earnings

---

between them. He cannot claim both." Lord Denning MR in *Anglia Television Ltd v Reed* [1972] 1 Q.B. 60 at 64. See too Evershed MR in *Cullinane v British "Rema" Manufacturing Co Ltd* [1954] 2 Q.B. 292 at 303 (statement, referring to reliance and expectation damages (though not by name), that plaintiff "may adopt one of two courses"); *New York Laser Clinic Ltd v Naturastudios Ltd* [2019] EWHC 2892 (QB) at [98] (Cavanagh J); and also *Sunshine Vacation Villas Ltd v Hudson's Bay Co* (1984) 58 BC.L.R. 33 at 39–42.

175 So held, explicitly, in *Kwik Fit Insurance Services Ltd v Bull Information Systems Ltd* (unreported 23 June 2000) at [75]–[76]. See too the earlier *Millar v Way* (1935) 40 Com. Cas. 204, where this was assumed (though the issue did not arise directly).

176 *Banks v Williams* (1910) 10 SR (NSW) 220. It is true that in the event a new trial was ordered; but this was only because the verdict had included some expenses that had not been irretrievably lost.

177 *TC Industrial Plant Pty Ltd v Roberts Queensland Pty Ltd* (1963) 37 A.L.J.R. 289, esp at 293.

178 [2006] EWCA Civ 161; [2006] P.N.L.R. 28.

179 *JP Morgan Chase Bank v Springwell Navigation Corp* [2006] EWCA Civ 161; [2006] P.N.L.R. 28 at [19].

180 [1904] 1 K.B. 725. Other examples are *Richard Holden Ltd v Bostock & Co Ltd* (1902) 18 T.L.R. 317; *Naughton v O'Callaghan* [1990] 3 All E.R. 191 (wasted expenditure on useless racehorse plus costs of feeding and keeping it until disposal); see too *Hydraulic Engineering Co v McHaffie* (1878) 2 Q.B.D. 670; *Snia Società v Suzuki & Co* (1924) 18 Ll L. Rep. 333 at 336–337, and *Millar's Machinery Co Ltd v Way & Sons Ltd* (1934–5) 40 Com. Cas. 204.

181 [1971] 1 W.L.R. 535.

resulting from the breach. And in *Malhotra v Choudhury*[182] consequential damages were awarded in addition to expectation damages, where the disappointed buyer of a doctor's surgery successfully obtained damages both for loss of bargain and also for consequential loss of profits. A more recent case confirming the possibility of this combination was *Louis Dreyfus Commodities Suisse SA v MT Maritime Management BV*,[183] where Males J, faced with the repudiation of a voyage charter, had no hesitation in upholding an arbitral decision awarding both the difference between the would-be and the actual freight during the time of the charter and in addition compensation for a profitable follow-on fixture lost as a result. On a similar basis it is submitted that a buyer of defective goods that damage other property of his will be entitled to both the difference in value and also to compensation for any other property destroyed.

21-058   Indeed, it is perfectly conceivable that a single breach of contract will give rise to claims of all three types. For example, suppose a buyer agrees to pay £80,000 for a vintage car which, at the time fixed for delivery, is worth £100,000. The buyer pays £8,000 in advance, and at the same time agrees to hire the car to a third party, X, for filming purposes as soon as he takes delivery. If the car is not delivered, the buyer will potentially have three claims. These are represented by: (i) an expectation loss of £20,000, being the difference between the value and the price of the car; (ii) reliance losses of £8,000, the amount of the prepayment; and (iii) consequential losses measured by any damages the buyer has to pay to X. None of these claims overlaps in the sense of covering the same loss more than once, and all should be recoverable. From this it follows that there should be no objection as such to combining two or more types of claim.

21-059   However, a note of caution is necessary: while there is no objection to combining different damage claims, there is every objection to compensating the same loss twice (a factor that may explain why it was long thought that such combination was not allowed at all). Suppose, for instance, that A agrees to sell securities to B for £1 million; that B agrees to sell them on to C at the same price; and that A fails to deliver them when they are worth £1.2 million. B has two claims against A for £200,000; consequential (i.e. the damages he will have to pay C), and expectation (the difference between £1 million and £1.2 million). But both represent essentially the same loss, from which it follows that in this case B must choose between them.

21-060   It is this point which, it is suggested, best explains the result, if not the reasoning, in *Cullinane v British "Rema" Manufacturing Co Ltd*.[184] Sellers of a clay pulveriser, in breach of contract, provided a machine that was useless for that purpose. Some years later, the buyers sued them, claiming (i) the costs of acquisition and erection of the useless device, and in addition (ii) the profits they would have made from using the machine had it worked. By a majority, the Court of Appeal held that they could not have both. It is true that the ostensible reason was that claims for lost profits and wasted expense could not be mixed.[185] But the real reason, it is suggested, was that (on the assumption that the machine would have depreciated by 100 per cent over its working life) the former costs would have had to be

---

[182] [1980] Ch. 52.
[183] [2015] EWHC 2505 (Comm); [2016] 1 Lloyd's Rep. 197
[184] [1954] 1 Q.B. 292.
[185] See [1954] 1 Q.B. 292 at 303–304, 306 (Evershed MR), 308 (Jenkins LJ).

incurred to make the profits, and hence to award both would have amounted to inadmissible double-counting.[186]

Expectation, reliance and consequential claims: independent claims?

With the old belief that different damage claims could not be combined there **21-061** often went another, related, idea. This was that they were independent claims, and that a claimant had an unfettered right to choose whichever gave him most, without reference to how he would have fared had he framed his claim differently, and in particular without having to give credit for any matters that might in that case have gone to reduce his loss.[187] But with the realisation that all contract damages support the same overriding principle— putting the claimant into the position he would have been in had the contract been fulfilled, but to no more—it is suggested that this must now be regarded as a heresy to be rejected. Hence in *CCC Films (London) Ltd v Impact Quadrant Films Ltd*[188] film distributors paid $12,000 for master copies of certain movies and a licence to distribute them, but never received the master copies. It was conceded that if the defendants could prove (which in the event they could not) that the distributors would actually have lost money in handling the movies, and hence that the breach of contract had actually saved them money,[189] then their claim to recover the $12,000 would be reduced accordingly.[190] And, sure enough, in the 2010 decision in *Omak Maritime Ltd v Mamola Challenger Shipping Co*,[191] a defendant successfully eliminated a claim for reliance loss on precisely this basis. Shipowners agreed to let a ship to charterers, at whose insistence they carried out expensive prior modifications. When the charterers threw up the charter, the owners' claim for the cost of the modifications rightly failed, the incontrovertible evidence being that the charter had in any case been a heavily unprofitable one for the owners at well below the market rate, and that its cancellation had allowed them to escape losses which in the event dwarfed the expenditure concerned.

Nevertheless, the idea of the claimant's right to choose between heads of **21-062** recovery retains one limited significance. In both *CCC Films*[192] and *Omak*

---

186 See the discussions by Buxton LJ in *J P Morgan Chase Bank v Springwell Navigation Corp* [2006] EWCA Civ 161; [2006] P.N.L.R. 28 at [8]–[9]; and by Richards J in *4 Eng Ltd v Harper* [2008] EWHC 915 (Ch.); [2009] Ch. 91 at [49]; and earlier by the High Court of Australia in *TC Industrial Plant Pty Ltd v Roberts Queensland Pty Ltd* (1963) 37 A.L.J.R. 289.

187 Often cited in favour of this view were Lord Denning MR's dicta in *Anglia Television Ltd v Reed* [1972] 1 Q.B. 60 at 63 and those of Evershed MR in the earlier *Cullinane v British "Rema" Manufacturing Co Ltd* [1954] 1 Q.B. 292 at 303.

188 [1985] Q.B. 16. For similar reasoning, see too *Milburn Services Ltd v United Trading Group (UK) Ltd* (1995) 52 Con L.R. 130, and the earlier Canadian decision in *Bowlay Logging Ltd v Domtar Ltd* (1978) 87 D.L.R. (3d) 325.

189 This is obviously essential. If the losses would have been suffered breach or no breach, no deduction falls to be made. See e.g. *Milburn Services Ltd v United Trading Group (UK) Ltd* (1995) 52 Con L.R. 130; and cf. *Times Newspapers Ltd v Weidenfeld & Nicolson Ltd* [2002] F.S.R. 29.

190 See [1985] Q.B. 16 at 32–41 (Hutchison J). Another case where a losing bargain was similarly alleged but not proved was *Grange v Quinn* [2013] EWCA Civ 24; [2013] 1 P. & C.R. 18. See generally D. Campbell and R. Halson, "Expectation and Reliance: One Principle or Two?" (2015) 32 JCL 231.

191 [2010] EWHC 2026 (Comm), [2010] 2 C.L.C. 194; A. Tettenborn, "Of damages, expenses and unprofitable charterparties" [2011] L.M. & C.L.Q. 1.

192 [1985] Q.B. 16. For similar reasoning, see too *Milburn Services Ltd v United Trading Group (UK) Ltd* (1995) 52 Con L.R. 130, and the earlier Canadian decision in *Bowlay Logging Ltd v Domtar Ltd* (1978) 87 D.L.R. (3d) 325.

Maritime,[193] it was accepted that if a defendant faced with a claim for reliance loss argued that the contract would have been a losing one, the burden of proof lay squarely on him. It follows that if no other evidence is available, the claimant's right to frame his claim as one for reliance loss is not only a matter of the claimant's own unfettered choice,[194] but also may still have considerable advantages.

IV. WAYS OF EXPRESSING THE LOSS RESULTING FROM NON-PERFORMANCE: "COST OF CURE" OR BALANCE-SHEET CALCULATION?

21-063   The idea that contract damages should, as far as possible, replicate in money the victim's position had he received performance is rightly fundamental. But it does not always give unambiguous results, especially where performance, or some near substitute, is still possible.[195] Suppose, for example, that a builder fails to do agreed home improvements, or does them badly: that the reasonable cost of getting the work done properly is £10,000; but that if done, the improvements will increase the value of the house by a mere £4,000.[196] Should the owner get (i) £10,000, the amount that will allow him to obtain the stipulated benefit in specie (sometimes called the "cost of cure"); or (ii) £4,000, the sum that will put him in the financial position, in terms of balance-sheet assets and liabilities, that he would have been in had the defendant performed (sometimes called the "diminution measure")? Both (i) and (ii) can plausibly be said to restore the would-be position had there been performance, and indeed on occasion the same might no doubt be said of some other measure too. But a choice clearly has to be made between them.[197]

Prima facie right to the cost of cure

21-064   On the modern authorities, despite occasional scepticism,[198] it seems clear that the presumptive measure of recovery is the cost of cure. And rightly so, it is suggested, for the simple reason that most people contract with a view to getting performance in specie rather than the abstract financial equivalent of it.[199] Hence Lord Cohen's lapidary pronouncement in *East Ham BC v Bernard Sunley & Sons*

---

[193] [2010] EWHC 2026 (Comm); [2010] 2 C.L.C. 194.

[194] See *C.C.C. Films (London) Ltd v Impact Quadrant Films Ltd* [1985] Q.B. 16 at 32 (Hutchison J).

[195] A. Loke, "Cost of Cure or Difference in Value? Toward a Sound Choice in the Basis for Quantifying Expectation Damages" (1996) 10 JCL 189.

[196] We are assuming, as is normally the case, that (i) is more than (ii). It can, of course, be less. In such a case, it is suggested that the issue will be regarded as one of mitigation, with the claimant prima facie bound to incur the cost of cure. On this question, see Lord Lloyd's comments in *Ruxley Electronics & Construction Ltd v Forsyth* [1996] A.C. 344 at 366.

[197] Hence, with great respect, Lord Mustill's comment in *Ruxley Electronics & Construction Ltd v Forsyth* [1996] A.C. 344 at 360, that in this connection "there are not two alternative measures of damage ... but only one, namely, the loss truly suffered by the promisee" is a little disingenuous. There is no such thing here as the "loss truly suffered by the promisee".

[198] Compare *Pegler Ltd v Wang (UK) Ltd* (unreported 25 February 2000 TCC), where Judge Bowsher QC denied any presumption in favour of the cost of cure.

[199] As Friedmann has put it in a perceptive article, damages rules should reflect the idea that contracts are made "to be performed": D. Friedmann, "The performance interest in contract damages" (1995) 111 L.Q.R. 628 at 629. See too *Ruxley Electronics & Construction Ltd v Forsyth* [1996] A.C. 344 at 360 (Lord Mustill, pointing out that householders contract for building work precisely to receive an extra degree of comfort, and must be entitled to compensation for not getting it); also *Tabcorp Holdings Ltd v Bowen Investments Pty Ltd* [2009] HCA 8; (2009) 83 A.L.J.R. 390 at [13]–[15].

Ltd,[200] a case involving defective building work where this measure was allowed:

> "There is no doubt that whenever it is reasonable for the employer to insist upon reinstatement the courts will treat the cost of re-instatement as the measure of damage."[201]

So too a series of cases at common law allows a landlord to recover restoration costs from an outgoing tenant who fails to deliver up in repair[202] (though this is now heavily qualified by statute).[203]

21-065 This approach, confirmed often since,[204] finds neat expression in the 1976 decision in *Radford v De Froberville*.[205] A west London householder sold off the far end of a long garden for building, the buyer promising among other things to construct a substantial dividing wall along the new boundary. The buyer having built house but no wall, the seller sued for the cost of getting the work done himself. His claim succeeded, despite the buyer's ingenious argument that on the evidence the absence of a physical boundary had no effect on the value of his own property. Oliver J was forthright. If, he said, a person

> "contracts for the supply of that which he thinks serves his interests, be they commercial, aesthetic or merely eccentric, then if that which is contracted for is not supplied ... I do not see why, in principle, he should not be compensated by being provided with the cost of supplying it through someone else or in a different way, subject to the proviso, of course, that he is seeking compensation for a genuine loss and not merely using a technical breach to secure an uncovenanted profit."[206]

Exceptions to the right to claim the "cost of cure"

21-066 The claimant's right to the cost of obtaining performance is nevertheless merely a prima facie right. It is not absolute and, in particular, is qualified in two cases. One is where the claimant does not in fact intend to—or for that matter now cannot—obtain the promised benefit. The other is where obtaining performance is entirely unreasonable, for reasons of disproportionate cost or otherwise.

21-067 **(i) Cases where cure impossible, or claimant has no intention to obtain it** If what a claimant contracted for is now unattainable,[207] the justification disappears for giving him the notional cost of getting it. In such a situation the courts are likely

---

200 [1966] A.C. 406.

201 [1966] A.C. 406 at 434 (see also Lord Upjohn at 445).

202 See e.g. *Joyner v Weeks* [1891] 2 Q.B. 31; *Eyre v Rea* [1947] K.B. 567 and more recently the carefully-reasoned *Tabcorp Holdings Ltd v Bowen Investments Pty Ltd* [2009] HCA 8; 83 A.L.J.R. 390.

203 See s.18 of the Landlord and Tenant Act 1927, referred to below.

204 See, for example, Steyn LJ in *Darlington Borough Council v Wiltshier Northern Ltd* [1995] 1 W.L.R. 68 at 79; Lords Jauncey and Lloyd in *Ruxley Electronics and Construction Ltd v Forsyth* [1996] A.C. 344 at 355–356, 366, 366; and Lord Goff in *Panatown Ltd v Alfred McAlpine Construction Ltd* [2001] 1 A.C. 518 at 548–549; and Leggatt LJ in *Endurance Corporate Capital Ltd v Sartex Quilts & Textiles Ltd* [2020] EWCA Civ 308; [2020] 1 C.L.C. 374 at [61]. See too the earlier Australian decision in *Bellgrove v Eldridge* (1954) 90 C.L.R. 613 at 618–619.

205 [1977] 1 W.L.R. 1262. See too the later *Dean v Ainley* [1987] 1 W.L.R. 1729; *Catlin Estates Ltd v Carter Jonas (A Firm)* [2005] EWHC 2315 (TCC), [2006] P.N.L.R. 15; and *Melhuish & Saunders Ltd v Hurden* [2012] EWHC 3119 (TCC).

206 [1977] 1 W.L.R. 1262 at 1270 (a statement later endorsed by Lord Goff in *Panatown Ltd v Alfred McAlpine Construction Ltd* [2001] 1 A.C. 518 at 551).

207 Or, more accurately, unattainable in substance. In *Radford v De Froberville* [1977] 1 W.L.R. 1262, above, Oliver J was unfazed by a pettifogging argument that the wall could not be built by the claim-

to fall back, *faute de mieux*, on the diminution in value measure. An example was given by Oliver J in *Radford v De Froberville*.[208] If a landowner A agrees with a neighbour B to construct an ornamental fountain on his land to improve the view from B's house, but the work is not done, there can be no justification of an award based on the cost of carrying it out (since this is now impossible without A's permission). Again, if A engages B to do work on A's house which B does badly, but A then sells the land to a third party, it is suggested that A is perforce limited to the diminution in value measure.[209]

21-068   A similar result applies where, even if performance is possible or a near substitute available, the claimant does not in fact intend to procure it.[210] Here too, notwithstanding the general rule that a court is not concerned with how a claimant spends his damages once he gets them,[211] the practice is to limit recovery to the diminution in the value of the claimant's assets due to the breach. So in *Wigsell v School for Indigent Blind*,[212] buyers of a plot of land who wished to put a school on it promised to circle it with a high wall to protect the amenity of the seller (who retained neighbouring land). In the event, however, although the plot was conveyed, the school was never built; and understandably, given the circumstances, neither was the wall. The seller failed in his suit for the cost of building a wall which he clearly had no intention of constructing; this sum, if awarded, would simply give him a windfall at the buyers' charge.[213] The same point in essence arose in *Ruxley Electronics & Construction Ltd v Forsyth*,[214] where a swimming pool was built a few inches too shallow and the owner sought the considerable cost of deepening it to the correct dimensions. The judge at first instance refused to make such an award, partly because he was unconvinced that the claimant would actually have the work done. In the House of Lords Lord Lloyd, who alone went into detail on the matter,

---

ant, as it should have been, on the defendants' side of the boundary: a wall a foot away on the claimant's side would, he said, be substantially the same thing. So too in the insurance case of *Endurance Corporate Capital Ltd v Sartex Quilts & Textiles Ltd* [2020] EWCA Civ 308; [2020] 1 C.L.C. 374 the Court of Appeal approved the award of the cost of putting up a modernised building on the site of a Victorian textile mill.

[208] [1977] 1 W.L.R. 1262 at 1269. See too Parke B's remark in *Pell v Shearman* (1855) 10 Ex 766 at 770 (promise to sink a mineshaft on defendant's land for benefit of claimant).

[209] Though American courts have occasionally, if perversely, decided the opposite: e.g. *American Standard, Inc v Schectman* 439 NYS 2d 1027 (1981).

[210] It is sometimes said that the claimant's intent to carry out the works goes merely to reasonableness: e.g. *Ruxley Electronics v Forsyth* [1996] A.C. 344 at 372 (Lord Lloyd); *St James's Oncology SPC Ltd v Lendlease Construction (Europe) Ltd* [2022] EWHC 2504 (TCC) at [339] and the insurance decision in *Endurance Corporate Capital Ltd v Sartex Quilts & Textiles Ltd* [2020] EWCA Civ 308; [2020] 1 C.L.C. 374 at [64]. But it is hard to think of any case where, assuming the cost of cure is higher, a court will give a claimant a windfall by awarding it despite the lack of any intent to carry out the works or anything equivalent to them. On this whole area, see however, S.Rowan, "Cost of cure damages and the relevance of the injured promisee's intention to cure" [2017] C.L.J. 616, where some scepticism is shown as to whether the claimant's intentions should in fact be relevant to the measure of recovery.

[211] Below, para.21-104.

[212] (1882) 8 Q.B.D. 357 (at least as subsequently interpreted by Megarry J in *Tito v Waddell (No.2)* [1977] Ch. 106 at 332–334 and Oliver J in *Radford v de Froberville* [1977] 1 W.L.R. 1262 at 1271).

[213] At least, this is how the case was subsequently interpreted by Megarry J in *Tito v Waddell (No.2)* [1977] Ch. 106 at 332–334 and Oliver J in *Radford v de Froberville* [1977] 1 W.L.R. 1262 at 1271).

[214] [1996] A.C. 344; see too *London Fire Authority v Halcrow Gilbert Associates Ltd* [2007] EWHC 2546 (TCC); (2008) 24 Const. L.J. 103. Generally, G. McMeel, "Common Sense on Cost of Cure: Ruxley Electronics and Construction v Forsyth" [1995] L.M.C.L.Q. 456.

agreed that he had been right to do so.[215] Despite reservations by another judge in the same case[216] Lord Lloyd's view now seems accepted as the correct one.[217] Thus a claimant who cannot demonstrate an intent to use any damages to carry out the work concerned will almost certainly either fail in his claim for the cost of doing so, or at the very least be made to undertake to use any damages for that purpose.[218]

(ii) Cases where incurring cost of cure unreasonable Even where curing the **21-069** defendant's breach is both possible and intended, the courts retain a jurisdiction, akin to but not identical with the doctrine of mitigation,[219] to prevent the claimant from claiming the cost of it where it would be disproportionate or unreasonable to incur it.[220] An early, if stark, example is a venerable American case, where builders engaged to construct a Long Island mansion wrongfully failed to use the stipulated brand of piping, substituting another make which, on the evidence, was equally good. The customer's argument that he was entitled to the substantial cost of its removal and replacement with the correct brand failed, as being "grossly and unfairly out of proportion" to any resulting benefit.[221] More recently, in *Tito v Waddell (No.2)*[222] Megarry V-C reached a similar decision over a defendant who stripmined land but then, in breach of contract with the owners, omitted to restore it to its original condition. Since the cost of restoration would be wildly disproportionate to any added value created (the land itself being worth very little even in pristine condition), he declined to award it as damages.[223] This result received the imprimatur of the House of Lords in *Ruxley Electronics & Construction Ltd v Forsyth*.[224] Faced with a swimming pool built marginally too shallow, their Lordships upheld the judge's refusal to award the £21,000 cost of digging it out on the basis that this would be "out of all proportion" or "wholly disproportionate",[225] and approved his order giving instead the modest sum of £2,500 in recognition of his failure to get what he had stipulated for.

In commercial cases, which as often as not involve construction contracts, the **21-070** prima facie remedy is in general still the cost of remediation. This is likely to be regarded as reasonable provided that the cost of it is not out of all proportion to the

---

[215] See [1996] A.C. 344 at 372–373 (a "mere pretence" to say this represented the claimant's loss).

[216] Lord Jauncey chose to leave the point open: [1996] A.C. 344 at 359.

[217] For a more recent example, see the shoddy building case of *Nordic Holdings Ltd v Mott Macdonald Ltd* (2001) 77 Const L.R. 88.

[218] As in *William Cory & Son Ltd v Wingate Investments (London Colney) Ltd* (1978) 17 B.L.R. 114.

[219] The distinction was emphasised by Lord Lloyd in *Ruxley Electronics and Construction Ltd v Forsyth* [1996] A.C. 344 at 369–370. Essentially it lies in the fact that nothing the claimant has done has increased his loss: see *Coles v Hetherton* [2012] EWHC 1599 (Comm); [2012] R.T.R. 33 at [37]–[40] (Cooke J). One important result of this distinction may lie in the burden of proof, it being up to the claimant to prove that the cost of cure is reasonable but up to the defendant to prove failure to mitigate.

[220] Compare the similar position in tort: e.g. *Taylor (CR) (Wholesale) Ltd v Hepworth* [1977] 1 W.L.R. 659; *Stow & Co Ltd v Lawrence Construction Ltd* (1992) 40 Con L.R. 27. Note that two or more different "costs of cure" may be in issue here, with one reasonable but the other regarded as wholly excessive: see *Melhuish & Saunders Ltd v Hurden* [2012] EWHC 3119 (TCC).

[221] See *Jacob & Youngs v Kent* 129 NE 889 at 891 (1921) (Cardozo J).

[222] [1977] Ch. 106

[223] See in particular [1977] Ch. 106 at 334; also Oliver J in *Radford v de Froberville* [1977] 1 W.L.R. 1262 at 1270 (similar statement of principle).

[224] [1996] A.C. 344. But cf. *Melhuish & Saunders Ltd v Hurden* [2012] EWHC 3119 (TCC) (house visibly badly built: cost of cure appropriate).

[225] See [1996] A.C. 344 at 344 (Lord Lloyd), 361 (Lord Mustill).

benefit to be obtained.[226] Especially when it comes to the timing of expenditure, commercial considerations may be relevant.[227]

21-071   Refusals to award costs of cure, based essentially on commercial reasonableness, are nevertheless by no means unknown in business contexts. Thus, while there is no absolute bar on awarding a commercial landlord the cost of undoing unauthorised but innocuous tenant's alterations,[228] such awards are uncommon. In *James v Hutton*,[229] for example, where landlords sought from outgoing lessees of a shop the cost of restoring an updated fascia to its original condition, Lord Goddard CJ observed that the restoration would not affect the quality or lettability of the shop, said it would be a "sheer waste of money", and awarded merely nominal damages. Again, the courts take the attitude that businesses or public authorities can be expected to take a fairly robust attitude to whether it is worth restoring premises after damage.[230] More recently, similar principles have been applied in non-land cases. Thus in the shipping context, where sellers have delivered,[231] or charterers redelivered,[232] vessels with non-contractual but relatively trifling defects, claimants have been limited to the amount, if any, by which these defects depreciated the open market value of the vessel concerned.

21-072   In non-commercial cases, by contrast, such decisions are somewhat exceptional, and courts are slow to second-guess what are, after all, often simple questions of aesthetic preferences. Lord Jauncey made the point forthrightly in the *Ruxley* case:[233]

> "If I contracted for the erection of a folly in my garden which shortly thereafter suffered a total collapse it would be irrelevant to the determination of my loss to argue that the erection of such a folly which contributed nothing to the value of my house was a crazy thing to do."[234]

So too the owner of a house is generally entitled to the cost of putting right aesthetic

---

[226] *East Ham Corp v Bernard Sunley & Sons* [1966] A.C. 406 at 434 and 445 (Lords Cohen and Upjohn); *Ruxley Electronics v Forsyth* [1996] A.C. 344 at 358, 360 and 367 (Lords Jauncey, Mustill and Lloyd); *Harrison v Shepherd Homes Ltd* [2011] EWHC 1811 (TCC) at [263] (Ramsey J); (2011) 27 Const. L.J. 709; *St James's Oncology SPC Ltd v Lendlease Construction (Europe) Ltd* [2022] EWHC 2504 (TCC) at [339] ff.

[227] See *Dodd Properties (Kent) Ltd v Canterbury City Council* [1980] 1 W.L.R. 433 and *Alcoa Minerals of Jamaica Inc v Broderick* [2002] 1 A.C. 371; [2000] 3 W.L.R. 23.

[228] See the decision of the High Court of Australia in *Tabcorp Holdings Ltd v Bowen Investments Pty Ltd* [2009] HCA 8; (2009) 83 A.L.J.R. 390 (cost of demolishing new foyer unlawfully added by tenant, even though no great effect on lettability).

[229] [1950] 1 K.B. 9.

[230] Cf. *London Fire Authority v Halcrow Gilbert Associates Ltd* [2007] EWHC 2546 (TCC); (2008) 24 Const. L.J. 103 (architects' negligence causes building to catch fire: unreasonable for claimants to reinstate rather than moving activities elsewhere). But see *OBS (Nominees1) v Lend Lease Construction (Europe) Ltd* [2017] EWHC 25 (TCC); (2017) 174 Con. L.R. 105 (replacement of defective glass cladding on tip-top City office building reasonable).

[231] *The Alecos M* [1991] 1 Lloyd's Rep. 120 (ship delivered to buyer without stipulated spare propeller: not vital item of equipment, and no claim for cost of obtaining another).

[232] *Channel Island Ferries Ltd v Cenargo Navigation Ltd* [1994] 2 Lloyd's Rep. 161 (wrongful, but essentially unimportant, damage to ship's equipment). See too *Sunrock Aircraft Corp Ltd v SAS* [2007] EWCA Civ 882; [2007] 2 Lloyd's Rep. 612 (similar re aircraft).

[233] [1996] A.C. 344.

[234] [1996] A.C. 358. See too Lord Mustill at 359–360; Oliver J. in *Radford v De Froberville* [1977] 1 W.L.R. 1262 at 1270. The example cited is an old one, dating back at least to 1871: see *Chamberlain v Parker* 45 NY 569 at 572 (1871).

defects without too close reference to any effect on the value of the property.[235] The reason is straightforward: as Lord Mustill put it, to allow the views of the community as a whole, rather than those of the individual contractor, to determine what was reasonable "would make a part of the promise illusory, and unbalance the bargain".[236]

(iii)   A statutory exception: Landlord and Tenant Act 1927, s.18   Under s.18   **21-073** of the Landlord and Tenant Act 1927, considerably modifying the common law rule,[237] damages for a tenant's failure to deliver up premises in repair are capped at the diminution in value of the reversion, and eliminated entirely if the premises are due to be demolished or remodelled.[238]

Cost of cure and diminution not only measures

In most cases the choice before the court is in practice limited to cost of cure or   **21-074** diminution in value. So in *Radford*'s case, referred to above,[239] the defendant suggested that even if the plaintiff could claim the cost of building a barrier to make good the defendant's omission he should recover only the cost of building the cheapest form of divider, such as a simple fence. Oliver J unhesitatingly discountenanced this suggestion. As he put it:

> "I know of no principle of damages which would dictate that a plaintiff who has stipulated for an article of a certain quality should be fobbed off with an inferior substitute merely because it is cheaper for a defendant who has broken his contract to supply it."[240]

However this is not always so, and there are cases where an intermediate award   **21-075** may be appropriate. In *Ruxley Electronics & Construction Ltd v Forsyth*[241] itself, for instance, the House actually gave neither the cost of obtaining full performance nor nominal damages, instead upholding an award of £2,500 by the trial judge, ostensibly for "loss of amenity". The award was not the subject of argument, but two of their lordships were prepared to justify it as marking the infringement of the non-commercial claimant's real, if intangible, interest in obtaining what he had contracted for, over and above any direct financial calculation.[242] Again, if a breach of contract leads to the destruction of property, it may be that a court may make an

---

235 *McGlinn v Waltham Contractors Ltd* [2007] EWHC 149 (TCC); 111 Con L.R. 1.
236 *Ruxley Electronics & Construction Ltd v Forsyth* [1996] A.C. 344 at 360.
237 See *Joyner v Weeks* [1891] 2 Q.B. 31, allowing full reinstatement costs as the presumptive measure.
238 On this, see *Latimer v Carney* [2006] EWCA Civ 1417; [2007] 1 P. & C.R. 13 and *Sunlife Europe Properties Ltd v Tiger Aspect Holdings Ltd* [2013] EWCA Civ 1656; [2014] 1 E.G.L.R. 30 esp at [16], making the point that the cost of repairs may still be a good guide to the depreciation in the reversion. Subject to this, the better view is that the general rules as to reasonableness in *Ruxley Electronics v Forsyth* [1996] A.C. 344 apply here too: see *Latimer v Carney*, above at [24] (Arden LJ) (though compare some scepticism expressed later in *Coldunell Ltd v Hotel Management International Ltd* [2022] EWHC 1290 (TCC) at [35]–[36]).
239 *Radford v De Froberville* [1977] 1 W.L.R. 1262.
240 [1977] 1 W.L.R. 1262 at 1284. See too *William Cory & Son Ltd v Wingate Investments (London Colney) Ltd* (1978) 17 B.L.R. 114 (promise to provide cement hardstanding: defendant not entitled to limit claim to lower cost of tarmac surface).
241 [1996] A.C. 344.
242 "Is there any reason why the court should not award by way of damages for breach of contract some modest sum, not based on difference in value, but solely to compensate the buyer for his disappointed expectations?" (Lord Lloyd at 374). See too Lord Mustill at 360-361. For subsequent decisions on similar principles see *Freeman v Nirumand* (unreported 8 May 1996) CA, and *Peebles v*

award based on the costs of restoration, but nevertheless award less than the full costs of literal restoration, if the latter are entirely disproportionate.[243]

V. Ways of Expressing the Loss Resulting From Non-Performance: Contracts Giving the Breaching Party a Choice as to How to Perform

21-076   Strictly speaking, the claimant's entitlement to be put in the position he would have occupied had the contract been performed is limited to the defendant's minimum obligation:[244] that is, to that performance to which he had an actual contractual entitlement.[245] It follows that, where the contract-breaker would have had a choice as to the mode or level of performance, any damages awarded against him presumptively fall to be reckoned on the basis of the minimum due from him consistently with the contract.[246] A straightforward instance is *Thornett & Fehr v Yuills Ltd*,[247] where sellers agreed to supply 200 tons of tallow plus or minus five per cent in their option. When they delivered substantially short, it was held that damages fell to be reckoned on the basis of an obligation to deliver only 190 tons, this being all the buyer was actually *entitled* to. Again, in the shipping case of *The Rijn*[248] charterers who repudiated a charter and refused to make the final voyage were held liable for damages based on the hire payable for that voyage, but it was held that those damages had to be reckoned on the hypothesis that it would have been made in ballast rather than laden, since that would have engendered the lowest hire payable. Yet again, it is this principle that lies behind the rule that in a wrongfully dismissed employee normally only recovers his salary during the relevant period of notice: beyond that time, whatever his factual expectations of continued employment, he had in law no right to it.[249] So too with a franchise or

---

Rembrand Builders Merchants Ltd [2017] SC DUN 28, commented on at L. Richardson, "Uneasy on the eye: determining the basis for contractual damages including non-pecuniary loss" (2018) 22 Edin. L.R. 289.

[243] Cf. the tort case of *Bryant v MacKlin* [2005] EWCA Civ 762 (mature trees destroyed: award of cost of replacement saplings, but not fully grown trees the expense of which would have been colossal).

[244] See M. Pratt, "Damages for Breach of Contracts with Alternative Performances" in J. Berryman and R. Bigwood (eds), *The Law of Remedies: New Directions in the Common Law*; also D. McLauchlan, "The Minimum Performance Rule in Contract Damages" [2019] L.M.C.L.Q. 75.

[245] As Scrutton LJ succinctly put it, it is contrary to principle to make a contractor liable in damages for not doing that which he was not obliged to do in the first place: see *Abrahams v Herbert Reiach Ltd* [1922] 1 K.B. 477 at 482.

[246] It must be presumed that the defendant "would have performed his legal obligation and no more": *The Mihalis Angelos* [1971] 1 Q.B. 164 at 203 (Davies LJ); cf. *Withers v General Theatre Co Ltd* [1933] 2 K.B. 536 at 551 (Scrutton LJ) and *Mackenzie v AA Ltd (formerly AA Plc)* [2022] EWCA Civ 901; [2022] I.C.R. 1362 at [28]–[35] (Bean LJ). See too the earlier *Robinson v Robinson (1851)* (1851) 1 De G.M. & G. 247 at 257, per Lord Cranworth: "When a man is bound by covenants to do one of two things and does neither, the measure of damages is in general the loss arising by reason of the covenantor having failed to do that which is least, not that which is most, beneficial to the covenantee." (This was actually a breach of trust case, but the principle is general.) For other early statements, see e.g. *Cockburn v Alexander* (1848) 6 C.B. 791 at 814 (Maule J); *Deverill v Burnell* (1872-73) L.R. 8 C.P. 475 at 481 (Bovill CJ).

[247] [1921] 1 K.B. 219.

[248] [1981] 2 Lloyd's Rep. 267.

[249] E.g. *Gunton v Richmond upon Thames LBC* [1981] Ch. 448 (dismissal in breach of disciplinary procedure: entitlement to salary only during would-be disciplinary procedure time and notice period of one month thereafter) and *Silvey v Pendragon Plc* [2001] EWCA Civ 784; [2001] I.R.L.R. 685; see too *Mackenzie v AA Ltd (formerly AA Plc)* [2022] EWCA Civ 901; [2022] I.C.R. 1362 (no account of bonus payments). Cf. *Hagen v ICI Chemicals & Polymers Ltd* [2002] I.R.L.R. 31; [2002]

services contract: if repudiated, the innocent party is generally only entitled to damages reckoned by any contractual notice period.[250]

21-077 For these purposes, it seems that the minimum performance to which the claimant is entitled is regarded as the performance least burdensome to the defendant, and not (if different) the one least beneficial to the claimant.[251]

21-078 It is a logical corollary of the "minimum performance" rule that, where it applies, the court is not concerned with the factual question of what the defendant would have done had he kept the contract. Thus the claimant in *Thornett & Fehr v Yuills Ltd*[252] would still have recovered in respect of only 190 tons even if it was clear that had the defendant kept the contract he would have delivered the full 200 tons or even more. So too in *The Rijn*,[253] Mustill J specifically refused to speculate whether in fact the final voyage would have been in ballast: he looked merely to the minimum the claimants were entitled to.

21-079 The "minimum performance" doctrine is nevertheless subject to a number of limits. This should not be surprising: in the light of its essentially counterfactual nature, it is not to be wondered at that the courts have been somewhat unwilling to extend it further than strictly necessary.

21-080 To begin with, it cannot be invoked merely because the duty in question is loosely defined, as is quintessentially the case with (for example) contractual duties to take care. Thus a defendant who breaks a duty to give careful advice on valuation is liable for damages based on what the court views as a reasonable valuation, and cannot reduce recovery to the amount of loss that would have been suffered had he shown the bare acceptable minimum of competence.[254]

21-081 Secondly, it seems that remote contingencies may be discounted, even if technically within the discretion of the defendant. An example is *Bold v Brough, Nicholson & Hall Ltd*,[255] where a wrongfully dismissed company director sued, among other things, for lost pension rights. He succeeded, despite the employer's ingenious plea that technically it could have chosen to wind up its entire pension

---

Lloyd's Rep. P.N. 288 and the *Canadian Hamilton v Open Window Bakery Ltd* (2002) 211 D.L.R. (4th) 443. In Scotland, it has been held that this principle does not apply as against a claimant who elects to keep the contract on foot rather than accepting a repudiatory breach (see *Dalton Group Ltd v City of Edinburgh Council* [2023] CSOH 4; 2023 S.L.T. 237). But with respect this seems doubtful.

[250] *HSS Hire Services Group Plc v BMB Builders Merchants Ltd* [2006] EWHC 3677 (QB). It has been said in Scotland that where the innocent party refuses to accept the repudiation this limitation does not apply: *Dalton Group Ltd v Edinburgh City Council* [2023] CSOH 4 (lost profits for whole period of waste disposal contract despite three-month termination provision). But with respect, it seems difficult to see why this should be.

[251] *Paula Lee Ltd v Robert Zehil Ltd* [1983] 2 All E.R. 390 at 393 (Mustill J). In other words, it will not be assumed that a defendant will "cut off his nose to spite his face" if a mode of performance more burdensome to him will reduce the benefit to the claimant still further: *Laverack v Woods of Colchester Ltd* [1967] 1 Q.B. 278 at 295–296 (Diplock LJ), and see too *Pacific Maritime (Asia) Ltd v Holystone Overseas Ltd* [2007] EWHC 2319 (Comm); [2008] 1 Lloyd's Rep. 371 at [39] (Christopher Clarke J).

[252] [1921] 1 K.B. 219.

[253] [1981] 2 Lloyd's Rep. 267. See too *Kaye SN Co Ltd v Barnett Ltd* (1932) 48 T.L.R. 440 (similar result re demurrage).

[254] See e.g. *Lion Nathan Ltd v C-C Bottlers Ltd* [1996] 1 W.L.R. 1438 (negligent overestimation of profits: no reduction of damages to take account of highest estimate that would not have been negligent). Similarly surveyors cannot minimise damages for overvaluation of real estate by reference to the highest possible non-negligent valuation: *Scotlife Homeloans v Kenneth James & Co* [1995] E.G.C.S. 70; *South Australia Asset Management Corp v York Montague Ltd* [1997] A.C. 191 at 221 (Lord Hoffmann).

[255] [1964] 1 W.L.R. 201.

scheme at any time and leave all its employees in the cold.[256] Another instance is the Australian decision in *TCN Channel 9 Ltd v Hayden Enterprises Ltd*.[257] Broadcasters, having reneged on an agreement to screen a chat show, sought to reduce or eliminate their liability to damages by invoking a clause in the relevant contract that their obligation to screen the show would terminate if they ceased to broadcast a certain other programme, which latter they were theoretically free to drop at any time. The argument once again failed: as a mere remote contingency whose chances of fulfilment were in practice nil, it could be discounted.

21-082   Thirdly, courts can avoid the problem by construing an apparent discretion over the mode of performance as implicitly requiring the defendant to act reasonably or non-arbitrarily. Thus wrongfully dismissed senior employees regularly recover for lost bonus rights on the basis that employers must, despite an apparently untrammelled right to withhold bonuses, treat their staff reasonably.[258] Again, a promise to buy wholesale clothing of the buyer's choice is regarded as a contract to buy a reasonable selection rather than uniformly bargain-basement items;[259] and, on a similar basis, in *Abrahams v Herbert Reiach Ltd*[260] damages for breach of a promise to publish a book were set on the basis of a reasonable print run. Notwithstanding a term which ostensibly left the publisher with complete discretion as to the manner and extent of publication, the court declined to set damages by reference to the smallest number of copies that might plausibly be called a "publication".

21-083   Fourthly, it is suggested that the "minimum performance" rule only applies to a breach committed (or a repudiation accepted) while the defendant still had the power to select the means of performance. Suppose a seller of soya beans has the option of shipping in August or September, but has to make an irrevocable election by July. If, having elected in July to make an August shipment, he then breaches, it is submitted that damages will be computed by reference to August values even if September shipment would have been less burdensome to him. And the result should be similar if he repudiates after the opportunity to make an August shipment has passed: by putting it out of his power to perform one option, he should be regarded as committed to the other, with damages quantified correspondingly.[261]

21-084   Fifthly, it must be remembered that only the defendant can invoke the rule. Where the option as to how to perform is in the claimant, no converse presumption ap-

---

[256] Of course, if it had in fact wound up the scheme the result would have been different. See *Lavarack v Woods of Colchester Ltd* [1967] 1 Q.B. 278 (wrongful dismissal: no claim for lost bonus where bonus scheme had actually been abandoned).

[257] (1989) 16 N.S.W.L.R. 130. See too the Canadian *MJB Enterprises Ltd v Defence Construction (1951) Ltd* [1999] 1 SCR 619 (invitor of tenders broke contract by accepting non-qualifying tender: liability in damages to submitter of qualifying tender unaffected by technical right to refuse to accept any tender at all).

[258] See e.g. *Clark v Nomura International Plc* [2000] I.R.L.R. 766; *Horkulak v Cantor Fitzgerald International* [2004] EWCA Civ 1287; [2005] I.C.R. 402. But the mere discretion to disapply a rule, such as a discretion to pay a bonus where none would normally be payable, is not within the rule: *Mackenzie v AA Ltd (formerly AA Plc)* [2022] EWCA Civ 901; [2022] I.C.R. 1362.

[259] *Paula Lee Ltd v Robert Zehil Ltd* [1983] 2 All E.R. 390. Analogous is *And So To Bed Ltd v Dixon* (unreported 21 November 2000) (damages against franchisee on basis that bound to operate business in commercially sensible way). Retailers' covenants to stay open are treated similarly: *Costain Property Developments Ltd v Finlay & Co Ltd* (1989) 57 P. & C.R. 345; see too *Douglas Shelf Seven Ltd v Co-operative Wholesale Society Ltd* [2007] CSOH 53, esp at [593].

[260] [1922] 1 K.B. 477 (the plaintiff being Harold Abrahams, of the film *Chariots of Fire* fame).

[261] This seems to follow from *McIlquham v Taylor* [1895] 1 Ch. 53 (contract to pay £1,000 or cause company to issue plaintiff with shares of a particular denomination with that face value: no qualifying shares in fact created: duty to pay £1,000).

plies in his favour. Thus in *Sudan Import & Export Co (Khartoum) v Societe Generale de Compensation*[262] sellers agreed to sell 2,000 tonnes of groundnuts plus or minus 10 per cent in their option. When the buyers repudiated, the Court of Appeal had no hesitation in quantifying damages by reference to what the sellers would in fact have shipped, and not the maximum quantity allowed under the contract.

VI.   FINANCIAL LOSS: QUESTIONS OF TIMING

In many cases damages for breach of contract are set by reference to some factor such as the cost, or the market value, of given assets or services: for example, the value of some asset that fell to be provided but was not, or the cost of making good the failure in performance. In any such case, this potentially raises a further question: at what time are the relevant figures to be taken?[263] The point can be immensely important in practice against a background of changes in the value of money, price volatility and legal delay.[264] It is also one where different kinds of claim may need separate treatment. In particular, it is suggested that expectation damages may fall to be treated differently in this context from reliance or consequential claims.

21-085

Timing: Expectation claims

(i)   In general   Where a contract is not properly performed, expectation damages are presumptively measured according to market values prevailing as at the time of breach.[265] In one case, indeed (namely, non-delivery or non-acceptance of goods agreed to be sold), this prima facie principle appears in statutory form.[266] But it equally applies at common law. So if a seller of land fails to convey, the normal measure of recovery is the difference between the value and the price at the time fixed for completion;[267] and the same applies to sales of intangibles such as securities.[268] Again, in the case of a sale of a business where (as is common) the seller warrants the truth of certain accounting or other statements, the measure of damages in the event of breach is taken as at the time of the sale, without refer-

21-086

---

[262] [1958] 1 Lloyd's Rep. 310. This is of course the mirror image of *Thornett & Fehr v Yuills Ltd* [1921] 1 K.B. 219, para.21-076.

[263] See generally S. Waddams, "The Date for the Assessment of Damages" (1981) 97 L.Q.R. 445.

[264] A point well made by Oliver J in 1977 at the end of a period of sustained inflation: *Radford v De Froberville* [1977] 1 W.L.R. 1262 at 1285.

[265] For statements of the rule see, e.g. *Jamal v Moolla Dawood Sons & Co* [1916] 1 A.C. 175 at 179 (Lord Wrenbury); *Miliangos v George Frank (Textiles) Ltd* [1976] A.C. 443 at 468 (Lord Wilberforce); *Johnson v Agnew* [1980] A.C. 367 at 400–401 (Lord Wilberforce); *Norden v Andre & Cie SA* [2003] 1 Lloyd's Rep. 287 at [43] (Toulson J); *Golden Strait Corp v Nippon Yusen Kaisha* [2007] UKHL 12; [2007] 2 A.C. 353 at [11] (Lord Bingham), [57] (Lord Carswell); *Maple Leaf Macro Volatility Master Fund v Rouvroy* [2009] EWHC 257 (Comm); [2009] 1 Lloyd's Rep. 475 at [315] (Andrew Smith J). See also *Dodd Properties (Kent) Ltd v Canterbury City Council* [1980] 1 W.L.R. 433 at 450–451, 454–455, 457; *County Personnel (Employment Agency) Ltd v Alan R Pulver & Co* [1987] 1 W.L.R. 916 at 925–926 (Bingham LJ).

[266] Sale of Goods Act 1979 ss.50(3), 51(3), reflecting the Common Law (*Williams v Reynolds* (1865) 6 B & S 495).

[267] *Diamond v Campbell-Jones* [1961] Ch. 22 at 36 (Buckley J).

[268] E.g. *Jamal v Moolla Dawood Sons & Co* [1916] 1 A.C. 175; *Oxus Gold Plc v Templeton Insurance Ltd* [2007] EWHC 770 (Comm); also *Bear Stearns Bank Plc v Forum Global Equity Ltd* [2007] EWHC 1576 (Comm) at [208].

ence to subsequent events.[269] In other words, the prima facie rule is that conditions prevailing at the time of breach, so to speak, "lock in" the measure of damages to the exclusion of subsequent events, such as a rise or fall in market prices, or events that would otherwise affect the claimant's loss.[270]

21-087   Where a contract is not simply broken but repudiated, the same rule applies, but with modifications. In cases of anticipatory repudiation, the time fixed for performance continues to be the operative one for damages purposes, even if the repudiation is accepted before that time and hence technically a right of action arises then. Thus where sellers repudiated a contract for the sale of cotton some weeks before delivery was due, and the buyers immediately accepted that repudiation, Bailhache J held that damages fell to be quantified as at the date fixed for delivery and not that of repudiation.[271] However, it seems that where a continuing contract, such as a service agreement or a seven-year charter of a ship, is repudiated during its currency, then the relevant date is when the repudiation is accepted by the innocent party.[272]

21-088   The "time of breach" rule makes considerable sense in cases where there is a market into which the claimant can go at, or shortly after, the breach. It thus works comparatively well with heavily traded commodities such as soya beans; with readily tradeable securities; and with such matters as ship charters, where market rates are often clearly and constantly documented. Indeed, it may also do substantial justice where there is a slightly more sluggish market, as with sales of land. Here, indeed, it dovetails to some extent with the rule of mitigation, under which a victim is expected to go into the market as soon as reasonably possible on breach,[273] with

---

[269] *Ageas (UK) Ltd v Kwik-Fit (GB) Ltd* [2014] EWHC 2178 (QB); [2015] Lloyd's Rep. I.R. 1 (a case involving a guarantor, but the same principles apply).

[270] For example, the fact that a seller faced with a defaulting buyer has since sold the goods at a premium (*Campbell Mostyn (Provisions) Ltd v Barnett Trading Co* [1954] 1 Lloyd's Rep. 65); or that a call option over securities which a seller ought to have granted has since become worthless because the stock price has collapsed (*Maple Leaf Macro Volatility Master Fund v Rouvroy* [2009] EWHC 257 (Comm); [2009] 1 Lloyd's Rep. 475).

[271] *Melachrino v Nickoll & Knight* [1920] 1 K.B. 693 (though on the facts the buyers recovered nothing because they had failed to mitigate). This remains so even where the date of delivery is in the buyer's control, the relevant date then being the last date at which the buyer might have demanded it: see *Tai Hing Cotton Mill Ltd v Kamsing Cotton Factory Ltd* [1979] A.C. 91 (rejecting suggestions that s.53 of the sale of Goods Act 1979, referring to the time of refusal to deliver, made a difference).

[272] See *Golden Strait Corp v Nippon Yusen Kaisha* [2007] UKHL 12; [2007] 2 A.C. 353, esp at [14]–[15] (Lord Bingham). For a spectacular demonstration of this idea, see *Turner v Superannuation & Mutual Savings Ltd* [1987] 1 N.Z.L.R. 218. This solution at least has the advantage of avoiding the complexities that would arise were the court to have to calculate damages based on prices that might fluctuate considerably over time.

[273] A requirement that can be fairly exacting: e.g. *Kaines (UK) Ltd v Österreichische Austrowaren GmbH* [1993] 2 Lloyd's Rep. 1 (duty of disappointed purchaser of oil to go into market within hours at latest).

the consequences of failure to do so being at his own risk[274] (though it should be noted that the parallel is not exact[275]).

Nevertheless, the rule has its limits. Where, at the time of breach, there is no **21-089** market at all to refer to, it is of necessity excluded. In such a case the claimant must simply prove his loss, using hindsight and giving credit where necessary to his duty to mitigate.[276] The point is neatly illustrated by a series of cases on repudiation of time charterparties. Where (as is normally the case) there is a functioning charter market at the time of repudiation, damages are based on the rate at which the vessel could then have been fixed for the remaining period of the charter,[277] without reference to subsequent changes in market values or the claimant's own later behaviour.[278] But if there is no such market (for example, because of extraordinary economic factors), then the court must simply compute as best it can what the claimant has actually lost, with subsequent developments very much in account.[279] So in *Glory Wealth Shipping Pte Ltd v Korea Line Corp*[280] charterers of a bulk carrier repudiated the charter with three years to run. There was then effectively no market for vessels of that sort, though some months later there was one, albeit very weak. It was held that profitable charters subsequently entered into by the owners had to be brought into account, even for the period after the market revived: absent a market at the time of breach, their only basis of claim could be their actual loss.

Furthermore, the problems are not limited to where there is no market. Even **21-090** where there is a market, the "time of breach" principle—for all its advantages as a simple rule of thumb—can cause injustice. For example, in times of inflation and fluctuating values damages awarded a long time after the event—even with pre-judgment interest superadded—are unlikely to enable a disappointed buyer to obtain a substitute, or to make up some defect in quality. For this and other reasons, the courts today regard the breach date principle more as a starting-point, and quite readily accept the possibility of departing from it where necessary. The modern approach is typified by the 1979 decision of the House of Lords in *Johnson v*

---

274 As Lord Brown pointed out in *Golden Strait Corp v Nippon Yusen Kaisha* [2007] UKHL 12; [2007] 2 A.C. 353 at [79]: "Essentially, [the breach date rule] applies whenever there is an available market for whatever has been lost and its explanation is that the injured party should ordinarily go out into that market to make a substitute contract to mitigate (and generally thereby crystallise) his loss." See too Lord Wrenbury in *Jamal v Moolla Dawood, Sons & Co* [1916] 1 A.C. 175 at 179; Oliver J in *Radford v De Froberville* [1977] 1 W.L.R. 1262 at 1272; and *Zodiac Maritime Agencies Ltd v Fortescue Metals Group Ltd* [2010] EWHC 903 (Comm) at [65] (David Steel J). See generally A. Dyson and A. Kramer, "There is no 'breach date rule': mitigation, difference in value and date of assessment" (2014) 130 L.Q.R. 259.

275 Since if it is a matter of mitigation, then logically the victim should receive time to go into the market; and if this is so, then the relevant time should be not the moment fixed for performance but the moment at which he could reasonably have done so (as in the UCC: see UCC, para.2.713). Cf. *Sharpe & Co Ltd v Nosawa* [1917] 2 K.B. 814 at 821, and the comments of Lord Scott in *Golden Strait Corp v Nippon Yusen Kaisha* [2007] UKHL 12; [2007] 2 A.C. 353 at [34].

276 See, for example, the sale of goods cases of *Thompson Ltd v Robinson (Gunmakers) Ltd* [1955] Ch. 177 and *Charter v Sullivan* [1957] 2 Q.B. 117 (seller's breach where no available market under Sale of Goods Act 1979 s.50(3)).

277 *The Elena D'Amico* [1980] 1 Lloyd's Rep. 75 at 87 (Goff J).

278 Though subject to the gloss in *Golden Strait Corp v Nippon Yusen Kaisha* [2007] UKHL 12; [2007] 2 A.C. 353: see para.21-097 below.

279 *The Griparion* [1994] 1 Lloyd's Rep. 533 at 537 (Rix LJ); *The Elbrus* [2009] EWHC 3394 (Comm); [2010] 1 C.L.C. 1 at [30] (Teare J); also *Zodiac Maritime Agencies Ltd v Fortescue Metals Group Ltd* [2010] EWHC 903 (Comm) at [63] (David Steel J).

280 [2011] EWHC 1819 (Comm); [2011] 2 Lloyd's Rep. 370. The result in *Zodiac Maritime Agencies Ltd v Fortescue Metals Group Ltd* [2010] EWHC 903 (Comm) was similar.

Agnew.[281] In that case, decided against the background of a highly volatile property market, house purchasers' wrongful failure to take the conveyance was followed by prolonged but ultimately fruitless attempts by the vendors to obtain specific performance. The vendors were thus forced to accept damages; and these, held Lord Wilberforce, fell to be calculated on the basis of the values obtaining after the attempt had failed (property prices having dropped in the meantime). In saying this, his Lordship made it clear that the breach date rule was

> "not an absolute rule: if to follow it would give rise to injustice, the court has power to fix such other date as may be appropriate in the circumstances".[282]

21-091   On this basis, courts, while accepting the breach date rule as a fall-back to be applied *faute de mieux*, have frequently been willing to quantify damages by reference to some other time (which normally, though not invariably, means the date of judgment or something close to it). This is especially so where the claimant, acting reasonably, could not have been expected to crystallise his loss at the time of breach. Thus, as in *Johnson v Agnew*,[283] where there are abortive proceedings for specific performance damages are likely to be reckoned as at the time when the prospect of performance disappears. Conversely, a disappointed buyer of land in times of steeply rising house prices may well receive damages as at the judgment date.[284] A similar rule applies where a buyer of goods continues to press for delivery despite apparent refusal by the seller to perform: damages, when ultimately awarded, may be assessed as at the time when the buyer finally gives up and cancels the contract.[285] Again, where a claimant claims as damages the price of obtaining something that a defaulting defendant ought to have provided, it will often be decided that full compensation demands an award based on the relevant price at judgment.[286]

21-092   **(ii)   Expectation damages: Later events reducing loss**   A corollary of the

---

[281] [1980] A.C. 367. See too the Western Australian decision in *Lords v Von Thomann (No 2)* [2014] WASC 320; 47 W.A.R. 473.

[282] [1980] A.C. 367 at 401. For other statements to much the same effect, see e.g. *County Personnel (Employment Agency) Ltd v Alan R Pulver & Co* [1987] 1 W.L.R. 916 at 924–925 (Bingham LJ); *Golden Strait Corp v Nippon Yusen Kaisha* [2007] UKHL 12; [2007] 2 A.C. 353 at [32] (Lord Scott); *Maple Leaf Macro Volatility Master Fund v Rouvroy* [2009] EWHC 257 (Comm); [2009] 1 Lloyd's Rep. 475 at [315] (Andrew Smith J). See too *Greenglade Estates Ltd v Chana* [2012] EWHC 1913 (Ch); [2012] 3 E.G.L.R. 99.

[283] [1980] A.C. 367. See too *Greenglade Estates Ltd v Chana* [2012] EWHC 1913 (Ch); [2012] 3 E.G.L.R. 99 (claim against auctioneers of land for breach of warranty of authority: values as at trial, since only then was it clear that vendor was not, and auctioneers were, liable in damages); also *Rahman v Rahman* [2020] EWHC 2392 (Ch).

[284] *Suleman v Shahsavari* [1988] 1 W.L.R. 1181; see too the earlier *Wroth v Tyler* [1974] Ch. 30 (award as at judgment on basis of Lord Cairn's Act, but since *Johnson v Agnew* [1980] A.C. 367 clearly justifiable at Common Law).

[285] For a straightforward example, see *Toprak Mahsulleri Ofisi v Finagrain Cie Commerciale* [1979] 2 Lloyd's Rep. 98; also *Aktion Maritime Corp'n v Kasmas & Bros Ltd* [1987] 1 Lloyd's Rep. 283. Old authority gave a similar result as regards defective goods, with damages regularly being awarded based on values when the defect should have been discovered: e.g. *Van den Hurk v Martens & Co Ltd* [1920] 1 K.B. 850.

[286] The most straightforward example is *Radford v De Froberville* [1977] 1 W.L.R. 1262 (cost of building wall left unconstructed by defendant). Similar: *Forster v Silvermere Golf & Equestrian Centre Ltd* (1981) 42 P. & C.R. 255A (promise to provide claimant with home). Compare the professional negligence case of *Maloney v Mundays LLP* [2021] EWHC 1324 (Ch) (negligent failure to ensure commercial purchaser got title to strip of land vital for dealings with the property: damages based on what it would cost purchaser to buy it in on discovery of the problem).

"breach date" rule is that, in so far as it applies, events subsequent to the breach are disregarded even if they go to reduce the claimant's actual loss. So, for example, if a seller of goods fails to deliver, it is generally irrelevant to the buyer's claim for the price-value differential that the goods would subsequently have been devalued in his hands, or that he would have sold them on for less than he had paid.[287] Conversely, a seller faced with wrongful non-acceptance can presumptively recover the relevant difference in value even if he has subsequently managed to sell the subject-matter advantageously elsewhere at well above the going rate.[288]

Nevertheless, this disregard of subsequent events is itself only a prima facie rule, **21-093** and it has been made subject to major inroads. One exception is covered above;[289] namely, the rule that acts by the claimant which go to reduce the loss flowing from the breach are in account if closely connected with it.[290] But there is also a second, less straightforward, qualification. In certain cases a court is entitled to invoke hindsight in order to take account of post-breach events which it is now known would have deprived the claimant, in whole or in part, of the right to receive the contractual performance concerned. This is covered in the following paragraphs.

The law relating to events that would have reduced a claimant's entitlement to **21-094** performance has seen a chequered history. For a long time such events were generally disregarded in assessing damages, on the basis that a right to sue for damages vested irrevocably in the claimant on breach, and that for that reason it was impermissible to reduce the amount recoverable by reference to events taking place later.[291] But recent developments have effectively reversed this position.

The new approach was first introduced in the situation where the event concerned **21-095** was predestined to happen, or virtually so, at the time the breach took place. The relevant decision was *The Mihalis Angelos*[292] in 1970. Charterers repudiated a voyage charter, on the basis that with three days to go before the deadline for delivery the chartered vessel was still unloading some 460 miles away, a process that would take many days, and thus that it was a physical impossibility that she could be made available on time. They were in the event held justified in doing so: but the Court of Appeal said that even if they had been in breach, damages would have been nominal: there was, it was pointed out, no reason to ignore the fact that in the event the owners would have suffered no loss at all from the repudiation since the charterers would have cancelled in any event.[293] Similarly, in a later decision where buyers repudiated a contract to buy a quantity of oil to be obtained from Saudi Arabia,

---

[287] See *Rodocanachi v Milburn* (1886) 18 Q.B.D. 67.
[288] See e.g. *Jamal v Moolla Dawood, Sons & Co* [1916] 1 A.C. 175; *Campbell Mostyn (Provisions) Ltd v Barnett Trading Co* [1954] 1 Lloyd's Rep. 65.
[289] See para.21-016 ff above.
[290] See, e.g. cases such as *Staniforth v Lyall* (1830) 7 Bing. 169 and *Pagnan & F'lli v Corbisa Industrial Agropacuaria Ltda* [1970] 1 W.L.R. 1306; and more recently *The Elbrus* [2009] EWHC 3394 (Comm); [2010] 1 C.L.C. 1.
[291] *Avery v Bowden* (1855) 5 E. & B. 714 at 727 (alleged repudiation of charterparty: if claim had been made out, damages would be unaffected by subsequent frustrating event); *Melachrino v Nickoll & Knight* [1920] 1 K.B. 693, 697 (Bailhache J); *The Mihalis Angelos* [1971] 1 Q.B. 164 at 178–183 (Mocatta J). This view remained tenable for surprisingly long: see e.g. *Chiemgauer Membran und Zeltbau GmbH v New Millennium Experience Co Ltd (No.2)* [2002] BPIR 42 (if anticipatory breach, apparently irrelevant to damages that claimant's subsequent insolvency and inability to pay would have exonerated defendant from any duty to perform when time for performance came). With respect, this must be regarded as extremely doubtful today.
[292] [1971] 1 Q.B. 164.
[293] See [1971] 1 Q.B. 164, 196–197 (Lord Denning MR), 201–203 (Edmund Davies LJ), 209–210 (Megaw LJ).

the sellers failed in their suit for substantial damages when it became clear that the application of certain Saudi export restrictions would inevitably have prevented them obtaining any oil to sell.[294] The principle in these cases was discussed, and upheld, in the 2013 decision in *Flame SA v Glory Wealth Shipping Pte Ltd*.[295] Charterers repudiated a long-term contract of affreightment; sued for damages, they alleged that the owners could not have provided the necessary shipping space and hence that any award should be nominal. Although in the event they failed to prove this (the proof being incumbent on them), Teare J had no doubt that the plea was in principle a good one.

21-096   *The Mihalis Angelos* and the other decisions referred to above involved what were in essence found to be inevitabilities.[296] This factor in a sense made an award of nominal damages entirely understandable, since in such a case it will be clear *even at the time of breach* that the claimant's contractual rights are in fact worthless. But what if the subsequent event is completely unexpected or fortuitous, such that at the time of breach the claimant seems to have suffered a loss, but later developments now make it clear that he has not? This point was not dealt with in *The Mihalis Angelos*; and indeed it was long thought that here a different rule applied, with unexpected or entirely adventitious subsequent developments continuing to be out of account in reckoning damages.[297]

21-097   However, in *Golden Strait Corp v Nippon Yusen Kaisha*[298] a bare majority of the House of Lords rejected any such limitation, and held that on principle any later event, whether bound to occur or entirely unexpected, could be relevant to the computation of damages. There, time charterers of a ship repudiated a seven-year charter priced at well above market rates when it still had four years to run. This would ordinarily have triggered a massive damages liability. However, 15 months after repudiation, but before the matter had been litigated, the 2003 Gulf War broke out; had the charter still been on foot, the charterer would at that point have been entitled to cancel, and would undoubtedly have done so. Observing that it made little sense for a court deliberately to ignore facts it now knew to be true,[299] the majority held that the owners had to be limited to only 15 months' lost earnings, this being the only contractual entitlement which it had actually lost. On the same basis, in the later decision in *Tele2 International Card Co SA v Post Office Ltd*,[300] where a distribution agreement was terminated by the distributor, it was held that had the termination been wrongful (which it was not), the claimants would not have recovered substantial damages because subsequent developments demonstrated that they would never have made any profits from it anyway. Indeed, it is now clear that

---

[294] *North Sea Energy Holdings NV v Petroleum Authority of Thailand* [1999] 1 Lloyd's Rep. 483. See too *Multi Veste 226 BV v NI Summer Row Unitholder BV* [2011] EWHC 2026 (Ch); (2011) 139 Con. L.R. 23 (breach of contract to participate in joint property development venture: nominal damages only when clear claimant himself could not have played his part).

[295] [2013] EWHC 3153 (Comm); [2014] Q.B. 1080

[296] A point made clear by Megaw LJ in *The Mihalis Angelos*: [1971] 1 Q.B. 164 at 209.

[297] See e.g. *The Noel Bay* [1989] 1 Lloyd's Rep. 361, 365 (Staughton LJ); *Chiemgauer Membran und Zeltbau GmbH v New Millennium Experience Co Ltd* [2002] BPIR 42 at [58] (Geoffrey Vos QC).

[298] [2007] UKHL 12; [2007] 2 A.C. 353; also the earlier *The Seaflower* [2000] 2 Lloyd's Rep. 37 and Q. Liu, "The date for assessing damages for loss of prospective performance under a contract" [2007] L.M.C.L.Q. 273.

[299] "With the light before him, why should [a judge] shut his eyes and grope in the dark?" Lord McNaghten in *Bwllfa & Merthyr Dare Steam Collieries (1891) Ltd v Pontypridd Waterworks Co* [1903] A.C. 426 at 431. See too *Curwen v James* [1963] 1 W.L.R. 748 at 753 (Harman LJ); *Mulholland v Mitchell* [1971] A.C. 666 at 680 (Lord Wilberforce).

[300] [2009] EWCA Civ 9.

the principle is of general application. Any matter that in retrospect would have reduced the innocent party's loss or deprived him altogether of the right to performance is relevant to damages. Thus in *Bunge SA v Nidera BV*[301] the *Golden Strait* principle was applied by the Supreme Court to a simple sale contract. Sellers of Russian wheat refused to perform before the event, citing an export ban (which would under a force majeure clause have exonerated them[302]); this was wrongful because they should have waited for the shipment date, by which time the ban might well have been lifted. In the event the ban did prove long-lasting and did indeed persist until the shipment date; and this, said the Supreme Court, was sufficient to reduce the buyers' damages to a nominal sum.

Reliance and consequential losses: Timing

The above discussion of the question of timing, it will be noted, has been limited **21-098** to expectation claims. Although the so-called "breach date rule" is sometimes referred to as if it extended equally to claims for other types of damage such as reliance or consequential losses,[303] on a close reading this makes little sense, if only because reliance losses often will, and consequential losses by definition must, occur *after* the relevant breach. Hence it is suggested that here it is not so much a matter of a presumptive "breach date" as an analogous "date of loss" rule. Damages, in other words, are presumptively measured according to values prevailing, not at the time of *breach*, but at the time of *loss*. Professional negligence cases involving bad advice illustrate the point nicely. For example, where a negligent survey causes a buyer to purchase an unsatisfactory house, then presumptively the difference in values is measured as at the time of the purchase,[304] that is, not the time of breach (which would be when the advice was received) but that when the loss was first incurred.[305]

Nevertheless, like the "breach date" rule, the "loss date" rule is itself merely a **21-099** prima facie position, applicable merely *faute de mieux* if no other date is clearly appropriate. Indeed, if anything it is even easier to displace. To begin with, it is subject to exceptions analogous to those applying to the breach date rule proper. For example, where misadvice causes a claimant to suffer a loss, then in so far as the claimant could not reasonably be expected to crystallise his loss immediately, a later date may be chosen than that of reliance. An instance is *Portman Building Society*

---

301 [2015] UKSC 43; [2015] 3 All E.R. 1082. See too the earlier *Novasen SA v Alimenta SA* [2013] EWHC 345 (Comm); [2013] 1 Lloyd's Rep. 648, and J. Carter, "Contract damages following discharge for repudiation — revisiting later events" (2016) 132 L.Q.R. 1.

302 The existence of a force majeure clause which for any reason would not have exonerated the defendant is, as one might expect, irrelevant. See *Classic Maritime Inc v Limbungan Makmur Sdn Bhd* [2019] EWCA Civ 1102; [2019] 4 All E.R. 1145.

303 For two instances, see *County Personnel (Employment Agency) Ltd v Alan R Pulver & Co* [1987] 1 W.L.R. 916 at 925–926 (Browne-Wilkinson LJ), and some of the cases cited by Lord Bingham in *Golden Strait Corp v Nippon Yusen Kaisha* [2007] UKHL 12; [2007] 2 A.C. 353 at [11].

304 See *Philips v Ward* [1956] 1 W.L.R. 471 at 475 (Denning LJ); *Perry v Sidney Phillips & Son* [1982] 1 W.L.R. 1297; *Holder v Countrywide Surveyors Ltd* [2003] P.N.L.R. 3. And similarly, it seems, with legal advice: *Charles v Hugh James Jones & Jenkins* [2000] 1 W.L.R. 1278 at 1290 (Swinton Thomas LJ) (solicitors' negligence deprives claimant of right of action: damages prima facie measured as at time cause of action lost).

305 True, in such cases the interval of time between breach and loss may be short. But not necessarily so: it may be a period of months covering substantial changes in property values.

v Bevan Ashford,[306] where negligent advice to a mortgage lender caused it to lend on second-rate security. Damages were computed on the basis of values obtaining, not at the time of the loan, but at the time when the lenders found out that the advice had been negligent and hence they had an opportunity to decide whether to maintain the loan or to try to mitigate their loss by taking steps to sell the property.

21-100   Furthermore, as regards reliance and consequential losses the "net loss only" principle is applied fairly strictly;[307] from which it follows that subsequent events going to reduce an initial loss are almost invariably taken into account. A classic instance is the decision in *British Westinghouse Electric Co Ltd v Underground Electric Rys Co of London*.[308] Large-scale electrical equipment was supplied to subway operators, which performed badly: the potential loss of profits was enormous. The buyers, however, replaced the entire machinery some years later with machinery whose operating efficiency was vastly greater. The House of Lords held that the extra profits thus generated must be taken into account. Where a claimant had taken such steps, said Lord Haldane, loss and gain had to be measured, and a balance struck: there was no reason why the buyers should be able to disregard matters that had in fact gone to reduce their damage.[309]

21-101   The point just referred to is further illustrated by a series of professional negligence cases, in which it has been held that courts must take notice of matters such as the later discharge of a non-performing loan when it was refinanced by the person in control of the original lender;[310] the later stabilisation of a house which at the time of purchase was apparently subsiding and for that reason almost worthless;[311] a subsequent change in the law removing a technical problem with a lease which solicitors had failed to spot;[312] and the eventual gratuitous discharge of a mortgage encumbering a property but which the buyers' solicitor had negligently failed to notice.[313]

The question of future losses

21-102   Most claims for damages for breach of contract are brought in respect of losses already suffered. But not all are. It is perfectly possible for a damages award to include an element meant to reflect prospective future losses. An obvious example is where a seller in breach of duty delivers defective goods and damages the buyer's future business prospects as regards the latter's own customers.[314] Others include the case where breach of a contract such as a charterparty or lease agreement

---

[306] [2000] P.N.L.R. 344 (disapproved, but not on this point, in *Hughes-Holland v BPE Solicitors* [2017] UKSC 21; [2018] A.C. 599). See also *London Congregational Union v Harriss & Harriss* [1985] 1 All E.R. 335; *Catlin Estates Ltd v Carter Jonas (a firm)* [2005] EWHC 2315 (TCC); [2006] P.N.L.R. 15; and the tort case of *Dodd Properties Ltd v Canterbury C.C.* [1980] 1 W.L.R. 433.

[307] As Nourse LJ put it in a consequential loss claim against negligent solicitors, "Compensation is a reward for real, not hypothetical, loss": *Kennedy v van Emden* [1996] P.N.L.R. 409 at 414.

[308] [1912] A.C. 673.

[309] [1912] A.C. 673 at 691.

[310] *Swynson Ltd v Lowick Rose LLP* [2017] UKSC 32; [2018] A.C. 313.

[311] *McKinnon v E Surv Ltd* [2003] EWHC 475 (Ch.); [2003] Lloyd's Rep. PN 174.

[312] *Kennedy v Van Emden & Co* [1996] P.N.L.R. 409 (negligent failure to advise buyer of residential lease that it would be illegal to charge premium for later assignment: law later changed to allow such charges).

[313] *Gregory v Shepherds* [2000] P.N.L.R. 769. So also with the later lifting of an otherwise disastrous planning restriction on a property bought for development: *Bacciottini v Gotelee & Goldsmith (A Firm)* [2016] EWCA Civ 170; [2016] P.N.L.R. 22.

[314] See, e.g. *Cointat v Myham & Son* [1913] 2 K.B. 220.

deprives a claimant of a future income stream, or where a breach of contract by an employer leaves an employee with reduced prospects of employment elsewhere.[315]

Generally speaking, future losses of this kind are treated in the same way as other **21-103** losses, though obviously they are in their nature more speculative. There are, however, two important distinctions. First, because future losses are necessarily speculative, they are generally awarded on a "loss of chance" basis. This is dealt with below.[316] Secondly, as with awards in tort where damages for loss of future earnings are in issue,[317] it is the practice of the courts in making such awards to recognise the time value of money by applying a discount reflecting the advantage to the claimant of receiving immediately money for which he would otherwise have had to wait. A straightforward illustration of this latter proposition is compensation for lost future earnings resulting from wrongful dismissal, where it is commonplace to reduce the amount recovered to reflect the value to the claimant of accelerated payment.[318] But the principle also applies in the commercial arena. So, for instance, damages that reflect the fact that a breach by the defendant has caused the claimant to be liable to make future payments to a third party will be awarded on a discounted basis.[319] Again, in *Overstone Ltd v Shipway*,[320] where a hire purchaser defaulted, the finance company's damages reflected in part the future instalments that would have been payable but for the default. The Court of Appeal correctly held that this element of loss, while indubitably recoverable, had to be discounted to take account of the fact that the owner was receiving them immediately rather than later:[321] and this point of principle was later confirmed by the House of Lords (albeit in a slightly different context from the present).[322] On a similar basis, damages that reflect the liability of the claimant to make future payments to a third party will equally be awarded on a discounted basis.[323]

VII. THE USE TO WHICH THE CLAIMANT PUTS DAMAGES

The fact that damages are awarded to make good a particular loss—for example, **21-104** the cost of repairs to property—is, as such, no guarantee that they will actually be used for that purpose. How far is it open to a court to take steps to ensure that they are so used? Or is it open to a claimant simply to receive the damages and pocket them, perhaps obtaining a windfall in the process?

In a few exceptional cases, the courts do indeed regard it as their function to **21-105** prevent a claimant using damages as a windfall, or for some purpose other than as

---

[315] An example being *Malik v Bank of Credit & Commerce International SA (in liquidation)* [1998] A.C. 20 (fraudulent operation of bank taints its employees in the eyes of other employers: recovery by employee for future hypothetical handicap in labour market).

[316] See para.24-034 ff below.

[317] See generally *Clerk & Lindsell on Torts*, 24th edn (London: Sweet & Maxwell, 2023), paras 28-28–28-33A.

[318] E.g. *Pugh v Cantor Fitzgerald International Ltd* [2001] EWCA Civ 307; [2001] C.P. Rep. 74.

[319] *Pennant Hills Restaurants Pty Ltd v Barrell Insurances Pty Ltd* (1981) 145 C.L.R. 625 (future third party liabilities for which plaintiffs personally liable due to insurance brokers' negligence).

[320] [1962] 1 W.L.R. 117. See too the earlier *Interoffice Telephones Ltd v Freeman & Co Ltd* [1958] 1 Q.B. 190 (damages for future telephone rentals).

[321] In consumer credit cases this is now irrelevant, since there is now a statutory scheme of allowances; see s.100 ff of the Consumer Credit Act 1974. But the point of principle remains good.

[322] *Christopher Moran Holdings Ltd v Bairstow* [2000] 2 A.C. 172 (in the context of statutory compensation under s.178 of the Insolvency Act 1986).

[323] *Pennant Hills Restaurants Pty Ltd v Barrell Insurances Pty Ltd* (1981) 145 C.L.R. 625 (future third party liabilities for which plaintiffs personally liable due to insurance brokers' negligence).

a genuine means of repairing the effects of a breach of contract. For example, we saw above that they will almost invariably[324] refuse to give "cost of cure" damages where it is clear that that cost will not in fact be incurred.[325]

21-106   Nevertheless, the position stated above is exceptional. The presumptive rule is the opposite: a claimant suffering a loss is entitled to have it made good in money, and thereafter it is "no concern of the law what the plaintiff proposes to do with his damages".[326] Thus, for example, it seems that where building work has been done badly, the notional cost of putting it right may generally be claimed from the constructor whether or not the claimant has any intention to use the money for that purpose.[327] So too, there is no general jurisdiction to condition an award of damages on an undertaking by the claimant to use the money in any particular way;[328] nor as a rule can the law, having awarded damages, exercise any subsequent control over what the claimant does with the money.[329] In so far as cases like *Ruxley* might seem to contradict these principles, they are better explained on the basis that a claimant with no intent to carry out given work cannot be heard to say that he has lost the cost of doing it in the first place, so that no question arises of questioning what he intends to do with any award made.[330]

VIII.   THE DEFINITION OF "LOSS": SOME PROBLEMATICAL CASES

21-107   In most cases it is relatively clear what counts as "loss" for the purpose of claims for financial losses. As good a working definition as any is that of Stephenson LJ in *Forster v Outred & Co*,[331] characterising a loss as

"any detriment, liability or loss capable of assessment in money terms ... [including] ... liabilities which may arise on a contingency, particularly a contingency over which the plaintiff has no control; things like loss of earning capacity, loss of a chance or bargain, loss of profit, losses incurred from onerous provisions or covenants in leases."

21-108   Nevertheless, there are a number of unusual or peripheral situations where the

---

[324] Perhaps not quite invariably, however: if costs of cure are *less* than diminution in value, a claimant may well be limited to them on mitigation grounds.

[325] *Ruxley Electronics & Construction Ltd v Forsyth* [1996] A.C. 344. See too *Wigsell v School for Indigent Blind* (1882) 8 Q.B.D. 357; *Radford v De Froberville* [1977] 1 W.L.R. 1262 at 1276–1277 (Oliver J); *Imodco Ltd v Wimpey Major Projects Ltd* (1987) 40 B.L.R. 1, 25 (Slade LJ); *Linden Gardens Developments Ltd v Lenesta Sludge Disposals Ltd* [1994] A.C. 85 at 97 (Lord Griffiths).

[326] *Darlington BC v Wiltshier Northern Ltd* [1995] 1 W.L.R. 68 at 80 (Steyn LJ). See too *Ruxley Electronics & Construction Ltd v Forsyth* [1996] A.C. 344 at 359 (Lord Jauncey), 372 (Lord Lloyd; also *Durley House Ltd v Firmdale Hotels Plc* [2014] EWHC 2608 (Ch), below). The principle is well-established in tort, especially with personal injury: e.g. *Daly v General SN Co Ltd* [1981] 1 W.L.R. 120.

[327] See *Darlington BC v Wiltshier Northern Ltd* [1995] 1 W.L.R. 68 at 80 (Steyn LJ).

[328] See *Scullion v Bank of Scotland Plc* [2010] EWHC 2253 (Ch), [2011] P.N.L.R. 5 at [68] ff (reversed on other grounds, [2011] EWCA Civ 693).

[329] See e.g. *Durley House Ltd v Firmdale Hotels Plc* [2014] EWHC 2608 (Ch) at [120] (damages for failure to pay claimant's debt to X without reference to what claimant actually did with the money); also the tort case of *Lim Poh Choo v Camden & Islington AHA* [1980] A.C. 184 at 191 (Lord Scarman). And cf. the Irish decision in *Dublin Corp'n v Building & Allied Trade Union* [1996] 1 IR 468 (money paid for reinstatement of damaged building to recipient who then demolished premises, sold the site and pocketed the considerable profits; held, no remedy available).

[330] See Kerr LJ in *Dean v Ainley* [1987] 1 W.L.R 1729 at 1737–1738; also *Nordic Holdings Ltd v Mott Macdonald Ltd* (2001) 77 Con L.R. 88 at [110].

[331] [1982] 1 W.L.R. 86 at 94.

definition of a "loss" for which damages are recoverable is less clear than it might seem. To these we now turn.[332]

"Buy-out" damages

A breach of contract may consist in the doing of some act that is otherwise **21-109** prohibited; for instance, building contrary to a promise not to do so, or publishing material having entered into a previous binding agreement not to publish. Very often breaches of this sort cause no direct loss to the victim, in that they make no difference to the value of his assets; and the general rule in such situations is that however much the defendant may have profited damages are merely nominal.[333] Nevertheless in a series of decisions damages have been awarded in such cases on a "buy-out" basis—that is, the sum that might reasonably have been demanded for a release of the obligation broken. The best-known instance concerns building in breach of a restrictive covenant;[334] but there are other examples too. In *Experience Hendrix LLC v PPX Enterprises Inc*,[335] the defendants published certain recordings in breach of a (contractual) compromise agreement, whereupon the Court of Appeal ordered payment on the basis of a reasonable royalty. And in another intellectual property case, *World Wide Fund for Nature v World Wrestling Federation Entertainment Inc*,[336] Peter Smith J was prepared to endorse a similar result in a dispute over the use of a name contrary to a previous agreement not to use it. Similarly, there is authority that a tenant who wrongfully sublets without permission may be amenable to damages measured by the amount that might reasonably have been negotiated for a licence to sublet.[337]

However, damages of this sort sit somewhat awkwardly between compensatory **21-110** and gain-based damages; and they will therefore be dealt with in more detail in Ch.26 below.

Breach of contract, but no ultimate effect on the claimant's wealth

The concept of "loss" at first sight implies, and certainly normally assumes, an **21-111** alteration of some kind in the claimant's balance sheet; or, put another way, it normally comports the idea that the claimant is worse off in financial terms than he would otherwise have been. It follows that, if no such change in the claimant's position can be shown, that is some indication that no loss has been suffered. Neverthe-

---

[332] See C. Webb, "Performance and compensation: an analysis of contract damages and contractual obligation" (2006) 26 OJLS 41, 53 ff; and cf. in the tort context, A. Tettenborn, "What is a Loss?" in Neyers (ed), *Emerging Issues in Tort Law* (2007), Ch.17.

[333] A point made abundantly clear by the Supreme Court in 2018 in *Morris-Garner v One Step (Support) Ltd* [2018] UKSC 20; [2019] A.C. 649.

[334] *Wrotham Park Estate Co Ltd v Parkside Homes Ltd* [1974] 1 W.L.R. 798. A contrary suggestion appears in *Surrey County Council v Bredero Homes Ltd* [1993] 1 W.L.R. 1361; but the better authority of *Wrotham Park* seems cemented by Lord Nicholls's approval of it in *Att Gen v Blake* [2001] 1 A.C. 268 at 283.

[335] [2003] EWCA Civ 323; [2003] F.S.R. 46.

[336] [2006] EWHC 184 (Ch.); [2006] F.S.R. 38 (reversed in the Court of Appeal on an interlocutory point at [2007] EWCA Civ 286; [2008] 1 W.L.R. 445, but no criticism of judge's decision on the substantive issue).

[337] See *Crestfort Ltd v Tesco Stores Ltd* [2005] EWHC 805 (Ch); [2005] L & TR 20 at [72]

less, the point can be one of some subtlety, and there is no reason to regard this as an absolute rule.[338] A number of instances may perhaps clarify the point.

21-112   To begin with, take the case of defective services or consumables. Suppose, for example, that an owner of valuable goods, having paid over the odds for their transport in a high-security armoured car, finds out that they have been carried by ordinary truck instead. Even if he cannot show that any of the goods were lost or stolen as a result, it is submitted that he has a claim for the difference in value between the two services.[339] And the same goes, it is suggested, for the ignorant restaurant diner who, having been promised some rare and costly wine, is served, and in innocence drinks, a cheaper vintage in lieu. Similarly, it seems that in certain other cases a buyer may be able to sue for damages for the supply of substandard goods of other sorts. This may arise if, for example, he has used or resold them in the same way as if they were perfect,[340] if any losses have in fact been recouped from his own customers,[341] or if his loss consists in a liability to a third party which in fact will never be paid because he is himself insolvent.[342] Moreover, a similar principle would seem to apply to damage to property: the victim can prima facie claim repair costs (which are presumptively taken to represent the diminution in value) without reference to whether he will ever actually pay them.[343]

21-113   It has been suggested, moreover, that this principle may extend a good deal further. *Linden Gardens Trust Ltd v Lenesta Sludge Disposals Ltd*[344] dealt with the not uncommon situation where a property owner A commissions building work from B on a site which he almost immediately sells to C. The House of Lords were agreed that were B to botch the work, A could recover at least the cost of making the defects good, even if any actual loss lay with C.[345] The majority were prepared

---

[338] To take a straightforward example, defendants have understandably been prevented from denying that a local authority has suffered loss of local taxation income merely because it had a right and duty to recoup the shortfall from its hapless ratepayers: *St Albans CC v International Computers Ltd* [1996] 4 All E.R. 481; [1997] F.S.R. 251. Compare too the old tort decision in *The Greta Holme* [1897] A.C. 596 (substantial damages for injury to property of Mersey Docks & Harbour Board despite statutory power and duty in Board to recoup losses from dues).

[339] So held, it seems, in *White Arrow Express Ltd v Lamey's Distribution Ltd* [1995] C.L.C. 1251: see H. Beale, "Damages for poor service" (1996) 112 L.Q.R. 205.

[340] *Slater v Hoyle & Smith Ltd* [1920] 2 K.B. 11 (substandard goods sold on). A similar principle applies to real property: *Newton Abbot Dev. Co Ltd v Stockman Bros* (1931) 47 T.L.R. 616 (houses jerry-built for developer: developer recovers from builder even though houses sold on for full value to purchasers), and also compare *Alfred McAlpine Construction Ltd v Panatown Ltd* [2001] 1 A.C. 518. Of course this does not mean the claimant will always recover, since there may be other reasons to limit his right to sue: compare cases such as *Bence Graphics International Ltd v Fasson UK Ltd* [1998] Q.B. 87, below, para.23-044 ff.

[341] See *Clark v Macourt* [2013] HCA 56; (2013) 304 A.L.R. 220 (useless sperm straws sold with business of AI clinic: recovery by buyer of price less value even though buyer could recoup losses by charging customers for new straws).

[342] *Total Liban SA v Vitol Energy SA* [2001] Q.B. 643. Not so apparently, however, in the converse case where the breach of contract makes the claimant liable *to* the insolvent but the debt will never be paid because of insolvency set-off: see *Biffa Waste Services Ltd v Maschinenfabrik Ernst Hese GmbH* [2008] EWHC 2210 (TCC); [2009] P.N.L.R. 5.

[343] Compare the tort case of *Burdis v Livsey* [2003] Q.B. 36. (car damaged: fact that owner exonerated from paying for repairs by vagaries of the Consumer Credit Act 1974 irrelevant to claim for damages based on repair costs); and see generally, for a discussion of the principle, *Coles v Hetherton* [2013] EWCA Civ 1704; [2015] 1 W.L.R. 160.

[344] [1994] 1 A.C. 85

[345] See too *GUS Property Management Ltd v Littlewoods Mail Order Stores Ltd* [1982] S.L.T. 533; *Offer-Hoar v Larkstore Ltd* [2006] EWCA Civ 1079; [2006] 1 W.L.R. 2926 at [69] (Mummery LJ);

to regard this as simply an exception to the need to prove loss;[346] but Lord Griffiths argued, with engaging simplicity, that there was no need for any such
exception. The claimant A had paid for good service and got bad; and that because
of this alone it had suffered a loss; and that it could therefore recover even if the
real effect had been felt elsewhere.[347] Admittedly Lord Griffiths' view was
controversial. But it did receive some support from the opinions of a majority of
the House of Lords in the later decision in *Alfred McAlpine Construction Ltd v
Panatown Ltd*.[348] A paid B to build on land that always had belonged to C; later,
however, A sought to claim substantial damages from B for building badly. To B's
plea of "no loss," Lords Goff, Millett and Browne-Wilkinson[349] gave the answer,
following Lord Griffiths in *Linden Gardens*, that B's bad workmanship was itself
sufficient loss. However, it must be remembered that Lords Goff and Millett were
actually in the minority in *Panatown*;[350] and that Lord Griffiths' approach remains
subject to a certain amount of scepticism.[351] At present the question whether it will
be generally followed remains open.

The above examples concerned defects in performance. But an analogous argu- **21-114**
ment can be made in respect of claims arising out of the provision by the claimant
of facilities or services. Even though a person providing services is no poorer as a
result (not having, for the sake of argument, in the course of providing the service
expended cash or foregone the opportunity to earn it), nevertheless there is no
reason why he should not be regarded as having suffered a loss calculated by reference to the reasonable value of what was provided. And this indeed appears to
represent the law. The point arose neatly in *Penarth Dock Engineering Co Ltd v
Pounds*,[352] where the owners of a pontoon in breach of contract allowed it to
overstay at the plaintiffs' wharf. The plaintiffs recovered a reasonable wharfage rate
for the excess period, despite the fact that the wharf was otherwise unused and
indeed due for demolition.[353] Similarly, it is suggested that where a breach of

---

Orchard Plaza Management Co Ltd v Balfour Beatty Regional Construction Ltd [2022] EWHC 1490
(TCC); [2022] P.N.L.R. 24 at [55].

[346] Namely the rule in *Dunlop v Lambert* (1839) 6 Cl & F 600; below, para.21-130 ff.

[347] See *Linden Gardens Trust Ltd v Lenesta Sludge Disposals Ltd* [1994] 1 A.C. 85 at 97. In *Palmali
Shipping SA v Litasco SA* [2020] EWHC 2581 (Comm) Foxton J held the principle to be limited to
cases where performance was generally for the benefit of the third party. See too *Swynson Ltd v
Lowick Rose LLP* [2017] UKSC 32; [2018] A.C. 313 at [14]–[17], [54], [101]–[108]; *BV
Nederlandse Industrie van Eiprodukten v Rembrandt Entreprises Inc* [2019] EWCA Civ 596; [2020]
Q.B. 551 at [55], [69]–[81]; and *Dr Jones Yeovil Ltd v Stepping Stone Group Ltd* [2020] EWHC 2308
(TCC).

[348] [2001] 1 A.C. 518

[349] See [2001] 1 A.C. 518 at 546, 577, 587–589.

[350] The case was decided on a different issue: namely, that even if A could sue on principle the
contractual nexus between A, B and C prevented them doing so.

[351] See e.g. *DRC Distribution Ltd v Ulva Ltd* [2007] EWHC 1716 (QB) at [69]–[79] (Flaux J); also the
Scots decision in *Royal Insurance (UK) Ltd v Amec Construction Scotland Ltd* [2006] P.N.L.R. 12;
[2005] CSOH 16. On the other hand, the "broad ground" in *Linden Gardens* has been enthusiasti-
cally accepted in Singapore: *Chia Kok Leong v Prosperland Pte Ltd* [2005] S.G.C.A. 12' [2005] 2
S.L.R. 484.

[352] [1963] 1 Lloyd's Rep. 359

[353] No doubt a hirer who kept goods for too long would simply be liable for a reasonable rate for the
extra period: cf. *Strand Electric & Engineering Co Ltd v Brisford Entertainments Ltd* [1952] 2 Q.B.
246.

contract on the part of A causes B to render services to C, then the measure of damages available to A will be the reasonable value of those services.[354]

Claims for overheads

21-115   Any business will incur overhead costs—salaries, building and equipment costs that must be paid however much or little the business is actually engaged in profitable activity. The question may then arise of whether overheads can ever be included as an element in a claim for consequential damages for breach of contract, or whether the defendant is able to deny liability by praying in aid the (undoubtedly true) fact that such costs would have been incurred in any case, whether or not there had been any breach. The answer, it is suggested, less one of strict logic than one of legal policy.[355]

Staff costs

21-116   Where the consequences of a breach of contract are such that the victim has to pay overtime to existing staff, hire in outside assistance,[356] or obtain professional advice to deal with the problems,[357] the amounts paid are (subject to proof and limits such as reasonableness) clearly recoverable from the defendant in breach.[358] But what about time spent by the claimant's own staff? As regards in-house professional services, the law has for some years unequivocally come down on the side of recoverability. Thus there is clear authority that a claimant can obtain the reasonable notional costs of work done by in-house lawyers[359] or valuers,[360] in so far as this was aimed at mitigating the consequences of the breach.[361]

21-117   Logically, the same should go for other staff time, since there is no clear reason to regard professionals as somehow special in this regard.[362] Admittedly some older cases denied this, on the basis that the claimant had incurred no *extra* wage costs,

---

[354]   An example might be where A, a head contractor, guarantees the workmanship of B, and A then has to correct poor work by B.

[355]   Hence one judge's characterisation of the issue in a staff costs case as involving "an accountants' theological debate": HH Judge Bowsher QC in *Horace Holman Group Ltd v Sherwood International Group Ltd* [2001] All E.R. (D) 83 (Nov) at [75].

[356]   E.g. *Balmoral Group Ltd v Borealis (UK) Ltd* [2006] EWHC 1900 (Comm); [2006] 2 Lloyd's Rep. 629 at [495].

[357]   *Portman Building Society v Bevan Ashford* [2000] 1 E.G.L.R. 81; [2000] P.N.L.R. 344 (disapproved, but not on this point, in *Gabriel v Little* [2017] UKSC 21; [2018] A.C. 599).

[358]   Moreover, this remains true even where services are bought in not independently but from an associated company: e.g. *Portman Building Society v Bevan Ashford* [2000] 1 E.G.L.R. 81; [2000] P.N.L.R. 344 (claim by mortgage lender: estate agency fees recoverable even though obtained from wholly-owned subsidiary).

[359]   Representative decisions include *Att Gen v Shillibeer* (1849) 4 Exch 606; *Henderson v Merthyr Tydfil UDC* [1900] 1 Q.B. 434; and *Portman Building Society v Bevan Ashford* [2000] 1 E.G.L.R. 81; [2000] P.N.L.R. 344. Compare too *Re Eastwood* [1975] Ch. 112.

[360]   *Portman Building Society v Bevan Ashford* [2000] 1 E.G.L.R. 81; [2000] P.N.L.R. 344.

[361]   So too with the value of the claimant's own time where he himself is the relevant professional: see *Stockler v Fourways Estates Ltd* (unreported 31 July 1985).

[362]   As the preponderance of American authority holds: e.g. *Convoy Co v Sperry-Rand Corp*, 672 F2d 781 at 785 (1982) (issue is "not whether Convoy would have paid the supervisors' salaries if the defendant had not breached the contract, but whether the breach deprived Convoy of the services it paid for."). See too *Dunn Appraisal Co v Honeywell Information Systems Inc*, 687 F2d 877 (1982).

and indeed managers were paid precisely to deal with problems of this sort.[363] Nevertheless, the point now seems to be established. In a series of tort cases it was progressively made clear that staff time was an acceptable head of loss, provided the actual amount of managerial resources used was properly quantified and proved;[364] and it is now clear that this reasoning extends to breach of contract too.[365] Thus in *Horace Holman Group Ltd v Sherwood International Group Ltd*,[366] staff time lost owing to a defendant's wrongful supply of useless computing facilities was compensated. The judge took a robust approach. "Every employer," he said, "values each employee at more than the employee is paid, otherwise there is no point in employing him."[367] Nor should any distinction be drawn between senior and junior employees, or between those working fixed and flexible hours: even in the case of the latter, it should be assumed that extra hours spent sorting out the consequences of a breach of contract resulted in lower productivity elsewhere.[368] It is nevertheless suggested that there is one qualification. Although it is clearly appropriate to assume, all else being equal, that the labourer is worthy of his hire and hence the employer loses out when his efforts are diverted, this ought to be regarded as merely a presumption in favour of the claimant. It should thus be open to a defendant to prove that the employees concerned were so under-employed that no actual loss was suffered as a result of their being occupied rather than idle.[369]

Other overheads

What goes for staff should logically go for other overheads: office expenses and **21-118** so on. Such authority as there is seems in favour of admitting claims of this sort,

---

[363] A New Jersey judge put this point of view succinctly, if sourly, when presented with a claim for alleged diversion of a corporate president's time: "That time does not represent a corporate loss. The president …, like presidents of all companies, manages the company. Part of that job entails handling the numerous problems that face a company each day, and presumably corporate presidents' salaries compensate them for performing not only routine tasks but unanticipated extraordinary ones as well." See *T & E Industries v Safety Light Co*, 587 A 2d 1249 at 1263–1264 (1990). In England see generally *Pearson v Sanders Witherspoon* [2000] P.N.L.R. 110 (Ward LJ) and *Admiral Management Services Ltd v Para-Protect Europe Ltd* [2002] EWHC 233 (Ch.); [2003] 2 All E.R. 1017; also *Standard Chartered Bank Ltd v Pacific Steam Navigation Co* [2001] EWCA 55 (Civ) at [49] (no claim for salary cost of senior manager dispatched abroad to sort out consequences of fraud on the claimants).

[364] The leading case was *Tate & Lyle Food Distribution Ltd v Greater London Council* [1982] 1 W.L.R. 149 at 151–152 (Forbes J). The case went to the House of Lords on another point: [1983] 2 A.C. 509. See too *Lonrho Plc v Fayed (No.5)* [1993] 1 W.L.R. 489 at 497 (Dillon LJ); *R+V Versicherung AG v Risk Insurance & Reinsurance Solutions SA* [2006] EWHC 42 (Comm) at [61]–[76] (Gloster J); and *Nationwide Building Society v Dunlop Haywards Ltd* [2009] EWHC 254 (Comm); [2009] 1 Lloyd's Rep. 447 at [15].

[365] The first such case being, it seems, the Scottish decision in *Euro Pools Plc v Clydeside Steel Fabrications Ltd*, 2003 S.L.T. 411 at [11]–[12].

[366] [2001] All E.R. (D) 83 (Nov).

[367] [2001] All E.R. (D) 83 (Nov) at [75]. See too *Balmoral Group Ltd v Borealis (UK) Ltd* [2006] EWHC 1900 (Comm); [2006] 2 Lloyd's Rep. 629 at [491]–[494] (same views expressed obiter).

[368] [2001] All E.R. (D) 83 (Nov) at [75].

[369] See *Firma C-Trade S.A. v Newcastle Protection & Indemnity Association* [1991] 2 A.C. 1 at 36 (Lord Brandon); also *Total Liban SA v Vitol Energy SA* [2001] Q.B. 643. See too the tort cases of *Aerospace Publishing Ltd v Thames Water Utilities Ltd* [2007] EWCA Civ 3; (2007) 110 Con L.R. 1 at [86] (Wilson LJ), and *The Charlotte C* [2005] EWHC 1974 (Comm); [2005] 2 Lloyd's Rep. 626 at [158]–[160] (Nigel Teare QC (now Teare J)).

provided a convincing formula can be found.[370] Similarly where a claimant is forced by a breach of contract to utilise spare equipment which he keeps for that purpose, the better view is that he can claim a proportionate part of the upkeep costs of the spare equipment.[371]

Liabilities to third parties

21-119   If a breach of contract causes the claimant to incur a legal liability to a third party and pay it, then (assuming the loss is not too remote) there is no difficulty: the liability is clearly an admissible head of damages. A seller of substandard goods must thus indemnify his buyer against liability to a sub-buyer arising out of the same defect;[372] charterers of a ship signing bills of lading contrary to instructions but nevertheless binding on the owners must indemnify the latter for any liability thus imposed on them;[373] and a seller without title must indemnify a buyer[374] or auctioneer[375] can sue for any sums paid to the true owner by way of damages for conversion. Moreover, in a suitable case the above principle applies not only to damages but also to costs[376] payable to the third party,[377] at least where the claimant acted reasonably in questioning his liability to the latter.[378]

Undischarged liabilities

21-120   This, however, leaves a further issue: is payment to the third party actually necessary? Two situations need to be distinguished. The first is where the liability has not been discharged yet, but it is clear that it will be (for example, out of any damages received). The second is where, for one reason or another, it is clear that discharge will never happen at all.

---

[370] See e.g. *JF Finnegan Ltd v Sheffield City Council* (1988) 43 B.L.R. 124; also the Canadian *Ellis-Don Ltd v Parking Authority of Toronto* (1978) 7 C.L.R. 82; (1978) 28 B.L.R. 98.

[371] Compare the tort case of *West Midlands Travel Ltd v Aviva Insurance UK Ltd* [2013] EWCA Civ 887; [2014] R.T.R. 10 (upkeep costs of spare bus when defendant's negligence put regular vehicle off the road).

[372] *Hammond & Co v Bussey* (1887) 20 Q.B.D. 79; *Biggin & Co Ltd v Permanite Ltd* [1951] 2 K.B. 314; *Dana UK Axle Ltd v Freudenberg FST GmbH* [2021] EWHC 1751 (TCC); [2021] T.C.L.R. 6. See too *Mowbray v Merryweather* [1895] 2 Q.B. 640 (third party liability for injury). Analogous is *Talbot Underwriting Ltd v Nausch, Hogan & Murray Inc (The Jascon 5)* [2006] EWCA Civ 889; [2006] 2 Lloyd's Rep. 195 (brokers' negligence failed to include co-assured: assured liable to co-assured in damages for lack of cover: liability recoverable from broker).

[373] See e.g. *The Imvros* [1999] 1 Lloyd's Rep. 848.

[374] *Butterworth v Kingsway Motors Ltd* [1954] 1 W.L.R. 1286.

[375] *Adamson v Jarvis* (1827) 4 Bing 66.

[376] At least where these do not exceed the amount that would have been awarded by a costs judge as between the third party and the claimant. Current authority doubts whether any more can be awarded (e.g. *British Racing Drivers' Club Ltd v Hextall Erskine & Co* [1996] 3 All E.R. 667; *The Tiburon* [1990] 2 Lloyd's Rep. 418, affirmed at [1992] 2 Lloyd's Rep. 26; and the tort case of *Dadourian Group International Inc v Simms (No.2)* [2007] EWHC 454 (Ch). But this authority has itself been regarded with some little judicial scepticism: see notably *National Westminster Bank Plc v Rabobank Nederland* [2007] EWHC 3163 (Comm); [2008] 1 All E.R. (Comm) 266 at [9] ff.

[377] *Hammond v Bussey* (1888) 20 Q.B.D. 79. See too *Agius v Great Western Colliery Co* [1899] 1 Q.B. 413 and *Butterworth v Kingsway Motors Ltd* [1954] 1 W.L.R. 1286.

[378] For cases where the claimant's liability was so clear-cut that it was held unreasonable to argue about it, see *The Wallsend* [1907] P 302 (expenses of raising ship). See too *Osman v J Ralph Moss* [1970] 1 Lloyd's Rep. 313 (insurance broker failed to arrange liability cover: successful claim by would-be insured for amount of liability, but not for costs, since liability clear).

In the first situation, it is clear that the claimant can sue:[379] it is not open to the **21-121** defendant to argue that the action is premature in the absence of evidence that the claimant has actually incurred expense in discharging the obligation.[380] This, moreover, is eminently sensible, since very often in practice the obligation cannot be discharged at all except out of the damages themselves as and when received.[381]

The second situation, that is where the third party liability will never be **21-122** discharged, is less easy. At first sight the argument against recovery looks unanswerable: even if a claimant has been technically made liable to a third party as a result of a breach by the defendant, why should he receive anything if on the evidence no actual payment has been, or ever will be, made to the third party? However, first appearances can be deceptive; and the law in fact takes a more nuanced and pragmatic approach here. Indeed, despite its counter-intuitive aura, the presumptive rule is that recovery is allowed in such a case. The leading decision is *Total Liban SA v Vitol Energy SA*.[382] A sold petrol to B, who resold it to C on back-to-back terms. The petrol was deficient; as a result A was liable to B, and B to C, for similar sums. B, however, was bankrupt. C, to avoid being left with a claim against an insolvent, took an assignment of B's claim against A and sued A in B's name. A pleaded that B (who could and would never have paid C) had suffered no loss and that C, who now stood in B's shoes, could fare no better. The court disagreed, holding that the fact of legal liability was enough to ground a claim for damages.[383]

Nevertheless, this is only a presumptive rule, and will not be applied if it would **21-123** result in a pure windfall.[384] Thus if the third party liability concerned has been compromised, it seems that compromise sum will limit any recovery,[385] unless presumably the compromise was part of a financially justified arrangement like that

---

[379] So held in *Randall v Raper* (1858) El. Bl. & El. 84. A similar principle applies in tort: see *Giles v Thompson* [1994] 1 A.C. 142 (hire charges claim where such charges to be paid out of damages) and the earlier *Allen v Walters & Co* [1935] 1 K.B. 200 (personal injury: incurred but as yet unpaid hospital charges). For future or as yet uncertain liabilities, a declaration that the claimant is entitled to an indemnity from the contract-breaker is often a sensible remedy: see e.g. *Dana UK Axle Ltd v Freudenberg FST GmbH* [2021] EWHC 1751 (TCC); [2021] T.C.L.R. 6.

[380] Compare the situation in the case of an indemnity clause, where the cause of action emphatically does arise only on payment: see *Collinge v Heywood* (1839) 9 A & E 633 (indemnity: limitation only starts to run on payment).

[381] So also an underwriter's duty to indemnify the assured against liability to a third party has been held to arise as soon as the amount of the liability is ascertained, whether or not it has been discharged (implicit in *Re Harrington Motor Co Ltd* [1928] Ch. 105, where it was held that an insolvent assured's right of indemnity passed to his creditors even though his liability to the victim remained undischarged).

[382] [2001] Q.B. 643. Cf. *Hydrocarbons GB Ltd v Cammell Laird Shipbuilders Ltd* (1991) 53 Build LR 84. A case where C had compromised its claim against A and A was suing B partly for the benefit of C, was *Mobil North Sea Ltd v PJ Pipe & Valve Co Ltd* [2001] EWCA Civ 741; [2001] 2 All E.R. (Comm) 289. Again, the "no loss" plea was rejected.

[383] [2001] Q.B. 643 at 663. See too *Palmali Shipping SA v Litasco SA* [2020] EWHC 2581 (Comm) at [31] (Foxton J).

[384] As emphasised in *Total Liban*: [2001] Q.B. 643 at 663. And note that where it might do so, it is also open to the court simply to declare a liability to indemnify, leaving quantification till later: see e.g. *Household Machines Ltd v Cosmos Exporters Ltd* [1947] K.B. 217, and *Deeny v Gooda Walker Ltd (No.3)* [1995] 1 W.L.R. 1206.

[385] See *Total Liban SA v Vitol Energy SA* [2001] Q.B. 643 at 663, discussing the earlier *Biggin v Permanite Ltd* [1951] 2 K.B. 314; also *Grebert-Borgnis v Nugent* (1885) 15 Q.B.D. 85 at 93 (Bowen LJ). No doubt this rule is an outlier of the principle in *British Westinghouse Electric & Mfg Co v Underground Electric Rys Co* [1912] A.C. 673 that the claimant who has taken steps to mitigate his damage must give credit for any gains obtained thereby.

in *Total Liban*.[386] And if the liability has been released or otherwise become ir-recoverable, that fact will be in account and will bar the action. A neat instance is *Biffa Waste Services Ltd v Maschinenfabrik Ernst Hese GmbH*.[387] Here, it was held that there would be no liability where A's breach of duty caused B to be liable to C, but C was insolvent owing huge sums to B and hence B's liability would not be discharged but would disappear in their rights to insolvency set-off.

Reasonable settlements of disputed claims

21-124   So far, we have assumed an actual third party liability. However, this is not neces-sarily essential. The law encourages commercial realism in the form of reasonable settlement of claims made,[388] and hence on principle sums reasonably paid to set-tle a doubtful claim can be recovered without reference to whether the money was strictly due.[389] The leading case is *Biggin & Co Ltd v Permanite Ltd*,[390] where buy-ers of allegedly defective roofing supplied it in turn to the Dutch government. The latter in due course made a claim for £55,000, which the buyers settled for £43,000. This sum the buyers successfully recovered from the sellers, it being said by Somervell LJ said that the amount of a reasonable settlement was generally recover-able irrespective of liability, the reasonableness to be shown by evidence to be produced by the now claimant, in the light of matters such as whether the settle-ment had been reached on competent legal advice.[391] Admittedly in *Biggin v Permanite* only the quantum of the third party claim was seriously in issue, li-ability being accepted: however, it is now clear that nothing turns on this, and that the principle applies equally to cases where liability itself is disputed.[392]

21-125   In the absence of proved liability, therefore, the question is simply one of reasonableness, which will depend on all the circumstances.[393] The claim must have been one which had a more than negligible prospect of success when he settled it:

---

[386] *Mobil North Sea Ltd v PJ Pipe & Valve Co Ltd* [2001] EWCA Civ 741; [2001] 2 All E.R. (Comm) 289. Moreover, it should be noted that if necessary the court can merely declare B liable to indemnify A, leaving the determination of quantum to a later stage.

[387] [2008] EWHC 2210 (TCC); [2009] P.N.L.R. 5. And compare the tort case of *Dimond v Lovell* [2002] 1 A.C. 384 (claim for cost of hiring car to replace damaged vehicle: no recovery, since replacement car hired on credit and credit agreement unenforceable against claimant under Consumer Credit Act 1974).

[388] Compare the comment of a Canadian judge on this: "What is relevant and material to the public inter-est is that an industrious and competent practitioner should not be unduly inhibited in making a deci-sion to settle a case by the apprehension that some Judge, viewing the matters subsequently, with all the acuity of vision given by hindsight, and from the calm security of the Bench, they tell him he should have done otherwise." *Karpenko v Paroian Courey Cohen & Houston* (1980) 117 D.L.R. (3d) 383 at 397–398 (Anderson J).

[389] For statements that actual liability need not be shown, see *Fisher v Val de Travers* (1876) 45 LJ N.S. 479; *Comyn Ching & Co (London) Ltd v Oriental Tube Co Ltd* (1979) 17 B.L.R. 47; *The Krapan J* [1999] 1 Lloyd's Rep. 688 at 696 (Colman J); *Hunt (John F) Demolition Ltd v ASME Engineering Ltd* [2007] EWHC 1507 (TCC); [2008] Bus. L.R. 558 at [60]–[61]. Note too *Codemasters Software Co Ltd v Automobile Club de l'Ouest* [2010] F.S.R. 12; [2009] EWHC 2361 (Ch), applying similar reasoning to an express contractual indemnity; and cf. the earlier *Smith v Compton* (1832) 3 B. & Ad. 407 (covenant for good title).

[390] [1951] 2 K.B. 314.

[391] See [1951] 2 K.B. 314 at 320–322; see also *Unity Insurance Brokers Pty Ltd v Rocco Pezzano Pty Ltd* (1998) 192 C.L.R. 603 at 608, 624–626, 652, 654 (a case of a claim for damages against insur-ance brokers, but raising essential the same issue).

[392] *Royal Brompton Hospital National Health Trust v Hammond* (1999) 66 Con L.R. 42.

[393] And a matter leaving a good deal of room for disagreement: hence the proper approach is to uphold a settlement as reasonable if within fairly wide bounds of plausibility. See *Siemens Building*

if it was manifestly bad, he will have no claim over.[394] Again, if the claimant or his advisers failed to take or argue a pertinent point in the negotiations leading to the settlement, the defendant may of course pray this in aid to reduce the amount of damages he has to pay.[395]

Although it might be thought that the need for a reasonable settlement was an **21-126** aspect of mitigation (an unreasonable settlement demonstrating failure to limit loss), this does not appear to be the case. Rather, the matter is regarded one of causation: in the absence of liability, an unreasonable settlement cannot be said to be caused by the defendant's breach at all. From this two things follow. First, the burden is on the now claimant to prove that the settlement is reasonable, and not (as would be the case with failure to mitigate[396]) on the defendant to show that it was not.[397] And secondly, if the settlement was unreasonable it seems that it is entirely out of account. Hence a claimant who settles unreasonably but cannot show that he was in fact liable obtains (somewhat counter-intuitively[398]) nothing at all; it is not open to him to argue that a smaller sum might have constituted a reasonable settlement and claim that instead, and not an amount representing what might have been a reasonable settlement.[399]

The case of loss suffered by third parties

Presumptively, and despite occasional doubts,[400] the general principle is that "a **21-127** plaintiff may only recover damages for a loss which he has himself suffered":[401] a loss suffered by a third party will not do. Thus breach by A of a promise made to B to pay a sum of money to C will not as such engender a claim for substantial dam-

---

Technologies FE Ltd v Supershield Ltd [2010] EWCA Civ 7; [2010] 1 Lloyd's Rep. 349 at [28] (Toulson LJ). For an example of un unreasonable settlement, see *Symrise AG v Baker & McKenzie (A Firm)* [2015] EWHC 912 (Comm); [2016] 1 All E.R. (Comm) 603.

[394] Since, no doubt, voluntary payment of a clearly bad claim breaks any chain of causation between the wrong and the payment. See generally *Comyn Ching & Co (London) Ltd v Oriental Tube Co Ltd* (1979) 17 B.L.R. 56 at 92 (Brandon LJ) (strictly concerning a contractual indemnity, but raising the same issue). Possibly this explains the decision in *Kiddle v Lovett* (1885) 16 Q.B.D. 605: see the comments on that case in *The Krapan J* [1999] 1 Lloyd's Rep. 688 at 695–696.

[395] See *The Sargasso* [1994] 1 Lloyd's Rep. 412 at 423 (Clarke J). Also *General Feeds Inc Panama v Slobodna Plovidba Yugoslavia* [1999] 1 Lloyd's Rep. 688 at 691, etc. (Clarke LJ); *P&O Nedlloyd Ltd v M & M Militzer Münch International Holding AG* [2002] EWHC 2622 (Comm), [2003] 1 Lloyd's Rep. 503 at [119]–[130]. More recently see *Symrise AG v Baker & McKenzie (A Firm)* [2015] EWHC 912 (Comm); [2016] 1 All E.R. (Comm) 603 (imprudent settlement with tax authorities bars claim for bad tax advice).

[396] *Geest Plc v Lansiquot* [2002] UKPC 48; [2002] 1 W.L.R. 3111; para.24-075 below.

[397] *DSL Group Ltd v Unisys International Services Ltd* (1994) 41 Con L.R. 33.

[398] So counter-intuitively, indeed, that this conclusion has been doubted in Australia: see *BNP Paribas v Pacific Carriers Ltd* [2005] NSWCA 72 at [258]–[263] (Giles JA).

[399] *Hunt (John F) Demolition Ltd v ASME Engineering Ltd* [2007] EWHC 1507 (TCC); [2008] Bus. L.R. 558; see too Ramsey J in *Siemens Building Technologies FE Ltd v Supershield Ltd* [2009] EWHC 927 (TCC); [2009] 2 All E.R. (Comm) 900 at [80] (not questioned on appeal at [2010] EWCA Civ 7; [2010] 1 Lloyd's Rep. 349).

[400] Most notably, see Lord Goff's studied scepticism concerning the "widely supposed" rule that "a party is only entitled to recover substantial damages for breach of contract in respect of his own loss, and not therefore in respect of loss suffered by a third party": *Panatown Ltd v Alfred McAlpine Construction Ltd* [2001] 1 A.C. 518 at 538. See too *Beswick v Beswick* [1968] A.C. 58 at 88 (Lord Pearce); *Woodar Investment Development Ltd v Wimpey Construction UK Ltd* [1980] 1 W.L.R. 277 at 284 (Lord Scarman), 300 (Lord Wilberforce).

[401] *Panatown Ltd v Alfred McAlpine Construction Ltd* [2001] 1 A.C. 518 at 522 (Lord Clyde).

ages by B;[402] and the same applies if a carrier A contracts with B to carry C's goods and damages them,[403] or A breaks a promise made to B to accept goods supplied by an associated company C.[404] Nevertheless, practicalities dictate that this rule cannot be taken absolutely *au pied de la lettre*, and there are a number of qualifications to it.

Agents and bailees

21-128   One exception concerns agents and bailees. For example, imagine that an agent contracts on terms that, contrary to the normal default rule,[405] he as well as the principal shall have the right to sue on the contract. In such a case, there is fairly consistent authority that the agent can not only sue, but can have substantial damages for any breach:[406] the technical fact that the party really at risk was the principal, and that conversely the agent is not prejudiced, is it seems ignored.[407] Again, it is suggested that a bailee who contracts for work to be done on the bailed property can make a substantial recovery if it is not done, or done defectively, even though the eventual loss falls on the bailor.[408]

Trustees and personal representatives

21-129   Another special case—which may admittedly be explained as a quirk of the difference between Common Law and Equity[409]—concerns trustees and personal representatives who contract as such. There is clear authority that personal representatives can recover substantial damages for breach of any such contract without reference to the fact that, because of their fiduciary position and right of indemnity from the trust property, they personally are not damnified in any way as

---

[402] *Beswick v Beswick* [1968] A.C. 58 (though see Lord Pearce at 88); *Woodar Investment Development Ltd v Wimpey Construction UK Ltd* [1980] 1 W.L.R. 277 at 293 (Lord Russell) (though with unease expressed by Lords Scarman and Wilberforce: see pp.284, 300). In so far as the result of the failure is to create or preserve an actual liability in the claimant to the relevant third party, the matter is of course different: see e.g. *Durley House Ltd v Firmdale Hotels Plc* [2014] EWHC 2608 (Ch).

[403] *The Albazero* [1977] A.C. 774

[404] *DRC Distribution Ltd v Ulva Ltd* [2007] EWHC 1716 (QB). So too with services: *Rolls-Royce Power Engineering Plc v Ricardo Consulting Engineers Ltd* [2003] EWHC 2871 (TCC), esp at [116].

[405] Which is that the agent has no title to sue at all: *Fairlie v Fenton* (1869) L.R. 5 Ex 169.

[406] The agent can "recover the damage suffered by him on the footing that he had been principal." See *Allen v O'Hearn* [1937] A.C. 213 at 218 (Lord Atkin). See in particular *Transcontinental Underwriting Agency SaRL v Grand Union Insurance Co* [1987] 2 Lloyd's Rep. 409; and *L/M International Construction Inc (now Bovis International Inc) v The Circle Ltd Partnership* (1995) 49 Con L.R. 12. Also the earlier *Atkinson v Cotesworth* (1825) 3 B & C 647, and the authorities listed in *Bowstead & Reynolds on Agency*, 21st edn (London: Sweet & Maxwell, 2019), para.9-013.

[407] See the statements of principle in *Woodar Investment Development Ltd v Wimpey Construction U.K. Ltd* [1980] 1 W.L.R. 277 at 283–284 (Lord Wilberforce) and *Alfred McAlpine Ltd v Panatown Ltd* [2001] 1 A.C. 518 at 522 (Lord Clyde).

[408] By analogy to the tort decision in *The Winkfield* [1902] P 42.

[409] "[I]n the eyes of the common law it is the trustee who sustains the loss. The fact that a court of equity will compel him to hold the benefit of the contract and any damages recovered for its breach in trust for the beneficiaries is neither here nor there": *Alfred McAlpine Ltd v Panatown Ltd* [2001] 1 A.C. 518 at 581 (Lord Millett).

a result of the breach;[410] and it seems that—as logic would suggest, and indeed has been held to be the case in tort[411]—the same applies to trustees too.[412]

Carriers and others: The rule in Dunlop v Lambert

The right of a claimant to recover in respect of another's loss is also established in at least two specialised commercial settings. **21-130**

One concerns carriage, where a carrier damages or loses goods neither owned by, nor at the risk of, the claimant.[413] Whatever the position in tort,[414] it was long assumed that the original consignor of the goods could recover the value of the goods in an action for breach of contract.[415] The early Scots case of *Dunlop v Lambert*[416] agreed, allowing the consignor of a cask of whisky shipped from Leith to Newcastle to recover its full value when it was lost overboard, even though at the time of the loss both title and risk had passed to a purchaser from the consignor. Admittedly the case is somewhat weak authority, since there the argument was over the availability of recovery, with its measure being conceded.[417] *Dunlop* was nevertheless held still to be good law over a hundred years later,[418] and confirmed by the House of Lords in 2000.[419] **21-131**

Dunlop v Lambert is now taken as establishing the limited proposition that a consignor may exceptionally[420] recover substantial damages for destruction of goods, albeit neither owned by him when lost nor at his risk, if (i) he himself contracted with the carrier, and (ii) it was never contemplated that anyone other than the claimant would get a direct contractual right against the carrier.[421] For these purposes the consignor is treated as though he has suffered a loss which in reality he has not,[422] being accountable over in the event that he does recover.[423] **21-132**

---

[410] See *Chappel v Somers & Blake* [2003] EWHC 1644 (Ch.); [2004] Ch. 19.

[411] See *Malkins Nominees Ltd v Société Financière Mirelis SA* [2004] EWHC 2631 (Ch).

[412] See *Chappel v Somers & Blake* [2003] EWHC 1644 (Ch.); [2004] Ch. 19 at [27]–[38] (Neuberger J): also *Lamb v Vice* (1840) 6 M & W 467, *Robertson v Wait* (1853) 8 Ex 299, *Lloyd's v Harper* (1880) 16 Ch. D. 290 at 315, 316–317, 321 (James, Cotton and Lush LJJ); and *Alfred McAlpine Ltd v Panatown Ltd* [2001] 1 A.C. 518 at 547 (Lord Goff). In *Rolls-Royce Power Engineering Plc v Ricardo Consulting Engineers Ltd* [2003] EWHC 2871 (TCC) at [116] it was said that this only applied where the existence of the trust was known to the defendant: but, with respect, this limitation seems hard to defend.

[413] See B. Coote, "Dunlop v Lambert: the Search for a Rationale" (1998) 13 JCL 91.

[414] Where prima facie only the owner could sue: *Coats v Chaplin* (1842) 3 Q.B. 483.

[415] E.g. *Davis v James* (1770) 5 Burr 2680; *Joseph v Knox* (1813) 3 Camp 320. But "assumed" is the operative word: the measure of damages was not in issue in either.

[416] (1839) 6 Cl & F 600.

[417] As Lord Diplock later pointed out: *The Albazero* [1977] A.C. 774 at 841.

[418] In *The Albazero* [1977] A.C. 774, above (where, however, it was distinguished). See too the earlier *Giampieri v Greek Petroleum (George Mamidakis) & Co* [1962] 1 W.L.R. 40.

[419] *Alfred McAlpine Ltd v Panatown Ltd* [2001] 1 A.C. 518.

[420] Lord Diplock stresses the exceptionality: see *The Albazero* [1977] A.C. 774 at 846. See too Lord Goff in *Alfred McAlpine Ltd v Panatown Ltd* [2001] 1 A.C. 518 at 539. For the main reason why it is exceptional, see the next note.

[421] See *The Albazero* [1977] A.C. 774 at 844 (Lord Diplock). In practice this means that almost all shipments where there is a bill of lading will be excluded, given the wide effect of the Carriage of Goods by Sea Act 1992 in giving the consignee a direct contractual right against the carrier.

[422] Hence Lord Goff's reference to it as involving a case of "transferred loss": see *White v Jones* [1995] 2 A.C. 207 at 267 (and H. Unberath, "Third Party Losses and Black Holes: Another View" (1999) 115 L.Q.R. 535).

Work on property of a third party

21-133   Closely related to *Dunlop v Lambert*[424] and to some extent derived from it is a similar rule concerning work on property. In *Linden Gardens Trust Ltd v Lenesta Sludge Disposals Ltd*[425] clients of a construction company sought to recover substantial damages from the latter for building defects, despite having disposed of the premises to buyers who in practice bore the loss. Lord Browne-Wilkinson, speaking for the majority, applied *Dunlop* to allow them to get over the plea that they had suffered no loss.[426] Following further support for this view from Lord Millett,[427] the professional negligence case of *Catlin Estates Ltd v Carter Jonas (A Firm)*[428] provided another example. There, incompetent supervision by architects allowed building work to be badly botched. However, by the time the clients sued the architects they had seemingly conveyed the land to an associated company for its full value. It was nevertheless held that, even if this were the case,[429] the original clients could recover under the *Dunlop* principle on behalf of the new owners.

Other cases: Claimant an investment vehicle for third parties

21-134   Apart from the specific examples above, the rule may well be more general. Thus in *Legal & General Mortgage Services Ltd v Underwoods*[430] the court smartly saw off a plea by a negligent valuer that the lender had no substantial claim against it because the moneys were provided, and the risk taken, by the lender's holding company. And so too with a lender under a syndication[431] or securitisation[432] agreement: in neither case is it open to a defendant to defend a suit by the lender that the real loss is that of the investors standing behind it.

---

[423]   *The Albazero* [1977] A.C. 774, 841; see too *Alfred McAlpine Ltd v Panatown Ltd* [2001] 1 A.C. 518 at 575 (Lord Browne-Wilkinson).

[424]   (1839) 6 Cl & F 600.

[425]   [1994] 1 A.C. 85.

[426]   See [1994] 1 A.C. 85 at 114.

[427]   In *Alfred McAlpine Construction Ltd v Panatown Ltd* [2001] 1 A.C. 518 at 588–589.

[428]   [2005] EWHC 2315 (Q.B.); [2006] P.N.L.R. 15.

[429]   Which in fact it was not, for reasons not relevant here.

[430]   [1997] P.N.L.R. 567.

[431]   See e.g. *Interallianz Finanz AG v Independent Insurance Company Ltd* [1997] EGCS 91; *Helmsley Acceptances Ltd v Lambert Smith Ltd* [2010] EWCA Civ 356.

[432]   *Titan Europe 2006-3 PLC v Colliers International UK PLC (In Liquidation)* [2015] EWCA Civ 1083; [2016] P.N.L.R. 7.

CHAPTER 22

DAMAGES: NON-PECUNIARY LOSS

For the purposes of damages in contract, as in tort, not all compensable losses **22-001** can be measured in money. This chapter is concerned with how far matters such as grief, disappointment, distress, inconvenience, humiliation and other matters not directly appraisable in financial terms can be made the subject of an action for damages for breach of contract.[1]

I. THE GENERAL RULE: NO RECOVERY

In English law, unlike many other systems[2] and in stark contrast to the tendency **22-002** in Europe as a whole,[3] the starting-point is straightforward. Damages for breach of contract are prima facie limited to loss measurable in economic terms. Non-pecuniary damages are the exception; if a claimant wishes to claim them he must show that his case falls within one of the exceptional areas where they are permitted. In particular, it has been emphasised repeatedly that it is not enough for him to establish, as it would be with consequential losses in general, that distress or disappointment was foreseeable as a result of the breach. Although in some other Commonwealth jurisdictions matters such as distress or disappointment are treated simply as a form of consequential loss, with recoverability depending on whether under the rule in *Hadley v Baxendale*[4] it was in the parties' contemplation,[5] this approach has been emphatically rejected in England.[6]

---

[1] *McGregor on Damages*, 21st edn (London: Sweet & Maxwell, 2020), para.5-023 ff; B. Jackson, "Injured feelings resulting from breach of contract" (1977) 26 I.C.L.Q. 502; N. Enonchong, "Breach of Contract and Damages for Mental Distress" (1996) 16 OJLS 616; E. MacDonald, "Contractual Damages for Mental Distress" (1994) 7 JCL 134; F. Dawson, "General Damages in Contract for Non-Pecuniary Loss" (1983) 10 NZULR 232.

[2] Compare, for example, French law, which regards it as axiomatic that if a defendant is liable in damages for breach, *dommage moral* has no more and no less claim to reparation than any other kind of *préjudice*. See e.g. C. Larroumet, *Droit Civil, Vol.3, Les Obligations: le contrat* (4th edn) (Paris: Economica, 2018), para.653. German law, by contrast, strictly limits the making good of *immaterieller Schaden*, in both contract and tort, to cases of injury to bodily integrity, health, freedom or sexual self-determination (BGB, para.253; *Münchener Kommentar BGB*, 5th edn, para.253, pp.9–20) plus limited protection to holidaymakers (BGB, para.651f). Generally W.H. Rogers and E. Baginska, *Damages for Non-Pecuniary Loss in a Comparative Perspective* (Vienna: Springer, 2001).

[3] Compare the *Principles of European Contract Law* (1999), which simply provide in para.9.501(2)(a) that damages for non-pecuniary loss are always on principle available in an action for breach of contract.

[4] (1854) 9 Exch 341.

[5] Notably in Canada: see *Fidler v Sun Life Assurance Co of Canada* (2007) 271 D.L.R. (4th) 1 and *Honda Canada Inc v Keays* 2008 SCC 39; [2008] 2 S.C.R. 362; and M. McInnes, "Contractual damages for mental distress – again" (2009) 125 L.Q.R. 16. This view is also prevalent in a number of

22-003   This approach to the award of damages is relatively recent in origin. Nineteenth-century authority was surprisingly mixed, sometimes accepting as a matter of course that non-pecuniary awards could be made where they seemed appropriate,[7] at other times taking a strikingly strict "money losses only" line.[8] It was not until *Addis v Gramophone Co Ltd*[9] in 1909 that the present position appeared in its final form. There the House of Lords held that damages for wrongful dismissal fell to be computed on the basis of the income lost to the claimant, and declined to accept that there could be any increase in the award on the ground that the dismissal in question had been highly unfair and humiliating. Although the gravamen of the decision seems to have been that punitive or aggravated damages were unavailable in a suit for wrongful dismissal,[10] there were clear statements in the judgments that as a general rule no damages for injury to feelings were available in an action for breach of contract.[11]

22-004   Whether on the basis of that case[12] or otherwise,[13] this position has now become orthodoxy. As Bingham LJ put it in 1991, in a proposition later approved twice in decisions of the House of Lords:[14]

> "a contract-breaker is not in general liable for any distress, frustration, anxiety, displeasure, vexation, tension or aggravation which his breach of contract may cause to the innocent party".[15]

22-005   On the basis just outlined, damages beyond proved financial loss have been regularly refused as a matter of law in respect of a large number of types of case.

American jurisdictions: e.g. *Lamm v Shingleton* 55 S.E.2d 810 (1949) and *Harris v Waikane Corp* 484 F. Supp. 372 at 381 (1980).

6   "This rule [i.e. against recovery for distress, etc] is not, I think, founded on the assumption that such reactions are not foreseeable, which they surely are or may be, but on considerations of policy": Bingham LJ in *Watts v Morrow* [1991] 1 W.L.R. 1421 at 1445; quoted with approval in *Farley v Skinner* [2001] UKHL 49; [2002] 2 A.C. 732 at [14] (Lord Steyn). See also *Ruxley Electronics v Forsyth* [1996] A.C. 344 at 374 (Lord Lloyd). For an attack on this idea, and a suggestion that English law should allow damages for non-pecuniary loss simply on the basis of foreseeability, see J. Hartshorne, "Damages for Contractual Mental Distress after Farley v Skinner" (2006) 22 JCL 118.

7   E.g. *Kemp v Sober* (1851) 1 Sim. N.S. 517 at 520.

8   E.g. *Hamlin v Gt Northern Rly Co* (1856) 1 H & N 408 at 411 (commercial traveller successfully sues when evening timetabled train not forthcoming, but entitled only to 5s [25p] out-of-pocket expenses).

9   [1909] A.C. 488.

10   The jury had given an overall verdict for £600, which on the evidence was clearly much more than the loss of earnings. The House of Lords reduced the verdict to the latter figure.

11   See [1909] A.C. 488 at 491 (Lord Loreburn), 492 (Lord James), 493 (Lord Atkinson), 501 (Lord Gorell), 504 (Lord Shaw).

12   For cases accepting the traditional interpretation of *Addis*, see e.g. *Bliss v South East Thames RHA* [1987] I.C.R. 700 at 717–718 (Dillon LJ); *Malik v Bank of Credit & Commerce International S.A.* [1998] A.C. 20 at 38 (Lord Nicholls); and *Vivian v Coca-Cola Export Corp* [1984] 2 N.Z.L.R. 289.

13   For other statements see *Watts v Morrow* [1991] 1 W.L.R. 1421 at 1443–1445 (Bingham LJ); *Johnson v Gore Wood & Co* [2002] 2 A.C. 1 at 42 ff (Lord Goff), 49 ff (Lord Cooke); *Channon v Lindley Johnstone (A Firm)* [2002] EWCA Civ 353; [2002] P.N.L.R. 41 at [50] (Potter LJ).

14   In *Johnson v Gore Wood & Co* [2002] 2 A.C. 1 at 37–38, (Lord Bingham), 48–50 (Lord Cooke), 56 (Lord Hutton), 68 (Lord Millett); and again in *Farley v Skinner (No.2)* [2001] UKHL 49; [2002] 2 A.C. 732 at 746 (Lord Steyn), 752–753 (Lord Clyde), 757 (Lord Hutton), 767 (Lord Scott).

15   *Watts v Morrow* [1991] 1 W.L.R. 1421 at 1443. To this should be added damage to reputation, at least where this cannot be expressed in cash terms: see *Groom v Crocker* [1939] 1 K.B. 194 (unauthorised admission of negligence by motorist's solicitor), though compare *Marbe v Edwardes* [1928] 1 K.B. 269 and *Malik v Bank of Credit & Commerce International SA* [1998] A.C. 20 (impairment on labour market compensable, since effect potentially financial).

These have included breach of contracts of insurance,[16] wrongful dismissal[17] and demotion[18] under contracts of employment;[19] breach of passenger carriage contracts;[20] breach of building contracts;[21] alleged wrongful failure by a university to admit a student;[22] and, importantly, professional negligence suits[23] against insurance brokers,[24] accountants,[25] surveyors,[26] financial advisers,[27] and solicitors, at least in respect of their conduct of essentially commercial or money claims.[28]

As regards essentially commercial transactions, the position remains as stated **22-006** above: damages for breach of contract can, it seems, never comport compensation for non-money losses. And, it is suggested, rightly so. The aim of most commercial transactions is to make money or to engender some other gain measurable in money; and, if so, there is little sense in appraising a contractor's interest in contractual performance at anything other than its pure money value.[29] As Staughton LJ once drily observed, it would be curious were a shipowner claiming freight or demurrage in the Commercial Court to be allowed to superadd a further claim for unquantified damages to cover his personal unhappiness at the defendant's breach of faith.[30]

Nevertheless, outside commercial cases the principle against damages for non- **22-007**

---

16 *Ukegheson v Gresham Insurance Co Ltd* [2020] EWHC 2903 (Comm) esp at [30].

17 See *Addis v Gramophone Co Ltd* [1909] A.C. 488 itself; also e.g. *Lavarack v Woods of Colchester Ltd* [1967] 1 Q.B. 278 at 299 (Russell LJ); and see too *Healthvision Corp v Killorn* (1997) 143 D.L.R. (4th) 477. Note, however, that the implicit identification of contracts of employment with other commercial contracts has not gone uncriticised. It has been rejected in New Zealand (see *Whelan v Waitaki Meats Ltd* [1991] 2 N.Z.L.R. 74 and *Stuart v Armourguard Security Ltd* [1996] 1 N.Z.L.R. 484) and was sharply questioned by Lord Cooke in *Johnson v Gore Wood* [2002] 2 A.C. 1 at 50.

18 *Bliss v South East Thames RHA* [1987] I.C.R. 700.

19 But note that as regards claims brought in employment tribunals for unfair dismissal under industrial relations legislation, the rule is otherwise: e.g. *Cleveland Ambulance NHS Trust v Blane* [1997] I.C.R. 851.

20 E.g. *Hobbs v London & South Western Rly Co* (1875) L.R. 10 Q.B. 111 at 122; *Wiseman v Virgin Atlantic Airways Ltd* [2006] EWHC 1566 (airline passenger "bumped"); *Graham v Thomas Cook Group UK Ltd* [2012] EWCA Civ 1355 (cancellation). But there is one apparently contrary decision in Scotland: see *O'Carroll v Ryanair Ltd*, 2009 S.C.L.R. 125 (upholding an award of some £500 for distress due to delayed baggage).

21 *Harrison v Shepherd Homes Ltd* [2011] EWHC 1811 (TCC); (2011) 27 Const. L.J. 709 (QBD (TCC)) (the point was not discussed on appeal at [2012] EWCA Civ 904; 143 Con. L.R. 69).

22 *Khan v University of Leeds* [2018] EWHC 912 (Ch).

23 The fact that tort liability, rather than breach of contract, is alleged in such a case makes no difference: see *Verderame v Commercial Union Assurance Co Plc* [1992] B.C.L.C. 793.

24 *Verderame v Commercial Union Assurance Co Plc* [1992] B.C.L.C. 793 (a tort case, but see the previous note).

25 E.g. *Pearce v European Reinsurance Consultants & Run-Off Ltd* [2005] EWHC 1493 (Ch), [2006] P.N.L.R. 8. So too with insolvency practitioners acting as trustees in bankruptcy: *Oraki v Bramston* [2017] EWCA Civ 403; [2018] Ch. 469 at [149]–[152].

26 *Watts v Morrow* [1991] 1 W.L.R. 1421 (though see *Farley v Skinner (No.2)* [2001] UKHL 49; [2002] 2 A.C. 732, referred to below).

27 *Seymour v Ockwell* [2005] EWHC 1137; [2005] P.N.L.R. 39.

28 E.g. *Hayes v James & Charles Dodds (A Firm)* [1990] 2 All E.R. 815 (commercial lease); *Johnson v Gore Wood & Co* [2002] 2 A.C. 1 (business deal); see too *Waraich v Ansari Solicitors (A Firm)* [2019] EWHC 1038 (Comm); [2019] P.N.L.R. 24 at [93]. For non-commercial transactions see below, para.22-009 ff.

29 Or, as Lord Cooke put it pithily in *Johnson v Gore Wood & Co* [2002] 2 A.C. 1 at 49, "Contract-breaking is treated as an incident of commercial life which players in the game are expected to meet with mental fortitude."

30 See *Hayes v James & Charles Dodds* [1990] 2 All E.R. 815 at 823.

pecuniary loss is less easy to justify; and no doubt for that reason it has been constrained by an increasing number of exceptions. To these we now turn.

II.   THE EXCEPTIONS TO THE GENERAL RULE

22-008   As the law has developed, there are now essentially three situations where, despite the decision in *Addis v Gramophone Co Ltd*[31] and the cases following it, damages may be awarded for distress, disappointment and other non-pecuniary affectations,[32] over and above any proved financial loss.[33] These are:

(1)   where a contract is of a type that is normally aimed, at least partly,[34] at providing (a) an element of fun or amusement, either in addition to or instead of a purely financial advantage; or (b) freedom from trouble or molestation; or (c) some other benefit of a social, aesthetic or otherwise essentially non-commercial sort;[35]

(2)   in certain cases, where the affectation consists in physical inconvenience;[36]

(3)   where a breach of contract causes personal injury, in which case the normal rules of personal injury apply, including the availability of damages for pain, suffering and loss of amenity.

In all these cases the court is prepared to regard non-pecuniary advantages as one of the contemplated end-results of performance, and to award a sum by way of rough and ready valuation of such advantages where they are not provided.[37]

Contracts aimed at amusement, freedom from trouble, etc

22-009   The reason why these cases are regarded as calling for different treatment is not difficult to see. If the object of contract damages is to compensate a claimant for not receiving what he has a right to, and his contractual entitlement consists in fun or something else not directly translatable into cash, then logically some element of damages for non-pecuniary loss must be allowable if that entitlement is not satisfied.

22-010   (i)   Contracts for pleasure, amusement or entertainment   The earliest reported

---

[31]   [1909] A.C. 488.

[32]   For a general statement of these, see Lord Steyn's speech in *Farley v Skinner (No.2)* [2001] UKHL 49; [2002] 2 A.C. 732 at [16] ff.

[33]   This is clear from two cases. In *Milner v Carnival Plc* [2010] EWCA Civ 389; [2011] 1 Lloyd's Rep. 374, a case of a disastrous cruise, substantial damages for distress and disappointment were awarded in addition to the "diminution in value" of the cruise provided. And in *Herrmann v Withers LLP* [2012] EWHC 1492 (Ch); [2012] P.N.L.R. 28, where solicitors failed through negligence to provide access to a communal garden, the client house-buyers recovered damages for both diminution in value and disappointment. In both cases the courts dismissed a very plausible argument that the prospect of enjoyment was already factored into the price of the good concerned: compare the tort case of *Raymond v Young* [2015] EWCA Civ 456; [2015] H.L.R. 41.

[34]   If a contract is partly for that purpose, that it seems will suffice: see *Farley v Skinner (No.2)* [2001] UKHL 49; [2002] 2 A.C. 732.

[35]   See *Johnson v Gore Wood & Co* [2002] 1 A.C. 1 at 49 (Lord Cooke), quoting and adding to Bingham LJ's dicta in the earlier *Watts v Morrow* [1991] 1 W.L.R. 1421 at 1445.

[36]   E.g. *Hobbs v London & South Western Ry Co* (1874–75) L.R. 10 Q.B. 111. In *Hart v Large* [2020] EWHC 985 (TCC) homebuyers recovered £15,000 damages for inconvenience where advised to buy a house that in the event required demolition and rebuilding. The case was appealed on other grounds in *Hart v Large* [2021] EWCA Civ 24; [2021] P.N.L.R. 13.

[37]   See, for a neat statement of this principle, *Morris-Garner v One Step (Support) Ltd* [2018] UKSC 20; [2019] A.C. 649 at [40] (Lord Reed).

decision explicitly to depart from the general rule and give damages in this respect was *Jarvis v Swans Tours Ltd*.[38] There the Court of Appeal, faced with a claim arising out of a drearily joyless package holiday whose provider had clearly been in breach of contract as regards the amenities available, not only returned the price to the plaintiff, but superadded a similar sum in addition to compensate him for the disappointment he had suffered. Lord Denning MR, giving the leading judgment, met the argument from precedent (i.e. *Addis v Gramophone Co Ltd*[39]) head-on. Despite regular rejection of claims for non-pecuniary loss in past contract cases, he held such damages unobjectionable provided that the contract in question was one classifiable as a "contract to provide entertainment and enjoyment", as in the case of a holiday or similar arrangement.[40]

Since *Jarvis*, damages of this sort in holiday cases have become normal and uncontroversial.[41] And the principle it embodies has been extended to cover loss of enjoyment in other cases, as where cruise providers fail to provide an agreed trip,[42] bungle the arrangements for shipboard pampering once the cruise has begun[43] or even allow the ship to sink beneath its hapless passengers;[44] where an apartment management company fails to provide contracted sports and leisure facilities;[45] where wedding photographers fail to provide the necessary festive pictures;[46] and where a film company breaks its promise to restore a period house to its former glory after the chaos of using it as a movie location.[47] There is also some authority that contracts to sell goods or supply services may fall into the same category where what is supplied is at least partly destined for pleasure rather than mere use,[48] and that the same may go in a few cases for conveyancing contracts, at least where

22-011

---

[38] [1973] Q.B. 233. See too *Jackson v Horizon Holidays Ltd* [1975] 1 W.L.R. 1468. Note, however, that there had been two similar but virtually unreported decisions in the 1950s: see *Stedman v Swans Tours Ltd* (1951) 95 SJ 727 and *Feldman v Allways Travel Service* [1957] CLY 934. And South Australia actually had an earlier reported decision: *Athens-Macdonald Travel Service Pty Ltd v Kazis* [1970] SASR 264.

[39] [1909] A.C. 488.

[40] See [1973] Q.B. 233 at 238; also *Bliss v South East Thames RHA* [1987] I.C.R. 700 at 718 (Dillon LJ), and *Farley v Skinner (No.2)* [2001] UKHL 49; [2002] 2 A.C. 732 at [34] (Lord Clyde).

[41] So much so that today a glance at most volumes of *Current Law* will yield a steady flow of decisions in the *Jarvis* mould, normally in the county court. The principle in *Jarvis's* case was upheld in *X v Kuoni Travel Ltd* [2021] UKSC 34; [2021] 1 W.L.R. 3910, where on the basis of it was held that the brutalisation of a guest by staff showing her the way through a hotel complex was held a breach of contract. The guiding of guests was determined to be part of the hotel's duty to provide an enjoyable experience.

[42] See the insurance case of *P&O Steam Navigation Co Ltd v Youell* [1997] 2 Lloyd's Rep. 136.

[43] *Milner v Carnival Plc* [2010] EWCA Civ 389; [2011] 1 Lloyd's Rep. 374.

[44] As in the Australian decision in *Baltic Shipping Co v Dillon* (1993) 67 A.L.J.R. 228.

[45] *Newman v Framewood Manor Management Co Ltd* [2012] EWCA Civ 159; [2012] 2 E.G.L.R. 45.

[46] *Diesen v Samson*, 1971 S.L.T. (Sh Ct) 49.

[47] *Haysman v Mrs Rogers Films Ltd* [2008] EWHC 2494 (QB).

[48] See *Freeborn v Marcal (t/a Dan Marcal Architects)* [2019] EWHC 454 (TCC) at [158] (botched design of home entertainment room); *Vyas v Goraya (t/a Taj Construction Roofing)* [2016] EWCA Civ 1095 (general house improvements badly bungled); also *Mitchell v Durham* [1998] CLY 1375 (badly-fitted double glazing) and the New Zealand case of *Rowlands v Collow* [1992] 1 N.Z.L.R. 178 (a badly laid domestic driveway). US authorities sometimes reach similar results: e.g. *Mitchell v Shreveport Laundries, Inc* 61 So.2d 539 (1952) (plaintiff's best suit lost, with result that he was forced to be married in a suit which was "noticeably soiled and unkempt in appearance": $350 damages for embarrassment). See too *Jackson v Chrysler Acceptances Ltd* [1978] R.T.R. 474, where the CA approved disappointment damages in the case of a car that malfunctioned and ruined a motoring holiday. But these cases may be better explained as involving the more general category of contracts to supply non-commercial benefits: see below, para.22-016 ff.

clients make clear to the professional concerned the importance of a particular amenity.[49]

22-012 (ii) **Contracts aimed at the avoidance of trouble or distress** As with the provision of pleasure or fun, so with its converse, the avoidance of disturbance or trouble. It is now clear that the principle in *Jarvis v Swans Tours Ltd*[50] also extends to cover contracts whose chief object is to provide peace of mind or lack of worry.[51] Although this category is not limited to professional liability,[52] the clearest examples concern solicitors. Thus damages for distress have been awarded against solicitors whose negligence (for example) has deprived a client of a non-molestation injunction which would have prevented harassment by an ex-boyfriend,[53] or allowed her estranged husband to kidnap her children and remove them abroad;[54] and Andrews J has refused to strike out a similar claim against a solicitor whose negligence had allegedly deprived a client of support at an inquest into the death of a loved one.[55]

22-013 As regards professionals other than solicitors, the position is somewhat haphazard. In *Watts v Morrow*[56] the Court of Appeal refused to regard a surveyor's obligation to take care in inspecting a house for a purchaser as one to save the client from disturbance so as to justify a *Jarvis*-style award for distress when the house transpired to be seriously decrepit and in need of substantial repairs. However, in 2001 the House of Lords, while accepting *Watts* as correctly decided,[57] held in *Farley v Skinner (No.2)*[58] that the result was different where the instructions to the professional concerned explicitly referred to a possible source of disturbance. So there an award of £10,000 was upheld against a surveyor who, told to report on possible aircraft noise affecting a country house uncomfortably close to Gatwick Airport, negligently dismissed it as a problem even though, as he ought to have known, the house was directly under the flight path. Again, while a simple misdesign claim against an architect may not engender a claim for distress, it seems that matters are different where he is instructed to design a particular feature into a house and fails to do so.[59]

---

[49] Notably because of the decision in *Herrmann v Withers LLP* [2012] EWHC 1492 (Ch); [2012] P.N.L.R. 28 (conveyancing solicitors, despite clear evidence that this was regarded by clients as vital, failed to ensure clients' access to London communal garden: award of £2,000).

[50] [1973] Q.B. 233.

[51] Thus Dillon LJ in *Bliss v South East Thames RHA* [1987] I.C.R. 700 at 718, explicitly referred to contracts "to provide peace of mind *or freedom from distress*". See too Bingham LJ in *Watts v Morrow* [1991] 1 W.L.R. 1421 at 1445 ("Where the very object of a contract is to provide pleasure, relaxation, peace of mind *or freedom from molestation* …"); *Farley v Skinner (No.2)* [2001] UKHL 49; [2002] 2 A.C. 732 at [34] (Lord Clyde: "where the contract is aimed at procuring *peace or pleasure* …") (italics supplied in all cases).

[52] See e.g. *Halcyon House Ltd v Baines* [2014] EWHC 2216 (QB) (breach of non-disparagement clause in agreement settling prior acrimonious litigation).

[53] *Heywood v Wellers* [1976] Q.B. 446. So too with a separated partner breaking a non-molestation covenant: see the old New South Wales decision in *Silberman v Silberman* (1910) 10 SR (NSW) 554.

[54] *Hamilton-Jones v David & Snape* [2003] EWHC 3147 (Ch), [2004] 1 W.L.R. 924.

[55] *Shaw v Leigh Day* [2017] EWHC 825 (QB); [2017] P.N.L.R. 26. (The claim later failed on the facts).

[56] *Watts v Morrow* [1991] 1 W.L.R. 1421.

[57] See [2001] UKHL 49; [2002] 2 A.C. 732 at [15] (Lord Steyn); [38]–[42] (Lord Clyde); [82] (Lord Scott).

[58] [2001] UKHL 49; [2002] 2 A.C. 732. And cf. the antique case of *Kemp v Sober* (1851) 1 Sim. N.S. 517 at 520, suggesting that a landowner who promised his neighbour not to set up a school on his land would, in the event of breach, be liable for any noise distress.

[59] *Knott v Bolton* (1995) 45 Con L.R. 127, to the opposite effect, was specifically disapproved in *Farley*

Nevertheless, despite *Farley v Skinner*[60] the courts have in general continued to **22-014** confine the category of contracts for the provision of pleasure or the avoidance of trouble within fairly narrow limits.[61] In particular, in the absence of specific instructions to deal with a particular amenity or source of difficulty they have consistently denied compensation for non-pecuniary losses in contracts with professionals to carry out commercial or property transactions even where the client is an individual and distress might be regarded as highly foreseeable. Thus they have refused distress damages against solicitors for mismanagement causing the collapse of a business deal;[62] for bungling a commercial lease so as to leave a small businessman with useless premises;[63] for loss of an ex-matrimonial home following mismanagement of ancillary relief litigation;[64] and for conveyancing mistakes leaving a family stuck in an undersized and unsaleable apartment.[65] Equally they have done the same in actions against surveyors for incompetence in failing to spot even highly vexing defects in residential properties.[66]

In addition to cases of professional negligence, damages for trouble and distress **22-015** have been given in a number of other situations, for example against airlines losing baggage.[67] And, while the authority is mixed, it also seems that contractual obligations of confidence may be treated similarly.[68] But once again, the category is kept within fairly narrow limits: it has not been applied, for example, to claims against residential landlords for breach of a covenant for quiet enjoyment.[69]

(iii) Other cases of non-commercial benefits Although the category of cases **22-016** giving rise to damages for non-pecuniary affectation is often thought of simply in terms of contracts for pleasure or peace of mind, logically there is no reason not to extend it more generally, to cover more generally cases of promised contractual benefits which are not fully reducible to money. Lord Cooke made this point, indeed, in *Johnson v Gore Wood & Co*,[70] where he said:

---

[60] *v Skinner (No.2)* [2001] UKHL 49; [2002] 2 A.C. 732. See also *Herrmann v Withers LLP* [2012] EWHC 1492 (Ch); [2012] P.N.L.R. 28 (access to communal garden).

[60] [2001] UKHL 49; [2002] 2 A.C. 732. And cf. the antique case of *Kemp v Sober* (1851) 1 Sim (NS) 517 at 520, suggesting that a landowner who promised his neighbour not to set up a school on his land would, in the event of breach, be liable for any distress resulting from the noise made by the scholars.

[61] Thus decisions such as *Fidler v Sun Life Assurance Co of Canada* [2006] 2 S.C.R. 3 (distress damages for wrongful denial of insurance cover) are almost inconceivable in England. Compare *Ukegheson v Gresham Insurance Co Ltd* [2020] EWHC 2903 (Comm) (claim against legal expenses insurer for wrongfully failing to fund court proceedings: even if claim good, no damages for distress resulting from policyholder having to conduct proceedings himself).

[62] *Johnson v Gore Wood & Co* [2002] 2 A.C. 1.

[63] *Hayes v James & Charles Dodds (A Firm)* [1990] 2 All E.R. 815.

[64] *Channon v Lindley Johnstone (A Firm)* [2002] EWCA Civ 353; [2002] P.N.L.R. 41. But the rule is not entirely consistent. In *Demarco v Bulley Davey* [2006] EWCA Civ 188; [2006] P.N.L.R. 27 distress damages were given against negligent insolvency practitioners for the stigma and distress of an unnecessary bankruptcy.

[65] *Wapshott v Davies Donovan* [1996] P.N.L.R. 361.

[66] *Watts v Morrow* [1991] 1 W.L.R. 1421. See too *Holder v Countrywide Surveyors Ltd* [2002] EWHC 856 (TCC); [2003] P.N.L.R. 3.

[67] See e.g. *O'Carroll v Ryanair Ltd*, 2009 S.C.L.R. 125.

[68] See the psychiatrist's case of *Cornelius v De Taranto* [2001] E.M.L.R. 12 at [65] ff (the point did not feature on appeal), declining to follow contrary suggestions by Scott J in *W v Egdell* [1990] 1 Ch. 359 at 398. But for an alternative explanation, see para.22-021 below.

[69] *Branchett v Beaney* [1992] 3 All E.R. 910.

[70] [2002] 1 A.C. 1.

"The exceptional category is not confined, in my view, to contracts to provide pleasure and the like. For example, breaches of contracts for status such as membership of a trade union or a club may carry damages for injured feelings."[71]

22-017   And indeed it is possible to find cases of just this sort where distress damages have been given.[72]

22-018   Similarly, where a contract concerns something of essentially sentimental value to a purchaser, there is authority that its non-provision may give rise to damages for disappointment and distress.[73] Yet again, in both Canada and the US there is a flourishing jurisprudence awarding such damages for such matters as bungled funerals and embalming.[74] Although some of the latter cases were decided simply on the basis that distress damages are recoverable if distress is foreseeable, which is a common view in the US[75] but does not represent English law,[76] no doubt contracts of this sort can be construed without too much difficulty as contracts aimed at peace of mind.

22-019   However, this category may be even wider than this. In particular, it arguably should be regarded as exemplified by an earlier case, namely the important decision in *Ruxley Electronics & Construction Co Ltd v Forsyth*.[77] There, builders hired to construct a swimming pool broke their contract by making it nine inches too shallow. The House of Lords, having declined to give the client the ruinous cost of digging it out to the proper depth, then had to decide whether the proper award was nil, reflecting the client's actual money loss, or whether the judge had been right to award him a fairly arbitrary sum of £2,500 to reflect the fact that, while technically not a penny poorer, he had not got what he wanted. They upheld the award. Lord Bridge bluntly denied that in such a case a court should be tied to purely financial criteria:

"[T]he court, in assessing the measure of the claimant's loss has ultimately to determine a question of fact, although the law has of course developed detailed criteria which are to be applied in ascertaining the appropriate measure of loss in a wide variety of commonly occurring situations. Since the law relating to damages for breach of contract has developed almost exclusively in a commercial context, these criteria normally proceed on the assumption that each contracting party's interest in the bargain was purely com-

---

[71]   [2002] 1 A.C. 1 at 49.

[72]   E.g. *Graham v Lakeside of Kilbirnie Bowling Club*, 1994 S.L.T. 1295 (£500 "solatium" for wrongful suspension from a smart sports club).

[73]   *Reed v Madon* [1989] Ch. 408 (burial plot). See too the bailment case of *Yearworth v North Bristol NHS Trust* [2009] EWCA Civ 37; [2010] Q.B. 1 (storage of sperm for later use in the same category, and hence damages could be had for distress at its destruction).

[74]   See *Mason v Westside Cemeteries Ltd* (1996) 135 D.L.R. (4th) 361 (deceased's ashes casually mislaid); also the decidedly unwholesome North Carolina case of *Lamm v Shingleton* 55 S.E.2d 810 (1949) (leaky coffin), and the New Mexico decision in *Flores v Baca* 871 P.2d 962 (1994) (incompetent embalming).

[75]   See D. Dobbs, *Law of Remedies*, 2nd edn (St Paul, MN: West Publishing Co, 1993) Vol.3, 112–117; and cf. J. Sebert, "Punitive and Nonpecuniary Damages in Actions based upon Contract", 33 UCLA L.Rev. 1565 (1986).

[76]   Above, para.22-002.

[77]   [1996] A.C. 344. For discussion, see B. Coote, "Contract Damages, Ruxley, and the Performance Interest" [1997] C.L.J. 537; also E. McKendrick, "Breach of Contract and the Meaning of Loss" [1999] CLP 37; and (a perceptive passage) Cartwright, "Compensatory Damages: Central Issues of Assessment", in A. Burrows and E. Peel (eds), *Commercial Remedies: Current Issues and Problems* (Oxford: Oxford University Press, 2003), 11 ff.

mercial and that the loss resulting from a breach of contract is measurable in purely economic terms. But this assumption may not always be appropriate."[78]

Lord Mustill argued on similar lines: **22-020**

"[T[he judges are well accustomed to putting figures to intangibles, and I see no reason why the imprecision of the exercise should be a barrier, if that is what fairness demands.... The judgment of the trial judge acknowledges that the employer has suffered a true loss and expresses it in terms of money."[79]

The tie between this reasoning and the other exceptions to the rule against non-   **22-021**
pecuniary compensation is reinforced by its subsequent approval in the House of Lords in *Farley v Skinner (No.2)*,[80] a case directly concerned with the established "peace of mind" exception. Not only does this neatly dovetail the result in *Ruxley Electronics* with other authority starting with *Jarvis v Swans Tours Ltd*.[81] It also makes it easier to understand the fact that damages have been awarded for non-money losses under contracts whose classification as contracts for pleasure or peace of mind might be regarded as implausible. These include not only construction contracts,[82] but also contracts for the sale of a car[83] and obligations to keep personal information confidential.[84]

(iv)   Contracts aimed at amusement, freedom from trouble, etc: The measure   **22-022**
of damages   As might be imagined, the quantification of damages under this head is an inexact science, and can at times verge on the impressionistic.[85] As a matter of principle, however, two points are clear. First, such damages ought to be moderate,[86] and awarded with one eye on non-pecuniary damages for distress elsewhere.[87] And secondly, the award of damages is an effort to quantify the claimant's disappointment: from which it follows that while the expectations raised by the defendant are relevant,[88] it is not legitimate to regard such damages as being in any

---

78   [1996] A.C. 344 at 353.
79   [1996] A.C. 344 at 361. See generally S. Mullen, "Damages for breach of contract: quantifying the lost consumer surplus" (2016) 36 O.J.L.S. 83.
80   See [2001] UKHL 49; [2002] 2 A.C. 732 at [48] (Lord Hutton), [77] ff (Lord Scott).
81   [1973] Q.B. 233.
82   Apart from the *Ruxley* case itself, see *Mitchell v Durham* [1998] CLY 1375 (distress damages for botched double glazing) and *Rowlands v Collow* [1992] 1 N.Z.L.R. 178 (badly constructed driveway).
83   *Jackson v Chrysler Acceptances Ltd* [1978] RTR 474 (holiday ruined when "lemon" car supplied).
84   See *Cornelius v De Taranto* [2001] EMLR 12 (appeal dismissed without reference to the point, [2001] EWCA Civ 1511; [2002] EMLR 6), where "distress" damages were awarded for breach of contractual confidence by a psychiatrist, and the dicta to the contrary in *W v Egdell* [1990] Ch. 359 at 398 doubted.
85   If only because the facts of particular cases vary, with the result that "comparables" from the like of *Current Law* are often of little help: see *Milner v Carnival Plc* [2010] EWCA Civ 389; [2011] 1 Lloyd's Rep. 374 at [35] (Ward LJ). But, to give some guidance, spoilt holidays tend to attract a global award to a family of between £1,000 and £5,000.
86   *Watts v Morrow* [1991] 1 W.L.R. 1421 at 1445 (Bingham LJ); *Farley v Skinner (No.2)* [2001] UKHL 49; [2002] 2 A.C. 732 at [28] (Lord Steyn). Although in *Ruxley Electronics & Construction Co Ltd v Forsyth* [1996] A.C. 344 the House of Lords upheld a trial judge's £2,500 award and in *Farley v Skinner* one for £10,000, in both cases the amounts caused distinctly raised judicial eyebrows.
87   *Milner v Carnival Plc* [2010] EWCA Civ 389; [2011] 1 Lloyd's Rep. 374 at [38] ff (Ward LJ).
88   In other words, a botched break in Benidorm is likely to attract lower damages than a mismanaged world cruise: see *Milner v Carnival Plc* [2010] EWCA Civ 389; [2011] 1 Lloyd's Rep. 374 at [43] (Ward LJ).

sense proportionally related to the price paid by the claimant.[89] It was on this basis that the Court of Appeal in 2010, faced with a seriously mismanaged world cruise, reduced an award to the wronged claimants of £15,000 to one of £8,500.[90]

Damages for inconvenience

22-023   In the view of English law,[91] physical inconvenience, while equally untranslatable into money terms, falls to be treated differently from distress.[92] The basis of the distinction is the somewhat unsatisfactory one that with inconvenience there is some physical outward manifestation, which is not a necessary component of mere distress.[93] The legal result is far-reaching and at times curious. Whereas the availability of damages for distress and disappointment is subject to the severe restrictions just mentioned, it seems that if a claimant can prove actual physical inconvenience he escapes these constraints. He can claim damages for it in the same way as for any other consequential loss: that is, he is entitled to compensation for any inconvenience that results from the breach, and in addition is not too remote.[94] The position was explained in the early railway case of *Hobbs v London & South Western Ry Co*,[95] where a passenger was, in breach of contract, deposited on a foul night at a station some miles short of his destination. As part of his damages he recovered £8 for the inconvenience of having to walk home. Mellor J drew just the distinction referred to: although "annoyance and loss of temper, or vexation" were "purely sentimental" and uncompensable, damages might be had where, as there, the inconvenience suffered by the plaintiff was "real and substantial".[96]

22-024   Narrow as it is, this distinction continues to apply today. So solicitors whose conveyancing bungle left a family sharing a house with in-laws were not liable for distress, but were liable for the physical chaos affecting their clients while there.[97] Similarly, surveyors who missed serious defects in a property escaped liability for pure distress and disappointment, but had to pay £1,500 on account of their clients having to live in a building site while the problems were sorted out.[98] And so too

---

[89] *Milner v Carnival Plc* [2010] EWCA Civ 389; [2011] 1 Lloyd's Rep. 374 at [59] (Ward LJ).

[90] *Milner v Carnival Plc* [2010] EWCA Civ 389; [2011] 1 Lloyd's Rep. 374.

[91] And of some jurisdictions in the US. See the New York decision in *Pollock v Holsa Corp* 470 NYS 2d 151 (1984) (inconvenience but not distress damages where motel guest wrongfully evicted in the early hours).

[92] For an explicit statement of this slightly queer distinction, see Lord Clyde in *Farley v Skinner* [2001] UKHL 49; [2002] 2 A.C. 732 at [34] ("In the ordinary case accordingly damages may be awarded for inconvenience, but not for mere distress"). See too *Watts v Morrow* [1991] 1 W.L.R. 1421 at 1445 (Bingham LJ).

[93] *Hobbs v London & South Western Ry Co* (1875) L.R. 10 Q.B. 111 at 122–123 (Mellor J), 124 (Archibald J); *Farley v Skinner (No.2)* [2001] UKHL 49; [2002] 2 A.C. 732 at [58] (Lord Hutton).

[94] *Hobbs v London & South Western Ry Co* (1875) L.R. 10 Q.B. 111 at 122–123 (Mellor J), 124 (Archibald J); *Bailey v Bullock* [1950] 2 All E.R. 1167 at 1170–1171 (Barry J); *Farley v Skinner (No.2)* [2001] UKHL 49; [2002] 2 A.C. 732 at [58] (Lord Hutton). See too the colourful early decision in *Burton v Pinkerton* (1867) L.R. 2 Ex 340 (British sailor objected to being co-opted to aid Peruvian revolutionaries when vessel in South America: as a result, employer in breach of contract simply abandoned him in Brazil: sailor entitled to "something under the head of general damage for some of the inconveniences and annoyances he had suffered").

[95] (1875) L.R. 10 Q.B. 111.

[96] See (1875) L.R. 10 Q.B. 111 at 122–123.

[97] *Bailey v Bullock* [1950] 2 All E.R. 1167.

[98] *Watts v Morrow* [1991] 1 W.L.R. 1421.

with jerry-builders[99] and incompetent architects who leave clients with serious damp problems.[100] Again, whereas it seems breach of a landlord's covenants in a lease, even a residential one, cannot give rise to damages for distress,[101] there can be recovery in similar circumstances for inconvenience.[102]

Nevertheless, the distinction between distress and inconvenience may be less **22-025** important than it seems at first sight. The line is not an easy one to draw and, at times, the difference between them almost reaches vanishing point: so much so, indeed, that in one case the House of Lords said that where a householder was plagued by the noise of low-flying aircraft, this amounted to both inconvenience and distress at the same time.[103] Since in many of the cases the claimant did recover for inconvenience even if not for distress, in practice the distinction between them seems to serve little purpose, save perhaps as a reminder that the amount of any damages in such cases should be kept fairly strictly limited.

Personal injury claims and other actions paralleling tort

Many actions for personal injury can be founded on the breach of a contractual **22-026** obligation to take care, either instead of, or in addition to, a duty of care in tort.[104] Where this is the case, damages fall to be computed in the same way as they would have been in tort, and may thus include elements for pain, suffering and loss of amenity.[105] It should be noted that this also extends to claims arising out of an employment relationship, whether for negligence or for breach of the duty of trust and confidence, in so far as this is not a disguised attempt to claim damages for the manner of dismissal.[106] To this extent, there is an exception to the general rule of non-recoverability of damages for non-pecuniary loss.[107] It is suggested that similar reasoning may well also apply to other actions paralleling tortious liability, such as those for damage to property: in so far as damage to property of sentimental value may give rise to damages for sentimental loss in tort, there seems no reason to apply a different rule merely because the claimant relies on the breach of a contractual duty.[108]

---

[99] *Melhuish & Saunders Ltd v Hurden* [2012] EWHC 3119 (TCC). Cf. *Buchanan v Newington Property Centre*, 1992 S.C.L.R. 583; also *Mack v Glasgow City Council* 2006 SC 543; [2006] CSIH 18 (landlord's duty to keep premises in habitable condition).

[100] *West v Ian Finlay & Associates* [2014] EWCA Civ 316; [2014] B.L.R. 324.

[101] *Branchett v Beaney* [1992] 3 All E.R. 910.

[102] *Uddin v Islington LBC* [2015] EWCA Civ 369; [2015] H.L.R. 28; *Moorjani v Durban Estates Ltd* [2015] EWCA Civ 1252; [2016] H.L.R. 6.

[103] See *Farley v Skinner (No.2)* [2001] UKHL 49; [2002] 2 A.C. 732 at [30].

[104] A straightforward example is employer's liability: *Matthews v Kuwait Bechtel Corp* [1959] 2 Q.B. 57. Another is occupiers' liability where a person enters land by virtue of a contract: Occupiers' Liability Act 1957 s.5.

[105] See A. Tettenborn and D. Wilby, *The Law of Damages*, 2nd edn (London: Butterworths, 2010), para.4.27; *Clerk & Lindsell on Torts*, 24th edn (London: Sweet & Maxwell, 2023), para.27-56 ff.

[106] See *Eastwood v Magnox Electric Plc* [2004] UKHL 35; [2005] 1 A.C. 503; *Monk v Cann Hall Primary School* [2013] EWCA Civ 826; [2013] I.R.L.R. 732. For the bar on such claims in the latter case see *Johnson v Unisys Ltd* [2001] UKHL 13; [2003] 1 A.C. 518 and *Edwards v Chesterfield Royal Hospital NHS Foundation Trust* [2011] UKSC 58; [2012] 2 A.C. 22.

[107] *Farley v Skinner (No.2)* [2001] UKHL 49; [2002] 2 A.C. 732 at [16] (Lord Steyn).

[108] Compare the gratuitous bailment decision in *Graham v Voigt* (1989) 95 FLR 146; also *Yearworth v North Bristol NHS Trust* [2009] EWCA Civ 37; [2010] Q.B. 1 at [59] (Lord Judge CJ).

CHAPTER 23

DAMAGES: REMOTENESS OF LOSS

I. REMOTENESS: THE RULE IN HADLEY V BAXENDALE

Generally

As soon as a legal system accepts that consequential damages should be al- **23-001**
lowed generally for any breach of contract, there must arise a risk of very extended
and possibly disproportionate liability:[1] a risk that carries with it the need for some
limitation device.[2] A number of methods are possible here: for example, manipula-
tion of the rules of causation (with remote consequences regarded as not really
caused by the breach[3]), or careful inquiry as to whether a particular loss was within
the ambit of the defendant's promise at all.[4] Both have at times been tried; neither,
however, has been found to provide a sufficiently reliable cap on liability. Hence
the courts have moved towards a general rule limiting recovery to those
consequences of a breach that might have been reasonably foreseen at the time of
contracting:[5] a development that culminated in the decision of the Court of

---

[1] Nicely illustrated by the reporter's slightly disconcerted tone in the seventeenth-century report in
Nurse v Barns (1674) T Ray 77: "The plaintiff declares, that the defendant in consideration of 10l.
promised to let him enjoy certain iron mills for six months; and it appeared that the iron mills were
worth but 20l. per annum, and yet damages were given to 500l. by reason of the loss of stock laid
in; and per curiam the jury may well find such damages, for they are not bound to give only the 10l.
but also all the special damages." Cf. Willes J's possibly spurious anecdote in *British Columbia
Sawmill Co Ltd v Nettleship* (1868) L.R. 3 C.P. 499 at 508 about the negligent blacksmith sued for
depriving his customer of an advantageous marriage to a fabulously rich heiress, the match being
lost owing to the laming of the horse that was to take the customer to the ceremony.

[2] For the history, see A.W.B. Simpson, "Innovation in Nineteenth Century Contract Law" (1975) 91
L.Q.R. 247 at 274; and for a modern international perspective, A. Komarov, "Limitation of Domestic
and International Contract Damages", 250 ff, in D. Saidov and R. Cunnington (eds), *Contract
Damages: Domestic and International Perspectives* (Oxford: Hart Publishing, 2008).

[3] A point sagely noted by Staughton LJ in *Total Transport Corporation v Arcadia Petroleum Ltd*
[1998] C.L.C. 90 at 96: There he pointed out that "the word 'remoteness' is often used to refer both
to causation and to the question whether loss was foreseeable or within the reasonable contemplation of the parties".

[4] For an example, see *Borradaile v Brunton* (1818) 8 Taunt 535 (anchor cable warranted good breaks,
causing loss of anchor: held, after discussion, loss properly within the scope of the warranty). Such
inquiries have recently been revived on a large scale, since the decision in *South Australia Asset
Management Corp v York Montague Ltd* [1997] A.C. 191 (on which, see below at para.24-008 ff).

[5] For an early example, see *Black v Baxendale* (1847) 1 Ex 401 at 411 (Parke J). Cf. *Waters v Towers*
(1853) 8 Ex 401. American writings had anticipated this development: *Sedgwick on Damages*, 1st
edn (1847), 64 ff. The CISG, in those jurisdictions where it governs international sales, has a similar
rule: see CISG, art.74 (damages "may not exceed the loss which the party in breach foresaw or ought

Exchequer in *Hadley v Baxendale*.[6] This case permanently established that this "limiting principle of policy"[7] applied to any claim for damages as a matter of law.[8]

23-002   In *Hadley* itself, Gloucester millers suffered a breakage in a worn-out crankshaft. As it happened, the shaft was a vital one, without which the mill was inoperable. They hired carriers to send it to London to have a replacement made to the same design: but the carriers delayed in delivering the replacement, with the result that the mill unnecessarily lost five days' production. A jury awarded £300 loss of profits for those five days, but this award was successfully overturned on appeal. Alderson B, having discussed mixed earlier authority,[9] laid down that damages recoverable for breach of contract were:

> "[S]uch as may fairly and reasonably be considered either arising naturally, ie according to the usual course of things, from such breach of contract itself, or such as may reasonably be supposed to have been in the contemplation of both parties, at the time they made the contract, as the probable result of the breach of it."[10]

Since in the actual case there was no indication either that the carriers had had reason to think that late delivery would leave the mill idle,[11] still less that this had been explicitly made clear to them, it followed that the loss of profits were irrecoverable as a matter of law.

23-003   Alderson B's formulation was quickly confirmed[12] and has been reiterated, in much the same terms, countless times since then.[13] In *Victoria Laundry (Windsor) Ltd v Newman Industries Ltd*,[14] Asquith LJ further elucidated it:

> "Everyone, as a reasonable person, is taken to know the "ordinary course of things" and

---

to have foreseen at the time of the conclusion of the contract, in the light of the facts and matters of which he then knew or ought to have known, as a possible consequence of the breach of contract.").

[6] (1854) 9 Ex. 341; *Chitty on Contracts*, 34th edn (London: Sweet & Maxwell, 2022), para.29-126 ff. See for the background F. Faust, "Hadley v Baxendale - an understandable miscarriage of justice" (1994) 15 J. Leg. Hist. 41 and R. Danzig, "Hadley v Baxendale: A Study in the Industrialization of the Law" (1975) 4 Journal of Legal Studies 249; also F.E. Smith, "The Rule in Hadley v. Baxendale" (1900) 16 L.Q.R. 275.

[7] This description is Goff J's: see *The Pegase* [1981] 1 Lloyd's Rep. 175 at 181.

[8] Remoteness of damage is to be regarded as a matter of law, unlike causation: see *Parsons (H) (Livestock) Ltd v Uttley Ingham & Co Ltd* [1978] Q.B. 791 at 801 (Lord Denning MR).

[9] Including American writings (*Sedgwick on Damages*, 1st edn (1847), 64 ff) and the then provision of the French *Code Civil*, art.1150 (*Le débiteur n'est tenu que des dommages et intérêts qui ont été prévus ou qu'on a pu prévoir lors du contrat, lorsque ce n'est point par son dol que l'obligation n'est point exécutée*) (now replaced by the similar Art.1231-3).

[10] See (1854) 9 Ex 341 at 354.

[11] As Alderson B remarked, "... in the great multitude of cases of millers sending off broken shafts to third persons by a carrier under ordinary circumstances, such consequences would not, in all probability, have occurred; and these special circumstances were here never communicated by the plaintiffs to the defendants": see (1854) 9 Ex 341 at 356.

[12] *Hadley* was an Exchequer Court decision (an appeal from the decision of an assize judge). *Smeed v Foord* (1859) 28 L.J.Q.B. 178 and *Wilson v Lancs & Yorks Ry Co* (1861) 30 L.J.C.P. 232 swiftly made it clear that the other two common law courts of the day would follow the Exchequer's lead.

[13] E.g. *Fletcher v Tayleur* (1855) 17 CB 21; *Hammond v Bussey* (1887) 20 Q.B.D. 79 at 87–88 (Lord Esher MR); *Agius v Gt Western Colliery Co* [1899] 1 Q.B. 413 at 419 (Lord Halsbury); *Hall (R & H) Ltd v W H Pim, Junr, & Co Ltd* (1928) 30 Ll L. Rep. 159 at 164 (Lord Shaw); *Monarch Steamship Co Ltd v Karlshamns Oljefabriker A/B* [1949] A.C. 196 at 220 (Lord Wright); *Victoria Laundry (Windsor) Ltd v Newman Industries Ltd* [1949] 2 K.B. 528 at 537 (Lord Asquith); *Jackson v Royal Bank of Scotland Plc* [2005] UKHL 3; [2005] 1 W.L.R. 377 at [25] (Lord Hope); *The Achilleas* [2008] UKHL 48; [2009] 1 A.C. 61 at [33] (Lord Hoffmann).

[14] [1949] 2 K.B. 528; C. Grunfeld (1949) 12 M.L.R. 504.

consequently what loss is liable to result from a breach of contract in that ordinary course
... . But to this knowledge, which a contract breaker is assumed to possess whether he
actually possesses it or not, there may have to be added in a particular case knowledge
which he actually possesses, of special circumstances outside the 'ordinary course of
things', of such a kind that a breach in those special circumstances would be liable to cause
more loss."

Although *Hadley v Baxendale* strictly speaking is a decision about the default **23-004**
measure of damages at common law, by analogy it may apply in other cases too.[15]
Thus at least some aspects of the statutory rules as to damages in ss.51–54 of the
Sale of Goods Act 1979 are to be regarded as codifying the Common Law and with
it the rule in *Hadley*'s case;[16] and with terms expressly making a party liable for
"loss suffered" or the like as a result of a breach of contract, the practice is generally to regard them as importing a similar limitation.[17]

Slightly more esoterically, it is also the courts' practice to read certain express **23-005**
contractual provisions in the light of *Hadley*'s case. So references in a contract to
"direct loss and/or damage" or some similar phrase[18] are normally—though of
course not conclusively—read as connoting losses falling under the first limb (i.e.
things resulting in the "ordinary course of things").[19] Conversely, common-form
clause excluding a party's liability for "consequential losses" will often be construed
as covering the second, but not the first, limb (i.e. events not generally foreseeable, but contemplated by the particular parties),[20] although the matter is always one
of interpretation[21] and courts are increasingly willing to look closely at the context
and where necessary depart from this limitation.[22]

Not surprisingly, the rule in *Hadley v Baxendale* is in a sense a default rule: if **23-006**
parties wish to exclude it they can and in some cases do. Collateral warranties in

---

[15] For example, a cross-undertaking in damages accompanying an interlocutory order: *Abbey Forwarding Ltd (in liquidation) v Hone (No.3)* [2014] EWCA Civ 711; [2015] Ch. 309, esp at [64].

[16] M. Bridge, "Markets and damages in sale of goods cases" (2016) 132 L.Q.R. 405 at 407. For state-
ments in the case-law to this effect, see e.g. *Cullinane Ltd v British "Rema" Manufacturing Co Ltd*
[1954] 1 Q.B. 292 at 301 (Evershed MR); *Bence Graphics International Ltd v Fasson UK Ltd* [1998]
Q.B. 87 at 93 (Otton LJ); *Saipol SA v Inerco Trade SA* [2014] EWHC 2211 (Comm) at [14] (Field
J); *Bunge SA v Nidera BV* [2015] UKSC 43; [2015] 3 All E.R. 1082 at [79] (Lord Toulson); *Euro-
Asian Oil SA v Credit Suisse AG* [2018] EWCA Civ 1720 at [67]; *McAlpine Grant ILCO Ltd v AFR
Refrigeration Ltd* [2020] EWHC 106 (QB) at [19] (Griffiths J).

[17] *The Eurus* [1998] 1 Lloyd's Rep. 351 ("responsible for any time, costs, delays, or loss suffered").

[18] For an example of a similar phrase, see *The Eurus* [1996] 2 Lloyd's Rep. 408, where the words "any
time, costs, delays, or loss suffered by Charterers due to failure to comply fully with Charterers' voyage instructions" appearing in an indemnity clause were held to be implicitly limited to foreseeable
consequences. Note too *The Kos* [2010] 1 Lloyd's Rep. 87 at 94 (Andrew Smith J).

[19] Examples include *Wraight Ltd v PH & T(Holdings) Ltd* (1968) 13 Build L.R. 26 at 34 and
Chiemgauer Membran und Zeltbau GmbH v New Millennium Experience Co Ltd [2002] BPIR 42

[20] See e.g. *Croudace Construction Ltd v Cawoods Concrete Products Ltd* [1978] 2 Lloyd's Rep. 55;
Deepak Fertilisers & Petrochemicals Corp Ltd v Davy McKee (London) Ltd [1999] 1 Lloyd's Rep.
387; and *McCain Foods GB Ltd v Eco-Tec (Europe) Ltd* [2011] EWHC 66 (TCC); [2011] C.I.L.L.
2989; also the *Australian Frank Davies Pty Ltd v Container Haulage Group Pty Ltd* (1989) 98 FLR
289 at 313 and *Environmental Systems Pty Ltd v Peerless Holdings Pty Ltd* [2008] VSCA 26; (2008)
19 VR 358.

[21] A point made clear in *Transocean Drilling UK Ltd v Providence Resources Plc* [2016] EWCA Civ
372; [2016] 2 Lloyd's Rep. 51 at n[14]–[20].

[22] See e.g. *The Star Polaris* [2016] EWHC 2941 (Comm); [2016] 2 C.L.C. 832 ("consequential loss"
exclusion against the background of an exhaustive guarantee). See too the earlier sceptical comments on the supposed "consequential loss" rule by Lord Hoffmann in *Caledonia North Sea Ltd v
British Telecommunications Plc* [2002] 1 Lloyd's Rep. 553 at 572.

the construction industry, for example, may explicitly oust it;[23] so too where a party to a contract gives an indemnity to another in respect of the consequences of a given event, the indemnity may expressly exclude considerations of remoteness; and even if it does not, an intention to do so may well be implied.[24]

Hadley v Baxendale: contract and tort

23-007   Until the 1960s it was arguable that the rule in *Hadley v Baxendale* was the relevant test of remoteness not only in contract but also in tort (or at least in those torts which did not involve deliberate wrongdoing).[25] However, it quickly became apparent that in practice a remarkably low level of foreseeability sufficed in order to make a defendant liable in negligence,[26] and that this was a far lower degree than was regularly applied in contract cases. It remained for Lord Reid in 1967 to draw the obvious conclusion from this, and to state in *Koufos v C. Czarnikow Ltd*[27] that while recovery was limited by foreseeability in respect of both the tort of negligence and breach of contract, the degree of foreseeability necessary, and hence the test for remoteness, differed in each case. In the law of tort a much lower degree sufficed.[28]

23-008   Unfortunately, this division caused a further difficulty: what if a defendant was concurrently liable in both contract and tort on the same facts? The point gained enormously in importance in the 1990s following the acceptance that in nearly all cases of professional malpractice a client had the option to sue in either contract or tort at his election, whereas previously he had been limited to claiming for breach of contract.[29] For a long time it was unclear whether this allowed the client to escape the restrictive rules in *Hadley v Baxendale* by the simple expedient of suing in tort. But in the solicitors' negligence case of *Wellesley Partners LLP v Withers LLP*[30] the Court of Appeal finally settled the point, and held unanimously that where there was concurrent liability in tort and contract there should be only one test of remoteness, and that should be the contractual one. The parties, said Floyd LJ, were

---

[23] See, for an example of a case where a JCT contract warranty was held to have this effect, *Orchard Plaza Management Co Ltd v Balfour Beatty Regional Construction Ltd* [2022] EWHC 1490 (TCC); [2022] P.N.L.R. 24 at [96].

[24] See *The Eurus* [1998] 1 Lloyd's Rep. 351 at 360 (Staughton LJ, stressing the importance of interpreting the clause concerned). Note, however, that a mere express agreement to pay a given loss does not necessarily exclude considerations of remoteness: *Parbulk A/S v Kristen Marine SA* [2010] EWHC 900 (Comm); [2011] 1 Lloyd's Rep. 220. Another example of exclusion may be the decision in *Supershield Ltd v Siemens Building Technologies FE Ltd* [2010] EWCA Civ 7; [2010] 1 Lloyd's Rep. 349, referred to below at para.23-013.

[25] E.g. *Sharp v Powell* (1872) L.R. 7 C.P. 253 at 258 (Bovill CJ); *Minister of Pensions v Chennell* [1947] K.B. 250 at 253 (Denning J). See too *The Wagon Mound (No 1)* [1961] A.C. 388 at 419 ff, where Viscount Simonds referred to the restrictive rule in *Hadley v Baxendale* as a good reason for introducing a rule in tort restricting recovery to these consequences that were foreseeable at the time of the tort.

[26] See e.g. *The Wagon Mound (No.2)* [1967] 1 A.C. 617 (very small, but nevertheless real, risk of fire sufficed for liability).

[27] [1969] 1 A.C. 350. See J. Pickering "The Remoteness of Damages in Contract" (1968) 31 M.L.R. 203.

[28] [1969] 1 A.C. 350 at 385–390. See too Lord Upjohn at 422; and later *The Achilleas* [2008] UKHL 48; [2009] 1 A.C. 61 at [31] (Lord Hoffmann) and *Wellesley Partners LLP v Withers LLP* [2015] EWCA Civ 1146; [2016] P.N.L.R. 19 at [145]–[146] (Roth J).

[29] See *Henderson v Merrett Syndicates Ltd* [1995] 2 A.C. 145, the decision that cemented this development, overruling decisions such as *Bagot v Stevens Scanlan & Co Ltd* [1966] 1 Q.B. 197.

[30] [2015] EWCA Civ 1146; [2016] P.N.L.R. 19; mildly criticised in M. Balen, "Concurrent Liability and Remoteness in Long-Term Relationships" [2016] L.M.C.L.Q. 187.

"assumed to be contracting on the basis that liability [would] be confined to damage of the kind which [was] in their reasonable contemplation".

In that case it made "no sense at all for the existence of the concurrent duty in tort to upset this consensus."[31]

Hadley v Baxendale: Two rules or one?

It will be noticed that in *Hadley* and *Victoria Laundry*, and in the cases follow- **23-009** ing them, the judges have been at pains to differentiate two categories of loss: first, damage likely to happen in the ordinary course of things and, secondly, damage specifically within the parties' contemplation. Largely as a result of this emphasis, the tendency is irresistible to think of *Hadley v Baxendale* in terms of a rule with two "limbs". For a loss to be recoverable, *either* it must have been so likely as to be foreseeable to any reasonable person in the defendant's position (the "first limb"); *or* alternatively its likelihood must in the particular circumstances have been clear to the parties (the "second limb").[32]

Analytically, this "two rules" approach can be unsatisfactory. In particular, taken **23-010** literally it might suggest that a claimant has an unfettered right to choose between them and invoke whichever limb is more advantageous to him: but it is now clear that this is not necessarily so, at least where a loss is foreseeable in principle but nevertheless entirely outside the parties' contemplation.[33] As a result it has been pointed out, with some plausibility,[34] that the correct approach is probably to regard the rule in *Hadley v Baxendale* as a "composite whole",[35] under which defendant is liable for any loss which was or may be regarded as having been in the parties' contemplation, in the light of any special knowledge they may or may not have had when contracting.[36]

Nevertheless, the fact remains that even with its defects the "two limbs" analysis **23-011**

---

[31] [2015] EWCA Civ 1146; [2016] P.N.L.R. 19 at [80]. See too [151]–[163] (Roth LJ) and [181]–[188]. Some earlier cases had foreshadowed this: e.g. *Matlock Green Garage Ltd v Potter Brooke-Taylor & Wildgoose* [2000] Lloyd's Rep. P.N. 935. See too the Canadian decision in *Asamera Oil Corp v Sea Oil & General Corp* [1979] 1 SCR 633 at 673; and generally A. Kramer, "Remoteness: New Problems with the Old Test", in D. Saidov and R. Cunnington (eds), *Contract Damages: Domestic and International Perspectives* (Oxford: Hart Publishing, 2008), Ch.12.

[32] Examples of cases explicitly referring to one or other "limb": *County Personnel (Employment Agency) Ltd v Alan R Pulver & Co* [1987] 1 W.L.R. 916 at 926 (Bingham LJ); *The Achilleas* [2008] UKHL 48; [2009] 1 A.C. 61 at [58] (Lord Hoffmann); *Sylvia Shipping Co Ltd v Progress Bulk Carriers Ltd* [2010] EWHC 542 (Comm); [2010] 1 C.L.C. 470 at [43] (Hamblen J).

[33] *Bence Graphics International Ltd v Fasson UK Ltd* [1998] Q.B. 87 at 99–100 (Otton LJ); below, para.23-044 ff.

[34] Especially since other systems show no trace of the "two rules" analysis: see, e.g. CISG, art.74 (referring simply to "the loss which the party in breach foresaw or ought to have foreseen at the time of the conclusion of the contract, in the light of the facts and matters of which he then knew or ought to have known, as a possible consequence of the breach of contract"), and also the French *Code Civil*, art.1231-3 (*dommages et intérêts qui ont été prévus ou qui pouvaient être prévus lors de la conclusion du contrat*).

[35] A phrase of Christopher Clarke J's in *The Achilleas* [2006] EWHC 3030 (Comm); [2007] 1 Lloyd's Rep. 19 at [49] (appealed to the HL on other grounds: [2008] UKHL 48; [2009] 1 A.C. 61).

[36] "I do not think that it was intended that there were to be two rules or that two different standards or tests were to be applied" (Lord Reid in *Koufos v C Czarnikow Ltd* [1969] 1 A.C. 350 at 384: see too Lord Upjohn at 421). For other expressions of the same idea, see e.g. *Hall (R & H) Ltd v W H Pim, Junr, & Co Ltd* (1928) 30 Ll L. Rep. 159 at 164 (Lord Shaw); *Jackson v Royal Bank of Scotland Plc* [2005] UKHL 3; [2005] 1 W.L.R. 377 at [49] (Lord Walker); *The Pegase* [1981] 1 Lloyd's Rep. 175 at 182 (Goff J); also *Baltic Shipping Co v Dillon* (1993) 176 C.L.R. 344 at 368 (Brennan J).

provides a convenient analytical device for judges, arbitrators and others in the majority of cases. For this reason, and also for ease of exposition, it will largely be adopted here.

The rationale of remoteness: Contemplation and responsibility

23-012   Although remoteness under *Hadley v Baxendale* is in theory a matter of reasonable contemplation or foreseeability, there is a modern tendency to take matters a stage further and regard this as a mere surrogate for a more fundamental idea: namely, that of accepted responsibility. On this argument, the real principle is that a contractor should be liable for consequences of breach if, and only if, he could reasonably have been regarded as accepting some kind of responsibility for them when contracting.

23-013   It is true that in most cases it does not matter much which view one takes. It is, after all, hardly unreasonable in the vast majority of situations to infer that contracts are aimed at making a contractor responsible for results of breach that could have been envisaged at the time of contracting, but not for others.[37] Nevertheless, on occasion the difference in approach may be important.[38] Thus a contract, if construed properly and in context, may inescapably indicate an aim to make one or other party responsible for consequences that, far from being foreseeable, are in fact fantastically unlikely: and if this is so, the courts will be inclined to decide accordingly.[39] Conversely, the fact that a consequence is something the defendant might have envisaged, while a very strong indication that a contractor accepts responsibility for it, is not always conclusive. As Lord Hoffmann said in the vital decision in *The Achilleas*.[40]

> "[T]he consequences for which the contracting party will be liable are those which 'the law regards as best giving effect to the express obligations assumed' and '[not] extending them so as to impose on the [contracting party] a liability greater than he could reasonably have thought he was undertaking.'"[41]

23-014   This is an important point, and its impact will be discussed further below.[42]

---

[37] A point made specifically by Hamblen J in *Sylvia Shipping Co Ltd v Progress Bulk Carriers Ltd* [2010] 1 C.L.C. 470 at [41].

[38] Sir Anthony Evans put this point succinctly in *Mulvenna v Royal Bank of Scotland Plc* [2003] EWCA Civ 1112 at [33]. "The authorities to which we were referred ... demonstrate that the concept of reasonable foreseeability is not a complete guide to the circumstances in which damages are recoverable as a matter of law."

[39] A straightforward example is contractual obligations to provide security against the unexpected. See e.g. *Supershield Ltd v Siemens Building Technologies FE Ltd* [2010] EWCA Civ 7; [2010] 1 Lloyd's Rep. 349 (anti-flood precautions: liability even for extremely unlikely flood). Note particularly Toulson LJ at [43].

[40] [2008] UKHL 48; [2009] 1 A.C. 61. In view of the agreement by Lords Hope and Walker with Lord Hoffmann's view, it seems that it must be regarded as representing the ratio of the decision: see *Sylvia Shipping Co Ltd v Progress Bulk Carriers Ltd* [2010] 1 C.L.C. 470 at [39]–[40]. In B. Coote, "Contract as Assumption and Remoteness of Damage" (2010) 26 JCL 211 it is suggested that *The Achilleas* represents acceptance of the idea that damages liability, as much as primary liability, is assumed rather than imposed: but this, respect, seems to be going too far.

[41] [2008] UKHL 48; [2009] 1 A.C. 61 at [16], partly quoting *South Australia Asset Management Corp v York Montague Ltd* [1997] A.C. 191 at 212.

[42] See para.23-027 ff.

Contemplation and timing

The relevant time for deciding whether a loss is within the parties' contempla- **23-015**
tion under *Hadley v Baxendale* is the time the contract is concluded,[43] with later
events transpiring between conclusion and breach being out of account.[44] This is
unsurprising: indeed, the most obvious reason for having a foreseeability rule at all
is that it gives a potential contractor the chance to weigh up his possible exposure
before irrevocably committing himself.[45]

One point should be noted, however. While the reasoning outlined above clearly **23-016**
suits one-off contracts, it is less ideal for long-term arrangements: for example,
those between banker and customer, or for supply of services such as
telecommunications. Such contracts can in general be terminated on reasonable
notice by either party; if so, then there is much to be said for reckoning foreseeability at a time shortly before the transaction giving rise to the breach, rather than
arbitrarily at the time, maybe many years previously, when the relationship first
commenced.[46] Similarly, where a long-term contract, such as a supply agreement,
can be terminated at particular intervals, it is suggested that the best solution may
well be to require foreseeability as at the time of the defendant's last opportunity
to cancel the contract before the transaction in question.

II.   HADLEY V BAXENDALE—THE FIRST "LIMB" (CONTEMPLATION OF PERSONS
GENERALLY)

The nature of foreseeability in general

Most questions of what forms of consequential loss count as "arising naturally, **23-017**
i.e. according to the usual course of things" within Alderson B's judgment in *Hadley
v Baxendale*[47] reduce to simple questions of fact on which extensive citation does
little if any good,[48] and where a holding at first instance is unlikely to be upset on
appeal. However, there are a few points of principle worth noting.

First, questions of what is foreseeable are reckoned objectively and not **23-018**
subjectively: more precisely, the issue is what, as reasonable actors, the contract-

---

[43] For authority, see e.g. *Hadley v Baxendale* (1854) 9 Ex 341 at 355 (Alderson B); *Victoria Laundry (Windsor) Ltd v Newman Industries Ltd* [1949] 2 K.B. 528 at 539 (Asquith LJ); and *Jackson v Royal Bank of Scotland Plc* [2005] UKHL 3, [2005] 1 W.L.R. 377 at [26], [36] (Lord Hope).

[44] So held in Australia: *Kollman v Watts* [1963] V.L.R. 396.

[45] A point clearly made by Lord Hope in *Jackson v Royal Bank of Scotland Plc* [2005] UKHL 3; [2005] 1 W.L.R. 377 at [36]; see too the comments of Lord Hoffmann in *The Achilleas* [2008] UKHL 48: [2009] 1 A.C. 61 at [12]-[13] (making the point that the price and other terms will be determined by the potential liabilities being undertaken).

[46] So held, apparently, in Victoria: see *National Australia Bank Ltd v Nemur Varity P/L* [2002] 4 V.R. 252 (cheque miscredited: in breach of contract action, relevant time for remoteness purposes was time of instructions to process the cheque, not of opening of account).

[47] (1854) 9 Ex 341.

[48] "The question of damages is a question of fact, and the only guidance the law can give is to lay down general principles which afford at times but scanty assistance in dealing with particular cases." Lord Haldane in *British Westinghouse Electric Co Ltd v Underground Electric Rlys Co of London* [1912] A.C. 673 at 688. See too Lord Shaw's excoriation of "ultra-analysis" of *Hadley's* case in *Hall (R & H) v Pim (WH) Jr & Co Ltd* (1928) 33 Com. Cas. 324 at 334; also Lord du Parcq in *A/B Karlshamns Oljefabriker v Monarch SS Co Ltd* [1949] A.C. 196 at 232.

ing parties might have been expected to foresee had they had breach in mind.[49] On this all the circumstances may on principle be in account, if they are matters of general knowledge, together with any reasonable inferences that should be taken from them. The point is illustrated by *A/B Karlshamns Oljefabriker v Monarch SS Co Ltd.*[50] In 1939 British shipowners were guilty of excessive delay in the course of carrying soya beans destined for Sweden; war having meanwhile broken out on 3 September, the ship, being still at sea, immediately ran for Glasgow. The consignees recovered the costs of on-shipment to Sweden, it having been common knowledge in the business that war was not unlikely and that no equivalent cargo would be available on the Swedish market.

23-019   Secondly the question whether a loss was, or should have been, contemplated as a possibility is viewed in a fairly expansive way. As in the law of tort,[51] what matters is whether an event of the broad type that gave rise to the loss could have been foreseen. The fact that no-one would have envisaged the precise circumstances which in fact occurred is irrelevant.[52] Davies LJ put this point clearly in *Christopher Hill Ltd v Ashington Piggeries Ltd*:[53]

> "in order to establish liability for the damage caused by a breach of contract, the party who has suffered damage does not have to show that the contract-breaker ought to have contemplated, as being not unlikely, the precise detail of the damage or the precise manner of its happening. It is enough if he should have contemplated that damage of that kind is not unlikely."[54]

23-020   Thirdly, courts are disinclined to allow a claimant to recover for consequences of a breach in so far as these result from his own particular circumstances. Thus, in *Hadley v Baxendale* itself, an important reason why the claim failed seems to have been that the loss arose out of the particular practice of the plaintiff in not having a spare shaft: as Alderson B put it:

> "it is obvious that, in the great multitude of cases of millers sending off broken shafts to

---

[49] See Cotton LJ in *McMahon v Field* (1881) 7 Q.B.D. 591 at 597 ("The parties never contemplate a breach, and the rule should rather be that the damage recoverable is such as is the natural and probable result of the breach of contract."). Similar statements: *Victoria Laundry (Windsor) Ltd v Newman Industries Ltd* [1949] 2 K.B. 528 at 540 (Asquith LJ); *A/B Karlshamns Oljefabriker v Monarch SS Co Ltd* [1949] A.C. 196 at 233 (Lord du Parcq).

[50] [1949] A.C. 196. So too if lawyers' incompetence causes a client to lose investment funds to fraud, it may well be foreseeable that if the client had been warned off the fraudulant scheme his lucre would otherwise have been profitably invested: *Leggett v Giambrone Law LLP* [2020] EWHC 724 (QB); [2020] P.N.L.R. 18.

[51] See *Hughes v Lord Advocate* [1963] A.C. 837; and generally *Clerk & Lindsell on Torts*, 24th edn (London: Sweet & Maxwell, 2023), para.2-154 ff.

[52] See e.g. *Rabilizirov v A2 Dominion London Ltd* [2019] EWHC 186 (QB) (breach of contract by builder causing water ingress to premises; rent lost owing to (unforeseeable) inability to improve premises pending resolution of the problem; loss recoverable nevertheless because of a foreseeable type). A similar case is *McAlpine Grant ILCO Ltd v AFR Refrigeration Ltd* [2020] EWHC 106 (QB) (defective refrigerator: liability for spoilt contents despite fact that user, unforeseeable, did not install alarm). So similarly a bank that fails to repay a foreign currency deposit on demand is liable for exchange losses, whether or not it could have foreseen the precise way they arose: *Khalifeh v Blom Bank SAL* [2021] EWHC 3399 (QB) at [255].

[53] [1969] 3 All E.R. 1496.

[54] [1969] 3 All E.R. 1496 at 1524 (appealed to the House of Lords on another issue: [1972] A.C. 441). Cf. too *The Rio Claro* [1987] 2 Lloyd's Rep. 173 at 175 (Staughton J); *Kpohraror v Woolwich Building Society* [1996] 4 All E.R. 119 at 126 (Evans LJ); *Abbey Forwarding Ltd (in liquidation) v Hone (No.3)* [2014] EWCA Civ 711; [2015] Ch. 309 at [72] (McCombe LJ); *Agouman v Leigh Day (A Firm)* [2016] EWHC 1324 (QB); [2016] P.N.L.R. 32 at [122] (Andrew Smith J).

third persons by a carrier under ordinary circumstances, such consequences would not, in all probability, have occurred".[55]

Similarly, in a more recent case convertible bond issuers who failed to issue the relevant shares on time were held liable for the shares' appreciation in market value in the relevant period, but not for trading profits on them which the holder claimed to have lost.[56] Again, solicitors who fail to provide a homebuyer with clear title are liable for the cost of perfecting that title, but not for his further expenses of long-distance commuting while matters are sorted out;[57] and while a tour company providing insanitary accommodation must pay for general inconvenience it is not liable if the unsatisfactory conditions make worse particular complaint suffered by the client.[58]

The degree of foreseeability

Just how foreseeable must an event be to count as something "arising naturally, i.e. according to the usual course of things, from such breach of contract"? Nineteenth-century decisions tended to be highly restrictive in this respect, Cockburn CJ at one point going so far as to limit liability to "immediate and necessary" results of a breach,[59] and other cases apparently ruling out recovery for certain types of consequential loss as almost a matter of law.[60] But attitudes later relaxed, largely as a result of two decisions of the House of Lords.   **23-021**

The first was *Hall (R & H) Ltd v Pim (WH) (Jr) & Co Ltd*[61] in 1927. There the House of Lords held a defaulting seller of wheat liable for the loss of a profitable subsale of the same cargo on the basis that such a loss was a distinct possibility, despite the fact that it had not been enormously likely. Having unhesitatingly rejected a suggestion that compensation was limited to losses that were more probable than not, Lord Shaw in that case suggested that on the contrary, any loss that was "not unlikely" could on principle be recovered.[62]   **23-022**

The liberalising process started in *Hall*'s case was confirmed in 1968 in what is currently the leading authority, namely *Koufos v C Czarnikow Ltd*.[63] The issue there was whether, in the case of delayed delivery of a cargo of sugar on a falling market, the commodity dealer to whom it was consigned could recover against the carrier for the resulting loss of sale value.[64] In holding that this damage was indeed not too remote, various members of the House of Lords chose to discuss more generally   **23-023**

---

55 See (1854) 9 Ex 341 at 356.
56 *Prakash Industries Ltd v Peter Beck Und Partner* [2022] EWHC 754 (Comm).
57 *Pilkington v Wood* [1953] Ch. 770. See too *Strategic Property Ltd v O'Se* [2009] EWHC 3512 (Ch) (defaulting buyer of land not liable when seller himself defaulted as against his buyer, thus incurring large damages bill).
58 See *Kemp v Intasun Holidays Ltd* [1987] F.T.L.R. 234.
59 See *Hobbs v London & SW Ry Co* (1875) L.R. 10 Q.B. 111 at 118 (passenger was ejected short of her destination on a wet night: no liability for resulting illness).
60 Examples: *The Parana* (1877) 2 P.D. 118 (on loss of market due to carrier's delay: finally overruled in *Koufos v C Czarnikow Ltd* [1969] 1 A.C. 350), and *Wilson v Lancashire & Yorkshire Ry Co* (1861) 9 CBNS 632 (on carriers' delay and lost resale profits).
61 (1927) 30 Ll. Rep. 159. For another lost profits case where there was no available market, see *Pascoe & Co Ltd v Holden's Motor Bodies Ltd* [1931] SASR 180.
62 (1927) 30 Ll. Rep. 159 at 333.
63 [1969] 1 A.C. 350.
64 An old case, *The Parana* (1876) L.R. 2 P.D. 118, having suggested—somewhat implausibly—that this could never be so.

how *Hadley v Baxendale* ought to be applied. Lord Reid, accepting that restrictions had loosened, put the necessary likelihood higher than that necessary for negligence liability in tort,[65] but certainly lower than 50 per cent.[66] A number of phrases received varying levels of approval: these included "not unlikely",[67] "quite likely",[68] a "real danger",[69] and a "serious possibility".[70]

23-024   The result of *Koufos v C Czarnikow Ltd*[71] was noticeably to reduce the burden on a claimant as regards consequential losses.[72] But it has also had another more important effect. Since then, with forms of words such as those appearing in *Koufos* as guidance but no more,[73] it has become clear that the question whether a given head of loss is too remote is simply one of fact in each case.[74] In particular there is now no room for the argument that there is a bar, as a matter of law, to the recovery of any particular kind of loss, whatever previous judges may have thought. For example, in *The Pegase*[75] consignees of ore sued carriers for late delivery, claiming loss of resale profits. Goff J refused to accept as determinative certain nineteenth-century authorities[76] suggesting that the claim had to fail, instead emphasising that what mattered was simply whether such losses arose in the ordinary course of things, and remitting the matter to the arbitrators to decide how far they did. Again, it has in recent years been made clear that there is no necessary bar on negligent conveyancing solicitors being held liable to purchasers for lost development profits in addition to any direct losses so caused.[77]

23-025   Nevertheless, at least in commercial cases, it remains the fact that the courts' expectations of what a person should foresee can be noticeably limited.[78] Thus while

---

[65]   [1969] 1 A.C. 350 at 384.
[66]   [1969] 1 A.C. 350 at 388.
[67]   [1969] 1 A.C. 350 at 390 (Lord Reid). See too *John Grimes Partnership Ltd v Gubbins* [2013] EWCA Civ 37; [2013] P.N.L.R. 17 at [17] (Sir David Keene).
[68]   [1969] 1 A.C. 350 at 390 (Lord Reid).
[69]   [1969] 1 A.C. 350 at 425 (Lord Upjohn).
[70]   [1969] 1 A.C. 350 at 390. See too the earlier *A/B Karlshamns Oljefabriker v Monarch SS Co Ltd* [1949] A.C. 196 at 233 (Lord du Parcq); and the later *Att Gen of the Virgin Islands v Global Water Associates Ltd* [2020] UKPC 18; [2021] A.C. 23 at [32] (although at para [28] their Lordships had made it clear that no form of words could be regarded as canonical).
[71]   [1969] 1 A.C. 350.
[72]   Thus (mirroring earlier suggestions by Parker LJ in *Interoffice Telephones Ltd v Robert Freeman & Co Ltd* [1958] 1 Q.B. 190 at 202), lost reasonable resale profits in commodity cases are now fairly consistently recoverable: see, e.g. *Contigroup Companies Inc v Glencore AG* [2005] 1 Lloyd's Rep. 241. Cf. too the important American decision in *Texas A & M v Magna Transportation* 338 F.3d 394 (2003) (transport of research equipment: foreseeable that late delivery might cause experiment to be aborted).
[73]   Hence the sage advice of Evans LJ in *Kpohraror v Woolwich Building Society* [1996] 4 All E.R. 119 at 127 not to treat interpretations of *Hadley v Baxendale* as a "straitjacket."
[74]   "[I]t becomes very largely a question of fact as to whether in any particular case a loss can 'fairly and reasonably' be considered as arising in the normal course of things"—Lord Morris in *Koufos v C Czarnikow Ltd* [1969] 1 A.C. 350 at 397.
[75]   [1981] 1 Lloyd's Rep. 175. See too the earlier *GKN Centrax Gears Ltd v Matbro Ltd* [1976] 2 Lloyd's Rep. 555 (similar decision re claim for loss of repeat orders following delivery of substandard components to industrialist).
[76]   For example, *Wilson v Lancashire & Yorkshire Ry Co* (1861) 9 CBNS 632.
[77]   See e.g. *Ladenbau (G & K) (UK) Ltd v Crawley & de Reya* [1978] 1 W.L.R. 266; also the more recent Scots decision in *Watts v Bell & Scott*, 2007 S.L.T. 665; [2007] CSOH 108.
[78]   On occasion a similar attitude appears in non-commercial cases: see e.g. the product liability case of *Busby v Berkshire Bed Co Ltd* [2018] EWHC 2976 (QB) (bed misconstructed with slight slope: fall from it onto the floor would require peculiar concatenation of circumstances, and not foreseeable).

contractors are generally fixed with knowledge of the facts of business life[79] and also with a fairly detailed familiarity with the minutiae of their own business, this is not so with others'; here the only expectation is that they will understand the "ordinary practices and exigencies of the other's trade or business".[80] This point is readily demonstrated by the Scottish decision in *Balfour Beatty Construction (Scotland) Ltd v Scottish Power Plc*.[81] Electricity suppliers broke their contract by wrongfully interrupting the power to a construction site. As luck would have it this happened during a critical pour of cement, necessitating the abandonment of an entire part structure incorporating that cement. The House of Lords, however, refused to charge this loss to the defenders: as Lord Jauncey put it:

> "It must always be a question of circumstances what one contracting party is presumed to know about the business activities of the other. No doubt the simpler the activity of the one, the more readily can it be inferred that the other would have reasonable knowledge thereof. However, when the activity of A involves complicated construction or manufacturing techniques, I see no reason why B who supplies a commodity that A intends to use in the course of those techniques should be assumed, merely because of the order for the commodity, to be aware of the details of all the techniques undertaken by A and the effect thereupon of any failure of or deficiency in that commodity."[82]

On a similar basis, a number of lost profit cases concerning sales of goods hold **23-026** that even if a claimant can recover, he is normally[83] limited to the usual level of profit concerned.[84] A defaulting commodity seller will thus not normally be liable for loss of profits that would have been made from a resale greatly above the market price;[85] and again, where a laundry boiler was delivered late, the laundry owners recovered for the ordinary profits that would be lost for lack of a suitable boiler, but not for the exceptional profits arising from a special and very lucrative contract which depended on the extra capacity that would have been provided. These latter would have been available only if the sellers had been made aware of their likelihood.[86]

Foreseeability vs acceptance of responsibility as a test of remoteness

As already mentioned above, it is possible to regard foreseeability not so much **23-027** as a criterion of liability in its own right, but as an indication that a contract should

---

[79] So that, for example, a shipowner is taken to be aware that cargo may be highly valuable, and if his ship breaks down large expenses for salvage and general average are apt to be incurred: *Mount Isa Mines Ltd v The Ship "Thor Commander"* [2018] FCA 1326 at [411]–[412].

[80] [1949] A.C. 196 at 224 (Lord Wright).

[81] 1994 SC (HL) 20. See P. Hood, "Remoteness of damage in contract revisited" (1996) 1 Edin. L.Rev. 127.

[82] 1994 SC (HL) 20 at 31–32.

[83] Though not invariably, See *R & H Hall Ltd v WH Pim (Junior) & Co Ltd* (1928) 30 Ll L. Rep. 159 (buyer foreseeably agrees to resell the very goods subject to the contract to a sub-buyer at an unusually high price: when seller defaults, profits held recoverable in the particular circumstances).

[84] In other words profits such as arise under "contracts in accordance with the market, not extravagant and unusual bargains"—*Hall (R & H) Ltd v Pim (WH) (Jr) & Co Ltd* (1928) 33 Com. Cas. 324 at 330 (Lord Dunedin). Cf. *North Sea Energy Holdings NV v Petroleum Authority of Thailand* [1997] 2 Lloyd's Rep. 418 (defaulting buyer of oil: seller cannot claim damages based on profit under unusually cheap supply contract).

[85] See the old case of *Williams v Reynolds* (1865) 6 B & S 495: now encapsulated in the Sale of Goods Act 1979 s.51(2); and cf. *Oxus Gold Plc v Oxus Resources Corp* [2007] EWHC 770 (Comm); [2007] All E.R. (D) 57 (Apr) at [80].

[86] See *Victoria Laundry (Windsor) Ltd v Newman Industries Ltd* [1949] 2 K.B. 528.

be regarded as putting, or not putting, the risk of loss caused by a given event on a particular party in breach. This possibility was referred to in passing in a number of decisions starting in the 1960s,[87] and is (it is suggested) closely related to the rule that a contract may be limited in the kinds of loss against which it is apt to protect the parties.[88]

23-028   After a period of obscurity, this idea was trenchantly vindicated in 2008 by the House of Lords in *The Achilleas*.[89] Time-charterers of a large bulk carrier miscalculated a final voyage and redelivered the vessel nine days late. As it happened, the market was then highly volatile, and the owners had some months earlier fixed a long-term follow-on charter at a rate much higher than that prevailing at the time of redelivery. Because of the delay, they lost this latter charter: and in due course they claimed for the enormous profits thus foregone. Although this loss was specifically found to have been foreseeable, the owners failed to recover their loss in the House of Lords, which (reversing the Court of Appeal[90]) limited their recovery to nine days' hire at the market rate less the charter rate. Lord Hoffmann explained why. It was only logical, he said,[91] that liability should be based on the intention of the parties: and, he went on:

> "If ... one considers what these parties, contracting against the background of market expectations found by the arbitrators, would reasonably have considered the extent of the liability they were undertaking, I think it is clear that they would have considered losses arising from the loss of the following fixture a type or kind of loss for which the charterer was not assuming responsibility. Such a risk would be completely unquantifiable, because although the parties would regard it as likely that the owners would at some time during the currency of the charter enter into a forward fixture, they would have no idea when that would be done or what its length or other terms would be."[92]

23-029   Although *The Achilleas* is a controversial decision,[93] the reasoning behind it has been applied in analogous situations,[94] and indeed in fairly different circumstances too. So a seller of land who breaks a warranty against hidden incumbrances is liable for the difference in value of the land and not for development profits lost, however foreseeably, since this is not the kind of loss for which he should be

---

[87] Notably by Lord Upjohn in *Koufos v C Czarnikow Ltd* [1969] 1 A.C. 350 at 421–422 and by Lord Denning MR and Bridge LJ in *GKN Centrax Gears Ltd v Matbro Ltd* [1976] 2 Lloyd's Rep. 555 at 574, 580.

[88] That is, the rule in *South Australia Asset Management Corp v York Montague Ltd* [1997] A.C. 191,

[89] [2008] UKHL 48; [2009] 1 A.C. 61; E. Peel, "Remoteness Revisited" (2009) 125 L.Q.R. 6; P. Wee, "Contractual interpretation and remoteness" [2010] L.M.C.L.Q. 150. See too *Pindell Ltd v Airasia Bhd* [2010] EWHC 2516 (Comm); [2012] 2 C.L.C. 1 (late return of aircraft under operating lease: loss of sale not a matter for which lessor took responsibility).

[90] [2007] EWCA Civ 901; [2007] 2 Lloyd's Rep. 555.

[91] [2008] UKHL 48; [2009] 1 A.C. 61 at [12]. See too Baroness Hale at [92] (question is "not only whether the parties must be taken to have had this type of loss within their contemplation when the contract was made, but also whether they must be taken to have had liability for this type of loss within their contemplation then. In other words, is the charterer to be taken to have undertaken legal responsibility for this type of loss?").

[92] See [2008] UKHL 48; [2009] 1 A.C. 61 at [23].

[93] The courts in Singapore have, for example, studiedly refused to follow it: *Out of the Box Pte Ltd v Wanin Industries Pte Ltd* [2013] SGCA 15; [2013] 2 S.L.R. 363. But the case was cited with apparent approval by Campbell JA in the New South Wales Court of Appeal in *Evans & Associates v European Bank Ltd* [2009] NSWCA 67; (2009) 255 A.L.R. 171 at [56]–[58].

[94] For example, in *The Great Creation* [2014] EWHC 3978 (Comm); [2015] 1 Lloyd's Rep. 315 Cooke J applied it by analogy to early redelivery of a time-chartered vessel, thus cutting out damages relating to the period after the relevant charter expired.

regarded as having taken responsibility;[95] and the issuer of a convertible bond accepts responsibility for differences in market value, but not for trading profits, in the event that it is tardy in allowing conversion.[96] Furthermore, on the correct basis that what is sauce for the goose should be sauce for the gander, the Court of Appeal has since *The Achilleas* made the obvious point that the principle contained in it may apply as much in favour of the claimant who wishes to increase the amount of any recovery as of the defendant who wishes to restrict it. It thus held that, by holding that, where a breach of contract consisted in failure to do something specifically aimed at reducing a given danger, there might be recovery despite a finding of fact that materialisation of the danger had been extremely unlikely.[97]

On the other hand, it is now clear that the decision in *The Achilleas* represents a **23-030** special case rather than any rule. The situations where it is applied are likely to be unusual ones where there is some specific reason to disapply the normal "contemplation" standard.[98] Thus in *Sylvia Shipping Co Ltd v Progress Bulk Carriers Ltd*[99] a vessel under time charter was delivered, rather than redelivered, late; the owners as a result lost a lucrative voyage charter. Although the case was in a sense the exact converse of *The Achilleas*, Hamblen J had no hesitation in upholding an arbitral award of damages for the lost profits. Regarding the *Achilleas* principle as best suited to

> "those relatively rare cases where the application of the general test leads or may lead to an unquantifiable, unpredictable, uncontrollable or disproportionate liability or where there is clear evidence that such a liability would be contrary to market understanding and expectations"[100]

he proceeded to find no such feature in the case before him to preclude recovery of an otherwise foreseeable loss. In similar vein, the Court of Appeal in *John Grimes Partnership Ltd v Gubbins*[101] approved this view when it upheld a decision that road contractors were liable in full when their delay in completing a relatively low-value contract caused a very costly, but nevertheless entirely foreseeable, delay to a housing development project. There was, said Sir David Keene,

---

[95] *Upton Park Homes Ltd v Macdonalds* [2009] CSOH 159; [2010] P.N.L.R. 12. See too *Midlothian Council v Bracewell Stirling Architects* [2017] CSOH 87; [2017] P.N.L.R. 33 at [34].

[96] *Prakash Industries Ltd v Peter Beck Und Partner* [2022] EWHC 754 (Comm) esp at [188].

[97] *Siemens Building Technologies FE Ltd v Supershield Ltd* [2010] EWCA Civ 7; [2010] 1 Lloyd's Rep. 349

[98] A point made trenchantly in *Sylvia Shipping Co Ltd v Progress Bulk Carriers Ltd* [2010] EWHC 542 (Comm); [2010] 1 C.L.C. 470 at [40] (Hamblen J). See too *Borealis AB v Geogas Trading SA* [2010] EWHC 2789 (Comm) at [48] (Gross LJ); also *The Amer Energy* [2009] 1 Lloyd's Rep. 293 at [17] and *John Grimes Partnership Ltd v Gubbins* [2013] EWCA Civ 37; [2013] P.N.L.R. 17 at [24], where Flaux J and Sir David Keene respectively denied that *The Achilleas* had introduced any revolutionary change; also *Louis Dreyfus Commodities Suisse SA v MT Maritime Management BV* [2015] EWHC 2505 (Comm); [2016] 1 Lloyd's Rep. 197 at [53]–[55] (Males J). In retrospect, the suggestion in E. Peel, "Remoteness Revisited" (2009) 125 L.Q.R. 6 at 12 that "[i]t may well be that the decision in *The Achilleas* does not have a profound effect in practice" has turned out prophetic.

[99] [2010] EWHC 542 (Comm); [2010] 1 C.L.C. 470

[100] [2010] EWHC 542 (Comm); [2010] 1 C.L.C. 470 at [40]. See too *The MTM Hong Kong* [2015] EWHC 2505 (Comm); [2016] 1 Lloyd's Rep. 197, refusing to cap damages for repudiation of a voyage charter by reference to the would-be duration of that charter.

[101] [2013] EWCA Civ 37; [2013] P.N.L.R. 17; see J. Goodwin, "A Remotely Interesting Case" (2013) 129 L.Q.R. 485.

"nothing to take this case out of the conventional approach to remoteness of damage in contract cases".[102]

III. HADLEY V BAXENDALE—THE "SECOND LIMB": LOSS IN THE CONTEMPLATION OF THE PARTIES

Generally

23-031   Alderson B in *Hadley*'s case, it will be remembered, said that a loss might be recoverable even if not foreseeable in the ordinary course of things, if it was

"such as may reasonably be supposed to have been in the contemplation of both parties, at the time they made the contract, as the probable result of the breach of it".[103]

23-032   So in an old case a carrier, having been told that goods were destined as samples to a trade fair, was liable for the loss of business when he failed to deliver them on time;[104] and in a more recent transport case another carrier was liable for loss of profits caused by late delivery of tender documents when, told of the circumstances, it assured its client of prompt delivery and then failed to provide it.[105] Again, if in a contract for the sale of goods the seller is told that the buyer is buying for resale to a particular person, this may suffice to make the seller liable for loss of profits on the subsale[106] or damages payable to the sub-buyer[107] in the event of non-delivery, or the costs of litigation incurred when the goods transpire to be substandard.[108] In the case of late delivery a seller may similarly be liable for loss of profit[109] or compensation payable to the sub-buyer.[110] So too where a construction contractor is late in clearing what it knows to be a development site, it will be liable for extra project finance and management costs incurred as a result.[111] Where a person is party to two associated contracts it is likely that the parties will have contemplated that breach of one will lead to non-performance of the other.[112]

23-033   The rationale for requiring loss otherwise unforeseeable to have been in the parties' contemplation in order to make it recoverable is not hard to see. A party want-

---

[102] [2013] EWCA Civ 37; [2013] P.N.L.R. 17 at [31].

[103] *Hadley v Baxendale* (1854) 9 Ex 341 at 356. See too, for other statements, *Victoria Laundry (Windsor) Ltd v Newman Industries Ltd* [1949] 2 K.B. 528 at 537–539 (Asquith LJ); *Koufos v C Czarnikow Ltd* [1969] 1 A.C. 350 at 421 (Lord Upjohn).

[104] *Simpson v London & NW Ry Co* (1876) 1 Q.B.D. 274. See too *Montevideo Gas Co v Clan Line Ltd* (1921) 37 T.L.R. 866 (knowledge by carriers that coal desperately needed by consignees to make gas).

[105] *Cornwall Gravel Co Ltd v Purolator Courier Ltd* (1979) 83 D.L.R. (3d) 267 (affd [1980] 2 SCR 118).

[106] E.g. *Patrick v Russo-British Grain Export Co* [1927] 2 K.B. 535; *Hall Ltd v Pim Junior & Co Ltd* (1927) 30 Ll. L.L. Rep. 159.

[107] E.g. *Grébert-Borgnis v Nugent* (1885) 15 Q.B.D. 85.

[108] See *Hammond & Co v Bussey* (1888) L.R. 20 Q.B.D. 79 at 87–90 (Lord Esher MR).

[109] *Hydraulic Engineering Co v McHaffie* (1878) 4 Q.B.D. 670 (where the goods were wanted for incorporation into goods being manufactured for the third party).

[110] E.g. *Contigroup Inc v Glencore AG* [2004] EWHC 2750 (Comm); [2005] 1 Lloyd's Rep. 241.

[111] *Barkby Real Estate Developments Ltd v Cornerstone Telecommunications Infrastructure Ltd* [2022] EWHC 1892 (TCC) at [101] ff.

[112] *Attorney General of the Virgin Islands v Global Water Associates Ltd* [2020] UKPC 18; [2021] A.C. 23 (two contracts by government with company: one to build an installation, the other to run it once built; breach of building contract held to carry liability for loss of profits from other contract). So too where the parties expressly contemplate assignment of the benefit of a contract, this may render recoverable damage foreseeably likely to be suffered by the assignee but not the assignor: *Orchard*

ing protection against losses not obviously in prospect in the event of breach can be expected to inform his co-contractor of the possibility that they may happen, and thus allow him to consider if he wants to contract at all and, if so, on what terms.[113] Thus in *Hadley v Baxendale*[114] itself the result might, it seems, have been different had the millers told the carriers before the contract was concluded that their mill would stand idle until the replacement shaft arrived.[115] Similarly, while damages for failure to convey or give good title to land will not normally include lost development profits or the like,[116] they may do so where the seller knows specifically what the buyer envisages doing.[117]

At first sight the second limb of *Hadley v Baxendale* seems neatly to parallel the **23-034** first. Indeed, in theory one can by juxtaposing them produce a single composite rule of remoteness: the criterion of liability is what might have been contemplated *taking into account the parties' actual knowledge of the specific circumstances*.[118] The practice, however, is not as straightforward as one might think.

In particular, while under the first limb of *Hadley's* case the foreseeability of a **23-035** particular loss is in practice normally determinative of its recoverability, in the second limb a good deal less weight is placed on fact of the parties' awareness of the surrounding facts even where proved. So as early as 1868, Willes J famously said that a lawyer travelling abroad to take up a well-paid brief could not simply by mentioning this fact at booking fix a shipping company with potential liability for the loss of the brief fee were he delayed:[119] and no doubt today the same would go for an interviewee seeking through a casual remark to make a taxi company liable for his failure to reach the interview on time and thereby land an enormously lucrative job.[120]

By way of illustration of the above, the courts have thus consistently held that **23-036** pretty specific knowledge must be shown for a claimant to be able to invoke the second limb, and that little short of this will do. For instance, in carriage contracts where late delivery will frustrate a very lucrative sale, it is not enough to mention that a sale may be aborted: the deal at risk must be described in considerable detail

---

Plaza Management Co Ltd v Balfour Beatty Regional Construction Ltd [2022] EWHC 1490 (TCC); [2022] P.N.L.R. 24 at [74] (Morris J).

113 A point well made in a number of cases: e.g. *Cory v Thames Ironworks Co* (1868) L.R. 3 Q.B. 181 at 190–191 (Blackburn J; also Pollock CB at 197); *British Columbia Sawmills v Nettleship* (1868) L.R. 3 C.P. 499 at 508 (Willes J) and *Seven Seas Properties Ltd v Al-Essa* [1993] 1 W.L.R. 1083 at 1088.

114 (1854) 9 Ex 341.

115 "[I]n the great multitude of cases of millers sending off broken shafts to third persons by a carrier under ordinary circumstances, such consequences would not, in all probability, have occurred; and these special circumstances were here never communicated by the plaintiffs to the defendants." (1854) 9 Ex 341 at 356.

116 *Diamond v Campbell-Jones* [1961] Ch. 22 and *Seven Seas Properties Ltd v Al-Essa* [1993] 1 W.L.R. 1083 being cases in point, as is the carefully-argued *Castle Constructions Pty Ltd v Fekala Pty Ltd* [2006] NSWCA 133; (2006) 65 N.S.W.L.R. 648 at [45]–[46]. So too, conversely, with a vendor's lost profits where the purchaser defaults: *Strategic Property Ltd v O'Se* [2009] EWHC 3512 (Ch).

117 Such cases are not very common: but one such is *Cottrill v Steyning & Littlehampton Building Society* [1966] 1 W.L.R. 753.

118 See Lord Walker's views in *Jackson v Royal Bank of Scotland Plc* [2005] UKHL 3; [2005] 1 W.L.R. 377 at [49]; and the other cases referred to at fn.36 above.

119 *British Columbia Sawmills Co v Nettleship* (1868) L.R. 3 C.P. 499 at 510. Cf. *Horne v Midland Ry Co* (1872) L.R. 7 C.P. 583; and also *Kemp v Intasun Holidays Ltd* [1987] F.T.L.R. 234.

120 Compare Akenhead J's similar *jeu d'esprit* in *Aldgate Construction Co Ltd v Unibar Plumbing & Heating Ltd* [2010] EWHC 1063 (TCC) at [22] (based on a journey to buy a lottery ticket). More generally see *Chitty on Contracts*, 34th edn (London: Sweet & Maxwell, 2022), para.29-142.

before the carrier will be liable for it.[121] Again, in the case of the delivery to a timber company of defective equipment, it has been held that even if the supplier does know the general use to which the equipment is to be put this will not without more make him liable if the equipment's failure causes the loss of very large logging profits.[122]

23-037   Similarly, a defaulting vendor of land will not be liable for the buyer's lost development profits merely because he knows the buyer is a property developer (and thus might be expected to infer that some such profits might be in the offing): the proposed deal must be made known to him in at least some detail. So in *Seven Seas Properties Ltd v Al-Essa*[123] a buyer who had agreed to resell a house in a back-to-back property transaction was unsuccessful in his claim for the gain lost when the vendor failed to convey despite the vendor's admitted knowledge that the buyer was in the property development business.

23-038   Why this restrictive attitude? Older cases on occasion suggested by way of explanation that liability for a given loss depended not so much on knowledge as on implicit agreement by the promisor to make it good in the event of breach;[124] but this view of the matter is somewhat illogical[125] and now rightly discountenanced.[126] A better explanation, it is suggested, can be derived from the relevance of acceptance of responsibility. In contrast to ordinary losses (where it is a fair inference that parties undertake responsibility for consequences of breach that are foreseeable to any reasonable contractor), with unusual losses the connection between contemplation and responsibility is less clear. It is simply less plausible to infer that, without more, a contractor is prepared to underwrite the consequences of all events that in the light of his knowledge he might have contemplated.

23-039   It is therefore suggested that the proper test is that propounded by Goff J in a 1981 case, as follows:

> "have the facts in question come to the defendant's knowledge in such circumstances that a reasonable person in the shoes of the defendant would, if he had considered the matter at the time of making the contract, have contemplated that, in the event of a breach by him, such facts were to be taken into account when considering his responsibility for loss suffered by the plaintiff as a result of such breach[?]"[127]

---

[121] See the old case of *Horne v Midland Ry Co* (1872) L.R. 7 C.P. 583. Contrast *Panalpina International Transport Ltd v Densil Underwear Ltd* [1981] 1 Lloyd's Rep. 187 (carriers told that goods required for Christmas market: liable for loss of that market when goods delayed).

[122] *Monroe Equipment Sales Ltd v Canadian Forest Products Ltd* (1961) 29 D.L.R. (2d) 730.

[123] [1993] 1 W.L.R. 1083; also the earlier (and very similar) *Diamond v Campbell-Jones* [1961] Ch. 22. Contrast, however, *Cottrill v Steyning & Littlehampton Building Society* [1966] 1 W.L.R. 753.

[124] For example, Willes J did in *British Columbia Sawmills Co v Nettleship* (1868) L.R. 3 C.P. 499 at 509 (must be "contemplated at the time of the contract that [the defendant] should be liable for all the consequences in the event of a breach.").

[125] Illogical because a contractor promises performance; payment of compensation in the event of lack of it is the subject matter not of a promise but of a secondary court-awarded remedy.

[126] See e.g. *Koufos v C Czarnikow Ltd* [1969] 1 A.C. 350 at 421–422 (Lord Upjohn), and *GKN Centrax Gears Ltd v Matbro Ltd* [1976] 2 Lloyd's Rep. 555 at 574, 580 (Lord Denning MR and Bridge LJ); *The Pegase* [1981] 1 Lloyd's Rep. 175 at 183–184 (Goff J). But note a rearguard action in A. Kramer, Remoteness: New Problems with the Old Test, in D. Saidov and R. Cunnington (eds), *Contract Damages: Domestic and International Perspectives* (Oxford: Hart Publishing, 2008), Ch.12.

[127] See *The Pegase* [1981] 1 Lloyd's Rep. 175 at 183 (Goff J). See too, for a similar formulation, *Supershield Ltd v Siemens Building Technologies FE Ltd* [2010] EWCA Civ 7; [2010] 1 C.L.C. 241 at [40] (Toulson LJ); and *Mulvenna v Royal Bank of Scotland Plc* [2003] EWCA Civ 1112; [2004] C.P. Rep. 8 at [24]–[26] Waller LJ).

This view of the matter was adopted in *Seven Seas Properties Ltd v Al-Essa*,[128]   **23-040**
where it was held that a vendor of property was not liable to the buyer for a lost
resale. The reason, it was said, was that it would have been necessary to show that
the loss was one the defendant

"was on notice might be occasioned by the breach *such that he may fairly be held, in
entering into his contract, to have accepted the risk*".[129]

Similarly, in a much earlier Canadian decision a timber company sought to
recover large sums in lost logging profits from the supplier of a defective tractor
on the basis of the latter's knowledge of the company's purpose in leasing it. The
claim failed, Miller CJ making the point that:

"Surely, no reasonable person could contemplate, under the circumstances of the renting
of this machine, that the lessor of one second-hand tractor was underwriting and virtually insuring the removal of all this pulpwood from the bush."[130]

The relevance of a defendant's acceptance of responsibility may also explain a   **23-041**
further point; namely that to be recoverable under the second limb of *Hadley v
Baxendale* loss must it seems be shown to be within the contemplation of both parties and not solely the contract-breaker.[131] Once one accepts that such acceptance
of responsibility must presumably be consensual, it is not hard to see why courts
should be reluctant to infer it from the knowledge of one party alone.

IV.   HADLEY V BAXENDALE: THE RELATION BETWEEN THE TWO LIMBS

The first limb as a presumptive measure

The rule in *Hadley v Baxendale* is all too easily seen as creating a crude   **23-042**
claimant's option: either the limited loss arising "naturally, according to the usual
course of things", or, if yielding a greater measure of recovery, any losses within
the parties' particular contemplation. Nevertheless, however useful as a rule of
thumb, this formulation is not strictly accurate. The proper analysis, it is now clear,
is one of a presumptive measure, open to displacement (among other cases) where,
given what the parties knew and envisaged, some different measure of recovery
must have been within their contemplation.

This is significant, in that it means that the choice of measure is the court's and   **23-043**
not the claimant's; from which it equally follows that the second limb—damage in
the parties' contemplation—may be invoked just as much as by the defendant who
wants to reduce exposure as by the claimant who wishes to increase recovery.
Devlin J made this point clearly in 1950:

"Damages which arise under the so-called 'second rule' in *Hadley v Baxendale* are
sometimes referred to as if they were an increased sum which the plaintiff could obtain
if he could show 'special circumstances', or as if the rule embodied a measure of dam-

---

[128] [1993] 1 W.L.R. 1083.
[129] [1993] 1 W.L.R. 1083 at 1088 (italics supplied); followed in *Strategic Property Ltd v O'Se* [2009]
EWHC 3512 (Ch) at [38].
[130] *Munroe Equipment Sales Ltd v Canadian Forest Products Ltd* (1961) 29 D.L.R. 2d 730 at 740.
[131] See *Quirk v Thomas* [1916] 1 K.B. 516 at 534 (Phillimore LJ); *Koufos v C Czarnikow Ltd* [1969] 1
A.C. 350 at 424 (Lord Upjohn); *Kpohraror v Woolwich Building Society* [1996] 4 All E.R. 119 at
127–128 (Evans LJ); *Jackson v Royal Bank of Scotland Plc* [2000] C.L.C. 1457 at [29] (Potter LJ).

age specially beneficial to the plaintiff which he could invoke if he fulfilled the necessary conditions. It is, no doubt, true that it generally operates in favour of a plaintiff rather than against him, but I think that it is capable of doing either."[132]

23-044   The Court of Appeal's decision in *Bence Graphics International Ltd v Fasson UK Ltd*[133] exemplifies this proposition. Buyers purchased plastic film which, as both parties knew perfectly well, was intended to be made into identification decals for sale to container owners. The sellers supplied inferior film worth much less than that stipulated: as it happened, however, the buyers were able to use it without mishap, and faced only sporadic and small claims from container owners. The buyers pressed for an award of the difference in value between sound film and that supplied, which they would normally be entitled to without regard to their subsequent use of the film.[134] However, it was held that any prima facie reason to award this amount had been displaced because of the parties' specific contemplation of the use to which the film was destined,[135] and that the proper measure of recovery was that under the second limb of *Hadley v Baxendale*: namely, the value of claims actually brought against the buyers.

The first limb: The problem of putative loss

23-045   It may well happen that a claimant's actual loss was neither foreseeable so as to come within the first limb of *Hadley v Baxendale*, nor within the parties' contemplation within the second; but that the defendant might nevertheless have contemplated some other, less unusual, damage that did not in fact occur. What should happen here? The position, it seems, is that the amount of the foreseeable loss may be recovered, despite the argument that it was never in fact suffered.

23-046   The issue arose straightforwardly in the early decision in *Cory v Thames Ironworks Co Ltd*.[136] In breach of contract, sellers delivered a floating derrick late. Unknown to the sellers, the buyers had wanted it for an unusual and unforeseeable—but very lucrative—purpose. It being clear that they could not recover in respect of this, they claimed instead for the profits that they could otherwise have made from a more normal use as part of a coal hulk. The claim succeeded. The later Court of Appeal decision in *Victoria Laundry (Windsor) Ltd v Newman Industries*

---

[132] *Biggin v Permanite Ltd* [1951] 1 K.B. 422 at 435–436. For other statements of this principle, see Lord Pearce in *Koufos v C Czarnikow Ltd* [1969] 1 A.C. 350 at 416, and Otton LJ in *Bence Graphics International Ltd v Fasson UK Ltd* [1998] Q.B. 87 at 99.

[133] [1998] Q.B. 87. See too *Louis Dreyfus Trading Ltd v Reliance Trading Ltd* [2004] EWHC 525 (Comm); [2004] 2 Lloyd's Rep. 243 at [25] (Andrew Smith J); and the perceptive N. Tamblyn, "Damages under string contracts for sale of goods" [2009] J.B.L. 1.

[134] See *Slater v Hoyle & Smith Ltd* [1920] 2 K.B. 11 (defective cloth supplied, but treated and resold by buyer at no discount: buyer still recovers difference in value).

[135] Thus, providing a possible distinction with *Slater v Hoyle & Smith Ltd* [1920] 2 K.B. 11, above, where (it is suggested) the absence of specific contemplation meant that the prima facie measure applied by default. See *Bence Graphics International Ltd v Fasson UK Ltd* [1998] Q.B. 87 at 99 (Otton LJ) and *Louis Dreyfus Trading Ltd v Reliance Trading Ltd* [2004] EWHC 525 (Comm); [2004] 2 Lloyd's Rep. 243 at [21] (Andrew Smith J) (though cf. the doubts of Auld LJ in *Bence*: [1998] Q.B. 87 at 102–103). That *Bence* is limited to where a particular subsale or subsequent use was specifically contemplated is suggested by Christopher Clarke J in *Choil Trading SA v Sahara Energy Resources Ltd* [2010] EWHC 374 (Comm) at [128] and seemingly decided by Moulder J in *BP Oil International Ltd v Glencore Energy UK Ltd* [2022] EWHC 499 (Comm) at [264].

[136] (1868) L.R. 3 Q.B. 181.

Ltd,[137] another late delivery case, raised much the same question. Sellers delayed in delivering a boiler to a laundry business, who in fact needed it to carry out a special and highly profitable contract. The laundry, while it could not recover for the loss of this contract, did recover the ordinary profits that it might have been expected to make from the boiler during the period of delay.[138]

V.   HADLEY V BAXENDALE: THE MEANING OF LOSS IN THE PARTIES' CONTEMPLATION

The degree of specificity required

It is now clear that, as in the case of tort,[139] what is required is foreseeability of **23-047** damage of the kind that has occurred:[140] the claimant does not have to go further and show that the defendant might have foreseen the precise form the loss took, nor the exact concatenation of events leading to it. The point is neatly illustrated by *Great Lakes SS Co v Maple Leaf Milling Co*.[141] In breach of contract, charterers failed to reduce the draught of a ship by lightering on arrival in shallow waters: as a result an abandoned anchor on the bottom fouled and damaged the ship. The Privy Council smartly saw off a plea that whereas ordinary grounding damage was foreseeable, this was not. "If," said Lord Carson, "grounding takes place in breach of contract, the precise nature of the damage incurred by grounding is immaterial."[142] So too, where contractors in breach of contract designed a building with over-inflammable cladding, they were held liable for maintaining a constant fire-watch while it was being replaced: it was enough that the necessity for fire precautions generally had been foreseeable.[143]

The extent of the damage

For many years the reach of *Hadley v Baxendale*, however straightforward in **23-048** general, remained unclear in one troublesome respect. In particular, did it apply to limit a defendant's liability where, although the *existence* of circumstances likely to cause a given head of loss might have been within the parties' contemplation, the *extent* or *seriousness* of the resulting damage was entirely unforeseeable? Logically it should, since a contractor's interest in avoiding unforeseeably extensive liability unless warned of the prospect of it was much the same whether what was involved was an entirely unforeseeable event or a foreseeable one with unforeseeably disastrous results. On the other hand, practicality clearly suggested otherwise. While deciding whether a given event was foreseeable was relatively easy, the factual difficulties of deciding just how much of a given loss was, or was not, foreseeable were, to say the least, formidable.

---

[137] [1949] 2 K.B. 528.

[138] See in particular [1949] 2 K.B. 528 at 542 (Asquith LJ).

[139] See *Clerk & Lindsell on Torts*, 24th edn (London: Sweet & Maxwell, 2023), para.2-154 ff and cases such as *Hughes v Lord Advocate* [1963] A.C. 837.

[140] *Parsons (H) (Livestock) Ltd v Uttley Ingham & Co Ltd* [1978] Q.B. 791 at 813 (Scarman LJ); also *Great Lakes SS Co v Maple Leaf Milling Co* [1924] 4 D.L.R. 1101 at 1106.

[141] [1924] 4 D.L.R. 1101.

[142] See [1924] 4 D.L.R. 1101 at 1106. *Compare McAlpine Grant ILCO Ltd v AFR Refrigeration Ltd* [2020] EWHC 106 (QB) (defective refrigerator: liability for spoilage of contents despite unforeseeable failure by user to install alarm).

[143] See *Martlet Homes Ltd v Mulalley & Co Ltd* [2022] EWHC 1813 (TCC) at [415]; 203 Con. L.R. 125.

23-049   For better or worse, it is now clear that the courts have chosen practicality over logic. What matters is whether the damage was foreseeable: the fact that in the event it was unforeseeably serious is irrelevant. The point was first established by Rees J in *Vacwell Ltd v BDH Ltd*.[144] There, suppliers of a volatile and potentially explosive chemical failed to provide adequate safety instructions to the buyers, who were industrialists. The result was an enormous explosion that largely destroyed the buyers' premises. Rees J, having made a clear finding of fact that while explosion was a foreseeable hazard, the kind of catastrophe that actually occurred was not, nevertheless held it appropriate to give judgment for the whole loss.[145] And in 1978 the Court of Appeal confirmed that this approach was the right one in *Parsons (H) (Livestock) Ltd v Uttley Ingham & Co Ltd*.[146] There it decided, on the basis of *Vacwell*, that where defectively constructed pig-feed hoppers carried a risk of causing illness in pigs, the suppliers were liable for all losses even though a group of pigs unforeseeably died as a result. What mattered, said Scarman LJ, was whether the parties had "contemplated as a serious possibility the type of consequence, not necessarily the specific consequence, that ensued upon breach".[147]

23-050   Since the above cases it has been taken as read that all that is necessary is that the "type or kind" of loss be within the parties' contemplation:[148] if it is the claimant recovers as a matter of course.[149] Thus where a bank breaks its customer's confidence in a way likely to affect the latter's profits, it will be liable for all such lost profits despite any argument that only short-term losses might strictly have been foreseeable;[150] and the same goes for negligent investment advice by a bank.[151] So too where a vendor fails to convey land and resale by the purchaser is foreseeable, the lost opportunity to resell at a premium to a special interest purchaser is compensable whether or not specifically in the parties' contemplation.[152]

23-051   Despite the clarification introduced by *Vacwell*,[153] one area remained uncertain until much later: if a claimant's loss resulting from a breach of contract was increased because his own impecuniosity, could this be something for which the defendant was liable? An old tort case, *The Liesbosch*,[154] suggested a negative answer, and despite the holding in *Vacwell* some contract cases followed suit[155]

---

[144] [1971] 1 Q.B. 88.

[145] "I am unable to find that because the damage to property was much greater than could have been reasonably foreseen, it was too remote to be recoverable in law": Rees J at [1971] 1 Q.B. 88 at 107.

[146] [1978] Q.B. 791.

[147] [1978] Q.B. 791 at 813. For a similar statement see *Asamera Oil Corp Ltd v Sea Oil & General Corp* [1979] 1 S.C.R. 633 at 655 (Estey J).

[148] The words are Staughton J's: *The Rio Claro* [1987] 2 Lloyd's Rep. 173 at 175.

[149] Representative cases: *Brown v KMR Services Ltd (formerly HG Poland (Agencies) Ltd)* [1995] 4 All E.R. 598 at 620–621 (Stuart-Smith LJ); *Banque Bruxelles Lambert SA v Eagle Star Insurance Co Ltd* [1995] Q.B. 375 at 405 (Bingham MR); *Homsy v Murphy* (1997) 73 P. & C.R. 26 at 45 (Hobhouse LJ); *Jackson v Royal Bank of Scotland* [2005] UKHL 3; [2005] 1 W.L.R. 377; *The Achilleas* [2008] UKHL 48; [2009] 1 A.C. 61 at [21] (Lord Hoffmann); and more recently, *Martlet Homes Ltd v Mulalley & Co Ltd* [2022] EWHC 1813 (TCC) at [416]; 203 Con. L.R. 125 (necessity for fire precautions foreseeable to fitter of flammable cladding: fact that very extensive, and expensive, measures necessary was irrelevant).

[150] *Jackson v Royal Bank of Scotland Plc* [2005] UKHL 3; [2005] 1 W.L.R. 377.

[151] *Rubenstein v HSBC Bank Plc* [2012] EWCA Civ 1184; [2012] 2 C.L.C. 747

[152] See *Homsy v Murphy* (1997) 73 P. & C.R. 26 (esp Hobhouse LJ at 45).

[153] *Vacwell Ltd v BDH Ltd* [1971] 1 Q.B. 88.

[154] [1933] A.C. 449

[155] E.g. *Ramwade Ltd v W J Emson & Co Ltd* [1987] RTR 72 (brokers who failed to insure truck

(though not all[156]). Logic, however, dictates that a defendant, whether in contract or tort, should take his unpredictably vulnerable victim as he finds him, and that the impecunious victim should not be in a special category as regards damages.[157] In 2003 this point was recognised in the tort context, and *The Liesbosch* finally discredited.[158] And, as with tort, so with contract: so in 2007 it was duly confirmed that a business furnished with inadequate business interruption cover because of its insurance brokers' breach of contract could recover all its losses, including those due to the parlous state of its own cash-flow.[159]

A further problem of principle remains, however. How can the courts' professed **23-052** disregard of the extent of a claimant's loss be reconciled with decisions like *Cory v Thames Ironworks Co Ltd*[160] or the *Victoria Laundry* case,[161] allowing recovery for ordinary but not extraordinary loss of profits? Why are extraordinary profits in such a case not regarded as just profits writ large? The answer, it is suggested, is that despite Alderson B's reference in *Hadley v Baxendale*[162] to "losses" in the contemplation of the parties, what is strictly relevant is whether the parties contemplated the *events* that caused a given loss.[163] Thus in *Victoria Laundry* the laundry failed to recover for its enhanced profits because they arose from an event outside the contemplation of the parties; namely, its intention to expand its operations by using the new boiler. By contrast, in *Parsons v Uttley Ingham*,[164] a typical case going the other way, the relevant event was the injurious affectation of the plaintiff's pigs, which was foreseeable. As a result the fact that the consequences might have been unforeseeably severe was irrelevant.

VI.   A Special Case: Interest and Late Payment of Money

It was once thought that, in the absence of a stipulation for interest, the only **23-053** pecuniary remedy for the late payment of money was statutory interest under what is now s.35A of the Senior Courts Act.[165] Today, however, this is no longer the case. Since 2007 it has been clear that if money is paid late in breach of contract, and the payee incurs actual interest payments (whether simple or compound) or loses deposit interest,[166] these sums may be recovered as damages, provided they fall

---

comprehensively not liable for costs of hiring replacement for uninsured vehicle, since these due to owners' impecuniosity).

[156] E.g. *Robbins of Putney Ltd v Meek* [1971] RTR 345 (where buyer repudiates sale, impecuniosity may justify seller in selling at otherwise inopportune time). Compare the similar sentiments of a then maverick Denning LJ 60 years ago: see *Trans Trust SpRL v Danubian Trading Co Ltd* [1952] 2 Q.B. 297 at 306.

[157] E.g. *Clippens Oil Co v Edinburgh & District Water Trustees* [1907] A.C. 291 at 303 (Lord Wright).

[158] See *Lagden v O'Connor* [2003] UKHL 64; [2004] 1 A.C. 1067, esp at [90].

[159] *Arbory Group Ltd v West Craven Insurance Services (A Firm)* [2007] P.N.L.R. 23.

[160] (1868) L.R. 3 Q.B. 181.

[161] *Victoria Laundry (Windsor) Ltd v Newman Industries Ltd* [1949] 2 K.B. 528.

[162] (1854) 9 Ex 341.

[163] Compare *Hall Ltd v Pim Junior & Co Ltd* (1927) 30 Ll. L.L. Rep. 159 at 162, where Lord Shaw said that where lost subsales were claimed against a seller in default, it had to be shown that the relevant contracts must be "contracts in accordance with the market, not extravagant and unusual bargains". The use of the word "contracts" is possibly instructive: it suggests that what mattered was not losses as such, but whether the contracts giving rise to those losses were foreseeable.

[164] [1978] Q.B. 791.

[165] Or its county court and arbitration equivalents, s.69 of the County Courts Act 1984 and s.49 of the Arbitration Act 1996.

[166] On what the claimant has to prove in this connection, see *Equitas Ltd v Walsham Brothers & Co Ltd*

within the appropriate *Hadley v Baxendale* limb.[167] This is significant, since (save in arbitration) the statutory power is limited to simple interest,[168] and it now seems clear that businessmen can be expected to foresee that business partners kept out of their money will in the ordinary course of things have to pay compound overdraft interest at a commercial rate applicable to their status.[169]

VII. DELIBERATE BREACHES AND LOSS DELIBERATELY CAUSED

23-054   Virtually every case decided under *Hadley v Baxendale*[170] has involved the consequences of an inadvertent breach of contract. Should deliberate or grossly negligent breaches be differently treated? It would seem that the answer is "no". Despite a respectable European tradition of doing just this,[171] there has never been any suggestion that the nature of the breach makes any difference in English law.

23-055   Nevertheless, even if deliberate *breaches* are not singled out for special treatment, it is arguable that deliberately caused *losses* should be. A potential defendant has no legitimate interest in being protected from extended liability here: and although there seems no authority on the matter, there is much to be said for extending into the law of contract the clear rule in tort[172] that a wrongdoer is liable in full for losses deliberately caused to a victim without regard to whether they were otherwise foreseeable.

[2013] EWHC 3264 (Comm); [2014] P.N.L.R. 8 at [107]–[126] and *Sagicor Bank Jamaica Ltd v Seaton* [2022] UKPC 48; [2023] 2 All E.R. 81. Essentially, actual financial loss must be established: the court will not allow the *Sempra* jurisdiction to be used to obtain interest as damages as of course.

[167] The process was twofold. In *Wadsworth v Lydell* [1981] 1 W.L.R. 598 the Court of Appeal allowed such claims under the second limb, where the likelihood of such losses was within the parties' specific contemplation; and in *Sempra Metals Ltd (formerly Metallgesellschaft Ltd) v Inland Revenue Commissioners* [2007] UKHL 34; [2008] 1 A.C. 561 at [92]–[100] the House of Lords extended the principle to cover claims under the first limb as well.

[168] And also excludes cases where the claimant pays in full before proceedings are issued: *President of India v La Pintada Cia Navegacion SA* [1985] A.C. 104.

[169] See e.g. *Peacock v Imagine Property Developments Ltd* [2018] EWHC 1113 (TCC).

[170] (1854) 9 Ex 341.

[171] Thus Art.1231-3 of the French Code Civil denies protection against unforeseeable losses where the defendant's breach is "*due à une faute lourde ou dolosive*". See too para.9.503 of the *Principles of European Contract Law*, denying protection to deliberate or grossly negligent contract-breakers.

[172] See particularly Lord Lindley in *Quinn v Leathem* [1901] A.C. 495 at 537 ("The intention to injure the plaintiff negatives all excuses and disposes of any question of remoteness of damage"); also *Ansett (Operations) Pty Ltd v Australian Federation of Air Pilots* [1991] 2 VR 636 at 649.

CHAPTER 24

DAMAGES: CAUSATION, MITIGATION AND THE CONDUCT OF THE CLAIMANT

Introduction This chapter deals with three important but related issues relating **24-001** to damages for breach of contract: causation, mitigation, and the effect of the claimant's own fault on the amount he can recover.

I. CAUSATION

The general rule: Recovery only for loss that would not have occurred but for the defendant's breach

Reflecting the function of damages as putting the claimant in the position it would **24-002** have occupied had the contract been performed,[1] a claimant seeking damages for breach of contract must, as is the case in tort,[2] show not only the breach and the loss, but a causal connection between the two.[3] Generally speaking this involves a showing that, but for the breach, the loss in respect of which he claims damages would not have been suffered. A neat example is the old decision in *The Europa*.[4] Sugar on a ship became contaminated owing to a cause for which the carriers were not responsible: the contamination was then made worse by the shipowners' breach of the contract of carriage in failing to provide a seaworthy ship with adequate facilities to remove the source of the contamination. The court held the carriers liable, but only to the extent of the further deterioration: this was the only loss that would not have occurred but for the defendants' breach. More recently, in *Tiuta International Ltd (In Liquidation) v De Villiers Surveyors Ltd*[5] a mortgage lender who refinanced real estate developers in reliance on a seriously negligent overvaluation had its damages reduced to reflect the fact that it had been refinancing its own debt, part of which would have been irrecoverable anyway.

Examples of the application of this principle are legion. Where a contract is **24-003** wrongfully terminated, for instance, the innocent party cannot sue for the profit he would have made in so far as it is shown that the defendant would have lawfully cancelled at a later date and thus he would have failed to make it even if there had

---

[1] That is, the rule in *Robinson v Harman* (1848) 1 Ex. 850, restated more recently in e.g. *Bunge SA v Nidera BV (formerly Nidera Handelscompagnie BV)* [2015] UKSC 43; [2015] 2 C.L.C. 120 at [14] and *Morris-Garner v One Step (Support) Ltd* [2018] UKSC 20; [2019] A.C. 649 at [31] ff.
[2] See e.g. *Barnett v Chelsea & Kensington HMC* [1969] 1 Q.B. 428.
[3] See *Chitty on Contracts*, 34th edn (London: Sweet & Maxwell, 2022), para.29-073 ff.
[4] [1908] P 84.
[5] [2017] UKSC 77; [2018] P.N.L.R. 12

been no breach.[6] Again, there are numerous professional negligence cases where a client has proved a breach of contract by a lawyer or other professional in providing careless advice, but has recovered nothing because he failed to prove that if advised properly he would have acted any differently.[7] Yet another illustration comes from the law of agency: in an action for breach of warranty of authority, nothing is recoverable if the principal himself is insolvent, since even if the warranty had not been broken the claimant would still have lost his money.[8]

24-004   Of course, in reckoning what losses result from a breach, care may have to be taken in determining what the precise obligation broken was, since on this depends the answer to the question what the state of affairs would have been had the contract been kept. Normally this is straightforward question to answer: but it can be less so. One example of some difficulty has already been described in Ch.21: where a defendant had a choice as to how to perform, as a matter of law the relevant comparison is generally speaking the situation that would have obtained had the defendant rendered the minimum performance permissible to him under the terms of the contract.[9] A more recent instance, this time depending on a matter of precise contract interpretation, came in the decision in *Maestro Bulk Ltd v Cosco Bulk Carrier Co Ltd*.[10] A ship was chartered under a contract requiring at least 18 days' notice of redelivery: she was in fact redelivered on only six days' notice. The charterer was clearly in breach of contract. But was the relevant obligation one to give earlier notice of the actual redelivery, or to redeliver later in accordance with the actual notice? If the former the owners' damages were large, since had earlier notice been given they could have made a highly profitable fixture; if the latter, much less. The court had to decide between the two, and chose the latter.

---

[6]   *The Mihalis Angelos* [1971] 1 Q.B. 164; see too *Golden Strait Corp v Nippon Yusen Kubishika Kaisha* [2007] UKHL 12; [2007] 2 A.C. 353; *Bunge SA v Nidera BV* [2015] UKSC 43; [2015] 3 All E.R. 1082. Note too also *Tele2 International Card Co SA v Kub 2 Technology Ltd* [2009] EWCA Civ 9 (wrongful termination of contract to buy telecommunications services: but clear in hindsight that provider could not have performed anyway, so no loss caused by breach).

[7]   E.g. *Sykes v Midland Bank Executor & Trustee Co Ltd* [1971] 1 Q.B. 113 (failure to advise lessee that terms ruinous, but lessee would have taken lease anyway); *Etridge v Pritchard Englefield* [1999] P.N.L.R. 839 (bad advice on implications of guarantee, but plaintiff would have signed in any case); *Beary v Pall Mall Investments* [2005] EWCA 415; [2005] P.N.L.R. 35 (failure to give proper financial advice, but would not have been followed); *Dancorp Developers Ltd v Auckland CC* [1991] 3 N.Z.L.R. 337 (failure to advise property developers of contamination, but developers would have built anyway).

[8]   See e.g. *Goodwin v Francis* (1870) L.R. 5 C.P. 295 at 308; *Re National Coffee Palace Co* (1883) 24 Ch. D. 367 at 372 (Brett MR); *Skylight Maritime SA v Ascot Underwriting Ltd* [2005] EWHC 15; [2005] P.N.L.R. 25 at [20] (Colman J).

[9]   Above, paras 21-75 ff.

[10] [2014] EWHC 3978 (Comm); [2015] 1 Lloyd's Rep. 315. A similar case in a different context was *Medsted Associates Ltd v Canaccord Genuity Wealth (International) Ltd* [2020] EWHC 2952 (Comm), where a financial institution, having agreed to pay an introducer for clients it provided, broke its contract by dealing directly with such clients. Was the relevant counterfactual (a) paying the introducer if it did business with the clients, or (b) not servicing such clients if it did not pay fees? The former was held correct, which meant substantial damages were payable.

Problems in causation: repudiation, breach of condition and claims for damages[11]

A repudiatory breach of contract gives the innocent party a right not only to claim **24-005** damages, but to put an end to the contract entirely.[12] Moreover, there is no doubt that termination on this basis leaves intact the victim's additional right to claim damages so as to be placed in the position he would have been in had he received full performance.[13] However, this principle is qualified in an important way. Where the contract is terminated, not on the basis of a repudiatory breach, but instead under an express provision for termination for a lesser breach, the innocent party loses the right to claim for any loss arising from failure to receive full performance. This is supposedly on causation grounds: namely, that in such a case the claimant's loss is treated as stemming from his own decision to terminate the contract, and not from the defendant's prior breach of it. So, in *Financings Ltd v Baldock*[14] a hire-purchase contract over a lorry permitted the financier to terminate it if any instalment was more than 10 days late. The financier, faced with such non-payment, exercised this power and retrieved the lorry. The Court of Appeal held that this action, while justified under the contract, barred any claim by the financier for the profits it would have made had the agreement run its course. In so far as they had lost any such profits, that loss resulted from their decision to exercise their option to terminate the contract, and not from the defendant's breach.[15] Most of the cases elucidating this principle arise from hire-purchase,[16] but it is not limited to such situations. In later cases it has been held that the same reasoning applies to distribution contracts terminated for stipulated cause,[17] and to a claim under a time-charter for loss of profits against a non-paying charterer (though on the facts the latter was found to have repudiated).[18]

The principle in *Baldock* is controversial.[19] On one view it seems highly arbitrary **24-006** that as a matter of law termination on the basis of an event stipulated by the parties in the contract itself should automatically sever the causal link breach and loss,

---

11 B. Opeskin, "Damages for breach of contract terminated under express terms" (1990) 106 LQR 293.
12 Above, para.9-012 ff.
13 See e.g. *The Raithwaite* [1921] 3 K.B. 420 and *Spar Shipping AS v Grand China Logistics Holding (Group) Co Ltd* [2015] EWHC 718 (Comm); [2015] 1 C.L.C. 356 (charters terminated for consistent non-payment); *Yeoman Credit Ltd v Waragowski* [1961] 3 All E.R. 145 and *Overstone Ltd v Shipway* [1961] 2 All E.R. 52 (hire-purchase); *And So To Bed Ltd v Dixon* (unreported 21 November 2000) (repudiation of franchise agreement); and cf. *Bunge Corp v Tradax Export S.A.* [1981] 2 All E.R. 513.
14 [1963] 2 Q.B. 104
15 See [1963] 2 Q.B. 104, esp at pp.111–113 (Lord Denning MR); also *Cavenagh v William Evans Ltd* [2012] EWCA Civ 697; [2013] 1 W.L.R. 238 at [51] (Tomlinson LJ).
16 See e.g. *Brady v St Margaret's Trust Ltd* [1963] 2 Q.B. 494 and *United Dominions Trust Ltd v Ennis* [1968] 1 Q.B. 54; also the Australian decision to the same effect in *AMEV-UDC Finance Ltd v Austin* (1987) 68 A.L.R. 185.
17 *Phones 4U Ltd (In Administration) v EE Ltd* [2018] EWHC 49 (Comm); [2018] 2 All E.R. (Comm) 315.
18 *Spar Shipping AS v Grand China Logistics Holding (Group) Co Ltd* [2016] EWCA Civ 982; [2016] 2 Lloyd's Rep. 447; E. Peel, "Withdrawal for late payment of hire under a charterparty" (2016) 132 L.Q.R. 177. Note too *The Astra* [2013] EWHC 865 (Comm); [2013] 2 Lloyd's Rep. 69, where it was accepted that the same principle applied.
19 It is supported in G. Treitel, "Damages on Rescission for Breach of Contract" [1987] L.M. & C.L.Q. 143, but its logic is attacked in J.English, "The nature of 'promissory conditions'" (2021) 137 L.Q.R. 630 at 655.

whereas termination for so-called repudiatory breach should leave it intact.[20] In any case, two matters reduce the importance of the *Baldock* decision. First, there seems no objection to its exclusion by suitable drafting: in other words, an express contractual stipulation that termination for non-repudiatory breach should leave intact the innocent party's claim for full expectation damages.[21] Although in the past such stipulations might have been regarded as unenforceable penalties,[22] it seems likely that they will now be upheld under the more relaxed regime applicable since 2015 to liquidated damages.[23] Secondly, it seems that it can equally be sidestepped by drafting. If a contract states that a given breach not only allows cancellation but shall be regarded as repudiatory, such a term will be given effect and the right to bargain damages will be preserved.[24]

Problems in causation: Scope of the defendant's duty and its relevance to the measure of damages

24-007   In a few situations the intended scope of the defendant's duty under a contract may affect the measure of damages available for breach of it.[25] It is true that in most cases this issues does not arise, and that the question is simply whether the loss would have been suffered if the contract had been kept. Other circumstances surrounding the breach, or the fact that the loss would not have happened had not some other unconnected factor combined with it, are generally irrelevant. This point is exemplified by *CTI Group Inc v Transclear SA*.[26] Sellers broke their contract by failing to supply Mexican buyers with cement f.o.b. Padang in Indonesia. Although there was plenty of other cement available at the contract price in Padang, these particular buyers were denied access to it because of pressure from hostile commercial interests in Mexico,[27] and had to buy elsewhere much more dearly. Field J unhesitatingly rejected a plea that this extra cost due to the claimants' peculiar commercial circumstances was somehow irrecoverable. Once it was shown that it resulted from the sellers' failure to supply, and foreseeably so, that was an end of the matter: recovery followed as a matter of course.

24-008   Nevertheless the principle just stated is not a universal rule, and there is one major exception to it. In the tort of negligence loss, in order to be recoverable, must be not only be foreseeable, but also within the scope of any duty of care owed by the defendant to the claimant.[28] And it now seems clear that, in cases where the

---

[20]   Hence the Supreme Court of Canada has refused to follow the case: *Langille v Keneric Tractor Sales Ltd* [1987] 2 S.C.R. 440.

[21]   For an example of such a clause, see cl.11 of the standard time charter form NYPE 2015.

[22]   As was held to be the case in *Baldock* itself: see [1963] 2 Q.B. 104 at 111 (Lord Denning MR).

[23]   I.e. since *Makdessi v Cavendish Square Holdings BV* [2015] UKSC 67; [2015] 3 W.L.R. 1373; below, para.25-012 ff. Essentially the criterion is whether the stipulation is wholly disproportionate to any legitimate interest the promisee has in making sure the defendant's obligations are performed: it seems very hard to argue that such a clause would be.

[24]   See *Lombard North Central Plc v Butterworth* [1987] Q.B. 527.

[25]   Compare, in the tort context, G. Williams, "Causation in the law" [1961] C.L.J. 62 at 71 ff; and J. Fraser and D. Howarth, "More Concern For Cause" (1984) 4 LS 131.

[26]   [2007] EWHC 2340; [2008] 1 Lloyd's Rep. 250 (the point was not mentioned in the CA: [2008] EWCA Civ 856; [2008] 2 Lloyd's Rep. 526).

[27]   The interests were those of a powerful Central American cartel: the reason for the pressure, that the claimants had been attempting to break it.

[28]   Notably *The Estrella* [1977] 1 Lloyd's Rep. 525 (ship collides in near-perfect visibility while as it happens negligently sailing in wrong part of traffic separation zone: this latter fact irrelevant to dam-

contractual duty broken consists in a duty to take care,[29] a similar rule applies to damages for breach of contract. This is the consequence of the important and controversial[30] decision in *South Australia Asset Management Corp v York Montague Ltd*,[31] as interpreted in the later decision in *Hughes-Holland v BPE Solicitors*.[32]

South Australia[33] involved valuers employed by mortgage lenders who negligently over-valued the proffered security by some £1.5 million. When the borrowers defaulted, however, the lenders lost well over £2 million, in part because of an intervening collapse in real estate values. Could the lenders recover the portion of their loss resulting from the depreciation in land prices, considerably over £0.5 million, on the basis that (as was accepted to be the case) it would not have been suffered but for the valuers' negligence, and in addition had been foreseeable?[34] Lord Hoffmann (who gave the only opinion in the House of Lords) said that they could not, and limited the valuers' exposure to the figure of £1.5 million representing the over-valuation. The reason was that the excess could not be said to have resulted *from the fact of misvaluation*. A person providing information which was wrong, he said, was: **24-009**

> "not generally regarded as responsible for all the consequences of that course of action. He is responsible only for the consequences of the information being wrong."[35]

Lord Hoffmann went on to imagine a doctor negligently advising a patient that a diseased knee was strong enough for mountaineering. If the patient followed the advice and mountaineered, the doctor's liability would be limited to injury caused by collapse of the knee: he would not be liable for any other harm suffered while mountaineering, however foreseeable, since this would be outside the scope of any advice given.[36] **24-010**

Since then, this principle—that a claimant cannot sue in respect of a loss outside the scope of the duty broken—has been applied to a number of cases involving **24-011**

---

ages, even though collision would not have happened had she not been sailing there). See too *Darby v National Trust* [2001] EWCA Civ 189; [2001] PIQR P27 (claimant drowned in pond on defendants' land: landowners' fault in failing to warn of danger of waterborne disease irrelevant, even if causative of claimant's decision to swim and hence, indirectly, of his death).

[29] A matter of particular significance in the case of professional negligence claims, as will appear below.

[30] It was accepted in New Zealand (see *Bank of New Zealand v New Zealand Guardian Trust Co Ltd* [1999] 1 N.Z.L.R. 664 at 682–683), but regarded with large scepticism in Australia (*Kenny & Good Pty Ltd v MGICA (1992) Ltd* (1999) 199 C.L.R. 413).

[31] [1997] A.C. 191. For a considered and critical view of this case, see J. Stapleton, "Negligent Valuers and Falls in the Property Market" (1997) 113 L.Q.R 1. These criticisms, and others, lie behind the doubts expressed over the correctness of the decision in the High Court of Australia in *Kenny & Good Pty Ltd v MGICA* (1992) Ltd (1999) 199 C.L.R. 413, esp at 444 ff (Gummow J).

[32] [2017] UKSC 21; [2018] A.C. 599 (esp at [20] ff).

[33] [1997] A.C. 191. The appeal was a portmanteau appeal, and the account here concerns the facts of just one of the cases, namely *Nykredit Mortgage Bank Plc v Edward Erdman*. See generally J. O'Sullivan, "Negligent Professional Advice and Market Movements" [1997] C.L.J. 19.

[34] Thus shutting out any plea of remoteness: see the same case below (sub nom *Banque Bruxelles Lambert S.A. v Eagle Star Insurance Co Ltd* [1995] Q.B. 375 at 405 (Bingham MR).

[35] [1997] A.C. 191 at 214.

[36] See [1997] A.C. 191 at 213. See too *Alexander v Cambridge Credit Corp Ltd* (1987) 9 N.S.W.L.R. 310 at 333 (Mahoney JA). But in Australia the preference is to argue simply that losses of this sort do not, in law, result from the breach, rather than to talk in terms of the scope of the duty broken: see e.g. *Trust Co of Australia Ltd v Perpetual Trustees WA Ltd* (1997) 42 N.S.W.L.R. 237 at 248–250 and *Kenny & Good Pty Ltd v MGICA* (1992) Ltd (1999) 199 C.L.R. 413.

breaches of contractual duties of care.[37] A neat example is *Andrews v Barnett Waddingham*.[38] A client took out a personal pension on the basis of negligent (and incorrect) information from his financial advisers that the pension benefited from a government guarantee against the provider's insolvency. This would clearly have given him a claim had the provider gone insolvent; but it was held not to do so when the pension turned out to be simply a disastrous investment, even though it might be clear that he would not have bought it but for the negligent advice. Similarly, in *Gabriel v Little*[39] solicitors negligently failed to tell an investor in a building project that the promoter had put no money into it himself. The investor lost his entire investment; but this was due not to the promoter's lack of support but to the utter unviability of the project as a whole. The solicitors, not having been employed to advise on the profitability of the transaction, escaped liability.

24-012   The same reasoning underlay *Lloyds Bank Plc v Crosse & Crosse*.[40] Mortgage lenders who lost money when their borrowers failed were held unable to recover their entire loss merely because they had been caused to lend by misinformation from their solicitors as to the existence of certain restrictive covenants over the subject property. Instead they were limited to the amount of the diminution in value due to the subsistence of the covenants. Similarly and more recently, it was held that where a bank's lawyers carelessly failed to tell it that loans it planned to make were ultra vires the borrowers, the lawyers escaped liability when the bank lost its money, not because of the borrowers' refusal to repay it, but because of their effective insolvency.[41] Yet again, it seems clear that where solicitors wrongly advise mortgage lenders that there are no junior charges affecting their security, or fail to draw lenders' attention to suspicious features of a transaction, the lenders will not normally recover the whole of their loss in so far as it is caused by such extraneous factors as a weak property market; this is outside the scope of any relevant breach of duty.[42]

24-013   Nevertheless, the *South Australia* constraint is of more limited application as regards damages for breach of contract than it might seem.

24-014   To begin with, it does not apply in the contractual context except to contractual obligations to take care. It is thus irrelevant to other contractual obligations, such as the strict duty to deliver goods under a contract of sale.[43]

24-015   Secondly, and equally importantly, even in the context of duties to take care the

---

[37]   Apart from the examples below, see too *Duncan Investments Ltd v Underwoods* [1998] P.N.L.R. 754; *HOK Sport Ltd (formerly Lobb Partnership Ltd) v Aintree Racecourse Co Ltd* [2002] EWHC 3094 (TCC); [2003] B.L.R. 155; *Freemont (Denbigh) Ltd v Knight Frank LLP* [2014] EWHC 3347 (Ch); [2015] P.N.L.R. 4; *Ahmad v Wood* [2018] EWHC 996 (QB); [2018] P.N.L.R. 28; *Manchester Building Society v Grant Thornton UK LLP* [2021] UKSC 20; [2022] A.C. 783; and *Bank of New Zealand v New Zealand Guardian Trust Co Ltd* [1999] 1 N.Z.L.R. 664. On the application of the South Australia principle to construction contracts, see *BDW Trading Ltd v URS Corp Ltd* [2021] EWHC 2796 (TCC) at [40]–[49]; and as regards surveyors' obligations, *Hart v Large* [2021] EWCA Civ 24; [2021] P.N.L.R. 13.

[38]   [2006] EWCA Civ 93; [2006] P.N.L.R. 24; see too *Broker House Insurance Services Ltd v OJS Law* [2010] EWHC 3816 (Ch); [2011] P.N.L.R. 23.

[39]   [2017] UKSC 21; [2018] A.C. 599 (esp at [20] ff).

[40]   [2001] EWCA Civ 366; [2001] P.N.L.R. 34.

[41]   *Haugesund Kommune v Depfa ACS Bank* [2011] EWCA Civ 33; [2011] 1 C.L.C. 166.

[42]   A number of authorities said there *would* be liability in such cases: see e.g. *Portman Building Society v Bevan Ashford (A Firm)* [2000] P.N.L.R. 344 and a number of the specific decisions (such as Steggles Palmer) encapsulated in *Bristol & West Building Society v Fancy & Jackson (a firm)* [1997] 4 All E.R. 582. But these were effectively overruled in *Gabriel v Little* [2017] UKSC 21; [2018] A.C. 599: see at [47] ff.

[43]   See the comments in *CTI Group Inc v Transclear SA* [2007] EWHC 2340; [2008] 1 Lloyd's Rep.

limitation applies only in limited circumstances. Lord Hoffmann made this point in *South Australia* itself:

> "The principle thus stated distinguishes between a duty to provide information for the purpose of enabling someone else to decide upon a course of action and a duty to advise someone as to what course of action he should take. If the duty is to advise whether or not a course of action should be taken, the adviser must take reasonable care to consider all the potential consequences of that course of action. If he is negligent, he will therefore be responsible for all the foreseeable loss which is a consequence of that course of action having been taken. If his duty is only to supply information, he must take reasonable care to ensure that the information is correct and, if he is negligent, will be responsible for all the foreseeable consequences of the information being wrong."[44]

However, to regard the relevant distinction as one between duties to inform and **24-016** to advise can be somewhat unhelpful, if only because that boundary is itself difficult to draw with any precision.[45] A better way of expressing it, appearing in more recent authority, depends on differentiating the function and comprehensiveness of the advice concerned. In so far as circumstances indicate that such advice has a limited ambit and that the claimant is acting as his own adviser and at his own risk in respect of matters outside that ambit, the *South Australia* principle applies, and losses springing from the latter factors will be outside the scope of the defendant's duty. By contrast, where the advice is effectively guiding the whole decision-making process, then on principle the person giving it will be regarded as potentially accepting responsibility for any consequences of reliance on the advice, provided that they are not too remote.[46]

Thus in contrast to the examples mentioned in para.24-011 above, there are a **24-017** large number of cases where full recovery obtains. For example, it was held in *Aneco Reinsurance Underwriting Ltd v Johnson & Higgins Ltd*[47] that where reinsurance brokers gave negligent advice to insurers as to whether certain risks were reinsurable, and thus in effect as to whether to accept them at all, they were liable for the whole loss suffered by the insurers as a result of reliance on the advice. Again, where more recently buyers of off-plan Italian villas relied on Italian lawyers to check title, ensure that guarantees were in place and handle the sales, it was held that the lawyers were liable when they failed to do so and the buyers lost their money because of the fraud of the developers.[48]

---

250 at [9] (Field J) (the point was not discussed on appeal at [2008] EWCA Civ 856; [2008] 2 C.L.C. 112).

[44] See [1997] A.C. 191 at 214.

[45] "Information given by a professional man to his client is usually a specific form of advice, and most advice will involve conveying information" (Lord Sumption in *Gabriel v Little* [2017] UKSC 21; [2018] A.C. 599 at [39]); also *Lloyds Bank Plc v McBains Cooper Consulting Ltd (No.2)* [2018] EWCA Civ 452; [2018] P.N.L.R. 23 at [33] (Longmore LJ).

[46] *Gabriel v Little* [2017] UKSC 21; [2018] A.C. 599 at [40]–[46] (Lord Sumption).

[47] [2001] UKHL 51; [2002] 1 Lloyd's Rep. 156.

[48] *Various Claimants v Giambrone & Law (A Firm)* [2017] EWCA Civ 1193; [2018] P.N.L.R. 2.

Problems in causation: Breach of contract as a concurrent cause of loss

24-018   The English law of tort has always been prepared to accept that one event can have two or more concurrent causes.[49] As regards the law of damages, the effect of this doctrine is straightforward and significant. In so far as the defendant's breach is a concurrent cause of a single loss,[50] the defendant is liable for the whole amount of it. The fact that there might have been some other cause as well is irrelevant (though if the other cause amounted to a wrong committed by a third party it may give rise to a right in the defendant to contribution from that third party).[51]

24-019   Most of the cases illustrating this principle are tort cases. So it is clear there that a defendant may be liable for the whole of a claimant's loss if his wrong, while not of itself sufficient to cause that loss, combines with other causes to produce that effect.[52] And similarly in cases of so-called "over-determination". If two wrongs, each of which would on its own be sufficient to cause the claimant's loss, in fact combine to do so, both wrongdoers are liable in full, and neither is allowed to argue that the loss would have occurred even had he not been guilty of any wrongdoing.[53]

24-020   Nevertheless, even though most cases concern tort, exactly similar principles govern claims for damages for breach of contract: if a cause is an effective cause, the fact that it combines with other factors is irrelevant.[54] One illustrative instance is the sea-carriage case of *Smith Hogg & Co Ltd v Black Sea & Baltic Insurance Ltd*.[55] There, the serious overloading of a vessel (a breach of contract for which the owners were responsible) combined with incompetent refuelling (for which, under the contract of carriage, they were not) to capsize her and cause the loss of the cargo. It was held that the carriers were liable for the loss. Another example, more recent, arises from the facts of the decision in *Saipol SA v Inerco Trade SA*.[56] A buyer bought differing quantities of vegetable oil from a number of different sellers; the various consignments of oil were then collected, commingled in a single large vessel and shipped to the buyer. In fact the oil was all seriously contaminated, and the

---

49   Compare Lord Reid's comment in the tort decision in *Stapley v Gypsum Mines Ltd* [1953] A.C. 663 at 681: "Sometimes it is proper to discard all but one [party's fault] and to regard that one as the sole cause, but in other cases it is proper to regard two or more as having jointly caused the accident." See too H. Hart & A. Honoré, *Causation in the Law* (1959), p.189 ff.

50   If the losses can be separated, then obviously this does not apply: see *The Europa* [1908] P 84, para.24-002 above, and compare the tort cases of *Thompson v Smiths Shiprepairers Ltd* [1984] Q.B. 405, esp at 441, and *Holtby v Brigham & Cowan (Hull) Ltd* [2000] 3 All E.R. 421.

51   Under s.1 of the Civil Liability (Contribution) Act 1978: see generally A. Tettenborn and D. Wilby (eds), *Law of Damages*, 2nd edn (London: Butterworths Law, 2010), para.8.53 ff.

52   See, e.g. *Pride of Derby Angling Association v British Celanese Ltd* [1953] Ch. 149; and *Rouse v Squires* [1973] Q.B. 889. *McGhee v National Coal Board* [1973] 1 W.L.R. 1 may well be another instance (though see *Fairchild v Glenhaven Funeral Services Ltd* [2002] UKHL 22; [2003] 1 A.C. 32 at [21]).

53   On which, see e.g.*Rahman v Arearose Ltd* [2001] Q.B. 351 at 361 ff (Laws LJ). See too the comments of Mason CJ in *March v Stramare Pty Ltd* (1991) 171 C.L.R. 506 at 516.

54   E.g. *Heskell v Continental Express Ltd* [1950] 1 All E.R. 1033 at 1047 (Devlin J); *British & Commonwealth Holdings Plc v Quadrex Holdings Inc* [1995] C.L.C. 1169 at 1230 (Staughton LJ); *Marshall v Rubypoint Ltd* (1997) 29 H.L.R. 850 at 855–856 (Peter Gibson LJ); *Symrise AG v Baker & McKenzie (A Firm)* [2015] EWHC 912 (Comm); [2016] 1 All E.R. (Comm) 603 at [58] (Burton J); *YJB Port Ltd v M&A Pharmachem Ltd* [2021] EWHC 42 (Ch) at [73] and *Beattie Passive Norse Ltd v Canham Consulting Ltd* [2021] EWHC 1116 (TCC); [2021] P.N.L.R. 22 at [106]–[112].

55   [1940] A.C. 997. (Strictly speaking this was a general average case; but the result turned on the question of the carrier's contractual liability to cargo.)

56   [2014] EWHC 2211 (Comm); [2015] 1 Lloyd's Rep. 26.

buyer suffered large losses as a result. Field J held that the buyer could sue any individual seller for the whole of its loss, on the basis that each had substantially contributed to the events giving rise to it. The fact that a given seller had not been exclusively responsible was irrelevant: any injustice could be remedied through contribution proceedings between the various sellers under the Civil Liability (Contribution) Act 1978.

Even here, however, a limitation needs to be noted: as in tort,[57] it must be shown **24-021** that the defendant's breach is a "substantial cause" of the loss suffered, rather than a mere marginal factor.[58] So in *Galoo Ltd v Bright Grahame Murray*,[59] a company's accountants had allegedly broken their contract by failing to report that the concern was unviable, with the result that the company was not wound up but continued trading, with disastrous results. A claim for these subsequent trading losses failed: the accountants' breach might in one sense have occasioned the loss, but could not be said to be a substantial cause of it.[60] Again, in *Weld-Blundell v Stephens*[61] the plaintiff wrote a defamatory letter about a third party to his accountant, which the latter in breach of contract mislaid; the subject of the letter, having discovered its existence, mulcted the plaintiff in large damages for libel. A claim against the accountant for the amount of those damages failed: the real cause of the plaintiff's loss was his own incautiousness in writing a libellous letter, not the defendant's loss of it.[62]

Causation and intervening factors: "Novus actus interveniens"[63]

Even if the defendant's breach of contract and the claimant's loss are causally **24-022** related in the sense above, an intervening event may nevertheless be regarded as, so to speak, wiping the slate clean.[64] The idea can be articulated in a number of ways—for example, by referring to a the factor as a *novus actus interveniens*,[65] or metaphorically to something "breaking the chain of causation"[66]—but the thinking is the same: when computing causative potency, an event may have such overwhelming significance as to justify ignoring an earlier breach of duty completely[67] and saying that it can no longer fairly be regarded as a cause of the loss.[68]

---

[57] *Bonnington Castings Ltd v Wardlaw* [1956] A.C. 613 at 620 ff (Lord Reid); *Sienkiewicz v Greif (UK) Ltd* [2011] UKSC 10; [2011] 2 A.C. 229 at [17] (Lord Phillips); *Chappel v Hart* (1998) 195 C.L.R. 232 at 244 (McHugh J).

[58] *Heskell v Continental Express Ltd* [1950] 1 All E.R. 1033 at 1047 (Devlin J); *Bluestorm Ltd v Portvale Holdings Ltd* [2004] EWCA Civ 289; [2004] L & TR 23 at [24] (Buxton LJ).

[59] [1994] 1 W.L.R. 1360.

[60] See [1994] 1 W.L.R. 1360 at 1369, 1374–1375, 1387, 1389.

[61] [1920] A.C. 956.

[62] See [1920] A.C. 956 at 981 (Lord Sumner).

[63] On the effect of which, see generally H.G. Beale (ed), *Chitty on Contracts*, 34th edn (London: Sweet & Maxwell, 2022), para.26-075 ff.

[64] *British & Commonwealth Holdings Plc v Quadrex Holdings Inc* [1995] C.L.C. 1169 at 1237.

[65] A phrase without much meaning, as observed by du Parcq LJ in the tort decision in *Ingram v United Automobile Services Ltd* [1943] 2 All E.R. 71 at 73.

[66] Or alternatively by referring to the Latin phrase *causae proximae non remotae spectantur*. For those interested, other choice metaphors can be found listed by Lord Sumner in *Weld-Blundell v Stephens* [1920] A.C. 956 at 986.

[67] Cf. *Clerk & Lindsell on Torts*, 24th edn (London: Sweet & Maxwell, 2023), para.2-110, referring to "an event of such impact that it 'obliterates' the wrongdoing of the defendant" and *Reeves v Commissioner of Police of the Metropolis* [2000] 1 A.C. 360 at 374 (Lord Jauncey). The graphic metaphor

24-023   Most of the cases concern the effect of the claimant's own actions. Often the action is one showing a high degree of fault, amounting to a reckless regard by the claimant of his own interests. A straightforward instance is *Lambert v Lewis*,[69] in which a buyer of a horse-box with a dangerously defective coupling continued to use it after discovering the problem. He was disabled from claiming from the sellers in respect of losses flowing from a subsequent accident caused by the defect. Other cases of continuing use of goods known to be defective have yielded similar results.[70] Similarly a claimant who knowingly courts danger may find himself regarded as responsible for any losses even if the danger is otherwise one for which the defendant is contractually liable,[71] as may one who, faced with a breach, takes some unforeseeable and very foolish action and suffers damage as a result.[72] On the other hand, there is no necessity that the claimant be at fault: any deliberate action on his part that may clearly lead to further loss may be sufficient. Thus where a buyer's surveyor over-values a property, the buyer who pays more than the value placed on the property by the surveyor is to that extent responsible for his own misfortune;[73] and a customer who complains that a spread-betting company has failed to close out his account at the proper time but is shown to have voluntarily continued to gamble on a volatile market has no claim in respect of the results of so doing.[74]

24-024   The plea of overriding cause, however, is not an easy one to make good in this connection.[75] Courts have taken the view that, absent highly exceptional circumstances, contractees are entitled to assume contracts will be performed and to rely on that assumption. Tomlinson J made the point neatly in *Vinmar International Ltd v Theresa Navigation SA*,[76] when he said that an event

---

of obliteration has not surprisingly been kept alive in contract cases: e.g. *Borealis AB v Geogas Trading SA* [2010] EWHC 2789 (Comm); [2011] 1 Lloyd's Rep. 482 at [44] (Gross LJ); *Hi-Lite Electrical Ltd v Wolseley UK Ltd* [2011] EWHC 2153 (TCC); [2011] B.L.R. 629 at [205] (Ramsey J); *Flanagan v Greenbanks Ltd (t/a Lazenby Insulation)* [2013] EWCA Civ 1702; 151 Con. L.R. 98 at [55] (Maurice Kay LJ).

[68]   A point succinctly made in the tort context by Lord Bingham: see *Corr v IBC Vehicles Ltd* [2008] UKHL 13; [2008] 1 A.C. 884 at [17]. In the contract context, see *County Ltd v Girozentrale* [1996] 3 All E.R. 834 at 849, 857 (Beldam and Hobhouse LJJ: if original event remains a cause, no break in causation).

[69]   [1982] A.C. 225.

[70]   E.g. *Beoco Ltd v Alfa Laval Co Ltd* [1995] Q.B. 137. See too the discussion in *Howmet Ltd v Economy Devices Ltd* [2014] EWHC 3933 (TCC) at [279]–[287] (upheld at [2016] EWCA Civ 847).

[71]   *Compania Naviera Maropan SA v Bowaters Lloyd Pulp & Paper Mills Ltd* [1955] 2 Q.B. 68 at 78 (Devlin J: if ship's master knowingly sails into highly dangerous port on charterer's (illegal) orders, arguably no action against charterer under safe port warranty).

[72]   *Quinn v Burch Bros. (Builders) Ltd* [1966] 2 Q.B. 370 (failure to provide ladder for working at height: plaintiff injured using highly unsafe home-made equipment).

[73]   *Hardy v Wamsley-Lewis* (1967) 203 E.G. 1039. So too a solicitor's client whose property is made unsaleable by negligent failure to register title can recover loss in value up to the time the problem becomes apparent, but not any later loss due to his own delay in selling: see the Irish decision in *Rosbeg Partners v LK Shields (A Firm)* [2018] IESC 23; [2018] P.N.L.R. 26.

[74]   *IG Index Ltd v Ehrentreu* [2015] EWHC 3390 (QB).

[75]   The burden being on the defendant who alleges it: *Brown v KMR Services Ltd* [1994] 4 All E.R. 385 at 398 (Gatehouse J).

[76]   [2001] EWHC 497 (Comm); [2001] C.L.C. 1035.

"cannot be regarded as breaking the chain of causation between the admitted breach of contract and the loss unless that conduct can be regarded as the sole cause of the loss to the exclusion of any efficacy of the breach."[77]

Courts have thus resisted the temptation to regard buyers as responsible for their own misfortune when they have failed, even negligently, to check whether goods bought have dangerous defects,[78] or to apply proper safety precautions when using them;[79] and similarly with insurance brokers' clients who have failed to take precautions in the face of doubts over whether the cover arranged is in fact appropriate.[80]   **24-025**

Moreover, a good deal of indulgence is shown to claimants in this situation: as has been rightly said, actions in this context "ought not to be weighed in nice scales at the instance of the party whose breach of contract has occasioned the difficulty".[81] Thus it has been held that, at least in the absence of blatantly obvious danger, a charterer who illegally orders a ship into an unsafe port remains liable for any resulting damage and cannot shift the blame to the master for obeying orders, even if the latter did know of a possible hazard.[82] And similarly, where a sea carrier in breach of contract failed to clean its vessel properly, thus contaminating a later cargo of ethylene, Tomlinson J had little time for the carrier's ingenious plea that the ship was so obviously filthy that the cargo owner in putting its cargo on board notwithstanding this fact was responsible for its own misfortune.[83] And yet again with reasonable reactions to a breach. So a government faced with large amounts of bogus currency in circulation due to its security printers' incompetence is justified in paying out good money to buy in the bad;[84] and landlords of a shopping mall faced with the wrongful withdrawal of an anchor store have been held able to recover for rent rebates voluntarily granted as a result to other stores in the same development: the decision may have been technically the landlords', but the occasion for that decision was indubitably the defendants' breach.[85]   **24-026**

These cases concern the effect of acts of the claimant himself. It is also possible, however, for the act of a third party, or an event that is due to no-one's fault,   **24-027**

---

[77] [2001] EWHC 497 (Comm); [2001] C.L.C. 1035 at [42]. Cf. Wright J's reference in a tort case to something "ultroneous, something unwarrantable, a new cause which disturbs the sequence of events, something which can be described as either unreasonable or extraneous or extrinsic": see *The Oropesa* [1943] P 32 at 39.

[78] See, e.g. *Trac Time Control Ltd v Moss Plastic Parts Ltd* [2004] EWHC 3298 (TCC) (failure by buyer to check goods for compliance with contract: no overriding cause shown); *Borealis AB v Geogas Trading SA* [2010] EWHC 2789 (Comm) (similar); cf. *Bank of Nova Scotia v Hellenic Mutual War Risks Association (Bermuda) Ltd, The Good Luck* [1992] 1 A.C. 233 at 266–267 (Lord Goff).

[79] *Hi-Lite Electrical Ltd v Wolseley UK Ltd* [2011] EWHC 2153 (TCC); [2011] B.L.R. 629, esp at [202]–[208] (culpable failure by fitter of electrical equipment to attach RCD device); see too *Howmet Ltd v Economy Devices Ltd* [2014] EWHC 3933 (TCC) at [279]–[287].

[80] *BP Plc v Aon Ltd (No.2)* [2006] EWHC 424 (Comm); [2006] 1 C.L.C. 881 (failure to insure on discovery that cover arranged by brokers inadequate: same result).

[81] See *Banco de Portugal v Waterlow & Sons Ltd* [1932] A.C. 452 at 506 (Lord Macmillan), quoted by Tomlinson J in *Vinmar International Ltd v Theresa Navigation SA* [2001] EWHC 497 (Comm); [2001] C.L.C. 1035 at [55].

[82] *Reardon Smith Line Ltd v Australian Wheat Board* [1956] A.C. 266 (chartered ship wrongfully ordered to unsafe port and damaged there: master's obedience to order not overriding cause, so charterers liable).

[83] *Vinmar International Ltd & Anor v Theresa Navigation SA* [2001] EWHC 497 (Comm); [2001] C.L.C. 1035.

[84] *Banco de Portugal v Waterlow & Sons Ltd* [1932] A.C. 452.

[85] *Transworld Ltd v Sainsbury Plc* [1990] 2 E.G.L.R. 255.

to amount to an overriding cause. Suppose, for example, that a buyer, having bought defective machinery, sends it for repair to a third party, but that owing to the repairers' unforeseeable incompetence the machinery suffers catastrophic damage when next used. The repairers' negligence will, it seems, overlay any liability of the sellers for loss of use after the attempted repair.[86] Again, where a plumbing subcontractor fits an anti-overflow valve incompetently he remains liable to the contractor for any flooding even if the latter would not have happened had proper drainage measures also been put in place by the building owner.[87] Similarly, it is suggested, if a defendant in breach of contract caused damage to a vehicle necessitating repairs lasting some weeks but the vehicle was then destroyed during repairs by an unavoidable accident, the defendant would also escape liability for any subsequent loss of use.[88]

24-028   Here too, however, the plea is hard to make out in practice. As in tort,[89] the mere fact that a third party's negligence combines with the defendant's breach and exacerbates its effects will not do. Thus a surveyor who negligently certifies a house to be suitable for a particular insulation treatment remains liable to the householder even though the fitter of the insulation is equally at fault in failing to make the necessary checks;[90] and a shipowner can sue a shipper of inflammable cargo for loss of the vessel where it catches fire, even though the ship was only lost because another very explosive cargo illegally shipped by a different shipper exploded: the act of the latter shipper would not be regarded as an overriding cause.[91] Only recklessness by the third party, or something close to it, will be regarded as sufficient to supplant the original breach as the cause of the loss. Furthermore, even if the third party's act is deliberate, if it is foreseeable or within the scope of the defendant's contractual obligation, then there will generally be liability.[92] Thus where tradesmen leave premises unsecured,[93] or landlords fail to carry out repairs necessary to proper security,[94] courts faced with claims for the resulting thefts have been unsympathetic to pleas that the thieves' actions broke the chain of causation. Indeed, even demonstrably illegal governmental acts have been left out of account where they were provoked by the act of one or other contracting party.[95]

Apportionment on the basis of causation

24-029   As will appear above, as between claimant and defendant causation in breach of contract cases is generally treated as an all-or-nothing issue. In so far as the

---

[86]   *Beoco Ltd v Alfa Laval Co Ltd* [1995] Q.B. 137, esp at 149 ff; see too the tort case of *The Sivand* [1998] C.L.C. 751.

[87]   *Supershield Ltd v Siemens Building Technologies FE Ltd* [2010] EWCA Civ 7; [2010] 1 C.L.C. 241.

[88]   Compare the tort case of *Carslogie SS Co Ltd v Royal Norwegian Government* [1952] A.C. 292; see too *Beoco Ltd v Alfa Laval Co Ltd* [1995] Q.B. 137.

[89]   See e.g. *Rahman v Arearose Ltd* [2001] Q.B. 351 and *Webb v Barclays Bank Plc* [2001] EWCA Civ 1141; [2002] PIQR P8 (cases of intervening medical negligence).

[90]   *Flanagan v Greenbanks Ltd* [2013] EWCA Civ 1702; (2013) 151 Con. L.R. 98

[91]   *Northern Shipping Co v Deutsche Seereederei GmbH* [2000] C.L.C. 933 at 951–952 (Auld LJ).

[92]   See the early tort decision in *Haynes v Harwood* [1935] 1 K.B. 146 (vandal startling unattended horse not overriding cause, since "[i]f what is relied upon as novus actus interveniens is the very kind of thing which is likely to happen if the want of care which is alleged takes place, the principle embodied in the maxim is no defence": Greer LJ at 156); and the discussion in the later tort decision in *Reeves v Metropolitan Police Comr* [2000] 1 A.C. 360.

[93]   *Stansbie v Troman* [1948] 2 K.B. 48.

[94]   *Marshall v Rubypoint Ltd* (1997) 29 HLR 850.

[95]   *Great Elephant Corp v Trafigura Beheer BV* [2013] EWCA Civ 905; [2013] 2 C.L.C. 185 at [45]–[46] (Longmore LJ).

defendant's breach of contract is a substantial cause of a particular loss suffered by the claimant, the defendant is liable for it in full. Such liability can be escaped only where there is some overwhelming interposed event amounting to a *novus actus interveniens*, in which case the causal link is severed and the defendant is not liable for the ensuing loss at all. The only qualification to this principle is the limited ability of a defendant in breach of a contractual duty of care to invoke the provisions of the Law Reform (Contributory Negligence) Act 1945, a matter dealt with below.[96]

However, the question may arise whether it open to a court to adopt a half-way **24-030** position here. Assuming the Law Reform (Contributory Negligence) Act 1945 does not apply, can it legitimately hold that where a given loss is the result partly of a defendant's breach of contract and partly of some act of the claimant, liability should be apportioned? In one case, *Tennant Radiant Heat Ltd v Warrington Development Corp*,[97] the Court of Appeal held this to be possible. A flood damaged the landlord's and tenant's parts of an industrial unit owing to an ingress of water caused by breaches by both parties of their mutual repair obligations. Each sued the other. Liability for the overall damage was apportioned according to the causative potency of each breach. Today, however, the validity this holding seems very doubtful. It is very hard to reconcile with a subsequent decision of the Court of Appeal that default of the claimant cannot affect contract damages outside the purview of the 1945 Act;[98] and in *Hi-Lite Electrical Ltd v Wolseley UK Ltd*[99] Ramsey J treated the precedential value of the *Tennant* case as confined to its own facts.

The proof of causation

(i) Burden on the claimant There is no doubt that as a general rule the claim- **24-031** ant bears the burden of proving, on a balance of probabilities, not only breach of contract and loss, but also the existence of a connection between them.[100] To this extent the position is the same in contract as it is in tort.[101] So in *Sykes v Midland Bank Executor & Trustee Co Ltd*,[102] solicitors' clients who had proved a negligent failure to warn them of highly disadvantageous clauses in a lease nevertheless failed

---

[96] Para.24-078 ff.

[97] (1988) 4 Const LJ 321. See too the first instance decision of *Lamb v J Jarvis & Sons Ltd* (1990) 60 Con LR 1 esp at [88]–[99].

[98] *Barclays Bank Plc v Fairclough Building Ltd* [1995] 1 Q.B. 214. See also May LJ's sceptical comments in *Bank of Nova Scotia v Hellenic Mutual War Risks Association (Bermuda) Ltd, The Good Luck* [1990] 1 Q.B. 818 at 904.

[99] [2011] EWHC 2153 (TCC); [2011] B.L.R. 629 at [228].

[100] See *Sykes v Midland Bank Executor & Trustee Co Ltd* [1971] 1 Q.B. 113 at 124–125, 127–128, 131–132 (Harman, Salmon and Karminski LJJ); *Etridge v Pritchard Englefield* [1999] P.N.L.R. 839 at 848 (Morritt LJ); *Bank of Credit and Commerce International SA (In Liquidation) v Ali (No.3)* [2002] EWCA Civ 82; [2002] 3 All E.R. 750 at [14] (Pill LJ). On what such proof involves see *Dana UK Axle Ltd v Freudenberg FST GmbH* [2021] EWHC 1751 (TCC); [2021] T.C.L.R. 6 at [227]–[245] (defective components supplied to buyer, followed by claims by sub-buyers alleging faults in manufactured goods: no need for exhaustive elimination of all possible other causes, merely a showing on the balance of probabilities).

[101] *Bonnington Castings Ltd v Wardlaw* [1956] A.C. 613 at 620 (Lord Reid); *Fairchild v Glenhaven Funeral Services Ltd* [2002] UKHL 22; [2003] 1 A.C. 32 at [8] (Lord Bingham). For discussion of this subject in the tort context, see Stapleton (1988) 108 L.Q.R 389; McLachlin, "Negligence Law—Proving the Connection" in N. Mullany and A. Linden (eds), *Torts Tomorrow, A Tribute to John Fleming* (North Ryde, NSW : LBC Information Services, 1998).

[102] [1971] 1 Q.B. 113.

to recover substantial damages when they failed to satisfy the court that they would have acted any differently if properly advised. Similarly, where a solicitor breaks his contract by giving negligent advice to a client, the client bears the burden of proving, on an all-or-nothing basis, that he would have followed proper advice, if given:[103] and again, where a solicitor negligently causes a client to be deprived of a cause of action, it is up to the client to prove that in the event he would have proceeded with the litigation had he been able to do so.[104]

24-032   The rule that the claimant must prove causation is subject to one possible uncertainty. In tort a number of older cases stated clearly that a defendant who alleged a discrete intervening event breaking the chain of causation bore the burden of proving it.[105] On the other hand, more recent authority is against this, suggesting merely that the relevant burden is evidential;[106] and it is suggested that today this view is more likely to be followed.

24-033   **(ii) Competing causes**   It follows from the above that if a claimant suffers a loss and can prove a breach by the defendant, but it is not clear whether the loss results from the breach or from some other cause for which the defendant is not liable, then the action will fail. For example, suppose an industrialist buys a chemical which is contaminated and proves disruption to his manufacturing process, but cannot prove whether that disruption was due to the impurity or to ambient pollution. Logically, in any action against the seller he must fail to recover substantial damages.[107] Alternatively, imagine that the same industrialist buys materials from two different suppliers; that the materials are defective in both cases; and that the industrialist again suffers disruption as a result of the defectiveness. It is suggested that an action against either supplier will fail, in the absence of proof that it was that supplier's material that caused the loss.[108]

24-034   **(iii) Causation and loss of a chance**   To say that a contract claimant bears the burden of proof of causation means that he must prove, on a balance of probabilities, that his loss would not have been incurred but for the defendant's breach of contract (or, in the case where two or more concurrent causes are in issue, that

---

[103] *Sykes v Midland Bank Executor & Trustee Co Ltd* [1971] 1 Q.B. 113.

[104] *Harrison v Bloom Camillin* [2001] P.N.L.R. 195, esp at 223.

[105] See in particular the shipping cases of *The Fritz Thyssen* [1967] 2 Lloyd's Rep. 199 at 203 (Willmer LJ); *The Zaglebie Dobrowskie (No.2)* [1978] 1 Lloyd's Rep. 573 at 574 (Brandon J).

[106] E.g. *Borealis AB v Geogas Trading SA* [2010] EWHC 2789 (Comm) at [43]–[45] (Gross LJ); see too *Trebor Bassett Holdings Ltd v ADT Fire & Security Plc* [2011] EWHC 1936 (TCC); [2011] B.L.R. 661 at [540] (Coulson J).

[107] Cf. *Clough v First Choice Holidays Ltd* [2006] EWCA Civ 15; [2006] PIQR P22 (contractual claim for injury: unclear whether injury due to breach by tour operator or other cause: no recovery). And see the tort case of *Wilsher v Essex Area Health Authority* [1988] A.C. 1074. On the other hand, if the claimant provides respectable evidence of a causal link and the defendant fails to answer that with evidence in favour of another cause, it will be proper to find causation proved: e.g. *Dana UK Axle Ltd v Freudenberg FST GmbH* [2021] EWHC 1751 (TCC).

[108] This seems a strong inference from *Fairchild v Glenhaven Funeral Services Ltd* [2002] UKHL 22; [2003] 1 A.C. 32. The rule laid down there, allowing a claimant in limited circumstances to claim despite being unable to prove which defendant injured him, is it seems to be regarded as exceptional (see [2002] UKHL 22; [2003] 1 A.C. 32 at [40], [68] and [74] (Lords Bingham and Hoffmann)), and possibly applicable only to a limited class of personal injury claims arising from asbestosis (see *Clough v First Choice Holidays & Flights Ltd* [2006] EWCA Civ 15; [2006] PIQR P22 at [43] and *International Energy Group Ltd v Zurich Insurance Plc* [2015] UKSC 33; [2016] A.C. 509 at [1] (Lord Mance)). If so, it presumably follows that in cases such as that referred to in the text the normal rule as to the burden of proof obtains.

the breach contributed in a substantial measure to that loss). If he does so, he recovers in full: if not, he obtains nothing. In particular, where this rule applies a court cannot in contract, any more than in tort,[109] choose to decide the matter according to the probability that the breach caused the loss, and award damages based on the amount of the loss, discounted so as to reflect the chance that it might not in fact have resulted from the breach.[110]

Nevertheless, the rule stated above is subject to one vital qualification. Even though a "loss of chance" analysis cannot be applied to proof that a loss was caused by the defendant's breach, it may apply to the *quantification* of a loss once causation has been proved.[111] Such will be the case in a situation where the essence of the claimant's complaint is that the defendant's breach of contract has deprived him of the opportunity to make a profit or to avoid some loss or damage. In practice, this is regarded as applying to two types of situation: (a) where the loss alleged by the claimant, and proved to have resulted from the defendant's breach, consists in the prospect of some future damage which may or may not materialise; and (b) where the question of how much the claimant has suffered as a result of a breach of contract depends on an assessment of the hypothetical actions of some given third party. **24-035**

(a) Future damage We can begin with future losses. The principle behind cases such as these was succinctly described by Lord Reid in the tort case of *Davies v Taylor*:[112] **24-036**

> "You can prove that a past event happened, but you cannot prove that a future event will happen and I do not think that the law is so foolish as to suppose that you can. All that you can do is to evaluate the chance. Sometimes it is virtually 100 per cent: sometimes virtually nil. But often it is somewhere in between. And if it is somewhere in between I do not see much difference between a probability of 51 per cent and a probability of 49 per cent."[113]

In the contract context, assume that a claimant proves that a breach of contract by a defendant has caused him to lose profits (or suffer losses). As regards past losses, it is up to the claimant to prove their amount.[114] But as for the future ones, the approach is to adopt the "loss of a chance" approach: that is, to ask whether **24-037**

---

[109] See *Hotson v East Berkshire Health Authority* [1987] A.C. 750 and *Gregg v Scott* [2005] UKHL 2; [2005] 2 A.C. 176, esp at [86]–[89] (Lord Hoffmann), [167]–[173] (Lord Phillips). See M. Stauch, "Causation, Risk and Loss of Chance in Medical Negligence" (1997) 17 OJLS 205.

[110] See *Sykes v Midland Bank Executor & Trustee Co Ltd* [1971] 1 Q.B. 113, a solicitors' negligence case where precisely this argument was rebuffed by the Court of Appeal. See also *Vasiliou v Hajigeorgiou* [2010] EWCA Civ 1475 (loss of restaurant profits due to breach of covenant), and the tort case of *The Vicky 1* [2008] EWCA Civ 101; [2008] 2 Lloyd's Rep. 45 (would-be profits of disabled supertanker).

[111] As Lord Hoffmann put it in *Gregg v Scott* [2005] UKHL 2; [2005] 2 A.C. 176 at [69]: "The rule against the recovery of uncertain damages is directed against uncertainty as to cause rather than as to extent or measure" (quoting Lord Guthrie in the earlier *Kenyon v Bell* 1953 SC 125 at 128). See generally H. Reece, "Losses of Chances in the Law" (1996) 59 M.L.R. 188; *McGregor on Damages*, 21st edn (London: Sweet & Maxwell, 2022), para.10-47 ff.

[112] [1974] A.C. 207.

[113] See [1974] A.C. 207 at 212–213. Also *Blue Circle Industries Ltd v Ministry of Defence* [1999] Ch. 289 (land irradiated: lost prospects of sale reckoned according to chances that sale attempt would now be unsuccessful).

[114] *Vasiliou v Hajigeorgiou* [2010] EWCA Civ 1475.

there was a more than negligible chance of making profits;[115] to quantify the amount of the profits that might have been made; and then to discount that figure to take account of contingencies.[116]

24-038 *(b)   The hypothetical action of a third party*   For at least 150 years, the courts have accepted the possibility of quantifying recovery by reference to "loss of a chance" reasoning where the answer to the question of what the claimant's position would have been but for the breach turns on some hypothetical decision that might have been taken by some third party.[117] Although there are other possible explanations,[118] the most convincing reason for this is that in so far as a contract refers to a matter subject to the decision of a third person, that is a strong (though not conclusive[119]) indication that if the contract is breached, what the innocent party has lost is best characterised as the chance of obtaining a decision favourable to his interests.[120]

24-039   Until 1995 awards of this type were somewhat sporadic. In the well-known 1910 case of *Chaplin v Hicks*[121] the Court of Appeal upheld a jury award of £100 representing, it would seem, the plaintiff's lost chance of winning a beauty contest from which the organisers had wrongfully excluded her.[122] And in *Kitchen v Royal*

---

[115] The law does not try to value negligible chances: *Webster v Sandersons Solicitors* [2009] EWCA Civ 830; [2009] P.N.L.R. 37 at [39]. And cf. the wrongful death case of *Davies v Taylor* [1974] A.C. 207 (prospect of future support negligible, so no Fatal Accidents Act recovery). In a suitable case there is no reason why a court should not instead order an indemnity: that is, declare that the claimant is entitled to be indemnified by the defendant for certain losses as and when they arise. This may be particularly appropriate where the claimant faces future claims from third parties arising from the defendant's breach: e.g. *Dana UK Axle Ltd v Freudenberg FST GmbH* [2021] EWHC 1751 (TCC).

[116] See *Allied Maples Group Ltd v Simmons & Simmons* [1995] 1 W.L.R. 1602 at 1610 (Stuart-Smith LJ); also *Sellars v Adelaide Petroleum NL* (1994) 179 C.L.R. 332. For instances, see e.g. *Salford City Council v Torkington* [2004] EWCA Civ 1646; [2004] 51 E.G. 89 (C.S.); *Trac Time Control Ltd v Moss Plastic Parts Ltd* [2004] EWHC 3286 (QB) (loss of future profits from supply of defective goods).

[117] For a very early instance, see *Inchbald v Western Neghilgerry Coffee Co* (1864) 17 CBNS 733 (agent deprived of chance to place shares in exchange for a payment of £400: £250 awarded, reduced to reflect chance that he might not have succeeded in placing them). But early authority was mixed, with some cases apparently denying that loss of a chance was an admissible head at all: e.g. *Sapwell v Bass* [1910] 2 K.B. 486 (no such recovery for breach of contract to serve brood mare with stallion).

[118] Compare Lord Hoffmann's speculation in *Gregg v Scott* [2005] UKHL 2; [2005] 2 A.C. 176 at [82], that the rule is due to an unstated belief that even if physical facts are predestined, human actions are not.

[119] This view has the advantage of accommodating the fact that some claims—notably claims for past lost profits—do depend on a view of the hypothetical third party actions (namely, those of potential customers), but are nevertheless not subject to a "loss of chance" analysis. See e.g. *Vasiliou v Hajigeorgiou* [2010] EWCA Civ 1475, and the discussion of the point in the tort case of *The Vicky I* [2008] 2 Lloyd's Rep. 45 at [68]–[74]. It is suggested that this remains the case despite the somewhat equivocal treatment of these decisions in *Wellesley Partners LLP v Withers LLP* [2015] EWCA Civ 1146; [2016] P.N.L.R. 19.

[120] The point may matter: what if the court has evidence from the third party as to what he would have done, so the element of unreckonability is not present (a point left open by David Richards J in *4Eng Ltd v Harper* [2008] EWHC 915 (Ch.); [2009] Ch. 91 at [57]–[58])? The better position, it is suggested (with *McGregor on Damages*, 21st edn (London: Sweet & Maxwell, 2018), para.10-69 ff) is that this should make no difference.

[121] [1911] 2 K.B. 786.

[122] The prize was one of 12, consisting of theatrical contracts paying between about £450 and £750 in total. The reader is left to calculate the plaintiff's chances of success as reckoned by the jury, who had (presumably) seen her.

Air Forces Ass'n[123] in 1957 the rule was authoritatively established, that where solicitors in breach of duty bungle litigation and as a result deprive the claimant of a cause of action, damages are assessed by reference to the amount the claimant would have got had the proceedings been competently and successfully prosecuted, discounted by the possibility that he would have lost. [124] This practice, moreover, fairly quickly spread to a number of other professional negligence situations.[125]

In the 1995 decision of *Allied Maples Group Ltd v Simmons & Simmons*,[126] the **24-040** Court of Appeal fused the previous authorities into a general principle. In that case, lawyers negotiating the purchase of a business for clients negligently failed to press for an adequate vendors' warranty against hidden liabilities. Substantial such liabilities having indeed materialised, the lawyers argued in answer to their clients' suit for negligence that even if they had been at fault no loss had been shown, since there was no proof that the vendors would have given any guarantee even if asked. The Court of Appeal disagreed, holding that the clients should recover the amount of the liabilities discounted by the chance that the vendors would have refused to grant the guarantee in question. The overall rule, said Stuart-Smith LJ, was that where the quantification of a loss depended on future events, or (in the case of wrongful omissions) on the hypothetical actions of third parties in the past (rather than that of the claimant or defendant themselves[127]), a "loss of chance" award was generally appropriate.[128]

Since *Allied Maples* the "loss of a chance" principle in it has been widely applied. **24-041** Although (as mentioned above) Stuart-Smith LJ limited its application to cases of wrongful omissions,[129] this limitation seems to have been ignored in most subsequent decisions. Thus, apart from bungled litigation, where it finds its commonest application, cases awarding "loss of chance" damages for breach of contract have included those involving hypothetical sales lost through a bank's breach of its obligation of confidentiality[130] or a lender's disregard of an exclusivity agreement;[131] reduced fire resistance in a misdesigned building which later burnt down;[132] profits lost to a developer when, in breach of contract, a contractor employed by him

---

[123] [1958] 1 W.L.R. 563. Cf. *Motor Crown Petroleum Ltd v SJ Berwin & Co* [2000] Lloyd's Rep. PN 438.

[124] See generally now *Perry v Raleys Solicitors* [2019] UKSC 5; [2019] 2 W.L.R. 636.

[125] Typical was *Everett v Hogg Robinson Ltd* [1973] 2 Lloyd's Rep. 217 (damages against insurance brokers for misrepresentations voiding cover). Cf. *O & R Jewellers Ltd v Terry* [1999] Lloyd's Rep. I.R. 436.

[126] [1995] 1 W.L.R. 1602. For very similar case and outcomes, see the later *Football League Ltd v Edge Ellison (A Firm)* [2006] EWHC 1462 (Ch.); [2007] P.N.L.R. 2; *Perkin v Lupton Fawcett* [2008] EWCA Civ 418; [2008] P.N.L.R. 30.

[127] See, e.g. *Harrison v Bloom Camillin* [2001] P.N.L.R. 195 (solicitors' negligence in allowing limitation to run: up to clients to prove that they would have prosecuted proceedings). The point was confirmed in *Perry v Raleys Solicitors* [2019] UKSC 5; [2019] 2 W.L.R. 636.

[128] See [1995] 1 W.L.R. 1602 at 1610 (Stuart-Smith LJ).

[129] See [1995] 1 W.L.R. 1602 at 1610.

[130] See *Jackson v Royal Bank of Scotland Plc* [2000] C.L.C. 1457 (middleman's banker revealing source of supply to middleman's customer: middleman lost the business: reversed in the HL on another matter: at [2005] UKHL 3; [2005] 1 W.L.R. 377). Analogous are *Stephenson (SBJ) Ltd v Mandy* [2000] I.R.L.R. 234 (sales lost through acts of disloyal employee) and *Take Ltd v BSM Marketing* [2007] EWHC 3513 (QB) (disloyalty of agent).

[131] *Bugsby Property LLC v LGIM Commercial Lending Ltd* [2022] EWHC 2001 (Comm). See too *Brooke Homes (Bicester) Ltd v Portfolio Property Partners Ltd* [2021] EWHC 3015 (Ch) (best efforts obligation to reach agreement).

[132] *Sainsbury Plc v Broadway Malyan* [1999] P.N.L.R. 286. The third party in question there was the

caused a project to be burnt down;[133] the opportunity of a very profitable sale of assets lost by reason of accountants' misvaluation of those assets;[134] an opportunity of a profitable investment abroad lost through solicitors' incompetence in drafting the necessary funding documentation;[135] and, in a series of cases, the opportunity for an early and profitable sale of realty lost through the negligence of solicitors in a slack market.[136]

24-042   The "loss of a chance" principle adumbrated in *Allied Maples Group Ltd v Simmons & Simmons*,[137] it should be noted, is a genuine rule of quantification of loss, rather than a mere amendment of the rules of proof. It follows that it cuts both ways: in a case where it is applicable, it can be invoked by the defendant as much as by the claimant. So where a third party's action is in point, even if a claimant can show a considerably more than evens chance that he would have benefited from that third party's action, he will still only recover discounted damages.[138]

24-043   Nevertheless, three important limits have been placed on the principle. First, it is important to remember that it applies only to the *hypothetical* decision of a third party. Where an actual decision has been taken, the normal rules of proof apply. Thus in *Bank of Credit and Commerce International SA (in liq) v Ali (No.3)*[139] ex-employees of a bank which the employers had, in breach of contract, used as a vehicle for fraud sued for damages reflecting their resulting handicap in the labour market. It was held that where (as was the case in many of the claimants) their complaint was that they had actually been refused employment, they had to prove on a balance of probabilities that their non-hiring had been influenced by their association with a tainted employer. Secondly, the lost chance must be substantial rather than negligible.[140] And thirdly, the principle has been held not to apply to loss of profit claims as such, despite the impeccably logical argument that all such claims ultimately depend on the hypothetical willingness of third parties—in this case, customers—to do business with the claimant.[141]

24-044   Where a loss of chance award is appropriate, its quantification is a com-

---

fire brigade, who might or might not have been able to contain the fire: see [1999] P.N.L.R. 286 at 325–326.

[133] *Aldgate Construction Co Ltd v Unibar Plumbing & Heating Ltd* [2010] EWHC 1063 (TCC), 130 Con L.R. 190

[134] *Dennard v PricewaterhouseCoopers LLP* [2010] EWHC 812 (Ch). Cf. the Canadian decision in *Multi-Malls Inc v Tex-Mall Properties Ltd* (1980) 108 D.L.R. (3d) 399 (loss of chance of profitable rezoning of plaintiffs' property).

[135] *Wellesley Partners LLP v Withers LLP* [2015] EWCA Civ 1146; [2016] P.N.L.R. 19

[136] *First Interstate Bank of California v Cohen Arnold & Co* [1996] C.L.C. 174; *Stovold v Barlows* [1996] C.L.C. 228; *Tom Hoskins Plc v EMW Law (A Firm)* [2010] EWHC 479 (Ch); [2010] ECC 20.

[137] [1995] 1 W.L.R. 1602. For very similar case and outcomes, see the later *Football League Ltd v Edge Ellison (A Firm)* [2006] EWHC 1462 (Ch), [2007] P.N.L.R. 2; *Perkin v Lupton Fawcett* [2008] EWCA Civ 418; [2008] P.N.L.R. 30.

[138] *Stovold v Barlows* [1996] C.L.C. 228 (loss of sale on a falling market caused by negligence of vendor's solicitors).

[139] [2002] 3 All E.R. 750.

[140] See e.g. the solicitors' cases of *Mount v Barker Austin* [1998] P.N.L.R. 493 at 510 (Simon Brown J); *Thomas v Albutt* [2015] EWHC 2187 (Ch); [2015] P.N.L.R. 29 at [461] (Morgan J). The figure of what chance is substantial seems to have stabilised at 10%: see Waksman J in *PCP Capital Partners LLP v Barclays Bank Plc* [2021] EWHC 307 (Comm) at [554]–[561] and also *Mackenzie v AA Plc* [2021] EWHC 1605 (QB) at [44].

[141] E.g. *Vasiliou v Hajigeorgiou* [2010] EWCA Civ 1475 (loss of restaurant profits due to breach of covenant). See the discussion of the point in *Wellesley Partners LLP v Withers LLP* [2015] EWCA Civ 1146; [2016] P.N.L.R. 19 at [90] ff (Floyd LJ).

monsense and at times fairly impressionistic matter.[142] If there is more than one contingency, discounting may be compound.[143] In a suitable case where the chances are extremely strong or overwhelming, a figure of 100 per cent may be justified.[144]

II. THE CONDUCT OF THE CLAIMANT: AVOIDABLE LOSS AND THE DUTY TO MITIGATE

The principle of mitigation of loss

The idea that the victim of a breach of contract should have to take reasonable steps to minimise his damage[145] is an old[146] and extensive[147] one. In England it seemingly originated as an extension of the law of causation.[148] Although this explanation has been strongly doubted[149] and other justifications at times been given for the doctrine,[150] it is suggested that this is still the best explanation.[151] In so far as a given loss has been incurred or increased by reason of the claimant's unreasonable

24-045

---

[142] In *Parabola Investments Ltd v Browallia Cal Ltd (formerly Union Cal Ltd)* [2010] EWCA Civ 486; [2011] Q.B. 477 at [25] Patten LJ referred to a judge "making a realistic and reasoned assessment of a variety of circumstances in order to determine what the level of loss has been." See too *Bugsby Property LLC v LGIM Commercial Lending Ltd* [2022] EWHC 2001 (Comm) at [224].

[143] See e.g. *Joyce v Bowman Law Ltd* [2010] EWHC 251 (Ch); [2010] P.N.L.R. 22 (three contingencies). But this assumes the contingencies are genuinely independent. If they are not, mechanistic multiplication is inappropriate: see *Hanbury v Hugh James Solicitors* [2019] EWHC 1074 (QB); [2019] P.N.L.R. 25 (unless contingencies genuinely independent, mechanistic multiplication of chances inappropriate).

[144] *Harrison v Bloom Camillin* [2001] P.N.L.R. 7 at [87] (Neuberger J). See too *Somatra v Sinclair Roche & Temperley (No 2)* [2003] EWCA Civ 1474; [2003] 2 Lloyd's Rep. 855 (solicitors' bad advice to insurance claimant led to settlement of claim at two-thirds, whereas it otherwise would have settled at 75 per cent: award of total difference upheld).

[145] See D. Feldman and D. Libling, "Inflation and Duty to Mitigate" (1979) 95 L.Q.R 270; M. Bridge, "Damages in Contract and the Meaning of Avoidable Loss" (1989) 105 L.Q.R 398; H. McGregor, "The Role of Mitigation in the Assessment of damages" in D. Saidov and R. Cunnington (eds), *Contract Damages; Domestic and International Perspectives* (Oxford: Hart Publishing, 2008), Ch.14.

[146] Its origins are, it seems, mid-nineteenth-century. One of the earliest instances is a dictum by Parke B in *Harries v Edmonds* (1845) 1 Car & Kir 686 at 687 (duty on defendant "to save the defendant from as much damage as he could"). Other early statements are in *Beckham v Drake* (1849) 2 HLC 599 at 607–608 (Erle J); *Frost v Knight* (1872) L.R. 7 Ex 111 at 115 (Cockburn CJ); and *Roper v Johnson* (1873) L.R. 8 C.P. 167 at 181–182 (Brett J).

[147] It applies in numerous cases outside English law, for example, in the CISG: see CISG, §77.

[148] Compare *Brace v Calder* [1895] 2 Q.B. 253 (technically dismissed employee refusing offer of continued engagement: damages nominal, since loss "his own fault.": see Lopes LJ at 261).

[149] See e.g. *McGregor on Damages*, 21st edn (London: Sweet & Maxwell, 2020), para.9-019; *Uzinterimpex JSC v Standard Bank Plc* [2008] EWCA Civ 819; [2008] 2 Lloyd's Rep. 456 at [56] (Moore-Bick LJ).

[150] Notably that it is an aspect of remoteness: see the suggestions of Diplock J in *Shindler v Northern Raincoat Co Ltd* [1960] 1 W.L.R. 1038 at 1048 and HHJ Newey in *Hospital for Sick Children v McLaughlin & Harvey Plc* (1987) 19 Con L.R. 25 at 94. But this is unconvincing: remoteness deals with what was foreseeable at the time of contracting, and there is no necessary connection between this and what amounts to reasonable conduct by the claimant at or after the time of breach.

[151] A view taken in a number of the decided cases. See e.g. *Lagden v O'Connor* [2003] UKHL 64; [2004] 1 A.C. 1067 at [99]–[100] (Lord Walker); also *Standard Chartered Bank v Pakistan National Shipping Corp* [2001] EWCA Civ 55; [2001] C.L.C. 825 at [41], where Potter L.J. described them as "two sides of the same coin".

behaviour,[152] to that extent the law refuses to regard it as a consequence of the defendant's breach.[153]

24-046 It should be noted, however, that even though causation and mitigation are closely connected and indeed often operate in tandem,[154] they are not today treated in quite the same way. Thus action (or inaction) by the claimant may, at least in practice, amount to an unreasonable failure to mitigate even if it would not otherwise be a *novus actus interveniens* or overriding cause in the law of causation generally. Conversely, while a reasonable decision taken by the claimant in response to a breach of contract cannot normally amount to failure to mitigate,[155] it may nevertheless on occasion be sufficient to negative any causal link between the resulting loss and the defendant's breach.[156]

24-047 The present rule on mitigation can be stated as follows. A claimant faced with a breach of contract is expected to take all such steps as are reasonable in his situation, to limit the loss suffered. While he is of course free not to do this,[157] to the extent that his loss is due to such failure, he is disabled from claiming in respect of it. This essentially reflects the summary of the rule given by James LJ in 1878 in *Dunkirk Colliery Co v Lever*:

> "What the plaintiffs are entitled to is the full amount of the damage which they have really suffered by a breach of the contract; the person who has broken the contract not being exposed to additional cost by reason of the plaintiffs not doing what they ought to have done as reasonable men, and the plaintiffs not being under any obligation to do anything not in the ordinary course of business."[158]

In other words, the damages available to the claimant who has unreasonably

---

[152] Only the actual claimant's behaviour is in account. So a subrogated insurance company suing in its assured's name is not bound to take advantage of an opportunity to mitigate available only to it: *Bee v Jenson (No.2)* [2006] EWHC 3359 (Comm); [2007] RTR 32 (affirmed [2007] EWCA Civ 923; [2008] RTR 7).

[153] See Toulson J in *Standard Chartered Bank Plc v Pakistan National Shipping Corp* [1999] 1 Lloyd's Rep. 747 at 758 ("The orthodox view is that the rule as to avoidable loss is merely an aspect of the fundamental principle of causation that a plaintiff can recover only in respect of damage caused by the defendant's wrong"); also *The Elena D'Amico* [1980] 1 Lloyds Rep. 75 at 88 (Goff J) and *Thai Airways International Ltd v KI Holdings Co Ltd* [2015] EWHC 1250 (Comm) at [33] (Leggatt J).

[154] Thus in *Lambert v Lewis* [1982] A.C. 225, where a buyer of defective and dangerous goods knowingly continued to use them, it was held that his claim for the resulting loss failed on causation grounds. But the result could equally well have been grounded on failure to mitigate.

[155] Below, para.24-056.

[156] As in *The Elena D'Amico* [1980] 1 Lloyd's Rep. 75 (breach of contract made chartered vessel unavailable: charterers' commercially reasonable decision not to charter replacement led to loss of lucrative market: even if not failure to mitigate, loss not caused by owners' breach).

[157] Hence the "duty" to mitigate is a misnomer. It is more accurately "a condition attached to the right to claim damages": see *The Solholt* [1981] 2 Lloyd's Rep. 574 at 580 (Staughton J). Note too *The Elena D'Amico* [1980] 1 Lloyd's Rep. 75 at 88 (Goff LJ), *Sembawang Corp Ltd v Pacific Ocean Shipping Corp (No.3)* [2004] EWHC 2743 (Comm) at [26] (same re express contractual duty to mitigate), and *Darbishire v Warran* [1963] 1 W.L.R. 1067 at 1075 (same re tort).

[158] (1878) 9 Ch. D. 20 at 25, approved by Lord Haldane in *British Westinghouse Electric Co Ltd v Underground Electric Rlys Co of London* [1912] A.C. 673 at 689. Similar formulations appear in *Jamal v Moolla Dawood* [1916] 1 A.C. 175 at 179 (Lord Wrenbury) and *Golden Strait Corp v Nippon Yusen Kubishika Kaisha* [2007] UKHL 12; [2007] 2 A.C. 353 at [10] (Lord Bingham). Or, as Leggatt J nicely put it, mitigation "is not in truth a duty but an assumption: damages are calculated on the assumption that the claimant has taken reasonable steps in mitigation whether it has in fact done so or not" (*Thai Airways International Ltd v KI Holdings Co Ltd* [2015] EWHC 1250 (Comm); [2015] 1 C.L.C. 765 at [34]).

failed to mitigate are reckoned on the (counterfactual) basis that he has in fact taken steps to do so.[159]

One important limitation to the duty to mitigate should be noted immediately: being concerned with the compensability of loss suffered by the claimant, it cannot apply except to actions for unliquidated damages.[160] It does not therefore affect claims of a restitutionary nature, such as claims for money paid by mistake or for a consideration that has failed, which do not depend on a showing of loss.[161] Nor does it apply to claims for liquidated damages, where the agreement on the amount of damages payable implicitly ousts any jurisdiction to reduce them on account of the claimant's acts.[162]

24-048

Nor, for the same reason, does it affect claims in debt. In the vital but controversial case of *White & Carter (Councils) Ltd v McGregor*,[163] advertisers agreed to renew an ongoing contract to publicise a client's business for a further three years. Before the three years had started the client changed its mind and repudiated: the advertisers, however, performed in full and then successfully claimed their fee. Although the case strictly did not turn on mitigation (concentrating instead on establishing that clients' unaccepted repudiation could not take away the advertisers' contractual rights), the essence of the clients' argument was that the advertisers had failed to mitigate, and it is implicit in the result in the claimants' favour that there is no room for the doctrine in claims for debt.[164]

24-049

The non-applicability of the duty to mitigate to debt claims can be significant in a number of cases. It means, for example, that where goods are sold and property and risk pass to the buyer, if the buyer thereafter refuses to collect them the seller can simply sue for the price, without reference to what might be reasonable efforts to mitigate loss.[165] On a similar basis it has been held that a lender can recover

24-050

---

[159] To take a straightforward example, where a seller repudiates a contract of sale and the buyer buys the same commodity later, the latter's damages are computed on the basis that he bought as soon as reasonably possible, and not at the date he actually bought in, if later: see *Kaines (UK) Ltd v Österreichische Waren HG Austrowaren GmbH* [1993] 2 Lloyd's Rep. 1. In the case of claims for defective services where the recipient unreasonably fails to accept an offer by the provider himself to correct matters, this can raise difficult issues as to the amount of recovery: see for example *Pearce & High Ltd v Baxter* [1999] C.L.C. 749 and *Woodlands Oak Ltd v Conwell* [2011] B.L.R. 365 at [23]–[25].

[160] Including claims for value-price differentials (for example, under ss.50 and 51 of the Sale of Goods Act 1979), despite a possible argument that these are not really claims for loss at all. See *Payzu Ltd v Saunders* [1919] 2 K.B. 581 (criticised on essentially this basis in M. Bridge, "Damages in Contract and the Meaning of Avoidable Loss" (1989) 105 L.Q.R 398 at 412–414).

[161] See *Kleinwort Benson Ltd v Birmingham City Council* [1997] Q.B. 380 at 395, 399 (Saville and Morritt LJJ) (appealed to the HL on another issue, [1999] 2 A.C. 349); G. Virgo, *Principles of the Law of Restitution*, 3rd edn (Oxford: Oxford University Press 2015), pp.705–707.

[162] *McGregor on Damages*, 21st edn (London: Sweet & Maxwell, 2020), para.16–025; *Abrahams v Performing Rights Society Ltd* [1995] I.C.R. 1028.

[163] [1962] A.C. 413; also *Anglo African Shipping Co of New York Inc v J Mortner Ltd* [1962] 1 Lloyd's Rep. 81. See W. Goodhart, "Measure of Damages When a Contract is Repudiated" (1962) 78 L.Q.R. 263; P. Nienaber [1962] C.L.J. 213; L.J. Priestley, "Conduct after Breach: the Position of the Party not in Breach" (1991) 3 JCL 218. The case is not uncontroversial; it has been rejected in Canada (see *Asamera Oil Corp v Sea Oil & General Corp* (1978) 89 D.L.R. (3d) 1), and American authority is predominantly against it (see the leading decision in *Rockingham County v Luten Bridge Co* 35 F.2d 301 (1929)). N. Andrews, *Contract Law*, p.529, is mildly critical.

[164] A point since regarded as settled: see, e.g. *Abrahams v Performing Right Society Ltd* [1995] I.C.R. 1028 and *Reichman v Beveridge* [2006] EWCA Civ 1659; [2007] 1 P. & C.R. 20.

[165] *Benjamin's Sale of Goods*, 11th edn (London: Sweet & Maxwell, 2020), para.16.022. But note Auld LJ's scepticism in *Habton Farms v Nimmo* [2003] EWCA Civ 68; [2004] Q.B. 1 at [128], where he

money lent without pursuing a credit insurer,[166] and a landlord can continue to claim rent from a tenant until the end of the lease, even when the latter has abandoned the premises, without any duty to take steps to regularise the position by terminating the lease.[167] And yet again, it seems that where an employer agrees to pay a dismissed employee a number of months' salary in lieu of notice, the employee can claim that sum without coming under any duty within that period to mitigate his loss by finding other employment.[168] Lastly, and highly significantly, it has been held that, because liquidated damages clauses analytically give rise to debt claims, no issue of mitigation can arise in connection with their enforcement.[169]

24-051   It should be noted, however, that the right to sue in debt is not entirely uncontrolled. Despite the decision in *White & Carter (Councils) Ltd v McGregor*[170] there are cases where the victim of a repudiation will be held to have no legitimate interest in suing in debt. In these cases, which are not part of the law of mitigation,[171] the claimant will be limited to such causes of action as he may have in damages. For details the reader is referred to para.19-037 ff, above.

When the duty to mitigate arises

24-052   The duty to mitigate is regarded as arising in response to a breach of contract by the defendant, or at the very least in response to an accepted repudiation. It follows that a claimant cannot be under any such duty unless and until the defendant is in fact in breach. Put another way, there is no such thing as an anticipatory duty to mitigate. *Wright v Dean*[172] makes this point abundantly clear. The grantor of an unregistered option over land sometime later sold the land, thereby defeating the option and breaking the contract. The grantee recovered full damages notwithstanding the grantor's observation that had he taken the obvious step of registering the option immediately he would have avoided the loss entirely. Although this was true, said Wynn-Parry J, this did not affect his claim; no duty to mitigate arose until breach, and breach had only occurred when the grantor sold elsewhere.[173]

24-053   It also follows that there can be no duty to mitigate when faced with a mere anticipatory repudiation. Unless and until accepted by the innocent party, it is a

suggests that a seller might, after a long time has passed, come under a duty to mitigate and sell elsewhere. Compare the provision in the UCC, para.2-709(1), which specifically limits the seller's right to claim the price of goods to cases where he is "unable after reasonable effort to resell them at a reasonable price", or they are lost or destroyed within a "commercially reasonable time".

166 *MTF Funding Ltd (In Liquidation) v Synergy Agroscience Ltd* [2023] EWHC 682 (Ch) at [126].
167 *Reichman v Beveridge* [2006] EWCA Civ 1659; [2007] 1 P. & C.R. 20. A lessor of chattels is in the same position: *FTAI AirOpCo UK Ltd v Olympus Airways SA* [2022] EWHC 1362 (Comm) at [258]. Cf. the less uncompromising attitude in Australia: *Vickers v Stichtenoth Investments Pty Ltd* (1989) 52 S.A.S.R. 90.
168 Held in *Abrahams v Performing Right Society Ltd* [1995] I.C.R. 1028. But note that this only applies if the employee has a right to such payment: a contract term allowing the employer to elect to pay a sum in lieu of notice is irrelevant. See *Cerberus Software Ltd v Rowley* [2001] EWCA Civ 78; [2001] I.C.R. 376.
169 *MSC Mediterranean Shipping Co SA v Cottonex Anstalt* [2015] EWHC 283 (Comm); [2015] 1 C.L.C. 143 at [70]–[71] (Leggatt J), provisionally approved on appeal by Moore-Bick LJ (see [2016] EWCA Civ 789 at [47]–[51]).
170 [1962] A.C. 413.
171 See *Reichman v Beveridge* [2006] EWCA Civ 1659; [2007] 1 P. & C.R. 20 at [12] (Lloyd LJ).
172 [1948] Ch. 686. See too *Hollington v Rhodes* [1951] 2 All E.R. 578 (Note), and the much earlier *Harries v Edmonds* (1845) 1 Car & Kir 686 (failure by charterer to ship cargo: no duty on shipowner to accept alternative cargo until laytime expired, since no breach until then).
173 See [1948] Ch. 686 at 696.

"thing writ in water":[174] a mere intimation of a possible future breach, otherwise without significance: thus the innocent party who chooses to ignore it, reasonably or otherwise, takes no risk as to damages.[175] So in 1874 it was held that where a seller repudiated before the date for delivery but the buyer ignored that repudiation, damages were to be set by reference to prices as at the delivery date even if the buyer could previously have mitigated his loss by buying equivalent goods for less.[176] And the principle was trenchantly restated in another context in 1959 in *Shindler v Northern Raincoat Co Ltd*.[177] A senior manager on a fixed term contract refused to accept a year's (wrongful) notice from his employers, and was duly dismissed at the end of the year. Even though he had admittedly taken no steps in the meantime to find another job, no reduction in his damages was made on that account. As Diplock J put it:

> "[I]t cannot be said that there is any duty on the part of the plaintiff to mitigate his damages before there has been any breach which he has accepted as such."[178]

On the other hand, the above statement is limited to *unaccepted* repudiations. **24-054** Once accepted, an anticipatory repudiation can be treated as a breach by the defendant as much as by the claimant: and hence it will thereafter trigger a duty to mitigate in the ordinary way. So in the sale of goods case of *Melachrino v Nicholl & Knight*[179] sellers of cotton repudiated some little time before delivery was due. Then, and at the time fixed for delivery, the market price was above the contract price, but in much of the intervening period it had been below it. The buyers were limited to nominal damages, on the basis that they had failed to minimise their loss by buying in at the lower price.

Not only can there be no question of an obligation to mitigate before breach: even **24-055** after breach, the fact that the victim's only obligation is to act reasonably means that it cannot affect him at any time before he has reason to know of it.[180] There are few breach of contract cases in point:[181] but the tort decision in *Twycross v Grant*[182] is as good an illustration as any. The defendant deceived the plaintiff into subscribing for shares in a worthless concern. Sued for the money paid, the defendant argued that the shares had had some value in the market for a time after the issue, and that the plaintiff ought to have mitigated by selling them then. This plea was seen off

---

[174] See Asquith LJ in *Howard v Pickford Tool Co Ltd* [1951] 1 K.B. 417 at 421; also *Heyman v Darwins Ltd* [1942] A.C. 356 at 361 (Lord Simon). The reference is to the epitaph on Keats's grave in the Protestant Cemetery in Rome: "Here lies one whose name was writ in water."

[175] *Brown v Muller* (1872) L.R. 7 Ex 319; *Shindler v Northern Raincoat Co Ltd* [1960] 1 W.L.R. 1038; *The Solholt* [1981] 2 Lloyd's Rep. 574 at 580 (Staughton J).

[176] *Brown v Muller* (1872) L.R. 7 Ex 319; also *Tredegar Iron & Coal Co Ltd v Hawthorn Bros* (1902) 18 T.L.R. 716.

[177] [1960] 1 W.L.R. 1038.

[178] [1960] 1 W.L.R. 1038 at 1048.

[179] [1920] 1 K.B. 693. For a similar later case see *Kaines (UK) Ltd v Österreichische Waren HG Austrowaren GmbH* [1993] 2 Lloyd's Rep. 1. Note too *Sudan Import & Export Co (Khartoum) v Societe Generale de Compensation* [1957] 2 Lloyd's Rep. 528 at 538.

[180] *Downs v Chappell* [1997] 1 W.L.R. 426 at 435 ff (Hobhouse LJ); also the tort decisions in *Smith New Court Ltd v Scrimgeour Vickers Ltd* [1997] A.C. 254 at 266 (Lord Browne-Wilkinson), and *Twycross v Grant* (1877) 2 CPD 469.

[181] But cf. *Hayes v James & Charles Dodd (A Firm)* [1990] 2 All E.R. 815 (solicitors' negligence leaves claimants with useless business premises: seemingly accepted that no duty to mitigate until negligence clear to claimants).

[182] (1877) 2 C.P.D. 469.

with the observation that no action could have been expected of the plaintiff before he had had notice of the fraud practised on him.

The content of the duty to mitigate

24-056 **(i) The principle of reasonableness** The claimant is not bound to take all possible steps to mitigate his loss. He is merely expected to act reasonably, taking into account the facts as apparent to him;[183] in Lord Haldane's words, the law

"does not impose on the plaintiff an obligation to take any step which a reasonable and prudent man would not ordinarily take in the course of his business".[184]

24-057 Moreover, and importantly, the courts have been at some pains to stress not only that the claimant must be shown to have acted (or failed to act) unreasonably,[185] but also that the doctrine should not be applied too demandingly against a contractor who has, after all, been put in the position he is now in by an admitted wrong on the other party's part.[186] As Lord Macmillan put it in 1931,

"the measures which [the claimant] may be driven to adopt in order to extricate himself ought not to be weighed in nice scales at the instance of the [wrongdoer]".[187]

24-058 What is reasonable is not a question of law, but rather a question of fact to be decided according to the different circumstances of each particular case.[188] Nevertheless, a number of indications as to what is likely to be regarded as reasonable in particular circumstances can be found in the case-law.

24-059 To start with, in the absence of unusual circumstances, commercial contract claimants are generally expected to take advantage of any easily available means of reducing their losses. A straightforward example is sales of commodities; if there is a ready market, the claimant is expected to go into it, and moreover to do so with some expedition as soon as he knows of the other party's breach.[189] Similarly, in more complicated transactions where hedging liabilities is standard practice, a

---

[183] See *Shindler v Northern Raincoat Co Ltd* [1960] 1 W.L.R. 1038 (senior manager dismissed: later offer of re-employment in fact genuine, but plaintiff still entitled to reject it owing to his own reasonable doubts about whether employer serious).

[184] *British Westinghouse Electric & Manufacturing Co Ltd v Underground Electric Rlys Co of London* [1912] A.C. 673 at 689 (Lord Haldane). For other statements, see *Dunkirk Colliery Co v Lever* (1878) 9 Ch. D. 20 at 25 (James LJ); *Jamal v Moolla Dawood, Sons & Co* [1916] 1 A.C. 175 at 179 (Lord Wrenbury), *London & South of England Building Society v Stone* [1983] 1 W.L.R. 1242 at 1262 (Stephenson LJ). Contract clauses expressly requiring a party to mitigate costs are similarly construed: *Sembawang Corp Ltd v Pacific Ocean Shipping Corp (No.3)* [2004] EWHC 2743 (Comm).

[185] "If there is more than one reasonable response open to the wronged party, the wrongdoer has no right to determine his choice. It is where, and only where, the wrongdoer can show affirmatively that the other party has acted unreasonably in relation to his duty to mitigate that the defence will succeed." Potter LJ in *Wilding v British Telecommunications plc* [2002] EWCA Civ 349; [2002] I.C.R. 1079 at [55]. See too *Thai Airways International Public Co Ltd v KI Holdings Co Ltd (formerly Koito Industries Ltd)* [2015] EWHC 1250 (Comm) at [38].

[186] See, e.g. *Banco de Portugal v Waterlow & Sons Ltd* [1932] A.C. 452 at 506; *London & South of England Building Society v Stone* [1983] 1 W.L.R. 1242 at 1262–1263 (Stephenson LJ); *Walker v Medlicott* [1999] 1 W.L.R. 727 at 743 (Simon Brown LJ); *Williams v Glyn Owen & Co* [2003] EWCA Civ 750; [2004] P.N.L.R. 20 at [68] (Jonathan Parker LJ).

[187] *Banco de Portugal v Waterlow & Sons Ltd* [1932] A.C. 452 at 506.

[188] See *Payzu Ltd v Saunders* [1919] 2 K.B. 581 at 588 (Bankes LJ).

[189] Cf. *Kaines v Österreichische Waren HG* [1993] 1 Lloyd's Rep. 1 (continuous and volatile market in oil: anticipatory breach by seller; duty in circumstances to buy in elsewhere within hours of ac-

claimant faced with breach may similarly be expected to take protective steps such as closing out his position.[190] Again, where a breach of contract by a defendant makes a claimant potentially liable to a third party for continuous or ongoing costs, he is expected to take reasonable steps to terminate or curtail them.[191] And a fortiori, a claimant is expected to keep any costs incurred as a result of the breach as low as reasonable.[192]

Nevertheless, even in the commercial context the standard expected of the victim **24-060** of breach is not put excessively high. In particular, he will not be penalised for failing to take measures that would be unusually difficult or troublesome. So in *Lesters Leather Co v Home & Overseas Brokers Ltd*,[193] buyers sued for loss of profits suffered as a result of their sellers' failure to deliver exotic snakeskins in England. On the evidence, while no alternative supplies of skins could be had at home, they were readily obtainable in India: nevertheless the buyers' hopeful contention that the sellers ought to have mitigated their loss by buying there was doomed to failure. As Lord Goddard CJ put it, "I cannot say that the buyers are bound to go hunting round the globe to find out where they can get skins."[194]

For similar reasons, a contract-breaker cannot generally expect a commercial **24-061** party to engage in damage limitation exercises that would require him further to hazard his own money or assets. The point, well-established in tort,[195] arose neatly in contract in *UCB Corporate Services Ltd v Edwin Watson & Son*.[196] Buyers, negligently misadvised by their surveyors, paid over the odds for certain properties and in due course sued for the excess. Their suit succeeded, despite a suggestion that they could have bought other properties in the same block, consolidated the freehold and sold the combined parcel at a profit. They could not, it was said, be criticised for declining to spend more of their own money in an attempt to save the interests of the defendants. Yet again, it has been said more recently that a buyer of commodities has no duty to take on further risk by entering into a hedging transaction against the effect of breach by his seller.[197]

In addition, it has been made clear that, in deciding what is reasonable, the **24-062** preservation of commercial reputation is a highly relevant factor. A spectacular

---

cepting it). It is often said that the market rule in contracts of sale is merely an aspect of mitigation: see e.g. A. Kramer and A. Dyson, "There Is No 'Breach Date' Rule: Mitigation, Difference in Value and Date of Assessment" (2014) 130 L.Q.R. 259 and cases such as *Hooper v Oates* [2014] Ch. 287 (sale of land) and *Bunge SA v Nidera BV* [2015] UKSC 43; [2015] 2 Lloyd's Rep. 469 at [17]. But this is doubtful, as is convincingly argued in M. Bridge, "Markets and damages in sale of goods cases" (2016) 132 L.Q.R. 405.

190 *Glencore Energy UK Ltd v Transworld Oil Ltd* [2010] EWHC 141 (Comm), [2010] 1 C.L.C. 284.
191 *Bulkhaul Ltd v Rhodia Organique Fine Ltd* [2008] EWCA Civ 1452; [2009] 1 Lloyd's Rep. 353 (long-term contract for lease of specialised tanks repudiated by lessee; lessor bound to take steps to cut his losses by selling them for what he could get). And cf. *County Personnel (Employment Agency) Ltd v Alan R Pulver & Co* [1987] 1 W.L.R. 916 (payment to buy out of disadvantageous lease regarded as potentially a reasonable step in mitigation and hence potentially claimable as damages).
192 Cf. the damages decision in *The Borag* [1981] 1 All E.R. 856; [1981] 1 W.L.R. 274 (costs of obtaining bank guarantee claimable as damages for wrongful arrest of ship, but not much greater costs of borrowing the necessary money on overdraft).
193 (1948) 64 T.L.R. 569.
194 *Lesters Leather Co v Home & Overseas Brokers Ltd* (1948) 64 T.L.R. 569.
195 *Jewelowski v Propp* [1944] K.B. 510, esp at 512.
196 Unreported 26 February 1999, Q.B.D.
197 See *Glencore Energy UK Ltd v Transworld Oil Ltd* [2010] EWHC 141 (Comm); [2010] 1 C.L.C. 284 at [79] (Blair J).

example is *Banco de Portugal v Waterlow & Sons Ltd*,[198] where British security printers, having printed a run of genuine Portuguese banknotes, allowed themselves in breach of contract to be duped into printing and releasing vast numbers of unauthorised ones.[199] The Portuguese government, concerned for the integrity of its currency, cashed large numbers of the spurious notes and sued for the amount so spent. The House of Lords had no doubt that this act, though voluntary, was not a culpable failure to minimise damage, and upheld the claim.[200] Similarly, in an action by buyers for damages in respect of a misdated bill of lading, it was shown that the buyers could in fact have reduced their loss to nil by forcing their goods on to sub-buyers under the terms of a subsale under which the latter were bound to accept them. Nevertheless, the Court of Appeal held that they were justified in not thus playing Shylock, and were not guilty of unreasonably failing to minimise their losses.[201]

24-063 Outside commercial contracts, the standards expected of a claimant are, if anything, even lower. A case in point is *Radford v De Froberville*,[202] where a buyer of a building plot at the bottom of a west London garden wrongfully failed to build a boundary wall between it and the seller's existing house. Sued for the cost of erecting the missing wall, she argued that a wooden fence would have been cheaper and just as effective, and hence the claim should be limited to the cost of that. Oliver J was having none of it. A fence, as he put it,

> "was not what the plaintiff stipulated for and what, in effect, he paid for when he sold the plot. I know of no principle of damages which would dictate that a plaintiff who has stipulated for an article of a certain quality should be fobbed off with an inferior substitute merely because it is cheaper for a defendant who has broken his contract to supply it".[203]

(ii)   The effect of offers by the defendant

24-064 *Offers by the defaulting party of substitute performance*   On principle, as in the law of tort,[204] the obligation to mitigate may apply on principle not only to extraneous opportunities for the claimant to minimise the effect of the breach, but also to offers by the wrongdoer himself to take steps to do so.[205] A straightforward example is *Brace v Calder*.[206] Owing to a change in the composition of a partnership of wine and spirits dealers, an employee of the firm found himself technically dismissed. His action for substantial damages nevertheless failed: the new partnership had been quite happy to continue to employ him and, because he had entirely unreasonably refused this offer, his losses from the dismissal were entirely his own fault. Such issues often arise in contracts for services, such as building contracts, where

---

[198] [1932] A.C. 452
[199] For the full story see M. Bloom, *The Man Who Stole Portugal* (1966).
[200] See particularly [1932] A.C. 452 at 471 (Viscount Sankey), 482 (Lord Warrington),
[201] See *Finlay (James) Ltd v NV Kwik Hoo Tong* [1929] 1 K.B. 400.
[202] [1977] 1 W.L.R. 1262.
[203] [1977] 1 W.L.R. 1262 at 1284.
[204] Cf. *Evans v TNT Logistics Ltd* [2007] Lloyd's Rep. IR 708 (claimant in traffic accident case expected to accept offer of cheap hire car at defendants' expense rather than hiring from third party).
[205] "[I]n commercial contracts it is general reasonable to accept an offer from the party in default": *Payzu Ltd v Saunders* [1919] 2 K.B. 581 at 589 (Scrutton LJ).
[206] [1895] 2 Q.B. 253.

employers pay third parties to have defects put right despite an offer by the builder to correct the defects for nothing.[207]

Moreover, this may equally apply to an offer of technically deficient **24-065** performance. Thus in *Payzu v Saunders*[208] sellers agreed to sell cloth on monthly credit but then wrongfully demanded cash on delivery. The buyers refused to accept the cloth on those terms, as they were entitled to do; but their claim for substantial damages for non-delivery was unsuccessful. It would have been straightforward for them to accept the cloth, pay cash then and subsequently claim the loss, if any, suffered.[209]

Similarly, and more controversially, the cancellation of an entire contract for a **24-066** mere technical breach, albeit under an express power to do so, may itself amount to a failure to mitigate so as to prevent the claimant recovering any expectation damages in respect of the performance he will not now receive. So in the ship sale case of *The Solholt*[210] a vessel was delivered a few days late to the buyers, who promptly rejected her. While the buyers had not as a matter of strict law acted wrongfully in doing this, they were nevertheless unsuccessful in their claim for the difference of about $500,000 between the market and contract prices. Acting reasonably, they ought to have accepted the late delivery: in so far as their loss resulted from failing to do so, it could not be charged to the sellers' account. Nevertheless, for this to occur the reason for rejection must be indeed technical. If there is a substantial justification, then rejection will it seems almost never be regarded as unreasonable failure to mitigate.[211]

Nonetheless, all mitigation cases turn on their facts; and while failure to accept **24-067** offers from the guilty party *may* constitute a failure to mitigate, in practice it very frequently will not. Nor is it hard to see why. An employee wrongfully dismissed may quite legitimately mistrust the good faith of his previous employer;[212] furthermore he may have justifiable feelings of *amour propre* against accepting alternative work involving loss of pay[213] or status,[214] or even possibly of a differ-

---

[207] In such cases the amount of recovery is normally the cost to the builder of rectifying the defect rather than the amount actually paid by the employer: see for example *Pearce & High Ltd v Baxter* [1999] C.L.C. 749 and *Woodlands Oak Ltd v Conwell* [2011] B.L.R. 365 at [23]–[25]. This is a little curious, since one would have thought that free rectification if accepted would reduce the loss to nil; but it does rough justice in preventing the builder profiting from his breach. See generally W. Courtney, "Offers to mitigate" (2020) 136 L.Q.R. 245.

[208] [1919] 2 K.B. 581 (criticised in M. Bridge, "Damages in Contract and the Meaning of Avoidable Loss" (1989) 105 L.Q.R 398 at 412–414). *Payzu* was followed in the land sale case of *Castle Constructions Pty Ltd v Fekala Pty Ltd* [2006] NSWCA 133, (2006) 65 N.S.W.L.R. 648; but there, unlike in *Payzu*, the claim was for consequential loss and not for the price-value differential).

[209] Presumably if the buyers had had no source of ready cash the result would have been different.

[210] [1983] 1 Lloyd's Rep. 605. See too the Australian *Shevill v Builders Licensing Board* (1982) 149 C.L.R. 620 (decided on different grounds, but arguably a mitigation case).

[211] See *Heaven & Kesterton Ltd v Établissements François Albiac & Cie* [1956] 2 Lloyd's Rep. 316, esp at 321 (Devlin J) (defective goods); and also *Truk (U.K.) Ltd v Tokmakidis GmbH* [2000] 1 Lloyd's Rep. 543, esp at 552 (similar).

[212] As in *Shindler v Northern Raincoat Co Ltd* [1960] 1 W.L.R. 1038 (scepticism as to seriousness of offer to re-engage). Presumably, since employment contracts require a degree of confidence on both sides, there may also be a justified unwillingness to work for a previous contract-breaker.

[213] E.g. *Jackson v Hayes Candy & Co Ltd* [1938] 4 All E.R. 587.

[214] *Yetton v Eastwoods Froy Ltd* [1967] 1 W.L.R. 104 (demotion from managing director to assistant managing director). Cf. *Clayton-Greene v de Courville* (1920) 36 T.L.R. 790 (offer of less important part to dismissed actor may be justifiably refused).

ent nature.[215] Again, while a buyer of simple goods that turn out defective might be obliged to accept an offer of substitute merchandise or a straightforward repair, it might not be the same where the goods were complex and the buyer had reason to mistrust the seller's competence.[216] Yet again, the victim of defective work is generally unlikely to be expected to accept an offer from the defendant to rectify the defects: if a contractor has once failed to do a proper job, it may well be reasonable to mistrust him in future.[217] But all cases are fact-sensitive. It might well, for example, make a difference in such a case were the offer by the supplier one to pay to have the work done by a subcontractor of unblemished reputation, if the matter was fully explained to the claimant, and it was clear that the work would solve the problem.[218]

24-068 *Offers to modify or cancel the contract* As with offers of substitute performance, so also with offers by the party in breach suggesting cancellation of the contract or something similar. In a simple case such an offer may have to be accepted. For example, if a seller of ordinary articles of commerce at market value offers to take back unsatisfactory items and refund the full price, the buyer should normally accept this offer rather than selling the articles elsewhere for less and then suing for the difference.[219] But it is only in simple cases such as this that the innocent party will be expected to give up his right to performance. The leading authority on the point is *Strutt v Whitnell*.[220] A seller of a house, finding himself unable to provide vacant possession, offered to repurchase it and cancel the deal; this offer being refused by the buyer, the seller alleged that the latter had unreasonably failed to mitigate his loss. This plea was unsuccessful, partly on the ground that the offer had required the buyer to abandon a good claim for expectation damages, but also because in any case the buyer could not legitimately be called on to give up the benefit of his right to retain the house if he so wished and claim damages for any deficiency.[221]

24-069 *Offers involving surrender of substantial rights* For obvious reasons, an offer requiring the innocent party actually to give up valuable rights is not one that the latter is bound to accept on pain of a charge of failure to mitigate. So in *Strutt v Whitnell*,[222] above, an offer to repurchase a house where vacant possession turned out to be unavailable was held unacceptable because its acceptance would have

---

[215] Cf. the colourful California decision in *Parker v Twentieth-Century Fox Film Corp* 474 P.2d 689 (1970) (no duty in film star to accept offer of part in rugged Western rather than musical romance).

[216] For an example, see *Manton Hire & Sales Ltd v Ash Manor Cheese Co Ltd* [2013] EWCA Civ 548 (fork-lift truck of wrong dimensions: seller's offer of ad hoc modifications to profile justifiably rejected).

[217] See *Mul v Hutton Construction Ltd* [2014] EWHC 1797 (TCC); [2014] B.L.R. 529 at [25] (Akenhead J). For an illustration, see *Connaught Restaurants Ltd v Indoor Leisure Ltd* [1992] 2 E.G.L.R. 252. Cf. *Gul Bottlers (PVT) Ltd v Nichols Plc* [2014] EWHC 2173 (Comm) (licensing agreement wrongfully terminated; serious acrimony and mistrust between parties; no duty to accept offer from licensor of new agreement).

[218] Uncertainty in this regard is a powerful argument against requiring the claimant to accept the defendant's offer. In *Manton Hire & Sales Ltd v Ash Manor Cheese Co Ltd* [2013] EWCA Civ 548, an important point was that the modification offered involved unproved technology.

[219] *Houndsditch Warehouse Co Ltd v Waltex Ltd* [1944] K.B. 579.

[220] [1975] 1 W.L.R. 870.

[221] See in particular [1975] 1 W.L.R. 870 at 873 (Cairns LJ); note too *Activa DPS Europe SàRL v Pressure Seal Solutions Ltd* [2012] EWCA Civ 943; [2012] 3 C.M.L.R. 33.

[222] [1975] 1 W.L.R. 870.

required the buyer not only to relinquish the property, but also to give up his accrued—and potentially profitable—right to claim damages for breach. Similar principles, too, lie behind a more recent vendor and purchaser case, *Velmore Estates Ltd v Roseberry Homes Ltd*.[223] A purchaser wrongfully refused to complete on time, but later offered to go ahead with the purchase in any case. The vendors declined the offer and sued for damages. The purchasers' argument that the vendor had failed to mitigate its loss was unsuccessful, the Court of Appeal making the obvious point that the offer would have had the effect of depriving the vendor of its existing right under the contract both to keep the deposit and in addition remarket the property in the hope of selling it on at a profit.

Delay, timing and mitigation

On occasion the duty to mitigate may raise delicate issues of timing.[224] As was mentioned above,[225] there is a presumption that expectation damages fall to be measured according to values prevailing at the time of breach;[226] and that for reliance and consequential damages the equivalent time is that when the loss is suffered.[227] But this is increasingly subject to displacement where justice demands that a later time be taken as the point of reference.[228]   **24-070**

At times, it has been suggested that the presumption in favour of values prevailing at the time of breach is merely an outgrowth of the duty to mitigate. Thus in 1976 Oliver J said that the reason for it   **24-071**

"appears to me to lie in the enquiry: at what date could the plaintiff reasonably have been expected to mitigate the damages by seeking an alternative to performance of the contractual obligation? In contracts for the sale of goods, for instance, where there is an available market, the date of non-delivery is generally the appropriate date because it is open to the plaintiff to mitigate by going into the market immediately."[229]

Whether the two rules can be amalgamated in this simple way, with the rule as to timing reduced to an aspect of mitigation, may nevertheless be regarded as doubtful, if only because if they were in reality one rule the date of breach or loss would have no part to play at all (the only relevant time would be when the claimant might have been expected to take steps to deal with the effects of the breach, which is not   **24-072**

---

[223] [2005] EWHC 3061 (Ch.); [2006] 2 P. & C.R. 10. Compare *Houndsditch Warehouse Co Ltd v Waltex Ltd* [1944] K.B. 579, where the offer had been made explicitly so as to preserve the innocent party's right to damages.

[224] See generally S. Waddams, "The Date for the Assessment of Damages" (1981) 97 L.Q.R. 445.

[225] See para.21-085 ff above.

[226] E.g. *Jamal v Moolla Dawood Sons & Co* [1916] 1 A.C. 175 at 179 (Lord Wrenbury); *Johnson v Agnew* [1980] A.C. 367 at 400–401 (Lord Wilberforce). See too Sale of Goods Act 1979 ss.50(3), 51(3), reflecting the common law (*Williams v Reynolds* (1865) 6 B & S 495).

[227] See *Philips v Ward* [1956] 1 W.L.R. 471 at 475 (Denning LJ); *Perry v Sidney Phillips & Son* [1982] 1 W.L.R. 1297; *Charles v Hugh James Jones & Jenkins* [2000] 1 W.L.R. 1278 at 1290 (Swinton Thomas LJ).

[228] E.g. *Johnson v Agnew* [1980] A.C. 367 at 401 (Lord Wilberforce); *County Personnel (Employment Agency) Ltd v Alan R Pulver & Co* [1987] 1 W.L.R. 916 at 924–925 (Bingham LJ); *Golden Strait Corp v Nippon Yusen Kaisha* [2007] UKHL 12; [2007] 2 A.C. 353 at [32] (Lord Scott).

[229] See *Radford v De Froberville* [1977] 1 W.L.R. 1262 at 1285. See too Mance J in *The Marine Star* [1994] 2 Lloyd's Rep. 629 at 635; *Golden Strait Corp v Nippon Yusen Kubishika Kaisha* [2007] UKHL 12; [2007] 2 A.C. 353 at [10] (Lord Bingham); S. Waddams, "The Date for the Assessment of Damages" (1981) 97 L.Q.R. 445.

the same thing).[230] Nevertheless, it is clear that there is a close relation between the two principles, and that the fact that the claimant has acted reasonably in delaying is a strong argument in favour of ignoring the date of breach or loss.[231]

An exception to the duty to mitigate: the claimant's right to claim against third parties

24-073   Frequently the victim of a wrong will have more than one potential defendant to pursue: in the particular context of breach of contract, the innocent party may well have a right to recoup all or some of his loss from some third party as well as from the contract-breaker himself. This fact is nevertheless neither a defence to the contract-breaker nor a matter going to reduce his liability. On the contrary: a claimant with two potential defendants has an unfettered choice which one to sue, and it does not lie in the mouth of either of them to say that it would have been more reasonable to pursue the other.[232] This rule, moreover, applies in the context of mitigation as it does elsewhere: despite some decisions assuming the contrary,[233] there can equally be no room for a defendant's plea that in failing to claim from a third party the claimant has failed to mitigate his loss.

24-074   *Peters v East Midlands Strategic Health Authority*[234] established this principle in tort. There the Court of Appeal decisively rejected an argument that failure to exercise a right to free state therapy could amount to relevant failure to mitigate in the case of an injured claimant who sought to recover the entire cost of private care from a negligent defendant. And, despite a number of earlier cases that had lost sight of the principle,[235] Tomlinson J in *Haugesund Kommune v DEPFA ACS Bank*[236] applied it to a contractual suit for legal malpractice. In that case Norwegian lawyers

---

[230]   Cf. *Sharpe & Co Ltd v Nosawa* [1917] 2 K.B. 814 at 821, and the comments of Lord Scott in *Golden Strait Corp v Nippon Yusen Kaisha* [2007] UKHL 12; [2007] 2 A.C. 353 at [34]. And compare the more realistic rule in the US: UCC, para.2.713 (difference in prices at the time buyer learns of the breach).

[231]   Sale of goods: see *Ogle v Vane (Earl)* (1867) L.R. 3 Q.B. 272 and *Hickman v Haynes* (1875) L.R. 10 C.P. 598. *Radford v De Froberville* [1977] 1 W.L.R. 1262 is a similar case: the claimant having acted reasonably in not obtaining substitute performance until the time of judgment, damages were set as at that time.

[232]   For statements of this principle, see *Haugesund Kommune v DEPFA ACS Bank* [2010] EWHC 227 (Comm); [2010] 2 Lloyd's Rep. 323 at [21] (Tomlinson J: reversed on appeal for other reasons, [2011] EWCA Civ 33; [2011] 1 C.L.C. 166); and the tort cases of *The Liverpool (No.2)* [1963] P 64 at 83 (Harman LJ); and *Peters v East Midlands Strategic Health Authority* [2009] EWCA Civ 145; [2010] Q.B. 48 at [33], [41] (Dyson LJ). The same presumptively applies with express duties to mitigate: *Equitix EEEF Biomass 2 Ltd v Fox* [2021] EWHC 2531 (TCC); (2021) 198 Con. L.R. 224.

[233]   Notably *London and South of England Building Society v Stone* [1983] 1 W.L.R. 1242 (negligent valuation of mortgaged property: potential duty in lender to pursue mortgagor personally for mortgage debt before suing valuer). Though it occasionally resurfaces (e.g. *Peregrine Aviation Bravo v Laudamotion GmbH* [2023] EWHC 48 (Comm) at [341]), this reasoning was effectively demolished by Dyson LJ in *Peters v East Midlands SHA* [2009] EWCA Civ 145; [2010] Q.B. 48 at [41] and should be seen as discredited. Another instance similarly open to reconsideration in the light of *Peters* is *Walker v Geo H Medlicott & Son* [1999] 1 W.L.R. 727 (disappointed legatee said to be potentially obliged to try to rectify will before suing negligent solicitor).

[234]   [2009] EWCA Civ 145; [2010] Q.B. 48. So too with failure to claim the benefits of insurance, whether one's own or another's: see *McMullan v Gibney* [1999] N.I.Q.B. 1 at [6] and *Salt v Helley* [2009] N.I.Q.B. 69 at [27] (failure to claim courtesy car from insurer no bar to claim against defendant for loss of use of car).

[235]   See *London & South of England Building Society v Stone* [1983] 1 W.L.R. 1242 and *Walker v Medlicott* [1999] 1 W.L.R. 727, above.

had negligently failed to advise lenders that certain loans to Norwegian municipalities were ultra vires and hence unenforceable against the borrowers. When sued, the lawyers argued that the sums lent, while irrecoverable as such, could be reclaimed from the municipalities themselves on the basis of unjust enrichment, and that in not taking steps to do this the lenders had failed to mitigate their loss. This plea was rejected as in effect an attempt to sidestep the claimants' right to choose which of two parties to claim against.[237]

The duty to mitigate: The burden of proof

Until 2001 there was room for doubt on the question of the burden of proof as regards mitigation: was it on the claimant to prove he had mitigated, or on the defendant to show that he had not?[238] It is now clear, however, since the Privy Council's decision in the tort case of *Geest Plc v Lansiquot*[239] that the burden is squarely on the defendant to show that the claimant has failed to take reasonable steps to mitigate.　**24-075**

Mitigation as a source of rights in the claimant

(i)　Costs incurred in mitigation　The doctrine of mitigation applies mainly as a protection for the contract-breaker. But this is not its only function: on occasion the claimant himself can invoke its benefit to increase his recovery. Thus where a claimant justifiably incurs expenses with a view to avoiding or reducing his loss, those costs are on principle recoverable[240]—always assuming that they are reasonable in the circumstances.[241] In *Lloyds & Scottish Finance Ltd v Cars & Caravans (Kingston) Ltd*,[242] for example, a buyer of goods from a seller who turned out to have had no title successfully sued to recover legal costs incurred in vainly resisting the true owner's claim. Similarly, where solicitors' negligence caused business partners to face risks of enormous expense if a company of their was wound up, expenditure to prop up the company and avoid this result was held recoverable on principle.[243] For these purposes, moreover, it does not matter whether the at-　**24-076**

---

[236] [2010] EWHC 227 (Comm); [2010] 2 Lloyd's Rep. 323.

[237] The decision was reversed on appeal on the issue of liability (see [2011] EWCA Civ 33; [2011] P.N.L.R. 14): but the point remains.

[238] Burden on the claimant: *Selvanayagam v University of the West Indies* [1983] 1 W.L.R. 585. On the defendant: *Roper v Johnson* (1873) L.R. 8 C.P. 167 at 178 (Keating J); *Mander v Commercial Union Assurance Co Ltd* [1998] Lloyd's Rep. IR 93 at 148 (Rix J); *Standard Chartered Bank v Pakistan National Shipping Corp* [2001] C.L.C. 825 at [38] (Potter LJ).

[239] [2002] UKPC 48; [2002] 1 W.L.R. 3111; see also *MSC Mediterranean Shipping Co SA v Cottonex Anstalt* [2015] EWHC 283 (Comm); [2015] 1 C.L.C. 143 at [59] (Leggatt J).

[240] See *Lloyds & Scottish Finance Ltd v Modern Cars and Caravans (Kingston) Ltd* [1966] 1 Q.B. 764 at 782 (Edmund Davies J); *The World Beauty* [1970] P 144 at 156 (Winn L.J); *Riyad Bank v Ahli United Bank (UK) Plc* [2005] EWHC 279 (Comm); [2005] 2 Lloyd's Rep. 409 at [167] (Moore-Bick J). So too in tort: e.g. *The Kingsway* [1918] P 344.

[241] For an example of costs not shown to be reasonable see *Riyad Bank v Ahli United Bank (UK) Plc* [2005] EWHC 279 (Comm); [2005] 2 Lloyd's Rep. 409 (appealed on other grounds at [2006] EWCA Civ 780; [2006] 1 C.L.C. 1007) (negligent investment advice to deposit-taker: costs of closing investment scheme not recoverable, since unreasonable).

[242] [1966] 1 Q.B. 764.

[243] *Xenakis v Birkett Long LLP (A Firm)* [2014] EWHC 171 (QB); [2014] P.N.L.R. 16. In fact the claim failed for other reasons.

tempt to reduce the loss was ultimately unsuccessful; its cost will be recoverable even if the attempt failed, provided that it was reasonable in the circumstances.[244]

24-077   **(ii)   Unsuccessful, but reasonable, efforts to mitigate**   It is only just that the principle of mitigation should cut both ways. If a claimant who fails to mitigate is liable to have any damages reduced to the extent that he failed to take steps to minimise any harm, by parity of reasoning a claimant who does take steps to mitigate should not suffer if in the event he actually increases his loss. Hence it is well-established that in such a case he can claim the whole increased loss from the person in breach. Most cases involve tort:[245] but the principle applies equally in contract. So in *Gebrüder Metelmann GmbH v NBR (London) Ltd*[246] buyers of sugar repudiated the contract before performance was due, whereupon the sellers immediately sold against them. As it happened this greatly increased the sellers' loss, since the market price had risen strongly by the delivery date. Nevertheless the sellers recovered damages based on the price obtained: there was no reason to penalise them, as against the contract-breaker, because of the subsequent change in the price.

III.   The Fault of the Claimant: Contributory Negligence and Damages for Breach of Contract

24-078   The doctrine of mitigation involves conduct by one who, faced with a loss for which someone else is liable, culpably fails to minimise the consequences of that loss. Contributory negligence, by contrast, involves culpable failure to prevent a loss being suffered in the first place—or, to put it another way, it invokes the idea that damages ought to reflect the fact that the person claiming them is, in whole or in part, at fault and thus responsible for his own misfortune. It will immediately be apparent that these doctrines have much in common:[247] so much, indeed, that in some jurisdictions little if any distinction is drawn between them.[248] In English contract law, however, the concepts have developed almost entirely separately, and to this day require different treatment.

24-079   In contract (as against tort[249]) the application of contributory negligence doctrine to the case where it was alleged to be the claimant's fault that he had suffered the loss at all was, until recently, highly unsettled.[250] Thus at common law it was on oc-

---

[244] As demonstrated by *Lloyds & Scottish Finance Ltd v Cars & Caravans (Kingston) Ltd* [1966] 1 Q.B. 764.

[245] For a classic example see *The Metagama* (1927) 29 Lloyd's LL Rep. 253.

[246] [1984] 1 Lloyd's Rep. 614. For another instance, see *Hoffburger v Ascot International Bloodstock Ltd, The Times* (unreported 29 January 1976) (buyer fails to accept racehorse: seller delays sale to get better price, but then incurs bills when horse falls ill: buyer liable for all loss); also the New South Wales decision in See too Samuels JA in *Simonius Vischer & Co v Holt & Thompson* [1979] 2 N.S.W.L.R. 322, especially at 355 ff.

[247] On the difficulties of distinguishing between them, see e.g. M. Bridge, "Mitigation of damages in contract and the meaning of avoidable loss" (1989) 105 L.Q.R 398 at 403–404.

[248] German lawyers, for example, regard both as instances of *Mitverschulden*—damage due to the fault of both parties—under BGB, para.254.2.

[249] On which, see *Clerk & Lindsell on Torts*, 22nd edn (London: Sweet & Maxwell, 2017), paras 3-57–3-102.

[250] On this, see generally G. Williams, *Joint Torts and Contributory Negligence* (1951), 214 ff; also J. Swanton, "Contributory Negligence as a Defence to Actions for Breach of Contract" (1981) 55 ALJ 278, and P. Chandler, "Contributory Negligence and Contract: Some Underlying Disparities" (1989) 40 NILQ 152.

casion held that the claimant recovered in full even if his loss was partly his fault.[251] But other decisions suggested a contrary approach, taking the view that, as was the case at common law in tort, contributory fault barred the action entirely.[252]

In 1945 Parliament passed the Law Reform (Contributory Negligence) Act 1945. **24-080** The operative wording of s.1 was as follows:

> "Where any person suffers damage as the result partly of his own fault and partly of the fault of any other person or persons, a claim in respect of that damage shall not be defeated by reason of the fault of the person suffering the damage, but the damages recoverable in respect thereof shall be reduced to such extent as the court thinks just and equitable having regard to the claimant's share in the responsibility for the damage."

By way of elucidation, "fault" was defined in s.4 as follows:

> "[N]egligence, breach of statutory duty or other act or omission which gives rise to a liability in tort or would, apart from this Act, give rise to the defence of contributory negligence."

These words were clearly aimed at getting rid of the common law rule that **24-081** contributory negligence barred an action in tort absolutely. Unfortunately, their application to contract claims is, to say the least, less than obvious. No doubt for that reason, up until 1989 decisions disagreed on whether claims for breach of contract could be reduced under the Act for comparative fault.[253]

The point about the application of the Act to contract claims finally arose directly **24-082** for decision in 1989 in *Forsikringsaktielskapet Vesta v Butcher*.[254] Reinsurance brokers were sued for breach of contract by the original underwriters of certain risks, the allegation being that the brokers had negligently failed to negotiate valid and effective reinsurance cover and thus left the underwriters fully exposed. The brokers, for their part, claimed the benefit of the 1945 Act, alleging that the underwriters themselves were partly to blame because they had failed to notice warning signs that their cover might be ineffective and take appropriate action. O'Connor LJ in the Court of Appeal held that this was a good plea. Essentially, he divided claims for breach of contract into two categories, according to whether the breach did, or did not, parallel a liability in tort. He then reasoned that, since the conduct of the defendant which was statutorily susceptible to reduction of damages had to be "negligence, breach of statutory duty or other act or omission which gives rise to a liability in tort", it followed that in the latter case there could be no apportionment.[255] But, his argument continued, this was not so in cases where (as in *Vesta* itself) liability existed in both contract and tort. In such a situation there was no difficulty in holding the Act applicable; furthermore, it would be highly

---

[251] See, e.g. *Vaile Bros v Hobson* (1933) 149 LT 283.

[252] E.g. *Morgan v Ravey* (1861) 6 H & N 265; *Burrows v March Gas Co* (1872) L.R. 7 Ex 96 (apparently). Cf. the later *Sole v WJ Hallt Ltd* [1973] Q.B. 574.

[253] Apportionment available: *Sayers v Harlow UDC* [1958] 1 W.L.R. 623; *Quinn v Burch Bros Ltd* [1966] 2 Q.B. 370; *De Meza v Apple* [1974] 1 Lloyd's Rep. 508 (appealed on other grounds: [1975] 1 Lloyd's Rep. 498). No statutory apportionment and recovery in full: *AB Marintrans v Comet Shipping Co* [1985] 1 W.L.R. 1270; *Basildon District Council v JE Lesser (Properties) Ltd* [1985] Q.B. 839. No statutory apportionment and contributory fault a total bar: *Sole v WJ Hallt Ltd* [1973] Q.B. 574. For discussion, see J. Swanton, "Contributory Negligence as a Defence to Actions for Breach of Contract" (1981) 55 ALJ 278.

[254] [1989] A.C. 852. In the House of Lords the issue of the application of the Act to contract claims had ceased to be in issue.

[255] See [1989] A.C. 852 at 866; also at 879 (Neil LJ). For later cases, see *Barclays Bank Plc v Fairclough*

undesirable in such a situation if a negligent claimant could prevent apportionment merely by electing to sue in contract rather than tort.[256]

24-083 Since *Vesta*, it is thus clear—at least in England[257]—that, while there will be apportionment in professional negligence and similar cases where there is no doubt that contractual and tortious liabilities exist in parallel,[258] most other contractual cases—including, importantly, cases where liability is not dependent on fault[259] and those rare cases where a contractual duty of care exists without a parallel tortious obligation—are excluded, with the result that the claimant recovers in full even if partly or even largely responsible for his own misfortune.[260] This is particularly significant in the case of obligations to supply satisfactory goods under the Sale of Goods Act 1979 ss.13-15 and (in the case of consumers) under ss.9-15 of the Consumer Rights Act 2015, since it means that damages for breach of these obligations are immune to reduction on the basis of the claimant's fault.[261]

Building Ltd [1995] Q.B. 214, *Raflatac Ltd v Eade* [1999] 1 Lloyd's Rep. 506, and *Anglian Water Services Ltd v Crawshaw Robbins & Co Ltd* (unreported 6 February 2001), Q.B.D.

[256] See [1989] A.C. 852 at 866–867.

[257] But the *Vesta* solution has not found favour everywhere. It was rejected, after extensive discussion, by the High Court of Australia in *Astley v Austrust Ltd* (1999) 161 A.L.R. 155, which held that even where there was liability in tort, a contract claimant could recover in full, without reduction (on which, see in turn M. Tilbury and J. Carter, "Converging Liabilities and Security of Contract: Contributory Negligence" (2000) 16 JCL 78. Some State legislation nevertheless gives statutory effect to the *Vesta* solution: e.g. Law Reform (Miscellaneous Provisions) Act 1965 (NSW) ss.8, 9.

[258] Since *Henderson v Merrett Syndicates Ltd (No.1)* [1995] 2 A.C. 145. This extends to most professional negligence claims and also to, for example, claims for breach of a bank's duty under *Barclays Bank Plc v Quincecare Ltd* [1992] 4 All E.R. 363: see *Singularis Holdings Ltd (In Liquidation) v Daiwa Capital Markets Europe Ltd* [2019] UKSC 50; [2020] A.C. 1189.

[259] But note one possible qualification. If a consumer buys a defective product from a manufacturer and is injured by it, the consumer's (strict) rights under the Sale of Goods Act 1979 are paralleled by a duty in tort—i.e. under Pt I of the Consumer Protection Act 1987. If so, it seems that logically there must be apportionment in the case of contributory negligence.

[260] See in particular *Bank of Nova Scotia v Hellenic Mutual War Risks Association (Bermuda) Ltd, The Good Luck* [1988] 1 Lloyd's Rep. 514 at 554–555 (Hobhouse J), and on appeal at [1990] 1 Q.B. 818 at 904 (May LJ); *Barclays Bank Plc v Fairclough Building Ltd* [1995] Q.B. 214 at 229 ff (Beldam LJ); *Hi-Lite Electrical Ltd v Wolseley UK Ltd* [2011] EWHC 2153 (TCC); [2011] B.L.R. 629. The decision in *Tennant Radiant Heat Ltd v Warrington Development Corp* (1988) 4 Const LJ 321 seems contrary to this: but for the reasons appearing in para.24-030 above, it is suggested that its correctness is open to doubt.

[261] See e.g. *Hi-Lite Electrical Ltd v Wolseley UK Ltd* [2011] EWHC 2153 (TCC); [2011] B.L.R. 629. The vital distinction between a strict obligation under sale of goods law and a mere duty of care to provide a service properly can at times be close: see e.g. *Trebor Bassett Holdings Ltd v ADT Fire & Security Plc* [2012] EWCA Civ 1158; [2012] B.L.R. 441 (design and fitting of a specialised fire suppression system).

CHAPTER 25

DAMAGES: AGREED DAMAGES AND OTHER REMEDIES FOR BREACH

I. LIQUIDATED DAMAGES CLAUSES

Having proved a breach of contract, under English law the victim is entitled on principle to the secondary remedy of damages. But the procedure of having these quantified by a court or arbitrator and arguing over the amount of any loss suffered is troublesome, risky and potentially costly for both sides. With this in mind, draftsmen frequently insert a "liquidated damages" clause[1] under which the parties agree, either absolutely or by way of some formula, the amount payable in the event of all or some breaches. Examples are legion. A construction contract, or a contract for the sale of commercial land, will often stipulate for payment of a fixed amount per day in the event of late completion.[2] Again, shipbuilding contracts ordinarily provide not only for this, but also for a sliding scale of damages for other breaches, such as failure by the vessel to meet its requirements for speed and capacity.[3] Yet again, in the context of shipping law a voyage charter invariably contains a clause requiring payment of a fixed sum per hour "demurrage" for excess time spent loading or unloading;[4] and so on.

25-001

The primary object of clauses of this sort is to give the victim of a breach the right simply to sue for the stipulated amount, without recourse to the general law on the measure of damages. In addition there may be other aims too. These may include saving the claimant and the defendant the trouble of arguing over what loss the claimant has suffered (and hence ultimately at reducing legal costs);[5] deterring breach by subjecting the defendant to a substantial fixed liability when establish-

25-002

---

[1] Or an analogous clause providing for transfer or forfeiture of money or other property. These matters will be dealt with at appropriate parts of this chapter. For a wide-ranging discussion, see L. Gullifer, "Agreed Remedies" in A. Burrows & E. Peel (eds), *Commercial Remedies: Current Issues and Problems* (Oxford: Oxford University Press, 2003), Ch.16.

[2] A case where nice issues can arise as to how long the liability to make per diem payments lasts, and to which breaches it applies: see in particular *Triple Point Technology Inc v PTT Public Co Ltd* [2021] UKSC 29; [2021] A.C. 1148 (clause applicable to work never done).

[3] S. Curtis, *Law of Shipbuilding Contracts*, 3rd edn (London: LLP Professional Publishing, 2002), pp.54–70. See, for a concrete example, the standard BIMCO NEWBUILDCON contract, paras 8–13.

[4] E.g. GENCON 1994, cll.6–7.

[5] As Lady Arden put it in *Triple Point Technology v PTT Public Company Ltd* [2021] UKSC 29; [2021] A.C. 1148 at [35]: "Parties agree a liquidated damages clause so as to provide a remedy that is predictable and certain for a particular event (here, as often, that event is a delay in completion). The employer does not then have to quantify its loss, which may be difficult and time-consuming for it to do." See too Lord Leggatt at [74]; and the earlier comments in *Clydebank Engineering & Shipbuilding Co Ltd v Don Jose Ramos Yzquierdo y Castaneda* [1905] A.C. 6 at 11 (Lord Halsbury) and *Robophone Facilities Ltd v Blank* [1966] 1 W.L.R. 1428 at 1449 (Diplock LJ).

ing recoverable loss might otherwise be awkward; or conversely capping the potentially unlimited exposure of a defendant to liability for consequential losses in exchange for a limited guaranteed payment to the victim.

25-003   Liquidated damages clauses are on principle valid, both in favour of the victim of the breach[6] and against him.[7] But their validity is not unqualified. They may be attacked on a number of grounds on the grounds of both inadequacy and excess. With the former, notably the effect of the Unfair Contract Terms Act 1977[8] and the Consumer Rights Act 2015,[9] we will not be concerned, and the reader is referred to works on contractual exemption and limitation clauses.[10] This chapter, by contrast, deals with controls based on excess; that is, with clauses which would be apt to give the claimant more than he would get in damages at common law. In particular it covers the doctrine of penalties; the rules against forfeiture; and a number of miscellaneous other legislative provisions having the effect of limiting the extent to which a contractor can stipulate for what is to happen in the event of non-performance by the other party.

II.   THE DOCTRINE OF PENALTIES

The historical background

25-004   The rules on penalty clauses form a rare, and closely limited, exception to the common law's uncompromising avowal of freedom of contract.[11] Equity from the seventeenth century, and later the common law itself, consistently prevented the enforcement of liquidated damages clauses where the sum stipulated to be paid was

---

[6]   As Tindal CJ put it in *Kemble v Farren* (1829) 6 Bing 141 at 148: "We see nothing illegal or unreasonable in the parties, by their mutual agreement, settling the amount of damages, uncertain in their nature at any sum upon which they may agree. In many cases, such an agreement fixes that which is almost impossible to be accurately ascertained; and in all cases, it saves the expense and difficulty of bringing witnesses to that point." See too *Betts v Burch* (1859) 4 H & N 506; *Dunlop Pneumatic Tyre Co Ltd v New Garage Co Ltd* [1915] A.C. 79 at 95 (Lord Atkinson), 97 (Lord Parker), 100 (Lord Parmoor); *Murray v Leisureplay Plc* [2005] EWCA Civ 963; [2005] I.R.L.R. 946 at [106] (Clarke LJ).

[7]   A point not beyond controversy (the German civil code explicitly allows damages above the agreed sum—BGB, para.340.2—and Art.1231-5 of the French Code Civil allows interference with a sum which is "manifestement dérisoire"). But in England it was finally cemented in *Cellulose Acetate Silk Co Ltd v Widnes Foundry (1925) Ltd* [1933] A.C. 20 (promise in construction contract to pay fixed sum for delay enforced even though actual loss greater). See too *Wall v Rederiaktiebolaget Luggude* [1915] 3 K.B. 66; *Leeds Shipping Co Ltd v Soc Francaise Bunge* [1957] 2 Lloyd's Rep. 183. Effectively this means that exemption and limitation clauses are subject simply to their own regime under (e.g.) the Unfair Contract Terms Act 1977 or the Consumer Rights Act 2015 (see *Chitty on Contracts*, 34th edn (London: Sweet & Maxwell, 2022), Ch.17).

[8]   In particular ss.2, 3 and 6.

[9]   See s.31.

[10]   *Chitty on Contracts*, 34th edn (London: Sweet & Maxwell, 2022), Ch.17. In *Eco World - Ballymore Embassy Gardens Co Ltd v Dobler UK Ltd* [2021] EWHC 2207 (TCC) at [97]–[116] the view was expressed, it is suggested correctly, that there was no reason why a clause that would be void as a penalty if sued on by the victim should not nevertheless take effect as a cap on liability if invoked by the contract-breaker.

[11]   "[T]he power to strike down a penalty clause is a blatant interference with freedom of contract and is designed for the sole purpose of providing relief against oppression for the party having to pay the stipulated sum. It has no place where there is no oppression": see *Elsey v J.G. Collins Insurance Agencies Ltd* (1978) 83 D.L.R. (3d) 1 at 15 (Dickson J), approved by the Privy Council in *Phillips Hong Kong Ltd v AG of Hong Kong* (1993) 61 B.L.R. 49 at 58; also *Cavendish Square Holding BV v Makdessi* [2015] UKSC 67; [2016] A.C. 1172 at [33] (Lords Neuberger and Sumption), [248] (Lord Hodge). See too *McGregor on Damages*, 20th edn (London: Sweet & Maxwell, 2018),

more than that required to protect the interests of the victim, such that it was unconscionable for the latter to rely on them. The practice originated[12] with conditional bonds, an old device under which a promise to pay a given sum was drafted as an obligation to pay a larger amount (normally double the original sum), subject to defeasance on prompt payment of the actual debt. Equity developed a practice,[13] later extended to the common law and embodied in legislation,[14] of preventing recovery of the penal sum if the defendant brought into court the genuine sum payable, together with interest.[15]

Whatever its origin, however, the penalties rule later became generalised as one of public policy.[16] It continues to apply today in such a way so as to strike down[17] any stipulation in a contract dealing with the consequences of breach where this is regarded as unconscionable or grossly disproportionate to any interest which the other party has a legitimate ground to protect. Most of the older cases concerned liquidated damages clauses, but (as will appear below) the doctrine is also apt to encompass other types of stipulations, such as retention funds and obligations to transfer money's worth rather than simply pay a cash sum.

    25-005

Before the Supreme Court's 2015 decision in *Cavendish Square Holding BV v Makdessi*,[18] the starting-point of any discussion of penalties was a House of Lords decision of exactly 100 years earlier: namely, *Dunlop Pneumatic Tyre Co Ltd v New Garage Co Ltd*.[19] Against the background of a then commonplace retail price maintenance scheme, retailers buying Dunlop tyres agreed not to resell them below list price, and to pay Dunlop the then considerable sum of £5 for every tyre discounted. The retailers argued that the sum of £5 per tyre was penal, being more than any conceivable loss caused to Dunlop by the sale of one cut-price tyre;[20] Dunlop countered with evidence that whatever the individual loss, wholesale discounting would cheapen the brand and deprive it of substantial, though unquantified, sales and profits. Reversing the Court of Appeal, the House of Lords supported Dunlop. Since there was evidence that mass discounting could cause

    25-006

Ch.16; E. Lanyon, "Equity and the Doctrine of Penalties" (1996) 9 J.C.L. 234; G. Miller, "Penalty clauses in England and France: a comparative study" (2004) 53 I.C.L.Q. 79.

[12] A useful summary of the history appears in A.W.B. Simpson, "The Penal Bond with Conditional Defeasance" (1966) 82 L.Q.R. 392 and *AMEV-UDC Finance Ltd v Austin* (1986) 162 C.L.R. 170 at 186–194 (Mason and Wilson JJ).

[13] E.g. *Tall v Ryland* (1670) 1 Ch. Cas 183 (promise not to molest neighbour and in default to pay £20: relief given where this was more than actual loss); also *Perkins v Kempland* (1776) 2 W. Bl. 1106 and *Sloman v Walter* (1783) 1 Bro CC 418.

[14] See 8 & 9 Will 3 (1696), c.11 ("An Act for the Better Preventing of Frivolous and Vexatious Suits"), s.8.

[15] See generally A.W.B. Simpson, *The History of the Common Law of Contract* (Oxford: Oxford University Press, 1987), p.183 ff; also *Wallis v Smith* (1882) 21 Ch. D. 243 (Jessel MR); *Dunlop Pneumatic Tyre Co Ltd v New Garage Co Ltd* [1915] A.C. 79 at 86, HL; *Jobson v Johnson* [1989] 1 W.L.R. 1026 at 1032 ff, 1039, CA (Dillon and Nicholls LJJ); *Cavendish Square Holding BV v Makdessi* [2015] UKSC 67; [2016] A.C. 1172 at [7] (Lord Neuberger).

[16] E.g. *Robophone Facilities Ltd v Blank* [1966] 1 W.L.R. 1428 at 1447–1448 (Diplock LJ); *Else (1982) Ltd v Parkland Holdings Ltd* [1994] 1 B.C.L.C. 130 at 135 (Evans LJ); *Cavendish Square Holding BV v Makdessi* [2015] UKSC 67; [2016] A.C. 1172 at [243] (Lord Hodge).

[17] The validity of a penal stipulation is an all-or-nothing issue. The clause is either effective and applicable in its entirety, or penal and thereby falling to be ignored. Unlike the situation in certain civil law jurisdictions (see e.g. Art.1231-5 of the French Code Civil), there is no curial discretion to vary its terms. See *Cavendish Square Holding BV v Makdessi* [2015] UKSC 67; [2016] A.C. 1172 at [84]–[87], [283] (Lords Neuberger, Sumption and Hodge).

[18] [2015] UKSC 67; [2016] A.C. 1172.

[19] [1915] A.C. 79.

[20] Especially since it actually exceeded the list price of the tyre involved, which was only £4 1s (£4.05).

substantial, albeit not precisely quantifiable, harm to Dunlop, and the sum stipulated was not entirely disproportionate, the stipulation for payment was legitimate. Lord Dunedin, who gave the leading judgment, reasoned as follows. His first, and unexceptionable, point was that any words used by the parties, such as "penalty", were far from conclusive, and that deciding whether a stipulation was penal was a matter of construction.[21] Secondly, and in the event more controversially, he went on to say that

> "[t]he essence of a penalty is a payment of money stipulated as *in terrorem* of the offending party; the essence of liquidated damages is a genuine covenanted pre-estimate of damage".[22]

He then listed some criteria that might "prove helpful": namely:

"(a)   It will be held to be penalty if the sum stipulated for is extravagant and unconscionable in amount in comparison with the greatest loss that could conceivably be proved to have followed from the breach. ...

(b)   It will be held to be a penalty if the breach consists only in not paying a sum of money, and the sum stipulated is a sum greater than the sum which ought to have been paid ....

(c)   There is a presumption (but no more) that it is penalty when 'a single lump sum is made payable by way of compensation, on the occurrence of one or more or all of several events, some of which may occasion serious and others but trifling damage'... .

(d)   It is no obstacle to the sum stipulated being a genuine pre-estimate of damage, that the consequences of the breach are such as to make precise pre-estimation almost an impossibility. On the contrary, that is just the situation when it is probable that pre-estimated damage was the true bargain between the parties."[23]

Another decision, dating back some 10 years earlier than *Dunlop*, also informed discussion. In *Clydebank Engineering & Shipbuilding Co v Don José Ramos Yzquierdo y Castaneda*,[24] a naval construction contract with the Spanish government for four torpedo boats provided for a "penalty" of £500 per week in the event of late delivery. In that case, which upheld the clause, Lord Halsbury, like Lord Dunedin in the later case, distinguished between an agreed sum for damages and a penalty to be held over the other party in terrorem;[25] and Lord Davey stressed the distinction between providing for liquidated damages and stipulating for a punishment irrespective of the damage caused.[26] However, Lord Halsbury also stressed, as a reason for upholding the clause, the extreme difficulty of proving loss in such a situation.[27]

25-007   Lord Dunedin's formulation of the penalty rule in *Dunlop*[28] was cited countless times later.[29] It was, however, less than satisfactory. The test of whether a stipulated sum amounted to a genuine pre-estimate of damage would not necessarily give the

---

[21]   See [1915] A.C. 79 at 86–87.
[22]   See [1915] A.C. 79 at 86; also *Clydebank Engineering & Shipbuilding Co v Don José Ramos Yzquierdo y Castaneda* [1905] A.C. 6 at 19 (Lord Robertson).
[23]   See [1915] A.C. 79 at 87–88.
[24]   [1905] A.C. 6.
[25]   [1905] A.C. 6 at 10.
[26]   [1905] A.C. 6 at 16.
[27]   [1905] A.C. 6 at 11–12.
[28]   *Dunlop Pneumatic Tyre Co Ltd v New Garage Co Ltd* [1915] A.C. 79.
[29]   See e.g. *Alder v Moore* [1961] 2 Q.B. 57 at 72; *Bridge v Campbell Discount Co Ltd* [1962] A.C. 600 at 615; *Lordsvale Finance Plc v Bank of Zambia* [1996] Q.B. 752 at 762; *Murray v Leisureplay Plc*

same result as the question whether it was in terrorem of the contract-breaker, which in turn was apt to yield a different answer from the question whether the agreed sum was extravagant and unconscionable in comparison with the greatest loss conceivably following from the breach.[30] Furthermore, the concept of a genuine pre-estimate of loss sat uncomfortably with the holding in *Dunlop* that one reason for upholding the stipulation there was that the loss there was virtually impossible to estimate with any accuracy.

Before *Dunlop*, and for some time afterwards, the tendency was generally to **25-008** stress the "genuine pre-estimate" criterion. Unfortunately the result was that, in many cases, the application of the penalty doctrine became almost a technical mathematical exercise.[31] For example, the inference was nearly always that a term was penal if under it the same sum was payable for different breaches, some of which would clearly result in loss less than the stipulated amount;[32] indeed the same might apply if the clause did reflect a loss, but that loss was regarded in law as not having been caused by the breach.[33]

As a result there were calls for a more nuanced approach based on the prevention **25-009** of oppression and unfair advantage-taking, and that the law should reflect this consideration.[34] Yet another approach sought to argue that the real issue was whether, assuming a clause did not reflect likely losses, it nevertheless had some

---

[2005] EWCA Civ 963; [2005] I.R.L.R. 946 at [38]. See too *Ringrow Pty Ltd v BP Australia Pty Ltd* (2005) 224 C.L.R. 656 at [10].

[30] A point not lost on Lord Mance in *Cavendish Square Holding BV v Makdessi* [2015] UKSC 67; [2016] A.C. 1172 at [152]; note also Arden LJ in *Murray v Leisureplay Plc* [2005] EWCA Civ 963; [2005] I.R.L.R. 946 at [15]. In *Paciocco v ANZ Banking Group Ltd* [2015] FCAFC 50, Allsop CJ at [25] was reduced to saying, in an apparent counsel of desperation, that "genuine pre-estimate" was merely a "descriptive phrase used to explain a sum paid upon breach of a term or pursuant to a collateral stipulation upon the failure of the primary stipulation that is not extravagant and not out of all proportion to the compensation for the breach or failure of the stipulation."

[31] "[The Court] assesses the common law damages which could be expected to flow from the breaches which trigger the allegedly penal clause. The assessment is hypothetical because the clause must be judged by reference to matters apparent at the time the contract was entered into and not in the light of subsequent events. If the amount set out in the clause exceeds the theoretical damages then the stipulation is a penalty." E. Lanyon, "Equity and the Doctrine of Penalties" (1996) 9 J.C.L. 234 at 237.

[32] "Where the sum which is to be a security for the performance of an agreement to do several acts, will, in case of breaches of the agreement, be, in some instances, too large and in others too small a compensation for the injury thereby occasioned, that sum is to be considered a penalty." (Bayley J in *Davies v Penton* (1827) 6 B & Cr 216 at 223). Examples of clauses struck on this basis were *Kemble v Farron* (1829) 6 Bing 141 (clause in a high-profile actor's contract fixing damages for any breach whatever at £1,000); *Willson v Love* [1896] 1 Q.B. 626 (agreement by farm tenant to pay £3 per ton for all hay and straw not ploughed in, once shown that the fertilising value of hay and straw was substantially different); *Ariston SRL v Charly Records Ltd* (1990) *Financial Times,* 21 March (bailee of recording paraphernalia to pay £600 in the event of late return of any item).

[33] *Financings Ltd v Baldock* [1963] 1 Q.B. 887 (minimum payment clause in hire purchase agreement requiring purchaser to make up two-thirds of the price if financier terminated the agreement: penal because might well result not from breach but from the financier's decision to terminate for breach).

[34] Cf. Dickson J in the Supreme Court of Canada in *Elsey v JG Collins Insurance Agencies Ltd* (1978) 83 D.L.R. (3d) 1 at 15: "It is now evident that the power to strike down a penalty clause is a blatant interference with freedom of contract and it is designed for the sole purpose of providing relief against oppression for the party having to pay the stipulated sum. It has no place where there is no oppression" (approved by the *Privy Council in Philips Hong Kong Ltd v Att Gen of Hong Kong* (1993) 61 B.L.R. 49 at 58); see too *Alfred McAlpine Capital Projects Ltd v Tilebox Ltd* [2005] EWHC 281 (TCC); [2005] B.L.R. 271 at [48] (Jackson J); *Murray v Leisureplay Plc* [2005] EWCA Civ 963; [2005] I.R.L.R. 946 at [114] (Buxton LJ).This is now common doctrine in Canada: e.g. *Liu v Coal Harbour Properties Partnership* (2006) 273 D.L.R. (4th) 508 at [24]. Mason and Wilson JJ

other legitimate commercial justification.[35] Arden LJ neatly summed up this view in the Court of Appeal decision in *Murray v Leisureplay Plc*[36] in 2005:

> "The real question is whether the sums for which the parties have provided to be paid on breach differ substantially from the sums that would be recoverable at common law *and whether there is shown to be no justification for that.*"[37]

25-010 The result in *Murray v Leisureplay* itself, involving a curious bid by employers to shelter behind the penalties rule when sued by their own employee for wrongful dismissal, neatly illustrated the approach. A senior executive on appointment negotiated a very generous severance package providing, in the event of wrongful dismissal, for a golden handshake vastly more than he would have received by way of damages at common law. The Court of Appeal upheld the clause; although it might give more than otherwise available, it was not unjustifiable or unconscionable in the context of executive employment practice generally.[38] In a similar vein, an employment agency's stipulation that refunds for unsuccessful placements were available only if payment had been made on time in the first place was held not penal within the rule, again on the basis of lack of unjustifiability: even if the agency might receive a windfall, it had, it was said, an entirely legitimate interest in maintaining its cash-flow.[39]

25-011 To confuse matters further, a further line of authority suggested that any clause aimed at punishing a defendant for breach was of itself an inadmissible penalty.[40] In the *Dunlop* case Lord Dunedin had after all singled out payments "stipulated as in terrorem of the offending party";[41] and in 1995 Colman J built on this, admitting the rule just referred to on commercial justification, but pointedly adding the

---

said much the same thing in the High Court of Australia in *AMEV UDC Finance Ltd v Austin* (1986) 162 C.L.R. 170 at 193. See too *Ringrow Pty Ltd v BP Australia Pty Ltd* (2005) 224 C.L.R. 656 at [32] (per curiam).

[35] Cf. Blair J's forthright comment in *Azimut-Benetti SpA v Healey* [2010] EWHC 2234 (Comm); (2010) 132 Con L.R. 113 at [21]: "[T]this does not imply that if the comparison between the amount payable on breach and the loss that might be sustained on breach discloses a discrepancy, it follows that the clause is a penalty. A particular clause might be commercially justifiable provided that its dominant purpose was not to deter the other party from breach." See too *General Trading Co (Holdings) Ltd v Richmond Corp Ltd* [2008] EWHC 1479 (Comm) at [128]; also Mason and Wilson JJ in *AMEV-UDC Finance Ltd v Austin* (1986) 162 C.L.R. 170 at 193 (account to be taken of both amount of agreed payment and relationship between contractors).

[36] [2005] EWCA Civ 963; [2005] I.R.L.R. 946.

[37] [2005] EWCA Civ 963; [2005] I.R.L.R. 946 at [46] (italics supplied). See too Colman LJ in *Lordsvale Finance Plc v Bank of Zambia* [1996] Q.B. 752 at 763–764: ("There would therefore seem to be no reason in principle why a contractual provision the effect of which was to increase the consideration payable under an executory contract upon the happening of a default should be struck down as a penalty if the increase could in the circumstances be explained as commercially justifiable") and *M & J Polymers Ltd v Imerys Minerals Ltd* [2008] EWHC 344 (Comm); [2008] 1 Lloyd's Rep. 541 at [46] (Burton J: if agreement not oppressive, commercially justifiable, entered into between equals and not penally intended, should be enforced). See too, for the requirement of unconscionability, *Ringrow Pty Ltd v BP Australia Pty Ltd* (2005) 224 C.L.R. 656, approved at E. Peden and J. Carter, "Agreed Damages Clauses—Back to the Future?" (2006) 22 JCL 189.

[38] [2005] EWCA Civ 963; [2005] I.R.L.R. 946 at [76] (Arden LJ) and [115] (Buxton LJ).

[39] *Euro London Appointments Ltd v Claessens International Ltd* [2006] EWCA Civ 385; [2006] 2 Lloyd's Rep. 436 (in fact obiter, since the penalty doctrine was held to have no application in any case).

[40] Cf. the old Scots decision in *Craig v M'Beath* (1863) 1 M 1020 at 1022, where Lord Inglis based the penalty jurisdiction on the idea that parties could not lawfully enter into an agreement that the one party should be punished at the suit of the other.

[41] *Dunlop Pneumatic Tyre Co Ltd v New Garage Co Ltd* [1915] A.C. 79 at 86.

words "provided always that its dominant purpose was not to deter the other party from breach"[42]

A new start: Cavendish v Makdessi[43]

Sensing the confusion and contradiction into which the penalties doctrine had **25-012** fallen, in 2015 the Supreme Court decided on a new start. *Cavendish Square Holding BV v Makdessi*[44] involved two conjoined appeals. *Cavendish Square v Makdessi*, a dispute between sophisticated business operators, involved the sale by the founder of an advertising and marketing company of a controlling interest in the business. The buyer agreed to pay up to $147 million in instalments; the precise amount depended on a calculation of the company profits, but it was accepted that a large element of it reflected goodwill. For an extended period after the sale the seller was understandably bound not to compete with the business he was selling. If he did, he agreed that he would forfeit all further payments and that the buyer would have an option to buy out his remaining shares at a price which disregarded the entire goodwill element. Found guilty of breaching the non-competition provision, the seller argued that these provisions were penal and not binding on him. The Court of Appeal agreed with him,[45] whereupon the buyer appealed. In the other appeal, *Parkingeye Ltd v Beavis*, a motorist parked in a private car park where notices prominently displayed stated that only two hours' free parking was available and that overstayers would be charged £85. In proceedings on behalf of the landowner to recover the £85, he argued that the stipulated charge was penal. The Court of Appeal held that that it was not,[46] and the motorist appealed. In the event, both clauses were held non-penal: hence the first appeal was allowed, and the second dismissed.

In reaching their decision, five of the seven members of the Supreme Court began **25-013** by repelling a frontal attack on the whole doctrine of penalty clauses, based on the argument that complete freedom of contract should prevail. None was receptive to this view; all agreed that the penalty rule should continue to exist. It was, it was pointed out, a doctrine accepted in every common law jurisdiction; most civil law jurisdictions had provision for some control over agreed remedies clauses; there was no challenge to other, parallel, cases of judicial control over terms such as forfeitures; and furthermore, the Law Commission had advocated not abolishing the penalty rule, but extending it. True, the legislation which is now s.63 of the Consumer Rights Act 2015 provided a good deal of protection in the consumer context; true also that there was a strong policy in favour of freedom of contract, with which the potential applicability of the penalty doctrine as between sophisticated businesses sat rather ill. Nevertheless, it was not appropriate to take the radical step of abolition, and there might well be non-consumer entities, such as small businesses, that still needed protection.[47] Nor was there any enthusiasm for

---

[42] *Lordsvale Finance Plc v Bank of Zambia* [1996] C.L.C. 1849; [1996] Q.B. 752 at 764 (see too Mance LJ in *Cine Bes Filmcilik ve Yapimcilik & Anor v United International Pictures* [2003] EWCA Civ 1669; [2004] 1 C.L.C. 401 at [15]).

[43] See J. Morgan [2016] C.L.J. 11 and B. Lindsay, "Penalty clauses in the Supreme Court: a legitimately interesting decision?" (2016) 20 Edin.L.Rev. 204.

[44] [2015] UKSC 67; [2016] A.C. 1172.

[45] [2013] EWCA Civ 1539; [2013] 2 C.L.C. 968.

[46] [2015] EWCA Civ 402; [2015] R.T.R. 27.

[47] *Cavendish Square Holding BV v Makdessi* [2015] UKSC 67; [2016] A.C. 1172 at [36]–[39] (Lords

cutting down the penalty rule and arbitrarily limiting it to non-commercial cases.[48] The emphasis in the *Cavendish* case was therefore on setting proper bounds to the rule and putting it on a convincing doctrinal footing.

The present rule on penalties: Clauses which act in proportionate defence of some legitimate interest are not penal

25-014   Four members[49] of the Court in *Cavendish Square Holding BV v Makdessi*[50] discussed at length the matter of the justification for, and proper extent of, the penalties doctrine. They all agreed that although Lord Dunedin's opinion in *Dunlop Pneumatic Tyre Co Ltd v New Garage Co Ltd*[51] had been repeatedly referred to, it had become bogged down in detail and did not give an adequately clear indication of what amounted to an unacceptable penalty clause.[52] Hence it should at best be regarded as a guide only.[53] In particular, little enthusiasm was shown for the criterion of a "genuine pre-estimate of loss" which had previously formed such a large part in discussions of the doctrine.[54]

25-015   Instead, what was favoured was a single interest-based analysis, under which a broad comparison fell to be drawn between, first, the burden placed on the contract-beaker by the clause in question and, secondly, the interest in performance of the innocent party which it served to protect. Only if the former was wholly disproportionate to the latter should the clause be struck down as obnoxious. Lords Neuberger and Sumption put the point elegantly:

> "The true test is whether the impugned provision is a secondary obligation which imposes a detriment on the contract-breaker out of all proportion to any legitimate interest of the innocent party in the enforcement of the primary obligation. The innocent party can have no proper interest in simply punishing the defaulter. His interest is in performance or in some appropriate alternative to performance."[55]

Lord Mance expressed a similar view:

> "What is necessary in each case is to consider, first, whether any (and if so what) legitimate business interest is served and protected by the clause, and, second, whether,

---

Neuberger and Sumption, with Lord Carnwath agreeing), [162]–[170] (Lord Mance), [256]–[268] (Lord Hodge).

[48] Such a solution was indeed explicitly ruled out by Lord Mance: *Cavendish Square Holding BV v Makdessi* [2015] UKSC 67; [2016] A.C. 1172 at [168] (Lord Mance).

[49] I.e. Lords Neuberger, Sumption, Mance and Hodge.

[50] [2015] UKSC 67; [2016] A.C. 1172.

[51] [1915] A.C. 79.

[52] "In our opinion, the law relating to penalties has become the prisoner of artificial categorisation, itself the result of unsatisfactory distinctions: between a penalty and genuine pre-estimate of loss, and between a genuine pre-estimate of loss and a deterrent. These distinctions originate in an over-literal reading of Lord Dunedin's four tests and a tendency to treat them as almost immutable rules of general application which exhaust the field": [2015] UKSC 67; [2016] A.C. 1172 at [31] (Lords Neuberger and Sumption).

[53] [2015] UKSC 67; [2016] A.C. 1172 at [21]–[22] (Lords Neuberger and Sumption), [139] (Lord Mance), [221] (Lord Hodge).

[54] See the highly critical discussion in the judgment of Lords Neuberger and Sumption: [2015] UKSC 67; [2016] A.C. 1172 at [31].

[55] [2015] UKSC 67; [2016] A.C. 1172 at [32].

assuming such an interest to exist, the provision made for the interest is nevertheless in the circumstances extravagant, exorbitant or unconscionable."[56]

So too with Lord Hodge, who concluded:

"the correct test for a penalty is whether the sum or remedy stipulated as a consequence of a breach of contract is exorbitant or unconscionable when regard is had to the innocent party's interest in the performance of the contract".[57]

On this criterion, it had to follow that neither of the cases before their lordships **25-016** involved clauses that offended against the rule. In *Cavendish* itself, the clauses disentitling the vendor of a business to further payment in the event of breach of a non-competition covenant, and requiring him to transfer his remaining shareholding at a price net of goodwill, supported a very legitimate interest in the purchaser to maintain the goodwill of the business it had bought. Since there was no evidence of any gross disproportion, it followed that they must be valid.[58] In the *Parkingeye* case, while it was true that the charge for overstaying was intended as a deterrent, and there was essentially no loss at all to the owner, the latter nevertheless had a legitimate interest in the orderly management of its facility, and the steps it had taken to protect that interest could not be castigated as wholly disproportionate.[59]

Penalties and legitimate interests: the application of the new rule

The most important conclusion to be drawn from the decision in *Cavendish* **25-017** *Square Holding BV v Makdessi*[60] is that it seems likely today that the regulation of penalty clauses will in practice be of a decidedly "light-touch" nature.[61] This is for two reasons. One is that the judgments make it clear that, before a clause existing to protect a given interest will be regarded as penal, there must be a *substantial* mismatch between its terms and the interest protected. The terms referred to above, such as "out of all proportion" and "extravagant, exorbitant or unconscionable", indicate that matters are unlikely to be weighed in nice scales: it is only in fairly egregious cases that the doctrine will bite at all.[62] It should also be remembered that *Cavendish* leaves untouched the well-established rule existing before 2015 that the burden of proving a clause penal lies on the party seeking to escape its effects.[63] In practice, moreover, this burden can be heavy. Well before *Cavendish*, the courts had

---

[56] [2015] UKSC 67; [2016] A.C. 1172 at [152].
[57] [2015] UKSC 67; [2016] A.C. 1172 at [255].
[58] [2015] UKSC 67; [2016] A.C. 1172 at [69]–[82] (Lords Neuberger and Sumption), [171]–[187] (Lord Mance), [269]–[282] (Lord Hodge).
[59] [2015] UKSC 67; [2016] A.C. 1172 at [97]–[101] (Lords Neuberger and Sumption), [188]–[199] (Lord Mance), [284]–[288] (Lord Hodge).
[60] [2015] UKSC 67; [2016] A.C. 1172.
[61] W. Day, "A Pyrrhic victory for the doctrine against penalties: Makdessi v Cavendish Square Holding BVI" [2016] JBL 115.
[62] Cf. the post-*Makdessi* case of *Purves v I P Solutions Group Ltd* [2016] EWHC 1835 (QB) at [85] (provision for expropriation of company director's shareholding in private company for £1 in event of material breach of director's duties not penal, since "nothing unconscionable in an arrangement arrived at between parties dealing at arms-length with the benefit of extensive expert advice"). See too *Triple Point Technology Inc v PTT Public Co Ltd* [2019] EWCA Civ 230; [2019] 1 W.L.R. 3549 at [69]–[72] (per diem delay sums in construction "modest" and clearly enforceable: reversed on other grounds, [2021] UKSC 29; [2021] A.C. 1148).
[63] See e.g. *Robophone Facilities Ltd v Blank* [1966] 1 W.L.R. 1428 at 1447–1448 (Diplock LJ); also *Philips Hong Kong Ltd v Att Gen for Hong Kong* (1993) 61 B.L.R. 41 at 59 (Lord Woolf). The point

recognised that quantifying remedies in advance made good business sense, and that the power to strike down an agreed provision as penal was a "blatant interference with freedom of contract",[64] very often inappropriate as between substantial commercial organisations.[65] For these and other reasons, Diplock LJ said in 1966 that courts

> "should not be astute to descry a 'penalty clause' in every provision of a contract which stipulates a sum to be payable by one party to the other in the event of a breach by the former".[66]

This is a view that has been frequently reiterated since.[67]

25-018   The second reason why most clauses are likely to pass the test in *Makdessi* is that the interests which a contractor may legitimately protect by agreed damages or other remedies clauses are broadly defined. In particular, it is now clear beyond doubt that there is no need for a direct link between the agreed payment and the financial consequences of the particular breach in question. This is implicit in the earlier decision in the *Dunlop* case,[68] where the obligation to pay £5 per tyre discounted was justified as non-penal by reference not to any immediate loss (of which there was none), but to Dunlop's overall reputation as a premium brand, which was indirectly threatened by the practice of mass discounting.[69] But the point was made explicit in *Makdessi* by Lords Neuberger and Sumption, when they confirmed that the interest the innocent party was entitled to protect was not necessarily limited to the mere recovery of compensation for a breach.[70] Lord Mance expanded on this point, when he said that a concern could

> "protect a system which it operates across its whole business by imposing an undertaking on all its counterparties to respect the system, coupled with a provision requiring payment of an agreed sum in the event of any breach of such undertaking"

and added that the impossibility of measuring loss from any particular breach was "a reason for upholding, not for striking down, such a provision".[71] This furthermore was reflected in the results in both appeals in *Makdessi*. The stipulations there were held to be justified by the general interest of the promisee in preserving its goodwill in *Makdessi* and the proper administration of the car park in *Parkingeye*, despite distinct uncertainty as to the loss directly caused to the promisee in the former and the entire lack of it in the latter.

25-019   It follows from the above that in all likelihood the pre-*Makdessi* cases in which agreed damages provisions were upheld would be decided the same way today.

---

was confirmed post-*Makdessi* by Sir Michael Burton in *De Havilland Aircraft of Canada Ltd v Spicejet Ltd* [2021] EWHC 362 (Comm) at [30].

[64] *Elsey v JG Collins Insurance Agencies Ltd* (1978) 83 D.L.R. (3d) 1 at 15.

[65] *Murray v Leisureplay Plc* [2005] EWCA Civ 963; [2005] I.R.L.R. 946 at [114] (Clarke LJ). Cf. the comments of Sackville AJA in *Arab Bank Australia Ltd v Sayde Developments Pty Ltd* [2016] NSWCA 328; (2016) 934 N.S.W.L.R. 231 at [7].

[66] *Robophone Facilities Ltd v Blank* [1966] 1 W.L.R. 1428 at 1447.

[67] E.g. *Philips Hong Kong Ltd v Att Gen of Hong Kong* (1993) 61 B.L.R. 41 at 59 (Lord Woolf); *Murray v Leisureplay Plc* [2005] I.R.L.R. 946 at [48] (Arden LJ); *Alfred McAlpine Capital Projects Ltd v Tilebox Ltd* [2005] B.L.R. 271 at [48] (Jackson J).

[68] *Dunlop Pneumatic Tyre Co Ltd v New Garage Co Ltd* [1915] A.C. 79.

[69] See [1915] A.C. 79 at 92–93 (Lord Atkinson).

[70] See [2015] UKSC 67; [2016] A.C. 1172 at [23].

[71] See [2015] UKSC 67; [2016] A.C. 1172 at [143].

Conversely, however, there are a number of other decisions striking down clauses as penal which may now have to be reconsidered.

Losses likely to be imponderable; "sliding scale" damages

Particular leeway has always been allowed where the claimant's loss is, in the **25-020** nature of things, likely to be imponderable.[72] Thus in the early decision in *Clydebank Engineering & Shipbuilding Co Ltd v Don José Ramos Yzquierdo y Castaneda*,[73] warships ordered from Glasgow shipbuilders by the Spanish Government for use in the 1898 Spanish-American War were delivered too late to fight seriously in it. The House of Lords had no hesitation in upholding a late delivery charge of £500 per week per vessel contained in the shipbuilding contract, precisely because damages would otherwise be highly difficult to predict or quantify. This would clearly be decided the same way today, on the basis that there is a very legitimate interest in avoiding arguments over imponderable damages:[74] indeed, clauses of this sort are commonplace in all standard shipbuilding contracts.[75]

Again, "sliding scale" damages of the sort in issue in *Clydebank Engineering*— **25-021** periodical payments for delay and the like—are generally likely to be upheld in all but exceptional cases. Thus in that case itself Lord Davey expressed the view that if agreed damages were

> "proportioned to the amount if I may so call it, or the rate of the non-performance of the agreement—for instance, if you find that it is so much per acre for ground which has been spoilt by mining operations, or if you find, as in the present case, that it is so much per week during the whole time for which the non-delivery of vessels beyond the contract time is delayed—then you infer that prima facie the parties intended the amount to be liquidate damages and not penalty."[76]

This is highly significant in practice: on the basis of this principle the courts even before *Makdessi* fairly consistently accepted periodic delay clauses in shipbuilding,[77] construction,[78] waste disposal[79] and similar[80] agreements, not to mention at

---

[72] "The courts have also long recognised the particular advantages of such clauses where the true amount of damages are uncertain and difficult to assess": Beatson J in *The Paragon* [2009] EWCA Civ 855; [2009] 2 Lloyd's Rep. 688 at [130].

[73] [1905] A.C. 6. See too *Webster v Bosanquet* [1912] A.C. 394 (breach of exclusive buying rights over part of Ceylon tea crop: liquidated damages provision upheld, partly because damages uncertain).

[74] See [2015] UKSC 67; [2016] A.C. 1172 at [143] (Lord Mance).

[75] Above, fn.3.

[76] See [1905] A.C. 6 at 12.

[77] Apart from the *Clydebank* case above, see, e.g. *Cenargo Ltd v Empresa Nacional Bazan de Construcciones Navales Militares SA* [2002] EWCA Civ 524; [2002] C.L.C. 1151 (standard liquidated damages provisions for deficiency in cargo spaces and speed).

[78] E.g. *Law v Redditch Local Board* [1892] 1 Q.B. 127, CA (£100 plus £5 per week); *JF Finnegan (J F) Ltd v Community Housing Assn Ltd* (1993) 34 Const L.R. 104 (£2,500 per week on a £1m project); *Alfred McAlpine Capital Projects Ltd v Tilebox Ltd* [2005] EWHC 281 (TCC), [2005] B.L.R. 271 (£45,000 per week for late completion of commercial development upheld); *Hall v van der Heiden* [2010] EWHC 586 (TCC) (£700 per week for late completion of works on home). The trend of American authority is similar: see the seminal Wisconsin decision in *Davis v La Crosse Hospital Assn* 99 NW 351 (1904) ($20 per day for late completion of hospital).

[79] *Elphinstone v Monkland Iron & Coal Co* (1886) 11 App Cas 332

[80] *Steria Ltd v Sigma Wireless Communications Ltd* [2008] EWHC 3454 (TCC); [2008] B.L.R. 79 (design services: one per cent of contract value per week of delay); see too the older *Elphinstone*

least some contracts for the sale of goods.[81] In *Philips Hong Kong Ltd v A-G for Hong Kong*,[82] for instance, highway contractors agreed with the Hong Kong government a complex system of daily payments for late completion, reckoned in a rough-and-ready way on the likely costs of any resulting traffic disruption. The Privy Council had no difficulty in deciding that this provision was enforceable: it had been agreed between sophisticated contractors with reference to possible losses, and the mere fact that it might lead to over-compensation was no reason to disapply it. The position remains similar post-*Makdessi*, at least where such clauses are agreed between relatively sophisticated commercial parties and are not wholly extravagant or unconscionable.[83]

25-022   In a few cases decided pre-*Makdessi*, clauses of this sort were struck down on the basis that they were perverse with regard to the victim's loss, and thus not a genuine pre-estimate of it. Thus in the car hire-purchase case of *Campbell Discount Ltd v Bridge*[84] a clause requiring a defaulting hirer to pay damages for "depreciation" by making up his total payments to two-thirds of the total due was held a penalty: as Lord Radcliffe put it, "It is a sliding scale of compensation, but a scale that slides in the wrong direction."[85] And although this point was not mentioned as such, similar thinking might well have lain behind the 2008 decision in *The Paragon*,[86] in which the Court of Appeal agreed that a clause in a time charterparty was penal which demanded a full month's hire for any late return: the less serious the breach, the more proportionately serious the consequences would be. However, the idea of a "genuine pre-estimate of loss" is now of vastly reduced importance. It may well be that such cases may have to be reconsidered. Financiers letting assets on hire-purchase may well have a legitimate interest in ensuring that arrangements are not prematurely terminated, and those chartering out vessels on time-charter have a very strong interest in ensuring timely redelivery to guarantee a smooth change-over of charterers: if so, then unless the sums involved are extortionate, such clauses would seem to have a good claim to validity.[87]

Commercial justification cases

25-023   In a series of cases dating from the 1990s, the view was expressed that the rule against penalties was not so much a rule against the victim of a breach of contract recovering more than he had lost, but a rule against his doing so without a good commercial reason. This position was well summed up in 1995 by Colman J:

(Lord) v Monkland Iron & Coal Co Ltd (1886) 11 App. Cas. 332 (promise to restore land after mining, with damages for failure fixed at £100 per acre).

[81]   *M & J Polymers Ltd v Imerys Minerals Ltd* [2008] EWHC 344 (Comm); [2008] 1 Lloyd's Rep. 541 ("take or pay" agreement).

[82]   (1993) 61 B.L.R. 41.

[83]   *GPP Big Field LLP v Solar EPC Solutions SL* [2018] EWHC 2866 (Comm); see esp at [67]. See too *Triple Point Technology Inc v PTT Public Co Ltd* [2019] EWCA Civ 230; [2019] 1 W.L.R. 3549 at [69]–[72] (similar). See too *Eco World - Ballymore Embassy Gardens Co Ltd v Dobler UK Ltd* [2021] EWHC 2207 (TCC); (2021) 197 Con. L.R. 108 (clause valid despite lack of provision for discount for collateral benefits to employer).

[84]   [1962] A.C. 600. The issue is now academic as regards virtually all consumer hire purchase and conditional sale cases: see the Consumer Credit Act 1974 s.100.

[85]   1962] A.C. 600 at 623.

[86]   [2009] EWCA Civ 855; [2009] 2 Lloyd's Rep. 688

[87]   It is worth noting that *Bridge v Campbell Discount* involved an element of consumer protection: but this has now been overtaken by both s.100 of the Consumer Credit Act 1974 and s.63 and Sch.2 of the Consumer Rights Act 2015.

"[T]he jurisdiction in relation to penalty clauses is concerned not primarily with the enforcement of inoffensive liquidated damages clauses but rather with protection against the effect of penalty clauses. There would therefore seem to be no reason in principle why a contractual provision the effect of which was to increase the consideration payable under an executory contract upon the happening of a default should be struck down as a penalty if the increase could in the circumstances be explained as commercially justifiable, provided always that its dominant purpose was not to deter the other party from breach."[88]

This is clearly reflected in the "legitimate interest" criterion in *Makdessi*, and hence cases decided on that basis will continue to be good law.

Instances of cases of this sort include a clause in a loan contract increasing the **25-024** interest rate payable by the borrower while the latter is in default, reflecting the fact that the demonstrably uncreditworthy present an increased credit risk;[89] a "take or pay" clause requiring a buyer of a commodity to pay for a minimum quantity whether it takes delivery of it or not, inserted to protect the seller's investment in arranging supply;[90] and a munificent "golden parachute" provision in a senior business executive's contract of employment, reflecting the fact that high pay can legitimately take many forms.[91] Other cases applying a similar principle have involved a clause allowing a bank providing credit card processing facilities to a merchant to deny reimbursement for prohibited transactions even if it personally suffered no loss from them;[92] a term requiring the purchaser of a superyacht to pay 20 per cent of its value if he did not accept and pay for it;[93] a provision depriving the seller of a business of £540,000 out of the price if it failed to procure a guarantee worth £240,000;[94] and a clause allowing an employment agency to refuse certain rebates to clients who failed to pay its charges on time, aimed at protecting the agency's positive cash-flow.[95] In Australia it has been held, on the basis of analogous reasoning, that a highway authority can legitimately provide for the compulsory and gratuitous takeover of a road contractor's plant to complete a job that the contractor has left undone;[96] and that an oil company can permissibly stipulate for a right

---

[88] *Lordsvale Finance Plc v Bank of Zambia* [1996] C.L.C. 1849; [1996] Q.B. 752 at 764. See too Mance LJ in *Cine Bes Filmcilik ve Yapimcilik v United International Pictures* [2003] EWCA Civ 1669; [2004] 1 C.L.C. 401 at [15]; and *Azimut-Benetti SpA v Healey* [2010] EWHC 2234 (Comm); (2010) 132 Con L.R. 113 at [21] (Blair J).

[89] *Lordsvale Finance Plc v Bank of Zambia* [1996] Q.B. 752; also the post-*Makdessi* cases of *ZCCM Investments Holdings Plc v Konkola Copper Mines Plc* [2017] EWHC 3288 (Comm) at [35]–[38] and *Cargill International Trading Pte Ltd v Uttam Galva Steels Ltd* [2019] EWHC 476 (Comm) But the court in all these cases stressed the modesty of the uplift, and the result may differ if it is immodest: see *Jeancharm Ltd (t/a Beaver International) v Barnet Football Club Ltd* [2003] EWCA Civ 58; (2003) 92 Con L.R. 26 (five per cent per week for late payment unacceptable), and the Australian *Elberg v Fraval* [2012] VSC 342 ($5,000 per day for late repayment of $250,000 loan: same result).

[90] *M&J Polymers Ltd v Imerys Minerals Ltd* [2008] EWHC 344 (Comm); [2008] 1 C.L.C. 276 esp at [46] (Burton J). Such clauses are very common in the oil and gas industry, and they also feature in analogous "ship or pay" provisions in contracts between oil and gas suppliers and pipeline companies.

[91] *Murray v Leisureplay Plc* [2005] EWCA Civ 963; [2005] I.R.L.R. 946, esp at [117] (Buxton LJ).

[92] *Lancore Services Ltd v Barclays Bank Plc* [2008] EWHC 1264 (Ch); [2008] 1 C.L.C. 1039.

[93] *Azimut-Benetti SpA v Healey* [2010] EWHC 2234 (Comm); (2010) 132 Con L.R. 113.

[94] *General Trading Co (Holdings) Ltd v Richmond Corp Ltd* [2008] EWHC 1479 (Comm).

[95] *Euro London Appointments Ltd v Claessens International Ltd* [2006] EWCA Civ 385; [2006] 2 Lloyd's Rep. 436.

[96] *Forestry Commission of N.S.W. v Stefanetto* (1976) 133 C.L.R. 507.

to buy back a service station if the owner breaks a solus agreement to sell only that company's fuel.[97]

25-025   Since the Supreme Court laid stress on the width of the interests open to protection through liquidated damages clauses, it is likely that successful attacks on the basis of "no interest" will be rare. Indeed, the effect of *Makdessi* may well be to put beyond attack a number of provisions that might previously have been of doubtful validity. For example, in 1962 it was said that where the terms of a contract allowed one party to withdraw for something short of a repudiatory breach, not only were damages for loss of bargain unavailable in such a case (since the loss would result from the decision to terminate and not from the breach) but any stipulation allowing them to be claimed would be penal.[98] And as late as 2013 Flaux J seems to have accepted that a clause in a charterparty allowing damages following withdrawal for a minor breach was penal, and to that end read it down so as to limit it to a breach of condition proper.[99] Yet it is difficult to say that a party has no interest in preserving its right to claim damages following termination under a power conferred by the contract itself,[100] and it is suggested that these authorities may well need to be reconsidered.

25-026   On the other hand, the characterisation of a clause as penal on the basis of lack of interest still cannot be ruled out. For example, in a one-off contract to buy goods where there is no serious prospect of consequential loss to the seller, it might well be that a stipulation for damages in noticeable excess of the ordinary measure available at common law would be regarded as an illegitimate penalty.[101] Another possible example would be where a contract to furnish the use of goods such as containers contained a clause requiring indefinite payment of demurrage even after it was clear that they were irretrievably lost.[102] Again, if it is true that the bargaining position of the parties is in account (a matter discussed below), an employer might have difficulty in showing that it had a legitimate interest in, for example, claiming anything more than its actual loss from an employee who left without giving proper notice.[103]

---

[97] *Ringrow Pty Ltd v BP Australia Pty Ltd* (2005) 224 C.L.R. 656.

[98] See the hire purchase case of *Financings Ltd v Baldock* [1963] 2 Q.B. 104 at 111 (Lord Denning MR).

[99] See *Kuwait Rocks Co v AMN Bulkcarriers Inc, The Astra* [2013] EWHC 865 (Comm); [2013] 1 C.L.C. 819.

[100] Indeed at least one of the standard time charter forms now allows exactly that: see NYPE 2015, cl.11(c).

[101] "The innocent party can have no proper interest in simply punishing the defaulter. His interest is in performance or in some appropriate alternative to performance. In the case of a straightforward damages clause, that interest will rarely extend beyond compensation for the breach, and we therefore expect that Lord Dunedin's four tests would usually be perfectly adequate to determine its validity": *Cavendish Square Holding BV v Makdessi* [2015] UKSC 67; [2016] A.C. 1172 at [32] (Lords Neuberger and Sumption). Cf. *Blu-Sky Solutions Ltd v Be Caring Ltd* [2021] EWHC 2619 (Comm) (vast charge for cancellation of mobile telephony provision contract unenforceable).

[102] Cf. *MSC Mediterranean Shipping Co SA v Cottonex Anstalt* [2015] EWHC 283 (Comm); [2015] 1 C.L.C. 143 at [106]–[116], where (admittedly before *Makdessi* was decided by the Supreme Court), Leggatt J thought such a clause would be penal.

[103] See *Girard UK Ltd v Smith* [2000] I.R.L.R. 763 (term requiring worker to forfeit four weeks' wages if he left without notice unenforceable). But possibly not where the worker was guilty of misconduct: see the "bad leaver" cases of *Richards v IP Solutions Group Ltd* [2016] EWHC 1835 (QB); [2017] I.R.L.R. 133 esp at [85] (effective forfeiture of shares if dismissed for misconduct) and *Gray v Braid Group (Holdings) Ltd* [2016] CSIH 68; 2017 S.C. 409 (transfer shares at a discount to other shareholders).

Penalties and proportionality

Since the Supreme Court laid stress on the width of the interests open to protec- **25-027**
tion through liquidated damages clauses, it is likely that most successful challenges to such clauses are likely to be on the basis of proportionality. This may well
be significant where there is a grotesque disparity between the stipulated sum and
any likely damages, or as Lord Dunedin put it in the *Dunlop* case, there is in issue
a provision "extravagant and unconscionable in amount in comparison with the
greatest loss that could conceivably be proved to have followed from the breach".[104]
Such a disparity will, it seems, suffice in and of itself. Lord Halsbury gave a clear,
if fantastic, instance in 1905: if, he said:

> "you agreed to build a house in a year, and agreed that if you did not build the house for
> £50, you were to pay a million of money as a penalty, the extravagance of that would be
> at once apparent".[105]

More recent actual examples include an obligation in a bailee of recording equipment, some of it of fairly negligible value, to pay a straight £600 for any delay,
however slight, in returning any of it,[106] and a provision for interest of five per cent
per week for late payment of a purchase price.[107]

In this connection, a difficult issue may arise as to the relevance of the bargain- **25-028**
ing power of the parties. In theory this used not to be in account. Lord Wright MR
said:

> "A millionaire may enter into a contract in which he is to pay liquidated damages, or a
> poor man may enter into a similar contract with a millionaire, but in each case the ques-
> tion is exactly the same, namely, whether the sum stipulated as damages for the breach
> was exorbitant or extravagant."[108]

However, the modern view is that some account may be taken of the parties'
bargaining position in reckoning whether a contractor is indeed merely using
proportionate means to protect his interests. Courts in Australia[109] and Canada[110]
have regarded relative bargaining power as a highly relevant matter, with the sup-

---

[104] See *Dunlop Pneumatic Tyre Co Ltd v New Garage & Motor Co Ltd* [1915] A.C. 79 at 87. See too
Lord Woolf in *Philips Hong Kong Ltd v Att-Gen of Hong Kong* (1993) 61 B.L.R. 41 at 59 ("totally
out of proportion to certain of the losses which may be incurred").

[105] *Clydebank Engineering & Shipbuilding Co Ltd v Don José Ramos Yzquierdo y Castaneda* [1905]
A.C. 6 at 10.

[106] *Ariston SRL v Charly Records Ltd* (1990) *Financial Times,* 21 March. Cf. *CMC Group Plc v Zhang*
[2006] EWCA Civ 408, [2006] All E.R. (D) 197 (Mar), CA (litigation settled for $40,000: term in
settlement agreement for repayment of entire amount on any breach of its terms).

[107] *Jeancharm Ltd (t/a Beaver International) v Barnet Football Club Ltd* [2003] EWCA Civ 58; (2003)
92 Con L.R. 26. So too, post-*Makdessi*, with interest at 12 per cent a month compounded monthly,
held to be obviously extravagant, excessive and oppressive in *Ahuja Investments Ltd v Victorygame
Ltd* [2021] EWHC 2382 (Ch).

[108] *Imperial Tobacco Co v Parslay* [1936] 2 All E.R. 515 at 523.

[109] *AMEV-UDC Finance Ltd v Austin* (1986) 162 C.L.R. 170 at 194 (Mason and Wilson JJ).

[110] "[T]he power to strike down a penalty clause ... is designed for the sole purpose of providing relief
against oppression for the party having to pay the stipulated sum. It has no place where there is no
oppression": see *Elsey v J.G. Collins Insurance Agencies Ltd* (1978) 83 D.L.R. (3d) 1 at 15 (Dickson
J); *Cavendish Square Holding BV v Makdessi* [2015] UKSC 67; [2016] A.C. 1172 at [33] (Lords
Neuberger and Sumption)

port of the Privy Council;[111] and this development has the imprimatur of at least some members of the Supreme Court in *Cavendish Square Holding BV v Makdessi*.[112] If so, then cases such as *Girard UK Ltd v Smith*,[113] striking down a term requiring a worker to forfeit four weeks' wages if he left without notice, might well be decided the same way today.

Relevance of the same sum being payable for different breaches

25-029　Prior to *Makdessi* there was venerable authority that

"Where the sum which is to be a security for the performance of an agreement to do several acts, will, in case of breaches of the agreement, be, in some instances, too large and in others too small a compensation for the injury thereby occasioned, that sum is to be considered a penalty."[114]

So, for example, in *Kemble v Farron*[115] a clause in a high-profile actor's contract fixing damages for any breach whatever at £1,000 was struck down; similarly in *Willson v Love*[116] an agreement by a farm tenant to pay £3 per ton for all hay and straw not ploughed in was similarly invalidated on a showing that the fertilising value of hay and straw was substantially different. It is respectfully suggested that this factor is now of limited, if any, importance. Provided the interest protected is legitimate and the sum is not extortionate, there seems no reason why this factor should prevent the enforcement of such clauses.[117]

The relevance of deterrence

25-030　Before *Makdessi* was decided, it seemed clear on the authorities that a stipulation which was not a genuine pre-estimate of recoverable loss was automatically invalid if predominantly aimed at deterring breach.[118] In the *Dunlop* case Lord Dunedin had specifically singled out as unenforceable payments of money "stipulated as *in terrorem* of the offending party";[119] and in 1995 Colman J, when stating the rule on commercial justification, pointedly added the words "provided always that its dominant purpose was not to deter the other party from breach".[120]

---

[111]　*Phillips Hong Kong Ltd v AG of Hong Kong* (1993) 61 B.L.R. 49 at 58 (Lord Woolf).

[112]　[2015] UKSC 67; [2016] A.C. 1172 at [35] (Lords Neuberger and Sumption). The same judges also stressed that on the facts of Makdessi the parties had been negotiating on roughly equal terms: see [66], as did Lord Hodge at [282].

[113]　[2000] I.R.L.R. 763. Compare, however, the pre-*Makdessi* decision in *Cleeve Link Ltd v Bryla* [2014] I.C.R. 264.

[114]　*Davies v Penton* (1827) 6 B & Cr 216 at 223 (Bayley J).

[115]　(1829) 6 Bing 141. The clause was not quite as outré as it looked. The case concerned the actor's late withdrawal from a long-term engagement of considerable moment, and as it was the theatre obtained a verdict for £750 damages at common law.

[116]　[1896] 1 Q.B. 626.

[117]　Indeed, this seems implicit from *Makdessi* itself, where in the *Parkingeye* case the court upheld a stipulation for £85 for overstaying, which applied whether the overage was five minutes or five hours.

[118]　Compare the old Scots decision in *Craig v M'Beath* (1863) 1 M 1020 at 1022, where Lord Inglis based the penalty jurisdiction on the idea that parties could not lawfully enter into an agreement that the one party should be punished at the suit of the other.

[119]　*Dunlop Pneumatic Tyre Co Ltd v New Garage Co Ltd* [1915] A.C. 79 at 86.

[120]　*Lordsvale Finance Plc v Bank of Zambia* [1996] C.L.C. 1849; [1996] Q.B. 752 at 764, and see too at 762 (also Mance LJ in *Cine Bes Filmcilik ve Yapimcilik & Anor v United International Pictures*

Thus in *The Paragon*[121] time-charterers agreed that in the event of late return the charter rate for the final month before the stipulated return date would be increased from the charter to the market rate; once this was found by the arbitrators to be intended to deter the charterers from ordering final voyages that risked late redelivery, the Court of Appeal peremptorily struck down the clause as penal. This authority must now, however, be regarded as superseded. Reference to deterrence as the mark of a penalty was deprecated in *Makdessi*;[122] and in the *Parkingeye* appeal a stipulation which was admittedly intended as a deterrent was nevertheless upheld.

The relevance of common law liability and causation

Under the pre-*Makdessi* regime, there was controversy over how far the concept **25-031** of a "genuine pre-estimate of loss" could take into account losses suffered but otherwise unrecoverable from the defendant at common law, for instance because they would have been too remote, outside the loss regarded in law as caused by the breach, or excluded because of the duty to mitigate. The accepted view was that the relevant figure was that of recoverable loss only,[123] and that a clause providing for payment of other losses did not represent a genuine pre-estimate.[124] Thus in one case it was definitively held that a liquidated damages clause including losses suffered but treated in law as not caused by the breach was a penalty.[125] On the other hand, Diplock LJ apparently saw no objection to express clauses allowing recovery of losses otherwise too remote under the rule in *Hadley v Baxendale*[126] in 1966;[127] and in 2005 Buxton LJ clearly suggested that it was entirely legitimate to use a liquidated damages clauses to pre-empt possibly protracted argument about whether a given loss could have been avoided or mitigated.[128]

Since *Makdessi*, it would seem that the wide scope given to legitimate interest **25-032** has resolved this conflict in favour of Buxton LJ's view. It is suggested that if, as is now clear, a contractor may legitimately protect some general interest of his

---

[2003] EWCA Civ 1669; [2004] 1 C.L.C. 401 at [13]–[15]; *Office of Fair Trading v Abbey National Plc* [2008] EWHC 875 (Comm) at [295] ff (Andrew Smith J); and *The Paragon* [2009] EWHC 551 (Comm), [2009] 1 Lloyd's Rep. 658 at [18]). The intent had to be predominant: see *M & J Polymers Ltd v Imerys Minerals Ltd* [2008] EWHC 344 (Comm), [2008] 1 Lloyd's Rep. 541 at [46] (Burton J).

121 [2009] EWCA Civ 855; [2009] 2 Lloyd's Rep. 688. For a more recent example, see *Fermiscan Pty Ltd v James* (2009) 261 A.L.R. 408 (clauses payable on breaches of settlement agreement).

122 "To describe [a term] as a deterrent (or, to use the Latin equivalent, in terrorem) does not add anything. A deterrent provision in a contract is simply one species of provision designed to influence the conduct of the party potentially affected. It is no different in this respect from a contractual inducement. Neither is it inherently penal or contrary to the policy of the law. The question whether it is enforceable should depend on whether the means by which the contracting party's conduct is to be influenced are 'unconscionable' ... by reference to some norm": [2015] UKSC 67; [2015] 3 W.L.R. 1373 at [31] (Lords Neuberger and Sumption). See too at [248] and [285] (Lord Hodge).

123 *The Paragon* [2009] EWCA Civ 855; [2009] 2 Lloyd's Rep. 688 at [22]. Contra, possibly, Diplock LJ in *Robophone Facilities Ltd v Blank* [1966] 1 W.L.R. 1428 at 1447–1448.

124 Cf. cases such as *Financings Ltd v Baldock* [1963] 1 Q.B. 887 and *Cooden Engineering Co v Stanford* [1953] 1 Q.B. 86 (losses caused essentially by claimant's own action).

125 *Financings Ltd v Baldock* [1963] 1 Q.B. 887.

126 (1854) 9 Exch. 341.

127 *Robophone Facilities Ltd v Blank* [1966] 1 W.L.R. 1428 at 1448.

128 See *Murray v Leisureplay Plc* [2005] EWCA Civ 963; [2005] I.R.L.R. 946 at [115] (a "golden parachute" provision attacked partly on the precise basis that it did *not* require the executive concerned to mitigate his loss by looking for another job).

despite a failure to show that it is directly harmed by the defendant's breach, he must a fortiori have a legitimate interest in being made good for a loss actually suffered in connection with the transaction concerned, whether or not he could actually have recovered in full from the defendant at common law.

25-033   A further point remains unanswered: can a contractor validly stipulate for a *measure* of recovery otherwise unavailable, such as an account of profits instead of damages? A Canadian court has said that such a clause would be penal and unenforceable:[129] it must remain an open question whether after *Makdessi* a contractor would be regarded as having a legitimate interest in insisting that any profits from a breach of contract went to him rather than the contract breaker.

A possible special case: Sums payable on late payment of a debt

25-034   The late payment of debts has always been a concern of the doctrine of penalties; indeed, as was stated above, an early function of the jurisdiction to relieve against penalties concerned penal bonds typified by the case where a debtor for £100 executed a bond for £200 defeasible on prompt payment of the original £100. From this, however, there had developed by the nineteenth century a highly specialised and inflexible rule. This was that, although a debtor could validly agree to pay periodic interest on sums paid late,[130] a promise to pay a fixed extra sum in the event of failure to discharge the original debt on time was invariably regarded as an unenforceable penalty.[131] Moreover, this provision was even stricter than the normal rule about penalties, in that—in parallel with the then general rule that there could be no damages for late payment[132]—the extra sum remained irrecoverable even if it did represent a loss likely to be suffered by the creditor as a result of being paid late.[133]

25-035   In addition to the rule about fixed sums, there developed another parallel and equally inflexible principle. Although it had always been regarded as permissible for a lender to increase the rate of interest payable by a borrower in respect of any period in which the latter was actually in default,[134] any term under which interest

---

[129]   *Clarke (HF) Ltd v Thermidaire Corp Ltd* (1974) 54 D.L.R. (3d) 385 (clause providing for surrender of gross profit in non-competition covenant held penal).

[130]   Though this interest, if extortionate, might itself amount to a penalty: see e.g. *Patel v Zukowski* (unreported, 18 December 1996), Q.B.D. (£5,000 per month on late payment of £85,000 struck down), and *Jeancharm Ltd v Barnet Football Club Ltd* [2003] EWCA Civ 58; (2003) 92 Con L.R. 26 (five per cent per week for late payment unacceptable). This remains a possibility (see e.g. *Ahuja Investments Ltd v Victorygame Ltd* [2021] EWHC 2382 (Ch)); though some fairly high rates have been tolerated, as in *Biosol Renewables UK Ltd v Lovering (t/a R & A Properties (A Partnership))* [2021] EWHC 71 (Comm) (1.5% per month).

[131]   See e.g. *Astley v Weldon* (1801) (1801) 2 B & P 346 at 353 (Heath J); *Wallis v Smith* (1882) 21 Ch. D. 243 at 256–257 (Jessell MR). *Dunlop Pneumatic Tyre Co Ltd v New Garage & Motor Co Ltd* [1915] A.C. 79 at 87 (Lord Dunedin).

[132]   See *London, Chatham & Dover Ry Co v South Eastern Ry Co* [1893] A.C. 429. The last vestiges of this foolish rule were only swept away in 2007: see *Sempra Metals Ltd v Inland Revenue Comm'rs* [2007] UKHL 34; [2008] 1 A.C. 561.

[133]   A point made (and sharply criticised) by Jessell MR in *Wallis v Smith* (1882) 21 Ch D 243 at 256–257.

[134]   As demonstrated by a number of cases on mortgages: e.g. *Herbert v Salisbury & Yeovil Ry Co* (1866) L.R. 2 Eq. 221. See too the later *David Securities Pty. Ltd v Commonwealth Bank of Australia* (1990) 93 A.L.R. 271.

became retrospectively payable, or payable at an increased rate, in the event of late payment of a capital sum was equally taken to be penal and unenforceable.[135]

These rules were, and are, arbitrary. But, as with many arbitrary rules, they were **25-036** balanced and mitigated by two equally inflexible converse principles. The first was that, while a promise to pay £110 if one was late in paying £100 was bad, a functionally indistinguishable promise to pay £110 with a £10 discount for prompt payment was good, on the reasoning that the loss of a discount could not count as a penalty.[136] The second principle was that while late payment could not give rise to an increase in the nominal sum owing, there was no objection to it accelerating an existing liability to pay. It followed that clauses were perfectly valid under which a capital debt originally payable by instalments became immediately due and owing in full if the debtor defaulted in paying any instalment[137] or a single debt payable on a particular date became payable early.[138]

Despite the more nuanced approach to penalty clauses generally dating from the **25-037** 1990s, in 1996 Colman J expressed no doubts about the old authorities preventing agreements to pay a greater sum for late payment of a smaller one, and agreements to increase interest backdated to a period before default;[139] and 11 years later the High Court accepted that obligations in the event of late payment to pay more than the capital sum outstanding fell to be struck down as penalties.[140]

Although no mention was made of these specific rules in *Makdessi*, their very **25-038** rigidity seems inconsistent with the flexible approach advanced in that case to the determination generally whether a clause is penal. It is respectfully suggested that they must now be open to reconsideration.[141]

The reach of the penalty clause doctrine

The archetypal object of the penalties rule is an obligation in a contractor who **25-039** is in breach of contract to pay a sum of money to the victim of the breach. Neverthe-

---

[135] *Holles (Lady) v Wyse* (1693) 2 Vern 289; see too *Wallingford v Mutual Society* (1880) 5 App Cas 685 at 702; *Kreglinger v New Patagonia Meat & Cold Storage Co Ltd* [1914] A.C. 25 at 35 (Lord Haldane).

[136] "It is a relaxation of the terms of that original contract, not taking it by way of penalty at all, but a relaxation of your contract which you would merit and purchase by paying at a definite and filed time" (Lord Hatherley in *Wallingford v Mutual Society* (1880) 5 App. Cas. 685 at 702). See too *Protector Endowment Loan & Annuity Co v Grice* (1880) 5 Q.B.D. 592 at 596 (Brett LJ). More recently this has been analysed on the basis that the duty to pay the £110 is a primary, not a secondary, obligation and thus outside the penalties doctrine: *Heritage Travel and Tourism Ltd v Windhorst* [2021] EWHC 2380 (Comm) at [89].

[137] See *Wallingford v Mutual Society* (1880) 5 App. Cas. 685. See too *Protector Endowment Loan & Annuity Co v Grice* (1880) 5 Q.B.D. 592; and, more recently, *The Angelic Star* [1988] 1 Lloyd's Rep. 122 and the post-*Makdessi* case of *ZCCM Investments Holdings Plc v Konkola Copper Mines Plc* [2017] EWHC 3288 (Comm), esp at [34]. However, nothing more than the original capital sum could be charged: anything more than that sum—for example, future interest liabilities—would cause it to be penal: *United Dominions Trust Ltd v Paterson* [1973] N.I. 142.

[138] See *Maple Leaf Macro Volatility Master Fund v Rouvroy* [2009] EWHC 257 (Comm); [2009] 1 Lloyd's Rep. 475, esp at [264]. This remains the case after *Makdessi*: see *Edgeworth Capital (Luxembourg) SàRL v Ramblas Investments BV* [2016] EWCA Civ 412.

[139] See *Lordsvale Finance Plc v Bank of Zambia* [1996] Q.B. 752 at 760–764.

[140] *County Leasing Ltd v East* [2007] EWHC 2907 (QB).

[141] Though note that the New South Wales Court of Appeal held in *Auzcare Pty Ltd v Idameneo (No 123) Pty Ltd* [2015] NSWCA 412; (2015) 91 N.S.W.L.R. 581 that a provision for a reviver of a debt in the event of breach of a compromise agreement was not penal.

less, the doctrine can go further than this, and some discussion is necessary of its precise boundaries.

25-040 **(i) Payments other than on breach: the problem of primary and secondary obligations** It is arguable that when equity first started to relieve against conditional bonds,[142] it did not limit its intervention to cases where the non-fulfilment of the condition amounted to a breach of contract.[143] Put another way, this means it is arguable that, in the light of its origins, the penalty doctrine should be capable of applying not only to secondary obligations arising on the non-performance of a contractual duty, but to primary obligations contained in the contract itself: for example, where a contractor was given an option to vary his performance, but only at an unconscionable price entirely disproportionate to any prejudice to the counterparty.[144] This view has been accepted in Australia, on the basis that any stipulation which operates in substance as security for contractual performance ought to be subject to control.[145] But it has been definitively rejected in England, with the rules on penalty clauses described above apply only to liabilities arising *on breach of contract* by the defendant.[146] As Lords Neuberger and Sumption put it in *Cavendish Square Holding BV v Makdessi*,[147] there is

> "a fundamental difference between a jurisdiction to review the fairness of a contractual obligation and a jurisdiction to regulate the remedy for its breach".

The former is not recognised, while the latter is.[148] It follows that, at least as a general rule, no relief can be given in respect of sums payable on other events,[149] even if the events triggering liability have the effect of depriving the claimant of

---

[142] Para.25-004.

[143] *Cavendish Square Holding BV v Makdessi* [2015] UKSC 67; [2016] A.C. 1172 at [7] (Lord Neuberger).

[144] For the arguments, see S. Stoljar, "The Contractual Concept of Condition" (1953) 69 LQR 485 and *Andrews v ANZ Banking Group Ltd* (2012) 247 C.L.R. 205 at [33]–[45].

[145] See *Andrews v ANZ Banking Group Ltd* (2012) 247 C.L.R. 205 at [33]–[45] (hefty charges levied by bank for dishonour of cheques and unarranged overdrafts subject to penalties doctrine, even though customers incurring them not in breach of contract); and *Cedar Meats Pty Ltd v Five Star Lamb Pty Ltd* (2013) 45 V.R. 79 ("take or pay" arrangement re services). The *Andrews* case is commented on in P. Davies and P. Turner, "Relief against penalties without a breach of contract" [2013] C.L.J. 21, and in J. Carter et al, "Contractual Penalties: Resurrecting the Equitable Jurisdiction" (2013) 30 J.C.L. 99.

[146] *Cavendish Square Holding BV v Makdessi* [2015] UKSC 67; [2016] A.C. 1172 at [13]–[14], [42] (Lords Neuberger and Sumption), [130] (Lord Mance), [241] (Lord Hodge). For earlier statements of this principle, see e.g. *Export Credits Guarantee Dept v Universal Oil Products Co* [1983] 1 Lloyd's Rep. 448 at 456, CA (Waller LJ) (decision upheld at [1983] 1 W.L.R. 399); also *EFT Commercial Ltd v Security Change Ltd*, 1992 SC 414 at 431 (Lord Hope) and *Jervis v Harris* [1996] Ch. 195 at 206 (Millett LJ); *Office of Fair Trading v Abbey National Plc* [2008] EWHC 875 (Comm); [2008] 2 All E.R. (Comm) 625 at [295]–[299] (Andrew Smith J) (the point was not taken on appeal at [2009] UKSC 6; [2010] 1 A.C. 696).

[147] [2015] UKSC 67; [2016] A.C. 1172.

[148] See [2015] UKSC 67; [2016] A.C. 1172 at [13].

[149] Before *Makdessi* it was held that where some of the events triggering an obligation to pay were breaches of contract but others were not, the penalties rule would apply where there had been a breach but not otherwise. See *Cooden Engineering Co Ltd v Stanford* [1953] 1 Q.B. 86 at 96 (Somervell LJ); *Maple Leaf Macro Volatility Master Fund v Rouvroy* [2009] EWHC 257 (Comm), [2009] 1 Lloyd's Rep. 475 at [262] (Andrew Smith J). But these may have to be reconsidered. In *Purves v I P Solutions Group Ltd* [2016] EWHC 1835 (QB) May J at [85] thought that where shareholders in a private company had to surrender their holding for £1 whenever they left, includ-

performance, and in addition the effect of enforcing the liability to pay is to over-compensate him for that deprivation.

The point most commonly arose in connection with attempts to create liabilities **25-041** consequent on the automatic termination of an agreement as a result of the supervening insolvency or incapacity of a party to it. For example, as early as 1942 it was held that the restrictions inherent in the penalty clause doctrine did not apply to agreed termination payments in hire-purchase agreements where termination was on the basis, not of breach, but of the hirer's insolvency;[150] and since then a steady stream of authority treated in a similar way minimum payment clauses in lease and analogous contracts,[151] not to mention provisions in financing agreements,[152] and more complicated financial transactions such as derivative swaps.[153] Since *Makdessi* it has been confirmed, on the basis of similar reasoning, that in respect of a financing agreement fees payable on events of default are outside the reach of the penalties doctrine.[154]

Provisions of the above sort, however, are not the only instance where the **25-042** requirement of a breach of contract prevents the application of the penalty doctrine. It is perfectly possible for other contractual provisions to be construed as binding a contracting party to pay over a sum of money, or to pay for something to be done, in circumstances where no question arises of the breach of any underlying contractual obligation. And where this happens, freedom of contract remains, with the result that the fact that the payee may obtain a windfall as a result of payment is irrelevant.[155] So where an injured professional footballer collected £500 under a disablement insurance policy but promised to return it if he ever returned to the professional game, the Court of Appeal understandably held the law on penalties irrelevant;[156] and where a banking contract imposed substantial charges for unauthorised overdrafts, Andrew Smith J decided that such charges could not be penal because the overdraft arose from the bank's honouring of an implicit request for accommodation and not from any breach by the customer.[157] Again, suppose a contract of sale contains a provision allowing the buyer to postpone the agreed

---

ing where they were guilty of breach of contract, this indicated that the provision was a primary obligation and thus entirely beyond the reach of the penalties jurisdiction.

[150] *Re Apex Supply Co Ltd* [1942] 1 Ch. 108. See too the similar *EFT Commercial Ltd v Security Change Ltd*, 1992 SC 414 and *Lombard North Central Plc v Brook* [1999] BPIR 701. See too *Transag Haulage Ltd (IAR) v Leyland DAF Finance Plc* [1994] BCC 356 (similar re provision for return of goods by hirer, though there relief against forfeiture granted).

[151] See e.g. *EFT Commercial Ltd v Security Change Ltd*, 1992 SC 414; *Lombard North Central Plc v Brook* [1999] BPIR 701; *Transag Haulage Ltd v Leyland DAF Finance Plc* [1994] BCC 356.

[152] *Maple Leaf Macro Volatility Master Fund v Rouvroy* [2009] EWHC 257 (Comm); [2009] 1 Lloyd's Rep. 475, esp at [260] (termination of funding agreement by lender if for any reason contemplated arrangements failed to materialise).

[153] See *Lomas v JFB Firth Rixson Inc* [2010] EWHC 3372 (Ch); *Lehman Bros Special Financing Inc v Carlton Communications Ltd* [2011] EWHC 718 (Ch) at [45]–[48].

[154] *Edgeworth Capital (Luxembourg) Sarl v Ramblas Investments BV* [2016] EWCA Civ 412. So also with a provision that share options remain exercisable by a departed business executive for a period after departure as long as he does not compete with his erstwhile employer: *Leiman v Noble Resources Ltd* [2020] SGCA 52.

[155] See, e.g., *Football Association Premier League Ltd v PPLive Sports International Ltd* [2022] EWHC 38 (Comm), esp at [120]–[121] (Fraser J) (payments to broadcast football matches scratched owing to Covid). Note that this may be so even if the payment is actually referred to in the contract as "liquidated damages": see *Fratelli Moretti SpA v Nidera Handelscompagnie BV* [1980] 1 Lloyd's Rep. 534 at 542 (Donaldson J).

[156] See *Alder v Moore* [1961] 2 Q.B. 57.

[157] See *Office of Fair Trading v Abbey National Plc* [2008] EWHC 875 (Comm); [2008] 2 All E.R.

delivery date on payment of a capital or periodic sum. Although in one sense this is concerned with the buyer's failure to perform as originally agreed, it is nevertheless clear that "carrying charges" of this sort are unaffected by the law on penalties.[158] Yet again, in a case decided after *Makdessi*, provisions in a private company's articles of association requiring surrender of employees' shareholdings for £1 if they left the company or were dismissed for misconduct were held to embody primary obligations and for that reason to be beyond the reach of the penalties rule.[159] What matters, therefore, is whether in substance[160] a provision is a sanction or remedy for non-performance (a secondary obligation), or genuinely a part of the agreed exchange concluded between the parties and hence a primary obligation.[161]

25-043   A difficult case arises where the event giving rise to the obligation to pay resembles in substance a breach of contract by the defendant, but the contract ostensibly characterises it instead as an option of non-performance available at a price. In *Associated Distributors Ltd v Hall*[162] the Court of Appeal upheld an attempt to invoke this somewhat unreal taxonomy. Thus where a hire purchase contract gave the defaulting hirer who could not afford to pay a *soi-disant* "option" to terminate the arrangement by returning the goods, and then went on to say that the exercise of this "option" triggered an obligation to pay a substantial minimum sum, no question of relief from penalties arose. Although in the later decision in *Bridge v Campbell Discount Ltd*[163] two members of the House of Lords correctly excoriated this interpretation as elevating form over substance and allowing clever draftsmen an end-run round the penalties rule,[164] two other Law Lords ac-

---

(Comm) 625 at [295] [299] (the point was not taken on appeal at [2009] UKSC 6; [2010] 1 A.C. 696, where the only issue concerned what is now the Consumer Rights Act 2015, Sch.2).

158   *Fratelli Moretti SpA v Nidera Handelscompagnie BV* [1980] 1 Lloyd's Rep. 534. A fortiori, of course, if the seller has to agree to such postponement: *Gonzalez (Thomas P) Corp v Waring (F.R.) (International) Pty Ltd* [1978] 1 Lloyd's Rep. 494.

159   See *Purves v I P Solutions Group Ltd* [2016] EWHC 1835 (QB) at [85]. See too *Longulf Trading (UK) Ltd v Niyazi Onen Gida Sanayi AS* [2019] EWHC 1573 (Comm), esp at [39].

160   "[T]he classification of terms for the purpose of the penalty rule depends on the substance of the term and not on its form or on the label which the parties have chosen to attach to it": *Cavendish Square Holding BV v Makdessi* [2015] UKSC 67; [2016] A.C. 1172 at [15] (Lords Neuberger and Sumption). On this question see generally the perceptive M.Phua, "Secondary obligations 'in substance'" (2021) 137 L.Q.R. 45.

161   On which the Singapore Court of Appeal has suggested a helpful test: does the provision exist "in order to secure some independent commercial purpose or end" over and above any response it prescribes for non-performance? If so it is in substance a primary obligation. See *Leiman v Noble Resources Ltd* [2020] SGCA 52; [2020] 2 S.L.R. 386 at [101].

162   [1938] 2 K.B. 83.

163   [1962] A.C. 600.

164   [1962] A.C. 600 at 629, 634 (Lords Denning and Devlin). American authority generally agrees: see *Restatement 2d of Contracts*, para.356, Comment c, and e.g. *Superfos Investments v First-Miss Fertilizer Co*, 821 F.Supp. 432 (1993). It should also be noted that the matter is now academic as regards regulated consumer credit agreements. Section 100 of the Consumer Credit Act 1974 regulates all minimum payment clauses however drafted, and effectively provides that the debtor can never be liable to make up payments to more than half the total price.

cepted it,[165] and save perhaps in one instance[166] it has not been seriously questioned since.[167]

In practice, however, the rule in *Associated Distributors Ltd v Hall*[168] is not very **25-044** significant, since it only applies where there is some act by the defendant that can be construed as a deliberate exercise of the option in question. With any other non-performance the stipulated payment will be treated as a secondary obligation in the normal way.[169] On this basis, for example, it is always accepted that a demurrage clause may be penal.[170] Analogous reasoning also applies in sale of goods cases. Thus, while a "carry-over" clause giving a buyer of goods the right expressly to opt to pay for the privilege of delaying acceptance of them is not potentially penal, the same will not go for a clause, however expressed, that simply provides for fixed sums to be paid in the event of delay.[171]

"Take or pay" agreements, under which a regular buyer of goods or services **25-045** agrees to pay periodically for a given quantity whether he takes it or not, are less straightforward. Before *Cavendish v Makdessi* it had been said that such clauses were subject to the penalties jurisdiction.[172] But there is a strong argument for saying that stipulations of this kind are not in substance concerned with breach at all, being aimed much more at protecting the cash-flow of the seller.[173]

---

[165] Lord Morton at [1962] A.C. 614 and, implicitly, Viscount Simonds at 613.

[166] See Lord Phillips in *Office of Fair Trading v Abbey National Plc* [2009] UKSC 6; [2010] 1 A.C. 696 at [83] (bank charges for unauthorised overdrafts: conceded that banks "could not convert what were in effect penalties into "price" simply by wording their contracts so as to ensure that the contingencies that triggered liability to pay the charges did not constitute breaches of contract."). It remains to be seen whether this concession is taken further.

[167] It was cited without adverse comment in *Fratelli Moretti SpA v Nidera Handelscompagnie BV* [1980] 1 Lloyd's Rep. 534 and also in *Lomas v JFB Firth Rixson Inc* [2010] EWHC 3372 (Ch). See too Andrew Smith J in *Office of Fair Trading v Abbey National Plc* [2008] 2 All E.R. (Comm) 625 at [295]–[324] (unauthorised overdraft charges not penalties, since no promise not to create unauthorised overdraft: but compare the dicta in the House of Lords on the same point at fn.156 above). Note, however, apparent scepticism in *Blu-Sky Solutions Ltd v Be Caring Ltd* [2021] EWHC 2619 (Comm) at [123], where the judge seemingly would have been prepared to apply penalty doctrine to a clause, whatever its form, that could not "in any meaningful way be described as a conditional primary obligation". But in the specific instance of hire-purchase contracts governed by the Consumer Credit Act 1974 it has been reversed legislatively: see Consumer Credit Act 1974 s.100.

[168] [1938] 2 K.B. 83

[169] See e.g. *Cooden Engineering Co v Stanford* [1953] 1 Q.B. 86 (mere default in hire purchase payments, triggering financier's right to terminate). Moreover, even where a defendant does state unequivocally that he is refusing to perform, it is open to a court to construe this as a simple statement that he intends to breach and not the exercise of any other option: see *Bridge v Campbell Discount Co Ltd* [1962] A.C. 600, where the House of Lords neatly sidestepped the issue of the lawfulness of a so-called minimum payment option by insisting that the hirer simply intended to break his contract and not to exercise his option.

[170] *Fratelli Moretti SpA v Nidera Handelscompagnie BV* [1980] 1 Lloyd's Rep. 534 at 542 (Donaldson J); Cooke et al, *Voyage Charters*, 4th edn (London: LLP Professional Publishing, 2014) 21.131. The point does not matter much in practice, since traditionally demurrage underestimates the loss to the shipowner anyway.

[171] *Fratelli Moretti SpA v Nidera Handelscompagnie BV* [1980] 1 Lloyd's Rep. 534 at 542 (Donaldson J).

[172] *M & J Polymers Ltd v Imerys Minerals Ltd* [2008] EWHC 344 (Comm); [2008] 1 Lloyd's Rep. 541 (though the clause there was held not penal on the facts). So too in Australia (*Cedar Meats Pty Ltd v Five Star Lamb Pty Ltd* (2013) 45 V.R. 79), but on a rather wider theory of the reach of the penalties rule. Clauses of this kind are commonplace in the oil and gas industries.

[173] Indeed they are often combined with an option in the buyer to take up any shortfall later, either free

25-046   **(ii)   Sums payable to or by third parties**   Reflecting the notion that the penalties doctrine is concerned with clauses dealing with what would otherwise be liability for breach of contract, it has been held that it does not apply in the case of liabilities to third parties, even if they are triggered by a breach of contract by the defendant. The leading case is *Export Credits Guarantee Dept v Universal Oil Products Co.*[174] The defendants had agreed to build an oil refinery in Canada. The claimants guaranteed payment by the buyer, but only the basis that they would not honour the guarantee, and that any monies already paid would be returnable, if it transpired that the defendants had committed any breach whatever of the construction contract. The buyers became insolvent; the claimants honoured their guarantee; but then it became clear that the defendants had indeed committed minor breaches of contract in the course of construction. On a demand by the claimants for repayment, the House of Lords rejected an argument that the obligation was penal and unenforceable. The penalties law, said Lord Roskill, existed to prevent grotesque over-recovery by victims of breach; here, by contrast, the defendant's argument was simply a plea to "relieve a party from the consequences of what may in the event prove to be an onerous or possibly even a commercially imprudent bargain".[175]

25-047   Although sums payable *to* third parties are generally outside the law of penalties, those payable *by* third parties are not. Thus if a particular provision on breach would otherwise be penal and unenforceable, it remains ineffective even if the promise to pay is that, not of the original contractor, but of a surety or guarantor: the creditor should not be allowed to get indirectly what he cannot obtain directly.[176] A fortiori, a provision allowing the victim of a breach of contract to draw down and keep a grotesquely excessive sum on a performance bond issued by a bank, which the contract-breaker must ultimately indemnify, is also apt to be struck down.[177]

25-048   **(iii)   Cases not involving promises to pay money**   Although most cases of penalties involve promises to pay money on breach, there is no doubt that the penalty doctrine goes further than this.[178]

25-049   *Non-money obligations*   First, the doctrine equally applies to non-money obligations.[179] In *Jobson v Johnson*,[180] for example, a contract for the sale of shares in a football club made the price of some £350,000 payable in instalments, and

---

or at a much reduced price. In such a case they share much in common with options to delay delivery, which are not penal.

[174] [1983] 1 W.L.R. 399. The case was cited with approval by Lords Mance and Hodge in *Cavendish Square Holding BV v Makdessi* [2015] UKSC 67; [2016] A.C. 1172 at [129] and [239].

[175] [1983] 1 W.L.R. 399 at 403.

[176] See *Citicorp Australia Ltd v Hendry* (1985) 4 N.S.W.L.R. 1 at 21; *Azimut-Benetti SpA v Healey* [2010] EWHC 2234 (Comm); (2010) 132 Con L.R. 113 at [24] (Blair J) (though in the latter case the sum was held non-penal). In the case of agreements governed by the Consumer Credit Act 1974, this principle is now partly statutory: see Consumer Credit Act 1974 s.113.

[177] So held by Morison J in *Cargill International SA v Bangladesh Sugar Corp* [1996] 4 All E.R. 563 at 573. When the same case went on appeal (see [1998] 1 W.L.R. 461), the point was not discussed.

[178] "The penalty rule has been seen to have application beyond the paradigm situation of a provision that requires the payment of a sum of money in the event of breach" (Beatson J in *General Trading Co (Holdings) Ltd v Richmond Corp Ltd* [2008] EWHC 1479 (Comm) at [113]). See too *Fermiscan Pty Ltd v James* (2009) 261 A.L.R. 408 (making conditional obligation unconditional).

[179] A point accepted in *Cavendish Square Holding BV v Makdessi* [2015] UKSC 67; [2016] A.C. 1172 at [16] (Lords Neuberger and Sumption), [157]–[158] (Lord Mance), [230]–[231] (Lord Hodge). See too *Egan v Railways Comr* (1978) 24 SASR 5 (forfeiture of contractor's equipment for breach); *Wollondilly Shire Council v Picton Power Lines Pty Ltd* (1994) 33 N.S.W.L.R. 551 at 555; *Amaltal Corp Ltd v Maruha (NZ) Corp Ltd* [2004] 2 N.Z.L.R. 614 at [61] (Blanchard J).

purportedly bound the buyer, in the event of failure, to pay any instalment, to reconvey the same shares to the seller for a mere £40,000. The Court of Appeal unhesitatingly refused to enforce the reconveyance obligation in its terms, on the basis that it was it was in essence a penalty since its effect, if enforced, was out of all proportion to the loss suffered by the seller.

Retentions   In many types of contract, most notably construction agreements,   **25-050**
provisions allow the client to retain a proportion of the due price in so far as the other party is in breach. Provisions of this sort are, it appears, subject to rules analogous to the penalties jurisdiction: in so far as the retention is gross or unconscionable, it may be struck down. The Privy Council held as much in 1906 in *Public Works Comrs v Hills*,[181] and the point was accepted in *Gilbert-Ash (Northern) Ltd v Modern Engineering Ltd*.[182] There, a term in a building sub-contract would, on one reading, have allowed the employers to refuse any payment whatever if the contractors were in breach of contract in any way. Although the House of Lords unanimously rejected this drastic interpretation of the contract, Lords Reid, Morris, Dilhorne and Salmon accepted that even if it had been right the clause concerned would have been ineffective as a penalty.[183] Although this holding was arguably obiter, Beatson J has since expressed agreement with it, applying the penalty doctrine to a provision in a contract for the sale of a business whose effect was to wipe out the buyer's liability to pay something over £500,000 if the seller failed to procure a guarantee worth £240,000.[184] In *Cavendish Square Holding BV v Makdessi*,[185] although one of the cases involved a deduction from the price in the event of breach, the issue of the application of the penalties doctrine did not arise directly, since the clause in question was not held penal in any case. Nevertheless, since Lords Neuberger, Sumption and Mance approved *Hills* and Lord Hodge cited it without disapproval,[186] it seems clear that the traditional view remains good law.

Forfeiture of accrued benefits   Parallel to the court's power to relieve against   **25-051**
forfeiture of property and analogous rights, referred to below, there is some authority that the law of penalties may affect a clause if its effect is to cancel a party's accrued claim to a particular benefit under it in the event of breach. Notably, in the

---

[180] [1989] 1 W.L.R. 1026.
[181] *Public Works Comm'rs v Hills* [1906] A.C. 368 (10 per cent withholding from price in rail construction contract disapplied as penal).
[182] [1974] A.C. 689. See too *Graham v Wagner* (1978) 89 D.L.R. (3d) 282 (80 per cent reduction in rent where lessor of parking spaces broke term of contract: held, penal and unenforceable).
[183] See [1974] A.C. 689 at 698, 703, 711 and 723. This view was supported, obiter, by Lord Hodge in *Cavendish Square Holding BV v Makdessi* [2015] UKSC 67; [2016] A.C. 1172 at [226]–[228]. Lords Neuberger, Sumption and Mance were more equivocal: see [73], 154]–[156].
[184] *General Trading Co (Holdings) Ltd v Richmond Corp Ltd* [2008] EWHC 1479 (Comm); [2008] 2 Lloyd's Rep. 275 at [109] ff. In fact the holding there too was obiter, and in any case the clause was held non-penal. But cf. *UK Housing Alliance (North West) Ltd v Francis* [2010] EWCA Civ 117; [2010] 3 All E.R. 519 (sale and lease-back of house; part of price ceased to be payable if lease prematurely terminated; apparently assumed could not be penalty).
[185] [2015] UKSC 67; [2016] A.C. 1172
[186] See [2015] UKSC 67; [2016] A.C. 1172 at [16], [156] and [219]. It should be noted, however, that Lords Neuberger and Sumption also stated, slightly oddly, that the relevant clause was not a liquidated damages provision but "in reality, a price adjustment clause". It is not entirely clear what the significance of this is.

insurance case of *The Fanti*[187] it was held in the Court of Appeal that this applied to a clause in a policy whose effect was retrospectively to withdraw accrued rights to claim in the event of failure by the assured to pay later premiums.[188] But to give rise to this rule, the benefits must have accrued: the withdrawal of the right to payment where performance is not complete is not capable of being penal,[189] and neither is a contingent benefit.[190]

25-052 On the other hand, the above cases on retention and forfeiture seem to represent an exceptional position, and must (it is suggested) be limited to the deprivation of rights that are in some sense already earned or vested. Elsewhere, it seems clear that the general rule is one of freedom of contract: as far as the law of penalties is concerned it is unobjectionable to make a benefit under a contract conditional on proper performance by the other side, however disproportionate this may be to the harm caused by the breach.[191] So in 1978 Mocatta J very smartly rebuffed an argument by a hopeful insured that a term depriving him of cover if he failed to give timeous notice of an incident could somehow be attacked as penal;[192] and in 1997 the Privy Council pointedly left a frustrated purchaser of real estate to its fate when, conformably to the clear terms of the contract, its seller rescinded on the basis that payment had been tendered 10 minutes late.[193] And other decisions have similarly declined to recognise any power to relieve against provisions making all benefits under a litigation funding agreement explicitly dependent on full and prompt payment of contributions;[194] making a moratorium on the payment of an admitted debt dependent on the delinquent debtor's observing the usual covenants;[195] conditioning an extension of time under a construction contract on the following of a given procedure;[196] making a guarantee of payment defeasible in the event of a breach by the creditor or lack of notice to the debtor;[197] or agreeing a rebate if a contract turns out unprofitable, but making that rebate dependent on due performance by the other side.[198]

25-053 **(iv) Penalties and forfeiture of monies paid** Agreed remedies for breach may operate in reverse, involving not a promise to pay on breach but a prepayment to be forfeited in the absence of proper performance. Examples include stipulations

---

187 [1989] 2 Lloyd's Rep. 239.

188 See [1989] 2 Lloyd's Rep. 239, esp at 262 at 265 (appealed to the HL on another point, [1992] A.C. 1). These statements were cited with approval by Beatson J in *General Trading Co (Holdings) Ltd v Richmond Corp Ltd* [2008] EWHC 1479 (Comm); [2008] 2 Lloyd's Rep. 275 at [112], and by Lord Hodge in *Cavendish Square Holding BV v Makdessi* [2015] UKSC 67; [2016] A.C. 1172 at [226].

189 *Interstar Wholesale Finance Pty Ltd v Integral Home Loans Pty Ltd* (2008) 257 A.L.R. 292.

190 *Imam-Sadeque v Bluebay Asset Management (Services) Ltd* [2012] EWHC 3511 (QB); [2013] I.R.L.R. 344 (future valuable fringe benefits accruing to dismissed employee). The above paragraph was cited with approval at [215].

191 See particularly H.G. Beale (ed), *Chitty on Contracts*, 34th edn (London: Sweet & Maxwell, 2022), para.29-247. Or, as Deane J pithily put it in *Acron Pacific Ltd v Offshore Oil NL* (1985) 157 C.L.R. 514 at 520, the "withdrawal of a mere incentive" cannot possibly be penal.

192 *The Vainqueur José* [1979] 1 Lloyd's Rep. 557.

193 *Union Eagle Ltd v Golden Achievement Ltd* [1997] A.C. 514.

194 *Nutting v Baldwin* [1995] 1 W.L.R. 201.

195 *Acron Pacific Ltd v Offshore Oil NL* (1985) 157 C.L.R. 514.

196 *City Inn Ltd v Shepherd Construction Ltd*, 2002 S.L.T. 781.

197 *Eshelby v Federated European Bank Ltd* [1932] 1 K.B. 423; and cf. *Export Credits Guarantee Dept v Universal Oil Products Co* [1983] 1 W.L.R. 399.

198 See *SCI (Sales Curve Interactive) Ltd v Titus SàrL* [2001] EWCA Civ 591; [2001] 2 All E.R. (Comm) 416; also *Euro London Appointments Ltd v Claessens International Ltd* [2006] EWCA Civ 385; [2006] 2 Lloyd's Rep. 436.

in an instalment sale or finance lease for forfeiture of prior payments in the case of
default, and also agreed deposits in connection with the sale of land or other assets.
There is no doubt that such stipulations are subject to control under the doctrine **25-054**
of relief from forfeiture,

> "an equitable remedy of great (sixteenth century) antiquity whereby the court grants relief
> against forfeiture when a strict and literal construction of the contractual terms would
> permit the plaintiff to retain or recover property by reason of the defendant's default in
> performance of the contract, but the court regards it as unconscionable to do so."[199]

Thus in a series of cases concerning sales of land[200] on the instalment basis, the
courts have held that notwithstanding anything in the contract a defaulting payer
who is nevertheless willing and able to perform may in the court's discretion obtain
specific performance if he tenders the amount owing,[201] or at least recover his
money if it is unconscionable for the seller to retain it.[202] Admittedly relief in such
cases has tended to go to claimants remaining able and willing to perform:[203] but
in *Stockloser v Johnson*[204] a majority of the Court of Appeal made it clear that it was
not limited to them. In that case defaulting buyers of machinery on an instalment
basis admitted that they had no chance of making good the promised payments but
nevertheless sought return of the instalments paid when the sellers cancelled the arrangements and repossessed the machinery. The sellers for their part sought to keep
the money on the basis that the terms of the contract allowed them to do exactly
that. The buyers were unsuccessful. Nevertheless the majority[205] confirmed that
relief was available in such cases, with Denning LJ summarising the jurisdiction
as follows: in order to invoke it, he said, a claimant had to show both that the
forfeiture would have a penal effect, and further that in the circumstances it would
be unconscionable for the defendant to retain the monies paid.[206]

Despite the superficial similarity of this principle to the penalties rule, there are **25-055**
two important differences.[207] First, whereas relief against penalty clauses is available as of right, the forfeiture jurisdiction is discretionary.[208] Thus in *Else (1982)*

---

[199] *Else (1982) Ltd v Parkland Holdings Ltd* [1994] 1 B.C.L.C. 130 at 135 (Evans LJ).

[200] And not only land: see *Else (1982) Ltd v Parkland Holdings Ltd* [1994] 1 B.C.L.C. 130 (shares in Sheffield United Football Club).

[201] As in *Starside Properties Ltd v Mustapha* [1974] 1 W.L.R. 816 and *Legione v Hateley* (1983) 152 C.L.R. 406. In Australia, though not in England, the court may even override a "time of the es- sence" clause here: compare *Legione v Hateley*, above, with *Steedman v Drinkle* [1916] 1 A.C. 275 and *Bidaisee v Sampath* [1995] N.P.C. 59.

[202] For discussion see, in particular, *Steedman v Drinkle* [1916] 1 A.C. 275 and *Legione v Hateley* (1983) 152 C.L.R. 406.

[203] And in *Mussen v Van Dieman's Land Co* [1938] Ch. 253 at 263–264 and *Galbraith v Mitchenall Estates Ltd* [1965] 2 Q.B. 473 was stated to be limited as a matter of law to such claimants.

[204] [1954] 1 Q.B. 476. See A. Diamond, "Equitable Relief for the Purchaser of Hire-Purchase Goods" (1956) 19 M.L.R. 498; E. Price, "Equitable Relief in the Law of Hire-Purchase" (1957) 20 M.L.R. 620.

[205] Denning and Somervell LJJ. Romer LJ would have denied any control over enforcement as such.

[206] See [1954] 1 Q.B. 476 at 489–492. These sentiments were trenchantly approved by the Supreme Court of Canada in *Dimensional Investments Ltd v R* [1968] S.C.R. 93 (though in the event relief was held barred by the terms of local legislation).

[207] See *Cavendish Square Holding BV v Makdessi* [2015] UKSC 67; [2016] A.C. 1172 at [160] (Lord Mance).

[208] See *Jobson v Johnson* [1989] 1 W.L.R. 1026 at 1041 (Nicholls LJ); CA; also *Else (1982) Ltd v Parkland Holdings Ltd* [1994] 1 B.C.L.C. 130 at 135, 146 (Evans and Hoffmann LJJ).

Ltd v Parkland Holdings Ltd[209] a would-be buyer of football club shares agreed to pay by instalments, and in addition in the event of serious default to forfeit both shares and money paid up to 50 per cent of the price. On his default the court nevertheless refused relief, and one reason for this was that because of his conduct—notably his previous cavalier attitude towards his contractual obligations—he did not deserve the benefit of the court's discretion. And secondly, whereas the enforceability of a penalty clause is judged as at the time of contracting, in deciding whether to exercise the discretion to relieve against a forfeiture the court takes account of the situation obtaining at the time relief is sought.[210] The *Else* case referred to above further illustrates this point. An additional reason why relief was refused there, quite apart from issues of discretion, was that the claimant had received benefits as a result of the arrangement (notably a prestigious position in the football world), and in the circumstances it was not unconscionable to allow the contractual stipulation its agreed effect.[211]

25-056   It is an open question whether a contractual right to forfeit a deposit may in suitable cases also be attackable as a penalty. Some earlier authorities saw deposit forfeiture clause as identical in substance to stipulations for payment on breach, and indeed on occasion actually referred to them as penalties;[212] and there is also more recent support for this view.[213] But it is not self-evidently true that they are functionally the same thing:[214] and there is also authority that the penalties doctrine does not apply to them,[215] including one recent clear decision to that effect.[216] In *Cavendish Square Holding BV v Makdessi*[217] Lords Mance and Hodge took the view, obiter, that the doctrines could co-exist;[218] the other members of the court expressed no concluded opinion, though Lords Neuberger and Sumption were inclined to agree.[219] Today, therefore, the better view seems to be that the same clause may be attackable under both heads.

---

[209] [1994] 1 B.C.L.C. 130.
[210] *Stockloser v Johnson* [1954] 1 Q.B. 476 at 488, 492 (Somervell and Denning LJJ); also *Else (1982) Ltd v Parkland Holdings Ltd* [1994] 1 B.C.L.C. 130 at 135 (Evans LJ).
[211] [1994] 1 B.C.L.C. 130 at 140 (Evans LJ).
[212] E.g. *Re Dagenham (Thames) Dock Co* (1873) 8 Ch App 1022 at 1025 (James LJ); *Kilmer v British Columbia Orchard Lands Ltd* [1913] A.C. 319 at 325 (Lord Moulton); also *Steedman v Drinkle* [1916] 1 A.C. 275 at 279 (Lord Haldane).
[213] See *BICC Plc v Burndy Corp* [1985] Ch 232 at 236–237 (Dillon LJ); Beatson J in *General Trading Co (Holdings) Ltd v Richmond Corp Ltd* [2008] EWHC 1479 (Comm) at [113]; also Deane J in *Legione v Hateley* (1983) 152 C.L.R. 406 at 445, regarding cases like *Steedman v Drinkle* as penalty cases.
[214] This is because it is psychologically easier to agree to pay large sums in the future than actually to put up such sums in the present with only an uncertain prospect of getting them back later. If so, then it follows that more protection is needed in the former than the latter case.
[215] See *Stockloser v Johnson* [1954] 1 Q.B. 476 at 488–489 (Denning LJ); *Jobson v Johnson* [1989] 1 W.L.R. 1026 at 1041, CA (Nicholls LJ); *Workers Trust & Merchant Bank Ltd v Dojap Investments Ltd* [1993] A.C. 573 at 578–579 (Lord Browne-Wilkinson); *Else (1982) Ltd v Parkland Holdings Ltd* [1994] 1 B.C.L.C. 130 at 139 (Evans LJ).
[216] *Cadogan Petroleum Holdings Ltd v Global Process Systems LLC* [2013] EWHC 214 (Comm); [2013] 1 C.L.C. 721: see Eder J at [33]–[34]. The decision in *Amble Assets LLP v Longbenton Foods Ltd* [2011] EWHC 3774 (Ch); [2012] 1 All E.R. (Comm) 764 seems to have proceeded on the same basis.
[217] [2015] UKSC 67; [2016] A.C. 1172.
[218] See [2015] UKSC 67; [2016] A.C. 1172 at [160]–[161], [227].
[219] See [2015] UKSC 67; [2016] A.C. 1172 at [18].

(v) Deposits on the sale of land[220] Deposits paid by buyers or would-be buy- **25-057**
ers of land, and other payments made purely as an earnest of performance, are
subject to a special rule of their own. In so far as they are normal and customary, it
seems they are regarded as immune to attack: as Lord Browne-Wilkinson put it in
the leading decision in *Workers Trust & Merchant Bank Ltd v Dojap Investments
Ltd*:[221]

> "Even in the absence of express contractual provision, it is an earnest for the performance
> of the contract: in the event of completion of the contract the deposit is applicable towards
> payment of the purchase price; in the event of the purchaser's failure to complete in ac-
> cordance with the terms of the contract, the deposit is forfeit, equity having no power to
> relieve against such forfeiture."

Hence the fact that that the vendor may have suffered no loss, or even benefited **25-058**
from the breach, is irrelevant.[222] Indeed, where the deposit is only part paid, there
is no bar on the vendor suing for the residue if the purchaser resiles.[223]

On the other hand, a deposit which is of more than the amount is, it seems, **25-059**
subject to the same rules referred to above as any other payment supposedly forfeit
for breach of contract. Thus in the *Workers Trust* case itself[224] the Privy Council,
while accepting that deposit in the customary figure of 10 per cent would be beyond
attack, peremptorily ordered the return of a 25 per cent deposit on the basis that is
"was not a true deposit by way of earnest", but "a plain penalty".[225]

In addition, it should be remembered that s.49(2) of the Law of Property Act 1925 **25-060**
provides a limited statutory discretion to order return of a deposit in a contract for
the sale of land.[226] But this is in practice exercised fairly sparingly: as Arden LJ has
remarked, however widely-drafted the provision is the courts must view it with one
eye on the fact that "the payment in question was a 'deposit', that is an earnest for
performance".[227] Thus the fact that the vendor has suffered no loss, or even made
a gain, from the purchaser's breach is not enough.[228] There is a need for "something
special or exceptional"[229] such as difficulties for the purchaser known to the
vendor[230] or where the vendor has in some way let the purchaser down.[231]

---

[220] See generally the very useful C. Harpum, "Relief against Forfeiture and the Purchaser of Land"
[1984] C.L.J. 134.

[221] [1993] A.C. 573 at 578–580 (approving Fry LJ in *Howe v Smith* (1884) 27 Ch. D. 89). And note the
earlier decision of the Privy Council in *Linggi Plantations Ltd v Jagatheesan* [1972] 1 Mal LJ 89.

[222] *Workers Trust v Dojap Investments Ltd* [1993] A.C. 573 at 578 (Lord Browne-Wilkinson); *Ng v
Ashley King (Developments) Ltd* [2010] EWHC 456 (Ch); [2011] Ch. 115 at [22] (Lewison J). But
the vendor, if he wishes to claim damages, must give credit for any deposit.

[223] A point put beyond doubt in *Hardy v Griffiths* [2014] EWHC 3947 (Ch); [2015] Ch. 417.

[224] [1993] A.C. 573. Compare the Hong Kong case of *Polyset Ltd v Panhandat Ltd* (2002) 5 HKCFAR
234.

[225] See [1993] A.C. 573 at 582. The case was inferentially approved by four Law Lords in *Cavendish
Square Holding BV v Makdessi* [2015] UKSC 67; [2016] A.C. 1172: see [16] (Lords Neuberger and
Sumption), [156] (Lord Mance) and [235] (Lord Hodge).

[226] For this jurisdiction, see G. Jones and A. Goodhart, *Specific Performance*, 2nd edn (London: Tottel, 1996), pp.304–305; *Emmet on Title*, 19th edn (London: Sweet & Maxwell 1985), para 7.028 (the
latter dated, but still useful). Relief may apparently be given on terms: see *Dimsdale Developments
(South East) Ltd v De Haan* (1983) 47 P. & C.R. 1 (deduction of vendor's losses).

[227] *Omar v El-Wakil* [2001] EWCA Civ 1090; [2002] 2 P. & C.R. 36 at [35].

[228] *Midill (97PL) Ltd v Park Lane Estates Ltd* [2008] EWCA Civ 1227; [2009] 1 W.L.R. 2460; also
Bidaisee v Sampath (1995) 46 WIR 461; [1995] N.P.C. 59.

[229] As Carnwath LJ put it in *Midill (97PL) Ltd v Park Lane Estates Ltd* [2008] EWCA Civ 1227; [2009]

The effect of a penal stipulation

25-061   Where a liquidated damages or other agreed remedies clause falls foul of the rules against penalties, the claimant cannot rely on it. Conversely the defendant may claim relief from it as of right; relief cannot be given on terms.[232] In effect this means that the claimant is relegated to any claim for damages that would exist apart from it. Although the view has been expressed that the clause remains effective, albeit only up to the amount that would otherwise have been recoverable[233]), it is now clear that as regards the claimant the clause is simply ignored.[234] By contrast, in cases where relief against forfeiture of sums paid is in issue, the court has a discretion as to any order for repayment. It may be appropriate to order the return of any sums over and above the actual loss suffered by the innocent party, but account may also be taken of other factors, such as the behaviour of the person seeking relief and any benefits gained by him.[235]

25-062   We have seen that if a liquidated damages clause is an unenforceable penalty, the defendant can disregard it and insist on limiting his liability to that arising at common law (assuming it is less). But can the invalidity of the clause be invoked by the claimant himself, so as to allow him to disregard it and recover a larger sum if that in fact represents the loss he has suffered? In at least one case it seems to have been assumed that the answer was Yes. In *Wall v Redeiaktiebolaget Luggude*[236] charterers failed to load under a charter which provided: "Penalty for non-performance of this agreement proved damages, not exceeding estimated amount of freight." The shipowner's loss in fact being more than the would-be freight, Bailhache J had no hesitation in holding that he could recover it: the clause, he said, could be disregarded as a *brutum fulmen*.[237] A number of subsequent cases reached the same conclusion on the same or similar wording.[238] It is, however, not clear whether this was on the basis that the clause was void as a penalty or simply that,

---

1 W.L.R. 2460 at [52], there is a need for "something special or exceptional" (Carnwath LJ). See too *Bidaisee v Sampath* (1995) 46 WIR 461; [1995] N.P.C. 59.

[230] As in *Universal Corp v Five Ways Properties Ltd* [1979] 1 All E.R. 552 (Nigerian purchasers facing exchange control problems).

[231] As by providing a defective, but technically contractually sufficient title: see *Midill (97PL) Ltd v Park Lane Estates Ltd* [2008] EWCA Civ 1227, [2009] 1 W.L.R. 2460 at [33]–[34] (Carnwath LJ).

[232] *Cavendish Square Holding BV v Makdessi* [2015] UKSC 67; [2016] A.C. 1172 at [87] (Lords Neuberger and Sumption), [160] (Lord Mance), [283] (Lord Hodge); *Else (1982) Ltd v Parkland Holdings Ltd* [1994] 1 B.C.L.C. 130 at 135 (Evans LJ). To this extent, *Jobson v Johnson* [1989] 1 W.L.R. 1026 was wrongly decided.

[233] "[T]he strict legal position is not that such a clause is simply struck out of the contract, as though with a blue pencil, so that the contract takes effect as if it had never been included therein. Strictly, the legal position is that the clause remains in the contract and can be sued upon, but it will not be enforced by the court beyond the sum which represents, in the events which have happened, the actual loss of the party seeking payment" (see Nicholls LJ in *Jobson v Johnson* [1989] 1 W.L.R. 1026 at 1040). This view has been accepted in Australia: *Andrews v Australia & New Zealand Banking Group Ltd* (2012) 247 C.L.R. 205 at [10] and *Paciocco v Australia & New Zealand Banking Group Ltd* [2015] FCAFC 50 at [27].

[234] *Cavendish Square Holding BV v Makdessi* [2015] UKSC 67; [2015] 3 W.L.R. 1373 at [85]–[87] (Lords Neuberger and Sumption).

[235] As in *Else (1982) Ltd v Parkland Holdings Ltd* [1994] 1 B.C.L.C. 130.

[236] [1915] 3 K.B. 66.

[237] [1915] 3 K.B. 66 at 72.

[238] Notably and *Leeds Shipping Co Ltd v Soc Francaise Bunge* [1957] 2 Lloyd's Rep. 183.

properly interpreted, it was not intended to limit the defendant's liability in any case.[239]

It is respectfully submitted that the better position is that this is all a matter of **25-063** interpretation. If the parties did not intend the clause to limit liability, it should indeed be disregarded: but if they did intend to provide for a maximum as well as a minimum award, to that extent it should be enforced in the ordinary way.[240] A number of authorities suggest this, albeit in obiter dicta;[241] and the Supreme Court of Canada agreed, for the best of reasons, in *Elsley v Collins Insurance Agencies Ltd*.[242] A non-competition covenant contained a penal stipulation for $1,000 to be paid in the event of breach. When it was broken, it was held that damages were limited to the $1,000: the fact that the promise to pay that sum was unenforceable against the defendant if the claimant had suffered a lower amount of loss was no reason whatever not to allow the defendant to take the benefit of it where the loss was greater.[243] By contrast, in the Privy Council decision in *Brown's Bay Resort Ltd v Pozzoni*[244] a lease stipulated that if owing to a breach of contract an interruption occurred, "then the party responsible will pay to the other party a penalty fee of US$4,000.00". This was construed as being a payment exigible independently of any damages and hence irrelevant to the quantum of the latter.

III. RELIEF AGAINST FORFEITURE[245]

Relief against forfeiture

Parallel to the law's power to relieve against penalties, equity has a separate and **25-064** very long-standing jurisdiction to relieve against stipulations having as their effect the unconscionable forfeiture of assets, even if agreed between the parties in an

---

[239] Compare Lords Finlay and Sumner in *Watts v Mitsui & Co* [1917] A.C. 227, where the latter apparently decided the clause was void as a matter of law and the former that it was inapplicable as a matter of interpretation. See [1917] A.C. 227 at 235 and 246 respectively. In *Luggude* itself Bailhache J seems to have regarded the matter as one of interpretation: see [1915] 3 K.B. 66 at 74 ("Clause 15 is a penal clause and not a limitation of liability clause"). The point was left open by Lord Atkin in *Cellulose Acetate Silk Co Ltd v Widnes Foundry Ltd* [1933] A.C. 20 at 26, by Lord Tomlin in *Pearl Assurance Co Ltd v Union of South Africa* [1934] A.C. 570 at 584, and by Diplock LJ in *Robophone Facilities Ltd v Blank* [1966] 1 W.L.R. 1428 at 1446–1447.

[240] Apart from anything else, to prevent such clauses limiting liability would simply duplicate the work of statutes such as the Unfair Contract Terms Act 1977 and the Consumer Rights Act 2015, and their equivalents in other common law jurisdictions.

[241] E.g. Lord *Elphinstone v Monkland Iron & Coal Co Ltd* (1886) 11 App. Cas. 332 at 346 (Lord Fitzgerald); *Public Works Commissioners v Hills* [1906] A.C. 368 at 385 (Lord Dunedin); *Eco World - Ballymore Embassy Gardens Co Ltd v Dobler UK Ltd* [2021] EWHC 2207 (TCC) at [97]–[116]; [2021] T.C.L.R. 7. See too *Jobson v Johnson* [1989] 1 W.L.R. 1026 at 1040 (clause "remains in the contract and can be sued on, but it will not be enforced by the court beyond the sum which represents the actual loss of the party seeking payment").

[242] (1978) 83 D.L.R. (3d) 1; approved in McBryde, "Remedies for breach of contract" (1996) 1 Edin. L.R. 43 at 75–76.

[243] As Dickson J put it (see (1978) 83 D.L.R. (3d) 1 at 15), the penalty rule existed "for the sole purpose of providing relief against oppression". There being no question of oppression exerted by the defendant against the plaintiff, it followed that "the normal rule of enforcement of contract should apply." See generally Hudson, "Penalties Limiting Damages" (1974) 90 L.Q.R. 30, "Penalties Limiting Damages" (1985) 101 L.Q.R. 480.

[244] [2016] UKPC 10.

[245] For a perceptive discussion, see L. Gullifer, "Agreed Remedies", in A. Burrows and E. Peel (eds), *Commercial Remedies: Current Issues and Problems* (Oxford: Oxford University Press, 2003), p.205 ff, suggesting rather wider grounds for relief than exist at present.

otherwise valid contract.[246] Traditionally this jurisdiction found its most common expression in the case of leases and mortgages. If a lessee failed to pay rent or was in breach of some other obligation, then even where the letter of the lease allowed the lessor to terminate it forthwith and re-enter, Equity had a jurisdiction to prevent termination if it was equitable to do so and the lessee paid a sum of money sufficient to make good any prejudice to the lessor.[247] Indeed, this jurisdiction is now statutory.[248] And similarly too with mortgages: Equity would readily protect a defaulting mortgagor's equity of redemption in so far as monies due and unpaid were brought into court.[249] The reasoning was that many covenants in mortgages or leases existed to preserve not so much the rights of mortgagor or lessor in the land itself, but rather their right (in the case of a lease) to profit from it, or (with a mortgage) to receive the payment secured on it. And, if so, then provided the mortgagor or lessor remained assured of getting his money there was obvious justice in preserving the mortgage or lease rather than allowing the land to be forfeit, with possibly disproportionate loss to one party and gain to the other.[250] Nevertheless, although most cases concern land, there is no doubt that the jurisdiction covers all types of property, real and personal.[251]

25-065   Not surprisingly, there were suggestions that similar reasoning might logically apply to simple cases of breach of contract. Contract-breakers, after all, might equally well be deprived of disproportionately valuable rights, and the victims of breach correspondingly and undeservingly enriched, if contractors were allowed free rein to stipulate for the right to cancel the contract or otherwise deprive the other party of benefits arising from it on any conditions they chose.[252] Surely, therefore (it was said), equity ought to have a power to intervene to prevent this in

---

[246] "There cannot be any doubt that from the earliest times courts of equity have asserted the right to relieve against the forfeiture of property": Lord Wilberforce in *Shiloh Spinners Ltd v Harding* [1973] A.C. 691 at 722. And, indeed, the twelfth of Francis's *Maxims of Equity*, dated 1728, states: "Equity suffers not advantage to be taken of a penalty or forfeiture, where compensation can be made." See too the discussion of the matter by Lord Briggs in *Manchester Ship Canal Co Ltd v Vauxhall Motors Ltd (formerly General Motors UK Ltd)* [2019] UKSC 46; [2020] A.C. 1161 at [17]–[23].

[247] The need to make good any loss has always been an important feature of the jurisdiction: e.g. *Davis v Thomas* (1830)1 Russ & M 506 at 507. But even this is not absolute. In *Çukurova Finance International Ltd v Alfa Telecom Turkey Ltd (Nos 3 to 5)* [2013] UKPC 20; [2015] 2 W.L.R. 875, where a lender peremptorily refused tender of repayment because it wished to appropriate certain shares hypothecated by the borrower, it was penalised by loss of interest from the time of the tender.

[248] See Law of Property Act 1925 s.146.

[249] E. Cousins, *Law of Mortgages*, 3rd edn (London: Sweet & Maxwell, 2010), paras 2-07–2.09. See also Lord Wilberforce's tour d'horizon of the whole subject in *Shiloh Spinnners Ltd v Harding* [1973] A.C. 691 at 722 ff.

[250] "The Court of Chancery gave relief against the strictness of the common law in cases of penalty or forfeiture for nonpayment of a fixed sum on a day certain, on the principle that the failure to pay principal on a certain day could be compensated sufficiently by payment of principal and interest with costs at a subsequent day." Rigby LJ in *Re Dixon* [1900] 2 Ch. 561 at 576. See too Greene MR in *Chandless-Chandless v Nicholson* [1942] 2 K.B. 321 at 323; and Lord Wilberforce in *Shiloh Spinners Ltd v Harding* [1973] A.C. 691 at 723.

[251] See *BICC Plc v Burndy Corp* [1985] Ch 232 at 252 (Dillon LJ); *Çukurova Finance International Ltd v Alfa Telecom Turkey Ltd (Nos 3 to 5)* [2013] UKPC 20; [2015] 2 W.L.R. 875 at [92]. Proprietary or possessory rights, moreover, are widely construed in this connection, including (for example) a right to discharge effluent which can only be effectuated through de facto control of the property onto which the discharge is to take place: see *Manchester Ship Canal Co Ltd v Vauxhall Motors Ltd* [2019] UKSC 46; [2020] A.C. 1161.

[252] These suggestions gained particular plausibility in the light of Lord Simon's incautious suggestion in the land case of *Shiloh Spinnners Ltd v Harding* [1973] A.C. 691 at 726 that there was an "unlimited and unfettered jurisdiction to relieve against contractual forfeitures and penalties".

so far as any prejudice caused by a breach could be adequately compensated in money.[253]

In 1983 the issue of whether the forfeiture jurisdiction could be extended in this way was directly raised for the first time. In *The Scaptrade*,[254] a case concerning a ship under time charter, the charterers argued that a term allowing cancellation for any lateness in payment of hire, however trivial, amounted to a potential forfeiture of valuable rights (particularly if freight rates had risen). And on this basis they contended that its operation ought to be susceptible to equitable intervention, if necessary by injunction, to prevent withdrawal of the vessel for inadequate reasons. However, the House of Lords forcefully disagreed. Giving the only substantial opinion, Lord Diplock provided three reasons for rejecting the charterers' position. First, he said, in a commercial charter case, unlike a lease or mortgage, no question arose of the loss of possessory or proprietary rights of the kind protectable by equitable orders of specific performance or injunction. All the charterer gained under a time charter, and hence all it stood to lose, was the personal contractual right to dictate the use of the vessel.[255] Secondly, since the vessel's owners retained possession and control of her, it was not true that their only substantial interest was financial, as would be the case with a mortgagee.[256] And thirdly, the need for commercial certainty, coupled with the lack of any pressing need for protection in either party, strongly supported the status quo.[257] A year later, moreover, the House of Lords once again confirmed this restrictive attitude, in denying relief to the holder of a mere contractual licence to use certain intellectual property rights. Protection against forfeiture, they reiterated, applied to existing possessory or proprietary interests; but there was no reason to project it any further.[258]

25-066

The result of *The Scaptrade* was to remove most commercial arrangements from the scope of any forfeiture doctrine. It did not decide, however, that commercial contracts were ipso facto immune to claims for relief. On the contrary, there remained at least limited scope for the doctrine where Lord Diplock's reasons for rejecting relief did *not* apply: namely, where (i) in contrast to the situation in *The Scaptrade* proprietary rights were in some way in issue, and (ii) the provision for their possible forfeiture was essentially security for payment of a sum of money or something similar to the innocent party. This point was duly taken up a couple of years later in *B.I.C.C. Plc v Burndy Corp*.[259] There, the Court of Appeal was in no doubt that it would have relieved against a clause in a joint venture agreement whose effect was to deprive one party of certain patent rights deriving from the venture if it failed to pay its allotted share of the expenses of the project.[260] This was, it was said, a case where the interests of the innocent party could be adequately

25-067

---

253 See, e.g. Lord Uthwatt in *Tankexpress A/S v Compagnie Financi£re Belge des Petroles S.A.* [1949] A.C. 76 at 100, Lord Simon in *The Laconia* [1977] A.C. 850 at 873–874 and Lloyd J in *The Afovos* [1980] 2 Lloyd's Rep. 469 (all suggesting a possible application to owners' rights to cancel charters for late payment); also Pennycuick J in *Barton Thompson & Co Ltd v Stapling Machines Co* [1966] Ch. 499 at 509 (doctrine might apply to commercial lease of machinery, though no case for relief there).

254 [1983] 2 A.C. 694. See too *UK Housing Alliance (North West) Ltd v Francis* [2010] EWCA Civ 117; [2010] HLR 28 at [11] (Longmore LJ).

255 [1983] 2 A.C. 694 at 700–702.

256 [1983] 2 A.C. 694 at 702.

257 [1983] 2 A.C. 694 at 703–704. See too Goff LJ in the CA: [1983] Q.B. 529 at 540–541.

258 *Sport Internationaal Bussum B.V v Inter-Footwear Ltd* [1984] 1 W.L.R. 776, esp Lord Templeman at 793–794.

259 [1985] Ch. 232.

260 In fact the party was held not in default owing to a set-off.

protected with a money award. It was also a case where proprietary rights were in issue; the fact that such rights were in personalty rather than land was no reason to deny them protection from forfeiture.[261]

Relief against forfeiture: The need for a proprietary interest

25-068   Since *The Scaptrade*[262] the courts have been careful to preserve the rule that the mere loss of a personal contractual right, unsupported by any proprietary interest or security, cannot amount to a relievable forfeiture.[263] Nevertheless, whether the necessary proprietary interest exists can often be a matter of impression rather than strict law; and in practice it has been held present in a fair number of situations. Essentially any proprietary or possessory interest over realty or personalty now suffices.[264] This has been held to have included, in particular, clauses depriving buyers of land,[265] and buyers of chattels in possession of them,[266] of the right to buy; and an agreement terminating a right to maintain drainage infrastructure on and discharge water over, someone else's land on non-payment of the relevant wayleave.[267] Relief has also been held to be available against stipulations stripping hirers,[268] including demise charterers of ships,[269] and hirers under finance leases[270] and hire-purchase agreements,[271] of their interests in goods on breach or insolvency. On a similar basis it has been held to apply to terms of the constitution of an association set up to co-ordinate litigation which have the effect of depriving members of the benefits otherwise available to them;[272] and a court has refused to strike out a claim that it equally applied to a term in a shareholders' agreement providing for complete or partial expropriation of one party's shares in the event of breach.[273]

Relief against forfeiture: Provisions acting merely as security for payment

25-069   Nevertheless, the twofold requirement of the forfeiture doctrine must be remembered: not only must there be deprivation of a proprietary interest, but in ad-

---

[261] See [1985] Ch. 232 at 251–252 (Dillon LJ); [1985] Ch. 232 at 253–254 (Kerr LJ).

[262] [1983] 2 A.C. 694.

[263] *Manchester Ship Canal Co Ltd v Vauxhall Motors Ltd (formerly General Motors UK Ltd)* [2019] UKSC 46; [2020] A.C. 1161 at [50]; cf. *UK Housing Alliance (North West) Ltd v Francis* [2010] EWCA Civ 117; [2010] 3 All E.R. 519.

[264] *Manchester Ship Canal Co Ltd v Vauxhall Motors Ltd (formerly General Motors UK Ltd)* [2019] UKSC 46; [2020] A.C. 1161;N.Tiverios, "The forfeiture of contractual rights" [2020] C.L.J. 17.

[265] E.g. *Hush Brasseries Ltd v RLUKREF Nominees (UK) One Ltd* [2022] EWHC 3018 (Ch) (option).

[266] *Transag Haulage Ltd (IAR) v Leyland DAF Finance Plc* [1994] BCC 356.

[267] *Manchester Ship Canal Co Ltd v Vauxhall Motors Ltd (formerly General Motors UK Ltd)* [2019] UKSC 46; [2020] A.C. 1161.

[268] *Celestial Aviation Trading 71 Ltd v Paramount Airways Private Ltd* [2010] EWHC 185 (Comm); [2011] 1 Lloyd's Rep. 9

[269] *The Jotunheim* [2004] EWHC 671 (Comm); [2005] 1 Lloyd's Rep. 181; *Courage Shipping Co v OCM Maritime Nile LLC* [2022] EWCA Civ 1091.

[270] *On Demand Information Plc v Michael Gerson (Finance) Plc* [2001] 1 W.L.R. 155; discussed Pawlowski [1999] Conv 426.

[271] *Transag Haulage Ltd (IAR) v Leyland DAF Finance Plc* [1994] BCC 356.The agreement in The *Jotunheim* [2004] EWHC 671 (Comm); [2005] 1 Lloyd's Rep. 181, though nominally a demise charter, was similar.

[272] *Nutting v Baldwin* [1995] 1 W.L.R. 201 (the proprietary right being members' potential equitable interest in any recoveries: see Rattee J at 208–209).

[273] *Kulkarni v Gwent Holdings Ltd* [2023] EWHC 484 (Ch).

dition that deprivation must be largely aimed at providing security to the other party. The rule will thus not apply in so far as the forfeiture serves some other substantial and legitimate purpose.[274] To put it another way, in all but specialised cases the principle of freedom of contract means that parties must be at liberty to make contractual benefits conditional, however arbitrarily or unfairly, without fear of court interference. In practice this has severely limited the application of the doctrine of relief. Thus it has been held that even if arbitrary cancellation of a contract for the sale of land amounts to a technical forfeiture of the buyer's equitable interest in it, this generally serves the buyer's interest in being able to deal freely with his property rather than being a security for the payment of money: it follows that it is outside control.[275] Similarly, whereas a lease which is essentially a finance lease or an arrangement analogous to a hire-purchase agreement is subject to the doctrine,[276] an ordinary lease of chattels is not: a right to terminate exists for many reasons other than the lessor's desire to secure payments due to him.[277] And on the same basis, where parties club together to fund litigation the courts will not second-guess their desire to provide that those who do not bear their share of risk by paying promptly should get nothing.[278]

Grant of relief against forfeiture

Unlike relief from the effect of penalty clauses, which is available as of right, relief from forfeiture, even where available, is in the discretion of the court. It can therefore be refused if, for example, the petitioner has previously been guilty of misconduct in the relevant litigation,[279] or shown a cavalier attitude to his contractual obligations,[280] or where there would in the court's view be no point in granting it.[281] **25-070**

IV. THE CONSUMER RIGHTS ACT 2015

In addition to the jurisdictions to strike down penalty clauses or relieve against a forfeiture, it should also be noted that in the context of consumer agreements, **25-071**

---

[274] Moreover, the relevant time for these purposes is that at which relief is sought. Even in the case of a finance lease, no relief will be given if the property has since been sold and so there is no lease to preserve any longer: see *On Demand Information Plc v Michael Gerson (Finance) Plc* [2001] 1 W.L.R. 155.

[275] See *Union Eagle Ltd v Golden Achievement Ltd* [1997] A.C. 514, esp at 520 (Lord Hoffmann) (cancellation permissible where price tendered 10 minutes late); cf. *Warnborough Ltd v Garmite Ltd* [2006] EWHC 10 (Ch); [2007] 1 P. & C.R. 2.

[276] See *On Demand Information Plc v Michael Gerson (Finance) Plc* [2001] 1 W.L.R. 155 and *The Jotunheim* [2004] EWHC 671 (Comm); [2005] 1 Lloyd's Rep. 181.

[277] *Celestial Aviation Trading 71 Ltd v Paramount Airways Private Ltd* [2010] EWHC 185 (Comm); [2011] 1 Lloyd's Rep. 9.

[278] *Nutting v Baldwin* [1995] 1 W.L.R. 201, esp at 210 (Rattee J).

[279] As in *Courage Shipping Co v OCM Maritime Nile LLC* [2022] EWCA Civ 1091 (repeated lies and evasions).

[280] As in *The Jotunheim* [2004] EWHC 671 (Comm); [2005] 1 Lloyd's Rep. 181 (repeated failure to pay sums due). This decision was regarded as "unsurprising" by the Privy Council in *Çukurova Finance International Ltd v Alfa Telecom Turkey Ltd (Nos 3 to 5)* [2013] UKPC 20; [2015] 2 W.L.R. 875 at [118].

[281] For example, where leased property has been sold: *On Demand Information Plc v Michael Gerson (Finance) Plc* [2001] 1 W.L.R. 155.

ss.62–63 and Sch.2 of the Consumer Rights Act 2015[282] may also be relevant. Ostensibly concerned with terms in consumer contracts which, "contrary to the requirement of good faith", cause a "significant imbalance in the parties' rights and obligations",[283] these regard as presumptively unfair and unenforceable any term "requiring a consumer who fails to fulfil his obligation to pay a disproportionately high sum in compensation".[284] This jurisdiction derives from EU Directive 93/13 on Unfair Terms in Consumer Contracts and requires complete non-enforcement of such terms,[285] if necessary of the court's own motion.[286] It seems curiously limited in some ways,[287] and will parallel the penalties jurisdiction in many consumer situations.[288] Nevertheless it may also go further.[289] Thus it may affect cancellation fees,[290] charges for late payment, including those expressed as rebates for payment on time, not covered by the penalties rule,[291] not to mention (at least on principle) interest charges for unauthorised overdrafts not previously arranged.[292]

V.   CREDIT AND HIRE PURCHASE: THE CONSUMER CREDIT ACT 1974

25-072   The rules as to penalties outlined above apply to hire purchase, conditional sale and finance leases as they apply to other contracts (subject now also to the provisions of the Consumer Rights Act 2015, referred to above). However, in regulated hire-purchase or conditional sale agreements within the Consumer Credit Act 1974—a term that, subject to a few exceptions, effectively means any case where

---

[282] Replacing broadly equivalent provisions in the Unfair Terms in Consumer Contracts Regulations 1999 (SI 1999/2083). It should be noted, however, that in one case it is wider. The 1999 Regulations, in reg.5(1), required that the term not have been individually negotiated. No such requirement appears in the 2015 Act.

[283] 2015 Act, s.62(4). Guidelines on the interpretation of the equivalent provision in the underlying Directive were provided by the ECJ in *Aziz v Caixa d'Estalvis de Catalunya, Tarragona i Manresa (Catalunyacaixa)* (Case C-415/11) [2013] 3 C.M.L.R. 5 at [76] and by the House of Lords in *Director General of Fair Trading v First National Bank Plc* [2002] 1 A.C. 481 at [17] and [54].

[284] 2015 Act, Sch.2, para.5.

[285] Thus it does not allow enforcement in part see *Banco Español de Crédito SA v Camino* (Case C-618/10) [2012] 3 C.M.L.R. 25 at [70]–[71] and *Unicaja Banco SA v Hidalgo Rueda* (Joined Cases C-482/13, C-484/13, C-485/13 & C-487/13) [2015] 2 C.M.L.R. 40.

[286] *Asbeek Brusse v Jahani BV* (Case C-488/11) [2013] 3 C.M.L.R. 45.

[287] Since it only applies, it seems, to money obligations, and has been suggested not to apply to forfeiture of rights to receive money: see *UK Housing Alliance (North West) Ltd v Francis* [2010] EWCA Civ 117; [2010] HLR 28 at [24] (Longmore LJ).

[288] Thus in *Cavendish Square Holding BV v Makdessi* [2015] UKSC 67; [2016] A.C. 1172 the overstayers' parking charge was also attacked under the predecessor to the 2015 Act. A majority held that this attack also failed. Lords Neuberger and Sumption held at [102]–[114] that because the charge was not wholly disproportionate and served a legitimate purpose, it could not be said to contravene the requirement of good faith. Lord Mance said (at [200]–[213]) that the charge was not disproportionate, clearly signed, and did not reflect a significant imbalance in the parties' obligations in the light of the two hours' free parking already offered. See too Lord Hodge at [289].

[289] *Cavendish Square Holding BV v Makdessi* [2015] UKSC 67; [2016] A.C. 1172 at [209] (Lord Toulson), pointing out the reversed burden of proof and the need for the supplier to be able to assume that the consumer would have agreed to it in individual negotiations on level terms.

[290] See *Clipper Ventures Ltd v Boyde*, 2013 S.C.L.R. 313 (where, however, the clause was upheld).

[291] As happened in *Munkenbeck & Marshall v Harold* [2005] EWHC 356 (TCC). See too *Bairstow Eves London Central Ltd v Smith* [2004] EWHC 263 (QB), [2004] 2 E.G.L.R. 25 (estate agents' commission rate supposedly halved for prompt payment: held, caught by regulations as if doubled for late payment). For the position at common law.

[292] See *Office of Fair Trading v Abbey National Plc* [2009] UKSC 6; [2010] 1 A.C. 696 (would have applied, save that on the facts covered by the exception in what is now s.64(1) of the 2015 Act); S. Whittaker, "Unfair contract terms, unfair prices and bank charges" (2011) 74 M.L.R. 106.

credit is granted by a business to an individual in his personal or business capacity, or to a small partnership[293]—further rights are given that are clearer, and in practice supplant the penalties jurisdiction. In particular, s.99 of that Act provides that the debtor is entitled to cancel the agreement at any time, and s.100 states that where he does so any liability of his is limited to making up his payments to half the total price. In addition the court is given a discretion to reduce that figure to the amount of actual loss suffered by the creditor if that is less.[294] It is also worth noting that in such contracts forfeitures are largely court-controlled by the provisions of ss.90 and 113 of the same Act.[295]

VI. Insolvency Law and the "Rule Against Deprivation"[296]

Although not strictly germane to this chapter, it should be remembered that, in addition to the above rules, insolvency law may sometimes affect agreed remedies where one or more parties are insolvent. In particular, the rule of public policy known as the "rule against deprivation" protects creditors' interests by in certain cases invalidating a stipulation aimed at depriving the insolvent of property or contractual rights and thus frustrating the normal rules of distribution on insolvency.[297] So, for instance, in *Ex p. Mackay*[298] the licensee of a patent agreed to pay over half the royalties to the licensor, but to keep the other half towards repayment of a loan made to the latter. A term providing that, if the licensor became bankrupt, the licensee's obligation to pay over any royalties at all should cease was struck down as "a clear attempt to evade the operation of the bankruptcy laws".[299] Similarly, a term in a building contract giving the employer the right to take over materials in the case of insolvency is ineffective;[300] and a claimant settling a claim cannot effectually agree that the settlement monies will cease to be payable to him if he becomes insolvent.[301]

25-073

But the reach of this principle is not unlimited. It only applies to provisions taking effect on insolvency: a divesting expressed to take effect on some event before

25-074

---

[293] See Consumer Credit Act 1974 s.8 and the Financial Services and Markets Act 2000 (Regulated Activities) Order 2001 (SI 2001/544), arts 60B, 60L. There is an exception for certain large loans that are not residential mortgages: see art.60H.

[294] See Consumer Credit Act 1974 s.100(3).

[295] More particularly, s.90 prevents the taking back of most goods subject to such agreements save by court order, thus giving the court effective control over what the debtor may be forced to forfeit. It is also worth noting the effect of s.113, which in essence prevents the creditor from obtaining more than he would otherwise be entitled to by the use of "security", a term presumably wide enough to cover money deposits.

[296] Well-outlined in R. Goode, *Principles of Corporate Insolvency Law*, 5th edn (London: Sweet & Maxwell, 2018), Ch.7 (though the principle itself is common to corporate and personal insolvency).

[297] See generally *Belmont Park Investments Pty Ltd v BNY Corporate Trustee Services Ltd* [2011] UKSC 38; [2012] 1 A.C. 383.

[298] (1873) L.R. 8 Ch. App 643.

[299] (1873) L.R. 8 Ch. App 643 at 648. The decision in *British Eagle International Airlines Ltd v Cie Nationale Air France* [1975] 1 W.L.R. 758, that netting arrangements could not deprive an insolvent party of a positive balance available against a single other debtor, was on a similar basis (though that has since been reversed in the netting context: see Financial Markets and Insolvency (Settlement Finality) Regulations 1999 (SI 2979/1999), Pt III.

[300] *Ex p. Jay* (1880) 14 Ch. D. 19.

[301] *Mayhew v King* [2011] EWCA Civ 328; [2011] B.C.C. 675.

then, while it may be open to attack on other grounds,[302] does not offend the pari passu principle since a trustee in bankruptcy or liquidator takes the insolvent's estate subject to all third party rights existing at the time of insolvency.[303] Furthermore, a limited right or interest, such as a licence to reproduce, may be issued on terms that it terminates on the licensee's insolvency without infringing the rule against deprivation.[304] And while an otherwise absolute obligation to pay for goods or services already supplied cannot be made to terminate on or after the creditor's insolvency,[305] the same does not apply where the debt envisages counter-performance that may not be forthcoming in the event of insolvency (as, for example, with interest rate swaps).[306] A fortiori, a provision for cancellation of a long-term contract, such as a 25-year contract of affreightment, on the insolvency of one party is not caught by the rule.[307]

---

[302] For instance, as an unregistered charge over corporate assets: e.g. *Re Cosslett (Contractors) Ltd (No.2)* [2001] UKHL 58, [2002] 1 A.C. 336.

[303] *Ex p. Newitt* (1881) 26 Ch. D. 522.

[304] *Belmont Park Investments Pty Ltd v BNY Corporate Trustee Services Ltd* [2011] UKSC 38; [2012] 1 A.C. 383.

[305] See *Ex p. Mackay* (1873) L.R. 8 Ch. App 643, above; also *Lomas v JFB Firth Rixson Inc* [2010] EWHC 3372 (Ch) at [108].

[306] *Lomas v JFB Firth Rixson Inc* [2012] EWCA Civ 419; [2012] 1 C.L.C. 713 at [80]–[94].

[307] *Re Pan Ocean Co Ltd* [2014] EWHC 2124 (Ch); [2014] Bus. L.R. 1041.

CHAPTER 26

DAMAGES: GAIN-BASED AWARDS

I. THE GENERAL PRINCIPLE

A contract-breaker may not only cause loss to his co-contractor: he may also **26-001** make a gain from his breach that exceeds that loss (or, at any rate, is easier for the claimant to prove). How far, if at all, may the victim of the breach lay a claim to that gain?[1]

The general rule is that, for the purposes of damages in contract, no such claim **26-002** will lie. However distasteful it might seem to allow a defendant to profit from his own wrong, the law presumptively limits any claim for damages for breach of contract to the amount of the claimant's losses due to the non-performance.[2] In so far as the defendant, having made good those losses, may still finish in profit, this is no concern of the law. The point of principle is neatly illustrated by *Tito v Waddell (No.2)*.[3] As part of a concession to strip-mine remote tropical islands for phosphates, defendants agreed that after they had finished they would restore the land to its previous condition. This they failed to do, thus making large savings for themselves (since restoration would have been very expensive) but causing comparatively little loss to the owners of the land, which had been almost worthless in any case. Megarry V-C made short work of the owners' claim to capture the defendants' savings in lieu of the comparatively negligible diminution in value of the land due to its non-restoration. "The question," he said, "is not one of making the defendant disgorge what he has saved by committing the wrong, but one of compensating the plaintiff."[4] So too in *One Step (Support) Ltd v Morris-Garner*[5] the seller of a business who agreed not to compete with the buyer and then did so was held liable only for the proved loss suffered by the latter. An attempt to quantify

---

[1] G. Jones, "The Recovery of Profits gained from a Breach of Contract" (1983) 99 L.Q.R. 443; R. O'Dair, "Restitutionary Damages for Breach of Contract and the Theory of Efficient Breach" [1993] C.L.P. 112; C. Mitchell, "Remedial Inadequacy in Contract and the Role of Restitutionary Damages" (1999) 15 J.C.L. 133; J. Edelman, *Gain-based Damages: Contract, Tort, Equity and Intellectual Property* (Oxford: Hart, 2002). See too E.A. Farnsworth, "My Loss or Your Gain? The dilemma of the disgorgement principle" (1985) 94 Yale L.J. 1339.
[2] "Damages are measured by the plaintiff's loss, not the defendant's gain":—*Att-Gen v Blake* [2001] 1 A.C. 268 at 278 (Lord Nicholls).
[3] [1977] Ch. 106. There is little older authority, but see the Scots *Teacher v Calder* [1899] A.C. 451 (no claim to profits from breaking promise to invest in pursuer's business in order to make greater gains elsewhere).
[4] *Tito v Waddell (No.2)* [1977] Ch. 106 at 332. There is a good deal of American authority on this point, mainly to the same effect. Typical is *Peevyhouse v Garland Coal & Mining Co,* 382 P.2d 109 (Okl. 1962).
[5] [2018] UKSC 20; [2019] A.C. 649. See C. Bartscherer, "Two steps forward, one step back: One Step (Support) Ltd v Morris-Garner and Another" (2019) 82 M.L.R. 367.

the damages by reference to the sum that might have been paid for a release of the covenant, and which had therefore been saved by the seller, was unhesitatingly rebuffed by the Supreme Court.

26-003   On a similar basis, a seller of shares in a private company who broke his contract by selling them to a third party was not amenable to an action by the original buyer for the extra profit thus generated;[6] and a distributor of surgical products was allowed to keep the substantial profits made by breaking faith with his supplier even after taking account of his liability for losses proved by the latter.[7] So too, at least as a matter of contract, employees have been held entitled to keep payments received for unauthorised outside work,[8] and for work done in breach of a non-competition agreement.[9]

II.   Qualifications to the General Rule

26-004   The principle just stated, however, is not absolute.[10] There are at least two classes of case in which the measure of recovery for breach of contract may reflect, to a greater or lesser extent, the defendant's gain from breach rather than the claimant's loss. These need to be dealt with in some detail.

26-005   First, since the decision in *Att-Gen v Blake*[11] in 2000 it is now absolutely clear that the rule stated in para.26-002 is not invariable. In highly exceptional situations a contract-breaker may be liable to pay over any profits derived from the breach, entirely independently of loss proved (or not proved) by the claimant, in much the same way as other wrongdoers, such as those in breach of fiduciary duty, may be amenable to an account of profits. And secondly, quite apart from an account of profits in the strict sense, awards are not infrequently made in a number of other situations which, at least de facto, have the effect of stripping the defendant of all or part of the profits of a contractual breach. This may be either because the distinction between loss to the claimant and gain to the defendant is often less clear-cut than it might seem, or for other reasons. The notable example of this latter is "buy-out" damages, referred to below.

Both these topics require fairly detailed coverage, which will be found below.

---

6   *Luxe Holding Ltd v Midland Resources Holding Ltd* [2010] EWHC 1908 (Ch) (though equivalent liability was established there on the basis of a constructive trust). So too with a shipowner breaking a charter agreement and chartering elsewhere at a princely rate: see the anonymised arbitration case reported under the name of *The Sine Nomine* [2002] 1 Lloyd's Rep. 805, and also dicta in *The Siboen* [1976] 1 Lloyd's Rep. 293 at 337 (Kerr J).

7   *Hospital Products Ltd v United States Surgical Corp* (1984) 156 C.L.R. 41.

8   *Nottingham University v Fishel* [2000] I.C.R. 1462 (illegally-moonlighting university professor). But the defendant there was in the event made to disgorge on the basis of a separate breach of fiduciary duty.

9   See *Lighthouse Carrwood Ltd v Luckett* [2007] EWHC 2866 (QB) at [58]; also *Clarke (H.F.) Ltd v Thermidaire Corp Ltd* (1974) 54 D.L.R. (3d) 385, and cf. *BGC Capital Markets (Switzerland) LLC v Rees* [2011] EWHC 2009 (QB). American authority is more equivocal here: compare *Vermont Electric Supply v Andrus,* 373 A.2d 531 (Vt 1975) (no claim for gain, as in England) and *Refrigeration Industries v Nemmers,* 880 S.W.2d 912 (Mo 1994) (plaintiff may strip defendant of gain).

10   See generally J. Edelman, *Gain-based Damages: Contract, Tort, Equity and Intellectual Property* (Oxford: Hart Publishing, 2002).

11   [2001] 1 A.C. 268.

Account of profits as a remedy for breach of contract

Account of profits is a troublesome topic in the law of contract.[12] Admittedly the **26-006** idea of a defendant's liability to surrender his gains from a civil wrong to the victim of that wrong is well-established as a remedy in a number of areas outside contract proper. This is notably true in the area of equitable and fiduciary obligations;[13] in the field of breach of confidence;[14] and in the case of the majority of intellectual property rights.[15] In addition, in a number of specific torts the victim in certain cases has the right to quantify his damages by reference to the defendant's gain rather than being strictly limited to being compensated for the prejudice to himself.[16] Until 2000, however, it was regarded as almost axiomatic that this reasoning could never extend to breach of contract as such,[17] unless the breach of contract also constituted another, concurrent, wrong where such relief was available, such as breach of fiduciary duty[18] or infringement of a legal or equitable property right.[19]

Nevertheless, in 2000 the House of Lords, while accepting the general principle **26-007** that damages for breach of contract were concerned with losses and not gains, created a clear exception to it. In *Att-Gen v Blake*[20] an erstwhile MI6 employee who had also spied for the Soviet Union as a double agent was due to receive £100,000 for a book about his experiences. The writing of the book was a blatant breach of his contract of employment with the Crown, but not technically a breach of confidence (the relevant information being by then in the public domain). The Crown having claimed the £100,000 but being otherwise unable to prove any loss, the House of Lords by a majority decided that it could do so, and this on the basis

---

12 J. Edelman, "Profits and Gains from Breach of Contract" [2001] L.M.C.L.Q. 9; M. Siems, "Disgorgement of profits for breach of contract: a comparative analysis" (2003) 7 Edin Law Rev 27; J. Edelman, *Gain-based Damages: Contract, Tort, Equity and Intellectual Property* (Oxford: Hart Publishing, 2002), pp.149–172; A. Gray, "Disgorgement Damages" [2013] J.B.L. 657.

13 G. Virgo, *The Principles of the Law of Restitution*, 3rd edn (Oxford: Oxford University Press, 2015), Ch.19.

14 G. Virgo, *The Principles of the Law of Restitution*, 3rd edn (Oxford: Oxford University Press, 2015), Ch.19.

15 L. Bently and B. Sherman, *Intellectual Property Law*, 4th edn (Oxford: Oxford University Press, 2014), p.1196.

16 *McGregor on Damages*, 21st edn (London: Sweet & Maxwell, 2022), para.15-029 ff. For examples, see *Ministry of Defence v Ashman* [1993] 66 P. & C.R. 195 and *Ramzan v Brookwide Ltd* [2010] EWHC 2453 (Ch); [2011] 2 All E.R. 38 (trespass). But the category is unlikely to be extended. See e.g. *Stoke-on-Trent CC v W. & J. Wass Ltd* [1988] 3 All E.R. 394 and *Forsyth-Grant v Allen* [2008] EWCA Civ 505; [2008] Env. L.R. 41 (no application to nuisance).

17 See, in particular, *Nottingham University v Fishel* [2000] I.C.R. 1462 at 1487–1488 (Elias J); also the Australian decision in *Hospital Products Ltd v United States Surgical Corp* (1984) 156 C.L.R. 41 (contractual distribution agreement broken: taken as given that no account of profits unless breach of fiduciary duty proved in addition). The strict position is defended in A.Gray, "Disgorgement Damages" [2013] J.B.L. 657.

18 Examples being *Nottingham University v Fishel* [2000] I.C.R. 1462, referred to above, and *Vercoe v Rutland Fund Management Ltd* [2010] EWHC 424 (Ch); [2010] Bus. L.R. D141 (both involving both contract and breach of equitable obligations); also, the earlier *Reid-Newfoundland Co v Anglo-American Telegraph Co Ltd* [1912] A.C. 555 (agency for transmission of messages).

19 As regards legal property, see the case of an overstaying tenant (as in *Swordheath Properties Ltd v Tabet* [1979] 1 W.L.R. 285 and *Ministry of Defence v Ashman* [1993] 66 P. & C.R. 195). For equitable property, the obvious instance is the vendor of land who sells twice over, thus infringing not only the first buyer's contractual rights but also his equitable interest in the property: see *Lake v Bayliss* [1974] 1 W.L.R. 1073.

20 [2001] 1 A.C. 268: see D. Fox, "Restitutionary damages to deter breach of contract" [2001] C.L.J. 33; P. Jaffey, "Disgorgement for breach of contract" (2000) 4 R.L.R. 578; J. Edelman, "Profits and gains from breach of contract" [2001] L.M.C.L.Q. 9.

that the payment represented the profits of a breach of contract. Lord Nicholls gave the leading judgment.[21] Though he emphatically supported a presumptive rule against account of profits,[22] there were, he thought, "many commonplace situations where a strict application of this principle would not do justice between the parties".[23] He went on to reason that in such cases restitutionary damages were exceptionally permissible; and that the facts of *Blake* itself embodied just such a situation.[24] Lord Steyn reasoned in much the same way, though with slightly more specificity: while there was "no or virtually no support for a general action for disgorgement of profits made by a contract breaker by reason of his breach",[25] the present case was exceptional, in that not only had the defendant blatantly broken a clear negative promise, but in addition an injunction would be of no use; if not a fiduciary he had been close to being one; and the Crown had had a "special interest over and above the hope of a benefit to be assessed in monetary terms" in suppressing such conduct.[26] It is now clear, moreover, that damages of this kind are different from, and available in different circumstances from, use-value and "buy-out damages"[27] referred to below.[28]

26-008   Unfortunately, besides confining the remedy of confiscation of profits to highly exceptional cases,[29] and saying that *Blake* was one of them, the majority gave little further guidance on what situations qualified as sufficiently unusual, besides stating, rather unhelpfully, that a court had to consider

> "all the circumstances, including the subject matter of the contract, the purpose of the contractual provision which has been breached, the circumstances in which the breach occurred, the consequences of the breach and the circumstances in which relief is being sought".[30]

Lord Nicholls did suggest, however, that a useful general guide might be whether the claimant would have had, besides any claim for breach, a legitimate interest in actually *preventing* the defendant from making a profit from the activity in

---

[21] In which Lords Goff and Browne-Wilkinson concurred, thus making it the majority view.
[22] [2001] 1 A.C. 268 at 285.
[23] [2001] 1 A.C. 268 at 278.
[24] [2001] 1 A.C. 268 at 286–287.
[25] [2001] 1 A.C. 268 at 291.
[26] [2001] 1 A.C. 268 at 291–292.
[27] These latter often referred to as "Wrotham Park damages" after the eponymous *Wrotham Park Estates Ltd v Parkside Homes Ltd* [1974] 1 W.L.R. 798. In *Morris-Garner v One Step (Support) Ltd* [2018] UKSC 20; [2019] A.C. 649 at [3] Lord Reed preferred "negotiating damages".
[28] See *Morris-Garner v One Step (Support) Ltd* [2018] UKSC 20; [2019] A.C. 649 at [73]–[82] (Lord Reed). Difficulties had previously arisen from some incautious remarks by Lord Nicholls in Blake itself suggesting that both categories involved a common principle: see *Att Gen v Blake* [2001] A.C. 268 at 283–285.
[29] See Lords Nicholls and Steyn in *Blake*: [2001] A.C. 268 at [285] and [291]. See too *World Wide Fund for Nature (formerly World Wildlife Fund) v World Wrestling Federation Entertainment Inc* [2002] F.S.R. 32 at [62] (Jacob J); (2001) 24(12) I.P.D. 24079; *Esso Petroleum Co Ltd v Niad Ltd* (unreported 22 November 2001) at [59]; and the Canadian *Atlantic Lottery Corp Inc v Babstock* 2020 SCC 19; [2020] 2 S.C.R. 420 at [61].
[30] [2001] 1 A.C. 268 at 285. See too Lord Steyn's equally uninformative justification at 292 that in the exceptional circumstances the remedy requested was in the interests of practical justice. The later pronouncement of Phillips J in *One Step (Support) Ltd v Morris-Garner* [2014] EWHC 2213 (QB); [2015] I.R.L.R. 215, that the House of Lords had "declined to set rigid parameters for the availability of an account of profits in breach of contract cases", is a masterpiece of refined understatement. The decision was reversed in the Supreme Court (see *Morris-Garner v One Step (Support) Ltd* [2018] UKSC 20; [2019] A.C. 649), but his Lordship remains correct.

question.[31] In the actual circumstances of *Blake*'s case, he regarded this criterion as satisfied, observing that the claim was similar to one for breach of fiduciary duty (which indubitably did engender a profits claim in equity), and that limiting the Crown to a damages claim based on its loss would be unrealistic and inadequate.[32]

Despite the deficiencies in the reasoning in *Att-Gen v Blake*,[33] it is suggested that **26-009** the principles described in the following paragraphs may form a workable basis for the jurisdiction described in it.[34]

We can begin negatively, with limitations. First, despite the result in *Blake* itself, **26-010** there is no doubt that such damages remain highly exceptional.[35] Attempts to extend such awards to ordinary breaches of contract, even deliberate and blatant ones, have since been consistently and rightly rebuffed.[36] Secondly, where it is permissible to award damages on a "buy-out" basis—that is, the amount that might notionally have been paid for a release of the relevant right, rather than complete disgorgement— then, if it comes to a choice between that and disgorgement, there should be a presumption in favour of the former.[37] Thirdly, it seems to be a precondition of disgorgement damages that no other possible remedy, such as compensatory damages or an injunction, would adequately protect or vindicate the claimant's rights in question;[38] and even if these criteria are met the award itself remains in the discretion of the court.[39] Fourthly, as was agreed by Lords Nicholls and Steyn in *Blake*, it is not enough that the breach is cynical or calculatedly lucrative.[40] Nor is it enough that it amounts to a dishonestly profitable but financially harmless breach, as where

---

[31] See [2011] 1 A.C. 268 at 285. But this itself is problematical. An employer presumably has a very legitimate interest in preventing his employees moonlighting for possible competitors, and yet under cases such as *Nottingham University v Fishel* [2000] I.C.R. 1462 this is *not* a case where account of profits is available.

[32] [2001] 1 A.C. 268 at 287–288. See too Lord Steyn at [2001] 1 A.C. 268 at 292.

[33] Which may be one reason why the Australian Federal Court has refused to follow it without the imprimatur of the High Court: *Hospitality Group Pty Ltd v Australian Rugby Union Ltd* (2001) 110 FCR 157.

[34] On this point see too E. McKendrick, "Breach of Contract, Restitution for Wrongs, and Punishment" in A. Burrows and E. Peel (eds), *Commercial Remedies: Current Issues and Problems* (Oxford: Oxford University Press, 2003), Ch.10; P. Collins, "Liability for profits in breach of contract: revisiting Attorney-General v Blake" [2015] R.L.R 44.

[35] As Lords Nicholls and Steyn pointed out in *Blake*: [2001] A.C. 268 at 285, 291. See too *World Wide Fund for Nature v World Wrestling Federation Entertainment Inc* (unreported 1 October 2001) Ch. D. (Jacob J); *WWF World Wide Fund for Nature (formerly World Wildlife Fund) v World Wrestling Federation Entertainment Inc* [2006] EWHC 184 (Ch); [2006] F.S.R. 38 at [63] (Jacob J); *Luxe Holding Ltd v Midland Resources Holding Ltd* [2010] EWHC 1908 (Ch) at [51] (Roth J). On occasion, unexceptionality has been put forward, without more, as a ground for refusing relief: e.g. *Experience Hendrix LLC v PPX Enterprises Inc* [2003] EWCA Civ 323; [2003] EMLR 25 at [55], and *One Step (Support) Ltd v Morris-Garner* [2014] EWHC 2213 (QB); [2015] I.R.L.R. 215 at [103] (the point was not taken on appeal at [2016] EWCA Civ 180; [2016] I.R.L.R. 435).

[36] E.g. *The Sine Nomine* [2002] 1 Lloyd's Rep. 805 at 809–810 (ship charter); *Vercoe v Rutland Fund Management Ltd* [2010] EWHC 424 (Ch); [2010] Bus. L.R. D141 at [337]–[343] (Sales J) (contractual obligation re corporate opportunity); *Luxe Holding Ltd v Midland Resources Holding Ltd* [2010] EWHC 1908 (Ch) at [47]–[56] (Roth J) (share sale agreement).

[37] *Vercoe v Rutland Fund Management Ltd* [2010] EWHC 424 (Ch); [2010] Bus. L.R. D141 at [341] (Sales J).

[38] See Lord Nicholls at [2001] 1 A.C. 268 at 285.

[39] See Lord Nicholls at [2001] 1 A.C. 268 at 284–285 ("discretionary remedy"). See too Peter Smith J in *WWF-World Wide Fund for Nature (formerly World Wildlife Fund) v World Wrestling Federation Entertainment Inc* [2006] EWHC 184 (Ch); [2006] F.S.R. 663 at [174] (though arguably this refers less to account of profits than to "buy-out" damages, referred to below).

[40] See [2001] 1 A.C. 268 at 286 (Lord Nicholls, making it clear that in his view the defendant's state of mind ought to be irrelevant).

a construction contractor skimps by using cheaper materials without causing any actual loss to the building owner,[41] the seller of a business shortly afterwards sets up and sells on a competing business in blatant breach of a non-competition covenant,[42] or a bank with more regard for its own profit figures than for commercial probity exploits for its own benefit a takeover opportunity for which a customer has applied for finance.[43] Fifthly, despite the suggestions by both Lords Nicholls and Steyn that non-fiduciary but fiduciary-like duties might attract such awards,[44] as a general rule the courts have shied away from allowing them simply because the claim in question bears some similarity to a complaint, such as one for breach of intellectual property rights, where such a remedy is admittedly available.[45] Sixthly, a disgorgement remedy is likely to be inappropriate where the defendant's wrong was merely one of a number of concurrent causes of his profitable activity, rather than the main cause.[46]

26-011   With these limitations in mind, it is nevertheless possible to delineate three kinds of case in which, it is suggested, a wholesale claim to disgorgement of profits on the lines of *Blake* is likely to lie.[47] These categories are: (i) contracts entered into in order to protect essentially public, aesthetic or altruistic interests not susceptible to valuation, (ii) contracts to avoid exploiting a given source of profit, entered into for the protection of some discrete and legitimate interest of the claimant, and (iii) contractual obligations reproducing what would otherwise be fiduciary obligations in any case.

26-012   **(i) Public, aesthetic or altruistic interests**   This category is (it is respectfully submitted) a straightforward application of *Blake* itself, where the litigation essentially concerned the judicial protection of a public good beyond valuation.[48] As a later judge put it,

---

[41] See [2001] 1 A.C. 268 at [286] and [291] (Lords Nicholls and Steyn, discountenancing suggestions by Lord Woolf MR in the Court of Appeal at [1998] Ch. 439 at 458). A different result has been reached in New Zealand in *Samson & Samson Ltd v Proctor* [1975] 1 N.Z.L.R. 655, and possibly in Canada in *Sunshine Exploration Ltd v Dolly Varden Mines Ltd (N.P.L.)* [1970] S.C.R. 2; but this must be very doubtful in England. Cf. the notorious American decision in *City of New Orleans v Firemen's Charitable Association*, 9 So. 486 (1891). Defendants paid to furnish a municipal fire service with a specified number of men and available hoses in fact provided a good deal less and pocketed the savings. Nevertheless, they had not failed to put out any fires as a result, and for this reason nominal damages only were awarded to the municipality.

[42] *One Step (Support) Ltd v Morris-Garner* [2014] EWHC 2213 (QB); [2015] I.R.L.R. 215 (the point was not raised on appeal at [2018] UKSC 20; [2019] A.C. 649). So also with a franchisor who in breach of contract sells to others in a franchisee's territory: see the Western Australian decision in *Dalecoast Pty Ltd v Guardian International Pty Ltd* [2003] WASCA 142.

[43] *CF Partners (UK) LLP v Barclays Bank Plc* [2014] EWHC 3049 (Ch) at [1168]–[1181].

[44] *Att-Gen v Blake* [2001] 1 A.C. 268 at 285 at 292; see also *CMS Dolphin Ltd v Simonet* [2001] 2 B.C.L.C. 704 at [142] (Lawrence Collins J).

[45] See *WWF-World Wide Fund for Nature v World Wrestling Federation Entertainment Inc* [2002] F.S.R. 32 at [63] (Jacob J: not enough that "a bit 'trademarkish' or 'IPish'"); also *Walsh v Shanahan* [2013] EWCA Civ 411; [2013] 2 P. & C.R. DG7 (while account of profits usual remedy for breach of fiduciary duty, not so once fiduciary duty comes to an end and claimant has to rely simply on a promise of confidentiality). However, cf. the comments of Mance LJ in *Experience Hendrix LLC v PPX Enterprises Inc* [2003] EWCA Civ 323; [2003] E.M.L.R. 25 at [32].

[46] *CF Partners (UK) LLP v Barclays Bank Plc* [2014] EWHC 3049 (Ch) at [1179] (Hildyard J).

[47] The term "wholesale disgorgement" is deliberately chosen. Separate considerations may apply to so-called "Wrotham Park", "negotiating" or "buy-out" damages, where the concentration is much more on the notional net profits of wrongdoing: see below.

[48] Cf. Lord Steyn's reference in *Blake* at [2001] 1 A.C. 268 at 291 to the Crown's "special interest over and above the hope of a benefit to be assessed in monetary terms".

"it may be more appropriate to award an account of profits where the right in question is of a kind where it would never be reasonable to expect that it could be bought out for some reasonable fee, so that it is accordingly deserving of a particularly high level of protection".[49]

In the nature of things, cases of this sort may well be few and far between, but a few possibilities come to mind. One would be an agreement entered into by a landowner to protect the aesthetics of a neighbourhood,[50] which the landowner then broke by carrying out unsightly but profitable development. Another might be where a person "buys" a promise whose justification is altruistic or otherwise not susceptible of valuation. Suppose, for instance, that an animal charity sold land to a farmer subject to a covenant by the purchaser not to use it for shooting or blood-sports, but to keep it as a wildlife sanctuary. Were the buyer to organise a commercial pheasant-shoot on the land for profit, there would be a strong case for allowing a claim in respect of that profit.

(ii) Legitimate private interests supporting a promise not to exploit a source of profit A promise to refrain from some given activity will not as such engender gain-based damages if it is broken.[51] But there may be exceptions. In particular, it is suggested that matters may possibly be different if the promisee can be said in some sense to have "bought" the promisor's undertaking to forgo some profitable activity in order to protect some entirely separate interest of his own. As Hildyard J said in 2014, *Blake* damages may be more appropriate where   26-013

> "the rights of the claimant are of a particularly powerful kind and/or such that his interest in full performance is particularly strong; and on whether those rights are asserted in an ordinary commercial context ('where a degree of self-seeking and ruthless behaviour is expected and accepted to a degree') or in the context of a relationship of special trust, such as was the case on *Blake* itself or such as in a fiduciary relationship (where 'self-seeking behaviour is required to be reined in on the grounds that special obligations ... have been assumed ...', and there is an enhanced importance of deterring abusive behaviour)."[52]

This seems the best explanation of the otherwise difficult decision in *Esso*   26-014
Petroleum Co Ltd v Niad Ltd.[53] Esso, as part of a corporate promotion aimed at consolidating its market share, paid a tied garage proprietor a sum in exchange for a promise by the latter not to sell petrol above a certain price. The retailer accepted the payment but did not discount his petrol. The Court of Appeal awarded damages against the retailer based on the whole of the extra profit made from its breach. The argument in favour of such an award was neither very clear nor entirely satisfactory:[54] nevertheless, it was, as Morritt V-C put it,

> "undoubted that [the defendant] obtained a benefit, in the form of the price support, to

---

[49] See *Vercoe v Rutland Fund Management Ltd* [2010] EWHC 424 (Ch); [2010] Bus. L.R. D141 at [340] (Sales J).
[50] For example, where the National Trust is involved: see the National Trust Act 1937 s.8, specifically empowering the Trust to enter into, and more importantly enforce, covenants of this sort with property owners whether or not it owns any land that would benefit from them.
[51] See *Att-Gen v Blake* [2001] 1 A.C. 268 at 286 (Lord Nicholls) for this obvious point.
[52] *CF Partners (UK) LLP v Barclays Bank Plc* [2014] EWHC 3049 (Ch) at [1172].
[53] [2001] All E.R. (D) 324.
[54] It is flatly rejected as wrong in E. McKendrick, "Breach of Contract, Restitution for Wrongs, and Punishment" in A. Burrows and E. Peel (eds), *Commercial Remedies: Current Issues and Problems*

which it was only entitled if it complied with its obligation to implement and maintain the recommended pump prices to be supported".[55]

It is not difficult to think of possible similar instances. For example, suppose an employment contract does not simply forbid "moonlighting" but specifically prohibits an employee from profiting on his own account from certain activities while employed and augments his salary in recognition of this fact;[56] or that telecommunication or other facilities are made available by a supplier to a client at a reduced rate on the understanding that they are not to be "sublet" to third parties for payment.[57] In such cases there is something to be said for enforcing the obligation concerned by making the defendant hand over any profit made in breach, whether or not any loss is shown.

26-015 **(iii)** **Obligations both fiduciary and contractual** Just as contractual and tortious liability may overlap, precisely the same obligation may on occasion be expressible either as a fiduciary duty or as a contractual requirement.[58] In such a case, it seems that an account of profits will be available in whichever guise the claim is formulated. As Lord Nicholls put it in *Blake* itself, to say that account of profits would be available for the breach of fiduciary duty, but not for breach of the identical duty expressed as a contractual obligation, would be "nothing short of sophistry".[59] And there has since been some support for this view: thus it has been said that a company director who steals a business opportunity from his employer will be liable to return any profit made whether the claim is made as one for breach of fiduciary duty or simple breach of contract.[60]

Cases other than account of profits: Usage fees, royalties and "buy-out damages"

26-016 So far, we have been dealing with wholly exceptional cases of an account of the profits of a breach of contract, where the court simply orders a defendant to disgorge his gains in their totality. But such cases, as pointed out, are very unusual. Much commoner are situations where for some other reason damages for breach of contract are reckoned, not by reference to any direct loss suffered by the claimant, but instead on the basis of the value of some service or facility which the defendant has been enabled to get for free from the claimant by virtue of his breach, or of some interest or right of the claimant which the defendant has infringed without causing the former any immediately obvious loss.

(Oxford: Oxford University Press, 2003), p.112; and also in A. Gray, "Disgorgement Damages" [2013] J.B.L. 657 at 663.

55 [2001] All E.R. (D) 324 at [64].

56 Thus, distinguishing it from that in *Nottingham University v Fishel* [2000] I.C.R. 1462. An instance might be an obligation by an employed commodities broker not to deal on his own account. It is suggested that this is different from a simple promise to devote the whole of one's time to one employer, since the employer here has a very real interest in preventing his employee entering into relations that might engender very awkward conflicts of interest.

57 On the telecommunications example, cf. the facts of *Reid-Newfoundland Co v Anglo-American Telegraph Co* [1912] A.C. 555. In that case the Privy Council held the defendant liable to account on the basis of breach of fiduciary duty: but since *Blake*, it is suggested that the same result could be reached at common law.

58 A straightforward example being an employee's duty not to misuse his employer's trade secrets: see, e.g. *Robb v Green* [1895] 2 Q.B. 315 at 319 (Kay LJ).

59 See *Att-Gen v Blake* [2001] 1 A.C. 268 at 285.

60 See *CMS Dolphin Ltd v Simonet* [2001] 2 B.C.L.C. 704 at [142] (Lawrence Collins J).

Cases of this sort, where damages de facto seem, at least to some extent, to reflect **26-017** a defendant's gain, vary considerably. Broadly, however, they fall into three categories. The first involves the use of property in breach of contract; the second the carrying on of an activity that might have been the subject of a royalty or similar agreement; and the third, the doing of some other act that infringes the claimant's contractual rights in circumstances where those rights might conceivably have been "bought out"—that is, released by the claimant on payment of some fee.[61]

(i) Use of property in breach of contract A long line of cases establishes that **26-018** the tortious use of someone else's land[62] or chattel[63] may trigger damages computed not by direct prejudice to the owner—which as often as not is nil—but by the value of the use obtained (or, put another way, the defendant has in such a case to pay over the amount he has saved as a result of not obtaining permission). In the nature of things, most such cases will concern tort: but there is no reason not to treat contract claims similarly, and on occasion this has indeed happened. A straightforward instance is *Penarth Dock & Engineering Ltd v Pounds*.[64] The defendants rented space at the plaintiff's wharf to store an unused pontoon for a limited period, but broke their contract by failing to remove it at the end of the agreed time. Even though the plaintiffs' docks were in decline and the wharf would otherwise have lain entirely derelict, and hence the overstay caused its owners no prejudice whatever, damages were set at a reasonable rate for the use of it during the excess period.

(ii) Royalty cases As with tangible property, so with intangibles. The use of **26-019** reasonable royalty payments is well-established as a guide to damages for tortious infringement of intellectual property rights;[65] and the parallel with contractual obligations to respect exclusive rights of the same sort has not been lost on the courts. Thus where a breach consists in carrying on some activity without the claimant's permission which might potentially have been made the subject of a

---

[61] See the summary by Lord Reed in *Morris-Garner v One Step (Support) Ltd* [2018] UKSC 20; [2019] A.C. 649 at [24] ff and [95] ff.

[62] See, for instance, the mining and similar cases of *Martin v Porter* (1839) 5 M & W 351, *Whitwham v Westminster Brymbo Coal & Coke Co* [1896] 2 Ch. 538 and *Bocardo SA v Star Energy UK Onshore Ltd* [2010] UKSC 35; [2010] 3 W.L.R. 654; also the right of way case of *Jaggard v Sawyer* [1995] 1 W.L.R. 269; and the overstaying tenant cases of *Swordheath Properties Ltd v Tabet* [1979] 1 W.L.R. 285 and *Inverugie Investments Ltd v Hackett* [1995] 1 W.L.R. 713.

[63] "If A, being a liveryman, keeps his horse standing idle in the stable, and B, against his wish or without his knowledge, rides or drives it out, it is no answer to A for B to say: 'Against what loss do you want to be restored? I restore the horse. There is no loss. The horse is none the worse; it is the better for the exercise": Lord Shaw in *Watson, Laidlaw, & Co Ltd v Pott, Cassels, & Williamson* 1914 S.C. (HL) 18 at 31. See generally *Strand Electric & Engineering Co Ltd v Brisford Entertainments Ltd* [1952] 2 Q.B. 246 at 253–255 (Denning LJ); and, more recently, *Brocket Hall (Jersey) Ltd v Kruger* [2019] EWHC 1352 (Ch).

[64] [1963] 1 Lloyd's Rep. 359 (wrongly stated to be a case of trespass in *Marathon Asset Management LLP v Seddon* [2017] EWHC 300 (Comm); [2017] 2 C.L.C. 182 at [172]). See too *Michael Gerson (Leasing) Ltd v Greatsunny Ltd* [2010] EWHC 1887 (Ch); [2010] 3 W.L.R. 1147 (hiring out of claimant's property: had this been in breach of contract, would have been award of reasonable hire charge).

[65] L. Bently, B. Sherman, D. Gamgjee & P. Johnson, *Intellectual Property Law*, 6th edn (Oxford: Oxford University Press, 2022), Ch.49. For examples, see *Pell Frischmann Engineering Ltd v Bow Valley Iran Ltd* [2009] UKPC 45; [2010] B.L.R. 73 (breach of confidence); *Blayney v Clogau St Davids Gold Mines Ltd* [2003] F.S.R. 360 (copyright); *General Tire & Rubber Co v Firestone Tyre & Rubber Co Ltd* [1975] 1 W.L.R. 819 (patent). But only where a plausible licence fee can be imagined: cf. *Experience Hendrix LLC v Times Newspapers Ltd* [2010] EWHC 1986 (Ch) at [137] (Sir William Blackburne).

royalty or similar payment, it has been repeatedly confirmed that the amount of any such hypothetical payment is an entirely acceptable way of measuring damages. For instance, in *Experience Hendrix LLC v PPX Enterprises Inc*,[66] the defendants compromised complex intellectual property litigation over musical rights by promising not to exploit certain recordings. Later, in clear breach of the compromise agreement, they exploited them in any case. The Court of Appeal had little hesitation in ordering payment of a reasonable royalty by way of damages. Similarly, in *WWF-World Wide Fund for Nature v World Wrestling Federation Entertainment Inc*,[67] another case of breach of a compromise agreement (this time not to use a given name) where the same point arose and was discussed at some length,[68] a royalty award was again held justified.

26-020 **(iii) "Buy-out" awards** Thirdly, even where neither of the above matters is in issue, similar reasoning can apply where there has been a breach of a restrictive covenant or some other promise to forgo some activity, and where there is some plausible way of calculating what would have been a reasonable price for release of the obligation concerned. Here the practice is well-established of basing damages on just such a reasonable "buy-out" price, such as would have been agreed between reasonable persons in the positions of claimant and defendant respectively.[69] The leading authority is *Wrotham Park Estates Ltd v Parkside Homes Ltd*.[70] Home Counties property developers built a small housing estate whose construction, as it turned out, infringed a restrictive covenant in favour of certain neighbouring land. There being no evidence of any devaluation in the market value of the dominant tenement, the issue arose as to what damages, if any, were available to the latter's owner. Brightman J, understandably disinclined to leave the defendants "in undisturbed possession of the fruits of their wrongdoing", instead awarded the claimants damages under Lord Cairns's Act[71] in the sum of five per cent of the defendants' profits from the development, this being in his judgment the sum that "might reasonably have been demanded ... as a quid pro quo for relaxing the covenant".[72] Similarly, in *Lunn Poly Ltd v Liverpool & Lancashire Properties Ltd*,[73] shop landlords in breach of their covenant for quiet enjoyment disrupted their ten-

---

[66] [2003] F.S.R. 46; [2003] EWCA Civ 323; see R. Cunnington, "A lost opportunity to clarify" (2007) 123 L.Q.R. 48.

[67] [2007] EWCA Civ 286; [2008] 1 W.L.R. 445. The claim in fact failed, but only for procedural reasons.

[68] See [2007] EWCA Civ 286; [2008] 1 W.L.R. 445 at [25]–[60] (Chadwick LJ). That the only justification for the award of royalty-style damages in *Hendrix* was the fact that in all but name it was an intellectual property case, was pointed out by Lord Reed in *Morris-Garner v One Step (Support) Ltd* [2018] UKSC 20; [2019] A.C. 649 at [88]–[89]. This also seems the only convincing justification of the decision in *Vercoe v Rutland Fund Management Ltd* [2010] EWHC 424 (Ch); [2010] Bus. L.R. D141, concerning misuse in breach of contract of information obtained in the course of a joint venture agreement: see *Morris-Garner* at [84].

[69] Again reflecting the practice in analogous tort cases, such as *Jaggard v Sawyer* [1995] 1 W.L.R. 269. The fact that no such buy-out would ever have been agreed is, of course, irrelevant: as has been repeatedly made clear, the quantification is a purely hypothetical exercise. See *Wrotham Park Estates Ltd v Parkside Homes Ltd* [1974] 1 W.L.R. 798 at 815; *Jaggard v Sawyer* [1995] 1 W.L.R. 269 at 282–283; *Pell Frischmann Engineering Ltd v Bow Valley Iran Ltd* [2010] B.L.R. 73; [2009] UKPC 45 at [49]; and *Morris-Garner v One Step (Support) Ltd* [2018] UKSC 20; [2019] A.C. 649 at [75].

[70] [1974] 1 W.L.R. 798. See too the almost identical *Bracewell v Appleby* [1975] Ch. 408.

[71] i.e. in lieu of an injunction, under what is now s.50 of the Senior Courts Act 1981. There was no doubt that such damages were available, the claimants having unsuccessfully sought injunctive relief.

[72] [1974] 1 W.L.R. 798 at 812, 815.

[73] [2006] EWCA Civ 430; [2007] L & TR 6.

ants' operations by moving a door. This being an operation that the tenants, like most tenants, would have permitted in exchange for a suitable douceur, damages—again awarded under Lord Cairns's Act—were set at the amount of such a payment. More recently, an award on the same basis was held appropriate in the case of a bank that, having received an application for a loan for a takeover project, mounted the takeover itself after the customer's bid had run into difficulties: the customer received what would have been a reasonable fee for broking the deal.[74]

It is important to note, however, that the damages in *Wrotham Park* and *Lunn* **26-021** *Poly* were awarded in lieu of an injunction under what is now s.50 of the Senior Courts Act 1981. The thinking was that it was the potential availability of specific enforcement that provided the occasion for a charge being made for non-enforcement, and that where this was not present there could be no scope (outside the property and royalty cases mentioned above) for any more general application of "buy-out damages" to claims for breach of contract at Common Law.[75] For a time some doubt was thrown on this view, and it was thought that "buy-out damages" were available more generally in breach of contract cases, independently of the availability of any other relief, where this was an appropriate way to quantify recovery.[76] In *One Step (Support) Ltd v Morris-Garner*,[77] however, the expansive view was rejected in the Supreme Court, and "buy-out" damages limited to cases where, owing to the availability of specific relief, or the neutralising of a valuable asset of the claimant as a result of the defendant's breach,[78] the concept of a buy-out made sense. Thus where the seller of a business had broken a covenant not to compete, a case which did not come within these categories and where there was no question of injunctive relief, a majority of the court held that the claimant was

---

[74] *CF Partners (UK) LLP v Barclays Bank Plc* [2014] EWHC 3049 (Ch); see especially at [1284]. Cf. *Brooke Homes (Bicester) Ltd v Portfolio Property Partners Ltd* [2021] EWHC 3015 (Ch) at [240] (breach of exclusivity agreement re property), and the breach of confidence case of *Primary Group (UK) Ltd v Royal Bank of Scotland Plc* [2014] EWHC 1082 (Ch); [2014] R.P.C. 26 (use of information from customer for own purposes: reasonable fee of £5,000 assessed). The *CF Partners* case is discussed in W. Day, "An application of Wrotham Park damages" (2015) 131 L.Q.R. 218.

[75] See the comments of the Court of Appeal in *Surrey County Council v Bredero Homes Ltd* [1993] 1 W.L.R. 1361, sidelining Wrotham Park on precisely this ground: on which, A. Burrows, "No Restitutionary Damages for Breach of Contract" [1993] L.M.C.L.Q. 453.

[76] E.g. *Experience Hendrix LLC v PPX Enterprises Inc* [2003] EWCA Civ 323; [2003] EMLR 25 at [58] (Peter Gibson LJ, suggesting that such damages were essentially available as a matter of discretion depending on the defendant's behaviour); *WWF v World Wrestling Federation Entertainment Inc* [2006] EWHC 184 at [164] (Peter Smith J, referring to "the flexibility of the court as to the calculation of the damages under the Wrotham principle when applied to the facts of the case"); and *Pell Frischmann Engineering Ltd v Bow Valley Iran Ltd* [2009] UKPC 45; [2011] 1 W.L.R. 2370 at [48] (Lord Walker: availability or otherwise of injunction irrelevant). See too in Canada *Smith v Landstar Properties Inc* 2011 BCCA 44; 14 B.C.L.R. (4th) 48 (borrower failed to provide security promised to lender; damages based on difference between secured and unsecured loan rates).

[77] [2018] UKSC 20; [2019] A.C. 649. For a recent case awarding negotiating damages following *Morris-Garner*, see *Mahmood v Big Bus Co Ltd* [2021] EWHC 3395 (QB), where defendants agreed not to set up in a particular business in Dubai unless the claimant was involved. Eady J held that this gave the claimant an effective right of veto over the starting of a business, and that when that veto was sidelined in breach of contract, negotiating damages were appropriate. With respect this seems a slightly generous interpretation of *Morris-Garner*.

[78] See the comment of Lord Reed in *Morris-Garner v One Step (Support) Ltd* [2018] UKSC 20 at [95]: "The rationale of such awards is that the person who makes wrongful use of property, where its use is commercially valuable, prevents the owner from exercising a valuable right to control its use, and should therefore compensate him for the loss of the value of the exercise of that right. He takes something for nothing, for which the owner was entitled to require payment." Note also the adherence of the Supreme Court to this restrictive view in the tort case of *Lloyd v Google LLC* [2021] UKSC 50; [2022] A.C. 1217 at [139]–[140].

limited to a claim for proved loss. Essentially this means that ordinary breach of contract cases will not normally now attract "buy-out" damages, even if the claimant will otherwise leave empty-handed because of the difficulty of proving loss in a more conventional way.[79] Indeed, since *One Step* it may well be that earlier cases allowing such damages in respect of such matters as breaches of joint venture agreements need to be regarded with some scepticism.[80]

26-022 The quantification of "buy-out" fees of this sort depends on issues of valuation and hypothetical outcomes of negotiations and, as such, can be highly impressionistic.[81] But there are some basic principles. The correct figure is that which in the court's view would have been agreed between more or less willing parties[82] at the time of the breach.[83] The fact that the claimant might have been able to extract a wholly disproportionate "ransom" payment had the defendant chosen to negotiate will not as such entitle him to claim that sum in damages.[84] Nevertheless, in general account can be taken of the actual position of the parties in assessing the appropriate sum, including in a general way the strengths and weaknesses of their would-be negotiating positions.[85] In a case where the calculation of a plausible "buy-out" fee is extremely difficult, a sum based on a fee for services may

---

79 For a recent decision applying the restrictive interpretation, see *Priyanka Shipping Ltd v Glory Bulk Carriers Pte Ltd* [2019] EWHC 2804 (Comm); [2019] 1 W.L.R. 6677 (seller of ship for scrap obtains injunction preventing return to normal use; but since the case involved no misuse of any asset of the claimant for the use of which payment might be required, would not have been entitled to gain-based damages for any extra profit gained). See too the Singapore decision in *Turf Club Auto Emporium Pte Ltd v Yeo Boong Hua* [2018] SGCA 44; [2018] 2 S.L.R. 655; and D.Xu, "Negotiating damages: rationalising the compensatory view" [2020] J.B.L. 561.

80 In particular the Privy Council decision in *Pell Frischmann Engineering Ltd v Bow Valley Iran Ltd* [2009] UKPC 45; [2011] 1 W.L.R. 2370 (breach of a co-operation agreement in developing an oil field). The only justification of the result seems to be an agreement there that damages should be reckoned as if awarded under Lord Cairns's Act.

81 Hence Peter Smith J's sage reference to "the flexibility of the court as to the calculation of the damages under the Wrotham principle when applied to the facts of the case": see *WWF v World Wrestling Federation Entertainment Inc* [2006] EWHC 184 at [164]. See too Hildyard J in *CF Partners (UK) LLP v Barclays Bank Plc* [2014] EWHC 3049 (Ch) at [1199]: "The exercise is artificial; and, despite the apparent precision of the figures and calculations deployed typically (and necessarily) on each side, it necessarily involves a question of impression." Generally, note the useful B. Mason, "Unravelling the Hypothetical Bargain" [2012] R.L.R. 75.

82 See *Pell Frischmann Engineering Ltd v Bow Valley Iran Ltd* [2009] UKPC 45; [2010] B.L.R. 73 (negotiations between willing parties, both assumed to act reasonably); also, the tort decision in *Lawson v Hartley-Brown* (1995) 71 P. & C.R. 242 at 250 (Aldous LJ).

83 See *AMEC Developments Ltd v Jury's Hotel Management (UK) Ltd* (2000) 82 P. & C.R. 286 at [11]–[13] (to be preferred, it is suggested, to the view of the Privy Council in *Horsford v Bird* [2006] UKPC 3; [2006] 15 E.G. 136 that the relevant time is that of the issue of proceedings). But exceptionally a different time may be taken; see *Lunn Poly Ltd v Liverpool & Lancashire Properties Ltd* [2006] EWCA Civ 430; [2007] L & TR 6, where there had been actual negotiations between the parties.

84 See the tort decision in *Jaggard v Sawyer* [1995] 1 W.L.R. 269 at 282–283 (Bingham LJ); and for a concrete example, another tort decision in *Wynn-Jones v Bickley* [2006] EWHC 1991 (Ch).

85 Claimant's position: see *Ryan v Al Harwood Building Services* [1997] CLY 1775, and cf. *Wynn-Jones v Bickley* [2006] EWHC 1991 (Ch). Defendant's position: see the tort decision in *Bocardo SA v Star Energy UK Onshore Ltd* [2010] UKSC 35; [2011] 1 A.C. 380 (oil unlawfully piped under claimant's land: fact that defendant could have got compulsory rites of passage reduces "buy-out" award).

be appropriate.[86] Account may, it seems, be taken of circumstances and knowledge obtaining not only at the time of infringement but also at the time of judgment.[87]

The nature of "buy-out" and similar damages

In a sense damages of this sort, whether based on royalty, use or "buy-out" value, do seem to be gain-based: the immediate reference is indeed to the saving to the defendant, not to the claimant's own impoverishment due to the breach. For this reason they have been judicially so described; for instance, Steyn LJ said in 1992 that they were awarded "not to compensate the plaintiffs for financial injury, but to deprive the defendants of an unjustly acquired gain".[88] But it now seems clear that this is wrong. When awarded, such damages are, it is submitted, best regarded for a number of reasons[89] as compensatory.[90] What they do is essentially to put a value—albeit a somewhat artificial one—on the claimant's right which has been set at nought by the defendant, and having done so to regard this as the amount that the claimant has lost.[91]

26-023

---

[86] *CF Partners (UK) LLP v Barclays Bank Plc* [2014] EWHC 3049 (Ch) (use of customer's information by bank for takeover: hypothetical brokerage fee awarded).

[87] *Morris-Garner v One Step (Support) Ltd* [2018] UKSC 20; [2019] A.C. 649 at [159] (Lord Carnwath, the other Justices in the majority not dealing in detail with the point); see too *Lunn Poly Ltd v Liverpool & Lancashire Properties Ltd* [2006] EWCA Civ 430; [2007] L & TR 6 at [29] (Neuberger LJ).

[88] *Surrey County Council v Bredero Homes Ltd* [1993] 1 W.L.R. 1361 at 1369. See too *Att-Gen v Blake* [2001] 1 A.C. 268 at 283–284 (Lord Nicholls, referring to *Wrotham* damages as involving "the benefit gained by the wrongdoer"). Powerful academic commentators support this view: see R. Cunnington and D. Saidov, *Contract Damages: Domestic and International Perspectives* (Oxford: Hart, 2008) Chs 7 and 9 (A. Burrows and R. Cunnington respectively); D. Harris, D. Campbell ad R. Halson, *Remedies in Contract and Tort*, 2nd edn (Cambridge: Cambridge University Press, 2002), pp.255–262; C. Rotherham, "Wrotham Park damages and accounts of profits: compensation or restitution?" [2008] L.M.C.L.Q. 25; and D. Xu, "Negotiating damages: rationalising the compensatory view" [2020] J.B.L., 561.

[89] One reason to reject the "gain" analysis is that the "gain" supposedly made by a defendant is itself largely artificial. If what was taken or used would not have been made available at any price, the suggestion that the defendant has saved what he could never have paid is somewhat unreal. Another is that if "buy-out" damages are gain-based, it is not immediately apparent why the defendant is not stripped of his whole gain, as in account of profits (cf. E. McKendrick, "Breach of Contract, Restitution for Wrongs, and Punishment" in A. Burrows and E. Peel (eds), *Commercial Remedies: Current Issues and Problems* (Oxford: Oxford University Press, 2003), p.114 and the judicial discussion in *Stadium Capital Holdings v St Marylebone Properties Co Plc* [2010] EWCA Civ 952).

[90] See *Morris-Garner v One Step (Support) Ltd* [2018] UKSC 20; [2019] A.C. 649 at [59] (Lord Reed). For earlier statements see *Att-Gen v Blake* [2001] 1 A.C. 268 at 298 (Lord Hobhouse): also *WWF-World Wide Fund for Nature v World Wrestling Federation Entertainment Inc* [2006] EWHC 184 (Ch); [2006] F.S.R. 38 at [137] (Peter Smith J) and the same case in the CA at [2007] EWCA Civ 286; [2008] 1 W.L.R. 445 at [42] (Chadwick LJ). The Singapore Court of Appeal has reached a similar conclusion: *Turf Club Auto Emporium Pte Ltd v Yeo Boong Hua* [2017] SGCA 21; [2017] 2 S.L.R. 12. Note too M. McInnes, Gain, Loss and the User Principle [2006] R.L.R. 76.

[91] Cf. the case in tort where a defendant converts or uses a chattel, such as a car, which the owner never used and would never have sold, but instead allowed to rot in a garage. There seems no objection on principle to awarding the owner the value of the item, despite the lack of any superficial loss to him.

CHAPTER 27

SPECIFIC RELIEF: THE GRANT OF SPECIFIC PERFORMANCE

I. THE NATURE OF SPECIFIC REMEDIES

The remedies of damages and debt referred to above[1] seek to compensate for the **27-001** effects of a breach of contract through a monetary award to the claimant (or, in the case of debt, to effectuate payment of a promised sum). By contrast, specific remedies are aimed at ensuring that the performance or other benefit to which the claimant is entitled is forthcoming in specie. For largely historical reasons, there are two forms of specific remedy in the English law of contract, depending on whether the obligation which it is sought to enforce is positive or negative. Broadly, orders of specific performance exist to effectuate positive obligations, whereas injunctions serve the function of enforcing negative stipulations.[2] Although many of the same principles apply to both, they are sufficiently different to justify separate treatment. Hence specific performance will be dealt with in this chapter, and injunctions in Ch.28.

Both injunctions and specific performance developed historically as equitable and **27-002** not as common law remedies.[3] Despite the effects of the Judicature Act reforms, this has had three results which are still relevant today.

The first is that, in contrast to the position in many civilian jurisdictions,[4] injunc- **27-003** tions and specific performance are regarded as secondary remedies. The primary remedy for any breach of contract, whether past or future, and whether performance remains possible or not, is the common law response of damages. Only if, for some reason, damages are regarded as inadequate will any question arise of awarding a specific remedy in equity.

Secondly, it must always be borne in mind that, in common with other equitable **27-004** remedies, neither injunctions nor specific performance are available as of right. Although clear practices have grown up as to when they will or will not be granted, they remain ultimately discretionary remedies, and may always on principle be

---

[1] Chs 19–26.
[2] Confusingly, there is also the possibility of a mandatory injunction, which can be almost indistinguishable from and indeed can at times be interchangeable with, an order of specific performance. See below, para.28-024.
[3] Generally I. Spry, *Equitable Remedies*, 9th edn (London: Sweet & Maxwell, 2013), Ch.3.
[4] See generally H. Lando and C. Rose, "On the enforcement of specific performance in Civil Law countries" (2004) 24 *International Review of Law & Economics* 473. But the contrast is not as stark as it looks, since even in civil law jurisdictions there are limits on specific enforcement, and indeed claimants often prefer money remedies. Nevertheless this has not prevented English judges occasionally regarding the difference as an important one: e.g. *Co-Operative Insurance Society Ltd v Argyll Stores (Holdings) Ltd* [1998] A.C. 1 at 11 (Lord Hoffmann).

refused entirely or, if granted, made available only on such terms as the court thinks fit.[5]

27-005   Thirdly, although in most cases the equitable remedies of injunctions and specific performance exist simply as parallel remedies to those available at common law, there are not a few situations where the equitable remedies are not available but common law ones are,[6] or vice versa.[7]

27-006   Because of the form taken by injunctions and specific performance, which are orders from the court physically to perform a contractual obligation (or refrain from breaching it) on pain of punishment for contempt, both injunctions and specific performance are on principle independent of the solvency of the defendant. In effect, therefore, the claimant who can establish his right to one or other of these remedies obtains a preferential claim in a defendant's insolvency. To that extent he is in a better position than a claimant who finds himself limited to a mere money award, since the latter must in effect tolerate the breach in the knowledge that all he will receive in respect of it is a worthless claim against a bankrupt defendant.[8] This feature of specific remedies is clearly highly important in practice: how far it actually affects the court's discretion to grant these remedies is discussed below.[9]

II.   THE NATURE OF SPECIFIC PERFORMANCE

27-007   The jurisdiction to order that a contract be performed in specie[10] is an ancient one, previously confined to the Court of Chancery but now available in all jurisdictions.[11] Specific performance normally[12] takes the form of an order by the court to the defendant to perform his contractual[13] obligation[14] (a term which, for these purposes, includes an arbitration award). The order operates in personam, and

---

[5]   A rule that, moreover, cannot be ousted by the parties: thus it has been held that the courts remain free to ignore even an express stipulation that a contract shall be specifically enforceable. See e.g. *Quadrant Visual Communications Ltd v Hutchinson Telephone (UK) Ltd* [1993] B.C.L.C. 442 at 451 at 452 (Stocker and Butler-Sloss LJJ).

[6]   For instance, in the case of employment contracts, where legislation forbids specific enforcement against the employee: below, para.27-079.

[7]   Notably in the case of relief against forfeiture and similar jurisdictions: see below, para.27-102.

[8]   This is particularly significant in the case of a pre-paying buyer of goods who has not yet become owner of them. If entitled to specific performance he obtains precisely what he sought: if not so entitled, then (subject today to s.20A of the Sale of Goods Act 1979) he loses everything. Cf. *Re Wait* [1927] 1 Ch. 606.

[9]   See para.27-086 ff.

[10]   It is sometimes suggested that the term "specific performance" should properly be reserved for orders to perform executory contracts, and that once a contract has been fully executed orders to ensure that one or other party receives his entitlement under it are merely orders analogous to specific performance: see R. Meagher, W. Gummow and J. Lehane, *Equity: Doctrines and Remedies*, 4th edn (London: LexisNexis, 2002), paras 20-005–20-020. But apart from taxonomical elegance, it is hard to see any reason to continue to draw this distinction, and it will be ignored here.

[11]   See now Senior Courts Act 1981 s.49; County Courts Act 1984 s.38. For the history, see G. Jones and W. Goodhart, *Specific Performance*, 2nd edn (London: Tottel, 1996), p.6 ff. Arbitrators presumptively have powers to order specific performance, save in regard to the transfer of land or an interest in it: Arbitration Act 1996 s.48(5)(b). Such orders may then if necessary be given effect by the court. Furthermore s.44 of the same Act allows courts to make interim orders in the nature of specific performance in certain circumstances in support of arbitrations.

[12]   Though not always. Thus, a right to specific performance may also be pleaded as a defence, for instance to a claim for possession of premises to which the defendant claims to be contractually entitled: e.g. *Kingswood Estate Co v Anderson* [1963] 2 Q.B. 169.

[13]   Obligations analogous to contracts may also be so enforced. The obvious example is arbitration awards: see R. Merkin, *Arbitration Law* (London: Informa, 2004) para.19.6, and e.g. *Blackett v Bates*

breach of it is a contempt, opening the defendant to a number of penalties including fines, imprisonment and sequestration.[15]

As with injunctions, an order in the nature of specific performance can in a suitable case be made on an interim basis. For example, the buyer of a ship may be ordered to release funds in order to protect the interests of the seller pending a final resolution of a claim by the latter for specific performance.[16] Conversely the buyer of a ship who may be entitled on one of two separate bases, involving payment of different amounts, may obtain an interim order for transfer of the vessel pending a decision on the parties' rights.[17]

27-008

In contrast to certain civil law jurisdictions,[18] there is no general power in the court to procure the physical results envisaged by the contract (for example, the forcible seizure by a state organ of an asset agreed to be sold followed by its delivery to the buyer); it follows that in theory an obstinate defendant prepared to go to prison can effectually prevent the claimant obtaining his contractual entitlement.

27-009

Nevertheless, in three ways this is now qualified. First, once a claimant has obtained an order of specific performance, then if the performance concerned is such as can be provided by a third party, rules of court allow the claimant, on further application to the court, to pay the third party to do what the defendant has been ordered to do and then recoup the cost incurred from the defendant as if it were a judgment debt.[19] Secondly, in so far as an order of specific performance involves an order to someone to execute a "conveyance, contract or other document", it can no longer be frustrated by a recalcitrant defendant, since the court now has the power to execute the necessary paperwork in the defendant's name.[20] And thirdly, there is authority that where a defendant is bound in certain events to agree to the

27-010

(1865) L.R. 1 Ch. App 117 and *Bremer Oeltransport GmbH v Drewry* [1933] 1 K.B. 753 at 759 (Slesser LJ). (On this subject generally, see the useful summary in *London Steam-Ship Owners' Mutual Insurance Association Ltd v Spain* [2021] EWCA Civ 1589; [2022] 1 W.L.R. 3434 at [107]–[121].) But there are other examples too, such as planning agreements (*Wycombe DC v Williams* [1995] 3 P.L.R. 19).

[14] It was once thought that only a contract as a whole could be specifically enforced, and that part only could not (e.g. *Merchants' Trading Co v Banner* (1871) L.R. 12 Eq 18 at 23 and *Kerr on Injunctions*, 6th edn (London: Sweet & Maxwell, 1927), p.409). But this view was flatly contradicted by a number of cases, such as *Lytton v Gt Northern Ry Co* (1856) 2 K & J 394 (enforcement of contract to build a railway spur, but not of parallel obligation to maintain it); and it now seems best regarded as a long-exploded heresy. See G. Jones and W. Goodhart, *Specific Performance*, 2nd edn (London: Tottel, 1996), pp.57–60 and *Rainbow Estates Ltd v Tokenhold Ltd* [1999] Ch. 64 at 73 (Lawrence Collins QC).

[15] See CPR 81.

[16] *The Messiniaki Tolmi (No.2)* [1982] Q.B. 1248 esp at 1265–1269 (Ackner LJ), the point being accepted as right in the House of Lords at [1983] 2 A.C. 787. See too the much earlier *Smith v Peters* (1875) L.R. 20 Eq. 511 (agreement to sell house at valuation: interim order to seller to let the valuer in).

[17] *Gravelor Shipping Ltd v GTLK Asia M5 Ltd* [2023] EWHC 131 (Comm).

[18] On which see K. Zweigert and H. Kötz, *Introduction to Comparative Law*, 3rd edn (Oxford: Clarendon Press, 1998) (tr. Tony Weir), pp.470–479. Original materials for English, Civil Law and other approaches are usefully provided in T. Kadner-Graziano, *Comparative Contract Law* (Basingstoke: Palgrave-Macmillan, 2009), pp.241–265.

[19] See CPR 70.2A.

[20] Senior Courts Act 1981 s.39. This is particularly significant in the case of land, the transfer of which invariably requires the execution of some such document. But it extends further: see, e.g. *Bank of Scotland Plc v Waugh (No.2)* [2014] EWHC 2835 (Ch) (court execution of deed necessary to turn equitable mortgage into legal charge), and *The Messiniaki Tolmi (No.2)* [1983] 2 A.C. 787 (execution in the defendant's name of document necessary to allow claimant to operate letter of credit).

release of funds held by a third party also before the court, then an order of the court requiring him to do so is self-executing. That is, it operates ipso facto as authority to the third party to release the funds.[21]

III. Specific Performance and Common Law Remedies

27-011   As mentioned above, the equitable remedy of specific performance is habitually referred to in England[22] as a secondary remedy, alternative to the right to recover damages for breach of contract, and available only if that right is inadequate to protect the claimant's interests. To some extent this is true. Thus if (for instance) the contract has been validly terminated together with all primary obligations arising under it, there can be no action for specific performance, for the simple reason that there is now nothing to enforce.[23] Nevertheless, as a matter of strict law the view just expressed is not entirely accurate. Technically, all that is required for equitable intervention is a contractual obligation regarded as valid and enforceable in equity.[24] Thus an order of specific performance may be issued, even though there has as yet been no breach of contract and hence there can be no action at law:[25] as an Australian court put it:

> "[P]roceedings for the specific performance of a contract which is of such a kind that it can be specifically enforced can be commenced as soon as one party threatens to refuse to perform the contract or any part thereof."[26]

27-012   And again, where relief against forfeiture is in issue, there may be specific performance on the basis that, even if the contract may have become ineffective at law, it remains valid in equity.[27]

27-013   Just as specific performance may be available where common law remedies are not, and vice versa, it is equally true that there is no objection as such to both be-

---

[21] *Tandrin Aviation Holdings Ltd v Aero Toy Store LLC* [2010] EWHC 40 (Comm); [2010] 2 Lloyd's Rep. 668 at [64], applying the maxim that equity regards as done that which ought to be done.

[22] Note that the approach in civilian Scotland (where the remedy is known as specific implement) is somewhat different. For a trenchant declaration of Scots independence on the matter, see Lord Rodger in *Highland & Universal Properties Ltd v Safeway Properties Ltd*, 2000 S.C. 297 at 299 ("in Scotland the breach of a contract for the sale of a specific subject such as landed estate gives the party aggrieved the legal right to sue for implement"); also *AMA (New Town) Ltd v Law* [2013] CSIH 61; 2013 S.C. 608 at [24] (Lady Dorrian). Some Scottish commentators go further and characterise specific implement as the primary remedy for refusal to perform (e.g. T. Smith, *A Short Commentary on the Law of Scotland* (Edinburgh: W. Green & Son Ltd., 1962), p.854): but the better view is that it is simply a remedy of co-ordinate status—see W. McBryde, *The Law of Contract in Scotland*, 3rd edn (Edinburgh: W. Green & Son Ltd., 2007), para.23–09.

[23] See, e.g. *Lavery v Pursell* (1888) L.R. 39 Ch. D. 508 (contract for sale of building salvage lawfully terminated: hence no specific performance).

[24] "It must be remembered that, although the remedy of specific performance is commonly applied in aid of a legal right, it extends to cases where, for one reason or another, there is no remedy at law, as well as to cases where the remedy at law is inadequate." See *J C Williamson Ltd v Lukey & Mulholland* (1931) 45 C.L.R. 282 at 297 (Dixon J).

[25] *Hasham v Zenab* [1960] A.C. 316 (order against vendor who repudiated almost before contractual ink was dry and well before conveyance due); *Airport Industrial GP Ltd v Heathrow Airport Ltd* [2015] EWHC 3753 (Ch); and also *Roy v Kloepfer Wholesale Hardware and Automotive Co Ltd* [1952] 2 S.C.R. 465. An action for damages will lie in such circumstances only if the claimant accepts the repudiation: for a rare example of where this happened, see *Grant v Dawkins* [1973] 1 W.L.R. 1406.

[26] *Turner v Bladin* (1951) 82 C.L.R. 463 at 472 (Williams, Fullagar & Kitto JJ).

[27] Below, para.27-102.

ing awarded concurrently. For example, it is open to a court to make parallel awards of damages and specific performance in respect of different obligations within the same contract, as where lessee under a lease requiring the lessor to carry out improvements seeks specific performance of the lease itself and also damages for breach of the obligation to build.[28] Again, where a purchaser of land has to resort to specific performance proceedings to obtain the property the subject of the contract, he can in addition recover damages for losses resulting from late conveyance,[29] or from the seller's failure to discharge incumbrances.[30]

On the other hand, there may be cases where an award of damages is logically **27-014** inconsistent with a concurrent order of specific performance. So, for instance, where a party to a contract for the sale of land seeks damages for loss of bargain based on the assumption that the contract will not be performed at all, then while he may combine this with a *claim* for specific performance, he will at the time of judgment be put to his election.[31] This is because persisting in a claim for damages of this sort is tantamount to putting an end to the parties' primary obligations under the contract and replacing them with obligations to compensate: and once the contract is gone, there is nothing left specifically to enforce. Even here, however, the principle does not work the other way round. Even if a claimant elects to take, and receives, an order of specific performance, this leaves the contract on foot.[32] It is thus always open to him if for some reason this becomes abortive to fall back on his right to terminate the contract and claim damages on that basis.[33]

IV. SPECIFIC PERFORMANCE AND THIRD PARTIES

Normally the only person against whom a decree of specific performance can be **27-015** made is the person liable to perform the contract or other obligation. However, in so far as a specifically enforceable contract to sell an asset creates an equitable interest in that asset in the buyer, that interest is on principle enforceable against anyone into whose hands the asset may come, unless the latter is a good faith purchaser without notice.[34] In the case of land, however, it must be noted that this is subject to the rules of the Land Registration Act 2002, under which a registered proprietor generally takes free of unregistered equitable interests, including agreements for

---

[28] See *Fennings v Humphery* (1841) 4 Beavan 1. More recently, compare *Airport Industrial GP Ltd v Heathrow Airport Ltd* [2015] EWHC 3753 (Ch) (specific performance of agreement to construct car park, plus order to pay damages for delay in finishing it).

[29] *Jaques v Millar* (1877) 6 Ch. D. 153: *Jones v Gardiner* [1902] 1 Ch. 191 at 195; *Ford Hunt v Singh* [1973] 1 W.L.R. 738. Also *Phillips v Lamdin* [1949] 2 K.B. 33 at 44 (Croom-Johnson J).

[30] *Grant v Dawkins* [1973] 1 W.L.R. 1406.

[31] *Johnson v Agnew* [1980] A.C. 367 at 392 at 398 (Lord Wilberforce); see too the earlier Australian *McKenna v Richey* [1950] V.L.R. 360.

[32] To put the matter in another way, the maxim *transit in rem judicatam*, while correctly describing the effect of an award of damages on the underlying obligation, does not apply to the award of specific performance. See *Austins of East Ham Ltd v Macey* [1941] Ch. 338 at 341 (Lord Greene MR); *Johnson v Agnew* [1980] A.C. 367 at 393 (Lord Wilberforce).

[33] *Johnson v Agnew* [1980] A.C. 367 at 398 (Lord Wilberforce); *Mahmut v Jones* [2017] EWCA Civ 2362; [2018] 1 W.L.R. 6051 at [18] (Lewison LJ).

[34] E.g. *Taylor v Stibbert* (1794) 2 Ves 437; *Wright v Dean* [1948] Ch. 686 at 693 (Wynn-Parry J); *Webb v Pollmount Ltd* [1966] Ch. 584, esp at 597 (Ungoed-Thomas J); *Jones v Lipman* [1962] 1 WLR 832. Most cases concern land, but the principle applies equally to personalty (e.g. *Graham v O'Connor* (1895) 73 LT 712 (shares)).

sale, even if he knows about them.[35] On principle the same applies to the increasingly rare case of unregistered land, by virtue of the Land Charges Act 1972, requiring contracts for the sale of land to be registered against the land and avoiding them as against a purchaser for value if unregistered.[36]

V. THE AVAILABILITY OF SPECIFIC PERFORMANCE

27-016   Specific performance is, it seems, available as a matter of jurisdiction[37] for all contractual obligations of any kind,[38] including those enforceable only by virtue of the Contracts (Rights of Third Parties) Act 1999,[39] and despite the fact that, for some reason or other, there may be no action available at law.[40] In a few cases its availability is specifically established by legislation.[41] There are, however, three exceptional cases where it may not be granted. First, it may be specifically excluded by statute.[42] Secondly, it now seems clear that parties can validly contract that it shall not be available.[43] And thirdly, the principle that equity will not assist a volunteer means that it is unavailable to enforce an obligation entered into by deed where no other consideration is present.[44]

27-017   Where a defendant has a choice as to how to perform a contract, then, in parallel with the rule that damages are awarded on the basis of the least burdensome performance that the claimant could have demanded,[45] any order of specific performance must be limited to "the very minimum of that which is expressed in the terms creating the obligation".[46]

27-018   It must be stressed, however, that the above statement goes to jurisdiction only. It does not deal with the practice of the court, and indeed and the main significance

---

[35]   Land Registration Act 2002, ss.20, 29(1). See e.g. *Groveholt Ltd v Hughes* [2012] EWHC 3351 (Ch); [2013] 1 P. & C.R. 20.

[36]   E.g. *Midland Bank Trust Co Ltd v Green* [1981] A.C. 513.

[37]   It is sometimes thought that there is no jurisdiction to grant the remedy if damages are adequate. But the better view is that this is a matter of discretion, not jurisdiction: e.g. *Dalgety Wine Estates Pty Ltd v Rizzon* (1979) 141 C.L.R. 552 at 560 (Gibbs J), 573–574 (Mason J).

[38]   For sale of goods contracts, see below, para.27-024 ff.

[39]   See s.1(5) of that Act.

[40]   Above, para.27-005.

[41]   For example, Companies Act 2006 s.740 (contract to underwrite debenture issue, on which see below, para.27-071); Employment Relations Act 1999 Sch.1, para.39(6) (duty to bargain collectively in certain cases); Consumer Rights Act 2015 s.58 (certain obligations of trader to consumer).

[42]   Notably in employment contracts against the employee (Trade Union and Labour Relations (Consolidation) Act 1992 s.236); and in all cases against the Crown and foreign sovereigns: see Crown Proceedings Act 1947 s.21(1)(a) and State Immunity Act 1978 s.13(2)(a). Another example is s.735(3) of the Companies Act 2006 (no specific performance of contract to redeem shares unless available distributable profits to pay for them).

[43]   *Mills v Sportsdirect.com Retail Ltd* [2010] EWHC 1072 (Ch); [2010] 2 B.C.L.C. 143; also the earlier dicta of Leggatt LJ in *Co-operative Insurance Society Ltd v Argyll Stores (Holdings) Ltd* [1996] Ch. 286 at 294. Note, however, that while agreement may oust the court's discretion to *grant* the remedy it cannot exclude the converse discretion to *refuse* it: see at 451–452 (Stocker and Butler-Sloss LJJ), and below, para.27-021.

[44]   *Colyear v Mulgrave (Countess)* (1836) 2 Keen 81; *Jefferys v Jefferys* (1841) 1 Cr. & Ph. 138. The question whether the presence of a nominal, but legally adequate, consideration makes any difference remains open: see *Mountford v Scott* [1975] Ch. 258 at 261 (Brightman J), *Philip Morris Products Inc v Rothmans International Enterprises Ltd (Preliminary Issues)* (unreported 7 March 2000), Neuberger J.

[45]   See above, para.21-076.

[46]   *Wilson v Northampton & Banbury Junction Ry Co* (1874) 9 L.R. Ch. App. 279 at 285 (Lord Selborne).

of the law consists in the circumstances in which the court will, and will not, exercise its discretion to grant the order concerned; and to this we now turn.

VI. THE COURT'S DISCRETION

Generally

As stated above, the court has *jurisdiction* to order specific performance of any **27-019** contractual obligation. But jurisdiction is not the same as court practice; specific performance is a discretionary remedy; and the question whether a claimant can persuade the court to exercise its discretion in his favour can be of vital importance as regards the balance of power between the parties. A claimant who gets an order of specific performance not only gets precisely what he wanted, but in addition is spared problems that all damages claimants face, such as the difficulty of proving loss, or the risks of an insolvent defendant.[47] Furthermore, it has to be remembered that wider considerations than those arising simply between the parties may be in account. For instance, an order of specific performance may have the effect of forcing performance of a contractual obligation where there is a grotesque disproportion between the cost to the defendant of giving, and the prejudice to the claimant in receiving, that performance, or where for some other reason it might be argued that non-fulfilment with payment of damages was more socially desirable or economically efficient.[48] These are matters which the courts have been known to take into account,[49] though not particularly often.[50]

In practice, the court's approach to the question whether or not to grant an order **27-020** of specific performance, while theoretically open-ended, depends on two factors. First, in line with the approach to specific performance as a secondary rather than a primary response to non-performance, it must be shown that damages would be an inadequate remedy.[51] As Lord Hoffmann put it:

---

[47] For a general discussion see D. Friedmann, "Economic Aspects of Damages and Specific Performance Compared", in Ch.2 of D. Saidov and R. Cunnington (eds), *Contract Damages: Domestic and International Perspectives* (Oxford: Hart Publishing, 2008). The American literature is immense: good starting points are A. Kronman, "Specific Performance", 45 U. Chi. L. Rev. 351 (1978) and B. Schwartz, "The Case for Specific Performance", 89 Yale LJ 271 (1979).

[48] The so-called theory of "efficient breach," which suggests that assets ought to be delivered to those who value them most even if this involves breaking a contract to deliver them to someone else. The literature is vast. See e.g. R. Posner, *Economic Analysis of Law*, 6th edn (Boston, MA: Little, Brown & Company, 1992), 4.12; M. Eisenberg, "Actual and virtual specific performance, the theory of efficient breach, and the indifference principle in contract law", 93 Cal. L.Rev. 975 (2005). This has at times been the subject of some judicial scepticism: compare *Butler v Countrywide Finance Ltd* [1993] 3 N.Z.L.R. 623 at 635 (Hammond J).

[49] Cf. *Co-Operative Insurance Society Ltd v Argyll Stores (Holdings) Ltd* [1998] A.C. 1 at 15 (potential imbalance between parties a reason not to enforce specifically a "stay-open" covenant). For an example of grotesque disproportion, see *Zinc Cobham 1 Ltd v Adda Hotels* [2018] EWHC 1025 (Ch); [2018] L. & T.R. 36 (tenant's obligation to landlord to operate hotels to Hilton institutional standards would cost £100 million to fulfil, as against a damage to the reversion of £2–3 million in the event of non-fulfilment: no order).

[50] For a sceptical comment (though in a slightly different context), see Lord Nicholls in *Att Gen v Blake* [2001] 1 A.C. 268 at 283 ("it is not clear why it should be any more permissible to expropriate personal [i.e. contractual] rights than it is permissible to expropriate property rights"). Cf. C. Warkol, "Resolving the Paradox between Legal Theory and Legal fact: The Judicial Rejection of the Theory of Efficient Breach", 20 Cardozo L.R. 321 (1998) (an American article, but relevant in the English context).

[51] Statements are legion. Apart from what appears below, see too, e.g. *Adderley v Dixon* (1824) 1 Sim

"Specific performance is traditionally regarded in English law as an exceptional remedy, as opposed to the common law damages to which a successful plaintiff is entitled as of right. There may have been some element of later rationalisation of an untidier history, but by the 19th century it was orthodox doctrine that the power to decree specific performance was part of the discretionary jurisdiction of the Court of Chancery to do justice in cases in which the remedies available at common law were inadequate. This is the basis of the general principle that specific performance will not be ordered when damages are an adequate remedy."[52]

And secondly, even if this is shown, there are a number of separate factors that will encourage or discline the courts to grant the remedy in the particular case before it. These are dealt with in detail below.[53]

27-021   Occasionally an agreement will contain an explicit provision that specific performance shall be available, or that damages are acknowledged to be an inadequate remedy for a particular kind of breach. It is clear, however, that the discretion whether to grant specific relief is that of the court, and cannot be ousted by mere agreement.[54] Nevertheless, agreements of this sort may in cases of doubt inform the court's discretion. So in the Australian decision in *Lionsgate Australia Pty Ltd v Macquarie Private Portfolio Management Ltd*,[55] where the issue was whether an agreement by a substantial minority shareholder to accept a bid should be specifically enforced, Barrett J said:

"The court must have regard to the circumstances as a whole. In doing so, it will recognise that [the defendant], which now seeks to resist specific performance, saw fit to give an express contractual acknowledgment of the inadequacy of damages as a remedy."[56]

Specific relief was duly granted there.

The adequacy of damages

27-022   In practice the answer to the first question in the previous paragraph—whether damages should be regarded as inadequate—depends very much on the type of

---

& St 607 at 610 ("Courts of Equity decree the specific performance of contracts ... because damages at law may not, in the particular case, afford a complete remedy"—Sir John Leach); *Wilson v Northampton & Banbury Junction Ry Co* (1874) L.R. 9 Ch. App. 279 at 284 ("the Court gives specific performance instead of damages, only when it can by that means do more perfect and complete justice": Lord Selborne); *Beswick v Beswick* [1968] A.C. 58 at 100 (Lord Upjohn); and *Société des Industries Metallurgiques SA v Bronx Engineering Co Ltd* [1975] 1 Lloyd's Rep. 465 at 468 (Lord Edmund-Davies). See too E. Macdonald, "The inadequacy of adequacy: the granting of specific performance" (1987) 38 N.I.L.Q. 244.

52   *Co-Operative Insurance Society Ltd v Argyll Stores (Holdings) Ltd* [1998] A.C. 1 at 11. See too the slightly curious formulation of Lord Neuberger in *Cavendish Square Holding BV v Makdessi* [2015] UKSC 67; [2016] A.C. 1172: the claimant must "have a legitimate interest extending beyond pecuniary compensation for the breach". One might have thought, with respect, that any promisee had a legitimate interest in receiving performance rather than a cheque.

53   See para.27-039 ff.

54   *Warner Bros Pictures Inc v Nelson* [1937] 1 K.B. 209 at 221 (Branson J), *Quadrant Visual Communications Ltd v Hutchinson Telephone (UK) Ltd* [1993] B.C.L.C. 442 at 451–452 (Stocker and Butler-Sloss LJJ), and generally R. Carroll, "Agreements to Specifically Perform Contractual Obligations" (2012) 29 J.C.L. 155. See too *Lionsgate Australia Pty Ltd v Macquarie Private Portfolio Management Ltd* [2007] NSWSC 371 at [63] (Barrett J). Nor can a defendant demand an order of specific performance against himself rather than damages in lieu if the claimant wishes the latter: see *Hunt v Optima (Cambridge) Ltd* [2013] EWHC 681 (TCC), esp at [241] (the point was not argued on appeal at [2014] EWCA Civ 714; [2015] 1 W.L.R. 1346).

55   [2007] NSWSC 371.

56   [2007] NSWSC 371 at [63].

contract involved. It is therefore necessary to discuss the position as regards a number of different categories of agreement.

(i) Contracts concerning land For contracts for the sale of land,[57] and for the **27-023** grant of leases over land (other than the most insubstantial), specific performance is generally available as of course, even if not as of right.[58] Although this is supposedly on the ground that all pieces of land are unique, and that damages are an inadequate remedy for breaches of contracts in relation to an asset of possible sentimental value to the claimant,[59] the principle is general and applies even where such considerations are not present. Thus it does not matter that the land concerned is a semi-detached house identical to hundreds next to it, or a nondescript workshop on a featureless industrial estate; nor that the transaction is purely for investment, with no element of sentiment involved.[60] Similarly it makes no difference that it is the seller or lessor, and not the buyer or lessee, seeking relief;[61] though here it is arguable that an interest in getting rid of a possible millstone round one's neck is itself an adequate ground for regarding damages as inadequate.[62]

---

[57] Including dispositions that are not strictly sales, such as exchanges, or promises of houses after death in exchange for looking after the old or infirm: e.g. *Wakeham v Mackenzie* [1968] 1 W.L.R. 1175. Since equity acts in personam, an order may refer to land outside the jurisdiction: see the antique decision in *Penn v Lord Baltimore* (1750) 1 Ves. Sen. 444, and a more up-to-date example in *Heslop v Heslop* [2021] EWHC 2957 (Ch); [2022] W.T.L.R. 137. Similarly a defendant may be ordered to perform an act outside the jurisdiction: for a recent example, see *Société Générale de Banque au Liban SAL* [2022] EWHC 669 (QB) (order to carry out banking transfer in Lebanon).

[58] "It is not in dispute that, like other equitable relief, the specific performance of contracts is a discretionary remedy; but, in the ordinary case of a sale of land or buildings, the court normally grants it as of course": Goulding J in *Patel v Ali* [1984] Ch. 283 at 286. See too *Sudbrook Trading Estates Ltd v Eggleton* [1983] 1 A.C. 444 at 478 (Lord Diplock); *McCrystal v O'Kane* [1986] N.I. 123 at 132 (Murray J); *Mungalsingh v Juman* [2015] UKPC 38; [2016] 1 P. & C.R. 7 at [32] (Lord Neuberger).

[59] *Adderley v Dixon* (1824) 1 Sim & St 607 at 610 ("damages at law ... may not be a complete remedy to the purchaser, to whom the land may have a peculiar and special value": Sir John Leach); *Mungalsingh v Juman* [2015] UKPC 38; [2016] 1 P. & C.R. 7 at [32] (Lord Neuberger: "In the context of a contract for the sale of land, damages have traditionally not been regarded as an adequate remedy on the basis that each piece of land is unique"). Compare *Sudbrook Trading Estate Ltdv Eggleton* [1983] 1 A.C. 444 at 478 (Lord Diplock) (if agreement to sell land at valuation, nominal damages clearly derisory remedy).

[60] See *Pianta v National Finance & Trustees Ltd* (1964) 180 C.L.R. 146 (nondescript land bought by developer for subdivision and onsale). This is a curiosity adverted to in G. Jones and W. Goodhart, *Specific Performance*, 2nd edn (London: Tottel, 1996), pp.32–33; see also J. Kirwan, "Appraising a presumption: a modern look at the doctrine of specific performance in real estate contracts" 47 William & Mary L.Rev. 697 (2005). There is some authority to the contrary in Canada (e.g. *Domowicz v Orsa Investments Ltd* (1993) 15 O.R. (3d) 661 and *Southcott Estates Inc. v Toronto Catholic District School Board* [2012] SCC 51; [2012] 2 S.C.R. 675), on which, see M. McInnes, "Specific performance and mitigation in the Supreme Court of Canada" (2013) 129 L.Q.R. 165 and P. Davies, "Being specific about specific performance" [2018] Conv 324. A minority of US jurisdictions are prepared to be more questioning (e.g. *Suchan v Rutherford*, 410 P.2d 434 at 438 (Idaho 1966)).

[61] E.g. *Walker v Eastern Counties Ry Co* (1848) 6 Hare 594; *Maskell v Ivory* [1970] Ch. 502. So too where a surety for a lessee agrees to take over the lease on the latter's default: *RVB Investments Ltd v Bibby* [2013] EWHC 65 (Ch). Where the sale price is payable by instalments, the order can be combined with a declaration of an equitable lien over the property for the unpaid portion of the price: *Nives v Nives* (1880) 15 Ch. D. 649.

[62] See *Eastern Counties Ry Co v Hawkes* (1855) 5 HL Cas. 331 at 373 (Lord Campbell) and the discussion in I. Spry, *The Principles of Equitable Remedies*, 9th edn (London: Sweet & Maxwell, 2014), pp.64–65. An alternative explanation based on "affirmative mutuality", or the rule that if one party can obtain specific performance so can the other, is unconvincing (see the same discussion).

SPECIFIC RELIEF: THE GRANT OF SPECIFIC PERFORMANCE

27-024   **(ii)   Contracts for the sale or lease of goods**   The court has an explicit statutory power under s.52 of the Sale of Goods Act 1979 specifically to enforce contracts for the sale of goods, if specific or ascertained, at the suit of the buyer. But this limited express power is not, it seems, exhaustive. This is for the very good reason that when this provision was first enacted[63] it was fairly clearly intended to supplement, rather than restrict, an inherent power to enforce such sales generally, by making it clear that sales of specific and ascertained goods could be enforced even if ownership had not passed to the buyer.[64] Hence there is now little doubt that specific performance may embrace agreements to deliver purely generic goods,[65] and in addition that orders may be granted to the seller of goods as much as to the buyer.[66] And there also seems no doubt that contracts of hire, at least of non-generic goods, can similarly be enforced.[67]

27-025   In contrast to contracts for the sale of land, however, the presumption in sale of goods cases is against specific enforcement,[68] particularly so in the case of an "ordinary article of commerce".[69] So in *Fothergill v Rowland*[70] a Rhondda coal-owner successfully resisted an order to continue the supply of fuel to a neighbouring ironmaster, the coal subject to the contract being coal "of a very ordinary description not alleged to be a peculiar coal", which could perfectly well be had elsewhere, albeit much less cheaply.[71] And since then the courts have adopted a consistently similar attitude.[72] On the other hand, the practice is not applied entirely mechanically. Thus where the same contract provides for the sale of land and certain

---

[63]   In the form of s.2 of the Mercantile Law Amendment Act 1856.

[64]   See G. Treitel, "Specific Performance in the Sale of Goods" [1966] J.B.L. 211; also Parker J in *Jones & Sons Ltd v Tankerville (Earl)* [1909] 2 Ch. 440 at 445.

[65]   See G. Treitel, "Specific Performance in the Sale of Goods" [1966] J.B.L. 211 at 216–217, and G. Jones and W. Goodhart, *Specific Performance*, 2nd edn (London: Tottel, 1996), p.144; also *VTB Commodities Trading DAC v JSC Antipinsky Refinery v Petraco Oil Co SA* [2020] EWHC 72 (Comm); [2020] 1 W.L.R. 1227 at [73]–[74].

[66]   See *The Messiniaki Tolmi (No.2)* [1983] 2 A.C. 787, esp 797 (Lord Roskill) (ship); also *Record v Bell* [1991] 1 W.L.R. 853 (chattels where vendor of house obtained relief).

[67]   This is implicit in cases such as *The Jotunheim* [2004] EWHC 671 (Comm); [2005] 1 Lloyd's Rep. 181, deciding that relief against forfeiture—itself dependent on a jurisdiction to give specific performance—is available in such cases (there a demise charter of a ship).

[68]   This means, of course, enforcement by an order of specific performance. If legal ownership has passed to the buyer, specific relief is available under the Torts (Interference with Goods) Act 1977 s.3(2)(a), and it has been said that, at least if the seller is insolvent, this remedy should be given almost as of course. See the discussion in *Re BA Peters Plc (In Administration)* [2008] EWHC 2205 (Ch); [2010] 1 B.C.L.C. 110 at [65].

[69]   "Speaking generally, courts of equity did not decree specific performance in contracts for the sale of commodities which could be ordinarily obtained in the market where damages were a sufficient remedy": Atkin LJ in *Re Wait* [1927] 1 Ch. 606 at 630. Cf. the old case of *Pearne v Lisle* (1749) Amb 75 (no enforcement in specie of contract to sell slaves, since "others are as good"); also *Whiteley v Hilt* [1918] 2 K.B. 808 at 819 (Swinfen Eady MR) (though this latter was strictly a case of a demand for specific restitution of property, not specific performance of a contract to sell it).

[70]   (1873) L.R. 17 Eq. 132 (Strictly speaking the claim was to an injunction, but Jessel MR was in no doubt that, since the injunction would if granted amount to specific performance under another name, the same principles applied). See too *Hills v Croll* (1845) 2 Ph. 60 (no specific performance of contract to supply acid; hence no injunction to prevent breach by buyer of exclusive purchasing agreement); also *Heathcote v North Staffordshire Ry Co* (1850) 2 Mac & G 100 at 112 (Lord Cottenham).

[71]   See (1873) L.R. 17 Eq.132 at 139 (Jessel MR).

[72]   E.g. *Dominion Coal Co Ltd v Dominion Iron & Steel Co Ltd* [1909] A.C. 293 at 310–311; *Re Wait.*[1927] 1 Ch. 606 at 620–621 (Lord Hanworth MR); *Société des Industries Metallurgiques SA v Bronx Engineering Co Ltd* [1975] 1 Lloyd's Rep. 465 at 469 (Buckley LJ); *VTB Commodities Trading DAC v JSC Antipinsky Refinery v Petraco Oil Co SA* [2020] EWHC 72 (Comm); [2020] 1 W.L.R.

chattels on it, then common sense prevails over logic: if the court grants specific relief in respect of the former, it will not refuse it for the latter.[73]

Unique chattels are, however, treated differently from articles of commerce. **27-026** Specific performance of contracts relating to their disposal may be available: and this is so whether they be traded for aesthetic reasons—as with a rare work of art,[74] or an Adam door[75] or other collectible item[76]—or used commercially, as with an aircraft[77] or ship,[78] or some equally massive and specialised chattel, such as a part of an oil-rig.[79] So too if a chattel has some specific legal attribute, such as a licence or permit, attached to it, so that supply is limited.[80] Similarly, there is no doubt that analogous chattel leases may be enforced, as with the demise charter of a ship,[81] or the lease of an aircraft.[82] It may also be that a chattel is, so to speak, negatively unique: that is, that it has some particularly costly or hazardous characteristic such as gives the claimant a special interest in getting rid of it, so as to justify specific relief against a purchaser who has agreed to take it off his hands.[83] Nevertheless, it is probably true that even with unique chattels, the grant of specific performance

---

1227 at [77]–[79]. In the last-named case Phillips LJ at [77] pointed out that one difficulty with orders in respect of generic goods was possible subversion of insolvency law. To be fair, however, exactly the same complaint can be raised in respect of ascertained goods where property has not passed, where orders are explicitly allowed under s.52. Furthermore the power of an insolvent estate to disclaim onerous property (see Insolvency Act 1986 ss.178, 315) may well mean that the problem is more apparent than real.

73   E.g. *Record v Bell* [1991] 1 W.L.R. 853.

74   *Falcke v Gray* (1859) 4 Drewry 651 (Chinese vases: appropriateness of specific relief accepted, though denied on the facts). See too *Robins v Zwirner*, 713 F.Supp. 2d 367 (NY 2010) (painting by abstract portraitist Marlene Dumas, though suit failed for other reasons).

75   *Phillips v Lamdin* [1949] 2 K.B. 33 (order to reinstate in leased premises). See too the vendor and purchaser case of *Taylor v Hamer* [2002] EWCA Civ 1130; [2003] 1 P. & C.R. DG6 (antique flagstones).

76   As often the best illustrations are American. See *Ruddock v First Nat. Bank of Lake Forest* 559 N.E.2d 483 (Ill 1990) (antique clock); also *Huddleston v Williams* 103 So.2d 809 (Ala 1958) and *Harris v Barcroft* 543 P.2d 656 (Ore 1975) (pedigree dogs). But a nice English example is *Gregor Fisken Ltd v Carl* [2021] EWCA Civ 792; [2021] 4 W.L.R. 91 (unique Ferrari gearbox).

77   *Bristol Airport Plc v Powdrill* [1990] Ch. 744 at 759; also, *Qatar Airways Group QCSC v Airbus SAS* [2022] EWHC 1247 (TCC) (refusal to strike claim for specific performance of contract to supply numerous Airbus airliners to claimants' specifications). But not invariably: cf. *Shilmore Enterprises Corp v Phoenix 1 Aviation Ltd* [2008] EWHC 169 (QB) at [39] (nothing very unique about ordinary executive jet, so no specific performance).

78   *Behnke v Bede Shipping Co* [1927] 1 K.B. 649; *The Star Gazer* [1985] 1 Lloyd's Rep. 370; also *The Oro Chief* [1983] 2 Lloyd's Rep. 509 at 521. So too Lord Roskill had no doubt that a court would be prepared to issue such an order against the buyer of a ship: see *The Messiniaki Tolmi (No.2)* [1983] 2 A.C. 787 at 797. Presumably, however, this is limited to types not readily available (e.g. bulk carriers rather than mass-produced yachts): and in any case the rule is not absolute: see *The Stena Nautica (No.2)* [1982] 2 Lloyd's Rep. 336 where damages were held adequate in respect of a fairly ordinary car ferry.

79   See *International Finance Corp v DSNL Offshore Ltd* [2005] EWHC 1844 (Comm); [2007] 2 All E.R. (Comm) 305, esp at [60]–[61] (Colman J) (equitable lien available, which itself depends on whether specific performance would be).

80   *Dougan v Ley* (1946) 71 C.L.R. 142 (licensed Sydney taxi when licences at a premium).

81   *The Scaptrade* [1983] 2 A.C. 694 at 702–703 (Lord Diplock). See too generally *The Stena Nautica (No.2)* [1982] 2 Lloyd's Rep. 336; also *The Jotunheim* [2004] EWHC 671 (Comm); [2005] 1 Lloyd's Rep. 181 (relief from forfeiture available, implying the same for specific performance).

82   See Browne-Wilkinson VC in *Bristol Airport Plc v Powdrill* [1991] Ch. 744 at 759 ("no doubt that a court will order specific performance of a contract to lease an aircraft, since each aircraft has unique features peculiar to itself"); also G. Watt, "The proprietary effect of a chattel lease" [2003] Conv 61.

83   E.g. *The Messianiki Tolmi (No.2)* [1983] 2 A.C. 787 (scrap ship: specific relief applicable against buyer); Cf. *P & O Nedlloyd BV v Arab Metals Co (No.2)* [2006] EWCA Civ 1717; [2007] 1 W.L.R.

is by no means assured. Courts remain prepared in practice to ask whether damages are in fact a sufficient remedy and to refuse specific remedies if so persuaded.[84]

27-027 The courts' habit of differentiating between ordinary items of commerce and unique chattels is largely based on the assumption that the former, but not the latter, are relatively easy to obtain elsewhere. It may be, however, that because of very particular circumstances, even something that would normally be regarded as an ordinary item of commerce is not in fact readily available. What then? The approach has varied. Where the difficulty is due simply to the fact that goods have to be laboriously made to individual order, this has been held insufficient to persuade a court to give specific relief. Thus in *Société des Industries Metallurgiques SA v Bronx Engineering Co Ltd*[85] producers of a very specialised manufacturing machine costing over £250,000 proposed, when it was nearly ready for a buyer who had waited nine months, to sell it to a third party. The Court of Appeal refused any order against the sellers, the machine being, albeit unavailable immediately or over the counter, "a type of machinery which is obtainable in the market in the ordinary course upon placing an order" and hence to be classed as an ordinary item of commerce.[86] On the other hand, in a nearly contemporary decision[87] Goulding J had little hesitation in holding that where temporary external events had made a commodity (in this case petrol) virtually unavailable, then damages would be a hollow remedy for a garage wrongfully deprived of supplies and specific relief should be ordered. More recently Goulding J's view received some support from Christopher Clarke J in *Thames Valley Power Ltd v Total Gas & Power Ltd*[88] when he said he would not have hesitated to enforce specifically a long-term gas supply contract against a supplier who sought to cut off supplies because of a substantial rise in world prices. It is not entirely easy to see the distinction between these cases and the *Bronx* case; and it is respectfully suggested that in so far as they are in conflict, the view of Goulding and Christopher Clarke JJ is the better one.[89]

27-028 **(iii)** **Contracts for the disposal of intangible assets** With intangible assets, as

---

2288 (contract to take delivery of mildly but inconveniently radioactive cargo: no strikeout of specific performance claim).

[84] See, e.g. *The Stena Nautica (No.2)* [1982] 2 Lloyd's Rep. 336 (no order where threatened disposal of ship in breach of contract to someone other than buyer); also *Blue Sky One Ltd v Blue Airways LLC* [2009] EWHC 3314 (Comm) at [313] (Beatson J).

[85] [1975] 1 Lloyd's Rep. 465.

[86] [1975] 1 Lloyd's Rep. 465 at 469 (Buckley LJ).

[87] *Sky Petroleum Ltd v V.I.P. Petroleum Ltd* [1974] 1 W.L.R. 576. Cf. *Dougan v Ley* (1946) 71 C.L.R. 142 (transfer of licensed taxi where these in short supply); also the property case of *Howard E Perry & Co v British Railways Board* [1981] 1 W.L.R. 1375 (strikebound steel, where strike itself made steel almost unobtainable).

[88] [2005] EWHC 2208 (Comm); [2006] 1 Lloyd's Rep. 441. See particularly [63]: "It would in my view be entirely unjust that TVPL [the claimants] should be confined to a remedy in damages. The basis of the [contract] was that TVPL would be assured of a source of supply from a first-rank supplier at an agreed price for a 15-year term in order that they might in turn contract with [Heathrow Airport] for a similar term. To confine them to a claim in damages would deprive them of substantially the whole benefit that the contract was intended to give them." In fact the suppliers had expressed willingness to continue supplying if legally bound to do so, so the point was moot. On the other hand, more recently Phillips LJ, sitting at first instance, has said that orders in respect of generic goods should be very exceptional: *VTB Commodities Trading DAC v JSC Antipinsky Refinery v Petraco Oil Co SA* [2020] EWHC 72 (Comm); [2020] 1 W.L.R. 1227 at [77]–[79].

[89] Compare the attitude of US courts, which are often more generous with items such as machinery: e.g. *Indiana Shovel & Supply Co v Castillo*, 234 N.E.2d 867 (Ind 1968) and *Stephan's Machinery & Tool, Inc v D & H Machinery Consultants, Inc*, 417 N.E.2d 579 (Ohio 1979). It may, however, make a difference where what is being asked for is supply of a range of goods over time; in such a

a general rule specific enforcement is available, provided the asset involved is unique or not readily obtainable elsewhere. Thus, while relief is not normally available for quoted securities, for the reason that such a commodity "is always to be had by any person who chooses to apply for it in the market",[90] matters are different with sales of unquoted shares or bonds,[91] and even for quoted ones where the contract is for wholesale quantities of them that would not be straightforwardly available in the market,[92] or a fortiori where the arrangement is intended to remove them from the market entirely.[93] The same is true for agreements to allot shares to the holder of a convertible note;[94] to sell the whole, or a substantial part, of the shares in a company in the course of a takeover bid;[95] and for sales of businesses by transfer of all the share capital of a given company.[96] Conversely, a contract is equally susceptible to enforcement in specie if it involves a purchase of shares not otherwise readily disposable,[97] or an underwriting arrangement.[98]

Most of the cases concern sales of securities. But there is no doubt that the court's **27-029** willingness to grant specific performance goes beyond this, and applies to sales of other intangibles, such as businesses[99] or intellectual property rights.[100]

(iv) Contracts to provide indemnity and security Some kinds of contracts **27-030** require one party to furnish a third party guarantee, indemnity or other security. The

---

case the courts may well be unwilling to force two parties into a collaborative exercise that one does not want. Cf. *Vibrant Doors Ltd v Rohden UK Ltd* [2018] EWHC 1761 (QB).

[90] As Shadwell V-C observed in *Duncuft v Albrecht* (1841) 12 Sim 189 at 199. See too *Re Schwabacher* (1907) 98 L.T. 127 at 128 and *Assenagon Asset Management SA v Irish Bank Resolution Corp Ltd* [2012] EWHC 2090 (Ch); [2013] Bus. L.R. 266 at [65]–[66]. It makes no difference, it seems, that the agreement relates to a specific holding: see *Chinn v Hochstrasser (Inspector of Taxes)* [1979] Ch. 447 at 470 (Goff LJ).

[91] *Duncuft v Albrecht* (1841) 12 Sim 189 (railway company shares not readily available); *Langen v Wind Ltd v Bell* [1972] Ch. 685 (remedy available, though refused for other reasons); *Baker v Potter* [2004] EWHC 1422 (Ch), [2005] BCC 855; *Marksans Pharma Ltd v Peter Beck & Partner VVW GmbH* [2015] EWHC 1608 (Comm); *ANZ Exors & Trees Ltd v Humes Ltd* [1990] VR 615.

[92] See *Duncuft v Albrecht* (1841) 12 Sim. 189 at 199 (Shadwell V-C); *Mills v Sportsdirect.com Retail Ltd* [2010] EWHC 1072 (Ch); [2010] 2 B.C.L.C. 143 at [75] (Lewison J). Cf. *ANZ Executors & Trustees Ltd v Humes Ltd* [1990] V.R. 615 (damages hard to estimate because shares would give claimant enormous advantages as a hold-out owner: specific performance would be available).

[93] *Assénagon Asset Management SA v Irish Bank Resolution Corp Ltd* [2012] EWHC 2090 (Ch); [2013] Bus. L.R. 266 at [66].

[94] *ANZ Executors Ltd v Humes Ltd* [1990] VR 615. So too, by statute, with agreements to subscribe for debentures (see Currently the Companies Act 2006 s.740), since otherwise underwriting agreements would be severely undermined.

[95] See Street J in *Rudder v George Hudson Holdings Ltd* [1972] 1 N.S.W.L.R. 529 at 535 (availability of specific performance used as foundation for equitable lien); also *Lionsgate Australia Pty Ltd v Macquarie Private Portfolio Management Ltd* [2007] N.S.W.S.C. 371.

[96] *MSAS Global Logistics Ltd v Power Packaging Inc* [2003] EWHC 1393 (Ch).

[97] See *Welshtown Corp NV v M Real Oyj* [2004] EWHC 859 (Ch) and *Gaetano Ltd v Obertor Ltd* [2009] EWHC 2653 (Ch). The same reasoning applies, as logically it must, to agreements for the exchange of such securities: *Assenagon Asset Management SA v Irish Bank Resolution Corp Ltd (formerly Anglo Irish Bank Corp Ltd)* [2012] EWHC 2090 (Ch); [2013] Bus. L.R. 266 at [65]–[66].

[98] *Odessa Tramways Co v Mendel* (1878) 8 Ch. D. 235.

[99] *MSAS Global Logistics Ltd v Power Packaging Inc* [2003] EWHC 1393 (Ch); *Timmerman v Norvina Industries Pty Ltd* [1983] 1 Qd.R. 1.

[100] E.g. *Printing & Numerical Registering Co v Sampson* (1875) L.R. 19 Eq 462; *British Nylon Spinners Ltd v Imperial Chemical Industries Ltd* [1953] Ch. 19 (patents); *Western Front Ltd v Vestron Inc* [1987] F.S.R. 66; *Griggs Group Ltd v Evans* [2004] EWHC 1088 (Ch); [2005] Ch. 153 (copyright).

security may be required to be given either to the other contracting party, or alternatively to a third person. In such cases it is normally accepted that damages are not an adequate remedy and that therefore, at least prima facie, an order of specific performance[101] is available. This the case where, for example, a construction contract may require the provision of a performance bond.[102] Again, a voyage charter not infrequently requires the owner to deliver without production of a bill of lading if the charterer so demands, against a promise by the latter to provide a letter of indemnity or to post security in the event of the vessel being arrested by a third party claimant. Such agreements are regularly specifically enforced.[103]

27-031   **(v)**   **Contracts to perform acts or provide services**   Although most specifically enforceable contracts involve promises to buy, sell or lease assets, there is no bar on principle to specific enforcement of a contract to do something or perform a particular service.[104] A case where orders are fairly readily granted is where the act is relatively formal or minor, such as the signing of a deed,[105] a contract[106] or a release,[107] the preparation of a document,[108] or alternatively the appointment of an expert or valuer,[109] or the physical admission of a valuer employed by the other party,[110] in order to determine the sale price of an asset. So too with duties to provide access to information as part of some wider contract or arrangement (for example, a professional's duty to a client[111] or a duty arising as part of the sale of a busi-

---

[101] Sometimes expressed as a mandatory injunction, but nothing turns on this.

[102] See e.g. *Liberty Mercian Ltd v Cuddy Civil Engineering Ltd* [2013] EWHC 4110 (TCC); [2014] C.I.L.L. 3469. In practice the grant of relief may well be quixotic, since a defendant of doubtful credit is likely to find compliance impossible (as happened in this very case: see *Liberty Mercian Ltd v Cuddy Civil Engineering Ltd (No 2)* [2014] EWHC 3584 (TCC); [2015] B.L.R. 242). But the remedy remains available.

[103] See e.g. *The Laemthong Glory (No.2)* [2004] EWHC 2738 (Comm); [2005] 1 Lloyd's Rep. 632, esp at [51]–[52] (Cooke J); *Harmony Innovation Shipping Pte Ltd v Caravel Shipping Inc* [2019] EWHC 1037 (Comm); *Trafigura Maritime Logistics PTE Ltd v Clearlake Shipping PTE Ltd* [2020] EWHC 726 (Comm); *NaviG8 Chemicals Pool Inc v Aeturnum Energy International Pte Ltd* [2021] EWHC 3132 (Comm).

[104] See generally G. Jones and W. Goodhart, *Specific Performance*, 2nd edn (London: Tottel, 1996), p.184 ff.; see too *Price v Strange* [1978] Ch. 337 at 359 (scepticism from Goff LJ on supposed rule that building contracts not specifically enforceable).

[105] *Bank of Scotland Plc v Waugh (No.2)* [2014] EWHC 2835 (Ch) (order to execute deed necessary to transform equitable mortgage into legal charge); see too *Westfields Homes Ltd v Keay Homes (Windrush) Ltd* [2020] EWHC 3368 (Ch) (subordination deed).

[106] *CH Giles & Co Ltd v Morris* [1972] 1 W.L.R. 307. This may apply even though the contract itself would *not* be specifically enforceable (see the same case). But the unlikelihood of any grant of specific performance of the contract itself may well tell against specifically ordering its execution as a matter of discretion (*Chelsfield Advisers LLP v Qatari Diar Real Estate Investment Co* [2015] EWHC 1322 (Ch) at [92]).

[107] *Starlight Shipping Co v Allianz Marine, Aviation Versicherungs AG, The Alexandros T* [2014] EWHC 3068 (Comm); [2014] 2 C.L.C. 503 at [69] (execution of formal release of claim abroad following binding English agreement to settle it).

[108] *The Messiniaki Tolmi (No.2)* [1983] 2 A.C. 787 (document to enable seller of ship to complete transaction by drawing on letter of credit).

[109] E.g. *Merer v Fisher* [2003] EWCA Civ 747. Older authority that a court would never compel the appointment of an arbitrator was discountenanced by the House of Lords in *Sudbrook Trading Estate Ltd v Eggleton* [1983] 1 A.C. 444.

[110] As in *Smith v Peters* (1875) L.R. 20 Eq. 511. Cf. *Bruce v Carpenter* [2006] EWHC 3301 (Ch) at [26] (provision of information to arbitrator).

[111] *Lee v South West Thames Regional Health Authority* [1985] 1 WLR 845 at 851 (Lord Donaldson MR) (doctor); *Yasuda Fire & Marine Insurance Co. of Europe Ltd. v Orion Marine Insurance*

ness[112]) and an employee's undertaking to return information entrusted to him.[113] Other examples where such orders have been granted include agreements to execute a document to give particular rights, for example a separation deed settling the rights of a divorced couple,[114] a collateral warranty in a construction contract,[115] a s.106 planning agreement in a contract for the sale of land[116] or a document necessary to allow a claimant properly to operate a letter of credit.[117]

Nevertheless, the possibility of specific relief goes a long way beyond merely **27-032** formal acts. Thus, despite occasional insistences that the thing is impossible,[118] such orders have been issued in respect of contracts to build,[119] whether these relate to small individual works,[120] underground facilities,[121] or very large projects,[122] where the court has believed damages an inadequate recompense. Similarly, the understandable desire of a claimant to have what he has contracted for rather than money in lieu has been held to justify specific performance of a leasehold repairing covenant against a landlord[123] or a tenant,[124] or a contract to service an apart-

---

Underwriting Agency Ltd [1995] Q.B. 174 (underwriting agent); *Transport for Greater Manchester v Thales Transport & Security Ltd* [2013] EWHC 149 (TCC); [2013] B.L.R. 339 (IT contractor).

[112] *Alfa Finance Holdings AD v Quarzwerke GmbH* [2015] EWHC 243 (Ch). So too with an informational duty attached to a waste disposal project agreement: *Bucks CC v FCC Buckinghamshire Ltd* [2021] EWHC 2867 (TCC) [107]–[115].

[113] *Personal Management Solutions Ltd v Brakes Bros Ltd* [2014] EWHC 3495 (QB).

[114] *Hart v Hart* (1880–81) L.R. 18 Ch. D. 670.

[115] *Northern & Shell Plc v John Laing Construction Ltd* (unreported 4 October 2002) Q.B.D. at [9].

[116] *Redrow Homes Ltd v Martin Dawn (Leckhampton) Ltd* [2016] EWHC 934 (Ch).

[117] *The Messiniaki Tolmi (No.2)* [1983] 2 A.C. 787.

[118] E.g. *Merchants' Trading Company v Banner* (1871) L.R. 12 Eq. 18 at 22 (Lord Romilly MR); also *Hill v Barclay* (1810) 16 Ves. 402 (no specific performance of repairing covenant). Indeed, as late as 1982 Lord Diplock incautiously said, referring to a decree for specific performance of a contract to render services, that "in respect of that category of contracts, even in the event of breach, this is a remedy that English courts have always disclaimed any jurisdiction to grant" (*The Scaptrade* [1983] 2 A.C. 694 at 701).

[119] Against both the builder, and possibly the underwriter of a collateral warranty who agrees to complete the works if the former does not: see *Parkwood Leisure Ltd v Laing O'Rourke Wales and West Ltd* [2013] EWHC 2665 (TCC); 150 Con. L.R. 93 at [29] (Akenhead J) and also *Toppan Holdings Ltd v Simply Construct (UK) LLP* [2022] EWCA Civ 823 at [47] (Coulson J). In *Hounslow LBC v Twickenham Garden Developments Ltd* [1971] Ch. 233 at 251 Megarry J apparently suggested that a builder could compel a landowner to allow him to build. Sed quaere.

[120] Most of the older cases concern railway works. See e.g. *Storer v Great Western Ry Co* (1842) 2 Y & CCC 48 (accommodation bridge to be built when railway crossed Wallingford landowner's park): *Lytton v Gt Northern Ry Co* (1856) 2 K & J 394 (siding); also *Greene v West Cheshire Ry* (1871) L.R. 13 Eq 44 (station). Two neat twenty-first century analogues are *Waltham Forest LBC v Oakmesh Ltd* [2009] EWHC 1688 (Ch); [2010] J.P.L. 249 (planning agreement to build a public footbridge) and *Airport Industrial GP Ltd v Heathrow Airport Ltd* [2015] EWHC 3753 (Ch) (airport car park). See too generally *Hounslow LBC v Twickenham Garden Developments Ltd* [1971] Ch. 233 at 251 (Megarry J).

[121] *Carpenters Estate Ltd v Davies* [1940] Ch. 160 (sewerage).

[122] *Wolverhampton Corp v Emmons* [1901] 1 Q.B. 515 (housing estate). In *Channel Tunnel Group Ltd v Balfour Beatty Construction Ltd* [1993] A.C. 334 the House of Lords plainly assumed that a major civil engineering contract might be similarly enforceable.

[123] *Jeune v Queens Cross Properties Ltd* [1974] Ch. 97; *Gordon v Selico* (1986) 18 HLR 219. This applies even to a mere ground rent landlord: *Blue Manchester Ltd v North West Ground Rents Ltd* [2019] EWHC 142 (TCC); [2019] L. & T.R. 13. In the case of residential tenancies this rule is now statutory: Landlord and Tenant Act 1985 s.17 (supplemented in Wales since December 2022 by s.100 of the Renting Homes (Wales) Act 2016, applicable to both landlords' and tenants' obligations).

[124] *Rainbow Estates Ltd v Tokenhold Ltd* [1999] Ch. 64 (discountenancing Lord Eldon's dicta in *Hill v Barclay* (1810) 16 Ves. 402 at 405. For discussion see J.Brown and M.Pawlowski, "Specific performance of repairing obligations" [1998] Conv 495; M.Pawlowski, "Can a landlord compel a

ment block with a porter.[125] Nor is the possibility limited to land cases: there has on occasion been such an order in respect of (for example) a contract by a publisher to publish,[126] a site owner to carry advertising,[127] a lessor to keep leased machinery in repair,[128] or a bank to transfer a customer's funds abroad.[129]

27-033   On the other hand, despite the above examples specific performance of contracts to provide services remains comparatively rare, and there is clear authority that courts are instinctively unwilling to grant it.[130] This is because in practice it is not unlikely that one or more of the other counter-indications will apply, such as difficulty of supervision, the impossibility of enforcing willing trust and co-operation, or the reluctance of courts to require the carrying on of a business under pain of criminal penalties.

27-034   In addition to the above, by statute the court now has a specific power, where a seller in breach of contract provides unsatisfactory goods to a consumer, to issue an order of specific performance at the suit of the buyer requiring the goods to be repaired or replaced.[131] Although the legislation is ostensibly directed to confirming that the court has jurisdiction to act in such a case,[132] rather at influencing its discretion whether in fact to issue such an order, it may well have an indirect effect on the latter. It would not be surprising if the courts were to take the statutory provision as an indication that they should not readily decline to enforce obligations of this sort at the buyer's request.

27-035   **(vi)   Contracts involving payment of money**   For obvious reasons, specific performance is normally irrelevant to contracts to pay money (and indeed such an award must generally be avoided against an insolvent defendant, since otherwise the insolvency regime could be subverted). In the vast majority of cases an action for damages, or as the case may be, in debt, will amply vindicate the claimant's rights.[133] Moreover, in many cases actions for specific performance of money obligations will fall foul of other bars, such as the prima facie rule that contracts to lend or borrow cannot form the subject of specific relief.

27-036   Nevertheless, there is no doubt that on principle the remedy is available for

---

tenant to repair?" (2021) 25 L & TR 111. In Wales this rule is statutory under s.100 of the Renting Homes (Wales) Act 2016, referred to in the previous note.

[125] *Posner v Scott-Lewis* [1987] Ch. 25.

[126] See *Barrow v Chappell & Co Ltd* (1951) [1976] RPC 355.

[127] *Sportfive UK Ltd v Nottingham Forest Football Club Ltd* [2022] EWHC 3522 (Comm). Strictly speaking this involved interlocutory relief but the court clearly thought it likely that final relief would be granted.

[128] *John Fairfax & Sons Ltd v Australian telecommunications Commission* [1977] 2 N.S.W.L.R. 400.

[129] See a trio of cases emerging from the financial chaos in Lebanon in 2019: *Bitar v Bank of Beirut SAL* [2022] EWHC 2163 (QB) at [149] and *Bitar v Banque Libano-Francaise SAL* [2023] EWHC 17 (KB); also *Manoukian v Societe Generale de Banque Au Liban Sal* [2022] EWHC 669 (QB).

[130] See e.g. *Clarke v Price* (1819) 2 Wils 157; *Ryan v Mutual Tontine Westminster Chambers Association* [1893] 1 Ch. 116 at 123 (Lord Esher MR); and more recently, *The Scaptrade* [1983] 2 A.C. 694 at 700–701 (Lord Diplock).

[131] Consumer Rights Act 2015 s.58(2) (referring to the obligation to repair or replace, or repeat services, created by ss.23, 43 or 55). This power implements EU Directive 1999/44/EC of 25 May 1999 but survives Brexit.

[132] Which it is submitted it does anyway: para.27-024 above.

[133] See *Macob Civil Engineering Ltd v Morrison Construction Ltd* [1999] C.L.C. 739 at 748 (Dyson J); also *Durley House Ltd v Firmdale Hotels Plc* [2014] EWHC 2608 (Ch) (promise by company to pay tenant's rent to landlord: no mandatory order requiring company to pay landlord direct, bercause monetary order in favour of tenant sufficient vindication).

money obligations.[134] It thus can be had in special cases where a simple action in debt or damages will not do, as with promises to pay annuities[135] and pensions,[136] and for agreements to pay money where the payment is intended to provide a vital injection of cash into a joint venture.[137] Any lingering doubts as to the propriety of such orders were dispelled in *Beswick v Beswick*,[138] where an order was made for payments to a third party. There a son, in consideration of a transfer to him of his father's business, agreed to pay a pension to his mother. After the father's death, it was held that the father's estate (represented by the mother) could specifically enforce payment, thus escaping a then[139] otherwise awkward issue of privity of contract. On a similar basis, it has been said that specific performance is available to an employee to force his employer to make contributions to his pension fund,[140] in the same way as it is available to the employer to compel contractual payments from the fund to the pensioner.[141]

In addition, where a principal debtor promises a surety to hold him harmless, **27-037** there is an ancient jurisdiction[142] to grant the surety an equitable remedy of exoneration, ordering the principal debtor to pay the debt.[143] This exists on the understandable basis that payment followed by a right to recoupment from a debtor of possibly doubtful solvency is no proper vindication of a right to be spared the necessity to pay in the first place.

Although most of the above cases concern special instances of obligations to pay **27-038** money, it nonetheless seems clear that the court may equally give an order of specific performance whose only effect is to require payment of a given sum by the defendant to the claimant, and indeed where an action of debt would lie just as well. Thus where a contract of sale is specifically enforceable at the suit of the purchaser, it is equally so enforceable at the instance of the vendor even if the latter has already performed, so that the only obligation left unperformed is payment of the price.[144] In the case of obligations to pay cryptocurrency, where there is some doubt whether

---

[134] See *Beswick v Beswick* [1968] A.C. 58; *Schorsch Meier GmbH v Hennin* [1975] Q.B. 416 at 425 (Lord Denning MR); *Miliangos v George Frank (Textiles) Ltd* [1976] A.C. 443 at 467 (Lord Wilberforce); *Durley House Ltd v Firmdale Hotels Plc* [2014] EWHC 2608 (Ch) at [123].

[135] *Swift v Swift* (1841) 3 Ir Rep Eq 267; *Peel v Peel* (1869) 17 WR 586 (the latter strictly speaking involving specific performance of an arbitral award which itself had ordered payment of an annuity: but the point is the same).

[136] *British Telecommunications Plc v Royal Mail Group Ltd* [2010] EWHC 8 (QB) at [38] (Edwards-Stuart J); see too the earlier *Beswick v Beswick* [1968] A.C. 58, below. Both cases involved promises to pay a third party: but a fortiori an order should be available to enforce payment where the claimant is the pensioner himself: see below.

[137] *Metrogem Ltd v Corrett* (unreported 22 May 2001) Chancery Division.

[138] [1968] A.C. 58. See too *Woodar Investment Ltd v Wimpey Construction UK Ltd* [1980] 1 W.L.R. 277 at 293.

[139] But not now: Contracts (Rights of Third Parties) Act 1999 s.1(1).

[140] *The Halcyon Isle (No.1)* [1977] Q.B. 14 at 24 (Brandon J) (though no order for other reasons).

[141] See *British Telecommunications Plc v Royal Mail Group Ltd* [2010] EWHC 8 (QB), above.

[142] Dating at least to the seventeenth century: *Ranelaugh v Hayes* (1683) 1 Vern 189.

[143] E.g. *Ascherson v Tredegar Dry Dock & Wharf Co Ltd* [1909] 2 Ch. 401; *Thomas v Nottingham FC* [1972] Ch. 596; *Moschi v Lep Air Services Ltd* [1973] A.C. 331 at 348 (Lord Reid). So too with a co-surety: *Wolmershausen v Gullick* [1893] 2 Ch. 514. See G.Andrews & R.Millett, *The Law of Guarantee*, 7th edn (London, Sweet & Maxwell, 2015) para.10-025 ff.

[144] See *Cogent v Gibson* (1864) 33 Beav. 557 (specific performance of obligation to pay for patent); *Turner v Bladin* (1951) 82 C.L.R. 463, esp at 473 (Williams, Fullagar and Kitto JJ) (price of land); R. Meagher, W. Gummow and J. Lehane, *Equity: Doctrines and Remedies*, 4th edn (London: LexisNexis, 2002), para. 20–045.

curial monetary remedies are available, it has been assumed, it is suggested correctly, that a court can in a suitable case award specific performance.[145]

Adequacy of damages: Other factors

27-039 **(i) The ability of the claimant to obtain the contracted benefit elsewhere** We have seen that in respect of contracts to buy, sell and lease property the question whether specific relief is available depends, to a greater or lesser extent,[146] on whether equivalent performance is available elsewhere. But the principle is general. Thus it applies to licences to use land, whose respect may be compelled, but only provided the claimant cannot obtain equivalent advantages elsewhere.[147] Similarly too with obligations to build. While performance is fairly readily compelled where the works are to take place on the defendant's land,[148] it is different with the claimant's land, since he can normally get the job done himself by someone else at the defendant's expense.[149] Reasoning of this sort may also explain why time and voyage charterparties are not specifically enforced in the case of ships:[150] however unique the ship, these are essentially contracts simply to provide carriage or shipping space, and these are generally available in the market at fairly short notice, albeit at considerable trouble and expense.

27-040 Just as a claimant who can procure the promised benefit elsewhere is likely to be refused specific performance, so also with the claimant who has another more straightforward means of enforcement of his rights. So mariners were refused an order against their employers to pay pension contributions, on the basis that they had a maritime lien against the ship for their wages, which included such payments, and could arrest her to enforce their rights.[151]

27-041 **(ii) Difficulties over the measure of damages** To the extent that damages would be unlikely properly to make good the effects of non-performance, thus far courts may infer that they are an inadequate remedy and hence specific enforcement is appropriate. This may be for a number of reasons. One is practical difficulties of quantification: thus in an old case where a buyer sought specific performance

---

[145] See the discussion in the Singapore case of *B2C2 Ltd v Quoine Pty Ltd* [2019] SGHC(I) 03; [2019] 4 S.L.R. 17 at [254]–[256], concerning a duty to pay Bitcoin. On the facts the remedy was refused and the claimant left to a remedy in damages. The issue was not argued on appeal at [2020] SGCA(I) 02; [2020] 2 S.L.R. 20. Note too the Law Commission's Consultation Paper No 256 on Digital Assets, para.19.16. But for a contrary view, asserting that this would amount to enforcing specifically a contract to provide a service, see A.Dickinson, *Cryptocurrencies and the Conflict of Laws*, in D.Fox and S.Green (eds), *Cryptocurrencies in Public and Private Law* (Oxford University Press 2019), para.5.92.

[146] Hence with land the presumption that this criterion is satisfied is much stronger: above, para.27-023 ff.

[147] See *Verrall v Great Yarmouth Borough Council* [1981] Q.B. 202 (use of central hall for political meeting); *Ryanair Ltd v SR Technics Ireland Ltd* [2007] EWHC 3089 (QB) (contract for use of hangar space, a commodity in short supply at Dublin Airport). See in particular Gray J at [170].

[148] Above, para.27-031. See, for a recent case where this feature was stressed, *Airport Industrial GP Ltd v Heathrow Airport Ltd* [2015] EWHC 3753 (Ch) (duty of lessee to construct car-park: lessor had no right of re-entry for failure to do so; order granted).

[149] See *North East Lincolnshire BC v Millenium Park (Grimsby) Ltd* [2002] EWCA Civ 1719 at [16] (Rix LJ).

[150] Effectively put beyond doubt in *The Scaptrade* [1983] 2 A.C. 694.

[151] *The Halcyon Isle (No.1)* [1977] Q.B. 14. But, with respect, this seems questionable: unless one means of enforcement is vastly easier than the other, it is arguable that the choice of which to employ ought to lie with the claimant.

of a contract to sell a German ship, Mellish LJ thought it a significant argument in favour of the remedy that it would be "almost impossible for him to prove in Hamburg how much the ship was worth".[152] Another is where the claimant's would-be loss more or less defies money quantification, as where the claimant is a public authority and the contractual benefit lost is social rather than pecuniary. Thus, the prejudice to a municipality when a speculative builder broke his promise to build a housing estate on land conveyed to him for the purpose was, it was said, something that "cannot adequately be estimated by pecuniary damages",[153] from which it was readily inferred that the case was one for specific performance.

Another factor in favour of specific performance is where the rules of damages, **27-042** at least without good reason,[154] distort the process of adequate compensation. *Beswick v Beswick*[155] is one obvious illustration. A father on retirement transferred the family business to his son, the latter agreeing to pay his mother a pension for life. On the father's death the son sought, in admitted breach of contract, to discontinue the pension. The rules of privity of contract as they then stood[156] meant that the mother herself could not sue at common law, and that if she sued for damages on behalf of the father's estate (of which she was executrix) the damages would be nominal, since the estate had suffered no loss. Members of the House of Lords variously referred to this as "grossly unjust" and "plainly inadequate"[157], and had no hesitation on that ground in awarding specific performance to the estate, thus compelling the son to continue paying.

(iii) The enforceability of a damages award: judgment-proof defend- **27-043** **ants** It now seems clear that the fact that the defendant may not be good for an award of damages may itself incline the court towards specific performance.[158] This in granting specific performance of a contract to provide security, Ransey J has said that "where, as here, the chances of a judgment being satisfied cannot be rated as other than questionable, damages would prima facie not be an adequate remedy;"[159] and the same conclusion was drawn more recently by Foxton J where the seller of a ship was a sanctioned Russian entity from whom extracting payment of any damages award would be problematical.[160]

(iv) Whether limiting the claimant to a claim in damages will deprive him of **27-044** **a substantial part of the contractual benefit** A contractual obligation may be entered into precisely to save the claimant expense or trouble: and if so, this seems

---

152 *Hart v Herwig* (1872–73) L.R. 8 Ch. App. 860 at 866. Cf. *ANZ Executors & Trustees Ltd v Humes Ltd* [1990] V.R. 615.
153 *Wolverhampton Corp v Emmons* [1901] 1 Q.B. 515 at 523 (A.L. Smith, MR).
154 Things are different if there is good reason. Thus if Parliament has put limits on abusive claims for damages for non-repair of demised premises, as in the Leasehold Property (Repairs) Act 1938 s.1(5), specific performance should not be used to subvert these limits: *Rainbow Estates Ltd v Tokenhold Ltd* [1999] Ch. 64 at 73.
155 [1968] A.C. 58. See para.27-035 above.
156 But no longer: see now the Contracts (Rights of Third Parties) Act 1999.
157 [1968] A.C. 58 at 73, 81 (Lords Reid and Hodson).
158 I. Spry, *The Principles of Equitable Remedies*, 9th edn (London: Sweet & Maxwell, 2014), pp.70–71.
159 See *Liberty Mercian Ltd v Cuddy Civil Engineering Ltd* [2013] EWHC 4110 (TCC) at [18]; compare the earlier *Evans Marshall & Co Ltd v Bertola SA (No.1)* [1973] 1 W.L.R. 349 at 380–381 (Lord Denning MR).
160 *Gravelor Shipping Ltd v GTLK Asia M5 Ltd* [2023] EWHC 131 (Comm) at [99].

to be a factor in favour of specific performance. Thus in *The Laemthong Glory*[161] charterers of a ship agreed that if she were arrested in certain circumstances (which in the event arose) they would provide bail. Cooke J had no hesitation in specifically enforcing this obligation: its object was to ensure the owners got their ship back and could continue to use it, and this would be largely defeated were they to be left to a remedy in damages. Again, this is the thinking behind the rule that a promise by a borrower to provide security will nearly always be enforced once the loan has been made:[162] and behind cases such as the unreported *Hurst-Bannister v New Cap Reinsurance Co Ltd*,[163] where it was said that there was every reason why a court should specifically enforce a contract by a payee to place monies received in a segregated *Quistclose* account[164] for the benefit of the payer.

27-045 **(v) Promises to provide security** Promises aimed creating security over a particular asset fall into a very special category,[165] since in the absence of specific enforcement—or at least the proprietary effect associated with specific enforceability—their object would be entirely defeated. The leading case is *Holroyd v Marshall*.[166] There a factory owner agreed to transfer to trustees for a creditor any future machinery he might put in. The House of Lords held that this gave the trustee a valid equitable security in the machinery as and when installed, good against the industrialists execution creditors. And the reason (according to Lord Westbury) was that the contract was "one of that class of which a Court of Equity would decree the specific performance".[167]

27-046 There is a strong argument that, despite Lord Westbury's view, the equitable security in such cases arises automatically from the agreement and has nothing to do with the law of specific performance.[168] Nevertheless, the orthodox view for the moment remains that, at least technically, the availability of specific relief remains essential to perfect the creditor's interest.[169] Hence where A promises to transfer an

---

161 [2004] EWHC 2738 (Comm); [2005] 1 Lloyd's Rep. 632.

162 E.g. *Hermann v Hodges* (1873) L.R. 16 Eq 18. See below, para.27-045.

163 Unreported 10 December 1999 Ch. D. See too *Lexington Insurance Co v Flashpoint Ltd* (unreported 19 January 2001) Comm Ct (obligation to place monies in accounts over which plaintiffs had security rights).

164 That is, a trust account pending the actual use of monies for the purpose for which they were paid over. See *Barclays Bank Ltd v Quistclose Investments Ltd* [1970] A.C. 567.

165 See generally J. Keeler, "Some Reflections on Holroyd v Marshall" (1969) 3 *Adelaide Law Review* 360.

166 (1862) 10 HL Cas 191.

167 (1862) 10 HL Cas 191 at 211. See too *Joseph v Lyons* (1884) L.R. 15 Q.B.D. 280 at 285 (Cotton LJ).

168 Compare Lord M'Naghten in *Tailby v Official Receiver* (1888) 13 App. Cas. 523 at 547. The argument is made by one of the present authors in A. Tettenborn, "Security over personalty: property, obligation and specific performance" (2022) 138 L.Q.R. 101.

169 See for example *Palmer v Carey* [1926] A.C. 703 at 706–707, referring to the "familiar doctrine of equity that a contract for valuable consideration to transfer or charge a subject matter passes a beneficial interest by way of property in that subject matter if the contract is one of which a Court of equity will decree specific performance", and the forthright statement of Mason CJ and Dawson J in *Bahr v Nicolay (No.2)* (1988) 164 C.L.R. 604 at 612 ("The existence and extent of the purchaser's equitable estate or interest in the property the subject of a contract of sale is commensurate with his ability to specifically enforce the contract."). And this was certainly the assumption behind cases such as *Thames Guaranty Ltd v Campbell* [1985] Q.B. 210.

asset to B by way of security for an obligation, B only obtains an effective security in so far as A's promise is specifically enforceable.[170]

However, it seems that once the underlying loan has been made, then specific **27-047** performance will run almost as of course, whatever kind of property is involved,[171] unless there is a specific reason not to grant it.[172] The point is that in such a case damages cannot be a sufficient remedy. As Cotton LJ put it, when enforcing a contract by a mortgagor to transfer certain chattels to a mortgagee to add to his security:

> "The mortgagee has performed his part of it by advancing his money on the faith of it, and the principle that damages are a sufficient remedy does not apply."[173]

Most cases of this sort deal with promises to mortgage or charge property: but **27-048** the principle is more general, and applies whenever equitable relief is necessary to perfect the claimant's agreed security. Thus a contract to transfer an asset to a creditor,[174] to provide him with security by using a particular asset or fund to pay him,[175] or to fund an escrow account,[176] will be specifically enforced to effectuate the creditor's security. And similar thinking underlies cases such as *Liberty Mercian Ltd v Cuddy Civil Engineering Ltd*,[177] where a contractor was ordered to provide a performance bond, and the unreported *Hurst-Bannister v New Cap Reinsurance Co Ltd*,[178] where it was said, for the same reason, that a court should specifically enforce a contract by a payee to place monies received in a segregated *Quistclose* account[179] for the benefit of the payer.

(vi) Promises in support of property rights A contractual obligation to do an **27-049**

---

170 E.g. *Re Clarke* (1887) L.R. 36 Ch. D. 348 at 352 (Collins LJ); J. Keeler, "Some Reflections on Holroyd v Marshall" (1969) 3 *Adelaide Law Review* 360 at 364 ff.

171 *Hermann v Hodges* (1873) L.R. 16 Eq 18; *Folgender Holdings Ltd v Letraz Properties Ltd* [2019] EWHC 2131 (Ch), esp at [18]. This includes property abroad: see *Re Scheibler* (1874) L.R. 9 Ch. App. 722 (promise to create security over house in Shanghai); cf. *Rayack Construction Ltd v Lampeter Meat Co Ltd* (1980) 12 B.L.R. 30 (injunction to compel creation by building employer of segregated retention fund). It also includes contracts to make property stand security for a debt owed to a third party: see *Re Lehman Brothers International (Europe) (in administration)* [2012] EWHC 2997 (Ch) at [43] (Briggs J).

172 An example being *Thames Guaranty Ltd v Campbell* [1985] Q.B. 210 (specific performance of husband's promise to charge matrimonial home would adversely affect wife).

173 *Re Clarke* (1887) 36 Ch. D. 348 at 352.

174 See *Man UK Properties Ltd v Falcon Investments Ltd* [2015] EWHC 1324 (Ch) (joint venture agreement; participant to transfer its interest in the venture to funder if it did not repay half sums advanced within 11 months of completion). See too *Re Grant Forest Products Inc* (2010) 101 O.R. (3d) 383.

175 *Palmer v Carey* [1926] A.C. 703 at 706–707 (Lord Wrenbury); *Swiss Bank Corp v Lloyds Bank Ltd* [1979] Ch. 548 (reversed on the facts, on a finding of no relevant agreement, at [1982] A.C. 584). For another example of the application of this principle, see *The Golfstraum* [1985] 2 All E.R. 669 (agreement to sell property and use proceeds to secure claim).

176 As in *Merthyr (South Wales) Ltd (formerly Blackstone (South Wales) Ltd) v Merthyr Tydfil CBC* [2019] EWCA Civ 526; [2019] J.P.L. 989.

177 [2013] EWHC 4110 (TCC); [2014] C.I.L.L. 3469. In fact the order was to use best endeavours because procuring a bond was likely to be difficult. In the end, it indeed proved impossible: see *Liberty Mercian Ltd v Cuddy Civil Engineering Ltd (No 2)* [2014] EWHC 3584 (TCC); [2015] B.L.R. 242.

178 Unreported 10 December 1999 Ch. D. See too *Lexington Insurance Co v Flashpoint Ltd*, Unreported January 19, 2001 Comm Ct, (obligation to place monies in accounts over which plaintiffs had security rights); and also *Rayack Construction Ltd v Lampeter Meat Co Ltd* (1980) 12 B.L.R. 30 and *Re Arthur Sanders Ltd* (1981) 17 B.L.R. 125 (obligation to create retention funds).

179 See *Barclays Bank Ltd v Quistclose Investments Ltd* [1970] A.C. 567.

act necessary to give effect to a claimant's property right is likely to be regarded as specifically enforceable. For instance, in *Puddephatt v Leith*[180] the mortgagee of shares contracted to vote them as directed by the mortgagor: when it became clear that he purposed not to do so, Sargant J had no hesitation in issuing the necessary mandatory order compelling him to keep his promise.

Factors telling against the grant of specific performance: general matters

27-050   The inadequacy of damages is a necessary condition for the grant of specific performance. But it is not a sufficient one. Even where it is shown, there are a number of factors that may incline a court against the grant of the remedy. It should be noted, however, that few of these are conclusive objections. Thus while a contract to lend money will not normally be enforced,[181] an obligation to sell realty will not cease to be specifically enforceable merely because a subsidiary term requires the vendor to leave part of the price outstanding on mortgage.[182] Again, in *C.H. Giles & Co Ltd v Morris*[183] vendors of a business agreed to sell shares in a company forming part of it and to appoint a particular person as a director. To a plea that the latter obligation was not one normally enforceable in specie, Megarry J. said:

> "the court may refuse to let the disadvantages and difficulties of specifically enforcing the obligation to perform personal services outweigh the suitability of the rest of the contract for specific performance, and the desirability of the contract as a whole being enforced. After all, pacta sunt servanda."[184]

27-051   **(i) Impossibility or futility**   Not surprisingly, specific performance will not be ordered of an obligation which the defendant cannot perform: equity, after all, does not act in vain. A court will not, for example, order a defendant on pain of imprisonment to allot shares which have already been allotted to someone else.[185] Nor, despite the courts' general lack of sympathy with those who enter into contracts without the means to perform them, will a court order a buyer to take and pay for a property which he has no chance whatever of finding the price for.[186] And similarly, while a court may specifically enforce the signing of a contract or other document, it is unlikely to order a defendant to sign a contract with the claimant if the contract itself would not be specifically enforceable.[187]

27-052   But cases of complete impossibility are rare. Much more common are cases

---

[180] [1916] 1 Ch. 200.

[181] Below, para.27-073.

[182] *Starkey v Barton* [1909] 1 Ch. 284.

[183] [1972] 1 W.L.R. 307.

[184] [1972] 1 W.L.R. 307 at 318.

[185] *Ferguson v Wilson* (1866–67) L.R. 2 Ch. App. 77. The fact that the impossibility is the fault of the defendant is irrelevant: *Seawell v Webster* (1859) 29 L.J. Ch. 71 at 73.

[186] See *Aranbel Ltd v Darcy* [2010] IEHC 272 (Clarke J: "I am satisfied that, as a matter of principle, where a purchaser demonstrates that … the purchaser concerned does not have the assets or borrowing capacity sufficient to allow them to purchase the property concerned at the contracted price, then a court should not make an order for specific performance for such an order would be in vain"); also *Titanic Quarter Ltd v Rowe* [2010] NI Ch. 14. But it is up to the defendant to show this, and the burden is a heavy one: cf. *Matila Ltd v Lisheen Properties Ltd* [2010] EWHC 1832 (Ch). The matter is discussed in A. Dowling, "Vendors' application for specific performance" [2011] Conv 208.

[187] *Chelsfield Advisers LLP v Qatari Diar Real Estate Investment Co* [2015] EWHC 1322 (Ch). So too

where performance may or may not be possible according to circumstances as yet unclear (for example where it depends on the action of a third party). And here the remedy is not necessarily barred: an order to use best endeavours may well be entirely appropriate.[188] So, for example, a person who has agreed to buy a leasehold interest whose assignment requires the landlord's consent will be ordered to take all reasonable steps to obtain that consent.[189] And, if the third party whose consent is essential is an entity controlled by the defendant—for instance, if it is a company in which he owns all the shares—then the court will have no compunction in ordering the defendant to procure that the third party do all that is necessary.[190]

Nevertheless, even here there are limits to the best endeavours that courts are prepared to demand. As Megarry J put it in *Wroth v Tyler*:[191]   **27-053**

"A vendor must do his best to obtain any necessary consent to the sale; if he has sold with vacant possession he must, if necessary, take proceedings to obtain possession from any person in possession who has no right to be there or whose right is determinable by the vendor, at all events if the vendor's right to possession is reasonably clear; but I do not think that the vendor will usually be required to embark upon difficult or uncertain litigation in order to secure any requisite consent or obtain vacant possession. Where the outcome of any litigation depends upon disputed facts, difficult questions of law, or the exercise of a discretionary jurisdiction, then I think the court would be slow to make a decree of specific performance against the vendor which would require him to undertake such litigation."

So in that case, where a divorcing husband agreed to sell the matrimonial home but his wife declined to leave, the court refused to order him to engage in litigation to evict the wife in order to provide vacant possession.

Not only will the court not compel performance of that which cannot be done: **27-054**
it will equally deny specific relief where a contemplated transaction as a whole cannot be completed even if the defendant's obligation technically can be. Hence where land agreed to be sold is subsequently expropriated so that the vendor will not be able to make title to it, then even though the contract remains technically valid at law[192] there will ordinarily be no order of specific performance against the purchaser: the contract was about the purchase of land, not a claim under the land compensation laws.[193] Again, where a purchaser agrees not to object to a possible defect in title and it later transpires that because of it the vendor cannot give pos-

---

the fact that a contract is determinable at short notice by the defendant is a strong reason against ordering its specific performance: see *Heppingstone v Stewart* (1910) 12 C.L.R. 126 at 129, 138.

[188] E.g. *Liberty Mercian Ltd v Cuddy Civil Engineering Ltd* [2013] EWHC 4110 (TCC); [2014] C.I.L.L. 3469. See also the Australian decision in *Dougan v Ley* (1946) 71 C.L.R. 142.

[189] For an example, see the Australian decision in *Kennedy v Vercoe* (1960) 105 C.L.R. 521. Similarly, where a contract of sale is subject to the consent of a government body: *McWilliam v McWilliams Wines Pty Ltd* (1964) 114 C.L.R. 656, and *Mount Kennett Investment Ltd v O'Mara* [2007] IEHC 420.

[190] *Jones v Lipman* [1962] 1 W.L.R. 832 (vendor's unsuccessful attempt to stymie specific performance by selling to controlled company: company characterised as "a device and a sham, a mask which he holds before his face in an attempt to avoid recognition by the eye of equity" and specific performance granted). The case was approved by Lord Sumption in *Prest v Petrodel Resources Ltd* [2013] UKSC 34; [2013] 2 A.C. 415 at [30].

[191] [1974] 1 Ch. 30 at 50. See too *Mean Machines Ltd v Blackheath Leisure (Carousel) Ltd* (1999) 78 P. & C.R. D36, where just this issue arose.

[192] The expropriation having taken place after risk has passed.

[193] *Cook v Taylor* [1942] Ch. 349; *Johnson & Co (Barbados) Ltd v N.S.R. Ltd* [1997] A.C. 400. But cf. *Kenney v Wexham* (1822) 6 Maddock 355 (specific performance of contract to buy annuity, though worthless because annuitant had meanwhile died).

session at all, the vendor will similarly be limited to his remedies at law.[194] Another example of the refusal of specific performance on grounds of futility was *Webb v Direct London & Portsmouth Ry Co*,[195] where a railway, having submitted to a landowner's predictably extortionate demands for payment for his land and agreed to buy it, abandoned the line altogether. The landowner's suit against the railway for specific performance was understandably dismissed.

27-055 **(ii) Unavailability of counter-performance** Whether or not the parties' mutual obligations under a contract are strictly interdependent at law, it is clear that a claimant will not get an order of specific performance unless he alleges and is prepared to prove that he is himself ready and willing to perform his own essential obligations.[196] But the word "essential" is important: as Barwick CJ said in the High Court of Australia:

> "The question as to whether or not the plaintiff has been and is ready and willing to perform the contract is one of substance not to be resolved in any technical or narrow sense. It is important to bear in mind what is the substantial thing for which the parties contract and what on the part of the plaintiff in a suit for specific performance are his essential obligations."[197]

27-056 So a buyer who, having had doubts about his ability to provide the price of land, convinces the court that he can provide it, albeit later than the contract demands, may be entitled to an order notwithstanding.[198] And conversely, a property developer is not barred from obtaining specific relief against a buyer merely because of small matters remaining uncompleted.[199]

27-057 **(iii) Lack of mutuality** In certain cases the decision whether to grant the claimant specific performance may depend on whether the defendant could himself have got it had he asked for it. In the nineteenth century the issue was regarded as a simple one: a contract, it was said, was in its nature specifically enforceable by both parties or by neither. It followed that if the defendant to a specific performance claim could not have obtained the remedy himself had the tables been turned then, whatever the equities might otherwise be, neither could the claimant.[200] But this view is now rightly rejected.[201] While mutuality of remedy is still relevant, its basis is changed. Today specific performance will be refused on this ground if, and only if, granting it would be unfair on the defendant at the time the action is brought,[202]

---

[194] *Re Scott and Alvarez's Contract* [1895] 2 Ch. 603.

[195] (1852) 1 De G M & G 521.

[196] E. Fry, *A Treatise on the Specific Performance of Contracts* (London: Stevens and Sons, 1921), 6th edn, p.435; *Ellis v Rogers* (1884) 29 Ch. D. 661 at 667; *Mehmet v Benson* (1965) 113 C.L.R. 295 at 314 (Windeyer J).

[197] *Mehmet v Benson* (1965) 113 C.L.R. 295 at 307.

[198] As in *Mehmet v Benson* (1965) 113 C.L.R. 295, referred to in the previous notes. See too dicta of Gresson P in *Gold v Penney* [1960] N.Z.L.R. 1032 at 1051 (enough if claimant demonstrates readiness to perform by time of judgment).

[199] *Matila Ltd v Lisheen Properties Ltd* [2010] EWHC 1832 (Ch).

[200] A view particularly associated with Sir Edward Fry: E. Fry, *A Treatise on the Specific Performance of Contracts* (London: Stevens and Sons, 1921), 6th edn, p.219.

[201] See *Price v Strange* [1978] Ch. 337 at 354 ff (Goff LJ), 361 at 367 (Buckley LJ).

[202] "What equity exacts today as a condition of relief is the assurance that the decree, if rendered, will operate without injustice or oppression either to plaintiff or defendant": *Epstein v Gluckin*, 233 NY 490 at 494 (1922) (quoted in I. Spry, *Equitable Remedies*, 9th edn (London: Sweet & Maxwell,

for example, by making him perform without adequate assurance of counter-performance from the claimant himself.[203]

The leading authority is *Price v Strange*.[204] The landlord of a London maisonette **27-058** agreed with his tenant that he would grant a new lease if the tenant carried out certain improvements, whereupon the tenant carried out the vast majority of the work. The landlord then repudiated his promise. Sued for specific performance, he objected to the grant of the remedy on the basis of the old rule of mutuality. The tenant, it was said, could not have been forced to perform his obligation to improve the premises;[205] and if so the remedy should equally be unavailable to enforce the landlord's obligation to lease. The Court of Appeal, in a very carefully argued decision, sided with the tenant. One reason was timing: the Court of Appeal stressed that the relevant time was not the making of the contract but rather the moment when the remedy was sought,[206] and here, whatever the situation had the contract been entirely executory, at the time of suit the tenant's side of it had been largely performed. It followed that, the only obligation remaining unfulfilled being one that was clearly enforceable specifically, there could be no objection to the requisite order. In addition, however, the court adumbrated the modern approach to mutuality. Quite apart from questions of timing, it limited refusal of relief to cases where there was a question of forcing one party to perform without assurance of performance from the other side; and in *Price* itself, this was plainly not the case.[207] Following *Price v Strange*, much the same issue arose, with a similar outcome, in *Turner v Turner*.[208] There a soon-to-be-divorced husband agreed to transfer the matrimonial home to his wife in exchange for the latter's promise to forgo any claim to maintenance. The wife having kept her part of the bargain, the court would have been willing[209] to enforce in specie her husband's promise to transfer the matrimonial home: by allowing the wife to perform, the husband had precluded himself from raising issues of mutuality.[210]

Conversely, a typical case where mutuality remains a bar, despite *Price v Strange*, **27-059** would be where A agrees to provide B with professional or personal services in exchange for advance payment in kind, for example shares in a private company. The effect of specifically enforcing the promise to transfer the shares would be unfairness to B, who would have no parallel guarantee of A's return performance, besides a potential right to sue A in damages.[211] It should nevertheless be noted that, even here the court retains a discretion. If the outstanding obligation is relatively

---

2014), p.98). See too *Price v Strange* [1978] Ch. 337 at 367–368 (Buckley LJ); also *J C Williamson Ltd v Lukey & Mulholland* (1931) 45 C.L.R. 282 at 298 (Dixon J).

[203] A view long accepted in the US: see, e.g. *Farnsworth on Contracts* (US: Wolters Kluwer, 2003), 3rd edn, para.12.7, and American cases such as *Sabin v Rauch* 258 P.2d 991 (1953). Some early English cases also reflect it: e.g. *Hills v Croll* (1845) 2 Ph. 60 (no injunction against breach of contract to buy all acid from plaintiff, because plaintiff's duty to supply not specifically enforceable: hence defendant would be compelled to perform with no assurance of return performance).

[204] [1978] Ch. 337.

[205] A proposition which itself seems open to some doubt: cf. para.27-031 ff above. But that is by-the-by.

[206] See [1978] Ch. 337 at 356 (Goff LJ), 367–368 (Buckley LJ); also, much earlier, *Eastern Counties Ry Co v Hawkes* (1855) 5 HL Cas. 331 at 364–365 (Lord Campbell).

[207] See [1978] Ch. 337 at 367 (Buckley LJ).

[208] [1984] Ch. 184.

[209] But for the fact that the contract, being aimed at sidelining the divorce jurisdiction, was against public policy.

[210] See [1984] Ch. 184 at 193.

[211] Compare the old cases of *Ogden v Fossick* (1862) 4 De G. F. & J. 426 (duty to employ in exchange

minor and damages would adequately remedy any breach, then an order may still be made.[212]

27-060 **(iv) Need for supervision** The courts once maintained an almost blanket ban on specifically enforcing obligations to provide continuing services, on the basis that policing any such order would require of them an exercise in constant supervision to ensure their orders were not being flouted. So, for instance, in 1893 it was held that a mansion block tenant could not compel the attendance of a resident porter and general servant according to the provisions in his tenancy agreement, on the simple basis that, as Lord Esher MR put it, this was "a long-continuing contract, to be performed from day to day", whose execution "would require that constant superintendence by the Court, which the Court in such cases has always declined to give".[213]

27-061 This restriction still obtains, at least in theory,[214] though it is rarely applied and is now more accurately and flexibly expressed as a practice of avoiding the need for "superintendence by the court to an unacceptable degree".[215] The leading recent authority is *Posner v Scott-Lewis*,[216] where tenants in another mansion block did succeed in enforcing an obligation to appoint and employ a porter. This order, said Mervyn Davies J, might require some supervision: but it did not on the facts involve any unacceptable need for supervision or hardship to the defendant, and hence there was no insuperable objection to it.

27-062 **(v) Need for willing co-operation which is now likely to be unforthcoming** Closely related to the question of supervision are obligations requiring willing co-operation and trust between the parties. In the nature of things, faith in one's co-contractor tends to evaporate concurrently with soured relations and the litigation that goes with them. In such a situation, specific relief may be denied on the very understandable basis that productive co-operation cannot be forcibly extracted from unwilling participants. One straightforward example is where it is sought to enforce an employment contract against the employer: although this is possible as

---

for commercial lease) and *Peto v Brighton, Uckfield & Tunbridge Wells Ry Co* (1863) 1 Hem & M 468 (railway construction contractor to be paid in stock). Similar, though technically involving an injunction, are *Measures Bros Ltd v Measures* [1910] 2 Ch. 248 and *Chappell v Times Newspapers Ltd* [1975] 1 W.L.R. 482 (see esp Lord Denning MR at 502).

[212] E.g. *Park Lane Ventures Ltd (In Administrative Receivership) v Locke* [2006] EWHC 1578 (Ch) (option to buy house coupled with obligation to carry out minor works on other premises).

[213] See *Ryan v Mutual Tontine Westminster Chambers Association* [1893] 1 Ch. 116 at 123. See too Dixon J in *J.C. Williamson Ltd v Lukey & Mulholland* (1931) 45 C.L.R. 282 at 297–298 ("Specific performance is inapplicable when the continued supervision of the court is necessary in order to ensure the fulfilment of the contract."). An instructive instance is *Powell Duffryn Steam Coal Co v Taff Vale Ry Co* (1874) L.R. 9 Ch. App. 331 (no specific enforcement of agreement to grant railway running powers, given the very detailed logistical and other operations involved).

[214] In *Co-Operative Insurance Society Ltd v Argyll Stores (Holdings) Ltd* [1998] A.C. 1 at 14 ff Lord Hoffmann was at some pains to discountenance suggestions by Megarry J in *C.H. Giles & Co Ltd v Morris* [1972] 1 W.L.R. 307 at 318 and *Tito v Waddell (No.2)* [1977] Ch. 106 at 321 that this had ceased to be an objection in its own right to the grant of specific relief.

[215] See *Rainbow Estates Ltd v Tokenhold Ltd* [1999] Ch. 64 at 70. The High Court of Australia has been more blunt, saying that this is "no longer an effective or useful criterion for refusing a decree of specific performance": see *Patrick Stevedores Operations (No.2) Pty Ltd v Maritime Union of Australia* (1998) 195 C.L.R. 1 at 46–47.

[216] [1987] Ch. 25.

a matter of law,[217] for precisely this reason no such order will in the ordinary course of things be granted.[218] Other similar cases include agreements to co-operate closely in property development;[219] to employ an advertising agency;[220] and to act as manager for a sportsman[221] or musician.[222] On a similar principle a contract to provide banking services will not be enforced in specie against a bank which, even wrongfully, insists on closing a customer's account.[223] In addition, there is little doubt that reasoning of this sort is a contributory factor in the general curial reluctance to enforce contracts to render services.[224]

Nevertheless, courts scrutinise pleas of this sort carefully, and may be prepared to discount such arguments in a suitable case as against the desirability of holding people to their bargains.[225]   **27-063**

(vi)   Uncertainty   On principle, no order of specific performance should be made   **27-064** if it cannot be made adequately clear what the defendant has to do in order to comply with it. This is for two reasons. First, there is the possibility of repeated and wasteful disputes over what amounts to obedience and whether it has taken place; and second, there is the fact that since the sanction for disobedience is the quasi-criminal one of committal for contempt, defendants are entitled to know what they must do to avoid punishment. As Lord Hoffmann put it in the leading decision in *Co-Operative Insurance Society Ltd v Argyll Stores (Holdings) Ltd*:[226]

> "If the terms of the court's order, reflecting the terms of the obligation, cannot be precisely drawn, the possibility of wasteful litigation over compliance is increased. So is the oppression caused by the defendant having to do things under threat of proceedings for contempt."

Thus in an old railway case a railway's promise to a landowner to open and oper-   **27-065** ate a "station", *tout court*, at a particular place was held too vague to be enforced

---

[217]   Since the Trade Union and Labour Relations (Consolidation) Act 1992 s.236, only bars the remedy against the employee. See too dicta at *Gregory v Philip Morris Ltd* (1988) 80 A.L.R. 455 at 481–482 (Ryan and Wilcox JJ).

[218]   E.g. *Chappell v Times Newspapers Ltd* [1975] 1 W.L.R. 482, esp at 492–493 (Megarry J), 501 (Lord Denning MR); *Geys v Société Générale* [2012] UKSC 63; [2013] 1 A.C. 523 at [77] (Lord Wilson); *Ashworth v Royal National Theatre* [2014] EWHC 1176 (QB); [2014] 4 All E.R. 238 at [25] (Cranston J). The same goes for orders that would have the same effect, such as injunctions or declarations: see *CCUK Finance Ltd v Barclays Bank Plc* [2018] EWHC 304 (Comm) at [27] and *Stobart Group Ltd v Tinkler* [2019] EWHC 258 (Comm) at [534]–[543]. See too the result in *Gregory v Philip Morris Ltd* (1988) 80 A.L.R. 455, above (no such order granted, despite admission of the theoretical possibility).

[219]   *BDW Trading Ltd v JM Rowe (Investments) Ltd* [2010] EWHC 1987 (Ch).

[220]   *More Group UK Ltd v Beat 106 Ltd* (unreported 7 August 2000) Q.B.D.

[221]   *Warren v Mendy* [1989] 1 W.L.R. 853 (an injunction case).

[222]   *Page One Records Ltd v Britton* [1968] 1 W.L.R. 157.

[223]   *Prosperity Ltd v Lloyds Bank Ltd* (1923) 39 T.L.R. 372.

[224]   See e.g. *Clarke v Price* (1819) 2 Wils 157; and more recently, *The Scaptrade* [1983] 2 A.C. 694 at 700–701 (Lord Diplock). Compare *Ashdown House School v JKL* [2019] UKUT 259 (AAC) at 220 ff (discussing the propriety of an order specifically to reinstate a private school pupil).

[225]   Compare the decisions in *Evans Marshall & Co Ltd v Bertola* [1973] 1 W.L.R. 349 and *Thomas Borthwick & Sons (Australasia) Ltd v South Otago Freezing Co Ltd* [1978] 1 N.Z.L.R. 538 (both condoning at least limited compulsion to perform distribution agreements).

[226]   [1998] A.C. 1 at 13. See too, for similar statements, *Wolverhampton Corp v Emmons* [1901] 1 K.B. 515 at 525 (Romer LJ); *Morris v Redland Bricks Ltd* [1970] A.C. 652 at 666 (Lord Upjohn).

specifically rather than by damages;[227] and in 1959 Harman J similarly refused peremptorily to order a publisher to publish an as yet unwritten, and hence editorially unapproved, article.[228] More recently still, the same reasoning was used to support denial of an order to keep a superstore "open for retail trade" in a shopping mall. Such an obligation, said Lord Hoffmann,

> "says nothing about the level of trade, the area of the premises within which trade is to be conducted, or even the kind of trade,"

and therefore was capable of providing "ample room for argument over whether the tenant is doing enough to comply with the covenant".[229]

27-066   **(vii)   Hardship**   If a contract would ordinarily be specifically enforceable, courts are normally unreceptive to pleas that compliance with an order would be financially or otherwise disastrous to the defendant.[230] Furthermore, hardship to the defendant even if proved has to be balanced against hardship to the claimant resulting from refusal of the remedy.[231] Nevertheless, even if a contract is indubitably valid and enforceable, there are cases where specific performance will be refused where its grant would cause excessive hardship to a defendant.[232] Thus where sellers of land promised the buyers to pay off all incumbrances, and it was later discovered that the land was subject to substantial negative equity, specific performance was denied and the buyer left to his remedy in damages.[233] Again, it has been held that even if damages are inadequate for the claimant, specific performance may be denied against the victim of crippling personal misfortune,[234] or where if granted it would forcibly embrangle the defendant in bitter family litigation.[235] And on a similar basis, in one scabrous 1900 case a vendor was denied specific performance when it transpired that, unknown to either party at the time

---

[227] *Wilson v Northampton & Banbury Junction Ry Co* (1874) 9 L.R. Ch. App. 279 at 285 (Lord Selborne). See too *Rushbrooke v O'Sullivan* [1908] 1 I.R. 232 (covenant in building lease to spend at least £600 in erecting buildings).

[228] *Joseph v National Magazine Co Ltd* [1959] Ch. 14. But it was different where the piece is complete and satisfactory: *Barrow v Chappell & Co Ltd* [1976] RPC 355.

[229] *Co-Operative Insurance Society Ltd v Argyll Stores (Holdings) Ltd* [1998] A.C. 1 at 16–17. See too *118 Data Resource Ltd v IDS Data Services Ltd* [2014] EWHC 3629 (Ch); [2016] F.S.R. 9 (no specific performance of imprecise undertaking to allow party to inspect records, since not sufficiently clear what facilities were to be afforded).

[230] For a recent instance, see *Matila Ltd v Clarke* [2010] EWHC 1832 (Ch) (order against purchasers of bijou flats despite property slump and disastrous effects on buyers). And compare *ANZ Executors & Trustees Ltd v Humes Ltd* [1990] V.R. 615 (specific enforcement of contract to issue shares fiscally disastrous to defendant: no sufficient hardship). But note Clarke J in the Irish High Court case of *Aranbel Ltd v Darcy* [2010] IEHC 272 ("I am satisfied that, as a matter of principle, where a purchaser demonstrates that … the purchaser concerned does not have the assets or borrowing capacity sufficient to allow them to purchase the property concerned at the contracted price, then a court should not make an order for specific performance for such an order would be in vain.").

[231] *Tamplin v James* (1880) 15 Ch. D. 215 at 221 (James LJ); *Eastes v Russ* [1914] 1 Ch. 468 at 480 (Swinfen Eady LJ); see too *Nicholas v Ingram* [1958] N.Z.L.R. 972 at 974.

[232] It has been said that the criterion is whether the defendant has shown that hardship amounting to an injustice would be inflicted on him, and that it would not be reasonable to do so. See *Suttor v Gundowda Pty Ltd* (1950) 81 C.L.R. 418 at 439.

[233] *Wedgwood v Adams* (1843) 6 Beav. 600.

[234] *Patel v Ali* [1984] Ch. 283.

[235] *Wroth v Tyler* [1974] Ch. 30 (need for husband to litigate to force unwilling wife to agree to sale of matrimonial home).

of the contract, the premises were happily in use as a brothel: it would, said Cozens-Hardy MR, be unfair to force on the buyer the obligation of suppressing such use.[236]

The above cases concerned events occurring, or appearing, after the time of the contract. But the hardship exception is a good deal wider that this, evidencing a well-established practice of denying specific performance if, even though the obligation which it is sought to enforce is otherwise valid at law,[237] there is some factor in or about its formation which in the circumstances makes it seriously unfair to enforce it in specie against the defendant. For instance, there are indications that a person who contracts in a state of disability such as drunkenness may be able to resist specific performance, even if the contract remains enforceable against him at law.[238]

27-067

(viii) Mistake   It is not uncommon for an error on the part of the defendant, even if not sufficient to vitiate the contract at law, to sway the court against giving specific relief against him. So where a term had been inadvertently omitted from a contract to lease commercial premises which was important to protect the lessor's interests, the lessee was refused specific relief;[239] and the result was the same where a seller at auction had been led to believe, with some reason, that the buyer was bidding as his agent and not on his own account.[240] Again, while a buyer of land cannot normally escape an order of specific performance with a simple plea that he was mistaken about the desirability of the plot he has agreed to buy,[241] it may be different with a mistake that was partly the fault of the claimant,[242] with a mistake in the heat of an auction about which precise lot he was bidding for,[243] or in a case where both parties had laboured under a fundamental error as to the size of the estate the subject of the sale.[244] And again, in 1993 when a university through a clerical error made an offer of admission to a patently underqualified student, the Court of Appeal, while accepting that the institution was in breach of contract by withdrawing the offer, had no doubt that it would not be right to order it to provide a place on pain of criminal punishment.[245]

27-068

(ix) Effect on human rights   Just as it seems that human rights and similar considerations may militate against the grant of an injunction,[246] the same may apply in respect of specific performance. Thus in *Ashworth v Royal National*

27-069

---

[236] *Hope v Walter* [1900] 1 Ch. 257.
[237] If it is not valid even at law, specific performance must a fortiori be refused because then there is nothing to enforce.
[238] *Cooke v Clayworth* (1811) Ves Jun 12 at 15 (Grant MR); *Blomley v Ryan* (1956) 99 C.L.R. 362 at 401 ff, 428 (Fullagar and Kitto JJ).
[239] *Garrard v Grinling* (1818) 1 Wils Ch. 460; see too *Wood v Scarth* (1855) 2 Kay & J 33.
[240] *Mason v Armitage* (1806) 13 Ves Jun 25.
[241] *Tamplin v James* (1880) 15 Ch. D. 215: see too *Fragomeni v Fogliani* (1968) A.L.J.R. 263 (buyer allegedly in error as to price agreed). So too with a seller unilaterally mistaken as to the terms on which he sells: *Slee v Warke* (1949) 86 C.L.R. 271.
[242] See *Baskcomb v Beckwith* (1869) L.R. 8 Eq. 100 and *Denny v Hancock* (1870) L.R. 6 Ch. App. 1 (both cases of ambiguous particulars of sale); also *Dell v Beasley* [1959] N.Z.L.R. 89 (sellers' unclarity as to planning status of land to be sold).
[243] *Malins v Freeman* (1837) 2 Keen 25.
[244] *Durham (Earl) v Legard* (1865) 34 Beav. 611 (estate believed to be 21,000 acres in fact only 11,000); on which see I. Spry, *Equitable Remedies*, 9th edn (London: Sweet & Maxwell, 2014), p.313.
[245] See *Moran v University College Salford (No.2)* [1994] ELR 187.
[246] See *London Regional Transport v Mayor of London* [2003] EMLR 4 at [45]–[46] (Robert Walker LJ); *Monckton v BBC* (unreported 31 January 2011) Q.B.D., below, para.28-022.

Theatre,[247] where actors were dismissed from a production in alleged breach of contract, one reason for the refusal of an order of specific performance requiring their reinstatement was that "the effect of the order sought would be to interfere with the National Theatre's right of artistic freedom" under Art.10 of the ECHR.[248]

27-070 **(x)** **Public law defences** It would seem that, on principle, a claim for specific performance should be denied in so far as its effect would be to force a public authority into unlawful action (for example, by fettering its discretion).[249] Conversely, in so far as a claim for specific performance by a public authority amounts to an abuse of power by the latter, the Court of Appeal confirmed in *Dudley Muslim Association v Dudley MBC*[250] that this might on principle be raised as a defence. Hence the defendants were allowed to argue that enforcement of a provision for reconveyance of certain land infringed their legitimate expectations (though on the facts in that case the defence failed).

27-071 **(xi)** **Adverse effects on third parties** Exceptionally, specific performance may be denied if its grant would adversely affect the rights or interests of, or otherwise cause hardship to, innocent third parties. So it has been said that there will be no specific performance of a contract of sale that would infringe a third party's right of pre-emption[251] or a contract to lease premises that would be contrary to a stipulation in a lender's charge.[252] Again, a contract by a lessee to sublet[253] or assign[254] will not be specifically enforced where such subletting would be contrary to the terms of the headlease and would thus deprive the head landlord of the protection of the relevant clause.[255] Similarly, where a sale by a person in a fiduciary position would possibly amount to a breach of trust prejudicing a beneficiary, the practice is to leave the purchaser to his rights at law against the fiduciary and refuse specific relief.[256] On the other hand, it should be noted that all these cases concerned *prior* obligations. The courts are less solicitous of the rights of subsequent promisees: thus where a borrower agrees successively to grant security over the same property to two different lenders, the first lender will normally obtain an order of specific performance as a matter of course.[257]

27-072 The above cases concerned cases where the rights of third parties were in issue.

---

247 [2014] EWHC 1176 (QB); [2014] 4 All E.R. 238. Compare the Australian decision in *Summertime Holdings Pty Ltd v Environmental Defender's Office Ltd* (1985) 45 N.S.W.L.R. 291 (no specific enforcement of promise to make apology, on free speech grounds).

248 [2014] EWHC 1176 (QB); [2014] 4 All E.R. 238 at [27] (Cranston J).

249 Compare the injunction case of *Shebelle Enterprises Ltd v Hampstead Garden Suburb Trust Ltd* [2014] EWCA Civ 305; [2014] 2 P. & C.R. 6.

250 [2015] EWCA Civ 1123; [2016] 1 P. & C.R. 10.

251 *Manchester Ship Canal Co v Manchester Racecourse Co* [1901] 2 Ch. 37 at 50–51 (Vaughan Williams LJ).

252 *Bower Terrace Student Accommodation Ltd v Space Student Living Ltd* [2012] EWHC 2206 (Ch)

253 *Warmington v Miller* [1973] Q.B. 877.

254 *Willmott v Barber* (1880) L.R. 15 Ch. D. 96.

255 Though presumably this is only a prima facie rule. It is suggested that things might be different if (say) the third party stood by and acquiesced in the new contract.

256 As where a single executor sells at what seems an undervalue: see *Sneesby v Thorne* (1855) 7 De G M & G 399 and *Colyton Investments Pty Ltd v McSorley* (1962) 107 C.L.R. 177, esp at 185. More recently, see *Downey v Stevens* [2021] EWHC 752 (Ch) (grounds for refusal of order where, if granted, its effect would have been to force club trustees to convey land in breach of trust); also *SMA Investment Holdings Ltd v Harbour Fund II LP* [2023] EWHC 428 (Comm) at [92] (no specific performance of contract by trustee to transfer securities in breach of trust).

257 *Folgender Holdings Ltd v Letraz Properties Ltd* [2019] EWHC 2131 (Ch) at [43].

As regards possible hardship to third parties, this is clearly more a matter of discretion: the hardship to the third party has to be weighed against the hardship to the claimant of being deprived of what would otherwise be his right. An example of a case where the former predominated was *Thames Guaranty Ltd v Campbell*.[258] A husband, without his wife's consent, purported in the name of both of them to borrow against the matrimonial home and to create a charge over it. No order was made at the lender's suit, even over the husband's share of the house. Even though this resulted in the loss of the lender's secured status, the hardship to the wife in possibly having the house sold over her head and the proceeds divided between her and the lender was held to be more significant. And, exceptionally, other matters may be in account, such as the likelihood of disorder affecting third parties, as where it is sought to enforce a contract to license premises to a group of activists with incendiary political views.[259]

Factors telling against the grant of specific performance: specific problematical types of contract

(i) Agreements to lend money "It would be quite new to me," said Sir John **27-073** Romilly in 1862, "to hear that this Court could specifically enforce a contract to lend money."[260] A consistent line of cases confirms this view: a contract to advance money to someone, or to make credit available to him, will not generally be enforced in specie.[261] Despite criticism,[262] and the fact that the normal reason given for this unwillingness (the adequacy of damages) is unconvincing,[263] there is much to be said for this principle, at least where simple loans are involved. If the circumstances of a would-be borrower have changed, it seems hard to compel a lender to commit his money to what he may see as certain loss, even if this is what he has promised to do. Furthermore, if the essence of the mutuality rule referred to above is that a party should not be forced to perform his side of a contract with no equivalent guarantee of counter-performance save a right to sue which may be of uncertain value,[264] then, as Lord Pearson put it in the Privy Council, there is

"an obvious objection in principle to granting specific performance of an unsecured loan. It would have a one-sided operation, creating a position of inequality. The borrower obtains immediately the whole advantage of the contract to him, namely the loan itself – a sum of money placed completely at his disposal. The lender on the other hand has to wait and hope for the payment of interest from time to time and for the eventual repayment of the capital. The Court has means of compelling a party to pay a sum of money if he is able to do so. But no writ of attachment or sequestration or other equitable process

---

[258] [1985] Q.B. 210; also *Watts v Spence* [1976] Ch. 165. And cf. the earlier *Thomas v Dering* (1837) 1 Keen 729 (sale by life tenant in prejudice of remaindermen).

[259] *Verrall v Great Yarmouth BC* [1981] Q.B. 202 (use of council premises by far-right politicians: possible disorder a relevant matter, though there the order was in fact granted).

[260] *Sichel v Mosenthal* (1862) 30 Beavan 371 at 377.

[261] See *Larios v Bonany* (1870) L.R. 5 C.P. 346; *Western Wagon Co v West* [1892] 1 Ch. 271 at 275 (Chitty J); *South African Territories Ltd v Wallington* [1898] A.C. 309 at 312, 315, 318 (Lords Halsbury, Herschell and M'Naghten); and the Privy Council decision in *Loan Corp of Australasia v Bonner* [1970] N.Z.L.R. 724.

[262] I. Spry, *The Principles of Equitable Remedies*, 9th edn (London: Sweet & Maxwell, 2014), pp.72–73.

[263] See e.g. *Sichel v Mosenthal* (1862) 30 Beavan 371 at 377. In fact, damages for failure to provide credit may in many cases be enormously difficult to prove.

[264] See above, para.27-055.

can compel the borrower to repay the loan, if when the time comes at the end of the period he has not enough assets to enable him to do so."[265]

27-074   Nevertheless, there are many different kinds of arrangement which technically amount to contracts to lend money, and a blanket ban on their specific enforcement can engender considerable commercial inconvenience. To some extent, indeed, allowance is made for this fact by exceptions to the general rule. Thus a contract to provide finance may be merely an ancillary part of a contract where specific relief can be had: and, if so, it will not stand in the way of the grant of such relief. An example is where there is an agreement to sell land with part of the price to remain outstanding on mortgage to the vendor. Despite the fact that granting the buyer specific performance will incidentally force the seller to lend, there is no doubt that the remedy is available here.[266] Again, since the application of the presumptive rule to agreements to subscribe to debentures[267] would prevent the proper enforcement of agreements to underwrite stock issues and leave the issuers at the mercy of possibly unscrupulous underwriters, statute now makes such contracts specifically enforceable.[268]

27-075   However, it is arguable that the exceptions do not go far enough. In particular, there is a strong case for a further relaxation in respect of agreements by banks and similar institutions to provide finance for particular projects. Although these are within the rule against specific performance,[269] this is a classic case where damages may well be an inadequate remedy. It has been recognised in Australia that the losses to a customer from sudden withdrawal of promised funding are likely to be serious, unpredictable and difficult to prove; that funding from elsewhere may well be difficult or impossible to obtain; and that for that reason damages may well be an inadequate remedy;[270] furthermore, the Privy Council has expressed the view that the rule against specific enforcement may be relaxed in "exceptional circumstances".[271] And, it is submitted, English courts should take note of these developments. True, there might be potential for injustice were specific performance to be granted after it became apparent that the borrower's credit or honesty was seriously in doubt. But (it is suggested) much of this could be neutralised by allowing a defence where the defendant could demonstrate such new knowledge, or some other relevant change in the circumstances, such as a drastic deterioration in the claimant's asset base or in the value of any security on offer.

27-076 (ii) Agreements to borrow money   Presumptively courts will not specifically

---

[265] *Loan Corp of Australasia v Bonner* [1970] N.Z.L.R. 724 at 735.

[266] *Starkey v Barton* [1909] 1 Ch. 284. But the loan portion must be truly subsidiary. A portmanteau contract to sell someone a house and in addition to lend them the money unsecured to buy it is not specifically enforceable: see the Privy Council decision in *Loan Corp of Australasia v Bonner* [1970] N.Z.L.R. 724.

[267] The point in issue in *South African Territories Ltd v Wallington* [1898] A.C. 309, referred to above.

[268] Currently the Companies Act 2006 s.740.

[269] *Larios v Bonany* (1870) L.R. 5 PC 346.

[270] See *Wight v Haberdan Pty Ltd* [1984] 2 N.S.W.L.R. 280 (where a financier was ordered to provide agreed finance, having stood by and allowed its customer to commit himself seriously to third parties: see esp pp.289–291); see too *Corpers (No.664) Pty Ltd v NZI Securities Australia Ltd* (1989) ASC 55–714, where Young J discountenanced the idea of any absolute bar, though on the facts specific performance was not ordered. A number of American decisions, while accepting the general rule, are similar in import: e.g. *Columbus Club v Simons,* 236 P 12 (Okla 1925) (promise of finance for new premises followed by extensive reliance); *Vandeventer v Dale Constr. Co,* 534 P.2d 183 (Ore 1975) (home finance).

[271] See *Loan Corp of Australasia v Bonner* [1970] N.Z.L.R. 724 at 735.

enforce contracts to borrow money any more than to lend it. Typical is *Rogers v Challis*.[272] The defendant reneged on an agreement to borrow £1,000 for a year at 10 per cent interest. The would-be lender sought to hold him to his bargain, but Sir John Romilly unhesitatingly left the lender to his claim in damages. It seems, however, that the case is different where the provision for the defendant to borrow is ancillary to some other contract otherwise susceptible to specific relief. An old-fashioned example is an agreement to buy property with part of the price remaining on mortgage to the vendor;[273] a more contemporary one might be an agreement by a corporation to buy a business or a property and to pay for it by issuing loan stock to the vendor.[274] Moreover, it must be remembered that the rule just stated is limited to cases where no advance has been made. As appears above, where a lender has advanced money but the borrower has failed to provide the stipulated security for it, specific performance issues as of course.

This rule has, like that relating to contracts to lend, been criticised,[275] but (it is suggested) with little reason. As was pointed out in *Rogers v Challis*,[276] it seems foolish and distasteful to compel a person to borrow money he does not want; and furthermore, damages for failure to borrow can fairly easily be computed. Moreover, they are likely to provide a perfectly adequate remedy. Rarely, if ever, will a claimant with money to invest have nowhere else he can lay it out at interest, subject to a claim against the would-be borrower for any difference in the return.[277]   **27-077**

(iii)   Agreements to carry on a business activity   Since the nineteenth century, courts have been disinclined to compel a defendant to carry on a particular business activity. Typical is the briefly reported *Hooper v Brodrick*[278] in 1840, where the lessor of a London hostelry sought to compel the lessee to keep open the demised premises as an inn, as covenanted. Shadwell V-C laconically discharged the order as clearly misconceived. The rule was well-established by the time of *Att Gen v Colchester Corp*[279] in 1955, when Lord Goddard CJ refused to compel a ferry operator to continue to run a ferry which had become a losing concern. And any doubts about its continued existence were conclusively dispelled by the House of Lords in *Co-Operative Insurance Soc Ltd v Argyll Stores (Holdings) Ltd*,[280] where it formed the main ground for their lordships' refusal to compel the major store in   **27-078**

---

[272] (1859) 27 Beavan 175.
[273] Such a contract was enforced at the purchaser's suit in *Starkey v Barton* [1909] 1 Ch. 284; and there seems no reason to think matters would have been different had the vendor been the claimant.
[274] Note that s.740 of the Companies Act 2006 does not apply here, since it renders specifically enforceable only agreements to *buy* debentures, not to *issue* them.
[275] I. Spry, *The Principles of Equitable Remedies*, 9th edn (Sweet & Maxwell, 2014), p.73.
[276] See (1859) 27 Beavan 175 at 178 (Sir John Romilly).
[277] See (1859) 27 Beavan 175 at 178–179.
[278] (1840) 11 Simons 47.
[279] [1955] 2 Q.B. 207. See too *Dowty Boulton Paul Ltd v Wolverhampton Corp* [1971] 1 W.L.R. 204 (no order to operate airfield); and *Braddon Towers Ltd v International Stores Ltd* [1987] 1 E.G.L.R. 209 at 213 (practice stated by Slade J to be "settled and invariable"). But an order not to refuse standardised services to one customer of many may be on a different footing: see the injunction case of *Sogexia SaRL v Raphael & Sons Plc* [2019] EWHC 2577 (Ch) (clearing services for one particular card issuer).
[280] [1998] A.C. 1. Not followed in Scotland: *Highland & Universal Properties Ltd v Safeway Properties Ltd (No.2)* 2000 S.C. 297. See A. Phang, "Specific performance—exploring the roots of 'settled practice'" (1998) 61 M.L.R. 421; A. Tettenborn, "Absolving the undeserving: shopping centres, specific performance and the law of contract" [1998] Conv 223; and the thoughtful D. Pearce, "Remedies for Breach of a Keep-Open Covenant" (2008) 24 JCL 199.

a shopping development to remain open, despite the extensive and at times uncertain losses this might cause to the mall's owners. The reason for the rule, said Lord Hoffmann, was essentially the same as that lying behind the "excessive supervision" ground: that faced with a person forced unwillingly to run a business against his commercial instincts court interventions might well have to be frequent and somewhat heavy-handed.[281] To this he might also have added the point that such an order may well cause hardship to a defendant, by forcing him on pain of serious penalties to risk his money and run the gauntlet of possibly open-ended losses. It should be added that in so far as the court will not compel the running of a business it will equally not compel its running to a particular standard.[282]

27-079 **(iv) Contracts of employment** By statute, reflective of the position in equity before legislative intervention,[283] there can be no specific performance of contracts of employment against the employee.[284] There is no converse bar on specific relief against the employer. Nevertheless, the practice is against awarding this in ordinary cases,[285] since it is normally inappropriate to force parties into relations demanding close personal trust and confidence.[286] Thus, to take an obvious example, employees engaging in industrial action against the employer's interests are likely to receive short shrift when seeking specific relief relating to their contracts of employment.[287] On the other hand, the refusal of specific relief is a practice and not a rule; in exceptional circumstances there is no doubt that such an award may be made. One case where it is appropriate is where, unusually, trust and confidence remain. Thus in the leading decision in *Hill v C.A. Parsons Ltd*[288] an employee threatened with instant (and wrongful) dismissal for refusal to join a trade union successfully sought relief[289] compelling his continued employment. Here the remedy was sought only for a relatively short time (its real aim was to secure the employee's position until a change in the law came into effect that improved his protection and enabled him to secure full pension rights); and the employer—importantly in the employment context—retained full confidence in his employee. Again, in *Powell v Brent LBC*[290] a worker wrongly demoted merely because of an internal procedural dispute obtained a similar remedy. Moreover, it is arguable that

---

[281] [1998] A.C. 1 at 11.

[282] *Zinc Cobham 1 Ltd v Adda Hotels* [2018] EWHC 1025 (Ch); [2018] L. & T.R. 36 (no compulsion to operate Hilton hotels to institutional standards).

[283] See e.g. *Firth v Ridley* (1864) 33 Beavan 516. But note the limits of a contract of personal service in this respect. A contract, for instance, to give a publisher first refusal on one's "next three books" is not: *Erskine MacDonald Ltd v Eyles* [1921] 1 Ch. 631.

[284] Trade Union and Labour Relations (Consolidation) Act 1992 s.236.

[285] Indeed, in the case of unfair dismissal there is no power in the Employment Tribunal to make any specifically enforceable order: *R. (on the application of Mackenzie) v University of Cambridge* [2019] EWCA Civ 1060.

[286] *Chappell v Times Newspapers Ltd* [1975] 1 W.L.R. 482, esp at 492–493 (Megarry J), 501 (Lord Denning MR); *Geys v Société Générale* [2012] UKSC 63; [2013] 1 A.C. 523 at [77] (Lord Wilson); *Ashworth v Royal National Theatre* [2014] EWHC 1176 (QB); [2014] 4 All E.R. 238 at [25] (Cranston J). See too *Gregory v Philip Morris Ltd* (1988) 80 A.L.R. 455. It should be noted that this bar on specific relief has been held ECHR-compliant: *MacKenzie v University of Cambridge* [2019] EWCA Civ 1060 at [32] (Underhill LJ) and *Steer v Stormsure Ltd* [2021] EWCA Civ 887; [2021] I.C.R. 1671.

[287] *Chappell v Times Newspapers Ltd* [1975] 1 W.L.R. 482.

[288] [1972] Ch. 305. See too *Irani v Southampton & South West Hampshire HA* [1985] I.C.R. 590 (dismissal on insistence of overbearing senior employee).

[289] Technically in injunctive form: but essentially equivalent to specific performance.

[290] [1988] I.C.R. 176.

similar arguments might be applied where, by reason of the fact that the employer is large and impersonal, the question of personal trust is in practice of little importance.[291] To take an obvious example, employees engaging in industrial action against the employer's interests are likely to receive short shrift when seeking specific relief relating to their contracts of employment.[292]

VII. GENERAL EQUITABLE BARS TO SPECIFIC PERFORMANCE

Specific performance being an equitable remedy, it is subject to the general bars **27-080** to equitable relief. In particular two are worth mentioning here: laches and the conduct of the claimant.

Laches

In contrast to actions for damages, there is no statutory limitation period for **27-081** specific performance claims.[293] Instead, the law looks to the more flexible doctrine of laches, under which an equitable right may be lost if it has not been exercised for a considerable time[294] and as a result either the defendant has either been prejudiced or it would for some other reason be unconscionable to allow enforcement of it.[295]

With executory contracts for the sale of land, it has been said that a claimant **27-082** must, on discovering that the other party is declining to perform, seek specific performance "within a reasonable time",[296] the reason being that:

"[N]o person is at liberty to hold an agreement for a purchase hanging over another's head for a great length of time and then to bring it forward...you must come speedily for a specific performance, or not at all."[297]

In practice, this means that delay of up to a year is likely to be tolerated, while **27-083** anything much longer may well call for explanation.[298] In so far as the defendant

---

[291] See *Powell v Brent LBC* [1988] I.C.R. 176 at 194 (Ralph Gibson LJ); *Geys v Société Générale* [2012] UKSC 63; [2013] 1 A.C. 523 at [78] (Lord Wilson); *Ashworth v Royal National Theatre* [2014] EWHC 1176 (QB); [2014] 4 All E.R. 238 at [22] (Cranston J).

[292] *Chappell v Times Newspapers Ltd* [1975] 1 W.L.R. 482.

[293] See Limitation Act 1980 s.36; *P & O Nedlloyd BV v Arab Metals Co* [2006] EWCA Civ 1717; [2007] 1 W.L.R. 2288 at [47]–[54] (Moore-Bick LJ). In the Australian decision in *Fitzgerald v Masters* (1956) 95 C.L.R. 420 a delay of some 26 years was condoned.

[294] "[A] party cannot call upon a court of equity for specific performance, unless he has shown himself ready, desirous, prompt, and eager" (Lord Alvanley MR in *Milward v Earl Thanet* (1801) 5 Ves 720n). For a recent example (failure to claim transfer of intellectual property rights for 10 years or so), see *Volumatic Ltd v Ideas for Life Ltd* [2019] EWHC 2273 (IPEC).

[295] Compare the delineation of when the doctrine will apply in the rescission case of *Lindsay Petroleum Co v Hurd* (1874) L.R. 5 C.P. 221 at 239–240 ("Where it would be practically unjust to give a remedy, either because the party has, by his conduct, done that which might fairly be regarded as equivalent to a waiver of it, or where by his conduct and neglect he has, though perhaps not waiving that remedy, yet put the other party in a situation in which it would not be reasonable to place him if the remedy were afterwards to be asserted").

[296] *Parkin v Thorold* (1852) 16 Beav. 59 at 73 (Lord Romilly MR).

[297] *Sharp v Milligan* (1856) 22 Beav. 606 at 612 (Romilly MR).

[298] See I. Spry, *The Principles of Equitable Remedies*, 9th edn (London: Sweet & Maxwell, 2014), pp.238–244 and cases there cited. For a recent discussion of what amounts to laches, see too *Wroth v Tyler* [1974] Ch. 30 at 53.

has changed his position, this may suffice to shorten the period,[299] as may the fact that the land forms part of a business, since here the parties have a legitimate right to expect that old agreements will not hamper future dealings.[300] Where the contract is no longer executory and a purchaser or lessee has gone into possession, then the period can be very extended, and laches correspondingly difficult to make out,[301] on the understandable basis that here the court is being asked not so much to activate an antique agreement as simply to regularise what has become the status quo.[302]

27-084   There is little authority as regards other contracts: but in so far as they involve commercial interests, it seems likely that relatively short periods may amount to laches, by analogy with agreements to dispose of business premises.

The conduct of the claimant

27-085   There is no doubt that the maxim that he who seeks equity must do equity[303] applies to specific performance.[304] One example is where the claimant has been guilty of non-disclosure: even if the contract is enforceable at law,[305] specific performance may be withheld at the court's discretion.[306] And the same goes for a claimant who has accepted an offer to sell property at an undervalue that any reasonable person would realise was the result of a mistake or miscalculation.[307] No doubt the result would be similar, and a court would be apt to refuse specific relief, if, say, the claimant had been guilty of deceiving the court or some similar misbehaviour.[308] But the mere fact that the claimant is a sharp business enterprise seeking to obtain an asset and then extract a major ransom value from it is not of itself enough.[309]

VIII.   Specific Performance and the Insolvent Defendant

27-086   As a remedy operating otherwise than by way of money claim, one effect of specific performance is to give the claimant an effective preference in the

---

[299] See the old case of *Reimers v Druce* (1857) 23 Beav. 145 (relevant papers astray).
[300] See *Huxham v Llewellyn* (1873) 21 W.R. 570 and *Glasbrook v Richardson* (1874) 23 W.R. 51 (business premises: five months and 3½ months amount to laches). The distinction between business and other premises was accepted by Denning LJ in *Williams v Greatrex* [1957] 1 W.L.R. 31 at 38 and Megarry J in *Wroth v Tyler* [1974] Ch. 30 at 53.
[301] *Williams v Greatrex* [1957] 1 W.L.R. 31 (10 years); see too *Sharp v Milligan* (1856) 22 Beav. 606 (12 years for claim against lessee in possession not excessive).
[302] The point was picturesquely put by an Irish judge thus: it was, he said, "nothing but a resting on the equitable estate by a person in possession, without clothing it with a legal title, which I think never was held to be that sort of laches that would prevent relief". See *Crofton v Ormesby* (1806) 2 Sch. & Lef. 583 at 604 (Lord Redesdale). Cf. the more recent Privy Council decision in *Hughes v La Baia Ltd* [2011] UKPC 9; [2011] 2 P. & C.R. DG7.
[303] I. Spry, *The Principles of Equitable Remedies*, 9th edn (London: Sweet & Maxwell, 2014), p.253 ff.
[304] See *Rosher v Williams* (1875) L.R. 20 Eq. 210 at 217 (Malins V-C); *Frasers Islington Ltd v Hanover Trustee Co Ltd* [2010] EWHC 1514 (Ch); [2010] 2 P. & C.R. DG20 at [29].
[305] A fortiori if it is voidable against the claimant, e.g. for breach of fiduciary duty: e.g. *Raso v Dionig* (1993) 100 D.L.R. (4th) 459.
[306] E.g. *Beyfus v Lodge* [1925] Ch. 350 (failure by vendor of leasehold to disclose dilapidations notice from landlord).
[307] *Webster v Cecil* (1861) 30 Beav. 62 (figure of £1250 for £2150, the mistake being apparent from previous negotiations).
[308] Compare the injunction case of *Armstrong v Sheppard & Short Ltd* [1959] 2 Q.B. 384.
[309] *ANZ Executors & Trustees Ltd v Humes Ltd* [1990] V.R. 615 (claim for shares of enormous value to one particular purchaser).

defendant's insolvency. This is most obviously the case with contracts to sell particular assets, where the existence of a specifically enforceable obligation is regarded, at least to some extent,[310] as constituting the vendor constructive trustee of the subject matter for the purchaser,[311] and there is clear authority that this trust can be enforced against a liquidator or similar officer.[312] But specific performance may on principle be granted against an insolvent defendant in respect of any obligation, whether or not a trust of this kind arises, and any order will bind the defendant as if he were solvent.[313]

Of itself, the insolvency of a defendant is not an argument against granting **27-087** specific relief in the case of a contract otherwise specifically enforceable, however beneficial to the defendant's creditors such refusal might be.[314] Thus the Court of Appeal pointedly had no objection to compelling a penniless and insolvent lessee formally to execute a lease with a view to activating a third party guarantee of the rent.[315] Where necessary, moreover, the jurisdiction to order specific performance with compensation can be prayed in aid here: so where a defendant promised to build housing on land and then convey it to the claimant, but then became insolvent before building, the buyer was able to obtain specific performance of the contract to convey with a reduction in price to reflect the fact that the land remained undeveloped.[316]

On the other hand, the insolvency of the defendant is by no means an irrelevant **27-088** factor. To begin with, permission from the court is required to commence any proceedings at all against an insolvent defendant,[317] and may be refused in so far as the claimant's case for relief is regarded as weak. Furthermore, it must be remembered that in both corporate and personal insolvency, there is a general power to disclaim onerous obligations so as to leave the obligee to prove for damages.[318] Although this power does not generally affect contracts to sell real property, on the basis that the purchaser has an equitable interest from the time of the contract which cannot be thus divested,[319] it allows escape from almost all other specifically

---

[310] For the nature of this trusteeship, which need not concern us here, see G. Jones and W. Goodhart, *Specific Performance*, 2nd edn (London: Tottel, 1996), p.17 ff; I. Spry, *The Principles of Equitable Remedies*, 9th edn (London: Sweet & Maxwell, 2014), pp.689–690.

[311] "It must, therefore, be considered to be established that the vendor is a constructive trustee for the purchaser of the estate from the moment the contract is entered into." *Lysaght v Edwards* (1876) 2 Ch. D. 499 at 510 (Jessel MR). See too *Shaw v Foster* (1872) L.R. 5 HL 321 at 333, 338, 349 (Lords Chelmsford, Cairns and O'Hagan).

[312] See *Re Scheibler* (1874) L.R. 9 Ch. App. 722; *Re Bastable* [1901] 2 K.B. 518; and more recently *Re A/Wear UK Ltd (In Administration)* [2013] EWCA Civ 1626; [2014] 1 P. & C.R. DG15 (agreement for company now insolvent to surrender lease and pay sum to landlord: landlord granted specific performance of agreement to surrender in order to trigger liability to pay).

[313] *AMEC Properties Ltd v Planning Research and Systems Plc* [1992] B.C.L.C. 1149 (specific performance of lease against insolvent lessee, with a view to engaging guarantor's liability).

[314] *Park Lane Ventures Ltd v Locke* [2006] EWHC 1578 (Ch).

[315] *AMEC Properties Ltd v Planning Research and Systems Plc* [1992] B.C.L.C. 1149. But where there is no good reason, then equity will not act in vain by decreeing specific performance against a penniless purchaser: *Aranbel Ltd v Darcy* [2010] IEHC 272.

[316] *Manchester & District Housing Association v Fearnley Construction Ltd (In Liquidation)* [2000] N.P.C. 94.

[317] Insolvency Act 1986 ss.126, 285. See I. Fletcher, *Law of Insolvency*, 5th edn (London: Sweet & Maxwell, 2017), paras 6-111, 22-006.

[318] Insolvency Act 1986 ss.178 (corporate), 315 (personal).

[319] See *Re Bastable* [1901] 2 K.B. 518.

enforceable obligations, including agreements to purchase property,[320] or to carry out work.[321] And even if the obligation has not been disclaimed when the action is brought, it is suggested that the court may well refuse specific relief on some other ground. For example, it is clear that relief will not be given in so far as it might subvert pari passu distribution.[322] Alternatively it may be refused as pointless, unless it relates to something that an insolvent defendant can do and the claimant has some other good reason (such as the preservation of a claim against a third party[323]) for claiming it.[324] In the case of a company in receivership, the power of disclaimer does not apply, but specific enforcement remains unlikely on the ground that it would act unfairly in making the receiver personally liable without his consent.[325]

27-089   Possibly more important is the converse question: if specific relief would not normally otherwise be granted, should the fact that a bankrupt defendant will not satisfy a damages award be relevant to the question whether damages are a sufficient remedy? The position of English law, in contrast to the prevailing rule in the US,[326] is that this factor is irrelevant: it does not make damages an inadequate remedy or otherwise provide a justification for ordering specific relief.[327] And, it is suggested, rightly so: in so far as a contractor has elected not to take security for performance, there is no reason to manipulate the law of specific performance to give him an assurance he never bargained for. As Goulding J put it in 1985:

> "[C]ommercial life would be subjected to new and unjust hazards if the court were to decree specific performance of contracts normally sounding only in damages simply because of a party's threatened insolvency."[328]

IX.   PARTICULAR APPLICATIONS OF SPECIFIC PERFORMANCE: SPECIFIC PERFORMANCE COUPLED WITH MONEY PAYMENTS

Unavailability of full performance: The possibility of specific performance with additional compensation to the claimant

27-090   If performance of an obligation is entirely impossible, albeit as a result of the defendant's breach, there can clearly be no order to carry it out in specie. But what if performance is partly possible? For example, a seller of realty may be able to convey the land, but only with an imperfect title, or without vacant possession.

---

[320] *Holloway v York* (1877) 25 WR 627.

[321] *Re Gough* (1927) 96 LJ Ch. 239.

[322] For instance, once insolvency has set in it is too late to compel creation of a retention fund in the hands of a bankrupt building employer, rights having crystallised on insolvency: see *MacJordan Construction Ltd v Brookmount Erostin Ltd* [1994] C.L.C. 581 at 588, approving *Re Jartray Developments Ltd* (1982) 22 B.L.R. 134.

[323] As in *AMEC Properties Ltd v Planning Research and Systems Plc* [1992] B.C.L.C. 1149.

[324] It should also be remembered that as a general rule dispositions of property after the onset of insolvency are ineffective (see e.g. Insolvency Act 1986 s.127); and the courts are unwilling to allow specific performance orders to subvert this principle: see *Re Wiltshire Iron Co* (1867–68) L.R. 3 Ch. App. 443.

[325] See the Scots decision in *McLeod v Alexander Sutherland Ltd* [1977] S.L.T. (N) 44.

[326] See *Restatement 2d of Contracts* §360(c) (1981); also cases such as *Roberts v Brewer*, 371 S.W.2d 424 (Tex. 1963).

[327] See *The Golfstraum* [1985] 2 All E.R. 669 at 674 (Goulding J); *AMEC Properties Ltd v Planning Research and Systems Plc* [1992] B.C.L.C. 1149 at 1152 (Balcombe LJ); *Park Lane Ventures Ltd v Locke* [2006] EWHC 1578 (Ch) at [119]. The apparent contrary suggestion in *The Oakworth* [1975] 1 Lloyd's Rep. 581 at 583 seems, with respect, heterodox.

[328] *The Golfstraum* [1985] 2 All E.R. 669 at 674.

Similarly, a seller of shares in a private company may be able to supply them, but only in short measure. Again, a seller of land may be able to convey a good title, but be guilty of some misdescription inducing the contract.

The law takes the view that this does not bar specific performance, but instead **27-091** allows the buyer, if he wishes, to claim in specie that performance which is possible, plus compensation[329] for that which is not.[330] The reasoning is simple: if a buyer is happy to take less than he contracted for with the remainder in money, that is his choice and it lies ill in the mouth of a contract-breaker to argue that he should not be allowed to do so.[331] This jurisdiction has nineteenth-century origins;[332] and although it has been somewhat sidelined since any court awarding specific performance now has powers to award damages in addition, either at Common Law or under Lord Cairns's Act,[333] it remains relevant on the question of when specific performance remains available at all in questions of partial impossibility.

Two typical examples are *Hill v Buckley*[334] in 1811, awarding specific **27-092** performance plus diminution in value where the amount of growing timber on land was grossly overstated, and *Grant v Dawkins*[335] in 1972, where sellers who wrongfully failed to clear two mortgages over the subject land were held amenable to specific performance coupled with compensation based on the cost of discharging the offending incumbrances. Other cases have concerned difficulties in the title to a one-third share of the subject matter of the sale,[336] and failure to provide technical vacant possession.[337]

Nevertheless, two limits must be noted to the purchaser's right. First, it seems **27-093** that the right to specific performance with compensation is limited to the purchaser who did not know of the defect in his vendor's title[338] (though the justification for denying relief against an admitted contract-breaker on this account is open to some doubt[339]).

Secondly, the rule does not apply to drastic or fundamental defects in the **27-094** defendant's title. The leading authority is the Court of Appeal's decision in *Rudd v Lascelles*.[340] In that case specific performance, even on terms, was refused to the buyer of investment properties which unexpectedly transpired to be affected by very

---

[329] Compensation under this jurisdiction is limited to the difference in value between that which is conveyed and that which should have been. It does not embrace damages for other breaches, such as late conveyance: see *Rutherford v Acton-Adams* [1915] A.C.866 and *King v Poggioli* (1923) 32 C.L.R. 222.

[330] For a useful, though not uncontroversial, account of this power, see C. Harpum, "Specific performance with compensation as a purchaser's remedy—a study in contract and equity" [1981] C.L.J. 47.

[331] See *Mortlock v Buller* (1804) 10 Ves 292 at 315–316 (Lord Eldon).

[332] It is summarised in, e.g. *Newham v May* (1824) 13 Price 749 at 752 (Alexander CB); and *Rudd v Lascelles* [1900] 1 Ch. 815 at 818 (Farwell J).

[333] See now Senior Courts Act 1981 s.50; also C. Harpum, "Specific performance with compensation as a purchaser's remedy—a study in contract and equity" [1981] C.L.J. 47 at 50–51.

[334] (1811) 17 Ves Jun 394. Other nineteenth-century examples include *Hughes v Jones* (1861) 3 De G & J 307 and *Hooper v Smart* (1874) L.R. 18 Eq 683.

[335] [1973] 1 W.L.R. 1406.

[336] *Basma v Weekes* [1950] A.C. 441. Cf. *Barnes v Wood* (1869) L.R. 8 Eq 424 (*soi-disant* freeholder who in the event had only estate *pur autre vie* bound to convey what he could).

[337] *Topfell Ltd v Galley Properties Ltd* [1979] 1 W.L.R. 446.

[338] *Castle v Wilkinson* (1870) L.R. 5 Ch. App. 534.

[339] It is noteworthy that in *Castle v Wilkinson*, above, the defect in title was in any case so serious that it would probably have barred relief under the principle in *Rudd v Lascelles* [1900] 1 Ch. 815 in any case.

[340] [1900] 1 Ch. 815; and see too the similar *Gander v Murray* (1908) 5 C.L.R. 575. For an earlier

awkward and unusual restrictive covenants. Farwell LJ limited the availability of the remedy to cases where, first, the amount of compensation could be "fairly ascertained", and, secondly, where the actual subject matter was "substantially the same as that stated in the contract".[341] Neither was the case there: the covenants gravely compromised the usability of the properties, and the reckoning of any difference in value was by no means a straightforward exercise. This effectively limits the jurisdiction to relatively small and straightforward defects in title.[342] In one sense such a view is open to criticism, on the basis that it should be up to a purchaser, rather than the court, to decide how serious a defect he is prepared to tolerate.[343] Such arguments may, however, be misplaced. Whatever the justice in minor defect cases of compelling a seller to convey with small adjustments, there is a strong case for allowing him to think again before forcing on him a sale of an inadvertently overvalued asset at a big discount which he might well have been most unwilling to accept.

Unavailability of full performance: Specific performance at the suit of the party in breach of his own obligations subject to counter-payment

27-095 The case where full performance is impossible may arise the other way round: that is, where it is the party himself in breach who seeks specific performance. Here, provided the breach is not a substantial one, and the defect in the property was not actually known to the vendor,[344] there is a parallel jurisdiction to give specific performance subject to the claimant (who is nearly always a vendor of realty[345]) compensating the defendant for any prejudice he may have suffered.[346] In *Rutherford v Acton-Adams*, Lord Haldane said:[347]

> "If a vendor sues and is in a position to convey substantially what the purchaser has contracted to get, the Court will decree specific performance with compensation for any small and immaterial deficiency."

27-096 But the operative words here are "small and immaterial". Any substantial breach will prevent this remedy being granted, and indeed will allow the other party to

---

example, see *Howell v George* (1815) 1 Maddock 1 (life tenant agreed to sell freehold: no order to convey life estate).

[341] See [1900] 1 Ch. 815 at 819–820.

[342] And may throw doubts on some earlier decisions, such as *Hooper v Smart* (1874) L.R. 18 Eq. 683 (remedy against seller with only a half-share).

[343] This is the thesis in C. Harpum, "Specific performance with compensation as a purchaser's remedy—a study in contract and equity" [1981] C.L.J. 47. See too W. Goodhart and G. Jones, *Specific Performance*, 2nd edn (London: Butterworths, 1996), p.294, describing it as "misconceived." For a recent case that seems hard to reconcile, see *Manchester & District Housing Association v Fearnley Construction Ltd (In Liquidation)* [2000] N.P.C. 94 (promise to build houses and then convey land: specific performance of promise to convey with compensation for lack of houses).

[344] See *Carlish v Salt* [1906] 1 Ch. 335 for this restriction.

[345] But not always: for a case of a purchaser obtaining specific performance despite arguable minor breaches on its part, see *Redrow Homes Ltd v Martin Dawn (Leckhampton) Ltd* [2016] EWHC 934 (Ch).

[346] For a typical case, see *Leyland v Illingworth* (1860) 2 De G. F. & J. 248 (misstatement as to cost of water supply: specific performance with compensation).

[347] [1915] A.C. 866 at 869–870.

rescind.[348] Thus in *Cato v Thompson*[349] in 1882 the Court of Appeal trenchantly refused specific performance to the vendor of a small housing development encumbered with restrictive covenants so savage as to amount to a virtual blot on the title. It was not the courts' business, said Jessel MR, to hold a buyers to a "bargain substantially different from that which the parties entered into",[350] which was the case here. Since then, it has been held that cases where what is on offer is "substantially different" from that promised includes a 50 per cent overestimate of the area of the land sold;[351] description of leasehold shops as "valuable business premises" when the lease very severely restricted the businesses that could be carried on there;[352] serious failures in the specification of upmarket apartments;[353] and failure to comply with pre-occupation planning conditions in respect of a new property.[354]

Logically similar to the above cases are those where a court relieves against a forfeiture, for example by disallowing the application of a term in a finance lease or commercial hire-purchase agreement permitting the lessor to deprive the lessee of a proprietary right in the event of non-payment of one or more instalments. Relief in such cases technically takes the form of the court expressing willingness to enforce the agreement specifically at the suit of the lessee, subject to the latter compensating the lessor for any prejudice suffered.[355] These matters are, however, closer to the law of penalties than to specific performance proper, and are dealt with at para.25-064 ff above. **27-097**

Conditional specific performance

Specific performance, being an equitable remedy, may be granted generally on terms: that is, subject to conditions other than the payment of compensation. For instance, in *Baskcomb v Beckwith*[356] ambiguous particulars of sale misled purchasers into believing that all the land for some distance around a high-class estate was covered by restrictive covenants against undesirable development, whereas in fact the purchasers retained a substantial plot not so restricted. The court's decision was that the vendors could obtain specific performance, but only if they were prepared to submit to similar restrictions on the use of their retained land. **27-098**

X.   A Specialised Case: Specific Performance Where No Liability at Law

Although generally equity follows the law in granting specific performance, in a few exceptional cases the remedy may be granted even if at law a contract is no **27-099**

---

[348] See generally *Flight v Booth* (1834) 1 Bing. N.C. 370.
[349] (1882) 9 Q.B.D. 616. See too Parker J in *Shepherd v Croft* [1911] 1 Ch. 521 at 527 ("I have to ask myself whether, if specific performance were granted, the defendant would be getting something different from that which the plaintiffs contracted to give her").
[350] (1882) 9 Q.B.D. 616 at 618.
[351] *Watson v Burton* [1957] 1 W.L.R. 19.
[352] *Charles Hunt Ltd v Palmer* [1931] 2 Ch. 287.
[353] *Donnelly v Weybridge Construction Ltd (No.2)* [2006] EWHC 2678 (TCC); (2006) 111 Con L.R. 112.
[354] *BDW Trading Ltd v Opticlife Ltd* [2010] EWHC 1951 (Ch).
[355] As explained by Lord Hoffmann in *Union Eagle Ltd Appellant v Golden Achievement Ltd* [1997] A.C. 514 at 518 ff. See cases such as *Transag Haulage Ltd (IAR) v Leyland DAF Finance Plc* [1994] BCC 356.
[356] (1869) L.R. 8 Eq. 100.

longer in effect. Two are worth mentioning here: stipulations as to time and forfeitures.

Stipulations as to time

27-100   At common law stipulations as to the time of performance were generally regarded, at least in contracts relating to land, as being of the essence; thus if they were not met the other party could cancel the contract and would not be amenable to a claim for damages or other common law relief.[357] Equity, however, took a different view and regarded late performance as curable, provided the other party was compensated for any loss.[358] The way the distinction was worked out was that even if the contract had been properly avoided at law for late performance, Equity retained a discretion to regard it as valid for its own purposes and, having done so, to enforce it specifically.[359]

27-101   The limits to this jurisdiction must be noted, however. First, Equity did not always decline to regard time as of the essence. On the contrary: the nature of some contracts was it did take time as of the essence and thus refused specific performance in the event of delay.[360] Secondly, a claimant who had repudiated a contract, or had committed some breach other than late performance allowing the other party to rescind, was not protected.[361] And thirdly, in a series of cases it was held that where a term in the contract expressly made time of the essence, that term could not be overridden; hence equity had no jurisdiction to award specific performance on the basis that it was unconscionable for a party to rely on an express right of cancellation.[362]

Forfeitures

27-102   As mentioned above,[363] equity has long professed a jurisdiction to relieve against contractual clauses which work as forfeiture. There are two conditions. First, the clause must be there not for its own sake but, in essence, to secure some other right,

---

[357] There is some doubt whether this remains the case after 1925, in the light of s.41 of the Law of Property Act 1925: see the controversial remarks by Lord Diplock in *United Scientific Holdings Ltd v Burnley BC* [1978] A.C. 904 at 926 ff. But this does not affect the general argument.

[358] *Parkin v Thorold* (1852) 16 Beavan 59 at 65 (Romilly MR); *Stickney v Keeble* [1915] A.C. 386 at 416 (Lord Parker).

[359] *Parkin v Thorold* (1852) 16 Beavan 59 at 67 (Romilly MR). That case is a classic example of such an award. For later instances, see *Starside Properties Ltd v Mustapha* [1974] 1 W.L.R. 816 and *Graham v Pitkin* [1992] 1 W.L.R. 403.

[360] E.g. *Tilley v Thomas* (1867) L.R. 3 Ch. App. 61 (urgent residential purchase); *Lock v Bell* [1931] 1 Ch. 35 (sale of business); *Hare v Nicoll* [1966] 2 Q.B. 130 (shares in private company). And if notice was given, it can make time of the essence even in equity: *King v Wilson* (1843) 6 Beav. 124, and cf. *Behzadi v Shaftesbury Hotels Ltd* [1992] Ch. 1. In practice, this is now dealt with expressly in many sales: see e.g. *Standard Conditions of Sale*, 5th edn, §6.8.

[361] I. Spry, *The Principles of Equitable Remedies*, 9th edn (London: Sweet & Maxwell, 2014), pp.210 ff, 220 ff.

[362] See *Steedman v Drinkle* [1916] 1 A.C. 275; *Brickles v Snell* [1916] 2 A.C. 599; and, more recently, *Union Eagle Ltd v Golden Achievement Ltd* [1997] A.C. 514. This development is attacked in C. Harpum, "Relief against Forfeiture and the Purchaser of Land" [1984] C.L.J. 134. It has been rejected as too narrow in Australia, where it has been held that even an express "time of the essence" clause cannot be invoked unconscionably (see *Legione v Hateley* (1983) 46 A.L.J.R. 1, though cf. *Tanwar Enterprises Pty Ltd v Cauchi* (2003) 217 C.L.R. 315 and J. Zerilli, "Accident in the Equitable Jurisdiction" (2008) 24 JCL 112).

[363] See para.25-064.

such as a right to payment.[364] And secondly, the provision must purport to deprive a party of some property right (as opposed to a mere contractual claim to performance).[365]

In most such cases, the mode of intervention in such cases is the same as where **27-103** equity declines to regard time as being of the essence: that is, by specifically enforcing the arrangement despite the fact that at law the operation of the forfeiture clause has deprived the claimant of any such right.[366] As a result, it is now clear that the only contracts where the doctrine can apply are those where equity would grant specific performance, or at the very least an injunction to prevent breach: if such a remedy is unavailable, there is simply no way in which equity can intervene.[367]

---

[364] *Shiloh Spinners Ltd v Harding* [1973] A.C. 691 at 723 (Lord Wilberforce); for an example, see *Warnborough Ltd v Garmite Ltd* [2006] EWHC 10 (Ch); [2007] 1 P. & C.R. 2 (pre-emption clause amounted to a genuine option, with whose exercise equity should not interfere).

[365] A point put beyond doubt by the House of Lords in *The Scaptrade* [1983] 2 A.C. 694.

[366] As typically with agreements to buy land with payment by instalments: e.g. *Kilmer v British Columbia Orchard Lands Ltd* [1913] A.C. 319. See too cases such as *Re Dagenham Dock Co* (1873) 8 Ch. App. 1022. But other kinds of contract may also be subject to the doctrine: see e.g. *Transag Haulage Ltd (IAR) v Leyland DAF Finance Plc* [1994] BCC 356 (vehicles); *Celestial Aviation Trading 71 Ltd v Paramount Airways Private Ltd* [2010] EWHC 185 (Comm); [2011] 1 Lloyd's Rep. 9 (aircraft); *The Jotunheim* [2004] EWHC 671 (Comm); [2005] 1 Lloyd's Rep. 181 (ship under demise charter).

[367] See *The Scaptrade* [1983] 2 A.C. 694 at 700 ff (Lord Diplock).

CHAPTER 28

SPECIFIC RELIEF: INJUNCTIONS AND BREACH OF CONTRACT

I. GENERALLY

In contrast to specific performance, the jurisdiction to issue injunctions, while on **28-001** principle covering any case of breach of contract, extends well beyond contract cases. It also covers torts, breaches of trust, and indeed any case where the court considers it "just and convenient" to issue an injunction,[1] assuming that the claimant can point to some legal or equitable right (in a wide sense) that needs to be protected.[2]

In the specific context of contractual rights, however, there are further distinc- **28-002** tions to be drawn. Injunctions come in a number of different forms, which are in many cases subject to different rules and practices.

First, there is the distinction between final injunctions (sometimes called **28-003** "perpetual" injunctions), aimed at disposing once and for all of the issues between the parties, and various types of interlocutory injunctions, whose object is the essentially procedural one of preserving the parties' position as best as can be done pending a final decision as to the parties' relative entitlements.[3] This chapter will largely be concerned with the former, final, version, and will not cover the latter in detail (though some mention will be made of them in passing). A further specialised type of injunction that will not be covered, though technically based on contract, is the procedural device of the anti-suit injunction, aimed at preserving the integrity of contractual arbitration or jurisdiction clauses against subversion by preventing the bringing of proceedings in a foreign jurisdiction in contravention of their terms.[4]

Secondly, while most final injunctions in the contractual context are prohibi- **28-004** tory—that is, in terms prohibiting a defendant from doing something or carrying on some activity that would infringe the claimant's rights—not all are. It is entirely possible for a court to issue a mandatory injunction requiring some action to be

---

[1] Senior Courts Act 1981 s.37(1), extended to the county court by the County Courts Act 1984 s.38(1).

[2] I. Spry, *The Principles of Equitable Remedies*, 9th edn (London: Sweet & Maxwell, 2014), p.342 ("any legal right whatever"); and, e.g. *Chief Constable of Kent v V* [1983] Q.B. 34 at 42, 45 (Donaldson and Slade LJJ). There is also a (fairly undefined) power under the section for a public authority to obtain an injunction to support its functions: e.g. *Broadmoor Special Hospital Authority v R* [2000] Q.B. 775. In addition, it now seems clear that injunctions may be issued in support of human rights, even if there is no other right in issue: *Venables v News Group Newspapers Ltd* [2001] Fam. 430 at 445–446.

[3] For details of interlocutory injunctions, the reader is referred to I. Spry, *The Principles of Equitable Remedies*, 9th edn (London: Sweet & Maxwell, 2014), p.462 ff; and S. Gee, *Commercial Injunctions*, 7th edn (London: Sweet & Maxwell, 2022), Ch.2 part (5) ff.

[4] See e.g. S. Gee, *Commercial Injunctions*, 7th edn (London: Sweet & Maxwell, 2020), Ch.14. An analogous form of order, which will also not be covered, is the anti-enforcement injunction aimed at preventing the enforcement of a judgment thus wrongfully obtained.

taken. Moreover, mandatory orders can themselves be divided into two categories. Most such orders are aimed at compelling the defendant to do some act actually required by the terms of the contract. But the court also has jurisdiction, at least in some cases, to issue what can be called restorative injunctions: that is, orders to undo the effect of some prior breach of contract.

II. PROHIBITORY INJUNCTIONS

28-005   In the contractual context, prohibitory injunctions can be regarded as a form of negative specific performance, aimed at compelling the observance of negative, as against positive, contractual obligations.[5] (Indeed, little would be lost were the separate terminology of injunctions and specific performance, which is largely due to history alone, to be abandoned, and a single term such as "mandatory orders" adopted.)

28-006   There is no doubt that a court has jurisdiction to interfere by injunction to compel a defendant to respect any negative stipulation in a contract.[6] This extends on principle to any case where contractual rights fall to be enforced. The point has been left open as to whether a mere anticipatory breach can be enjoined before performance itself is due:[7] it is submitted, however, that the better view is that it can. There is clear authority that in equity orders of specific performance can be issued before the claimant has a cause of action at law on the contract;[8] and there seems no reason to treat injunctions any differently.

Limitations to prohibitory injunctions

28-007   Like specific performance, prohibitory injunctions are an equitable remedy, secondary to damages and other common-law remedies. It follows that they are theoretically available only in so far as the remedies available at common law are inadequate for the protection of the claimant's rights.[9] In addition they are subject

---

[5]   "[A] prohibition, preventing the commission of an act may as effectually perform an agreement as an order for the performance of the act agreed to be done": *Lumley v Wagner* (1852) 1 De G M & G 604 at 615–616 (Lord St Leonards).

[6]   See *Doherty v Allman* (1878) 3 App. Cas. 709 at 719–720 (Lord Cairns); *Attorney General v Barker (Worldwide Injunction)* [1990] 3 All E.R. 257 at 260; *Insurance Co v Lloyd's Syndicate* [1995] 1 Lloyd's Rep. 272 at 277 (Colman J); *Dyson Technology Ltd v Pellerey* [2016] EWCA Civ 87; [2016] I.C.R. 688 at [16]–[17] (Sir Colin Rimer).

[7]   See the discussion in *Berkeley Community Villages Ltd v Pullen* [2007] EWHC 1330 (Ch).

[8]   Compare *Hasham v Zenab* [1960] A.C. 316 and *Roy v Kloepfer Wholesale Hardware and Automotive Co Ltd* [1952] 2 S.C.R. 465, both holding that orders of specific performance were available in such circumstances.

[9]   See generally, in the non-contractual context, *Shelfer v City of London Electric Lighting Co (No.1)* [1895] 1 Ch. 287 at 322–333 (A.L. Smith LJ).

to the general discretion of the court,[10] and also to general equitable defences such as laches[11] and acquiescence.[12]

As with specific performance, it is suggested that, whereas the jurisdiction to *refuse* an injunction in support of contractual rights is the court's and cannot be excluded by contract,[13] there is no reason why an agreement should not be able validly to exclude the *grant* of such relief.[14]   **28-008**

The inadequacy of damages as a remedy[15]

In theory the courts adhere to the view that there can be no injunction against a   **28-009** breach of contract unless it is shown that damages, or some other common law remedy, are inadequate to protect the claimant's interests.[16] To this extent, indeed, injunctions are in theory equated to orders of specific performance.[17] In practice, however, the presumption is strongly in favour of compelling performance of negative stipulations, if there are no clear countervailing features: indeed, in such cases, it is now true to say that an injunction is available virtually as of course.[18] The reasons are not hard to see. There is a strong interest in ensuring that contracts are kept.[19] Furthermore, the fact that contractual obligations are voluntarily assumed means that the fine balancing of parties' interests and the public weal which is often

---

[10]   "[I]n this as much as in any other area of the law an injunction is a discretionary remedy, whose grant or refusal, especially at an interlocutory stage, depends on the infinitely variable facts of the individual case. Although statements of the principles on which the discretion ought to be exercised in some particular area are often authoritative, they are principles of practice rather than of law, whose application may be rendered inappropriate by the finest of factual variations between one case and another": Nourse LJ in *Warren v Mendy* [1989] 1 W.L.R. 853 at 860. See too Branson J in *Warner Bros Pictures Inc v Nelson* [1937] 1 K.B. 209 at 217; and *Araci v Fallon* [2011] EWCA Civ 668 at [33] (Jackson LJ).

[11]   E.g. *Jaggard v Sawyer* [1995] 1 W.L.R. 269, esp at 287 (Millett LJ).

[12]   E.g. *Gafford v Graham* (1999) 77 P. & C.R. 73.

[13]   This is certainly the case with specific performance (*Quadrant Visual Communications Ltd v Hutchinson Telephone (UK) Ltd* [1993] B.C.L.C. 442 at 451–452 (Stocker and Butler-Sloss LJJ)), and there is no conceivable reason to think the position any different as regards injunctions.

[14]   In the case of arbitrators there is clear authority to this effect (see *Vertex Data Science Ltd v Powergen Retail Ltd* [2006] EWHC 1340 (Comm); [2006] 2 Lloyd's Rep. 591 at [28]): but this arguably depends on the principle encapsulated in the Arbitration Act 1996 s.48, that the arbitrator has such remedial powers, and only such powers, as the parties may agree. Nevertheless, the position stated in the text clearly represents the law in the analogous area of specific performance (see *Mills v Sportsdirect.com Retail Ltd* [2010] EWHC 1072 (Ch); [2010] 2 B.C.L.C. 143 and the earlier dicta of Leggatt LJ in *Co-Operative Insurance Society Ltd. v Argyll Stores (Holdings) Ltd* [1996] Ch. 286 at 294); and there seems no reason to treat injunctions any differently.

[15]   D. Bean, I. Parry & A. Burns, *Injunctions* (14th ed, Sweet & Maxwell, 2021), para.2-09–2-15; L. Aitken, "When are Damages an Adequate Remedy?" (2004) 78 ALJ 544.

[16]   E.g. *Donnell v Bennett* (1883) L.R. 22 Ch. D. 835 at 837–838 (Fry J); see too *Araci v Fallon* [2011] EWCA Civ 668; [2011] L.L.R. 440 at [42].

[17]   Compare I. Spry, *The Principles of Equitable Remedies*, 9th edn (London: Sweet & Maxwell, 2014), p.591 ff, referring to the underlying assumption that there is no general divergence between the principles applying to the specific enforcement of positive and negative stipulations.

[18]   See *Doherty v Allman* (1878) 3 App Cas 708 at 720 (Lord Cairns); *Insurance Co v Lloyd's Syndicate* [1995] 1 Lloyd's Rep. 272 at 277 (Colman J); *SDI Retail Services Ltd v Rangers Football Club Ltd* [2018] EWHC 2772 (Comm) at [46] (Teare J); *Priyanka Shipping Ltd v Glory Bulk Carriers Pte Ltd* [2019] EWHC 2804 (Comm); [2019] 1 W.L.R. 6677 at [97]. Of course if it can be positively shown that damages would not do a claimant justice, so much the better for the claimant: see *Araci v Fallon* [2011] EWCA Civ 668 (jockey contracted to ride claimant's horse in the Derby; injunction against riding rival horse, partly because damages difficult in their nature to estimate).

[19]   "[D]amages are inadequate if they cannot satisfy the demands of justice, and that justice to a promisee might well require that a promisor perform the promise": *Zhu v Treasurer of the State of*

necessary in tort cases is of vastly less significance.[20] Conversely, the issues of oppressiveness or impossibility of supervision which often bedevil specific performance claims are less likely to arise where it is the defendant's inaction, rather than action, which the court is being called on to compel.

28-010   The accepted position is nicely demonstrated by the classic decision in *Lumley v Wagner*,[21] where an opera star agreed to sing for the plaintiff theatre owner and for no-one else, but then later expressed her intention of performing for a competitor. Although there was no possibility of specific performance of the obligation to sing for the plaintiff, Lord St Leonards had no hesitation in interfering by injunction to stop her performing for anyone else: Equity, he said,

"operates to bind men's consciences, as far as they can be bound, to a true and literal performance of their agreements; and it will not suffer them to depart from their contracts at their pleasure, leaving the party with whom they have contracted to the mere chance of any damages which a jury may give".[22]

28-011   Lord Cairns in the later case of *Doherty v Allman*[23] was even more forthright:

"If parties, for valuable consideration, with their eyes open, contract that a particular thing shall not be done, all that a Court of Equity has to do is to say, by way of injunction, that which the parties have already said by way of covenant, that the thing shall not be done; and in such case the injunction does nothing more than give the sanction of the process of the court to that which already is the contract between the parties. It is not then a question of the balance of convenience or inconvenience, or of the amount of damage or of injury."[24]

Although this almost certainly goes too far in so far as it suggests that the injunction is somehow available as of right rather than at the court's discretion,[25] as an emphasis of the attitude of the courts to such stipulations it is entirely correct.

---

[20]   *New South Wales* [2004] HCA 56; (2004) 218 C.L.R. 530 at [129] (per curiam). See too *Araci v Fallon* [2011] EWCA Civ 668 at [70], where Elias LJ said that the adequacy of damages was "not generally a relevant consideration" in such cases. *Dyson Technology Ltd v Pellerey* [2016] EWCA Civ 87; [2016] I.C.R. 688 at [13]–[17] (Sir Colin Rimer). In that case, concerning an ordinary confidentiality covenant, the Court of Appeal regarded as of limited significance in contract the Supreme Court's decision in in *Coventry v Lawrence* [2014] UKSC 13; [2014] A.C. 822, where that court substantially re-drew the boundaries of injunctive relief in nuisance and more generally in tort.

[21]   (1852) 1 De G M & G 604. See too the much earlier *Martin v Nutkin* (1724) 2 P. Wms. 266; and, for a case with a more contemporary slant, where the defendant was a TV presenter, *Curro v Beyond Productions Ltd* (1993) 30 N.S.W.L.R. 337.

[22]   (1852) 1 De G M & G 604 at 619; R. Stevens, "Involuntary Servitude by Injunction" [1921] *Cornell LQ* 235; also the useful comments in D. Harris, D. Campbell and R. Halson, *Remedies in Contract and Tort*, 2nd edn (London: Butterworths, 2001), pp.205–206. For the application of these principles to interlocutory injunctions, see *Hampstead & Suburban Properties Ltd v Diomedous* [1969] 1 Ch. 248.

[23]   (1878) 3 App. Cas. 709.

[24]   (1878) 3 App. Cas. 709 at 720. See too *McEacharn v Colton* [1902] A.C. 104; also, *Osborne v Bradley* [1903] 2 Ch. 446 (same doctrine applicable to restrictive covenants). The passage from *Doherty* has been fairly frequently quoted: for some more recent examples, see e.g. *Att Gen v Barker* [1990] 3 All E.R. 257 at 261–262 (Nourse LJ) and *Araci v Fallon* [2011] EWCA Civ 668 at [36] and [70] (Jackson and Elias LJJ).

[25]   *Priyanka Shipping Ltd v Glory Bulk Carriers Pte Ltd* [2019] EWHC 2804 (Comm); [2019] 1 W.L.R. 6677 at [64]–[79]; *Dalgety Wine Estates Pty Ltd v Rizzon* (1979) 141 C.L.R. 552 at 560 (Gibbs J), 573 (Mason J); *Lucas Stuart Pty Ltd v Hemmes Hermitage Pty Ltd* [2010] NSWCA 283 at [5] (Campbell JA); I. Spry, *The Principles of Equitable Remedies*, 9th edn (London: Sweet & Maxwell, 2014), p.597 ff.

Since then, this doctrine has been applied to a vast variety of cases of negative **28-012** covenants, both express and implied.[26] Decisions have involved such diverse matters as promises by railways not to put traffic across any but a particular company's line;[27] by sellers not to sell their output to anyone other than one buyer;[28] by buyers not to take supplies from anyone else other than a given seller;[29] by sellers of growing timber not to prevent the buyer collecting the timber;[30] by employees not to work for their employers' competitors[31] or divulge their secrets;[32] by employers not to discipline employees except through proper contractual channels;[33] and by the buyer of a ship for scrap not to return it to active trade;[34] not to mention a promise by a retained jockey not to ride for any other owner.[35] Indeed, by 1973 the tendency to grant injunctions in respect of straightforward negative stipulations was so pronounced that Sachs LJ was able to say this:

> "The standard question in relation to the grant of an injunction, 'Are damages an adequate remedy?', might perhaps, in the light of the authorities of recent years, be rewritten: 'Is it just, in all the circumstances, that a plaintiff should be confined to his remedy in damages?'"[36]

In keeping with this, the Court of Appeal has declined to regard the fact that parties have agreed to liquidated[37] or capped[38] damages as a convincing reason not to grant an injunction where that would otherwise be appropriate.

Reasons against granting prohibitory injunctions

The effect of *Lumley v Wagner* and the cases following it is that an injunction to **28-013** prevent a breach of contract will very seldom be refused on the basis that the breach

---

[26] On the application to implied covenants, see *Wolverhampton & Walsall Railway Co v London & NW Ry Co* (1873) L.R. 16 Eq. 433 at 440; also *Jones & Sons Ltd v Tankerville (Earl)* [1909] 2 Ch. 440, and *Bower v Bantam Investments Ltd* [1972] 1 W.L.R. 1120. Note, however, the suggestion by Lindley LJ in *Mortimer v Becket* [1920] 1 Ch. 571 at 578 that the equities were marginally less in favour of the claimant with an implied than with an express stipulation, since the latter had been more explicitly agreed on.

[27] *Wolverhampton & Walsall Ry Co v London & NW Ry Co* (1873) L.R. 16 Eq. 433.

[28] *Donnell v Bennett* (1883) L.R. 22 Ch. D. 835.

[29] *Metropolitan Electric Supply Co Ltd v Ginder* [1901] 2 Ch. 799.

[30] *Jones & Sons Ltd v Tankerville (Earl)* [1909] 2 Ch. 440.

[31] *Marco Productions Ltd v Pagola* [1944] 1 K.B. 111, esp at 113–114 (Hallett J); *Dyson Technology Ltd v Strutt* [2005] EWHC 2814 (Ch).

[32] See e.g. the colourful *Att Gen v Barker* [1990] 3 All E.R. 257 (revelations from employee in royal household).

[33] See, e.g., *Edwards v Chesterfield Royal Hospital NHS Foundation Trust* [2011] UKSC 58; [2012] 2 A.C. 22 and *Chhabra v West London Mental Health NHS Trust* [2013] UKSC 80; [2014] I.C.R. 194; also the Irish decision in *O'Donovan v Over-C Technology Ltd* [2020] IEHC 291.

[34] *Priyanka Shipping Ltd v Glory Bulk Carriers Pte Ltd* [2019] EWHC 2804 (Comm); [2019] 1 W.L.R. 6677

[35] *Araci v Fallon* [2011] EWCA Civ 668; [2011] L.L.R. 440. Cf. *Curro v Beyond Productions Ltd* (1993) 30 N.S.W.L.R. 337.

[36] *Evans Marshall & Co Ltd v Bertola SA* [1973] 1 W.L.R. 349 at 379; also (verbatim) Jackson LJ in *Araci v Fallon* [2011] EWCA Civ 668; [2011] L.L.R. 440 at [42].

[37] *Bath & North East Somerset District Council v Mowlem Plc (Note)* [2004] EWCA Civ 115; [2015] 1 W.L.R. 785 at [14] (Mance LJ).

[38] *AB v CD* [2014] EWCA Civ 229; [2015] 1 W.L.R. 771. See too *London EV Co Ltd v Optimas OE Solutions Ltd* [2022] EWHC 2525 (Comm).

is better compensated with damages.[39] Nevertheless, even accepting that damages will not normally be regarded as a sufficient remedy for claimant faced with a threatened breach of a negative stipulation, it is clear that a number of other considerations will militate more or less strongly against the grant of injunctive relief.

28-014　**(i)**　**No adequate purpose served**　Even where there has been a breach of a clear negative stipulation, in very clear cases the courts will still be prepared to say that the claimant has no legitimate interest in enforcing the term specifically, or that no adequate purpose would be served by so doing. Indeed, it is often forgotten that the above-mentioned decision in *Doherty v Allman*[40] was itself just such a case. There, the House of Lords upheld the Irish courts' refusal to prevent a long leaseholder developing derelict military buildings for housing in breach of a technical covenant against it in the lease, on the basis that stifling the development of the land would serve no useful purpose: reasoning that has been applied since in other cases concerning innocuous redevelopment in similar circumstances.[41] So too, where land has been sold subject to contract and subject to an agreement by the seller not to negotiate with anyone else, the latter promise will not normally be enforced by injunction, since the claimant has no right that it be sold to him and preventing negotiation with anyone else would sterilise it.[42] Again, in *Hammersmith London Borough Council v Creska Ltd*[43] a tenant insisted on preventing its landlord entering to carry out repairs to the heating system that were inconvenient and largely unnecessary. Despite the landlord technically being within its rights, Jacob J refused an injunction: even if the negative covenant principle applied, this was a breach that saved the tenant great inconvenience, caused the landlord little if any loss, and could be easily cured with a payment of damages.

28-015　**(ii)**　**Certainty**　Just as the defendant in an action for specific performance is entitled to know precisely what he is to do, hence precluding the enforcement of vague or open-ended obligations,[44] so also with injunctions. Hence it is clear that a court may refuse injunctive relief in respect of an admittedly valid contractual obligation on the basis that its precise content is uncertain, as (for example) with an unparticularised duty of "good faith",[45] or an implied obligation on a buyer of land not to frustrate a given development and indeed to use its best endeavours to procure it.[46]

28-016　**(iii)**　**Lack of assurance of counter-performance**　Where a claimant seeks an

---

[39]　See Elias LJ in *Araci v Fallon* [2011] EWCA Civ 668 at [70] (adequacy of damages "not generally a relevant consideration" in such cases).

[40]　(1878) 3 App. Cas. 709.

[41]　E.g. *British Glass Manufacturers Confederation v Sheffield University* [2003] EWHC 3108 (Ch); [2004] L. & T.R. 14. See too *Sharp v Harrison* [1922] 1 Ch. 502 (insertion of wholly innocuous window in breach of covenant).

[42]　*Tye v House* [1997] 2 E.G.L.R. 171.

[43]　[2000] L & TR 288.

[44]　See para.27-064.

[45]　See Warby J in the employment case of *Elsevier Ltd v Munro* [2014] EWHC 2648 (QB) at [83] ("I agree with the Defendant's submission that the Claimant's claim for an injunction to restrain a breach of the duty of good faith is unsound, because the wording is too vague and uncertain").

[46]　*Bower v Bantam Investments Ltd* [1972] 1 W.L.R. 1120. Compare another "best endeavours" case, *Charters-Ancaster College v Girls' Public Day School Trust (1872)* [1996] ELR 123 (obligation as regards preservation of school ethos).

injunction to prevent a breach of contract, it is normally a condition of relief (as it is with specific performance[47]) that in so far as some essential performance is still due from himself, he is ready and able to provide it. *Measures Bros Ltd v Measures*,[48] a case where counter-performance would clearly never be provided at all, illustrates the point neatly. A company director under a seven-year contract entered into a non-competition covenant expressed to last so long as he should be employed, and for seven years thereafter. Made redundant on his employers' receivership six years later, he successfully resisted the receiver's plea for an injunction to enforce the covenant. Even if (it was said) the covenant remained binding at law even in the event of premature dismissal, the fact that the insolvent company could no longer do its part by employing the defendant disentitled it to any equitable relief in support of it.[49] More recently, and on a similar basis, it has been held that in so far as an injunction preventing a building contractor from terminating a contract would leave the contractor locked into a relationship with an entirely unreliable and untrustworthy counterparty, that will be a strong argument in favour of refusing it.[50]

Moreover, the cases also suggest that an injunction may on occasion be denied **28-017** if, however willing and apparently able the claimant to provide counter-performance, the defendant would be left without adequate assurance of actually receiving it (as against a right to sue for damages, with the attendant credit risk). So in *Hills v Croll*,[51] a requirements case where a seller agreed to supply a buyer with all the acid he required in exchange for the buyer's promise not to buy from anyone else, the seller failed in his quest for an injunction to enforce the buyer's undertaking. The ground was akin to mutuality: the court, said Lord Cottenham, "has no power to compel the Plaintiff to supply the Defendant with acids" and, for that reason, it would be unfairly one-sided to compel the defendant alone to observe the contract *in specie*. But this principle is limited: once the defendant has obtained some benefit from the claimant's performance, the lack of assurance of future benefits may well be outweighed by the court's reluctance to allow a defendant to get something for nothing.[52] Hence in *Regent International Hotels (UK) Ltd v Pageguide Ltd*,[53] where a management company agreed to manage the Dorchester Hotel in London for a fixed period, the Court of Appeal upheld an injunction against wrongful termination: the managers having in effect enabled the defendants to acquire and profit from the hotel, should not be deprived of the fruits of their labour by being left to a doubtful claim in damages.

(iv) Relationships of trust Where a commercial relationship has broken down, **28-018** an injunction will often be refused if its effect would be to compel continuing relations between those who can no longer realistically work together. Thus, even if a bank acts in breach of contract in closing a customer's account it will not normally

---

[47] Para.27-055 ff.

[48] [1910] 2 Ch. 248.

[49] Contra, however, where it is the employee who resigns, since here the equities are almost wholly in favour of the employer: *Standard Life Health Care Ltd v Gorman* [2009] EWCA Civ 1292; [2010] I.R.L.R. 233.

[50] *Ferrara Quay Ltd v Carillion Construction Ltd* [2009] B.L.R. 367. See too *Vertex Data Science Ltd v Powergen Retail Ltd* [2006] EWHC 1340 (Comm); [2006] 2 Lloyd's Rep. 591 esp at [46].

[51] (1845) 2 Ph. 60

[52] See *Dietrichsen v Cabburn* (1846) 2 Ph. 52 at 57 (Lord Cottenham); *Regent International Hotels (UK) Ltd v Pageguide Ltd* (1985) *The Times*, 13 May.

[53] (1985) *The Times*, 13 May.

be ordered to keep it open;[54] and a company that wrongfully dismisses a service provider in acrimonious circumstances will generally not be ordered to reinstate it.[55]

28-019 **(v) Rights of innocent third parties** A court is not prevented from granting an injunction solely because a third party's rights may thereby be compromised.[56] However, injunctive relief may be refused as a matter of discretion in such a case, at least where the third party is innocent and without notice.[57] Thus, once a lender has contracted to sell a mortgaged property to a third party without notice following non-payment by the mortgagor, no injunction will normally issue to prevent the completion of the sale even if it is otherwise wrongful, for example because it is at an undervalue.[58]

28-020 **(vi) Hardship** Although hardship to the defendant is a well-established factor in the decision whether to grant an injunction in property or tort cases,[59] courts are generally, and very understandably, unsympathetic to the parallel argument in contract. Protestations by a contractor that he would suffer hardship as a result of being compelled passively to abide by a promise he himself made are in their nature unconvincing.[60] Nevertheless, it is now clear that the court does retain a discretion even here to refuse it where any hardship to the defendant vastly outweighs the harm that would be suffered by the claimant if refused specific relief.[61]

28-021   Similarly, an injunction may apparently be refused where, despite the lack of any strict legal wrong on the claimant's part, its award would have an entirely one-sided result. This, at least, seems to be the result of *Shell UK Ltd v Lostock Garage Ltd*.[62] Having obtained an agreement from a garage to buy petrol exclusively from them, Shell failed to support the garage during a petrol price war (though they did

---

[54] *Prosperity Ltd v Lloyds Bank Ltd* (1923) 39 T.L.R. 372.

[55] *Vertex Data Science Ltd v Powergen Retail Ltd* [2006] EWHC 1340 (Comm); [2006] 2 Lloyd's Rep. 591.

[56] *SDI Retail Services Ltd v Rangers Football Club Ltd* [2018] EWHC 2772 (Comm) at [59] (Teare J).

[57] Hence in *SDI Retail Services Ltd v Rangers Football Club Ltd* [2018] EWHC 2772 (Comm), when Teare J prevented a football club performing a merchandising contract with a third party concluded in breach of the claimant's exclusive rights, he was at some pains to emphasise that the third party had when contracting been fully aware of the risks involved. See at [59].

[58] *Buwule v MT Finance Ltd* [2021] EWHC 1725 (QB). A similar rule applies in specific performance: *Warmington v Miller* [1973] Q.B. 877.

[59] I. Spry, *The Principles of Equitable Remedies*, 9th edn (London: Sweet & Maxwell, 2014), p.413 ff; and see generally *Sharp v Harrison* [1922] 1 Ch. 502.

[60] *Doherty v Allman* (1878) 3 App. Cas. 709 at 719–720 (Lord Cairns); see too *Araci v Fallon* [2011] EWCA Civ 668 (tough, but not excessive hardship, on jockey contracted to claimant to be prevented from riding for rival on Derby Day). In *De Mattos v Gibson* (1859) 4 De G. & J 276 at 299 Lord Chelmsford suggested that hardship was simply irrelevant: but this almost certainly goes too far.

[61] *Sutton Housing Trust v Lawrence* (1987) 19 H.L.R. 520 at 522 (Kerr LJ) (plea admissible, though ultimately unsuccessful, where social landlord sought injunction preventing disabled tenant keeping a dog in breach of lease); also *Insurance Co v A Lloyd's Syndicate* [1995] 1 Lloyd's Law Reports 272 at 276–277 (Colman J). The court in *Sutton* followed the suggestion to that effect in what is now I. Spry, *The Principles of Equitable Remedies*, 9th edn (London: Sweet & Maxwell, 2014), pp.608–609. See too *Provident Financial Group Ltd v Hayward* [1989] 3 All E.R. 298 (no injunction, as a matter of discretion, against other employment during employee's "gardening leave" where clear other employment in other business entirely unconnected with employer's), and *GFI Group Inc v Eaglestone* [1994] I.R.L.R. 119. The fact that the grant of an injunction would put the defendant in breach of contract is also an argument against its grant: see *Buwule v MT Finance Ltd* [2021] EWHC 1725 (QB) (no injunction against sale of property where sale to third party already arranged in good faith).

[62] [1976] 1 W.L.R. 1187.

support its competitors, which they also supplied, by granting them rebates and other benefits). Faced with a threat born of desperation to buy supplies elsewhere, they then sought to enforce the solus tie by injunction. Denning and Ormrod LJJ, despite finding that the garage was in breach of contract, nevertheless thought that this was a case for refusing an injunction: Shell, having in effect thrown the defendant to the economic wolves and reduced the benefit of the contract to it to nil, had excluded themselves from the protection of equity.[63]

(vii) Effect on the defendant's human rights On some occasions the European   **28-022**
Convention on Human Rights may be relevant to the decision whether to enjoin a breach of contract. For example, it is now clear that Art.8 of the Convention, which protects the home, may limit public authorities' rights under private law in respect of properties they own;[64] this may be relevant where, for example, injunctions are sought to enforce terms of residential tenancies. Again, before the Human Rights Act 1998, it was accepted that publication of information in breach of contract was no different from any other breach of a negative contractual stipulation: notwithstanding the Convention right to free speech in Art.10, an injunction therefore issued almost as of course.[65] Whether this remains the case since the 1998 Act has never been decided, but it seems doubtful. Under s.12 of that Act a court must, in deciding whether to grant any relief that might affect the defendant's rights to freedom of speech, have regard to the possible public interest in allowing journalistic, literary or artistic material to be published. The section draws no distinction being drawn between contractual and other restrictions in this connection, from which it presumably follows that here too a balancing exercise must now be undertaken,[66] even if in practice the courts are likely to be more willing to draw the balance in favour of the claimant in contractual than non-contractual cases.[67]

(viii) General equitable defences The injunction against a breach of contract   **28-023**
being an equitable remedy, it is subject to all the general equitable defences,[68] such as laches[69] and the rule that he who comes to equity must do equity.[70]

---

[63] See [1976] 1 W.L.R. 1187 at 1199, 1202.
[64] See *Manchester City Council v Pinnock* [2010] UKSC 45; [2010] 3 W.L.R. 1441. On the effect of the ECHR on private landlords' rights, which is more questionable, see *McDonald v McDonald* [2016] UKSC 28; [2017] A.C. 273.
[65] *Att Gen v Barker* [1990] 3 All E.R. 257 (disclosures by royal household employee).
[66] See *London Regional Transport v Mayor of London* [2001] EWCA Civ 1491, [2003] E.M.L.R. 4 at [45]–[46] (Robert Walker LJ); *Monckton v BBC* (unreported 31 January 2011) Q.B.D. The point equally seems to have been assumed in *HRH Prince of Wales v Associated Newspapers Ltd* [2006] EWCA Civ 1776, [2008] Ch. 57.
[67] *Campbell v Frisbee* [2002] EWCA 1374; [2003] E.M.L.R. 3 at [22] (Lord Phillips); *Att Gen v Parry* [2002] EWHC 3201 (Ch); [2004] E.M.L.R. 13 at [14] (Lewison J); *HRH Prince of Wales v Associated Newspapers Ltd* [2006] EWCA Civ 1776, [2008] Ch. 57 at [28]–[30] (Lord Phillips); *ABC v Telegraph Media Group Ltd* [2018] EWCA Civ 2329; [2019] 2 All E.R. 684 at [11]–[24].
[68] I. Spry, *The Principles of Equitable Remedies*, 9th edn (London: Sweet & Maxwell, 2014), p.607.
[69] There seems no case of laches barring enforcement of a straight contractual obligation: but the jurisdiction is well-established in the analogous case of restrictive covenants (e.g. *Osborne v Bradley* [1903] 2 Ch. 446; *Gafford v Graham* (1999) 77 P. & C.R. 73). And note Jacob J in *WWF-World Wide Fund for Nature v World Wrestling Federation Entertainment Inc* [2002] F.S.R. 504 at 526–527.
[70] E.g. *Maythorne v Palmer* (1865) 11 Jur N.S. 230 (employer who writes untrue reference cannot injunctively enforce non-competition covenant). Cf. *Shell UK Ltd v Lostock Garage Ltd* [1976] 1 W.L.R. 1187 at 1199 (Lord Denning MR).

III.   MANDATORY INJUNCTIONS TO ENFORCE CONTRACTUAL OBLIGATIONS

28-024   Mandatory injunctions in contract are in practice normally granted at the interlocutory stage, to prevent the position being prejudiced by the defendant's inaction pending final determination of the parties' rights.[71] Such orders are, however, sparingly made,[72] will not be made where they may cause serious inconvenience or difficulty,[73] and are only generally available where a claimant shows a very clear prospect of success at trial.[74]

28-025   Quite apart from the interlocutory stage, however, on occasion a claimant may require an order that a particular positive contractual obligation be performed; and in such a case the court may issue a final mandatory injunction to achieve that end. Examples are where a mortgagee of shares agrees to vote them as directed by the mortgagor;[75] where the buyer of an asset promises to release an escrow deposit to the seller in the event of his own default;[76] where a charterparty requires a charterer to provide security if the vessel is arrested in respect of a charterer's liability;[77] where an insurance broker agrees with an underwriter to set up a premium trust account;[78] where a bank refuses to make a contractually-agreed money transfer;[79] where a contract contains a term requiring one party to grant access to information or documentation;[80] where a building contract requires the client to be admitted to the site to carry out tests there;[81] and where the terms of a lease require a landlord to repair[82] or tenants to co-operate with repairers appointed by the lessor.[83]

28-026   In practice orders of this sort tend to refer to discrete and relatively minor obligations within a contract. Not surprisingly in view of the similarity of such orders to

---

[71]   For examples, see e.g. *Sky Petroleum Ltd v VIP Petroleum Ltd* [1974] 1 W.L.R. 576 (argument as to whether petrol company bound to continue supplying station: injunction to continue supplies in the interim); *The Messiniaki Tolmi (No.2)* [1982] Q.B. 1248 (ship sale dispute: order to buyers to release price into escrow account pending determination); *N v S* [2015] EWHC 3248 (Comm) (carrying out of banking instructions where account peremptorily frozen with no good reason).

[72]   For discussion, see *Locabail International Finance Ltd. v Agroexport* [1986] 1 W.L.R. 657 at 664–665 (Mustill LJ) and I. Spry, *The Principles of Equitable Remedies*, 9th edn (London: Sweet & Maxwell, 2014), p.594 ff.

[73]   For example, where requiring the readmission to university of a student suspended for alleged sexual impropriety would create feelings of unsafety among other students: see *AB v University of XYZ* [2020] EWHC 206 (QB), esp at [110]–[115].

[74]   See, e.g. *Films Rover Ltd v Canon Film Sales Ltd* [1987] 1 W.L.R. 570; *Nottingham Building Society v Eurodynamics Systems* [1993] F.S.R. 468.

[75]   *Puddephatt v Leith* [1916] 1 Ch. 200. Why an order of this sort is not referred to as one of specific performance is not entirely clear.

[76]   *Tandrin Aviation Holdings Ltd v Aero Toy Store LLC* [2010] EWHC 40 (Comm); [2010] 2 Lloyd's Rep. 668.

[77]   See e.g. *The Laemthong Glory (No.2)* [2004] EWHC 2738 (Comm); [2005] 1 Lloyd's Rep. 632, esp at [51]–[52] (Cooke J); *Harmony Innovation Shipping Pte Ltd v Caravel Shipping Inc* [2019] EWHC 1037 (Comm); *Trafigura Maritime Logistics Pte Ltd v Clearlake Shipping Pte Ltd* [2020] EWHC 726 (Comm); and *NaviG8 Chemicals Pool Inc v Aeturnum Energy International Pte Ltd* [2021] EWHC 3132 (Comm).

[78]   *AmTrust Europe Ltd v Trust Risk Group SpA* [2014] EWHC 4169 (Comm).

[79]   E.g. *Manoukian v Societe Generale de Banque Au Liban Sal* [2022] EWHC 669 (QB). The order was referred to as one of specific performance, but in essence what was granted was a mandatory injunction.

[80]   E.g. *Honeywell Control Systems Ltd v Multiplex Constructions (UK) Ltd* [2007] EWHC 390 (TCC) (building contract); *Banca Generali SpA v CFE (Suisse) SA* [2022] EWHC 1450 (Ch) (details of receivables comprised in securitisation).

[81]   *Newcastle NHS Foundation v Healthcare Support (Newcastle) Ltd* [2015] EWHC 2777 (TCC).

[82]   E.g. *Parker v Camden London Borough Council* [1986] Ch. 162.

[83]   *Metropolitan Properties Ltd v Wilson* [2002] EWHC 1853 (Ch).

orders of specific performance,[84] it is often the case that analogous practices apply to those obtaining there.[85] Thus a mandatory order will not be granted if, for instance, it would effectively require a defendant to carry on a line of business[86] or engage in dealings requiring the continued operation of a closely co-operative relationship,[87] or if the acts or omissions ordained cannot be defined with sufficient certainty.[88] Conversely, it seems it will be granted in respect of an obligation existing to provide the claimant with security.[89] But absent some such ground of objection, there is nineteenth-century authority that courts will award mandatory injunctions for contractual obligations fairly readily, and certainly more so than in the case of tort.[90]

IV. MANDATORY RESTORATIVE INJUNCTIONS

Mandatory orders may be available not only before the event, to force performance of an as yet unperformed contractual obligation, but also afterwards, in order to compel the undoing of the effects of a past breach. Most of the cases are not strictly contract cases, involving instead the closely analogous situation where a landowner claims an order for the undoing of building work done on land in breach of a restrictive covenant.[91] But there are some contract cases too. One such is *Charrington v Simons & Co Ltd*.[92] There, sellers of land, who retained other land which they needed to safeguard for their business of fruit farming, took a covenant from the buyers not to resurface a road so as to raise its level and risk flooding. When the buyers broke this covenant, the Court of Appeal held that they should be ordered to undo the work and restore the pre-breach position. Conversely, in *Carter v Cole*[93] a vendor of land planted shrubs on retained land which obstructed road visibility, rendered the plot sold useless for the purpose intended and amounted to a derogation from grant: they were ordered to remove the offending growths. Nor is

28-027

---

[84] Compare *NaviG8 Chemicals Pool Inc v Aeturnum Energy International Pte Ltd* [2021] EWHC 3132 (Comm) at [67], where in the context of that case the remedies were said to be "one and the same".

[85] Above, Ch.27.

[86] On the principle enunciated in *Co-Operative Insurance Society Ltd v Argyll Stores (Holdings) Ltd* [1998] A.C. 1; above, para.27-078: see *Flogas Ltd v Warrington (t/a Robin Sutton Gases)* [2007] EWHC 1303 (QB) (resale and promotion of claimant's goods). But an order not to cease providing a standardised business to one customer of many may be different: cf. *Sogexia SaRL v Raphael & Sons Plc* [2019] EWHC 2577 (Ch).

[87] *Ross v Stanbridge Earls School* [2002] EWHC 2255 (QB); [2003] E.L.R. 400 (no order to readmit school pupil); *Akai Holdings Ltd v RSM Robson Rhodes LLP* [2007] EWHC 1641 (Ch) (no order to forensic accountants not to terminate retainer); *Vertex Data Science Ltd v Powergen Retail Ltd* [2006] EWHC 1340 (Comm); [2006] 2 Lloyd's Rep. 591 (complex building contract). Note also *Hayes v Pack* [2022] EWHC 2508 (KB) at [65] (doubtful if injunction appropriate to force readmission to political party after breakdown of relationship, even if expulsion wrongful). See generally above, para.27-062.

[88] *Vertex Data Science Ltd v Powergen Retail Ltd* [2006] EWHC 1340 (Comm); [2006] 2 Lloyd's Rep. 591 at [46] (Tomlinson J). See too the earlier *Bower v Bantam Investments Ltd* [1972] 1 W.L.R. 1120.

[89] *Rayack Construction Ltd v Lampeter Meat Co Ltd* (1980) 12 B.L.R. 30 (contract by building employer to set up segregated retention fund).

[90] *Att Gen v Mid-Kent Ry Co* (1867) 3 Ch. App. 100 at 104 (Rolt LJ). See too *Manners (Lord) v Johnson* (1875) 1 Ch. D. 673 at 680 (Hall V-C).

[91] A straightforward, and extensively-argued, example being *Shepherd Homes Ltd v Sandham* [1971] Ch. 340 (action, in the event unsuccessful, to compel removal of a fence erected by a householder on an open-plan estate). See too the later *Wakeham v Wood* (1982) 43 P. & C.R. 40.

[92] [1971] 1 W.L.R. 598.

[93] [2009] EWCA Civ 410; [2009] 2 E.G.L.R. 15.

the principle confined to land: it may apply equally well in other contexts.[94] Indeed, in a suitable case not only the other party to the contract, but in addition any third party involved in the breach, is susceptible to such an order.[95]

28-028 Outside contract (and related cases such as restrictive covenants), there is no doubt that orders of this sort are given very sparingly indeed.[96] In contract, by contrast, it is suggested that the courts may well be slightly more generous.[97] Even here, however, it is clear that the open-handed practice characterised by *Doherty v Allman*[98] does not apply; the courts remain chary of granting relief, and the decision whether to give it is much more fact-sensitive. Buckley J usefully summed up the position in 1969:

> "Different considerations may, I think, arise in a case where the court has to consider whether a defendant should be compelled by a mandatory order to remedy a breach of contract which he has committed from those which would arise if the question were whether the court should restrain a threatened breach of contract. To the latter case the principle enunciated by Lord Cairns LC in *Doherty v Allman* ... may apply in its full rigour. Where a mandatory order is sought the court must consider whether in the circumstances as they exist after the breach a mandatory order, and, if so, what kind of mandatory order, will produce a fair result. In this connection the court must, in my judgment, take into consideration amongst other relevant circumstances the benefit which the order will confer on the plaintiff and the detriment which it will cause the defendant."[99]

28-029 Mandatory orders are also subject to the same general defences, such as laches[100] or unconscionable conduct by the claimant,[101] as other injunctions.

V.   INJUNCTIONS AND INDIRECT SPECIFIC PERFORMANCE

28-030 The relation between injunctions and specific performance can at times be an uneasy one. This can be particularly true in the case of prohibitory injunctions, where the highly claimant-friendly principle in *Doherty v Allman*,[102] under which negative covenants are very readily enforced by injunction, contrasts starkly with the courts' otherwise highly cautious attitude to granting positive orders of specific performance of contracts as a whole.

---

[94] e.g. *Youatwork Ltd v Motivano Ltd* [2003] EWHC 1047 (Ch); [2004] Masons Comp.L.R. 25 (website moved in breach of contract from one host to another: order to restore situation).

[95] *Esso Petroleum Co Ltd v Kingswood Motors (Addlestone) Ltd* [1974] Q.B. 142 (land containing petrol station collusively conveyed away in breach of contract with a view to defeating petrol solus tie: order to both vendor and purchaser to reverse conveyance). See too *Hemmingway Securities Ltd v Duraven Ltd* [1995] 1 E.G.L.R. 61 (tenant subleases in breach of covenant; lessor entitled to injunction ordering both tenant and subtenant to undo the arrangement); also *SDI Retail Services Ltd v Rangers Football Club Ltd* [2021] EWCA Civ 790 (order not only to refrain from enforcing, but to unwind, marketing deals made with third parties in clear breach of exclusive marketing agreement).

[96] For discussion, see *Redland Bricks Ltd v Morris* [1970] A.C. 652 (a nuisance case concerning removal of support).

[97] Compare *Att Gen v Mid-Kent Ry Co* (1867) 3 Ch. App. 100 at 104 (Rolt LJ), referred to above. Although that dictum referred to a mandatory injunction to enforce a legal right rather than remove a legal wrong, the reasoning remains convincing here.

[98] (1878) 3 App. Cas. 709.

[99] *Charrington v Simons & Co Ltd* [1970] 1 W.L.R. 725 at 730 (Buckley J) (reversed on the application of those principles at *Charrington v Simons & Co Ltd* [1971] 1 W.L.R. 598). See too *Shepherd Homes Ltd v Sandham* [1971] Ch. 340 at 346 (Megarry J).

[100] Cf. *Shepherd Homes Ltd v Sandham* [1971] Ch. 340 (a restrictive covenant case, but still in point).

[101] *Harris v Williams-Wynne* [2006] EWCA Civ 104; [2006] 2 P. & C.R. 27.

[102] (1878) 3 App. Cas. 709: above, para.28-011.

The starting point in finding an accommodation between these two principles is **28-031** straightforward. Since insisting on observance of a specific negative covenant in a contract is a more limited, and less intrusive, exercise than compelling performance of the contract as a whole, it follows that the mere fact that the contract concerned is not specifically enforceable is of itself no bar to the grant of an injunction restraining the defendant from breaking a negative stipulation contained in it.[103] So in the leading decision in *Lumley v Wagner*,[104] a theatre owner successfully obtained an injunction preventing his star performer singing anywhere else, even though her promise not to do so appeared in a contract of employment which was admittedly not specifically enforceable. Lord St Leonards summed the matter up thus:

> "It was objected that the operation of the injunction in the present case was mischievous, excluding the Defendant J. Wagner from performing at any other theatre while this Court had no power to compel her to perform at Her Majesty's Theatre. It is true that I have not the means of compelling her to sing, but she has no cause of complaint if I compel her to abstain from the commission of an act which she has bound herself not to do, and thus possibly cause her to fulfil her engagement. The jurisdiction which I now exercise is wholly within the power of the Court, and being of opinion that it is a proper case for interfering, I shall leave nothing unsatisfied by the judgment I pronounce."[105]

Since then, the principle referred to by Lord St Leonards has been applied not **28-032** only to exclusivity clauses in contracts of employment,[106] but to provisions limiting the right to remove an employee from the payroll;[107] to exclusivity obligations in contracts for the sale of chattels;[108] to agreements to preserve the exclusivity of a sales agency;[109] to conflict of interest obligations undertaken by professional accountants;[110] and to a clause limiting a shipowner's right to time-charter her outside the membership of a particular pool.[111]

Nevertheless, the courts remain aware that care must be taken to prevent the use **28-033** of this principle as a means of wholesale subversion of the rules concerning specific

---

[103] "Wherever this Court has not proper jurisdiction to enforce specific performance, it operates to bind men's consciences, as far as they can be bound, to a true and literal performance of their agreements";—Lord St Leonards in *Lumley v Wagner* (1852) 1 De G M & G 604 at 619. See too *Donnell v Bennett* (1883) 22 Ch. D. 835 at 838 (Fry J); *Warner Bros Pictures Inc v Nelson* [1937] 1 K.B. 209 at 215 (Branson J); *Lauritzencool AB v Lady Navigation Inc* [2005] EWCA Civ 579; [2005] 1 W.L.R. 3686 at 3694 (Mance LJ).

[104] (1852) 1 De G M & G 604.

[105] (1852) 1 De G M & G 604 at 619.

[106] *Warner Bros Pictures Inc v Nelson* [1937] 1 K.B. 209 (similar facts to *Lumley v Wagner*, the defendant there being the Hollywood diva Bette Davis). See too *Marco Productions Ltd v Pagola* [1945] K.B. 111 (another entertainment case: injunction granted despite no showing of likely damage from breach of negative covenant). Cf. *Araci v Fallon* [2011] EWCA Civ 668 (exclusive agreement by jockey).

[107] *Irani v Southampton and South West Hampshire Health Authority* [1985] I.C.R. 590; *Gryf-Lowczowski v Hinchingbrooke Healthcare NHS Trust* [2005] EWHC 2407 (QB); [2006] I.C.R. 425; and cf. the earlier *Hill v CA Parsons & Co Ltd* [1972] Ch. 305.

[108] *Donnell v Bennett* (1883) 22 Ch. D. 835 (contract not to sell waste fish to anyone other than the plaintiff).

[109] *Decro-Wall International S.A. v Practitioners in Marketing Ltd* [1971] 1 W.L.R. 361 at 371 (Salmon LJ).

[110] *Akai Holdings Ltd v RSM Robson Rhodes LLP* [2007] EWHC 1641 (Ch) (injunction against merger in so far as it would compromise obligations, even though no injunction against termination of retainer).

[111] *Lauritzencool AB v Lady Navigation Inc* [2005] EWCA Civ 579; [2005] 1 W.L.R. 3686. Time-charters are as such not specifically enforceable: see *The Scaptrade* [1983] 2 A.C. 694 at 702–703 (Lord Diplock).

performance. For this reason, it is subject to one obvious exception. An injunction which, though negative in form, in substance amounts to an order to perform the positive obligations in the contract is treated as an instance of specific performance under another name, and is granted only subject to the same restrictions.[112] Examples of such negative orders pregnant with affirmative compulsions are injunctions against dismissal;[113] against withdrawing supplies of petrol under a long-standing contract;[114] against withdrawing a ship under time-charter;[115] or against terminating a professional retainer.[116]

28-034   More difficult are cases where an injunction may have the effect of forcing performance, but only indirectly so. For example, if an employee under a fixed-term contract containing an exclusivity clause is enjoined from working for anyone other than his present employer, then unless he has private means he is effectively being given the choice between performance and penury, which in practice may amount to forcing him into a form of salaried slavery.[117] Again, if a seller of a complex chattel is enjoined from supplying it to anyone other than the agreed buyer, the choice will often be the somewhat unreal one of allowing it to moulder in his workshop or supplying it under the terms of the original contract.[118]

28-035   For a long time, such cases of indirect compulsion were consistently treated in the same way as orders in form negative but in substance positive, and hence regarded as a general exception to *Doherty v Allman*.[119] The point was illustrated mainly by a line of employment cases typified by *Whitwood Chemical Co v Hardman*.[120] There the Court of Appeal discharged an injunction against an employee working elsewhere during the time of his employment: as Lindley LJ tellingly put it:

> "What injunction can be granted in this particular case which will not be, in substance and effect, a decree for specific performance of this agreement? It appears to me the difficulty of the Plaintiffs is this, that they cannot suggest anything which, when examined, does not amount to this, that the man must either be idle, or specifically perform the agreement into which he has entered."[121]

A long series of very similar employment cases followed.[122] Similarly, barring exceptional cases, the courts regularly denied injunctions in cases where their ef-

---

[112] "The mere fact that a covenant which the Court would not enforce, if expressed in positive form, is expressed in the negative instead, will not induce the Court to enforce it." Branson J in *Warner Bros Pictures Inc v Nelson* [1937] 1 K.B. 209 at 219.

[113] See *Chappell v Times Newspapers Ltd* [1975] 1 W.L.R. 482. This practice was upheld in *Steer v Stormsure Ltd* [2021] EWCA Civ 887; [2021] I.C.R. 1671 and *Union of Shop, Distributive and Allied Workers (USDAW) v Tesco Stores Ltd* [2022] EWCA Civ 978; [2022] I.C.R. 1573 (see Bean LJ at [55]–[56]). In the *Steer* case it was also held ECHR-compliant.

[114] *Sky Petroleum Ltd v V.I.P. Petroleum Ltd* [1974] 1 W.L.R. 576.

[115] *The Scaptrade* [1983] 2 A.C. 694 at 701 (Lord Diplock); *Lauritzencool AB v Lady Navigation Inc* [2005] EWCA Civ 579; [2005] 1 W.L.R. 3686 at [10] (Mance LJ).

[116] *Akai Holdings Ltd v RSM Robson Rhodes LLP* [2007] EWHC 1641 (Ch).

[117] As William Jowitt KC once nicely put it in argument: "Slavery is not the less slavery because the chains are gilded" (*Warner Bros Pictures Inc v Nelson* [1937] 1 K.B. 209 at 211).

[118] Cf. *Société des Industries Metallurgiques SA v Bronx Engineering Co Ltd* [1975] 1 Lloyd's Rep. 465, discussed below.

[119] (1878) 3 App. Cas. 709.

[120] [1891] 2 Ch. 416.

[121] [1891] 2 Ch. 416 at 427.

[122] E.g. *Ehrman v Bartholomew* [1898] 1 Ch 671; *Kirchner & Co v Gruban* [1909] 1 Ch. 413; *Rely-A-Bell Burglar & Fire Alarm Co Ltd v Eisler* [1926] Ch. 609; *Kapp v BC Lions Football Club* (1967) 64 D.L.R. (2d) 426; cf. *Warren v Mendy* [1989] 1 W.L.R. 853.

fect would be to give the defendant no choice but to employ, or use the confidential services of, the claimant: for example, where a manager sought an injunction against a sportsman[123] or musician[124] preventing the latter from using someone else's services. Moreover, in *Société des Industries Metallurgiques SA v Bronx Engineering Co Ltd*[125] analogous reasoning was applied by the Court of Appeal in refusing an injunction to prevent delivery of a complex machine tool made to the claimant's order to anyone other than to the claimant, on the basis that such an order would amount to indirect specific performance of a contract not so enforceable, and to that extent would be impermissible.

More recently, however, it has become clear that no such general rule exists, and **28-036** that whatever the situation with employment contracts and the like, a more nuanced approach is necessary. The leading decision today is *Lauritzencool AB v Lady Navigation Inc*.[126] In that case, the owners of two ships under time charter to a shipping pool purported to withdraw them in breach of contract; the charterers, who administered the pool, thereupon sought an injunction preventing any disposition of the vessels to third parties inconsistent with their rights under the charter. They succeeded at first instance; and, even though it was abundantly clear that the order given would have had the effect of forcing continued performance (since otherwise the vessels would have to remain idle at ruinous and unproductive expense to their owners), and despite it being equally clear that specific performance would never be granted of a time charter,[127] the Court of Appeal unhesitatingly upheld the judge's order. While accepting the results in the employment cases referred to above, Mance LJ was firmly convinced that there was no call to generalise from them to contracts generally. In particular, there was (he thought) no reason to say on principle that an injunction ought to be refused whenever, if granted, it would incidentally pressurise a contractor into performing a contract not otherwise specifically enforceable. On the contrary: inflexible prohibitions were generally foreign to the law of injunctions;[128] a number of earlier cases had acquiesced in orders effectively forcing performance of non-specifically-enforceable contracts;[129] and the employment cases were special in that they involved potentially undesirable interference with the personal freedom of workers and employers.[130] The result, said his Lordship, was that no injunction could be resisted on the ground, without more, that if granted the "only realistic commercial course" left to the defendant would be to perform a contract not otherwise specifically enforceable.[131]

Since the radical change in attitude engendered by *Lauritzencool AB v Lady* **28-037** *Navigation Inc*,[132] it is not entirely clear how far the "indirect specific performance" defence will continue to apply. The best view, it is suggested, is that it will now

---

123 *Warren v Mendy* [1989] 1 W.L.R. 853.
124 *Page One Records Ltd v Britton* [1968] 1 W.L.R. 157.
125 [1975] 1 Lloyd's Rep. 465.
126 [2005] EWCA Civ 579; [2005] 1 W.L.R. 3686. Note, however, that the decision was not entirely without precedent: see e.g. dicta in the much earlier *Le Blanch v Granger* (1865) 35 Beav. 187 at 188 (Lord Romilly).
127 Because of the House of Lords' decision in *The Scaptrade* [1983] 2 A.C. 694, esp at 702–703.
128 [2005] EWCA Civ 579; [2005] 1 W.L.R. 3686 at [25].
129 See in particular *De Mattos v Gibson* (1859) 4 De G & J 276 at 299 (Lord Chelmsford); *The Lord Strathcona* [1926] A.C. 108 at 125; *Regent International Hotels (UK) Ltd v Pageguide Ltd* (1985) *The Times*, 13 May.
130 [2005] EWCA Civ 579; [2005] 1 W.L.R. 3686 at [24].
131 [2005] EWCA Civ 579; [2005] 1 W.L.R. 3686 at [33].
132 [2005] EWCA Civ 579; [2005] 1 W.L.R. 3686.

depend on the reason why specific performance would be denied. In so far as denial would be on the basis of oppression or hardship to the defendant, or a fortiori where statute forbids such an order at all (of which the classic example is enforcement of an employment contract against the employee[133]), then it seems clear that the argument must remain available.[134] It will probably also be the same where the effect of the injunction will be to lock the parties into a continuing relationship involving mutual trust. Thus, the old cases denying injunctions to employees against dismissal[135] and to managers and agents against their clients[136] are likely to remain good law.[137] But otherwise, it is submitted that the courts will generally be prepared to award injunctions without undue concern as to whether they amount to "back-door" specific performance. In particular, cases such as *Société des Industries Metallurgiques SA v Bronx Engineering Co Ltd*[138] should now be regarded as open to some doubt. If courts are prepared to enjoin a defendant so as indirectly to enforce a charterparty not otherwise specifically enforceable, it is hard to see why they should act differently as regards a contract for the sale of goods.

28-038 In cases where the "indirect specific performance" principle exceptionally continues to obtain, notably in the field of employment, it should nevertheless be noted that even here a fairly sophisticated approach falls to be taken, with all factors in account. It is not enough, for example, to show simply that the grant of an injunction against an employee is likely to exert very strong pressure to work for the employer: it must be shown that there is effectively no choice at all. So, in *Warner Bros Pictures Inc v Nelson*[139] Branson J had no difficulty in enjoining a film star from working elsewhere in the motion picture business. She was, he said, "a person of intelligence, capacity and means", "able to employ herself both usefully and remuneratively in other spheres of activity", and the fact that she could not earn as much there was beside the point.[140] As his lordship pithily put it:

> "She will not be driven, although she may be tempted, to perform the contract, and the fact that she may be so tempted is no objection to the grant of an injunction."[141]

Again, it may well be that an employer seeking to prevent an employee working for a competitor can circumvent the principle by a so-called "garden leave" clause; that is, by an agreement to pay the employee for not working, so avoiding

---

[133] Trade Union and Labour Relations (Consolidation) Act 1992 s.236.

[134] Hence cases such as *Whitwood Chemical Co v Hardman* [1891] 2 Ch. 416, referred to in para.28-035 above, remain good law.

[135] *Chappell v Times Newspapers Ltd* [1975] 1 W.L.R. 482.

[136] See *Page One Records Ltd v Britton* [1968] 1 W.L.R. 157 and *Warren v Mendy* [1989] 1 W.L.R. 853, above.

[137] As held in *Vertex Data Science Ltd v Powergen Retail Ltd* [2006] EWHC 1340 (Comm); [2006] 2 Lloyd's Rep. 591. Cf too *Woods Building Services v Milton Keynes Council* [2015] EWHC 2172 (TCC); [2015] B.L.R. 591 (no order to contract with claimant for long-term asbestos removal, despite successful challenge to tendering process under which contract awarded to competitor).

[138] [1975] 1 Lloyd's Rep. 465. It should be noted that there is now some authority that contracts for goods not otherwise readily obtainable are specifically enforceable anyway: see *Thames Valley Power Ltd v Total Gas & Power Ltd* [2005] EWHC 2208 (Comm); [2006] 1 Lloyd's Rep. 441 at [63] (Christopher Clarke J).

[139] [1937] 1 K.B. 209. The defendant was the late Bette Davis (whose married name was Ruth Elizabeth Nelson).

[140] [1937] 1 K.B. 209 at 219. See too the earlier *William Robinson & Co Ltd v Heuer* [1898] 2 Ch. 451 (employee enjoined from working elsewhere in the same, but not a different, business). A similar assumption is, of course, implicit in *Lumley v Wagner* (1852) 1 De G M & G 604.

[141] [1937] 1 K.B. 209 at 219–220.

the "work or starve" dilemma that might otherwise apply.[142] Conversely, an employee may be able to obtain an injunction against the employer if either the employer retains full faith in the employee (the wrongful dismissal being due, for example, to third party pressure)[143] or even if he does not have such faith, if the injunction is for a limited period to enable (for instance) proper disciplinary proceedings to be gone through.[144]

VI.   INJUNCTIONS AND THE INSOLVENT DEFENDANT

As with specific performance, it is suggested that the fact that a defendant is insolvent is no bar as such to the award of an injunction. For example, there seems no reason why an ex-employee should be able to flout a valid non-competition covenant or non-disclosure agreement merely because he is bankrupt. On the other hand, those seeking injunctions against insolvent defendants face a number of other difficulties. Leave is required to commence any proceedings against an insolvent defendant in the first place.[145] In both corporate and personal insolvency, onerous obligations may be disclaimed and the obligee left to prove for damages—a remedy that clearly excludes the possibility of an injunction.[146] And even if this does not apply, the court may well refuse specific relief on some other ground. For example, it is clear that an injunction will not be granted in so far as it might subvert the general principle of pari passu distribution in insolvency.[147]

28-039

---

[142] *Evening Standard Co Ltd v Henderson* [1987] I.C.R. 588. A fortiori, the employer can prevent the employee from working for someone else while suspended following alleged misbehaviour: *Standard Life Health Care Ltd v Gorman* [2009] EWCA Civ 1292; [2010] I.R.L.R. 233.

[143] See e.g. *Hill v C.A. Parsons & Co Ltd* [1972] Ch. 305 and *Powell v Brent London Borough Council* [1988] I.C.R. 176 (both interlocutory injunction cases, but in point).

[144] *Irani v Southampton & South West Hampshire Health Authority* [1985] I.C.R. 590; *Gryf-Lowczowski v Hinchingbrooke Healthcare NHS Trust* [2006] I.C.R. 425.

[145] Insolvency Act 1986 ss.126, 285(3); I. Fletcher, *Law of Insolvency*, 5th edn (London: Sweet & Maxwell, 2017), para.22-005 ff.

[146] Insolvency Act 1986 ss.178 (corporate), 315 (personal).

[147] For instance, once insolvency has set in it is too late to compel creation of a retention fund in the hands of a bankrupt building employer, rights having crystallised on insolvency: see *MacJordan Construction Ltd v Brookmount Erostin Ltd* [1994] C.L.C. 581 at 588, approving *Re Jartray Developments Ltd* (1982) 22 B.L.R. 134.

INDEX

LEGAL TAXONOMY
FROM SWEET & MAXWELL

This index has been prepared using Sweet & Maxwell's Legal Taxonomy. Main index entries conform to keywords provided by the Legal Taxonomy except where references to specific documents or non-standard terms (denoted by quotation marks) have been included. These keywords provide a means of identifying similar concepts in other Sweet & Maxwell publications and online services to which keywords from the Legal Taxonomy have been applied. Readers may find some minor differences between terms used in the text and those which appear in the index. Suggestions to *sweetandmaxwell.taxonomy@tr.com*.

Also Available:

Duress, Undue Influence and Unconscionable Dealing, 4th Edition

Professor Nelson Enonchong

9780414110557
Publication date: May 2023
Formats: Hardback/ProView eBook/Westlaw UK

Duress, undue influence and unconscionable dealing are grounds on which a contract can be set aside because the claimant was induced to enter into it by means which the law considers unacceptable. Professor Enonchong provides a detailed and rigorous analysis of the circumstances where an otherwise valid transaction can be avoided on each of these grounds. The 4th edition is completely up-to-date and contains detailed discussion of important decisions since the last edition.

Estoppel by Conduct and Election, 3rd Edition

The Hon Patrick Keane AC KC

9780414110878
Publication date: November 2022
Formats: Hardback/ProView eBook

Estoppel by Conduct and Election, originally written by the Honourable K.R. Handley, has been comprehensively reviewed and updated in this 3rd edition by the Honourable Patrick Keane. The book examines estoppel in the context of commercial transactions and property dealings. It examines election in relation to commercial dealings. It provides a comprehensive but accessible exposition of general principles including a discussion of the particular relationships in which these principles have been applied and developed by the courts. With the concerns of practising lawyers who advise upon and litigate issues of estoppel in mind, the general principles are stated and illustrated in their application by reference to leading decisions of the higher courts of the Commonwealth of Nations. Where steps in the judicial development remain controversial in point of authority, the controversy is identified and explicated by an in-depth examination of the leading cases.

Damages for Breach of Contract, 2nd Edition

Professor Katy Barnett

9780414110878
Publication date: November 2022
Formats: Hardback/ProView eBook

This new work on *Damages for Breach of Contract*, written by new author an
remedies law leading expert, Professor Katy Barnett, provides authoritativ
and practical guidance on the nature, extent and limitations of damage
individuals and companies can claim in the event of breach of contrac
The book deals primarily with English law, but also considers othe
jurisdictions (such as Australia and Singapore) when relevant. Clearly settin
out what the law is, this new title is written with practitioners in mind. It wi
also be of real value to students and academics as it considers some of th
theoretical debates surrounding this topic.

Exclusion Clauses and Unfair Contract Terms, 13th Edition

Professor Neil Andrews

9780414110908
Publication date: November 2022
Formats: Hardback/ProView eBook/Westlaw UK

Fully revised and updated by Professor Neil Andrews to take account
important case law developments of the last five years, this new editic
examines, in a detailed, practical and incisive manner, th
important area of contract law. It provides guidance to t
practitioner on drafting and using exclusion clauses effective
within the formative phase of a contract. Additionally, it offe
commentary on the possibility of challenging an exclusion claus
The text deals with exclusion clauses and unfair contract terms in the conte
of both commercial and consumer contracts, considering the legal tests whi
are applied to determine whether the exclusion clause has been successfu
incorporated, how it should be interpreted, and the extent to which it mig
be invalidated at common law and under statute.